Readings in Object-Oriented
Database Systems

THE MORGAN KAUFMANN SERIES IN
DATA MANAGEMENT SYSTEMS

Series Editor, Jim Gray (Tandem Computers, Inc.)

Readings in Object-Oriented Database Systems
Edited by Stanley B. Zdonik (Brown University) and
David Maier (Oregon Graduate Center)

Database Programming Languages
Proceedings of the Second International Workshop
Edited by Richard Hull (University of Southern California)
David Stemple (University of Massachusetts)
Ron Morrison (University of St. Andrews)

Readings in Database Systems
Edited by Michael Stonebraker (University of California, Berkeley)

Deductive Databases and Logic Programming
By Jack Minker (University of Maryland)

Readings in Object-Oriented Database Systems

Edited by

Stanley B. Zdonik
Brown University

and

David Maier
Oregon Graduate Center

MORGAN KAUFMANN PUBLISHERS, INC.
SAN MATEO, CALIFORNIA

Sponsoring Editor *Bruce Spatz*
Production Manager *Shirley Jowell*
Production Assistant *John Galbraith*
Copy Editor *Lyn Dupre*
Indexer *Frances Bowles*
Cover Designer *Jo Jackson*
Typesetter *Technically Speaking Publications*
Cover Illustration *Maureen Flores*

Library of Congress Cataloging-in-Publication Data
　　Readings in object-oriented database systems.

　　Includes bibliographical references
　　Includes index
　　1. Data base management.　2.　Object-oriented data bases.
　　3.　Programming languages.　I. Zdonik, Stanley Benjamin.
　　II.　Maier, David, 1953 -

QA76.9.D3R42　1990　　　　　005.75　　　　　88-35776

　　ISBN 0-55860-000-0
　　ISSN 1046-1698

Morgan Kaufmann Publishers, Inc.
Editorial Office: 2929 Campus Drive, San Mateo, California 94403
Order from: P.O. Box 50490, Palo Alto, California 94303-9953
© 1990 by Morgan Kaufmann Publishers, Inc.

94 93 92 91 90　　5 4 3 2

Preface

We decided to prepare this collection of readings to provide anyone who has a basic background in computer science with a view of the young field of object-oriented databases. We believed that to write a textbook would be premature. Researchers are actively defining the field and deciding which of the variations on this theme will endure. The field is in flux; at this time, the best we can do is to assemble a representative collection of readings. The papers in the field appear in many different and sometimes difficult-to-find sources. By putting together this book, we hope to provide easy access to these ideas.

We have tried to create a volume that will provide any reader with a deeper understanding of this field. We hope that its interest extends beyond the academic. A thorough reading of these papers should give the reader a clear picture of what the issues and problems in the area are, and should provide some notion of how people are currently approaching the solutions. We have also included some editorial material that is intended to guide the reader.

We extend a special thanks to Jim Gray, Roger King, Frank Manola, and Fred Maryanski for their careful and thoughtful reviews of the introductory chapter on *Fundamentals of Object Oriented Databases*. They asked us hard questions, and we hope that the final product shows the benefits of their advice. We also thank Bruce Spatz, our editor, for being so helpful and understanding during some of the more difficult moments. We thank Sandy Heiler for telephoning to make sure we were working.

Electronic mail and Federal Express facilitated our working together at a distance. There were times, however, when we needed to have extended conversations to reconcile different points of view. In these cases, it was essential to be in the same location. Luckily, we often found ourselves attending the same conference or visiting a company or university on each other's coast. We thought that it would be fun to make a list of all of the places and occasions that we could remember where we worked together on this book. The result was surprising in its variety, so we thought that we would share it with you.

- Oregon Graduate Center

- Brown University, Computer Science Department (old and new buildings)

- Train from Bad Muenster to Mainz in Germany

- Cupertino Inn (twice) when we were visiting Apple

- Asilomar Conference Center, Pacific Grove, California

- Car from Asilomar to Cupertino Inn

- Stan's kitchen

- Dave's picnic table

- VLDB, Long Beach
- Chicago SIGMOD (with room-service lunch courtesy of Bruce Spatz)
- Bus ride to O'Hare (with Stan's ears ringing from too much blues)
- Washington DC, Expert Database Systems Conference
- Lounge in the Portland Inn, Portland, Oregon
- Miami Beach, ONR Workshop on Directions in Programming Languages
- OOPSLA, Orlando, Florida
- Airplane from Portland to Chicago
- Bill Weihl's office at MIT

- Backstage at the Hatch Shell in Boston (during a Boston Bluegrass Union Festival)
- Database Engineering Conference in Los Angeles
- Napa, California, Workshop on Software CAD
- Harvard Square (at Dave's hotel)
- Xerox Advanced Information Technology (they let us use their Macintoshes—Thanks!)
- Portland SIGMOD
- Hot tub at Salishan Lodge, Oregon coast.

We wish that we could share all these wonderful places with you. In their stead, we offer you the result of our writing, arguing, and rewriting. We hope you learn from it as much as we did from the process.

Dave Maier
Beaverton, OR

Stan Zdonik
Providence, RI

Contents

Chapter 9 *Applications*

Fundamentals of

Object-Oriented Databases

1. Introduction

The field of object-oriented databases has emerged as the convergence of several research threads. The fields of programming languages, artificial intelligence, and software engineering all have contributed to the use of object-oriented technology in the database area. The challenge from the database side is to integrate these threads into a single system design that maintains desired features from each field. If the result is to remain a database system, it must retain the central features of modern databases, including persistence, concurrency control, recovery, consistency, and a query language.

Object-oriented database systems is an active area at present. Although no common definition for "the" object-oriented *data model* has emerged, there is some agreement over what features are expected in an object-oriented *database system*. Moreover, there is a large set of applications for which this technology holds promise. These applications tend to center on high-performance graphics workstations and environments that support computer-aided design.

This introductory chapter sketches the dimensions of this field. We will describe some of the decisions in designing any object-oriented database system. We will try to enumerate the choices at these decision points and to discuss the relative tradeoffs of these choices. We propose a reference model that takes a position on these issues to illustrate how some of these choices might fit together.

The papers included in this volume are a selection from the growing literature on this subject. They were chosen primarily for their coverage. They are intended not to describe all of the good work underway, but rather to illustrate the main ideas and approaches. They should present the reader with a good overview of the field. We asked ourselves what papers would we want any new graduate student who was entering the field to read. This compilation is our answer to that question.

There are some specialized topics that we left out because of space limitations, such as schema modification. We provide some references to works on these subjects in this general introduction and in the chapter introductions.

2.   Who Needs Object-Oriented Databases?

The design of traditional database systems has largely been determined in response to the needs of typical business applications. Before commercial database-management systems were introduced, each application program owned its own set of files, each of which had its own idiosyncratic format and structure. Data in these file-based systems often were stored redundantly and, as a result, were difficult to keep consistent. Creation of new applications required difficult extractions of information from many disparate sources. Programs were dependent on the structures of the stored data, making these structures difficult to change.

Database systems have improved the application-development process in large data-intensive environments by providing a single, uniform view of data expressed in structure-independent terms. Their high-level linguistic features and their facilities for controlled sharing make it possible to create integrated applications more easily than before. Other benefits accrue. Integrity of the data is controlled by the database system, rather than being the responsibility of each application program. Furthermore, there is one set of highly tuned routines for data formatting and access, rather than separate sets of routines, of varying quality, in each application.

2.1   Computer-Aided Design

The availability of high-performance graphics workstations has increased the breadth and complexity of data-intensive applications that are being attempted. Examples are computer-aided design (CAD), computer-aided software enginering (CASE), and office information systems (OIS). If we look at electrical CAD as an example, the software systems that make up a typical design environment include tools such as schema-capture editors, design-rule checkers,

and circuit-layout programs. All these sub-systems, like their data-processing predecessors, require massive numbers of persistent data; however, the level of complexity of these programs and of these data has grown far beyond what traditional database systems are prepared to handle.

Currently, the application programs in design environments store their data in application-specific file structures. The state of the art here is roughly at the same stage that existed before the emergence of database technology in the data-processing world. There is wide agreement that what is needed is an extension of database technology that can provide the same boost for developing these complex applications that occurred in the commercial data-processing world. The development of object-oriented databases, to a large extent, has been driven by this need.

These design applications place many demands on conventional database technology, including the ability to model very complex data and the ability to evolve without disruptive effects on the current application base. These demands in turn place a requirement on the system to provide an appropriate level of extensibility to capture easily application-specific data semantics and mechanisms for incremental development of the database structures. Extensibility is discussed further in later sections.

2.2   Software Engineering Support for Data-Intensive Applications

Although it is tempting to say that object-oriented databases are databases that are designed to address the problems of design environments, their applicability extends beyond this narrow market niche. Design environments are just a first example of a broader category of applications that we might characterize as *data-intensive programming in the large*.

A data-intensive program is one that produces and/or requires large numbers of data—so many that they might not all fit at one time into the virtual memory of the program. *Programming in the large* refers to the software-engineering process required for multiple programmers to produce very large and complex programs. *Data-intensive programming in the large*, then, refers to the production of very large, complex software systems that also require large numbers of data. Computer-aided design tools are examples of such applications.

The complexity of these systems shows up not only in the programs that manipulate the data, but also in the data themselves. For example, the data that are used in an electrical design application contain many complex interconnections with many complex constraints on the way these interconnections can be made.

Object-oriented databases address both sources of complexity by including facilities to manage the software-engineering process (e.g., data abstraction and inheritance), and features for capturing more directly some of the interconnections and constraints in the data (e.g., properties, relationships, and complex objects).

2.3 Impedance Mismatch

One problem in developing database applications is the *impedance mismatch* between the data-manipulation language (DML) of the database, and the general-purpose programming language in which the rest of the application is written [Bancilhon and Maier]. There are two aspects of this mismatch. One is the difference in programming paradigms; for example, between a declarative DML such as SQL, and an imperative programming language such as PL/I. The other aspect is the mismatch of type systems. A loss of information occurs at the interface, if the programming language is unable to represent database structures, such as relations, directly. Furthermore, since there are two type systems, there is no automatic way to type check the application as a whole. Some early systems like LEAP [Feldman and Rovner] actually had a single type system, but only triples were persistent, thereby not meeting the orthogonal persistence criterion.

Why are two languages necessary in the first place? Neither one alone possesses the features required for the full application. The DML lacks the computational completeness to express the non–data-manipulation parts of the application. The general-purpose language has persistent data only in the form of files. It is missing a sophisticated model of persistent memory that includes high-level types, constraints, and queries.

Database programming languages solve the impedance mismatch problem by making more of the data types of a general-purpose language persistent, or by adding database types, such as lists or relations, to the type system of the language. However, when we access the data from other languages, the impedance mismatch still exists. Application generators and fourth generation languages (4GLs) might be considered database-programming languages of a sort. Certain kinds of applications can be specified with these tools, and the specifications are in terms of the database schema. These tools, in some cases, emit code for the application in a combination of DML and a general-purpose

language, but the application developer is shielded from the boundary between the two.

Object-oriented databases (OODBs) try to ameliorate the impedance mismatch by extending the DML so that more of an application can be written in the DML. Although few current OODBs can express complete applications by themselves, with more of the application in the database, the interface between database and general-purpose language is crossed less frequently. (Note that computational completeness is not enough to ensure that an OODB can express an entire application. The OODB must also be able to access the necessary resources, such as the user's display and print output devices.)

3. Contributing Technology

To meet the demands of these new applications, the next generation of databases is incorporating technology from other fields—notably from software engineering, programming languages, and artificial intelligence. What technology in particular is showing up in object-oriented database systems?

Most of these systems allow some form of database extension by supplying additional code. If this code is to evolve, we are immediately faced with software-engineering concerns, in that good organization via modularity must be enforced at the system level. We might, therefore, say that one of the principal advantages of an object-oriented database is that it supports the software-engineering process for complex applications that require large numbers of persistent data.

Object-oriented databases contain some features in common with modern abstraction-based programming languages. Since most object-oriented databases provide a computationally complete data-manipulation language, it is possible to include more of the execution of the application in the database itself. This inclusion presents an opportunity for using the knowledge of the database structures in the optimization and intelligent processing of the application code.

From artificial intelligence (AI), we see powerful knowledge-representation techniques appearing in object-oriented databases. Examples are classification and specification hierarchies, delegation of behavior, and modifiable meta-information. We also see implementation techniques common in AI languages, such as dynamic binding of messages to methods, automatic garbage collection, and structured virtual memory.

4.   Running Example

We outline the following application to illustrate later points. Consider a company, **Media Storage Services** (MSS), that offers safe storage for computer disks and tapes. MSS has a fleet of vans that pick up and deliver magnetic media of clients throughout the city. MSS wants to build a database to help in planning the best routes for the drivers to take each day. Thus, the database must have information about the road network in the city, the locations of the clients, pickup and delivery requests, and the planned routes. The database will be used each night by route planners to plan the next day's routes, and will also generate a route map for each driver.

The main entities in the street network are *roads*, *road segments*, and *intersections*. Intersections divide a road into a sequence of road segments. Each road segment has a beginning and ending intersection. Each intersection represents the convergence of two or more road segments. Each road is described as an alternating sequence of road segments and intersections.

Each road has a name and a road type (street, avenue, etc.). Each road segment knows to which road it belongs. Road segments have a shape, for display purposes, which may be either a straight line or an arc. Each road segment also has an address range, a side for odd-numbered addresses, and a direction (two-way or one-way). Intersections have an associated position in coordinates relative to a map. We can summarize this information as follows, using no particular schema language:

Road
>   name: **String**
>   roadType: {**road, avenue, boulevard, lane,** ...}
>   segmentList: **sequence of RoadSegment or Intersection**

RoadSegment
>   inRoad: **Road**
>   segmentShape: **Arc or Line**
>   start: **Intersection**
>   end: **Intersection**
>   direction: {**one-way-SE, one-way-ES, two-way**}
>   addressRange: (**StreetNumber, StreetNumber**)
>   oddSide: {**left, right**}

Intersection
>   incomingSegs: **set of RoadSegment**
>   position: **Coordinate**

Here, **Coordinate, StreetNumber, Arc**, and **Line** are types assumed defined elsewhere.

MSS also wants a digitized image of a map of the city. The application for aiding route planners will display requested stops and routes being planned by overlaying them on this map image, and the coordinates are relative to the map image. The composite image will also be used in generating route maps for use by the drivers. Each client will have a company name, an address (including the road segment and street address), possibly a standing request for pickups at regular times, and a collection of individual requests for pickups and deliveries. We have the following hierarchy:

>   Request
>   **PickupRequest**
>   >   StandingRequest
>   **DeliveryRequest**

A Route is much like a road, being represented by a sequence segmentList of alternating road segments and intersections. A route has a list of stops, which can involve a pickup, a delivery, or both:

>   **Stop**
>   >   **Pickup**
>   >   >   **PickupAndDeliver**
>   >   **Delivery**
>   >   >   **PickupAndDeliver**

There is an **initialLoad** associated with the route which is what the driver loads into the van in the morning. The route also identifies the **vehicle** for the route. Vehicles have varying capacities, and a constraint on a route is that the vehicle never be loaded past capacity. We assume that all pickups and deliveries are in terms of **Bins**, so the capacity of a vehicle is a number of bins, a stop lists bins to pickup or deliver, and the initial load for a route is a set of bins.

5.   What Makes An OODB a Database?

We will shortly describe the linguistic basis for object-oriented data models. We must be careful to understand that an *object-oriented* database-management system (DBMS) must first of all be a DBMS, and as such must provide the features and functionality that we have come to expect from modern database systems. These features are typically not found in the current breed of object-oriented programming languages (e.g., Smalltalk).

We define here what we mean by a DBMS. Our description has three parts: the features we consider essential to a DBMS, the features that are frequently present, and the features that are sometimes present.

5.1 Essential Features

Model and Language. A DBMS has a non-trivial model and language. That is, the DBMS understands some structure on the data (the data model) it contains, and provides a language for manipulating structured data. Usually, the model provides for records and some sort of grouping of records, such as sets, trees, or lists. The operations often include creation, destruction, and modification of records; inserting and deleting of records in the grouping construct; and a mechanism for searching a group for records with a given value. These requirements exclude a system that supports only uninterpreted strings of bytes as the only data items. However, they admit a system that uses a data structure of, say, matrices, and a language that provides matrix operations.

Relationships. A DBMS can represent relationships between entities, the relationships can be named, and the language can query those relationships. There are many ways the relationships might be captured: as binary associations of entities, as *n*-way associations, as physical links from one entity to another, or as logical links. A physical link is one where one data item contains a reference that denotes the location of another data item in storage. A logical link is one where one data item contains a *value* that identifies another data item by one of its properties. The requirement for named relationships excludes systems that support that data item's only undifferentiated binary links, as might be found in a hypertext system (although most hypertext systems do have a means for labeling links).

Permanence. A DBMS provides a persistent and stable store. By *persistent* we mean that data are accessible past the end of the process that creates them. By *stable*, we mean that data have some resiliency in the face of process failure, system failure, and media failure. In process failure, a program using the database terminates abnormally. In system failure, the computer on which the DBMS resides crashes because of an operating- or database-system software error or a hardware error. In media failure, the storage medium for the data, usually magnetic disk, is corrupted. Most DBMSs cope with process and system failure with a *recovery* mechanism, which writes information about changes to the database to secondary storage, and uses this information to make corrections to the data after a failure. The system deals with media failures by duplicating storage devices or by writing information on database state or updates to tape.

Sharing. A DBMS permits data to be shared. At a simple level, a DBMS allows data created by one user or program to be used by another. This requirement excludes a system that simply stores snapshots of individual user workspaces, if a program cannot access two workspaces simultaneously, or if individual data items cannot be exported between workspaces. The sharing must permit simultaneous use of the database by multiple users, although not necessarily of the same data items at once. Conventional DBMSs have a *concurrency-control* mechanism that prevents users from executing inconsistent actions on the database, usually by locking data items when they are read or written. Concurrency control is generally coupled with a transaction mechanism that provides *atomicity*: A group of related operations for one user gets executed in an all-or-nothing manner. Thus, the database is never left partially updated, and partial changes are not visible to other users.

Arbitrary Size. The address space of a DBMS is not constrained by limitations in the physical processor. Thus, the size of a database should not be limited by the amount of main memory, or by the address range of virtual memory.

5.2 Frequent Features

The following items are present in some form in almost all mainframe database products. We do not, however, think that they are as central to the definition of a DBMS as are the foregoing items. We list them separately so as not to exclude a priori from the domain of DBMSs certain new approaches, such as persistent programming languages.

Integrity Constraints. A DBMS can help to ensure the correctness and consistency of the data it contains by *enforcing integrity* constraints which are statements that must always be true for data items in the database. Some common kinds of constraints are *domains* for fields in records, which specify the range of legal values for a field; *keys*, which say that certain data values serve to identify uniquely items in a collection (for example, that the map coordinates uniquely identify each intersection in a city); and *referential* integrity constraints, which assert that a reference in one data item indeed leads to another data item (e.g., when a road segment refers to the road it is in, a data item for that road actually exists). Some DBMSs provide *triggers* to help in constraint enforcement: Actions can be initiated on access to particular data items, either to check that constraints hold or to perform additional updates to bring the database to a state of consistency. For example, deleting a road might trigger deleting all its road segments.

Authorization (also called access control). Most DBMSs support ownership of data by particular users, and give the owner a mechanism to permit selective access to data by other users. In our example, the route planners might have permission to update route information, but be able only to read road information and not to update it.

Querying (a declarative query language and associative access support). Especially in relational DBMSs, there is a facility to express the desired query or update on the database without requiring that the query writer give the details of how the answer is to be derived. For instance, such a query might be, "Find all roads with a segment such that at least one end of the segment is southeast of coordinate (1336, 871)." The user says *what*, the q*uery processor* determines the particular *how*. Many of the queries expressed in such a language are *associative*: They request retrieval of data items based on a property of the items or on their relationship to other items, as in the previous example. Thus, many DBMSs support creation and maintenance of *auxiliary structures* for access of data, such as indices and inverted files, that give alternative paths to locate data associatively. The query processor then chooses whether to use such structures to answer a particular query.

The query language exists typically in two versions: one for expressing queries embedded in programs and another for users to type in their requests directly. The latter is often called an *ad hoc query language*. For us, the salient attributes of an ad hoc query language are that it be high level, that query processing for it be reasonably efficient, and that it be *generic*: Once a new type of data item is defined, the language can query items of that type.

Separate Schema. Most DBMSs maintain a central *schema*, a catalog of the types defined in the database and the names of objects declared to be of those types. Different programs and users share this *meta-information*. Contrast this situation to the one in programming languages, where each program contains its own definitions of types and declarations of variables. We do not insist on a separate schema as an absolute requirement for a DBMS, to allow a system where each data item knows its own type directly. The schema for a database is often itself represented as data in the database, and is hence accessible through the query mechanism for regular data.

Another distinction is that there is no notion in a database system of a "compile time" after which type definitions and variable declarations are fixed, unlike the majority of programming languages. New type definitions, and new named instances of types, can be added throughout the life of a database. (However, programming languages with recursion support the creation of new instances of local variables at runtime, and heap-based languages can allocate new instances of types, although generally without the abilitiy to create new names for the instances.)

Views. This feature allows definition of virtual data, which are not stored explicitly, but rather are computed from stored data. Views are used to give selective access to data, to present data in a form more easily understood by users, and to provide a stable interface to part of the database even though the logical structure might change. For example, we might want to present a view of road segments in which the segments contain information on the location of their endpoints derived from the start and end intersections. A closely related feature is *derived fields*, which are fields in records computed from other information on demand.

Database Administration. A special interface for the database administrator to perform data-management functions. These functions include:

- Reorganizing: changing the logical or physical structure of the data

- Statistic monitoring: gathering statistics on frequently used queries and data sets

- Auditing: keeping track of usage of data for security or accounting reasons

- Adding and removing users

- Archiving: copying or removing part of the database

5.3 Less Frequent Features

Report and Form Management. Since many database applications involve data entry as well as report, chart, and graph formatting, many database vendors include or sell as an option a facility to generate forms and reports from high-level specifications.

Data Dictionary. A data dictionary is an extension of the database schema. It gives not just the format of data, but also documentation, information on timeliness or reliability of data, procedures to validate data on entry, procedures to format data on output, and information about parts of database applications outside the DBMS, such as which application programs access which data.

Distribution. The latest commercial offerings support distributed databases. The data may be distributed over multiple computers (called *sites*), which are often geographically distant. The reason for distribution is generally improved performance or increased availability.

Shared data are placed at the site where they are used most, but the DBMS still supports queries that use data from multiple sites. A related feature is access to external DBMSs.

6. Basic Object-Oriented Concepts and the Threshold Model

This section introduces some basic terminology and concepts that pervade the literature on object-oriented databases. It also describes what we consider to be a threshold model that delineates those features that we believe must be present in order for a database system to call itself object-oriented.

6.1 Object-Oriented Terminology

An *object* is an abstract machine that defines a *protocol* through which users of the object may interact. The object can have a state that is stored in an encapsulated piece of memory. This hiding of an object's stored state is a crucial feature of an object-oriented langauge. As such, we might say that object-oriented languages are distinguished from previous memory-oriented languages, in which new types were defined as templates for memory structures.

The protocol of an object is typically defined by a set of *messages* (i.e., operations) with typed *signatures*. A message can be sent to an object (called the *receiver*) to perform some action. As long as the types of the parameters match the signatures, the object is guaranteed to interpret this message and to carry out the action. Therefore, a message is just like a procedure call in which one argument (the receiver) is distinguished. A message is implemented by a *method,* which is a piece of code that accomplishes the desired effect. Thus, a method is like a procedure body. A method has special privileges in that it is able to access the private memory representation of the object to which the corresponding message was sent. A message name can be overloaded with many possible method implementations. The object-oriented type system contains rules for determining the correct one to use at run-time based on the type of the receiver (see Section 7.1, Dispatching).

A *class* (sometimes called a *type*) is a template for its *instances*. Often the terms *type* and *class* are used interchangeably, but when the two terms are used in the same system, *type* usually refers to specifications, whereas *class* refers to the extension (i.e., all current instances) of the corresponding type. Every object is an instance of some class. This class defines all the messages to which the object will respond, as well

as the way that objects of this class are implemented. Classes are typically arranged in a directed graph, with the edges connecting *superclasses* to their *subclasses*. These edges are often called *is-a links*. They express a compatibility relationship between the classes. That is, a subclass inherits all the behavior defined by its superclass and may define additional behavior of its own. Instances of the subclass are completely substitutable in contexts (i.e., expressions) that expect instances of the superclass.

Here are some examples of these concepts. One piece of information a route planner wants is an estimate of the time it takes to follow a given route. Time is spent driving along road segments, stopped at intersections, and stopped at a client's facility. We can think of each component of a route as contributing a delay. Thus, to capture some of the behavioral semantics of the application, we can define a **delay** message that **RoadSegment**, **Intersection**, and **Stop** all understand. In every case, the message will return the elapsed time, but the method used for each class will be different. The method for **RoadSegment** probably will make an estimate based on the length of the segment. The **Intersection** might just return a constant. **Stop** and its subtypes could all use different methods, and base the estimate on the number of bins involved.

As an example of the subtype concept with message overloading, we might have two classes describing intersections. **Class Controlled_Intersection** is a subclass of class **Intersection,** and both of these classes define the **delay** message. **Controlled_Intersection** also defines a message that returns the traffic signal object that is associated with that intersection. The **delay** method for **Intersection** returns a constant (as previously described), whereas the **delay** method for **Controlled_Intersection** computes the **delay** as a function of the cycle time of the associated traffic signal. If we had a variable i that was declared to be of class **Intersection,** we could legally assign a **Controlled_Intersection** object to it. If we then sent the **delay** message to the variable i, the system would choose which **delay** method to invoke based on the class of the object to which i currently referred.

6.2 Complex State

An object has a state that is expressed by the results of functions (i.e., messages or operations) that are defined for it. The values of these functions are other objects. We say that one object x *refers* to another object y when there exists a function f defined on x such that $f(x) = y$.

It is possible for more than one object to refer to the same object. This ability for objects to share related components is often called *aliasing* in the programming-language world. Aliasing is a useful capability, since it reflects any changes in the shared subcomponent in both of the containing objects. Consider two **RoadSegment** objects with a shared **Intersection**. Any change to the **Intersection** through one of the **RoadSegments** will be seen as a change to the **Intersection** in the context of the other **RoadSegment**.

Sometimes, additional semantics are placed on these functional relationships. For example, some of them might be designated as part of relationships, such as to express the fact that the **Intersection** is a part of the **RoadSegment.** Any such relationships might bear additional meaning in that operations on one object might have a side effect on the other. For example, deleting the container might have the effect of deleting the part, or vice versa. We will discuss other such distinguished relationships in Section 8.6.

6.3 Types and Encapsulation

One goal of research on object-oriented databases is to provide a system in which the basic modeling primitives are *extensible*, because new applications involve unpredictably complex forms of data and because these forms will evolve over time. That is, a fixed set of data-structuring primitives is not sufficient in a platform to support arbitrary new design data. An extension should provide new functionality to the data model that is indistinguishable from built-in functionality.

One of the principal techniques for providing extensions is through the creation of new *types* [Batory, et al. 1988]. A principal use of types in the programming-language world is type checking. *Type checking* ensures that the types of expressions match the context in which they are used. For example, the type of an expression that is used as an actual parameter to a function must match the type of the formal parameter in the function definition. An important question about the design of a type system is whether or not this type checking can be done at compile-time, or whether some or all of it must be deferred to run-time.

Although the idea of creating new types is not new to the database field, the view that a type is really an abstract data type [Liskov, 1977; 1.2] that encapsulates its implementation is rather new. Earlier database models provided the user with a fixed set of built-in types and a small set of type constructors (e.g., record). New types could be built with the type constructors, but these new types did not allow for operations that were different from the operations defined for the type constructor. For example, for a record the operations are the basic get- and set-value operations on its fields, plus record creation. In other words, there is no way to hide the representation of a new type.

Encapsulation is a powerful system-structuring technique in which a system is made up of a collection of modules, each accessible through a well-defined interface. The abstract data-type approach defines the interface by a set of strongly typed operation (also called message) signatures. It also requires that each type define a representation (an instance of some existing data type) that is allocated for each of its instances. This representation is used to store the state of the object. Only the methods implementing operations for the objects are allowed to access the representation, thereby making it possible to change the representation without disturbing the rest of the system. Only the methods would need to be recoded.

Encapsulation represents a software-engineering methodology that makes a sharp distinction between the specification of a module and the code and data structures that are used to implement this specification. Specifications can be designed and used independently of the implementation techniques. When we look at subtyping in Section 8.2, Hierarchies, we will have to distinguish these two aspects.

Some object-oriented models do not provide a strong view of encapsulation. These models have been called *structurally object-oriented*. In a structural model, we are able to construct new types, but the underlying representation of the type is visible. This feature is shared with a class of models, called *semantic data models* [Hammer, 1981; 2.3], that was popular in the late seventies.

Some systems treat types as first-class objects. That is, a type is an instance of some other type (i.e., *metatype*) that describes how types behave. In this view, types can be passed as values to programs and can be manipulated just like any other object or value. This feature provides a great deal of uniformity and power in the data model, but makes operations such as compile-time type checking difficult.

Another distinction between type models is whether a type is a specification (i.e., intension) or a set of objects (i.e., extension). An intensional specification is a template specifying all possible objects with a given structure. For example, the definition of the type **RoadSegment** specifies all possible road segments. Some systems view types as intensions (e.g., ENCORE [Hornick, 1987; 4.3]), whereas others view them as extensions (e.g., SDM [Hammer, 1981; 2.3]). Still other systems (e.g., GALILEO [Albano, 1985; 2.5]) support both notions by having types separate from collections or classes. Viewing a type as a collection of instances provides a basis for a name space over which queries are possible and natural. We might ask for all employees who make more than $20K. This query is made over the class of all employees. The existence of a class of all instances of a given type can, however, lead to problems. For example, if there is a class of all arrays, then it might be possible to access an array that was being used as a representation for some other type (e.g., **stack**), thereby breaking the encapsulation of the latter type.

6.4 Identity

Object-oriented data models are also characterized by the ability to make references through an *object identity*. This capability requires that there be something about the object that remains invariant across all possible modifications of the object's value. Most modern programming languages can capture object identity, as can some early database models (e.g., CODASYL). The current generation of database models (e.g., relational, functional), however, tends to be value-based. In a value-based model, an object is identified by a subset of its attributes, called its *key*. This approach leads to simpler computational structures, but makes some kinds of information difficult to express. Suppose a **RoadSegment** referred to its containing **Road** by its **name** and **RoadType**. If the name of a **Road** changes, its constituent **RoadSegments** would no longer refer to it. If, however, the **RoadSegments** held the identity of the **Road**, a change to the **Road** would not break the connections to its **RoadSegment**.

The identity of an object must be immutable. There is no operation that can ever change the correspondence between an object and its identity. (Smalltalk contains such an operation, **become**, which exchanges the identity of two objects. To what such an operation would correspond in the real world is unclear. It is largely an implementation mechanism in Smalltalk, used, for example, to increase the size of an object.) The identity will persist until the object is destroyed.

Identity allows us to express the notion of shared structure. We can distinguish between the idea of referring to two things that are alike and that of referring to two things that are in fact the same (see cartoon). That is, two objects x and y can each have a subcomponent c which, in fact, is the same object. A change to c will be reflected in both x and y. For example, there could be an in-tersection shared by two road segments. A change in the position of the intersection would be reflected in both of the road segments. Alternatively, the two road segments could reference two intersections that had equal state (same coordinates, same incoming segments) but were distinct objects. Here, a change in one intersection would not change the other, and would result in the two intersections being unequal.

We also point out that the set of permissible object references might be larger than the set of object identifiers. Whereas we posit a one-to-one correspondence between identifiers and objects, there may be a many-to-one mapping from references to identifiers. For example, object space might be partitioned into segments such that, within a single segment, interobject references can be shorter than full object IDs, and full objects IDs are necessary only for references between segments.

In many current databases, it is possible to delete data items (i.e., records). In the object-oriented case, if we delete an object x, there might be other objects that have stored the identity of x. The deletion can lead to dangling references or to references that, when dereferenced, yield some undefined piece of storage. The wisdom of deletion semantics in an object-oriented database is questionable. Instead, we might prefer to adopt the semantics of garbage-collected languages, in which objects cannot be deleted, but, instead, references to objects are destroyed. When all references to an object have been removed, the system reclaims the storage occupied by that object.

Although object-oriented databases are based on the notion of identity, it is important to note that the way in which objects are related may or may not be based on this feature. References that make use of an object's identity directly are much like pointers in conventional programming languages. In an object-oriented database, it is possible to relate an object x to another object or set of objects S by storing the identity of S (or of the members of S) in x. Since all access to an object x is through the messages defined on its type, however, computing the association between x and S must be done by a method. This method can make use of a stored identity, or it can use a value-based expression, as in a relational query language (e.g., SQL). In this way, object-oriented databases provide a framework for unifying value-based and identity-based access.

An often-asked question is whether a primary key in a relational database is the same as an object identity. The answer is no. Primary keys are not unique systemwide; they are unique only within a single relation. Object identities are unique across the database. Such uniform references to objects make it easy to create collections with objects of heterogeneous types, such as a set of **RoadSegments** and **Intersections**. In the relational model, a systemwide reference would require a relation name *and* key value. Yet few relational languages have the ability to extract a relation name from a field, then to turn around and use that name to search the relation. Some relational systems use systemwide tuple identifiers (tids) in their implementation, and make tids available in the data manipulation language. However, tids are usually tied to the physical location of tuples, and are not guaranteed immutable over updates in the database.

Another problem with keys is that, if they represent information from the real world, they are subject to change. For example, consider road names as a key for **Road** objects. Even if a road's name serves to distinguish that road within a given town (a questionable assumption), roads do get renamed. Of course, system-generated surrogates for tuples would not have to change.

Keys still have a place in object-oriented databases. A key is a property or set of properties that uniquely identifies an object within a collection. A key is not something that is associated with a type, since the uniqueness of the key is guaranteed only with a given collection of objects. For example, the map-coordinate position of an intersection could be a key within the set of all intersections on a particular map, but between maps coordinates of intersections could be duplicated. Different collections over the same type might have different keys. We might have one set of **RoadSegment** objects keyed on **start** and **end** intersections, and another set keyed on **inRoad** and **addressRange**.

We can imagine a type for which some value for the states of instances functionally determines the identity of those instances. Call such a type a *singular type*. For example, in Smalltalk, the class **Symbol** consists of character-string objects such that no two objects have the same string. The advantage of a singular type is that comparison for state equality reduces to identity comparisons. The expense generally involves maintaining a collection of all instances of the type, and checking that no object creation or update operation causes the state of another instance of the type to be duplicated.

6.5 Inheritance and Type Hierarchies

Another frequent feature of object-oriented models in general is a typing scheme that includes some form of inheritance. *Inheritance* is a term that has come to describe many different mechanisms in which type definitions or implementations can be related to one another through a partial order. The basic notion is that we can modify type definitions incrementally by adding subtype definitions that somehow modify the original type. The combination of the supertype definition and the subtype modifications produces a completely defined new type.

Many variations on this idea have been proposed in the literature. We must be careful when discussing or comparing different languages with respect to the semantics of their subtyping mechanisms that the same kind of inheritance is being described. We say more on inheritance hierarchies in Section 8.2.

6.6 The Threshold Model

We present a threshold model that can be used as a yardstick to determine whether or not a given system should be considered to be an object-oriented database. These characteristics are essential to the spirit of object-oriented databases. It is likely that any real system would include many other features.

An object-oriented database must, at a minimum, satisfy the following requirements:

1. It must provide *database* functionality. As such, it should include all the essential features listed earlier in Section 5.1.

2. It must support *object identity*.

3. It must provide *encapsulation*. This encapsulation should be the basis on which all abstract objects are defined.

4. It must support objects with *complex state*. The state of an object may refer to other objects, which in turn may have incoming references from elsewhere.

Inheritance is not on our list. Although we believe that inheritance is a useful tool to support software reuse, and we would probably like any system that we used in practice to support some form of it, we do not think it is definitional. That is, an object-oriented database could exist without it.

We exclude inheritance from the threshold model for a number of reasons. First, the term is used in so many ways in the literature that it would be necessary to distinguish exactly which aspects of inheritance we were talking about. Second, many of the capabilities of inheritance mechanisms can be simulated with other language features. For example, the ability to add code to a subtype can be simulated with a facility that copies code bodies from the scope of one type definition to another. Third, we believe that encapsulation of storage is more fundamental and is what we require to cross the line from storage-oriented to object-oriented systems. Fourth, as we do not require typing or explicitly stored collections, it is difficult to talk about inheritance.

Typing also is not on the list. We admit a system in which each object records its own representation and its own methods. This approach can provide encapsulation, but since there is not necessarily any commonality among objects, it does not require types.

7. Further Concepts

Numerous additional features show up frequently in object-oriented systems. We shall discuss several of the more common ones in this section.

7.1 Dispatching

One of the unique aspects of object-oriented languages is the ability to overload message names by providing an implementation method for the message for more than one type along a path through the type lattice. When any such message is sent to an object, the lowest-level subtype of the receiver is used to determine which of the method definitions to use. In the single inheritance case (i.e., when the subtype graph is a tree), the method definition that is closest to the lowest-level subtype of the receiver is used. We call this case *simple dispatching*. In the multiple inheritance case (i.e., when the subtype graph is a DAG), some search method (e.g., left-to-right, depth-first) is used to locate a unique method to use.

Dispatching based on the type of the receiver is most common. However, other kinds of dispatching can be useful. For example, if a language allows multiple representations for a type, it would be necessary to dispatch to a particular method, depending on the representation of the receiver. Imagine an **Array** data type with two different implementations, sparse arrays and dense arrays. A *sparse array* is stored as a list of elements with their indices, whereas a *dense array* is a preallocated block of slots with one slot for every indexed position in the array. For each of the messages to an array, there would be two implementations, one for the sparse representation and one for the dense case. When a message was sent to an array, the

system would have to look at the representation and dispatch to the appropriate method at run-time.

The dispatching mechanism we have described can be generalized to depend on more than just the type of the receiver. It can depend on the types of some subset or all of the message arguments. We call this case *multiargument dispatching*. For example, we might have one method for the Add message if the first argument is a real and the second is an integer, and we might have a different method for the case in which they are both integers. Some LISP-based object extensions have this kind of dispatching. A problem with this generalization is that the total number of cases that would have to be described is the product of the numbers of possible types for each argument position on which dispatching depends.

Describing all of these cases is tedious. Also, there is no simple framework to organize them within the context of the type lattice (as there is in simple dispatching). We can imagine defining methods for some subset of the points in this cross-product space. Any case that was not specifically defined but that specialized one of the explicit cases would resolve to that case. This procedure has problems, however, as can be seen by the following example. If we had a method for **int X number** and a different one for **number X int**, it would not be clear which of these to use for a call with arguments of the form **int X int**.

Dispatching is a special case of a concept that we call *resolution*. Resolution is an interpretation process that happens at run-time to select a value from a (possibly ambiguous) set of values. For dispatching, the set of values is all the possible methods that could be used to implement a named message. Additional information from the context is used to make the selection. Similarly, we could have a reference to a set of object versions, and a resolution procedure could pick one based on the context—for example, the latest one, or one that belongs to the current configuration.

Dispatching does not necessarily entail an unbounded search at run-time. It is often possible to determine from the context at compile-time what method will be used. If we send a message to a variable of a leaf type in the hierarchy, no dispatching is required, because we know at run-time that the type of the value of the variable cannot be a subtype of the declared type. If the type hierarchy will change frequently, we can compile a *dispatch vector* into the code that avoids literally doing a search up the hierarchy. A dispatch vector is essentially a branch table or case statement based on an object's type. In these optimizations, however, it would be necessary to recompile the code whenever the type hierarchy was modified or a new method was inserted on some type.

It is possible to accommodate general *database operations* that are not associated with any single type in the same system that also supports polymorphism and dispatching. A database operation involves arguments of multiple types such that it would be unnatural to associate that operation with any one of the arguments. In this case, there is no receiver and no dispatching. It is just like a subroutine call.

7.2 Polymorphism of Code

In object-oriented systems, it is possible to have code that is polymorphic; that is, it will work on objects of different forms. We will distinguish two different kinds of polymorphism:

1. **Extension polymorphism.** Here, an operation is defined on two or more record structures with some common fields. As such, these record structures are said to be subtypes of each other. Consider **RecA** = (*a*: **A**, *b*: **B**) and **RecB** = (*a*: **A**, *b*: **B**, *c*: **C**, *d*: **D**), with **RecB** a subtype of **RecA**. Code that is defined to work on objects of type **RecA** will also work on objects of type **RecB** by simply ignoring the fields that are in the extension (e.g., *c* and *d*) that the subtype provides. This kind of polymorphism deals more with representations of objects than with their abstract protocol.

2. **General polymorphism.** This kind of polymorphism allows code that works on different abstract types. A code body can use an operation that will perform differently based on the type of its argument (see Section 7.1). The code body is written once and will perform correctly regardless of the types of the objects that it encounters.

In our roads example, we could use extension polymorphism to model a **Controlled_ Intersection**. An **Intersection** has a position field and a field holding a set of incoming **RoadSegments**. A **Controlled_Intersection** might extend this structure with a field that stored the traffic signal that controlled the traffic flow through the intersection. Any methods defined on the representation of **Intersections** will work on **Controlled_Intersections** by simply ignoring the extra field.

Our example also could make use of general polymorphism to construct a piece of code that calculated the total elapsed time for a route by summing the delay times for each of the route's components. This piece of code is easy to write if both the **RoadSegment** type and the **Intersection** type support the **delay** message that takes an object of the appropriate type and returns an integral number of minutes.

7.3 What Can Be Typed?

In an OODB, there are a variety of things with which to associate typing information. In programming languages, types are typically associated with identifiers: variables, named constants, procedure names. This information gives us the basis to reason about the types of larger syntactic units, such as expressions, at compile time. Having such typing information can prevent run-time errors that involve applying an operation to an argument of the wrong type. (Languages that prevent such an occurrence are called *strongly typed*.) Such information can sometimes also help with storage allocation and code optimization.

In an object-oriented language, it is common to associate types with objects themselves. This information can be used to make the language strongly typed, although the test is made at run-time (dynamic type checking) rather than at compile-time (static type checking). In the absence of types on variables (e.g., Smalltalk), this information can be used to do type checking (i.e., testing that messages are applied to arguments of the appropriate type). Note that type information *must* be associated with objects to do dynamic binding of messages to methods based on types.

OODBs can support both typing of objects and typing of variables, although the type systems for the two may not be the same. In Vbase, the type system for fields is more expressive than the type system for objects. For example, a field can be declared as a union of two types, but an object may not be created as an instance of a union type.

Another place to include type information is in object identifiers and references. Such type information might be used for efficiency reasons: The type of an object can be checked without the state of the object being accessed. It can also support type casting. For example, to treat a **Controlled_Intersection** as an **Intersection** object, the database might convert a reference of **Controlled_Intersection** type to a reference of **Intersection** type. Access to the **Controlled_Intersection** object through the **Intersection** reference would mask the part of the state of a **Controlled_Intersection** not in common with **Intersection**.

7.4 What Makes Objects Persist?

A fundamental question about the persistence of objects is, *How is persistence indicated*? That is, what makes an object persistent or transitory? Different systems make different choices on this issue, thereby having fundamental effects on the design of the data and schema languages.

Some choices for the point at which to indicate persistence follow:

1. **When an object is created**. There can be some parameter associated with all creation operations or with a pair of creation operations for each type (e.g., **create_persistent_array** and **create_temporary_array**) that indicates whether to create a persistent or a temporary object of the type.

2. **When an object is connected to some persistent structure**. Sometimes, there is a persistent root object (e.g., the database object). Any object that is reachable from this persistent root is also persistent. In this scheme, an object can be made persistent at any time in its lifetime, and can later lose its persistence.

3. **When an object is stored in persistent storage**. Here, there is a storage space that is defined to be persistent, and every variable names a location in persistent storage or in regular storage. Any object that is written into a persistent variable becomes persistent as long as it remains in the variable.

4. **When an object is issued an explicit message to make itself persistent**. This operation coerces the receiver to be a persistent object.

5. **When the object is instantiated from a persistent type**. Some types are designated as persistent, whereas others are designated as temporary. Any instance of a persistent type is automatically persistent. The E language [Carey, 1989; 7.3] uses this approach; as a result, one often maintains two parallel hierarchies, one with the temporary types and one with corresponding persistent types.

8. The Reference Model

The threshold model set forth minimal requirements for a system to be called an object-oriented DBMS. A system with only those features, however, would not give powerful support for developing data-based applications. Each of the systems we include in the chapter on object-oriented database systems has capabilities well beyond those required by the threshold model. In this section, we set out a reference model for OODBMSs, which we think has the level of capabilities that a competitive commercial product might support.

It is not our purpose to proclaim the reference model as the "standard" for object-oriented DBMSs. Rather, we use it to introduce a variety of features that will be common in future OODBMSs, to show how the features interact, and to discuss alternatives to those features. We state here briefly what the features are, but leave it for later subsections to elaborate on features not discussed already.

The reference model subsumes the threshold model. Thus, it supports complex objects, identity, and encapsulation, as well as essential data management features. Beyond those capabilities, it adds the following:

1. **Structured representations for objects**. The threshold model requires that the state of an object be shielded from direct access by encapsulation with the operations for the object. The reference model goes beyond that in allowing the state of an object to be a compound data structure, with nested application of constructors.

2. **Persistence by reachability.** The reference model stipulates that persistence is by reachability from a distinguished root object in each database. We require that objects of any type be able to persist—that is, persistence is *orthogonal* to typing.

3. **Typing of objects and variables**. Every object instance knows its type (it can respond to a message asking for its type). Further, every variable and argument in a method definition has a type, as do the slots in data structures used for representations of objects. We distinguish the *declared type* of a variable from its *immediate type* at any point in execution: the type of the object that is the current value of the variable. We want static type checking of methods to ensure that, at run-time, the immediate type of a variable is always a subtype of its declared type. (Here, we consider a type to be a subtype of itself.) We also want to ensure that every message is sent to an object of a type that understands the message. Further, each type definition associates input and output types with all its messages—the *signature* for the message—and all methods in the implementation for the type are checked for compliance with the corresponding message signature.

4. **Three hierarchies**. The reference model supports three separate hierarchies of groupings of objects: a specification hierarchy of types, an implementation hierarchy of representations and methods, and a classification hierarchy of explicit collections of objects.

5. **Polymorphism**. The reference model supports polymorphism through dispatching. The actual method executed at run-time for a message expression is dependent on the type of the receiver of the message—not that this dynamic binding of messages to methods does not conflict with static type checking. In an expression such as *message1(V)*, static type checking determines that *message1* is part of the protocol of the declared type T of V; hence, *message1* is part of the protocol of any subtype of T. However, type T, and its subtypes, may use different methods to implement *message1*, so the correct method must be determined (in general) dynamically from the immediate type of T.

6. **Collections**. The reference model has built-in types for aggregate objects, such as sets, lists, and arrays. These types are distinct from the constructors for object reps, although those constructors could certainly be used to implement aggregate types. All set-based querying is against explicit collection objects; the reference model does not automatically provide the current extension of a type. Collections can also be *keyed*, which means elements are distinguishable by some part of their states.

7. **Name spaces**. The reference model provides persistent variables of any type. These variable names are made available in a structured name space (e.g., a hierarchical name space).

8. **Queries and indexes**. The reference model requires a query language that is of high level and is amenable to optimization. It also requires that indexes can be created on collections that the query-evaluation system can use. Queries are rooted at persistent variables in the name space, which can hold aggregate or regular objects.

9. **Relationships**. Named relationships are supported beyond just one-way links.

10. **Versions**. The reference model provides for accessing versions of an object's state, and for assembling configurations of consistent versions of objects.

8.1 Structured Representations and Constructors

Each type defines a *representation* that is used to store the state of its instances. The representation of a type T is a data structure that is available only to the methods of T. Creating an instance of a type allocates an instance of that type's representation and then initializes it according to the parameters in the call to the create operation. We shall call the instance of the representation for an object the *rep* of the object.

The rep may contain references to other objects, but the other objects are not considered to be a part of the rep. They are distinct objects with their own identity that can be freely referenced from other objects. For example, the **RoadSegment** type might define its representation to be a record. This record might have a field called **inRoad** that contains a reference to the object that represents the road in which the segment lies. The record is the rep for a **RoadSegment** object, but the referenced **Road** object is not part of the rep.

To allow more complex structures, we distinguish objects from values. An object possesses the ability to be referenced from any context, whereas a value is private to some rep. If we define a rep as

Define type RoadSegment
  rep: record (inRoad: **Road**
      segmentShape: **value Arc**
      start: Intersection ...)

then the **segmentShape** field of the rep refers to a value. That is, the value that fills this field cannot be referenced from any context other than the **RoadSegment** rep that is pointing to it. We can, therefore, rely on this fact, and we need never be concerned with the possibility that other objects might contain references to these values. Therefore, if we delete an object, it is always possible to delete any values that it includes without causing dangling references.

This scheme creates two address spaces, one based on object identifiers and another based on virtual memory addresses. In this way, the rep is that part of an object's state that is available only to the object's methods, even if it consists of several pieces. These rep pieces could be referenced from one another by addresses from the private rep address space.

Changes to the rep do not necessarily reflect a corresponding change in the abstract state of an object. An object's abstract state changes only if there exists an operation to observe the change. For example, if we use an **Ordered_Set** as the representation for **Set**, an insertion into a **Set** might change the ordering present in the rep.

Although the presence of the inserted element would be visible from the **Set** interface, the new ordering of the **Ordered_Set** rep would not be visible.

The reference model provides several built-in type constructors for producing structured reps. They are **set**, **array**, and **tuple**. A **set** is an unordered collection of homogeneous objects, an **array** is an indexed collection of homogeneous objects, and a **tuple** is an indexed (by name) collection of heterogeneous objects. We think that at least these three rep constructors are necessary, because it is difficult to encode any one in terms of the other two. For example, representing an array with sets and tuples involves storing an explicit field giving ordering information. This representation is slow to access and difficult to update.

8.2   Hierarchies

Type hierarchies play an important role in object-oriented programming systems. The notion of inheritance pervades the literature of this field. It allows for incremental modification of type definitions, thereby providing capability for such things as extension of previous definitions and reuse of code. These modifications to types are limited to those that can be made without disturbing dependencies between the preexisting types and programs that use them. For example, adding a message to a subtype has no effect on previous definitions or preexisting code. Subtyping captures these nondisruptive changes.

We believe that past discussions of this notion contain many variations that are not always clearly distinguished from one another. The many design variations for inheritance mechanisms all can be traced to sound methodological bases. We need to understand the goals of a given design and to select carefully among the possible features that an inheritance mechanism might have.

It can also be the case that certain desirable features for a type hierarchy do not combine in a consistent way. Consider the following example. We can list four features of a subtyping mechanism that all seem to be desirable, yet, as we shall show, it is not possible to combine them in a single type system. The four features are

1. Substitutability
2. Static type checking
3. Mutability
4. Specialization via constraints

The following paragraphs will define these concepts more precisely.

To say that B is a subtype of A typically means that any context that is expecting an instance of type A must also accept an instance of type B. We call this the principle of *substitutability*. For example, a function f that is defined on an input argument of type A must legally accept an instance of type B. That is, for the following three definitions:

B is subtype of A
define $f(a:A)$
declare $x:B$

$f(x)$ should be allowed. Assignments of expressions of type B to variables of type A must also be allowed.

By *static type checking*, we mean that all reasoning based on information expressed on types is checkable at compile-time. In other words, there is no need to check type compatibility at run-time. This property is clearly desirable, since it means that there is no need to insert expensive run-time checks in the resulting code, and also the coder can be assured that a certain class of errors can never occur. Static type checking is a simple kind of formal verification of programs.

It is possible to interact with an object only via its available messages or operations. We call the set of operations that are defined for instances of type T, Ops(T). Intuitively, an object supports a state that can be observed by some subset of its operations. We call the operations that report on an object's state *observers* or *reporters,* and denote the set of such operations $O_r(T)$. Some types might also support operations that will alter the state of its instances; we denote the set of mutators $O_m(T)$. We assume that reporters and mutators are disjoint.

An operation m is a mutator for type T if, for some instance x of T and for some r in O_r, it is possible to execute the following code fragment such that, at the end, a is not equal to b.

$a = r(x); m(x); b = r(x);$

That is, if m is to be a mutator, it must be possible to observe its effect on some object. A type system incorporates *mutability* if it is possible to construct a type T with some operation that is a mutator.

It is often useful to allow subtypes to be defined by restricting some aspect of the supertype. This is a reflection of the fact that some models [Hammer, 1981; 2.3] use a class hierarchy to express application-specific constraints. If **RoadSegments** have directions that can be **one-way-SE**, **one-way-ES**, or **two-way**, we would like to define **OneWaySegment** as a subtype of **RoadSegment** with direction **one-way-SE** or **one-way-ES**.

Constraints of this kind can be viewed as a restriction on the parameters of the operations of the subtype. For example, the type **RoadSegment** and the type **OneWaySegment** would have corresponding operations to set their direction with the following signatures:

set_direction (*S*: RoadSegment, dir: {one-way-SE, one-way-ES, two-way})

set_direction (*OS*: OneWaySegment, dir: {one-way-SE, one-way-ES})

Assume that Ops(*T*: Type) is a function that returns the legal operations (i.e., messages) that are defined on the given type *T*. Also, assume that messages can be redefined (overloaded) on a subtype. *Specialization via constraints* happens whenever the following is permitted:

B subtype_of *A* and *T* subtype_of *S* and
f(. . . *b*: *T* . . .) returns *r*: *R* in Ops(*B*) and
f(. . . *b*: *S* . . .) returns *r*: *R* in Ops(*A*) and

That is, specialization via constraints occurs whenever the operation redefinition on a subtype constrains one of the arguments to be from a smaller value set than the corresponding operation on the supertype.

All four of these properties seem to be desirable, and various languages and databases have incorporated one or more of them. We submit, however, that it is impossible to have all four of them in the same type system. This conflict can be illustrated with the following example, in which the type **OneWaySegment** is defined by specialization from **RoadSegment**, as before.

S: RoadSegment
OS: OneWaySegment
. . .
S := OS;
. . .
set_direction (*S*, two-way);

The assignment statement must be allowed if **O n e W a y S e g m e n t** is a subtype of **RoadSegment**, and if we have substitutability and mutability. The **set_direction** operation would type check at compile-time, since the signature for **s e t _ d i r e c t i o n** on type **RoadSegment** matches this invocation. Of course, since a **OneWaySegment** is being passed to the **set_direction** operation, the actual invocation will fail even though the compile-time check determined that it was all right.

We observe that any three of the four features seem to work just fine. No one of them is obviously the one that must be discarded, but in any type system, at least one of them must be sacrificed to achieve consistency with the others.

We respond to this observation in the reference model by reducing our ability to do static type checking. We do, however, retain the ability to do some compile-time checking and to separate those constraints that must be checked at run-time into a separate hierarchy (the classification hierarchy).

In fact, the reference model distinguishes three separate hierarchies. Each of them is responsible for a separate function that is often folded into a single subtyping mechanism in existing languages. We believe that separating them allows us to have a cleaner semantics. The three hierarchies are

1. Specification hierarchy: compatibility of predicates

2. Implementation hierarchy: code sharing

3. Classification hierarchy: subsets and constraints

By *hierarchy*, we mean a partial order (e.g., a DAG conveniently represents this). The specification hierarchy expresses consistency among type specifications in such a way as to allow for substitution of instances of a subtype in contexts that are expecting an instance of a supertype. To achieve this property, we allow subtypes to add behavior only to their supertypes. They cannot restrict the values of the input arguments to any of the methods of the supertype. In this way, the specification hierarchy supports static type checking.

The *implementation hierarchy* provides for code sharing among types. It is a pragmatic mechanism that supports the software-engineering principle of code reuse. It allows some of the operations on a type to be inherited (i.e., reused) and others to be redefined. The redefined methods overload the name of the operations, and the proper code body is selected at run-time based on the type of a distinguished argument. Redefinition of operations allows us to reuse what is similar between an old type and a new type, and to modify the behavior of that part of an old type definition that must be different. This hierarchy need not mirror the specification hierarchy.

Note that the strict inheritance of operation signatures in the specification hierarchy permits formulating queries over a set that consists of instances of a type and its subtypes. If the query restricts itself to the operations on the type, those operations are sure to be defined on the subtypes. However, the same cannot be said for implementation. Thus, structural query (on the representation of objects) over the same set could well be ill-defined, as we do not dictate that a type and its subtypes stand in any particular relationship in the implementation hierarchy. Thus, instances of a subtype could have a structure radically different from that of instances of the type.

The *classification hierarchy* describes collections of objects and the containment relationship among these collections. The collections can be defined by enumeration or by a predicate. For example, **Dangerous_ Intersections** might be defined (by enumeration) as the subset of **Intersections** that are deemed dangerous by the safety council. **Boulevards** are defined (by a predicate) as a subset of **Roads** such that the **roadType** property is equal to **boulevard**.

Once we have defined a containment hierarchy of these collections or classifications, we might want to constrain the members of the collections by a set of predicates that must be maintained over the membership. As an example of predicates as constraints, we might have classes **Segments** and **OneWaySegments**, both of which contain **RoadSegment** objects. Placement of an object in **OneWaySegments** is done explicitly; but once done, the **direction** value of the object must always be **one-way-SE** or **one-way-ES**. This constraint must be checked when an object is moved into **OneWay- Segments**, and every time the object is updated, until it is removed from the class **OneWaySegments**. (Note that objects can change classes, but we do not allow objects to change types.) An example of predicates as characterizing class membership would be if all elements of **Segments** with direction equal to **one-way-SE** or **one-way-ES** were automatically made members of **OneWaySegments**, and a **RoadSegment** left **OneWaySegments** if its direction changed to **two-way**.

In a classification, certain updates might be disallowed. For example, the collection **Boulevards** is a subset of the collection **Roads**. We might wish to constrain the **segmentList** property for any member of the **Boulevards** collection to only take **two-way RoadSegments**.

8.3 Collections

Collections play an important role in object-oriented databases. A *collection* is a way of aggregating related objects. Query (i.e., search) is performed over some type of collection. We must determine how collections fit into a given object-oriented data model. Are the collections treated as objects, or are they some metalinguistic construct? If they are objects, they must be described by some type. What is the nature of the types that describe collections?

Often, the type of a collection is related to the type of the objects that it is allowed to contain.

Thus, the type **Set_of_Intersections** is different from the type **Set_of_RoadSegments**. This distinction is often captured by *parameterized types* (see Section 10.1). In our example, the two set types share a protocol (i.e., set of messages) that is of a similar form except for the types of their parameters. That is, **Set[Intersection]** supports the message *insert (si: Set[Intersection], i: Intersection)*, whereas **Set[RoadSegment]** supports the analogous message *insert (sr: Set[RoadSegment], r: RoadSegment)*. We say that **Set[Intersections]** and **Set[RoadSegments]** are two different parameterizations of the parameterized type **Set[T: Type]**. As such, a given set of **RoadSegments** would be an instance of the type **Set[RoadSegments]**.

Another question that arises concerning collections is: When are two collections equal? In some models, two collections are *equal* if they contain the same values. In others, it is possible to have two collections that contain the same values but that are, nevertheless, different objects. This distinction is often useful for more precise modeling. If we have two trucks that are always driven by the same set of people, we might like to have the two truck objects refer to (i.e., share) the same set of drivers. Adding or deleting drivers from this set through one of the truck objects will be visible through the other truck object. This situation models the constraint that these sets will always be constrained to be the same. Alternatively, we might like to have two different set objects that represent the drivers of the two trucks. These sets might serendipitously contain the same members at some point in time; however, we might like to be able to ask whether the two sets are the same and to have the answer be no. This situation models the fact that the two sets are independent.

There are other kinds of equality that can be defined for sets. We say that two objects are *identically equal* if they are, in fact, the same entity (i.e., they cannot ever be told apart). *Shallow equality* holds for two sets that are themselves not identically equal but whose members are identically equal. *Deep equality* holds for two sets that are themselves not identically equal but for which, if we were to traverse recursively the structures that the elements of these sets define to their leaves, we would find those leaves to be identically equal.

In some data models, any denotable collection can be used to form a query; in others, there are distinguished collection types that are used to construct queries. An example of this resticted class of collections is relations in the relational model.

Keys still have a place in object-oriented databases. A *key* is a property or set of properties that uniquely identifies an object within a set. The key is not something that is associated with a type, since the uniqueness of the key is guaranteed for only a given aggregation of objects. The reference model includes keyed collections.

8.4   Name Spaces

As mentioned in Section 5.2, most databases support names for data items. These names are in effect "persistent variables": variables whose values endure within the database system from one session to the next. These named items serve as the starting points in query expressions. However, in conventional database systems, the kinds of data items that can be named are limited. For example, in relational systems, the only items with persistent names are relations and virtual relations (views). Tuples and scalar values do not have persistent names, typically. Although tuple or column variables may appear in data manipulation statements, and the interface to the application program can support cursors, these variables are transitory and do not persist past the end of a user session. (The effect of a scalar variable can be simulated with a 1-column, 1-tuple relation, although that is a lot of mechanism for simply remembering an integer.)

Another limitation on persistent variables or names in relational systems is that declaring a name is bound up with defining a type. One "create relation" statement, from a programming-language view, simultaneously defines a type, declares a variable of that type, and creates an instance of that type associated with the variable. (A notable exception is Pascal/R, where a relation type is defined, then multiple variables are declared of that type, and those variables may take on different relations as their values at different times.) Finally, in most database systems, a "database" constitutes a single domain of names. Within a single database, different users may not reuse a single name.

For the reference model, we posit persistent names in the form of *database variables*. A database variable may be declared of any type, and there may be any number of variables of the same type. In our roads example, we might want a database variable **HeadquartersInt** of type **Intersection** that holds the object that represents the intersection nearest MSS headquarters. Another variable, **GarageInt**, might hold the **Intersection** nearest to the garage where MSS vehicles are housed. As we describe in the next section, database variables are the *starting points* for queries against the database. Most often, queries will start from database variables that

contain collections—for example, a variable **UnderConstr** that contains a set of **RoadSegments** with construction work underway. However, a query could as well start from an object that is a collection. For example, a query could begin from **GarageInt** and then perhaps inquire about the **RoadSegments** that enter the intersection.

We also specify in the reference model that the name spaces for database variables be structured so as to permit control on sharing and visibility of names. Thus, a user, application, or group can have a private name space of database variables that can duplicate variables names in other private name spaces. Public name spaces can exist with various degrees of visibility. Some may be visible to all users of the database, whereas others may be shared with a limited set of users.

Both GemStone and Vbase support structural name spaces. GemStone supports a list of symbol tables for each user, some of which can be shared with other users. Vbase provides a rich set of facilities in the type-definition language (which is also a "name-declaration language") for scoping and sharing of names.

8.5   Querying and Indexing

Queries are a high-level specification of a set of objects of interest from the database. They are usually specified in a language that allows for describing what must be retrieved without requiring a statement of how to go about doing it. The query processor figures out the most efficient plan for the retrieval. Query languages (i.e., fourth-generation languages) and their associated optimizers have been one of the major achievements of the relational approach.

Queries in the object-oriented model can be cast as expressions over special methods defined on the types that are defined for aggregating objects (e.g., **Set**, **List**, **Tree**). As a simple example, the type **Set** would define a method

Select (S1: **Set**(T), P: Predicate) **returns** S2: Set(T).

The predicate is a function of the form **P: T -> Boolean**. The output argument **S2** is a subset of all the elements of the first input argument **S1** such that they satisfy the Predicate P. Notice that it is possible to pass a function (i.e., the predicate) as an argument, and that these functions in no way violate the encapsulation of the type. **Select**(S, P) = { s | s in S and P(s) }. The **Select** operation would be part of a query language, and is similar to the **Select** operation in the relational algebra.

Why is querying in an object-oriented model any different from querying in the relational model? As mentioned, we can construct an algebra for expressing queries over sets of objects. One problem involves the optimization of these expressions. In the relational model, queries are cast in terms of well-defined operators over very simple structures (i.e., normalized relations). In the object-oriented models, queries can involve operators for newly defined abstract data types. Each new type, by introducing operations, creates a new algebra whose properties are unknown to the query optimizer. When the algebraic properties of these new operators are not known, it is difficult to transform query expressions into alternative equivalent forms.

Another problem involves the information hiding presented by abstract types. Even if we can produce transformed versions of queries, we need to be able to determine the relative costs of processing these query expressions. Processing costs are typically dependent on the underlying storage structures for the objects and their aggregates. For example, if a given set S is implemented by a B-tree on some attribute A, then retrievals over S on attribute A probably will be relatively inexpensive. Knowing about the existence of such storage structures seems to be a violation of encapsulation. Although encapsulation is a principle of good software structuring that is important to preserve between application-level modules, the query optimizer is a trusted component of the database system and can be allowed to look inside an abstract data type and to determine the implementation. There is still a question about how this can be managed effectively if the implementation can involve arbitrary data structures and algorithms.

A query language for an object-oriented database might be based on or be compiled into an object-oriented algebra. This algebra would consist of a set of operations that could be performed on aggregate types, and a set of operators that could be used to form predicates over abstract types based on the abstract properties defined by these types. An example of such an algebra that we will adopt in our reference model is the following:

Operations on Sets:
    Select (C, p) -> { x | x in C and p(x) }
    Image (C, f) -> { f(x) | x in C }
    Merge (C1, C2, f(x: C1, y: C2),
      p(x: C1, y: C2)) ->
        { f(x,y) | x in C1, y in C2, p(x, y) }
    Union (C1, C2) -> { x | x in C1 Or x in C2 }
    Intersection (C1, C2) -> { x | x in C1 And
      x in C2 }
    Difference (C1, C2) -> { x | x in C1 And
      Not (x in C2) }

Predicate Formers:
    For_all (S, P) = true if (for_all s in S) P(s), otherwise false
    For_some (S, P) = true if (there_exists_an s in S) P(s), otherwise false
    And, Or, Not (Boolean connectives)
    =, <, >, . . . (Comparison operators)
    x in S
    S1 in S2

Merge is similar to the join in the relational algebra. It is exactly the same when *C1* and *C2* are sets of tuples, and if f is a function of two tuples that produces the concatenation of those two tuples as a result. Although the gestalt of an object-oriented model is to use type definitions whose complete behavior is specified in advance, the **Merge** operation can be used to compute relationships between objects that were not prespecified.

Suppose we have two maps that give adjacent regions—say, Boston and Brookline—and some intersections at the boundary are modeled by two **Intersection** objects, one in each collection of intersections for each map. Call the two collections **BostonInts** and **BrooklineInts**. Suppose that a boundary **Intersection** only contains the incoming road segments that appear on its corresponding map. For each intersection that appears on both maps, suppose we want to create a single **Intersection** object with all the road segments from the two equivalent **Intersection** objects in **BostonInts** and **BrooklineInts**. We can do this task with **Merge**.

We will combine intersections by finding pairs that are at the same location. Suppose the offset between the coordinate systems of the Boston map and the Brookline map is 770 units in the x direction and 15 units in the y direction. Then, for a section predicate we can use the function,

    p(i1, i2) == **plus(coords(***i2***), (770,15)) =
      coords(***i1***)**

assuming a **Coordinate** object interprets **plus** as elementwise sum, and (770, 15) is a literal. For the combining function we use

    f(*i1***, *i2***) == newIntersect(coords(***i1***),
      Union(segs(***i1***), segs(***i2***)))**

where **newIntersect** creates a new **Intersection** object from a coordinate position and a set of road segments.

We can then get the set of new intersections we want with

    **Merge(BostonInts, BrooklineInts,
      f(***i1***, *i2***), p(***i1***, *i2***))**

Note that the new **Intersections** in the result of the **Merge** will have coordinate positions relative to the Boston map.

Not all of these operators are primitive, since some of them can be expressed in terms of the others. For example,

> **Image** (S, f: S -> T) =
>   **Select** (T, **lambda** (t)
>   **For_some** (S, **lambda** (s) f(s) = t))

We include the larger set of operators because these operators' existence simplifies query optimization. We can use the wider set in transformation rules to simplify the matching of subexpressions.

Query optimization is an important aspect of a query facility. One approach takes expressions in an algebra such as the one we have proposed and applies transformation rules on them to obtain equivalent expressions. If we can find expressions that are both equivalent and cheaper to evaluate, then we have improved our situation.

It is possible to discover transformation rules that can generally be applied to query expressions. Like query optimization in relational systems, we can use these transformations to get new query expressions that have lower expected costs. The following three rules are examples:

1. **Select** (S1, **lambda** (s) s.p **in** S2) =
   Image (S2, **inverse** (p))

2. **Union** (**Select** (S, P1), **Select** (S, P2)) =
   Union (**Select** (S, P1 or P2))

3. **Select** (S1, **lambda** (s) s.p1.p2 **in** S3) =
   Select (S1, **lambda** (s) s.p1 **in**
        Select (S2, **lambda** (s) s.p2 **in** S3))

These rules depend on only the fact that all aggregates support the operations **Select**, **Image**, and **Union**, and that there are well-defined operators that support the notion of properties. For a property p defined on a type T with a value of type S, these operators are **get_p:** $T \rightarrow S$ and **set_p:** $T \times S \rightarrow T$. We also know other characteristics of these operators; for example, **get_p** has no side effects.

As an example, consider the sets Trucks and Drivers and the following query.

> **Select** [Trucks, **lambda** (t) t.driver_of.name = "Fred"]

The naive way to process this query is to take each truck, to follow the *driver_of* property to get a driver, and to follow the *name* property on this driver to get a string. For each truck t that results in the string "Fred," place t in the result set.

If we know that the property *drives* on drivers is the inverse of the property *driver_of* on trucks, we can use transformation rule 1 to transform the original query into the following query:

> **Image** [**Select** [Drivers, **lambda** (d) d.name = "Fred"], drives]

Furthermore, if the set of drivers that have name equal to "Fred" is supported by an index (i.e., the drivers can be located quickly), then the second query probably will be less expensive to process than the first.

How do we know whether one expression is less expensive to evaluate than another? One way is to notice that one expression uses an auxiliary access path such as an index, whereas the other does not. An index is like a precomputed query. By looking up the desired answer in the index, we find the objects (tuples) that would have yielded that answer, thereby eliminating the need to do a search. Indexes for abstract types are based on the return values of messages. An index on the **Position** message for **Intersections** would tell us which **Intersection** objects in some set of **Intersections** would yield a given value for the **Position** message. Notice that the index is associated with a given set. Indexing is an implementation alternative for set types.

An index can always be constructed for any message that returns a value. Maintaining the correctness of an index when the state of an object that is being indexed is allowed to change presents a problem. It requires that we know all possible changes that could affect the result of the message. In general, it is possible to index on any message whose method does not go beyond an object's representation. That is, as long as the bodies of all methods for a type do not depend on any object outside the representation of that object, we can successfully maintain an index on that type of object, since the events that could affect the index are limited.

As an example, suppose that we have a set of **Intersections** whose reps are records with a field called **position** that holds a **Coordinate** value. The type **Intersection** defines a *positionOf* message that returns a copy of the **Coordinate** value that is in the **position** field. Further suppose that we construct an index on the *positionOf* message for the set of **Intersections**. As long as the **Coordinate** value is part of the rep of an **Intersection**, and can be changed only by messages to an **Intersection** object, we can place triggers in the methods for **Intersection** messages. Those triggers will update the index on any change that affects the result of the *positionOf* message. Note that, if the position field were a **Coordinate** *object*, with other references possible, there could be messages that changed the **Coordinate** object that did not go through an **Intersection** object. Thus, triggers on methods for **Intersection** would not suffice for index maintenance.

8.6 Relationships

A *relationship* is a named correspondence between objects. Much work in data modeling has focused on understanding the many types of relationships that naturally surface in any application. Relationships are one of the most fundamental parts of any data model. From one point of view, they are what distinguish databases from file systems.

The most common type is a binary relationship that relates two objects. For example, the *inRoad* relationship is a binary relationship that relates a **RoadSegment** to a **Road**. Notice that this relationship has some implied directionality. That is, we can use the *inRoad* relationship to determine a **Road** given a **RoadSegment**, but we cannot use it to go the other way. If we draw an arrow between the **RoadSegment** and the **Road** in the direction of this relationship, we call the object at the tail of the arrow the *subject* of the relationship, and the object at the head of the arrow the *object* of the relationship (as in English syntax).

To move from a **Road** to a **RoadSegment**, we would need another binary relationship (perhaps called *segments_of*) that relates a **Road** to a set of **RoadSegments**. We call this pair of relationships *inverses*. Some models allow the type definer to declare an inverse relationship between two relationships, and then the system maintains the correspondence between them. An update to one side of the relationship automatically gets reflected in the other. That is, if we change a **RoadSegment's** Road, the value of the *segments_of* relationship for that Road will be updated automatically.

This example also illustrates the distinction between *single-valued* and *multivalued* *relationships*. Some relationships (e.g., *inRoad*) can be constrained to have a single object as their value, whereas others (e.g., *segments_of*) can be allowed to have a set of objects as their value. Again, these predeclared constraints can be enforced by the database system.

Symmetric relationships are inherently bidirectional. That is, a symmetric relationship such as *spouse_of* can be applied to either party and will yield the other. Often the term *relationship* is used to mean symmetric relationship, whereas the directional relationship is termed a *property*.

Note that a relationship or property is an abstract idea that should be specifiable

independently of the way in which it is stored. Therefore, we should not confuse relationships with slots or instance variables (à la Smalltalk). Slots are a reflection of the *stored state* of an object, whereas relationships express something about the *abstract state* of an object. For example, a **RoadSegment** might have a property called *length* that is not stored in the underlying representation. Instead, this value is computed from the positions of the start and end intersections, which are stored. It is impossible to distinguish this *derived property* from one that is stored.

Another question that arises in modeling relationships is whether or not properties and relationships are objects themselves. If relationships are objects, then there must be types that describe the behavior or message protocol of properties. Also, if they are objects, then it is possible to ascribe all of the characteristics of objects in general to properties. One of these characteristics is that objects can have properties. Thus, if properties are objects, they can have properties of their own. This is useful for semantic accuracy to express facts such as *Joe advises Fred since June 1*. Here there is a relationship between Joe and Fred called *advises*, and the *advises* property has a property called *started_on* with a value of June 1.

As objects, however, properties have some unusual semantics. For example, it might not be possible to instantiate a relationship object apart from some base object to which it attaches. If the type **RoadSegment** defines an *inRoad* property, it makes no sense to create an instance of the *inRoad* property without first creating the **RoadSegment** to which it is anchored. Property instances are implicitly created when an instance of the base type is created. When an object is deleted, any properties that are attached to that object are also deleted.

The subject and the object of a given relationship type are in some sense a key for the set of all such relationship instances, because it is impossible to have two relationship instances of the same name with the same subject and object.

Although relationships appear to be like ordered pairs, it is not possible to implement them as pair objects, where one position in the pair refers to the subject and the other refers to the object. Although this implementation allows us to ask the relationship instance for the subject or the object, it does not allow us to navigate from the subject to the object, the most common kind of access. This is because, unless the set of all such relationships (extent) is maintained, it is not possible to look through all instances of the named relationship to find the one that has the subject of interest as its first component.

Normally, we implement properties by embedding a pointer in the subject. It is also possible to implement a property by embedding the object of the property inside the subject. This technique does not allow shared references.

Complex objects are objects that are built out of other objects. For example, a van is really an object that contains an engine, four fenders, a chassis, and a body (among other things). An engine is an object that contains things such as a carburetor (primitive technology), some pistons, and a crankshaft. The relationship between the parts and the whole can be modeled with a special relationship called *contains*. The *contains* relationship might have some special semantics; for example, deleting the whole might also delete the parts, or locking the container might generate locks on the parts.

Some models support n-way relationships as a way of modeling a relationship among a group of more than two objects. If a **Delivery** is made to a **Client** by an **Agent**, the relationship among all three of these objects might be modeled by a single relationship type, possibly called *delivers*. An n-way relationship can be diagrammed as an n-pointed star.

Our reference model will support the notion of named, binary relationships such that they support navigation from either direction (i.e., subject to object and object to subject). They are private objects (conceptually like pairs) in the sense that there can be no reference to them from another object other than the subject and the object. They must be many-to-many in that they can relate an object to a group of objects (also in both directions).

8.7 Versions

We often find discussions about versions and configuration management in the context of object-oriented databases. This has less to do with the model than with the kinds of applications for which the model was developed. As we have mentioned earlier, object-oriented databases have emerged largely as a response to the problems of design applications. These same applications require support for managing the evolution of objects over time. Version management addresses these needs, but this work might also be cast in terms of other models (e.g., relations).

Versions are a way to record the history of an object. In our reference model, an object is a partially ordered set of versions. Consider an instance x of the type T. Each version of x is a read-only value of type T. The object x is actually a set of values of type T, which we shall call a *version set*. References to this version set typically select a single version.

Version sets impose a partial order on the individual versions so that they can accommodate alternative states of an object. This capability is useful when two or more designers decide that they want to create competing versions of the same object for experimental reasons. A given version can, therefore, have several successors as well as several predecessors. The latter case is used for merging competing versions into a single agreed-on combined form. Given a version v, it should always be possible to ask for its successor(s) (unless v is a leaf version) and its predecessor(s) (unless v is the root version).

The interaction between versions and the referencing mechanisms of the language provide interesting design problems. Most often, a program wants to refer to an object without having to worry about which version of the state is required. A context can be set up once such that the dereferencing mechanism will always retrieve the correct version with respect to the current context. A context can be established globally, or it can be established for each reference.

The reference model supports two kinds of references: static and dynamic. A *static* reference always points to the same version within a version set for all time. A *dynamic* reference can point to different versions within a version set at different points in time. A dynamic version is a query over the members of the version set. An example of a dynamic reference would be a Latest-Version-Reference. As new versions are added to the version set, the referent of a dynamic reference can change. That is, dereferencing it at one point in time can give results different from those obtained when dereferencing takes place at another time.

Another problem in managing versions arises when we access several objects at different times. It is possible for a program to obtain versions of these objects that never existed together. They are each snapshots of the object at times that might be inconsistent with one another. This situation is especially likely to occur with dynamic references, since the referents to a set of references might diverge seriously as time passes. We allow for the specification of a global time parameter that essentially qualifies all subsequently dereferenced references. This time parameter is a time interval that is implicitly appended to all references. It limits the versions in a version set that qualify as possible results. For example, a Latest-Version-Reference that is evaluated with the global interval of last week will return a version different from that returned by the evaluation of the same reference with the global interval set to this week.

A selection of a set of mutually consistent versions is normally referred to as a *configuration.* In a program-development environment, a configuration is one version of each of the modules in a system such that that set of versions produces a consistent system. The problem of selecting this set of versions, either manually or automatically, is referred to as *configuration management.*

The problem of automatic propagation of values is related to the problem of version and configuration management. Adding a new version of a component of a larger object might cause a new version of the larger object to be generated. This information propagation or triggering is called *percolation.* The ability to support percolation in our version mechanism is related to configuration management. By percolating changes up the containment hierarchy, we automatically get new configurations that record the state of the container over time. In the reference model, we allow for the definition of properties that support percolation (e.g., *part_of*). This percolation happens at transaction-commit-time. That is, all the new versions created by the transactions are installed at one time, and the resulting percolation creates a single new version of the container.

Transaction managers typically allow one writer at a time. Long transactions (e.g., as seen in design applications) often require multiple writers. A version mechanism could be used by a concurrency-control manager to handle conflicts caused by two transactions. If transaction $T1$ changes the value of x, when transaction $T2$ attempts either to read or to write x, it can be allowed to do so by forking alternative versions for all objects written by $T2$. This technique delays the effect of the conflict. It is reasonable if the conflict is not likely to cause inconsistencies that cannot be negotiated later. The philosophy behind this type of concurrency-control mechanism is a "pay-me-later" scheme that requires that the users sort out the inconsistencies during the process of merging those alternatives. The normal scheme that causes transactions that would cause a conflict to wait or be aborted might be characterized as a "pay-me-now" scheme.

9. Differences from Previous Models

The relational model is well accepted as the state of the art in the commercial-database field. It is worth understanding how object-oriented databases differ from these systems. We have already indicated some of the technical features that underlie the object-oriented approach. Features such as identity and encapsulation distinguish object-oriented DBMSs, but how do these features affect how these systems can be optimally used?

Relational databases present a view of the persistent data space to the programmer consisting of primitive values of integers, reals, and strings and requiring that all aggregate objects be represented as tuples or as sets of tuples (i.e., relations) over these primitive values. This rather high-level view of data is convenient for data-processing applications that are principally concerned with producing reports. It is a hindrance, however, for systems programs that are at roughly the same level of complexity as is an operating system or a compiler. These programs require tight control over how storage is used. They need data structures such as stacks, queues, and streams of bytes. An object-oriented database allows programmers to create abstractions that match the data structures that are needed for complex applications.

The relational data model is *value-based,* as opposed to earlier data models, such as CODASYL, which could be called *identity-based.* This distinction arises from the mechanisms that a data model provides for relating objects to each other, a fundamental part of the modeling capability for any database system. A value-based system expresses the relationship between two objects by embedding the same (or a similar) value in two or more related objects. An identity-based model can relate two or more objects independently of their embedded values.

Object-oriented database systems are identity-based like network models such as CODASYL. However, this one similarity is not enough to equate the models. The object-oriented models add a notion of typing and extensibility that is considerably different from their network predecessors. They add abstraction based on behavioral encapsulations and usually an incremental modification mechanism in the form of inheritance.

Although object-oriented systems provide the capability to form references based on identity, identity is not the sole basis for relationships in the model. A model such as ENCORE [Hornick, 1987; 4.3] can relate objects by means of *properties.* A property is a reflection of the abstract state of an object. As such, a property *p* relates an object *x* to a set of objects *S* without making any statement about how this relationship is realized. It could be computed by a direct reference to the identity of *S* (or its members), or it could be computed by a matching of values for some other properties, as with a relational join. Consider the following type definition:

Define Type Intersection

Properties
　　InComingSegments: **Set of** RoadSegments
　　position: Coordinate

Define Type RoadSegment

We could implement the *location* property, which expresses the location of a given intersection, by imbedding the object identifier for a coordinate pair in the representation for an intersection. If the representations for both the **Intersection** and the **RoadSegment** types are tuples in a relation, the *has* property could be implemented by a relational query of the form

has (i) = **Project**$_{RoadSegment}$ (**Select**

　　(**Join** (Intersection, RoadSegment),
　　　　lambda (ir) ir.id = i.id))

An object-oriented database is based on the ability to define new abstractions and to control the implementation of these abstractions. From the preceding example, we can see that it is possible to combine both identity-based and value-based relationships at the implementation level while retaining the same abstraction at the logical level.

10. Other Useful Features

The features discussed in this section are by no means unique to object-oriented databases. They make sense in most database systems, but we include them here because they either have special aspects when considered in object-oriented databases or can be supported in new ways.

10.1 Parameterized Types

Parameterized types provide a way to define a template for a set of types whose members behave in a similar way. The parameter in a parameterized type is usually bound to some other type; when this parameter is bound to some value, a new type is generated. The parameterized type is much like a metatype, as defined in Smalltalk [Goldberg, 1983].

Although the notion of parameterized types is a general one, it plays a special role in object-oriented databases, since it is typically used to define the aggregate types. For example, the type **Set** is usually parameterized by some other type that describes the type of the elements of any instance of the type. In this way, we might have Set[T] as a parameterized type that defines the

general notion of sets. When we bind T to another type, such as **Truck**, we produce a new type, **Set[Truck]**, which is constrained to contain only trucks.

Different parameterizations of a parameterized type produce different types. **Set[Road]** is not equivalent to **Set[RoadSegment]**. Many examples of parameterized types have the parameter as another type (e.g., Set[T: Type]). The parameter could be of any other type. For example, the length of an array could be considered a parameter of the parameterized type **Array[len: Int]**. In this way **Array[100]** is a different type from **Array[200]**.

The implementations for the methods of a parameterized type also contain references to the parameter. When a value is bound to the parameter, a new method body is produced for each of the methods of the parameterized type. This allows us to represent a family of type definitions and implementations with a single parameterized definition.

The parameterizations can share implementations. On the other hand, it is useful to allow different parameterizations to be implemented differently. **Set(Truck)** might be implemented as a B-tree based on the key property *Vehicle_Identification_Number*, whereas **Set(Road)** might be implemented as a hash table on the *County_Road_Number* property of **Roads.**

10.2 Schema Update

Design environments are characterized by continual change. The designs themselves are constantly being revised to amend bugs and to alter the design to fit more accurately the specifications of the application. The type definitions (or schema) are also likely to change as designers arrive at a better understanding of their problem and its solution. Conventional database systems have only limited facilities to accommodate changes at the level of the types. Some work has been done in the field of object-oriented databases to try to make schema updates less painful.

There are two changes that we might like to accommodate:

1. **Same interface with new representation.** In this case, data abstraction relieves us of the burden of having to recode programs that used the modified type; however, it is necessary to convert all the old instances that have been stored in the database to have the new representation. This conversion can be done automatically, but it requires that we write a conversion program.

2. **New interface with the same representation**. This kind of change is more problematic. Many programs are written to depend on the interface to a type. Allowing this kind of change requires either recoding any programs that used this type, or having some mechanism that intervenes at run-time to make old instances look like new instances, and vice versa.

10.3 Active and Derived Data

Active data provide that an access to one data item can cause other activities to happen. For example, we might want the removal of an **Intersection** object from a **Road** object to cause the removal of the **RoadSegment** objects entering that intersection. We distinguish between *active data* and *active databases*. The distinction is based on whether the caused changes can affect processes outside the database. A DBMS can support active data, but have the database itself be passive, as the entailed changes happen only to other data items in the database. By *passive DBMS*, we mean a DBMS that communicates with an application program only in response to a direct call. An active database is one where a change to the data could cause a message to be sent to a process outside the database. Such a facility is sometimes called a *notifier* or *alerter*.

The most common mechanism for providing active data is a *trigger*. A trigger is a monitor placed on a data item that initiates an action on access to the item. It is a logical notion that can be thought of as a pattern–action pair. When the pattern becomes true, the action is executed. The trigger might be sensitive to the kind of operation being performed (e.g., only on read or only on write). There are a number of ways to implement triggers. They can be handled by special bits in the representation of the data item, in which case the storage manager detects them and fires the appropriate action. They can be realized with special kinds of locks, in which case the lock manager fires actions. OODBs provide another implementation option, which is by method modification. Since methods are the only way to access data, the method compiler or interpreter can detect expressions that access monitored data, and can insert additional code to accomplish the triggered action. Note that the technique of query modification used in relational systems to handle authorization and views does not work well with triggers, as most relational-query languages cannot express in a single command an operation that does both a retrieval operation and an update, or that updates multiple relations at once.

Related to active data are *derived data*. Views in conventional systems are one form of derived data. The other common form is fields in data structures whose values are computed from other data. Methods can provide derived fields, if the interface to fields in an object is always through messages. Users of a field cannot tell whether an access is a lookup or a computation. However, other mechanisms for derived fields exist [Hudson, 1986; 6.4]. The derived field can be computed and stored, then updated when the data on which it depends changes. (Or it can be lazily updated the next time it is accessed after a change.) The advantage here over methods is that, if the derived field is accessed many times between changes of its value, time is not expended to compute it repeatedly.

Rules are a high-level mechanism used with both active and derived data. In simple form, they have a body, which is a pattern against the database, and a head, which is another pattern. The intent is that, whenever the body matches the database, the head should too. (There can be variables bound in matching the body that are used by the head.) For active data, when a match of the body occurs, the head indicates changes to existing data to make it match. With derived data, the head specifies new data to create when the body matches. Deductive databases, which typically use large rule sets, can be viewed conceptually as defining a large number of derived data from an explicitly stored base. Rather than materializing all the implied data, however, query processsors for deductive databases attempt to materialize parts of them on demand to answer a specific query.

10.4 Integrity Constraints

Integrity constraints are predicates on the state of the database that the database system is responsible for enforcing. We have seen examples of constraints—keys and referential integrity—in previous sections. Neither of those is unique to object-oriented databases. However, there is a type of constraint—*instance-level constraints*—that fits especially well with object-oriented models.

Almost all constraints that current DBMSs support are *schema-level constraints*. They are defined relative to entities in the schema, and apply to all instances of a type or to all elements of a collection. For design applications in particular, it is useful to have constraints that apply to a single object. In the roads example, we might be constructing **Route** objects that contain a sequence of **RoadSegments** and **Stops** making up a route for one of the drivers. Suppose one particular driver only works three-quarters time. For the **Route** object for that driver, we want to attach the constraint that the elapsed time for the route is no more than 6 hours.

We know of no current system that supports an instance-level constraint mechanism directly. There are, however, ready means to simulate such constraints in some OODBs. A special subtype for the constrained object can be created that checks the constraint during updates. Some OODB models have been proposed where individual objects can override method definitions. Thus, a constrained object can have its own methods that check for the constraint. A third possibility is to interpose a "handler" object between the constrained object and the reference to that object. All messages to the constrained object actually go to the handler object, which checks whether they are permissible. One problem with all three techniques, however, is that the constraint checking is done immediately when the object is updated. In commercial systems it is usually possible to designate that a constraint be checked only at transaction boundaries, and not after every operation, allowing subsequent operations in the transaction to satisfy the constraint.

10.5 Transactions in Object-Oriented Databases

To preserve the correctness of the database in the face of concurrently executing processes, database systems define a concept of *atomic transactions*. Transactions are units of work that, when allowed to proceed concurrently, are guaranteed to produce results that are equivalent to the results produced by some serial execution. We say that any interleaving of operations that preserves this equivalence is *serializable*.

There have been many implementations proposed that are guaranteed to produce serializable executions. These are largely based on read-write semantics. That is, reads and writes on a data item x are both defined to conflict with other writes on x. The data manager can then make decisions (e.g., when to schedule a read or write) that will ensure serializability.

Object-oriented databases present an opportunity to provide more concurrency than more traditional approaches allow [Weihl, 1985; 5.1]. In the object-oriented approach, the database system knows more about the operations that are being performed. They are not simply reads or writes, but rather have more semantics. For example, for a queue data type, we would have operators such as enqueue and dequeue. From some point of view, these operators can be considered a write and a read, respectively, but if we take the special semantics of these operators

into account, we can achieve a higher degree of concurrency.

If we have a queue object Q and two transactions $T1$ and $T2$, and $T1$ has done an enqueue on Q, then $T2$ will be prevented from doing a dequeue on Q by common read–write semantics until $T1$ has committed. However, if we notice that, for nonempty queues, these two operations do not affect each other's result, we can allow them to proceed without a conflict. However, implementing the queue in a way that allows each of the transactions possibly to abort and undo its action is nontrivial.

For cooperative applications, such as those seen in design environments, the notion of serializability is too strong a correctness criterion. Serializability is founded on an assumption that transactions should not interact in the middle of their execution. Cooperative design, however, is based on the notion that the units of work must interact so that the results are usable together. This observation has led to a new area of research, often based in object-oriented technology, that is exploring new models of concurrency control for cooperative transactions.

10.6 Distributed Databases

Object-oriented databases have been designed to support complex applications, such as engineering, that will largely run on high-performance workstations. Each designer will have a workstation that will interact with other workstations and with a few larger server machines through a local-area network. Some data will be stored on shared data servers, whereas other data will reside locally on the secondary storage of the workstation. It is also unlikely that a single server will supply all the data storage needs of a large design environment. We must therefore confront the additional problems presented by an environment that is naturally suited to a distributed database.

To simplify programming and to preserve data independence, existing distributed database implementations have as one goal *transparent distribution*. That is, it should be possible to name the data items in the same way as in centralized databases. The system is responsible for locating the required data items and for updating them atomically. Thus, programmers need to worry about only logical issues. As the data are redistributed through the network, the programs remain invariant, and the system can produce new optimizations for processing queries that require data from different sites.

Distributed databases have been discussed in the literature for some time, and they are now becoming a commercial reality. Previous discussion was largely in the context of relational systems. It is worthwhile to ask whether the object-oriented approach raises any additional problems or facilitates any new solutions. For example, most conventional models of distribution have considered multiple server machines. In object-oriented databases, we see more talk of distribution in work-station/server environments.

One opportunity for better performance in an object-oriented framework derives from the fact that programs (i.e., methods) are objects. As such, they can be moved around in the distributed database just like any other object. In performing a computation or processing a query, the system has the choice of moving the data to the programs, or of moving the programs to the data. Often, for executing a method M on a very large object x, it is more reasonable to move the method M to the machine on which x resides than it is to transfer x to M's site.

Most database systems require that the schedule produced by a set of transactions be serializable [Bernstein, 1987]. Achieving this condition often requires a great deal of communication. At the end of each transaction, all objects that have been touched must be written back to the server. Sacrificing some of the benefits of serializability may be necessary to achieve high performance in applications such as interactive design environments.

Caching strategies are also relevant in a distributed system. As objects move from machine to machine, retaining local copies for some period can often shorten subsequent retrievals.

The interpretive nature of object-oriented systems can create performance problems that are particularly acute in the distributed environment if object placement is not done carefully. Late binding of messages to methods requires looking at several objects. By judicious placement of the objects required to interpret a message, we can minimize the required communication to access multiple objects on different machines.

A major problem imposed by the application environment is one of interoperability among heterogeneous systems. This problem is exacerbated in a distributed environment, because there is little control over the characteristics of the participating systems. This heterogeneity can take several forms. There can be differences in the underlying data formats of the participating tools and systems, differences in the languages used for developing applications, differences in the underlying operating systems, and differences in the way that designers need to share information.

Object-oriented databases can address some of these problems of interoperability. Their abstraction mechanisms can be used to build bridges to existing data repositories. An existing data-storage system becomes the implementation vehicle for new abstract types. The representation for this new type would be some data structure that is supported by the foreign data repository. Whenever a method of this new type was invoked, the method code would make a call to this repository in order to access the external representation. Old applications would access and update persistent data in the same way as they have always done, but new applications would access persistent data through abstract types that were defined in the object-oriented schema (see Figure 1). Although this process might be somewhat slow, the ability to access data across different storage systems is a valuable functionality.

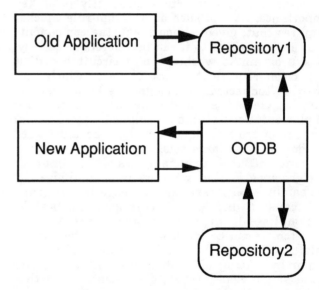

Figure 1. Interoperability

11. Architecture and Implementation Considerations

It is common to see an object-oriented database implemented as an interpreter on top of a basic storage manager. The storage manager is responsible for movement of objects from the disk into main memory, for buffer management, and for some low-level transaction and recovery tasks. The interpreter is responsible for providing the facilities required to provide the view of objects, types, and methods.

This architecture appears in some relational database systems. For example, System R, IBM's relational prototype, had a storage manager, called RSS, that supported the basic relational run-time system, called RTS.

The degree of semantics built into the storage manager is an important architectural design decision. Some systems, such as ObServer [Hornick, 1987; 4.3], put very little semantics in the storage manager. The advantages of this approach include simplicity, the ability to support multiple external models, and the fact that the semantic functions are handled in one place—the higher-level interpreter. On the other hand, some systems, such as GemStone [Maier, 1987; 3.1], put a high level of semantics in the storage manager. The GemStone storage manager includes information about the classes, typing, and indices. The advantages of this approach include the potential for more optimization, the efficient enforcement of constraints, and the ability to maintain auxiliary access paths.

For many design applications, being able to traverse a graph structure efficiently is of key importance. A tool such as a design-rule checker requires that, given a component, the components that are connected to it can be referenced quickly. If a program is working on a circuit board, it will often require the back plane to which that board is connected. Although this kind of access can be viewed as a degenerate query, other implementation techniques might be more useful for it than are techniques that have been designed for queries over large sets.

One of the principal ways to improve performance in this situation is to minimize the probability that traversing an edge in the graph will cause a disk fault. This goal can best be accomplished with *intelligent prefetching*. Prefetching can be implemented either by putting related things on the same physical unit of transfer or by getting more than one unit of transfer for a single read. Often, a scheme is used that allows applications to create arbitrary-sized collections of objects, called *segments,* that are stored contiguously on the disk. Whenever any object in a segment is accessed, the entire segment is read (prefetched) into the memory of the application. If the segments are set up properly, this strategy will reduce the number of disk faults. Determining how to configure automatically a set of segments for a particular pattern of accesses requires more research.

The anticipated environment for these databases is a network of workstations. Typically, one of these workstations, or some bigger machine (or machines), is designated as an object server that supplies objects to the workstations and to their application programs as needed. Communication between the work-stations and the server must be minimized.

Another classic way to improve the performance of a database is to introduce auxiliary access methods that can be used to limit the amount of search that needs to be done. We have already discussed the idea of abstract indices in Section 8.5 on query optimization. Index structures can be useful for managing large collections of objects or for handling single very large objects (e.g., bitmaps). The EXODUS storage system [Carey, 1989; 7.3] constructs a tree for large objects, thereby increasing the efficiency of retrieving smaller pieces. The tree structure allows us to access a sequence of bytes from the middle without having to read the entire object, and to update a fragment of the object without reading or writing the entire object.

12. Directions for the Field

It took roughly 15 years, from 1970 to 1985, for relational databases to be developed from a concept to a commercial product available on nearly all computing platforms. The initial concepts for object-oriented databases seemed to arrive on the coattails of Smalltalk and PS-Algol in the early 1980s. However, the technology seems to be developing more rapidly, and commercial OODBs could be widely available in 1993. There are several reasons for the more rapid emergence of OODBs. For one, database technology as a whole is more advanced now than it was in the 1970s, and the better understanding of transactions, recovery, memory management, indexing schemes, and so forth makes designing the architecture for any database system a less daunting problem. Second, in many cases, OODBs are supporting applications where no database system was in use formerly. Relational systems for the most part went head to head with hierarchical and network databases that were already in use. Third, object-oriented languages are rapidly gaining acceptance, and OODBs are seen as better able to take care of the persistent data needs of these languages than are record-based models. In addition, much of the conceptual and language-design work from object-oriented programming languages (OOPLs) carries over easily to OODBs.

We expect that the first wide use of OODBs as part of delivered applications will be embedded OODBs as part of CAE and CASE environments. These systems are likely to be persistent versions of, or heavily biased toward, a single OOPL, such as C++. OODBs that are more like current systems—supporting linkages to multiple programming languages and ad hoc querying by users—will emerge strongly a little later, probably for office applications, such as document processing, task management, and organization modeling. Eventually, OODBs will appear that are slanted toward the engineering-simulation and scientific-computing markets—areas characterized by their extensive use of ordered and graph-structured data, such as vectors, tensors, matrices, and finite-element grids. We also expect to see many object-oriented features brought into record-based systems—support for complex structures with record-valued fields, hierarchies of record types, a wider variety of base types and type constructors, and more procedural material stored in the database.

The research and development work on OODBs is far from complete. No commercial OODB or prototype now supports all the features of our reference model. Some of the work to be done is conceptual, such as gaining a better understanding and better formalization of persistence, inheritance, and typing. Other work is system engineering, such as determining how to merge features, or how to make OODB implementations more efficient and reliable. Finally, there is still much to learn about how to map applications onto OODBs.

The following sections indicate which areas we believe will be most active in OODB research over the next 3 to 5 years.

12.1 Conceptual

The exact role of *types* in OODBs is hotly contested. Types in programming languages are mainly a tool for determining program correctness, whereas in databases they have traditionally been more a modeling tool. Should they incorporate the notion of extensions for querying? Should they be bound up with implementation, or only concern specification? Should they subsume constraints, or should constraints be separate? One problem is that the type system is often the only part of a programming system that is formalized enough to reason about, and the tendency is to load types with any aspect of the system one wants to reason about.

Query languages for OODBs are still rough. There is a tension between encapsulation and the structural view of data characteristic of query languages such as SQL and QUEL.

Version and configuration models are still rudimentary. If OODBs are to serve design applications, there should be some system support for managing versions of components and configurations of those versions. However, too detailed or rigid a model is likely to be seen as dictating what should be site- or application-specific policies on configuration management.

An active area in database-systems research is *deductive* or *logic databases*. These are relationallike databases with query languages based on logic-programming languages or other logic formalisms, particularly the Prolog language. They provide much more expressive query capabilities than do current relational query languages, as they are able to express recursion. They also possess a much cleaner semantics than do typical object-oriented languages, making queries more amenable to transformation, analysis, and optimization. However, they are currently lacking in support for useful modeling concepts such as object identity, inheritance, and update abstractions. Researchers are currently trying to extend the logic formalism with these features.

12.2 System Engineering

Optimization technology for object-oriented systems lags behind that of relational systems considerably. One problem is that there is more variety in the data structures used for object representations; thus, optimization has the added complexity of such things as nested structures and arrays. Also, languages in OODBs are currently more procedural than declarative, mixing update with retrieval, and thus limiting the transformations available on expressions. A third problem is that encapsulation hides the big picture for what is going on in a query; no object has a vantage point to see a description of all the processing steps involved in evaluating an expression. Researchers are attacking all these problems. For example, the last problem can be dealt with through a trusted system component to which objects reveal behavior of messages.

Storage management for OODBs is in its infancy. There is still an enormous design space to explore in terms of clustering, object assembly in main memory, and replication and distribution. A particular problem with replication and distribution of objects is that the objects' methods must also be distributed if an object is to be accessible at its local site.

Parallelism has been a major topic in database research throughout the 1980s, both in the design of database machines and in query processing on general-purpose parallel computers. Most of the parallelization attempts have concentrated on set-oriented operations, such as join and select, where the arguments can be partitioned and the processing for one operation can be subdivided among several processors. OODBs admit the possibility of messages to objects as units of parallel processing. However, it may be that a single method-evaluation is too small a unit of work relative to the overhead of scheduling it.

Other developments in database system building that may influence OODB development include the emergence of *nonstandard architectures* for database systems. The advent of optical storage technology makes thinkable databases that never remove old versions of data, which would support no-deletion semantics without the need for garbage collection (but would require migration of data from magnetic to optical storage). Main-memory databases may couple well with object-oriented models to support design checking and simulation.

12.3 Applications

The distinguishing feature among commercial database systems that seem to influence buying decisions most is the collection of *application-development tools*. These include schema editors, report and form generators, browsers, and data dictionaries. The offerings with current OODBs are minimal, and will have to be expanded if OODBs are to compete directly with relational systems. Also, *design methodology* for OODBs is still a black art. Object-oriented schema design is more complex than is design of record-based databases, because behavior must be modeled, and its partitioning between classes must be decided.

Hypertext systems share features with OODBs, leading to suggestions that OODBs are the obvious choice for database support for hypertext (and also to suggestions that hypertext databases might be storage managers for object-oriented databases). Still, there is no direct mapping from hypertext to OODBs. Hypertext systems support links that can be established between objects of arbitrary kinds, which would make the endpoints of a **Link** object difficult to assign a type. Also, links can be attached in the middle of objects in some hypertext models, such as to a substring or character position within a block of text. OODBs do not typically support references into the middle of objects, unless the reference is to an identifiable subobject. Hypertext links also are more personal than are shared data; they indicate the connections that particular individual thinks are interesting or important. Two users might want to maintain entirely different linkage structures on the same corpus of text.

Finally, OODBs are good candidates for supporting environments for *cooperative work*. They support sharing of artifacts at multiple levels of granularity, appear to be able to support versions and alternatives reasonably well, and can capture the mass of management information that goes along with any multiperson project—such as schedules, task dependencies, memoranda, annotations, records

of design decisions, and even project-specific policies.

13. Summary

The papers in this book represent a snapshot of the current object-oriented database landscape. Work to firm up this new technology is ongoing. Some of this work is intended to obtain a deeper understanding of object-oriented principles like inheritance and incremental change; other research is aimed at the pragmatic aspects of building usable, efficient systems. Still other work is investigating how these systems can best be used in nonstandard applications.

This introduction is intended to give the reader a grounding in the basic concepts, and to make it possible for her or him to approach the research literature as represented by this volume.

14. References

S. Abiteboul and N. Bidoit. Non First Normal Form Relations to Represent Hierarchically Organized Data. *Proceedings of the ACM Symposium on Principles of Database Systems*. Waterloo, Ontario, 1984.

J.R. Abrial. Data Semantics. In *Data Management Systems*. J.W. Klimbie and K.L. Koffeman, eds. North Holland, 1974.

H. Ait-Kaci and R. Nasr. Logic and Inheritance. *ACM Symposium on Principles of Programming Languages*. St. Petersburg, FL, January 1986.

T.M. Atwood. An Object-Oriented DBMS for Design Support Applications. *Proceedings IEEE COMPPINT 85*, 1985.

F. Bancilhon, T. Briggs, S. Khoshafian, and P. Valduriez. FAD, a Powerful and Simple Database Language. *Proceedings of the XIII International Conference on Very Large Databases*. Brighton, England, 1987. Morgan Kaufmann Publishers, San Mateo, CA.

F. Bancilhon and S. Khoshafian. A Calculus for Complex Objects. *Proceedings of the ACM SIGACT-SIGMOD Symposium on Principles of Database Systems*. Boston, March 1986.

F. Bancilhon with D. Maier. Multilanguage Object-Oriented Systems: New Answer to Old Database Problems? *Future Generation Computer*

II. K. Fuchi and L. Kott eds. North Holland, Amsterdam, 1988.

J. Banerjee, H.T. Chou, J. Garza, W. Kim, D. Woelk, and N. Ballou. Data Model Issues for Object-Oriented Applications. *ACM Transactions on Office Information Systems.* 5(1), 1987.

J. Banerjee, H.J. Kim, W. Kim, and H.F. Korth. Schema Evolution in Object-Oriented Persistent Databases. *Proceedings of the Sixth Advanced Database Symposium*, August 29-30, 1986.

D.S. Batory, J.R. Barnett, J.F. Garza, K.P. Smith, K. Tsukuda, B.C. Twitchell, and T.E. Wise. GENESIS: An Extensible Database Management System. *IEEE Transactions on Software Engineering.* 14(11), 1988.

P. Bernstein, V. Hadzilacos, and N. Goodman. *Concurrency Control and Recovery in Database Systems.* Addison-Wesley, Reading, MA, 1987.

M.L. Brodie. On Modeling Behavioral Semantics of Data. *Proceedings of the VII International Conference on Very Large Databases.* Florence, Italy, September 1981. Morgan Kaufmann Publishers, San Mateo, CA.

H.-T. Chou and W. Kim. A Unifying Framework for Version Control in a CAD Environment. *Proceedings of the XII International Conference on Very Large Databases.* Kyoto, Japan, 1986. Morgan Kaufmann Publishers, San Mateo, CA.

S. Christodoulakis and C. Faloutsos. Design and Performance Considerations for an Optical Disk-Based, Multimedia Object Store. *IEEE Computer*, December 1986.

U. Dayal, and J.M. Smith. PROBE: A Knowledge-Oriented Database Management System. In *On Knowledge Base Management Systems,* M.L. Brodie and J. Mylopoulos, eds. Springer-Verlag, New York, 1986.

D. Decouchant. Design of a Distributed Object Manager for the Smalltalk-80 System. *OOPSLA* 86, September–October, 1986.

K.R. Dittrich, W. Gotthard, and P.C. Lockemann. DAMOKLES—A Database System for Software Engineering Environments. *Proceedings IFIP Workshop on Advanced Programming Environments.* Trodheim, June 1986, Lecture Notes in Computer Science, Springer-Verlag, New York.

C.M. Eastman. System Facilities for CAD Databases. *17th Design Automation Conference,* June 1980. *or* Database Facilities for Engineering Design. *Proceedings IEEE* 69:10, October 1981.

D.J. Ecklund, E.F. Ecklund, B.O. Eifrig, and F.M. Tonge. DVSS: A Distributed Version Storage Server for CAD Applications. *Proceedings of the XIII International Conference on Very Large Databases.* Brighton, England, September 1987. Morgan Kaufmann Publishers, San Mateo, CA.

A. Goldberg and D. Robson. *Smalltalk-80: The Language and Its Implementation.* Addison-Wesley, Reading, MA, 1983.

S. Heiler and A. Rosenthal. G-Whiz, a Visual Interface for the Functional Model with Recursion. *Proceedings of the XI International Conference on Very Large Databases.* Stockholm, Sweden, August 1985. Morgan Kaufmann Publishers, San Mateo, CA.

S.E. Hudson and R. King. A Generator for Direct Manipulation Office Systems. *ACM TOOIS*, 4:2, April 1986.

R. Katz and T. Lehman. Database Support for Versions and Alternatives of Large Design Files. *IEEE Transactions on SE* 10:2, March 1984.

W. Kim, J. Banerjee, H.-T. Chou, J. F. Garza, and D. Woelk. Composite Object Support in an Object-Oriented Database System. *Proceedings of the ACM Conference on Object-Oriented Programming, Systems, Languages, and Applications.* Orlando, FL, October 1987.

H. Korth, W. Kim, and F. Bancilhon. Towards a Theory of Complex Objects. *Proceedings of the International Conference on the Management of Data*, ACM, 1986.

G.S. Landis. Design Evolution and History in an Object-Oriented CAD/CAM Database. *31st IEEE COMPCON*, March 1986.

R. Lorie and W. Plouffe. Complex Objects and Their Use in Design Transactions. *Proceedings ACM Workshop on Engineering Design Applications.* San Jose, CA, May 1983.

P. Lyngbaek and W. Kent. A Data Modeling Methodology for the Design and Implementation of Information Systems. *1986 International Workshop on Object-Oriented Database Systems.* Pacific Grove, CA, September 1986.

B.J. MacLennan. *A View of Object-Oriented Programming*. Naval Postgraduate School, NPS52-83-001, February 1983.

D. Maier, P. Nordquist, and M. Grossman. Displaying Database Objects. *Proceedings of the First International Conference on Expert Database Systems*. Charleston, SC, April 1986.

F. Maryanski, J. Bedell, S. Hoehlscher, S. Hong, L. McDonald, J. Peckman, and D. Stock. The Data Model Compiler: A Tool for Generating Object-Oriented Database Systems. In *Proceedings International Workshop on Object-Oriented Database Systems*, K.R. Dittrich and U. Dayal, eds. Pacific Grove, CA, September 1986.

E. Moss. *An Introduction to Nested Transactions*. University of Massachusetts at Amherst, Computer and Information Science Technical Report 86 41, September 1986.

P. O'Brien, B. Bullis, and C. Schaffert. Persistent and Shared Objects in Trellis/OWL. *1986 International Workshop on Object-Oriented Database Systems*. Pacific Grove, CA, September 1986.

H.B. Paul, H.J. Schek, M.H. Scholl, G. Weikum, and U. Deppisch. Architecture and Implementation of the Darmstadt Database Kernel System. *ACM Proceedings of the International Conference on the Management of Data*. San Francisco, CA, June 1987.

M.A. Roth and H.F. Korth. The Design of ~1NF Relational Databases into Nested Normal Form. *ACM Proceedings of the International Conference on the Management of Data*. San Francisco, CA, June 1987.

W.B. Rubenstein, M.S. Kubicar, and R.G.G. Cattell. Benchmarking Simple Database Operations. *Proceedings ACM-SIGMOD International Conference on Management of Data*. San Francisco, CA, May 1987.

J. Schmidt. Typed Database Views. *Proceedings of the Workshop on Database Programming Languages*. Roscoff, France, September 1987.

P. Schwarz, W. Chang, J.C. Freytag, G. Lohman, J. McPherson, C. Mohan, and H. Pirahesh. Extensibility in the Starburst Database System. *International Workshop on Object-Oriented Database Systems*. Pacific Grove, CA, September 1986.

T.W. Sidle. Weaknesses of Commercial Data Base Management Systems in Engineering Applications. *17th Design Automation Conference*, June 1980

A.H. Skarra and S.B. Zdonik. Management of Changing Types in an Object-Oriented Database. *Proceedings of the ACM Conference on Object-Oriented Programming, Systems, Languages, and Applications*. Portland, OR, September 1986.

J.M. Smith and D.C.P. Smith. Database Abstractions: Aggregation and Generalization. *ACM Transactions on Database Systems*, 2(2), June 1977.

J.W. Stamos. Static Grouping of Small Objects to Enhance Performance of a Paged Virtual Memory. *ACM Transactions on Computer Systems*, 1984.

J. Stein and D.J. Penny. Class Modification in the GemStone Object-Oriented DBMS. *ACM Proceedings of the Conference on Object-Oriented Programming, Systems, Languages, and Applications*. Orlando, FL, October 1987.

M. Stonebraker. *Readings in Database Systems*. Morgan Kaufmann Publisher, San Mateo, CA, 1988.

M. Stonebraker and L. Rowe. The Design of Postgres. *ACM-SIGMOD Proceedings of the International Conference on the Management of Data*. Washington, D.C., May 1986.

W. Weihl. Data-dependent Concurrency Control and Recovery. *Proceedings of the Second Annual ACM Symposium on Principles of Distributed Computing*. Toronto, Ontario, August 1988.

C. Zaniolo. The Database Language GEM. *Proceedings of the ACM-SIGMOD International Conference on Management of Data*. San Jose, CA, May 1983.

R. V. Zara and D. R. Henke. Building a Layered Database for Design Automation. *Design Automation Conference*.

Chapter 1

Object-Oriented Fundamentals

Introduction

This chapter introduces some of the fundamental concepts in what has become known as *object-oriented technology*. Some of these ideas have already been discussed in the introduction to this volume. The four papers here provide a deeper insight and historical perspective for those ideas.

Khoshafian and Copeland [KC86] discuss object identity, a fundamental difference between relational database systems and object-oriented database systems. This concept has been known for some time, but this paper emphasizes its importance and points out some design implications faced by any system that supports identity.

The idea of identity in object-oriented systems is shared with the earlier network-based data models (e.g., CODASYL). Note, however, that there are many other features that are required for object-oriented database systems that are not present in network models. For example, the earlier network models had not considered support for behavioral encapsulation (a part of our threshold model) or for any sort of inheritance or type hierarchy (a wide-spread feature of OODB's).

As the introduction to this volume points out, relational systems are value-based. By this, we mean that a given tuple from relation $R1$ can refer to another tuple in relation $R2$ only by embedding a user-visible key value from $R2$ in the tuples of $R1$. In an identity-based system (e.g., an object-oriented database system), the token that represents an object's identity is not accessible from the interface. This hiding makes the boundaries of an object less clear. In the relational (i.e., value-based) case, the tuple is flat, and not directly linked to any other tuple. In the identity-based case, however, the object can be viewed as inextricably bound to its related (e.g., component) objects. The logical boundaries could therefore include with the object components that it references.

Expanded object boundaries lead to more complex notions of *object equality* than one would find in a relational system. Khoshafian and Copeland discuss several of these. For example, they define *identical*, *shallow-equal*, and *deep-equal* as three different equivalence relations on objects. Shallow- and deep-equal are based on the substructure of extended objects. An object can have other objects as components. The equivalence of two objects, then, can be based on the identity of the top-level objects or on the identities of the subcomponents. Shallow-equal is based on the identity of the objects one level away from the top-level objects, and deep-equal is based on the identity of the lowest-level object.

The extended view of objects leads to differences in other operations, such as copy, delete, or lock. The general question for each of these operations is: Should the operation be applied to just the top-level object, or to that object and all its subparts? Khoshafian and Copeland discuss corresponding variants for the copy operation, called shallow-copy and deep-copy.

They also discuss several distinct schemes for implementing object identity. In any identity-based system, the identity must be represented by some symbol or surrogate. The form that is chosen for this surrogate influences the performance and capabilities of the system. For example, if the surrogate codes a physical disk location for the object, then it becomes difficult to move the object once space for it has been allocated. It is then difficult to expand the size of an object.

Many programming languages include identity in the form of pointers and call by reference. The problems of aliasing that have been studied in the programming-language context are relevant to object-oriented databases. If we wish to combine programming languages and databases, a clean semantics for identity and persistent objects is certainly required.

We have identified data abstraction through encapsulation as one of the key characteristics of an object-oriented database. The CLU [LS+77] programming language introduced abstraction into a language with strong, static type checking. The central concept in CLU is the *cluster* (thereby, the name CLU). A cluster is a data abstraction that has a representation of some other type and an interface as defined by a set of operations. Only these operations have the privilege of accessing the representation of objects of the type.

CLU associates operations with representations in a somewhat different way from that in an object-oriented language such as Smalltalk. In Smalltalk, the operations (or messages) are logically associated with single objects. When an object x is sent a message m, the method code that implements m can access only the instance variable (i.e., the rep) of the receiving object x. If there are other objects of the same type as x (i.e., the receiver) in the argument list, the method code cannot access their reps. In CLU, however, the operations are logically associated with the type. If an operation is defined on a type **T**, then the operation can access the rep of any arguments of type **T** that are in the parameter list to that operation.

The CLU paper also describes some other important abstraction mechanisms. These include iteration abstraction and parameterized types. Iteration abstraction (embodied as *iterators*) provides a way to define an operation on an aggregate type that can be called multiple times and that will return a different member each time. Iteration abstraction is important in databases, since we are concerned with being able to provide access to potentially very large sets. Systems such as EXODUS have incorporated iterators as in CLU, although EXODUS extends the notion to simultaneous iteration over multiple aggregates.

Parameterized types are a way to define a family of types with a single definition. This parameterized definition captures the commonality in a set of types and expresses the differences in terms of a set of type parameters. By binding the parameters to values, CLU generates new types. Sets are a classic example of how parameterized types can be used. A set of pickup requests is much like a set of deliveries. We can capture the commonality by defining *Set[T:Type]* with its associated operations (i.e., *insert (Set[T], x: T)*, *delete (Set[T], x: T)*, etc.) and instantiate *T* for the different variety of sets needed.

Although CLU has no support for type hierarchies, parameterized types are a step in that direction. Much like subtypes, they express commonality between types. We know that any parameterization of **Set[T]** will support an insert operation. In our example, both **Set[Request]** and **Set[Delivery]** will support an insert operation.

As pointed out by Cardelli [Ca88], however, we must be careful not to assume that two parameterizations of the same type will be subtypes of each other simply because the parameters are subtypes of each other. Even though **Delivery** is a subtype of **Request**, **Set[Delivery]** cannot be viewed as a subtype of **Set[Request]** if the **Set[T]** type supports mutators (i.e., operations that can change the state of the object). **Set[T]** supports *insert*, which in most situations would be defined as a mutator. The subtyping relationship isn't satisfied because of the substitutability requirement of subtypes. Consider the following code:

```
sd: Set[Delivery];
sr: Set[Request];
r: Request;
sr := sd;          //legal by substitutability
insert (sr, r);    //correctly type checks at
                   //compile-time
```

This code type checks; however, the *insert* operation will actually receive a **Set[Delivery]** and a generic Request (which could be a **Pickup**). The existence of the mutator *insert* is causing this problem. This, of course, is not a problem in CLU, since CLU has no facility for subtypes.

Assignment semantics in CLU is by reference or pointer. This semantics is the same as identity in the Khoshafian and Copeland paper, since it allows us to construct structures with shared components.

The CLU programming methodology is strongly based on specifications. It should be possible to understand each type (cluster) solely by inspecting its interface specification. A type specification is typically given in terms of the syntactic signatures and the pre- and post-conditions on its operations. Each operation must also specify any exceptions that can be raised during its execution. This assumption is also a part of the object-oriented paradigm, yet it is not often stated explicitly.

If taken seriously, the specification-oriented view can complicate the addition of other database features to an object-oriented type system. For example, when we add declarative constraints to an object-oriented database system, we must consider how the interface specifications to the types are affected by such constraints. Adding a new constraint is equivalent to adding exceptions to the operations. How is a constraint decomposed into the corresponding modifications to the type interfaces?

Two papers in this chapter discuss inheritance. Cardelli looks at inheritance in a structural type system, whereas Snyder [Sn86] looks at the problems of inheritance in the context of encapsulation and data abstraction.

In Cardelli's view, the structure of the data determines its type, in contrast to type models that are based on name equivalence. Cardelli's model also views subtyping as a relationship that can be inferred from the structure of types.

Cardelli covers a number of fundamental properties of static type checking in a model with subtypes. He discusses the important contravariance rule for function subtypes. If function signatures are viewed as types for functions, then a function type G can be viewed as a subtype of a function type F if and only if the inputs to F are subtypes of the inputs to G and the result type of G is a subtype of the result type of F. This rule has been adopted by the Trellis/Owl language [S+86].

Snyder uncovers several fundamental breeches of encapsulation in some object-oriented languages. For example, Smalltalk allows the instance variables (i.e., the representation) of a supertype S to be inherited by any subtype T of S. That breaks the encapsulation principle that a language such as CLU enforces, which says that each type is a separate module that can be maintained independently of any other type. In the Smalltalk case, if any change is made to the instance variables of S, each subtype of S and any subtypes of those subtypes, and so on, may need to be recoded.

To provide safe access to the instance variable of a supertype S from a subtype T, we should allow the methods of the subtype to access the abstract interface of the supertype just like any other type. This restriction maintains the proper independence between the implementation's subtypes and supertypes.

The principle that is at work in the preceding discussion is that a module should have an interface that is as narrow as possible and should expose as little as possible to other modules that make use of this interface. In other words, it is good design to limit the dependencies that can occur between modules. Dependencies make evolution difficult.

Snyder is in essence arguing for types as independent modules that can be maintained and understood on their own. The Smalltalk case views modules (i.e., types) as containing other modules. The type **Car** contains the type **Toyota** in the sense that **Toyota** is dependent on the internal structure of **Car**.

Another kind of dependency that Snyder points out is the dependency of a program on the particular structure of the inheritance hierarchy. A type should provide an interface that is not dependent on how that interface came to be. It should not be possible to write code that depends on the fact that **B** is a subtype of **A**.

As pointed out in the introduction, type hierarchies can be used to achieve several different ends. Snyder points out the distinction between the use of hierarchy for specification (subtypes) and for implementation.

Many of the ideas represented in this chapter have been discussed from the point of view of programming languages. Designers of object-oriented databases are trying to incorporate these notions into a framework of a sharable persistent space that has been established for databases. Therefore, questions about how to incorporate queries and transactions into a data model based on abstraction, inheritance, and identity pervade the current research. It is at questions such as these that the rest of this book is aimed.

References

[Br85] R. J. Brachman. I Lied About the Trees — Or, Defaults and Definitions in Knowledge Representation. *AI Magazine*, 6(3):80–93, 1985.

• [Ca88] L. Cardelli. A Semantics of Multiple Inheritance. *Information and Computation*, 26(2/3):138–164, 1988.

[DT88] S. Danforth and C. Tomlinson. Type Theories and Object-Oriented Programming. *ACM Computing Surveys*, 20(1):29–72, 1988.

• [KC86]   S. Khoshafian and G.P. Copeland. Object Identity. *Proceedings of the ACM Conference on Object-Oriented Programming Systems, Languages, and Applications*, Portland, OR, September 1986.

• [LS+77]   B. Liskov, A. Snyder, R. Atkinson, and C. Schaffert. Abstraction Mechanisms in CLU. *Communications of the ACM*, 20(8):564–576, 1977.

[LZ75]   B.H. Liskov and S.N. Zilles. Specification Techniques for Data Abstractions. *IEEE Transactions on Software Engineering*, SE-1:7–19, 1975.

[Pa72]   D.L. Parnas. Information Distribution Aspects of Design Methodology. *Information Processing*, 71(1)339–344, North Holland, Amsterdam, 1972.

[S+86]   C. Schaffert et al. An Introduction to Trellis/ Owl. *Proceedings of the ACM Conference on Object-Oriented Programming Systems, Languages, and Applications*, Portland, OR, September 1986.

• [Sn86]   A. Snyder. Encapsulation and Inheritance in Object-Oriented Programming Languages. *Proceedings of the ACM Conference on Object-Oriented Programming Systems, Languages, and Applications*, Portland, OR, September 1986.

[SS77]   J. Smith and D. Smith. Database Abstractions: Aggregation and Generalization. *ACM Transactions on Database Systems*, 2(2):105–133, June 1977.

• indicates article included in this volume

Object Identity

Setrag N. Khoshafian and George P. Copeland

Microelectronics And Computer Technology Corporation
9430 Research Blvd.
Austin, Texas 78759

Abstract

Identity is that property of an object which distinguishes each object from all others. Identity has been investigated almost independently in general-purpose programming languages and database languages. Its importance is growing as these two environments evolve and merge.

We describe a continuum between weak and strong support of identity, and argue for the incorporation of the strong notion of identity at the conceptual level in languages for general purpose programming, database systems and their hybrids. We define a data model that can directly describe complex objects, and show that identity can easily be incorporated in it. Finally, we compare different implementation schemes for identity and argue that a surrogate-based implementation scheme is needed to support the strong notion of identity.

1 Introduction

With the advent of increased efficiency of computer systems, the sophistication and demand of the users of these systems has been increasing. We have seen some significant changes in both general-purpose programming and database languages. In general-purpose programming, we went from assemblers to high-level languages and, more recently, to logic, functional and object-oriented languages. In database languages, we went from navigational to more declarative relational models. In more novel applications, such as CAD/CAM, document retrieval, expert systems and decision support systems, we are realizing that there are a host of powerful data modeling concepts which need to be introduced in both programming languages and database models. One of these concepts is the need to model arbitrarily complex and dynamic objects with versions. A more specific need in this representation is the ability to distinguish objects

from one another regardless of their content, location or addressability, and to be able to share objects. In this paper we concentrate on a powerful concept called object identity which enables us to realize this goal.

Every language must have some way to tell one object from another. Identity is that property of an object which distinguishes it from all other objects. Most programming and database languages use variable names to distinguish temporary objects, mixing addressability and identity. Most database systems use identifier keys (i.e., attributes which uniquely identify a tuple) to distinguish persistent objects, mixing data value and identity. Both of these approaches compromise identity. Object-oriented languages employ separate mechanisms for these concepts, so that each object maintains a separate and consistent notion of identity regardless of how it is accessed or how it is modeled with descriptive data. This paper focuses on the identity aspects of languages that model both temporary and persistent data.

Section 2 describes the importance of identity in both programming and database environments, as well as the need to have a consistent notion of identity in environments which attempt to merge temporary and persistent data. A continuum between weak and strong support of identity is described, and an argument is made for the importance of incorporating the strong notion of identity at the conceptual level. Section 3 defines an object model that can directly describe complex objects, and shows that identity can easily be incorporated in it. Section 4 compares the various implementation techniques for identity based on how well they preserve identity when objects are modified and physically moved, and argues that a surrogate-based implementation scheme is needed to support the strong notion of identity. Implementation of the object model using surrogates is discussed. Section 5 provides a summary.

2 The Importance Of Object Identity

Identity has been investigated almost independently in general-purpose programming languages and database languages. Its importance is growing as these two environments evolve and merge.

This section describes a continuum between weak and strong support of identity. We argue for the incorporation of the strong notion of identity at the conceptual level in languages for general-purpose programming, database systems and their hybrids.

2.1 Degrees Of Support Of Identity

There are at least two dimensions involved in the support of identity, the representation dimension and the temporal dimension. Figure 1 illustrates this identity space, populated with some example languages. Note that when a language includes a stronger support of identity in either dimension, it is not repeated at the weaker levels.

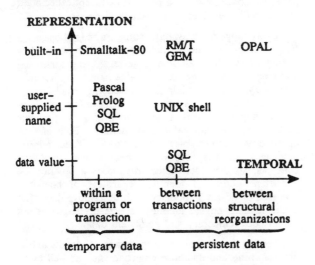

FIGURE 1: Languages In The Identity Space

The representation dimension distinguishes languages based on whether they represent the identity of an object by its value (e.g., identifying employees by social security number), by a user-defined name (e.g., variable names, user-defined file names, etc.), or built into the language (e.g., Smalltalk-80 [Goldberg and Robson 1983]). Going upward in this dimension indicates stronger support of identity. A language providing a stronger notion of identity in this dimension must maintain its representation of identity during updates, use identity in the semantics of its operators, and provide operators to manipulate identity.

The temporal dimension distinguishes languages based on whether they preserve their representation of identity within a single program or transaction, between transactions, or between structural reorganizations. An example of structural reorganization is schema reorganization in databases [Sockut 1985]. Going to the right in this dimension indicates stronger support of identity. A language providing stronger identity in the temporal dimension must employ more robust implementation techniques to preserve its representation of identity.

2.2 Identity In Programming Languages

Most general-purpose programming languages are designed without the notion of persistent data in mind. For this reason, they provide weak support of identity in the temporal dimension. As far as the language is concerned, data lives only during the execution of a program. A file system, which is not part of the language, is used for any persistent data. Input and output is usually designed for user interaction, that is, to a screen or printer, or from a keyboard or mouse. Then this same input and output model is applied, as an afterthought, to file system transfers. The structures supported in the virtual address space of the program are usually not supported in the file system.

Programming languages vary in their support of identity in the representation dimension. Most programming languages and file systems employ user-defined names (i.e., variables in languages and file names in files systems) to represent identity. The actual binding of an object to its name could be either dynamic (i.e., at run-time) or static. Figure 1 includes Pascal [Wirth 1971] and Prolog [Colmerauer 1975] as representatives of these languages. This approach mixes addressability and identity, although the concepts are quite different. Addressability is external to an object. Its purpose is to provide a way to access to an object within a particular environment and is therefore environment dependent. Identity is internal to an object. Its purpose is to provide a way to represent the individuality of an object independently of how it is accessed. An address-based identity mechanism compromises identity. Object-oriented languages, such as Smalltalk-80, provide separate mechanisms for these concepts so that neither is compromised.

There are practical limitations to the use of variable names without some built-in representation of identity and operators to test and manipulate this representation at an abstract level. One problem is that a single object may be accessed in different ways and bound to different variables without having a way to find out if they refer to the same object [Saltzer 1978]. For example, an employee object may be accessed as the vice president of sales and bound to the variable X. The same employee object may be accessed as an employee with a salary>\$60,000 who is stationed in Austin and bound to the variable Y. Smalltalk-80 provides a simple identity test with the expression X==Y, which is different from the equality test X=Y. Unix [Ritchie and Thompson 1974] has a built-in representation for file identity to support links between files, but provides no way to test directly whether two files arrived at by different paths are the same.

Given that such built-in support for identity is provided, adequate operators to manipulate identity are needed. For example, two objects with separate identity may later be discovered to be the same (the murderer is the butler!) and therefore need to be merged. Codd [1979] has argued for a "coalescing" operator in RM/T which merges identity. Different copy operators are also needed to indicate the degree of copying vs. sharing. Smalltalk-80 provides a "shallow copy" operator and a "deep copy" operator in addition to simple assignment. For example, suppose the value of Y is a set. Assigning Y to X causes X to share the same set object as Y. Assigning a shallow copy of Y to X causes X to be a new set object with its own identity, whose elements are shared with those in Y. Assigning a deep copy of Y to X causes X to be a new set object with its own identity, whose elements are new objects with their own identity, but which have the same values as those of Y.

2.3 Identity In Database Languages

Database languages are designed to support large and persistent data that models large and persistent real-world systems. These characteristics require strong support of identity in both the representation and temporal dimensions.

Every real-world object is an individual. That is, there is something unique about everything. We have often heard this pointed out about humans, as well as such simple and plentiful objects as leaves, grains of sand, blades of grass and snow flakes. When we model real-world objects with some particular purpose in mind, however, we only include some subset of that object's description in the model. This subset may not be complete enough to capture the object's uniqueness. In some cases uniqueness is external (e.g., an object is unique if it has some local attribute values and belongs to a different set, or is related to a different object). This problem arises in databases, as well as in many other computer systems, because they attempt to model real-world systems. Smith and Smith [1978] have argued for the principle of individual preservation for databases, which states that "every user-invokeable update operation must preserve the integrity of individuals". If the concept of identity is ·built into a language, then an object's uniqueness is modeled even though its description is not unique.

Codd [1970] introduced the notion of user-defined identifier keys to represent the identity of an object. An identifier key is some subset of the attributes of an object which is unique for all objects in the relation. This representation of identity is supported in many existing database systems. For example, Figure 1 includes SQL [Chamberlin and Boyce 1974] and QBE [Zloof 1975] as representatives of these systems. Both languages use identifier keys to identify persistent objects. SQL uses tuple variables and QBE uses domain variables, as does Prolog, to identify temporary objects. There are several problems with identifier keys which are due to the fact that the concepts of data value and identity are mixed.

One problem is that identifier keys cannot be allowed to change, even though they are user-defined descriptive data. For example, a department's name may be used as the identifier key for that department and replicated in employee objects to indicate where the employee works. But the department name may need to change under a company reorganization, causing a discontinuity in identity for the department as well as update problems in all objects which refer to it.

A second problem is that identifier keys cannot provide identity for every object in the relational model. Each attribute or meaningful subset of attributes cannot have identity. For example, an employee object may have an attribute describing the employee's spouse by his or her first name. Later, the spouse also becomes an employee, causing a discontinuity in identity for the spouse.

A third problem is that the choice of which attribute/s to use for an identifier key may need to change. For example, RCA may use an employee numbers to identify employees, while General Electric may use social security numbers for the same purpose. A merger of these two companies would require one of these to change, causing a discontinuity in identity for the employees of one of the companies.

A fourth problem is that the use of identifier keys causes joins to be used in retrievals instead of path expressions, which are simpler, as in GEM [Zaniolo 1983] and OPAL [Copeland and Maier 1984]. For example, suppose we have an employee relation employee[name, SS#, birthdate, assignment] and a department relation department[name, budget, location], and the assignment attribute establishes a relationship between an employee and a department. Using identifier keys, assignment would have as its value the identifier key of the department, say name. A retrieval involving both tuples would require a join between the two tuples. Using tuple variables, a retrieval might be

SELECT E.name, D.location WHERE
E.assignment=D.name
& E IN employee & D IN department,

where E and D are tuple variables. Using domain variables, the retrieval would be

[X, Z] <== employee[X, -, -, Y], department[Y, -, Z],

where X, Y and Z are domain variables. Using built-in identity, assignment would have as its value a department tuple. Unlike strict hierarchical database systems, the department tuple could also be the value of other objects without either being owned by any object or being replicated, forming a directed graph structure. Using tuple variables, the retrieval would be

SELECT E.name, E.assignment.location WHERE E IN
employee.

Using domain variables, the retrieval would be

[X, Z] <== employee[X, -, -, department[-, -, Z]].

The identifier key approach requires explicitly introducing the additional tuple variable D or domain variable Y for the join. The built-in identity approach has some of the advantages of the universal relation approach (i.e., no joins for entity relationships) but without the disadvantages of requiring unique attribute names (because nested names are used) and occasionally having ambiguous paths (since paths are specified) [Kent 1981, Maier et al. 1984]. Note that with built-in identity, hierarchical structures are possible without the undesirable insertion and deletion anomalies described by Codd [1971].

Kent [1978] describes many other problems with using descriptive data for identity. The solution calls for built-in support for identity in the language which is independent of its external descriptive data, so that the system can provide a strong notion of identity in both the representation and temporal dimensions. Strong support is provided in the representation dimension because identity is built-in. Strong support is provided in the temporal dimension because identity is preserved between transactions, regardless of changes in data or structure. RM/T and GEM provide built-in identity for some persistent objects. These languages are not fully object-oriented because they lack a uniform treatment of all objects, providing identity only for persistent tuples. OPAL [Copeland and Maier 1984] provides built-in identity for all temporary and persistent objects.

Several researchers have argued for a temporal data model [e.g., Copeland 1980 and 1982, Ben-Zvi 1982, Clifford and Warren 1983, Katz and Lehman 1984, Copeland and Maier 1984]. The reason is that most real-world organizations deal with histories of objects, but they have little support from existing systems to help them in modeling and retrieving historical data. Strong support of identity in the temporal dimension is even more important for temporal data models, because a single retrieval may involve multiple historical versions of a single object. Such support requires the database system to provide a continuous and consistent notion of identity throughout the life of each object, independently of any descriptive data or structure which is user modifiable. This identity is the common thread that ties together these historical versions of an object.

Database systems must provide efficient access to large data. To deal with this, database languages usually provide the capability to map the user's conceptual schema onto an internal schema, which describes the way that data is actually stored [ANSI/X3/SPARC 1975]. An internal schema may have multiple copies of the conceptual schema and may further partition the attributes of an object of the conceptual schema. Some way of relating these multiple copies and attribute partitions to the same conceptual object is needed. The object's identity provides a convenient way of doing this.

2.4 The Hybrid Environment

Programming with persistent data has always been difficult because programming language environments and database systems are each designed within different cultures. They are usually built on different concepts for typing, computation and identity. Typing systems in programming languages typically include arrays, lists and atomic types, while typing systems in database languages typically include sets, records and atomic types. Computational models in programming languages are typically rich in manipulation capability, while computational models in database languages typically include only search and simple update capability. The notion of identity in programming languages is typically weaker than that of database systems.

The interfaces between programming and database languages are usually crude because of these differing concepts and because they are usually designed as an afterthought. This causes what some have called an "impedance mismatch" [Copeland and Maier 1984], because much of the meta information (e.g., structures and operations) in either system is reflected back at the interface rather than passing through it. This meta information must be defined redundantly in both languages. Also, transformations must be defined whenever data or operations need to pass through the interface.

There is a growing trend to merge programming and database languages into a hybrid environment which includes a language with a unified typing and computation. Some researchers have approached the problem by making programming language data types persistent. Some examples of this approach are PS-algol [Atkinson et al. 1983], Amber [Cardelli 1984], Poly [Matthews 1985] and Galileo [Albano et al. 1985]. These languages extend the file system to support the same types as in the language and provide type checking when file objects are imported into a program. Others have approached the problem by combining programming and database language data types and database transactions. Some examples of this are PASCAL/R [Schmidt 1977] which combines PASCAL with relational data types, PLAIN [Wasserman 1979] and RIGEL [Rowe and Shoens 1979] each of which combines a new programming language with relational data types, and OPAL [Copeland and Maier 1984] which combines Smalltalk-80 and a set data type with predicate calculus.

Regardless of how one approaches this merging of programming and database capability, the end result should be a language with a uniform treatment of types, computation and identity. Data instances of any type should be capable of being either temporary or persistent. Any computation should apply uniformly to either temporary or permanent data, although computations which cause state changes of shared persistent data should be enveloped by a transaction. All types should employ the same notion of identity.

3 An Object Model

This section provides an object model which incorporates object identity. Much of this model is similar to the Smalltalk-80 [Goldberg and Robson 1983] and FAD [Bancilhon et al. 1985] languages. Our purpose is not to present a complete language, but rather to demonstrate how the strong notion of identity in the representation dimension (i.e., built-in) can be incorporated into an object model. We concentrate on the definition of object structures and those operators which manipulate identity. Although this model includes only atomic and two structured types, its generalization to other structured types is straightforward.

3.1 Object Structure

The object structure is very similar to the object structure of FAD [Bancilhon et al. 1985]. We assume we are given a set of attribute names A, a set of identifiers I, a collection of base atomic types.

An *object* O is a triple (*identifier, type, value*) where

a) The identifier is in I. The identifier of an object O is denoted O.identity.

b) The type is in {*atom, set, tuple*}. We provide only single-level typing for simplicity. A more complete typing system would be desirable for a full language (for example, a set of tuples whose attribute values are typed). .

c) The value is one of the following:

1) If the object is of the type atom, then the value is an element of a user-defined domain of atoms, each of which has no subparts.

2) If the object is of the type set, then the value is a set of distinct identifiers from I.

3) If the object is of the type tuple, then the value is of the form
[A1:I1, A2:I2, ..., An:In], where the Ai's are distinct attribute names, and the Ii's are distinct identifiers from I. Ii is the value taken by the object O on attribute Ai and is denoted O.Ai.

Note that this model allows us to have objects of arbitrary nestings and graphical structure. For example, we can have nested relations [Jaeske and Schek 1982] and nested tuples [Zaniolo 1985].

Objects can be represented graphically. We represent an atomic object by a node labeled by its value, a tuple object O = [A1:O1, ..., An:On] by a node labeled by its identifier such that there is an arc labeled Ai which goes from O to Oi, and a set O = {O1, ..., On} by a node labeled by its identifier such that there is an unlabeled arc going from O to every Oi. As an example, suppose we have a database which consists of employees and students, where each has a name, consisting of first name and last name, and an age. Then an instance of the database could be represented as in Figure 2.

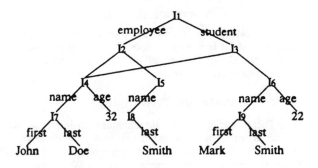

FIGURE 2: Object Model Example

An *Object System* is a set of objects. An object system is *consistent* if

(a) No two distinct objects have the same identifiers (unique identifier assumption). In other words, the identifier functionally determines the type and the value of the object.

(b) For each identifier present in the system there is an object with this identifier (no dangling identifier assumption).

All object systems will be assumed consistent throughout this paper. This definition of objects allows a directed-graph structure. An object can belong to multiple objects through set membership or attribute assignment without being replicated and without being owned by any object.

3.2 Operators With Object Identity

In the previous section we defined object structure with identity. In this section, we define several operators which compare or manipulate objects with identity, and give an informal semantics for each operator.

Definition: *identity predicate (identical)*

Given two objects, O1 and O2 the predicate identical(O1, O2) will return true if O1 and O2 are the same. Therefore, identical(O1, O2) is true if O1.identity = O2.identity.

Definition: *shallow equality predicate (shallow-equal)*

Two objects are shallow-equal if their values are identical. Note that this definition is not recursive, i.e., two set objects whose elements have pairwise equal values are not necessarily shallow-equal or two tuples whose attributes have pairwise equal values are not necessarily shallow-equal.

Definition: *deep equality predicate (deep-equal)*

Object *deep equality* is defined as follows:

(a) Two atomic objects are deep-equal if their values are the same (note that deep-equal and shallow-equal are the same for atomic objects).

(b) Two set objects are deep-equal if the they have the same cardinality and the elements in their values are pairwise deep-equal.

(c) Two tuple objects are deep-equal if the value they take on the same attributes are deep-equal.

This shows that we have three flavors of "equality":

(1) Identical, which checks if the two objects are the same object.

(2) Shallow, which goes 1 level deep, comparing values of the components of the object.

(3) Deep, which recursively traverses the objects, comparing equality of corresponding components.

Each is an equivalence relation on objects: (3) refines (2) and (2) refines (1). Therefore, two identical objects are always shallow-equal and deep-equal. Furthermore, two shallow-equal objects are always deep-equal.

Next, we discuss two kinds of operators which are used to update tuple and set objects. Atomic objects are not updatable.

Definition: *assigning an object to an attribute of a tuple (assign)*

To assign an object to an attribute of a tuple we use:

assign(<tuple object>, <attribute name>, <object>).

The effect of this operator is to assign the <object> to <tuple object>.<attribute name>. For example, if X = [name:O_1, age:O_2], then assign(X, salary, O_3) will yield X = [name:O_1, age:O_2, salary:O_3]. The identities of X, O_1, O_2 and O_3 are not changed. If X.salary was defined before the assignment, O_3 will replace the old X.salary.

Definition: *adding an element to a set (add-element)*

The second operation on sets adds an element to a set. Therefore,

add-element(<set object>, <object>)

will add <object> as an element of <set object>. The set or any of its existing elements are not affected. Note that if the object already exists in the set, the effect of the add-element update operator is null. However, if the set already contains an object which is either shallow-equal or deep-equal to the object to be added (but not identical to it), the object will still be added to the set. Below, we shall introduce an operator which eliminates duplicates based on values.

Definition: *removing an element from a set (remove-element)*

The third operator on sets removes an element from a set. Therefore,

remove-element(<set object>, <object>)

will remove <object> from <set object>, if the object is there.

Definition: *value elimination from a set (value-eliminate)*

We already alluded to the problem of the existence of value based duplicates in a set. This problem becomes important if we want to generate a final result showing only the content (i.e., the values) of the set object without any duplicates. If an operation is interested in only manipulating unique values (e.g., count the different colors of parts), without value elimination we might have redundant information accessed and manipulated. Therefore, the fourth operator on sets performs value based duplicate elimination:

value-eliminate(<set object>).

If O is a set object, value-eliminate(O) will create a new set object whose elements are new objects and whose values are the same as in O but without duplicate values. That is, there will be no two distinct elements O_1 and O_2 in value-eliminate(O) that are deep-equal. The existence of identity and value elimination allows the option of either objects or values to be manipulated.

Definition: *merging two objects into one (merge)*

Another operator which is useful for systems that support object identity merges two objects and makes them a single object. In other words, if we realize that two similarly structured objects are really the same we could have

merge(O_1, O_2),

which will merge the two objects and henceforth they will be one and the same object. Note that this is an updating operation. The semantics and support of this operation could be tricky and expensive. The simplest approach is to require the two objects to have the same type and be deep-equal. Then all that we need is to ensure all the references to the old objects and their sub-components now refer to the merged object and its sub-components. However, it is possible to make merging more sophisticated and provide support for merging differently structured objects. This is a very useful concept in statistical databases called record-linking [Wrigley 1973, Howe and Lindsay 1981], where an attempt is made to merge information which was gathered by different sources and which contain different sorts of information about the same objects.

Finally, similar to the different flavors of equality, there are two flavors of object copying, called shallow-copy and deep-copy.

Definition: *shallow copying (shallow-copy)*

The shallow-copy operator will copy its first argument into the second, such that the resulting object will be shallow-equal to the first and the two objects will have different identity. Therefore,

shallow-copy(O_1, O_2)

will generate a new object O_2 such that O_2.identity is not equal to O_1.identity but shallow-equal(O_2, O_1) is true.

Definition: *deep copying (deep-copy)*

The deep-copy operator will copy its first argument into the second, such that the resulting object will be deep-equal to the first and the two objects will have different identity. Therefore,

deep-copy(O_1, O_2)

will generate a new object O_2, with all new sub-parts, such that, if O_1 is a set or a tuple, O_2 is not shallow-equal to O_1, but O_2 is deep-equal to O_1. Deep-copy should also preserve co-referencing.

4 Implementation Techniques

There have been several techniques for implementing object identity both in databases and in programming languages. In this section, we first provide a taxonomy of identity implementation techniques. We draw our examples from programming languages, distributed file systems and database management systems. Then, we describe how the object system in Section 3 can be implemented using surrogates, which is the most powerful of these techniques.

4.1 Implementation Taxonomy

The power of each implementation technique can be measured by the degree of value, structure and location independence it provides. Data independence means that identity is preserved through changes in either data values or structure. Location independence means that identity is preserved through movement of objects among physical locations or address spaces. Both of these are important when implementing objects with the strong notion of identity in both the representation and temporal dimensions as described in Section 2.

Figure 3 describes where these implementation techniques lie in the two dimensional space provided by this taxonomy. Some of the details of these techniques are described below.

address implementation allows only whole pages of objects, not individual objects, to be moved within one virtual address space, providing minimal location independence. However, because objects cannot be moved between address spaces, object sharing among multiple programs is limited. Both real physical address and virtual address implementations provide data independence, unless such modifications cause the object to be moved within the address space due to size differences.

Identity Through Indirection

In Smalltalk-80 [Goldberg and Robson 1983], an oop (object–oriented pointer) is used to implement identity. An oop is an entry in an object table. Therefore, identities are implemented through a level of indirection.

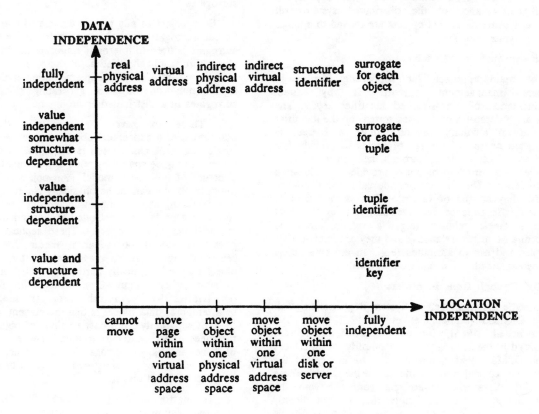

FIGURE 3: Implementation Taxonomy

Identity Through Physical Address

Perhaps the simplest implementation of the identity of an object is the physical address of the object. This physical address could be the real or the virtual address of the object (if the object system is operating in a virtual memory environment). For example, in PASCAL the "identity" of a record (i.e., the pointer to the record) is implemented through a virtual heap address. Physical address implementation does not permit an object to be moved, so that there is no location independence. Virtual

In LOOM [Kaehler and Krasner 1983], it is shown that this scheme could be used to support secondary-storage resident objects, providing support for a much larger number of objects. Indirect physical or virtual address implementations allow individual objects to be moved within one address space, providing stronger location independence than direct address implementation but not allowing sharing of objects among multiple programs. Indirect address implementations provide full data independence.

Identity Through Structured Identifier

In some distributed systems, such as the Cambridge File Server [Dion 1980] and the LOCUS system [Popek et al. 1981], the identifiers of files (the objects of the systems) are structured, where part of the structure captures an aspect of the location of the object, such as a disk or server. For example, in LOCUS part of the identifier of a file identifies a (logical) volume where the file is located. Structured identifiers provide full data independence. Structured identifiers allow individual objects to be moved within one disk or server, although movement among multiple address spaces is possible so that objects can be shared among multiple programs.

One reason why movement of object is desirable is due to the load balancing in a distributed systems. In other words, if a server contains many "hot" objects, the overall performance of the distributed system will improve if some of the hot objects are moved to another site (e.g., volume or site).

Identity Through Identifier Keys

The main approach for supporting identity in database management systems is by direct implementation of user-supplied identifier keys. The tuples are ordered (in most cases sorted) on the identifier key and an auxiliary structure (e.g., a B-tree) is constructed on top of the set of tuples to provide fast access to objects retrieved through their identifier keys. Identifier key implementations provide full location independence. They do not provide value independence because they consist of values. They do not provide structure independence because they are unique only within a single relation (e.g., a relation may be restructured into two relations) and they are applied only to tuples and not to attributes (e.g., an attribute object may be expanded into a tuple on its own).

Identity Through Tuple Identifiers

In some systems, such as System R [Astrahan et al. 1976], INGRES [Stonebraker et al. 1976] and WiSS [Chou et al. 1985], internal tuple identifiers are introduced in the internal layer to simplify the interfaces of the DBMS layering scheme and to implement the concurrency control/recovery module of the DBMS. These tuple identifiers should not be confused with the implementation of identity, since they do not directly correspond to any conceptual notion of identity. Tuple identifiers can, however, be used to implement identity. They are system-generated identifiers which are unique for all tuples within a single relation and have no relationship to physical location. Tuple identifiers provide full location independence. They also provide full value independence. They do not provide full structure independence since they are unique only within a single relation and they are applied only to tuples and not to attributes.

Identity Through Surrogates

The most powerful technique for supporting identity is through *surrogates* [Abrial 1974, Hall et al. 1976, Kent 1978, Codd 1979]. Surrogates are system-generated, globally unique identifiers, completely independent of any physical location. Leach et al. [1982] argue for the use of surrogates in distributed systems. The arguments of location independence presented therein are also valid for distributed database management systems. Surrogates provide full location independence. If surrogates are associated only with some objects, such as tuples in RM/T [Codd 1979] and GEM [Tsur and Zaniolo 1984], then they provide value independence but not full structure independence. If surrogates are associated with every object as in OPAL [Maier et al. 1985], then they provide full data independence.

4.2 Implementing The Object Model With Surrogates

This section provides a more detailed description of how to realize the object model in Section 3 using surrogates.

Each object of any type is associated with a globally unique surrogate at the instant it is instantiated. This surrogate is used to internally represent the identity of its object throughout the lifetime of the object. Leach et al. [1982] discusses several implementation issues involved in the non-trivial task of generating globally unique surrogates in a distributed environment.

There are several reasons why the physical description of a conceptual object may not be stored in a single location. One reason is that some of the parts of an object may be shared by other objects due to the graph structure of the object model. An object referenced by multiple objects cannot be physically stored with each of its referencing objects without uncontrolled replication. A second reason is that controlled replication may be used to facilitate data recovery. These replicates must be physically stored on separate media for maximum recoverability. A third reason is that the parts of an object may be physically partitioned based on frequency of use together to improve performance for disk-resident data [Hoffer 1975]. A fourth reason pertaining to support of a temporal data model is that the current version may be kept separately from past versions of objects, so that the speed of access to current data is not reduced. For all of these, an object's surrogate provides a convenient way to relate these separately stored replicates or parts of the single conceptual object.

Testing for identity (i.e., O1.identity = O2.identity) is required to support identity and shallow-equal predicates. This is accomplished by testing surrogate equality (i.e., O1.surrogate = O2.surrogate).

The remove-element operator requires checking for dangling identifiers to insure consistency of the object system. That is, there should not be any references to an object that does not exist. This could be implemented by searching for dangling surrogates each time such an update is made. This is similar to the technique used in databases which allow foreign identifier key declaration with referential integrity enforcement.

The assign operator may cause the last reference to an object to disappear, so that it is no longer accessible and its storage can be freed. This could be implemented by keeping a reference count for each object (i.e., the number of references to an object), which is updated each time a reference is added or removed. When the reference count of an object goes to zero, garbage collection is invoked. This is important for temporary data and is used in the Smalltalk-80 system [Goldberg and Robson 1983].

The merge operator causes two objects to become one. This could be implemented by maintaining an equivalence relationship between the two surrogates.

To support systems that form a hybrid of programming languages and database systems, it is important to maintain a consistent and continuous notion of identity throughout the lifetime of an object. Let us consider an object that is first created as a temporary and later made persistent. Although the strong notion of identity in both the representation and temporal dimensions is most important to persistent objects, this ability to change status means that the same implementation representation of identity should apply to both temporary and persistent objects.

5 Summary

Most programming and database languages mix the concepts of addressability and identity, using variable names as the only way to distinguish temporary objects. Most database languages mix the concepts of data value and identity, using identifier keys as the only way to distinguish persistent objects. Both of these concepts compromise identity. Object-oriented languages distinguish these concepts, providing a stronger notion of identity which is independent of how an object is accessed or described with data values.

We discussed the importance of identity in both programming and database languages as well as languages which combine the power of both these disciplines. Strong identity involves two dimensions, representation and temporal. The representation dimension distinguishes languages based on whether they represent the identity of an object by its value, by a user-defined name, or built into the language. The temporal dimension distinguishes languages based on whether they preserve their representation of identity within a single program or transaction, between transactions, or between structural reorganizations. Strong identity in the representation dimension is important for both temporary and persistent objects. Strong identity in the temporal dimension is important for persistent objects. For hybrid languages which merge programming and database functionality, a strong identity in both dimensions is important due to the need for a uniform treatment of all objects, because their status may change between temporary and persistent.

We defined a data model, including structures and operations, which supports complex objects with strong identity. Although structures included only atomic types and two structured types (i.e., set and tuple), its generalization to other structured types is straight forward. The operators serve as the building blocks of a data manipulation language based on this object model with identity.

We compared different implementation techniques for identity using a taxonomy which is based on data and location independence. Value and structure independence means that identity is preserved through changes in either data values or structure. Location independence means that identity is preserved through movement of objects among physical locations or address spaces. The most robust of these techniques is surrogates, which provides full independence in both dimensions. We described how the object model could be implemented using surrogates.

Acknowledgments

Thanks to David Maier of OGC for his many suggestions concerning both the content and presentation of this paper.

References

J.R. Abrial, "Data Semantics," in Data Base Management, J.W. Klimbie and K.L. Koffeman, eds., North-Holland Publishing Co., New York (1974).

A. Albano, G. Ghelli and R. Orsini, "The Implementation Of Galileo's Values Persistence," Proceedings Of The Appin Workshop on Persistence And Data Types, University Of Glasgow (August 1985).

M.M. Astrahan, M.W. Blasgen, D.D. Chamberlin, K.P. Eswaran, J.N. Gray, P.P. Griffiths, W.F. King, R.A. Lorie, P.R. McJones, J.W. Mehl, G.R. Putzolu, I.L. Traiger, B.W. Wade and V. Watson, "System R: Relational Approach To Database Management," Transactions On Database Systems, ACM, Vol. 1, No. 2 (June 1976).

ANSI/X3/SPARC, Study Group On Data Base Management Systems Interim Report 75-02-08, FDT Bulletin, Vol. 7, No. 2 (February 1975).

M.P. Atkinson, P.J. Bailey, W.P. Cockshott, K.J. Chisholm and R. Morrison, "An Approach To Persistent Programming," Computer Journal, Vol. 26, No. 4 (1983).

F. Bancilhon, S. Khoshafian and P. Valduriez, "FAD, A Database Machine Language, Formal Description," personal communications (1985).

J. Ben-Zvi, "The Time Relational Model," Ph.D. Dissertation, UCLA (1982).

L. Cardelli, "Amber," AT&T Bell Labs Technical Memorandum 11271-840924-10TM (1984).

D.D. Chamberlin and R.F. Boyce, "SEQUEL: A Structured English Query Language," Proceedings of the SIGMOD Workshop On Data Description, Access And Control, ACM, Ann Arbor (May 1974).

H.T. Chou, D.J. DeWitt, R. Katz, and A. Klug, "Design And Implementation of The Wisconsin Storage System," Software Practice And Experience, Vol. 15, No. 10 (October 1985).

J. Clifford and D.S. Warren, "Formal Semantics For Time In Databases," Transactions On Database Systems, ACM, Vol. 8, No. 2 (June 1983).

E. F. Codd, "A Relational Model Of Data For Large Shared Data Banks," Communications of the ACM, Vol. 13, No. 6 (June 1970).

E. F. Codd. "Further Normalization Of The Data Base Relational Model," in Data Base Systems, Courant Institute Computer Science Symposia 6, R. Rustin (ed.), Prentice-Hall, Inc., Englewood Cliffs, New Jersey (May 1971).

E. F. Codd, "Extending The Database Relational Model To Capture More Meaning," Transactions On Database Systems, ACM, Vol. 4, No. 4 (December 1979).

A. Colmerauer, "Les Grammaires De Metamorphose," Groupe d'Intelligence Artificielle, Marseille-Luminy (November 1975).

G.P. Copeland, "What If Mass Storage Were Free?," Proceedings Of The Fifth Workshop On Computer Architecture For Non-Numeric Processing, ACM, Pacific Grove, California (March 1980); a revised version appears in Computer, IEEE Computer Society, Vol. 15, No. 7 (July 1982).

G.P. Copeland and D. Maier, "Making Smalltalk A Database System," Proceedings of the SIGMOD Conference, ACM, Boston (June 1984).

J. Dion, "The Cambridge File Server," Operating Systems Review, ACM SIGOPS, Vol. 14, No. 4 (October 1980).

A. Goldberg and D. Robson, Smalltalk-80: The Language And Its Implementation, Addison-Wesley Publishing Co., Reading, Massachusetts (1983).

P.A.V. Hall, J. Owlett and S.J.P. Todd, "Relations And Entities," In Modeling In Data Base Management Systems, G.M. Nijssen, ed., North-Holland Publishing Co., New York (1976).

J.A. Hoffer, "A Clustering Approach To The Generation Of Subfiles For The Design Of A Computer Database," Ph.D. dissertation, Cornell University (January 1975).

G.R. Howe and J. Lindsay, "A Generalized Iterative Record Linkage Computer System For Use In Medical Follow-up Studies," Computers And Biomedical Research, Vol. 14 (1981).

G. Jaeske and H. Schek, "Remarks On The Algebra Of Non First Normal Form Relations," Proceedings of the Symposium On Principles Of Database Systems, ACM SIGACT-SIGMOD, Los Angeles (March 1982).

T. Kaehler and G. Krasner, "LOOM—Large Object-Oriented Memory For Smalltalk-80 Systems," in Smalltalk-80: Bits Of History, Words Of Advice, Addison-Wesley Publishing Co., Reading, Mass. (1983).

R.H. Katz and T.J. Lehman, "Database Support For Versions And Alternatives Of Large Design Files," Transactions On Software Engineering, IEEE, Vol. SE-10. No. 2 (March 1984).

W. Kent, Data And Reality, North-Holland Publishing Co., New York (1978).

W. Kent, "Consequences Of Assuming A Universal Relation," Transactions On Database Systems, ACM, Vol. 6, No. 4 (December 1981).

P.J. Leach, B.L. Stumpf, J.A. Hamilton and P.H. Levine, "UIDS As Internal Names In A Distributed File System," Proceedings of the First Symposium On Principles Of Distributed Computing, ACM, Ottawa (August 1982).

D. Maier, J.D. Ullman and M.Y. Vardi, "On The Foundations Of The Universal Relation Model," Transactions On Database Systems, ACM, Vol. 9, No. 2 (June 1984).

D.C.J. Matthews, "An Overview Of The Poly Programming Language," Proceedings Of The Appin Workshop on Persistence And Data Types, University Of Glasgow (August 1985).

D. Maier, A. Otis and A. Purdy, "Object-Oriented Database Development At Servio Logic," Database Engineering, IEEE, Vol. 8, No. 4 (December 1985).

G. Popek, B. Walker, J. Chow, D. Edwards, C. Kline, G. Rudisin and G. Thiel, "LOCUS: A Network Transparent, High Reliability Distributed System," Proceedings of the Eight Symposium On Operating Systems Principles, (December 1981).

D.M. Ritchie and K. Thompson, "The Unix Time-Sharing System," Communications Of The ACM, Vol. 17, No. 7 (July 1974).

L. Rowe and K. Shoens, "Data Abstraction, Views And Updates In RIGEL," Proceedings of the SIGMOD Conference, ACM, Boston (May 1979).

J.H. Saltzer, "Naming And Binding Of Objects," in Lecture Notes In Computer Science, Goos and Hartman, eds., Springer-Verlag, (1978).

J.W. Schmidt, "Some High Level Language Constructs For Data Type Relation," Transactions On Database Systems, ACM, Vol. 2, No. 3 (September 1977).

G.H. Sockut, "A Framework For Logical-Level Changes Within Database Systems," Computer, IEEE Computer Society, Vol. 18, No. 5 (May 1985).

M. Stonebraker, E. Wong and P. Kreps, "The Design And Implementation Of INGRES," Transactions On Database Systems, ACM, Vol. 1, No. 3 (September 1976).

J.M. Smith and D.C.P. Smith, "Principles Of Database Conceptual Design," Proceedings Of The NYU Symposium On Database Design, New York (May 1978).

S. Tsur and C. Zaniolo, "An Implementation Of GEM—Supporting A Semantic Data Model On A Relational Back-End," Proceedings of the SIGMOD Conference, ACM, Boston (June 1984).

A.I. Wasserman, "The Data Management Facilities Of PLAIN," Proceedings of the SIGMOD Conference, ACM, Boston (May 1979).

N. Wirth, "The Programming Language PASCAL," Acta Informatica 1, Vol. 1 (May 1971).

E.A. Wrigley (ed.), Identifying People In The Past, Edward Arnold. London (1973).

C. Zaniolo, "The Database Language GEM," Proceedings of the SIGMOD Conference, ACM, San Jose (May 1983).

C. Zaniolo, "The Representation And Deductive Retrieva' Of Complex Objects," Proceedings of the International Conference on Very Large Data Bases, Stockholm (August 1985).

M.M. Zloof, "Query By Example," Proceedings of the NCC, AFIPS Press, Montvale, N.J. (May 1975).

Language Design for   S.L. Graham
Reliable Software   Editor

Abstraction Mechanisms in CLU

Barbara Liskov, Alan Snyder,
Russell Atkinson, and Craig Schaffert
Massachusetts Institute of Technology

CLU is a new programming language designed to support the use of abstractions in program construction. Work in programming methodology has led to the realization that three kinds of abstractions — procedural, control, and especially data abstractions — are useful in the programming process. Of these, only the procedural abstraction is supported well by conventional languages, through the procedure or subroutine. CLU provides, in addition to procedures, novel linguistic mechanisms that support the use of data and control abstractions. This paper provides an introduction to the abstraction mechanisms in CLU. By means of programming examples, the utility of the three kinds of abstractions in program construction is illustrated, and it is shown how CLU programs may be written to use and implement abstractions. The CLU library, which permits incremental program development with complete type checking performed at compile time, is also discussed.

Key Words and Phrases: programming languages, data types, data abstractions, control abstractions, programming methodology, separate compilation

CR Categories: 4.0, 4.12, 4.20, 4.22

This research was supported in part by the Advanced Research Projects Agency of the Department of Defense, monitored by the Office of Naval Research under contract N00014-75-C-0661, and in part by the National Science Foundation under grant DCR74-21892.

A version of this paper was presented at the SIGPLAN/SIG-OPS/SICSOFT Conference on Language Design for Reliable Software, Raleigh, N.C., March 28-30, 1977.

Authors' address: Laboratory for Computer Science, Massachusetts Institute of Technology, 545 Technology Square, Cambridge, MA 02139.

1. Introduction

The motivation for the design of the CLU programming language was to provide programmers with a tool that would enhance their effectiveness in constructing programs of high quality — programs that are reliable and reasonably easy to understand, modify, and maintain. CLU aids programmers by providing constructs that support the use of abstractions in program design and implementation.

The quality of software depends primarily on the programming methodology in use. The choice of programming language, however, can have a major impact on the effectiveness of a methodology. A methodology can be easy or difficult to apply in a given language, depending on how well the language constructs match the structures that the methodology deems desirable. The presence of constructs that give a concrete form for the desired structures makes the methodology more understandable. In addition, a programming language influences the way that its users think about programming; matching a language to a methodology increases the likelihood that the methodology will be used.

CLU has been designed to support a methodology (similar to [6, 22]) in which programs are developed by means of problem decomposition based on the recognition of abstractions. A program is constructed in many stages. At each stage, the problem to be solved is how to implement some abstraction (the initial problem is to implement the abstract behavior required of the entire program). The implementation is developed by envisioning a number of subsidiary abstractions (abstract objects and operations) that are useful in the problem domain. Once the behavior of the abstract objects and operations has been defined, a program can be written to solve the original problem; in this program, the abstract objects and operations are used as primitives. Now the original problem has been solved, but new problems have arisen, namely, how to implement the subsidiary abstractions. Each of these abstractions is considered in turn as a new problem; its implementation may introduce further abstractions. This process terminates when all the abstractions introduced at various stages have been implemented or are present in the programming language in use.

In this methodology, programs are developed incrementally, one abstraction at a time. Further, a distinction is made between an abstraction, which is a kind of behavior, and a program, or *module*, which implements that behavior. An abstraction isolates use from implementation: an abstraction can be used without knowledge of its implementation and implemented without knowledge of its use. These aspects of the methodology are supported by the CLU *library*, which maintains information about abstractions and the CLU modules that implement them. The library permits separate compilation of modules with complete type checking at compile time.

To make effective use of the methodology, it is necessary to understand the kinds of abstractions that are useful in constructing programs. In studying this question, we identified an important kind of abstraction, the data abstraction, that had been largely neglected in discussions of programming methodology.

A data abstraction [8, 12, 20] is used to introduce a new type of data object that is deemed useful in the domain of the problem being solved. At the level of use, the programmer is concerned with the *behavior* of these data objects, what kinds of information can be stored in them and obtained from them. The programmer is *not* concerned with how the data objects are represented in storage nor with the algorithms used to store and access information in them. In fact, a data abstraction is often introduced to delay such implementation decisions until a later stage of design.

The behavior of the data objects is expressed most naturally in terms of a set of operations that are meaningful for those objects. This set includes operations to create objects, to obtain information from them, and possibly to modify them. For example, push and pop are among the meaningful operations for stacks, while meaningful operations for integers include the usual arithmetic operations. Thus a data abstraction consists of a set of objects and a set of operations characterizing the behavior of the objects.

If a data abstraction is to be understandable at an abstract level, the behavior of the data objects must be *completely* characterized by the set of operations. This property is ensured by making the operations the *only direct means* of creating and manipulating the objects. One effect of this restriction is that, when defining an abstraction, the programmer must be careful to include a sufficient set of operations, since every action he wishes to perform on the objects must be realized in terms of this set.

We have identified the following requirements that must be satisfied by a language supporting data abstractions:

1. A linguistic construct is needed that permits a data abstraction to be implemented as a unit. The implementation involves selecting a representation for the data objects and defining an algorithm for each operation in terms of that representation.

2. The language must limit access to the representation to just the operations. This limitation is necessary to ensure that the operations completely characterize the behavior of the objects.

CLU satisfies these requirements by providing a linguistic construct called a *cluster* for implementing data abstractions. Data abstractions are integrated into the language through the data type mechanism. Access to the representation is controlled by type checking, which is done at compile time.

In addition to data abstractions, CLU supports two other kinds of abstractions: procedural abstractions and control abstractions. A procedural abstraction performs a computation on a set of input objects and produces a set of output objects; examples of procedural abstractions are sorting an array and computing a square root. CLU supports procedural abstractions by means of procedures, which are similar to procedures in other programming languages.

A control abstraction defines a method for sequencing arbitrary actions. All languages provide built-in control abstractions; examples are the **if** statement and the **while** statement. In addition, however, CLU allows user definitions of a simple kind of control abstraction. The method provided is a generalization of the repetition methods available in many programming languages. Frequently the programmer desires to perform the same action for all the objects in a collection, such as all characters in a string or all items in a set. CLU provides a linguistic construct called an *iterator* for defining how the objects in the collection are obtained. The iterator is used in conjunction with the **for** statement; the body of the **for** statement describes the action to be taken.

The purpose of this paper is to illustrate the utility of the three kinds of abstractions in program construction and to provide an informal introduction to CLU. We do not attempt a complete description of the language; rather, we concentrate on the constructs that support abstractions. The presence of these constructs constitutes the most important way in which CLU differs from other languages. The language closest to CLU is Alphard [24], which represents a concurrent design effort with goals similar to our own. The design of CLU has been influenced by Simula 67 [4] and to a lesser extent by Pascal [23] and Lisp [15].

In the next section we introduce CLU and, by means of a programming example, illustrate the use and implementation of data abstractions. Section 3 describes the basic semantics of CLU. In Section 4, we discuss control abstractions and more powerful kinds of data abstractions. We present the CLU library in Section 5. Section 6 briefly describes the current implementation of CLU and discusses efficiency considerations. Finally, we conclude by discussing the quality of CLU programs.

2. An Example of Data Abstraction

This section introduces the basic data abstraction mechanism of CLU, the cluster. By means of an example, we intend to show how abstractions occur naturally in program design and how they are used and implemented in CLU. In particular, we show how a data abstraction can be used as structured intermediate storage.

Consider the following problem: given some document, we wish to compute, for each distinct word in the document, the number of times the word occurs and its frequency of occurrence as a percentage of the total number of words. The document will be represented as a sequence of characters. A word is any nonempty sequence of alphabetic characters. Adjacent words are separated by one or more nonalphabetic characters such as spaces, punctuation, or newline characters. In recognizing distinct words, the difference between upper and lower case letters should be ignored.

The output is also to be a sequence of characters, divided into lines. Successive lines should contain an alphabetical list of all the distinct words in the document, one word per line. Accompanying each word should be the total number of occurrences and the frequency of occurrence. For example:

a	2	3.509%
access	1	1.754%
and	2	3.509%

Specifically, we are required to write the procedure *count_words*, which takes two arguments: an *instream* and an *outstream*. The former is the source of the document to be processed, and the latter is the destination of the required output. The form of this procedure will be

count_words = **proc** (i: instream, o: outstream);

. . .

end count_words;

Note that *count_words* does not return any results; its only effects are modifications of *i* (reading the entire document) and of *o* (printing the required statistics).

Instream and *outstream* are data abstractions. An *instream* *i* contains a sequence of characters. Of the primitive operations on *instreams*, only two will be of interest to us. *Empty* (*i*) returns **true** if there are no characters available in *i* and returns **false** otherwise. *Next* (*i*) removes the first character from the sequence and returns it. Invoking the *next* operation on an empty *instream* is an error.[1] An *outstream* also contains a sequence of characters. The interesting operation on *outstreams* is *put_string* (*s*, *o*), which appends the string *s* to the existing sequence of characters in *o*.

Now consider how we might implement *count_words*. We begin by deciding how to handle words. We could define a new abstract data type *word*. However, we choose instead to use strings (a primitive CLU type), with the restriction that only strings of lower case alphabetic characters will be used.[2]

Next we investigate how to scan the document. Reading a word requires knowledge of the exact way in which words occur in the input stream. We choose to isolate this information in a procedural abstraction, called *next_word*, which takes in the *instream* *i* and returns the next word (converted to lower case charac-

ters) in the document. If there are no more words, *next_word* must communicate this fact to *count_words*. A simple way to indicate that there are no more words is by returning an "end of document" word, one that is distinct from any other word. A reasonable choice for the "end of document" word is the empty string.

It is clear that in *count_words* we must scan the entire document before we can print our results, and therefore we need some receptacle to retain information about words between these two actions (scanning and printing). Recording the information gained in the scan and organizing it for easy printing will probably be fairly complex. Therefore we defer such considerations until later by introducing a data abstraction *wordbag* with the appropriate properties. In particular, *wordbag* provides three operations: *create*, which creates an empty *wordbag*; *insert*, which adds a word to the *wordbag*; and *print*, which prints the desired statistical information about the words in the *wordbag*.[3]

The implementation of *count_words* is shown in Figure 1. The "%" character starts a comment, which continues to the end of the line. The "~" character stands for boolean negation. The notation *variable: type* is used in formal argument lists and declarations to specify the types of variables; a declaration may be combined with an assignment specifying the initial value of the variable. Boldface is used for reserved words, including the names of primitive CLU types.

The *count_words* procedure declares four variables: *i*, *o*, *wb*, and *w*. The first two denote the *instream* and *outstream* that are passed as arguments to *count_words*. The third, *wb*, denotes the *wordbag* used to hold the words read so far, and the fourth, *w*, the word currently being processed.

Operations of a data abstraction are named by a compound form that specifies both the type and the operation name. Three examples of operation calls appear in *count_words*: *wordbag$create*( ), *wordbag$insert* (*wb*, *w*) and *wordbag$print* (*wb*, *o*). The CLU system provides a mechanism that avoids conflicts between names of abstractions; this mechanism is discussed in Section 5. However, operations of two different data abstractions may have the same name; the compound form serves to resolve this ambiguity. Although the ambiguity could in most cases be resolved by context, we have found in using CLU that the compound form enhances the readability of programs.

The implementation of *next_word* is shown in Figure 2. The *string$append* operation creates a new string by appending a character to the characters in the string argument (it does *not* modify the string argument). Note the use of the *instream* operations *next* and *empty*. Note also that two additional procedures have been used: *alpha* (*c*), which tests whether a character is alphabetic or not, and *lower_case* (*c*), which returns the lower case version of a character. The implementations

---

[1] The CLU error handling mechanism is discussed in [10].

[2] Sometimes it is difficult to decide whether to introduce a new data abstraction or to use an existing abstraction. Our decision to use strings to represent words was made partly to shorten the presentation.

[3] The *print* operation is not the ideal choice, but a better solution requires the use of control abstractions. This solution is presented in Section 4.

Fig. 1. The *count_words* procedure.

```
count_words = proc (i: instream. o: outstream);
   % create an empty wordbag
   wb: wordbag := wordbag$create ( );
   % scan document, adding each word found to wb
   w: string := next_word (i);
   while w ~= " " do
      wordbag$insert (wb. w);
      w := next_word (i);
      end;
   % print the wordbag
   wordbag$print (wb. o);
   end count_words;
```

Fig. 2. The *next_word* procedure.

```
next_word = proc (i: instream) returns (string);
   c: char := '';
   % scan for first alphabetic character
   while ~alpha (c) do
      if instream$empty (i)
         then return " ";
         end;
      c := instream$next (i);
      end;
   % accumulate characters in word
   w: string := " ";
   while alpha (c) do
      w := string$append (w. c);
      if instream$empty (i)
         then return (w);
         end;
      c := instream$next (i);
      end;
   return (w);      % the nonalphabetic character c is lost
   end next_word;
```

of these procedures are not shown in the paper.

Now we must implement the type *wordbag*. The cluster will have the form

```
wordbag = cluster is create. insert. print;
    . . .
    end wordbag;
```

This form expresses the idea that the data abstraction is a set of operations as well as a set of objects. The cluster must provide a representation for objects of the type *wordbag* and an implementation for each of the operations. We are free to choose from the possible representations the one best suited to our use of the *wordbag* cluster.

The representation that we choose should allow reasonably efficient storage of words and easy printing, in alphabetic order, of the words and associated statistics. For efficiency in computing the statistics, maintaining a count of the total number of words in the document would be helpful. Since the total number of words in the document is probably much larger than the number of distinct words, the representation of a *wordbag* should contain only one "item" for each distinct word (along with a multiplicity count), rather than one "item" for each occurrence. This choice of representation requires that, at each insertion, we check whether

the new word is already present in the *wordbag*. We would like a representation that allows the search for a matching "item" and the insertion of a not previously present "item" to be efficient. A binary tree representation [9] fits our requirements nicely.

Thus the main part of the *wordbag* representation consists of a binary tree. The binary tree is another data abstraction, *wordtree*. The data abstraction *wordtree* provides operations very similar to those of *wordbag*: *create* ( ) returns an empty *wordtree*; *insert* (*tr*, *w*) returns a *wordtree* containing all the words in the *wordtree tr* plus the additional word *w* (the *wordtree tr* may be modified in the process); and *print* (*tr*, *n*, *o*) prints the contents of the *wordtree tr* in alphabetic order on *outstream o* along with the number of occurrences and the frequency (based on a total of *n* words).

The implementation of *wordbag* is given in Figure 3. Following the header, we find the definition of the representation selected for *wordbag* objects:

rep = **record** [contents: wordtree. total: **int**];

The reserved type identifier **rep** indicates that the type specification to the right of the equal sign is the representing type for the cluster. We have defined the representation of a *wordbag* object to consist of two pieces: a *wordtree*, as explained above, and an integer, which records the total number of words in the *wordbag*.

A CLU record is an object with one or more named components. For each component name, there is an operation to select and an operation to set the corresponding component. The operation *get_n* (*r*) returns the *n* component of the record *r* (this operation is usually abbreviated *r.n*). The operation *put_n* (*r*, *x*) makes *x* the *n* component of the record *r* (this operation is usually abbreviated *r.n* := *x*, by analogy with the assignment statement). A new record is created by an expression of the form type$\{name_1: value_1, \ldots \}$.

There are two different types associated with any cluster: the abstract type being defined (*wordbag* in this case) and the representation type (the record). Outside of the cluster, type checking ensures that a *wordbag* object will always be treated as such. In particular, the ability to convert a *wordbag* object into its representation is not provided (unless one of the *wordbag* operations does so explicitly).

Inside the cluster, however, it is necessary to view a *wordbag* object as being of the representation type, because the implementations of the operations are defined in terms of the representation. This change of viewpoint is signalled by having the reserved word **cvt** appear as the type of an argument (as in the *insert* and *print* operations). **Cvt** may also appear as a return type (as in the *create* operation); here it indicates that a returned object will be changed into an object of abstract type. Whether **cvt** appears as the type of an argument or as a return type, it stipulates a "conversion" of viewpoint between the external abstract type

Fig. 3. The *wordbag* cluster.

```
wordbag = cluster is
    create,      % create an empty bag
    insert,      % insert an element
    print;       % print contents of bag
    rep = record [contents: wordtree, total: int];
create = proc ( ) returns (cvt);
            return (rep${contents: wordtree$create ( ), total: 0});
            end create;
insert = proc (x: cvt, v: string);
            x.contents := wordtree$insert (x.contents, v);
            x.total := x.total + 1;
            end insert;
print = proc (x: cvt, o: outstream);
            wordtree$print (x.contents, x.total, o);
            end print;
end wordbag;
```

and the internal representation type. **Cvt** can be used only within a cluster, and conversion can be done only between the single abstract type being defined and the (single) representation type.[4]

The procedures in *wordbag* are very simple. *Create* builds a new instance of the **rep** by use of the record constructor

rep${contents: wordtree$create ( ), total: 0}

Here *total* is initialized to 0 and *contents* to the empty *wordtree* (by calling the *create* operation of *wordtree*). This **rep** object is converted into a *wordbag* object as it is being returned. *Insert* and *print* are implemented directly in terms of *wordtree* operations.

The implementation of *wordtree* is shown in Figure 4. In the *wordtree* representation, each node contains a word and the number of times that word has been inserted into the *wordbag*, as well as two subtrees. For any particular node, the words in the "lesser" subtree must alphabetically precede the word in the node, and the words in the "greater" subtree must follow the word in the node. This information is described by

node = **record** [value: **string**, count: **int**,
                  lesser: wordtree, greater: wordtree];

which defines "node" to be an abbreviation for the information following the equal sign. (The reserved word **rep** is used similarly as an abbreviation for the representation type.)

Now consider the representation of *wordtrees*. A nonempty *wordtree* can be represented by its top node. An empty *wordtree*, however, contains no information. The ideal type to represent an empty *wordtree* is the CLU type **null**, which has a single data object **nil**. So the representation of a *wordtree* should be either a node or **nil**. This representation is expressed by

rep = **oneof** [empty: **null**, non_empty: node];

Just as the record is the basic CLU mechanism to

form an object that is a collection of other objects, the *oneof* is the basic CLU mechanism to form an object that is "one of" a set of alternatives. Oneof is CLU's method of forming a discriminated union, and is somewhat similar to a variant component of a record in Pascal [23].

An object of the type **oneof** $[s_1: T_1 \ldots s_n: T_n]$ can be thought of as a pair. The "tag" component is an identifier from the set $\{s_1 \ldots s_n\}$. The "value" component is an object of the type corresponding to the tag. That is, if the tag component is s_i, then the value is some object of type T_i.

Objects of type **oneof** $[s_1: T_1 \ldots s_n: T_n]$ are created by the operations $make\_s_i(x)$, each of which takes an object x of type T_i and returns the pair $\langle s_i, x \rangle$. Because the type of the value component of a oneof object is not known at compile time, allowing direct access to the value component could result in a run-time type error (e.g. assigning an object to a variable of the wrong type). To eliminate this possibility, we require the use of a special **tagcase** statement to decompose a oneof object:

tagcase e
    tag s_1 (id$_1$: T$_1$):   statements . . .
                    . . .
    tag s_n (id$_n$: T$_n$):   statements . . .
    end;

This statement evaluates the expression *e* to obtain an object of type **oneof** $[s_1: T_1 \ldots s_n: T_n]$. If the tag is s_i, then the value is assigned to the new variable id$_i$ and the statements following the ith alternative are executed. The variable id$_i$ is local to those statements. If, for some reason, we do not need the value, we can omit the parenthesized variable declaration.

The reader should now know enough to understand Figure 4. Note, in the *create* operation, the use of the construction operation *make_empty* of the representation type of *wordtree* (the discriminated union **oneof** [empty: **null**, nonempty: node]) to create the empty *wordtree*. The **tagcase** statement is used in both *insert* and *print*. Note that if *insert* is given an empty *wordtree*, it creates a new top node for the returned value, but if *insert* is given a nonempty *wordtree*, it modifies the given *wordtree* and returns it.[5] The *insert* operation depends on the dynamic allocation of space for newly created records (see Section 3).

The *print* operation uses the obvious recursive descent. It makes use of procedure *print_word* (w, c, t, o), which generates a single line of output on *o* consisting of the word *w*, the count *c*, and the frequency of occurrence derived from *c* and *t*. The implementation of *print_word* has been omitted.

We have now completed our first discussion of the

---

[4] **Cvt** corresponds to Morris' seal and unseal [16] except that **cvt** represents a change in viewpoint only; no computation is required.

[5] It is necessary for *insert* to return a value in addition having a side effect because in the case of an empty *wordtree* argument side effects are not possible. Side effects are not possible because of the representation chosen for the empty *wordtree* and because of the CLU parameter passing mechanism (see Section 3).

Fig. 4. The *wordtree* cluster.

```
wordtree = cluster is
   create,      % create empty contents
   insert,      % add item to contents
   print;       % print contents
   node = record [value: string, count: int,
                    lesser: wordtree, greater: wordtree];
   rep = oneof [empty: null, non_empty: node];
create = proc ( ) returns (cvt):
   return (rep$make_empty (nil));
   end create;
insert = proc (x: cvt, v: string) returns (cvt);
   tagcase x
      tag empty:
               n: node := node${ value: v, count: 1,
                                 lesser: wordtree$create ( ),
                                 greater: wordtree$create ( )};
               return (rep$make_non_empty (n));
      tag non_empty (n: node):
         if v = n.value
                  then n.count := n.count + 1;
            elseif v < n.value
                  then n.lesser := wordtree$insert (n.lesser, v);
            else n.greater := wordtree$insert (n.greater, v);
            end;
            return (x);
      end;
   end insert;
print = proc (x: cvt, total: int, o: outstream);
   tagcase x
      tag empty: ;
      tag non_empty (n: node):
         wordtree$print (n.lesser, total, o);
         print_word (n.value, n. count, total, o);
         wordtree$print (n.greater, total, o);
      end;
   end print;
end wordtree;
```

court_words procedure. We return to this problem in Section 4, where we present a superior solution.

3. Semantics

All languages present their users with some model of computation. This section describes those aspects of CLU semantics that differ from the common Algol-like model. In particular, we discuss CLU's notions of objects and variables and the definitions of assignment and argument passing that follow from these notions. We also discuss type correctness.

3.1 Objects and Variables

The basic elements of CLU semantics are *objects* and *variables*. Objects are the data entities that are created and manipulated by CLU programs. Variables are just the names used in a program to refer to objects.

In CLU, each object has a particular *type*, which characterizes its behavior. A type defines a set of operations that create and manipulate objects of that type. An object may be created and manipulated only via the operations of its type.

An object may *refer* to objects. For example, a record object refers to the objects that are the components of the record. This notion is one of logical, not physical, containment. In particular, it is possible for two distinct record objects to refer to (or *share*) the same component object. In the case of a cyclic structure, it is even possible for an object to "contain" itself. Thus it is possible to have recursive data structure definitions and shared data objects without explicit reference types. The *wordtree* type described in the previous section is an example of a recursively defined data structure. (This notion of object is similar to that in Lisp.)

CLU objects exist independently of procedure activations. Space for objects is allocated from a dynamic storage area as the result of invoking constructor operations of certain primitive CLU types. For example, the record constructor is used in the implementation of *wordbag* (Figure 3) to acquire space for new *wordbag* objects. In theory, all objects continue to exist forever. In practice, the space used by an object may be reclaimed when the object is no longer accessible to any CLU program.[6]

An object may exhibit time-varying behavior. Such an object, called a *mutable* object, has a state which may be modified by certain operations without changing the identity of the object. Records are examples of mutable objects. The record update operations (*put_s* (r, v), written as $r.s := v$ in the examples), change the state of record objects and therefore affect the behavior of subsequent applications of the select operations (*get_s* (r), written as $r.s$). The *wordbag* and *wordtree* types are additional examples of types with mutable objects.

If a mutable object m is shared by two other objects x and y, then a modification to m made via x will be visible when m is examined via y. Communication through shared mutable objects is most beneficial in the context of procedure invocation, described below.

Objects that do not exhibit time-varying behavior are called *immutable* objects, or *constants*. Examples of constants are integers, booleans, characters, and strings. The value of a constant object can not be modified. For example, new strings may be computed from old ones, but existing strings do not change. Similarly, none of the integer operations modify the integers passed to them as arguments.

Variables are names used in CLU programs to *denote* particular objects at execution time. Unlike variables in many common programming languages, which *are* objects that *contain* values, CLU variables are simply names that the programmer uses to refer to objects. As such, it is possible for two variables to denote (or *share*) the same object. CLU variables are much like those in Lisp and are similar to pointer variables in other languages. However, CLU variables are *not* objects; they cannot be denoted by other variables or

---

[6] An object is accessible if it is denoted by a variable of an active procedure or is a component of an accessible object.

referred to by objects. Thus variables are completely private to the procedure in which they are declared and cannot be accessed or modified by any other procedure.

3.2 Assignment and Procedure Invocation

The basic actions in CLU are *assignment* and *procedure invocation*. The assignment primitive $x := E$, where x is a variable and E is an expression, causes x to denote the object resulting from the evaluation of E. For example, if E is a simple variable y, then the assignment $x := y$ causes x to denote the object denoted by y. The object is *not* copied; after the assignment is performed, it will be *shared* by x and y. Assignment does not affect the state of any object. (Recall that $r.s := v$ is not a true assignment, but an abbreviation for $put\_s\ (r, v)$.)

Procedure invocation involves passing argument objects from the caller to the called procedure and returning result objects from the procedure to the caller. The formal arguments of a procedure are considered to be local variables of the procedure and are initialized, by assignment, to the objects resulting from the evaluation of the argument expressions. Thus argument objects are shared between the caller and the called procedure. A procedure may modify mutable argument objects (e.g. records), but of course it cannot modify immutable ones (e.g. integers). A procedure has no access to the variables of its caller.

Procedure invocations may be used directly as statements; those that return objects may also be used as expressions. Arbitrary recursive procedures are permitted.

3.3 Type Correctness

Every variable in a CLU module must be declared; the declaration specifies the type of object that the variable may denote. All assignments to a variable must satisfy the variable's declaration. Because argument passing is defined in terms of assignment, the types of actual argument objects must be consistent with the declarations of the corresponding formal arguments.

These restrictions, plus the restriction that only the code in a cluster may use **cvt** to convert between the abstract and representation types, ensure that the behavior of an object is indeed characterized completely by the operations of its type. For example, the type restrictions ensure that the only modification possible to a record object that represents a *wordbag* (Figure 3) is the modification performed by the *insert* operation.

Type checking is performed on a module by module basis at compile time (it could also be done at run time). This checking can catch all type errors—even those involving intermodule references—because the CLU library maintains the necessary type information for all modules (see Section 5).

4. More Abstraction Mechanisms

In this section we continue our discussion of abstraction mechanisms in CLU. A generalization of the *wordbag* abstraction, called *sorted_bag*, is presented as an illustration of parameterized clusters, which are a means for implementing more generally applicable data abstractions. The presentation of *sorted_bag* is also used to motivate the introduction of a control abstraction called an *iterator*, which is a mechanism for incrementally generating the elements of a collection of objects. Finally, we show an implementation of the *sorted_bag* abstraction and illustrate how *sorted_bag* can be used in implementing *count_words*.

4.1 Properties of the Sorted_bag Abstraction

In the *count_words* procedure given earlier, a data abstraction called *wordbag* was used. A *wordbag* object is a collection of strings, each with an associated count. Strings are inserted into a *wordbag* object one at a time. Strings in a *wordbag* object may be printed in alphabetical order, each with a count of the number of times it was inserted.

Although *wordbag* has properties that are specific to the usage in *count_words*, it also has properties in common with a more general abstraction, *sorted_bag*. A bag is similar to a set (it is sometimes called a multiset) except that an item can appear in a bag many times. For example, if the integer 1 is inserted in the set {1, 2}, the result is the set {1, 2}, but if 1 is inserted in the bag {1, 2}, the result is the bag {1, 1, 2}. A *sorted_bag* is a bag that affords access to the items it contains according to an ordering relation on the items.

The concept of a *sorted_bag* is meaningful not only for strings but for many types of items. Therefore we would like to parameterize the *sorted_bag* abstraction, the parameter being the type of item to be collected in the *sorted_bag* objects.

Most programming languages provide built-in parameterized data abstractions. For example, the concept of an array is a parameterized data abstraction. An example of a use of arrays in Pascal is

array 1..n **of integer**

These arrays have two parameters, one specifying the array bounds (1..n) and one specifying the type of element in the array (integer). In CLU we provide mechanisms allowing user-defined data abstractions (like *sorted_bag*) to be parameterized.

In the *sorted_bag* abstraction, not all types of items make sense. Only types that define a total ordering on their objects are meaningful since the *sorted_bag* abstraction depends on the presence of this ordering. In addition, information about the ordering must be expressed in a way that is useful for programming. A natural way to express this information is by means of operations of the item type. Therefore we require that the item type provide less than and equal operations (called *lt* and *equal*). This constraint is expressed in the header for *sorted_bag*:

sorted_bag = **cluster** [t: **type**] **is** create, insert, . . .
   where t **has**
    lt, equal: **proctype** (t, t) **returns** (**bool**);

The item type *t* is a *formal parameter* of the *sorted_bag* cluster; whenever the *sorted_bag* abstraction is used, the item type must be specified as an *actual parameter*, e.g.

sorted_bag[**string**]

The information about required operations informs the programmer about legitimate uses of *sorted_bag*. The compiler will check each use of *sorted_bag* to ensure that the item type provides the required operations. The **where** clause specifies exactly the information that the compiler can check. Of course, more is assumed about the item type *t* than the presence of operations with appropriate names and functionalities: these operations must also define a total ordering on the items. Although we expect formal and complete specifications for data abstractions to be included in the CLU library eventually, we do not include in the CLU language declarations that the compiler cannot check. This point is discussed further in Section 7.

Now that we have decided to define a *sorted_bag* abstraction that works for many item types, we must decide what operations this abstraction provides. When an abstraction (like *wordbag*) is written for a very specific purpose, it is reasonable to have some specialized operations. For a more general abstraction, the operations should be more generally useful.

The *print* operation is a case in point. Printing is only one possible use of the information contained in a *sorted_bag*. It was the only use in the case of *wordbag*, so it was reasonable to have a *print* operation. However, if *sorted_bags* are to be generally useful, there should be some way for the user to obtain the elements of the *sorted_bag*; the user can then perform some action on the elements (for example, print them).

What we would like is an operation on *sorted_bags* that makes all of the elements available to the caller in increasing order. One possible approach is to map the elements of a *sorted_bag* into a sequence object, a solution potentially requiring a large amount of space. A more efficient method is provided by CLU and is discussed below. This solution computes the sequence one element at a time, thus saving space. If only part of the sequence is used (as in a search for some element), then execution time can be saved as well.

4.2 Control Abstractions

The purpose of many loops is to perform an action on some or all of the objects in a collection. For such loops, it is often useful to separate the selection of the next object from the action performed on that object.

Fig. 5. Use and definition of a simple iterator.

```
count_numeric = proc (s: string) returns (int);
    count: int := 0;
    for c: char in string_chars (s) do
        if char_is_numeric (c)
            then count := count + 1;
            end;
        end;
    return (count);
    end count_numeric;
string_chars = iter (s: string) yields (char);
    index: int := 1;
    limit: int := string$size (s);
    while index < = limit do
        yield (string$fetch (s, index));
        index := index + 1;
        end;
    end string_chars;
```

CLU provides a control abstraction that permits a complete decomposition of the two activities. The **for** statement available in many programming languages provides a limited ability in this direction: it iterates over ranges of integers. The CLU **for** statement can iterate over collections of any type of object. The selection of the next object in the collection is done by a user-defined *iterator*. The iterator produces the objects in the collection one at a time (the entire collection need not physically exist); each object is consumed by the **for** statement in turn.

Figure 5 gives an example of a simple iterator called *string_chars*, which produces the characters in a string in the order in which they appear. This iterator uses string operations *size*(*s*), which tells how many characters are in the string *s*, and *fetch* (*s*, *n*), which returns the *n*th character in the string *s* (provided the integer *n* is greater than zero and does not exceed the size of the string).[7]

The general form of the CLU **for** statement is

for declarations **in** iterator_invocation **do**
   body
   end;

An example of the use of the **for** statement occurs in the *count_numeric* procedure (see Figure 5), which contains a loop that counts the number of numeric characters in a string. Note that the details of how the characters are obtained from the string are entirely contained in the definition of the iterator.

Iterators work as follows: A **for** statement initially invokes an iterator, passing it some arguments. Each time a **yield** statement is executed in the iterator, the objects yielded[8] are assigned to the variables declared in the **for** statement (following the reserved word **for**)

---

[7] A **while** loop is used in the implementation of *string_chars* so that the example will be based on familiar concepts. In actual practice, such a loop would be written by using a **for** statement invoking a primitive iterator.

[8] Zero or more objects may be yielded, but the number and types of objects yielded each time by an iterator must agree with the number and types of variables in a **for** statement using the iterator.

in corresponding order, and the body of the **for** statement is executed. Then the iterator is resumed at the statement following the **yield** statement, in the same environment as when the objects were yielded. When the iterator terminates, by either an implicit or explicit **return**, the invoking **for** statement terminates. The iteration may also be prematurely terminated by a **return** in the body of the **for** statement.

For example, suppose that *string_chars* is invoked with the string "a3". The first character yielded is 'a'. At this point, within *string_chars*, *index* = 1 and *limit* = 2. Next the body of the **for** statement is performed. Since the character 'a' is not numeric, *count* remains at 0. Next *string_chars* is resumed at the statement after the **yield** statement, and when resumed, *index* = 1 and *limit* = 2. Then *index* is assigned 2, and the character '3' is selected from the string and yielded. Since '3' is numeric, *count* becomes 1. Then *string_chars* is resumed, with *index* = 2 and *limit* = 2, and *index* is incremented, which causes the **while** loop to terminate. The implicit **return** terminates both the iterator and the **for** statement, with control resuming at the statement after the **for** statement, and *count* = 1.

While iterators are useful in general, they are especially valuable in conjunction with data abstractions that are collections of objects (such as sets, arrays, and *sorted_bags*). Iterators afford users of such abstractions access to all objects in the collection without exposing irrelevant details. Several iterators may be included in a data abstraction. When the order of obtaining the objects is important, different iterators may provide different orders.

4.3 Implementation and Use of Sorted_bag

Now we can describe a minimal set of operations for *sorted_bag*. The operations are *create*, *insert*, *size*, and *increasing*. *Create*, *insert*, and *size* are procedural abstractions that, respectively, create a *sorted_bag*, insert an item into a *sorted_bag*, and give the number of items in a *sorted_bag*. *Increasing* is a control abstraction that produces the items in a *sorted_bag* in increasing order; each item produced is accompanied by an integer representing the number of times the item appears in the *sorted_bag*. Note that other operations might also be useful for *sorted_bag*, for example, an iterator yielding the items in decreasing order. In general, the definer of a data abstraction can provide as many operations as seems reasonable.

In Figure 6, we give an implementation of the *sorted_bag* abstraction. It is implemented by using a sorted binary tree, just as *wordbag* was implemented. Thus a subsidiary abstraction is necessary. This abstraction, called *tree*, is a generalization of the *wordtree* abstraction (used in Section 2), which has been parameterized to work for all ordered types. An implementation of *tree* is given in Figure 7. Notice that both the *tree* abstraction and the *sorted_bag* abstraction place the same constraints on their type parameters.

Fig. 6. The *sorted_bag* cluster.

```
sorted_bag = cluster [t: type] is create, insert, size, increasing
    where t has equal, lt: proctype (t, t) returns (bool);
    rep = record [contents: tree[t], total: int];
create = proc ( ) returns (cvt);
    return (rep${contents: tree[t]$create ( ), total: 0});
    end create;
insert = proc (sb: cvt, v: t);
    sb.contents := tree[t]$insert (sb.contents, v);
    sb.total := sb.total + 1;
    end insert;
size = proc (sb: cvt) returns (int);
    return (sb.total);
    end size;
increasing = iter (sb: cvt) yields (t, int);
    for item: t, count: int
        in tree[t]$increasing (sb.contents) do
            yield (item, count);
            end;
    end increasing;
end sorted_bag;
```

Fig. 7. The *tree* cluster.

```
tree = cluster [t: type] is create, insert, increasing
    where t has equal, lt: proctype (t, t) returns (bool);
    node = record [value: t, count: int,
                      lesser: tree[t], greater: tree[t]];
    rep = oneof [empty: null, non_empty: node];
create = proc ( ) returns (cvt);
    return (rep$make_empty (nil));
    end create;
insert = proc (x: cvt, v: t) returns (cvt);
    tagcase x
        tag empty:
            n: node := node${value: v, count: 1,
                              lesser: tree[t]$create ( ),
                              greater: tree[t]$create ( )};
            return (rep$make_non_empty (n));
        tag non_empty (n: node):
            if t$equal (v, n.value)
                    then n.count := n.count + 1;
                elseif t$lt (v, n.value)
                    then n.lesser := tree[t]$insert (n.lesser, v);
                else n.greater := tree[t]$insert (n.greater, v);
                end;
            return (x);
        end;
    end insert;
increasing = iter (x: cvt) yields (t, int);
    tagcase x
        tag empty: ;
        tag non_empty (n: node):
            for item: t, count: int
                in tree[t]$increasing (n.lesser) do
                    yield (item, count);
                    end;
            yield (n.value, n.count);
            for item: t, count: int
                in tree[t]$increasing (n.greater) do
                    yield (item, count);
                    end;
        end;
    end increasing;
end tree;
```

An important feature of the *sorted_bag* and *tree* clusters is the way that the cluster parameter is used in places where the type **string** was used in *wordbag* and *wordtree*. This usage is especially evident in the implementation of *tree*. For example, *tree* has a representation that stores values of type *t*: the *value* component of a *node* must be an object of type *t*.

In the *insert* operation of *tree*, the *lt* and *equal* operations of type *t* are used. We have used the compound form, e.g. *t$equal* (*v*, *n.value*), to emphasize that the *equal* operation of *t* is being used. The short form, *v* = *n.value*, could have been used instead.

The *increasing* iterator of *tree* works as follows: first it yields all items in the current tree that are less than the item at the top node; the items are obtained by a recursive use of itself, passing the *lesser* subtree as an argument. Next it yields the contents of the top node, and then it yields all items in the current tree that are greater than the item at the top node (again by a recursive use of itself). In this way it performs a complete walk over the tree, yielding the values at all nodes, in increasing order.

Finally, we show in Figure 8 how the original procedure *count_words* can be implemented in terms of *sorted_bag*. Note that the *count_words* procedure now uses *sorted_bag*[**string**] instead of *wordbag*. *Sorted_bag*[**string**] is legitimate since the type **string** provides both *lt* and *equal* operations. Note that two **for** statements are used in *count_words*. The second **for** statement prints the words in alphabetic order, using the *increasing* iterator of *sorted_bag*. The first **for** statement inserts the words into the *sorted_bag*; it uses an iterator

words = **iter** (i: instream) **yields** (string);
          . . .
          end words;

The definition of *words* is left as an exercise for the reader.

5. The CLU Library

So far, we have shown CLU modules as separate pieces of text, without explaining how they are bound together to form a program. This section describes the CLU library, which plays a central role in supporting intermodule references.

The CLU library contains information about abstractions. The library supports incremental program development, one abstraction at a time, and, in addition, makes abstractions that are defined during the construction of one program available as a basis for subsequent program development. The information in the library permits the separate compilation of single modules with complete type checking of all external references (such as procedure invocations).

The structure of the library derives from the fundamental distinction between abstractions and implementations. For each abstraction, there is a *description unit* which contains all system-maintained information about that abstraction. Included in the description unit are zero or more modules that implement the abstraction.[9]

The most important information contained in a description unit is the abstraction's *interface specification*, which is that information needed to type-check uses of the abstraction. For procedural and control abstractions, this information consists of the number and types of parameters, arguments, and output values, plus any constraints on type parameters (i.e. required operations, as described in Section 4). For data abstractions, it includes the number and types of parameters, constraints on type parameters, and the name and interface specification of each operation.

An abstraction is entered in the library by submitting the interface specification; no implementations are required. In fact, a module can be compiled before any implementations have been provided for the abstractions that it uses; it is necessary only that interface specifications have been given for those abstractions. Ultimately, there can be many implementations of an abstraction; each implementation is required to satisfy the interface specification of the abstraction. Because all uses and implementations of an abstraction are checked against the interface specification, the actual selection of an implementation can be delayed until just before (or perhaps during) execution. We imagine a process of binding together modules into programs, prior to execution, at which time this selection would be made.

An important detail of the CLU system is the method by which CLU modules refer to abstractions. To avoid problems of name conflicts that can arise in large systems, the names used by a module to refer to abstractions can be chosen to suit the programmer's convenience. When a module is submitted for compilation, its external references must be bound to description units so that type checking can be performed. The binding is accomplished by constructing an *association list*, mapping names to description units, which is passed to the compiler along with the source code when compiling the module. The mapping in the association list is stored by the compiler in the library as part of the module. A similar process is involved in entering interface specifications of abstractions, as these will include references to other (data) abstractions.

When the compiler type-checks a module, it uses the association list to map the external names in the module to description units and then uses the interface specifications in those description units to check that the abstractions are used correctly. The type correctness of the module thus depends upon the binding of names to description units and the interface specifications in those description units, and could be invalidated if changes to the binding or the interface specifications were subsequently made. For this reason, the process of compilation permanently binds a module to the abstractions it uses, and the interface description of an abstraction, once defined, is not allowed to change. (Of course, a new description unit can be created to describe a modified abstraction.)

---

[9] Other information that may be stored in the library includes information about relationships among abstractions, as might be expressed in a module interconnection language [5, 21].

Fig. 8. The *count_words* procedure using iterators.

```
count_words = proc (i: instream, o: outstream);
  wordbag = sorted_bag[string];
  % create an empty wordbag
  wb: wordbag := wordbag$create ( );
  % scan document, adding each word found to wb
  for word: string in words (i) do
    wordbag$insert (wb, word);
    end;
  % print the wordbag
  total: int := wordbag$size (wb);
  for w: string, count: int in wordbag$increasing (wb) do
    print_word (w, count, total, o);
    end;
  end count_words;
```

6. Implementation

This section briefly describes the current implementation of CLU and discusses its efficiency.

The implementation is based on a decision to represent all CLU objects by *object descriptors*, which are fixed-size values containing a type code and some type-dependent information.[10] In the case of mutable types, the type-dependent information is a pointer to a separately allocated area containing the state information. For constant types, the information either directly contains the value (if the value can be encoded in the information field, as for integers, characters, and booleans) or contains a pointer to separately allocated space (as for strings). The type codes are used by the garbage collector to determine the physical representation of objects so that the accessible objects can be traced; they are also useful for supporting program debugging.

The use of fixed-size object descriptors allows variables to be fixed-size cells. Assignment is efficient: the object descriptor resulting from the evaluation of the expression is simply copied into the variable. In addition, a single size for variables facilitates the separate compilation of modules and allows most of the code of a parameterized module to be shared among all instantiations of the module. The actual parameters are made available to this code by means of a small parameter-dependent section, which is initialized prior to execution.

Procedure invocation is relatively efficient. A single program stack is used, and argument passing is as efficient as assignment. Iterators are a form of coroutine; however, their use is sufficiently constrained that they are implemented using just the program stack. Using an iterator is therefore only slightly more expensive than using a procedure.

The data abstraction mechanism is not inherently expensive. No execution-time type checking is necessary. Furthermore, the type conversion implied by **cvt** is merely a change in the view taken of an object's type and does not require any computation.

A number of optimization techniques can be applied to a collection of modules if one is willing to give up the flexibility of separate compilation. The most effective such optimization is the inline substitution of procedure (and iterator) bodies for invocations [18]. The use of data abstractions tends to introduce extra levels of procedure invocations that perform little or no computation. As an example, consider the *wordbag$insert* operation (Figure 3), which merely invokes the *wordtree$insert* operation and increments a counter. If data abstractions had not been used, these actions would most likely have been performed directly by the *count_words* procedure. The *wordbag$insert* operation is thus a good candidate for being compiled inline. Once inline substitution has been performed, the increase in context will enhance the effectiveness of conventional optimization techniques [1–3].

7. Discussion

Our intent in this paper has been to provide an informal introduction to the abstraction mechanisms in CLU. By means of programming examples, we have illustrated the use of data, procedural, and control abstractions and have shown how CLU modules are used to implement these abstractions. We have not attempted to provide a complete description of CLU, but, in the course of explaining the examples, most features of the language have appeared. One important omission is the CLU exception handling mechanism (which does support abstractions); this mechanism is described in [10].

In addition to describing constructs that support abstraction, previous sections have covered a number of other topics. We have discussed the semantics of CLU. We have described the organization of the CLU library and discussed how it supports incremental program development and separate compilation and type checking of modules. Also we have described our current implementation and discussed its efficiency.

In designing CLU, our goal was to simplify the task of constructing reliable software that is reasonably easy to understand, modify, and maintain. It seems appropriate, therefore, to conclude this paper with a discussion of how CLU contributes to this goal.

The quality of any program depends upon the skill of the designer. In CLU programs, this skill is reflected in the choice of abstractions. In a good design, abstractions will be used to simplify the connections between modules and to encapsulate decisions that are likely to change [17]. Data abstractions are particularly valuable for these purposes. For example, through the use of a data abstraction, modules that share a system database rely only on its abstract behavior as defined by the database operations. The connections among these modules are much simpler than would be possible if they shared knowledge of the format of the database and the relationship among its parts. In addition, the database abstraction can be reimplemented without affecting the code of the modules that use it. CLU encourages the use of data abstractions and thus aids the programmer during program design.

[10] Object descriptors are similar to capabilities [11].

The benefits arising from the use of data abstractions are based on the constraint, inherent in CLU and enforced by the CLU compiler, that only the operations of the abstraction may access the representations of the objects. This constraint ensures that the distinction made in CLU between abstractions and implementations applies to data abstractions as well as to procedural and control abstractions.

The distinction between abstractions and implementations eases program modification and maintenance. Once it has been determined that an abstraction must be reimplemented, CLU guarantees that the code of all modules using that abstraction will be unaffected by the change. The modules need not be reprogrammed or even recompiled; only the process of selecting the implementation of the abstraction must be redone. The problem of determining what modules must be changed is also simplified because each module has a well-defined purpose — to implement an abstraction — and no other module can interfere with that purpose.

Understanding and verification of CLU programs is made easier because the distinction between abstractions and implementations permits this task to be decomposed. One module at a time is studied to determine that it implements its abstraction. This study requires understanding the behavior of the abstractions it uses, but it is not necessary to understand the modules implementing those abstractions. Those modules can be studied separately.

A promising way to establish the correctness of a program is by means of a mathematical proof. For practical reasons, proofs should be performed (or at least checked) by a verification system, since the process of constructing a proof is tedious and error-prone. Decomposition of the proof is essential for program proving, which is practical only for small programs (like CLU modules). Note that when the CLU compiler does type checking, it is, in addition to enforcing the constraint that permits the proof to be decomposed, also performing a small part of the actual proof.

We have included as declarations in CLU just the information that the compiler can check with reasonable efficiency. We believe that the other information required for proofs (specifications and assertions) should be expressed in a separate "specification" language. The properties of such a language are being studied [7, 13, 14, 19]. We intend eventually to add formal specifications to the CLU system; the library is already organized to accommodate this addition. At that time various specification language processors could be added to the system.

We believe that the constraints imposed by CLU are essential for practical as well as theoretical reasons. It is true that data abstractions can be used in any language by establishing programming conventions to protect the representations of objects. However, conventions are no substitute for enforced constraints. It is inevitable that the conventions will be violated — and

are likely to be violated just when they are needed most, in implementing, maintaining, and modifying large programs. It is precisely at this time, when the programming task becomes very difficult, that a language like CLU will be most valuable and appreciated.

Acknowledgments. The authors gratefully acknowledge the contributions made by members of the CLU design group over the last three years. Several people have made helpful comments about this paper, including Toby Bloom, Dorothy Curtis, Mike Hammer, Eliot Moss, Jerry Saltzer, Bob Scheifler, and the referees.

References
1. Allen, F.E., and Cocke, J. A catalogue of optimizing transformations. Rep. RC 3548. IBM Thomas J. Watson Res. Ctr., Yorktown Heights, N.Y., 1971.
2. Allen, F.E. A program data flow analysis procedure. Rep. RC 5278, IBM Thomas J. Watson Res. Ctr., Yorktown Heights, N.Y., 1975.
3. Atkinson, R.R. Optimization techniques for a structured programming language. S.M. Th., Dept. of Electr. Eng. and Comptr. Sci., M.I.T., Cambridge, Mass., June 1976.
4. Dahl, O.J., Myhrhaug, B., and Nygaard, K. The SIMULA 67 common base language. Pub. S-22. Norwegian Comptng. Ctr., Oslo, 1970.
5. DeRemer, F., and Kron, H. Programming-in-the-large versus programming-in-the-small. Proc. Int. Conf. on Reliable Software, SIGPLAN Notices 10, 6 (June 1975), 114–121.
6. Dijkstra, E.W. Notes on structured programming. *Structured Programming, A.P.I.C. Studies in Data Processing No. 8*. Academic Press, New York, 1972, pp. 1–81.
7. Guttag, J.V., Horowitz, E., and Musser, D.R. Abstract data types and software validation. Rep ISI/RR-76-48. Inform. Sci. Inst., U. of Southern California, Marina del Rey, Calif., Aug. 1976.
8. Hoare, C.A.R. Proof of correctness of data representations. *Acta Informatica 4* (1972), 271–281.
9. Knuth, D. *The Art of Computer Programming. Vol. 3: Sorting and Searching*. Addison Wesley, Reading, Mass., 1973.
10. Laboratory for Computer Science Progress Report 1974–1975. Comput. Structures Group. Rep. PR-XII, Lab. for Comptr. Sci., M.I.T. To be published.
11. Lampson, B.W. Protection. Proc. Fifth Annual Princeton Conf. on Inform. Sci. and Syst., Princeton U., Princeton, N.J., 1971, pp. 437–443.
12. Liskov, B.H., and Zilles, S.N. Programming with abstract data types. Proc. ACM SIGPLAN Conf. on Very High Level Languages, SIGPLAN Notices 9, 4 (April 1974), 50–59.
13. Liskov, B.H., and Zilles, S.N. Specification techniques for data abstractions. *IEEE Trans. Software Eng.*, SE-1 (1975), 7–19.
14. Liskov, B.H., and Berzins, V. An appraisal of program specifications. Comput. Structures Group Memo 141, Lab. for Comptr. Sci., M.I.T., Cambridge, Mass., July 1976.
15. McCarthy, J., et al. *LISP 1.5 Programmer's Manual*. M.I.T. Press, Cambridge, Mass., 1962.
16. Morris, J.H. Protection in programming languages. *Comm. ACM 16*, 1 (Jan. 1973), 15–21.
17. Parnas, D.L. Information distribution aspects of design methodology. Information Processing 71, Vol. 1, North-Holland Pub. Co., Amsterdam, 1972, pp. 339–344.
18. Scheifler, R.W. An analysis of inline substitution for the CLU programming language. Comput. Structures Group Memo 139, Lab. for Comptr. Sci., M.I.T., Cambridge, Mass., June 1976.
19. Spitzen, J., and Wegbreit, B. The verification and synthesis of data structures. *Acta Informatica 4* (1975), 127–144.
20. Standish, T.A. Data structures: an axiomatic approach. Rep. 2639, Bolt, Beranek and Newman, Cambridge, Mass., 1973.
21. Thomas, J.W. Module interconnection in programming systems supporting abstraction. Rep. CS-16, Comptr. Sci. Prog., Brown U., Providence, R.I., 1976.
22. Wirth, N. Program development by stepwise refinement. *Comm. ACM 14*, 4 (1971), 221–227.
23. Wirth, N. The programming language PASCAL. *Acta Informatica 1* (1971), 35–63.
24. Wulf, W.A., London, R., and Shaw, M. An introduction to the construction and verification of Alphard programs. *IEEE Trans. Software Eng.* SE-2 (1976), 253–264.

A Semantics of Multiple Inheritance

Luca Cardelli[1]

AT&T Bell Laboratories, Murray Hill, NJ 07974

1. Introduction

There are two major ways of structuring data in programming languages. The first and common one, used for example in Pascal, can be said to derive from standard branches of mathematics. Data is organized as cartesian products (i.e. record types), disjoint sums (i.e. unions or variant types) and function spaces (i.e. functions and procedures).

The second method can be said to derive from biology and taxonomy. Data is organized in a hierarchy of classes and subclasses, and data at any level of the hierarchy *inherits* all the attributes of data higher up in the hierarchy. The top level of this hierarchy is usually called the class of all *objects*; every datum *is an* object and every datum *inherits* the basic properties of objects, e.g. the ability to tell whether two objects are the same or not. Functions and procedures are considered as local actions of objects, as opposed to global operations acting over objects.

These different ways of structuring data have generated distinct classes of programming languages, and induced different programming styles. Programming with taxonomically organized data is often called *object-oriented programming*, and has been advocated as an effective way of structuring programming environments, data bases, and large systems in general.

The notions of inheritance and object-oriented programming first appeared in Simula 67 [Dahl 66]. In Simula, objects are grouped into classes and classes can be organized into a subclass hierarchy. Objects are similar to records with functions as components, and elements of a class can appear wherever elements of the respective superclasses are expected. Subclasses inherit all the attributes of their superclasses. In Simula, the issues are somewhat complicated by the use of objects as coroutines, so that communication between objects can be implemented as *message passing* between processes.

Smalltalk [Goldberg 83] adopts and exploits the idea of inheritance, with some changes. While stressing the message-passing paradigm, a Smalltalk object is not usually a separate process. Message passing is realized by function calls, although the association of message names to functions (called *methods*) is not straightforward. With respect to Simula, Smalltalk also abandons static scoping, to gain flexibility in interactive use, and strong typing, allowing it to implement system introspection and to introduce the notion of meta-classes.

[1]Present address: DEC SRC, 130 Lytton Ave, Palo Alto, CA 94301.

Inheritance can be single or multiple. In the case of single inheritance, as in Simula or Smalltalk, the subclass hierarchy has the form of a tree, i.e. every class has a unique superclass. A class can sometimes be considered a subclass of two incompatible superclasses; then an arbitrary decision has to be made to determine which superclass to use. This problem leads naturally to the idea of multiple inheritance.

Multiple inheritance occurs when an object can belong to several incomparable superclasses: the subclass relation is no longer constrained to form a tree, but can form a dag. Multiple inheritance is more elegant than simple inheritance in describing class hierarchies, but it is more difficult to implement. So far, it has mostly been considered in the context of type-free dynamically-scoped languages and implemented as Lisp or Smalltalk extensions [Borning 82, Bobrow 83, Hullot 83, Steels 83, Weinreb 81], or as part of knowledge representation languages [Attardi 81]. Exceptions are Galileo [Albano 85] and OBJ [Futatsugi 85] where multiple inheritance is typechecked.

The definition of what makes a language object-oriented is still controversial. An examination of the differences between Simula, Smalltalk and other languages suggest that inheritance is the only notion critically associated with object-oriented programming. Coroutines, message-passing, static/dynamic scoping, typechecking and single/multiple superclasses are all fairly independent features which may or may not be present in languages which are commonly considered object-oriented. Hence, a theory of object-oriented programming should first of all focus on the meaning of inheritance.

The aim of this paper is to present a clean semantics of multiple inheritance and to show that, in the context of strongly-typed, statically-scoped languages, a sound typechecking algorithm exists. Multiple inheritance is also interpreted in a broad sense: instead of being limited to objects, it is extended in a natural way to union types and to higher-order functional types. This constitutes a semantic basis for the unification of functional and object-oriented programming.

A clean semantics has the advantage of making clear which issues are fundamental and which are implementation accidents or optimizations. The implementation of multiple inheritance suggested by the semantics is very naïve, but does not preclude more sophisticated implementation techniques. It should be emphasized that advanced implementation techniques are absolutely essential to obtain usable systems based on inheritance [Deutsch 84].

The first part of this paper is informal, and presents the basic notations and intuitions by means of examples. The second part is formal: it introduces a language, a semantics, a type-inference system and a typechecking algorithm. The algorithm is proved sound with respect to the inference system, and the inference system is proved sound with respect to the semantics [Milner 78].

2. Objects as records

There are several ways of thinking of what objects *are*. In the pure Smalltalk-like view, objects recall physical entities, like boxes or cars. Physical entities are unfortunately not very useful as semantic models of objects, because they are far too complicated to describe formally.

Two simpler interpretations of objects seem to emerge from the implementations of object-oriented languages. The first interpretation derives from Simula, where objects are essentially records with possibly functional components. Message passing is achieved by simple field selection (of functional record components) and inheritance has to do with the number and type of fields possessed by a record.

The second interpretation derives from Lisp. An object is a function which receives a message (a string or an atom) and dispatches on the message to select the appropriate *method*. Here message passing is achieved by function application, and inheritance has to do with the way messages are dispatched.

In some sense these two interpretations are equivalent because records can be represented as functions from labels (messages) to values. However, to say that objects are functions is misleading, because we must qualify that objects are functions over messages. Instead, we can safely assert that objects are records, because labels are an essential part of records.

We also want to regard objects as records for typechecking purposes. While a (character string) message can be the result of an arbitrary computation, a record selection usually requires the selection label to be known at compile-time. In the latter case it is possible to statically determine the set of messages supported by an object, and a compile-time type error can be reported on any attempt to send unsupported messages. This property is true for Simula, but has been lost in all the succeeding languages.

We shall show how the objects-as-records paradigm can account for all the basic features of objects, provided that the surrounding language is rich enough. The features we consider are multiple inheritance, message-passing, private instance variables and the concept of *self*. However, the duality between records and functions remains: in our language objects are records, but the semantics interprets records as functions.

3. Records

A *record* is a finite association of values to labels, for example:

    {a = 3, b = true, c = "abc"}

This is a record with three fields a, b and c having as values an integer 3, a boolean true and a string "abc" respectively. The *labels* a, b and c belong to a separate domain of labels; they are not identifiers or strings, and cannot be computed as the result of expressions. Records are unordered and cannot contain the same label twice.

The basic operation on records is field selection, denoted by the usual dot notation:

    {a = 3, b = true, c = "abc"} . a = 3

An expression can have one or more types; we write

    e : τ

to indicate that expression e has type τ.

Records have *record types* which are labeled sets of types with distinct labels, for example we have:

    {a = 3, b = true} : {a : int, b : bool}

In general, we can write the following informal typing rule for records:

[Rule1]   if $e_1 : \tau_1$ and ... and $e_n : \tau_n$ then $\{a_1 = e_1, ..., a_n = e_n\} : \{a_1 : \tau_1, ..., a_n : \tau_n\}$

This is the first of a series of informal rules which are only meant to capture our initial intuitions about typing. They are not supposed to form a complete set or to be independent of each other.

There is a *subtype* relation on record types which corresponds to the *subclass* relation of Simula and Smalltalk. For example we may define the following types (type definitions are prefixed by the keyword type):

    type any   = {}
    type object   = {age: int}
    type vehicle = {age: int, speed: int}
    type machine = {age: int, fuel: string}
    type car   = {age: int, speed: int, fuel: string}

Intuitively a vehicle *is* an object, a machine *is* an object and a car *is* a vehicle *and* a machine (and therefore an object). We say that car is a subtype of machine and vehicle; machine is a subtype of object; etc. In general a record type τ is a subtype (written $\leq$) of a record type τ' if τ has all the fields of τ', and possibly more, and the common fields of τ and τ' are in the $\leq$ relation. Moreover, all the basic types (like int and bool) are subtypes of themselves:

[Rule2]   • $\iota \leq \iota$ (ι a basic type)
            • $\tau_1 \leq \tau'_1, ..., \tau_n \leq \tau'_n \Rightarrow \{a_1 : \tau_1, ..., a_{n+m} : \tau_{n+m}\} \leq \{a_1 : \tau'_1, ..., a_n : \tau'_n\}$

Let us consider a particular car (value definitions are prefixed by the keyword value):

    value mycar = {age = 4, speed = 140, fuel = "gasoline"}

Of course mycar: car (mycar has type car), but we might also want to assert mycar: object. To obtain this, we say that when a value has a type τ, then it has also all the types τ' such that τ is a subtype of τ'. This leads to our third informal type rule:

[Rule3]   if $a : \tau$ and $\tau \leq \tau'$ then $a : \tau'$

If we define the function:

    value age(x: object): int = x.age

we can meaningfully compute age(mycar) because, by [Rule3], mycar has the type required by age. Indeed mycar has the types car, vehicle, machine, object, the empty record type and many other ones.

When is it meaningful to apply a function to an argument? This is determined by the following rules:

[Rule4]   if $f : \sigma \to \tau$ and $a : \sigma$ then $f(a)$ is meaningful, and $f(a) : \tau$
[Rule5]   if $f : \sigma \to \tau$ and $a : \sigma'$, where $\sigma' \leq \sigma$ then $f(a)$ is meaningful, and $f(a) : \tau$

[Rule5] is just a consequence of [Rule3] and [Rule4]. From [Rule3] and $a : \sigma'$ we can deduce that $a : \sigma$; then it is certainly meaningful to compute $f(a)$ as $f : \sigma \to \tau$.

The conventional *subclass* relation is usually defined only on objects or classes. Our *subtype* relation extends naturally to functional types. Consider the function

    serial_number: int $\to$ car

We can argue that serial_number returns vehicles, as all cars are vehicles. In general, all car-valued functions are also vehicle-valued functions, so that for any domain type t we can say that t→car (an appropriate domain of functions from t to car) is a subtype of t→vehicle:

    t $\to$ car $\leq$ t $\to$ vehicle   because   car $\leq$ vehicle

Now consider the function:

    speed: vehicle $\to$ int

As all cars are vehicles, we can use this function to compute the speed of a car. Hence speed is also a function from car to int. In general every function on vehicles is also a function on cars, and we can say that vehicle→int is a subtype of car→int:

    vehicle $\to$ t $\leq$ car $\to$ t   because   car $\leq$ vehicle

Something interesting is happening here: note how the subtype relation is inverted on the left hand side of the arrow. This happens because of the particular meaning we are giving to the → operator, as explained formally in the following sections. (Semantically, we work in a universal value domain V of all computable values. Every function f is a function from V to V, written f: V -> V, where -> is the conventional continuous function space. By f: $\sigma \to \tau$ we indicate a function f: V -> V which whenever given an element of $\sigma \subseteq V$ returns an element of $\tau \subseteq V$; nothing is asserted about the behavior of f outside σ).

Given any function f: $\sigma \to \tau$ from some domain σ to some codomain τ, we can always consider it as a function from some smaller domain $\sigma' \subseteq \sigma$ to some bigger codomain $\tau' \supseteq \tau$. For example a function f: vehicle→vehicle can be used in the context age(f(mycar)), where it is used as a function f: car→object (the application f(mycar) makes sense because every car is a vehicle; v = f(mycar) is a vehicle; hence it makes sense to compute age(v) as every vehicle is an object).

The general rule of subtyping among functional types can be expressed as follows:

[Rule6]   if $\sigma' \leq \sigma$ and $\tau \leq \tau'$ then $\sigma \to \tau \leq \sigma' \to \tau'$

As we said, the subtype relation extends to higher types. For example, the following is a definition of a function mycar_attribute which takes any integer-valued function on cars and applies it to my car.

    value mycar_attribute(f: car → int): int = f(mycar)

We can then apply it to functions of any type which is a subtype of car→int, e.g., age:object→int. (Why? Because car is a subtype of object, hence object→int is a subtype of car→int by [Rule6], hence (mycar_attribute: (car→int)→int)(age: object→int) makes sense by [Rule5]).

    mycar_attribute(age)   ≡ 4
    mycar_attribute(speed)   ≡ 140

Up to now we proceeded by assigning certain types to certain values. However the subtype relation has a very strong intuitive flavor of *inclusion* of types considered as sets of objects, and we want to justify our type assignments on semantic grounds.

Semantically we could regard the type vehicle as the set of all the records with a field age and a field speed having the appropriate types, but then cars would not belong to the set of vehicles as they have three fields while vehicles have two. To obtain the inclusion that we intuitively expect, we must say that the type vehicle is the set of all records which have *at least* two fields as above, but may have other fields. In this sense a car is a vehicle, and the set of all cars is included in the set of all vehicles, as we might expect. Some care is however needed to define these "sets", and this will be done formally in the following sections.

We conclude this section with a pragmatic consideration about record notation. Record types can have a large number of fields, hence we need some way of quickly defining a subtype of some record type, without having to list again all the fields of the record type. The following three sets of definitions are equivalent:

```
type object    = {age: int}
type vehicle   = {age: int, speed: int}
type machine   = {age: int, fuel: string}
type car       = {age: int, speed: int, fuel: string}


type object    = {age: int}
type vehicle   = object and {speed: int}
type machine   = object and {fuel: string}
type car       = vehicle and machine


type object    = {age: int}
type car       = object and {speed: int, fuel: string}
type vehicle   = car ignoring fuel
type machine   = car ignoring speed
```

The and operator forms the union of the fields of two record types; if two record types have some labels in common (like in vehicle and machine), then the corresponding types must match. At this point we do not specify exactly what *match* means, except that in the example above *matching* is equivalent to *being the same*. In its full generality, and corresponds to a meet operation on type expressions, as explained in a later section.

The ignoring operator simply eliminates a component from a record type. Both and and ignoring are undefined on types other than record types.

4. Variants

The two basic non-functional data type constructions in denotational semantics are cartesian products and disjoint sums. We have seen that inheritance can be expressed as a subtype relation on record types, which then extends to higher types. Record types are just labeled cartesian products, and by analogy we can ask whether there is some similar notion deriving from labeled disjoint sums.

A labeled disjoint sum is called here a *variant*. A variant type looks very much like a record type: it is an unordered set of label-type pairs, enclosed in brackets:

```
type int_or_bool = [a: int, b: bool]
```

An element of a variant type is a labeled value, where the label is one of the labels in the variant type, and the value has a type matching the type associated with that label. An element of int_or_bool is either an integer value labeled **a** or a boolean value labeled **b**.

```
value an_int      = [a = 3] : int_or_bool
value a_bool      = [b = true] : int_or_bool
```

The basic operations on variants are is, which tests whether a variant object has a particular label, and as, which extracts the contents of a variant object having a particular label:

```
an_int is a   ≡ true
an_int is b   ≡ false
an_int as a   ≡ 3
an_int as b   does not have a value
```

A variant type σ is a subtype of a variant type τ (written $\sigma \leq \tau$) if τ has all the labels of σ and correspondingly matching types. Hence int_or_bool is a subtype of [a: int, b: bool, c: string].

When the type associated to a label is unit (the trivial type, whose only defined element is the constant unity), we can omit the type altogether; a variant type where all fields have unit type is also called an *enumeration* type. The following examples deal with enumeration types.

```
type precious_metal    = [gold, silver]            (i.e. [gold: unit, silver: unit])
type metal             = [gold, silver, steel]
```

A value of an enumeration type, e.g. [gold = unity], can similarly be abbreviated by omitting the "= unity" part, e.g. [gold].

A function returning a precious metal is also a function returning a metal, hence:

$$t \rightarrow \text{precious\_metal} \leq t \rightarrow \text{metal} \quad \text{because} \quad \text{precious\_metal} \leq \text{metal}$$

A function working on metals will also work on precious metals, hence:

$$\text{metal} \rightarrow t \leq \text{precious\_metal} \rightarrow t \quad \text{because} \quad \text{precious\_metal} \leq \text{metal}$$

It is evident that [Rule6] holds unchanged for variant types. This justifies the use of the symbol $\leq$ for both record and variant subtyping. Semantically the subtype relation on variants is mapped to set inclusion, just as in the case of records: metal is a set with three defined elements [gold], [silver] and [steel], and precious_metal is a set with two defined elements [gold] and [silver].

There are two ways of deriving variant types from previously defined variant types. We could have defined metal and precious_metal as:

```
type precious_metal    = [gold, silver]
type metal             = precious_metal or [steel]
```

or as:

```
type metal             = [gold, silver, steel]
type precious_metal    = metal dropping steel
```

The or operator makes a union of the cases of two variant types, and the dropping operator removes a case from a variant type. The precise definition of these operators is contained in a later section.

5. Inheritance idioms

In the framework described so far, we can recognize some of the features of what is called *multiple inheritance* between objects, e.g. a car has (inherits) all the attributes of vehicle and of machine. Some aspects are however unusual; for example the inheritance relation only depends on the structure of objects and need not be declared explicitly.

This section compares our approach with other approaches to inheritance, and shows how to simulate a number of common inheritance techniques. However we are not trying to *explain* existing inheritance schemes (e.g. Smalltalk) in detail, but rather trying to present a new perspective on the issues.

Some differences between this and other inheritance schemes result in net gains. For example, we are not aware of languages where typechecking coexists with multiple inheritance and higher order functions, with the exception of Galileo [Albano 85] and Amber [Cardelli 86] which were developed in conjunction with this work. Typechecking provides compile-time protection against obvious bugs (like applying the speed function to a machine which is not a vehicle), and other less obvious mistakes. Complex type hierarchies can be built where "everything is also something else", and it can be difficult to remember which objects support which messages.

The subtype relation only holds on types, and there is no similar relation on objects. Thus we cannot model directly the *subobject* relation used by, for example, Omega [Attardi 81], where we could define the class of gasoline cars as the cars with fuel equal to "gasoline".

However, in simple cases we can achieve the same effect by turning certain sets of values into variant types. For example, instead of having the fuel field of a machine be a string, we could redefine:

```
type fueltype     = [coal, gasoline, electricity]
type machine      = {age: int, fuel: fueltype}
type car          = {age: int, speed: int, fuel: fueltype}
```

Now we can have:

```
type gasoline_car      = {age: int, speed: int, fuel: [gasoline]}
type combustion_car    = {age: int, speed: int, fuel: [gasoline, coal]}
```

and we obtain gasoline_car ≤ combustion_car ≤ car. Hence a function over combustion cars, for example, will accept a gasoline car as a parameter, but will give a compile-time type error when applied to electrical cars.

It is often the case that a function contained in a record field has to refer to other components of the same record. In Smalltalk this is done by referring to the whole record (i.e. object) as *self*, and then selecting the desired components out of that. In Simula there is a similar concept called *this*.

This self-referential capability can be obtained as a special case of the rec operator which we are about to introduce. The rec operator is used to define recursive functions and data. For example, the recursive factorial function can be written as:

```
rec fact: int → int. λn: int. if n=0 then 1 else n*fact(n-1)
```

(This is an expression, not a declaration.)

The body of rec is restricted to be a *constructor*; this is a vague term indicating that, in an implementation, computation can be temporarily suspended thereby avoiding some looping situations [Morris 80]. In the language we are considering, a constructor is either a constant, a record, a variant, a function or a rec expression obeying this restriction.

Examples of circular data definitions are extremely common in object-oriented programming. In the following example, a functional component of a record refers to *its* other components. The functional component d, below, computes the distance of *this* active_point from any other point.

```
type point =
    {x: real, y: real}
type active_point =
    point and {d: point → real}
value make_active_point(px: real, py: real): active_point =
    rec self: active_point.
        {x = px, y = py,
         d = λp: point. sqrt((p.x - self.x)**2 + (p.y - self.y)**2)}
```

Objects often have *private* variables, which are useful to maintain and update the local state of an object while preventing arbitrary external interference. Here is a counter object which starts from some fixed number and can only be incremented one step at a time. cell n is an updatable cell whose initial contents is n; a cell can be updated by := and its contents can be extracted by get (side-effects will not be treated in the formal semantics). Here, $\lambda().e$ is an abbreviation for $\lambda x{:}unit.e$, where x does not occur in e, and let x = a in b introduces a new variable x (initialized to a) local to the scope of b, whose value is returned.

```
type counter =
    {increment: unit → unit, fetch: unit → int}
value make_counter(n: int): counter =
    let count = cell n
    in   {increment = λ(). count := (get count)+1,
          fetch = λ(). get count}
```

Private variables are obtained in full generality by the above well known static scoping technique.

In the presence of side-effects, it can be useful to cascade operations on objects. For example we might want to define a different kind of counter, which could be used in the following way (where f() is an abbreviation for f(unity)):

```
make_counter(0).increment().increment().fetch()  ≡  2
```

In this case, a local record operation must be able to return *its* record. This requires both recursive objects and recursive types:

```
type counter =
    rec counter. {increment: unit → counter, fetch: unit → int}
value make_counter(n: int): counter =
    let count = cell n
    in   rec self: counter.
             {increment = λ(). count := (get count)+1; self,
              fetch = λ(). get count}
```

where ";" is sequencing of operations. (Recursive types will not be treated in the formal semantics; we believe they can be dealt with, but the complications would distract us from the major topic of this paper.)

In Smalltalk terminology, a subclass automatically inherits the methods of all its superclasses. A subclass can also redefine inherited methods. In any case all the objects created as members of a particular class or subclass will share the same methods. Here is an example where a class called Class_A is defined to have methods f and g; a make_A function creates objects of class Class_A by forming records with f and g components.

```
type Class_A            = {f: X → X', g: Y → Y'}
value fOfA(a: X): X'    = ...
value gOfA(a: Y): Y'    = ...
value make_A(): Class_A = {f = fOfA, g = gOfA}
```

Now we define a subclass of Class_A, called A_Subclass_B, which has an extra h method. The make_B function assembles objects of the subclass from the f component of the superclass, explicitly inheriting it, a newly defined g component, modifying an inherited method, and a new h component, local to the subclass.

```
type A_Subclass_B             = Class_A and {h: Z → Z'}
value gOfB(a: Y): Y'          = ...
value hOfB(a: Z): Z'          = ...
value make_B(): A_Subclass_B  = {f = fOfA, g = gOfB, h = hOfB}
```

Contrarily to Simula and Smalltalk, nothing prevents us from having totally different methods in different objects of the same class, as long as those methods have the prescribed type.

Both Simula and Smalltalk allow objects to access methods of their superclasses. This cannot be simulated in any general and direct way in our framework, partially because of the presence of multiple superclasses.

6. Typechecking anomalies

The style of inheritance typechecking we have presented has a few unexpected aspects. These have to do with the lack of parametric polymorphism and with side-effects.

Consider the following identity function on records having an integer component a:

```
type A           = {a: int}
value id(x: A): A = x
```

It is possible to apply id to a subtype B of A, but type information is lost in the process, as the result will have type A, not B. For example, the following expression will not typecheck:

```
(id({a = 3, b = true})).b
```

While this does not have serious consequences in practice, one is forced to adopt a less polymorphic style than one would like: in the previous example it is necessary to write many identity functions for different types.

The following example shows that inheritance polymorphism can sometime achieve the effect of parametric polymorphism, but not quite:

```
type anyList          = rec list. [nil: unit, cons: {rest: list}]
type intList          = rec list. [nil: unit, cons: {first: int, rest: list}]
type intPairList      = rec list. [nil: unit, cons: {first: int, second: int, rest: list}]

value rest(l: anyList): anyList            = (l as cons).rest
value intFirst(l: intList): int            = (l as cons).first
value intSecond(l: intPairList): int       = (l as cons).second

value rec length(l: anyList): int =
    if l is nil then 0 else (1 + length(rest l))
```

Here intPairList is a subtype of intList, which is a subtype of anyList. The rest operator can work on any of these lists, and it can be used to define a polymorphic length function. But it is not possible to define a polymorphic first operator. The intFirst function above works on intList and intPairList, and intSecond works only on intPairList. A solution to this problem is proposed in [Cardelli 85], where multiple inheritance and parametric polymorphism are merged.

Inheritance typechecking has to be restricted to preserve soundness in presence of side-effects. Parametric polymorphism also has to be restricted in order to deal with side-effects, but the problem seems to be rather different in nature. Consider the following example (due to Antonio Albano), where we assume that it is possible to update record fields by a := operator (this is a different update mechanism than the one used in the previous section):

```
value f(r: {a: {}}): unit =
    r.a := {}
value r =
    {a = {b = 3}}
f(r)
r.a.b
```

The last expression will cause a run-time error, as the a component of r has been changed to {} by f. To prevent this, it is sufficient to distinguish syntactically between updatable and non-updatable record fields, and to require type equivalence (instead of type inclusion) while checking inclusion of updatable fields. Again, this discussion is informal; side-effects will not be dealt with in the rest of the paper.

7. Expressions

We now begin the formal treatment of multiple inheritance. First, we define a simple applicative language supporting inheritance. Then a denotational semantics is presented, in a domain of values V. Certain subsets of V are regarded as types, and inheritance corresponds directly to set inclusion among types. A type inference system and a typechecking algorithm are then presented. The soundness of the algorithm is proved by showing that the algorithm is consistent with the inference system, and that the inference system is in turn consistent with the semantics.

Our language is a variant of the typed lambda calculus with type inclusion, recursion and a data domain including records and variants. The following notation is often used for records (and similarly for record and variant types):

$$\{a_1 = e_1, \ldots, a_n = e_n\} \equiv \{a_i = e_i\} \quad i \in 1..n$$
$$\{a_1 = e_1, \ldots, a_n = e_n, a'_1 = e'_1, \ldots, a'_m = e'_m\} \equiv \{a_i = e_i, a'_j = e'_j\} \quad i \in 1..n, j \in 1..m$$

Here is the syntax of expressions and type expressions:

$e ::=$		expressions
$x \mid$		identifiers
$b \mid$		constants
if e then e else $e \mid$		conditionals
$\{a_i = e_i\} \mid e.a \mid$	$(i \in 1..n, n \geq 0)$	records
$[a = e] \mid e$ is $a \mid e$ as $a \mid$		variants
$\lambda x{:}\tau . e \mid e\ e \mid$		functions
rec $x{:}\tau . e \mid$		recursive data
$e{:}\tau \mid$		type specs
(e)		
$\tau ::=$		type expressions
$\iota \mid$		type constants
$\{a_i : \tau_i\} \mid$	$(i \in 1..n, n \geq 0)$	record types
$[a_i : \tau_i] \mid$	$(i \in 1..n, n \geq 0)$	variant types
$\tau \rightarrow \tau \mid$		function types
(τ)		

where $i \neq j \Rightarrow a_i \neq a_j$
take $\iota_0 = $ unit, $\iota_1 = $ bool, $\iota_2 = $ int, etc.

Syntactic restriction: the body e of rec $x{:}\tau . e$ can only be a constant, a record, a variant, a lambda expression, or another rec expression obeying this restriction.

Labels a and identifiers x have the same syntax, but are distinguishable by the syntactic context. Among the type constants we have unit (the domain with one defined element), bool and int. Among the constants we have unity (of type unit), booleans (true, false) and numbers (0, 1, ...).

Instead of the two operations is and as on variants, one could use a single case construct. The former are more direct and illustrate the semantic handling of exceptions, while the latter is more elegant (one construct instead of two) and avoids dealing with exceptions.

Standard abbreviations are (the last two can only appear after a let):

let x: τ = e in e'	for	(λx: τ . e') e
f(x: τ): τ' = e	for	f: $\tau \to \tau'$ = λx: τ . (e: τ')
rec f(x: τ): τ' = e	for	f: $\tau \to \tau'$ = rec f: $\tau \to \tau'$. λx: τ . e

Record and variant type expressions are unordered, so for any permutation $\pi(n)$ of 1..n, we identify:

$$\{a_i : \tau_i\} \equiv \{a_{\pi(n)(i)} : \tau_{\pi(n)(i)}\} \; i \in 1..n$$
$$[a_i : \tau_i] \equiv [a_{\pi(n)(i)} : \tau_{\pi(n)(i)}] \; i \in 1..n$$

8. The semantic domain

The semantics of expressions is given in the recursively defined domain V of *values*. The domain operators used below are disjoint sum (+), cartesian product ($\times$), and continuous function space (->).

$$V = B_0 + B_1 + ... + R + U + F + W$$
$$R = L \to V$$
$$U = L \times V$$
$$F = V \to V$$
$$W = \{w\}$$

where L is a flat domain of character strings, called *labels*, and B_i are flat domains of basic values. We take:

$$B_0 \equiv O \equiv \{\perp_O, \text{unity}\}$$
$$B_1 \equiv T \equiv \{\perp_T, \text{true, false}\}$$
$$B_2 \equiv N \equiv \{\perp_N, 0, 1, ...\}$$

b_{ij} is the j-th element of the basic domain B_i

W is a domain which contains a single element w, the *wrong* value. The value w is used to model run-time *type errors* (e.g. trying to apply an integer as if it were a function) which we want a compiler to trap before execution. It is not used to model run-time *exceptions* (like trying to extract the head of an empty list); in our context these can only be generated by the as operator. The name wrong is used to denote w as a member of V (instead of simply a member of W). Run-time exceptions should be modeled by an extra summand of V, but for simplicity we shall instead use the undefined element of V, $\perp_V$ (often abbreviated as $\perp$).

$R = L \rightarrow V$

is the domain of *records*, which are associations of values to labels.

$U = L \times V$

is the domain of *variants* which are pairs <l,v> with a label l and a value v.

$F = V \rightarrow V$

is the domain of the continuous functions from V to V, used to give semantics to lambda expressions.

9. Semantics of expressions

The semantic function is $\mathbb{E} \in Exp \rightarrow Env \rightarrow V$, where Exp are syntactic expressions according to our grammar, and $Env = Id \rightarrow V$ are environments for identifiers. The semantics of basic values is given by $\mathbb{B} \in Exp \rightarrow V$, whose obvious definition is omitted.

Using the conventions below, we define:

$\mathbb{E}[\![x]\!]\eta = \eta[\![x]\!]$

$\mathbb{E}[\![b_{ij}]\!]\eta = \mathbb{B}[\![b_{ij}]\!]$

$\mathbb{E}[\![\text{if } e \text{ then } e' \text{ else } e'']\!]\eta =$

    if $\mathbb{E}[\![e]\!]\eta \, \varepsilon \, T$ then (if $(\mathbb{E}[\![e]\!]\eta \mid T)$ then $\mathbb{E}[\![e']\!]\eta$ else $\mathbb{E}[\![e'']\!]\eta$) else wrong

$\mathbb{E}[\![\{a_1 = e_1, \dots , a_n = e_n\}]\!]\eta =$

    (λb. if b=a_1 then $\mathbb{E}[\![e_1]\!]\eta$ else ... if b=a_n then $\mathbb{E}[\![e_n]\!]\eta$ else wrong) in V

$\mathbb{E}[\![e.a]\!]\eta = $ if $\mathbb{E}[\![e]\!]\eta \, \varepsilon \, R$ then $(\mathbb{E}[\![e]\!]\eta \mid R)(a)$ else wrong

$\mathbb{E}[\![[a = e]]\!]\eta = <a, \mathbb{E}[\![e]\!]\eta>$ in V

$\mathbb{E}[\![e \text{ is } a]\!]\eta = $ if $\mathbb{E}[\![e]\!]\eta \, \varepsilon \, U$ then $(\text{fst}(\mathbb{E}[\![e]\!]\eta \mid U) = a)$ in V else wrong

$\mathbb{E}[\![e \text{ as } a]\!]\eta =$

    if $\mathbb{E}[\![e]\!]\eta \, \varepsilon \, U$ then (let <b,v> be $(\mathbb{E}[\![e]\!]\eta \mid U)$ in if b = a then v else $\perp$) else wrong

$\mathbb{E}[\![\lambda x{:}\tau . e]\!]\eta = (\lambda v. \mathbb{E}[\![e]\!]\eta\{v/x\})$ in V

$\mathbb{E}[\![e \, e']\!]\eta =$

    if $\mathbb{E}[\![e]\!]\eta \, \varepsilon \, F$ then (if $\mathbb{E}[\![e']\!]\eta \, \varepsilon \, W$ then wrong else $(\mathbb{E}[\![e]\!]\eta \mid F)(\mathbb{E}[\![e']\!]\eta))$ else wrong

$\mathbb{E}[\![\text{rec } x{:}\tau . e]\!]\eta = Y(\lambda v. \mathbb{E}[\![e]\!]\eta\{v/x\})$

$\mathbb{E}[\![e{:}\tau]\!]\eta = \mathbb{E}[\![e]\!]\eta$

Comments on the equations:

- d in V (where $d \in D$ and D is a summand of V) is the injection of d in the appropriate summand of V . Hence d in $V \in V$. This is not to be confused with the let ... be ... in ... notation for local variables.

- $v \, \varepsilon \, D$ (where $v \in V$ and D is a summand of V) is a function yielding: $\perp_T$ if v = $\perp_V$; true if v = d in V for some $d \in D$; false otherwise.

- $v \mid D$ (where D is a summand of V) is a function yielding: d if v = d in V for some $d \in D$; $\perp_D$ otherwise.

- if ... then ... else ... is syntax for a function cond: $T \rightarrow V \rightarrow V \rightarrow V$ mapping $\perp_T$ to $\perp_V$.

- equality in L yields $\perp_T$ whenever either argument is $\perp_L$.
- fst extracts the first element of a pair, snd extracts the second one.
- Y is the fixpoint operator of type $(V \to V) \to V$.
- $\mathbb{E}$ defines a call by value semantics, but it allows circular structures to be built.

Intuitively, a well-typed program will never return the wrong value at run-time. For example, consider the occurrence of wrong in the semantics of records. The typechecker will make sure that any record selection will operate on records having the appropriate field, hence that instance of wrong will never be returned. A similar reasoning applies to all the instances of wrong in the semantics: wrong is a run-time type error which can be detected at compile-time. Run-time exceptions which cannot be detected are represented as $\perp$; the only instance of this in the above semantics is in the equation for e as a.

Having defined $\mathbb{E}$ so that it satisfies the above intuitions about run-time errors, we procede in the following sections by interpreting "e is semantically well-typed" to mean "$\mathbb{E}[\, e\,]\eta \neq$ wrong", and finally we give an algorithm which statically checks well-typing.

10. Semantics of type expressions

The semantics of types is given in the *weak ideal model* [MacQueen 86] $\Im(V)$ (the set of non-empty left-closed subset of V which are closed under least upper bounds of increasing sequences and do not contain wrong). $\Im(V)$ is a lattice of domains, where the ordering is set inclusion. $\Im(V)$ is closed under intersections and finite unions, as well as the usual domain operations.

Here $\mathbb{D} \in \textbf{\textit{TypeExp}} \to \Im(V)$:

$\mathbb{D}[\![\, u_i\,]\!] = B_i$ in V

$\mathbb{D}[\![\, \{a_i : \tau_i\}\,]\!] = \bigcap_i \{r \in R \mid r(a_i) \in \mathbb{D}[\![\, \tau_i\,]\!]\}$ in V \qquad (where $\mathbb{D}[\![\, \{\}\,]\!] = R$ in V)

$\mathbb{D}[\![\, [a_i : \tau_i]\,]\!] = (\{\langle \perp_L, v \rangle \mid v \in V\} \cup \bigcup_i \{\langle a_i, v \rangle \in U \mid v \in \mathbb{D}[\![\, \tau_i\,]\!]\})$ in V

$\mathbb{D}[\![\, \sigma \to \tau\,]\!] = \{f \in F \mid v \in \mathbb{D}[\![\, \sigma\,]\!] \Rightarrow f(v) \in \mathbb{D}[\![\, \tau\,]\!]\}$ in V

where D in $V = \{d$ in $V \mid d \in D\} \cup \{\perp_V\}$

Theorem ($\mathbb{D}$ properties)

$\forall \tau.\ \mathbb{D}[\![\, \tau\,]\!]$ is an ideal (hence $\perp \in \mathbb{D}[\![\, \tau\,]\!]$)

$\forall \tau, v.\ v \in \mathbb{D}[\![\, \tau\,]\!] \Rightarrow v \neq$ wrong

The wrong value is deliberately left out of the type domains so that if a value has a type, then that value is not a run-time type error. Another way of saying this is that wrong has no type.

11. Type inclusion

A subtyping relation can be defined syntactically on the structure of type expressions. This definition formalizes our initial discussion of subtyping for records, variants and functions.

$$\iota \leq \iota$$

$$\{a_i : \sigma_i, a_j : \sigma_j\} \leq \{a_i : \sigma'_i\} \quad \text{iff} \quad \sigma_i \leq \sigma'_i \qquad (i \in 1..n, n \geq 0; \ j \in 1..m, m \geq 0)$$

$$[a_i : \sigma_i] \leq [a_i : \sigma'_i, a_j : \sigma'_j] \quad \text{iff} \quad \sigma_i \leq \sigma'_i \qquad (i \in 1..n, n \geq 0; \ j \in 1..m, m \geq 0)$$

$$\sigma \to \tau \leq \sigma' \to \tau' \quad \text{iff} \quad \sigma' \leq \sigma \text{ and } \tau \leq \tau'$$

no other type expressions are in the $\leq$ relation

Proposition

$\leq$ is a partial order.

It is possible to extend type expressions by two constants anything and nothing, such that nothing $\leq \tau \leq$ anything for any τ. Then, $\leq$ defines a lattice structure on type expressions, which is a sublattice of $\mathfrak{I}(V)$. Although this is mathematically appealing, we have chosen not to do so in view of our intended application. For example, the expression if x then 3 else true, should produce a type error because of a conflict between int and bool in the two branches of the conditional. If we have the full lattice of type expression, it is conceivable to return anything as the type of the expression above, and carry on typechecking. This is bad for two reasons. First, no use can be made of objects of type anything (at least in the present framework). Second, type errors are difficult to localize as their presence is only made manifest by the eventual occurrence of anything or nothing in the resulting type.

As we said, the ordering of domains in the $\mathfrak{I}(V)$ model is set inclusion. This allows us to give a very direct semantics to subtyping, as simple set inclusion of domains.

Theorem (Semantic Subtyping)

$$\tau \leq \tau' \quad \Leftrightarrow \quad \mathbb{D}[\tau] \subseteq \mathbb{D}[\tau'].$$

The proof is by induction on the structure of τ and τ'. We shall only need the $\Rightarrow$ direction in the sequel.

12. Type inference rules

In this section we formally define the notion of a *syntactically well-typed expression*. An expression is well-typed when a type can be deduced for it, according to a set of type rules forming an *inference system*. If no type can be deduced, then the expression is said to contain type errors.

In general, many types can be deduced for the same expression. Provided that the inference system is consistent, all those types are in some sense compatible. A typechecking algorithm can then choose any of the admissible types as *the* type of an expression, with respect to that algorithm (in some type systems there may be a *best*, or *most general*, or *principal* type). Inference systems may be shown to be consistent with respect to the semantics of the language, as we shall see at the end of this section.

Here is the inference system for our language. It is designed so that (1) it contains exactly one type rule for each syntactic construct; (2) it satisfies the intuitive subtyping property expressed by the syntactic subtyping theorem below; and (3) it satisfies a semantic soundness theorem, relating it to the semantics of the language.

The use of the subtyping predicate $\leq$ is critical in many type rules. However it should be noted that subtyping does not affect the fundamental λ-calculus typing rules, [ABS] and [COMB]. This indicates that our style of subtyping merges naturally with functional types.

[VAR]
$$A.x: \tau \vdash x: \tau' \qquad \text{where } \tau \leq \tau'$$

[BAS]
$$A \vdash b_{ij} : \iota_i$$

[COND]
$$\frac{A \vdash e: \text{bool} \quad A \vdash e': \tau \quad A \vdash e'': \tau}{A \vdash (\text{if } e \text{ then } e' \text{ else } e''): \tau}$$

[RECORD]
$$\frac{A \vdash e_1 : \tau_1 \quad ... \quad A \vdash e_n : \tau_n}{A \vdash \{a_1 = e_1, ... , a_n = e_n\} : \{a_i : \tau_i\}} \qquad \text{where } i \in I \subseteq 1..n$$

[DOT]
$$\frac{A \vdash e: \{ ... a: \tau ... \}}{A \vdash e.a : \tau}$$

[VARIANT]
$$\frac{A \vdash e: \tau}{A \vdash [a = e] : [... a: \tau ...]}$$

[IS]
$$\frac{A \vdash e: [...]}{A \vdash (e \text{ is } a) : \text{bool}}$$

[AS]
$$\frac{A \vdash e: [... a: \tau ...]}{A \vdash (e \text{ as } a) : \tau}$$

[ABS]
$$\frac{A.x: \sigma \vdash e: \tau}{A \vdash (\lambda x: \sigma. e) : \sigma \rightarrow \tau}$$

[COMB]
$$\frac{A \vdash e: \sigma \rightarrow \tau \quad A \vdash e': \sigma}{A \vdash (e\ e') : \tau}$$

[REC]
$$\frac{A.x: \sigma \vdash e: \rho}{A \vdash (\text{rec } x: \sigma . e): \tau} \qquad \text{where } \rho \leq \sigma \text{ and } \rho \leq \tau$$

[SPEC]
$$\frac{A \vdash e: \sigma}{A \vdash (e: \sigma) : \tau} \qquad \text{where } \sigma \leq \tau$$

Some comments on the rules:

- A (called a set of assumptions) is a finite mapping of variables to types; A(x) is the type associated with x in A; A.x:τ is the set of assumptions A extended with the association x:τ, i.e. it maps x to τ and any other y to A(y).
- If there are some non-trivial inclusions in the basic types (e.g. int ≤ real) then [BAS] must be changed to $A \vdash b_{ij} : \tau$ where $\iota_i \leq \tau$.
- In [RECORD], the derived record type can have fewer fields than the corresponding record object.
- In [VARIANT], the derived variant type can have any number of fields, as long as it includes a field corresponding to the variant object.
- The [IS] rule assumes that the set of basic types does not contain a supertype of bool, otherwise a more refined rule is needed. Similarly, [COND] assumes that there are no subtypes of bool.

The basic syntactic property of this inference system is expressed in the syntactic subtyping theorem below: if an expression has a type τ, and τ is a subtype of τ', then the expression has also type τ'. The lemma is required to prove the [ABS] case of the theorem. Both the lemma and the theorem are proved by induction on the structure of the derivations.

Lemma (Syntactic Subtyping)

$A.x: \sigma \vdash e: \tau$ and $\sigma' \leq \sigma \Rightarrow A.x: \sigma' \vdash e: \tau$.

Theorem (Syntactic Subtyping)

$A \vdash e: \tau$ and $\tau \leq \tau' \Rightarrow A \vdash e: \tau'$.

The next theorem states the soundness of the type system with respect to the semantics: if it is possible to deduce that e has type τ, then the value denoted by e belongs to the domain denoted by τ. A set of assumptions A agrees with an environment η if for all x in the domain of A, A(x) = τ implies $\eta[x] \in D[\tau]$.

Theorem (Semantic Soundness)

if $A \vdash e: \tau$ and A agrees with η then $B[e]\eta \in D[\tau]$.

The proof is by induction on the structure of the derivation of $A \vdash e: \tau$, using the semantic subtyping and D-properties theorems.

In words, if e is syntactically well-typed (i.e. for some τ, $A \vdash e: \tau$), then it is also semantically well-typed (i.e. for some η such that A agrees with η, $B[e]\eta \in D[\tau]$, which implies that $B[e]\eta \neq$ wrong).

13. Join and meet types

In the examples at the beginning of the paper we used the and and or type operators, and we are now going to need them in the definition of the typechecking algorithm. However those operators are not part of the syntax of type expressions, nor are ignoring and dropping.

This is because the above operators only work on restricted kinds of type expressions. Applied to arbitrary type expressions they either are undefined, or can be eliminated by a normalization process. If we have a type expression containing the above operators we can process the expression checking that the operators can indeed be used in that context, and in such case we can normalize them away obtaining a normal type expression.

The and operator is interpreted as a (partial) *meet* operation on types (written ↓), and or is interpreted as (partial) *join* (written ↑). Joins and meets are taken in the partial order determined by ≤, when they exist.

The definition of the operators also immediately defines the normalization process which eliminates them:

$$u \uparrow u = u$$
$$\{a_i : \tau_i, b_j : \sigma_j\} \uparrow \{a_i : \tau'_i, c_k : \rho_k\} = \{a_i : \tau_i \uparrow \tau'_i\}$$
$$\quad \text{if all } \tau_i \uparrow \tau'_i \text{ are defined} \quad (\forall j,k.\ b_j \neq c_k)$$
$$[a_i : \tau_i, b_j : \sigma_j] \uparrow [a_i : \tau'_i, c_k : \rho_k] = [a_i : \tau_i \uparrow \tau'_i, b_j : \sigma_j, c_k : \rho_k]$$
$$\quad \text{if all } \tau_i \uparrow \tau'_i \text{ are defined} \quad (\forall j,k.\ b_j \neq c_k)$$
$$(\sigma \to \tau) \uparrow (\sigma' \to \tau') = (\sigma \downarrow \sigma') \to (\tau \uparrow \tau')$$
$$\tau \uparrow \tau' \qquad \text{undefined otherwise}$$

$$u \downarrow u = u$$
$$\{a_i : \tau_i, b_j : \sigma_j\} \downarrow \{a_i : \tau'_i, c_k : \rho_k\} = \{a_i : \tau_i \downarrow \tau'_i, b_j : \sigma_j, c_k : \rho_k\}$$
$$\quad \text{if all } \tau_i \downarrow \tau'_i \text{ are defined} \quad (\forall j,k.\ b_j \neq c_k)$$
$$[a_i : \tau_i, b_j : \sigma_j] \downarrow [a_i : \tau'_i, c_k : \rho_k] = [a_i : \tau_i \downarrow \tau'_i]$$
$$\quad \text{if all } \tau_i \downarrow \tau'_i \text{ are defined} \quad (\forall j,k.\ b_j \neq c_k)$$
$$(\sigma \to \tau) \downarrow (\sigma' \to \tau') = (\sigma \uparrow \sigma') \to (\tau \downarrow \tau')$$
$$\tau \downarrow \tau' \qquad \text{undefined otherwise}$$

$$\{a_i : \tau_i\} \text{ ignoring } a = \{a_j : \tau_j\} \qquad (i \in 1..n,\ j \in 1..n - \{k \mid a_k = a\})$$
$$\tau \text{ ignoring } a \qquad \text{undefined otherwise}$$

$$[a_i : \tau_i] \text{ dropping } a = [a_j : \tau_j] \qquad (i \in 1..n,\ j \in 1..n - \{k \mid a_k = a\})$$
$$\tau \text{ dropping } a \qquad \text{undefined otherwise}$$

Note that ↑ may be undefined even if there is a least upper bound with respect to ≤ for its operands; similarly for ↓.

Proposition (↑ and ↓ properties)

If $\sigma \uparrow \tau$ is defined, then it is the smallest ρ (w.r.t. ≤) such that $\sigma \leq \rho$ and $\tau \leq \rho$.

If $\sigma \downarrow \tau$ is defined, then it is the largest ρ (w.r.t. ≤) such that $\rho \leq \sigma$ and $\rho \leq \tau$.

Let S be the set of ideals denoted by ordinary type expressions (without $\downarrow$ (and) and $\uparrow$ (or) operators) where r/a = (λb. if b = a then $\perp$ else r(b)).

Proposition

$\mathbb{D}[\![\sigma$ and $\tau]\!]$ = the largest ideal in S contained in $\mathbb{D}[\![\sigma]\!] \cap \mathbb{D}[\![\tau]\!]$
  when defined

$\mathbb{D}[\![\tau$ ignoring a$]\!]$ = {r $\in$ R | ((r / a) in V) $\in \mathbb{D}[\![\tau]\!]$} in V
  when defined

$\mathbb{D}[\![\sigma$ or $\tau]\!]$ = the smallest ideal in S containing $\mathbb{D}[\![\sigma]\!] \cup \mathbb{D}[\![\tau]\!]$
  when defined

$\mathbb{D}[\![\tau$ dropping a$]\!]$ = $\mathbb{D}[\![\tau]\!]$ − ({<a, v> $\in$ U} in V)
  when defined.

14. Typechecking

The (partial) typechecking function is $T \in Exp \rightarrow TypeEnv \rightarrow TypeExp$, where Exp and $TypeExp$ are respectively expressions and type expressions according to our grammar, and $TypeEnv = Id \rightarrow TypeExp$ are type environments for identifiers.

The following description is to be intended as a scheme for a program that returns a type expression denoting the type of a term, or fails in case of type errors. The fail word is a global jump-out: when a type error is detected the program stops. Similarly, typechecking fails when the $\uparrow$ and $\downarrow$ operations are undefined. When we assert that $T[\![e]\!]\mu = \tau$, we imply that the typechecking of e does not fail.

$T[\![x]\!]\mu = \mu[x]$

$T[\![b_{ij}]\!]\mu = \iota_j$

$T[\![$ if e then e' else e" $]\!]\mu$ = if $T[\![e]\!]\mu$ = bool then $T[\![e']\!]\mu \uparrow T[\![e"]\!]\mu$ else fail

$T[\![\{a_1 = e_1, \dots , a_n = e_n\}]\!]\mu = \{a_1 : T[\![e_1]\!]\mu, \dots , a_n : T[\![e_n]\!]\mu\}$

$T[\![e.a]\!]\mu$ = if $T[\![e]\!]\mu = \{ \dots a : \tau \dots \}$ then τ else fail

$T[\![[a = e]]\!]\mu = [a : T[\![e]\!]\mu]$

$T[\![e$ is a $]\!]\mu$ = if $T[\![e]\!]\mu = [\dots a : \tau \dots]$ then bool else fail

$T[\![e$ as a $]\!]\mu$ = if $T[\![e]\!]\mu = [\dots a : \tau \dots]$ then τ else fail

$T[\![\lambda x : \tau . e]\!]\mu = \tau \rightarrow T[\![e]\!]\mu\{\tau / x\}$

$T[\![e\ e']\!]\mu$ = if $T[\![e]\!]\mu = (\tau \rightarrow \tau')$ and $T[\![e']\!]\mu \leq \tau$ then τ' else fail

$T[\![$ rec x: σ . e $]\!]\mu$ = if $T[\![e]\!]\mu\{\sigma / x\} = \tau$ and $\tau \leq \sigma$ then τ else fail

$T[\![e : \sigma]\!]\mu$ = if $T[\![e]\!]\mu = \tau$ and $\tau \leq \sigma$ then σ else fail

This typechecking algorithm is correct with respect to the type inference system: if the algorithm succeeds and returns a type τ for an expression e, then it is possible to prove that e has type τ. A type environment μ agrees with a set of assumptions A if for every x in the domain of A, $\mu[x] = A(x)$.

Theorem (Syntactic Soundness)

if $T[\![e]\!]\mu = \tau$ then μ agrees with some A such that A $\vdash$ e: τ .

The proof of the theorem is by induction on the structure of e, using the properties of ↑, ↓ and ≤.

Combining the syntactic soundness, semantic soundness and 𝔻-properties theorems we immediately obtain:

Corollary (Typechecking prevents type errors):

if $\mathcal{T}[\![e]\!]\mu = \tau$ then $\mathcal{E}[\![e]\!]\eta \neq$ wrong   (when $\eta[\![x]\!] \in \mathcal{D}[\![\mu[\![x]\!]]\!]$ for all x).

i.e. if e can be successfully typechecked, then e cannot produce run-time type errors.

The typechecking algorithm is intentionally more restrictive than the type inference system; it is possible to deduce A.x:bool ⊢ if x then {a=true} else {a=3} : {}, but in practice we want this to be a type error for the same reasons that made us rule out the anything type. This restriction is enforced by the definitions of ↑ and ↓ . Similarly, one can infer any type for [a=3] as b, while the typechecker fails; this is justified since [a=3] as b will always fail at run-time.

For these reasons, we do not have a (perhaps desirable) syntactic completeness theorem of the form: if A ⊢ e: τ and μ agrees with A, then $\mathcal{T}[\![e]\!]\mu$ is defined and $\mathcal{T}[\![e]\!]\mu$ ≤ τ. One could strive for syntactic completeness by using the (partial) ∨ and ∧ (w.r.t. ≤) instead of ↑ and ↓ in the typechecking algorithm (then the modified algorithm computes $\mathcal{T}[\![$if x then {a=true} else {a=3}$]\!]\mu$ = {}), and by replacing the is and as primitives by a case construct.

15. Conclusions

This work originated as an attempt to justify the multiple inheritance constructs present in the Galileo data base language [Albano 85] and to provide a sound typechecking algorithm for that language. The Amber language [Cardelli 86] was then devised to experiment, among other things, with inheritance typechecking. I believe this paper adequately solves the basic problems, although some practical and theoretical issues may require more work.

Parametric polymorphism has not been treated in this paper. The intention was to study multiple inheritance problems in the cleanest possible framework, without interaction with other features. Side-effects and circular types should also be integrated in a full formal treatment.

Some confusion may arise from the fact that languages like Smalltalk are often referred to as polymorphic languages. This is correct, if by polymorphism we mean that an object or a function can have many types. However it now appears that there are two subtly different kinds of polymorphism: inheritance polymorphism, based on type inclusion, and parametric polymorphism, based on type variables and type quantifiers.

These two kinds of polymorphism are not incompatible. We have seen here that inheritance can be explained in the semantic domains normally used for parametric polymorphism. Moreover the technical explanation of polymorphism is the same in both cases: domain intersection. Merging these two kinds of polymorphism does not seem to introduce new semantic problems. The interactions of inheritance and parametric polymorphism in typechecking are addressed in [Cardelli 85].

There are now several competing (although not totally independent) styles of parametric polymorphism, noticeably in [Milner 78], [Reynolds 74, McCracken 84] and [MacQueen 86]. Inheritance is orthogonal to all of these, so it seems better to study it independently, at least initially. However, the final goal is to achieve full integration of parametric polymorphism and multiple inheritance, merging functional programming with object-oriented programming at the semantic and typing levels; this problem is currently receiving much attention.

16. Related work and acknowledgements

I would like to mention here [Reynolds 80, Oles 84] which expose similar semantic ideas in a different formal framework, [Ait-Kaci 83] again exposing very similar ideas in a Prolog-related framework, [Mitchell 84] this time presenting different, but related, ideas in the same formal framework, and [Futatsugi 85] whose OBJ system implements a first-order multiple inheritance typechecker, and whose subsorts have much to do with subtypes.

Finally, I would like to thank David MacQueen for many discussions, John Reynolds and the referees for detailed suggestions and corrections, and Antonio Albano and Renzo Orsini for motivating me to carry out this work.

References

[Ait-Kaci 83] H.Ait-Kaci: **Outline of a calculus of type subsumptions**, Technical report MS–CIS-83-34, Dept of Computer and Information Science, The Moore School of Electrical Engineering, University of Pennsylvania, August 1983.

[Albano 85] A.Albano, L.Cardelli, R.Orsini: **Galileo: a strongly typed, interactive conceptual language**, IEEE Transactions on Database Systems, June 1985.

[Attardi 81] G.Attardi, M.Simi: **Semantics of inheritance and attributions in the description system Omega**, M.I.T. A.I. Memo 642, August 1981.

[Bobrow 83] D.G.Bobrow, M.J.Stefik: **The Loops manual**, Memo KB–VLSI-81-13, Xerox PARC.

[Cardelli 85] L.Cardelli, P.Wegner: **On understanding types, data abstraction and polymorphism**, *Computing Surveys*, Vol 17 n. 4, pp 471-522, December 1985.

[Cardelli 86] L.Cardelli: **Amber**, *Combinators and Functional Programming Languages, Proc. of the 13th Summer School of the LITP*, Le Val D'Ajol, Vosges (France), May 1985. Lecture Notes in Computer Science n. 242, Springer-Verlag, 1986.

[Dahl 66] O.Dahl, K.Nygaard: **Simula, an Algol-based simulation language**, Comm. ACM, Vol 9, pp. 671-678, 1966.

[Deutsch 84] P.Deutsch: **An efficient implementation of Smalltalk-80**, Proc. POPL '84.

[Futatsugi 85] K.Futatsugi, J.A.Goguen, J.P.Jouannaud, J.Meseguer: **Principles of OBJ2**, Proc. POPL '85.

[Goldberg 83] A.Goldberg, D.Robson: **Smalltalk-80. The language and its implementation**, Addison-Wesley, 1983.

[Hullot 83] J-M.Hullot: **Ceyx: a Multiformalism programming environment**, IFIP 83, R.E.A.Mason (ed), North Holland, Paris 1983.

[McCracken 84] N.McCracken: **The typechecking of programs with implicit type structure**, in *Semantics of Data Types*, Lecture Notes in Computer Science n.173, Springer-Verlag 1984.

[MacQueen 86] D.B.MacQueen, G.D.Plotkin, R.Sethi: **An ideal model for recursive polymorphic types**, Information and Control 71, pp. 95-130, 1986.

[Milner 78] R.Milner: **A theory of type polymorphism in programming**, Journal of Computer and System Science 17, pp. 348-375, 1978.

[Oles 84] F.J.Oles: **Type algebras, functor categories, and block structure**, in *Algebraic semantics*, M.Nivat and J.C.Reynolds ed., Cambridge University Press 1984.

[Reynolds 74] J.C.Reynolds: **Towards a theory of type structure**, in *Colloquium sur la programmation* pp. 408-423, Springer-Verlag Lecture Notes in Computer Science, n.19, 1974.

[Reynolds 80] J.C.Reynolds: **Using category theory to design implicit type conversions and generic operators**, in *Semantics-directed compiler generation*, Lecture Notes in Computer Science 94, pp. 211-258, Springer-Verlag 1980.

[Morris 80] L.Morris, J.Schwarz: **Computing cyclic list structures**, Conference Record of the 1980 Lisp Conference, pp.144-153.

[Steels 83] L.Steels: **Orbit: an applicative view of object-oriented programming**, in: *Integrated Interactive Computing Systems*, pp. 193-205, P.Degano and E.Sandewall editors, North-Holland 1983.

[Weinreb 81] D.Weinreb, D.Moon: **Objects, Message Passing, and Flavors**, chapter 20 of *Lisp machine manual*, Fourth Edition, Symbolics Inc., 1981.

Encapsulation and Inheritance
in
Object-Oriented Programming Languages

Alan Snyder
Software Technology Laboratory
Hewlett-Packard Laboratories
P.O. Box 10490
Palo Alto CA 94303-0971
(415) 857-8764

Abstract

Object-oriented programming is a practical and useful programming methodology that encourages modular design and software reuse. Most object-oriented programming languages support *data abstraction* by preventing an object from being manipulated except via its defined external operations. In most languages, however, the introduction of *inheritance* severely compromises the benefits of this encapsulation. Furthermore, the use of inheritance itself is globally visible in most languages, so that changes to the inheritance hierarchy cannot be made safely. This paper examines the relationship between inheritance and encapsulation and develops requirements for full support of encapsulation with inheritance.

Introduction

Object-oriented programming is a practical and useful programming methodology that encourages modular design and software reuse. One of its prime features is support for data abstraction, the ability to define new types of objects whose behavior is defined abstractly, without reference to implementation details such as the data structure used to represent the objects.

Most object-oriented languages support data abstraction by preventing an object from being manipulated except via its defined external operations. Encapsulation has many advantages in terms of improving the understandability of programs and facilitating program modification. Unfortunately, in most object-oriented languages, the introduction of *inheritance* severely compromises encapsulation.

This paper examines the issue of encapsulation and its support in object-oriented languages. We begin by reviewing

the concepts of encapsulation and data abstraction, as realized by most object-oriented languages. We then review the concept of inheritance and demonstrate how the inheritance models of popular object-oriented languages like Smalltalk [Goldberg83], Flavors [Moon86], and Objective-C [Cox84] fall short in their support of encapsulation. We examine the requirements for full support of encapsulation with inheritance.

Object-Oriented Programming

Object-oriented programming is a programming methodology based on the following key characteristics:

- Designers define new classes (or types) of objects.

- Objects have operations defined on them.

- Invocations operate on multiple types of objects (i.e., operations are generic).

- Class definitions share common components using inheritance.

In this paper, we use the following model and terminology: An object-oriented programming language allows the designer to define new *classes* of objects. Each object is an *instance* of one class. An object is represented by a collection of *instance variables*, as defined by the class. Each class defines a set of named *operations* that can be performed on the instances of that class. Operations are implemented by procedures that can access and assign to the instance variables of the target object. Inheritance can be used to define a class in terms of one or more other classes. If a class *c* (directly) inherits from a class *p*, we say that *p* is a *parent* of *c* and that *c* is a *child* of *p*. The terms *ancestor* and *descendant* are used in the obvious way.[1]

---

[1] We avoid the traditional terms *subclass* and *superclass* because these terms are often used ambiguously to mean both direct and indirect inheritance.

Encapsulation

Encapsulation is a technique for minimizing interdependencies among separately-written modules by defining strict external interfaces. The external interface of a module serves as a contract between the module and its clients, and thus between the designer of the module and other designers. If clients depend only on the external interface, the module can be reimplemented without affecting any clients, so long as the new implementation supports the same (or an upward compatible) external interface. Thus, the effects of compatible changes can be confined.

A module is *encapsulated* if clients are restricted by the definition of the programming language to access the module only via its defined external interface. Encapsulation thus assures designers that compatible changes can be made safely, which facilitates program evolution and maintenance. These benefits are especially important for large systems and long-lived data.

To maximize the advantages of encapsulation, one should minimize the exposure of implementation details in external interfaces. A programming language supports encapsulation to the degree that it allows *minimal* external interfaces to be defined and enforced.[2] This support can be characterized by the kinds of changes that can safely be made to the implementation of a module. For example, one characteristic of an object-oriented language is whether it permits a designer to define a class such that its instance variables can be renamed without affecting clients.

Data Abstraction

Data abstraction is a useful form of modular programming. The behavior of an abstract data object is fully defined by a set of abstract operations defined on the object; the user of an object does not need to understand how these operations are implemented or how the object is represented.

Objects in most object-oriented programming languages are abstract data objects. The external interface of an object is the set of operations defined upon it. Most object-oriented languages limit external access to an object to invoking the operations defined on the object, and thus support encapsulation.[3] Changes to the representation of an object or the implementation of its operations can be made without affecting users of the object, so long as the externally-visible behavior of the operations is unchanged.

A class definition is a module with its own external interface. Minimally, this interface describes how instances of the class are created, including any creation parameters. In many languages, a class is itself an object, and its external interface consists of a set of operations, including operations to create instances.

To summarize, objects in most object-oriented programming languages (including class objects) are encapsulated modules whose external interface consists of a set of operations; changes to the implementation of an object that preserve the external interface do not affect code outside the class definition.[4] If it were not for inheritance, the story would end here.

Inheritance

Inheritance complicates the situation by introducing a new category of client for a class. In addition to clients that simply instantiate objects of the class and perform operations on them, there are other clients (class definitions) that inherit from the class. To fully characterize an object-oriented language, we must consider what external interface is provided by a class to its children. This external interface is just as important as the external interface provided to users of the objects, as it serves as a contract between the class and its children, and thus limits the degree to which the designer can safely make changes to the class.

Frequently, a designer will want to define different external interfaces for these two categories of clients. Most object-oriented languages respond to this need by providing a much less restricted external interface to children of a class. By doing so, the advantages of encapsulation that one associates with object-oriented languages are severely weakened, as the designer of a class has less freedom to make compatible changes. This issue would be less important if the use of inheritance were confined to individual designers or small groups of designers who design families of related classes. However, systems designers have found it useful to provide classes designed to be inherited by large numbers of classes defined by independent applications designers (the class *window* in the Lisp Machine window system [Weinreb81] is a good example); such designers need the protection of a well-defined external interface to permit implementation flexibility.

We will begin our examination of inheritance with the issue of access to inherited instance variables.

Inheriting Instance Variables

In most object-oriented languages, the code of a class may directly access all the instance variables of its objects, even those instance variables that were defined by an ancestor class. Thus, the designer of a class is allowed full access to the representation defined by an ancestor class.

This property does not change the external interface of individual objects, as it is still the case that the instance

---

[2] One can always improve the encapsulation support provided by a language by extending it with additional declarations (in the form of machine readable comments, say) and writing programs to verify that clients obey these declarations. However, the effective result of this approach is that a new language has been defined (in a way that happens to avoid changing the existing compiler); the original language has not become any less deficient.

[3] Most practical languages provide escapes from strict encapsulation to support debugging and the creation of programming environments. For example, in Smalltalk the operations instVarAt: and instVarAt:put: allow access (by numeric offset) to any named instance variable of any object [Goldberg83, p. 247]. Because these escapes are not normally used in ordinary programming, we ignore them in this analysis.

[4] In C++ [Stroustrup86], an operation performed on one object of a class can access the internals of other objects of the class; thus, the set of objects of a class is an encapsulated module rather than each individual object. We ignore this distinction in this paper as it does not affect our analysis.

variables of an object are accessible only to operations defined on that object. However, it does change the external interface of the class (as seen by its descendants), which now (implicitly) includes the instance variables.

Permitting access to instance variables defined by ancestor classes compromises the encapsulation characteristics stated above: Because the instance variables are accessible to clients of the class, they are (implicitly) part of the contract between the designer of the class and the designers of descendant classes. Thus, the freedom of the designer to change the implementation of a class is reduced. The designer can no longer safely rename, remove, or reinterpret an instance variable without the risk of adversely affecting descendant classes that depend on that instance variable.

In summary, permitting direct access to inherited instance variables weakens one of the major benefits of object-oriented programming, the freedom of the designer to change the representation of a class without impacting its clients.

Accessing Inherited Variables Safely

To preserve the full benefits of encapsulation, the external interfaces of a class definition should not include instance variables. Instance variables are protected from direct access by users of an object by requiring the use of operations to access instance variables. The same technique can be used to prevent direct access by descendant classes.

Additional language support is required to permit instance variable access operations to be used effectively by descendant classes. Ordinary operation invocation on self[5] is inadequate, as it may invoke the wrong operation (if the operation is redefined by the class or one of its descendants). Instead, a way is needed to directly invoke (on self) an operation as defined by a parent class. Smalltalk provides a mechanism in the context of single inheritance: the pseudo-variable super. Performing an operation on super is like performing an operation on self, except that the search for the operation to invoke starts with the parent of the class in which the invocation appears, instead of with the class of self. Equivalent features using compound names (parent and operation) to specify the desired operation are provided by CommonObjects [Snyder85a], Trellis/Owl [Schaffert86], extended Smalltalk[6] [Borning82], and C++ [Stroustrup86]. Because the search for the proper operation starts at a statically known class, invoking an operation in this manner can be more efficient than normal operation invocation; in some implementations, no run-time lookup is required.

There are several possible objections to using operations to access inherited instance variables. Most of these objections also apply to the ordinary case of using operations to access the instance variables of an object, and they can be

resolved the same way: Syntactic abbreviations allow the inheriting class to use ordinary variable reference syntax to invoke these operations [Snyder85a].[7] Inline substitution avoids the overhead of invoking a procedure (at the cost of requiring recompilation of the client if an ancestor class is incompatibly changed).

The most serious objection to this solution is that it requires the cooperation of the designer of the ancestor class that defines the instance variable (as well as the designers of all intervening ancestors), since no access to an inherited instance variable is possible unless appropriate operations have been provided. We claim this is as it should be. If you (as designer of a class) need access to an inherited instance variable and the appropriate operations are not defined, the correct thing to do is to negotiate with the designer(s) of the ancestor class(es) to provide those operations.[8]

One problem with this scenario is that the instance variable operations defined on a class for the benefit of its descendants may not necessarily be appropriate for users of instances of the class, yet they are publically available. A convenient solution (provided by Trellis/Owl) is to declare that some operations are available only for direct invocation (on self) by descendant classes, but are not part of the external interface of objects of the class. This notion is a generalization of the "private operations" provided by various languages, including Trellis/Owl and C++. It gives the designer fine-grained control over the external interfaces provided to the two categories of clients of a class.

If instance variables are not part of the external interface of a parent class, then it is not proper to merge inherited instance variables with instance variables defined locally in a class (as is done by Flavors). Clearly, if a local instance variable and an inherited instance variable with the same name wind up as a single instance variable, then changing the name of the instance variable in the parent is likely to change the behavior of the child class. It is also inappropriate to signal an error if a class defines an instance variable with the same name as an inherited instance variable (as is done by Smalltalk), as changing the name of an instance variable could make a descendant class illegal. Similar objections apply to merging instance variables defined by multiple parents (as is done by Flavors), or signalling an error if multiple parents define instance variables with the same name (as is done by extended Smalltalk).

The Visibility of Inheritance

A deeper issue raised by inheritance is whether or not the use of inheritance itself should be part of the external interface (of the class or the objects). In other words, should

---

[5] In Smalltalk and many of its derivatives, self is used within an operation to refer to the object that the operation is being performed on. Names used in other languages for the same purpose include me and this.

[6] We use the term "extended Smalltalk" to refer to the multiple inheritance extension to Smalltalk defined by Borning and Ingalls.

[7] This option is a special case of a general construct which we call *pseudo variables* [Snyder85b]. A pseudo variable looks like an ordinary lexical variable, but the effect of referencing or assigning to the variable is to execute arbitrary (possibly user-specified) code.

[8] A software development environment might allow you to circumvent this restriction, say by temporarily defining those operations yourself. However, if you seriously intend to leverage off someone else's code, such negotiation is essential.

clients of a class (necessarily) be able to tell whether or not a class is defined using inheritance?

If the use of inheritance is part of the external interface, then changes to a class definition's use of inheritance may affect client code. For example, consider a class that is defined using inheritance. Suppose the designer of that class decides that the same behavior can be implemented more efficiently by writing a completely new implementation, without using the previously inherited class. If the previous use of inheritance was visible to clients, then this reimplementation may require changes to the clients. The ability to safely make changes to the inheritance hierarchy is essential to support the evolution of large systems and long-lived data.

This issue raises the fundamental question of the purpose of inheritance. One can view inheritance as a private decision of the designer to "reuse" code because it is useful to do so; it should be possible to easily change such a decision. Alternatively, one can view inheritance as making a public declaration that objects of the child class obey the semantics of the parent class, so that the child class is merely *specializing* or *refining* the parent class. This question is addressed in the context of knowledge representation in [Brachman85].

Our position is that being able to use inheritance without making a public commitment to it in the external interface of a class is valuable, and we will analyze how existing object-oriented languages support this option. We will begin by considering only the single inheritance case, i.e., where the inheriting class (the *child*) directly inherits from a single class (the *parent*). Multiple inheritance introduces additional problems and will be discussed below.

Excluding Operations

Most object-oriented languages promote inheritance as a technique for specialization and do not permit a class to "exclude" an inherited operation from its own external interface. However, if inheritance is viewed as an implementation technique, then excluding operations is both reasonable and useful.

For example, consider the abstractions *stack* and *deque*, where a *stack* is a queue that permits elements to be added or removed from one end, and a *deque* is a queue that permits elements to be added or removed from either end. The external interface of a *deque* is a superset of the external interface of a *stack*: a *deque* has two additional operations for adding and removing elements from the "back end".

The simplest way to implement these two abstractions (at least for prototyping purposes) is to define the class *stack* to inherit from the class *deque*, and exclude the extra operations. *Stack* inherits the implementation of *deque*, but is not a specialization of *deque*, as it does not provide all the *deque* operations.

The ability for a class to exclude operations defined by its parents is provided in CommonObjects. Of course, this effect can be achieved in any object-oriented language simply by redefining the operation in the child class to signal an error when invoked. Doing so, however, fails to take full

advantage of static type checking (in languages like Trellis/Owl and C++) and can lead to unnecessary name conflicts involving the "excluded" operations.

Even if a child excludes an inherited operation from its external interface, it is useful to be able to invoke the operation (on **self**) within the child. Ordinary operation invocation cannot be used, because the operation is not defined on instances of the child. However, as described above in the section on accessing inherited instance variables, several languages (including CommonObjects) provide the required ability to directly invoke an operation defined by a parent class.

Subtyping

One way in which inheritance can appear in the external interface of a class is *subtyping*, the rules by which objects of one type (class) are determined to be acceptable in contexts expecting another type (class). In statically-typed languages like Trellis/Owl, Simula [Dahl66], and C++, subtyping rules are of critical importance because they determine the legality of programs. In dynamically-typed languages like Common Lisp [Steele84], subtyping rules affect the results of type predicates.

Many object-oriented languages relate subtyping and inheritance. For example, in Trellis/Owl, Simula, and C++ a class *x* is a subtype of a class *y* if and only if *x* is a descendant of *y*. If the designer should reimplement class *x* so that it inherits from class *z* instead of *y*, client programs that assume *x* is a subtype of *y* would no longer be legal, even if the *intended* external interface of *x* (the operations) is unchanged. Thus, the use of inheritance is exposed via the subtyping rules.[9]

To avoid this problem, subtyping should not be tied to inheritance. Instead, subtyping should be based on the behavior of objects. If instances of class *x* meet the external interface of class *y*, then *x* should be a subtype of *y*. The example above demonstrates that the implementation hierarchy need not be the same as the type hierarchy (as defined by object behavior) [Canning85]. In that example, *stack* inherits from *deque* but is not a subtype of *deque*, and *deque* is a subtype of *stack* but does not inherit from *stack*.

Behavioral subtyping cannot be deduced without formal semantic specifications of behavior. Lacking such specifications, one can deduce subtyping based solely on syntactic external interfaces (i.e., the names of the operations) [Cardelli84]. Alternatively (or in addition), one can allow the designer of a class to specify which other classes it is a subtype of. The default may be that a class is a subtype of each of its parents. However, as demonstrated by the example, the designer must be able to specify that the class is not a subtype of a parent or that the class is a subtype of an unrelated class (not its parent). The first case arises when

---

[9] It should be noted that although equating subtyping of classes with inheritance entails a loss of flexibility, it has significant implementation advantages in statically-typed languages like those mentioned, where the cost of performing an operation involves at most an extra level of indirection.

the behavior of the objects is incompatible with the interface of parent objects. The second case arises when the class is supporting the external interface of another class without sharing its implementation.

CommonObjects, an object-oriented extension to Common Lisp, is an example of a language that allows the designer to specify the type hierarchy independently of the inheritance hierarchy. In Common Lisp, type checking is defined in terms of a predicate typep that takes two arguments, an object and a type specification, and returns true if and only if the object is a member of the specified type. CommonObjects classes are integrated into the Common Lisp type system such that if the object given to typep is an instance of a class and the type specification is a class name, then the :typep operation is performed on the object (with the type specification as the argument) to determine the result of typep. The designer of a class can write an arbitrary predicate for this operation, although a default is provided.[10]

The following operations would be used in the above example:

```
(define-method (stack :typep) (the-type)
  (equal the-type 'stack))

(define-method (deque :typep) (the-type)
  (or (equal the-type 'deque)
      (equal the-type 'stack)
  ))
```

This primitive mechanism is sufficient, but is neither convenient nor reliable. A better solution would explicitly represent subtyping relationships and ensure transitivity.

Attribute Visibility

If the use of inheritance is not part of the external interface of a class, then clients of the class may not directly refer to ancestors of the class. Specifically, a class may refer to its parents, but not its more distant ancestors.

As mentioned above, it is useful for a class to be able to invoke an operation defined by a parent. In most languages that support this feature, the desired operation is specified by a compound name consisting of the name of the parent class and the name of the operation. This solution is sufficient: To access an operation of a more distant ancestor without violating encapsulation, that operation must be passed down via all intervening ancestors including at least one parent. Trellis/Owl and extended Smalltalk allow a class to directly name an operation of a non-immediate

---

[10] Smalltalk defines an operation isKindOf: on all objects that tests whether the object is an instance of a class or one of its descendants; however, it is not clear that this operation can usefully be redefined.

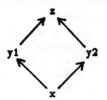

Figure 1: Example of multiple inheritance.

---

ancestor. As a result, in these languages, the names of ancestor classes are unavoidably part of the external interface of a class.

Multiple Inheritance

Multiple inheritance means that a class can have more than one parent. One can view a class (call it the *root class*) as forming the root of a directed (acyclic) graph, which we will call an *inheritance graph*, where each class is a node and there is an arc from each class to each of its parents. Figure 1 shows an inheritance graph with multiple inheritance. In this example, class *x* is the root class. Class *x* inherits from classes *y1* and *y2*, and classes *y1* and *y2* both inherit from class *z*.

There are two strategies in common use for dealing with multiple inheritance. The first strategy attempts to deal with the inheritance graph directly. The second strategy first flattens the graph into a linear chain, and then deals with that chain using the rules for single inheritance.

Graph-Oriented Solutions

Trellis/Owl and extended Smalltalk are examples of object-oriented languages whose semantics model the inheritance graph directly. In these languages, operations are inherited along the inheritance graph until redefined in a class. If a class inherits operations with the same name from more than one parent, the conflict must be resolved in some way. One way is to redefine the operation in the child class; the new definition can invoke the operations defined by the parent classes. To invoke all definitions of an operation in the inheritance graph (e.g., all display operations), each class could define an operation that invokes the operation on each of its parents and then performs any local computation, resulting in a depth-first traversal of the inheritance graph. Extended Smalltalk provides a convenient syntax for invoking an operation on each parent of a class.

In these languages, the interesting issues arise when the graph is not a tree, i.e., when a single class is reachable from the root class by multiple paths (as in Figure 1). Trellis/Owl and extended Smalltalk adopt similar solutions for resolving the conflict when a class attempts to inherit an operation from more than one parent: It is an error[11] if a class inherits operations with the same name from two or

---

[11] Trellis/Owl signals an error at compilation time; extended Smalltalk creates an operation for the class that signals an error when invoked.

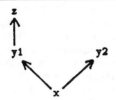

Figure 2: Altering the inheritance structure.

more parents, but *only* if the operations are actually different. In other words, if the *same* operation (from the same class) is inherited by a class via different paths through the inheritance graph, it is not an error.

This same-operation exception is motivated by convenience, as operation conflicts are inevitable when there is merging in the inheritance graph. Although this exception may at first glance seem innocuous, it forces the use of inheritance to be part of the external interface.

Consider further the example shown in Figure 1. If an operation o is defined (only) by the class z, it will be inherited by $y1$ and $y2$ and then by x (with no error). Now suppose the class $y2$ is reimplemented so that it no longer inherits from z (see Figure 2) but still supports the same behavior. Class x will now be in error, because it is inheriting two *different* operations named o, one from class z via class $y1$ and one from class $y2$. (The operations are different yet have equivalent behavior on objects of their respective classes.) Thus, the change to class $y2$ to stop inheriting from z was visible to class x, a client of class $y2$. The external interface of $y2$ was therefore changed, even though the external interface of its instances remains unchanged (the instances have the same externally-visible behavior).

To prevent the use of inheritance from necessarily becoming part of the external interface of a class, one must abandon the convenient same-operation exception to the rule regarding operation conflict. An alternative conflict resolution technique that avoids this problem is to select the operation from the "first" parent that defines one (based on the textual order in which the parents are named); this alternative is undesirable because it fails to warn the designer about unintentional conflicts.

Another attribute of the graph-oriented solution is that only one set of instance variables is defined for any ancestor class, regardless of the number of paths by which the class can be reached in the inheritance graph. For example, in Figure 1, an instance of x contains one of each instance variable defined by z, not two.

While this result is usually desirable, it introduces potential problems. For example, using a depth-first traversal (as described above) on an inheritance graph with merging will result in some operations being invoked more than once on the same set of instance variables. As a result, a designer cannot change the use of inheritance within a class without the danger of breaking some descendant class.

Consider the structure shown in Figure 2. Suppose the operation o is defined by classes z, $y2$, and x, where the definition of o in class x invokes operation o on both parents.

Now suppose the designer of class $y2$ decides to reimplement $y2$ to inherit from z in a manner that preserves the external behavior of objects of class $y2$; assume that class $y2$ will either inherit o from z or will revise its definition of o to invoke o as defined by z. The operation o on class x will now have the effect of invoking the operation o on class z twice, on the same set of instance variables. If o on z has side-effects, the result might not be acceptable. Thus, in this example, a change to the use of inheritance by a class ($y2$) has broken one of its clients (x), even though its operations have the same external behavior; the use of inheritance is therefore (implicitly) part of the external interface of the class $y2$.

Linear Solutions

The second strategy for dealing with multiple inheritance is to first flatten the inheritance graph to a linear chain, without duplicates, and then treat the result as single inheritance. This strategy is used by Flavors (as recently revised) [Moon86] and CommonLoops [Bobrow86]. These languages use similar algorithms for creating a total ordering that preserves the ordering along each path through the inheritance graph (a class never appears after one of its ancestors). Flavors attempts as well to preserve the relative ordering of the parents of a class (the first parent of a class never appears after the second, etc.); an error is signalled if no total ordering exists that satisfies all such constraints.

While the relative ordering of a class and its ancestors is preserved in the total ordering, unrelated classes can be

Figure 3: Linearized multiple inheritance.

inserted between a class and its parent. For example, the inheritance graph shown in Figure 1 would be transformed into the chain shown in Figure 3. Note that the class $y2$ now appears between class $y1$ and its parent class z. Thus, although these languages treat the computed inheritance chain as single inheritance, the computed inheritance chain has the unusual property that the "effective parent" of a class c may be a class of which the designer of class c has absolutely no knowledge.

One problem with this solution is that in the case of operation conflicts (two or more parents defining the same operation), one operation will be selected even if there is no clearly "best" choice. Consider the above example: If operation o is defined only by classes $y1$ and $y2$, then class x will inherit the operation defined by class *y1*. This selection assumes that the ordering of parents in a class definition is significant. Although such conflicts are likely to be unintentional, no warning is given.

Another problem involves the ability of a class to reliably communicate with its "real" parents. CommonLoops allows a class to invoke its "effective parent" (its parent in the computed inheritance chain) using a notation similar to super in Smalltalk. Flavors provides a declarative mechanism called method combination that is essentially equivalent. These mechanisms avoid the problem of unintentional multiple invocations of operations that can occur using graph-oriented solutions. However, these mechanisms make it difficult for a class to reliably set up private communication with a parent, given the interleaving of classes that can occur when the inheritance chain is computed.

In the above example, suppose that class *y1* wants to communicate privately with its parent *z*; specifically, it wants to invoke (public) operations defined by *z* without being affected by redefinitions of those operations by other classes. This kind of private communication is easily arranged in the graph-oriented languages (Trellis/Owl and extended Smalltalk) by directly naming the operations of *z*. However, using super or its equivalent, class *y1* can directly invoke only operations of its "effective parent", which in this case is *y2*; if *y2* happened to redefine the operation in question, the "wrong" operation (from *y1*'s point of view) would be invoked. This example demonstrates that to correctly use *y1* as a parent, one must understand details of its internal design regarding its use of its parent *z*.

Unlike the graph-oriented languages, neither Common-Loops nor Flavors allows a class to designate an operation by the name of the defining parent. Adding this feature would allow one to simulate the semantics of the graph-oriented languages. However, its use would be error-prone, as mixed use of the two different styles (linear or graph) would probably produce undesirable results.

Tree Solutions

We are exploring in CommonObjects [Snyder85a] a third strategy for handling multiple inheritance that avoids the problems of the graph-oriented and linear solutions. Like the graph-oriented solutions of Trellis/Owl and extended Smalltalk, the semantics of CommonObjects models the inheritance graph. However, there are two key differences: (1) An attempt to inherit an operation from more than one parent is always an error, regardless of the source(s) of the operation. This change plugs the "leak" described above. (2) The inheritance graph is converted into a tree by duplicating nodes. In other words, each parent of each class defines a completely separate set of inherited instance variables; if a class is reachable by multiple paths through the inheritance graph, a separate set of instance variables will be created for each such path. For example, in Figure 1, an instance of *x* contains two of each instance variable defined by *z*. This change avoids situations where an operation is accidentally invoked multiple times on the same set of instance variables or where two classes conflict in their use of an inherited class.

The tree solution used by CommonObjects avoids exposing the use of inheritance, but radically changes the semantics of inheritance graphs with shared nodes. Applications in other languages that use shared ancestors would almost certainly have to be redesigned in CommonObjects (and vice versa). Shared ancestors typically arise when inheriting multiple "base" classes, where a "base" class is one that defines a "complete" set of operations and is generally designed to be instantiated. An alternative is to inherit a single "base" class and one or more "mixin" classes, where a "mixin" class [Weinreb81] defines a set of operations related to one particular feature and is designed only to be inherited from ("mixed into" a class). Using this strategy, designers will be encouraged to create more, and more general, "mixin" classes. Further experimentation is needed to determine the practicality of this alternative programming style.

Inheritance in ThingLab [Borning81] uses a modified tree solution: it differs from CommonObjects in two major ways: in ThingLab, each parent (called a *part*) is an object in its own right, and the ThingLab *merge* capability can explicitly induce merging in the inheritance hierarchy.

Summary

We have identified two areas where most object-oriented languages are deficient in their support for encapsulation. One area is the encapsulation of instance variables, a significant feature of most object-oriented languages. Many popular object-oriented languages (e.g., Smalltalk, Flavors, and Objective-C) allow free access to inherited instance variables by descendant classes, thus denying the designer the freedom to compatibly change the representation of a class without affecting clients. It is encouraging that several newer languages (CommonObjects, Trellis/Owl, and C++) correct this deficiency by restricting access to inherited instance variables. Where access to inherited instance variables is needed, it should be provided in the form of operations. Language support is needed to permit classes to directly invoke parent operations (on self) and to permit such operations to be made available in this manner but not via ordinary operation invocation. Furthermore, the implicit by-name merging of instance variables defined in separate classes is inconsistent with the goals of encapsulation.

The other area is the visibility of inheritance itself. Inheritance is a useful mechanism for reusing code; the decision by the designer to use inheritance for this purpose should be private and easily changed. To permit the use of inheritance to be private, a class must be able to exclude operations defined on its parents. A class must not refer to ancestors other than its parents. A language cannot define a subtyping relation based solely on inheritance. Conflicts in operation inheritance between multiple parents must be reported regardless of the source(s) of the operation(s).

The two models of multiple inheritance in common use both require knowledge about the use of inheritance by a class to understand how to correctly inherit that class. CommonObjects provides an alternative form of multiple inheritance that supports encapsulated class definitions whose external interface is fully defined by a set of operations; further experimentation is needed to evaluate and refine this programming style.

The challenge for language designers is to provide the means by which the designer of a class can express an interface to inheriting clients that reveals the minimum information needed to use the class correctly.

References

[Bobrow86] Danny Bobrow, et al. *CommonLoops: Merging Common Lisp and Object-Oriented Programming.* Proc. ACM Conference on Object-Oriented Systems, Languages, and Applications. Portland, Oregon, Sept. 1986.

[Borning81] Alan Borning. The Programming Language Aspects of ThingLab, a Constraint-Oriented Simulation Laboratory. *ACM Transactions on Programming Languages and Systems* 3:4 (Oct. 1981), 353-387.

[Borning82] Alan Borning and Daniel Ingalls. Multiple Inheritance in Smalltalk-80. Proc. AAAI 1982, 234-237.

[Brachman85] Ronald J. Brachman. "I Lied about the Trees" – Or, Defaults and Definitions in Knowledge Representation. *AI Magazine* 6:3 (Fall 1985), 80-93.

[Canning85] Peter Canning. Personal communication.

[Cardelli84] Luca Cardelli. The Semantics of Multiple Inheritance. *Proceedings of the Conference on the Semantics of Datatypes.* Springer-Verlag Lecture Notes in Computer Science, June 1984, 51-66.

[Cox84] Brad Cox. Message/Object Programming: An Evolutionary Change in Programming Technology. *IEEE Software* 1:1 (Jan. 1984), 50-61.

[Dahl66] O.-J. Dahl and K. Nygaard. Simula – An Algol-based Simulation Language. *Comm. ACM* 9:9 (Sept. 1966), 671-678.

[Goldberg83] Adele Goldberg and David Robson. *Smalltalk-80: The Language and its Implementation.* Addison-Wesley, Reading, Massachusetts, 1983.

[Moon86] David A. Moon. *Object-Oriented Programming with Flavors.* Proc. ACM Conference on Object-Oriented Systems, and Applications. Portland, Oregon, Sept. 1986.

[Schaffert86] Craig Schaffert, et. al. *An Introduction to Trellis/Owl.* Proc. ACM Conference on Object-Oriented Systems, and Applications. Portland, Oregon, Sept. 1986.

[Snyder85a] Alan Snyder. *Object-Oriented Programming for Common Lisp.* Report ATC-85-1, Software Technology Laboratory, Hewlett-Packard Laboratories, Palo Alto, California, 1985.

[Snyder85b] Alan Snyder, Michael Creech, and James Kempf. *A Common Lisp Objects Implementation Kernel.* Report STL-85-08, Software Technology Laboratory, Hewlett-Packard Laboratories, Palo Alto, California, 1985.

[Steele84] Guy L. Steele, Jr. *Common Lisp – The Language.* Digital Press, 1984.

[Stroustrup86] Bjarne Stroustrup. *The C++ Programming Language.* Addison-Wesley, Reading, Massachusetts, 1986.

[Weinreb81] Daniel Weinreb and David Moon. *Lisp Machine Manual.* Symbolics, Inc., 1981.

Chapter 2

Semantic Data Models and Persistent Languages

Introduction

This chapter can be viewed as historical background for the object-oriented model. In addition to being interesting in its own right, this research has laid the groundwork for what we now call *object-oriented databases*.

We can divide the five systems represented in this chapter into two groups: semantic data models and persistent programming languages. SDM and DAPLEX are semantic data models; TAXIS, GALILEO, and PS/Algol are persistent languages.

Interest in semantic data models began in the middle seventies and was, to some extent, a reaction to the simplicity of the relational model. In this model, any semantics that could not be expressed directly in terms of relations would have to be embedded in the application code. The semantic data models include higher-level modeling constructs so that a database designer can assert more information about the data in a way that the database system understands.

There were no commercial implementations of these semantic data models during the period of active research. However, semantic data models have had a strong historical influence on object-oriented databases, for which there is currently a strong commercial interest.

Semantic data models include object identity and usually a type hierarchy. They do not commonly include the notions of data abstraction or

of user-defined operations (i.e., methods). It is the addition of these last two features that distinguish object-oriented data models from semantic data models. It is data abstraction and operations that allow object-oriented models to be extended in arbitrary ways. Semantic data models have at times been called structurally object-oriented (as opposed to behaviorally object-oriented). Because they lack data abstraction and operations, they are not extensible models. As a result, we see many modeling facilities built in.

One of the goals of semantic data model research was to produce a semantically accurate data model. That is, for each entity or idea in the application space, there should be a single natural choice of modeling construct.

The Semantic Data Model (SDM) was designed for implementation as a more expressive interface over a relational system. The designers attempted to distill their experience in designing databases to select the most common data semantics, and to incorporate them into a single data model. It is only recently that a subset of SDM has been made into a product by Unisys called SIM.

A toy implementation was used by Dennis McLeod to build an Interaction Formulation Advisor Program (IFAP). It presumes that some users do not have sufficient knowledge of the database contents to form an SQL query. The IFAP leads the user through a dialog about information stored in the database through questions about the user's interest. This dialog is driven by the high degree of semantics captured in an SDM schema. In this way, the SDM schema and the IFAP interface provide a very convenient semantic data dictionary for its users. The SDM schema provides documentation about the database structure that can be exploited by a conversational interface. It is worth looking at the appendix of McLeod's thesis [Mc78] to see a sample interaction with the IFAP.

The SDM defines classes that can be related to each other through a class hierarchy. The model supports many ways to define an *interclass connection,* which is a relationship between two classes. One important kind of interclass connection involves the definition of a subclass by means of a predicate. It also inherits all of the attributes defined for its superclass. This kind of subclassing is related to the notion of *classification* that was discussed in *Fundamentals of Object-Oriented Databases.* Subclasses can be defined by enumeration, intersection (such as multiple inheritance), and difference (not generally present in the object-oriented models).

Another kind of interclass connection is created by the *grouping class.* A grouping class on a class C defines a new class G with elements that are sets of elements drawn from C, and establishes a relationship between C and G. This is a higher-order notion and corresponds loosely to the notion of metatype in object-oriented models. The grouping class can contain classes as elements and in this way is similar to a metatype (i.e., type of a type).

DAPLEX [Sh81] was developed at Computer Corporation of America as a response to models like the SDM. It attempts to express concepts like those introduced in the SDM in a concise conceptual framework. In other words, it uses a notation of mathematical functions as the basis upon which higher-level semantic concepts can be built. The DAPLEX view is that everything is a function. Even persistent names of data items are modeled as functions. For example, the name **Intersections** is a zero-argument function that evaluates to a set of **Intersections**. DAPLEX adopts this view to introduce simplicity and uniformity into a complex modeling environment like that proposed by the SDM.

The DAPLEX query language is cast in terms of a built-in set of iterators that apply a predicate to a set of values. The two basic iterators are FOR EACH and FOR SOME. FOR EACH takes a set S and a predicate P and returns the subset of S that satisfies P. FOR SOME is a predicate that takes a set S and a predicate P and returns *true* if any member of S satisfies P.

It should be noted that although SDM and DAPLEX were both data models and not full programming languages, they each inspired a database programming language based on them. DIAL was a language that extended SDM, and ADAPLEX was a programming language based on ADA and DAPLEX.

Galileo was developed as a complete programming language based on the language ML. It is strongly typed and incorporates a model of data that is much like that of the semantic data models. It embeds this model in the type system of a programming language with many of the features of modern object-oriented languages, such as abstract types and type hierarchies. It allows structural types and abstract types to coexist, while the more common approach in object-oriented languages allows for only abstract types. Unlike object-oriented languages, Galileo does not treat types as denotable values. The Galileo paper [ACO85] does not discuss query language issues, but it does briefly describe a transaction scheme.

Developed during the same period as the other semantic models, TAXIS [MBW80] also has several built-in, high-level modeling primitives (e.g., properties, classes, and subclasses), but it adds other concepts that bear a striking similarity to object-oriented systems.

Like many object-oriented languages, TAXIS treats many of its constructs as objects. Classes are objects and as such must be described by other classes, called *metaclasses* (much like Smalltalk). SDM [HM81] also treats classes as objects in that they can be entities in a grouping class. An SDM class definition can define member attributes (attributes that are available on the instances) and class attributes (attributes that are available on the class itself). The definition of the class attributes accompanies the class definition itself. It is not necessary to talk about the metaclass, but we can think of class-attribute definitions as inducing a metaclass that defines the class attributes.

TAXIS also treats transactions as objects. This is similar to the object-oriented notion that operations are objects and are therefore describable by types. Functional languages adopt a similar view in which the type of a function is related to the types of its inputs and output. The TAXIS view of transaction types is that they have a time-varying extension for which the instances are executions of the operation (like activation records).

TAXIS also treats constraints and exceptions as objects. This characteristic is present in the Vbase object-oriented database. Constraints in TAXIS show up as prerequisites (i.e., preconditions) on transactions.

TAXIS supports an *is-a* relationship between classes. This relationship forms a strict hierarchy (i.e., one parent, many children) and allows subclasses to add properties and refine properties that are defined on a supertype. The refinement of a property P allows the value class V of P to be replaced by any subclass of V.

As an example, the class **Roads** might define a property called *#lanes* with a value class of **Integer**. In TAXIS, we could define subclasses **Highway** with *#lanes* ≥ 4 and **County-Road** with *#lanes* ≤ 3. We can see from the discussion in the Introduction to this volume that this capability requires run-time type checking.

TAXIS differs from its object-oriented counterparts in that its classes are not based on data abstraction. The active part of the model (i.e., the transaction) is not fundamentally associated with a class. Therefore, it does not support the disambiguation of overloaded function names by the types of the actual parameters.

PS-Algol [AB+83] is an attempt to add persistence as an abstraction to a language. *Persistent data* are data that outlive the program that created them. PS-Algol adopts a few important design principles. First, programs should be insensitive to whether or not the objects they manipulate are persistent. Second, persistence should be orthogonal to other aspects of the language. For example, if arrays can store any type, they should be able to store persistent objects as well as temporary objects.

Reachability is the basis for deciding which objects persist. In this scheme, there is a persistent root object, and any other objects in the transitive closure of references from this root are automatically made persistent. PS-Algol has a simple transaction mechanism at the level of the database. A program can open a database for reading or writing. There can be only one writer for a database. When a writer closes the database, any objects that are reachable from the database root are made persistent.

The motion of objects from the persistent store into the heap is invisible to application programs. The techniques used by PS-Algol to achieve this are relevant for the implementation of object-oriented databases.

References

[Ab74]   J.R. Abrial. Data Semantics. In Data Management Systems. J.W. Klimbie and K.L. Koffeman, eds. North Holland, 1974.

•[ACO85]   A. Albano, L. Cardelli, and R. Orsini. Galileo: A Strongly-Typed, Interactive Conceptual Language. ACM Transactions on Database Systems, 10(2):230–260, 1985.

•[AB+83]   M.P. Atkinson, P.J. Bailey, K.J. Chisholm, W.P. Cockshott, and R. Morrison. An Approach to Persistent Programming. The Computer Journal, 26(4), 1983.

•[HM81]   M. Hammer and D. McLeod. Database Description with SDM: A Semantic Data Model. ACM Transactions on Database Systems, 6(3), 1981.

[Mc78]   D. McLeod. A Semantic Database Model and its Associated Structured User Interface. Technical Report TR-214, MIT, Lab for Computer Science, Cambridge, MA, 1978.

•[MBW80]   J. Mylopoulos, P. Bernstein, and H.K.T. Wong. A Language Facility for Designing Interactive Database-Intensive Applications. *ACM Transactions on Database Systems*, 5(2):185–207, 1980.

[OBS86]   P. O'Brien, B. Bullis, and C. Schaffert. Persistent and Shared Objects in Trellis/OWL. *1986 International Workshop on Object-Oriented Database Systems*, Pacific Grove, CA, September, 1986.

•[Sh81]   D. Shipman. The Functional Data Model and the Data Language DAPLEX. ACM TODS, 6:1, March, 1981.

[SS77]   J.M. Smith and D.C.P. Smith. Database Abstractions: Aggregation and Generalization. *ACM Transactions on Database Systems*, 2(2), 1977.

• indicates article included in this volume

The Functional Data Model and the Data Language DAPLEX

DAVID W. SHIPMAN
Computer Corporation of America

DAPLEX is a database language which incorporates:

(1) a formulation of data in terms of entities;
(2) a functional representation for both actual and virtual data relationships;
(3) a rich collection of language constructs for expressing entity selection criteria;
(4) a notion of subtype/supertype relationships among entity types.

This paper presents and motivates the DAPLEX language and the underlying data model on which it is based.

Key Words and Phrases: database, language, functional data model
CR Categories: 4.22, 4.33

1. INTRODUCTION

1.1 The Goals of the Language

DAPLEX is a data definition and manipulation language for database systems, grounded in a concept of data representation called the functional data model. DAPLEX may be considered to be a syntactic embodiment of the functional data model and throughout this paper the two terms will be used interchangeably.

A fundamental goal of DAPLEX is to provide a "conceptually natural" database interface language. That is, the DAPLEX constructs used to model real-world situations are intended to closely match the conceptual constructs a human being might employ when thinking about those situations. Such conceptual naturalness, to the extent it has been achieved, presumably simplifies the process of writing and understanding DAPLEX requests, since the translation between the user's mental representation and its formal expression in DAPLEX is more direct.[1]

[1] To some extent this "naturalness" has been a goal of other data models. For example, the "simplicity" which is often cited as an objective of the relational data model [7] is similar to naturalness in some respects, but it also includes the notions of minimality (i.e., a small number of data constructs) and nonredundancy (i.e., representation of a single "fact" only once in the database). These latter attributes of the relational model are almost certainly not characteristic of the way humans model the world. DAPLEX is prepared to sacrifice these goals in favor of a more natural representation.

Author's present address: Massachusetts Institute of Technology, Research Laboratory of Electronics, Room 36-597, Cambridge, MA 02139.
© 1981 ACM 0362-5915/81/0300-0140 00.75

The basic constructs of DAPLEX are the *entity* and the *function*. These are intended to model conceptual objects and their properties. We may, for example, model a particular student and the courses he is taking as entities, with the function "course of" defined to map one to the other. (A DAPLEX function, in general, maps a given entity into a *set* of target entities.)

Often some properties of an object are derived from properties of other objects to which it is related. For example, assume that courses have an "instructor of" property. We may then consider an "instructors of" property which relates students to their instructors. Such a property would be based on the "instructor of" property of those courses in which the student is enrolled. The principle of conceptual naturalness dictates that it be possible for users to treat such derived properties as if they were primitive. This follows, for example, from the observation that properties which are "derived" in one database formulation may be "primitive" in another, even though the same real-world situation is being modeled. Such alternative representations of the same facts are modeled in DAPLEX by the notion of *derived function*.

The problem of database representation is complicated by the fact that no single model of reality may be appropriate for all users and problem domains. The properties which are considered relevant and the mechanisms by which they are most naturally referenced vary across differing world views. Even the decision as to what constitutes an object depends on the world view assumed. Some users might prefer, for example, to view the enrollment of a student in a course as an entity having its own properties, while for others, dealing with enrollments as objects would be unnatural and awkward. To cope with these issues, DAPLEX provides for the construction of separate user *views* of the database. Because user views are specified in terms of derived functions, complex interrelationships among views may be accommodated.

In short, the DAPLEX language is an attempt to provide a database system interface which allows the user to more directly model the way he thinks about the problems he is trying to solve.

1.2 A Quick Look at DAPLEX

Consider the query,

"What are the names of all students taking EE courses from assistant professors?"

In DAPLEX this is expressed as

```
FOR EACH Student
  SUCH THAT FOR SOME Course(Student)
    Name(Dept(Course)) = "EE" AND
    Rank(Instructor(Course)) = "ASSISTANT PROFESSOR"
  PRINT Name(Student)
```

(DAPLEX requests can be read in an English-like manner: "For each student such that, for some course of the student, the name of the department of the course is EE and the rank of the instructor of the course is assistant professor, print the name of the student.")

Figure 1 is a graphic representation of the data description for the database against which this query is issued. The rounded enclosures indicate entity types which the course is offered. "Name" is a function which may be applied to "Department" entities to return the STRING entity which indicates the name of the department. This STRING entity is compared to the string "EE".

1.3 Relation to Previous Work

Data modeling has been one of the major themes of database research over the past ten years. DAPLEX is an outgrowth of this work. As extensive summaries of the field appear elsewhere [1, 10, 12], only particularly relevant research will be discussed here.

The notion of a functional data model was first introduced by Sibley and Kershberg [15]. This work explored the use of the functional approach as a tool for modeling the data structures representable under the three dominant data models (hierarchical, relational, and network). However, the payoff resulting from the concept of derived functions was not recognized.

The semantic data model of McLeod and Hammer [9, 12] does recognize the potential inherent in the notion of derived data. In addition, this work includes a great deal of pioneering research into the descriptive capabilities needed to represent, in the database, useful semantic properties of the real world being modeled. This work, however, has not concentrated on extracting the underlying primitives of the proposed model or on expressing its ideas within a concise notational framework. To a large extent, DAPLEX is an attempt to provide such a framework for many of the ideas in this model.

In a concurrent effort, Buneman [5] has developed a functional notation for data which incorporates many of the concepts underlying the functional data model proposed here. His notation is based on the functional programming (FP) notation advocated by Backus [4]. While Buneman's notation is not entirely suitable as a user interface language, it may well be useful as an internal representation for portions of the DAPLEX syntax.

In addition, some reference should be made to the work of Smith and Smith [16], whose explorations of the issues of generalization and aggregation lead directly or indirectly to many of the concepts embodied in DAPLEX; to the work of Bachman [3], whose role model bears many similarities to the use of types in DAPLEX; and to the work of Kent [11], who argues persuasively of the disadvantages of record-based data modeling. Rowe and Shoens [14] introduced the notion of procedural encapsulation of view updates. System R [2] and INGRES [17] both employ data dictionaries defined in terms of the native data model.

Many, if not most, of the ideas incorporated in DAPLEX have been adapted from previous work in database management. What is significant about DAPLEX is the fact that these ideas have been integrated into a single framework, the functional data model, and expressed in a syntax which tends to avoid unnecessary awkwardness.

The remainder of this paper includes sections describing data definition, data manipulation, derived data, metadata, and applications examples. It should be pointed out that the study of the DAPLEX language and its implications is a continuing effort and that details of the design should be considered preliminary. No implementation currently exists. The appendix presents the complete specification of the language as it stands.

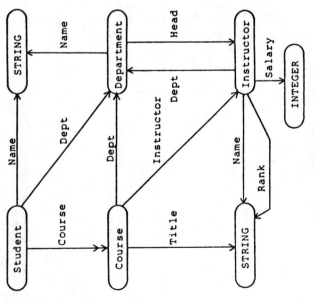

Fig. 1. The university database.

and the arrows depict functions mapping their argument types into their result types.[2]

In this example the FOR EACH statement iterates over a set of entities of type "Student", executing its for-body, the PRINT statement, for each member of the set. Here, the set of entities under consideration has been qualified by a SUCH THAT clause. SUCH THAT will consider all "Student" entities, testing them against a qualifying predicate. The qualification here further involves quantification as indicated by the phrase "FOR SOME Course(Student)". Within this phrase, the variable "Student" refers to the particular student under consideration by SUCH THAT. "Course" is a function defined over students that returns a set of course entities. If the following Boolean predicate is true for at least one of the courses, then the student entity will pass the SUCH THAT qualification. This Boolean predicate consists of two comparisons joined by the Boolean operator AND. Notice the nested functional notation here. In the expression "Name(Dept(Course))", "Course" refers to the particular "Course" entity under consideration by the FOR SOME phrase. When the "Dept" function is applied to this entity, the result is a "Department" entity indicating the department under

---

[2] The formal DAPLEX description of this database is given in the following section. Readers familiar with the AI literature will recognize that we are essentially dealing with a form of *semantic net* [13]. It should also be pointed out that the simple graphical notation indicated here is not adequate to represent the full power of the data description capability.

2. DATA DEFINITION

2.1 The DECLARE Statement

Figure 1 illustrates the data definition statements needed to express the data structure which is graphically presented in Figure 1. All of the statements shown here are DECLARE statements. They establish functions in the system. Functions are used to express both entity types and what we have been calling the "properties" of an entity.

Let us consider a number of the statements in this description. First, we look at

DECLARE Name(Student) → STRING

This states that "Name" is a function which maps entities of type "Student" to entities of type STRING. STRING is one of a number of entity types provided by the system along with such other types as INTEGER and BOOLEAN. The statement

DECLARE Dept(Student) → Department

states that "Dept" is a function which applied to a "Student" entity returns an entity of type "Department". It is important to remember that when the "Dept" function is applied, a department entity itself is returned, not a department number or other identifier. These two functions are called *single-valued* as they always return a single entity. (Strictly speaking, single-valued functions return a set of entities consisting of a single element.) Single-valued functions are indicated by use of a single-headed arrow (→) in their definition. An example of a *multivalued* function, indicated by the double-headed arrow (⟹), is

DECLARE Course(Student) ⟹ Course

Here the "Course" function, applied to a "Student" entity, returns a set of entities of type "Course". A multivalued function may return the empty set.

DECLARE Student ( ) ⟹ ENTITY
DECLARE Name (Student) → STRING
DECLARE Dept (Student) ⟹ Department
DECLARE Course (Student) ⟹ Course

DECLARE Course ( ) ⟹ ENTITY
DECLARE Title (Course) → STRING
DECLARE Dept (Course) → Department
DECLARE Instructor (Course) ⟹ Instructor

DECLARE Instructor ( ) ⟹ ENTITY
DECLARE Name (Instructor) → STRING
DECLARE Rank (Instructor) → STRING
DECLARE Dept (Instructor) → Department
DECLARE Salary (Instructor) → INTEGER

DECLARE Department ( ) ⟹ ENTITY
DECLARE Name (Department) → STRING
DECLARE Head (Department) → Instructor

Fig. 2. Data description.

All function applications evaluate to sets of entities in the mathematical sense; that is, the sets are considered unordered and do not contain duplicates.[3]

The functions we have examined so far take a single argument. It is also possible for functions to take no arguments. For example,

DECLARE Student ( ) ⟹ ENTITY

Here the function "Student" evaluates to a set of entities. ENTITY is the system-provided type of all entities. By convention, zero-argument functions define entity types. Thus the statement above has a dual purpose; it declares the function "Student" and it defines the entity type "Student". All and only those entities returned by the "Student" function are of type "Student".

Multivalued functions are initialized to return the empty set. Single-valued functions must be explicitly initialized by the user.[4] Further instantiation of functions takes place through update statements, discussed in Section 3.4.

2.2 Multiple Argument Functions

We have just considered functions of zero and one argument. However, functions taking any number of arguments may be declared. For example, we could augment the data description of Figure 2 with the statement

DECLARE Grade(Student, Course) → INTEGER

The "Grade" function might return the grade which "Student" obtained in "Course".

Other data modeling mechanisms often force the creation of new entity types in such a situation, for example, [6]. In these systems it is necessary to view, for example, the enrollment of a student in a course as a conceptual object, and then to assign a "grade of" property to that "object." With DAPLEX, the mandatory creation of such potentially unnatural entity types is avoided.

A difficulty with the function declaration above is that it specifies the function "Grade" as well defined for every "Student"–"Course" pair, while in fact the function should only exist for those courses in which the student is enrolled. The more sophisticated declaration that follows circumvents this problem:

DECLARE Grade(Student, Course(Student)) → INTEGER

2.3 Function Inversion

The reader may be concerned that DAPLEX functions map in only one direction. Thus, given a "Course" entity, we may apply the function "Instructor" to obtain the instructor of the course. But, given an "Instructor" entity, how do we determine the courses he teaches? This problem is solved through the use of function inversion, as illustrated by

DEFINE Course(Instructor) ⟹
INVERSE OF Instructor(Course)

---

[3] As we see later, however, the language does include facilities which allow the user to associate orders with certain sets of entities.

[4] Formally, single-valued functions are initialized to a particular entity which is only of type ENTITY. Because the value of the function is of the wrong type, any reference to the function will cause a run-time error. Further, the transaction (i.e., top-level DAPLEX statement) will abort if the function has not been properly initialized by the end of the transaction (see Appendix, Section A2.2.2).

```
DECLARE Person ()  ⟹ ENTITY
DECLARE Name (Person) → STRING

DECLARE Student () ⟹ Person
DECLARE Dept (Student) → Department
DECLARE Course (Student) ⟹ Course

DECLARE Employee () ⟹ Person
DECLARE Salary (Employee) → INTEGER
DECLARE Manager (Employee) → Employee

DECLARE Instructor () ⟹ Employee
DECLARE Rank (Instructor) → STRING
DECLARE Dept (Instructor) → Department
```

Fig. 3. Subtypes.

We now have a function "Course" which can be applied to "Instructor" entities. In so doing, we have entered the domain of derived functions (notice the keyword DEFINE has replaced DECLARE). Section 4 is devoted to the definition and use of derived data, and in that section the subject of function inversions is taken up again.

2.4 Subtypes and Supertypes

Rather than declare "Student" and "Instructor" entities, as is done in Figure 2, the more general specification given in Figure 3 might be used. Here, by defining students as persons and instructors as employees, who in turn are persons, we have implied a number of *subtype* and *supertype* relationships.

In Figure 3 the "Student" function is defined to return a set of "Person" entities. That is, the set of "Student" entities is a subset of the set of "Person" entities. This implies that any "Student" entity also has the "Name" function defined over it since it is necessarily a "Person" entity as well.

Similar comments apply to the specification of the "Employee" type, as well as to the "Instructor" type, a subtype of the type "Employee". An "Instructor" entity has "Name", "Salary" and "Manager" functions specified over it as well as "Rank" and "Dept".

The mechanisms discussed above organize types into a hierarchy. However, use of the INTERSECTION OF or UNION OF operators, described in Section 4, results in a lattice of entity types.

2.5 Function Names

A single entity may be a member of several types. A particular "Student" entity, for example, may be an "Instructor" entity as well. This can give rise to potential ambiguities in function invocation. Earlier, the "Course" function was defined over "Instructor" entities to return the courses the instructor teaches. But the "Course" function was also declared above to map a "Student" entity into the courses the student is taking. When we apply the function "Course" to an entity which is both a "Student" and an "Instructor", which courses do we get?

The resolution of this dilemma lies in the fact that the two "Course" functions *are different functions*. Consequently they are given different *internal names* even though their *external names* are the same. Such a situation is generally referred to as "function name overloading." The internal name of a function is generated by enclosing in square brackets the external function name and the argument types over which it was originally specified. Thus the internal names of our two functions are [Course(Instructor)] and [Course(Student)].

Which function is chosen depends on the role the argument entity plays in the user's request. If the entity is currently being viewed as a student, then [Course(Student)] is applied. If it is being viewed as an instructor, then [Course(Instructor)] is applied instead.

The formal notion of *role*, discussed in Section 3.6, is used to achieve these results. Briefly, role associates an entity type with every expression in the language. External function names are disambiguated by determining the role of their argument expressions.

2.6 Ordered Data

Order forms a natural part of a user's conception of reality and consequently has been incorporated into the design of DAPLEX. An explicit ordering facility eliminates the need for the artificial "ordering attributes" sometimes required with other data models.

Any multivalued function may have an order associated with the members of the set it returns. In particular, types may be ordered by associating an order with the zero-argument function which defines the type.

Orders may be system maintained or user maintained. A system-maintained ordering is based on the evaluation of expressions defined over the elements of the set to be ordered. An example would be the ordering of instructors by rank and salary, or the ordering of students by the number of courses which they are taking. User-maintained orders are defined explicitly via update statements in the language. Examples might include the ordering of the musical notes in a melody, the ordering of the stops on a subway line, or the ordering of statements in a computer program.

The syntax relevant to orders is rather conventional. The reader is directed to the appendix for further details.

3. DATA MANIPULATION

3.1 Expressions and Statements

The basic elements of the DAPLEX syntax are statements and expressions. Statements direct the system to perform some action and include the data definition statements and FOR loops. Expressions, which always appear within statements, evaluate to a set of entities. As seen in the example query of Section 1, expressions may involve qualification, quantification, Boolean operators, and comparisons. Figure 4 presents a decomposition and labeling of the syntactic units of this query according to the syntax specification of the appendix.

3.2 Some Syntactic Tricks

This section discusses two syntactic devices, namely, nested function calls and implicit looping variables, which are designed to increase the "conceptual conciseness" of DAPLEX. A conceptually concise language is one which reduces the need for introducing artificial elements when formally specifying a query.

In the later query, the symbol "Employee" is used in two distinct senses. In the first line, it refers to the entity type "Employee" and references the entire set of "Employee" entities.[5] In succeeding lines the symbol "Employee" is a looping variable. It is bound successively to the members of the iteration set, as is the symbol "X" in the former query.

Each set expression in DAPLEX has associated with it a reference variable. Operators which iterate over the set, such as FOR EACH and SUCH THAT in the preceding example, successively bind this variable to the entities in the iteration set. The reference variable typically appears in the body of the iterating operator and references the particular entity being considered in the current iteration. By using the IN operator, the user is able to explicitly specify the reference variable associated with a set. Otherwise the reference variable is implicitly declared, usually to be the same symbol as the first identifier in the set expression.[6]

Although the implicit variable declaration results in more readable requests, the explicit form is provided in DAPLEX for two reasons. The first is that this syntax is expected to be easier for a database front end (such as a natural language front end) to generate. The second is that there are circumstances in which two or more variables must range over the same set of entities and in which implicit variable declarations would assign both variables the same name. Such usage is illustrated in the following (exceedingly) awkward rendition of the preceding query.

```
FOR EACH X IN Employee
  SUCH THAT FOR SOME Y IN Employee
    Y = Manager (X) AND
    Salary (X) > Salary (Y)
  PRINT Name (X)
```

It is important to note, however, that it is almost never necessary to use explicit reference variables. Through such techniques as nested functional notation, DAPLEX eliminates the need for multiple variables ranging over the same set in nearly all cases. In fact, a good rule of thumb is that whenever explicit ranging variables must be specified, the query is probably poorly formulated.

3.3 Aggregation

Aggregation functions include AVERAGE, TOTAL, COUNT, MAXIMUM, and MINIMUM. Consider the request, "How many instructors are in the EE department?"

```
PRINT COUNT (Instructor
  SUCH THAT Name (Dept(Instructor)) = "EE")
```

The argument to the COUNT function is a set of "Instructor" entities, and COUNT simply returns the cardinality of that set.

---

[5] "Employee" here is equivalent to "Employee()." In general, a symbol which is a type name evaluates to the set of entities of that type, *unless* the symbol has been already bound in the local context to a particular entity. Such binding of symbols occurs, for example, with formal parameters (see Section 4.1) and with the explicit and implicit looping variables discussed in this section.

[6] The precise rules for implicit declaration of reference variables are given in the appendix. Note that although this symbol is often a type name, it need not be.

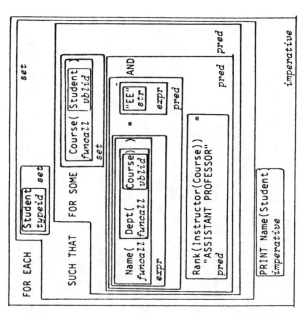

Fig. 4. Anatomy of a request.

The functional notation readily lends itself to functional nesting. Consider the following predicate from Figure 4:

```
Rank(Instructor(Course)) = "ASSISTANT PROFESSOR"
```

The advantage of such a construct is that it is not necessary to introduce the additional instructor variable which would be required if function nesting were not permitted. In languages without function nesting, the above predicate would have to be expressed as something analogous to the following:

```
FOR SOME Instructor
  Instructor(Course) = Instructor AND
  Rank(Instructor) = "ASSISTANT PROFESSOR"
```

Another way the language is made conceptually concise is through the use of implicitly declared looping variables. Consider the query, "Which employees earn more than their managers?" This could be expressed in DAPLEX as

```
FOR EACH X IN Employee ()
  SUCH THAT Salary (X) >
    Salary(Manager (X))
  PRINT Name(X)
```

However, the following semantically equivalent rendition is preferred, since it avoids the introduction of the explicit looping variable "X":

```
FOR EACH Employee
  SUCH THAT Salary(Employee) >
    Salary(Manager(Employee))
  PRINT Name(Employee)
```

The set orientation of DAPLEX presents a problem for aggregation in general. Assume we wish to know the average salary of instructors in the EE department. We cannot take the average of the *set* of such salaries because the set notion does not allow duplicates. (The average of $15,000, $25,000, and $15,000 would be $20,000 if we simply took the average of the set of salaries.) The following notation resolves this problem. "What is the average salary of instructors in the EE department?"

PRINT AVERAGE (Salary(Instructor) OVER Instructor
SUCH THAT Name (Dept(Instructor)) = "EE")

The semantics of this query are as follows. The OVER operator takes a set specification and an expression defined over members of that set. Here the set involved is a particular set of "Instructor" entities. This set does not contain duplicates. For each member of this set, the given expression is evaluated. (Note that "Instructor" in this expression is an implicit looping variable.) Each resulting value is included in the average independent of whether or not duplicate values are present. Strictly speaking, the OVER expression evaluates not to a set but to a bag.[7] The cardinality of the bag is the same as the cardinality of OVER's set operand.

3.4 Updating

Update statements are used to specify the value returned by a function when applied to particular entities. Some examples illustrate the syntax involved. "Add a new student named Bill to the EE department and enroll him in 'Systems Analysis' and 'Semiconductor Physics',"

```
FOR A NEW Student
BEGIN
LET Name (Student) = "Bill"
LET Dept (Student) = THE Department SUCH THAT
    Name (Department) = "EE"
LET Course (Student) =
    (THE Course SUCH THAT Name (Course) =
        "Systems Analysis",
    THE Course SUCH THAT Name (Course) =
        "Semiconductor Physics")
END
```

The following illustrates the incremental updating of multivalued functions. "Drop 'Introductory Physics' from John's courses and add 'Organic Chemistry',"[8]

```
FOR THE Student SUCH THAT Name (Student) = "John"
BEGIN
EXCLUDE Course (Student) =
    THE Course SUCH THAT Name (Course) =
        "Introductory Physics"
INCLUDE Course (Student) =
    THE Course SUCH THAT Name (Course) =
        "Organic Chemistry"
END
```

[7] A *bag*, sometimes called a *multiset*, is a set which may contain duplicate elements.

[8] A less awkward version of this request is presented in Section 4.1.

3.5 Function Evaluation

Update statements set the value a function is to return when it is applied to particular arguments. In the context of a DAPLEX expression, however, a function's arguments are not always individual entities but rather sets of entities. This is simply a result of the fact that the argument to a function is an expression, and expressions, in general, evaluate to a set. When a function is evaluated, the result is the union of all entities returned by the function applied to all members of its argument set. Thus, "List all courses taken by EE students,"

```
FOR EACH
    Course (Student SUCH THAT Dept (Student) = "EE")
    PRINT Title (Course)
```

The argument to the "Course" function here is a set of "Student" entities. The evaluation of the function returns the set of all courses taken by any of these students. Note that each course is listed only once.[9]

A corollary to the function evaluation convention is that functions with null set arguments evaluate to the null set.

3.6 Value, Role, and Order

We are now ready to consider some of the more subtle aspects of expression evaluation in DAPLEX. Three components are associated with every expression evaluation. These are the expression *value*, the expression *role*, and the expression *order*. The expression value is the set of entities returned by evaluating the expression. The expression role is the entity type under which these entities are to be interpreted when resolving external function name ambiguities. The expression order is the ordering associated with these entities.

So far in our discussions we have been almost exclusively concerned with expression value. Clearly, it is the most important aspect of expression evaluation.

An expression's role is used only in determining internal function names (see Section 2.5). The role of an expression can always be determined by a static analysis of the request and the data description; accessing of the actual database is not required.

An expression's order is only relevant when the expression is used with the operator FOR EACH...IN ORDER, with expressions involving the keywords PRECEDING and FOLLOWING and with predicates which compare two entities based on their order. Otherwise the order is ignored.

The value, role, and order of an expression are calculated from the value, role, and order, respectively, of its subexpressions. The appendix gives complete rules for obtaining value, role, and order for each of the expression types in DAPLEX. The following example illustrates the use of expression role. "Among the students who are also instructors, list those who are taking a course which

[9] Had we, for some reason, desired duplicate courses to be listed, the query would have been expressed as

```
FOR EACH Student SUCH THAT Dept (Student) = "EE"
    FOR EACH Course (Student)
        PRINT Title (Course)
```

they teach,"

FOR EACH Student SUCH THAT
  SOME Course (Student) =
    SOME Course (Student AS Instructor)
PRINT Name (Student)

The operator AS converts the role of an expression without affecting its value or order. In the first use of the function name "Course", the argument to the function has the role "Student". Therefore, the internal function name for this invocation is [Course (Student)]. In the second use of the function name "Course", the argument to the function has been converted to have the role "Instructor". Consequently, the internal function name for this invocation is [Course (Instructor)]. It should also be noted that the AS expression evaluates to the null set (and consequently the qualifying predicate evaluates to FALSE) when the current "Student" is not of type "Instructor".

3.7 General-Purpose Operators and Control Structures

It is intended that DAPLEX be embedded in a general-purpose high-level language. Consequently, syntax for general-purpose operators and control structures are not specified here, as this would be supplied by the high-level language. Nonetheless, the examples here have made use of such constructs (e.g., PRINT, AND, BEGIN ... END are all assumed to be supplied by the high-level language). The semantics in these cases should be cl.

4. DERIVED DATA

4.1 The DEFINE Statement

The use of derived data dramatically extends the naturalness and usability of a database system. In the context of the functional data model, "derived data" is interpreted to mean "derived function definitions." Essentially we are defining new properties of objects based on the values of other properties. Derived functions are specified by means of DEFINE statements.[10]

To define a function "Instructor" over "Student" entities which returns the instructors of courses the student is taking, use

DEFINE Instructor(Student) ⟹
  Instructor(Course(Student))

The function "Instructor" may now be used in queries exactly as if it had been a primitive function. The user need not be aware that it is derived data.
As another example, assume we wish to define a "grade point average" property of students:

DEFINE GradePointAverage(Student) ⟹
  AVERAGE(Grade(Student, Course)
  OVER Course(Student))

[10] Derived functions behave as if their values were recomputed on each access. This does not imply, however, that they actually need be. An implementation strategy which stored the derived function values would be perfectly acceptable so long as it produced the same values as a recompute-on-each-access strategy. This would involve updating a stored value when the values on which it is based have changed.

"Student" is being used as a formal parameter within the body of the DEFINE statements above. When the derived function is evaluated, this variable is bound to the actual argument supplied. In cases where a function takes more than one argument of the same type, the IN operator can be used.[11] Thus, to define a Boolean function which compares two students on the basis of their respective grade point averages, use

DEFINE Brighter(S1 IN Student, S2 IN Student) ⟹
  GradePointAverage(S1) > GradePointAverage(S2)

Derived functions may also be defined over the system-supplied entity types. For example,

DEFINE Student(STRING) ⟹ INVERSE OF Name(Student)
DEFINE Course(STRING) ⟹ INVERSE OF Title(Course)

These functions map a STRING into a set of "Students" or "Courses", respectively. The update request presented earlier in Section 3.4 can now be written more straightforwardly as follows: "Drop 'Introductory Physics' from John's courses and add 'Organic Chemistry',"[12]

FOR THE Student("John")
  BEGIN
  EXCLUDE Course(Student) =
    THE Course("Introductory Physics")
  INCLUDE Course(Student) =
    THE Course("Organic Chemistry")
  END

4.2 Conceptual Abstractions

Consider the query, "Which instructors earn over twice the average salary for instructors in their departments?" In the DAPLEX rendition that follows, the query is broken into three parts. First, a function mapping departments to their instructors is defined. Next, a property of "instructors' average salary" is defined for departments. Finally, this property is used to find the desired instructors.

DEFINE Instructor(Department) ⟹
  INVERSE of Department(Instructor)

DEFINE InstAvgSal(Department) ⟹
  AVERAGE (Salary(Instructor)
  OVER Instructor(Department))

FOR EACH Instructor
  SUCH THAT
    Salary(Instructor) >
    2·InstAvgSal(Dept(Instructor))
  PRINT Name(Instructor)

This request illustrates a profound capability of derived functions: the ability to specify and name conceptual abstractions. This ability is the essence of structured programming, abstract data types, and subroutines. It lies at the core

[11] This is not a special case but follows from the fact that the function arguments specified in DECLARE and DEFINE statements may be arbitrary DAPLEX expressions (see the appendix).
[12] Yet another version of this request appears in Section 4.4.

of good software engineering practice. Derived data provides this capability in DAPLEX.

4.3 User Views

For reasons of convenience a user may not wish to see the database as depicted in Figures 1 and 2, but rather as it is depicted in Figure 5. Here, the only user-defined entity type is "StudentName", a subtype of STRING, and all of the functions over "StudentName" return STRING entities. The derived function definitions that follow convert the original database to this new view:

DEFINE StudentName( ) ⇒ Name(Student( ))

DEFINE DeptName(StudentName AS STRING) ⇒
Name(Dept(THE Student (StudentName)))

DEFINE CourseName(StudentName AS STRING) ⇒
Title(Course(THE Student(StudentName)))

These definitions provide the user with access to the functions he desires. For example, "What department is Mary in?" can be expressed as[13]

PRINT DeptName("Mary")

User views are often for purposes of security as well as convenience. That is, not only may it be desirable for the user to have access to the new definitions but also for him to be prevented from directly invoking the underlying functions. To accomplish this, the new user view is defined in a different name space (i.e., different "module" or "package") from the old view.[14] A secure system, then, would only allow the user to access the name space in which the new view is defined. In addition to this security consideration, the name space distinction is needed when certain function renamings take place. For example, if the new view were to reference the course titles of a student with a function called "Course" rather than one called "CourseName," separate name spaces would be needed to distinguish this new "Course" function from the original one.

4.4 Updating Derived Data

Suppose we have the following update request expressed over the view constructed in the preceding section, "Change Jack's department to Biology",

LET DeptName("Jack") = "Biology"

There are several conceivable interpretations of this request in terms of the underlying primitive functions. The first, and most plausible, is that Jack is to be registered in the Biology department; that is,[15]

LET Dept(THE Student("Jack")) = THE Department("Biology")

The second, somewhat less plausible, is that the name of Jack's current department, say the Mathematics department, is to be changed to "Biology"; that is,

LET Name(Dept(THE Student("Jack"))) = "Biology"

Yet a third alternative, similar to the proposal of Dayal [8] for updating views in the relational data model, would be to create a new department which is given the name "Biology" and to which Jack is assigned; that is,

FOR A NEW Department
BEGIN
LET Name(Department) = "Biology"
LET Dept(THE Student("Jack")) = Department
END

It is not possible for the system to intuit which of these three meanings is desired.

In DAPLEX, the semantics for updating derived data are explicitly provided by the user. This is accomplished with the PERFORM ... USING construct. For example, updates to the derived function "CourseName" might reasonably be defined as follows:

PERFORM
INCLUDE CourseName(StudentName AS STRING) = Title
USING
INCLUDE Course(THE Student(StudentName)) =
THE Course(Title)

PERFORM
EXCLUDE CourseName(StudentName AS STRING) = Title
USING
EXCLUDE Course(THE Student(StudentName)) =
THE Course(Title)

With these update specifications, the request presented earlier in Sections 3.4

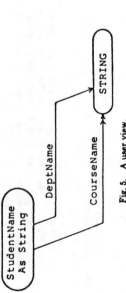

Fig. 5.   A user view.

---

[13] Some discussion of the use of the AS STRING phrase in the preceding definitions is in order. As the example illustrates, these functions are not defined over entities of type "StudentName" but rather over entities of type STRING (but only those STRING entities which also happen to be names of students). That is, the internal names of these functions are [DeptName(STRING)] and [CourseName(STRING)]. Had we instead used

DEFINE DeptName(StudentName) ⇒
Name(Dept(THE Student(StudentName)))

a function with internal name [DeptName(StudentName)] would have been defined and then we would have had to express "What department is Mary in?" as

PRINT DeptName("Mary" AS StudentName)

Since an AS phrase must be used somewhere, it is preferable to include it once in the definition of the function rather than require it every time the function appears in a request.

[14] The "package" or "module" facility is assumed to be provided by the high-level language (see Section 3.7).

[15] We are assuming for these examples a previous definition,

DEFINE Department(STRING) ⇒ INVERSE of Name(Department)

and 4.1 may be expressed even more succinctly, "Drop 'Introductory Physics' from John's courses and add 'Organic Chemistry'",

EXCLUDE CourseName("John") = "Introductory Physics"
INCLUDE CourseName("John") = "Organic Chemistry"

The PERFORM ... USING statement directs the system to execute the body of the statement whenever the indicated update operation is performed. It is important to point out that this facility merely allows users to provide the *illusion* of derived data updating. The system does not, for example, validate the PERFORM ... USING statement to ensure that it results in the intended derived data update. Finally, it should be noted that a derived data update is illegal unless an appropriate PERFORM ... USING directive has been declared.

4.5 Some Special Operators for Defining Functions

In this section we examine the operators INVERSE OF, TRANSITIVE OF, INTERSECTION OF, UNION OF, DIFFERENCE OF, and COMPOUND OF. These operators are used only in function definitions.

To invert the function [Instructor(Course)], we could use

DEFINE Course(Instructor) ⟹ Course SUCH THAT
  Instructor = Instructor(Course)

It is more convenient, however, to define this function as

DEFINE Course(Instructor) ⟹
  INVERSE OF Instructor(Course)

A simple modification of this syntax allows us to define transitive closures. For example,

DEFINE Superior(Employee) ⟹
  TRANSITIVE OF Manager(Employee)

The function [Superior(Employee)] returns the set containing the manager of the employee, the manager's manager, the manager's manager's manager, etc. The INTERSECTION OF, UNION OF, and DIFFERENCE OF operators may be used to form set intersections, unions, and differences. They are most useful in creating new types. For example,

DEFINE StudentTeacher( ) ⟹
  INTERSECTION OF Student, Instructor

The COMPOUND OF operator is used to create derived entities corresponding to the elements of the Cartesian product of its operands. As an example, assume that we wish to view the enrollment of a given student in a particular course as a "thing" designated by an entity. We could define the set of enrollment entities by

DEFINE Enrollment( ) ⟹
  COMPOUND OF Student, Course(Student)

In addition to defining the set of "Enrollment" entities and the "Enrollment" entity type, the system implicitly defines the two functions "Student" and "Course" to operate over entities of type "Enrollment". These return the "Stu-

dent" and "Course" entities upon which the compound entity was based. The entity is fully specified by the values of these system-defined functions. That is, no two "Enrollment" entities correspond to the same "Student"–"Course" entity pair. If the set of students or their courses are altered, the set of enrollments automatically reflects this change.

4.6 Constraints

Assume we wish to enforce the constraint that a department's head must come from within the department. We could define the following function over "Department" entities:

DEFINE NativeHead(Department) ⟹
  Dept(Head(Department)) = Department

This function will evaluate to TRUE for those departments which satisfy the desired constraint and to FALSE for those which do not. By inserting the keyword CONSTRAINT, we define a *constraint* which instructs the system to abort any update transactions which leave the function value FALSE for any department. Thus

DEFINE CONSTRAINT NativeHead(Department) ⟹
  Dept(Head(Department)) = Department

Constraints may also be specified over the database as a whole. For example, to ensure that the number of managers is always less than the number of nonmanagement employees, use

DEFINE Manager( ) ⟹ Manager(Employee( ))
DEFINE NonManager( ) ⟹ DIFFERENCE OF Employee, Manager
DEFINE CONSTRAINT TooManyChiefs( ) ⟹
  COUNT(Manager( )) < COUNT(NonManager( ))

The *trigger* capability is related to that for constraints. When a trigger has been installed over a function definition, a specified imperative is executed whenever the function changes from FALSE to TRUE. To inform the department head whenever more than 45 students are enrolled in a class, we might use[16]

DEFINE Student(Class) ⟹ INVERSE OF Class(Student)
DEFINE TRIGGER Overbooked(Class) ⟹
  COUNT(Student(Class)) > 45
  SendMessage(Head(Dept(Class)), "Overbooked:",
    Title(Class))

5. DATABASE SYSTEM CONSIDERATIONS

5.1 Data Description as Data

The data description is itself data. In a DAPLEX system implementation, the data description can be queried as ordinary data. The design of the data description for the data description, that is, the metadescription, is not specified here and depends, to some extent, on the details of system implementation. In any

---

[16] In this request "SendMessage" is a procedure defined in the high-level language.

case, of course, it is possible for individual users to define their own view of the data description.

The metadescription includes entities of type FUNCTION. A special system function APPLY is also provided. APPLY takes one or more arguments, the first of which is a function entity, and returns the value of that function applied to the remaining arguments.

Access to metadata is especially useful in building sophisticated interfaces (e.g., natural language front ends) for the naive user, who is often unfamiliar with the structure of the database he is using.

5.2 Updating Metadata

Metadata is normally updated using DECLARE and DEFINE statements. It is also possible for users to update the data description using update statements operating over entities of type FUNCTION. Such updates do not directly update the metadata but instead manipulate a system-provided metadata user view. PERFORM ... USING statements trap updates to the metadata user view and perform whatever system-internal measures are necessary (such as allocating storage or establishing indices) to effect the desired metadata update.

5.3 Storage Attributes

Storage attributes are associated with each function as metadata. The storage attributes direct the system as to how the data are to be physically organized on the storage medium. Like other metadata, storage attributes may be updated via the metadata user view. These storage attributes indicate how functions are to be internally represented, which data items are to be located near each other, and whether indexed access via function values is to be provided. For derived functions, the storage statements can indicate whether the function values are to be physically stored or recomputed each time they are referenced. A general discussion of storage considerations is beyond the scope of this paper.

6. EXAMPLE APPLICATIONS

6.1 DAPLEX Front Ends

The data modeling capabilities of DAPLEX incorporate those of the hierarchical, relational, and network models, the principal database models in use today. This suggests the possibility of DAPLEX front ends for existing databases and database systems.

As an example, consider a relational version of the database of Figures 1 and 2. This is illustrated in Figure 6. Figure 7 shows the isomorphic DAPLEX description. It is clear that the relational model is a subset of the functional model since the isomorphic DAPLEX description of any relational database will be subject to the following limitations:

(1) No multivalued functions are allowed.
(2) Functions cannot return user-defined entities.
(3) Multiple-argument functions are not allowed.
(4) There are no subtypes.

Having specified the isomorphic description, and assuming the existence of a

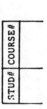

STUDENT

STUD#	NAME	DEPT#

COURSE

COURSE#	TITLE	DEPT#	INSTRUCTOR#

ENROLLMENT

STUD#	COURSE#

INSTRUCTOR

INSTRUCTOR#	NAME	RANK	DEPT#	SALARY

DEPARTMENT

DEPT#	NAME	HEAD#

Fig. 6. Relational data description.

suitable data manipulation translator, DAPLEX requests can be written against the relational database. However, the full benefits of the DAPLEX approach will not be available because of the limitations in the underlying data model. What is needed is to define derived functions which provide a more convenient view of the database. The additional definitions in Figure 8 transform the description of Figure 7 to conform to that of the original DAPLEX example of Figure 2. Having specified these functions, we may now write DAPLEX queries as if we were working with the DAPLEX database.

The derived functions of Figure 8 can be thought of as adding semantic information which is not expressible in the relational data model. Figure 9 shows the steps for transforming a DAPLEX request into a relational request in the data language QUEL [8]. Figure 9a shows the original request. After the substitutions indicated by derived function definitions are performed, the query will

DECLARE Student( ) ⟹ ENTITY
DECLARE Stud#(Student) → INTEGER
DECLARE Name(Student) → STRING
DECLARE Dept#(Student) → INTEGER

DECLARE Course( ) ⟹ ENTITY
DECLARE Course#(Course) → INTEGER
DECLARE Title(Course) → STRING
DECLARE Dept#(Course) → INTEGER
DECLARE Instructor#(Course) → INTEGER

DECLARE Enrollment( ) ⟹ ENTITY
DECLARE Stud#(Enrollment) → INTEGER
DECLARE Course#(Enrollment) → INTEGER

DECLARE Instructor( ) ⟹ ENTITY
DECLARE Instructor#(Instructor) → INTEGER
DECLARE Name(Instructor) → STRING
DECLARE Rank(Instructor) → STRING
DECLARE Dept#(Instructor) → INTEGER
DECLARE Salary(Instructor) → INTEGER

DECLARE Department( ) ⟹ ENTITY
DECLARE Dept#(Department) → INTEGER
DECLARE Name(Department) → STRING
DECLARE Head#(Department) → INTEGER

Fig. 7.   The relational description in DAPLEX.

DEFINE Dept(Student) → Department SUCH THAT
    Dept.#(Department) = Dept#(Student)

DEFINE Course(Student) → Course SUCH THAT
  FOR SOME Enrollment
    Stud#(Student) = Stud#(Enrollment) AND
    Course#(Enrollment) = Course#(Course)

DEFINE Dept(Course) → Department SUCH THAT
    Dept.#(Course) = Dept#(Department)

DEFINE Instructor(Course) → Instructor SUCH THAT
    Instructor#(Instructor) = Instructor#(Course)

DEFINE Dept(Instructor) → Department SUCH THAT
    Dept.#(Instructor) = Dept#(Department)

DEFINE Head(Department) → Instructor SUCH THAT
    Instructor#(Instructor) = Head#(Department)

Fig. 8.   Definitions for the functional view.

(a)
FOR EACH Student SUCH THAT
  FOR SOME Course(Student)
    Name(Dept(Course)) = "EE" AND
    Rank(Instructor(Course)) = "ASSISTANT PROFESSOR"
  PRINT Name (Student)

(b)
FOR EACH Student SUCH THAT
  FOR SOME (Course SUCH THAT
  FOR SOME Enrollment
    Stud#(Student) = Stud#(Enrollment) AND
    Course#(Enrollment) = Course#(Course))
  (FOR SOME (Department SUCH THAT
    Dept#(Department) = Dept#(Course))
    Name(Department) = "EE")
  AND
  (FOR SOME (Instructor SUCH THAT
    Instructor#(Instructor) = Instructor#(Course))
    Rank(Instructor) = "ASSISTANT PROFESSOR")
  PRINT Name(Student)

(c)
FOR EACH Student SUCH THAT
  FOR SOME Course
  FOR SOME Enrollment
  FOR SOME Department
  FOR SOME Instructor
    Stud#(Student) = Stud#(Enrollment) AND
    Course#(Enrollment) = Course#(Course) AND
    Dept#(Department) = Dept#(Course) AND
    Name(Department) = "EE" AND
    Instructor#(Instructor) = Instructor#(Course) AND
    Rank(Instructor) = "ASSISTANT PROFESSOR"
  PRINT Name(Student)

(d)
RANGE OF S IS Student
RANGE OF C IS Course
RANGE OF E IS Enrollment
RANGE OF D IS Department
RANGE OF I IS Instructor
RETRIEVE S. Name WHERE
  S.Stud# = E.Stud# AND
  E.Course# = C.Course# AND
  D.Dept# = C. Dept# AND
  D.Name = "EE" AND
  I.Instructor# = C.Instructor# AND
  I.Rank = "ASSISTANT PROFESSOR"

Fig. 9.   Steps in request translation.

appear as shown in Figure 9b. This query can be reorganized using simple syntactic transformations to arrive at the representation in Figure 9c. The corresponding QUEL query is shown in Figure 9d.

6.2 Database Networks

The notion of DAPLEX front ends can be adapted to provide an interface to a network of dissimilar database management systems, as illustrated in Figure 10. An isomorphic DAPLEX description is written for each of the local databases in

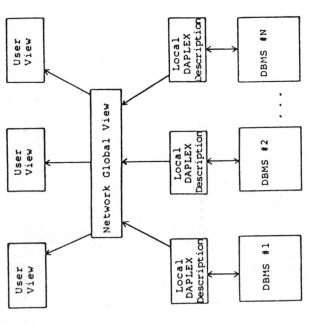

Fig. 10. Networked databases.

the network. These are then converted, via view mechanisms, into a common unified view of the entire network database. DAPLEX provides the global language by which this database is accessed. Individual user views may be defined over the global database as necessary.

7. CONCLUSION

The principal characteristics of DAPLEX can be summarized as follows:

(1) Data is modeled in terms of entities. Database entities are meant to bear a one-to-one correspondence to the "real-world" entities in the user's mental conception of reality.

(2) Relationships between data are expressed as functions, exploiting an established programming metaphor. Identical functional notation is used to reference both "primitive" and "derived" relationships. Conceptual conciseness is enhanced through the use of nested function reference. Functions may be multivalued, returning sets of entities.

(3) The request language is based on the notion of looping through entity sets. Expressions in the language are, in general, set valued. Sets are specified using the functional notation with special operators for qualification and quantification. A simple aggregation semantics, also based on looping, is incorporated. Looping variables are typically declared implicitly.

(4) Computational power is provided through the general-purpose operators of a high-level language. While not emphasized in this paper, this capability is crucial to the development of realistic applications systems.

(5) Derived functions allow users to represent arbitrary entity relationships directly by defining them in terms of existing relationships. We have seen one example request (in Sections 3.4, 4.1, and 4.4) become progressively simpler through the introduction of appropriate derived functions. In effect, the derived function capability allows application semantics to be encoded into the data description, thereby allowing requests to be expressed directly in terms of those semantics. Updating of derived relationships is supported through procedures explicitly supplied by the user.

(6) Entity types are defined as functions taking no arguments. Notions of subtype and supertype follow naturally from this formulation.

(7) User views are implemented in terms of derived functions. It was shown how DAPLEX views may be constructed over existing databases represented in terms of traditional models, thus lending support to the use of DAPLEX as a "universal" database language for heterogeneous networked databases.

APPENDIX. SPECIFICATION OF DAPLEX

A1. Syntax

The DAPLEX syntax is described in terms of the syntax specification language proposed by Wirth [18]. To quote the original proposal describing the specification language:

This meta language can therefore conveniently be used to define its own syntax, which may serve here as an example of its use. The word *identifier* is used to denote *nonterminal symbol*, and *literal* stands for *terminal symbol*. For brevity, *identifier* and *character c*flare not defined in further detail.

syntax = {*production*}.
production = *identifier* "=" *expression* ".".
expression = *term* {"|" *term*}.
term = *factor* {*factor*}.
factor = *identifier* | *literal* | "(" *expression* ")" | "[" *expression* "]" | "{" *expression* "}".
literal = """"*character* {*character*}"""".

Repetition is denoted by curly brackets, i.e. {a} stands for ε|a|aa|aaa| ... Optionality is expressed by square brackets, i.e. [a] stands for a|ε. Parentheses merely serve for grouping, e.g. (a|b)c stands for ac|bc. Terminal symbols, i.e. literals, are enclosed in quote marks (and, if a quote mark appears as a literal itself, it is written twice), which is consistent with common practice in programming languages.

In Figure 11 we define the DAPLEX syntax itself.

A2. Semantics

A2.1 *Expressions*

expr = *set* | *singleton*.

Expressions evaluate to either singletons or sets.

A2.1.1 Sets. The properties of a *set* are its value, role, order, and reference variable. Value, role, and order are discussed in Section 3.6. The reference variable is used as the formal parameter or looping variable corresponding to the *set*. In the syntactic specifications that follow, digit suffixes may be appended to symbols for purposes of reference.

set = *mvfuncall*.
Value: the *set* returned by the multivalued function application
Role: that of *mvfuncall*
Order: that of *mvfuncall*
Reference Variable: the *funcid* in the *mvfuncall*

set = *typeid*.
Value: the *set* of entities of this type (this usage is vald only when the *typeid* identifier is not currently bound as a reference variable)
Role: *typeid*
Order: that of the type
Reference Variable: *typeid*

set = "(" *singleton* {"," *singleton* } ")".
Value: a *set* consisting of the listed *singletons* (All *singletons* must have the same type)
Role: the type of the *singletons*
Order: the listed order
Reference Variable: none (if a reference variable is desired it must be explicitly declared using the IN operator)

set = *set1* "SUCH" "THAT" *pred*.
Value: those members of *set1* for which *pred* is true (in evaluating *pred*, the reference variable is bound to the member of *set1* being tested)
Role, order, reference variable: that of *set1*

set = *set1* *comp* *singleton*.
Value: those members of *set1* bearing the *comp* relationship to the *singleton*
Role, order, reference variable: that of *set1*

set = *set1* *comp* *quant* *set2*.
Value: those members of *set1* bearing the *comp* relationship to the specified quantity of members of *set2* (in evaluating *set2*, the reference variable of *set1* is bound to the member under consideration)
Role, order, reference variable: that of *set1*

set = *identifier* "IN" *set1*.
Value, role, order: that of *set1*
Reference Variable: identifier

set = *expr* "AS" *typeid*.
Value: those members of *expr* which are of the specified type
Role: *typeid*
Order, reference variable: that of *expr*

```
program = {statement}.
statement = declarative | imperative.
declarative = "DECLARE" funcspec ("=" | "=>") expr [order] |
    (expr |
    "INVERSE" "OF" funcspec |
    "TRANSITIVE" "OF" expr |
    "COMPOUND" "OF" tuple |
    ("INTERSECTION" | "UNION") "OF" expr {"," expr} |
    "DIFFERENCE" "OF" expr "," expr |
    ) [order] .
    "DEFINE" "CONSTRAINT" funcspec "=" boolean |
    "DEFINE" "TRIGGER" funcspec "=" boolean imperative |
    "PERFORM" update "USING" imperative.
funcspec = funcid "(" [tuple] ")".
tuple = expr {"," expr}.
expr = set | singleton.
set = mvfuncall | typeid |
    "(" [singleton {"," singleton}] ")" |
    set "SUCH" "THAT" pred |
    set comp {singleton | quant set} |
    identifier IN set | expr AS typeid |
    "(" set ")" | gpset.
singleton = constant | vblid | svfuncall | aggcall | pred |
    "THE" set | "A" "NEW" typeid |
    "THE" set ("PRECEDING" | "FOLLOWING") singleton |
    "(" singleton ")" | gpsingleton.
svfuncall = funcall.
mvfuncall = funcall.
funcall = funcid "(" [tuple] ")".
aggcall = aggid "(" bag ")".
bag = expr | singleton "OVER" tuple.
pred = boolean |
    "FOR" (singleton | quant set) pred |
    (singleton | quant set) comp (singleton | quant set) |
    quant set ("EXIST" | "EXISTS").
comp = ">" | "<" | "=" | "EQ" | "NE" | "LT" | "GT" | "LE" | "GE".
quant = "SOME" | "EVERY" | "NO" |
    ("AT" ("LEAST" | "MOST") | "EXACTLY") integer.
integer = singleton.
string = singleton.
boolean = singleton.
constant = int | str | bool.
int = digit {digit}.
str = "'" character {character} "'".
bool = "TRUE" | "FALSE".
imperative = forloop | update | gpimperative |
forloop = "FOR" "EACH" set [order] imperative |
    "FOR" singleton imperative.
order = "IN" "ORDER"
    ("BY" [("ASCENDING" | "DESCENDING")] singleton).
update = "LET" svfuncall "=" singleton |
    ("LET" | "INCLUDE" | "EXCLUDE") mvfuncall "=" expr |
    "INSERT" mvfuncall "=" (singleton | set [order])
    ("PRECEDING" | "FOLLOWING") singleton |
vblid = identifier.
typeid = identifier.
funcid = identifier.
aggid = identifier.
```

Fig. 11. DAPLEX syntactic specification.

set = "(" *set1* ")".
Value, role, order, reference variable: that of *set1* (this construct is used only for syntactic grouping)

set = *gpset.*
gpset is a *set*-valued expression in the general-purpose syntax. Value, role, order, and reference variable are not specified here.

A2.1.2 *Singletons.* Only value, role, and reference variable need be specified for *singletons*, as the order is trivial.

singleton = *constant.*
Value: that of the *constant*
Role: the type of the *constant*
Reference Variable: none

singleton = *vblid.*
Value: *vblid* must be bound to a particular entity
Role: that of the *expr* for which this is the reference variable
Reference Variable: *vblid*

singleton = *svfuncall* | *aggcall.*
Value: the entity returned by the single-valued function or aggregation application
Role: that of *svfuncall* or *aggcall*
Reference Variable: the *funcid* in the *svfuncall* or *aggid* in *aggcall*

singleton = *pred.*
Value, role, reference variable: that of *pred*

singleton = "THE" *set.*
Value: The single member of *set* (if *set* evaluates to more than one member an error is flagged)
Role, reference variable: that of *set*

singleton = "A" "NEW" *typeid.*
Value: a new entity of the specified type
Role: *typeid*
Reference Variable: *typeid*

singleton = "THE" *set* ("PRECEDING" | "FOLLOWING") *singleton.*
Value: the member of *set* preceding or following *singleton* according to the order of *set* (*singleton* must be a member of *set*)
Role, reference variable: that of *set*

singleton = "(" *singleton* ")".
Value, role, reference variable: that of *singleton*

singleton = *gpsingleton.*
gpsingleton is an entity valued expression in the general-purpose syntax. Value, role, order, and reference variable are not specified here.

A2.1.3 *Predicates.* The role of all predicates is BOOLEAN, and there is no reference variable, thus only value needs to be specified.

pred = *boolean.*
Value: that of the *boolean* constant or expression

pred = "FOR" *singleton pred1.*
Value: that of *pred1* evaluated with *singleton*'s reference variable bound to the value of *singleton*

pred = "FOR" *quant set pred1.*
Value: TRUE if *pred1* evaluates to true for the specified quantity of members of *set*, FALSE otherwise

pred = *singleton1 comp singleton2.*
Value: TRUE if *singleton1* bears the *comp* relation to *singleton2*, FALSE otherwise (the reference variable of *singleton1* is bound to the value of *singleton2*)

pred = *singleton comp quant set.*
Value: TRUE if *singleton* bears the *comp* relation to the specified quantity of members of *set*, FALSE otherwise (the reference variable of *singleton* is bound to the value of *singleton* during evaluation of *set*)

pred = *quant set comp singleton.*
Value: TRUE if the specified quantity of members of *set* bear the relation *comp* to *singleton*, FALSE otherwise (the reference variable of *set* is bound to the member under consideration during the evaluation of *singleton*)

pred = *quant set1 comp quant set2.*
Value: TRUE if the specified quantity of members of *set1* bears relation *comp* to the specified quantity of members of *set2*, FALSE otherwise (the reference variable of *set1* is bound to the member under consideration during the evaluation of *set2*, the scope of the first quantifier extends over that of the second)

pred = *quant set* ("EXIST" | "EXISTS").
Value: TRUE if the specified quantity of members of *set* exist, FALSE otherwise (note that this predicate is vacuously TRUE for the quantifier EVERY)

comp = ">" | "<" | "=" | "EQ" | "NE" | "LT" | "GT" | "LE" | "GE".
The comparators >, <, LT, GT, LE, and GE require that their operands have the same role. In such cases the comparisons are with respect to that role's order. The operators =, EQ, and NE do not require their operands to have the same role. In such cases, the comparison is based solely on the values of the operands.

quant = "SOME" | "EVERY" | "NO" | ("AT" ("LEAST" | "MOST") | "EXACTLY") *integer.*
The quantifier semantics should be self-evident.

A2.1.4 Miscellaneous Expressions

svfuncall = funcall.
mvfuncall = funcall.
funcall = funcid "(" [tuple] ")".
tuple = expr {"," expr}.

svfuncalls are those invoking single-valued functions, mvfuncalls those invoking multivalued functions. The value returned by the funcall is the union of the results obtained by applying the function to each element of tuple. The elements of tuple are constructed in the following way. This method allows exprs in tuple to contain the reference variables of preceding exprs. First, the first expr is evaluated to return a set of entities. Then, for each member of the set, the reference variable for the first expr is bound to the member of the set and the second expr is evaluated. This continues until all of the constituent exprs have been processed. Note that when reference variables of preceding exprs are not present, tuple simply evaluates to the cross product of the expr sets. Example: The tuple "Student(),Course(Student)" refers to those student-course pairs for which the course is a course of the student.

The funcid and the roles of the argument exprs specify a particular internal function name. It is this function which is applied to the argument values. The internal function name is determined in the following manner in order to avoid ambiguous reference. First, the set is constructed consisting of all internal names which have the specified funcid and proper number of arguments and which are defined over the types or the supertypes of the types which are the roles of the argument expr. If this set is empty, the funcall is illegal (undefined). The designated internal name is that member, M, of this set such that, for every argument position, there exists no other member defined over some subtype of the type over which M is defined at that argument position. If there is no such M, then the function reference is illegal (ambiguous). Example: If "expr1" has role "type1," "expr2" has role "type2," "super1" is a supertype of "type1" but not of "type2," "super2" is a supertype of "type2" but not of "type1," and the only internal names are "[F(type1,super2)]" and "[F(super1,type2)]", then the reference "F(expr2,expr1)" is illegal (undefined) and the reference "F(expr1,expr2)" is illegal (ambiguous).

aggcall = aggid "(" bag ")".
bag = expr | singleton "OVER" tuple.

In the case of expr, each element of the set is passed to the aggregator specified by aggid. In the case of an OVER phrase, singleton is evaluated for each element of tuple and the result is passed to the aggregator. During evaluation of singleton, the reference variables for each constituent expression of tuple are bound to the corresponding element of the expression value.

A2.1.5 Typed Expressions and Constants

integer = singleton1.
string = singleton2.
boolean = singleton3.
constant = int | str | bool.

int = digit {digit}.
str = "''''" character {character} "''''".
bool = "TRUE" | "FALSE".

singleton1 must be of type INTEGER. singleton2 must be of type STRING. singleton3 must be of type BOOLEAN. ints have type INTEGER, strs STRING and bools BOOLEAN.

A2.2 Statements

program = {statement}.
statement = declarative | imperative.

programs consist of statements which are either declaratives or imperatives.

A2.2.1 Declaratives

declarative =
"DECLARE" funcspec ("→"|"⇒") expr [order].
funcspec = funcid "(" [tuple] ")".

This declares primitive functions, which are directly updatable. If "→" is used, the function is single-valued; if "⇒", it is multivalued. If the function takes arguments, the type of the function is the role of expr. If there are no arguments, the funcid is implicitly declared to be a typeid and the function has type funcid, which is considered a subtype of the role of expr. The order of the function is determined by order. The internal name of the function is constructed from the funcid and the roles of the exprs in tuple.

declarative =
"DEFINE" funcspec ("→"|"⇒") expr [order].

This declares a derived function. The value of a derived function is computed on each invocation by evaluating expr. This evaluation is done with the reference variables of the exprs in funcspec bound to the corresponding actual arguments. Type, order and internal function name are determined as for actual primitive functions. It is not possible to directly update a derived function, however the PERFORM ... USING construct allows such updates to be simulated.

declarative = "DEFINE" funcspec ("→"|"⇒")
"INVERSE" "OF" funcspec2 [order].

funcspec1 and funcspec2 must specify one-argument functions. The role of the argument expr in funcspec1 must be the same as the type of funcspec2. The value of a funcall on the new function will be those entities which, when supplied as arguments to the function specified by funcspec2, return the actual argument in the funcall. The type of funcspec1 is the role of the expr argument in funcspec2, and the default order is the order of that type.

declarative = "DEFINE" funcspec ("→"|"⇒")
"TRANSITIVE" "OF" expr [order].

funcspec must involve exactly one argument which must have the same role as expr. expr must contain the reference variable for the formal argument in funcspec. The value of the defined function is the union of the values of expr evaluated with the reference variable bound to the actual function argument and to all other values which the function returns.

declarative = "DEFINE" *funcspec* ("⟶"|"⟹") "COMPOUND" "OF" *tuple* [*order*].

funcspec must specify a zero-argument function. The new type being defined will be a subtype of ENTITY and will include one entity for each element of *tuple*. For each *expr* component of *tuple*, the system will implicitly define an access function. The access function will map entities of the new type into the corresponding component of the tuple associated with the entity. The *funcid* of the access function is the reference variable of the corresponding *expr* in *tuple*.

declarative = "DEFINE" *funcspec* ("⟶"|"⟹") ("INTERSECTION"|"UNION") "OF" *expr* {"," *expr*} [*order*].
declarative = "DEFINE" *funcspec* ("⟶"|"⟹") "DIFFERENCE" "OF" *expr* "," *expr* [*order*].

A derived function is declared. If the function takes arguments, then each of the *exprs* must be of the same type which becomes the type of the function. If the function takes no arguments, a new type is being defined. The function is of that type, which is considered to be a subtype of each of the roles of the *exprs*. The value of the function is the intersection, union or difference of the sets obtained by evaluating the *exprs*. In the case of functions which take arguments, this evaluation takes place with the reference variables of the *funcspec* arguments bound to the corresponding actual values.

declarative = "DEFINE" "CONSTRAINT" *funcspec* "⟶" *boolean*.

The function is defined as if the keyword CONSTRAINT were not present. In addition, if any top-level statement (i.e., a program statement) completes with the function having the value FALSE for any arguments, the statement is aborted; that is, any updates it had performed are undone.

declarative = "DEFINE" "TRIGGER" *funcspec* "⟶" *boolean imperative*.

The function is defined as if the keyword TRIGGER and the *imperative* were not present. In addition, whenever the function becomes TRUE for any arguments, *imperative* is executed. This execution is performed with the reference variables of the *funcspec* arguments bound to the entities for which the function has become true. When multiple triggers are activated, the order of execution of the corresponding *imperatives* is arbitrary.

declarative = "PERFORM" *update* "USING" *imperative*.

update specifies a statement which updates a derived function. *update* will contain a *funcspec* and a *vblid* which formally represents the value to which the derived function is to be set. *imperative* typically contains this *vblid* as well as the reference variable for the formal arguments of the *funcspec*. When an update statement is executed which corresponds to the format of update, then these variables are bound to the actual parameters appearing in the update statement and *imperative* is executed. The *imperative* would presumably effect the desired update to the derived function but this is not guaranteed nor is it checked for. Use of the A NEW operator against a derived type will have the effect of INCLUDEing the new entity in that type and all its supertypes. These implicit INCLUDEs also trigger a matching PERFORM ... USING imperative.

A2.2.2 Imperatives

imperative = *forloop* | *update* | *gpimperative*.

The *gpimperatives* are imperative statements in the general-purpose language and are not further specified here.

forloop = "FOR" "EACH" *set* [*order*] *imperative*.

The *imperative* is executed for each member of *set* with the reference variable for *set* bound to that member. If *order* is supplied without any BY-phrases then the members of *set* are processed according to the order associated with *set*. If *order* is supplied with BY-phrases then the members of *set* are processed in the order specified by the BY-phrases. Otherwise, the order of processing is arbitrary.

forloop = "FOR" *singleton imperative*.

imperative is executed with the reference variable of *singleton* bound to the value of *singleton*.

update = "LET" *svfuncall* "=" *singleton*.

The value returned by the function referenced by *svfuncall* when applied to the actual arguments in *svfuncall* is changed to the value of *singleton*. The role of *singleton* and that of *svfuncall* must be the same.

update = ("LET"|"INCLUDE"|"EXCLUDE") *mvfuncall* "=" *expr*.

The value returned by the function referenced by *mvfuncall* when applied to the actual arguments in *mvfuncall* is changed. For LET, it becomes the value of *expr*. For INCLUDE, it becomes the union of the current value of *mvfuncall* and that of *expr*. For EXCLUDE, it becomes the difference of the current value of *mvfuncall* and that of *expr*. The role of *expr* and that of *mvfuncall* must be the same. If an update statement has the effect that some *funcall* returns an incorrect type, that *funcall* is illegal, and the situation must be corrected before the *program statement* is exited. No update statement for explicitly deleting entities from the database is provided, since entities are effectively deleted when they can no longer be referenced. This is typically done by excluding the entity from all of the types in which it participates.

update = "INSERT" *mvfuncall* "=" (*singleton1* | *set* [*order*]) ("PRECEDING"|"FOLLOWING") *singleton2*.

mvfuncall must refer to an explicitly ordered function. The value of the *mvfuncall* becomes the union of its previous value and the value of *singleton1* or *set*. If a *set* is specified, the elements are partially ordered with respect to *singleton2* (which must be a current value of *mvfuncall*) as indicated by the

PRECEDING/FOLLOWING keyword. If *order* is supplied, then it specifies their new relative order within *mufuncall*, otherwise they are mutually unordered. If any inserted elements are already being returned by *mufuncall*, then they are reordered. The roles of *expr*, *singleton* and *mufuncall* must be the same.

A2.2.3 Orders

order = "IN" "ORDER" ("BY" [("ASCENDING"|"DESCENDING")] *singleton*}.

The order syntax is used to specify a partial order for a *set*. When used in a function declaration or definition, the absence of a BY-phrase indicates that an explicitly ordered function is being defined. When used in a FOR EACH or INSERT statement, the absence of a BY-phrase indicates that the existing order associated with the *set* is to be used. When multiple BY-phrases are included, the first is the primary ordering, the second the secondary ordering, the third the tertiary ordering, etc. The partial order for each BY-phrase is determined by evaluating *singleton* for each member of the *set* with the reference variable for the *set* bound to that member. The relative order of the members of *set* is that of the relative order of the corresponding values of *singleton* relative to the order associated with *singleton*'s role. While *order* may specify a total order, it in general specifies a partial order. In the case of the FOR EACH statement and expressions involving PRECEDING/FOLLOWING or the *comp* operators, however, a total order is required. In these cases, the system supplies an arbitrary total order which conforms to the partial order. However, this total order is guaranteed not to change during the execution of any single statement.

ACKNOWLEDGMENTS

The author wishes to thank the many members of the Cambridge area database community for their helpful discussions and criticisms of the DAPLEX design. Special thanks are due Jim Rothnie for helping the author develop an understanding of the significance of the proposed approach and for his long-standing personal encouragement.

REFERENCES

1. SPECIAL ISSUE ON DATA-BASE MANAGEMENT SYSTEMS. *ACM Comput. Surv. 8*, 1 (March 1976), 1-151.
2. ASTRAHAN, M.M., ET AL. System R: Relational approach to database management. *ACM Trans. Database Syst. 1*, 2 (June 1976), 97-137.
3. BACHMAN, C.W., AND DAYA, M. The role concept in database models. *Proc. Int. Conf. Very Large Databases*, Tokyo, Japan, Oct. 1977, pp. 464-476.
4. BACKUS, J. Can programming be liberated from the von Neumann style? A functional style and its algebra of programs. *Commun. ACM 21*, 8 (Aug. 1978), 613-641.
5. BUNEMAN, P., AND FRANKEL, R.E. FQL—A functional query language. *Proc. ACM SIGMOD Conf.*, Boston, Mass., May-June 1979, pp. 52-58.
6. CHEN, P.P.S. The entity-relationship model: Toward a unified view of data. *ACM Trans. Database Syst. 1*, 1 (March 1976), 9-36.
7. CODD, E.F. A relational model of data for large shared data banks. *Commun. ACM 13*, 6 (June 1970), 377-387.
8. DAYAL, U., AND BERNSTEIN, P.A. On the updatability of relational views. *Proc. 4th Int. Conf. Very Large Databases*, Berlin, West Germany, Sept. 1978, pp. 368-377.
9. HAMMER, M. AND McLEOD, D. The semantic data model: A modelling mechanism for database applications. *Proc. 1978 SIGMOD Conf.*, Austin, Tex., May 1978, pp. 26-35.
10. KENT, W. *Data and Reality.* North-Holland, Amsterdam, 1978.
11. KENT, W. Limitations of record-based information models. *ACM Trans. Database Syst. 4*, 1 (March 1979), 107-131.
12. McLEOD, D. A semantic data base model and its associated structured user interface. Ph.D. Dissertation, Dep. Electrical Engineering and Computer Science. M.I.T., Cambridge, Mass., 1978.
13. QUILLIAN, H.R. Semantic memory. In *Semantic Information Processing*, M. Minsky, Ed. M.I.T. Press, Cambridge, Mass., 1968.
14. ROWE, L., AND SHOENS, K. Data abstraction views and updates in RIGEL. *Proc. ACM SIGMOD Conf.*, Boston, Mass., May-June 1979, pp. 71-81.
15. SIBLEY, E.H., AND KERSHBERG, L. Data architecture and data model considerations. *Proc. AFIPS Nat. Computer Conf.*, Dallas, Tex., June 1977, pp. 85-96.
16. SMITH, J.M., AND SMITH, D.C.P. Database abstractions: Aggregation and generalization. *ACM Trans. Database Syst. 2*, 2 (June 1977), 105-133.
17. STONEBRAKER, M., WONG, E., KREPS, B., AND HELD, G. The design and implementation of INGRES. *ACM Trans. Database Syst. 1*, 3 (Sept. 1976), 189-222.
18. WIRTH, N. What can we do about the unnecessary diversity of notation for syntactic definitions? *Commun. ACM 20*, 11 (Nov. 1977), 822-823.

Received March 1979; revised November 1979; accepted August 1980

A Language Facility for Designing Database-Intensive Applications

JOHN MYLOPOULOS
University of Toronto
PHILIP A. BERNSTEIN
Harvard University
and
HARRY K. T. WONG
IBM Research Laboratory

TAXIS, a language for the design of interactive information systems (e.g., credit card verification, student-course registration, and airline reservations) is described. TAXIS offers (relational) database management facilities, a means of specifying semantic integrity constraints, and an exception-handling mechanism, integrated into a single language through the concepts of *class*, *property*, and the *IS-A* (generalization) *relationship*. A description of the main constructs of TAXIS is included and their usefulness illustrated with examples.

Key Words and Phrases: applications programming, information system, relational data model, abstract data type, semantic network, exception handling
CR Categories: 3.70, 3.73, 4.22, 4.29, 4.33, 4.34, 4.39

1. INTRODUCTION

1.1 Motivation

A primary goal of database management is the reduction of software costs by promoting data independence. In the database literature, practical aspects of the development of applications software that use a database system are often treated as peripheral to the main thrust of database research. Until recently, applications programming has usually been considered in the context of a data sublanguage embedded in a conventional applications programming language. Some of the better examples of this approach include papers by Date [5] and Schmidt [17].

A more recent trend is to design the programming language with database facilities as a single unit [16, 22]. This paper takes a step along this path by presenting an applications programming language that tightly integrates data with the procedures that use it (in the style, say, of SIMULA [4]).

Our language, called TAXIS,[1] is designed primarily for applications systems that are highly interactive and make substantial use of a database. These applications, which we call interactive information systems (IIS), are characterized by their handling of large volumes of transactions that are short, of predictable structure, and update intensive. Examples include credit card verification, student-course registration, and airline reservations. By applying our tools to a more limited domain, we can customize them to the domain. Also, by defining our problem more narrowly than that of "applications systems," it will be easier to evaluate the efficacy of our approach.

In the future, we see TAXIS at the center of a programming system that would permit a designer to interactively build an IIS with the help of specialized text-editing and graphics facilities. The system would include a relational database management system (DBMS). The DBMS provides an interface into which the database operations of the IIS can be compiled.

1.2 Design Principles

TAXIS is eclectic, combining concepts from three areas of computer science research: artificial intelligence (AI), programming languages, and database management. From AI we have used the concept of semantic network for data and procedure modeling [2, 11]. From programming languages we have borrowed the concept of abstract data type [12, 18] and exception handling [21]. Finally, from database management we have built on the concept of a relational database [8].

These ideas are married to form a concise language framework, yielding a novel and powerful collection of facilities. First, the semantic network modeling constructs represent a qualitative improvement in abstraction mechanisms over conventional programming languages. Database operations can work on hierarchies of objects, instead of independent tuples and relations (similar to [20]). Data can thereby be manipulated at varying levels of abstraction. We extend our semantic structures beyond relations and apply them equally to procedures, integrity constraints, and exception handling.

Second, by associating operations with the data they use, the semantics of the *database* can be represented in the applications program. This is in contrast to the sharp distinction between DDL and DML in most database languages. The semantic information can be used by the compiler to solve many integrity, security, and concurrency problems at compile time.

Finally, since the application is described in a formal semantic model, "meta-level" commands allow the application description itself to be manipulated by programming language commands. This permits database administrator functions to peruse the logical design on-line.

Four principles guided much of the TAXIS design:

(1) The language must offer relations and associated operations for database

---

[1] Taxis (τάξις): Greek noun meaning order as in "law and order" or class as in "social class," "university class," etc.

This work was supported in part by the National Science Foundation under Grant ENG77-05720, in part by the National Research Council of Canada, and in part by the Division of Applied Sciences at Harvard University.
Authors' addresses: J. Mylopoulos, Department of Computer Science, University of Toronto, Toronto, Ont., M5S 1A7, Canada; P.A. Bernstein, Aiken Computation Laboratory, Harvard University, Cambridge, MA 02138; H.K.T. Wong, IBM Research Laboratory, San Jose, CA.
© 1980 ACM 0362-5915/80/0600-0185 $00.75

management, transactions for the specification of application programs, and exception-handling facilities to enhance the development of interactive systems.

(2) Each conceptual object represented in the language must have associated semantics that involve both a behavioral and a structural component. These semantics are expressed in terms of the notions of class, property, and the IS-A hierarchy (cf. "generalization" in [20]).

(3) As much of the language as possible should be placed into the framework of classes, properties, and the IS-A hierarchy.

(4) The schema (i.e., the collection of classes, along with their properties and the associated IS-A hierarchy) should be compilable into a language such as Pascal, enriched with a relation data type and associated operations (as proposed, for instance, in [17]).

The first principle is a consequence of the intended scope of the language. The second reflects our belief that much of the difficulty of designing and implementing IISs (usually translated into high costs of initial implementation and maintenance) is due to the lack of appropriate programming constructs in "conventional" languages (e.g., Cobol and PL/I) for handling the semantics of any one application. The third and fourth principles are the results of our concern for linguistic uniformity and efficiency. We consider both of them quite important given the multiplicity of sources of ideas and the complexity of the problem at hand.

Section 2 of the paper discusses the basic entities that constitute a TAXIS program. Section 3 describes the *IS-A* hierarchy as an organizational principle (abstraction mechanism) for the classes constituting a program. In Section 4 we present more details about the different categories of classes. Concluding remarks and directions for further research appear in Section 5.

The presentation of the language is rather informal and necessarily sketchy due to space limitations. The interested reader is referred to [14, 25] for more details.

2. OBJECTS AND PROPERTIES

There are three types of objects in TAXIS: *tokens*, which represent constants; *classes*, which describe collections of tokens; and *metaclasses*, which describe collections of classes.

2.1 Tokens and Classes

Tokens are the constants of a TAXIS program. For example, *john-smith* (representing the particular person called John Smith), 'SMITH,JOHN,B' (representing the string SMITH,JOHN,B), and 7 (representing the number 7) are all tokens. Tokens are denoted throughout the paper by identifiers in lowercase letters and numerals; strings are delimited by single quotes.

A class is a collection of tokens sharing common properties. If a token *t* is an element of the collection associated with a class C we say that *t is an instance of* C. It may be helpful for the reader to compare TAXIS classes with SIMULA classes or programming language types as points of reference.

Some sample classes are *PERSON*, whose instances are tokens such as *john-smith*, representing particular persons, *PERSON-NAME*, whose instances are

(string) tokens, such as 'SMITH,JOHN,B' that can serve as proper names, and *INTEGER*, whose instances are integers such as 7. We use identifiers in uppercase letters to denote classes.

We call the collection of all tokens which are instances of a class C *the extension of C*.

2.2 Properties

Classes and tokens have properties through which they can be related to other classes and tokens. Some of the properties that may be associated with the class *PERSON* represent the following information:

"each person has a name, an address, an age, and a phone number"
"each person's name consists of a first and last name and possibly a middle initial"

For tokens, properties represent specific facts rather than abstract rules such as those presented above. Thus, *john-smith* will have properties expressing facts such as

"*john-smith*'s name is 'SMITH,JOHN,B', his address is 38 Boston Dr., Toronto, his age is 32, and his telephone number is 762-4377"

Properties are triples consisting of one or more *subjects*, an *attribute*, and a *property value* (or *p-value*). For example, *PERSON* may have the following properties:

⟨*PERSON, name, PERSON-NAME*⟩
⟨*PERSON, address, ADDRESS-VALUE*⟩
⟨*PERSON, age, AGE-VALUE*⟩
⟨*PERSON, phone#, PHONE-VALUE*⟩

The same applies for properties of tokens, i.e.,

(*john-smith, name,* 'SMITH,JOHN,B')
(*john-smith, address, john-smith's-address*)
(*john-smith, age,* 32)
(*john-smith, phone#,* 7624377)

Note that the properties of *PERSON* provide information about the structure of instances of that class, while the properties of *john-smith* specify the structure of the token itself. This distinction was already made in the notation just introduced for properties, with the properties of a class delimited by angular brackets and those of a token by parentheses. We call the former type of property *definitional* and the latter *factual*.

Some properties may have more than one subject. For example,

⟨(*FLIGHT#, DATE*)*, flt, FLIGHT*⟩

defines a (definitional) *complex property* with subjects the classes *FLIGHT#* and *DATE* and *p*-value the class *FLIGHT*. This property may represent the information:

"each combination of a flight number and a date has an associated flight"

As the reader may have suspected, there is a strong relationship between the definitional properties of a class and the factual properties of its instances. The relationship may be expressed in terms of the following property induction principle.

Property Induction Principle. The definitional properties of a class induce factual properties for its instances.

If classes $C_1, \ldots, C_n$ are the subjects of a definitional complex property with attribute p, the TAXIS expression $(C_1, \ldots, C_n)..p$ (or $C_1..p$ if $n=1$) returns the p-value of that property. For example, $PERSON..age$ returns the class $AGE\text{-}VALUE$, while $(FLIGHT, DATE)..flt$ returns $FLIGHT$. In other words, ".." is a "schema selector" and allows the traversal of the schema defined with a TAXIS program by its classes and their definitional properties. For the ".." operator to be unambiguous, no two definitional properties can have the same subject(s) and attribute.

Turning to factual properties, if $((C_1, \ldots, C_n), p, C)$ is a definitional property and t_i is an instance of C_i, $1 \le i \le n$, then $((t_1, \ldots, t_n), p, p)$ (or $t_1.p$ if $n=1$) evaluates to an instance of C, say t, such that $((t_1, \ldots, t_n), p, t)$ is a factual property. Thus $john\text{-}smith.age$ returns 32 while $(802, may\text{-}1\text{-}1979).flt$ returns the particular flight associated with those two tokens through the flt property (i.e., the property with attribute "flt").

2.3 Metaclasses

If one wishes to represent the information

> "the average age of (known) persons is 28"

or

> "the number of (known) flights is 473"

he may be tempted to express these facts by

> $(PERSON, average\text{-}age, 28)$
> $(FLIGHT, cardinality, 473)$

However, this representation is incorrect since definitional properties represent information about the structure of instances of a class, not the class itself. Instead, factual properties must be used to represent these facts:

> $(PERSON, average\text{-}age, 28)$
> $(FLIGHT, cardinality, 473)$

But to be consistent with the property induction principle, these factual properties must be induced by definitional properties which have the classes *PERSON* and *FLIGHT* as instances. This observation leads to the introduction of a third type of TAXIS object called *metaclass*. A metaclass is similar to a class in every respect, except that its instances are classes rather than tokens. For instance, the metaclass *PERSON-CLASS* may be defined with instances of all classes whose instances denote persons (e.g., *PERSON, STUDENT, EMPLOYEE, MAN-AGER*). Then the definitional property

> $(PERSON\text{-}CLASS, average\text{-}age, AGE\text{-}VALUE)$

allows the association of an *average-age* factual property with every instance of PERSON-CLASS.

> $(PERSON, average\text{-}age, 28)$
> $(STUDENT, average\text{-}age, 19)$, etc.

We refer to the relationships between a token (class) and the class (metaclass) it is an instance of as the *INSTANCE-OF* relationship.

Generally, a TAXIS program includes tokens which can only have factual properties associated with them, classes which can have factual and definitional properties, and metaclasses which can only have definitional properties. For a more sophisticated treatment of the *INSTANCE-OF* relationship which allows an arbitrary number of levels of metaclasses, see [11] and [19]. We expect that the three levels allowed in TAXIS will suffice for most practical situations. For metaclasses, we use identifiers in uppercase letters which end in *-CLASS*. As with classes, the collection of all instances of a metaclass is called its extension.

2.4 Examples

Classes and metaclasses are defined by specifying their name and their simple properties. For example, the metaclass *PERSON-CLASS* can be defined by

```
metaclass PERSON-CLASS with
    attribute-properties
        average-age: AGE-VALUE;
end
```

Here *PERSON-CLASS* is defined to have one simple (i.e., noncomplex) property

> $(PERSON\text{-}CLASS, average\text{-}age, AGE\text{-}VALUE)$

The metaclass definition also specifies that the property defined is of the attribute-property category which means that the *average-age* factual property of an instance of *PERSON-CLASS* may change with time. Generally, every definitional property defined in a TAXIS program is classified into a unique *property category* at the time of its definition, which determines the functional and operational characteristics of the property.

Property categories allow the specification of information such as that the function defined by a property is time varying or 1-1 or should be used in a particular manner when instances of its subject(s) are created. The following examples illustrate the different uses of property categories.

The class *PERSON* can now be defined as an instance of the metaclass *PERSON-CLASS* by

```
PERSON-CLASS PERSON with
    keys
        person-id: (name, address);
    characteristics
        name: PERSON-NAME;
        address: ADDRESS-VALUE;
        phone: PHONE-VALUE;
    attribute-properties
        age: AGE-VALUE;
        status: STATUS-IN-CANADA;
end
```

According to this definition, *PERSON* has two attribute (i.e., time-varying) properties and three characteristic properties which are time invariant. The key property described in the definition of *PERSON* specifies the complex property

((*PERSON-NAME, ADDRESS-VALUE*), *person-id, PERSON*)

Thus (*SMITH, JOHN, B', john-smith's-address*).*person-id* returns the person with '*SMITH, JOHN, B*' as name and *john-smith's-address* as address, if any. If there is none, the expression returns the special TAXIS token *nothing*.
The class *FLIGHT* can be defined in a similar fashion:

VARIABLE-CLASS FLIGHT with
keys
    flt: (*flight#, date*);
characteristics
    flight#: (|1::999|)
    departure: [|*city*: *CITY, country*: *COUNTRY*|];
    destination: [|*city*: *CITY, country*: *COUNTRY*|];
    aircraft: *AIRCRAFT-TYPE*;
    date: *DATE-VALUE*;
attribute-properties
    seats-left: *NONNEGATIVE-INTEGER*;
end

Here *VARIABLE-CLASS* stands for a special metaclass whose instances can have their collections of tokens changed in terms of explicit insertions or removals. Thus, since *FLIGHT* is an instance of *VARIABLE-CLASS*, it can have tokens added to or removed from its collection of instances. Clearly, variable classes behave very much like relations [3]. *PERSON* can also be made an instance of the metaclass *VARIABLE-CLASS*, in addition to its being an instance of *PER-SON-CLASS*, by relating the metaclasses *PERSON-* and *VARIABLE-CLASS* through the *IS-A* relationship. This is discussed in more detail in Section 3.

The class defined by {|1::999|} is *finitely defined* in the sense that it has a finite, time-invariant collection of instances which includes all integers from 1 to 999. Since this class does not have an associated name, it can only be referenced through expressions such as *PERSON*..*flight#*.

The class defined by [|*city*: *CITY, country*: *COUNTRY*|] has as instances all tuples with the first component an instance of *CITY* and the second an instance of *COUNTRY*. Classes such as this are instances of the special metaclass *AGGREGATE-CLASS*. Generally, an instance of *AGGREGATE-CLASS*, say *A*, has a collection of instances which is the cross product of the collections of instances of classes that serve as *p*-values of *A*'s characteristic properties. In this respect, aggregate classes are quite different from variable classes.

In other words, if aggregate class *C* has characteristic properties $p_1, \ldots, p_n$ with *p*-values $C_1, \ldots, C_n$, respectively, and if the extensions of these classes are $\text{ext}(C_1, \sigma), \ldots, \text{ext}(C_n, \sigma)$ in some database state σ, then

$$\text{ext}(C, \sigma) = \text{ext}(C_1, \sigma) \times \text{ext}(C_2, \sigma) \times \cdots \times \text{ext}(C_n, \sigma).$$

The class [|*city*: *CITY, country*: *COUNTRY*|] could have been defined separately.

AGGREGATE-CLASS LOCATION with
characteristics
    city: *CITY*;
    country: *COUNTRY*;
end

with *LOCATION* replacing [|*city*: *CITY, country*: *COUNTRY*|]. If that second method were used,

FLIGHT..*departure* = *FLIGHT*..*destination*

With the original definition of *FLIGHT*, however, the above equality does not hold. In other words, each class definition that appears in a TAXIS program causes the introduction of yet another class in the schema described by the program.
Turning to some of the classes mentioned in the definitions presented so far, let us first define *PHONE-VALUE* as

FORMATTED-CLASS PHONE-VALUE with
    (|'('|) @ *REPEAT*(*DIGIT*, 3) @ (|')'|) @ *REPEAT*(*DIGIT*, 7)
end

Formatted classes (i.e., instances of *FORMATTED-CLASS*) have as instances all strings which are consistent with a given string pattern. In particular, *PHONE-VALUE* instances have the format '(*ddd*)*ddddddd*' where *d* is any digit. Here (|')'|) defines a class with only instance the string ')', and *A @ B* defines a class with instances strings obtained by concatenating an instance of *B* to an instance of *A*. Moreover,

REPEAT(*A*, *n*) = *A @ A @ ··· @ A* (*n* times)

Finally, *DIGIT* is assumed to be the class {|'0', '1', ..., '9'|}.
It was mentioned in the introduction that all TAXIS constructs are treated within the framework described so far. Thus transactions are classes too. For example, the transaction *RESERVE-SEAT* may be defined as follows:

TRANSACTION-CLASS RESERVE-SEAT with
parameter-list
    reserve-seat: (*p, f*);
locals
    p: *PERSON*;
    f: *FLIGHT*;
    x: *INTEGER*;
prereqs
    seats-left?: *f. seats-left* > 0;
actions
    make-reservation:
        insert-object in *RESERVATION* with
            person ← p, flight ← f;
        decrement-seats: *f. seats-left ← f. seats-left* − 1;
        assign-aux variable: *x ← f. seats-left*;
returns
    rtrn: *x*;
end

The above definition specifies the parameter list of *RESERVE-SEAT* through the parameter-list property which defines a complex property

((*PERSON, FLIGHT*), *reserve-seat, RESERVE-SEAT*)

Local properties (locals) define either parameters or local variables of the transaction. The body of the transaction is given in terms of zero or more prerequisite, action, and result properties (prereqs, actions, result, respectively) whose *p*-values are invariably expressions. Finally, the returns property (returns) associates with a transaction an expression to be evaluated when execution of the body of the transaction has been completed. The value of the expression is also the value returned by the transaction.

It is assumed in the definition of *RESERVE-SEAT* that *RESERVATION* has already been defined as a variable class and that it has two characteristics with attributes *person* and *flight*, respectively. Thus the insert-object expression inserts another instance into the extension of this class and sets its two characteristic properties to *p* and *f*, respectively. The other two action properties decrement the *seats-left* property of *flight f* by 1 and set the local variable *x* to the value to be returned by the transaction.

A transaction class is similar to a variable class in that it has a time-varying extension. When an expression involving a call to *RESERVE-SEAT* is evaluated, a new token is first created and added to the extension of *RESERVE-SEAT*. This token is essentially an execution instance of *RESERVE-SEAT*, and the factual properties associated with it indicate the values of local variables at any one time. In fact, for the expressions which appear inside the transaction, mention of a local variable or parameter, i.e., *p, f,* or *x* for *RESERVE-SEAT*, is interpreted as equivalent to *self.p, self.f, self.x,* where *self* denotes the execution instance with respect to which these expressions are evaluated. Something analogous applies to prereqs, actions, result, and returns properties which initially have *p*-value unknown (another special TAXIS token), until the corresponding property is the value returned by the expression. Thus if the identifier *make-reservation* appears in an expression, before the *make-reservation* action property is evaluated its value is unknown, while after it is evaluated, it is the value returned by the insert-object expression.

As mentioned earlier, execution of a transaction begins by adding a token to the extension of the transaction (class). Execution then proceeds by evaluating each prerequisite *p*-value expression to make sure that it returns the value true. If any of the prerequisite expressions are found to have a value other than true, an *exception* is said to arise and execution is suspended. Otherwise, action expressions and then result expressions, which must also return true values, are evaluated. Thus prerequisite and result properties can be thought of as preconditions and postconditions which must be satisfied if execution of the transaction is to be meaningful. If they are not, an exception is raised and an exception-handling transaction is called to correct the situations. The exception-handling mechanism of TAXIS is discussed in Section 4.4.

When the *p*-value of a definitional property $((C_1,\ldots,C_n),p,T)$ is a transaction, the meaning of the property changes in that T specifies not the type of *p*-values of factual properties induced by $((C_1,\ldots,C_n),p,T)$, but rather an algorithm for

getting them. For example, suppose the property

(*PERSON, birthdate, COMPUTER-BIRTHDATE*)

is added to the definition of *PERSON* where

TRANSACTION-CLASS COMPUTE-BIRTHDATE with
  parameter-list
    birthdate: (*p*);
  returns
    rt: this-year - p.age;
end

and *this-year* is an identifier that denotes the current year. Clearly, to every particular person this property associates not an instance of *COMPUTE-BIRTH-DATE*, but rather a token returned by the *p*-value of the *rt* property.

This convention of treating transactions as a means for obtaining *p*-values rather than as types of *p*-values is consistent with the SIMULA class concept. Thus in TAXIS

p.birthdate = *COMPUTE-BIRTHDATE*(*p*)

where *p* is an instance of *PERSON*. Similarly, for the parameter-list complex property associated with *RESERVE-SEAT*,

(*prsn, flt*).*reserve-seat* = *RESERVE-SEAT*(*prsn, flt*)

3. THE *IS-A* HIERARCHY

We envision a TAXIS program as a large collection of tokens, classes, and metaclasses interconnected through their properties. Perhaps the most important feature of TAXIS is the facility it provides for organizing the collection of classes and metaclasses into a hierarchy (taxonomy).

3.1 Preliminaries

The *IS-A* (generalization) relationship is defined over classes and metaclasses. Informally, we say that (*A IS-A B*) where *A, B* are both classes (metaclasses) if every instance of *A* is an instance of *B*. For example, (*ADULT IS-A PERSON*) specifies that every adult is a person and (*CHILD IS-A PERSON*) that every child is a person.

If (*A IS-A B*) then every definitional property of *B* is also a definitional property of *A*. Moreover, *A* can have additional properties that *B* does not have at all, or it can redefine some of the properties of *B*. For example, the class *ADULT* inherits the *name, address,* and *phone#* properties of *PERSON* but must redefine the *age* property by restricting *age p*-values to instances of the class *OVER-18*. Similar remarks apply for *CHILD* which, in addition, has the *guardian* property that *PERSON* does not have at all. In defining the classes *ADULT* and *CHILD*, one need not mention the properties these classes share with *PERSON*:

VARIABLE-CLASS ADULT is-a *PERSON* with
  attribute-properties
    age: OVER-18;
end
VARIABLE-CLASS CHILD is-a *PERSON* with
  attribute-properties
    age: UNDER-18;
    guardian: ADULT;
end

Properties cannot be redefined arbitrarily. For example, redefinition of *age* only makes sense if (*UNDER-18 IS-A AGE-VALUE*). As the reader may have suspected, the *IS-A* relationship referred to above is the reflexive transitive closure of the relationship **is-a** used in class definitions.

3.2 *IS-A* Relationship Postulates

The formal properties of the *IS-A* relationship can be summarized in terms of the following postulates:

I. All classes (metaclasses) constituting a TAXIS program are organized into an *IS-A* hierarchy in terms of the binary relation *IS-A* which is a partial order.

II. There is a most general (maximum) and a most specialized (minimum) class with respect to *IS-A* called, respectively, *ANY* and *NONE*. Similarly, there is a most general and a most specialized metaclass called, respectively, *ANY-CLASS* and *NO-CLASS*.

III. (Extensional *IS-A* Constraint) If (*C IS-A D*) for classes (metaclasses) *C* and *D*, then every instance of *C* is also an instance of *D*.

IV. (Structural *IS-A* Constraint) If (*A IS-A B*) and *B* is the subject of a definitional property $((C_1, \ldots, B, \ldots, C_n), p, D)$, then *A* is also the subject of a definitional property $((C_1, \ldots, A, \ldots, C_n), p, E)$ and moreover (*E IS-A D*).

Note that these postulates define *necessary* not sufficient conditions for the *IS-A* relationship to hold.

It is assumed that there exist classes *ANY-FORMATTED, ANY-VARIABLE, ANY-TRANSACTION,* etc., which are specializations of *ANY* and below which one finds all formatted classes, variable classes, etc. For example, the definition given earlier

VARIABLE-CLASS FLIGHT with
  ...
end

places *FLIGHT* below *ANY-VARIABLE* and is therefore equivalent to

VARIABLE-CLASS FLIGHT is-a *ANY-VARIABLE* with
  ...
end

For metaclasses the *IS-A* hierarchy must be defined explicitly by the TAXIS user. For example, the metaclass *PERSON-CLASS* should be a specialization of *VARIABLE-CLASS*, as suggested in Section 2.4, and for this purpose its definition should be changed to

metaclass *PERSON-CLASS* is-a *VARIABLE-CLASS* with
  ...   (as before)
end

After this change, all instances of *PERSON-CLASS* are also instances of *VARIABLE-CLASS* according to Postulate III, and therefore *PERSON* is a variable class.

The Hasse diagram of the *IS-A* relationship need not be a tree. For example, the definition

PERSON-CLASS MALE-STUDENT is-a *MALE, STUDENT* with
  ...
end

makes *MALE-STUDENT* a specialization of *MALE* and *STUDENT* which may not be *IS-A*-comparable.

The class *ANY* has as instances all tokens available to a TAXIS program, while *NONE* has no instances at all. Similarly, *ANY-CLASS* has all classes as instances, while *NO-CLASS* has no instances at all.

3.3 More on Seat Reservations

We return to the world of persons, flights, and seat reservations to illustrate the use of the *IS-A* hierarchy.

First, let us define a few specializations of previously defined classes.

INTERNATIONAL-FLIGHT# := (|500::999|) is-a *FLIGHT..flight#*
FLIGHT#-WITHIN-CANADA := (|1::499|) is-a *FLIGHT..flight#*

places the finitely defined classes with extensions the ranges 500::999 and 1::499, respectively, below *FLIGHT..flight#* (= (|1::999|)) on the *IS-A* hierarchy. Similarly,

CANADA:= (|'CANADA'|) is-a *COUNTRY*

makes *CANADA* a class with a single instance. Presumably, *COUNTRY* has as instances many other strings such as 'USA', 'CHINA', and 'GREECE', in addition to 'CANADA'.

It is now possible to define two specializations of *FLIGHT*

VARIABLE-CLASS INTERNATIONAL-FLIGHT is-a *FLIGHT* with
characteristics
  flight#: INTERNATIONAL-FLIGHT#;
end

VARIABLE-CLASS FLIGHT-WITHIN-CANADA is-a *FLIGHT* with
characteristics
  flight#:FLIGHT#-WITHIN-CANADA;
  departure: [|*country: CANADA*|]) is-a *FLIGHT..departure;*
  destination: [|*country: CANADA*|]) is-a *FLIGHT..destination;*
end

When a class is defined "on-line" in terms of the match-fix operators (|,|) or [|,|], one can place it at the same time on the *IS-A* hierarchy, as illustrated in the *departure* and *destination* properties of *FLIGHT-WITHIN-CANADA*. Of course, since the aggregate class defined by [|*country: CANADA*|] is a specialization of *FLIGHT..departure* (= [|*city: CITY, country: COUNTRY*|]), it has two (not one) characteristic properties, as *city* is inherited.

According to the definition of *RESERVE-SEAT*, the definitional complex property

((*PERSON, FLIGHT*), *reserve-seat, RESERVE-SEAT*)

is part of the TAXIS program being constructed. It follows then from Postulate IV (the structural *IS-A* constraint) that any combination of specializations of the classes *PERSON* and *FLIGHT* must have a *reserve-seat* complex property whose *p*-value, a transaction, is a specialization of the transaction *RESERVE-SEAT*. Intuitively, this means that the *reserve-seat* for, say, *CHILD,* and *INTERNATIONAL-FLIGHT* must have at least the prerequisites, actions, and results of *RESERVE-SEAT* and possibly more of each. For example, suppose that we wish to enforce a (rather conservative) constraint whereby each child must be accompanied by his/her guardian on an international flight. This is clearly a constraint concerning the transaction (*CHILD, INTERNATIONAL-FLIGHT*)..*reserve-seat*. It can be added to that transaction as a prerequisite as follows:

prereq *accompanied-by-guardian?* on
(*CHILD, INTERNATIONAL-FLIGHT*)..*reserve-seat* is
not ((*p.guardian, f*).*reservation* = nothing)

This definition adds *accompanied-by-guardian?* as a prerequisite property of the transaction (*CHILD, INTERNATIONAL-FLIGHT*)..*reserve-seat*, which, of course, also inherits all properties of *RESERVE-SEAT*. The expression (*p.guardian, f*).*reservation* has value nothing when there is no instance identified by the key value (*p.guardian, f*) in the (variable) class *RESERVATION*; otherwise, it returns the instance of *RESERVATION* identified by that key value.

As another example, suppose that any person (adult or child) entering Canada must be a citizen, landed-immigrant, or visitor:

prereq *can-enter-canada?* on
(*PERSON, INTERNATIONAL-FLIGHT*)..*reserve-seat* is
p.status instance-of (|'*CITIZEN*', '*LANDED-IMMIGRANT*', '*VISITOR*'|)
or not *f.destination.country* = '*CANADA*'

As a final example of how specializations of *RESERVE-SEAT* might be modified to suit particular combinations of specializations of *PERSON* and *FLIGHT*, suppose that the income tax office must be notified for any citizens or landed immigrants leaving Canada:

action *notify-income-tax-people* on
(*ADULT, INTERNATIONAL-FLIGHT*)..*reserve-seat* is
if (*p.status* = '*CITIZEN*' or *p.status* = '*LANDED-IMMIGRANT*'
and *f.departure.country* = '*CANADA*'
and not (*f.destination.country* = '*CANADA*')
then *NOTIFY-INCOME-TAX-PEOPLE*(*p, f*)

This action has no effects if its Boolean condition is not true.

Once these properties have been added to their corresponding transactions, the expression (*p, f*).*reserve-seat* has quite different meaning depending on whether *p* is an adult, a child, or just a person and *f* is an international or local flight. Generally,

(*p, f*).*reserve-seat* = (*Type*(*p*), *Type*(*f*))..*reserve-seat*(*p, f*)

where *Type*(*x*) returns (one of) the least general class that has *x* as an instance. If there is more than one such class, then it is assumed that choosing between them does not affect the value or the side effects caused by the call.

The examples presented illustrate the following points about the *IS-A* relationship.

(1) It is not only data objects that can be organized into an *IS-A* hierarchy but also semantic integrity constraints, expressed as prerequisites, results, and database actions.

(2) Parts of the *IS-A* hierarchy determine the structure of other parts through the definition of properties. For example, the part of the *IS-A* hierarchy which appears below the transaction *RESERVE-SEAT* is structurally homomorphic to the cross product of the *IS-A* hierarchies which appear below *PERSON* and *FLIGHT*. This is a direct consequence of Postulate IV (the structural *IS-A* constraint) and it can serve as a powerful guiding principle for the construction of a TAXIS program.

4. MORE ON CLASSES AND METACLASSES

We return to the topic of classes and metaclasses in order to provide additional details about them.

4.1 Variable Classes

The built-in metaclass *VARIABLE-CLASS* has the special feature that only its instances can have their extensions altered through the expressions insert-object, remove-object. For example,

VARIABLE-CLASS PASSENGERS with
  p: PERSON
end

defines an instance of *VARIABLE-CLASS* which initially has no instances of its own. However,

insert-object in *PASSENGERS* with *p* ← *john-smith*

adds a new token to the extension of *PASSENGERS* with "*p*" *p*-value the person *john-smith*, and returns that new token as value. A token *x* can be removed from the extension of a class *C* through the expression

remove-object *x* from *C*

Note that when a token is added to the extension of a class, it is also added to the extensions of all its generalizations, and when it is removed from a class, it is removed from the extensions of all its specializations. Thus Postulate III for the *IS-A* relationship is never violated as a result of an insertion or removal of a token.

In addition to insert-object and remove-object, TAXIS provides three other QUEL-like ([7]) expressions which allow general searches of the extension of one or more variable classes. Thus the expression

for *x* in *EMPLOYEE*
for *y* in *MANAGER*
  retrieve into *FATCATS* with *name* ← *x.name, sal* ← *x.sal*
  where *x.dept* = *y.dept* and *x.sal* > *y.sal*

retrieves into the variable class *FATCATS* employees making more than one of their managers. Note that the assumption (*MANAGER IS-A EMPLOYEE*) implies that *MANAGER* has the properties of *EMPLOYEE*, in particular, *sal* and *dept*.

In addition to retrieve, append and delete expressions are also provided and are similar in form and semantics to retrieve (or corresponding QUEL commands).

Variable classes are the only classes which are allowed to have key properties. Going from a key to the corresponding token is handled in terms of the mechanisms already introduced. Thus if *address-1* is a particular address,

(*SMITH, JOHN, B', address-1*).*person-id*

returns either the person identified by this key or nothing.

The attribute factual properties of a variable class instance can be changed through the *update operator* "←". For instance, john-smith.age ← 35

changes john-smith's age from whatever it was to 35.

4.2 Aggregate Classes

A second important category of classes consists of instances of the built-in metaclass *AGGREGATE-CLASS*. The extension of an aggregate class is determined at all times by the cross product of the extensions of its *p*-values. For example, the extension of the aggregate class [|*city*: *CITY*, *country*: *COUNTRY*|] is the cross product of the extensions of *CITY* and *COUNTRY*. The only way to change the extension of an aggregate class is to change the extension of one of its *p*-values.

Instances of aggregate classes can be referenced but never created or destroyed. Thus

[*city*: *TORONTO*, *country*: '*CANADA*']

references a tuple which is an instance of any aggregate class whose extension includes the tuple ('*TORONTO*', '*CANADA*'). We call the tokens referenced through the matchfix operators [.] *aggregates*.

All the simple properties of an aggregate class are characteristic properties and cannot be changed for any one aggregate. However, there is an expression in TAXIS which allows the identification of an aggregate related to a given one with respect to some of its components. For example, if x is the aggregate [('*TORONTO*', '*CANADA*'] then the expression

x but *city* ← '*MONTREAL*'

identifies the tuple obtained from x by replacing its *city* *p*-value with '*MON-TREAL*'.

4.3 Finitely Defined Classes

Instances of the built-in metaclass *FINITELY-DEFINED-CLASS* have their extensions specified once and for all at the time they are defined, e.g.,

CANADIAN-METROPOLES := (|'*MONTREAL*', '*TORONTO*', '*VANCOUVER*'|)

or

INTERNATIONAL-FLIGHT# := (|500 :: 999|) is-a *FLIGHT#*

Finitely defined classes are very similar to Pascal scalar types. For instance, the functions *succ* and *pred* return the successor or predecessor of an instance in the ordering of instances specified by the class definition. Similarly, there are special relations *lt, gt, le, ge* which compare two instances of a finitely defined class with respect to this ordering.

4.4 Test-Defined Classes

Aggregate, finitely defined, and formatted classes are all special cases of the general collection of *test-defined classes*. Such classes are characterized by the fact that membership in their extension is determined by a transaction defined for this purpose:

((*ANY*, *TEST-DEFINED-CLASS*), *test*, *TEST-TRANSACTION*)

This complex property specializes for aggregate classes to

((*ANY-AGGREGATE*, *AGGREGATE-CLASS*), *test*, *TEST-AGGREGATE*)

where *AGGREGATE* is a specialization of *ANY* with all possible aggregates as instances. Similarly, we have

((*ANY-FINITELY-DEFINED*, *FINITELY-DEFINED-CLASS*), *test*, *FINITE-TEST*))

and

((*STRING*, *FORMATTED-CLASS*), *test*, *FORMAT-TEST*)

where *STRING*'s extension contains all strings and *TEST-AGGREGATE*, *FI-NITE-TEST*, and *FORMAT-TEST* are all specializations of *TEST-TRANS-ACTION*. The essence of these three transactions was already given in the discussion of aggregate, finitely defined, and formatted classes. For instance, *TEST-AGGREGATE*(x, *C*) checks that the components of aggregate x are instances of the *p*-values of *C*'s attribute properties. *FINITE-TEST*(x,*C*), on the other hand, checks whether x is one of the tokens defined to be in the extension of *C*. Generally, if *C* is a test-defined class, then

x instance-of *C* = (*Type*(x), *Type* (*C*)) .. *test* (x,*C*)

Not all test transactions are predetermined as they are for aggregate, finitely defined, and formatted classes. For example, we can define the metaclass

metaclass *TRAVELER-TO-CANADA-CLASS* is-a *TEST-DEFINED-CLASS*

and then the transaction

TRANSACTION-CLASS TEST-TRAVELER-TO-CANADA is-a *TEST-TRANSACTION* with parameter-list

```
test:(p, class);
locals
    p: PERSON;
    class: TRAVELER-TO-CANADA-CLASS;
returns
    rtrn: not (nothing =
        get-object x from RESERVATION
        where (x.person = p and
            x.flight.destination.country = 'CANADA'))

end
```

thereby setting up the definitional property

((*PERSON*, *TRAVELER-TO-CANADA-CLASS*), *test*, *TEST-TRAVELER-TO-CANADA*)

Now, the class defined by

TRAVELER-TO-CANADA-CLASS TRAVELER-TO-CANADA is-a *PERSON*

has as instances all persons who have booked a reservation for a flight with a destination in Canada.

4.5 Expressions

Expressions can only appear in TAXIS programs as *p*-values of prerequisite, action, result, or return properties.[2]

Conditional, block, and looping constructs are provided in the language for the construction of compound expressions from simpler ones.

Expressions are classes and can have definitional properties of their own (which associate exceptions with them). However, expressions are special types of classes

---

[2] This discussion does not apply to expressions involving @, [|,|], and ((,|)) which define new classes and are evaluated at compilation time.

in two respects:

(1) their extension is invariably empty;

(2) their IS-A hierarchy is determined by the following rule: If $\langle T, p, E\rangle$ and $\langle T', p, E'\rangle$ and $(T$ IS-A $T')$, then $(E$ IS-A $E')$, where T, T' are transactions, and E, E' are expressions.

Thus there is no need to specify explicitly the IS-A hierarchy of expression classes since that is determined by the transactions to which they are attached.

The fact that expression classes have empty extensions means that Postulate III (the extensional IS-A constraint) is trivially satisfied for expressions. As a replacement we propose the following postulate.

III' (Behavioral IS-A Constraint) (a) If E, E' are Boolean expressions and $(E$ IS-A $E')$, then it must be that $E \to E'$ (E implies E') and E causes at least the side effects of E'.

(b) If E, E' are non-Boolean expressions and $(E$ IS-A $E')$, then it must be that when *value* $(E) \neq$ *nothing*, *value* $(E) =$ *value* (E') and moreover E causes at least the side effects of E'.

Consider, for example, a specialization of the *RESERVE-SEAT* transaction, say T, for which the prerequisite *seats-left?* must be redefined. It makes sense, according to the Postulate III' (the behavioral IS-A constraint), to redefine it as

    prereq seats-left? on T is f.seats-left > 10,

since $(f.seats\text{-}left > 10) \to (f.seats\text{-}left > 0)$. The redefinition, however,

    prereq seats-left? on T is f.seats-left > 0 or p.age < 2

is inappropriate because

$$(f.seats\text{-}left > 0 \text{ or } p.age < 2) \not\to f.seats\text{-}left > 0)$$

Similarly, the block expression E defined by

```
begin
    insert-object in RESERVATIONS with
        person ← p, flight ← f;
    insert-object in PASSENGERS with p ← p;
end
```

can be made a specialization of *RESERVE-SEAT .. make-reservation* because its side effects, which involve two insertions, include those of *RESERVE-SEAT .. make-reservation*. The same statement is not true if the first insert-object expression is deleted from E.

Postulate III' (the behavioral IS-A constraint) is formalized in [25] and its consequences are discussed.

4.6 Transactions

We have already presented the basic categories of properties one can associate with a transaction. Through prerequisites, actions, and results, the TAXIS user can "factor out" a transaction body into semi-independent constraint checks and actions that may be associated with a transaction directly, during its definition, or indirectly, through inheritance.

4.7 Exceptions

We have adapted Wasserman's [21] procedure-oriented exception-handling mechanism with modifications that allow exceptions and exception-handling to be treated within the framework of classes, properties, and the IS-A relationship.

Exception classes are defined and organized into an IS-A hierarchy, like all other classes. The built-in metaclass *EXCEPTION-CLASS* has as instances all exception classes which are also specializations of the built-in class *ANY-EXCEPTION*. For a particular TAXIS program, or a collection thereof, we may have below *ANY-EXCEPTION* the classes *SECURITY-EXCEPTION*, *CONSTRAINT-EXCEPTION*, etc. Below these, one may wish to attach exception classes such as

```
EXCEPTION-CLASS NO-SEATS-LEFT is-a CONSTRAINT-EXCEPTION with
attribute-properties
    pers: PERSON;
    flt: FLIGHT;
end
```

When an instance of this exception class is created (i.e., is *raised*), its factual properties are assigned p-values through which one can obtain information about the circumstances under which the exception was raised.

Exceptions are raised when a prerequisite or result expression evaluates to a value other than true. To specify which exception is raised, one must associate with a prerequisite or result p-value, which is always an expression class, an exception class. For *RESERVE-SEAT*, for example, this can be done either by replacing the *seats-left?* property of the transaction with

```
TRANSACTION-CLASS RESERVE-SEAT with
...
seats-left?: f.seats-left > 0 exc
    NO-SEATS-LEFT (pers: p, flt: f);
...
end
```

or by adding a definitional property to the p-value of the *seats-left?* property with

```
exception-property exc on RESERVE-SEAT .. seats-left? is NO-SEATS-LEFT (pers:
p, flt: f)
```

In both cases, the associations *pers: p, flt: f* indicate the p-values to be assigned to the factual properties of the *NO-SEAT-LEFT* instance raised when the prerequisite *seats-left?* fails.

When an exception is raised within a transaction T, it is up to the caller of T to specify what should be done to handle it. Such specifications come in the form of complex properties called *exception-handlers* that take as subjects an expression E and an exception *EXC* and p-value an exception-handling transaction T_h. When an instance of *EXC* is raised during the evaluation of E, then T_h is called with the exception raised as its only argument. Suppose, for example, that the transaction *CALLER* calls *RESERVE-SEAT* or one of its specializations during the execution of one of its actions, say *act*. To indicate that the transaction *FIND-ALTERNATIVE* should be called if the exception *NO-SEATS-LEFT* is raised, we write

```
TRANSACTION-CLASS CALLER with
...
actions
    act: RESERVE-SEAT(p1, f1) is
        exc-handler eh for NO-SEATS-LEFT is
            FIND-ALTERNATIVE
    ...
end
```

which defines the complex property

((RESERVE-SEAT(p1, f1), NO-SEAT-LEFT), eh, FIND-ALTERNATIVE)

Now, if an instance of *NO-SEATS-LEFT* is raised during the evaluation of *RESERVE-SEAT* (p1, f1), *FIND-ALTERNATIVE* will be called with the newly created exception instance as argument. From the properties of this instance, *FIND-ALTERNATIVE* will determine the circumstances of the exception and, we hope, what should be done.

Treating exceptions and exception-handling in terms of classes, properties, and data the *IS-A* relationship means that the already existing *IS-A* hierarchy of data classes and transactions can be used to structure exception-handling within any one TAXIS program. We illustrate this point by extending the example we have used so far so that if a *NO-SEATS-LEFT* instance is raised for a child, it is not only for the child that an alternative is found but also for his or her guardian. First, we create a specialization of *NO-SEATS-LEFT*:

EXCEPTION-CLASS NO-SEAT-FOR-CHILD is-a *NO-SEATS-LEFT* with
attribute-properties
    guardian: ADULT;
end

Then we redefine the exception property *exc* of the *seats-left?* prerequisite for the transaction (*CHILD, INTERNATIONAL-FLIGHT*) .. *reserve-seat*

exception-property *exc* on (*CHILD, INTERNATIONAL-FLIGHT*) ..
    reserve-seat .. seats-left? is
    NO-SEAT-FOR-CHILD (*pers: p, flt: f, guardian: p.guardian*)

Finally, we augment the exception handler *FIND-ALTERNATIVE* for the exception-handling property *eh* of *CALLER .. act* and *NO-SEAT-FOR-CHILD*:

action *find-alternative-for-guardian-too* on
(*CALLER .. act, NO-SEAT-FOR-CHILD*) .. *eh* is
/*remove the child's guardian from the flight *flt* and reserve a seat for him or her as well on the alternative flight selected*/

According to this, another action property is added to the (transaction) class specified by the expression (*CALLER .. act, NO-SEAT-FOR-CHILD*) .. *eh. CALLER .. act* evaluates to the expression class *RESERVE-SEAT*(p1, f1) (see definition of *CALLER*), and *RESERVE-SEAT*(p1, f1), *NO-SEATS-LEFT* have a complex property *eh* whose *p*-value is the (exception-handling) transaction *FIND-ALTERNATIVE*. It follows then that the expression (*CALLER .. act, NO-SEAT-FOR-CHILD*) .. *eh* evaluates to a specialization of *FIND-ALTERNATIVE* which inherits all the actions of that transaction in addition to the new action defined by the *find-alternative-for guardian-too* action.

We will not present code for the new action defined for the exception-handler of *NO-SEATS-LEFT* exceptions. It is worth noting, however, that the *IS-A* hierarchy of exception-handlers is patterned after that of *PERSON, FLIGHT*, and their specializations, along with the transactions that operate on them.

When an exception-handling transaction completes its execution, control returns to the point where the exception was raised and the expression following the prerequisite or result where the exception was raised is evaluated. Thus each prerequisite or result expression E can be interpreted as a conditional expression

if E then nil else...

where the blank is filled by the caller of the transaction where E appears.

5. CONCLUSIONS

Several other research efforts are related and/or have influenced our work. PLAIN [22] is one of the few examples of a language designed with goals similar to those of TAXIS. The main difference between the two languages is that PLAIN does not use the *IS-A* relationship as a structuring construct for data or procedures. We have adapted PLAIN's exception-handling mechanism, but modified it to make it consistent with the TAXIS framework. Moreover, due to the structure of transactions, we have managed to restrict the kind of situation under which an exception is raised to failure of a prerequisite or a result.

A recent proposal in [13] for the use of type hierarchy is basically identical to the *IS-A* hierarchy described in this paper. Our work seems to differ from Mealy's only in that his is applied to ELI data structuring mechanisms [23] rather than the design of an application language.

Our *IS-A* hierarchy is also similar to the generalization hierarchy proposed in [20], although we do not use the "unique key" assumption they impose on their hierarchy, nor do we use their notion of image domains which defines a particular implementation of the *IS-A* relationship within a relational database framework. Another difference between *IS-A* and the generalization hierarchy proposed by the Smiths is that it is possible to redefine a property for a specialization of a class in TAXIS (subject to Postulate IV structural *IS-A* constraint), but that is not the case for the generalization hierarchy. We consider this ability to redefine properties (by specializing their *p*-values) an important component of the structuring mechanism offered by the *IS-A* relationship. Hammer and McLeod [6] and Lee and Gerritzen [9] have also proposed data models which offer an *IS-A* relationship.

The treatment of the *INSTANCE-OF* relationship in TAXIS is based on the treatment this relationship receives in PSN (procedural semantic network formalism) described in [10, 11]. However, PSN allows an arbitrary number of metaclass levels, as well as the possibility for a class to be an *INSTANCE-OF* itself. We have avoided such a scheme because experience has taught us that two levels of classes are sufficient for most situations. Lee [8] and Smith and Smith [19] also offer proposals concerning the *INSTANCE-OF* relationship.

The high-level relational database operations of QUEL (e.g., retrieve [7]) are very similar to the compound expressions used to manipulate variable classes. Obviously, variable classes share many features with relations of the relational model. In embedding variable classes in a programming language we have taken a very different approach from that described in [17] which treats relations as data objects that can be created dynamically as results of relational operations. Instead, in TAXIS no classes (variable or otherwise) can be created as results of run-time operations. We rejected Schmidt's proposal very early in our work because it raises a design dilemma for which we do not have a good solution: either we allow the inclusion of classes in TAXIS programs that do not have the usual TAXIS semantics (i.e., properties and a position on the *IS-A* hierarchy), contrary to design principle (2) of Section 1, or we include run-time facilities for obtaining the TAXIS semantics for derived classes, as done in [15], contrary to design principle (4).

Finally, Abrial's work [1] has been very influencial in directing us toward "data models" or "representation schemes" [26] which offer procedural as well as data-oriented facilities for the definition of a model.

From an AI point of view, our work is a direct descendant of PSN, with much of the power of the formalism left out to accommodate the design principles of TAXIS.

As far as contributions are concerned, we believe that this paper has provided evidence on how a framework involving classes, properties (of classes), the IS-A relationship, and to a lesser extent the INSTANCE-OF relationship, can be used to account not only for data-oriented (declarative, to use the terminology in [26]) aspects of a model of some enterprise, but also procedural ones, e.g., expressions, exceptions, and transactions.

Acceptance of the TAXIS framework for the design of IISs can have far-reaching consequences:

(1) It provides a methodology for dealing with semantic integrity constraints, which in TAXIS are treated as prerequisite and result properties of transactions and are organized into an IS-A hierarchy consistent with those defined for data classes and operations on them.

(2) It provides a general design methodology based on "stepwise refinement by specialization" as opposed to "stepwise refinement by decomposition" [24], which has been the main design tool used so far in program development. For data structures, an account of what stepwise refinement by specialization means and how it relates to stepwise refinement by decomposition has already been given in [20]. TAXIS proposes a similar framework for all aspects concerning a program design, not just its data structures. Further evidence for the importance of this notion is provided in [25].

There are four directions along which research on TAXIS is proceeding:

(1) Formalization. TAXIS offers some unusual constructs and a formal definition of what they mean appears highly desirable. Wong [25] provides an axiomatization of the language as well as a denotational semantics to account for these constructs. A by-product of this work is the ability to prove TAXIS programs correct with respect to some logical specification.

(2) Definition of Input/Output Facilities. TAXIS does not offer input/output facilities at this time. To extend it in order to have it provide such facilities, we are considering the possibility of using the same framework (classes et al.) for the definition of all syntactic and pragmatic aspects of a user interface.

(3) Implementation. A TAXIS parser and code generator, and possibly an interactive system through which a designer can use TAXIS, is an important step toward testing the language. Also, there are important theoretical problems such as the mapping of variable and transaction classes into relations and procedures, respectively.

(4) Applications. Apart from the design of individual IISs in TAXIS, we wish to explore the possibility of extending TAXIS to make it suitable for the design of IISs from one particular applications area, say, accounting or inventory control.

ACKNOWLEDGMENTS
We would like to thank Teresa Miao for typing this paper.

REFERENCES

1. ABRIAL, J.R. Data semantics. In Data Management Systems, J.W. Klimbie and K. L. Koffeman (Eds.). North Holland Pub. Co.. Amsterdam, 1974.
2. BRACHMAN, R. On the epistemological status of semantic networks. In Associative Networks, N. Findler (Ed.), Academic Press, New York, 1979.
3. CODD, E.F. A relational model for large shared data banks. Commun. ACM 13, 6 (June 1970), 377-387.
4. DAHL, O.J., AND HOARE, C.A.R. Hierarchical program structures. In Structured Programming, O.J. Dahl, E. Dijkstra, and C.A.R. Hoare (Eds.), Academic Press, New York, 1972.
5. DATE, C.J. An architecture for high level language database extension. Proc. 1975 ACM SIGMOD Conf., pp. 101-122.
6. HAMMER, M., AND MCLEOD, D. The semantic data model: A modeling mechanism for database applications. Proc. 1978 ACM SIGMOD Conf., pp. 26-36.
7. HELD, G., STONEBRAKER, M., AND WONG, E. INGRES: A relational data base system. Proc. Nat. Computer Conf., Anaheim, Calif., 1975, pp. 19-22.
8. LEE, R., On the semantics of instance in database modeling. Working Paper, Dep. Decision Sci., Wharton School, Univ. Pennsylvania, Philadelphia, 1978.
9. LEE, R., AND GERRITZEN, R. A hybrid representation for database semantics. Tech. Rep. 78-01-01, Dep. Decision Sci., Wharton School, Univ. Pennsylvania, Philadelphia, 1978.
10. LEVESQUE, H. A procedural approach to semantic networks. M.Sc. thesis (Tech. Rep. 105), Dep. Computer Sci., Univ. Toronto, Toronto, Canada, 1977.
11. LEVESQUE, H., AND MYLOPOULOS, J. A procedural semantics for semantic networks. In Associative Networks, N. Findler (Ed.), Academic Press, New York, 1979.
12. LISKOV, B., SNYDER, A., ATKINSON, R., AND SCHAFFERT, C. Abstraction mechanisms in CLU. Commun. ACM 20, 8 (Aug. 1977), 564-576.
13. MEALY, G. Notions. In Current Trends in Programming Methodology, vol. 2, R. Yeh (Ed.). Prentice-Hall, Englewood Cliffs, N.J., 1977.
14. MYLOPOULOS, J., BERNSTEIN, P., WONG, H.K.T. A preliminary specification of TAXIS: A language for interactive systems design. Tech. Rep. CCA-78-02, Computer Corp. of America, 1978.
15. ROUSSOPOULOS, N. A semantic network model of databases. Ph.D. dissertation (Tech. Rep. 104), Dep. Computer Sci., Univ. Toronto, Toronto, Canada, 1976.
16. ROWE, L.A., AND SHOENS, K.A. Data abstraction, views and updates in RIGEL. Proc. 1979 ACM SIGMOD Conf.
17. SCHMIDT, J.W. Some high level language constructs for data of type relation. ACM Trans. Database Syst. 2, 3 (Sept. 1977), 247-261.
18. SHAW, M., WULF, W.A., AND LONDON, R.L. Abstraction and verification in ALPHARD: Defining and specifying iteration and generators. Commun. ACM 20, 8 (Aug. 1977), 553-563.
19. SMITH, J., AND SMITH, D.C.P. A database approach to software specification. Tech. Rep. CCA-79-17, Computer Corp. of America, 1979.
20. SMITH, J., AND SMITH, D.C.P. Database abstractions: Aggregation and generalization. ACM Trans. Database Syst. 2, 2 (June 1977), 105-133.
21. WASSERMAN, A.I. Procedure-oriented exception-handling. Tech. Rep. 27, Lab. Medical Inf. Sci., Univ. California, San Francisco, 1977.
22. WASSERMAN, A.I., SHERTZ, D.D., AND HANDA, E.F. Report on the programming language PLAIN. Lab. Medical Inf. Sci., Univ. California, San Francisco, 1978.
23. WEGBREIT, B. The treatment of data-types in EL1. Commun. ACM 17, 5 (May 1974), 251-264.
24. WIRTH, N. Program development by step-wise refinement. Commun. ACM 14, 4 (April 1971), 221-227.
25. WONG, H.K.T. Design and verification of interactive information systems. Ph.D. dissertation, Dep. Computer. Sci., Univ. Toronto, Toronto, Canada. To appear.
26. WONG, H.K.T., AND MYLOPOULOS, J. Two views of data semantics: Data models in artificial intelligence and database management. INFOR 15, 3 (Oct. 1977), 344-382.

Received April 1978; revised November 1979; accepted December 1979

Database Description with SDM: A Semantic Database Model

MICHAEL HAMMER
Massachusetts Institute of Technology
and
DENNIS McLEOD
University of Southern California

SDM is a high-level semantics-based database description and structuring formalism (database model) for databases. This database model is designed to capture more of the meaning of an application environment than is possible with contemporary database models. An SDM specification describes a database in terms of the kinds of entities that exist in the application environment, the classifications and groupings of those entities, and the structural interconnections among them. SDM provides a collection of high-level modeling primitives to capture the semantics of an application environment. By accommodating derived information in a database structural specification, SDM allows the same information to be viewed in several ways; this makes it possible to directly accommodate the variety of needs and processing requirements typically present in database applications. The design of the present SDM is based on our experience in using a preliminary version of it.

SDM is designed to enhance the effectiveness and usability of database systems. An SDM database description can serve as a formal specification and documentation tool for a database; it can provide a basis for supporting a variety of powerful user interface facilities, it can serve as a conceptual database model in the database design process; and, it can be used as the database model for a new kind of database management system.

Key Words and Phrases: database management, database models, database semantics, database definition, database modeling, logical database design
CR Categories: 3.73, 3.74, 4.33

Permission to copy without fee all or part of this material is granted provided that the copies are not made or distributed for direct commercial advantage, the ACM copyright notice and the title of the publication and its date appear, and notice is given that copying is by permission of the Association for Computing Machinery. To copy otherwise, or to republish, requires a fee and/or specific permission.
This research was supported in part by the Joint Services Electronics Program through the Air Force Office of Scientific Research (AFSC) under Contract F44620-76-C-0061, and, in part by the Advanced Research Projects Agency of the Department of Defense through the Office of Naval Research under Contract N00014-76-C-0944. The alphabetical listing of the authors indicates indistinguishably equal contributions and associated funding support.
Authors' addresses: M. Hammer, Laboratory for Computer Science, Massachusetts Institute of Technology, Cambridge, MA 02139; D. McLeod, Computer Science Department, University of Southern California, University Park, Los Angeles, CA 90007.
© 1981 ACM 0362-5915/81/0900-0351 $00.75

1. INTRODUCTION

Every database is a *model* of some real world system. At all times, the contents of a database are intended to represent a snapshot of the state of an *application environment*, and each change to the database should reflect an event (or sequence of events) occurring in that environment. Therefore, it is appropriate that the structure of a database mirror the structure of the system that it models. A database whose organization is based on naturally occurring structures will be easier for a database designer to construct and modify than one that forces him to translate the primitives of his problem domain into artificial specification constructs. Similarly, a database user should find it easier to understand and employ a database if it can be described to him using concepts with which he is already familiar.

The global user view of a database, as specified by the database designer, is known as its (*logical*) *schema*. A schema is specified in terms of a database description and structuring formalism and associated operations, called a *database model*. We believe that the data structures provided by contemporary database models do not adequately support the design, evolution, and use of complex databases. These database models have significantly limited capabilities for expressing the meaning of a database and to relate a database to its corresponding application environment. The *semantics* of a database defined in terms of these mechanisms are not readily apparent from the schema; instead, the semantics must be separately specified by the database designer and consciously applied by the user.

Our goal is the design of a higher-level database model that will enable the database designer to naturally and directly incorporate more of the semantics of a database into its schema. Such a semantics-based database description and structuring formalism is intended to serve as a natural application modeling mechanism to capture and express the structure of the application environment in the structure of the database.

1.1 The Design of SDM

This paper describes *SDM*, a database description and structuring formalism that is intended to allow a database schema to capture much more of the meaning of a database than is possible with contemporary database models. SDM is designed to provide features for the natural modeling of database application environments. In designing SDM, we analyzed many database applications, in order to determine the structures that occur and recur in them, assessed the shortcomings of contemporary database models in capturing the semantics of these applications, and developed strategies to address the problems uncovered. This design process was iterative, in that features were removed, added, and modified during various stages of design. A preliminary version of SDM was discussed in [21]; however, this initial database model has been further revised and restructured based on experience with its use. This paper presents a detailed specification of SDM, examines its applications, and discusses its underlying principles.

SDM has been designed with a number of specific kinds of uses in mind. First, SDM is meant to serve as a formal specification mechanism for describing the meaning of a database; an SDM schema provides a precise documentation and communication medium for database users. In particular, a new user of a large and complex database should find its SDM schema of use in determining what information is contained in the database. Second, SDM provides the basis for a variety of high-level semantics-based user interfaces to a database; these interface facilities can be constructed as front-ends to existing database management systems, or as the query language of a new database management system. Such interfaces improve the process of identifying and retrieving relevant information from the database. For example, SDM has been used to construct a user interface facility for nonprogrammers [28]. Finally, SDM provides a foundation for supporting the effective and structured design of databases and database-intensive application systems.

SDM has been designed to satisfy a number of criteria that are not met by contemporary database models, but which we believe to be essential in an effective database description and structuring formalism [22]. They are as follows.

(1) The constructs of the database model should provide for the explicit specification of a large portion of the *meaning* of a database. Many contemporary database models (such as the CODASYL DBTG network model [11, 47] and the hierarchical model [48]) exhibit compromises between the desire *to* provide a user-oriented database organization and the need to support efficient database storage and manipulation facilities. By contrast, the relational database model [12, 13] stresses the separation of user-level database specifications and underlying implementation detail (data independence). Moreover, the relational database model emphasizes the importance of understandable modeling constructs (specifically, the nonhierarchic relation), and user-oriented database system interfaces [7, 8].

However, the *semantic expressiveness* of the hierarchical, network, and relational models is limited; they do not provide sufficient mechanism to allow a database schema to describe the meaning of a database. Such models employ overly simple data structures to model an application environment. In so doing, they inevitably lose information about the database; they provide for the expression of only a limited range of a designer's knowledge of the application environment [4, 36, 49]. This is a consequence of the fact that their structures are essentially all record-oriented constructs; the appropriateness and adequacy of the record construct for expressing database semantics is highly limited [17, 22–24, 27]. We believe that it is necessary to break with the tradition of record-based modeling, and to base a database model on structural constructs that are highly user oriented and expressive of the application environment. To this end, it is essential that the database model provide a rich set of features to allow the direct modeling of application environment semantics.

(2) A database model must support a *relativist* view of the meaning of a database, and allow the structure of a database to support alternative ways of looking at the same information. In order to accommodate multiple views of the same data and to enable the evolution of new perspectives on the data, a database model must support schemata that are flexible, potentially logically redundant, and integrated. *Flexibility* is essential in order to allow for multiple and coequal views of the data. In a *logically redundant* database schema, the values of some database components can be algorithmically derived from others. Incorporating such derived information into a schema can simplify the user's manipulation of a database by statically embedding in the schema data values that would otherwise have to be dynamically and repeatedly computed. Furthermore, the use of derived data can ease the development of new applications of the database, since new data required by these applications can often be readily adjoined to the

existing schema. Finally, an *integrated* schema explicitly describes the relationships and similarities between multiple ways of viewing the same information. Without a degree of this critical integration, it is difficult to control the redundancy and to specify that the various alternative interpretations of the database are equivalent.

Contemporary, record-oriented database models do not adequately support relativism. In these models, it is generally necessary to impose a single structural organization of the data, one which inevitably carries along with it a particular interpretation of the data's meaning. This meaning may not be appropriate for all users of the database and may furthermore become entirely obsolete over time. For example, an association between two entities can legitimately be viewed as an attribute of the first entity, as an attribute of the second entity, or as an entity itself; thus, the fact that an officer is currently assigned as the captain of a ship could be expressed as an attribute of the ship (its current captain), as an attribute of the officer (his current ship), or as an independent (assignment) entity. A schema should make all three of these interpretations equally natural and direct. Therefore, the conceptual database model must provide a specification mechanism that simultaneously accommodates and integrates these three ways of looking at an assignment. Conventional database models fail to adequately achieve these goals.

Similarly, another consequence of the primacy of the principle of relativism is that, in general, the database model should not make rigid distinctions between such concepts as entity, association, and attribute. Higher-level database models that do require the database designer to sharply distinguish among these concepts (such as [9, 33]) are thus considered somewhat lacking in their support of relativism.

(3) A database model must support the definition of schemata that are *based on abstract entities.* Specifically, this means that a database model must facilitate the description of relevant *entities* in the application environment, *collections* of such entities, *relationships* (associations) among entities, and *structural interconnections* among the collections. Moreover, the entities themselves must be distinguished from their syntactic identifiers (*names*); the user-level view of a database should be based on actual entities rather than on artificial entity names.

Allowing entities to represent themselves makes it possible to directly reference an entity from a related one. In record-oriented database models, it is necessary to cross reference between related entities by means of their identifiers. While it is of course necessary to eventually represent "abstract" entities as symbols inside a computer, the point is that users (and application programs) should be able to reference and manipulate abstractions as well as symbols; internal representations to facilitate computer processing should be hidden from users.

Suppose, for example, that the schema should allow a user to obtain the entity that models a ship's current captain from the ship entity. To accomplish this, it would be desirable to define an attribute "Captain" that applies to every ship, and whose value is an officer. To model this information using a record-oriented database model, it is necessary to select some identifier of an officer record (e.g., last name or identification number) to stand as the value of the "Captain" attribute of a ship. For example, using the relational database model, we might have a relation SHIPS, one of whose attributes is Officer_name, and a relation

OFFICERS, which has Officer_name as a logical key. Then, in order to find the information about the captain of a given ship, it would be necessary to join relations SHIPS and OFFICERS on Officer_name; an explicit cross reference via identifiers is required. This forces the user to deal with an extra level of indirection and to consciously apply a join to retrieve a simple item of information.

In consequence of the fact that contemporary database models require such surrogates to be used in connections among entities, important types of semantic integrity constraints on a database are not directly captured in its schema. If these semantic constraints are to be expressed and enforced, additional mechanisms must be provided to supplement contemporary database models [6, 16, 19, 20, 45]. The problem with this approach is that these supplemental constraints are at best ad hoc, and do not integrate all available information into a simple structure. For example, it is desirable to require that only captains who are known in the database be assigned as officers of ships. To accomplish this in the relational database model, it is necessary to impose the supplemental constraint that each value of attribute Captain_name of relation SHIPS must be present in the Captain_name column of relation OFFICERS. If it were possible to simply state that each ship has a captain attribute whose value is an officer, this supplemental constraint would not be necessary.

The design of SDM has been based on the principles outlined above which are discussed at greater length in [22].

2. A SPECIFICATION OF SDM

The following general principles of database organization underlie the design of SDM.

(1) A database is to be viewed as a collection of *entities* that correspond to the actual objects in the application environment.

(2) The entities in a database are organized into *classes* that are meaningful collections of entities.

(3) The classes of a database are not in general independent, but rather are logically related by means of *interclass connections*.

(4) Database entities and classes have *attributes* that describe their characteristics and relate them to other database entities. An attribute value may be derived from other values in the database.

(5) There are several primitive ways of defining interclass connections and derived attributes, corresponding to the most common types of information redundancy appearing in database applications. These facilities integrate multiple ways of viewing the same basic information, and provide building blocks for describing complex attributes and interclass relationships.

2.1 Classes

An *SDM database* is a collection of entities that are organized into classes. The structure and organization of an SDM database is specified by an *SDM schema*, which identifies the classes in the database. Appendix A contains an example SDM schema for a portion of the "tanker monitoring application environment"; a specific syntax (detailed in Appendix B) is used for expressing this schema. Examples in this paper are based on this application domain, which is concerned

with monitoring and controlling ships with potentially hazardous cargoes (such as oil tankers), as they enter U.S. coastal waters and ports. A database supporting this application would contain information on ships and their positions, oil tankers and their inspections, oil spills, ships that are banned from U.S. waters, and so forth.

Each class in an SDM schema has the following features.

(1) A *class name* identifies the class. Multiple synonymous names are also permitted. Each class name must be unique with respect to all class names used in a schema. For notational convenience in this paper, class names are strings of uppercase letters and special characters (e.g., OIL_TANKERS), as shown in Appendix A.

(2) The class has a collection of *members*: the entities that constitute it. The phrases "the members of a class" and "the entities in a class" are thus synonymous. Each class in an SDM schema is a homogeneous collection of one type of entity, at an appropriate level of abstraction.

The entities in a class may correspond to various kinds of objects in the application environment. These include objects that may be viewed by users as:

(a) concrete objects, such as ships, oil tankers, and ports (in Appendix A, these are classes SHIPS, OIL_TANKERS, and PORTS, respectively);

(b) events, such as ship accidents (INCIDENTS) and assignments of captains to ships (ASSIGNMENTS);

(c) higher-level entities such as categorizations (e.g., SHIP_TYPES) and aggregations (e.g., CONVOYS) of entities;

(d) names, which are syntactic identifiers (strings), such as the class of all possible ship names (SHIP_NAMES) and the class of all possible calendar dates (DATES).

Although it is useful in certain circumstances to label a class as containing "concrete objects" or "events" [21], in general the principle of relativism requires that no such fixed specification be included in the schema; for example, inspections of ships (INSPECTIONS) could be considered to be either an event or an object, depending upon the user's point of view. In consequence, such distinctions are not directly supported in SDM. Only name classes (classes whose members are names) contain data items that can be transmitted into and out of a database, for example, names are the values that may be entered by, or displayed to, a user. Nonname classes represent abstract entities from the application environment.

(3) An (optional) textual *class description* describes the meaning and contents of the class. A class description should be used to describe the specific nature of the entities that constitute a class and to indicate their significance and role in the application environment. For example, in Appendix A, class SHIPS has a description indicating that the class contains ships with potentially hazardous cargoes that may enter U.S. coastal waters. Tying this documentation directly to schema entries makes it accessible and consequently more valuable.

(4) The class has a collection of attributes that describe the members of that class or the class as a whole. There are two types of attributes, classified according to *applicability*.

(a) A *member attribute* describes an aspect of each member of a class by logically connecting the member to one or more related entities in the same or another class. Thus a member attribute is used to describe each member of some class. For example, each member of class SHIPS has attributes Name, Captain, and Engines, which identify the ship's name, its current captain, and its engines (respectively).

(b) A *class attribute* describes a property of a class taken as a whole. For example, the class INSPECTIONS has the attribute Number, which identifies the number of inspections currently in the class; the class OIL_TANKERS has the attribute Absolute_legal_top_speed which indicates the absolute maximum speed any tanker is allowed to sail.

(5) The class is either a *base class* or a *nonbase class*. A base class is one that is defined independently of all other classes in the database; it can be thought of as modeling a primitive entity in the application environment, for example, SHIPS. Base classes are mutually disjoint in that every entity is a member of exactly one base class. Of course, at some level of abstraction all entities are members of class "THINGS"; SDM provides the notion of base class to explicitly support cutting off the abstraction below that most general level. (If it is desired that all entities in a database be members of some class, then a single base class would be defined in the schema.)

A nonbase class is one that does not have independent existence; rather, it is defined in terms of one or more other classes. In SDM, classes are structurally related by means of *interclass connections*. Each nonbase class has associated with it one interclass connection. In the schema definition syntax shown in Appendix A, the existence of an interclass connection for a class means that it is nonbase; if no interclass connection is present, the class is a base class. In Appendix A, OIL_TANKERS is an example of a nonbase class; it is defined to be a subclass of SHIPS which means that its membership is always a subset of the members of SHIPS.

(6) If the class is a base class, it has an associated list of groups of member attributes; each of these groups serves as a logical key to uniquely identify the members of a class (*identifiers*). That is, there is a one-to-one correspondence between the values of each identifying attribute or attribute group and the entities in a class. For example, class SHIPS has the unique identifier Name, as well as the (alternative) unique identifier Hull_number.

(7) If the class is a base class, it is specified as either *containing duplicates* or *not containing duplicates*. (The default is that duplicates are allowed: in the schema syntax used in Appendix A, "duplicates not allowed" is explicitly stated to indicate that a class may not contain duplicate members.) Stating that duplicates are not allowed amounts to requiring the members of the class to have some difference in their attribute values; "duplicates not allowed" is explicit shorthand for requiring all of the member attributes of a class taken together to constitute a unique identifier.

2.2 Interclass Connections

As specified above, a nonbase class has an associated interclass connection that defines it. There are two main types of interclass connections in SDM: the first allows subclasses to be defined and the second supports grouping classes. These interclass connection types are detailed as follows.

2.2.1 *The Subclass Connection.* The first type of interclass connection specifies that the members of a nonbase class (S) are of the same basic entity type as those in the class to which S is related (via the interclass connection). This type of interclass connection is used to define a subclass of a given class. A *subclass S* of a class C (called the *parent class*) is a class that contains some, but not necessarily all, of the members of C. The very same entity can thus be a member of many classes, for example, a given entity may simultaneously be a member of the classes SHIPS, OIL_TANKERS, and MERCHANT_SHIPS. (However, only one of these may be a base class.) This is the concept of "subtype" [21, 25, 31, 32, 41] which is missing from most database models (in which a record belongs to exactly one file).

In SDM, a subclass S is defined by specifying a class C and a predicate P on the members of C; S consists of just those members of C that satisfy P. Several types of predicates are permissible.

(1) A predicate on the member attributes of C can be used to indicate which members of C are also members of S. A subclass defined by this technique is called an *attribute-defined subclass*. For example, the class MERCHANT_SHIPS is defined (in Appendix A) as a subclass of SHIPS by the member attribute predicate "where Type = 'merchant'"; that is, a member of SHIPS is a member of MERCHANT_SHIPS if the value of its attribute Type is "merchant." (A detailed discussion of member attribute predicates is provided in what follows. The usual comparison operators and Boolean connectives are allowed.)

(2) The predicate "where specified" can be used to define S as a *user-controllable subclass* of C. This means that S contains at all times only entities that are members of C. However, unlike an attribute-defined subclass, the definition of S does not identify which members of C are in S; rather, database users "manually" add to (and delete from) S, so long as the subclass limitation is observed. For example, BANNED_SHIPS is defined as a "where specified" subclass of "SHIPS"; this allows some authority to ban a ship from U.S. waters (and possibly later rescind that ban).

An essential difference between attribute-defined subclasses and user-controllable subclasses is that the membership of the former type of subclass is determined by other information in the database, while the membership of the latter type of subclass is directly and explicitly controlled by users. It would be possible to simulate the effect of a user-controllable subclass by an attribute-defined subclass, through the introduction of a dummy member attribute of the parent class whose sole purpose is to specify whether or not the entity is in the subclass. Subclass membership could then be predicated on the value of this attribute. However, this would be a confusing and indirect method of capturing the semantics of the application environment; in particular, there are cases in which the method of determining subclass membership is beyond the scope of the database schema (e.g., by virtue of being complex).

(3) A subclass definition predicate can specify that the members of subclass S are just those members of C that also belong to two other specified data-

base classes (C_1 and C_2); this provides a class *intersection* capability. To insure a type-compatible intersection, C_1 and C_2 must both be subclasses of C, either directly or through a series of subclass relationships. For example, the class BANNED_OIL_TANKERS is defined as the subclass of SHIPS that contains those members common to the classes OIL_TANKERS and BANNED_SHIPS.

In addition to an intersection capability, a subclass can be defined by class *union* and *difference*. A union subclass contains those members of C in either C_1 or C_2. For example, class SHIPS_TO_BE_MONITORED is defined as a subclass of SHIPS with the predicate "where is in BANNED_SHIPS or is in OIL_TANKERS_REQUIRING_INSPECTION." A difference subclass contains those members of C that are not in C_1. For example, class SAFE_SHIPS is defined as the subclass of SHIPS with the predicate "where is not in BANNED_SHIPS."

The intersection, union, and difference subclass definition primitives allow *set-operator-defined subclasses* to be specified; these primitives are provided because they often represent the most natural means of defining a subclass. Moreover, these operations are needed to effectively define subclasses of user-controllable subclasses. For example, class intersection (rather than a member attribute predicate) must be used to define class SHIPS_TO_BE_MONITORED; since BANNED_SHIPS and OIL_TANKERS_REQUIRING_INSPECTION are both user-controllable subclasses, no natural member attributes of either of these classes could be used to state an appropriate defining member attribute predicate for SHIPS_TO_BE_MONITORED.

(4) The final type of subclass definition allows a subclass S to be defined as consisting of all of the members of C that are currently values of some attribute A of another class C. That is, class S contains all of the members of C that are a value of A. This type of class is called an *existence subclass*. For example, class DANGEROUS_CAPTAINS is defined as the subclass of OFFICERS satisfying the predicate "where is a value of Involved_captain of INCIDENTS"; this specifies that DANGEROUS_CAPTAINS contains all officers who have been involved in an incident.

2.2.2 The Grouping Connection. The other type of interclass connection allows a class to be defined, called a *grouping class* (G), whose members are of a higher-order entity type than those in the underlying class (U). A grouping class is *second order*, in the sense that its members can themselves be viewed as classes; in particular, they are classes whose members are taken from U.

The following options are available for defining a grouping class.

(1) The grouping class G can be defined as consisting of all classes formed by collecting the members of U into classes based on having a common value for one or more designated member attributes of U (an *expression-defined grouping class*). A *grouping expression* specifies how the members of U are to be placed into these groups. The groups formed in this way become the members of G, and the members of a member of G are called its *contents*. For example, class SHIP_TYPES in Appendix A is defined as a grouping class of SHIPS with the grouping expression "on common value of Type". The members of

SHIP_TYPES are not ships, but rather are groups of ships. In particular, the intended interpretation of SHIP_TYPES is as a collection of types of ships, whose instances are the contents (members) of the groups that constitute SHIP_TYPES. This kind of grouping class represents an abstraction of the underlying class. That is, the elements of the grouping class correspond in a sense to the shared property of the entities that are its contents, rather than to the collection of entities itself.

If the grouping expression used to define a grouping class involves only a single-valued attribute, then the groups partition the underlying class; this is the case for SHIP_TYPES. However, if a multivalued attribute is involved, then the groups may have overlapping contents. For example, the class CARGO_TYPE_GROUPS can be defined as a grouping class on SHIPS with the grouping expression "on common value of Cargo_types"; since Cargo_types is multivalued, a given ship may be in more than one cargo type category.

Although the grouping mechanism is limited to single grouping expressions (namely, on common value of one or more member attributes), complex grouping criteria are possible via derived attributes (as discussed in what follows).

It should be clear that the contents of a group are a subclass of the class underlying the grouping. The grouping expression used to define a grouping class thus corresponds to a collection of attribute-defined subclass definitions. For example, for SHIP_TYPES, the grouping expression "on common value of Type" corresponds to the collection of subclass member attribute predicates (on SHIPS) "Type = 'merchant'," "Type = 'fishing'," and "Type = 'military'." Some or all of these subclasses may be independently and explicitly defined in the schema. In Appendix A, the class MERCHANT_SHIPS is defined as a subclass of SHIPS, and it is also listed in the definition of SHIP_TYPES as a class that is explicitly defined in the database ("groups defined as classes are MERCHANT_SHIPS"). In general, when a grouping class is defined, a list of the names of the groups that are explicitly defined in the schema is to be included in the specification of the interclass connection; the purpose of this list is to relate the groups to their corresponding subclasses in the schema.

(2) A second way to define a grouping class G is by providing a list of classes (C_1, C_2, ..., C_n) that are defined in the schema; these classes are the members of the grouping class (an *enumerated grouping class*). Each of the classes (C_1, C_2, ..., C_n) must be explicitly defined in the schema as an (eventual) subclass of the class U that is specified as the class underlying the grouping. This grouping class definition capability is useful when no appropriate attribute is available for defining the grouping and when all of the groups are themselves defined as classes in the schema. For example, a class TYPES_OF_HAZARDOUS_SHIPS can be defined as "grouping of SHIPS consisting of classes BANNED_SHIPS, BANNED_OIL_TANKERS, and SHIPS_TO_BE_MONITORED."

(3) A grouping class G can be defined to consist of user-controllable subclasses of some underlying class (a *user-controllable grouping class*). In effect, a user-controllable grouping class consists of a collection of user-controllable subclasses. For example, class CONVOYS is defined as a grouping of SHIPS "as specified." In this case, no attribute exists to allow the grouping of ships into convoys and individual convoys are not themselves defined as classes in the schema; rather, each member of CONVOYS is a user-controllable group of ships that users may

add to or delete from. This kind of grouping class models simple "aggregates" over a base class: arbitrary collections of entities manipulated by users.

2.2.3 Multiple Interclass Connections. As specifed above, each nonbase class in an SDM schema has a single interclass connection associated with it. While it is meaningful and reasonable in some cases to associate more than one interclass connection with a nonbase class, the uncontrolled use of such multiple interclass connections could introduce undesirable complexity into a schema. In consequence, only a single interclass connection (the most natural one) should be used to define a nonbase class.

To illustrate this point, consider for example the class RURITANIAN_OIL_TANKERS. Clearly, this class could be specified as an attribute-defined subclass of OIL_TANKERS (by the interclass connection "subclass of OIL_TANKERS where Country.Name = 'Ruritania'"), or as a subclass of RURITANIAN_SHIPS (by the interclass connection "subclass of RURITANIAN_SHIPS where Cargo_types contains 'oil'"); these definitions are, in a sense, semantically equivalent. The possibility of allowing multiple (semantically equivalent) interclass connections to be specified for a nonbase class was considered, but it was determined that such a feature could introduce considerable complexity. The mechanism could be used to force two class definitions that are not semantically equivalent to define classes with the same members. For example, one could associate interclass connections that define the class of all Ruritanian ships and the class of all dangerous ships with a single class, intending to force the sets of members of these two possibly independent collections to be the same. In sum, without a carefully formulated and powerful notion of semantic equivalence [30], it was determined that multiple interclass connections for a nonbase class should not be allowed in SDM. Of course, multiple class names and judiciously selected class descriptions can be used to convey additional definitions, for example, naming a class BANNED_SHIPS and RURITANIAN_OIL_TANKERS to indicate that the two sets of ships are intended to be one and the same.

2.3 Name Classes

Entities are application constructs that are directly modeled in an SDM schema. In the real world, entities can be denoted in a number of ways; for example, a particular ship can be identified by giving its name or its hull number, by exhibiting a picture of it, or by pointing one's finger at the ship itself. Operating entirely within SDM, the typical way of referencing an entity is by means of an entity-valued attribute that gives access to the entity itself. However, there must also be some mechanism that allows for the outside world (i.e., users) to communicate with an SDM database. This will typically be accomplished by data being entered or displayed on a computer terminal. However, one cannot enter or display a real entity on such a terminal: it is necessary to employ representations of them for that purpose. These representations are called SDM *names*. A name is any string of symbols that denotes an actual value encountered in the application environment; the strings "red," "128," "8/21/78," and "321-004" are all names. A name class in SDM is a collection of strings, namely, a subclass of the built-in class STRINGS (which consists of all strings over the basic set of alphanumeric characters).

Every SDM name class is defined by means of the interclass connection "subclass." The following methods of defining a class *S* of names are available.

(1) The class *S* can be defined as the intersection, union, or difference of two other name classes.

(2) The class *S* can be defined as a subclass of some other name class *C* with the predicate "where specified," which means that the members of *S* belong to *C*, but must be explicitly enumerated. In Appendix A, class COUNTRY_NAMES is defined in this way.

(3) A predicate can be used to define *S* as a subclass of *C*. The predicate specifies the subset of *C* that constitutes *S* by indicating constraints on the format of the acceptable data values. In Appendix A, classes ENGINE_SERIAL_NUMBERS, DATES, and CARGO_TYPE_NAMES are defined in this way. CARGO_TYPE_NAMES has no format constraints, indicating that all strings are valid cargo type names. ENGINE_SERIAL_NUMBERS and DATES do have constraints that indicate the patterns defining legal members of these classes. Note that for convenience, the particular name classes NUMBERS, INTEGERS, REALS, and YES/NO (Booleans) are also built into SDM; these classes have obvious definitions. (Further details of the format specification language used here are presented in [26].)

2.4 Attributes

As stated above, each class has an associated collection of attributes. Each attribute has the following features.

(1) An *attribute name* identifies the attribute. An attribute name must be unique with respect to the set of all attribute names used in the class, the class's underlying base class, and all eventual subclasses of that base class. (As decribed in [30], this means that attribute names must be unique within a "family" of classes; this is necessary to support the attribute inheritance rules described in what follows.) As with class names, multiple synonymous attribute names are permitted. For notational convenience in this paper, attribute names are written as one uppercase letter followed by a sequence of lowercase letters and special characters (e.g., the attribute Cargo_types of class SHIPS), as shown in Appendix A.

(2) The attribute has a *value* which is either an entity in the database (a member of some class) or a collection of such entities. The value of an attribute is selected from its underlying *value class*, which contains the permissible values of the attribute. Any class in the schema may be specified to be the value class of an attribute. For example, the value class of member attribute Captain of SHIPS is the class OFFICERS. The value of an attribute may also be the special value *null* (i.e., no value).

(3) The *applicability* of the attribute is specified by indicating that the attribute is either:

(a) a member attribute, which applies to each member of the class, and so has a value for each member (e.g., Name of SHIPS); or

(b) a class attribute, which applies to a class as a whole, and has only one value for the class (e.g., Number of INSPECTIONS).

(4) An (optional) *attribute description* is text that describes the meaning and purpose of the attribute. For example, in Appendix A, the description of Captain of SHIPS indicates that the value of the attribute is the current captain of the ship. (This serves as an integrated form of database documentation.)

(5) The attribute is specified as either *single valued* or *multivalued*. The value of a single-valued attribute is a member of the value class of the attribute, while the value of a multivalued attribute is a subclass of the value class. Thus, a multivalued attribute itself defines a class, that is, a collection of entities. In Appendix A, the class OIL_TANKERS has the single-valued member attribute Hull_type and the multivalued member attribute Inspections. (In the schema definition syntax used in Appendix A, the default is single valued.) It is possible to place a constraint on the size of a multivalued attribute, by specifying "multivalued with size between X and Y," where X and Y are integers; this means that the attribute must have between X and Y values. For example, attribute Engines of SHIPS is specified as "multivalued with size between 0 and 10"; this means that a SHIP has between 0 and 10 engines.

(6) An attribute can be specified as *mandatory*, which means that a null value is not allowed for it. For example, attribute Hull_number of SHIPS is specified as "may not be null"; this models the fact that every SHIP has a Hull_number.

(7) An attribute can be specified as *not changeable*, which means that once set to a nonnull value, this value cannot be altered except to correct an error. For example, attribute Hull_number of SHIPS is specified as "not changeable."

(8) A member attribute can be required to be *exhaustive* of its value class. This means that every member of the value class of the attribute (call it A) must be the A value of some entity. For example, attribute Engines of SHIPS "exhausts value class," which means that every engine entity must be an engine of some ship.

(9) A multivalued member attribute can be specified as *nonoverlapping* which means that the values of the attribute for two different entities have no entities in common; that is, each member of the value class of the attribute is used at most once. For example, Engines of SHIPS is specified as having "no overlap in values," which means that any engine can be in only one ship.

(10) The attribute may be related to other attributes, and/or defined in terms of other information in the schema. The possible types of such relationships are different for member and class attributes, and are detailed in what follows.

2.4.1 *Member Attribute Interrelationships.* The first way in which a pair of member attributes can be related is by means of inversion. Member attribute A_1 of class C_1 can be specified as the *inverse* of member attribute A_2 of C_2 which means that the value of A_1 for a member M_1 of C_1 consists of those members of C_2 whose value of A_2 is M_1. The inversion interattribute relationship is specified symmetrically in that both an attribute and its inverse contain a description of the inversion relationship. A pair of inverse attributes in effect establish a binary association between the members of the classes that the attributes modify. (Although all attribute inverses could theoretically be specified, if only one of a

pair of such attributes is relevant, then it is the only one that is defined in the schema, that is to say, no inverse specification is provided.) For example, attribute Ships_registered_here of COUNTRIES is specified in Appendix A as the inverse of attribute Country_of_registry of SHIPS; this establishes the fact that both are ways of expressing in what country a ship is registered. This is accomplished by

(1) specifying that the value class of attribute Country_of_registry of SHIPS is COUNTRIES, and that its inverse is Ships_registered_here (of COUNTRIES);
(2) specifying that the value class of attribute Ships_registered_here of COUNTRIES is SHIPS, and that its inverse is Country_of_registry (of SHIPS).

The second way in which a member attribute can be related to other information in the database is by *matching* the value of the attribute with some member(s) of a specified class. In particular, the value of the match attribute A_1 for the member M_1 of class C_1 is determined as follows.

(1) A member M_2 of some (specified) class C_2 is found that has M_1 as its value of (specified) member attribute A_2.
(2) The value of (specified) member attribute A_3 for M_2 is used as the value of A_1 for M_1.

If A_1 is a multivalued attribute, then it is permissible for each member of C_1 to match to several members of C_2; in this case, the collection of A_3 values is the value of attribute A_1. For example, a matching specification indicates that the value of the attribute Captain for a member S of class SHIPS is equal to the value of attribute Officer of the member A of class ASSIGNMENTS whose Ship value is S.

Inversion and matching provide multiple ways of viewing n-ary associations among entities. Inversion permits the specification of binary associations, while matching is capable of supporting binary and higher degree associations. For example, suppose it is necessary to establish a ternary association among oil tankers, countries, and dates, to indicate that a given tanker was inspected in a specified country on a particular date. To accomplish this, a class could be defined (say, COUNTRY_INSPECTIONS) with three attributes: Tanker_inspected, Country, and Date_inspected. Matching would then be used to relate these to appropriate attributes of OIL_TANKERS, COUNTRIES, and DATES that also express this information. Inversions could also be specified to relate the relevant member attributes of OIL_TANKERS (e.g., Countries_in_which_inspected), COUNTRIES (e.g., Tankers_inspected_here), DATES, and COUNTRY_INSPECTIONS (see Figure 1).

The combined use of inversion and matching allows an SDM schema to accommodate relative viewpoints of an association. For instance, one may view the ternary relationship in the above example as an inspection entity (a member of class COUNTRY_INSPECTIONS), or as a collection of attributes of the entities that participate in the association. Similarly, a binary relationship defined as a pair of inverse attributes could also be viewed as an association entity, with matching used to relate that entity to the relevant attributes of the associated entities [30].

OFFICERS that is the value of Captain for S. In this case, the attributes Captain of SHIPS and Name of OFFICERS are single valued; in general, this need not be the case. For example, consider the mapping for SHIPS "Engines. Serial_number." Attribute Engines is multivalued which means that "Engines. Serial_number" may also be multivalued. This mapping evaluates to the serial numbers of the engines of a ship. Similarly, the mapping for SHIPS "Captain.Superiors.Name" evaluates to the names of all of the superiors of the captain of a ship. This mapping is multivalued since at least one of the steps in the mapping involves a multivalued attribute. The value of a mapping "X.Y.Z," where X, Y, and Z are multivalued attributes, is the class containing each value of Z that corresponds to a value of Y for some value of X.

2.4.1.3 *Member Derivation Primitives.* The following primitives are provided to express the derivation of the value of a member attribute; here, attribute A_1 of member M_1 of class C_1 is being defined in terms of the relationship of M_1 to other information in the database.

(1) A_1 can be defined as an *ordering* attribute. In this case, the value of A_1 denotes the sequential position of M_1 in C_1 when C_1 is ordered by one or more other specified (single-valued) member attributes (or mappings) of C_1. Ordering is by increasing or decreasing value (the default is increasing). For example, the attribute Seniority of OFFICERS has the derivation "order by Date_commissioned." The OFFICER with the earliest date commissioned will then have Seniority value of 1. Ordering within groups is also possible: "order by A_2 within A_3" specifies that the value of A_1 is the sequential position of M_1 within the group of entities that have the same value of A_3 as M_1, as ordered by the value of A_2. (A_2 and A_3 may be mappings as well as attributes.) For example, attribute Order_for_tanker of INSPECTIONS has the derivation "order by decreasing Date within Tanker," which orders the inspections for each tanker. The value class of an ordering attribute is INTEGERS.

(2) The value of attribute A_1 can be declared to be a Boolean value that is "yes" (true) if M_1 is a member of some other specified class C_2, and "no" (false) otherwise. Thus, the value class of this *existence* attribute is YES/NO. For example, attribute Is_tanker_banned? of class OIL_TANKERS has the derivation "if in BANNED_SHIPS."

(3) The value of attribute A_1 can be defined as the result of combining all the entities obtained by recursively tracing the values of some attribute A_2. For instance, attribute Superiors of OFFICERS has the derivation "all levels of Commander"; the value of the attribute includes the immediate commander of the officer, his commander's superiors, and so on. Note that the value class of Commander is OFFICERS; this must be true for this kind of recursive attribute derivation to be meaningful. It is also possible to specify a maximum number of levels over which to repeat the recursion, namely, "up to N levels" where N is an integer constant; this would be useful, for example, to relate an officer to his subordinates and their subordinates.

(4) When a grouping class is defined, the derived multivalued member attribute *Contents* is automatically established. The value of this attribute is the

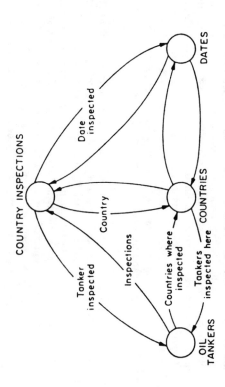

COUNTRY INSPECTIONS

Date inspected

Country

Inspections

Tanker inspected

Countries where inspected

Tankers inspected here   COUNTRIES

DATES

OIL TANKERS

Fig. 1. Multiple perspectives on the "Country Inspections" association. Circles denote classes and are labeled with class names. Arrows denote member attributes, labeled by name, with the arrowhead pointing to the attribute's value class. For brevity, only some of the possible attributes are named (as would be the case in many real SDM schemata).

2.4.1.1 *Member Attribute Derivations.* As described above, inversion and matching are mechanisms for establishing the equivalence of different ways of viewing the same essential relationships among entities. SDM also provides the ability to define an attribute whose value is calculated from other information in the database. Such an attribute is called *derived*, and the specification of its computation is its associated *derivation.*

The approach we take to defining derived attributes is to provide a small vocabulary of high-level attribute derivation primitives that directly model the most common types of derived information. Each of these primitives provides a way of specifying one method of computing a derived attribute. More general facilities are available for describing attributes that do not match any of these cases: A complex derived attribute is defined by first describing other attributes that are used as building blocks in its definition and then applying one of the primitives to these building blocks. For example, attribute Superiors of OFFICERS is defined by a derivation primitive applied to attribute Commander, and in turn, attribute Contacts is defined by a derivation primitive applied to Superiors and Subordinates. This procedure can be repeated for the building block attributes themselves, so that arbitrarily complex attribute derivations can be developed.

2.4.1.2 *Mappings.* Before discussing the member attribute derivation primitives, it is important to present the concept of *mapping.* A mapping is a concatenation of attribute names that allows a user to directly reference the value of an attribute of an attribute. A mapping is written, in general, as a sequence of attribute names separated by quotation marks. For example, consider the mapping "Captain.Name" for class SHIPS. The value of this mapping, for each member S of SHIPS, is the value of attribute Name of that member O of collection of members (of the class underlying the grouping) that form the contents of that member. For example, each member of the grouping class SHIP_TYPES has as the value of its Contents attribute the class of all ships of the type in question.

(5) The value of a member attribute can be specified to be derived from and equal to the value of some other attribute or mapping. For instance, attribute Date_last_examined of OIL_TANKERS has the derivation "same as Last_inspection.Date." (Note that this, in effect, introduces a member attribute as shorthand for a mapping.)

(6) Attribute A_1 can be defined as a *subvalue* attribute of some other (multivalued) member attribute or mapping (A_2). The value of A_2 is specified as consisting of a subclass of the value of A_1, that satisfies some specified predicate. For example, attribute Last_two_inspections of OIL_TANKERS is defined as "subvalue of Inspections where Order_for_tanker ≤ 2."

(7) The value of a member attribute can be specified as the intersection, union, or difference of two other (multivalued) member attributes or mappings. For example, attribute Contacts of OFFICERS has the definition "where is in Superiors or is in Subordinates," indicating that its value consists of an officer's superiors and subordinates.

(8) A member attribute derivation can specify that the value of the attribute is given by an arithmetic expression that involves the values of other member attributes or mappings. The involved attributes/mappings must have numeric values, that is, they must have value classes that are (eventual) subclasses of NUMBERS. The arithmetic operators allowed are addition ("+"), subtraction ("−"), multiplication ("•"), division ("/"), and exponentiation ("↑"). For example, attribute Top_speed_in_miles_per_hour of OIL_TANKERS has the derivation "= Absolute_top_speed/1.1" (to convert from knots).

(9) The operators "maximum," "minimum," "average," and "sum" can be applied to a member attribute or mapping that is multivalued; the value class of the attributes involved must be an (eventual) subclass of NUMBERS. The maximum, minimum, average, or sum is taken over the collection of entities that comprise the current value of the attribute or mapping.

(10) A member attribute can be defined to have its value equal to the number of members in a multivalued attribute or mapping. For example, attribute Number_of_instances of SHIP_TYPES has the derivation "number of members in Contents." "Number of unique members" is used similarly. "Number of members" and "number of unique members" differ only when duplicates are present in the multivalued attribute involved.

2.4.1.4 *The Definition of Member Attributes.* We now specify how these derivation mechanisms for derived attributes may be applied. The following rules are formulated in order to allow the use of derivations while avoiding the danger of inconsistent attribute specifications.

(1) Every attribute may or may not have an inverse; if it does, the inverse must be defined consistently with the attribute.

(2) Every member attribute A_1 satisfies one of the following cases.

(a) A_1 has exactly one derivation. In this case, the value A_1 is completely specified by the derivation. The inverse of A_1 (call it A_2), if it exists, may not have a derivation or a matching specification.

(b) A_1 has exactly one matching specification. In this case, the value of A_1 is completely specified by its relationships with an entity (or entities) to which it is matched (namely, member(s) of some class C). The inverse of A_1 (call it A_2), if it exists, may not have a derivation. It can have a matching specification, but this must match A_2 to C in a manner consistent with the matching specification of A_1.

(c) A_1 has neither a matching specification nor a derivation. In this case, it may be the case that the inverse of A_1 (call it A_2) has a matching specification or a derivation; if so, then one of the above two cases ((a) or (b)) applies. Otherwise, A_1 and A_2 form a pair of primitive values that are defined in terms of one another, but which are independent of all other information in the database.

With regard to updating the database, we note that in case (c), a user can explicitly provide a value for A_1 or for A_2 (and thereby establish values for both of them). In cases (a) and (b), neither A_1 nor A_2 can be directly modified; their values are changed by modifying other parts of the database.

2.4.2 *Class Attribute Interrelationships.* Attribute derivation primitives analogous to primitives (5)–(10) for member attributes can be used to define derived class attributes, as these primitives derive attribute values from those of other attributes. Of course, instead of deriving the value of a member attribute from the value of other member attributes, the class attribute primitives will derive the value of a class attribute from the value of other class attributes. In addition, there are two other primitives that can be used in the definition of derived class attributes.

(1) An attribute can be defined so that its value equals the number of members in the class it modifies. For example, attribute Number of INSPECTIONS has the derivation "number of members in this class."

(2) An attribute can be defined whose value is a function of a numeric member attribute of a class; the functions supported are "maximum," "minimum," "average," and "sum" taken over a member attribute. The computation of the function is made over the members of the class. For example, the class attribute Total_spilled of OIL_SPILLS has the derivation "sum of Amount_spilled over members of this class."

2.4.3 *Attribute Predicates for Subclass Definition.* As stated earlier, a subclass can be defined by means of a predicate on the member attributes of its parent class. Having described the specifics of attributes, it is now possible to detail the permissible types of attribute predicates. In particular, an attribute predicate is a simple predicate or a Boolean combination of simple predicates; the operators used to form such a Boolean combination are "and," "or," and "not." A simple predicate has one of the following forms:

(1) MAPPING SCALAR_COMPARATOR CONSTANT;
(2) MAPPING SCALAR_COMPARATOR MAPPING;
(3) MAPPING SET_COMPARATOR CONSTANT;

(4) MAPPING SET_COMPARATOR CLASS_NAME;

(5) MAPPING SET_COMPARATOR MAPPING.

Here, MAPPING is any mapping (including an attribute name as a special case); SCALAR_COMPARATOR is one of "=", "≠", ">", "≥", "<", and "≤"; CONSTANT is a string or number constant; SET_COMPARATOR is one of: "is contained in," "is properly contained in," "contains," and "properly contains"; CLASS_NAME is the name of some class defined in the schema. For illustration, an example of each of these five forms is provided below along with an indication of its meaning; the first two predicates define subclasses of class OFFICERS, while the third, fourth, and fifth apply to class SHIPS:

(1) Country_of_license = 'Panama' (officers licensed in Panama);

(2) Commander.Date_commissioned > Date_commissioned (officers commissioned before their commander);

(3) Cargo_types contains 'oil' (ships that can carry oil);

(4) Captain is contained in DANGEROUS_CAPTAINS (ships whose captain in the class containing officers that are bad risks);

(5) Captain.Country_of_license is contained in Captain.Superior.Country_of_license (ships commanded by an officer who has a superior licensed in the same country as he).

2.4.4 *Attribute Inheritance.* As noted earlier, it may often be the case that an entity in an SDM database belongs to more than one class. SDM classes can and frequently do share members, for example, a member of OIL_TANKERS is also a member of SHIPS; a member of OIL_SPILLS is also in INCIDENTS. As a member of a class C, a given entity E has values for each member attribute associated with C. But in addition, when viewed as a member C, E may have additional attributes that are not directly associated with C, but rather are *inherited* from other classes. For example, since all oil tankers are ships, each member T of the class OIL_TANKERS inherits the member attributes of SHIPS. In addition to the attributes Hull_type, Is_tanker_banned, Inspections, Number_of_times_inspected, Last_inspection, Last_two_inspections, Date_last_examined, and Oil_spills_involved_in, which are explicitly associated with OIL_TANKERS, T also has the attributes Name, Hull_number, Type, etc.; these are not mentioned in the definition of OIL_TANKERS but are inherited from SHIPS (a superclass of OIL_TANKERS). The value of each inherited attribute of tanker T is simply the value of that attribute of T when it is viewed as a member of SHIPS; the very same ship entity that belongs to OIL_TANKERS belongs also to SHIPS, so that the value of each such inherited attribute is well defined.

The following specific rules of attribute inheritance are applied in SDM.

(1) A class S that is an attribute-defined subclass of a class U, or a user-controllable subclass of U, inherits all of the member attributes of U. For example, since RURITANIAN_OIL_TANKERS is an attribute-defined subclass of OIL_TANKERS, RURITANIAN_OIL_TANKERS inherits all of the member attributes of OIL_TANKERS; in turn, members of OIL_TANKERS inherit all of the member attributes of SHIPS. Class attributes describe properties of a class taken as a whole and so are not inherited by an attribute-defined or user-controllable subclass. In order for an attribute to be inherited from class U by class S, both its meaning and its value must be the same for U and S. This is not true in general for class attributes. Although a subclass may have a similar class attribute to one defined for its parent class, for example, Number_of_members, their values will in general not be equal.

(2) A class S defined as an intersection subclass of classes U_1 and U_2 inherits all of the member attributes of U_1 and all of the member attributes of U_2. For example, the class BANNED_OIL_TANKERS, defined as containing all members of SHIP that are in both BANNED_SHIPS and OIL_TANKERS, inherits all attributes of BANNED_SHIPS as well as all of the attributes of OIL_TANKERS. This follows since each member of BANNED_OIL_TANKERS is both an oil tanker and a banned ship and so must have the attributes of both. Note that since BANNED_SHIPS and OIL_TANKERS are themselves defined as subclasses, they may inherit attributes from their parent classes which are in turn inherited by BANNED_OIL_TANKERS.

(3) A class S defined as the union of classes U_1 and U_2 inherits all of the member attributes shared by U_1 and U_2. For example, the class SHIPS_TO_BE_MONITORED inherits the member attributes shared by BANNED_SHIPS and OIL_TANKERS_REQUIRING_INSPECTION (which turn out to be all of the member attributes of SHIPS).

(4) A subclass S defined as the difference of classes, namely, consisting of all of the members in a class U that are not in class U_1, inherits all of the member attributes of U. This case is similar to (1), since S is a subclass of U.

These inheritance rules determine the attributes associated with classes that are defined in terms of interclass connections. These rules need not be explicitly applied by the SDM user; they are an integral part of SDM and are automatically applied wherever appropriate.

2.4.4.1 *Further Constraining an Inherited Member Attribute.* An important constraint may be placed on inherited attributes in an SDM schema. This constraint requires that the value of an attribute A inherited from class C_1 by class C_2 be a member of a class C_3 (C_3 is a subclass of the value class of A). To specify such a constraint, the name of the inherited attribute is repeated in the definition of the member attributes of the subclass, and its constrained value class is specified. For example, attribute Cargo_types is inherited by MERCHANT_SHIPS from SHIPS; its repetition in the definition of MERCHANT_SHIPS indicates that the value class of Cargo_types for MERCHANT_SHIPS is restricted to MERCHANT_CARGO_TYPE_NAMES. Values of attribute Cargo_types of SHIPS must satisfy this constraint. If the value being inherited does not satisfy this constraint, then the attribute's value is null.

2.5 Duplicates and Null Values

As specified above, an SDM class is either a set or a multiset: It may or may not contain duplicates. If a class has unique identifiers, then it obviously cannot have duplicates. If unique identifiers are not present, then the default is that duplicates are allowed. However, a class can be explicitly defined with "duplicates not allowed." Duplicates may also be present in attribute values, since attribute derivation specifications and mappings can yield duplicates.

In point of fact, the existence or nonexistence of duplicates is only of importance when considering the number of members in a class or the size of a multivalued attribute. On most occasions, the user need not be concerned with whether or not duplicates are present. Consequently, the only SDM primitives that are affected by duplicates are those that concern the number of members in a class and the size of an attribute. The SDM interclass connections and attribute derivation primitives are defined so as to propagate duplicates in an intuitive manner. For example, attribute-defined and user-controllable subclasses contain duplicates if and only if their parent class contains duplicates; and, if the class underlying a grouping has duplicates, the contents of the groups will similarly contain duplicates. Further details of this approach to handling duplicates are provided in [27].

As stated above, any attribute not defined as "mandatory" may have "null" as its value. While the treatment of null values is not a simple issue, we state that for the purposes here null is treated just like any other data value. A detailed discussion of null value handling is beyond the scope of this paper (see [14] for such a discussion).

2.6 SDM Data Definition Language

As noted above, this paper provides a specific *database definition language* (*DDL*) for SDM. The foregoing description of SDM did not rely on a specific DDL syntax although the discussion proceeded through numerous examples expressed in a particular sample DDL syntax. Many forms of DDL syntax could be used to describe SDM schemas, and we have selected one of them in order to make the specification of SDM precise.

The syntax of SDM DDL is presented in Appendix B, expressed in Backus–Naur form style. The particular conventions used are described at the beginning of Appendix B. For the most part, the syntax description is self-explanatory; however, the following points are worthy of note.

(1) Syntactic categories are capitalized (with no interspersed spaces, but possibly including "___"s). All lowercase strings are in the language itself, except those enclosed in "•"s; the latter are descriptions of syntactic categories whose details are obvious.

(2) Indentation is an essential part of the SDM DDL syntax. In Appendix B, the first level of indentation is used for presentation, while all others indicate indentation in the syntax itself. For example, MEMBER_ATTRIBUTES is defined as consisting of "member attributes," followed by a group of one or more member attribute items (placed vertically below "member attributes").

(3) Many rules that constrain the set of legal SDM schemata are not included in the syntax shown in the figure. For example, in SDM, the rule that attributes of different applicability (member attributes and class attributes) must not be mixed in is not included in the syntax, as its incorporation therein would be too cumbersome. A similar statement can be made for the rules that arithmetic expressions must be computed on attributes whose values are numbers, that a common underlying class must exist for classes defined by multiset operator interclass connections, and so forth.

2.7 Operations on an SDM Database

An important part of any database model is the set of operations that can be performed on it. The operations defined for SDM allow a user to derive information from a database, to update a database (adding new information to it or correcting information in it), and to include new structural information in it (change an SDM schema) [27]. Note that operations to derive information from an SDM schema are closely related to SDM primitives for describing derived information (e.g., nonbase classes and derived attributes). There is a vocabulary of basic SDM operations that are application environment independent and predefined. The set of permissible operations is designed to permit only semantically meaningful manipulations of an SDM database. User-defined operations can be constructed using the primitives. A detailed specification of the SDM operations is beyond the scope of this paper.

3. DISCUSSION

In this paper, we have presented the major features of SDM, a high-level data modeling mechanism. The goal of SDM is to provide the designer and user of a database with a formalism whereby a substantial portion of the semantic structure of the application environment can be clearly and precisely expressed. Contemporary database models do not support such direct conceptual modeling, for a number of reasons that are summarized above and explored in greater detail in [22]. In brief, these conventional database models are too oriented toward computer data structures to allow for the natural expression of application semantics. SDM, on the other hand, is based on the high-level concepts of entities, attributes, and classes.

In several ways, SDM is analogous to a number of recent proposals in database modeling, including [1, 3, 5, 9, 14, 31, 33, 34, 39–41, 43, 46]. Where SDM principally differs from these is in the extent of the structure of the application domain that it can capture and in its emphasis on relativism, flexibility, and redundancy. An SDM schema does more than just describe the kinds of objects that are captured in the database; it allows for substantial amounts of structural information that specifies how the entities and their classes are related to one another. Furthermore, it is a fundamental premise of SDM that a semantic schema for a database should directly support multiple ways of viewing the same information, since different users inevitably will have differing slants on the database and even a single user's perspective will evolve over time. Consequently, redundant information (in the form of nonbase classes and derived attributes) plays an important role in an SDM schema, and provides the principal mechanism for expressing multiple versions of the same information.

3.1 The Design of SDM

In the design of SDM, we have sought to provide a higher level and richer modeling language than that of conventional database models, without developing a large and complex facility containing a great many features (as exemplified by some of the knowledge representation and world modeling systems developed by the artificial intelligence community, e.g., [35, 51]). We have sought neither absolute minimality, with a small number of mutually orthogonal constructs, nor a profusion of special case facilities to precisely model each slightly different type of application. There is a significant trade-off between the complexity of a modeling facility and its power, naturalness, and precision. If a database model contains a large number of features, then it will likely be difficult to learn and to apply; however, it will have the potential of realizing schemata that are very sharp and precise models of their application domains. On the other hand, a model with a fairly minimal set of features will be easier to learn and employ, but a schema constructed with it will capture less of the particular characteristics of its application.

We have sought a middle road between these two extremes, with a relatively small number of basic features, augmented by a set of special features that are particularly useful in a large number of instances. We adhere to the principle of the well-known "80-20" rule; in this context, this rule would suggest that 80 percent of the modeling cases can be handled with 20 percent of the total number of special features that would be required by a fully detailed modeling formalism. Thus, a user of SDM should find that the application constructs that he most frequently encounters are directly provided by SDM, while he will have to represent the less common ones by means of more generic features. To this end, we have included such special facilities as the inverse and matching mechanisms for attribute derivation, but have not, for example, sought to taxonomize entity types more fully (since to do so in a meaningful and useful way would greatly expand the size and complexity of SDM). We have also avoided the introduction of a huge number of attribute derivation primitives, limiting ourselves to the ones that should be of most critical importance. For example, there does not exist a derivation primitive for class attributes to determine what percentage the members of the class constitute of another class. Such special cases would be most usefully handled by means of a general-purpose computational mechanism.

SDM as presented in this paper is neither complete nor final. SDM as a whole is open to any number of extensions. The most significant omission in this paper is that of the operations that can be applied to an SDM database: the database manipulation facility associated with the database definition facility presented here. Such a presentation would be too lengthy for this paper and can be found in [27]. In brief, however, the design of SDM is strongly based on the duality principle between schema and procedure, as developed in [21]. From this perspective, any query against the database can be seen as a reference to a particular virtual data item; whether that item can easily be accessed in the database, or whether it can only be located by means of the application of a number of database manipulation operations, depends on what information has been included in the schema by the database designer. Frequently retrieved data items would most likely be present in the schema, often as derived data, while less commonly requested information would have to be dynamically computed. In both cases, however, the same sets of primitives should be employed to describe the data item(s) in question, since dynamic data retrieval and static definitions of derived data are fundamentally equivalent, differing only in the occasions of their binding. Thus the SDM database manipulation facility strongly resembles the database facilities described above for computing nonbase classes and derived attributes. Among other beneficial consequences, this duality allows for a natural evolution of the semantic schema to reflect changing patterns of use and access: As certain kinds of requests become more common, they can be incorporated as derived data into the schema and thereby greatly simplify their retrieval.

3.2 Extensions

Numerous extensions can be made to SDM as presented here. These include extending SDM by means of additional general facilities, as well as tailoring special versions of it (by adding application environment specific facilities). For example, as it currently is defined, derived data is continuously updated so as always to be consistent with the primitive data from which it is computed. Alternative, less dynamic modes of computation could be provided, so that in some cases derived data might represent a snapshot of some other aspect of the database at a certain time. Similarly, a richer set of attribute inheritance rules, possibly under user control, might be provided to enable more complex relationships between classes and their subclasses. In the other direction, a current investigation is being conducted with the goal of simplifying SDM and accommodating more relativism [30]. Further, an attempt is currently under way to construct a version of SDM that contains primitives especially relevant to the office environment (such as documents, events, and organization hierarchies), to facilitate the natural modeling and description of office structures and procedures.

3.3 Applications

We envision a variety of potential uses and applications for SDM. As described in this paper, SDM is simply an abstract database modeling mechanism and language that is not dependent on any supporting computer system. One set of applications uses SDM in precisely this mode to support the process of defining and designing a database as well as in facilitating its subsequent evolution. It is well known that the process of logical database design, wherein the database administrator (DBA) must construct a schema using the database model of the database management system (DBMS) to be employed, is a difficult and error-prone procedure [10, 30, 31, 37, 38, 42, 44, 50]. A primary reason for this difficulty is the distance between the semantic level of the application and the data structures of the database model; the DBA must bridge this gap in a single step, simultaneously conducting an information requirements analysis and expressing the results of his analysis in terms of the database model. What is lacking is a formalism in which to express the information content of the database in a way that is independent of the details of the database model associated with the underlying DBMS. SDM can be used as a higher-level database model in which the DBA describes the database prior to designing a logical schema for it. There are a number of advantages to using the SDM in this way:

(1) An SDM schema will serve as a specification of the information that the database will contain. All too often, only the most vague and amorphous English language descriptions of a database exist prior to the database design process. A formal specification can more accurately, completely, and consistently communicate to the actual designer the prescribed contents of the database. SDM provides some structure for the logical database design process. The DBA can first seek to describe the database in high-level semantic terms, and then reduce that schema to a more conventional logical

design. By decomposing the design problem in this way, its difficulty as a whole can be reduced.

(2) SDM supports a basic methodology that can guide the DBA in the design process by providing him with a set of natural design templates. That is, the DBA can approach the application in question with the intent of identifying its classes, subclasses, and so on. Having done so, he can select representations for these constructs in a routine, if not algorithmic, fashion.

(3) SDM provides an effective base for accommodating the evolution of the content structure, and use of a database. Relativism, logical redundancy, and derived information support this natural evolution of schemata.

A related use of SDM is as a medium for documenting a database. One of the more serious problems facing a novice user of a large database is determining the information content of the database and locating in the schema the information of use to him. An SDM schema for a database can serve as a readable description of its contents, organized in terms that a user is likely to be able to comprehend and identify. A cross-index of the schema would amount to a semantic data dictionary, identifying the principal features of the application environment and cataloging their relationships. Such specifications and documentation would also be independent of the DBMS being employed to actually manage the data, and so could be of particular use in the context of DBMS selection or of a conversion from one DBMS to another. An example of the use of SDM for specification and documentation is [15].

On another plane are a number of applications that require that SDM schema for a database be processed and utilized by a computer system. One such application would be to employ SDM as the conceptual schema database model for a DBMS within the three-schema architecture of the ANSI/SPARC proposal [2]. In such a system, the conceptual schema is a representation of the fundamental semantics of the database. The external views of the data (those employed by programmers and end-users) are defined in terms of it, while a mapping from it to physical file structures establishes the database's internal schema (storage and representation). Because of its high level and support for multiple views, SDM could be effectively employed in this role. Once occupying such a central position in the DBMS, the SDM schema could also be used to support any number of "intelligent" database applications that depend on a rich understanding of the semantics of the data in question. For example, an SDM schema could drive an automatic semantic integrity checker, which would examine incoming data and test its plausibility and likelihood of error in the context of a semantic model of the database. A number of such systems have been proposed [16, 19, 20, 45], but they are generally based on the use of expressions in the first-order predicate calculus that are added to a relational schema. This approach introduces a number of problems, ranging from the efficiency of the checking to the modularity and reliability of the resulting model. By directly capturing the semantics in the schema rather than in some external mechanism, SDM might more directly support such data checking. Another "semantics-based" application to which SDM has been applied is an interactive system that assists a naive user, unfamiliar with the information content of the database, in formulating a query against it [28].

It might even be desirable to employ SDM as the database model in terms of which all database users see the database. This would entail building an SDM DBMS. Of course, a high-level database model raises serious problems of efficiency of representation and processing. However, it can also result in easier and more effective use of the data which may in the aggregate dominate the performance issues. Furthermore, SDM can be additionally extended to be more than just a database model; it can serve as the foundation for a total integrated database programming language in which both the facilities for accessing a database and those for computing with the data so accessed are combined in a coherent and consistent fashion [18]. And, SDM can provide a basis for describing and structuring logically decentralized and physically distributed database systems [22, 29].

APPENDIX A. AN SDM SCHEMA FOR THE TANKER MONITORING APPLICATION ENVIRONMENT

SHIPS
description: all ships with potentially hazardous cargoes that
  may enter U.S. coastal waters
member attributes:
Name
  value class: SHIP_NAMES
Hull_number
  value class: HULL_NUMBERS
  may not be null
  not changeable
Type
  description: the kind of ship, for example, merchant or fishing
  value class: SHIP_TYPE_NAMES
Country_of_registry
  value class: COUNTRIES
  inverse: Ships_registered_here
Name_of_home_port
  value class: PORT_NAMES
Cargo_types
  description: the type(s) of cargo the ship can carry
  value class: CARGO_TYPE_NAMES
  multivalued
Captain
  description: the current captain of the ship
  value class: OFFICERS
  match: Officer of ASSIGNMENTS on Ship
Engines
  value class: ENGINES
  multivalued with size between 0 and 10
  exhausts value class
  no overlap in values
Incidents_involved_in
  value class: INCIDENTS
  inverse: Involved_ship
  multivalued
identifiers:
Name
Hull_number

INSPECTIONS
description: inspections of oil tankers
member attributes:
  Tanker
    description: the tanker inspected
    value class: OIL__TANKERS
    inverse: Inspections
  Date
    value class: DATES
  Order__for__tanker
    description: the ordering of the inspections for a tanker
    with the most recent inspection having value 1
    value class: INTEGERS
    derivation: order by decreasing Date within Tanker
class attributes:
  Number
    description: the number of inspections in the database
    value class: INTEGERS
    derivation: number of members in this class
identifiers:
  Tanker + Date

COUNTRIES
description: countries of registry for ships
member attributes:
  Name
    value class: COUNTRY__NAMES
  Ships__registered__here
    value class: SHIPS
    inverse: Country__of__registry
    multivalued
identifiers:
  Name

OFFICERS
description: all certified officers of ships
member attributes:
  Name
    value class: PERSON__NAMES
  Country__of__license
    value class: COUNTRIES
  Date__commissioned
    value class: DATES
  Seniority
    value class: INTEGERS
    derivation: order by Date__commissioned
  Commander
    description: the officer in direct command of this officer
    value class: OFFICERS
  Superiors
    value class: OFFICERS
    derivation: all levels of values of Commander
    inverse: Subordinates
    multivalued
  Subordinates
    value class: OFFICERS
    inverse: Superiors
    multivalued
  Contacts
    value class: OFFICERS
    derivation: where is in Superiors or is in Subordinates
identifiers:
  Name

ENGINES
description: ship engines
member attributes:
  Serial__number
    value class: ENGINE__SERIAL__NUMBERS
  Kind__of__engine
    value class: ENGINE__TYPE__NAMES
identifiers:
  Serial__number

INCIDENTS
description: accidents involving ships
member attributes:
  Involved__ship
    value class: SHIPS
    inverse: Incidents__involved__in
  Date
    value class: DATES
  Description
    description: textual explanation of the accident
    value class: INCIDENT__DESCRIPTIONS
  Involved__captain
    value class: OFFICERS
identifiers:
  Involved__ship + Date + Description

ASSIGNMENTS
description: assignments of captains to ships
member attributes:
  Officer
    value class: OFFICERS
  Ship
    value class: SHIPS
identifiers:
  Officer + Ship

OIL__TANKERS
description: oil-carrying ships
interclass connection: subclass of SHIPS where Cargo__types contains 'oil'
member attributes:
  Hull__type
    description: specification of single or double hull
    value class: HULL__TYPE__NAMES
  Is__tanker__banned?
    value class: YES/NO
    derivation: if in BANNED__SHIPS
  Inspections
    value class: INSPECTIONS
    inverse: Tanker
    multivalued
  Number__of__times__inspected
    value class: INTEGERS

        derivation: number of unique members in Inspections
    Last_inspection
        value class: MOST_RECENT_INSPECTIONS
        inverse: Tanker
    Last_two_inspections
        value class: INSPECTIONS
        derivation: subvalue of inspections where
            Order_for_tanker ≤ 2
        multivalued
    Date_last_examined
        value class: DATES
        derivation: same as Last_inspection.Date
    Oil_spills_involved_in
        value class: INCIDENTS
        derivation: subvalue of Incidents_involved_in
            where is in OIL_SPILLS
        multivalued
    class attributes:
    Absolute_top_legal_speed
        value class: KNOTS
    Top_legal_speed_in_miles_per_hour
        value class: MILES_PER_HOUR
        derivation: = Absolute_top_legal_speed/1.1

RURITANIAN_SHIPS
    interclass connection: subclass of SHIPS where
        Country.Name = 'Ruritania'

RURITANIAN_OIL_TANKERS
    interclass connection: subclass of OIL_TANKERS where
        Country.Name = 'Ruritania'

MERCHANT_SHIPS
    interclass connection: subclass of SHIPS where Type = 'merchant'
    member attributes:
    Cargo_types
        value class: MERCHANT_CARGO_TYPE_NAMES

OIL_SPILLS
    interclass connection: subclass of INCIDENTS where
        Description = 'oil spill'
    member attributes:
    Amount_spilled
        value class: GALLONS
    Severity
        derivation: = Amount_spilled/100,000
    class attributes:
    Total_spilled
        value class: GALLONS
        derivation: sum of Amount_spilled over members of this class

MOST_RECENT_INSPECTIONS
    interclass connection: subclass of INSPECTIONS where
        Order_for_tanker = 1

DANGEROUS_CAPTAINS
    description: captains who have been involved in an accident
    interclass connection: subclass of OFFICERS where is a value of Involved_captain of
        INCIDENTS

BANNED_SHIPS
    description: ships banned from U.S. coastal waters
    interclass connection: subclass of SHIPS where specified
    member attributes:
    Date_banned
        value class: DATES

OIL_TANKERS_REQUIRING_INSPECTION
    interclass connection: subclass of OIL_TANKERS where specified
        is in BANNED_SHIPS and is in OIL_TANKERS

BANNED_OIL_TANKERS
    interclass connection: subclass of SHIPS where
        is in BANNED_SHIPS and is in OIL_TANKERS

SAFE_SHIPS
    description: ships that are considered good risks
    interclass connection: subclass of SHIPS where is not in BANNED_SHIPS

SHIPS_TO_BE_MONITORED
    description: ships that are considered bad risks
    interclass connection: subclass of SHIPS where is in BANNED_SHIPS
        or is in OIL_TANKERS_REQUIRING_INSPECTION

SHIP_TYPES
    description: types of ships
    interclass connection: grouping of SHIPS on common value of Type
        groups defined as classes are MERCHANT_SHIPS
    member attributes:
    Instances
        description: the instances of the type of ship
        value class: SHIPS
        derivation: same as Contents
        multivalued
    Number_of_ships_of_this_type
        value class: INTEGERS
        derivation: number of members in Contents

CARGO_TYPE_GROUPS
    interclass connection: grouping of SHIPS on common value of
        Cargo_types

TYPES_OF_HAZARDOUS_SHIPS
    interclass connection: grouping of SHIPS consisting of classes
        BANNED_SHIPS, BANNED_OIL_TANKERS,
        SHIPS_TO_BE_MONITORED

CONVOYS
    interclass connection: grouping of SHIPS as specified
    member attributes:
    Oil_tanker_constituents
        description: the oil tankers that are in the convoy (if any)
        value class: SHIPS
        derivation: subvalue of Contents where is in OIL_TANKERS
        multivalued

CARGO_TYPE_NAMES
    description: the types of cargo
    interclass connection: subclass of STRINGS

MERCHANT_CARGO_TYPE_NAMES
    interclass connection: subclass of CARGO_TYPE_NAMES
        where specified

COUNTRY_NAMES
    interclass connection: subclass of STRINGS where specified

ENGINE_SERIAL_NUMBERS
    interclass connection: subclass of STRINGS where format is

(3) Syntactic categories are capitalized while all literals are in lowercase.
(4) { } means optional.
(5) [ ] means one of the enclosed choices must appear; choices are separated by a ";" (when used with "{ }") one of the choices may optionally appear).
(6) ( ) means one or more of the enclosed can appear, separated by spaces with optional commas and an optional "and" at the end.
(7) ⟨ ⟩ means one or more of the enclosed can appear, vertically appended.
(8) • • encloses a "meta"-description of a syntactic category (to informally explain it).

```
SCHEMA ←
    ⟨(CLASS)⟩
CLASS ←
    (CLASS_NAME)
    {description: CLASS_DESCRIPTION}
    {[BASE_CLASS_FEATURES; INTERCLASS_CONNECTION]}
    {MEMBER_ATTRIBUTES}
    {CLASS_ATTRIBUTES}
CLASS_NAME ←
    •string of capitals possibly including special characters•
CLASS_DESCRIPTION ←
    •string•
BASE_CLASS_FEATURES ←
    {[duplicates allowed; duplicates not allowed]}
    {(⟨IDENTIFIERS⟩)}
IDENTIFIERS ←
    [ATTRIBUTE_NAME; ATTRIBUTE_NAME + IDENTIFIERS]
MEMBER_ATTRIBUTES ←
    member attributes:
    ⟨(MEMBER_ATTRIBUTE)⟩
CLASS_ATTRIBUTES ←
    class attributes:
    ⟨(CLASS_ATTRIBUTE)⟩
INTERCLASS_CONNECTION ←
    [SUBCLASS; GROUPING_CLASS]
SUBCLASS ←
    subclass of CLASS_NAME where SUBCLASS_PREDICATE
GROUPING ←
    [grouping of CLASS_NAME on common value of (ATTRIBUTE_NAME)
    {groups defined as classes are ⟨CLASS_NAME⟩};
    grouping of CLASS_NAME consisting of classes ⟨CLASS_NAME⟩;
    grouping of CLASS_NAME as specified]
SUBCLASS_PREDICATE ←
    [ATTRIBUTE_PREDICATE;
    specified;
    is in CLASS_NAME and is in CLASS_NAME;
    is not in CLASS_NAME;
    is in CLASS_NAME or is in CLASS_NAME;
    is a value of ATTRIBUTE_NAME of CLASS_NAME;
    format is FORMAT]
ATTRIBUTE_PREDICATE ←
    [SIMPLE_PREDICATE; ⟨ATTRIBUTE_PREDICATE⟩;
    not ATTRIBUTE_PREDICATE;
```

"H"
    number where integer and ≥1 and ≤999
"_"
    number where integer and ≥0 and ≤999999
DATES
    description: calendar dates in the range "1/1/75" to "12/31/79"
    interclass connection: subclass of STRINGS where format is
    "/"
    month: number where ≥1 and ≤12
    "/"
    day: number where integer and ≥1 and ≤31
    "/"
    year: number where integer and ≥1970 and ≤2000
    where (if (month = 4 or = 5 or = 9 or = 11) then day ≤30)
    and (if month = 2 then day ≤29)
    ordering by year, month, day
ENGINE_TYPE_NAMES
    interclass connection: subclass of STRINGS where specified
GALLONS
    interclass connection: subclass of STRINGS where format is
    number where integer
HULL_NUMBERS
    interclass connection: subclass of STRINGS where format is
    number where integer
HULL_TYPE_NAMES
    interclass connection: subclass of STRINGS where specified
    description: single or double
INCIDENT_DESCRIPTIONS
    description: textual description of an accident
    interclass connection: subclass of STRINGS
KNOTS
    interclass connection: subclass of STRINGS where format is
    number where integer
MILES_PER_HOUR
    interclass connection: subclass of STRINGS where format is
    number where integer
PORT_NAMES
    interclass connection: subclass of STRINGS
PERSON_NAMES
    interclass connection: subclass of STRINGS
SHIP_NAMES
    interclass connection: subclass of STRINGS
SHIP_TYPE_NAMES
    description: the names of the ship types, for example, merchant
    interclass connection: subclass of STRINGS where specified

APPENDIX B. SYNTAX OF THE SDM DATA DEFINITION LANGUAGE

The following list is given to clarify and define some of the items and terms used in this appendix.

(1) The left side of a production is separated from the right by a "←".
(2) The first level of indentation in the syntax description is used to help separate the left and right sides of a production; all other indentation is in the SDM data definition language.

= MAPPING_EXPRESSION;
[maximum; minimum; average; sum] of MAPPING;
number of (unique) members in MAPPING]
MEMBER-SPECIFIC_DERIVATION ←
[order by [increasing; decreasing] (MAPPING)
(within (MAPPING));
if in CLASS_NAME;
[up to CONSTANT; all] levels of values of ATTRIBUTE_NAME;
contents]
CLASS-SPECIFIC_DERIVATION ←
[number of (unique) members in this class;
[maximum; minimum; average; sum] of ATTRIBUTE_NAME over
members of this class]
MAPPING EXPRESSION ←
[MAPPING; (MAPPING); MAPPING NUMBER_OPERATOR MAPPING]
NUMBER OPERATOR ←
[+; -; ×; /; ↑]

ATTRIBUTE_PREDICATE and ATTRIBUTE_PREDICATE;
ATTRIBUTE_PREDICATE or ATTRIBUTE_PREDICATE]
SIMPLE_PREDICATE ←
[MAPPING SCALAR_COMPARATOR [CONSTANT; MAPPING];
MAPPING SET_COMPARATOR [CONSTANT; CLASS_NAME; MAPPING]]
MAPPING ←
[ATTRIBUTE_NAME; MAPPING.ATTRIBUTE_NAME]
SCALAR_COMPARATOR ←
[EQUAL_COMPARATOR; >; ≥; <; ≤]
EQUAL_COMPARATOR ←
[=; ≠]
SET_COMPARATOR ←
[is (properly) contained in; (properly) contains]
CONSTANT ←
•a string or number constant•
FORMAT ←
•a name class definition pattern•
(see [26])
MEMBER_ATTRIBUTE ←
(ATTRIBUTE_NAME)
(ATTRIBUTE_DESCRIPTION)
value class:CLASS_NAME
[inverse:ATTRIBUTE_NAME]
[[match:ATTRIBUTE_NAME of CLASS_NAME on ATTRIBUTE_NAME];
derivation:MEMBER_ATTRIBUTE_DERIVATION])
(single valued; multivalued [with size between CONSTANT and CONSTANT])
(may not be null)
(not changeable)
(exhausts value class)
(no overlap in values)
CLASS_ATTRIBUTE ←
(ATTRIBUTE_NAME)
(ATTRIBUTE_DESCRIPTION)
value class:CLASS_NAME
derivation:CLASS_ATTRIBUTE_DERIVATION])
(single valued; multivalued [with size between CONSTANT and CONSTANT])
(may not be null)
(not changeable)
ATTRIBUTE_NAME ←
•string of lowercase letters beginning with a capital and possibly
including special characters•
ATTRIBUTE_DESCRIPTION ←
•"string."
MEMBER_ATTRIBUTE_DERIVATION ←
[INTERATTRIBUTE_DERIVATION;
MEMBER-SPECIFIC_DERIVATION]
CLASS_ATTRIBUTE_DERIVATION ←
[INTERATTRIBUTE_DERIVATION;
CLASS-SPECIFIC_DERIVATION]
INTERATTRIBUTE_DERIVATION ←
[same as MAPPING;
subvalue of MAPPING where [is in CLASS_NAME; ATTRIBUTE_PREDICATE];
where [is in MAPPING and is in MAPPING; is in MAPPING or is in MAPPING;
is in MAPPING and is not in MAPPING];

ACKNOWLEDGMENTS

The authors wish to thank the following persons for their comments on the current or earlier versions of this paper, SDM, and related work: Antonio Albano, Arvola Chan, Peter Chen, Ted Codd, Dennis Heimbigner, Roger King, Peter Kreps, Frank Manola, Paula Newman, Diane and John Smith. In particular, Diane and John Smith helped the authors realize some of the weaknesses of an earlier version of SDM vis-a-vis relativism. Ted Codd's RM/T model has also provided many ideas concerning the specifics of SDM. DAPLEX (of Dave Shipman) and FQL (of Peter Buneman and Robert Frankel) have aided us in formulating various SDM constructs (e.g., mapping). Work performed at the Computer Corporation of America (under Frank Manola) and at the Lockheed California Company (under Don Kawamoto) has provided valuable input regarding the practical use of SDM. Finally, the referees provided many helpful comments concerning both the substance and presentation of this paper; their observations and suggestions are gratefully acknowledged.

Note: Because of the lack of neuter personal pronouns in English, the terms "he," "his," etc., are used throughout this paper to refer to an individual who may be either male or female.

REFERENCES
1. ABRIAL, J.R. Data semantics. In Database Management. J. Klimbie and K. Koffeman. Eds. North-Holland, Amsterdam, 1974.
2. ANSI/X3/SPARC (Standards Planning and Requirements Committee). Interim report from the study group on database management systems. FDT (Bulletin of ACM SIGMOD) 7, 2 (1975).
3. BACHMAN, C.W. The role concept in data models. In Proc. Int. Conf. Very Large Databases. Tokyo, Japan, Oct. 1977.
4. BILLER, H., AND NEUHOLD, E.J. Semantics of databases: The semantics of data models. Inf. Syst. 3 (1978), 11–30.
5. BUNEMAN, P., AND FRANKEL, R.E. FQL—A functional query language. In Proc. ACM SIGMOD Int. Conf. Management of Data, Boston, Mass. 1979.

6. BUNEMAN, P., AND MORGAN, H.L. Implementing alerting techniques in database systems. In *Proc. COMPSAC'77*, Chicago, Ill., Nov. 1977.

7. CHAMBERLIN, D.D. Relational database management systems. *Comput. Surv. 8*, 1 (March 1976), 43–66.

8. CHANG, C.L. A hyper-relational model of databases. IBM Res. Rep. RJ1634, IBM, San Jose, Calif., Aug. 1975.

9. CHEN, P.P.S. The entity-relationship model: Toward a unified view of data. *ACM Trans. Database Syst. 1*, 1 (March 1976), 9–36.

10. CHEN, P.P.S. The entity-relationship approach to logical database design. Mono. 6, QED Information Sciences, Wellesley, Mass., 1978.

11. CODASYL COMMITTEE ON DATA SYSTEM LANGUAGES. Codasyl database task group report. ACM, New York, 1971.

12. CODD, E.F. A relational model of data for large shared data banks. *Commun. ACM 13*, 6 (June 1970), 377–387.

13. CODD, E.F. Further normalization of the database relational model. In *Database Systems*, Courant Computer Science Symposia 6, R. Rustin, Ed. Prentice-Hall, Englewood Cliffs, N.J., 1971, pp. 65–98.

14. CODD, E.F. Extending the database relational model to capture more meaning. *ACM Trans. Database Syst. 4*, 4 (Dec. 1979), 397–434.

15. COMPUTER CORPORATION OF AMERICA. DBMS—Independent CICIS specifications. Tech. Rep. CCA, Cambridge, Mass., 1979.

16. ESWARAN, K.P., AND CHAMBERLIN, D.D. Functional specifications of a subsystem for database integrity. In *Proc. Int. Conf. Very Large Databases*, Framingham, Mass., Sept. 1975.

17. HAMMER, M. Research directions in database management. In *Research Directions in Software Technology*, P. Wegner, Ed. The M.I.T. Press, Cambridge, Mass., 1979.

18. HAMMER, M., AND BERKOWITZ, B. DIAL: A programming language for data-intensive applications. Working Paper, M.I.T. Lab. Computer Science, Cambridge, Mass., 1980.

19. HAMMER, M., AND McLEOD, D. Semantic integrity in a relational database system. In *Proc. Int. Conf. Very Large Databases*, Framingham, Mass., Sept. 1975.

20. HAMMER, M., AND McLEOD, D. A framework for database semantic integrity. In *Proc. 2nd Int. Conf. Software Engineering*, San Francisco, Calif., Oct. 1976.

21. HAMMER, M., AND McLEOD, D. The semantic data model: A modelling mechanism for database applications. In *Proc. ACM SIGMOD Int. Conf. Management of Data*, Austin, Tex., 1978.

22. HAMMER, M., AND McLEOD, D. On the architecture of database management systems. In *Infotech State-of-the-Art Report on Data Design*. Pergamon Infotech Ltd., Berkshire, England, 1980.

23. KENT, W. *Data and Reality*. North-Holland, Amsterdam, 1978.

24. KENT, W. Limitations of record-based information models. *ACM Trans. Database Syst. 4*, 1 (March 1979), 107–131.

25. LEE, R.M., AND GERRITSEN, R. Extended semantics for generalization hierarchies. In *Proc. ACM SIGMOD Int. Conf. Management of Data*, Austin, Tex. 1978.

26. McLEOD, D. High level definition of abstract domains in a relational database system. *J. Comput. Languages 2*, 3 (1977).

27. McLEOD, D. A semantic database model and its associated structured user interface. Tech. Rep., M.I.T. Lab. Computer Science, Cambridge, Mass. 1978.

28. McLEOD, D. A database transaction specification methodology for end-users. Tech. Rep., Computer Science Dep. Univ. Southern California, Los Angeles, Calif., 1980.

29. McLEOD, D., AND HEIMBIGNER, D. A federated architecture for database systems. In *Proc. ACM SIGMOD Int. Conf. Management of Data*, Austin, Tex. 1978.

30. McLEOD, D., AND KING, R. Applying a semantic database model. In *Proc. Int. Conf. Entity-Relationship Approach to Systems Analysis and Design*. Los Angeles, Calif., Dec. 1979.

31. MYLOPOULOS, J., BERNSTEIN, P.A., AND WONG, H. K. T. A language facility for designing interactive database-intensive applications. In *Proc. ACM SIGMOD Int. Conf. Management of Data*, Austin, Tex. 1978.

32. PALMER, I. Record subtype facilities in database systems. In *Proc. 4th Int. Conf. Very Large Databases*. Berlin, West Germany, Sept. 1978.

33. PIROTTE, A. The entity-property-association model: An information-oriented database model. Tech. Rep., M.B.L.E. Res. Lab., Brussels, Belgium, 1977.

34. ROUSSOPOULOS, N. Algebraic data definition. In *Proc. 6th Texas Conf. Computing Systems*, Austin, Tex. Nov. 1977.

35. SCHANK, R.C. Identification of conceptualizations underlying natural language. In *Computer Models of Thought and Language*, R.C. Schank and K.M. Colby, Eds. W.H. Freeman, San Francisco, Calif. 1973.

36. SCHMID, H.A. AND SWENSON, J.R. On the semantics of the relational data model. In *Proc. ACM SIGMOD Int. Conf. Management of Data*, San Jose, Calif. 1975.

37. SENKO, M.E. Information systems: Records, relations, sets, entities, and things. *Inf. Syst. 1*, 1 (1975), 3–14.

38. SENKO, M.E. Conceptual schemas, abstract data structures, enterprise descriptions. In *Proc. ACM Int. Computing Symp.*, Belgium, April 1977.

39. SHIPMAN, D. W. The functional data model and the data language DAPLEX. *ACM Trans. Database Syst. 6*, 1 (March 1981), 140–173.

40. SMITH, J.M., AND SMITH, D.C.P. Database abstractions:Aggregation. *Commun. ACM 20*, 6 (June 1977), 405–413.

41. SMITH, J.M., AND SMITH, D.C.P. Database abstractions:Aggregation and generalization. *ACM Trans. Database Syst. 2*, 2 (June 1977), 105–133.

42. SMITH, J.M., AND SMITH, D.C.P. Principles of conceptual database design. In *Proc. NYU Symp. Database Design*, New York, May 1978.

43. SMITH, J.M., AND SMITH, D.C.P. A database approach to software specification. Tech. Rep. CCA-79-17, Computer Corporation of America, Cambridge, Mass., April 1979.

44. SOLVBERG, A. A contribution to the definition of concepts for expressing users' information system requirements. In *Proc. Int. Conf. Entity-Relationship Approach to Systems Analysis and Design*, Los Angeles, Calif., Dec. 1979.

45. STONEBRAKER, M.R. High level integrity assurance in relational database management systems. Electronics Res. Lab. Rep. ERL-M473, Univ. California, Berkeley, Calif. Aug. 1974.

46. Su, S.Y.W., AND Lo, D.H. A semantic association model for conceptual database design. In *Proc. Int. Conf. Entity-Relationship Approach to Systems Analysis and Design*, Los Angeles, Calif. Dec. 1979.

47. TAYLOR, R.W. AND FRANK, R.L. CODASYL database management systems. *Comput. Surv. 8*, 1 (March 1976), 67–104.

48. TSICHRITZIS, D.C. AND LOCHOVSKY, F.H. Hierarchical database management:A survey. *Comput. Surv. 8*, 1 (March 1976), 105–124.

49. WIEDERHOLD, G. *Database Design*. McGraw-Hill, New York, 1977.

50. WIEDERHOLD, G., AND EL-MASRI, R. Structural model for database design. In *Proc. Int. Conf. Entity-Relationship Approach to Systems Analysis and Design*, Los Angeles, Calif. Dec. 1979.

51. WONG, H.K.T. AND MYLOPOULOS. J. Two views of data semantics:A survey of data models in artificial intelligence and database management. *INFOR 15*, 3 (Oct. 1977), 344–382.

An Approach to Persistent Programming

M. P. Atkinson†, P. J. Bailey*, K. J. Chisholm†, P. W. Cockshott† and R. Morrison*

†Department of Computer Science, University of Edinburgh, Mayfield Rd., Edinburgh EH9 3JZ, UK
*Department of Computational Science, University of St. Andrews, North Haugh, St. Andrews KY16 8SX, UK

This paper presents the identification of a new programming language concept and reports our initial investigations of its utility. The concept is to identify persistence as an orthogonal property of data, independent of data type and the way in which data is manipulated. This is expressed by the principle that all data objects, independent of their data type, should have the same rights to persistence or transience. We expect to achieve persistent independent programming, so that the same code is applicable to data of any persistence. We have designed a language PS-algol by using these ideas and constructed a number of implementations. The experience gained is reported here, as a step in the task of achieving languages with proper accommodation for persistent programming.

INTRODUCTION

The long term storage of data has been of concern to programming language designers for some time. Traditional programming languages provide facilities for the manipulation of data whose lifetime does not extend beyond the activation of the program. If data is required to survive a program activation then some file I/O or database management system interface is used. Two views of data evolve from this. Data can either be classed as short term data and would be manipulated by the programming language facilities or data would be long term data in which case it would be manipulated by the file system or the database management system (DBMS). The mapping between the two types of data is usually done in part by the file system or the DBMS and in part by explicit user translation code which has to be written and included in each program.

These different views of data are highlighted when the data structuring facilities of programming languages and database management systems are compared. Database systems have developed relational, hierarchical, network and functional data models[1-5] whereas programming languages may have arrays, records, sets, monitors[6] and abstract data types.[7]

That there are two different views of data has certain disadvantages. Firstly in any program there is usually a considerable amount of code, typically 30% of the total,[8] concerned with transferring data to and from files or a DBMS. Much space and time is taken up by code to perform translations between the program's form of data and the form used for the long term storage medium. This is unsatisfactory because of the time taken in writing and executing this mapping code and also because the quality of the application programs may be impaired by the mapping. Frequently the programmer is distracted from his task by the difficulties of understanding and managing the mapping. The translation merely to gain access to long term data should be differentiated from translations from a form appropriate to one use of the data to a form suitable for some other algorithms. Such translations are justified when the two forms cannot coexist and there is a substantial use of both forms. The second major disadvantage is that the data type protection offered by the programming language on its data is often

lost across the mapping. The structure that might have been exploited in a program to aid comprehension is neither apparent nor protected, and is soon lost.

We seek to eliminate the differences between the DBMS and programming language models of data. This can be done by separating the issue of what data structures are best from the issue of identifying and managing a property of data we call persistence. This is the period of time for which the data exists and is useable. A spectrum of persistence exists and is categorized by

1. transient results in expression evaluation
2. local variables in procedure activations
3. own variables, global variables and heap items whose extent is different from their scope
4. data that exists between executions of a program
5. data that exists between various versions of a program
6. data that outlives the program.

The first three persistence categories are usually supported by programming languages and the second three categories by the DBMS, whereas filing systems are predominantly used for categories 4 and 5. We report here on the PS-algol system which is a step in the search for language and database constructs which meet the needs of persistent data and hence obviate the need for the programmer to cope with the problems described above. PS-algol uniformly supports programming for an increased range of persistence. The system is implemented and is being actively used in a number of projects. Here we will describe the language design decisions in implementing persistence, the underlying implementation problems, the results obtained and some thoughts for the future.

THE LANGUAGE DESIGN METHOD

As a first attempt at producing a system to support persistence we hypothesized that it should be possible to add persistence to an existing language with minimal change to the language. Thus the programmer would be faced with the normal task of mastering the programming language but would have the facility of persistence for little or no extra effort.

The language chosen for this was S-algol,[9,10] a high level Algol used for teaching at the University of St Andrews. This decision was made by the University of Edinburgh team after some trouble with attempts at Algol 68[11] and Pascal,[12] and resulted in the two teams collaborating on the project.

S-algol stands somewhere between Algol W[13] and Algol 68. It was designed using three principles first outlined by Strachey[14] and Landin.[15] These are

1. The principle of correspondence.
2. The principle of abstraction.
3. The principle of data type completeness.

The application of the three principles in designing S-algol is described elsewhere.[16] The result is an orthogonal language whose 'power is gained from simplicity and its simplicity from generality'.[17] Here we are interested in data and the S-algol universe of discourse can be defined by

1. The scalar data types are integer, real, boolean, string, picture and file.
2. For any data type T, $*T$ is the data type of a vector with elements of type T.
3. The data type pointer comprises a structure with any number of fields, and any data type in each field.

The world of data objects can be formed by the closure of rule 1 under the recursive application of rules 2 and 3.

The unusual features of the S-algol universe of discourse are that it has strings as a simple data type,[18] pictures as compound data objects[19] and run time checking of structure classes. The picture facility allows the user to produce line drawings in an infinite two dimensional space. It also offers a picture building facility in which the relationship between different subpictures is specified by mathematical transformations. A basic set of picture manipulating facilities along with a set of physical drawing attributes for each device is defined. A pointer may roam freely over the world of structures. That is a pointer is not bound to a structure class. However, when a pointer is dereferenced using a structure field name, a run time check occurs to ensure that the pointer is pointing at a structure with the appropriate field.

Together with our hypothesis of minimal change to the programming language we recognize certain principles for persistent data.

1. Persistence independence: the persistence of a data object is independent of how the program manipulates that data object and conversely a fragment of program is expressed independently of the persistence of data it manipulates. For example, it should be possible to call a procedure with its parameters sometimes objects with long term persistence and at other times only transient.
2. Persistence data type orthogonality: in line with the principle of data type completeness all data objects should be allowed the full range of persistence.
3. The choice of how to provide and identify persistence at a language level is independent of the choice of data objects in the language.

A number of methods were investigated to identify persistence of data. Some involved associating persistence with the variable name or the type in the declaration. Under the rule of persistence independence these were disallowed. S-algol itself helped to provide the solution. Its data structures already have some limited notion of persistence in that the scope and extent of these objects need not be the same. Such structures are of course heap items and their usability depends on the availability of legal names.

This limited persistence was extended to allow structures to persist beyond the activation of the program. Their use is protected by the fact that the structure accesses are already dynamically checked in S-algol. Thus we have achieved persistence and retained the protection mechanism. Of course, in implementing this we had to devise a method of storing and retrieving persistent data as well as a description of its type and a method of checking type equivalence when data is reused in different programs. This was not a trivial task.

The choice of which data items persist beyond the lifetime of a program was next. We argued, by preaching minimum change, that the system should decide automatically. Such decisions are already taken in a number of languages like S-algol when garbage collection is involved and we therefore felt that reachability, as in garbage collection, was a reasonable choice for identifying persistent objects. However a new origin for the transitive closure of references, under explicit user control, which differentiates persistent data and transient data is introduced. Thus when a transaction is committed we can identify a root object from which we can find all the persistent data in the program. This data we preserve for later use.

PS-ALGOL

Given the constraint of minimal change to S-algol the simplest way to extend the facilities of the language is by adding standard functions and PS-algol is implemented as a number of functional extensions to S-algol. In this way the language itself does not change to accommodate persistence. Thus, the population of S-algol programmers could now use PS-algol with very little change to their programming style. In fact an S-algol program will run correctly with little diminution of speed in the PS-algol run time environment.

The functions added to support persistence are:

procedure *open · database*(**string** *database · name*,
  password, mode → **pntr**)

This procedure attempts to open the database specified by *database · name* (which in general is a path down a tree of directories, terminating in the database's name) in the mode (read or write) specified by *mode*, quoting *password* to establish this right. If the open fails the result is a pointer to an error record. If it succeeds the result is a pointer to a table (see below) which contains a set of name-value pairs and is the root from which preserved data is identified by transitive closure of reachability. A table is chosen so as to permit programs which use one route to the data to be independent of programs using other routes. Many databases may be open for reading, but only one may be open for writing so that the destination for new persistent data may be deduced. If this is the first successful *open · database* then a transaction is started.

procedure *commit*

This procedure commits the changes made so far to the databases open for writing. The program may continue to make further changes. Only changes made before the last commit will be recorded, so that not performing a commit is equivalent to aborting the transaction.

procedure *close · database*(**string** *database · name*)

This procedure closes the specified database making it available for other users who wish to write to it (multiple readers are allowed). It takes effect immediately. An implicit close database is applied to every database open at the end of the program. When a database has been closed references to objects not yet imported may remain accessible as may any imported data. An error is detected if the programmer tries to access any data that has not been imported from the closed database. A program may reopen a database it has closed but to avoid inconsistency between data that was held in the program and the database, it may only do so if there has not been an intervening write to that database.

These three procedures are those concerned with managing persistence, but there are also a set of procedures to manipulate tables, a mechanism for associative lookup, implemented as B-trees[20] or equivalent algorithms. A table is an ordered set of pairs. Each pair consists of a key and a value. At present the key may be an integer or string value, and the value is a pointer to a structure instance or table. The basic library for tables is:

procedure *table*(→ **pntr**)

This procedure creates an empty table represented by an instance of the structure class Table.

procedure *s · lookup*(**string** *key*; **pntr** *table* → **pntr**)
procedure *i · lookup*(**int** *key*; **pntr** *table* → **pntr**)

These procedures take a given key and considering only the pairs within the table return the last value stored by a call of *s · enter* or *i · enter* for this key, or **nil** if there is no such pair.

procedure *s · enter*(**string** *key*; **pntr** *table*, *value*)
procedure *i · enter*(**int** *key*; **pntr** *table*, *value*)

These procedures store in the given table a pair or if the supplied value is **nil** delete the previously stored value for the given key.

procedure *s · scan*(**pntr** *table*, *environment*;
           (**string**, **pntr**, **pntr** → **bool**) *user* → **int**)
procedure *i · scan*(**pntr** *table*, *environment*;
           (**int**, **pntr**, **pntr** → **bool**) *user* → **int**)

These procedures provide iteration over tables. The function *user* is applied to every pair with a key of the appropriate type, in ascending order of integers or lexical order of strings, until either it yields **false** or the whole table has been scanned. The first parameter supplied to the function *user* is the key, the second is the corresponding value and the third parameter the value given as *environment*. The result of these scan procedures is the number of times *user* is applied. An example of their use is given in Fig. 3.

procedure *cardinality*(**pntr** *table* → **int**)

This procedure returns the current number of entries in the given table.

The table facilities were envisaged as a way of packaging index constructions. For example singly and multiple indexed relations can readily be constructed using them. They have also proved very popular as a dynamic data structure constructor. We present as an example of their use three PS-algol programs to maintain a simple address list. The program in Fig. 1 adds an new person, that in Fig. 2 looks up the telephone number of a person and that in Fig. 3 finds the longest telephone number.

```
structure person(string name, phone.no ; pntr addr. other)
structure address(int no ; string street, town ; pntr next.addr)
let db = open.database("Address.list", "Morwenna", "write")
if db is error.record then write "Can't open database" else
begin
        write "Name :"            ; let this.name  = read.a.line
        write "Phone number :"    ; let this.phone = read.a.line
        write "House number :"    ; let this.house = readi
        write "Street :"          ; let this.street = read.a.line
        write "Town :"            ; let this.town = read.a.line
        let p = person(this.name, this.phone, address (this.house, this.street,
                         this.town, nil), nil)
        let addr.list = s.lookup("addr.list.by.name", db)
        s.enter(this.name, addr.list, p)
        commit
end
```

Figure 1. A program to add one new person to a database containing an address list.

```
structure person(string name, phone.no ; pntr addr. other)
let db = open.database("Address.list", "Kernow", "read")
if db is error.record do{write "Can't open database"; abort}
let addr.list = s.lookup ("addr.list.by.name", db)
write "Name :"            ; let this.name = read.a.line
let this.person = s.lookup(this.name, addr.list)
if this.person = nil then write "Person not known" else
    write "Phone number is :", this.person(phone.no)
```

Figure 2. A program to look up the telephone number of one person from the address list.

```
structure person(string name, phone.no ; pntr addr, other)
let db = open.database("Address.list", "Kernow", "read")
if db is error.record do{write "Can't open database"; abort}
let addr.list = s.lookup("addr.list.by.name", db)
structure env(int max ; string longest)
let el = env(0, "")
procedure phone(string name ; pntr val, el → bool)
begin
        let number = val(phone.no)
        let len = length(number)
        if len > el(max) do{el(max) := len; el(longest) := number}
        true
end
let count = s.scan(addr.list, el, phone)
if count = 0 then write "Nobody in the list yet" else
write "Longest telephone number is : ", el(longest)
```

Figure 3. A program to find the longest telephone number in the address list.

Note that in these examples the declared data structures are different. This identifies which parts of the data each program may touch, and so behaves like a simple database view mechanism. Only those quoted will be matched against the stored set of data descriptions when they are first used. Paths to other data, e.g. alternative addresses via *next · addr* and extra information about people via *other* have not been used. They are there to give access to data pertinent to other programs or to future needs and they do not clutter programs which do not use them. Similarly the standard table is used to name access paths and only those used need be considered in a particular program. Figure 4 shows a program to introduce a new access path to the address list. With these disciplines. which we find useful, data design and programs can grow together. These examples illustrate the ease with which small programs operating on persistent data may be composed to provide a complete system. In this example one would imagine other programs: to start an address list, to delete it, to remove entries, amend addresses, print lists etc. We believe this method of constructing software tools to be an attractive way of building such systems.

As well as showing these features of persistence the programs illustrate features of the parent language S-algol. For example, the type of a name is deduced from the initializing expression, this leads to conciseness. The freedom to place declarations where they are needed means'that constant names are common and programs may be read without searching far for declarations.

```
structure person(string name, phone.no ; pntr addr, other)
let db = open.database("Address.list", "Morwenna", "write")
if db is error.record do{write "Can't open database"; abort}
let addr.list = s.lookup("addr.list.by.name", db)
let phone.number.table = table          ! create a new empty table
procedure put.it.in.phone.number.table(string name ; pntr val, env → bool)
    {s.enter(val(phone.no), phone.number.table, val); true}
let count = s.scan(addr.list, nil, put.it.in.phone.number.table)
s.enter("addr.list.by.phone.number", db, phone.number.table)
```

Figure 4. A program to construct a new index onto the address list, by phone number.

THE PERSISTENT OBJECT MANAGEMENT SYSTEM

The persistent object management system is concerned with the movement of data between main store and backing store. This is controlled by the run time support system where transactions are implemented by Challis' algorithm.[21] The movement of data is achieved as follows.

(a) Movement of data on to the heap

Data may be created on the heap during a transaction or it may migrate there as a copy of some persistent data object. The second mechanism is invoked when a pointer being dereferenced is a persistent identifier (**PID**). The presistent object manager is called to locate the object and place it on the heap, possibly carrying out minor translations. The initial pointer which is a **PID** is that yielded by *open · database* and subsequent pointers will be found in the fields of structures reached from that reference.

(b) Movement from the heap

When a transaction is committed, all the data on the heap that is reachable from the persistent objects used during the transaction are transferred back to the disk. Some anticipation of these transfers may be necessary if the heap space is insufficient for the whole transaction.

The algorithms and data structures used to implement this data movement are described elsewhere.[22,23] Since the database may be shared by many programs, the binding of the names of persistent data must be dynamic and symbolic. In PS-algol this binding is performed automatically when the object is accessed for the first time. There is no overhead in accessing local objects.

Type checking is also performed by the system. Remember that a pointer may roam over the domain of structure classes. Thus. when a pointer is dereferenced to yield a value the system must check that the pointer points to a structure with the correct field name. The field name and the structure incarnation must carry around type information to enable this checking to be performed.

To extend this type checking to persistent structures it is sufficient to ensure that the type information migrates with the structure itself. This is accomplished by making the type information an implicit field of the structure thus guaranteeing that the type information will persist.

DESIGN ISSUES IN PERSISTENT OBJECT MANAGEMENT

There are a number of tradeoffs to consider when designing the persistent object manager used to implement the data migration. Some of these are illustrated here. We may choose between making all references suitable as disc references (as in Smalltalk[24]), translating every time or we may (and usually do) economize by storing a mapping and translating less often. Then a choice exists as to when to build up the map. Do we make an entry when a reference is first introduced or when it is first dereferenced? Similarly do we make all references go via this map? There are problems of how to store the map so that it grows on demand rather than causing a high initial overhead. We require access to the map to be fast in both directions. These decisions interact with store management. We wish to avoid putting data on disc if we can determine it is not reachable. We may use these transfer mechanisms to avoid space exhaustion after garbage collection. When virtual memory[25] is available it interacts with these algorithms and may be exploited if the operating system permits. On the other hand we would like a run time system which is portable.

The design of the address structure for the persistent data allows interaction between addressability and the cost of disc garbage collection. This influences attempts to make the address structure extensible, to make it space efficient and to make it address sufficient data. Placement strategies, data compression techniques and variations on the method of implementing transactions again interact and have significant effect on performance. The choice of a particular implementation is therefore a choice of a particular point in an extensive and many dimensional space. Our present choice described below is empirical and pragmatic rather than being based on systematic evaluation of this space or the optimization of some abstract model.

Thus venturing into this approach to providing presistence has provoked many research issues concerning implementation which we have only just begun to explore and which will be the topics of other papers, the first of which is in preparation.[26]

AN IMPLEMENTATION OF PERSISTENCE

Our earliest implementation of persistence used a linear table of PIDS and local addresses, with entries for every pointer in imported objects (objects that had been brought in from the database). Hashing was used to accelerate lookups of a PID (needed when a object is being imported to translate pointers to objects already imported). In the next implementation the position in this table was referred to as the local object number LON, and all references in all objects were represented by their LON. This cost an indirection in every reference (using an addressing mode on the VAX11) but meant that the local address to PID translation, needed on transferring data to the database (export) was merely indexing the table. Hash coding accelerated PID to LON translation and Bloom filters[27] were used to reduce the cost of discovering that a PID had not yet been encountered. The main disadvantage of this was that an entry in the PIDLAM was needed for every active object, so this table grew large. That implementation achieved good performance by using the virtual memory mechanisms of VAX, implementing Challis' algorithm as page tables stored at the start of the file and arranging that altered pages were paged to a new site.

Our present implementation, POMS (persistent object management system), is designed to overcome many of the deficiencies of the earlier systems, it is described in detail elsewhere.[28] Briefly, the design depends on adaptive structures for all the addressing mechanisms, to avoid the problems of a high fixed overhead, or a small limit to the maximum volume of data that can be accommodated. The PIDLAM is now two hashing structures which grow as necessary, one from PIDs to local addresses, the other from local addresses to PIDs, for only the pointers which have been both imported and dereferenced. Translation is done when a reference is first used to minimize the size of these tables.

To avoid a large number of transfers on startup, the logical to physical disc address mapping is itself mapped, using its own mapping and a bootstrap. So this map may grow as the database grows and is loaded incrementally. To avoid dependence on particular operating system features and the problem found when implementing transactions that file operations and database operations can get out of step, we include our own directory mechanism for databases. Depending on this strategy and writing most of the code for POMS in PS-algol itself, we believe we have achieved reasonable portability.

The objects are clustered by type in the database pages, so that the type description information may be factored out. The order of transfers during import is not under POMs control since it depends on the order in which the program accesses structures. During the routines for commit, when data is exported, the total set of data which cannot become reachable from the root is identified from local information and discarded. The imported objects that have been changed and the newly created objects reachable from them, then have to be exported. This list of exports is sorted to minimize transfers and head movement, before write-back. The combination of these tactics, which we continue to refine, gives reasonable performance. Better performance may be achievable by exploiting segmentation hardware within the operating system.

EXPERIENCE USING PS-ALGOL

At first sight the set of facilities provided by PS-algol may look fairly primitive. Notice however that the programmer never explicitly organizes data movement but that it occurs automatically when data is used. Notice also that the language type rules are strictly enforced and that the programmer uses a method already familiar to him to preserve data. That is by the usual naming convention where the preservation of data is a consequence of arranging that there is a way of using the data. Thus we have achieved persistence by minimal change allowing the programmer to use all his familiar techniques of problem solving.

The effect on programs written in PS-algol has been quite dramatic. We have some early results of tests comparing programs written in PS-algol with programs written in Pascal with explicit database calls. These programs implemented a DAPLEX[5] look-alike, a relational algebra and various CAD and demonstration programs. We have found that there is a reduction by a factor of about three in the length of the source code. These are of course early results and will need further confirmation. However it is the sort of result we expected.

We have also found that the coding time for these programs is reduced by at least the same factor. We suspect that the maintenance of the programs will be easier. We avoid the layering costs associated with calls to successive levels of a DBMS as data is brought into the normal program from the heap. Consequently we have observed a reduction in CPU requirements for equivalent programs even though we are still interpreting. Whether there is an overall increase in speed depends on the data structures and the algorithms over them and we hope to investigate performance further.

EVALUATION OF PERSISTENCE AS AN ABSTRACTION

The abstraction of persistence has been so successful that we would recommend that other language designers consider it for the languages they design. It identifies significant aspects of common programming tasks, consequently reducing the effort required by the programmer to accomplish those tasks. It abstracts away much detail commonly visible to the programmer so that programs produced using it are simpler to understand and to transport. It is feasible to implement.

Persistence has also appeared as an orthogonal

property of data in the work of Albano et al.[29] In an attempt to accommodate longer term persistence they make contexts proper objects which can be manipulated, as we suggest for an identified subset of contexts in our language proposals NEPAL.[30] In another group of languages PASCAL/R,[31] RIGEL[32] and PLAIN[33] the designers have chosen not to adopt the principle of data type completeness, and have only allowed instances of type relation to have longer term persistence. It is interesting to note that in PASCAL/R the construct DATABASE has a form like a PASCAL record, and if its fields were allowed to take any of the PASCAL data types then that language would be consistent in allowing data structures of any type to have any persistence. ADAPLEX[34] is constructed by merging a given database model, DAPLEX[5] and an existing language ADA,[35] with the inevitable consequence of restrictions on which data types can have which persistence. When casting program examples to assess languages[36] we have found it particularly irksome if data types which can persist cannot also have temporary instances. We conclude, therefore, that the consistency of our form of persistence is of advantage to the programmer.

CONCLUSIONS

The abstraction achieved by treating persistence as an orthogonal property of data has been shown to have many interesting properties. It is clear that it favourably affects program length, program development time and program maintainability. Demonstration implementations of a particular flavour of this idea have shown it to be practicable for reasonable amounts of data. This particular flavour does not have concurrency other than at database level. This may be a limitation which prevents its application to simple transactions on large database systems, but this leaves the very substantial number of programs which run against conventional files which implement complex interactions as in CAD, or use personal databases as uses of this language.

Acknowledgements

The work at Edinburgh was supported in part by U.K. SERC grant GRA 86541. It is now supported at Edinburgh by U.K. SERC grants GRC 21977 and GRC 21960 and at St Andrews by U.K. SERC grant GRC 15907. The work is also supported at both Universities by grants from ICL.

REFERENCES

1. F. H. Lochovsky and D. C. Tsichritizis, Data Models. Prentice Hall, London (1982).
2. E. F. Codd, A relational model for large shared databases. Comm. ACM 13 (6), 377–387 (1970).
3. F. H. Lochovsky and D. C. Tsichritizis, Hierarchical database management systems. ACM Computing Surveys 8 (1), 105–123 (1978).
4. R. C. Taylor and R. L. Frank, CODASYL database management systems. ACM Computing Surveys 8 (1), 67–103 (1976).
5. D. W. Shipman, The functional data model and the data language DAPLEX. ACM TODS 6 (1), 140–173 (1981).
6. C. A. R. Hoare, Monitors: an operating system structuring concept. Comm. ACM 17 (10), 549–557 (1974).
7. B. H. Liskov et al. Abstraction mechanisms in CLU. Comm. ACM 20 (8), 564–576 (1977).
8. IBM report on the contents of a sample of programs surveyed. San Jose, California (1978).
9. R. Morrison, S-algol Language Reference Manual. University of St Andrews CS/79/1 (1979).
10. A. J. Cole and R. Morrison, An Introduction to Programming with S-algol, Cambridge University Press (1982).
11. A. van Wijngaarden et al. Report on the algorithmic language Algol 68. Numerische Mathematik 14, 79–218 (1969).
12. N. Wirth, The programming language Pascal. Acta Informatica 1, 35–63 (1971).
13. N. Wirth and C. A. R. Hoare, A contribution to the development of algol. Comm. ACM 9 (6), 413–431 (1966).
14. C. Strachey, Fundamental Concepts in Programming Languages. Oxford University Press (1967).
15. P. J. Landin, The next 700 programming languages. Comm. ACM 9 (3), 157–164 (1966).
16. R. Morrison, Towards simpler programming languages: S-algol. IUCC Bulletin 4 (3), (October 1982).
17. A. van Wijngaarden, Generalised algol. Annual Review of automatic programming 3, 17–26 (1963).
18. R. Morrison, The string as a simple data type. ACM Sigplan Notices 17 (3) (1982).
19. R. Morrison, Low cost computer graphics for micro computers. Software—Practice and Experience 12, 767–776 (1982).
20. B. Bayer and A. McCreight, Organisation and maintenance of large ordered indexes. Acta Informatica 1, 173–189 (1972).
21. M. P. Challis, Data Consistency and integrity in a multi-user environment. In Databases: Improving Usability and Responsiveness, Academic Press, 245–270 (1978).
22. M. P. Atkinson, K. J. Chisholm and W. P. Cockshott, CMS—A chunk management system. Software—Practice and Experience 13, 273–285 (1983).
23. M. P. Atkinson, K. J. Chisholm, W. P. Cockshott and R. M. Marshall, Algorithms for a persistent heap. Software—Practice and Experience 13, 259–271 (1983).
24. T. Kaehler, Virtual memory for an object-oriented language. Byte, 378–387 (1982).
25. I. L. Traiger, Virtual memory management for database systems. ACM Sogops 16 (4), 26–48 (1982).
26. M. P. Atkinson, K. J. Chisholm and W. P. Cockshott, An exploration of various strategies for implementing persistence as an orthogonal property of data. In preparation.
27. B. H. Bloom, Space/time tradeoffs in hash coding with allowable errors. Comm. ACM 13 (7), 422–426 (1970).
28. M. P. Atkinson, P. J. Bailey, K. J. Chisholm, W. P. Cockshott and R. Morrison, The persistent object management system. To be published in Software—Practice and Experience (1983).
29. A. Albano, L. Cardelli and R. Orsini, Galileo: a strongly typed interactive conceptual language, to be published.
30. M. P. Atkinson, K. J. Chisholm and W. P. Cockshott, NEPAL—The New Edinburgh Persistent Algorithmic Language. DATABASE Infotech State of the Art Report 9 (8), 299–318 (1982).
31. J. W. Schmidt, Some high level language constructs for data of type relation. ACM TODS 2 (3), 247–261 (1981).
32. L. A. Rowe, Reference manual for the programming language RIGEL. Department of Computer Science, University of California, Berkeley.
33. A. I. Wasserman, D. D. Sheretz, M. L. Kersten and R. D. van de Reit, Revised report on the programming language PLAIN. ACM Sigplan Notices 16 (5), (1981).
34. J. M. Smith, S. Fox and T. Landers, Reference Manual for ADAPLEX. Computer Corporation of America, Cambridge, Massachusetts (1981).
35. Ichbiah et al. Rationale of the design of the programming language Ada. ACM Sigplan Notices 14 (6), (1979).
36. M. P. Atkinson and P. Buneman, Survey paper on persistent languages. In preparation.

Received March 1983

Galileo: A Strongly-Typed, Interactive Conceptual Language

ANTONIO ALBANO
Universita' di Pisa

LUCA CARDELLI
AT&T Bell Laboratories

AND

RENZO ORSINI
Universita' di Pisa

Galileo, a programming language for database applications, is presented. Galileo is a strongly-typed, interactive programming language designed specifically to support semantic data model features (classification, aggregation, and specialization), as well as the abstraction mechanisms of modern programming languages (types, abstract types, and modularization). The main contributions of Galileo are (a) a flexible type system to model database structure and semantic integrity constraints; (b) the inclusion of type hierarchies to support the specialization abstraction mechanisms of semantic data models; (c) a modularization mechanism to structure data and operations into interrelated units (d) the integration of abstraction mechanisms into an expression-based language that allows interactive use of the database without resorting to a new stand-alone query language.

Galileo will be used in the immediate future as a tool for database design and, in the long term, as a high-level interface for DBMSs.

Categories and Subject Descriptors: D.3.3 [**Programming Languages**]: Language Constructs—*abstract data types; data types and structures*; H.2.1 [**Database Management**]: Logical Design—*data models; schema and subschema*; H.2.3 [**Database Management**]: Languages—*data description languages (DDL); data manipulation languages (DML); query languages*

General Terms: Design, Languages

Additional Key Words and Phrases: Type hierarchy, database semantics, integrity constraints, exception handling.

1. INTRODUCTION

1.1 Motivation

If complex applications utilizing DBMS technology are to be developed, the crucial aspects of these applications must be designed in a high-level language with features that differ considerably from those supported by traditional DBMSs

[18, 34, 35, 38, 54]. Let us call this activity *conceptual modeling*, its result a *conceptual schema*, and the language used the *conceptual language*.

There are many opinions as to the role of the conceptual schema during the design process. These ideas, which are reflected in the features of the conceptual language, are briefly outlined below.

(1) The conceptual schema documents the database structure in terms very similar to those employed by users to describe an application. It is therefore a model that will be used during the entire life cycle of the database for considerations on the logical data structure and to verify informally that this structure can adequately satisfy user requirements, before the implementation begins. As the conceptual schema is only used for documentation, it does not have to be given in an executable language. The schema is automatically processed only to provide useful reports. An early significant example of this approach is the PSL/PSA design environment [50].

(2) A second class of proposals extends the previous approach in a direction that more closely resembles the software specification problem. This perspective is particularly interesting because of the reciprocal influences of techniques and methodologies [1, 19, 21, 48]. The rationale behind this approach is that since a complex database implementation is a long-term evolving activity, it is essential that the conceptual schema be carefully designed and tested to reduce logical errors in the implementation, and to safely incorporate the new requirements which will arise during the operational phase. The features of the conceptual language are at present still under discussion. In particular, attention is being given to operational aspects, besides the structure of data. However, in addition to abstract specifications, there are a number of pragmatic reasons why a high-level, executable language should be used in conceptual design. In fact, such a language could also be used to test the adequacy of the conceptual schema, if we do not care about execution efficiency [16, 26, 34, 39].

(3) A third class of proposals considers a conceptual language as a tool that is much more than a mere step on the way to implementing a database application. To design complex, interactive computerized information systems, a programming language with abstraction mechanisms to model databases is needed.

There are a few proposals that have adopted the last approach, although general agreement has been reached only with regard to certain basic features of the language [22, 31, 32, 37, 49]. Such a language should provide constructs to aid the designer in expressing, as far as possible, the semantics of the application in the conceptual schema, rather than in the application programs. At the least it should provide the following features:

(a) data defined both declaratively, with abstraction mechanisms (aggregation, classification, and specialization), and procedurally (derived data);

(b) semantic integrity constraints, both standard (such as keys and mandatory values) and those described by a general-purpose constraint specification language;

(c) operations to give the behavioral semantics of the data in the schema; and

(d) a sound mathematical foundation for the language.

1.2 Assumptions

This paper describes the features of the conceptual language Galileo, a programming language that supports semantic data model features. It therefore belongs to the third approach outlined above. The features presented here have been partially implemented [4]. These are the first results of a project that aims at designing and implementing a prototype system, Dialogo, to experiment with a stand-alone programming environment and to support the development and testing of database design [2].

The approach adopted in designing Galileo takes into account the requirements previously described, but also assumes that a conceptual language should provide

(a) a set of independent constructs to be used in any combination to achieve simplicity and expressiveness;

(b) features to design and test the solution incrementally;

(c) a modularization mechanism to decompose the design into meaningful modular units that correspond to a description of the database at different levels of successive refinements, or to application-oriented views of the database.

1.3 Relation to Previous Work

The design of Galileo has been influenced by two areas of research: conceptual modeling and programming languages. Although these areas have a number of overlapping issues, there are problems to be solved if the results from both areas are to be successfully integrated [18, 20].

Galileo applies results from the conceptual modeling sector for features related to object-oriented databases, declarative definitions of constraints, multiple descriptions of objects, and view modeling [11, 13, 17, 31–33, 35, 37, 42, 45, 47, 49, 53].

Galileo borrows features such as data types, abstract types, and modularization from the programming language area [44]. Although the utility of such features is recognized both pragmatically and theoretically, they have mainly been studied for applications to temporary data (i.e., not involving databases).

The database proposals that have most influenced the design of Galileo are TAXIS, DIAL, and ADAPLEX. TAXIS is notable for introducing the basic knowledge representation mechanisms of semantic networks on data, transactions, and exceptions and for its approach to user dialogue modeling [12]. DIAL, which has evolved from SDM [32], uses data types, classes, derived classes, the "port" mechanism to deal with user interaction, and features to control concurrency at the conceptual level [31]. Finally, ADAPLEX uses semantic data model features in a strongly-typed programming language, namely, Ada [49].

The main contributions of Galileo are

(1) the integration of features to support semantic data model abstraction mechanisms within an expression-based, strongly-typed programming language;

(2) a systematic use of both concrete and abstract types to model structural and behavioral aspects of a database;

(3) the inclusion of type hierarchies to support the specialization abstraction mechanism of semantic data models as well as a software development methodology by data specialization [5, 14];

(4) the proposal of another abstraction mechanism, modularization, to organize a conceptual scheme in meaningful and manageable units, so as to deal with data persistence without resorting to specific data types such as files of data programming languages, and to deal with application-oriented views of data in a similar way to the view mechanism of DBMSs [7];

(5) a small number of independent primitive features that can be applied orthogonally, that is, in any combination.

The basic ideas of Galileo have been investigated in ELLE, a programming language designed to deal uniformly with temporary and persistent complex data, that is, without resorting to special data type constructors to deal with permanent data [3]. Both ELLE and Galileo borrow many of their features from the functional programming language ML [29]. A comparison of ADAPLEX, DIAL, Galileo, and TAXIS is reported in [15].

1.4 Structure of the Paper

The purpose of this paper is to illustrate the features of Galileo. The schema fragments used as examples are intended only to illustrate the main concepts, and do not cover all the language features. A complete description of Galileo exists as a technical report [6]. The semantics of Galileo are described informally, but its formalization, using a denotational approach, is reported in [24, 41]. Pragmatic aspects of Galileo (schema design methodology and designers' reactions to the language) are also beyond the scope of this paper; they are currently being studied in the context of a joint project by a group of Italian universities and companies sponsored by the Italian National Research Council (CNR) [27]. The goal of the project is the development of a database design methodology, together with a set of integrated computer-assisted tools covering all aspects of the design process, including application analysis, conceptual modeling, and logical and physical design in both centralized and distributed environments.

The next section presents the basic data modeling features of Galileo. Section 3 describes the operators that affect the environment used to evaluate expressions. Section 4 describes the type system of the language, and Section 5 the notion of type hierarchies. Section 6 presents the class mechanism used to build an object-oriented view of a database, with classification, aggregation, and specialization abstraction mechanisms. Section 7 presents the modularization mechanism to structure a schema and to deal with persistent data. Section 8 illustrates the failure-handling mechanism together with transactions modeling. In the conclusions, we comment upon the implementation now underway and on our future plans.

2. OVERVIEW OF GALILEO

Galileo supports the following abstraction mechanisms for database modeling:

Classification. Entities being modeled which share common characteristics are gathered into *classes*. All elements of a class have the same type. The name of the class denotes the elements present in the database. The elements of a class are represented uniquely, that is, only one copy of each element is allowed.

Aggregation. Elements of classes are aggregates; that is, they are abstractions having heterogeneous components, and may have elements of other classes as checker is not able to ascribe a type to an expression, the user must specify the type with the notation "Expression: Type". The language has been designed to be statically type-checkable for two reasons: first, for the considerable benefits in testing and debugging; second, because programs can be safely executed disregarding any information about types at run time. Execution time testing will be required for constraints only. Finally, static type checking allows a typechecker to give the correct meaning to overloaded operators (i.e., operators that can be used with operands of different types).

(6) Class elements possess an abstract type and are the only values which can be destroyed. Predefined assertions on classes are provided and, if not otherwise specified, the operators for including or eliminating elements of a class are automatically defined.

(7) A control structure is provided for failures and their handling.

The following simple schema illustrates Galileo. The example concerns departments and employees in a firm. The definitions are collected in the Organization schema.

```
Organization := (
rec Departments class
    Department ↔
        (Name: string
        and Budget: num
        and Address: Address
        and Manager: var Employee
        and Employees: var seq Employee)
        key (Name)

and Employees class
    Employee ↔
        (Name: string
        and Salary: var num
        and NameOfDept :=
            derived Name of
                get Departments with this isin (at Employees))
        key (Name)

and NewEmployee(AName: string, ASalary: num): Employee :=
    mkEmployee (Name := AName and Salary := var ASalary)

and VipEmployees subset of Employees class
    VipEmployee ↔
        (is Employee
        and VipProperty: string)

and type Address :=
    (Street: string
    and Zip: string
    and City: string)

    drop mkEmployee
```

The rec is used for recursive functions or for mutually dependent types, such as Department and Employee.

components. Associations among entities are represented by aggregations in a Galileo database. Components of aggregates can be collections of homogeneous values to represent, for example, multivalued associations among entities. Because of the unique representation of elements of classes, any modification of an element is reflected everywhere that element appears as a component.

Generalization. Elements of a class can be described in different ways by means of subclasses. Subclasses are derived from classes by using a predefined set of operators. Elements of a subclass also belong to their parent class. The type of the elements of a subclass is a subtype of the type of elements of the parent class. The subclass mechanism includes the IS-A hierarchy of semantic networks and semantic data models.

Modularization. Data and operations can be partitioned into interrelated modules. A complex schema can therefore be structured into smaller units. For instance, a unit may model a user view or a description of the schema produced by a stepwise refinement methodology.

Galileo also has the following features:

(1) It is an expression language; each construct is applied to values to return a value.

(2) It is an interactive language; the system repeatedly prompts for inputs and reports the results of computations; this interaction is said to happen at the top level of evaluation. At the top level one can evaluate expressions or perform declarations. This feature allows the interactive use of Galileo without a separate query language.

(3) It is higher order, in that functions are denotable values of the language. Therefore, a function can be embedded in data structures, passed as a parameter, and returned as a value.

(4) Every denotable value of the language possesses a type:

(a) A type is a set of values sharing common characteristics, together with the primitive operators which can be applied to these values.

(b) The predefined types of the language are bool, num, string, equipped with the usual operators, and the type null, which is a singleton set with the element nil equipped with the equality operator.

(c) The type constructors available to define new types, from predefined or previously defined types, are tuple (record), sequence, discriminated union (variant), function, modifiable value (reference), and abstract types. There are two constructors for abstract types: ⇔ and ↔. The former is similar to CLU clusters, ALPHARD forms, or Euclid modules: it is used to define a new type together with the available operations. The latter is similar to the type constructor of Ada: it defines a new type which inherits the primitive operations of the representation type.

(d) The type system supports the notion of type hierarchy; if a type t is a subtype of a type t', then a value of t can be used as argument of any operation defined for values of t', but not vice versa, because the subtype relation is a partial order.

(5) Every Galileo expression has a type. The meaning of "an expression e having type t" is that the value of e possesses the type t. In general, any expression has a type that can be statically determined, so that every type violation can be detected by textual inspection (static type checking). However, if the type

Departments and Employees are examples of base classes, while **key** is an example of predefined class constraint to assert that the elements of the classes must differ in the value of the Name attribute.

An attribute of an element of a class may be *primitive* or *derived*. A primitive attribute is one that is subject to direct initialization and updating. The value of a derived attribute is automatically computed from other information in the database and cannot be updated: every time the value of the attribute is used, it is as if the associated expression were evaluated to derive the value. An example of a derived attribute is NameOfDept in Employees, where "this" is bound to the current element of the class.

An attribute can be modified if and only if it is defined as type **var**, otherwise it is constant, and any attempt to update the value is detected statically.

The function NewEmployee is an example of a defined operation included in the schema. It is the only operation that can be used to create new elements of the class Employees, since the **drop** operator prevents the predefined mk-Employee operation from being exported outside the schema definition. For Departments and VipEmployees, the functions mkDepartment and mkVipEmployee are available.

VipEmployees is an example of a subclass. It contains all those employees who are believed to be very important. The elements of a subclass must have a type that is a subtype of the elements of the parent class. For instance, the type of the elements of VipEmployees is that of Employee with the additional attribute VipProperty.

This example shows how classes are used to deal with sets of related objects. The approach has some similarity to that adopted for relational databases: in both cases the associations among data are described by means of the value of an attribute. However, in relational databases, data are tuples of simple values collected in relations, and associations among them are represented by assigning as value to an attribute the key value of another tuple. To represent associations in Galileo, the mechanism of "data sharing" is used instead, so that an element of a class can be shared as a component by many others.

3. THE BASIC ENVIRONMENT OPERATORS

An important notion in Galileo is that of *environment*, as it used in the denotational semantics description of programming languages [51]. It is useful to distinguish between the definition of an environment and its run-time interpretation.

An *environment definition* is a map from identifiers to definitions of types or values; it is used to typecheck declarations and expressions before their evaluation.

A *run-time environment* is a map from identifiers to denotable values of the language, obtained by evaluating an environment expression. The evaluation of any expression takes place in the context of an environment, which specifies what the identifiers in use denote. Types are not present in run-time environments since they are not denotable values; that is, types cannot be produced as the result of expressions.

An environment definition is given with the following operators, where A and B stand for environment expressions.

Id := Term	Introduces a new binding between the identifier Id and Term, which is the definition of a value or a type.
A and B	introduces the bindings of A and B, but the bindings of A cannot be used in B and vice versa.
A ext B	introduces the bindings of B and those of A not redefined in B. The bindings of A can be used in B, but not vice versa. In other words, A is extended with B.
rec A	introduces the bindings of A which can be used recursively in A.
type A	introduces the bindings between identifiers and types defined in A.
A drop Id	introduces the bindings of A, except the one with binder Id.
A take Id	introduces only the binding with binder Id defined in A.
A rename Id by NewId	introduces the bindings of A, but the binder Id is renamed as NewId.

For instance

```
type b := int
ext rec fact(x:b):b :=
  if x = 0 then 1 else x*fact(x − 1)
ext a := fact(3)
ext c := fact(4)
```

The binders defined are b, *fact*, a, and c bound respectively to the type int, the factorial function, the expression fact(3), and the expression fact(4). Once this environment expression has been evaluated, it denotes the set of associations (a, 6), (c, 24), and (fact, the internal representation of the function).

The expression "use A in Expression" evaluates "Expression" in the current environment temporarily extended with the bindings of A.

```
use a := 3
and b := 4
in a + b      yields 7
```

Other environment operators will be introduced in the sequel to this paper.

4. THE TYPE SYSTEM

All denotable values of the language possess a type. A *type* is a set of values, possibly infinite, together with the primitive operations that can be applied to these values. The predefined types of the language are **bool**, **num**, and **string**, equipped with the usual operators, and **null**, which is a singleton set whose only element is **nil**, equipped with the equality operator.

Type constructors exist to define a type for the following values: tuples, discriminated unions, sequences, modifiable values, functions, and abstract values.

4.1 Tuples

The data structure tuple, such as the records of programming languages and traditional database models, consists of a set of (identifier (attribute or label), denotable value) pairs. The order of the pairs is unimportant. Examples of denotations of tuples are

PaulBrown :=
(Name := "Paul"
and Surname := "Brown"
and BirthDate := "06/12/1941")
Department :=

(Name := "Computer Science"
and NumOfEmployee := 10
and Chairman :=
(Name := "John"
and Surname := "Moore"
and Salary := 80))

We say that a value is associated with an identifier when it appears in a pair together with that identifier.

Tuples are equipped with the **of** operator which returns the value associated with an identifier (**of** is right associative):

Name, of
(Surname := "Moore"
and Name := "John"
and Salary := 80)   yields "John".

A tuple type consists of an unordered set of pairs (identifiers, type). Two tuple types are equal if they have equal sets of pairs.

Tuples in Galileo are just environments constructed with any environment operators except **type**, although we continue to use the two terms to indicate their use as a data structure (tuple) or as a binding in which evaluation takes place (environment). The following example shows how to construct and use circular data with the operators **rec**, **and**, and **use**:

use rec Cs :=
(Name := "Computer Science"
and Budget := 100
and Chairman := Smith)
and Smith :=
(Name := "John"
and Salary := 100
ext Deductions := Salary* 0.1
and Department := Cs)
in
Deductions of Chairman of Cs   yields 10

A discriminated union, or variant, type consists of a set of alternative values. It is different from the mathematical union of sets in that each value retains an inspectable *tag*, indicating the alternative to which it belongs. Two variant types are equal if the sets of their pairs ⟨tag, type⟩ are equal. An example of variant type is

type Employee :=
⟨Technician: (Name: string and Skill: string)
or Secretary: (Name: string and TypingSpeed: string)⟩

Values of such a type are denoted by giving the expected tag:

JohnSmith := ⟨Secretary := (Name := "John Smith" and TypingSpeed := "High")⟩
MarySmith := ⟨Technician := (Name := "Mary Smith" and Skill := "Analyst")⟩

Two basic operators are defined on variants: **is**, to test the **tag** of a variant value, and **as**, to get the value contained in the variant. Suppose w denotes a value of type Employee, then a legal Galileo expression is

if w is Technician
then Skill of (w as Technician)
else TypingSpeed of (w as Secretary)

The case construct is a convenient form to test the tag of a variant and to bind the value to a local identifier:

case w when
⟨Technician := x. Skill of x
or Secretary := y. TypingSpeed of y⟩

The Pascal-like enumeration type ⟨Id or ... or Id⟩ is an abbreviation for ⟨Id:null or ... or Id:null⟩, and values of such a type can be denoted with ⟨Id⟩ instead of ⟨Id := nil⟩. "optional t" is an abbreviation for ⟨bound: t or unbound: null⟩. If x is a value of type "optional t", it can be used in any expression as an abbreviation for "x as bound".

4.2 Sequences

A sequence is a finite ordered collection of homogeneous elements (i.e., data with the same type). Sequences differ from sets in the ordering and multiplicity of elements.

[3; 4; 6*3; 4]   is a sequence of integers
[(Name := "Jim" and Age := 20);
(Name := "Alice" and Age := 31)]   is a sequence of tuples

A sequence type is denoted by **seq** followed by the type of the elements. For instance, the following are the types of the above sequences:

seq num
seq (Name: string and Age: num)

Since each expression must have a type that is statically determinable, empty sequences must be followed by their types, as in

[]: seq num
[]: seq (Name: string and Age: num)

Two sequences are equal when they meet three conditions: they have the same element types, the same cardinality, and their elements are pairwise equal, in the correct order. Two sequence types are equal if they have equal element types. The following examples show some operators on sequences:

first [2;3;2]	yields 2
rest [2;3;2]	yields [3;2]
[1;2] **append** [3;4;2]	yields [1;2;3;4;2]
setof [1;2;2;1]	yields [1;2]
3 **isin** [2;3;5]	yields true
emptyseq [2]	yields false

first and **rest** generate a failure when applied to an empty sequence.

all x **in** [2;3;2;3;6] **with** x > 2   yields [3;3;6]
all p **in** [(Name := "Jim" **and** Age := 20); (Name := "Alice" **and** Age := 31)]
with Age **of** p > 20   yields [(Name := "Alice" **and** Age := 31)]

The following semantically equivalent expression is preferred for sequences of tuples, since it avoids the introduction of the explicit binder:

all [(Name := "Jim" **and** Age := 20); (Name := "Alice" **and** Age := 31)]
with Age > 20   yields [(Name := "Alice" **and** Age := 31)]

To evaluate an expression for each element of a sequence, such as "Select the names of persons aged more than 20", the following expression can be used:

for [(Name := "Jim" **and** Age := 20);(Name := "Alice" **and** Age := 31)]
with Age > 20 **do** Name   yields the sequence ["Alice"]

The conventional aggregate functions sum, average, and so on, are available for sequences of numbers.

4.3 Modifiable Values

Values associated with the previous types cannot be modified. To introduce "modifiability" in the language, for example, to modify the value of a tuple pair or to change the value associated with an identifier in the environment, a new kind of value, the *location*, is introduced. Its name and meaning is one that is commonly used in the denotational semantics description of programming languages [51]. Locations reside in a time-varying structure, the store, and are associated with values of any type, including other locations, since they are also denotable values. The expression "**var** 3" denotes a new location which is associated in the store with the value 3. The type of "**var** Expression" is "**var** TypeOfExpression", and two location types are equal if and only if their associated types are equal.

The operations on locations are getting the associate value, that is, that content of the location; replacing the associated value with a new value of the same type (assigning a value); and testing for equality between locations. For instance,

use x := **var** 3
in at x + 1   yields 4

The evaluation of **at** x gives the value associated with the declared location.

The assignment operator ← is an infix binary operator. The value of the left operand must be a location, while the value of the right operand must be a value of the same type as the previous content of the location. This operation modifies the store replacing the old value of the location and returns **nil**. For example,

use x := **var** 3
in (x ← **at** x + 1; x)   yields 4

where (E1; ...; En) evaluates all expressions Ei sequentially and returns the value of the last one.

4.4 Functions

Functional types are built by the operator →. The type $(tx \rightarrow ty)$ consists of all the functions that map values of type tx to the result of type ty. The expression "**fun**(x: tx): ty **is** Expression" denotes a function with a formal parameter x and a body Expression that returns a value of type ty. The function possesses a type $(tx \rightarrow ty)$. To define a function f with formal parameter x and body Expression,

one performs the declaration "f(x: t): t' := Expression", equivalent to "f := **fun**(x: t): t' **is** Expression". To apply f to an actual parameter p, one evaluates the expression "f(p)". The body of f is evaluated in the environment where f is defined (static scoping) and extended with the bindings (formal parameters, value of the actual parameter). The value of the body is returned as the result of the application. The control structures available to define compound expressions are sequencing, selection, repetition, and failure handling; these will be discussed in Section 8.

4.5 Abstract Types

The types of the values presented so far depend on the structure of the values only. That is, the type compatibility rule adopted is the so-called *structural equivalence* rule. User-defined type names are used as abbreviations for the structures they represent. These types are called *concrete*, in contrast with a new kind of type, called *abstract*. Two user-defined abstract types are always different (i.e., the type compatibility rule adopted for them is the so-called *name equivalence* rule).

Abstract types are not abstract in the sense of algebraic abstract types, but rather are analogous to CLU clusters, ALPHARD forms, and Euclid modules. They are mechanisms to abstract representations of the data from their behavior. Such behavior is defined by the designer in terms of the operations that can manipulate the data. However, an abstract type can be used like any other type in all the contexts where a type is expected. That is, user-defined abstract types have the same status as primitive types, which can be regarded as predefined abstract types provided by the language.

The main reason for introducing abstract types is protection, that is, to provide a mechanism to define a new type together with the operations available on values of that type. Thus, values of different abstract types are not compatible, even though they have the same representation (e.g., a weight is different from a height, although both are represented by integers). In this way, it is possible to tailor unique operations for each type, which cannot be used for objects of other types. For example, a function that tests a height and an age against a table of standards cannot be misused by applying it to a weight and an age. Another important protection introduced by abstract types is that programs are independent of changes in data representation as long as the primitive operations are the same.

To define abstract types, Galileo offers the following environment operator:

type Id ↔ Type [**assert** [**with** "Name"] BoolExpr]

This environment expression introduces the following bindings:

(1) Id is bound to a new type with a domain isomorphic to the domain of the representation type, Type, possibly restricted by the assertions.
(2) The identifiers mkId and repId are bound to two primitive functions, declared automatically, to map values of the representation type into the abstract one and vice versa:

mkId: Type → Id
repId: Id → Type

If an **assert** clause is present, BoolExpr is a Boolean expression on the values of the type. The assertions impose constraints on data values, which are controlled at execution time, when the data is created. If an assertion is violated, the operation fails with the name of the operation or with the name of the assertion, if present.

type Time ⟷ (hrs: num **and** mins: num)
assert use this
in hrs within (0,23) **And** mins within (0,59)

This declaration defines an abstract type Time, together with the primitive functions mkTime and repTime. As an abbreviation, constraints on a property can be specified directly in the corresponding pair declaration:

type Time ⟷
(hrs: num **this** within (0,23)
and mins: num **this** within (0,59))

To define an abstract type with the representation hidden, but with user-defined operations, the following definition might be used:

type Time ⟷
(hrs: num **this** within (0,24)
and mins: num **this** within (0,60))
with Hours(t: Time): num :=
hrs **of** repTime(t)
and Minutes(t: Time): num :=
mins **of** repTime(t)
and MakeTime(x: num, y: num): Time :=
mkTime((hrs := x **and** mins := y))

This declaration exports an abstract type Time, together with three functions MakeTime, Hours, and Minutes. The two primitive functions mkTime and repTime are only available in the definitions that appear in the **with** part, but they are not exported in the scope of the type declaration. The **with** construct is not a special syntax for abstract types, but it is another environment operator: A **with** B means that the types in A can be used in B, and they are exported together with the definitions in B; the values in A (like mkTime and repTime) can be used in B, but they are not exported. Abstract types are obtained from the interaction of two orthogonal features: the isomorphism constructor ⟷ and the environment operator **with**. Mutually dependent types can be defined with the expression:

type rec
(u ⟷ ...
and v ⟷ ...
. . . . .
and z ⟷ ...)
w,ih op(...) := ...
. . . . .
and op(...) := ...

To define new types, Galileo provides an additional environment operator:

type Id ⟷ Type |**assert** [Name]BoolExpr|

This operator introduces the following bindings:

(1) A new type that *inherits* the primitive operators on the representation type. The primitive operators retain their names, but this overloading does not introduce ambiguities because the typechecker can infer the meaning of an operator from the type of the operands. To restrict the set of operators to be

inherited, the operators **drop** or **take** on the representation type might be used.

(2) The identifiers mkId and repId, as for the ⟷ operator.

This environment operator has been included, since, in many cases, most of the primitive operators on the representation type are also needed for the abstract type, especially in database applications. The protection required is that the operators must never be applied to values of different types; and this is the effect of introducing a new type with this operator. When all the operators on the representation type are inherited, this operator is equivalent to the type constructor in Ada, where user-defined types are always different.

type PersonAge ⟷ num **this** within (0,150)
drop mod,*

This declaration introduces:

(1) The new type PersonAge with a domain isomorphic to a subset of numbers.
(2) The primitive functions mkPersonAge and repPersonAge.
(3) The predefined operators on numbers translated on the type PersonAge, except mod and *. The operators incorporate the control of the assertion, so the expression "mkPersonAge(10) + mkPersonAge(1)" is equivalent to mkPersonAge(10 + 1).

For example, another definition of Time, which introduces a new type equipped with the selector operators "Hours **of**" and "Minutes **of**" and the functions mkTime and repTime, is

type Time ⟷
(Hours: num **this** within (0,23)
and Minutes: num **this** within (0,59))

In defining a new tuple type with the operator ⟷, it is possible to declare a pair as *default* or *derived*:

Type Product
(Code: string
and SaleTax: **default** 0.06
and Price: var num
and Cost: var num
ext Profit:= **derived**(Price − Cost))

This declaration has the following meanings:

(1) In the parameter of the function mkProduct, the derived attributes are ignored, and if default attributes are omitted, the specified value is assumed.
(2) Every time the selector "Profit **of**" is used on a value of type Product, the associated expression is evaluated and its result is returned. If the derived attribute is defined with the **ext** operator, the expression is evaluated extending the definition environment temporarily with the pairs of the tuple. When the **and** operator is used, the function is evaluated in the definition environment.

5. TYPE HIERARCHIES

An important property of the Galileo type system is the notion of subtype: if a type u is a subtype of a type v ($u \subseteq v$), then a value of type u can be used in any context where a value of type v is expected, but not vice versa. The subtype relation is a partial order. For instance, if a function f has a formal parameter of type v, then an application of f to a value of type u is correctly typechecked because no run-time errors can occur. It is important to stress the point that since Galileo has a secure type system, the notion of type hierarchies is related to that of well-typed expressions [24, 28]: expressions that are syntactically well typed are always semantically well typed (i.e., such expressions do not cause run-time type errors, and give a value of the correct type). In Milner's words, "well-typed expressions do not go wrong" also [36] apply to hierarchies among types.

This notion of type hierarchies is different from the subtype concept of Ada, but is similar to the subclass mechanisms of Simula 67 and Smalltalk. In Galileo, this notion is extended to all the types, in the sequel explained in the sequel to this paper, while preserving two important properties: the language is still strongly-typed and the functions need not be recompiled in order to be used on parameters of any subtype.

With this mechanism Galileo supports the notion of *programming by data specialization*, originally introduced in Simula 67 and generalized in TAXIS to all the constituents of a database application: data, transactions, assertions, and scripts [14]. Complex software applications, especially those related to databases, can be designed and implemented incrementally. Once a set of functions has been designed and tested for the most general data, it can be used with data of any subtype introduced later on in the software development process. Moreover, new functions on the subtypes can be defined in terms of the old functions.

The subtype relation is automatically inferred by the typechecker for concrete types, but it must be declared explicitly among abstract types. The rules followed by the typechecker are

(1) For any type t, $t \subseteq t$.

(2) If r and s are tuple types, then $r \subseteq s$ iff:
  (a) the set of identifiers of r *contains* the set of identifiers of s, and
  (b) If r' and s' are the types of a common identifier, then $r' \subseteq s'$.

For instance, if

```
type (Address :=
    (Street: string
    and Zip: string)
    and VipAddress :=
    (Street: string
    and Zip: string
    and Country: string)
    and Person :=
    Name: string
    and Address: Address)
    and Student :=
    (Name: string
    and Address: Address
    and School: string)
    and VipPerson :=
    (Name: string
    and Address: VipAddress))
```

then

$$\text{Student} \subseteq \text{Person}$$
$$\text{VipPerson} \subseteq \text{Person}$$

while it is false that

$$\text{Person} \subseteq \text{VipPerson},$$
$$\text{Person} \subseteq \text{Student},$$
$$\text{Student} \subseteq \text{VipPerson and}$$
$$\text{VipPerson} \subseteq \text{Student}.$$

(3) If r and s are variant types, then $r \subseteq s$ iff:
  (a) the set of tags of r is *contained* in the set of tags of s, and
  (b) if r' and s' are the types of a common tag, then $r' \subseteq s'$.

For instance, if

```
type (Day :=
    (Monday or Tuesday
    or Wednesday or Thursday
    or Friday or Saturday
    or Sunday)

and Weekend := (Saturday or Sunday))
```

then

$$\text{Weekend} \subseteq \text{Day}.$$

(4) If r and s are sequence types with elements of types r' and s', then $r \subseteq s$ iff $r' \subseteq s'$.

(5) A modifiable type "var r" is a subtype of another type "var s" iff r and s are the same type.

To clarify the reason for this rule, consider the following expression evaluated in an environment containing the previous type definitions.

```
use type Traveler :=
    (Name: string
    and Address: var Address)
ext Agnelli :=
    (Name:= "Gianni Agnelli"
    and Address :=
    var (Street:= "200 Bloor St, Toronto"
    and Zip:= "M4V 2H5"
    and Country:= "Canada"))
and ChangeAddress (x :Traveler, y: Address) :=
    Address of x ← (Street:= Street of y and Zip:= Zip of y);
in
    (ChangeAddress(Agnelli,
    (Street:= "New Address"
    and Zip := "New Zip"
    and Country:= "New Country"));
Country of at (Address of Agnelli)
```

The application of ChangeAddress is not well typed according to the above rule because the type of Agnelli is not a subtype of Traveler. If, for instance, a different rule had been adopted, say that two types var r and var s are in the $\subseteq$ relation if $r \subseteq s$, then the previous expression would have been accepted by the typechecker, but it would no longer be true that "well-typed expressions do not go wrong": the last expression will generate a run-time error because the tuple Agnelli has lost the pair with attribute Country! This is a consequence of the assignment operation in the ChangeAddress function: it assigns a new data value of type (Street: string and Zip: string) to the Address of the actual parameter.

(6) If $(r \rightarrow s)$ and $(r' \rightarrow s')$ are function types, then $(r \rightarrow s) \subseteq (r' \rightarrow s')$ iff $r' \subseteq r$ and $s \subseteq s'$.

Note the inversion of the subtype relation between the domains of the functions. To clarify the reason for this rule, consider the following expression (a parameter of type $(r \to s)$ means that the actual parameter can be any function mapping values of type r to values of type s):

```
use type
  (Person := (Name: string)
   and Student :=
     (Name: string
      and School: string)
   and ForeignStudent :=
     (Name: string
      and School: string
      and Country: string))
and John :=
  (Name := "John")
and JohnStudent :=
  (Name := "John"
   and School := "UofT")
and AnItalian:=
  (Name := "Mario"
   and School: "UofT"
   and Country: "Italy")
and NameOfPerson (x: Person): string :=
  Name of x
and CountryOfForeignStudent (x: ForeignStudent): string :=
  Country of x
and StringFromStudent (g: Student → string, x: Student): string :=
  g(x)
in
  (StringFromStudent (CountryOfForeignStudent,JohnStudent);
   StringFromStudent (NameOfPerson, AnItalian))
```

For the above rule, the first application of StringFromStudent is not well typed because the type of CountryOfForeignStudent (ForeignStudent → string) is not a subtype of (Student → string). In fact, if it were executed, a run-time error would occur because of the use of the selector "Country of" in the function CountryOfForeignStudent on a value of type Student. In contrast, the second application of StringFromStudent is instead well typed.

(7) A type Id ↔ t(the same rule applies to ↔) is a subtype of another type Id' ↔ t', with primitive types considered as predefined abstract types, when the subtype relation is declared explicitly to the typechecker as follows:

Id is Id' ↔ t"NewAssertions", and $t \subseteq t'$

Note that the assertions on Id are those of Id' plus "NewAssertions".

```
type (PersonAddress := (HomeAddress: string)
  and StudentAddress :=
    (HomeAddress: string
     and College: string)
  and Person ↔
    (Name: string
     and Age: num this within (0,150)
     and Address: PersonAddress)
  and Student is Person ↔
    (Name: string
     and Age: num this within (6,25)
```

```
     and School: string
     and Address: StudentAddress))
```

The following abbreviation, used when the representation type is a tuple type, makes evident that the subtype Student inherits attributes and assertions of the type Person:

```
type Student ↔
  (is Person
   and School: string
   ext Address: StudentAddress
   assert use this in Age within (6,25)
```

In the abbreviated notation, the **ext** operator must be used to redefine the type of Address. A derived attribute cannot be redefined in a subtype.

Finally, multiple hierarchies are declared as "Id is Id', Id" ↔ t', where $t \subseteq t'$, and $t \subseteq t''$, or in the abbreviated form "Id ↔ is Id', Id"". Note that in the abbreviated form, if a common identifier is presented with type tr' in t' and tr'' in t'', then tr' must be a subtype of tr'' or vice versa. In the representation of type Id, the identifier will have the most specialized type.

6. CLASSES

Classes provide a mechanism for representing a database by means of sequences of modifiable interrelated objects. An element of a class is an object that is the computer representation of certain facts of an entity of the world that is being modeled. An object-oriented view of a database is characterized by the following [14, 33, 35]:

(1) There is a one-to-one correspondence between objects in the database and entities of the world that is being modeled.

(2) The objects of the database are all distinct, and they might not have an external reference, such as a key, that stands for them.

(3) Associations among entities are modeled by relating the corresponding objects and not the external references. Moreover, only objects that exist in the database can be used to model associations.

A class is characterized by a name and the type of its elements. The name of a class denotes the elements of the class currently present in the database, while the type gives the structure of the elements. The type of the class elements must be abstract, therefore two elements of different classes are always of different types, although they may be defined with the same representation.

Elements of classes are the only values in Galileo that can be created and destroyed. Moreover, they are uniquely represented, and when updated their modification is reflected in all other objects in which they appear as components.

Each class can be either a *base* class or a *subclass*. A base class is defined independently of other classes, while a subclass is defined in terms of other classes. As in SDM [32], a base class is used to model a primitive collection of entities, while a subclass is used to model alternative ways of looking at the same entities.

6.1 Base Classes

A base class is defined by the environment operator **class**, as shown in the following example with two mutually defined classes:

```
rec Departments class
    Department ↔
        (Name: string
        and Budget: num
        and Address: string
        and Manager: optional Employee
        and Employees: var seq Employee)
        key (Name)

and Employees class
    Employee ↔
        (Name: string
        and Salary: num
        and NameOfDept :=
            derived Name of
            get Departments with this isin (at Employees)
        key (Name)
```

The **class** operator introduces the following bindings:

(1) The identifiers Department and Employee are bound to new types isomorphic to tuples.
(2) The class identifiers Departments and Employees are bound to modifiable sequences of values of type Department and Employee, respectively.
(3) The identifiers mkDepartment and mkEmployee are bound to two primitive functions, automatically declared, which differ from similar functions for abstract types in that every time they are applied, new objects are created and automatically inserted in front of the associated sequences if the specified constraints are not violated. The constructed elements are also the values returned by these functions.

The above declaration defines the structure of the objects together with a few constraints, some of which are predefined constraints on sequences, to be tested when an instance is created or modified:

(1) The **key** constraint asserts that elements of a class must differ in the value of certain constant attributes. Note that if the **key** constraint is not specified, the insertion will be made even though the values of the attributes are equal to those of another object already present in the class. That is, elements of classes are always distinct objects, but the construction of an element will fail when the constraints are violated.

Other constraints are specified directly in the definition of the element type:

(2) Only attributes with a **var** type can be modified.
(3) Only modifiable attributes with an **optional** type can be left unspecified when an element is created.
(4) A derived attribute such as NameOfDept is used to model a mapping from the employees to the department where they are employed, while the property Employees in Departments is used to model a *part-of* relationship, which implies the following dependency constraint: an employee cannot be eliminated from the database as long as he or she belongs to a department.

Since the name of a class denotes the sequence of all the current elements present in the database, all the operators on sequences can be applied to classes.

In addition to these operators, the following is also provided:

get ClassId **with** Condition

This is another operator on sequences: it returns the only element in a sequence which satisfies the condition. Otherwise, a failure is generated.

6.2 Subclasses

Subclasses and type hierarchies are the features provided by Galileo to support the abstraction mechanism of IS-A hierarchies, originally proposed in the context of semantic networks, and considered nowadays as an essential requirement for a language supporting semantic data model features [35].

There are, however, differences between IS-A hierarchies and the type hierarchies introduced in the previous section:

(1) The subtype notion in Galileo refers to a static aspect of the language, and has been introduced to establish a compatibility rule among all the possible values of a type and those of its supertypes.
(2) An IS-A hierarchy (e.g., Students IS-A Persons) involves two different notions. First, it establishes an existence constraint among the elements of the database: the elements of Students are always a subset of the elements of Persons (extensional notion). Second, it establishes a subtype hierarchy between the type of the elements of Students and Persons. Therefore, an element of Students can be used as an argument of any operation defined for elements of Persons (intensional notion).

In Galileo, the two notions behind the IS-A hierarchy are expressed with two distinct mechanisms: the type hierarchy, to deal with the intensional aspect, and the subclass, to deal with the extensional aspect. This distinction increases the modeling capability of the language because it allows the use of the type hierarchy independently of the subclass mechanism.

There are three ways of defining subclasses: by *subset, partition,* or *restriction.*

A *subset* class with elements of type T contains those elements of the parent class that have been included explicitly in the subclass with the proper operator in T.

A *partition* object is like a subset class, but it enforces the additional constraint that its elements are not included in another subclass of the same partition.

A *restriction* class contains all the elements of the parent class that satisfy some predicate, which is evaluated at the time of element construction. This predicate cannot be defined over modifiable or derived values.

In all cases, when a new element is added to a subclass it then also becomes an element of the parent class. In the case of restriction classes, a new element must also satisfy the restriction predicate.

Finally, the operator

remove Expression1,..., ExpressionN

is provided to eliminate objects from a class and from its subclasses, and return the value nil only if the objects are not used as components of other elements. Otherwise, a failure is generated. "Expression i" must evaluate to a sequence of elements.

The type of the elements of a subclass must be a subtype of the element type of the parent class. New attributes can be added with the **and** operator or old attributes can be redefined with the **ext** operator, but the following restrictions must be satisfied:

(1) Nonoptional attributes may be added only when a subclass is defined as a subset or partition.

(2) When a subclass is defined by restriction, then only derived, optional, or default attributes can be added.

Subclasses can also be defined from more than one parent class, with the restriction that the type of the elements must be a subtype of the element type of each parent class. An element of a subclass is always an element of all its parent classes. Some examples follow to clarify these points:

PublicEmployees restriction of Employees class
PublicEmployee ↔ is Employee

The elements are the same as the Employee class.

DowntownDepartments restriction of Departments
with Address = "Downtown"
class
DowntownDept ↔
(is Department
ext ManagerSalary := derived Salary of (at Manager))

The elements of the DowntownDepartments class are all the departments in Downtown.

Managers partition of Employees
with Secretaries, Craftsmen class
Manager ↔ (is Employee and Bonus: num)

Secretaries partition of Employees
with Managers, Craftsmen class
Secretary ↔ is Employee

Craftsmen partition of Employees
with Secretaries, Managers class
Craftsman ↔ is Employee

Carpenters subset of Craftsmen class
Carpenter ↔ is Craftsman

Bricklayers subset of Craftsmen class
Bricklayer ↔ is Craftsman

The Employees are partitioned into three disjoint subsets, while the Craftsmen have been refined into two overlapping subsets of instances. In all the above cases, the classes must be populated explicitly.

The predicate **alsoIn** is provided to check whether or not an object of one class also belongs to a subclass:

Expression alsoIn Subclass

Expression must evaluate to an object of a class.
The following operator is used to include an element of a class in a subclass with elements of type T:

inT (Expression1, Expression2)

Expression1 must evaluate to the object to be included in the subclass, while Expression2 must evaluate to a value of the representation type T. The operator checks that the values of the corresponding attributes of Expression1 and Expression2 are the same. Expression2 can be omitted when an object of a subclass has the same attributes as an object of the superclass.

Finally, to operate on an object of a parent class as if it were the element of a subclass, the object must be retyped with the following operator:

Expression likeIn Subclass

Expression must evaluate to an object of a class. The result is the object as member of Subclass. This operator is needed due to the static type checking discipline.

7. ENVIRONMENTS AS A MODULARIZATION MECHANISM

The languages hitherto proposed for conceptual modeling do not provide features to help the designer to develop and test a schema incrementally or to express the overall structure of a schema in terms of smaller related parts. This issue has been addressed in Galileo by using the environment, which is a denotable value, as a modularization mechanism [5]. As will be shown in the sequel to this paper, the environment operators previously defined can be used to structure a schema in a way similar to that suggested for theories by Burstall and Goguen in their specification language Clear [23].

Another use of environments is to deal with data and operations as a single unit which can be accessed by programs. This problem has also been addressed in ADAPLEX with a specialized form of Ada packages [49]. In fact, a drawback to commercial DBMSs is that no kind of procedural knowledge can be described in the schema, whether "derived" information or application domain oriented operations. In other words, in these systems data can be shared, but the procedural knowledge cannot: it must be embedded in the applications. The inclusion of the operations in the schema has the following advantages:

(1) The same operations on the database are not duplicated in all the programs that need them.

(2) The database schema does reflect all the knowledge available about the application domain. In particular, the schema contains not only the description of the structure of the objects and the constraints, but also the operations on the objects, which complete their semantics.

(3) It is possible to constrain user programs to operate on the database through a set of predefined operations, especially designed to include critical design choices, such as integrity preservation.

Environments also have other useful applications. First, it is the mechanism used by Galileo to deal with persistence without resorting to specific data types, such as files of programming languages. Second, to deal with evolving applications, the environment is used to establish explicitly the way in which new applications interact when they use common data. Finally, the environment is used to define application-oriented views of data in a similar way to the view mechanisms of DBMSs.

7.1 Persistence

Temporary values exist in the system only during the execution of the expression in which they are defined. None of the abstraction mechanisms described previously have the property of defining persistent values. For instance, user programs may also contain class definitions, if temporary classes must be kept while running an application. To deal with persistence, a global environment is assumed in which all values are automatically maintained. Such an environment is managed by the system that supports the language. For other approaches to the treatment of persistence as an orthogonal property of data, see [10].

The global environment is extended by adding new bindings with the command use. In fact, for user protection, a warning is generated if use is used with identifiers already bound in the current environment. Instead of having a single set of unrelated definitions and values, as imposed by the interactive approaches of LISP top level and APL workspace, the user can fruitfully employ the environment mechanism to structure the global environment. For instance, the following is the definition, at top level, of an environment Personnel with two permanent classes (for brevity, defined operations are omitted):

```
use
Personnel :=
(rec Departments class
   Department ↦
      (Name: string
      and Manager: var Employee
      and Budget: num)
      key (Name)
   and Employees class
   Employee ↦
      (Name: string
      and Salary: num
      and Dept: var Department)
      key (Name));
```

Each expression is evaluated inside an environment, initially the global one, called the *current environment*. Any environment that can be accessed from the global environment can become the current one with the command **"enter Environment"**, while to return to the global environment there is the command **quit**. Since the language is expression-based, it is possible in the current environment to evaluate any expression by simply typing it. For example, assuming that the classes in Personnel have already been populated, a simple interactive session is:[1]

enter Personnel:

To get the names of all the employees with a salary less than the average salary of their department:

```
for x in Employees
   with Salary of x
      < avg(for y in Employees
         with at Dept of x = at Dept of y
         do Salary of y)
do Name of x;
```

To add a new employee to the Research department:

```
mkEmployee
   (Name := "Brown"
   and Salary := 4
   and Dept := get Departments with Name = "Research");
```

7.2 Encapsulation

Another use of the environment mechanism is to model a schema as a set of interrelated units. Each unit encapsulates data and operations that are closely related. For instance, let us assume that we are interested in describing as distinct units data relevant to the planning and administration departments of our hypothetical firm, although these departments share data of the environment Personnel:

```
use Planning :=
(Personnel
and Projects class
   Project ↦
      (Name: string
      and Budget: num)
      key (Name));

use Administration :=
(Personnel
and Suppliers class
   Supplier ↦
      (Name: string
      and Address: var string
      and Credit: var num)
      key (Name));
```

Note that, because of the semantics of environment operators, the Personnel environment is shared by Planning and Administration, so that any updating of a class in any environment will be reflected in all the others.

7.3 Refinements

It is possible to start with one environment and to generate others by extending the environment with new definitions. Thus, data concerning the same application are visible at different levels of detail.

```
use DetailedPersonnel :=
(Personnel
and Branches class
   Branch ↦
      (Name: string
      and Address: string
      and Other: string)
      key (Name)
```

---

[1] A more elaborate session is reported in [4].

ext Special Employees subset of Employees class
    SpecialEmployee ↔
        (is Employee
        and PrivateData: string));

7.4 View Modeling

To provide controlled access to the database, it is possible to give a different view of an environment by excluding some of its data or operations.

use OnlyDepartments := Personnel drop Employees

In OnlyDepartments, Employees are not visible, while in the following environment only the names of the employees and the names of the departments where they work can be accessed:

use EmployeesView :=
    (use Personnel
    in Employees :=
        derived for e in Employees
        do (e ext NameOfDept := Name of Dept)
        drop Dept, Salary);

The expression "Id := derived Expression" denotes an environment in which the only association is between the Id and a virtual value, which is obtained by evaluating Expression every time the value of Id is requested. All the operators used to query a class can be applied to Employees, which therefore behaves like a view of relational database.

7.5 Logical Independence

The environment operators allow the designer to make applications independent from changes in an environment, as long as the old view of the database is derivable from the redefined environment. For instance, let us assume that an application program was designed to work in the DetailedPersonnel environment on Branches of a certain area, "Downtown", to retrieve data. The database was then extended to include Branches in other areas, with the elements type redefined as

Branch ↔
    (Name: string
    and Address: string
    and Area: string
    and Other: string)

In order to make the old program independent of these changes, it can be used in the following environment:

use NewDetailedPersonnel :=
    (DetailedPersonnel
    ext Branches :=
        derived for b in Branches
        with Area = "Downtown"
        do b drop Area);

8. TRANSACTIONS AND FAILURE HANDLING

Every top level Galileo expression is a *transaction*. That is to say, it is considered an atomic action against the database: once invoked, it either completes all its operations or behaves as if it were never invoked. Transactions may fail due either to a hardware or software failure or to a run-time program error. In Galileo it is possible to cause such an event, and also to sense its occurrence so as to perform an appropriate action. The failure of a transaction causes an interruption of the normal control flow, and, in addition, all updatings from the beginning of the transaction are undone.

A transaction can be either *simple* or *compound*. Each expression typed in at top level by the user is a simple transaction. Therefore, if the expression fails, the persistent data are unaffected. However, if more than one top level expression must be considered as a single transaction, the expressions must be enclosed in "transaction brackets": **transaction** and **end transaction**. A compound transaction is a sequence of top level expressions enclosed in such brackets.

Since any operation whether predefined or defined that is accessible to the user may be applied as a simple transaction, whenever the schema designer defines operations, he or she is in fact defining transactions. As a consequence, transactions can be nested by defining a new function as a composition of predefined ones: an action, atomic at a higher level of abstraction, may be decomposed into subatomic actions to perform, for example, a stepwise updating of the database [30]. A failure of inner transactions can be controlled, and alternative transactions can be started to achieve the desired effect. Consider, for example, the case of booking a tour with an airline reservations system. Even if the reservation of single parts of the tour succeeds, unless all the tour has been reserved, the effects of previous operations must be revoked, and a new attempt could be made with a different airline, or with a different schedule. The different attempts should be treated as alternative transactions, and the outermost one should fail only if all attempts fail. Another important advantage of nested transactions is the ability to define transactions not knowing the context in which they might be used [9].

The linguistic construct for handling failures has a block structure, unlike the usual proposed **commit** and **abort** statements [30]: "Expression **if_fails** Expression". If the first expression fails, its effects are undone, and the value of the whole construct is that of the second expression. Otherwise, it is that of the first one with the effects preserved.

Failures have associated with them a string that can be used for a selective handling of failures with the **case_fails** construct. For failures which occur during the execution of primitive operations, the string returned is the name of the operation. The user can generate a failure with the expression "**failwith** string" or with **fail**, which is equivalent to "**failwith** "fail"". When a failure occurs, the normal execution path is interrupted, control is passed to the first surrounding failure handler, and the effects are undone. If no handler is present, the top level expression fails, all its effects are undone, an error message is printed, and the execution terminates. Let us consider an example with the of the system, called Dialogo, which presently supports a significant subset of Galileo [4]. Tools are available to edit a conceptual schema, query the definitions, and load and query test data. An interesting feature of Dialogo is that it is based on a top level cycle in which a Galileo expression from the user is accepted, executed, and the result displayed while the effect of the user expression on the database is permanently preserved. An expression may be the invocation of a single predefined function or any complex expression of the language. Future studies on Galileo will proceed along the following lines:

(1) *Extensions.* We will extend the language to provide (a) a form-oriented, input/output interface; (b) a process construct to model interactions with the users and database evolution, with an approach similar to that adopted in TAXIS.

(2) *Implementation.* The Dialogo system is being reimplemented by extending the present implementation of the ML compiler, available on a VAX 11/780 running the UNIX² operating system.

(3) *Applications.* With the new implementation of Dialogo, it will be possible to effectively experiment with the design of database applications using Galileo. This will also provide the opportunity to test the tools available in our designer's workbench against the demands of specific user environments.

ACKNOWLEDGMENTS

We are indebted to M. E. Occhiuto, who contributed to the design of a preliminary version of Galileo, and to the members of the Galileo Project, M. Capaccioli, F. Giannotti, B. Magnani, D. Pedreschi, and M. L. Sabatini, for their constructive criticisms. Also, many thanks to A. Borgida, S. Gibbs, D. Lee, A. Mendelzon, J. Mylopoulos, B. Nixon, and I. Reichstein for their helpful suggestions in improving a previous version of this paper, at the time A. Albano was visiting professor at the Computer Science Department of the University of Toronto. The paper has also benefited from the constructive comments made by the referees.

REFERENCES

1. ABRIAL, J.R. Data semantics. In *Data Management Systems*, J. K. Klimbie and K. L. Koffeman, Eds., North-Holland, Amsterdam, 1974, 1–60.

2. ALBANO, A., AND ORSINI, R. An interactive integrated system to design and use data bases. In *Proceedings Workshop on Data Abstraction, Data Bases and Conceptual Modelling, ACM SIGMOD Special Issue 11*, 2 (1981), 91–93.

3. ALBANO, A., OCCHIUTO, M.E., AND ORSINI, R. A uniform management of persistent and complex data in programming languages. In *Infotech State of Art Report on Databases*, M.P. Atkinson, Ed., Series 9, No. 4, Pergamon Infotech, 1981, 321–344.

4. ALBANO, A., AND ORSINI, R. Dialogo: An interactive environment for conceptual design in Galileo. In *Methodology and Tools for Database Design*, S. Ceri, Ed., North-Holland, Amsterdam, 1983, 229–253.

5. ALBANO, A. Type hierarchies and semantic data models. *ACM Sigplan '83: Symposium on Programming Language Issues in Software Systems* (San Francisco, 1983), 178–186.

6. ALBANO A., CAPACCIOLI, M., AND ORSINI, R. La definizione del Galileo (Versione 83/6). Rapporto Tecnico DATAID N.20, Pisa, 1983.

² UNIX is a trademark of Bell Laboratories.

selective failure handler:

```
Employee class
Employee ↔
    (Name: string
    and Salary: num
    and Dept: Department)
key (Name)
    assert with "LowPay" Salary < Minimum
    assert with "HighPay" Salary < (Budget of Dept)/10
ext rec NewEmployee(AName: string, ASalary: num, ADept: string):Employee :=
mkEmployee
    (Name := AName
    and Salary := ASalary
    and Dept := get Departments with Name = ADept)
case_fails
    ["LowPay"]
        NewEmployee(AName, Minimum, ADept)|
    ["HighPay"]
        NewEmployee(AName,
            (Budget of get Departments with Name = ADept)/10,
            ADept)
```

9. CONCLUSIONS

A strongly-typed programming language for database applications has been presented. Unlike other proposals, which integrate a relational data model into a conventional, general-purpose programming language, e.g., Pascal, [8, 40, 43, 46, 52], we have integrated into the framework of the programming language Edinburgh ML [29], a strongly-typed interactive language, features to support semantic data model abstraction mechanisms (classification, aggregation, and specialization) as well as abstraction mechanisms of modern programming languages (types, abstract types, and modularization).

The approach adopted is therefore closer to that of ADAPLEX, which extends Ada with new features to support databases modeling [49]; although the features included in Galileo, notably the type hierarchies, are not ad hoc for databases, but can be used independently. This approach was preferred for two reasons.

First, we were interested in studying a uniform approach towards the design of a modern strongly-typed programming language, which would include features to support semantic data models. We believe that this paper provides evidence of how types, abstract types, type hierarchies, classification, aggregation, specialization, and modularization can be integrated in an expression-based language that is statically type-checkable. In particular, we have shown the effectiveness of the environment, a novel abstraction mechanism, in the context of conceptual modeling, for structuring complex applications and for view modeling.

Second, we were interested in developing an interactive database designer's workbench, which would integrate a set of tools for creating, testing, and implementing on a traditional DBMS a database design [2]. Since, in the short term, we have mainly been interested in using this aid for conceptual modeling, we have found it more convenient to design a new language for dealing with the specific problems in this area. We have already implemented a prototype version

7. ALBANO, A., CAPACCIOLI, M., OCCHIUTO, M.E., AND ORSINI, R. A modularization mechanism for conceptual modeling. In *Proceedings 9th International Conference on VLDB* (Florence, Italy, 1983), 232–240.

8. AMBLE, T., BRATBERGSENGEN, K., AND RISNES, O. ASTRAL, a structured and unified approach to database design and manipulation. In *Data Base Architecture*, G. Bracchi and G.M. Nijssen, Eds., North-Holland, Amsterdam, 1979, 240–257.

9. ATKINSON, M.P., CHISHOLM, K.J., AND COCKSHOTT, W.P. The new Edinburgh persistent algorithmic language. In *Infotech State of Art Report on Databases*, M.P. Atkinson, Ed., Series 9, No. 4, Pergamon Infotech, 1981, 299–318.

10. ATKINSON, M.P., BAILEY, P.J., CHISHOLM, K.J., COCKSHOTT, W.P., AND MORRISON, R. An approach to persistent programming. *Comput. J. 26*, 4 (1983), 360–365.

11. BALTZER, R. An implementation methodology for semantic database models. In *Entity Relationship Approach to System Analysis and Design*, P.P. Chen, Ed., North-Holland, Amsterdam, 1980, 433–444.

12. BARRON, J. Dialogue organization and structure for interactive information systems. M.Sc. thesis, Dept. of Computer Science, Univ. of Toronto, 1980.

13. BILLER, H. AND NEUHOLD, E.J. Semantics of databases: The semantics of data models. *Inf. Syst. 3* (1978), 1–30.

14. BORGIDA, A.T., MYLOPOULOS, J., AND WONG, H.K.T. Methodological and computer aids for interactive information systems design. *Automated Tools for Information System Design*, H.J. Schneider and A. Wasserman, Eds., North-Holland, Amsterdam, 1982.

15. BORGIDA, A. Features of languages for the development of information systems at the conceptual level. *IEEE Softw.* (1984), to appear.

16. BREUTMAN, B., FALKENBERG, E., AND MAUER, R. CSL: A language for defining conceptual schemas. In *Data Base Architecture*, G. Bracchi and G.M. Nijssen, Eds., North-Holland, Amsterdam, 1979, 237–256.

17. BRODIE, M.L. The application of data types to database semantic integrity. *Inf. Syst. 5*, 4 (1980), 287–296.

18. BRODIE, M.L., AND ZILLES, S.N. Eds. *Proceedings Workshop on Data Abstraction, Data Bases, and Conceptual Modelling, ACM SIGMOD Special Issue 11*, 2 (1981).

19. BRODIE, M.L. On modeling behavioral semantics of databases. In *Proceedings 7th International Conference on VLDB* (Cannes, 1981), 32–42.

20. BRODIE, M.L., MYLOPOULOS, J., AND SCHMIDT, J.W. Eds. *On Conceptual Modeling: Perspectives from Artificial Intelligence, Databases, and Programming Languages*, Springer Verlag, New York, 1984.

21. BUBENKO, J.A. Information modeling in the context of system development. In *IFIP Congress 1980*, North-Holland, Amsterdam, 1980, 395–411.

22. BUNEMAN, P., AND FRANKEL, R.E. FQL—a functional query language. In *Proceedings of ACM SIGMOD Conference* (Boston, Mass., 1979), 52–58.

23. BURSTALL, R.M., AND GOGUEN, J.A. Putting theories together to make specifications. In *Proceedings IJCAI* (Boston, Mass., 1977), 1045–1058.

24. CAPACCIOLI, M. La Semantica Denotazionale del Galileo. Tesi di laurea in Scienze dell'Informazione, Univ. di Pisa, Italy, 1983.

25. CARDELLI, L. A semantics of multiple inheritance. In *Semantics of Data Types*, G. Kahn, D.B. MacQueen, and G. Plotkin, Eds., Lecture Notes in Computer Science, Vol. 173, Springer Verlag, New York, 1984, 51–67.

26. CERI, S., PELAGATTI, G. AND BRACCHI, G. Structured methodology for defining static and dynamic aspects of data base applications. *Inf. Syst. 6*, 1 (1981), 31–45.

27. CERI, S., Ed. *Methodology and Tools for Database Design*, North-Holland, Amsterdam, 1983.

28. GORDON, M. *The Denotational Description of Programming Languages. An Introduction*, Springer Verlag, New York, 1979.

29. GORDON, M., MILNER, R., AND WADSWORTH, C. *Edinburgh LCF*, Lecture Notes in Computer Science, Vol. 78, Springer Verlag, New York, 1979.

30. GRAY, J. The transaction concept: Virtues and limitations. In *Proceedings 7th International Conference on VLDB* (Cannes, 1981), 144–154.

31. HAMMER, M., AND BERKOWITZ, B. DIAL: A programming language for data intensive applications. In *Proceedings of ACM SIGMOD Conference*, (Santa Monica, Calif., 1980), 75–92.

32. HAMMER, M., AND MCLEOD, D. Database description with SDM: A semantic database model. *ACM Trans. Database Syst. 6*, 3 (1981), 351–386.

33. KENT, W. Limitations of record-based information models. *ACM Trans. Database Syst. 4*, 1 (1979), 107–131.

34. LUM, V., ET AL. 1978 New Orleans Data Base Design Workshop Report. In *Proceedings 5th International Conference on VLDB* (Rio de Janeiro, 1979), 328–339.

35. MCLEOD, D. AND KING, R. Semantic database models. In *Principle of Database Design*, S.B. Yao, Ed., Prentice-Hall, 1984.

36. MILNER, R. A theory of type polymorphism in programming. *J. Comput. Syst. Sci. 17*, (1978), 348–375.

37. MYLOPOULOS, J., BERNSTEIN, P.A., AND WONG, H.K.T. A language facility for designing database-intensive applications. *ACM Trans. Database Syst. 5*, 2 (1980), 185–207.

38. NAVATHE, B.S. Information modeling tools for data base design. Panel on Logical Database Design (Fort Lauderdale, Fla. 1980).

39. ROUSSOPOULOS, N. CSDL: A conceptual schema definition language for the design of data base applications. *IEEE Trans. Softw. Eng. SE-5*, 5 (1979), 481–496.

40. ROWE, L.A., AND SHOENS, K.A. Data abstraction, views and updates in RIGEL. In *Proceedings ACM SIGMOD Conference* (Boston, Mass., 1979), 71–81.

41. SABATINI, L. La Semantica Statica del Galileo. Tesi di laurea in Scienze dell'Informazione, Univ. di Pisa, Italy, 1982.

42. SCHMIDT, J.W. Type concepts for database definition. In *Database: Improving Usability and Responsiveness*, B. Schneidermann, Ed., Academic Press, New York, 1978, 215–244.

43. SCHMIDT, J.W., AND MALL, M. *Pascal/R Report*. Univ. of Hamburg, Fachbereich Informatik, Rep. 66, Jan. 1980.

44. SHAW, M. The impact of abstraction concerns on modern programming languages. *Proc. IEEE 68*, 9 (1980), 1119–1130.

45. SHIPMAN, D.W. The functional data model and the data language DAPLEX. *ACM Trans. Database Syst. 6*, 1 (1980), 140–173.

46. SHOPIRO, J.E. A programming language for relational databases. *ACM Trans. Database Syst. 4*, 4 (1979), 493–517.

47. SMITH, J.M., AND SMITH, D.C.P. Database abstraction: Aggregation and generalization. *ACM Trans. Database Syst. 2*, 2 (1979), 105–133.

48. SMITH, J.M., AND SMITH, D.C.P. A database approach to software specifications. In *Software Development Tools*, W.E. Riddle and R.E. Fairley, Eds., Springer Verlag, Berlin, 1979, 176–200.

49. SMITH, J.M., FOX, S., AND LANCERS, T. Reference manual for ADAPLEX. Tech. Rep. CCA-81-02, Computer Corporation of America, Jan. 1981.

50. TEICHROEW, D., AND HERSHEY, E.A. PSL/PSA: A computer-aided technique for structured documentation and analysis of information processing systems. *IEEE Trans. Softw. Eng. SE-3*, 1 (1977), 41–49.

51. TENNENT, R.D. *Principles of Programming Languages*. Prentice-Hall International, London, 1981.

52. WASSERMAN, A.I. The data management facilities of PLAIN. In *Proceedings of the ACM SIGMOD Conference* (Boston, Mass., 1979), 60–70.

53. WEBER, H. A software engineering view of data base systems. In *Proceedings 4th International Conference on VLDB* (Berlin, 1978), 36–51.

54. YAO, S.B., NAVATHE, S.B., AND WELDON, J.L. An integrated approach to logical database design. In *Proceedings NYU Symposium on Data Base Design*, (1978), 1–14.

Received April 1984; revised January 1985; accepted February 1985

Chapter 3

Object-Oriented Database Systems

Introduction

This chapter describes several object-oriented data models. It provides a good study of the differences in these models, which on the surface may seem to be much the same.

We have only included examples of behaviorally object-oriented systems. We do not cover structurally object-oriented systems, as they do not meet the threshold-model requirement of encapsulated behavior. The semantic data models also have this property. Other structural models include [AB84], [DPS86], [DGL86], and [Pa+87]. These systems have the functionality of a storage manager plus a query language. Often, a semantic layer is built on the top of one of these models to provide application-specific objects (e.g., CASE, geographic data).

The structural systems raise the question of whether behavior should be embedded at the database level or in a layer outside the database. By putting the behavior inside the database, can we achieve any performance improvement? The structural systems were running their semantic layer in the workstation before the interpreters and storage managers of behavioral systems were running on multiple machines. Therefore, distributed applications were running on structural systems earlier than they were on behavioral systems.

GemStone [MS87] has one of the simplest object-oriented models. It is based on Smalltalk, with very few extensions. Orion [Ba+87] also has a Smalltalk-like model, but with many more extensions. For example, it has a facility for complex objects that is built in and that affects the

semantics of fundamental notions such as creation and deletion. An important issue in the design of such a model is how much semantics is needed in the database interpreter, and how much should be built out of the interpreter's primitives at the application level.

GemStone is a commercial product. It incorporates object identity and encapsulation via data abstraction that defines an external interface as a set of messages. It also suports inheritance. Section 3 of [MS87] on the GemStone Model and the OPAL language is a good summary of message-passing syntax. What does GemStone add to Smalltalk to create a database? It is disk-based, and it provides concurrency control and recovery, constraints, secondary storage management, queries, index support, authorization, and a structured name space.

GemStone incorporates a query language, but queries are formed over the instance variables of an object. Although this approach avoids some of the problems of querying abstract types, it violates the principle of encapsulation. It should not be possible to write any external programs, including queries, that depend on the representation (i.e., instance variables) of an object.

Indices are also available on the instance variables (i.e., their internal structure). This idea per se is not a breach of encapsulation, since the presence of indices does not need to show through the interface. In GemStone, however, queries can name instance variables and there is a special syntax to indicate that the system should try to use the available indices. The problem of maintaining an index in the presence of encapsulation was discussed in *Fundamentals of Object-Oriented Databases* in this volume.

Issues arise involving what can be indexed. GemStone allows indexing on arbitrary collections, whereas Orion indexes only classes. Also, there is a question about whether to support indices on simple properties or on paths of properties. GemStone does the latter.

Vbase [AH87] is a commercial product whose data model was influenced substantially by CLU. It emphasizes strong typing and the use of abstract data types. Vbase attempts to do all type checking at compile-time, but when it can not accomplish this it defers the checks to run-time. GemStone does not have typed program variables; it has only typed objects. Thus, it must do all of its type checking dynamically.

Like GemStone, Vbase has a definite separation between interface and implementation. Unlike GemStone, for which the interface is a set of messages, a Vbase interface consists of a set of operations (messages) and a set of properties. The properties express the abstract state of an object and do not necessarily imply anything about the representation or stored state. A property definition implies the existence of both a *get* and a *set* operation, which respectively, observe and modify the property's value.

Vbase has database variables (persistent names) for objects of any type. In standard record-based models, only certain types of objects can have persistent names. For example, in the relational model, a relation can have a name, whereas an integer cannot have one.

The other systems represented in this chapter associate all operations with some type. Vbase supports free operations that are not associated with any type. This raises the question of whether or not these operations are necessary in an application that has been decomposed using proper object-oriented methodology.

In Vbase, TDL is the specification language; COP is the language for implementation. TDL is a special syntax for creating type-defining objects and for declaring database variables and constraints. It is much like the type-definition and variable-declaration portion of a language such as Pascal. TDL supports block scoping of names. TDL also has enumeration, union, variant, and parameterized types.

TDL also supports exceptions as objects that contain detailed information about the exception for use by the exception handler. This last feature is much like TAXIS [My+80].

Vbase has inverse relationships, a feature that we see in many of the semantic data models. GemStone and Orion do not have inverses. Inverses can be simulated with the use of an index.

Orion is also a Smalltalk derivative. Among its many features, it has default values for instance variables and multiple inheritance.

Orion has a type **SetOfT** for every type **T** in the type hierarchy. This creates a parallel hierarchy of **Set** types. If **S** is a subtype of **T**, then Orion has **SetOfS** as a subtype of **SetOfT**. As discussed in the introduction to this volume and in Chapter 1, this relationship can cause problems if we have a program that applies an update method (e.g., insert) on a variable of type **SetOfT**, and the value of that variable at run-time is actually a **SetOfS.** This situation is allowed by substitutability. If the system does not check at run-time, it might be possible to insert a giraffe into a set of elephants through an expression that type checks correctly at compile-time.

Another issue raised is the existence of a **SetOfSetOfT** type. Since **SetOfT** is a perfectly good type, it seems reasonable to postulate the existence of **SetOfSetOfT**, **SetOfSetOfSetOfT**, and so on.

Vbase deals with typed sets by a **Set[T]** parameterized type. This approach is different from that of Orion, in that the Set types are not manifest until they are needed. GemStone has set instances that can be constrained to have objects of a particular type.

Orion supports automatic type extents. That is, for any type **T**, the system maintains the set of all **T**s. Systems vary substantially in this regard. GemStone, for example, does not support automatic extents. Other languages, such as O$_2$, will support them optionally.

Orion has concentrated on the area of schema evolution and has produced a set of rules that must be obeyed in order for a type hierarchy to remain consistent in the face of change. Other work in this area includes [Pa+87] and [SZ86]. It has also produced results in the area of composite objects—the ability to model objects that are built out of other objects. This area is treated in more detail in Chapter 6.

PDM [MD86] from Computer Corporation of America (now Xerox Advanced Information Technology) is based on DAPLEX [Sh81]. It has an algebraic data model with special extensions for spatial and temporal data. The PDM algebra is related to the relational algebra, but it has been extended with operators that directly allow for the application of multiargument functions to objects. Instead of a join operator, PDM includes an APPLY_APPEND operator that models function composition.

In PDM, everything is a function. It accommodates both stored and computed functions in a uniform framework. A stored function is viewed as a table. APPLY_APPEND applies a function (either stored or computed) to a function stored in another table.

Objects in PDM are explicitly added to types. This is in contrast to a system such as Vbase, in which objects are created of some type and their properties and operations are determined by this creation type. In PDM, objects are allowed to enter and leave types dynamically. They will acquire new functions as they do so.

PDM supports a way to view a table as a family of functions. For example, a table with three columns can be treated as a one-input, two-output, or two-input, one-output, or no-input, three-output, or three-input, Boolean output function. This usage is similar to a PROLOG predicate and to the IRIS system.

IRIS [FB+87], an experimental system from Hewlett-Packard, is the most relational of all the approaches represented in this chapter. It was designed to support persistence in multiple programming languages, whereas O_2 was designed to support multiple database languages for writing methods.

IRIS uses a relational storage manager similar to the Relational Storage System (RSS) component of System R [AS+76]. It supports a separate query language, based on SQL, called OSQL. An issue here is whether queries should be captured by a separate language as in IRIS or whether they should be a part of a single language, as in GemStone.

The IRIS model is based on objects, types and operations. Types are collections of objects. Other models treat types as a protocol specification (e.g., Vbase). This distinction leads to interesting differences in a system's view of inheritance as discussed in the introduction to this volume. Within the IRIS type hierarchy, it is possible to constrain a set of subtypes to be mutually exclusive. Such a constraint is not a typical programming-language feature for types (e.g., Vbase and GemStone do not support it). It is a feature that is most similar to knowledge-representation languages.

IRIS allows several types of functions. A *stored function* is a table that explicitly records the mappings between the input objects and the output. It is like the stored function in PDM. A *derived function* is specified as a query whose result is a virtual table. The query is evaluated whenever the function is invoked. In this way, derived functions are similar to views. A *foreign function* is written in some programming language such as C or LISP. These last functions are outside the control of the system and can, therefore, have arbitrary side effects.

IRIS allows the type graph to change dynamically. Types can be added or deleted, and objects can change their type. This kind of capability is

useful for modeling real-world situations, but it introduces safety problems with respect to type checking. For example, assignment of an object of type T to a variable x defined to be of type T might not guarantee that x will contain a T at some time in the future.

IRIS will support multimedia databases by accessing specialized data managers. This illustrates an architectural decision that distinguishes these systems. Some systems store all objects (of any type) in a single storage system, whereas others, such as IRIS, allow access to external sources. The latter approach is often taken in systems whose goal is to integrate diverse, separately created, and controlled data sources (e.g., engineering information systems).

O_2 [LRV88] is the most formally described of these systems. It supports identity, types with encapsulation, inheritance, and operation overloading with dynamic binding. Ait-Kaci and Nasr [AN86] also present a formal model, but that one does not make a type–instance distinction.

The authors define O_2 by first describing a consistent set of objects (i.e., no dangling references and only one object with a given id). Next, they define a type structure and what it means for that to be consistent. Finally, they provide an interpretation that maps each type to a subset of objects.

O_2 makes a distinction between values and objects. Objects have identity and can, therefore, be referenced from many contexts, whereas values do not. A value can be embedded in an object or in another value, and as such is guaranteed to have no outside reference.

Data objects are (id, value) pairs, and values are basic (i.e., primitive), tuple, or set. Update is supported by changing the id-to-value binding. Tuples and sets can refer to other object ids.

In O_2, a type describes a minimal behavior for an object. An object that is an instance of type T must support all the behavior associated with T, but might actually support more. For example, ("John", 20) is an instance of the type **tuple (name: String, age: Int)** and also an instance of the type **tuple (name: String)**. Subtypes are defined explicitly. That is, the system does not infer the subtype relationship by looking at the signatures for the types. The user must declare this fact which asserts that the subtype extension is a subset of the supertype extension.

Classes and methods are not objects. This situation is in contrast to many object-oriented systems (e.g., GemStone) in which everything is an object, including the metadata.

The O_2 view of storage is that objects cannot be deleted explicitly. Instead, only references can be deleted, and objects that cannot be reached are garbage collected. This viewpoint is relatively unusual for a database system, but it leads to a clean semantics by not allowing dangling pointers.

O_2 supports multiple languages for writing methods. Currently, BASIC, C, and LISP are available, but others can be added if an O_2 layer is defined for each language. That software layer must provide a way to declare types of values and classes of objects, to manipulate complex values, and to pass messages to objects.

References

[AB84]   S. Abiteboul and N. Bidoit. Non First Normal Form Relations to Represent Hierarchically Organized Data. *Proceedings of the ACM Symposium on Principles of Database Systems*, Waterloo, Ontario, 1984.

• [AH87]   T. Andrews and C. Harris. Combining Language and Database Advances in an Object-Oriented Development Environment. *Proceedings of the ACM Conference on Object-Oriented Programming Systems, Languages, and Applications*, Orlando, FL, October 1987.

[AN86]   H. Ait-Kaci and R. Nasr. Logic and Inheritance. *ACM Symposium on Principles of Programming Languages*, St. Petersburg, FL, January 1986.

[As+76]   M.M. Astrahan, et al. System R: A Relational Database Management System. *ACM Transactions on Database Sytems*, 1(2):97–137, 1976.

• [Ba+87]   J. Banerjee, et al. Data Model Issues for Object-Oriented Applications. *ACM Transactions on Office Information Systems*, 5(1), 1987.

[DGL86]   K.R. Dittrich, W. Gotthard, and P.C. Lockemann. DAMOKLES—A Database System for Software Engineering Environments. *Proceedings of the IFIP Workshop on Advanced Programming Environments*. Trodheim, June 1986. Lecture Notes in Computer Science, Springer-Verlag, New York.

[DPS86]   U. Deppisch, H.B. Paul, and H.J. Schek. A Storage System for Complex Objects. In K. Dittrich and V. Dayal, eds. *International Work-shop on Object-Oriented Database Systems*, Pacific Grove, CA, September 1986.

• [FB+87]   D. H. Fishman, et al. IRIS: An Object-Oriented Database Management System. *ACM Transactions on Office Information Systems*, 5(1), 1987.

•[HZ87]   M. Hornick and S. Zdonik. A Shared Segmented Memory System for an Object-Oriented Database. *ACM Transactions on Office Information Systems*, 5(1):70–95, January 1987.

• [LRV88]   C. Lecluse, P. Richard, and F. Velez. O_2, an Object-Oriented Data Model. *ACM International Conference on the Management of Data*, Chicago, May 1988.

• [MD86]   F. Manola and U. Dayal. PDM: An Object-Oriented Data Model. *International Workshop on Object-Oriented Database Systems*, Pacific Grove, CA, September 1986.

• [MS87]   D. Maier and J. Stein. Development and Implementation of an Object-Oriented DBMS. In B. Shriver and P. Wegner, eds. *Research Directions in Object-Oriented Programming*, 355–392, MIT Press, Cambridge, MA, 1987.

[My+80]   J. Mylopoulus, et al. A Language Facility for Designing Interactive Database-Intensive Systems. *ACM Transactions on Database Systems*, 5(2):185–207, 1989.

[Pa+87]   H.B. Paul, et al. Architecture and Implementation of the Darmstadt Database Kernel System. *Proceedings of the International Conference on the Management of Data*, San Francisco, CA, 1987.

•[Sh81]   D. Shipman. The Functional Data Model and the Language DAPLEX. *ACM Transactions on Database Systems*, 6(1), 1989.

[SZ86]   A.H. Skarra and S.B. Zdonik. Management of Changing Types in an Object-Oriented Database. *Proceedings of the ACM Conference on Object-Oriented Programming Systems, Languages, and Applications*, Portland, OR, September 1986.

• indicates article included in this volume

Development and Implementation of an Object-Oriented DBMS

David Maier
Jacob Stein

1   Introduction

The GemStone database system is the result of a development project started three years ago at Servio [CM84, MOP85, MS86, MSOP86]. GemStone merges object-oriented language concepts with those of database systems, and provides an object-oriented database language called OPAL which is used for data definition, data manipulation and general computation.

Conventional record-oriented database systems often reduce application development time and improve data sharing among applications. However, these DBMSs are subject to the limitations of a finite set of data types and the need to normalize data [Eas80, Sid80]. In contrast, object-oriented languages [GR83, Kra83] offer flexible abstract data-typing facilities and the ability to encapsulate data and operations via the message metaphor.

Our premise was that combining object-oriented language capabilities with the storage management functions of a traditional data management system would result in a system that reduces application development efforts and increases modeling power. The extensible data-typing facility of the system facilitates storing information not suited to normalized relations. In addition, we believe that an object-oriented language is complete enough to handle database design, database access, and applications. Object-like models have long been popular in CAD [BBD*84, CFHL83, EM83, Kat82, Kat83, LP81, MNBR83, SMF86, Tho86] and seem well suited to supporting programming environments [MBH*86, PL83], hypermedia systems [Mey86], knowledge bases [DK84], and office information systems [ABB*83, MBH*86, Zdo84]. Other groups are in the process of implementing object model database systems [DKL85, MD86, Nie85, OBS86, SZR86, Wie86, ZW86].

In Section 2, we discuss the choice of Smalltalk as a database management language. In Section 3, we briefly introduce the GemStone model. Extensions to Smalltalk that are needed in a DBMS are discussed in Section 4. Our approach to providing these extensions is discussed in Section 5. In Section 6, we take an in-depth look at indexing in GemStone.

Initially, we developed a predominantly declarative query language. However, we felt it deficient in the procedural capabilities needed to model the behavior of real-world entities. Given the problems entailed in providing procedural extensions and educating users to a completely new language, we decided to use an existing object-oriented language, Smalltalk-80 [GR83], as the basis for product development. Below, we discuss those aspects of Smalltalk that led to this choice.

Other object-oriented language and programming systems support many of the same features as Smalltalk. Some of the main reasons we chose Smalltalk over the alternatives are:

2   The Choice of Smalltalk

1. *Available Literature:* The body of texts and papers, particularly introductory pieces, is larger for Smalltalk than for the alternatives.

2. *Virtual Machine Model:* Previous work on Smalltalk implementations has produced a conceptual abstraction called the *virtual machine* that provides a good framework for implementation. In particular, the virtual machine concept makes a clean split between *object memory*, which stores objects and provides structural access, and the *interpreter*, which understands the semantics of the data model and procedure evaluation.

3. *Scheme/Instance Distinction:* Some object-oriented systems do not distinguish rigidly between the "subtype of" and the "instance of" relationships. Smalltalk does. We felt the distinction was important in the database world, where programmers are used to a clear distinction between scheme and data.

2.1   Object Identity

Smalltalk supports *object identity* [KC86, Mac83]. A data object retains its identity through arbitrary changes in its own state. Entities with information in common can be modeled as two objects with a shared subobject containing the common information. Such sharing reduces the "update anomalies" that exist in the relational data model. In the relational model, the properties of an entity must be sufficient to distinguish it from all other entities. In order for one entity to refer to another, there must be some fields that uniquely and immutably identify the other entity. Using department names to identify department tuples is fine until a department's name changes. Making up unique department numbers puts an added burden on the application developer and introduces artifacts into the database scheme not present in the world being modeled. Some extensions to the relational model incorporate forms of identity [Cod79, Zan83].

2.2   Modeling Power

Smalltalk supports modeling of complex objects and relationships directly and organizes classes of objects into an inheritance hierarchy. A single entity is modeled as a single object, not as multiple tuples in multiple relations [HL82, JSW83, LP83, PKLM84]. Properties of entities need not be simple data values, but can be other entities of arbitrary complexity. The home address component of an employee object need not be just a text string: in Smalltalk it can be a structured object, itself having components for street number, street and city, and its own defined behavior (Figure 1). Smalltalk directly supports set-valued entities without the encoding required in the relational model. Furthermore, sets can have arbitrary objects as elements and need not be homogeneous. Smalltalk provides the physical data independence of relational databases without their limitations on modeling power.

2.3   Object Behavior

Smalltalk supports modeling of the *behavior* of real-world entities, not only their structure. Data manipulation commands in conventional systems are oriented towards machine representations: "modify field," "insert tuple," "get next within parent." For an office management system, several applications might reserve a room. In a conventional database system, each application would contain statements to test for room availability, insert or change a record to indicate the reservation, and perhaps create another record for the appointment calendar of the reserver. Changes to the structure of the database or the company policy for reserving rooms may require locating and modifying every application that makes use of the database. In Smalltalk, on the other hand, one can define a reserveRoom message that takes a date and a time as parameters and performs all the necessary checks and updates to the database to reserve a room.

Of course, in a conventional system we could factor out this functionality into a separate procedure which multiple application programs could use. However, none of those applications is forced to use the procedure to access the room reservation data. In Smalltalk, the state of an object is accessible only through its message interface. Thus, the designer of a class controls the access and use of the data in objects of that class. Smalltalk has the further advantage that it organizes the messages along with the structural descriptions of objects. In conventional systems, a common procedure would typically reside on a file system external to the database, rather than being a part of the database.

The Smalltalk procedure or method that implements a message can execute any number of database queries and updates, with many advantages. Applications are more concise: sending one message takes the place of many database operations. The code is more reliable, as every application that

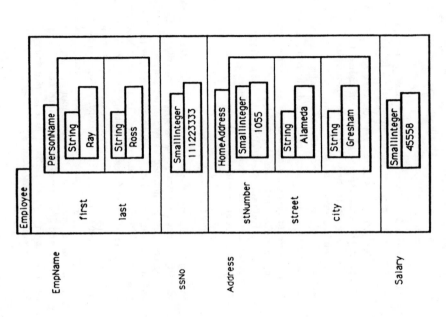

Figure 1. An employee object.

reserves a room uses exactly the same procedure — the method associated with the reserveRoom message. If the structure of the database or the policy on reserving rooms changes, modifying the single method for reserveRoom means that all applications that make reservations will have the changed behavior. The linkage of message to method occurs at runtime in Smalltalk, so applications need no recompiling to make the changed behavior available. Further, messages can protect the integrity of the database by consistency checks in their methods. The reserveRoom message can make checks to forestall double-booking of rooms. Applications cannot modify the room reservation data directly, which might lead to an inconsistent booking schedule if they did not include the checks that reserveRoom performs.

2.4 Classes

The class structure of Smalltalk makes it possible to produce new data types and helps organize database schemes. Smalltalk comes with a large complement of classes implementing frequently used data types, which database designers can use to represent the internal state of objects they define. Class definitions are the analogue to schemes in database systems, but classes also package operations with the structure, to encapsulate behavior. Smalltalk partially orders classes in an inheritance hierarchy. Whereas a class helps organize data, the class hierarchy helps organize the classes. The subclass inheritance mechanism allows a database scheme to capture similarities among various classes of entities that are not totally identical in structure or behavior. Subclassing also provides a means to handle special cases without cluttering up the definition of the normal case [MBW80].

2.5 Associating Types with Objects

Unlike most programming languages that support abstract data types, Smalltalk associates types with values, not the slots holding the values. Below, we consider some of the advantages of such typing. In a later section, we consider the disadvantages.

We want to help database designers to model application domains they previously may have shied away from because of complexity or lack of regular structure. However, modeling an enterprise for the first time is a very different undertaking from building a database application for an area that has already been modeled but has not yet been computerized. The basic modeling for financial record keeping was done long before computers, and the structure of the information involved readily fits into standard record-based data models. A development schedule based on scheme definition, application writing, database population and debugging is reasonable. Not so with a CAD task being modeled for the first time or a database to support an expert system. The application area has not been modeled before, and there will be many iterations of the database scheme before the application is mature [ACO85, AO84, MP84]. Being able to start writing database routines without completely specifying the structure and behavior of every class of entities can be of great advantage.

In particular, the type of a field can be initially just Object, the most general class, meaning there is no constraint on the values that occupy the field. As the model stabilizes, more and more specific types can be associated with the field, for integrity or efficiency. We are currently developing tools to update instances that do not conform to a modified class definition.

By not associating types with variables, unanticipated cases (say, a company car might be assigned to a department as well as an employee) can be more easily handled. A method makes assumptions about the protocol of the objects that are its arguments, not their class. An instance variable that has a value whose class is not among those anticipated during design does not necessarily invalidate a method using that instance variable. As long as the value responds to the same messages as objects of the "expected" classes, the message will continue to function. For example, if every object responds to the printString message to return a string representing itself, then a method can be written for Set that prints a string representation of the entire set regardless of the classes of the elements. Similarly, detecting messages sent to objects where there is no method for the message points out places where data modeling is incomplete.

2.6 A Unified Language

Smalltalk is much more powerful than standard data manipulation languages. It is a database programming language (like RIGEL [RS79], Pascal/R [Sch73], and Galileo [ACO85]), not just a data manipulation language. It is computationally complete and easily supports almost all the computation required in an application. Completeness helps avoid the problem of impedance mismatch, arising when information must pass between two languages that are semantically and structurally different (such as a declarative data sublanguage and an imperative general-purpose language). Smalltalk stresses uniformity of access to all system objects and functions, using the same mechanisms as for regular data objects. What would be external operating system commands in most programming languages are messages to special system objects in Smalltalk.

3 The GemStone Model

This section outlines the GemStone data model and OPAL programming language. The reader familiar with Smalltalk can safely skip this section.

The three principal concepts of the GemStone model and language are object, message, and class. They correspond roughly to record, procedure call, and record type in conventional systems (see Figure 2 for other correspondences). An object is a chunk of private memory with a public interface. Objects communicate with other objects by passing messages, which are requests for the receiving object to change its state or return a result. The set of messages an object responds to is called its protocol (its "public interface"). An object may be inspected or changed only through its protocol. The means by which an object responds to a message is a method, an OPAL

3.1 Objects

Internally, most objects are divided into fields called *instance variables*. Each instance variable can hold a value, which is another object. Figure 1 shows an Employee object with four instance variables: **empName**, **ssNo**, **address**, and **salary**. The empName instance variable holds an object that is an instance of the PersonName class. Not all objects are internally

procedure that is invoked when an object receives a particular message. So that each object need not carry around its own methods, objects with the same internal structure and methods are grouped together into a class and are called *instances* of the class. The methods and structure are in a single object describing the class, the *class-defining object* or CDO, and all instances of the class contain a reference to the class-defining object. Unlike some other object models, an object is an instance of exactly one class, although it can inherit behavior from superclasses of its class.

divided into instance variables. Certain basic types such as SmallInteger and Character are not further decomposed. The instance variables in the Employee object are called *named instance variables*. An object can have *indexed instance variables*, which can be viewed as instance variables with numbers instead of names. Indexed instance variables are used mainly for implementing ordered collections such as arrays.

3.2 Messages

The basic form of all message expressions is <receiver><message>. The <receiver> part is an identifier or expression denoting an object that receives and interprets the message. The <message> part gives the *selector* of the message and possibly *arguments* to the message. Every message returns a result to the *sender*, which is usually another object. There are three kinds of messages: *unary, binary and keyword*.

Unary messages have no arguments and have selectors that are a single identifier. Assume that emp is a variable holding an Employee object. If we have a unary message firstName to retrieve the first name of the employee, then

    emp firstName

returns a string that is the first name of emp. *Binary message* expressions have a receiver, one argument, and a message selector that is one or two non-alphanumeric characters. To multiply 8 by 3, we send to 8 the message "Multiply yourself by 3":

    8 * 3

Here * is the binary selector for the multiplication message. Comparisons are also handled with binary messages. In

    (emp1 salary) <= (emp2 salary)

the receiver and argument of the <= binary message are both results of unary message expressions. *Keyword messages* have one or more arguments and have multipart selectors composed of alphanumeric characters and colons. To set the third component of an array held in anArray to 'Ross' we use

    anArray at: 3 put: 'Ross'

The same effect is accomplished in other languages by

    anArray[3] := 'Ross'

The message selector here has two parts, at: and put:; since it takes two arguments, the array index and the object to be stored at that index. We refer to a message by the concatenation of its parts: at:put:.

Approximate Equivalences

GemStone	Conventional
object	record instance, set instance
instance variable	field, attribute
instance variable constraint	field type, domain
message	procedure call
method	procedure body
class-defining object	record type, relation scheme
class hierarchy	database scheme
class instance	record instance, tuple
collection class	set, relation

Figure 2. The correspondence between object-oriented and conventional database systems.

3.3 Methods

To construct a method we need to know what objects are visible within its scope. All the named instance variables of the receiver are available via their names. Thus, in a method for class Employee, as defined in Figure 1, the instance variables empName, ssNo, address and salary are accessible. A method may also have temporary variables, which are declared between vertical bars at the beginning of the method: |temp1 temp2|. Each user has one or more dictionaries of global variables, and those global variables can appear in methods. There are two other operators we need before we can write methods: the assignment operator, :=, and the operator ^ that returns the value of the expression as the result of a method:

For a unary message wholeName in class PersonName that returns the first and last name concatenated with a space between, we can use the following method:

```
wholeName
    |temp|
    temp := first.
    temp := temp + ' ' + last.
    ^ temp
```

The first statement, temp := first, assigns the value of the instance variable first in the receiver (a PersonName object) to the temporary variable temp. The statement

```
temp := temp + ' ' + last
```

concatenates the value of temp, a blank, and the contents of the instance variable last of the receiver (+ is the binary message for concatenation of strings). The result of the concatenations is assigned to temp. Finally, the statement ^temp returns the value of temp as the result of the message wholeName. (This particular message could be implemented with the single message expression

```
^ first + ' ' + last
```

with no need for a temporary variable.) A method can also change the state of the receiver, by assigning new values to instance variables. Suppose objects of class Department have a budget instance variable. The following method increases a department's budget by a certain percentage, up to a limit:

```
increaseBudgetBy: aPercentage upTo: aLimit
    budget := budget + (budget * (aPercentage / 100)).
    (budget > aLimit) ifTrue: [budget := aLimit].
    ^ budget
```

The increaseBudgetBy:upTo: message takes two arguments represented by variables aPercentage and aLimit. This method changes the budget instance variable of the Department object that receives the increaseBudgetBy:upTo: message. In the second line of the method we see a keyword message ifTrue: that functions as a conditional control construct. The receiver of this message is a Boolean value. The argument of the message is a *block*. A block is a sequence of one or more OPAL statements within brackets, and is a first-class object in GemStone. The effect of a message aBoolean ifTrue: aBlock is to perform the code in aBlock if aBoolean is true. The third line of the method returns the new value of budget.

OPAL includes messages for iterative control structures, using blocks with arguments. Block arguments are declared at the beginning of a block. For example,

```
[:n | (2 * n) - 1]
```

is a block with one argument, n. For this block to be evaluated, it needs a value for the argument. The value: message provides the argument and causes execution. A block returns the value of its last expression when executed. Thus,

```
[ :n | (2 * n) - 1 ] value: 7
```

returns 13. In general, given a value of N, this block returns the Nth odd number.

All methods we have seen so far have been defined in terms of other messages. The definitions of methods are not completely circular, however: at the bottom of everything is a handful of *primitive methods*. When the OPAL interpreter encounters a message that has a primitive method, it executes a piece of machine code rather than an OPAL method. Primitive methods exist for arithmetic, comparisons, object creation and copying, array selection, string manipulation, and set functions. The set of primitive methods in GemStone cannot be augmented by a GemStone programmer, although such an extension could be provided [BM86].

3.4 Classes

Every class is represented by a *class-defining object* (CDO) that describes the structure and behavior of instances of the class, as well as the position of the class in the class hierarchy. Any object returns the CDO for its class in response to the message class. Suppose that the variable assoc holds an object of class Association (an Association is a key-value pair used in building dictionaries). The assignment

```
ac := assoc class
```

causes ac to be assigned the CDO for class Association. CDOs respond to messages just as all other objects do. For example, CDOs respond to the name message. The result of the expression

Classes	Instances
PersonName	—— 'Ray Ross'
TitledName	—— 'Dr. Ray Ross'
TitledNameWithLetters	—— 'Dr. Ray Ross, OBE'

Class	InstanceVariables	Messages
PersonName	first last	first first: last last: fullName
TitledName	(above) + title	(above) + titledName
TitledNameWithLetters	(above) + letters	(above) + titledName (new Method)

Figure 4. A portion of the class hierarchy.

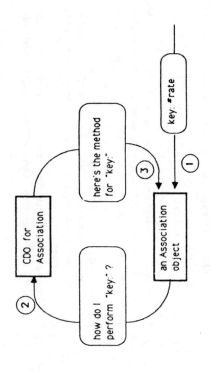

Figure 3. Determining the method for a message.

assoc class name

is #Association. (Symbols are indicated by a prefixed #.)

The instance variable names and methods for instances of a class are stored in the CDO for the class. CDOs also store the methods that instances execute in response to various messages. When an object receives a message, it consults the CDO to find out how to execute that message (see Figure 3).

OPAL provides a *class hierarchy* to exploit similarities in structure and behavior of entities. A subclass inherits structure and behavior from its superclass. Structure is inherited in that all named instance variables in the superclass are also present in any subclass. Suppose we want objects that represent person names with titles. We can create a subclass TitledName of PersonName. Instances of TitledName automatically have instance variables first and last. We add an instance variable, title, to TitledName to hold the title (see Figure 4).

A subclass inherits methods from its superclass. Thus, if fullName is a message for PersonName, instances of TitledName respond to that message by using the method from PersonName. The look-up process to determine which method corresponds to a message starts in an object's class. If the message is not defined in that class, the search proceeds to the class's superclass, the superclass of that class, and so forth.

A subclass can implement messages of its own. For TitledName we might want a message that returns a string containing the full name with

title:

    titledName

        ^ title + ' ' + self fullName

A new feature in this example is self, a special variable whose value is always the receiver of the message. A subclass can reimplement an inherited message. Suppose we define a class TitledNameWithLetters as a subclass of TitledName. This subclass adds an instance variable letters that holds the letters after a person's name, as in Dr. Ray Ross, OBE. We can reimplement the titledName message in TitledNameWith-Letters to include the letters after the name.

4 Turning Smalltalk into a DBMS

Smalltalk is implemented as a single-user, memory-based, single-processor system. It does not meet the requirements for a database system. While Smalltalk provides a powerful user interface and many tools for application development, it is oriented to a single-user workstation. To meet the requirements for a database system, the following enhancements are needed.

4.1 Support of a Multi-User, Disk-Based Environment

The database must be intelligent about staging objects between disk and memory. It should try to group objects accessed together onto the same disk pages, try to anticipate which objects in main memory are likely to be used again soon, and organize its query processing to minimize disk traffic.

Since GemStone data is shared by multiple users, the system must provide concurrent access. Each user should see a consistent version of the database, even with other users running simultaneously. A related requirement is management of multiple name spaces. Smalltalk assumes a single user per image and so provides a single global name space. It is unreasonable to expect either that GemStone users share a single global name space, or that user name spaces are disjoint.

Current Smalltalk implementations use a single processor for both display processing and object management. We expect GemStone to support multiple interactive applications. Hence, it does not seem wise to use the same processor for secondary storage management as for display processing at the end-user interface.

4.2 Data Integrity

Various kinds of failures (program, processor, media) and violations (consistency, access, typing) can compromise the validity and integrity of a database. A database system must be able to cope with failure by restoring the database to a consistent state, and should prevent violations from occurring.

By "program failure" we mean that an application program may fail to complete, say, because of a run-time error. Database systems provide for multiple updates to be performed through the use of transactions. A transaction is used to mark a section of processing so that all its changes are made permanent (the transaction commits) or none are made permanent (the transaction aborts). By "processor failure", we mean that the processor handling GemStone storage management fails. For such failures, the database must be kept intact. Recovering from program and processor failure implies that master copies of objects on secondary storage must be updated carefully. By "media failure" we mean that disk flaws may cause committed data to be lost. No strategy can provide complete protection against media failure. We wanted GemStone to provide for both periodic backup and dynamic replication: by the latter, we mean keeping multiple online copies of a database, all of which are updated on every transaction.

Turning to violations, database consistency can be violated if transactions from multiple users interleave their updates. GemStone must support serializability of transactions: the net effect of concurrent transactions on the database must be equivalent to some serial execution of those transactions. The integrity of a database can also be violated if a user accesses data that he or she should not be permitted to see. In Smalltalk, all objects are available to the user. Gemstone must assign ownership and access privileges to every object. Integrity constraints, such as uniqueness keys and referential integrity (that is, referenced objects exist), are assertions that a priori exclude certain states of the database. At a minimum, the database should support constraints that require subparts of an entity or collections to belong to a certain class. We note that referential integrity comes "for free" in GemStone. One object refers directly to another object, not to a name for that object. The reference cannot be created if the other object does not exist. GemStone has no explicit deletion mechanism. The space for an object is reclaimed only if no other object references that object. Thus once a reference exists, it will continue to be valid.

4.3 Large Object Space

Gemstone must store both large numbers of objects and objects that are large in size. The first Smalltalk-80 implementations had a limit of 2^{15} objects, 2^{15} instance variables in any object, and 2^{20} total words of object memory [GR83, KK83]. Large disk-based objects require new storage techniques. Some objects will be too large to fit in main memory and must be paged in. While virtual-memory implementations page large objects, we felt we must get away from linear representations of long objects, since requiring large objects to be laid out contiguously in secondary storage will lead to unacceptable fragmentation or expensive compaction passes.

In Smalltalk, to "grow" an object such as an array, a new, larger object is created and the contents of the smaller object are copied into it. If the object to be grown is a Set or subclass thereof, then rehashing every element of the set may be required. We want the time required to update or extend an object to be proportional to the size of the update or extension, *not* to the size of the object being updated. Simple hashing does not scale up to handle sets of the size that a DBMS must be able to represent efficiently. The basic operations of union, intersection and difference become prohibitively expensive. Additionally, Smalltalk hashes set elements by value, not identity, and provides no trigger mechanism to rehash an object in the set(s) to which it belongs when the object's value changes. Nor does a trigger mechanism exist to change the position of an object within an ordered collection when the object's value changes in a way that alters its position in the collection. For these reasons we felt that Smalltalk's repertoire of basic storage representations was inadequate for supporting large collections. Thus, GemStone needs a basic storage type for large collections, both in ordered and unordered form.

Most Smalltalk implementations include a become: message which interchanges the identity of two objects. For example, after executing A become: B, all references to A refer to B and vice versa. Its primary use is in growing objects, changing the class of an object and atomic update. For example, to cause an instantaneous update of a displayed object C, a Smalltalk method would make a copy D of C, perform changes on D, then execute C become: D. The side effects of become: are difficult to anticipate and control, in particular with regard to maintaining constraints such as instance variable typing. GemStone does not support the become: message, but uses other mechanisms to support its functionality. Instances of collection classes can grow and shrink in GemStone, unlike in Smalltalk. GemStone also supports a protocol to change the class of an object. Finally, GemStone's transaction support ensures that changes from one session become visible in an all-or-nothing manner to other sessions.

Finally, searching a long collection by a sequential scan will give unacceptable performance with a disk-based object. Searching for elements should be at most logarithmic in the size of the collection, rather than linear. Thus, GemStone should support associative access on elements of large collections: It should supply storage representations and auxiliary structures to support locating an element by its internal state. This requirement reinforces the need for typing on collections and instance variables. To index a collection E of employees on the value of the salary instance variable, the system needs assurances that every element in E has a salary entry. Furthermore, if that index is to support range queries on salary, the system needs a declaration that all salary values will be comparable according to some total order.

Along with storage-level support for associative access, OPAL must have language constructs that allow associative access.

4.4 Physical Storage Management

GemStone must provide features for managing the physical placement of objects on disk. Smalltalk is a memory-resident system and so there is not much need to say where an object goes. The database administrator, or a savvy application programmer, should be able to hint to GemStone that certain objects are often used together and so should be clustered on the disk. The administrator should be able to take objects off line, say for archiving, and bring them back on line later.

4.5 Access From Other Systems

While OPAL goes much further than conventional database languages in providing a single language for database application programming, we concentrated our initial efforts on storage management issues rather than user interfaces. Thus, GemStone provides for access to its facilities from other programming languages. We want to support an application development environment for OPAL along the lines of the Smalltalk programming environment [Gra84], but we recognize that the application development environment may not be the same as the environment in which the finished application runs. We provide a procedural interface to C and are developing an interface to Smalltalk [PMS87, Sch86].

5 Our Approach

This section addresses how we provided the enhancements needed to Smalltalk to make it a database system. We start with an overview of the architecture of GemStone.

5.1 GemStone Architecture

Figure 5 shows the major pieces of the GemStone system. Stone and Gem correspond roughly to the object memory and the virtual machine of the standard Smalltalk implementation [Gra84]. Stone provides secondary storage management, concurrency control, authorization, transactions, recovery, and support for associative access. Stone also manages workspaces for active sessions. Stone uses unique surrogates called object-oriented pointers (OOPs) to refer to objects and an object table to map an OOP to a physical location. Other object-oriented systems use direct references between objects to cut down access time. We chose the object-table approach because it gives us the flexibility to move objects around in secondary storage (which is important when objects change size) and permits an easy implementation of our shadowing scheme for recovery. Stone is built upon the underlying VMS file system. The data model that Stone provides is simpler than the full GemStone model, and provides only operators for structural update and access. An object may be stored separately from its subobjects, but the OOPs for the values of an object's instance variables are grouped together. Others have considered decomposed representations of objects [CDF*82, CK85], and more clustered representations of objects [DPS86].

Gem sits atop Stone and elaborates Stone's storage model into the full GemStone model. Gem also adds the capabilities of compiling OPAL methods into bytecodes and executing that code, user authentication, and session control. (OPAL bytecodes are similar, but not identical, to the bytecodes used in Smalltalk.) Part of the Gem layer is the virtual image: the collection of OPAL classes, methods and objects that is supplied with every manipulation needs to happen near the end user, while GemStone is optimized toward maintaining large numbers of persistent objects. The programming environment classes are replaced by a browser application that runs on a separate processor, which we describe in a later subsection. We have added classes and methods to make the data management functions of transaction control, accounting, ownership, authorization, replication, user profiles and index creation controllable from within OPAL.

The *procedural interface module* (PIM) is a set of routines to facilitate communication from other programs in other languages running on processors (possibly) remote from Gem. The PIM currently supports calls from C programs running on an IBM-PC for session and transaction control, sending messages to GemStone objects, executing a sequence of OPAL statements, compiling OPAL methods, and error explanation. In addition, the PIM provides "structural access" calls for determining an object's size, class, and implementation, accessing an object's state and creating new objects.

Information passes between the PIM and Gem in the form of bytes and GemStone object pointers. Certain objects have predefined object pointers, such as instances of Boolean, Character and SmallInteger. Instances of Float and String are passed as byte sequences. Instances of other classes must be decomposed into instances of the classes mentioned, in order to pass their internal structure between the PIM and Gem. However, the identity of any object can be passed between the PIM and Gem, regardless of its complexity.

Gem, Stone and the PIM are structured as separate processes. Our current mapping of processes to processors has Gem and Stone running on on a VAX under VMS. While a GemStone system has a single Stone process, it maintains a separate Gem process for each active user, and the PIM handles communication on a per-application basis.

5.2 Multiple Users

Stone supports multiple concurrent users by providing each user session with a workspace that contains a *shadow copy* of the object table derived from the most recently committed object table, called the *shared table*. Whenever a session modifies an object, a new copy of that object is created and placed on a page that is inaccessible to other sessions. The shadow copy of the object table is updated so that the object's OOP references the new copy. One of the advantages of shadowing over logging is that several consistent versions of the database may be accessed simultaneously. A alternative approach to shadowing in an object-oriented database system is given by Thatte [Tha86].

Conceptually, the shadow object table for a workspace is a complete copy of the version of the shared table when the session starts. Actually, we do not make a copy all at once. Object tables are represented as B-trees, indexed on OOPs. For a shadow object table, we need copy only the top

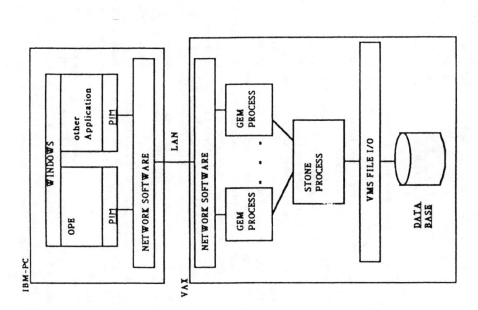

Figure 5.   The architecture of GemStone.

GemStone system.

In going from the Smalltalk hierarchy to GemStone's virtual image, we have removed classes for file access, communication, screen manipulation and the programming environment. The file classes are unnecessary, as we have persistent storage for all GemStone objects. Computation for screen

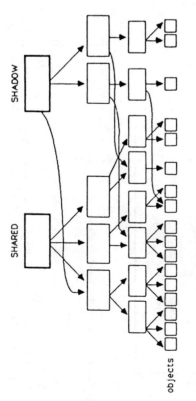

Figure 6. Shared and shadow object tables.

node of the committed object table. As the objects are changed in a session, the shadow object table adds new nodes that are copies of its shared object table with the proper changes. Figure 6 shows the state of a shadow object table after the alteration of a single object. Multiple paths have been copied since several objects may have been on the same page as the altered object.

We chose an optimistic concurrency control scheme: one in which access conflicts are checked at commit time, rather than prevented from occurring through locking. For each transaction, Stone keeps track of which objects the transaction has read or written. At commit time, Stone checks for read-write and write-write conflicts with transactions that have committed since the time the transaction began. If there are none, the transaction commits. For a commit, the shadow object table of the session is treated as if it were "transparent" on the entries that have not been modified, and is overlaid on the most recent version of the shared table. In this way, the changes made by the committing session are merged with those of other transactions that committed after the committing session began. If the current transaction fails to commit, the changes in its shadow table are discarded, after using the table to reclaim pages used for new copies of objects.

This optimistic scheme ensures that read-only transactions never conflict with other transactions. Such a transaction gets a consistent copy of the database state, does its reading, and has no changes to make to the shared table on commit. This scheme never deadlocks, as a session experiences no contention with other sessions before a commit point. However, it is possible that an application that writes a large portion of the database may fail to commit any transactions for an arbitrarily long time. Therefore, there may be situations where a pessimistic (locking) scheme is desirable over an

optimistic one. We believe it is easier to implement a pessimistic scheme over an optimistic one than vice versa, and are currently exploring the implementation of locking and versioning on top of our shadow scheme [PSM87].

5.3 Efficiency Considerations

One problem with recording all the objects a session reads or writes is that the list can grow quite long. One optimization is that certain classes of objects that contain immutable instances need not be recorded for concurrency control. Even excluding these objects, however, single objects are just of too fine a granularity for concurrency control. Thus, we introduced the notion of *segments*, which are logical groupings of objects that are the unit of concurrency control in GemStone, much like the segments of the Adaplex LDM [CFLR81]. A segment may contain any number of objects. GemStone keeps a list of just the segments read or written by a session, rather than all objects. Segments are visible from within OPAL through the class Segment. Users can control placement of objects in segments, to group objects so as to try to avoid conflict. System objects that are shared by many users but are almost never updated can be placed on a single segment, so that the concurrency mechanism need record one entry for a transaction, no matter how many of these objects it uses.

5.4 Name Spaces

Gem manages multiple name spaces. The virtual image has a class UserProfile that is used to represent properties of each user, including a list of dictionaries used to resolve symbols when compiling OPAL code for that user. When an identifier is encountered in OPAL code and that identifier is neither an instance variable nor a class variable, the dictionaries are searched in order to find an object corresponding to that identifier. There may be any number of dictionaries for a user, to accommodate various degrees of sharing. For example, a programmer's first dictionary may contain objects and classes for his or her portion of a project, the second may be for objects shared with other programmers working on the same project, and the third could contain system objects.

5.5 Transactions and Recovery

To reiterate, every session gets a shadow copy of the shared object table when it begins and installs its shadow copy as the shared copy when it successfully commits a transaction. Further, a session always writes changed and new objects into pages that are not accessible to any other transaction. Thus, aborting a transaction means throwing away its shadow object table, and committing means replacing the shared table with a shadow copy. The only issue that needs more elaboration is atomicity — that the changes of a transaction are made, apparently, all at once. When a shadow table is to replace the shared table, the new table can replace the old by simply overwriting the root of the shared object table with the root of the new object table (recall that object tables are represented as B-trees). Rewriting the root is the only place where any part of the shared copy of the database is overwritten.

Our unit of recovery is a transaction. Changes made by committed transactions are kept, changes not yet committed are lost. Since the shared version of the database is never overwritten, we need almost nothing in the way of logs to bring the database to a consistent state, since it never leaves one. To handle the eventuality of a crash while writing the root of the object table, we keep two copies of the root. To restore a consistent state of the database after the crash, we simply check those two pages. If they are different, we copy one that can be determined to be uncorrupted over the other. The real work on recovery is garbage collection: removing the detritus of the transactions that had not committed before the crash.

To guard against media failure, we have introduced a structure called a *repository*. A repository is the unit of replication and also the unit of storage that can be taken off line. A repository may be taken off line, which means all its objects become inaccessible. Repository is an OPAL class providing internal representatives of repositories. A Repository instance can respond to a message replicate, which means two copies of the repository will be maintained (at increased cost in time and space). The copies know about each other, and if the medium for one fails, the other is still available.

5.6 Authorization

Segments are also the unit of ownership and authorization. Every user has at least one segment, and when he or she creates new objects, they go in an owned segment. A user may grant read or write permission on a segment to other users. Such grants must always come from the original owner. Read or write permission on a segment implies the same permission on all objects assigned to the segment.

Read and write permission introduce some subtleties in an object model. First, having the identity of an object (its OOP) is not the same as reading the object. Second, having permission on an object does not imply permission on all its subobjects. So, for example, an Employee object, along with the values for instance variables empName, ssNo, and address, could reside in one segment. By putting a SalaryHistory object in another segment, authorization can be granted to just a portion of an employee's personnel information. If a user cannot find an object, he or she cannot read the object.

5.7 Large Object Space

In designing GemStone, we have tried to always set limits on object numbers and sizes so that physical storage limits will be encountered first. A GemStone system can support 2^{31} objects (2^{32} counting instances of SmallInteger) and an object can have up to 2^{31} instance variables. Segments have no upper bound on the number of objects they can contain other than the number of objects in the system.

When an object is larger than a page, it is broken into pieces and organized as a tree spanning several pages. A large object can be accessed and updated without bringing all the pages of an object into a workspace. The tree structure of large objects makes it possible to update pieces of them without rewriting the whole object, much as for the object table. Since pages of a large object need not be contiguous in secondary storage, such objects can grow and shrink with no need to recopy the entire object.

Stone supports five basic storage formats for objects, *self-identifying* (e.g., SmallInt, Character, Boolean), *byte* (e.g., String, Float), *named*, *indexed* and *non-sequenceable collections*. The byte format is used for classes whose instances may be considered atomic. The named format supports access to the components of an object by unique identifiers, instance variable names. The indexed format supports access to the components of an object by number, as in instances of class Array. This format supports insertions of components into the middle of an object, and can grow to accommodate more components. The non-sequenceable collection (NSC) format is used for collection classes, such as Bag and Set, in which instance variables are *anonymous*: members of such collections are not identified by name or index, but a collection can be queried for membership and have members added, removed, or enumerated.

We feel that main- and virtual-memory-based Smalltalk systems could benefit from the extensions GemStone has made to the basic object storage model. Smalltalk implementations with increased numbers of OOPs already exist. Supporting objects that can grow or shrink dynamically avoids a great deal of the copying that current Smalltalk implementations do. As applications require larger and larger objects, the overhead for copying will become more and more onerous.

The basic data formats that an object management system provides should support reasonably direct and efficient use of user-defined data types. We feel that at least three types of basic data structuring mechanisms are required for efficient applications: sequencing (records), iteration (arrays) and collections (sets). Our thesis is that no two of these structuring primitives can efficiently simulate the third. Relational database systems support only sequencing and collections and must encode arrays. Smalltalk supports sequencing and iterations, and encodes sets. GemStone supports all three.

6 Indexing

In GemStone, the basic problem is to select efficiently from a collection those members meeting a selection criterion. For example, we may want to find all objects that contain a given object as the value of a particular instance variable. GemStone does not support direct navigation from an object O to objects for which O is the value of an instance variable, as an object may be the value of an instance variable in several objects. No object assumes that it makes a unique reference to any of its instance variables' values. (Such a constraint would be enforced by the method that updates the field.) For example, the same Department instance can fill the worksIn variable for many Employee objects. All GemStone objects are *independent*: no object's existence is constrained to depend on the existence of another object.

One should be able to index on instance variables that are nested several levels deep in an object to be indexed, such as the manager variable of the Department object that fills an Employee's worksIn variable. The manager of a Department object can change with no change being apparent in an Employee object that references that Department object. This localization of change influences the complexity of index maintenance.

In GemStone, a class defines the structure of its instances, but rarely keeps track of all those instances. Instead, collection objects — Arrays, Bags, Sets — serve to group those instances. An object may belong to more than one collection (unlike relational, hierarchical or network models, where a record belongs to a single relation, parent or set). Such multiple membership is allowed in the hybrid relational-network model of Haynie [Hay81].

6.1 The Problems and Solutions

In this section we elaborate on the problems the GemStone model presents with respect to associative access and indexing.

6.1.1 Language Issues

The two issues here are when to invoke auxiliary access paths for associative searching, and whether indexes should be keyed on an object's structure or on its protocol.

How should we indicate or permit the use of indexes in the OPAL language? One solution is to do nothing with the language and simply provide system classes in the virtual image for building and using indexes. Drawbacks to this approach are that application programs must perform index maintenance and no longer have physical data independence. At the other extreme, we could go without modifications to the language and treat every OPAL expression as a candidate for use of indexing structures in evaluation. OPAL is not just a query language: much OPAL code operates on single objects, where an index has no likely benefit. Indexes are helpful only for operations iterated over members of a large collection.

Some more moderate positions are to designate certain messages as the only ones for which index use will be attempted, or to add a data sublanguage to OPAL for expressing associative searches. Adding a sublanguage complicates the language and introduces the danger of an "impedance mismatch". If the sublanguage route is chosen, the question is, what kind of sublanguage? A calculus-like language could support associative searching, extraction of subparts of objects and creation of new objects as the answer to a query. Allowing a query to assemble new objects arbitrarily would mean creating classes on the fly. Another problem is whether variables in calculus queries range over classes or collections. Allowing a variable to range over all instances of a class means that a collection of those instances must be maintained. Having variables range over collections introduces a problem with binding the query to the specific collections. If the actual collections are not determined until run time, little preprocessing of the query can take place.

A disadvantage to a full calculus sublanguage is that a query must be translated before it can be processed. A more restricted declarative language might support only selection, avoiding the need to create new classes for the results of queries. The selection conditions could be arbitrary blocks of OPAL code, or have some restrictions. A problem with arbitrary blocks of code is that such code can have side effects on the objects being examined. A sublanguage could be more procedural, but still encapsulate iteration — an algebra for collections of objects. Some of the required operations are already present in GemStone, mainly Boolean operations on sets.

However, forming such a language by simply adding messages to collection classes for performing analogues of selection, projection and join would have limited power. To really exploit an algebra, the system must be able to take an expression involving several algebraic operators and transform it into an equivalent expression to optimize its performance. It must also have multiple methods to evaluate each operation and choose a particular method for an operation in the context of a larger expression. Changes in the evaluation mechanism in GemStone are needed if expressions in the sublanguage are to be treated as single units for optimization and execution planning.

While algebras have been proposed for non-1NF relations, we have yet to see a workable algebra for complex objects with identity. The non-1NF algebras operate on relations that are strict hierarchical structures. An algebra for objects would have to deal with shared subparts and resolve whether answers to a query are copies of or references to database objects.

The other major issue regarding languages is whether indexes are based on the structure (the instance variables) of objects, or on the protocol (the responses to messages). If indexes are based on message notation, we must know which structural changes in an object can influence the result of a message, so that we know when to update the appropriate indexes. Also, a method can change the state of an object, and we need assurances that a message will yield the same answer twice in a row if the structure of the object has not been explicitly changed. The method for a message can be overridden in a subclass, which presents problems in allowing kinds of a class into a message-based index along with instances of the class (an object O is a *kind of* its class and its class's superclasses). Indexing based on structure has the advantage that it can be supported at the Stone level, while message-based indexing requires access to the execution model at the Gem level. Indexing on structure violates the privacy of objects, as it bypasses an object's protocol.

6.1.2   Index Structure

If we want to index objects on their internal structure, one question is, how deep to index? Do we index only the immediate instance variables of an object, or do we allow indexes on instance variables of instance variables? With a one-level index, we always have the object in hand when a change occurs that can affect its position in an index. With a multilevel index, such as anEmp.worksIn.manager, we have the problem that an object's position in an index can be invalidated by a change in a subobject that is not manifested in the object itself (a Department gets a new manager).

If we do index on paths with multiple links (multiple instance variables), we have the choice of a single index for the whole path or several indexes, one for each link. For anEmp.worksIn.manager, we could have one index on worksIn.manager mapping managers directly to the employees they manage, or we can have one index on worksIn mapping departments to employees, and another on manager mapping managers to departments. With a single index on the entire path, there are fewer indexes to maintain and fewer consultations needed for an associative lookup. Indexing by links means that prefixes of a path are indexed as well: indexing ability on anEmp.worksIn.manager implies ability ou anEmp.worksIn. Supporting a path index as multiple link indexes also allows sharing between path indexes with a common prefix.

Since GemStone associates types with objects rather than identifiers, we cannot tell a priori that an object supports a certain path or know the class of the object at the end of the path. Further, if the index is to be ordered, we need to know that the last values in a path hold comparable values, such as Strings. We need typing on collection elements and instance variables to support indexes.

Additionally, we need to consider the following questions on indexing strategy:

1. What construct do we use to denote the type of a field: a class, a kind (a class plus all of its subclasses), or something more abstract? A more abstract denotation for a type might be a template giving the internal structure of an object, or a protocol description giving messages an object understands and the types of their results. The choice depends greatly on whether indexing is based on the structure or protocol of an object. Another consideration is how heterogeneous the elements of a collection can be and still allow an index on the collection. The more abstract type descriptions allow indexing on collection that have some similarity in structure or protocol, while being of incomparable classes. An example is an index for a collection of Company and Person objects on address.zip. Classes as types are easiest to check at the Stone level, since an object carries a reference to its class.

2. Is nil a member of every type? What about nil values along a path? Should selection conditions be given the semantics that the existence of the path is presumed? That is, should both

        anEmp.name.last = 'Ross'

   and

        anEmp.name.last ~= 'Ross'   (not equal)

   be false if anEmp.name is nil?

3. Should an index be based on identity of key objects or their values? An identity index is immune to changes in the key object's state. However, an identity index on Strings will not support range queries. On the other hand, if we build an index on String objects sorted on their contents, we must detect the case where some method changes the characters of one of those Strings.

4. If range indexes are allowed, what comparison operators are allowed for the sort order? If the programmer supplies a method for the comparison, how do we know it is transitive?

6.1.3   Indexing on Classes Versus Collections

Another decision to be made in designing associative access is which to index, classes or collections? Several applications can use instances of the same class and store them in different collections. For example, if an application wants to index Employee objects on their last names, should it build one index on all instances of Employee or individual indexes on each collection of Employee objects it uses? If an application that uses only a subset of the Employee objects builds an index on the whole Employee class, then any other application that uses Employee objects pays the overhead of maintaining the index on updates, even if that index is useless to the other application. Also, the applications that needed the index see some performance degradation, because the objects of interest to the application are "diluted" by the rest of the Employee objects.

Indexing a collection allows the possibility that instances of subclasses be included in a collection that is indexed. For example, a last-name index could be built on a collection of instances of Person and its subclasses, such as Employee, StockHolder and Manager. Indexing on a class basis makes it easier to trace changes to the state of an object that could cause the class-based index to be positioned differently within an index. The implementation of a class-based index could include triggers on methods that update instance variables relevent to the index. Whenever the method was invoked on an object, the index would be notified, so that the index could inspect the object for changes affecting its placement in the index. In this manner, individual objects would not need to be tagged with the indexes they participate in.

Notice that with a class-based index, if a query is posed against a collection, then there is an added operation of intersecting the collection with the result of an indexed access. Another consideration with class-based indexing is whether the index includes subclasses. For example, should a last-name index on Person include all Employee and StockBroker objects? Having a separate index for each class would complicate access when a user wanted to query over the combined classes. A single combined index imposes performance overhead on a query against instances of a single class.

Indexing on individual collections also introduces complications. One object may belong to multiple collections and hence may be referenced from multiple indexes. It seems necessary to keep track, on an object-by-object basis, of what indexes an object participates in.

6.2   Path Expressions and Typing in OPAL

In this section and the next, we outline the actual choices made on language design and indexing strategy in GemStone. In order to facilitate associative access, both paths and instance variable typing have been introduced into OPAL.

6.2.1   Path Expressions

A *path expression* (or simply a *path*) is a variable name followed by a sequence of zero or more instance variable names called *links*. The variable name appearing in a path is called the *path prefix*; the sequence of links, the *path suffix*. The value of a path expression $A.L_1.L_2 \cdots L_n$ is defined as follows:

1. If $n = 0$, then the value of the path expression is the value of A.

2. If $n > 0$, then the value of the path expression is the value of instance variable L_n within the value of $A.L_1.L_2. \cdots .L_{n-1}$ if $A.L_1.L_2. \cdots .L_{n-1}$ is defined and L_n is an instance variable in the value of $A.L_1.L_2. \cdots .L_{n-1}$. Otherwise, the value of the path expression is undefined.

A path suffix S is *defined with respect to* a path prefix P if the value of $P.S$ is defined.

Consider a variable anEmp whose value is an instance of Employee. The value of the path anEmp.name is defined if name is an instance variable defined in Employee. Its value would be the value of anEmp's name instance variable. The value of anEmp.name.first is defined if the value of anEmp.name is defined and first is an instance variable in the value of anEmp.name. Its value would be the value of instance variable first in the value of anEmp.name.

Path expressions may be used anywhere in OPAL that an expression is allowed, but normally appear only in associative selection queries.

6.2.2   Typing

In OPAL, constraints on the values of named instance variables may be specified when creating classes. Each named instance variable may be constrained by declaring a class-kind for the variable. In an object of class C, each named instance variable for which a class-kind is specified in C may have only a value that is either nil or a kind of the class-kind specified for the instance variable in C. Consider the class Employee discussed above. Suppose the instance variable name's class-kind is PersonName and PersonName has an instance variable first; then in any Employee object anEmp where anEmp.name is not nil, the path suffix name.first is defined.

Class-kind constraints are inherited through the class hierarchy and can be made more restrictive in a subclass. If Manager is a subclass of Employee, then the class-kind of name could be TitledPersonName if titledPersonName was a subclass of PersonName.

A class-kind constraint may be specified for an NSC class such as Bag or Set. An NSC instance may contain only members that are nil or match the specified class-kind. Such a constraint is declared in the class of the NSC, which means a subclass of Bag or Set must be created to support instances with typed elements. Consider the class Employee discussed above. By creating a subclass EmpSet of Set whose class-kind is Employee, NSCs can be created that contain only nil and objects that are a kind of Employee. Class-kind constraints for NSCs are inherited by subclasses. In the same manner as for named instance variables, class-kind constraints can be made more restrictive in subclasses of an NSC class. For example, a class SetOfEmployee whose class-kind is Employee can have a subclass SetOfManager whose class-kind is Manager, since Manager is a subclass of Employee.

6.3   Indexing in OPAL

6.3.1   Design Considerations

In OPAL, only NSCs support indexes, and only when proper typing exists for the path being indexed (for further details see [MS86]). By requiring type information in this way, the access path that an index represents can be determined at the time of index creation, using only class objects; there is no need to recompute the access path represented by a path expression for each element of an NSC.

OPAL supports two kinds of indexes: identity and equality indexes. Since the identity of an object is independent of its class, identity indexes support only the search operators == (identical to) and ~~ (not identical to). Equality indexes support the search operators =, ~=, <, <=, > and >=. Not every class supports these operators, which means that constraints on paths for equality indexes are stricter than those for identity indexes. Thus, for an equality index, we must be able to determine the type of every object along a path, whereas for an identity index, the final link on a path may be untyped. Additionally, so that the associative access routines need not execute arbitrary methods to test the search operators, paths for equality indexes must lead to a Boolean, Character, DateTime, Float, Fraction, Integer, Number, String, or subclasses thereof.

Consider the class Employee discussed above. In addition to the instance variable name, let address be an instance variable defined in Employee that is constrained to Address. Further, in Address let state be an instance variable constrained to String and let zip be an instance variable constrained to SmallInteger. In SetOfEmployee objects, either identity or equality indexes can be created on the suffixes name.first, address.state and address.zip. Identity indexes can be created on address, name, the empty path and possibly other paths.

Even in the absence of indexes, OPAL takes advantage of typing information in evaluating queries against NSCs. By being able to apply the same access strategy to each element of an NSC for a given path and being able to evaluate the comparison operator without the use of message sends, conditions that use a path expression and an operator that the path supports can be evaluated efficiently.

6.3.2   Implementation

Indexes on paths are implemented by a sequence of index components, one for each link in the path suffix. For an index into a SetOfEmployees object on name.last, there would be an index component from name values of elements of the SetOfEmployee object to those elements, and a component from last values of PersonName objects to those objects for which any PersonName object that is the name value of some element of the SetOfEmployee object. By our method of implementing indexes, creating either an identity or equality index on a path suffix $L_1.L_2.\cdots.L_n$ implicitly creates an identity index on $L_1.L_2.\cdots.L_i$, for $1 \le i < n$.

All data structures used in implementing indexes are stored in object space, and so are managed by Stone. In this manner, OPAL's concurrency control mechanism handles concurrency conflicts on index structures.

Every NSC object has a named instance variable, NSCDict, that is not accessible to the user. If the NSC is indexed, then NSCDict is an *index dictionary* containing one or more *dictionary entries*. An dictionary entry contains the following information about an index for the NSC:

1. whether it is an identity or an equality index

2. for an equality index, the type of the last object along the indexed path

3. the number of links in the path

4. for each link in the path, the offset of the corresponding instance variable in the object and the index component for that link.

Index components are currently implemented using B$^+$-trees ordered on the type of the corresponding link. The component for the last link in an identity index is ordered by OOPs. In the component for the last link in an equality index, the ordering of key values is determined by the class-kind of the key values. The index component for the first link requires special treatment, because it indexes into the NSC object. If the path suffixes of two or more indexes into an NSC have a common prefix, then the indexes will share the index components on the common prefix. For example, if there were address.state and address.zip indexes into an EmployeeBag object, then both indexes would share the component from Address objects to elements of the NSC object. The paths are merged, in essence, into a tree structure.

Objects in GemStone may be tagged with a *dependency list*. For every index component in which an object appears as a key, the object's dependency list will contain a pair of values consisting of the OOP of an index component and an offset. The pair indicates that if the value at the specified offset is updated then the corresponding index component must be modified.

6.3.3   Indexed Lookups

The evaluation of an indexed lookup begins with a lookup for the last link in a path. If the indexed path is of length one, then the lookup is complete. Otherwise, the following sequence is repeated $n-1$ times for a path of length n. The result of the previous lookup is sorted by OOP and, using the sorted list, a lookup is performed on the index component for the preceding link in the path.

Consider the evaluation of the condition `A.name.last = an` equality index on `name.last`. By using the index for the second component of the indexed path, all those `PersonNameObject` with a `last` value of `'Jones'` are found. These `personName` objects are then sorted by OOP. By performing an incremental search of the B-tree for the name links, with the sorted list of `PersonName` objects as lookup keys, the elements of `A` whose name values have a `last` value of `'Jones'` are found.

Since we do not have index entries for `nil` elements of an NSC and do not propagate entries for `nil` key values to next-components, indexed lookup never returns elements of the NSC for which a path is undefined. Thus, to find those elements of an NSC for which a path is undefined, one forms an NSC containing the values present in the first index component of the path and performs a set difference of it from the indexed NSC.

6.3.4   The Query Language

We have chosen to provide associative access through a limited calculus sublanguage. However, we have been careful in constructing the language so that associative queries can be viewed as procedural OPAL code. We support selection on collections with NSC implementations — subclasses of `Set` and `Bag`. Selection conditions are conjunctions of comparisons, where the comparisons are between path expressions and other path expressions or literals. While simple conjunctive selections might seem limited, we note that about the same support for associative access is supplied at the logical level in Cypress [Cat83] and in the internal representation of Adaplex queries [CFLR81], although those systems, like some others [ZW86], select from classes rather than collections. In an object-oriented model, there is no need for many of the joins used in relational systems, as these joins often serve to recompose entities that were decomposed for data normalization. Entities are not decomposed in the first place in an object-oriented model; most joins are replaced by path-tracing, which we support.

An associative query is a variation on a `select` expression. Suppose an Employee object also has a `worksIn` instance variable whose class-kind is Department. Then the following query will make use of all indexes available on the paths in the condition:

```
Emps select:
   {anEmp | anEmp.name.last = 'Jones' &
            anEmp.salary > anEmp.worksIn.manager.salary}
```

We have extended all of OPAL to allow path expressions. The meaning of the above query is the same as for the corresponding OPAL expression within a regular block:

```
Emps select:
   [anEmp | anEmp.name.last = 'Jones' &
            anEmp.salary > anEmp.worksIn.manager.salary]
```

Thus there is little impedance mismatch between OPAL and its query sublanguage.

7   Related Work

Experimental extensions of System/R to support complex design objects have dealt with the problem of indexing [HL82, LP81, MS86]. There, complex objects are built of a root tuple plus a tree of component tuples. The resulting object model differs from ours in that the component tuples are dependent on the root tuple. Those component tuples are removed when the root tuple is removed and are not shared with other complex objects. (Later versions of the work allow external references to component objects, but do not enforce referential integrity [Dat83] for such references.) The notion of dependent component objects shows up in other models [BB84, Gra84, Nie85, Wei85].

Each complex object is composed from tuples of several relations; these relations can be indexed on values actually stored in the tuple. In the hierarchy of component tuples, each tuple has a reference to its parent tuple and may have references to other component tuples in the same object or to roots of other objects. Further, each root tuple maintains an index to its component tuples at all levels, to aid in traversing from parent to child tuple and in moving or copying the entire object. The techniques for indexing complex objects in System/R are not directly applicable to our problem, since component objects in GemStone can be arbitrarily shared and are not dependent.

Adaplex [CDF*82, CFLR81] provides a model similar to GemStone but again with a significant difference. Entities (objects) may belong to multiple types (classes), unlike GemStone where every object is an instance of a single class. Other models share this multiple-membership property with Adaplex [DKL85, Zdo84, Zdo85]. Since an entity can acquire mappings (attributes) from all the various types it belongs to, the Adaplex designers have chosen to decompose the storage representation of an entity into a logical record for each type to which the entity belongs. Each connected component of the type hierarchy has an entity dictionary — much like our object table — which maps entity identifiers to logical records. The collection of logical records for a given type can be indexed, but on data values only (not entities) and hence not on the substructure of entities. Adaplex allows declarations that two mappings invert each other (such as manages and manager between Employee and Department) to support access from an entity to all other entities containing the first entity as the value for a particular mapping. Note that the individual link indexes in GemStone in essence maintain such an inverse mapping for all objects in a collection, although the inverse mapping is not named.

We also note that Adaplex tightly couples its procedural data language to the host language at the expression level, but preprocesses the host language to extract data accesses and encapsulate them in non-procedural "envelopes". In Cypress [Cat83], entities are maintained separately from information about entities (relationships). Entities in a domain (class) are indexed by identity, and relationships can also be indexed. Further, a linked list can be maintained for an entity and all relationship records in which it appears.

An extension to Ingres allows a programmer to add new data types and index support for them [SRG83]. However, Ingres treats instances of those types as uninterpreted sequences of bits, so instances of such types cannot reference other database entities directly. A successor to Ingres, Postgres [SR85], makes some provision for objects, but does so through storing QUEL and C procedures as attribute values. Since complex objects are something the application designer implements on top of Postgres, it is hard for the system to give any direct support to indexing complex objects. DROID is an experimental object-oriented design database based on LISP flavors. Its goal is to allow multiple VLSI design tools to access shared design objects at a level of granularity finer than files.

8 Future Work

While we feel that our initial efforts substantially meet the goals outlined in Sections 2 and 4, we see several potential areas for future research and development. Locking implemented on top of our shadowing scheme could be used to insure that transactions, particularly long ones, are not aborted. Versioning, possibly built on top of our shadowing scheme, could be used to maintain past states of objects. More robust means of handling schema changes would be useful during schema development, and as a database, or the application it models, evolves. Nested transactions would provide a means of restoring a user's shadow copy of the object table to an internally consistent state during error recovery, and would provide for a finer granularity of transaction management. Extending the query language to allow more operations to be specified declaratively would allow better optimization and use of indexes. Making use of instance variable typing in compiled methods to allow earlier binding may reduce execution time.

9 Acknowledgements

The authors would like to thank the following people for their contributions to the GemStone project: Ken Almond, quality and change control; Robert Bretl, Stone object manager; John Bruno, browser; Maureen Drury, virtual image; Jack Falk, documentation; Lynn Gallinat, virtual image; Larry Male, OPE editor; Daniel Moss, PC/VAX communications; Allen Otis, project manager; Alan Purdy, system architecture; Bruce Schuchardt, OPE implementation, bulk loader and dumper; Harold Williams, Gem implementation; Rich McCain, VAX system support; Monty Williams, quality and support implementation; Mike Nastos, documentation and bug hunting; Rick Nelson, VAX system manager; D. Jason Penney, Stone implementation, process scheduler; Mun Tuck Yap, Gem object manager, PC/VAX communications.

References

[ABB*83] M. Ahlsen, A. Bjornerstedt, S. Britts, C. Hutten and L. Suderland: An Architecture for Object Management in OIS. *ACM TOOIS* 2:3 (July 1983).

[ACO85] A. Albano, L. Cardelli and R. Orsini: Galileo: A Strongly-Typed Interactive Conceptual Language. *ACM TODS* 10:2 (June 1985).

[AO84] A. Albano and R. Orsini: A Prototyping Approach to Database Applications Development. *Database Engineering* 7:4 (December 1984).

[BM86] M. Ballard and D. Maier: QUICKTALK: A Smalltalk-80 Dialect for Defining Primitive Methods. *Proc. ACM Conference On Object-Oriented Programming Systems, Languages and Applications*, September 1986.

[BB84] D. Batory and A. Buckman: Molecular Objects, Abstract Data Types and Data Models: A Framework. *Proc. Conference on Very Large Databases*, 1984.

[BBD*84] M. Brodie, B. Blaustein, U. Dayal, F. Maniola and A. Rosenthal: CAD-CAM Database Management. *Database Engineering* 7:2 (June 1984).

[Cat83] R. G. Catell: Design and Implementation of a Relationship-Entity-Datum Model. Xerox CSL 83-4, May 1983.

[CDF*82] A. Chan, A. Danberg, S. Fox, W.-T. K. Lin, A. Nori and D. Ries: Storage and Access Structures to Support a Semantic Data Model. *Proc. Conference on Very Large Databases*, September 1982.

[CFHL83] K. C. Chu, J. P. Fishburn, P. Honeyman and Y. E. Liem: Vdd — A VLSI Design Database. *Engineering Design Application Proceedings* from *SIGMOD Database Week*, May 1983.

[CFLR81] A. Chan, S. A. Fox, W.-T. K. Lin and D. Ries: Design of an ADA Compatible Local Database Manager (LDM). TR CCA 81-09, Computer Corporation of America, November 1981.

[Cod79] E. F. Codd: Extending the Relational Database Model to Capture More Meaning. *ACM TODS* 4:4 (December 1979).

[CK85] G. Copeland and S. N. Koshafian: A Decomposition Storage Model. *Proc. ACM/SIGMOD International Conference on the Management of Data*, 1985.

[CM84] G. Copeland and D. Maier: Making Smalltalk a Database System, *Proc. ACM/SIGMOD International Conference on the Management of Data*, 1984.

[Dat83] C. J. Date: *An Intoduction to Database Systems, Volume 2.* Addison-Wesley, 1983.

[DPS86] U. Deppish, H. B. Paul and H. J. Scheck: A Storage System for Complex Objects. *Proc. International Workshop on Object-Oriented Database Systems*, September 1986.

[DK84] D. R. Dolk and B. R. Konsynski: Knowledge Representation for Model Management Systems. *IEEE Transactions on Software Engineering* 10:6 (November 1984).

[DKL85] N. Derret, W. Kent, P. Lynbaek: Some Aspects of Operations in an Object-Oriented Database. *Database Engineering* 8:4 (December 1985).

[Eas80] C. M. Eastman: System Facilities for CAD Databases. *Proc. IEEE 17th Design Automation Conference*, June 1980.

[EM83] J. C. Emond and G. Marechad: Experience in Building ARCADE, a Computer-Aided Design System Based on a Relational DBMS. *Engineering Design Application Proceedings from SIGMOD Database Week*, May 1983.

[GR83] A. Goldberg and D. Robson: *Smalltalk-80: The Language and Its Implementation.* Addison-Wesley, 1983.

[Gra84] Gray, M.: Databases for Computer-Aided Design. In *New Applications of Databases*, G. Garadarin and E. Gelenbe (eds.), Academic Press, 1984.

[Hay81] M. N. Haynie: The Relational/Network Hybrid Data Model for Design Automation Databases. *Proc. IEEE 18th Design Automation Conference*, 1981.

[HL82] R. L. Haskin and R. A. Lorie: On Extending the Functions of a Relational Database System. *Proc. ACM/SIGMOD International Conference on the Management of Data*, 1982.

[JSW83] H. R. Johnson, J. E. Schweitzer and E. R. Warkentire: A DBMS Facility for Handling Structural Engineering Entities. *Engineering Design Application Proceedings from SIGMOD Database Week*, May 1983.

[Kat82] R. H. Katz: A Database Approach for Managing VLSI Design Data. *Proc. IEEE 9th Design Automation Conference*, 1982.

[Kat83] R. H. Katz: Managing the Chip Design Database. *IEEE Computer* 16:12 (December 1983).

[KC86] S. N. Khoshafian and G. P. Copeland: Object Identity. *Proc. ACM Conference On Object-Oriented Programming Systems, Languages and Applications*, September 1986.

[KK83] T. Kaehler and G. Krasner: LOOM — Large Object-Oriented Memory for Smalltalk-80 Systems. In [Kra83].

[Kra83] G. Krasner: *Smalltalk-80: Bits of History, Words of Advice.* Addison-Wesley, 1983.

[LP81] M. La Croix and A. Pirotte: Data Structures for CAD Object Description. *Proc. IEEE 18th Design Automation Conference*, 1981.

[LP83] R. Lorie and W. Plouffe: Complex Objects and Their Use in Design Transactions. *Engineering Design Application Proceedings from SIGMOD Database Week*, May 1983.

[Mac83] B. J. MacLennan: A View of Object Oriented Programming. Naval Postgraduate School NPS52-83-001, February 1983.

[MBH*86] F. Maryanski, J. Bedell, S. Hoelscher, S. Hong, L. McDonald, J. Peckman and D. Stock: The Data Model Compiler: A Tool for Generating Object-Oriented Database Sytems. *Proc. International Workshop on Object-Oriented Database Systems*, September 1986.

[MBW80] J. Mylopoulos, P. A. Bernstein and H. K. T. Wong: A Language Facility for Designing Database-Intensive Applications. *ACM TODS* 5:2 (June 1980).

[MD86] Manola, F. and U. Dayal: PDM: An Object-Oriented Data Model. *Proc. International Workshop on Object-Oriented Database Systems*, September 1986.

[Mey86] N. Meyrowitz: Intermedia: The Architecture and Construction of an Object-Oriented Hypermedia System and Application Framework. *Proc. ACM Conference On Object Oriented Programming Systems, Languages and Applications*, September 1986.

[MNBR83] D. McLeod, K. Narayanaswamy and K. V. Bapa Rao: An Approach to Infomation Management for CAD/VLSI Applications.

Engineering Design Application Proceedings from *SIGMOD Database Week*, May 1983.

[MOP85] D. Maier, A. Otis and A. Purdy: Object-oriented Database Development at Servio Logic. *Database Engineering* 18:4 (December 1985).

[MP84] D. Maier and D. Price: Data Model Requirements for Engineering Applications. *Proc. International Workshop on Expert Database Systems*, 1984.

[MS86] D. Maier and J. Stein: Indexing in an Object-Oriented DBMS. *Proc. International Workshop on Object-Oriented Database Systems*, september 1986.

[MSOP86] D. Maier, J. Stein, A. Otis and A. Purdy: Development of an Object-Oriented DBMS. *Proc. ACM Conference On Object-Oriented Programming Systems, Languages and Applications*, September 1986.

[Nie85] O. M. Nierstrasz: Hybrid: A Unified Object-Oriented System. *Database Engineering* 8:4 (December 1985).

[OBS86] P. O'Brien, B. Bullis and C. Schaffert: Persistent and Shared Objects in Trellis/Owl. *Proc. International Workshop on Object-Oriented Database Systems*, September 1986.

[PSM87] D. J. Penney, J. Stein and D. Maier: Mixed Mode Concurrency Control in the GemStone Object-Oriented DBMS. Manuscript in preparation.

[PKLM84] W. Plouffe, W. Kim, R. Lorie and D. McNabb: A Database System for Engineering Design. *Database Engineering* 7:2 (June 1984).

[PL83] M. L. Powell and M. A. Linton: Database Support for Programming Environments. *Engineering Design Application Proceedings* from *SIGMOD Database Week*, May 1983.

[PMS87] A. Purdy, D. Maier and B. Schuchardt: Integrating an Object Server with Other Worlds. To appear: *ACM TOOIS*.

[RS79] L. A. Rowe and K. A. Shoens: Data Abstraction, Views and Updates in RIGEL. *Proc. ACM/SIGMOD International Conference on the Management of Data*, 1979.

[Sch73] J. W. Schmidt: Some High Level Language Constructs for Data of Type Relation. *ACM TODS* 2:3 (September 1973).

[Sch86] B. Schuchardt: GemStone to Smalltalk Interface, Servio Logic Development Corp. Technical Report, Sept. 1986.

[Sid80] T. W. Siddle: Weaknesses of Commercial Data Base Management Systems in Engineering Applications. *Proc. IEEE 17th Design Automation Conference*, June 1980.

[SMF86] D. L. Spooner, M. A. Milican and D. B. Fatz: Modelling Mechanical CAD Data with Data Abstractions and Object-Oriented Techniques. *Proc. 2nd International Conference on Data Engineering*, February 1986.

[SRG83] M. Stonebraker, B. Rubenstein and A. Guttman: Applications of Abstract Data Types and Abstract Indices to CAD Data Bases. *Engineering Design Application Proceedings* from *SIGMOD Database Week*, May 1983.

[SR85] M. Stonebraker and L. Rowe: The Design of POSTGRES. Berkeley TR ERL 85/95, November 1985.

[SZR86] A. H. Skarra, S. B. Zdonik and S. P. Reiss: An Object Server For an Object-Oriented System. *Proc. International Workshop on Object-Oriented Database Systems*, September 1986.

[Tha86] S. M. Thatte: Persistent Memory: A Storage Architecture for Object-Oriented Database Proc. *International Workshop on Object-Oriented Database Systems*. September 1986.

[Tho86] C. Thompson: Object-Oriented Databases. *Texas Instruments Engineering Journal*, 3:1 (Jan-Feb 1986).

[Wei85] S. P. Weisner: An Object-Oriented Protocol for Managing Data. *Database Engineering*, 8:4 (December 1985).

[Wie86] D. Wiebe: A Distributed Repository for Immutable Persistent Objects. *Proc. ACM Conference On Object-Oriented Programming Systems, Languages and Applications*, September 1986.

[Zan83] C. Zaniolo: The Database Language GEM. *Proc. ACM/SIGMOD International Conference on the Management of Data*, May 1983.

[Zdo84] S. B. Zdonik: Object Management Systems Concepts. *Proc. ACM SIGOA Conference on Office Information Systems*, 1984.

[Zdo85] S. B. Zdonik: Object Management Systems for Design Environments. *Database Engineering* 8:4 (December 1985).

[ZW86] S. B. Zdonik and P. Wegner: Language and Methodology for Object-Oriented Database Environments. *Proc. Nineteenth Annual Hawaii International Conference on System Science*, January 1986.

Trademarks

Combining Language and Database Advances in an Object-Oriented Development Environment

Timothy Andrews & Craig Harris

Ontologic, Inc.
47 Manning Road
Billerica, MA 01821

"You're both right. It's a dessert topping and a floor wax!"
– Chevy Chase

Abstract

Object-oriented languages generally lack support for persistent objects—that is objects that survive the process or programming session. On the other hand, database systems lack the expressiblity of object-oriented languages. Both persistence and expressibility are necessary for production application development.

This paper presents a brief overview of VBASE, an object-oriented development environment that combines a procedural object language and persistent objects into one integrated system. Language aspects of VBASE include strong datatyping, a block structured schema definition language, and parameterization, or the ability to type members of aggregate objects. Database aspects include system support for one-to-one, one-to-many, and many-to-many relationships between objects, an inverse mechanism, user control of object clustering in storage for space and retrieval efficiency, and support for trigger methods.

Unique aspects of the system are its mechanisms for custom implementations of storage allocation and access methods of properties and types, and free operations, that is operations that are not dispatched according to any defined type.

During the last several years, both languages and database systems have begun to incorporate object features. There are now many object-oriented programming languages. [Gol1983, Tes1985, Mey1987, Cox1986, Str1986]. Object-oriented database management systems are not as prevalent yet, and sometimes tend to use different terms (Entity-Relationship, Semantic Data Model), but they are beginning to appear on the horizon [Cat1983, Cop1984, Ston1986, Mylo1980]. However, we are not aware of any system which combines both language and database features in a single object-oriented development platform. This is essential since a system must provide both complex data management and advanced programming language features if it is to be used to develop significant production software systems. Providing only one or the other is somewhat akin to providing half a bridge: it might be made structurally sound, perhaps, but it is not particularly useful to one interested in getting across the river safely.

Object-oriented languages have been available for many years. The productivity increases achievable through the use of such languages are well recognized. However, few serious applications have been developed using them. One reason has been performance, though this drawback is being eliminated through the development of compiled object languages. The remaining major negative factor, in our view, is the lack of support for persistence; the lack of objects that survive the processing session and provide object sharing among multiple users of an application.

Database management systems, in contrast, suffer from precisely the opposite problem. While having excellent facilities for managing large amounts of data stored on mass media, they generally support only limited expression capabilities, and no structuring facilities.

Both language and database systems usually solve this problem by providing bridges between the systems. Thus the proliferation of 'embedded languages', allowing language systems to access database managers. These bridges are usually awkward, and still provide only restricted functionality. Both performance and safety can be enhanced through a tighter coupling between the data management and programming language facilities.

It is this lack of a truly integrated system which provided our inspiration at Ontologic, Inc. This paper reviews Ontologic's VBASE Integrated Object System and describes how it combines language and database functionality.

1. General System Overview

The single overriding consideration which drove the design and development of VBASE was to provide a complete development system for practical production applications based on object-oriented technology.

Two goals flowing from this motivation were:

1) To integrate a procedural language with support for persistent objects. This support should be as transparent as possible to users of the system.

2) To take maximum advantage of strong typing inherent in object systems in both the language and database.

The system derives its heritage from many precursors. Probably the single most important language influence was the CLU programming language developed at MIT[Lis1981]. Thus, VBASE is based around the abstract data type paradigm, rather than the object/message paradigm. This orientation manifests itself in many areas. For example, in typical object/message systems, all access to object behavior is through a uniform message syntax. In VBASE, object behavior is elicited by a combination of properties and operations. Properties represent static behavior; operations represent dynamic behavior. Property definition and access are syntactically differentiated from those of operations. This provides a more natural model of object behavior. It also saves the programmer from writing trivial code to get and set the values of properties. In VBASE, these operations are normally generated by the system, further increasing programmer productivity.

In fact, the fundamental emphasis on a strong separation between the specification of a system and the implementation of a system is common to abstract data type and object/message systems. VBASE uses this methodology at several levels to provide an extremely flexible architecture. (The overall architecture is shown in figure 1.)

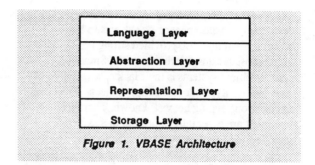

Figure 1. VBASE Architecture

The language layer contains compilers for defining and implementing the behavior of objects. The abstraction layer implements the object meta-model, providing support for inheritance, operation dispatching, method combination, and property manipulation. The representation layer is the locus of our reference semantics. The storage layer is responsible for object persistence.

Each layer of VBASE is implemented within VBASE itself. Thus each layer has a VBASE specification and a VBASE implementation. Consequently, we realize many of the advantages of the system in the implementation of the system itself. Chief among these has been the ability to implement the total system quickly and then tune performance by replacing or enhancing various implementations. As the specifications were unaffected, effort could be concentrated where it was needed, allowing a good deal of performance work to be completed on the system at an early date.

As mentioned previously, support for persistent objects, or objects that survive process lifetimes and programming sessions was a key motivation. This requires 'database' support; that is, handling of storage on stable media such as disks. There are some further capabilities implied by 'database' support:

1) sharing of object data among multiple processes/users.

2) handling large numbers of objects and consequently handling a large object storage space.

3) software stability so that the object space is maintained in a consistent state in the face of system or media failure.

We had a further desire: to provide 'seamless' support for persistent objects through a natural syntax. We particularly wished to avoid the 'embedded language' approach. The goal was to integrate persistent objects completely into the language as pseudo-standard variables. This makes the entire expression processing capability of the language layer available to the persistent objects.

The last of the primary motivations directing the design and development of VBASE was to build an object system that also provided strong typing. One of the most serious drawbacks of the Smalltalk class of object systems is their lack of any notion of type specificity. There are simply objects. The benefits of strong typing are well known. There are three that are especially important in a system intended for commercial development.

First, strong typing resolves many more errors at compile time than weakly-typed systems. Since objects' main claim to fame is productivity gain, the resolution of errors at an earlier time in the software lifecycle is significant. It should also be noted that compile time errors are generally easier to analyze and correct than errors of type mismatch that occur at run time.

Second, strong typing of object data structures provides superior specification of the system. Rather that relying on user-constructed naming conventions to convey type information (aFruit, anApple, aCar, etc), data structure type declarations provide a clear and exploitable specification since the type declarations are all part of the system specification. Thus, one can examine the declaration aFruit: Fruit, and then examine the Fruit definition for further information. This process can be applied recursively to any desired level of detail, and is not dependent on adoption of any conventions by the system implementors.

One final issue regarding strong typing is its effect on system performance. A strongly typed system allows the language processor to do far more analysis at compile time. This analysis can often reduce the need for runtime type checks, as well as allow methods to be statically bound. Our experience to date indicates that 90% of all type checking and method binding can be done at compile time. This eliminates the performance degradation frequently resulting from object systems' need to dynamically bind all method code to achieve object/message behavior. Thus VBASE exhibits the functionality of dynamic method binding based on a hierarchy of types, as do all object systems. However, it does so with performance comparable to a compiled, statically bound system.

There are, in fact, many more optimizations that the language processor can do based upon its knowledge of the semantics of the types and objects in the system, and the amount of work that can be done is proportional to the amount of information that is contained in the definitions. This is yet another argument for a strongly typed system.

While VBASE supports strong typing, the VBASE type system also provides a great deal of flexibility.

Through the use of subtyping and parameterized types and operations, VBASE provides a high degree of static type checking. There are cases, however, where static type checking is impossible or undesirable. Explicit run-time type checking can then be used to achieve the same expressive capability as an untyped object system. Thus, in VBASE, the tradeoff between compile-time optimization and run-time flexibility is controlled by the application developer.

2. System Components

VBASE is currently implemented on top of Sun OS 3.2 UNIX. There are presently two language interfaces: TDL (for Type Definition Language) and COP (for C Object Processor). TDL is used to specify a data model. That is, it is used to define data types and specify their associated properties and operations. COP is used in two roles. It is used to write the code to implement the operations. It is used to write the applications programs. There is also a set of tools to assist development. These include a debugger, interactive object editor, and a verifier program that checks consistency of the physical layout of the object data space.

TDL is a proprietary language. It is block structured, with features in common with such languages as Pascal, Modula, and Algol. Types are the most common entities defined in TDL. A type serves as the nexus for behavior of its instances. It determines the properties for which its instances supply values and it defines operations which may be performed on its instances.

The current version of the system allows only one supertype to be specified; this supertype places the type definition in the type hierarchy. Behavior is inherited via the type hierarchy in the expected manner. A type is also a block scope in TDL, and consequently may contain other arbitrary definitions along with its central property and operation definitions.

COP is a strict superset of the C language as defined by Kernighan and Ritchie. Any program which compiles with standard C will compile with COP. It contains syntactic extensions to the C language to allow typed declarations of variables, access to properties of objects, and invocation of operations on objects. COP is used to write the actual code that implements the operations and properties and other behaviors specified in TDL. It is currently implemented as a preprocessor which emits standard

C code.

The debugger allows source line debugging of the COP source code. The object editor allows interactive traversal of type and object definitions, assignment of object property values, and invocation of operations. The storage verifier examines the physical layout of the database and verifies its structural integrity.

3. Interesting Language Aspects

VBASE incorporates most of the standard object technology. There is a taxonomy of types, with subtypes inheriting both properties and operations from their supertype. Subtypes can add more specific behavior by specifying additional properties or operations, and can also refine existing behavior of inher-

ited properties or operations. When an operation is invoked, it is dispatched according to the type of the object of the invocation. Thus in COP one writes:

Entity$print (someObject);

which means find the print operation of the type closest in the type hierarchy to the direct type of someObject. Of course, there is complete type extensibility, with the user being able to define and use whatever types are desired.

3.1 Strong Typing

The most important language influence—strong typing—is unusual among current object systems. In TDL, the following definition illustrates the typing aspects:

```
define Type Part
    supertypes = {Entity};

properties = {
    partID: Identifier;
    name: optional String;
    components: distributed Set[Part]
        inverse componentOf;
    componentOf: Part inverse components;
}
operations = {
    display (p:Part)
        raises (NoDisplayImage)
        method (Part_Display);

    isComponentOf (p1: Part, p2:Part)
        raises (IsRootComponent)
        method (Part_IsComponentOf)
        returns (Boolean);

    connect (p: Part, to: Part,
        keywords
            optional using: Connector)
        raises (BadConnect)
        method (Part_Connect)
        returns (Part);

    iterator components (p: Part)
        yields (p: Part)
        method (Part_Components);

    refines delete (p: Part)
        triggers (Part_deleteTrigger);
    };

    PRIVATE
    properties = {
        displayImage: optional Image;
        isRootComponent: Boolean := False;
        };

end Part;
```

```
define Type Pipe
    supertypes = {Part};

    properties = {
        length: Integer := 0;
        diameter: Integer := 0;
        leftConnection: Part;
        rightConnection: Part;
        threadtype: optional ThreadType :=
            Thread ype$ScrewThread;
        isInsulated: optional Boolean:= False;
    };
        operations = {
        refines connect (p: Pipe, to: Part,
            keywords
                optional usingConnector: Connector)
            raises (ThreadtypeMisMatch,
                IncompatibleMaterials)
            method (Pipe_Connect)
            returns (Part);

        materialsCompatible(p1:Pipe, p2:Pipe)
            method (Pipe_MaterialsCompatible)
            returns (Boolean);

        refines delete (p: Pipe)
            raises (CannotDelete)
            triggers (Pipe_deleteTrigger);
        };
    end Pipe;

    define Type ThreadType is enum (ScrewThread,
    PolThread);
```

Figure 2. TDL code for two type definitions is shown. Type Part is a generic definition used for all parts in this hypothetical engineering design database. It is the supertype of type Pipe which inherits all the behavior of parts and adds behavior specific to pipes.

Note that all definitions are associated with a type. This applies at all levels. At the topmost level, the 'define Type Part' fragment says that Part is of type Type. In a similar manner, properties are defined in terms of their data type, as are operation arguments, return values, and exception specifications. The type information contained in the TDL specifications is then used to generate a schema for an object database. In practice, VBASE provides a substantial kernel schema. TDL is then used to augment this schema with user extensions. Thus TDL can be described as an incremental schema compiler.

After the datatypes are defined, COP code is written and compiled against the object database. The COP compiler is a database application, and uses the

---

Figure 3. COP code for the Pipe_Connect method. This method implements the operation defined in Type Pipe in figure 2.

```
method
obj Part
Pipe_Connect (aPipe, toPart, usingConnector)

obj Pipe aPipe;
obj Part toPart;
keyword obj Connector usingConnector;

{
   obj Part connectedPart;
   obj Pipe toPipe;
   int j;

   if (hasvalue (usingConnector))
   {
     connectedPart = Pipe$Connect
        (aPipe, usingConnector);
     return (Part$Connect (connectedPart, toPart,
using: usingConnector));
   }

   toPipe = assert (toPart, obj Pipe);
   except (ia: IllegalAssert)
   {
     PipeSystem$ErrorPrint (aPipe, toPart, "can only
connect Pipes to Other Pipes");
   }
   if (aPipe.threadtype != toPipe.threadtype)
     raise (ThreadTypeMisMatch);

   if (! Pipe$MaterialsCompatible (aPipe, toPipe))
     raise (IncompatibleMaterials);

   aPipe.leftConnection = toPipe;
   toPipe.rightConnection = aPipe;

   connectedPart = $$ (aPipe, aPart);

   return (connectedPart);
}
```

type information of the database to do what type checking is possible at compile time. When static type checking is not possible, the check is deferred to runtime.

Operations in the type definition are implemented by methods written in COP. Figure 3 shows the code to implement the Pipe_Connect method.

Note that all object variables are declared with the additional keyword obj. This allows the program variables to be associated with types in the schema, and COP can then do type checking based on the schema information. Therefore the assignment:

aPipe.leftConnection = toPipe;

is allowed since the leftConnection property of type Pipe is of type Part, and the declared type of the variable toPipe is Pipe. These are compatible since Pipe is a subtype of Part. All operation invocations and their arguments are similarly checked.

When it is not possible to determine type compatibility at compile time, the programmer uses the assert statement. The assert statement defers type checking until runtime. This allows handling assignment of a more general type to a more specific type without violating strict compile-time type checking in most cases, an invaluable productivity win in large, complex systems. In the method example in figure 3, assert is used for two purposes.

First, this simple implementation assumes that pipes can only be connected to pipes; thus the assert does a runtime type check for the programmer, while allowing the code to be written for the more general case of connecting a pipe to any other part.

Second, the statement:

toPipe.rightConnection = aPipe;

will not compile if the declared type of toPipe is Part. This is because Part does not define the property rightConnection. rightConnection is defined by Pipe. Thus while it is quite possible that, since part is pipe's supertype, a given part is a pipe, it is not guaranteed by the declarations of the program. This is a very common type violation in object systems, and this is what VBASE prevents. The assert alerts the implementor that the actual type of the object toPipe must be pipe (or a subtype of pipe) in order for this assignment to be valid.

This is in stark contrast to Smalltalk-like object systems.

3.2 A Block-structured Schema Definition Language

Another notable feature of TDL is that it is a block

structured language. This is different from most object systems, and certainly very different from most schema definition languages of DBMS's. It gives TDL the kind of complex name environment that most structured programming languages have, with the concommitant reduction of name conflicts. It also means that the system supports pathnames, allowing simple grouping of names, and relative names as well as global names.

The '$' is the pathname component separator. Thus the name 'Threadtype$Screwtype' refers to the name Screwtype within the block defined by the name Threadtype. Analogously, in the COP fragment, a name such as 'Pipe$Connect' refers to the name Connect within the Pipe scope. Names which begin with a '$' are considered absolute relative to the root scope maintained by VBASE. Names in the root include such things as kernel type names, system exception types, etc. New type definitions, unless contained within a scope, are placed in the root. A file is not considered a scope. This last point is generally not true of present systems, and has the pleasant side effect that many definitions can be placed in a single file or set of files without affecting the desired scoping.

3.3 Constant & Variable Definitions in TDL

Another programming language capability available in TDL is defining constants and variables. This allows user-customized constants to be placed in the object database. For instance:

```
define Constant myDefault := Null;
define Constant No := False;
define Constant Yes := True;
define Variable background: Color := Colors$Gray;
```

As in other languages, constants are immutable, while variables can have their bindings reassigned.

3.4 Enumeration, Union, and Variant Types

Along similar lines, TDL allows the definition of enumerations, unions and variants. Type definitions such as these are rarely supported in object systems or database systems. This is certainly unfortunate, as their uses are well known. For instance:

```
define type Day Is enum (Monday, Tuesday, ...);
```

Unions and variants are especially important in object systems, particulary those which do not support multiple inheritance. These definitional abilities allow any type of polymorphism desired to be expressed without circumventing the type safety of the system. Rather than having to declare any variable that can potentially hold objects of types which are disjoint in the type hierarchy as Entity, one can restrict the set of types to only those which can actually occur:

```
define type BlockScope Is union (Type, Module, Environment, Directory, ...);
```

This allows common mistakes to be ferreted out at compile time. Thus:

```
obj BlockScope scope;
....
scope = Day$Monday;
```

will fail at compile time. If, instead, the variable's scope had to be declared of type Entity (the root of the type hierarchy), this mistake would go unnoticed during compilation.

3.5 Parameterization

Another significant capability of VBASE is what is sometimes referred to as parameterization: the ability to specify the type of the objects contained inside aggregate objects. This ability is often not even available in procedural languages. Thus one can write:

```
obj Array[Animal] myZoo;
```

VBASE will type check all insertions into and assignments from the aggregate just as it checks standard types. The lack of such checking is a serious shortcoming of present systems as aggregates are widely used to store critical system information. Often this information is typed, but there is no way to enforce proper use short of writing expensive runtime checks of the elements of the aggregate. Thus:

```
{
    obj Array[Animal] myZoo;
    obj Fruit aKiwi;

    aKiwi = myZoo[3];
}
```

fails at compile time.

Once again, it must be emphasized that this does not limit the programmer. If the programmer actually wishes an 'untyped' Array:

```
obj Array[Entity] myUntypedArray;
```

will suffice. However, as most system implementors can testify, this is rarely the case. More usually,the appropriate types cannot be defined within the confines of the chosen system, and the programmer must circumvent the system in order to accomplish the task with reasonable efficiency.

3.6 Method Combination

The above paragraphs have described some of the more interesting 'data definition' (to use the term rather loosely) capabilities of VBASE. There are also some very interesting runtime features in VBASE. Perhaps the most notable of these is the VBASE approach to method combination. Method combination in object systems results when a refining method invokes its refinee. In Smalltalk, for example, one uses the pseudo-variable 'super' for this purpose. VBASE uses '$$' for this purpose. This notation, rather than super or some derivative thereof, was chosen because of the novel view of operations behavior that VBASE takes.

Operations are viewed as being implemented by a series of executable code fragments. The number of fragments is arbitrary, and is the sum of all triggers and methods defined in the operation. Reviewing the TDL figure 2, note that each operation definition can include a method clause, and a triggers clause. Each operation is therefore potentially associated with one method, called the base method, and an arbitrary number of trigger methods. The execution sequence begins with the first trigger in the triggers clause. The '$$' syntax transfers execution to the next code fragment: either the next trigger, or if no more are specified, to the method specified in the method clause. Once these fragments are executed, '$$' transfers execution to the refinee operation at the supertype level.

Thus, in the case where only a base method is defined, '$$' functions exactly as 'super' in Smalltalk. However, when triggers are used, this is not the case. Consequently, VBASE avoids the super syntax in favor of the '$$' syntax to avoid the impression of moving up the supertype chain. Rather, '$$' simply transfers execution to the next code fragment, whatever that may be.

Functionally, '$$' behaves like a function call. Thus, the placement of the '$$' in the code allows implementation of pre-processing, post-processing, or both: wrapper processing.

One interesting subject regarding this implementation of method combination is the compatibility of operation specifications in a chain of operation refinements. In a strongly typed system such as VBASE this is an important issue. The approach we have taken focusses on guaranteeing a conformance relation.

Methods are checked by the COP compiler for conforming to their specification defined by the operation. Refinements of inherited specifications are verified by the TDL compiler for conforming to the original specifications. The specific criteria for conformance have been motivated by the work of Cardelli[CAR1984].

3.7 Exceptions

In many languages, there are no specific exception handling mechanisms. Thus code to detect and handle exceptions must be explicitly inserted at each point in a program where an exception might occur. This not only forces the writing of a great many short, repetitive code fragments, it also places an additional burden on the establishment of extra-language applications conventions and creates numerous opportunities for lapses in programming discipline.

In VBASE, we included a specific exception handling mechanism. Exception conditions detected during the execution of an operation raise an exception. That is, they transfer control to a pre-defined exception handling routine rather than return control to the caller.

Once again, referring to figure 3, note the except and raise statements. These statements allow graceful handling of abnormal events that occur during processing, and are variations on a fairly standard theme. What is notable is that in VBASE, exceptions are types. This means that all of the behavior definition mechanisms available to types are available to exceptions. One consequence is that the implementor can define a hierarchy of exceptions. Thus exceptions can be generalized just like types are generalized. For example, a memory allocation operation might raise the exception OutOfMemory. A refinement of the operation, say one which allocates memory for strings, might raise a more specific exception, say StringSpaceFull. StringSpaceFull could be implemented as a subtype of OutOfMemory. As a subtype of OutOfMemory, it could be used in any context where OutOfMemory itself would be expected.

The second implication of exceptions as types is that one can define properties and /or operations of exceptions. Properties can be extremely useful. In the previous example, one could add the property AmountRequested to the exception type OutOfMemory. For example, assume the raising routine returned:

```
raise OutOfMemory (AmountRequested: 4000000);
```

The 'catching' program could then issue a meaningful error message or do something else appropriate. For example:

```
except (o: OutOfMemory)
{
    printf ("The amount of memory: %d, requested is not available\n", o.AmountRequested);
}
```

One can thus consider each actual raising of an exception as creating an instance of the exception. This instance is available to the catching program, which can treat it like any other object, accessing its properties, etc.

4. Interesting Database Aspects

VBASE supports most of the expected functionality of a DBMS. Objects can be shared among multiple processes concurrently, backup and recovery facilities are provided, and simple access control is available. A first version of an object query language is also under development for inclusion in the first version of VBASE. Beyond this, there are many notably different aspects of VBASE that derive from database influences.

4.1 Persistence

Persistence of objects is clearly the most notable difference between VBASE and most current object systems. Any time an object is created, either by a TDL definition or an invocation of a create operation in COP, it is considered permanent and continues to exist until it is explicitly deleted by a delete operation. The ability to deal with persistent objects without any special effort is an enormous advantage of VBASE.

4.2 Clustering

Another database influence apparent in the system is the ability to cluster objects on disk and in memory. Every create operation allows the invoker to specify a previously-existing clustering object. The new object is then clustered in the same segment as the clustering object. Since segments are the unit of transfer to and from secondary storage in VBASE, whenever any one of the objects in the cluster is accessed, the segment is transferred to memory (if it is not already there). Thus any subsequent references to one of the clustered objects will not require a disk access.

This has numerous applications. For instance, objects contained within an array can be clustered with the array. It is also very useful for a-part-of, or component, hierarchies, which are extremely common in engineering and text management applications. In this case, all the component objects can be clustered. Therefore only one disk access is required to transfer the entire hierarchy into memory. Clustering also provides space saving benefits, as there is less overhead when objects are stored in one segment.

4.3 Inverse Relationships

Reviewing the TDL definition of the type Part (figure 2) points out a further database influence in VBASE—the support for inverse relationships. Note the components and componentOf property definitions. These properties are declared as inverses. This means that whenever a modification is made to one of these properties, the other property is modified accordingly. This construct solves one of the more vexing problems in database management systems, particularly relational database systems. One-to-one, one-to-many, and many-to-many relationships between objects can all be supported and maintained automatically using the inverse capability. Thus, such common relationships as Parts–Suppliers or Employees–Departments can be implemented directly with no additional definitions or code. This is a dramatic improvement over most current database systems, and is not available in current object systems.

4.4 Protecting the Object Database from Process Failure

A last database style aspect of VBASE is the support of a minimal protection scheme. Current object systems are entirely memory resident and generally ignore the issue of corruption due to process failure. However, this has long been a standard issue of database systems since large amounts of important data are being manipulated. Some degree of safety and resilience must be offered. VBASE will offer concurrency control and recovery in its first release.

4.5 Triggers

The availability of triggers, discussed previously, can be considered both a language and a database influence. Many database systems talk about triggers, few implement them. Their utility is obvious. Triggers can be attached to properties as well as operations to generate whatever behavior is desired. These behaviors include standard ones such as 'when my QuantityOnHand property falls under twenty, issue a new order for a hundred more', to more esoteric patterns such as keeping audit trails of property and operation access for security purposes.

In VBASE the triggers are often used to augment creation and deletion methods. The use of triggers can insure, for instance that, upon creation of an object, all important referent objects are created as well. Delete triggers reverse this to delete all referent objects. Consider the example in figure 4.

When a PipeConnector object is created, one would also like to create an Array for the bolts property of the connector, perhaps initializing it from a set of Bolts passed to the Create operation. The use of a trigger on the standard create operation provides this functionality.

```
method obj PipeConnector
PipeConnector_CreateTrigger
    (aType, numberOfBolts, boltSet)

obj Type aType;/* must always take a Type arg when
    doing a create */
obj Integer numberOfBolts;
obj List[Bolt] boltSet;
{
  obj PipeConnector newConnector;   /* the result of
      the creation process */
  obj Bolt aBolt;        /* range variable for bolt set */
  Int j = 0;               /* standard C variable */
  newConnector = $$ (aType);
        /* create the new object by invoking the
              standard system create operation */

  /* create the referent object */
  newConnector.boltSet =
    Array$Create ($Array, numberOfBolts);

  /* initialize the referent object */
  iterate (aBolt = boltSet)
    newConnector.bolts[j++] = aBolt;

  return (newConnector);
}
```

Figure 4. Triggers can add behaviors to a create operation. The trigger method is shown above, the type definition is in the shaded block at right.

```
define Type PipeConnector
    supertypes = {Part};

    properties = {
        bolts: Array[Bolt];
        ...
    };
end PipeConnector;
```

Two aspects of the system should be noted in passing. First is the arbitrary combination of C program variables with object variables. This, as stated, was an important goal: a truly integrated language. The language processor does all necessary conversion to assure a correct program is produced. The second factor is the iterate statement. Drawn from CLU, this statement processes all members of a database aggregate an element at a time without requiring the writing of a 'for' loop. This is yet another productivity gain of the system, as it is unnecessary to compute the boundaries for a for loop. Perhaps more importantly, iterators provide access to the elements of an aggregate abstractly, without exposing (or requiring knowlege of) the underlying implementation.

4.6 Access To Meta Level Information

The final attribute of VBASE drawn from DBMS's is the availability of meta information. VBASE is entirely self-describing: all system characteristics except the lowest layers of storage management are imple-mented using types. The properties and operations of these system types are freely available to programmers to use to their advantage. This makes system development easier, and allows implementors to create customized tools of their own while taking advantage of system tools already in existence.

5. Some Further Unique Aspects

5.1 Customized Property Implementations

Object systems are known for their ability to allow users to create customized abstractions. VBASE provides users with the unique ability to customize implementations as well. This ability is available at two levels.

In the simpler case, an implementor can provide customized access to a property by replacing the default get and set operations for the property by customized ones. For instance, the property 'age' in the following example has such customized operations specified.

```
define Type Person
    supertypes = {Mammal};
    properties = {
        age: Integer define set
            method (Person_SetAge)
            define get
            method (Person_GetAge);
    };
end Person;
```

This specification will cause the user defined routines to be invoked whenever access to the age property occurs as in:

```
{
obj Person aPerson;
obj Integer theAge;
....
theAge = aPerson.age;
....
}
```

What is different here from most systems is that when both a get and set operation are specified, no storage is allocated. Thus the programmer truly takes over the implementation, including storage allocation. The user may choose to calculate the value (in the case of age, it is common to calculate the value as the difference between the person's birth-date and the current system date), in which case no storage is needed. If storage is necessary, the implementor may allocate it wherever he/she desires. For example, in a design application one might store large bitmap graphic images using a compression algorithm, and write customized code to read and write the image. In a similar vein, in a CASE system one might store fragments of source code in standard operating system files so that the various language processors will recognize the fragments. Finally, data from alien databases can be imported and exported transparently by using customized properties. The get and set operations are used to call the appropriate database routines on the foreign database to read and write the data.

5.2 Customized Type Implementations - MasterTypes

The use of custom routines for handling property implementation still incurs the overhead of a standard object. There is space overhead for the default representation, and the overhead of the system routines for dispatching to the user's custom routines. For sophisticated users wishing to avoid even this overhead, VBASE allows the complete implementation of customized types. Since VBASE provides the complete specification of all system types including type Type, a complete customization of a type is possible. It requires substantially more work than a custom property, but this is to be expected.

Customized types are actually handled as a subtype of type Type, called MasterType. The most significant characteristic of a MasterType is that it takes over the dereferencing operation. VBASE insists on strong reference semantics. That is, objects are always represented by a reference, and these references appear uniform from the outside. Thus, the 'every object is a first class object' semantics is maintained; even integers, single characters, and booleans are true first class objects. However, the types Integer, Character and Boolean are also MasterTypes. They implement their own creation, deletion, and dereferencing operations. This allows types such as Integer to store their value within their reference, and for types such as Real to make use of special hardware to implement arithmetic operations. MasterTypes must implement a create routine which fabricates and returns a reference, an appropriate dereferencing routine, routines for property access and operation dispatching and invocation, etc. However, once the complete specification has been met, these MasterTypes behave exactly like all other types to users, and all of the attributes of the VBASE environment can be used with them.

Implementors can therefore use the MasterType feature to create extremely customized types. No space or time overhead is incurred because the user implementation handles everything. MasterTypes are very useful for implementing custom access methods which require special data formats. This is a unique aspect of VBASE: the ability to tune access to special data formats such as large blocks of text or graphics, while remaining within the basic system.

Another use for MasterType implementations is the construction of efficient integration databases. A model of a complex data structure is created through the definition of the appropriate types, properties and operations. This data, which is actually stored in existing foreign databases, is accessed through MasterTypes which transfer the data to and from the alien databases. The use of MasterTypes allows a relatively efficient interface to the foreign database system to be implemented, while the processing and data modeling can be done in VBASE, with the attendant increase in modeling power and ease of implementation.

5.3 Free Operations

VBASE defines free operations: operations that are not associated with a type, and consequently, are not invoked via the standard dispatching means. In object message systems, every message is dispatched; that is, the type of the object being sent the message is used to find the method which implements the message. Free operations in VBASE, in contrast, do not have a distinguished argument. They are simply procedures free of type association.

Summary

VBASE has, we hope, achieved all of the goals we set for ourselves, at least to some extent. It is a relatively complete development system with language processors and development tools. It is object based, strongly typed, and provides support for persistent objects. It also allows custom implementations for improved efficiency. VBASE contains many interesting features from both the language and database spheres. In fact, the most interesting aspect of VBASE is that it cannot be strictly classified as a language or a database system.

References

BOR1982 Borning, Alan H. and Ingalls, Daniel H. H.; "A Type Declaration and Inference System for Smalltalk"; Conference Record of the Ninth Annual ACM Symposium on Principles of Programming Languages, pp 133-139, 1982.

CAR1984 Cardelli, Luca; "A Semantics of Multiple Inheritance"; Lecture Notes in Computer Science. Springer-Verlag, New York, 1984, pp 51-67.

CAR1986 Cardelli, Luca and Wegner, Peter; "On
Understanding Types, Data Abstraction, and Poly-
morphism"; Computing Surveys, Vol. 17, No. 4,
December 1985

CAT1983   Cattell, R.G.G.; "Design and Implementation of a Relationship-Entity-Datum Data Model"; Xerox Corporation, 1983

COP1984   Copeland, George and Maier, David;
"Making Smalltalk a Database System;" Sigmod
'84, Sigmond Record Volume 14, Number 2, pp
316-324, Association for Computing Machinery,
1984

COX1986   Cox, Brad J.; *Object-Oriented Programming: An Evolutionary Approach;* Addison-Wesley, Reading, MA 1986

GEM1986   *GemStone Product Overview, Gem-
Stone Version 1.0;* Servio Logic Development Corporation. March, 1986

GOL1983   Goldberg, Adele and Robson, David;
*Smalltalk-80: The Language and its Inplementa-
tion;* Addison- Wesley, Reading, MA, 1983

JOH1986 Johnson, Ralph; "Type Checking
Smalltalk"; in Proceedings of ACM Conference
on Object-Oriented Programming Systems, Languages and Applications; pp 315-321; Portland,
OR; September 29-October 2, 1986

LIS1981   Liskov, Barbara; Atkinson, Russell;
Bloom, Toby; Moss, Eliot; Schaffert, J. Craig;
Scheifler, Robert and Snyder, Alan; *Lecture Notes
in Computer Science;* Springer-Verlag, New
York, NY 1981

MEY1986   Meyer, Bertrand; "Genericity versus
inheritance"; in *Proceedings of ACM Conference
on Object-Oriented Programming Systems, Languages and Applications;* pp 391-405, Portland,
OR; September 29-October 2, 1986

MEY1987   Meyer, Bertrand; "Eiffel: Programming for Reusability and Extendibility;" SIG-
PLAN, Notices, vol 22, no 2, pp 85-94; February
1987

MYLO1980   Mylopoulos, John, Bernstein; Philip
A., and Wong Harry K.T.; "A Language Facility
for Designing Database-Intensive Applications",
Transactions on Database Systems; Vol 5, No 2.
pp 185-207; Association for Computing Machinery; June, 1980

STON1986   Stonebraker, Michael and Rowe,
Lawrence A. "The Design of Postgres"; Sigmond
Record, vol 15, no. 2, pp 340-355; Association for
Computing Machinery; June 1986

STR1986   Stroustrup, Bjarne L.; *The C++ Programming Language;* Addison-Wesley; Reading,
MA, 1986

TES1985   Tesler, Larry; "Object Pascal Report";
Structured Langauage World, vol 9, no.3, 1985

Data Model Issues for Object-Oriented Applications

JAY BANERJEE, HONG-TAI CHOU, JORGE F. GARZA, WON KIM, DARRELL WOELK, and NAT BALLOU

MCC

and

HYOUNG-JOO KIM

University of Texas

Presented in this paper is the data model for ORION, a prototype database system that adds persistence and sharability to objects created and manipulated in object-oriented applications. The ORION data model consolidates and modifies a number of major concepts found in many object-oriented systems, such as objects, classes, class lattice, methods, and inheritance. These concepts are reviewed and three major enhancements to the conventional object-oriented data model, namely, schema evolution, composite objects, and versions, are elaborated upon. Schema evolution is the ability to dynamically make changes to the class definitions and the structure of the class lattice. Composite objects are recursive collections of exclusive components that are treated as units of storage, retrieval, and integrity enforcement. Versions are variations of the same object that are related by the history of their derivation. These enhancements are strongly motivated by the data management requirements of the ORION applications from the domains of artificial intelligence, computer-aided design and manufacturing, and office information systems with multimedia documents.

Categories and Subject Descriptors: H.1.2 [Models and Principles]: User/Machine Systems—human information processing; H.2.1 [Database Management]: Logical Design—data models; H.4.1 [Information Systems Applications]: Office Automation

General Terms: Design, Theory

Additional Key Words and Phrases: Composite object, object-oriented database, schema evolution, version management

1. INTRODUCTION

In recent years, object-oriented programming has gained a tremendous popularity in the design and implementation of emerging data-intensive application systems. These include artificial intelligence (AI), computer-aided design and manufacturing (CAD/CAM), and office information systems (OIS) with multimedia

Authors' addresses: J. Banerjee, H.-T. Chou, J. F. Garza, W. Kim, and D. Woelk, Database Program, MCC, 3500 West Balcones Center Drive, Austin, TX 78759. N. Ballou, AI/KBS Program, MCC, 3500 West Balcones Center Drive, Austin, TX 78759; H.-J. Kim, Department of Computer Sciences, University of Texas, Austin, TX 78712.

documents [2, 8, 15]. Object-oriented programming offers a number of important advantages for these applications over traditional control-oriented programming. One is the modeling of all conceptual entities with a single concept, namely, objects. An *object* represents anything from a simple number, say, the number 25, to a complex entity, such as an automobile or an insurance agency. The state of an object is captured in the *instance variables*. The behavior of an object is captured in *messages* to which an object responds. The messages completely define the semantics of an object.

Another advantage of object-oriented programming is the notion of a *class hierarchy* and *inheritance* of properties (instance variables and messages) along the class hierarchy. The class hierarchy captures the IS-A relationship between a class and its *subclass* (equivalently, a class and its *superclass*). All subclasses of a class inherit all properties defined for the class and can have additional properties local to them. The notion of property inheritance along the hierarchy facilitates top-down design of the database, as well as applications.

We are presently prototyping an object-oriented database system, called ORION, to support the data management needs of object-oriented applications from the CAD/CAM, AI, and OIS domains. The intended applications for ORION impose two types of requirements: advanced functionality and high performance. The ORION architecture has been designed to satisfy these requirements. ORION will provide a number of advanced features that conventional commercial database systems do not, including version control and change notification [7], storage and presentation of unstructured multimedia data [31], and dynamic changes to the database schema [4]. For high performance, ORION will support appropriate access paths and techniques for query processing, buffer management, and concurrency control.

To derive an object-oriented application interface to ORION, our initial plan was simply to use a data model from some of the existing object-oriented systems [28] or object-oriented data models [1, 3, 24]. However, two major problems rendered this approach impossible. One was that there is no consensus about the object-oriented model; different object-oriented systems support different notions of objects. We had to extract and consolidate a number of major concepts found in many object-oriented systems and use them as the basis for our data model.

Another problem was that most existing object-oriented systems are programming language systems [6, 13, 20, 21, 22, 29]. As such, their data models completely ignore many important database issues, such as deletions of persistent objects, dynamic changes to the database schema, and predicate-based query capabilities. They also lack concepts that are important to applications, such as *composite objects* and *aggregate objects* for defining and manipulating complex collections of related objects. Further, they do not include version control, which most application systems in the CAD/CAM and OIS domains require. We had to augment the basic set of object concepts with these additional concepts and capabilities.

In Section 2, we provide a review of the fundamental object-oriented concepts, including approaches to the problem of conflict resolution, which arises when a class inherits properties from one or more superclasses, and our own approach to supporting predicate-based queries against the database. In Section 3 we introduce a formal framework for understanding the taxonomy and semantics of schema change operations that we allow, including changes to the class definitions and the class lattice structure. In Section 4 we define the semantics of composite objects and show their integration into the object-oriented data model. Section 5 shows the integration of our model of versions into the object-oriented data model.

2. OBJECT-ORIENTED CONCEPTS

Existing object-oriented systems exhibit significant differences in their support of the object-oriented paradigm; Stefik and Bobrow [28] provide an excellent account of different variations of the object concepts. In this section we review the basic object concepts, and, where appropriate, show how we have refined them to suit the requirements of our applications in a database environment.

2.1 Basic Concepts

In object-oriented systems, all conceptual entities are modeled as objects. An ordinary integer or string is as much an object as is a complex assembly of parts, such as an aircraft or a submarine. An object consists of some private memory that holds its state. The private memory is made up of the values for a collection of instance variables. The value of an instance variable is itself an object and therefore has its own private memory for its state (i.e., its instance variables). A primitive object, such as an integer or a string, has no instance variables. It only has a value, which itself is an object. More complex objects contain instance variables, which, in turn, contain other instance variables. Further, two objects may have instance variables that refer to a common object. For example, the value of the Manufacturer instance variable of a vehicle may be an object that represents a certain auto company, and that same auto company may also be the value of the Employer instance variable of a person.

The behavior of an object is encapsulated in *methods*. Methods consist of code that manipulates or returns the state of an object. Methods are a part of the definition of the object. Methods, as well as instance variables, however, are not visible from outside of the object. Objects can communicate with one another through messages. Messages, together with any arguments that may be passed with the messages, constitute the public interface of an object. For each message understood by an object, there is a corresponding method that executes the message. An object reacts to a message by executing the corresponding method and returning an object in response.

A program may create and reference a large number of objects. A database may contain an even larger collection of objects. If every object is to carry its own instance variable names and its own methods, the amount of information to be specified and stored can become unmanageably large. For this reason, as well as for conceptual simplicity, "similar" objects are grouped together into a *class*. All objects belonging to the same class are described by the same instance variables and the same methods. They all respond to the same messages. Objects that belong to a class are called *instances* of that class. A class describes the form (instance variables) of its instances and the operations (methods) applicable to its instances. Thus, when a message is sent to an instance, the method that implements that message is found in the definition of the class.

ORION supports two features to further reduce redundant storage and specification of objects: shared-value and default-value instance variables. For such variables, a value must be specified. For a *shared-value variable* of a class, all instances of the class take on the specified value. This is similar to the class variable concept in Smalltalk [13]. For a *default-value variable*, those instances of a class whose value for the instance variable is not specified take on the specified default value. It is certainly possible for the user to implement the concept of default values through the use of a special-purpose instance creation method for each class. However, for ORION applications that use default values extensively, the provision of the default value concept as a modeling feature makes the creation of classes considerably simpler.

For example, we may define instance variables Medium and TakeoffDistance for the class Aircraft. The instance variable Medium may be shared valued and take on the same value for every aircraft. The instance variable TakeoffDistance, on the other hand, may have a default value of 300. In case a new aircraft is created and its takeoff distance is not specified, the value of that variable is 300.

In ORION, as in most object-oriented systems, both classes and instances are viewed as objects. This is necessary mainly for uniformity in the handling of messages. Messages are sent to objects. In most cases messages are sent to instance objects. However, how can one, for example, create an instance object in the first place? Since the instance does not exist, it cannot be sent a message to create itself. This problem is solved by treating a class as a (class) object. To create an instance of a class, a message is sent to the corresponding class object. There are also many other situations in which it is necessary to send messages to class objects, including inquiry of the definition of a class, changing the definition of a class, and so on.

Grouping objects into classes helps avoid the specification and storage of much redundant information. The concept of a *class hierarchy* extends this *information hiding* capability one step further. A class hierarchy is a hierarchy of classes in which an edge between a node and a child node represents the IS-A relationship; that is, the child node is a specialization of the parent node (and conversely, the parent node is a generalization of the child node [27]). For a parent-child pair of nodes on a class hierarchy the parent is called the superclass of the child, and the child is called the subclass of the parent. The instance variables and methods (collectively called properties) specified for a class are shared (inherited) by all its subclasses. Additional properties also may be specified for each of the subclasses. A class needs to inherit properties only from its immediate superclass. Since the latter inherits properties from its own superclass, it follows by induction that a class inherits properties from every class in its *superclass chain*.

Smalltalk [12] originally restricted a class to only a single superclass. In other words, the class hierarchy was limited to being a tree. Most other object-oriented systems, as well as the recent version of Smalltalk, have relaxed this restriction. In these systems (and in ORION) a class can have more than one superclass. Thus the class hierarchy is generalized to a lattice. (We borrow the term *lattice* from the literature on object-oriented systems to mean a directed acyclic graph structure.)

Aircraft instance. This definition overrides any definition that may be inherited from any superclass.

The approach used in many systems to resolve name conflicts among superclasses of a given class is as follows. If an instance variable or a method with the same name appears in more than one superclass of a class C, the one chosen by default is that of the first superclass in the list of (immediate) superclasses for C. For example, as shown in Figure 1, the class Submarine has to inherit an instance variable Size either from the superclass WaterVehicle (which defines Size) or from NuclearPoweredVehicle (which inherits Size from its superclass MotorizedVehicle). If, in the definition of the class Submarine, NuclearPoweredVehicle is specified as the first superclass, Size will be inherited from NuclearPoweredVehicle.

Since this default conflict resolution scheme hinges on the permutation of the superclasses of a class, unlike most other systems, ORION allows the user to explicitly change this permutation at any time. Further, ORION provides two ways in which a user can override the default conflict resolution.

(1) The user may explicitly inherit one instance variable or method from among several conflicting ones. For example, in Figure 1, the user who defines the class Submarine may choose to inherit the instance variable Size from WaterVehicle rather than from NuclearPoweredVehicle, even if Nuclear-PoweredVehicle is the first superclass in the list of superclasses of Submarine.

(2) The user may explicitly inherit one or more instance variable or method that have the same name and rename them within the new class definition. For example, the definer of the class Submarine may specify that the instance variable Size be inherited from WaterVehicle with the new name CrewSize, and also from NuclearPoweredVehicle with the name Size (ORION ensures that all names inherited or defined within a class are distinct).

2.3 ORION Class Lattice and the Set Class

We mentioned earlier that the capability of issuing predicate-based queries against a large database of persistent objects is an important requirement in a database environment. A few operational object-oriented database systems support associative queries [3, 24]. However, most existing object-oriented systems are programming language systems, and as such they do not support associative queries. In this section we provide our simple extension to the existing notion of a class lattice as a formal basis for allowing queries against unnamed instances of classes.

As in any object-oriented system, ORION defines a class called OBJECT as the root of the class lattice. The class lattice includes not only all user-defined classes, but also all system-defined classes. Figure 2 shows all ORION-defined classes as subclasses of the OBJECT class. The class PType provides the basis for defining all classes that can be used as primitive domains of instance variables. The class Collection consists of objects that are collections of other objects. A subclass of Collection is the class Set, each of whose instances is a set (a collection of objects with no duplicates) [9, 13]. Whereas the class Collection supplies messages for iterating over the elements in a collection object, the class Set supplies further messages for searching the elements of a set, adding an element

We emphasize, however, that ORION still requires instance objects to belong to only one class. Sometimes, it is useful to allow an instance object to belong to more than one class. That is, an instance object, such as "my-car," may belong to two different classes, say, LandVehicle and PetroleumFueledMotorizedVehicle. We have concluded that the consequences of this generality are lower performance and a large increase in system complexity. This results from the fact that the structure of an instance object is completely variable; since it can belong to any number of classes, its instance variables cannot be determined a priori, and the identifiers of all classes to which an instance belongs must be stored with each and every instance. Only by examining the content of an instance object and determining the classes to which it belongs will it be possible to determine its instance variables and methods. To model "my-car" in the above example, the ORION user must create a new class called Automobile with two superclasses LandVehicle and PetroleumFueledMotorizedVehicle. All instances of cars, including "my-car," then belong to the Automobile class, rather than to two different classes.

It is often desirable not to require the value of an instance variable to belong to a particular class, that is, not to bind the possible values of the instance variable to any single class. This means that two different instances of the same class may reference objects from two different classes, through the same instance variable. For example, the VehicleId of one aircraft may be an integer object, and that of another aircraft may be a string object. In other words, the class definition for Aircraft does not bind the possible values of VehicleId to either the integer class or the string class.

However, for the purposes of integrity control, it is also desirable to bind the domain (called data type in conventional programming languages, such as Pascal and C) of an instance variable to a specific class (and therefore implicitly to all subclasses of the class). For example, the Manufacturer instance variable of the Aircraft class may be bound to the class Company. Thus a manufacturer is a company. Further, if the Company class has subclasses, the Manufacturer instance variable may also take on as its value an instance of any subclass of Company. Thus ORION supports both typing and no typing.

2.2 Class Lattice and Conflict Resolution

The class lattice simplifies data modeling and often requires fewer classes to be specified than are required with a class hierarchy. In a class lattice, however, a class has multiple superclasses and thus inherits properties from each of the superclasses. This feature is often referred to as *multiple inheritance* [21, 28]. In a class lattice, two types of conflicts may arise in the names of instance variables and methods. One is the conflict between a class and its superclass (this type of problem also arises in a class hierarchy). Another is between the superclasses of a class; this is the consequence of multiple inheritance. In this section we discuss approaches to resolving these two types of inheritance conflicts.

In all systems we are aware of, name conflicts between a class and its superclasses are resolved by giving precedence to the definition within the class over that in its superclasses. For example, if the class definition for a class Aircraft specifies an instance variable VehicleId, it is the definition used for every

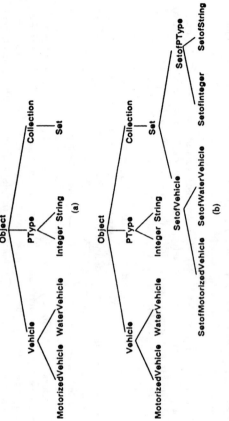

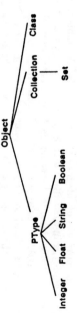

Fig. 3. Expansion of a class hierarchy (a) with set classes (b). (a) Primitive class hierarchy. (b) Class hierarchy expanded with set classes.

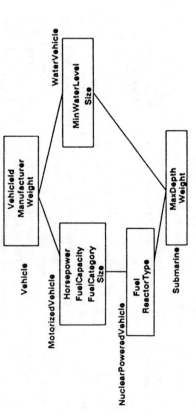

Fig. 1. Resolution of name conflicts among instance variables.

Fig. 2. Primitive class hierarchy in ORION.

to a set, etc. We may define subclasses of the Collection class later in order to add additional capabilities on lists of objects, such as doubly linked lists, stacks, and queues. Each class object belongs to a class, the system-defined class Class. All class objects are instances of this class. To create a new class, a message needs to be sent to the Class class.

For each user-defined class and for the class PType and its subclasses, ORION implicitly defines a corresponding class, a Set-Of class, as a subclass (immediate or indirect) of the Set class. These Set-Of classes form a lattice parallel to the lattice of user-defined classes. For example, the class lattice of Figure 3a is implicitly expanded to the lattice of Figure 3b.

One special instance of the Set-Of class of a user-defined class C is the set of all instances of the class C. Another special instance of the Set-Of class of a user-defined class C is the set of all instances of C or its subclasses. The notion of a set object is particularly important for a database of persistent objects, which outlive programs that created them. While a program is in execution, objects created by a program can be referenced through symbols that point to them. A program's symbol table provides handles into objects. However, a newly started program has direct reference to instances of classes through its symbol table. Instead, the program can refer to the two special set objects in the Set-of class of a class C, thereby referring either to all instances of C, or to all instances of C and its subclasses. A simple naming convention may be used to refer to these

objects, for example, the name C to refer to the set object that contains all instances of the class C, and the name C* to refer to the set object that contains all instances of C and its subclasses. Predicate-based queries are messages to these set objects and return subsets of these sets.

For example, for the class MotorizedVehicle, the system defines a class SetofMotorizedVehicle, which has at least one instance, the set object containing all instances of the class MotorizedVehicle. This special set object provides a handle into the instances of the class MotorizedVehicle. Individual instances of MotorizedVehicle may be referenced as elements of this set.

Another motivation for the automatic generation of the Set-Of classes corresponding to user-defined classes is that instance variables often require values that are sets of objects. Just as any other object, set objects must belong to some class. Without the notion of implicitly defined Set-Of classes to which such objects can belong, the user will either have to create a class explicitly to capture the structure and semantics of these objects or treat them as instances of the class OBJECT, thereby losing their semantics.

3. SCHEMA EVOLUTION

ORION applications require considerable flexibility in dynamically defining and modifying the database schema, that is, the class definitions and the inheritance structure of the class lattice [19, 31]. Existing object-oriented systems support only a few types of changes to the schema, without requiring system shutdown. This is the consequence of the fact that existing object-oriented systems are programming language systems. We note that even existing conventional database systems allow only a few types of schema changes: For example, SQL/DS only allows the dynamic creation and deletion of relations (classes) and the addition of new columns (instance variables) in a relation [14]. This is because the applications they support (conventional record-oriented business applications) do not require more than a few types of schema changes; also the data models they support are not as rich as object-oriented data models.

In this section we first provide a taxonomy of schema change operations supported in ORION. We then present a framework for understanding and enforcing the semantics of each of the schema change operations. The framework consists of the set of properties, which we call *invariants of the class lattice*, and a set of rules for resolving ambiguities in enforcing the invariants. Finally, we describe the semantics of some of the schema change operations to illustrate the application of the schema evolution framework. We refer the reader to our earlier work [4] for more detailed discussions of the contents of this section. A graphics-based schema editor has been implemented to validate the semantics of schema evolution. A detailed presentation of the schema editor will be given in a forthcoming paper.

3.1 Taxonomy of Schema Evolution

Changes to the class lattice can be broadly categorized as (1) changes to the contents of a node, (2) changes to an edge, and (3) changes to a node. ORION allows all three types of changes. These changes can be classified further. In particular, changing the contents of a node implies adding or dropping instance variables or methods, or changing the properties of existing instance variables or methods. The schema change taxonomy is as follows:

(1) Changes to the contents of a node (a class)
  (1.1) Changes to an instance variable
    (1.1.1) Add a new instance variable to a class
    (1.1.2) Drop an existing instance variable from a class
    (1.1.3) Change the Name of an instance variable of a class
    (1.1.4) Change the Domain of an instance variable of a class
    (1.1.5) Change the inheritance (Parent) of an instance variable (inherit another instance variable with the same name)
    (1.1.6) Change the Default value of an instance variable
    (1.1.7) Manipulate the Shared value of an instance variable
      (1.1.7.1) Add a Shared value
      (1.1.7.2) Change the Shared value
      (1.1.7.3) Drop the Shared value
  (1.2) Changes to a method
    (1.2.1) Add a new method to a class
    (1.2.2) Drop an existing method from a class
    (1.2.3) Change the Name of a method of a class
    (1.2.4) Change the Code of a method in a class
    (1.2.5) Change the inheritance (Parent) of a method (inherit another method with the same name)
(2) Changes to an edge
  (2.1) Make a class S a superclass of a class C
  (2.2) Remove a class S from the superclass list of a class C
  (2.3) Change the order of superclasses of a class C
(3) Changes to a node
  (3.1) Add a new class
  (3.2) Drop an existing class
  (3.3) Change the name of a class

3.2 Invariants of Schema Evolution

In this section we summarize the properties of the class lattice that we can extract from our data model. We call these properties *invariants of the class lattice*. Any changes to the class definitions and to the structure of the class lattice must preserve these properties.

3.2.1 *Class Lattice Invariant*. The class lattice is a *rooted and connected directed acyclic graph* with labeled edges. The directed acyclic graph (DAG) has exactly one root, the class OBJECT. The DAG is connected; that is, there are no isolated nodes. Edges are labeled such that all edges directed to any given node have distinct labels (the edges are used to aid conflict resolution, as we show in Section 3.3).

3.2.2 *Distinct Name Invariant*. All instance variables and methods of a class, whether locally defined or inherited, must have distinct names.

3.2.3 *Distinct Identity Invariant*. All instance variables and methods of a class have distinct origin. For example, referring back to Figure 1, the class Submarine can inherit the instance variable Weight from either the class WaterVehicle or the class NuclearPoweredVehicle. In both these superclasses, however, Weight has the same origin, namely, the instance variable Weight of the class Vehicle, where Weight was originally defined. Therefore, the class Submarine must have only one occurrence of the instance variable Weight.

3.2.4 *Full Inheritance Invariant*. A class must inherit all instance variables and methods from each of its superclasses. There is no selective inheritance, unless the full inheritance invariant should lead to a violation of the distinct name and distinct identity invariants.

3.2.5 *Domain Compatibility Invariant*. If an instance variable V_2 of a class C is inherited from an instance variable V_1 of a superclass of C, then the domain of V_2 must either be the same as that of V_1, or a subclass of V_1. For example, if the domain of instance variable Manufacturer in the Vehicle class is the Company class, then the Manufacturer of a MotorizedVehicle can be a Company or a subclass of Company, for example, a MotorizedVehicleCompany.

3.3 Rules of Schema Evolution

The invariants of the class lattice hold at every quiescent state of the schema, that is, before and after a schema change operation. They guide the definition of the semantics of every meaningful schema change operation by ensuring that the change does not leave the schema in an *inconsistent* state (one that violates an invariant). Occasionally, however, several meaningful ways of interpreting a schema change will result in a consistent schema. To select one that is semantically the most meaningful, we need *rules* that govern our schema change semantics. The rules fall into three categories: default conflict resolution rules, property propagation rules, and DAG manipulation rules.

3.3.1 Default Conflict Resolution Rules.

The following three rules select a single inheritance option whenever there is a name or identity conflict. They ensure that the distinct name and distinct identity invariants are satisfied in a deterministic way. The user may override the default conflict resolution rules by explicit requests to resolve conflicts differently.

Rule 1. If an instance variable is defined within a class C, and its name is the same as that of an instance variable of one of its superclasses, the newly defined instance variable is selected over the conflicting instance variable of the superclass.

Rule 2. If two or more superclasses of a class C have instance variables with the same name, but distinct origin, the instance variable selected for inheritance is that from the first superclass (corresponding to the node with the lowest labeled edge coming into C) among conflicting superclasses.

Rule 3. If two or more superclasses of a class C have instance variables with the same origin, the instance variable with the most specialized (restricted) domain is selected for inheritance. However, if the domains are the same, or if one domain is not a superclass of the other, the instance variable inherited is that of the first superclass among conflicting superclasses.

For example, in Figure 1, if the domain of Manufacturer of Nuclear-PoweredVehicle is Company, and the domain of Manufacturer of WaterVehicle is WaterVehicleCompany, which is a subclass of Company, the instance variable inherited into the class Submarine is the Manufacturer instance variable from the class WaterVehicle.

3.3.2 Property Propagation Rules.

The properties of an instance variable, once defined or inherited into a class, can be modified in a number of ways. In particular, its name, domain, default value, or shared value may be changed. Also, an instance variable that is not presently a shared value can be made one, or vice versa. Further, the properties of a method belonging to a class may be modified by changing its name or code. The following rule provides guidelines for supporting all changes to the properties of instance variables and methods.

Rule 4. When the properties of an instance variable or method in a class C are changed, the changes are propagated to all subclasses of C that had inherited them, unless these properties were previously redefined within the subclasses.

For example, if the instance variable Weight of the class Vehicle has its default value changed to 2000, then the same must be done to Weight in all subclasses of Vehicle. However, if Weight had earlier been explicitly assigned a default value of 1000 in the class MotorizedVehicle (which is a subclass of Vehicle), then MotorizedVehicle will not accept the change. Consequently, the change will also not be propagated to the subclasses of MotorizedVehicle that had inherited Weight from MotorizedVehicle.

Rule 4 requires that changes to names of instance variables and methods also be propagated. However, the propagation of name changes or of newly added instance variables or methods of a class may introduce new conflicts in the subclasses. We take the position that name changes are made primarily to resolve conflicts and as such should not introduce new conflicts. By a similar reasoning, we take the view that new instance variables and methods that give rise to new conflicts should not be propagated. Hence we have the following rule, which modifies Rule 4.

Rule 5. A name change or a newly added instance variable or method is propagated to only those subclasses that encounter no new name conflicts as a consequence of this schema modification. A subclass that does not inherit this modification does not propagate it to its own subclasses. For the purposes of propagation of changes to subclasses, Rule 5 overrides Rule 2.

3.3.3 DAG Manipulation Rules.

We need a set of rules that govern the addition and deletion of nodes and edges from the class lattice. The following rule ensures that drastic changes are avoided when a new edge is added to a class lattice.

Rule 6. (*Edge Addition Rule*). If a class A is made a superclass of a class B, then A becomes the last superclass of B. Thus any name conflicts that may be triggered by the addition of this superclass will not require any default resolution; that is, name conflicts can be ignored. If a newly inherited instance variable causes an identity conflict, Rule 3 must be applied to resolve the conflict.

The deletion of an edge from node A to node B may cause node B to become isolated in the case in which class A is the only superclass of class B. The following rule is necessary to prevent such a violation of the class lattice invariant, which requires that the DAG be connected.

Rule 7 (*Edge Removal Rule*). If class A is the only superclass of class B, and A is removed from the superclass list of B, then B is made an immediate subclass of each of A's superclasses. The ordering of these new superclasses of B is the same as the ordering of superclasses of A (clearly, A and B will now have the same collection of superclasses).

The addition of a new node should not violate the class lattice invariant. If the new node has no superclasses, it becomes an isolated node, violating the class lattice invariant. Hence we have the following rule.

Rule 8 (*Node Addition Rule*). If no superclasses are specified for a newly added class, the root class OBJECT is the default superclass of the new class.

The deletion of a node A is a three-step operation: first the deletion of all edges from A to its subclasses, then the deletion of all edges directed into A from its superclasses, and finally the deletion of node A itself. We need the following rule to ensure the preservation of the class lattice invariant when deleting a node.

Rule 9 (*Node Removal Rule*). For the deletion of edges from A to its subclasses, Rule 7 is applied if any of the edges is the only edge to a subclass of A. Further, no system-defined classes can be deleted.

3.4 Semantics of Schema Evolution

In this section we provide a description of the semantics of some of the schema change operations, to illustrate the application of the invariants of the class lattice and the schema change rules. We note that there is one very important aspect of schema evolution that the discussions of this section do not properly address. It concerns methods of a class containing references to inherited instance variables. For example, when an instance variable V is dropped from a class S, a method defined in a class C, a subclass of S, that references V will no longer be operable. It is possible to efficiently detect methods that may become inoperable as a result of schema change operations. However, we defer to a forthcoming paper detailed discussions of how we address this and other problems with methods in the context of schema evolution.

(1) *Define a new class C.* The new class C may be created as a specialization of an existing class or classes. The latter classes can be specified as the superclasses of the new class. As discussed earlier, the instance variables specified for C will override any conflicting instance variables inherited from the superclasses that C inherits from its superclasses, default conflict resolution rules 2 and 3 are used, unless the user explicitly overrides the default rules.

The class C may also be defined without any superclasses. In this case, C is made a subclass of Object (rule 8). The user may, at a later time, add superclasses for C, in which case Object will no longer be an immediate superclass of C.

(2) *Add a new instance variable to a class C.* The new instance variable, in case of a conflict with an already inherited instance variable, will override the inherited variable (rule 1). In that case, the inherited instance variable must be dropped from C and replaced with the new instance variable, and existing instances of C will take on the value nil or user-specified default for the new instance variable.

If C has subclasses, they will inherit the new instance variable of C. If there is a conflict with an instance variable that they have already defined or inherited, the new variable is ignored (rule 5). If there is no conflict, the subclasses inherit the new instance variable, together with a default value, if any.

(3) *Drop a class C.* Whenever a class definition is dropped, all its instances are deleted automatically, since instances cannot exist outside of a class. However, subclasses of C, if any, are not dropped; subclasses of C will lose C as their superclass. However, if C was their only superclass, they will gain C's superclasses as their immediate superclasses (rule 9).

Further, when a class C is dropped, its subclasses will lose the instance variables (and methods) that they had previously inherited from C. If, in the process, a subclass of C loses an instance variable V that was selected over a conflicting instance variable in another superclass of that subclass, it will now inherit the alternate definition of V (to maintain the full inheritance invariant). Consequently, the instances of any such subclass will lose their present values for V and inherit the default value (or nil) under the new definition of V.

When an instance of the class C is dropped, all objects that reference it will now be referencing a nonexistent object. The user will need to modify those references when they are encountered. ORION will not automatically identify references to nonexistent objects because of the performance overhead.

If the class C being dropped is presently the domain of an instance variable V_1 of some other class, V_1's domain becomes the first superclass of the class C. Of course, the user has the choice of specifying a new domain for V_1.

(4) *Drop an instance variable V from a class C.* The instance variable V is dropped from the definition (and from the instances) of the class C. To maintain the full inheritance invariant, C will inherit V from another superclass if there has been a name conflict involving V. All subclasses of C will also be affected if they have inherited V. If C or a subclass of C has methods that refer to V, such methods will now become invalid. The user can either delete these methods or redefine them to make all references consistent with the new definition of C and its subclasses.

(5) *Change the domain of an instance variable V of a class C.* The domain of an instance variable is itself a class. The domain, class D, of an instance variable V of a class C may only be changed to a superclass of D. The values of existing instances of the class C are not affected in any way. If the domain of an instance variable V must be changed in any other way, V must be dropped, and a new instance variable V must be added in its place.

4. COMPOSITE OBJECTS

Many applications require the ability to define and manipulate a set of objects as a single logical entity [3, 9, 15, 19, 23, 28, 31]. For example, a vehicle is an object that contains a body object, which has a set of door objects, and each door has a position object and a color object. In other words, a body object exclusively belongs to (is a part of) a vehicle instance, and a set of doors, in turn, belongs to a body, and so on. In general, a complex object, such as a vehicle, forms a hierarchical structure of exclusive component objects. We define a *composite object* as an object with a hierarchy of exclusive component objects, and refer to the hierarchy of classes to which the objects belong as a *composite object hierarchy*.

The object-oriented data model, in its conventional form, is sufficient to represent a collection of related objects. However, it does not capture the IS-PART-OF relationship between objects; one object simply *references*, but does not own, other objects. A composite object hierarchy captures the IS-PART-OF relationship between a parent class and its component classes, whereas a class hierarchy represents the IS-A relationship between a superclass and its subclasses.

Composite objects add to the integrity features of an object-oriented data model through the notion of dependent objects. A *dependent object* is one whose existence depends on the existence of other objects and that is owned by exactly one object. For example, the body of a vehicle is owned by one specific vehicle and cannot exit without the vehicle that contains it. As such, a dependent object cannot be created if its owner does not already exist. This means that a composite object hierarchy must be instantiated in a top-down fashion; the root object of a composite object hierarchy must be created first, then the objects at the next level, and so on. When a constituent object of a composite object is deleted, all its dependent objects must also be deleted.

We note that an object may contain references to both dependent objects and independent objects, or to only dependent or independent objects. We use the term *aggregate object* to refer to such a general collection of objects. A composite object is a special case of an aggregate object.

The definition of a set of objects as a composite object also offers an opportunity for performance improvement. ORION considers a composite object as a unit for clustering related objects on disk. This is because, if an application accesses the root object, it is often likely to access all (or most) dependent objects as well. Thus it is advantageous to store all constituents of a composite object as close to one another as possible on secondary storage.

The notion of composite objects has been investigated by various researchers. It has been called a complex object in IBM's experimental extension to SQL/DS [14] and a composite object in LOOPS [5]. Our contribution in this paper is in showing the integration of the data modeling concept of composite objects into an object-oriented data model. In particular, after a formal definition of composite objects, we specify our semantics of composite objects and relate them to object-oriented concepts. We then illustrate the composite object semantics in terms of schema definition, and creation and deletion of composite objects. We also indicate our approach to implementing composite objects, including enforcement of the semantics of composite objects, and physical clustering.

4.1 Definitions

A composite object can be defined in BNF as follows:

⟨Composite Object⟩ ::= ⟨Composite Object Root⟩ (⟨Linked Dependent⟩*),
⟨Linked Dependent⟩ ::= ⟨Instance Variable⟩ ⟨Dependent Object⟩,
⟨Dependent Object⟩ ::= ⟨Leaf Object⟩
    | ⟨Dependent Object Root⟩ (⟨Linked Dependent⟩*)
    | {⟨Dependent Object⟩*}.

In the above definition, the * is a metasymbol that denotes an indefinite number of occurrences. A composite object has a special instance object, called the *root object*. The root of the composite object is connected to multiple *dependent objects*, each through an instance variable in the root object. Each dependent object can be a simple object (with no dependent objects), or it can itself be the root of a hierarchical structure. A dependent object can also be a set of objects. In a composite object, the same instance object cannot be referenced more than once. Thus the definition of a composite object is a hierarchy of instance objects (and not a general digraph). However, all instance objects within a composite object can be referenced by instance objects that do not belong to the composite object, and these references can have the complete generality of a digraph, including digraphs with cycles.

The instance objects that constitute a composite object belong to classes that are also organized in a hierarchy. This hierarchical collection of classes is called a *composite object schema*. A nonroot class on a composite object schema is called a *component class*. Each nonleaf class on a composite object schema has one or more instance variables that serve as links, called *composite links*. We call instance variables that serve as composite links *composite instance variables*.

In Figure 4, we illustrate a composite object schema for vehicles. The classes that are connected by bold lines form the composite object schema. The *root class* is the class Vehicle. Through instance variables Body, Drivetrain, and Color, vehicle instances are linked to their dependent objects, which belong to classes AutoBody, AutoDrivetrain, and String. (An instance variable with a primitive domain, such as Integer or String, can always be considered a composite link. A value from a primitive domain can be freely copied; hence every reference to such an object can be exclusive. Thus two vehicles can have the color red because each vehicle refers to a separate string object "red.") The Vehicle class has another instance variable called Manufacturer, but it is not a link to dependent objects. The instances of AutoBody and AutoDrivetrain, in turn, are connected to other dependent objects. A vehicle composite object then is an instance of the class Vehicle, together with an instance of each of the classes AutoBody, Auto-Drivetrain, and String (for Color). The brace in the figure indicates a set object. The instance variable Doors of the class AutoBody represents a set of Door instances, each of which has a Position and Color.

4.2 Semantics of Composite Objects

In this section we define the semantics of composite objects within an object-oriented framework. First, the semantics of a composite link are as follows: If there is a composite link from a class A to a class B through an instance variable V_a of A, an instance of B can be referenced through V_a by only one instance of A. There can be other instance objects that can also reference this instance of B, but any such reference cannot be through another composite link. In other words, if an instance object is referenced through a composite link, it must be the only composite link to the object. For example, an instance of the class Vehicle can have a composite link to an instance of the class AutoBody through the instance variable Body. No other instance of Vehicle can refer to this instance of AutoBody through the instance variable Body. Further, if an instance of some other class, say Inventory, has a reference to this instance of AutoBody, the reference must be through an instance variable that is not a composite link.

The composite link property of an instance variable of a class is inherited by subclasses of that class. For example, if the class Automobile is a subclass of Vehicle, it inherits the instance variable Body from Vehicle. Further, because Body is a composite link in the Vehicle class, it will also be a composite link in the Automobile class.

A composite instance variable may later be changed to a noncomposite instance variable, that is, it may lose the composite link property. If a class A has a composite link to a class B through an instance variable V and V becomes a noncomposite instance variable, then the class B may become the root class of a composite object schema through its composite links to other classes.

However, we do not allow a noncomposite instance variable to acquire the composite link property later. An instance object may be referenced by any number of instances of a class through a noncomposite instance variable. However, a dependent object of a composite object may be referenced by only one instance of a class through a composite instance variable of the class. Therefore, to change a noncomposite instance variable to a composite instance variable makes it necessary to verify that existing instances are not referenced by more than one instance through the instance variable. This, in turn, makes it necessary to maintain a list of reference counts for each instance object, one reference count for each instance variable through which the instance object may be referenced.

Next, composite objects can further enhance information hiding through the notion of *value propagation* [5]. Default values can be propagated from an instance object to all its dependent objects, thereby simplifying the definition of dependent objects. For example, the color of the body of a vehicle is, by default, the color of the vehicle. We note that value propagation refers to the sharing of the value of an instance variable between instance objects, whereas inheritance is the sharing of the name of an instance variable (and method) between classes.

Values can be propagated only if an object has an instance variable that has the same name as some instance variable of a higher level object. Propagation of a value to a lower level object takes place from the lowest level containing object that has an appropriate value. Further, if the default value of a higher level object is changed, the new value is propagated as the default value of the dependent objects. As an example, in Figure 4 the default color of the doors can be the same as that of the vehicle's body or of the vehicle. If a vehicle's body did not have an instance variable named Color, or (if it did have such an instance variable, but) if the instance variable had no value assigned to it, then every door can assume its default color from the vehicle (bypassing the vehicle's body).

Value propagation is not automatic; it must be specified in the definition of the composite object schema. For example, unless indicated in the definition, the body of a vehicle does not assume the color of the vehicle. Once value propagation is specified, it takes precedence over inheritance from superclasses. For example, let us assume in Figure 4 that the domain of the instance variable Body of the class Vehicle is the class AutoBody, and that AutoBody inherits the instance

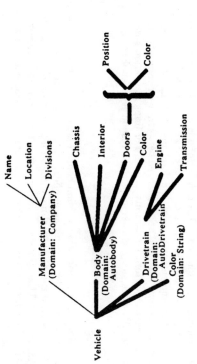

Fig. 4. Vehicle composite hierarchy.

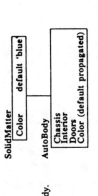

Fig. 5. The class hierarchy of AutoBody.

variable Color from its superclass SolidMatter. This class hierarchy is shown in Figure 5. Let us also assume that the default value of Color in SolidMatter is "blue." The color of a vehicle's body will not be blue; instead, it will assume the color of its containing vehicle.

4.3 Schema Definition, Creation, and Deletion of Composite Objects

A composite object schema is created through composite instance variables. These instance variables have component classes as their domains. For example, the class Vehicle in Figure 4 has a composite link to the class AutoBody through the instance variable Body. The instance variable Body has as domain the class Autobody, and it has the composite link property. The Vehicle class has another instance variable Drivetrain, whose domain is the class AutoDrivetrain, and which is also a composite link. The classes AutoBody and AutoDrivetrain similarly have composite instance variables.

Although Autobody is the domain of the composite instance variable Body of the class Vehicle, it may be used as the domain of other instance variables, including other composite instance variables. In fact, if Vehicle has two subclasses Car and Truck, they both inherit the instance variable Body, along with its domain (AutoBody) and the composite link property. However, an instance of AutoBody can be referenced by only one instance object through a composite instance variable. A particular instance of AutoBody cannot simultaneously be a part of both a Car and a Truck.

An instance object can be made a part of a composite object only at the time of creation of that instance object. The integrity requirement for composite objects is that any instance object within a composite object cannot be referenced through more than one composite link. This integrity requirement is easily enforced. The only way in which a nonnull value can be assigned to a composite instance variable is by simultaneously creating that value (a dependent instance object). Any attempt to assign a nonnull value to a composite instance variable separately is rejected, because in our implementation instance objects within a composite object do not carry the identifer of the composite object to which they belong. Thus, for example, if an existing Body instance were to be separately assigned to a Vehicle instance, it would be prohibitively expensive to determine whether that body is already a part of some other vehicle. If that body were indeed a part of another vehicle, it would then have two parents, violating the integrity constraint on vehicle composite objects.

An instance object, once it is created as a dependent object, cannot have independent existence. Therefore, if any instance object within a composite object is deleted, it causes a recursive deletion of instances that depend on the object. The parent of this instance object now has a dangling reference. On a subsequent attempt to access an object through such a dangling reference, the application may choose to replace it with a null value.

A dependent object remains a dependent object throughout its existence, unless a composite link is redefined in the schema as a noncomposite link. The only way in which a composite link between instance objects can be severed is by either deleting the dependent object or making it a part of some other composite object through an ExchangePart message.

4.4 Clustering of Composite Objects

In ORION all instances of the same class are placed in the same storage segment. Thus a class is associated with a single segment, and all its instances reside in that segment. The user does not have to be aware of segments; ORION automatically allocates a separate segment for each class. For clustering composite objects, however, it is often advantageous to store instances of multiple classes in the same segment. User assistance is required to determine which classes should share the same segment.

The user may issue a message, a Cluster message, as a hint for ORION to cluster instances of a class with instances of other classes. A Cluster message specifies a list of class names, ListofClassNames. Instances of classes listed in the ListofClassNames are to be placed in a single segment. The initial size of the segment and any later increments to that size may be specified optionally. The user may sometimes need to cluster a new class C with some existing classes that have already been allocated a segment. In such case the user needs to issue a Cluster message, in which the ListofClassNames is a pair, namely, the class C and any of the existing classes with which C should share a segment. C will then share the same segment with the existing classes.

As we have seen already, a dependent object is linked to its parent when it is created; as such, a dependent object can be stored close to its parent. Ideally, the constituents of a composite object should be stored clustered at all times. In general, this requirement is not a difficult one. A composite object can be stored in a sequence of linked pages. If the composite object increases in size, a new page can be acquired and linked in the manner of a B-tree. If a composite object shrinks in size, pages may be released or compacted. The only difficulty seems to arise with the implementation of the ExchangePart message. When two dependent objects (two subtrees) are exchanged between two parent objects, they really should exchange storage positions as well. For implementation simplicity, however, ORION does not recluster objects in response to an ExchangePart message.

5. VERSIONS

There is a general consensus that version control is one of the most important functions in various data-intensive application domains, such as integrated CAD/CAM systems and OISs dealing with compound documents [3, 10, 11, 16-18, 25, 26, 30]. Users in such environments often need to generate and experiment with multiple versions of an object before selecting one that satisfies their requirements.

In this section, we show our approach to integrating version concepts into an object-oriented data model, including some of the salient implementation issues. A full description of our model of versions, along with a preliminary consideration of its implementation, is given in Chou [7]. The model is appropriate for a federated system of a central server and a number of autonomous workstations sharing objects through the server.

5.1 Version Semantics

In our current prototype we distinguish two types of versions on the basis of the types of operations that may be allowed on them. They are transient versions and working versions.

A *transient version* has the following properties:

(1) It can be updated by the user who created it.
(2) It can be deleted by the user who created it.
(3) A new transient version may be derived from an existing transient version. The existing transient version then is "promoted" to a working version.

A *working version* has the following properties:

(1) It is considered stable and cannot be updated.
(2) It can be deleted by its owner.
(3) A transient version can be derived from a working version.
(4) A transient version can be "promoted" to a working version. Promotion may be explicit (user specified) or implicit (system determined).

We impose the update restriction on the working version because it is considered stable, and thus transient versions can be derived from it. If a working version is to be directly updated after one or more transient versions have been derived from it, we need a set of careful update algorithms (for insert, delete, update) that will ensure that the derived versions will not see the updates in the working version.

5.2 Version Name Binding

There are two ways to *bind* an object with another versioned object: static and dynamic. In *static binding*, the reference to an object includes the full name of the object, the object identifier, and the version number. In *dynamic binding* [3, 11, 18], the reference needs to specify only the object identifier and may leave the version number unspecified. The system selects the default version number. Clearly, dynamic binding is useful, since transient or working versions that are referenced may be deleted and new versions created.

We need to examine the issue of selecting default versions for dynamic binding. In other proposals, the default selected is often the "most recent" version. This simple defaulting scheme is not appropriate in our model. One difficulty is that in our model version history is represented in a hierarchy, the *version-derivation hierarchy*. In particular, we allow more than one transient version to be derived from a working version. In a linear-derivation scheme, where only one version may be derived from any version [10], the most recent version has the implicit meaning that it is the "most correct" or "most complete." However, a version-derivation hierarchy, in which any number of new versions may be derived from any node on the hierarchy any time, potentially has any number of "most recent" versions in this sense. Therefore, we need to allow the user to specify a particular version on the version-derivation hierarchy as the default version. In the absence of a user-specified default, the system selects the version with the "most recent" timestamp as the default.

5.3 Implementation

Because of the performance overhead in supporting versions, we require the application to indicate whether a class is *versionable*. When an instance of a versionable class is created, a *generic object* for that instance is created, along with the first version of that instance. A generic object is essentially a data structure for the version-derivation hierarchy of an instance of a versionable class. It is deleted when the version-derivation hierarchy for its instance contains no versioned object. A generic object consists of the following system-defined instance variables:

(1) an object identifier,
(2) a default version number,
(3) a next-version number,
(4) a version count, and
(5) a set of version descriptors, one for each existing version on the version-derivation hierarchy of the object.

The default version number determines which existing version on the version-derivation hierarchy should be chosen when a partially specified reference is dynamically bound. The next-version number is the version number to be assigned to the next version of the object that will be created. It is incremented after being assigned to the new version.

A version descriptor contains control information for each version on a version-derivation hierarchy. It includes

(1) the version number of the version,
(2) the version number of the parent version,
(3) the identifier of the versioned object, and
(4) the schema version number associated with the version

The version of schema used for version V_i of an object may be different from that used for version V_j derived from V_i. For example, after a transient version is derived, the user may modify the schema for the transient version. Then the original version and the transient version will use different schemas. This is the reason for including the schema version number for each versioned object. We note, however, that a version of schema for an object X is in general shared by multiple versions of X. For example, if a transient version is derived from a working version, both versions may use the same version of schema. A detailed discussion of our proposal for supporting versions of schemas will be given in a forthcoming paper.

A generic object is also an object and as such has an object identifier. Each version of an instance object of a versionable class contains three system-defined instance variables. One is the identifier of the generic object. The others are the version number of the version and the version status (transient or working). The generic object identifier is required, so that, given a version of an instance object, any other versions of the instance object may be efficiently found. The version number is needed simply to distinguish a version of an instance object from other versions of the instance object. The version status is necessary so that the system may easily reject an update on working versions.

A versioned object is created initially by the *create* command, which creates the generic-object data structure for the object. The *derive* command is used to derive a new transient version and allocate a new version number for it. If the parent was a transient version, it is automatically promoted to a working version. The *replace* operation causes the contents of a transient version to be replaced by a work-space copy the user specifies. A transient version is explicitly promoted to a working version, making the version nonupdatable, through the *promote* command. The user may delete a version or an entire version-derivation hierarchy using the *delete* command. If the delete is against a generic object, all versions of the instance for which the generic object was created are deleted. If a working version is deleted from which other versions have been derived, the version is deleted, but the fact that the version existed is not deleted from the generic object. The user uses the *set_default* command to specify the default version on a version-derivation hierarchy of an object. A specific version number or the keyword "most-recent" may be specified as the default.

6. CONCLUDING REMARKS

In this paper we first provided a brief review of the basic object-oriented concepts that we extracted from existing object-oriented systems to form the basis of an object-oriented data model. Then we elaborated on three major enhancements to the conventional object-oriented data model. First was schema evolution, or the capability of making a wide variety of changes to the database schema, including class definitions and the structure of the class lattice, without requiring a database reorganization or system shutdown. We provided a taxonomy for schema changes that an object-oriented database system should allow and introduced a framework for understanding the semantics of the schema changes. Second was the concept of composite objects. A composite object is a collection of objects that recursively captures the IS-PART-OF relationship between pairs of objects. Composite objects should be used for enforcing this IS-PART-OF relationship and, as units of storage clustering and retrieval for improving system performance. We elaborated on the semantics of composite objects and showed their integration into an object-oriented data model in terms of schema definition and creation and clustering of composite objects. Third was version control. We discussed the semantics of versions and showed how they are integrated into the object-oriented data model.

The basic object-oriented concepts and the three enhancements we discussed in this paper, as well as a number of other important features, are presently being incorporated into ORION. ORION is a prototype object-oriented database system under implementation in the Database Program at MCC as a research vehicle for developing a database technology for object-oriented applications from the

CAD/CAM, AI, and OIS domains. The system is intended to directly support some of the applications under development in the AI/KBS (knowledge base system) Program at MCC and to receive feedback about the performance and functionality of the system from them. Because the AI/KBS applications are being implemented in Common LISP, in order to be closely coupled with them, we are implementing ORION in Common LISP to execute on the Symbolics LISP machines. The application interface to ORION then is an object-oriented extension to LISP, much as Flavors [29] and ObjectLISP [22] are, and includes message passing protocol, class lattice, and property inheritance along the class lattice. We are integrating ORION message-passing protocol with LISP function calls so that, to the extent possible, ORION applications can view both ORION objects and LISP structures without having to move from one programming environment to another.

ACKNOWLEDGMENTS

We thank Fred Lochovsky, editor of this issue, and the reviewers for their constructive comments on an earlier draft of this paper. They helped us to correct some technical inaccuracies and improve the overall presentation of the paper.

REFERENCES

1. AFSARMANESH, H., KNAPP, D., MCLEOD, D., AND PARKER, A. An object-oriented approach to VLSI/CAD. In *Proceedings of the 11th International Conference on Very Large Data Bases* (Stockholm, Sweden, Aug.). VLDB Endowment, Saratoga, Calif, 1985.

2. AHLSEN, M., BJORNERSTEDT, A., BRITTS, S., HULTEN, C., AND SODERLUND, L. An architecture for object management in OIS. *ACM Trans. Office Inf. Syst. 2*, 3 (July 1984), 173–196.

3. ATWOOD, T. M. An object-oriented DBMS for design support applications. In *Proceedings of IEEE First International Conference on Computer-Aided Technologies 85* (Montreal, Canada, Sept.). IEEE, New York, 1985, pp. 299–307.

4. BANERJEE, J., KIM, H. J., KIM, W., AND KORTH, H. F. Schema evolution in object-oriented persistent databases. In *Proceedings of the 6th Advanced Database Symposium* (Tokyo, Japan, Aug.). Information Processing Society of Japan's Special Interest Group on Database Systems, 1986, pp. 23–31.

5. BOBROW, D. G., AND STEFIK, M. *The LOOPS Manual.* Xerox PARC, Palo Alto, Calif., 1983.

6. BOBROW, D. G., KAHN, K., KICZALES, G., MASINTER, L., STEFIK, M., AND ZDYBEL, F. *CommonLoops: Merging Common Lisp and Object-Oriented Programming,* Intelligent Systems Laboratory Series ISL-85-8. Xerox PARC, Palo Alto, Calif., 1985.

7. CHOU, H. T., AND KIM, W. A unifying framework for version control in a CAD environment. In *Proceedings of the 12th International Conference on Very Large Data Bases* (Kyoto, Japan). VLDB Endowment, Saratoga, Calif, 1986, pp. 336–344.

8. CHRISTODOULAKIS, S., VANDERBROEK, J., LI, J., WAN, S., WANG, Y., PAPA, M., AND BERTINO, E. Development of a multimedia information system for an office environment. In *Proceedings of the 10th International Conference on Very Large Data Bases* (Singapore, 1984). VLDB Endowment, Saratoga, Calif., pp. 261–271.

9. COPELAND, G., AND MAIER, D. Making Smalltalk a database system. In *Proceedings of the ACM SIGMOD International Conference on the Management of Data* (June 18–21, Boston, Mass.). ACM, New York, 1984, pp. 316–325.

10. DADAM, P., LUM, V., AND WERNER, H. Integration of time versions into a relational database system. In *Proceedings of the 10th International Conference on Very Large Data Bases* (Singapore, Aug. 1984). VLDB Endowment, Saratoga, Calif. pp. 509–522.

11. DITTRICH, K., AND LORIE, R. Version support for engineering database systems. IBM Research Rep. RJ4769, IBM Research, San Jose, Calif., July 1985.

12. GOLDBERG, A. Introducing the Smalltalk-80 system. *BYTE 6*, 8 (Aug. 1981), 14–26.

13. GOLDBERG, A., AND ROBSON, D. *Smalltalk-80: The Language and Its Implementation.* Addison-Wesley, Reading, Mass., 1983.

14. IBM CORPORATION. SQL/Data System: Concepts and Facilities. GH24-5013-0, File No. S370-50, IBM Corporation, San Jose, Jan. 1981.

15. IEEE. *Database Eng. 8*, 4 (Dec. 1985), Special Issue on Object-Oriented Systems, F. Lochovsky, Ed. IEEE, New York.

16. KAISER, G., AND HABERMANN, A. An environment for system version control. Tech. Rep. Dept. of Computer Science, Carnegie-Mellon University, Pittsburgh, Pa, Nov. 1982.

17. KATZ, R., AND LEHMAN, T. Database support for versions and alternatives of large design files. *IEEE Trans. Softw. Eng. SE-10*, 2 (Mar. 1984), 191–200.

18. KATZ, R., CHANG, E., AND BHATEJA, R. Version modeling concepts for computer-aided design databases. In *Proceedings of the ACM SIGMOD International Conference on Management of Data* (Washington, D.C., May 28–30). ACM, New York 1986.

19. KIM, W. CAD database requirements. Tech. Rep, MCC, Austin, Tex., July 1985.

20. KRASNER, G., Ed. *Smalltalk-80: Bits of History, Words of Advice.* Addison-Wesley, Reading, Mass., 1983.

21. LMI, INC. *Lisp Machine Manual.* LMI, Cambridge, Mass., 1983.

22. LMI, INC. *ObjectLISP User Manual.* LMI, Cambridge, Mass., 1985.

23. LORIE, R., AND PLOUFFE, W. Complex objects and their use in design transactions. In *Proc. ACM Database Week: Eng. Design Appl.* (May 1983), 115–121.

24. MAIER, D., STEIN, J., OTIS, A., AND PURDY, A. Development of an object-oriented DBMS. Tech. Rep. CS/E-86-005, Oregon Graduate Center, Beaverton, Oreg., Apr. 1986.

25. MCLEOD, D., NARAYANASWAMY, K., AND BAPA RAO, K. An Approach to Information Management for CAD/VLSI Applications. In *Proceedings of the Conference on Databases for Engineering Applications, Database Week 1983* (ACM, May). ACM, New York, 1983, pp. 39–50.

26. ROCHKIND, M. The source code control system. *IEEE Trans. Softw. Eng. SE-1*, 4 (Dec. 1975), 364–370.

27. SMITH, J., AND SMITH, D. Database abstractions: Aggregation and generalization. *ACM Trans. Database Syst. 2*, 2 (June 1977), 105–133.

28. STEFIK, M., AND BOBROW, D. G. Object-oriented programming: Themes and variations. *AI Magazine* (Jan. 1986), 40–62.

29. SYMBOLICS, INC. *FLAVObjects, Message Passing, and Flavors.* Symbolics, Cambridge, Mass., 1984.

30. TICHY, W. Design implementation, and evaluation of a revision control system. In *Proceedings of the 6th IEEE International Conference on Software Engineering* (Sept.). IEEE, New York, 1982.

31. WOELK, D., KIM, W., AND LUTHER, W. An object-oriented approach to multimedia databases. In *Proceedings of ACM SIGMOD Conference on the Mangement of Data* (Washington, D.C., May 28–30). ACM, New York, 1986.

Received August 1986; revised November 1986; accepted December 1986

PDM: An Object-Oriented Data Model *

Frank Manola, Umeshwar Dayal

Computer Corporation of America
Cambridge, Massachusetts U.S.A.

Abstract

This paper describes the development of the data model of PROBE, a knowledge-oriented DBMS being developed at CCA [DAYA85, DAYA86]. The data model, called PDM, is an extension of the Daplex functional data model [SHIP81, FOX84] that illustrates an integration of functional, relational, and object-oriented approaches. The extensions are primarily those required to handle the requirements of new database applications, such as engineering applications and cartography, having spatial or temporal semantics.

1. Introduction

The application of database technology to new applications, such as CAD/CAM, geographic information systems, software engineering, and office automation, is an extremely active area of database research. Many of these new applications deal with highly structured objects that are composed of other objects. For example, a part in a part hierarchy may be composed of other parts; an integrated circuit module may be composed of other modules, pins, and wires; a geographic feature such as an industrial park may be a complex composed of other features such as buildings, smokestacks, and rail lines; and so forth. Moreover, many of the objects dealt with in these applications have spatial or temporal properties, or have conventional properties that vary in time or space. For example, a mechanical part has a geometric shape; the altitude of the earth's surface varies with the latitude and longitude.

A number of papers have proposed extensions to conventional record- or tuple-oriented data models to deal with these applications, e.g., [LORI83]. However, another approach has been the development of entity- or object-oriented data models for these applications [LOCH86]. This paper describes the development of the data model of PROBE, a knowledge-oriented DBMS being developed at CCA [DAYA85, DAYA86]. Our approach has been to start from DAPLEX, an entity-oriented functional data model and query language [SHIP81, SMIT81] which already provides some of the necessary basic features, and to enhance DAPLEX to meet the requirements of these new database applications. We refer to the enhanced model as

* This work was supported by the Defence Advanced Research Projects Agency and by the Space and Naval Warfare Systems Command under Contract No. N00039-85-C-0263. The views and conclusions contained in this paper are those of the authors and do not necessarily represent the official policies of the Defense Advanced Research Projects Agency, the Space and Naval Warfare Systems Command, or the U.S. Government.

PDM (PROBE Data Model).

Our interest in starting with DAPLEX was due not only to our prior experience with both the design of DAPLEX and its implementation in several DBMS systems (e.g., LDM [CHAN82]). It was also because DAPLEX incorporates many of the features generally associated with object-oriented models, and considered as advantages in the new DBMS applications, including:

- the concept of an *entity* or *object* that has existence independent of any properties or relationships with other entities it might have.

- object- and set-valued properties of entities (in DAPLEX, entity- and set-valued *functions*); this in turn allows the structure of complex objects to be modeled directly.

- an entity class or type concept, together with generalization (subtype) hierarchies among classes with property inheritance.

- a method for incorporating entity behavior and derived properties in the model; this is provided by functions in DAPLEX (these correspond to messages in other object-oriented models).

The implementation of the basic DAPLEX model, including support for entities, functions (typically implemented by pointers), referential integrity, and generalization hierarchies, has been described in [CHAN82].

Our specific goals for PDM extensions were to provide:

- a smooth incorporation of multiargument functions and computed functions (general procedures) into the model.

- an algebra-based formal data model definition (along the lines of the relational model) for use as a foundation for query optimization, view mapping, and query language development studies.

- a clean way of extending the model with objects having nonconventional semantics, particularly spatial and temporal semantics.

Multiargument and computed functions are important as representations for time- and space-varying entity properties, and in the integration of derived data, general procedures, and operations into the model. A variant of relational algebra has been used previously as an informal target interpretation of Daplex in the study of query optimization techniques (e.g., [RIES83]). It was felt that a more explicit definition of such an algebra would be useful for PDM.

The structure of this paper is as follows. First, we describe the basic characteristics of the model. We then describe an algebraic definition of the model and some issues related to the definition. Next, we briefly describe other facilities of the model, such as rule facilities and recursion, and finally we describe current work in progress. Our intent is to describe the general characteristics of PDM objects. We do not consider in this paper the special characteristics of particular object classes that have been investigated for PROBE, such as spatial/temporal entities, or their functions (for a description of such entities and functions, see [MANO86]).

2. PDM — Data Objects

2.1 Entities

There are two basic types of data objects in PDM, *entities* and *functions*. An *entity* is a data object that denotes some individual thing. The basic characteristic of an entity that must be preserved in the model is its distinct identity. An entity is represented by a surrogate.

In PDM, entities are grouped into collections called *entity types*. Examples of entity types might be PERSON (representing people) and MATERIAL (representing types of materials). An entity is not "typed" in the sense that it necessarily has a representation distinct from that of other types. An entity must be asserted to be of one or more types by operations. The types of an entity serve to define what functions may be applied with the entity as a parameter value.

Generalization hierarchies may be defined among entity types, as in Daplex, with the usual function inheritance semantics. This allows inheritance of operations as well as properties. The same entity may be associated with one or more entity types in the database, as defined by database declarations, and may move in and out of types as a result of database operations. Thus, one might define STUDENT and INSTRUCTOR as subtypes of PERSON. An entity that is a STUDENT is also a PERSON, and any function that is defined for an entity of type PERSON may also be applied to an entity of type STUDENT. Moreover, an entity might move from subtype STUDENT to INSTRUCTOR (e.g., if a former STUDENT was hired as an INSTRUCTOR).

2.2 Functions

Properties of entities, relationships between entities and operations on entities are represented in PDM by *functions* (operations). In order to access properties and relationships of an entity, one must evaluate a function over the entity, rather than imagining that the properties and relationships are "there", as in a record-oriented approach. In Daplex, a function is a mapping from entities to either individual entities, sets of entities, or scalar values. Thus, for type STUDENT, one might define:

AGE(STUDENT) → INTEGER
ADVISOR(STUDENT) → INSTRUCTOR

PDM generalizes this concept by defining a function as a relationship between collections of entities and scalar values. For example, one might define:

QUANTITY_ON_HAND(DEPOT, →
   (MATERIAL, INTEGER)
or FINITE_ELEMENT_ANALYSIS(MODEL,LOADS,
   OPTION) → DEFORMED_MODEL

Functions may be defined that have no input arguments. For example, an entity type is, in some contexts, considered as a function of no arguments that returns all entities of that type (see below). Also, functions can be defined that have only boolean (truth valued) results.

The PDM generalization of Daplex functions allowing multiple input and output arguments has a number of notational and semantic effects. First, because it is possible for functions to have more than one output argument, the function name and its input parameters do not always denote a single output value, as in conventional functional languages: sometimes it denotes a *tuple* of output argument values. Because it is necessary to be able to refer to individual output values within such a tuple, PDM functional notation provides each argument with a label. This acts as a formal parameter name as in a procedure defined in a programming language.

Second, because of the way PDM functions are defined as relationships between *collections* of entities and scalar values, it is possible to have function arguments that serve as both input and output parameters. For example, given a 3-ary relationship QUANTITY-ON-HAND between depots, materials, and amounts of materials stored at depots, one could imagine both the functions

QUANTITY_ON_HAND_1(DEPOT,MATERIAL) →
   INTEGER
and QUANTITY_ON_HAND_2(DEPOT) →
   (MATERIAL,INTEGER)

being useful, even though they are based on the same 3-ary relationship. This notation appears to define two different functions, but the only real difference is that MATERIAL is an input variable in one and an output variable in the other. The PDM notation for the above two functions would be:

QUANTITY_ON_HAND(D: in DEPOT,
               M: in out MATERIAL,
               QUAN: out integer)

This notation is essentially that used in declaring an Ada* subprogram, using "in" and "out" declarations to specify how the parameter may be used, as well as giving a parameter label and the required parameter type. (As in Ada, parameters may be supplied to functions using either "keyword" or positional references). The general notation is:

function_name(label1: {*in/out/in out*} type1,...
            ,labeln: {*in/out/in out*} typen)...

(This notation applies to the concrete syntax being used to define the PDM model. A query language based on the model might very well adopt a different convention).

Using this notation, general procedures can be included in the model, e.g.,

function FE_ANALYSIS(MODEL: in FE_MODEL,
               LOADS: in FE_LOAD,
               OPTION: in integer,
               DEFORMED_MODEL: out FE_MODEL)

---

* Ada is a trademark of the Department of Defense (Ada Joint Program Office).

The definition of this function indicates that parameters labeled MODEL, LOADS, and OPTION are input-only parameters, while DEFORMED_MODEL is an output-only parameter. Similarly, a conventional entity property might be defined by:

function AGE(PERSON: in out PERSON,
            RESULT: in out integer)

a function in which either argument can be an input or output parameter (note in this notation that the first appearance of PERSON is a formal parameter name, the second is an entity type). In this case, the function may be invoked with a value for either parameter, to produce a value for the other. Functions can also be used to model arbitrary operations on entity types. Examples of such operations are "the center of gravity of a part" (computed from the shape of the part), and "rotate part X through angle A."

2.3 Computed versus Stored Functions

PDM functions may either be intensionally-defined (with output values computed by procedures) or extensionally-defined (having stored database extents, as is usually the case in conventional Daplex). If the function is intensionally-defined, the body of the function is stored in the DBMS metadata. If the function has a stored extent, the extent is conceptually a stored table (a database relation) containing a tuple for each combination of legal input and output values. Set-valued functions are viewed as being "flattened" into tuples in such relations in the normal relational style. Conceptually, the column names of this table are the labels of the parameters defined in the function definition.

In PDM, references to all functions are treated syntactically as if they were references to computed functions, even when a stored extent exists, rather than either treating all functions as if they corresponded to stored relations, or treating the two classes of functions differently. (The next section describes the effect this has on the definition of algebraic operations). This functional interpretation matches the functional syntax intended for query languages based on the model (similar to Daplex) more closely than a relational interpretation would. It has also assisted in understanding problems related to integrating computed functions into the model (discussed in the next section).

Effectively, the difference between the two classes of functions is that, if a function has a stored extent, the function can actually be evaluated with any combination of input or output arguments assigned values. This is reflected in parameters of stored functions being generally declared as "in out".

It may be observed that mathematically these "functions" are relations, and those with stored extents are relations in the sense of the conventional tabular view of relations in the relational data model. We will continue to refer to these objects as "functions", because syntactically they will be "applied" like (computed) functions. However, as the definition of the algebra will make clear, what has been defined here can be considered a form of "entity relational" model, along the lines of RM/T [CODD79].

3. PDM Algebra

3.1 Relationship to Relational Algebra

An algebra can be formed for the objects (entities and functions) defined in the last section by adopting a "functional interpretation" for operations of a modified relational algebra, and considering these operations as built-in operations (functions) on function objects. (For functions with stored extents, this interpretation is consistent with the one normally associated with the relational model). These operators are viewed as operating on functions and returning functions (effectively relations, as noted above). The arguments of these returned functions are defined in terms of the input functions in the same way as columns of output relations are defined for conventional relational algebra operations. In addition, operators are provided for creating and destroying entities.

To illustrate the "functional interpretation" of relational operators, the projection of F(X,Y) on X can be interpreted as asking "what values of argument X are defined for function F(X,Y)?" It is possible to imagine that in some cases projection would be defined for intensionally-defined functions as well as for conventional relations. Metadata specifications can be used to indicate whether or not such a built-in function applies to a given function in the database.

In PDM algebra, both functions with stored extents and functions with computed extents are treated as subroutines. Instead of a join operation, an "apply and append" operation is provided that applies a function to arguments contained in tuples of another function. The result is a new function formed conceptually by appending columns to the argument function containing the results of the function evaluation. In the case of functions with stored extents, the interpretation of an "apply and append" is that of a relational join of the relation containing the arguments (the argument function) to the relation representing the function extent.

The appearance of a function in an algebraic expression is a call for its evaluation, using actual parameters substituted for its formal parameters. The form for this is: function-name(Li1:Lo1,...,Lin:Lon), where Li is a formal parameter label. For input parameters, Lo will be the label of an existing column in the argument function that contains the values to be supplied for that parameter. For output parameters, Lo will be the label to be assigned to that output parameter for use within the result function.

An advantage of including function application within an algebraic framework like this is that the resulting function "built up" by an algebraic expression serves as a context for the evaluation of subsequent functions. In particular, it retains associations (possibly indirect) between input and output arguments that can be useful in constructing complex results, such as those found in view definitions and other types of computed functions. The result appears to be an effective integration of strictly functional capabilities such as those in [BUNE82] with relational and object-oriented ones. The identification of functional and object-oriented capabilities with relational ones is particularly important in suggesting implementation strategies and query-optimization techniques.

The algebra contains operations for projection, Cartesian product, and set operations (and their "outer" variants [CODD79]). The usual union-compatibility constraints apply. Any columns containing entities are considered union-compatible (allowing formation of new generalizations). Selection is defined as in the relational algebra, where the selection condition may be either a Boolean function evaluation (which may be nested), including such functions as the usual predicates allowed in relational Θ-joins, logical connectives, or function arguments ("columns") containing truth values.

To illustrate these ideas, consider the following example (in a Daplex-like query language):

print(NAME({P in PERSON where AGE(P) < 10}))

PDM algebra:

T1:   apply_append(,PERSON:P)
T2:   apply_append(T1,AGE(PERSON:P,RESULT:A))
T3:   select(T2,LT(A,10))
T4:   apply_append(T3,NAME(PERSON:P,RESULT:N))
T5:   print(T4,N)

(The operations have been separated for clarity). The sequence of operations is similar to that which would be used in the relational algebra in an RM/T-like database, except for the use of "apply_append" instead of join. The initial "apply_append" in T1 denotes the evaluation of entity type PERSON as a 0-argument function returning a set (column) of entities of that type. The functional interpretation of this is that each new "apply_append" of a user-defined function appends additional columns to the function denoted by the algebraic expression, as a relational join would do to a relation.

3.2 Function Application

The more interesting operations of the algebra are those involving function application, and those involving individual entities. The primary operation of interest here is "apply (function) and append". This plays a role in the PDM algebra corresponding to that of join in the relational algebra (and for functions having stored extents, the intended interpretation is the same). The generic version of "apply and append" is defined as follows:

apply and append — Given a function P having an existing set of labels LIi (the "input" labels), a set of column labels LOi (the "output" labels) not currently defined in P, and a function F(L1,L2,...,Ln) where the Li are formal parameter labels, and LIi is type-compatible with Li, the application of F to P,

apply_append(P, F(..., Lj:LIj, ... , Lk:LOk, ...))

is the set of tuples t such that t is the concatenation of a tuple t1 of P and a distinct tuple of values labeled LOk returned by evaluating the function using parameters taken from the LIi columns of t1. If, for a given set of parameter values, function F is set-valued, each member of the set will be concatenated with t1 to produce a new tuple t.

If computed functions are to be integrated into PDM algebra with the same generality that relational algebras such as that found in [CODD79] provide for relations, a number of issues must be addressed. These include issues relating to the semantics of partial functions and incomplete information. The issues can be identified in functional terms as follows:

a. what should be the result when the function is not defined for a particular tuple of input arguments?

b. what should be the result when the function is defined for tuples of input arguments that are not actually supplied as arguments?

c. should the function return both the input argument values and results, or just results?

d. how are functions to be updated (primarily of concern for stored functions).

These issues have been partially dealt with in the relational model by providing different types of joins, and by adding null values and "outer" operations. In addition, Codd has noted that the differences between "closed world" and "open world" assumptions about relations could be dealt with in the model by determining which of two types of null values should be returned by outer joins [CODD79]. Codd has suggested that this be determined on a per-relation basis, although the type of null could also be indicated by a parameter or by different operation variants. Provision of these join variants gives the user control over the appropriate interpretation of the functions represented by relations, and what the user intends to happen under various circumstances. For completeness, similar capabilities must either be provided for computed functions, or their absence explicitly recognized, and dealt with. That is why the above definition of "apply and append" was referred to as "generic": like join, a number of variants have been identified, and are defined in the model. Note that one always has the option to "construct" appropriate results using more conventional operations, rather than defining multiple "apply" options. Again, this is just like the outer join case: the results of outer joins can be constructed using more conventional operations, but it is often more convenient to have the special operations.

Case (a) refers, in relational terms, to the choice between an ordinary join and a "left outer join" (using terminology from [MERR84]). In a conventional join, the input tuple for which the function was undefined would be eliminated. However, even though this might be desirable, it would be an unconventional side effect of trying to apply a computed function to a set of arguments. A more normal result for computed functions would be that the function aborts in some way. This can currently occur in Daplex if, for example, STUDENT and INSTRUCTOR entities are defined as subtypes of PERSON, ADVISOR(STUDENT) → INSTRUCTOR is defined, and one attempts to evaluate ADVISOR over a set of PERSON entities, some of which are not students. A third possible result would be for the function to return some form of null value, as in an outer join. This allows the user to ensure that the result contains all the original arguments, and that the query does not abort in the middle of a set-oriented expression.

To support the requirements of these operations, two types of "null values" are currently supported, as described in [MERR84]. The *"don't care" null*, denoted * here, behaves like a special value, with properties similar to those of non-null values. Thus, every domain contains * as a potential value, and a three-valued logic is not required. The *"don't know" null*, denoted ? here, can be used as the default value of stored functions for which no explicit value has been supplied. The use of the ? null requires the definition of a three-valued logic. The one currently being considered is that defined in [MERR84], although this is under investigation.

Case (b) refers, in relational terms, to the choice between an ordinary join and a "right outer join". In a conventional join, the effect would be the "normal" one: the function is unevaluated for that argument tuple. However, an option corresponding to a right outer join might apply here too, i.e. supplying "null columns" of input arguments for unsupplied arguments for which the function is defined. (This would certainly be required for stored functions). Cases (a) and (b) also involve the choice of what kind of null would be returned if that were required.

Case (c) refers, in relational terms, to the choice between a natural join and a Θ-join. For computed functions, the problem is relatively straightforward for equijoins, but is less so for other forms of Θ-join. The obvious solution here, as in the previous cases, is to forbid forms of function application that make no sense for specific functions. The point is that all these variants are useful for stored functions (relations), and it is these sorts of *semantic* distinctions that create problems in trying to hide the fact that certain functions are computed.

Case (d) refers to a number of problems. For example, if a multiargument function is intended to be a total function, i.e., defined for all possible values of the input arguments, this means that all possible n-tuples of input arguments would ordinarily have to be present in a stored extent. Moreover, when a user added a new argument value involved in such a function, the user would theoretically have to supply a value for each combination of that value with all combinations of the other arguments, in order to comply with the requirement that the stored extent reflect the "totalness" of the function. This is clearly unrealistic, from both the user and implementation perspectives. One solution would be to allow functions to be declared as either partial or total. A function declared as total might then have a less-than complete extent, and would by default generate ? nulls if applied with input argument values not present in its stored extent. The same function declared as partial, with the same stored extent, would generate * nulls under similar circumstances.

The general problem of updating functions in the model is coextensive with that of updating views. In general, functions may be defined that are partially stored and partially computed. For example, the function

ALTITUDE(LAT,LONG) → HEIGHT

in a geographic database would typically be defined by interpolation over a set of (LAT, LONG, HEIGHT) tuples, while using a stored value where one existed for a particular latitude and longitude.

In addition to the forms of functions described already, PDM also supports various other forms, such as aggregate functions. Again, the techniques used borrow heavily from those familiar in the relational model.

3.3 Other Operations

Operations for operating on single entities are also provided in the model. For example:

Createobj — Given a function P(L1,...,Ln), createobj(P,L) returns a function P1(L1,...,Ln,L) obtained by concatenating each tuple of P with a new entity (surrogate) in column L.

Duplicates Removal (Unique) — Given a function P, one of its labels L1 denoting a column containing entity surrogates, and a set of labels Li denoting other columns of P, the removal of duplicates among the entities labeled L1 in P is denoted by unique(P,L1,Li). It is the function obtained by replacing all entities in the same label L1 position in tuples having the same values for columns Li by a single entity.

It should be noted that using "createobj" to form a new entity (or a column of new entities in a function) effectively constructs a dynamically-created entity type (since all an entity type is in PDM is a set of entities). Such entities may exist in algebraic expressions without functions that can be applied to them (these would have to be created by separate operations).

Metadata is represented using entities and functions, so that PDM algebra can also be used in operating on metadata. Currently, the structure of this metadata is a hybrid between that used in the LDM [CHAN82] and RM/T [CODD79], although there is obviously a great deal more potential flexibility in the use of an object-oriented approach for metadata. The need for some of the special operators defined in RM/T for use in mixed metadata/data queries is currently being investigated. Unlike RM/T, which requires operators to translate between names and relations, PDM allows direct functions between metaentities and extensional objects (e.g., database entities). Thus, some of these operators may not be needed. The full model definition also includes operations for updating database entity types and functions (where this is permissable).

3.4 Algebra Power

The algebra as currently defined is powerful enough to perform arbitrary manipulations of PDM databases, including formation of generalization hierarchies, new entity types, and multiargument functions. A number of examples have been worked out, although space precludes presenting one here. The technique is essentially that used in performing database "restructuring" in the relational model. Existing entity types and functions can be combined into complex functions using apply_append or Cartesian product, and "new" entity types and functions can be projected from those functions.

4. Other PDM Capabilities

4.1 Extensibility

New data types and operations can be added by defining them as new entity types and functions. The physical realization of these types and their operations may be made invisible to the users through an abstract data type mechanism (as in [STON83]). Essentially this provides a straightforward way of interfacing specialized hardware or software processors to the DBMS. The data types and operations implemented by these processors are defined in the schema as entity types and functions that can be used in queries and transactions exactly like the entity types and functions that are "directly" implemented by the DBMS.

Recognizing that many of the objects that occur in the applications to be supported by PROBE deal with spatial and temporal data, we have given special treatment to spatial and temporal semantics. This is accomplished through the definition of special entity types (which are subtypes of the generic type ENTITY), with special behavior, to model spatial and temporal properties of objects. How this works in general is shown in the following simplified (spatial) example. A thorough discussion can be found in [MANO86].

entity PART
function PART#(PT: in PART,NUM: out integer)
function SHAPE(PT: in PART,SHP: out PTSET)
function COLOR(PT: in PART,EXTENT: in PTSET,
                 CLR: out COLORVALUE)

entity PTSET
function CONTAINS(P:PTSET,Q:PTSET)

Briefly, entities of type PTSET that have the semantics of points or point sets (such as lines, areas, or volumes) are defined in the model. These serve as the values of spatial attributes, such as "shape" or "boundary", of ordinary database entities, such as "parts". Subtypes of PTSET can be defined to represent general classes of point sets (e.g., 2D and 3D point sets), and specific types of objects within those general classes (e.g., 2D lines and curves, 3D solids). (Points and intervals can also be defined in the same way to represent temporal objects). For each subtype, appropriate functions can be defined to represent the properties and operations appropriate to the type of object being represented. Note that both spatial and non-spatial attributes (such as "PART#") to be associated with the same database entities in a straightforward way.

Attributes, such as COLOR or DENSITY, that vary over the shape of the part may be handled in two ways. First, the attribute, e.g. COLOR, can be defined as a multiargument function (in this case, as taking a part and a portion of its boundary, and returning a color value). Alternatively, a separate entity could be defined. In this model, object versions (which have received special treatment in some models) are treated as temporal objects. The model is general enough to support many different notions of space and time.

Our approach to implementing spatial objects is to use simple approximate geometric representations (based on space-filling curves) and corresponding fast query processing algorithms that produce approximate answers to spatial queries. These approximate techniques work with a set of objects at a time and can dramatically reduce the amount of work that must subsequently be done by specialized processors that work with one or two objects at a time and manipulate more detailed representations to refine the approximate answers. Temporal data is handled as a one-dimensional special case [OREN86].

Since metadata is also represented by entities and functions, extensibility can also be applied to metadata. This might be used to create multiple metadata-data levels, although this has not yet been investigated in any great detail.

4.2 Rule Specification

A general mechanism for specifying rules is also included in the PROBE data model and language. This mechanism is used to specify rules for propagating changes to derived functions, rules for propagating operations on some entities to other entities to which they are related (hence, for propagating operations from a complex object to its components, and vice versa), rules for specifying how and when to check constraints, rules for invoking exception handlers, etc.

Constraints themselves are specified either as rules that assert some invariants over the database or indirectly through procedures that check whether some desired conditions are satisfied.

4.3 Recursion

The inclusion of recursion in DBMSs, especially to support PROLOG-style deduction over relational databases, has become an extremely active area of research. Rather than adding general recursive PROLOG-style rule processing, which is potentially inefficient and not guaranteed to terminate, to a DBMS, we have identified a special class of recursion, called *traversal recursion*, that has two crucial properties. First, it is powerful enough to express the recursive computations needed for complex objects. Second, very efficient algorithms, based on graph traversal, exist for performing these computations. Traversal recursions generalize transitive closure computations on the database viewed as a graph.

Our implementation approach is to tailor fast graph traversal algorithms for various flavors of traversal recursion, which differ depending upon properties of the graph (is it acyclic or cyclic? is it disjoint or not?), properties of the functions (e.g., whether they are monotonic, whether components are spatially enclosed within their parent objects), and properties of the computations, which are gleaned from the user's query and the metadata. See [ROSE86] for details of these techniques.

Specific forms of recursion are integrated into the model as multiargument functions. These functions can then be invoked in the usual way. The parameters for these functions, and their semantics, are given by the "recursion templates" defined in [ROSE86].

4.4 Global Query Optimization

Query optimization in PROBE will adopt a compromise between the approach to query optimization in distributed optimizers [DANI82], which can obtain some knowledge of the file structures, query processing algorithms, and cost statistics of the individual local processors, and the pure abstract data type approach or object-oriented approach, in which the implementation of every abstract type and its operations is a black box to the optimizer. In the PROBE design, while the implementations of the abstract types and their operations are, indeed, hidden from the end user, each abstract type definition includes an interface to the global optimizer in which some information is revealed. This information includes the algebraic properties of the operations supported (e.g., commutativity, associativity, distributivity), and cost and result size estimates. The global optimizer will utilize this information in constructing efficient global execution plans. This will make the system extensible, in that new types and new operations can be added easily, while at the same time permitting the exploitation of new functionally specialized components for improved performance. Another area of interest is the optimization of the multiple related queries that can result during the construction of complex output objects using the "restructuring" capabilities of the algebra.

4.5 Contexts

The PDM view mechanism involves a generalization that we

call "contexts". The motivation for the facility is that adding spatial/temporal capabilities may greatly increase database sizes and their structural complexity. It is felt that an improved method of organizing this data for users will be required. For example, in a conventional database system, only "current" data is available. Using PDM temporal facilities, data about the state at multiple points in time will be available. The simultaneous availability of data as of multiple points in time may prove rather confusing. Similar comments apply regarding multiple spatial perspectives about the same entities.

In our approach, a context is a generalization of the conventional database view facility that allows switching between views during operations, while retaining some data and metadata from previous views in subsequent ones. There are similarities with the "consult" facility in Prolog. At various points in a Prolog program, new rules and facts may be read into the active database of the program by specifying "consult(filename)" in a rule. These new facts and rules constitute additions (or changes) to the "knowledge" available.

Thus, at any time, a user would be operating in a specific "context". This context is a collection of data and metadata that defines, for that user:

a. what entities exist;
b. what functions can be applied to them;
c. what the definitions of those functions are;

Users may change contexts, and in doing so acquire access to additional or different entities, additional functions that may be applied to entities, or changed definitions of various functions. For example, an entity may be in one type in one context, and in a different type in another. A context change could be used, for example, to change the scale of a map, or to zoom in on a portion of it. In this case, the same entities might exist in both contexts, but the definitions of their functions having spatial values (and thus the values themselves) would change. Also, new entities (representing features not visible in the first scale) might "become visible" in the new context.

The context facility is currently under development. It requires at minimum the ability to define contexts and relationships between them, and to switch contexts during database operations.

5. Other Current Work

Work related to PDM is ongoing in a number of areas, some of them mentioned in previous sections. We are continuing to investigate the semantics of function application in the context of set-oriented queries. We feel particularly that being able to deal consistently with partial functions will be of assistance in integrating user-defined extensions (including functions defined for individual objects as opposed to whole types) into the framework. A breadboard implementation of the Probe Data Model and algebra, and of some query processing algorithms, is under way. This involves the definition of a number of specific extended entity types involving spatial semantics [MANO86].

Acknowledgements

We express our thanks to Alex Buchmann, David Goldhirsch, Sandra Heiler, Jack Orenstein, and Arnie Rosenthal for their contributions to the development of PDM.

6. References

[BUNE82]
Buneman, P., R.E. Frankel, and R. Nikhil, "An Implementation Technique for Database Query Languages," *ACM Trans. Database Systems*, 7, No. 2 (June 1982).

[CHAN82]
Chan, A., et al, "Storage and Access Structures to Support a Semantic Data Model," *8th Intl. Conf. on Very Large Data Bases*, Mexico City, 1982.

[CODD79]
Codd, E.F., "Extending the Database Relational Model to Capture More Meaning," *ACM Trans. Database Systems, 4*, No. 4 (December 1979).

[DANI82]
Daniels, D., et. al., "An Introduction to Distributed Query Compilation in R*," *Proc. 2nd Intl. Symp. on Distributed Databases*, Berlin, September 1982.

[DAYA85]
Dayal, U., et.al., "PROBE — A Research Project in Knowledge-Oriented Database Systems: Preliminary Analysis," Technical Report CCA-85-03, Computer Corporation of America, July 1985.

[DAYA86]
Dayal, U., and J.M. Smith, "PROBE: A Knowledge-Oriented Database Management System," to appear in M.L. Brodie and J. Mylopoulos (eds.), *On Knowledge Base Management Systems: Integrating Artificial Intelligence and Database Technologies*, Springer-Verlag, 1986.

[LOCH86]
Lochovsky, F. (ed.), *Database Engineering*, Vol. 8, No. 4, Special Issue on Object-Oriented Systems, 1986.

[LORI83]
Lorie, R.A., and W. Plouffe, "Complex Objects and Their Use in Design Transactions,," Proc. 1983 ACM Engineering Design Applications, San Jose, CA (May 1983).

[MANO86]
Manola, F.A., and J.A. Orenstein, "Toward a General Spatial Data Model for an Object-Oriented DBMS," *Proc. Twelfth Intl. Conf. on Very Large Data Bases*, Kyoto, August 1986.

[MERR84]
Merrett, T.H., *Relational Information Systems*, Reston, 1984.

[OREN86]
Orenstein, J., "Spatial Query Processing in an Object-Oriented Database System," *Proc. 1986 ACM-SIGMOD Intl. Conf. on Management of Data*.

[RIES83]
Ries, D.R., et. al., "Decompilation and Optimization for ADAPLEX: A Procedural Database Language", Technical Report CCA-82-04, Computer Corporation of America, September 1983.

[ROSE86]
Rosenthal, A., et al., "A DBMS Approach to Recursion," *Proc. 1986 ACM-SIGMOD Intl Conf. on Management of Data*.

[SHIP81]
Shipman, D., "The Functional Data Model and the Data Language DAPLEX," *ACM Trans. Database Systems*, 6,1 (March 1981).

[SMIT81]
Smith, J.M., et al., "ADAPLEX Rationale and Reference Manual," Technical Report CCA-83-08, Computer Corporation of America (May 1983).

[STON83]
Stonebraker, M., B. Rubenstein, and A. Guttman, "Application of Abstract Data Types and Abstract Indices to CAD Databases," *Proc. Database Week: Engineering Design Applications*, IEEE Computer Society, 1983.

Iris: An Object-Oriented Database Management System

D. H. FISHMAN, D. BEECH, H. P. CATE, E. C. CHOW, T. CONNORS, J. W. DAVIS, N. DERRETT, C. G. HOCH, W. KENT, P. LYNGBAEK, B. MAHBOD, M. A. NEIMAT, T. A. RYAN, and M. C. SHAN

Hewlett-Packard Laboratories

The Iris database management system is a research prototype of a next-generation database management system (DBMS) intended to meet the needs of new and emerging database applications, including office information and knowledge-based systems, engineering test and measurement, and hardware and software design. Iris is exploring a rich set of new database capabilities required by these applications, including rich data-modeling constructs, direct database support for inference, novel and extensible data types, for example, to support graphic images, voice, text, vectors, and matrices, support for long transactions spanning minutes to many days, and multiple versions of data. These capabilities are, in addition to the usual support for permanence of data, controlled sharing, backup, and recovery.

The Iris DBMS consists of (1) a query processor that implements the Iris object-oriented data model, (2) a Relational Storage Subsystem (RSS) -like storage manager that provides access paths and concurrency control, backup, and recovery, and (3) a collection of programmatic and interactive interfaces. The data model supports high-level structural abstractions, such as classification, generalization, and aggregation, as well as behavioral abstractions. The interfaces to Iris include an object-oriented extension to SQL.

Categories and Subject Descriptors: D.3.3 [**Programming Languages**]: Language Constructs—*abstract data types*; *data types and structures*; H.2.1 [**Database Management**]: Logical Design—*data models*; H.2.3 [**Database Management**]: Languages—*data description language (DDL)*; *data manipulation language (DML)*; *query languages*; H.2.4 [**Database Management**]: Systems—*query processing*; *transaction processing*; I.2.4 [**Artificial Intelligence**]: Knowledge Representation Formalisms and Methods—*relation systems*; *representation languages*; *semantic networks*; I.2.5 [**Artificial Intelligence**]: Programming Languages and Software

General Terms: Languages

Additional Key Words and Phrases: Iris DBMS, LISP, object-oriented DBMS. OSQL persistent objects, SQL

1. INTRODUCTION

The Iris database management system is a research prototype of a next-generation database management system (DBMS). We are exploring new database features and capabilities through a series of increasingly more capable systems, of which the current Iris prototype is the first. In this paper we present a snapshot of the current system and discuss its capabilities and those we are exploring for future implementations.

The Iris DBMS is intended to meet the needs of new and emerging database applications, such as office information and knowledge-based systems, engineering test and measurement, and hardware and software design. These applications require a rich set of capabilities that are not supported by the current generation of DBMSs. In addition to the usual requirement for permanence of data, controlled sharing, backup, and recovery, the new capabilities that are needed include rich data modeling constructs, direct database support for inference, novel data types (graphic images, voice, text, vectors, matrices), lengthy interactions with the database spanning minutes to many days, and multiple versions of data. The Iris DBMS is being designed to meet these needs.

Figure 1 is a depiction of the layered architecture of Iris. In the middle of the system is the Iris Object Manager, the query processor of the DBMS. The Object Manager implements the Iris Data Model [13, 14], which falls into the general category of object-oriented models that support high-level structural abstractions, such as classification, generalization/specialization, and aggregation [1, 7, 18, 26, 30, 31], as well as behavioral abstractions [5, 21, 28]. The query processor translates Iris queries and operations into an internal relational algebra format, which is then interpreted against the stored database. Instead of inventing a totally new formalism on which to base the correct behavior of our system, we rely on the relational algebra as our theory of computation. The capabilities of the Object Manager are discussed in Section 2.

The Iris Storage Manager is (currently) a conventional relational storage subsystem. It is very similar to the Relational Storage Subsystem (RSS) in System R [3]. The capabilities supported by the storage manager include the dynamic creation and deletion of relations, transactions with "savepoints" and "restores to savepoints," concurrency control, logging and recovery, archiving, indexing, and buffer management. It provides tuple-at-a-time processing, with commands to retrieve, update, insert, and delete tuples. Indexes and threads allow users to access the tuples of a relation in a predefined order. Additionally, a predicate over column values can be used to qualify tuples during retrieval. Our plans to modify and extend this subsystem to support the additional requirements noted above are discussed in Section 4.

Like most other database systems, Iris is designed to be accessible from any number of programming languages, and by stand-alone interactive interfaces. Construction of interfaces is made possible by a set of C language subroutines that defines, indeed *is*, the object manager interface. Currently, two lexically oriented interactive interfaces are supported. One of these, called OSQL, for Object SQL, is an object-oriented extension to SQL. We have chosen to extend SQL rather than invent a totally new language because of the prominence of SQL in the database community, and because, as we explored the possibility, the extensions seemed fairly natural. The other interactive interface, called the Inspector, is an extension of a LISP structure browser. This interface allows the user to explore interactively the Iris metadata (type) structures, as well as the interobject connection structures defined on a given Iris database. Although the Inspector currently offers only a lexical style of interface, it is a precursor to a graphical interface.

Authors' address: Hewlett-Packard Laboratories, 1501 Page Mill Road, Palo Alto, CA 94304.

Therefore, referential integrity [11] can be supported. This is a major advantage over record-oriented data models in which the objects, represented as records, can be referred to only in terms of their attribute values.

Objects are described by their behavior and can only be accessed and manipulated in terms of predefined operations. As long as the semantics of the operations remains the same, the database can be physically, as well as logically, reorganized without affecting application programs. This provides a very high degree of data abstraction and data independence.

Objects have the following characteristics:

—Objects are classified by type. Objects that share common properties belong to the same type.

—Objects may serve as arguments to operations and may be returned as results of operations.

The Iris data model distinguishes between *literal objects*, such as character strings and numbers, and *nonliteral* objects, such as persons and departments. Literal objects are directly representable, whereas nonliteral objects are represented internally in the database by surrogate identifiers. A nonliteral object may be referenced either in terms of its property values, for example,

the person named "Randy Newman"

or in terms of its relationships with other objects, for example,

the spouse of the person named "Sandy Newman."

The Object Manager provides operations for explicitly creating and deleting nonliteral objects, and for assigning values to their properties. Referential integrity is supported in the current prototype by allowing objects to be deleted only if they are not being referred to.

Note that by a "property" of an object we mean a *function* (a kind of operation) that returns a value when applied to that object. Thus we model properties or attributes of Iris objects with functions. This is discussed further in the section on operations.

2.2 Types and Type Hierarchies

Types are named collections of objects. Objects belonging to the same type share common properties. For example, all the objects belonging to the Person type have a Name and an Age property. Properties are operations (functions) defined on types (see Section 2.3); they are applicable to the instances of the types. In effect, therefore, types are constraints. Objects are constrained by their types to be applicable to only those properties (functions) that are defined on the types.

Types are organized in a type structure that supports generalization and specialization. A type may be declared to be the subtype of another type. In that case all instances of the subtype are also instances of the supertype. However, a supertype may have instances that do not belong to its subtype. Properties defined on the supertype are also defined on the subtype. We say that the properties are *inherited* by the subtype.

The Iris type structure is a directed acyclic graph (DAG). A given type may have multiple subtypes and multiple supertypes. Figure 2 illustrates a type graph

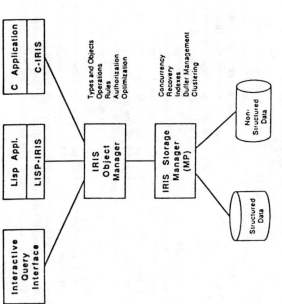

Fig. 1. Iris system structure.

As already noted, access to Iris is facilitated by a set of C language subroutines. In addition, we are exploring three kinds of LISP programmatic interfaces. The first kind is a straightforward embedding of OSQL into LISP. This has been done with minor syntactic modifications to OSQL, including a generous dose of parenthetization. Another kind of interface is the encapsulation of the Iris DBMS as a programming language *object* [10, 32, 35] whose methods correspond to the functions in the C subroutine interface to the Iris Object Manager. The third kind of interface is part of a longer term investigation into *persistent objects*, the intent of which is to make programming language objects transparently persistent and sharable across applications and languages. The various Iris interfaces are discussed in Section 3.

2. IRIS OBJECT MANAGER

The Iris Object Manager implements the Iris data model by providing support for schema definition, data manipulation, and query processing. The data model, which is based on the three constructs *objects*, *types*, and *operations*, supports inheritance and generic properties, constraints, complex or nonnormalized data, user-defined operations, version control, inference, and extensible data types. The roots of the model can be found in previous work on DAPLEX [30] and its extensions [22] and on the Taxis language [28].

2.1 Objects

Objects represent entities and concepts from the application domain being modeled. They are unique entities in the database, with their own identity and existence, and they can be referred to regardless of their attribute values.

and existing types deleted, and objects may gain or lose types throughout their lifetimes. In the current implementation a type may be deleted only if it has no subtypes and no instances. Furthermore, new subtype/supertype relationships among existing types cannot be created.

2.3 Operations and Rules

An Iris operation is a computation that may or may not return a result. Operations are defined on types and are applicable to the instances of the types. Currently all Iris operations do return results, and so we use the words *operation* and *function* interchangeably. The Iris data model and its current prototype support user-defined operations that are stored and executed under the control of the database management system.

2.3.1 Functions for Retrieving Information. The specification of an Iris operation consists of two parts, a *declaration* and an *implementation*. A declaration specifies the name of the operation and the number and types of its parameters and results. An implementation specifies just that, how the operation is implemented.

For example,

NEW FUNCTION marriage(p/Person) = (spouse/Person, date/Charstring)

declares a function called marriage. A function can return a compound result, as in the above example, where the result of the function contains both the spouse and the date of the marriage. This function can be called as follows:

(s, d) = marriage(bob)

A function may also return multiple results, for example,

NEW FUNCTION children(p/Person) = c/Person

which returns the set of children of a person.

The function declaration is also used to specify upper and lower bound constraints on the number of occurrences of each parameter and result value. For example, a function result value may be specified to be REQUIRED, which means that a result value must exist for each possible parameter value, or it may be UNIQUE, which means that distinct parameter values will be mapped onto distinct result values.

The operation *implementation* may be specified in various ways, which we discuss below.

2.3.2 Stored Functions. One way to implement a function is to store it as a table, mapping input values to their corresponding result values. Such a table may be implemented and accessed using standard relational database techniques. The STORE operation allows the user to specify that a function is to be implemented in this way. Thus

STORE marriage

causes the Object Manager to create a table with, in the case of the above declaration, three columns for the person, spouse, and date.

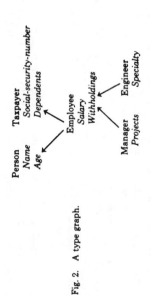

Fig. 2. A type graph.

with five types, each having a number of properties. The Employee type is a direct subtype of the Person and Taxpayer types, and the Employee type itself has two direct subtypes, Manager and Engineer.

Instances of type Employee belong to the Taxpayer and Person types as well. The properties defined on Person and on Taxpayer are inherited by Employee. Thus Employee objects have all of the six properties Salary, Withholdings, Name, Age, Social-security-number, and Dependents.

Instances of Engineer also belong to the Employee, Person, and Taxpayer types, and Engineer objects have the six properties of Employees, as well as the Specialty property. If Manager and Engineer are declared to be *disjoint*, Manager objects are guaranteed not to belong to the Engineer type. If Engineer and Manager are declared to be *overlapping*, Manager objects may belong to the Engineer type. Thus two types that are declared to be disjoint cannot be supertypes of a common subtype.

Properties may be *generic*; that is, properties defined on different types may have identical names even though their definitions may differ. Thus a database designer can introduce a property in its most general form by defining it on a general type and later refine the property definition for the more specialized subtypes. For example, the Employee type may have a general Salary property, whereas the Manager and Engineer types have Salary properties that are specific to the two job categories. This approach to design is called stepwise refinement by specialization [28]. The rules for property selection are not yet finalized.

When a generic property is applied to a given object, a single specific property must be selected at the time of application. The specific property is determined not only by the name of the generic property, but also by the type of the object to which it is applied. If the object belongs to several types that all have specific properties of the given name, the property of the most specific type is selected. If a single most specific type cannot be found, user-specified rules for property selection will apply. These rules are specified for families of functions that share the same names.

The type Object is the supertype of all other types and therefore contains every object. Types are objects themselves, and their relationships to subtypes, supertypes, and instances are expressed as functions in the system [25].

In order to support graceful database evolution, the Object Manager allows the type graph to be changed dynamically. For example, new types may be created

The mappings of several functions may be stored together in a single table. For example,

```
STORE name ON person, age ON person
```

would create a table containing persons with their names and ages. Restrictions have been introduced to ensure that such a table is in normal form.

2.3.3 *Derived Functions.* The definition of a function may be specified in terms of other functions, for example,

```
DEFINE manager(e/employee) = FIND m/employee
  WHERE m = department-manager(department(e))
```

This simple definition specifies how the manager of an employee may be derived. In general, function definitions may contain arbitrary queries. These definitions are compiled by the Object Manager into an internal relational algebra representation that is interpreted when the function is invoked.

A function definition may contain calls to several other derived functions, for example,

```
DEFINE important-manager = FIND m/employee
  WHERE FORSOME d/department
  m = department-manager(d) AND department-size(d) > 20
```

In this case the relational algebra expressions for the functions that are called in the definition are combined into a larger relational expression, with selections and joins as appropriate.

2.3.4 *Foreign Functions.* It is desirable to be able to add new data types, together with their associated operations, to a database system. For example, we might want to add a matrix or a vector data type, with associated addition and multiplication operators. In order to do this, it must be possible to link such operations into the database system and invoke them from the query processor. The current Iris prototype allows the user to define new types and operations, but only if they can be defined using the types and operations already supplied in the database system. We plan to allow privileged users to add to the database operations that are written in a traditional programming language such as C. This facility is important, both for extending the functionality of the database system and for efficient computation on rich object structures or data types.

2.3.5 *Compound Operations.* We are currently working on extensions to our model to allow the user to define operations containing sequences of operations. This requires changes to the Iris query compiler and interpreter.

2.3.6 *Rules.* Rules in the Iris model are simply functions. For example, given a *parent* function, we can define a *grandparent* function as follows:

```
DEFINE grandparent(p/Person) = FIND gp/Person
  WHERE gp = parent(parent(p))
```

A more complex rule may be defined as follows:

```
DEFINE older-cousin(p/Person) = FIND c/Person
  WHERE c = child(sibling(parent(p))) AND age(c) > age(p)
```

We note that the nested-function notation used in Iris function definitions dispenses with the variables needed in, for example, Prolog [8], to carry results from one function call to the next. Variables can, however, be used in Iris function bodies, if required.

An important difference between C functions and Prolog rules (taking C and Prolog as examples of a traditional programming language and a rule-based language) is that the C function returns a single result, whereas the rule returns a stream of results. Iris functions can return multiple results, and a nested function call returns the concatenation of the sets of results obtained from calling the inner function. For example, the function call

```
children(members(sales-dept))
```

returns all of the children of all of the members of the sales department.

Like Prolog, Iris makes the closed-world assumption: Any fact that is not deducible from the data in the database is assumed to be false.

The current Iris prototype supports only conjunctive, nonrecursive rules, but disjunction, negation, and recursion are being studied.

2.3.7 *Update Operations.* An update operation in Iris changes the future behavior of a database function. For example, the operation

```
SET department-manager(sales-dept) = john
```

will cause the department-manager function to return the value john in a future invocation with the parameter sales-dept.

If a function is multivalued, then we can add the extra values

```
ADD member(sales-dept) = bill
```

which adds bill to the set of members of the department. Similarly, we can say

```
REMOVE member(sales-dept) = james
```

The REMOVE operation also applies to single-valued functions.

The current implementation of updates requires single argument and result values to be explicitly specified. The prototype is being extended to support the specification of updates to sets of objects. An example of such an update would be to increase the salary of all engineers by 10 percent.

Each function in Iris may have up to four compiled representations: one each for GET, SET, ADD, and REMOVE. In the case of a simple function, the implementation of the update can be deduced by the system, but for more complex functions, such as a function involving a join, it is necessary for the function definer to specify the implementation. Currently, only simple functions can be updated.

2.3.8 *Relationships and Attributes.* A database may wish to group together database operations in either of two ways:

(1) grouping according to argument types, for example, collecting together all of the operations on persons—this gives the sense of defining the properties of objects and is the traditional object-oriented approach;

(2) grouping by relationships, for example, collecting together functions and their inverses—this gives the sense of defining families of semantically related operations and is the traditional relational approach.

Either of these ways of grouping operations together is valid in its context, and the Iris data model does not insist on one or the other. Rather than introduce two concepts, however, we have chosen one.

Information about objects is modeled in Iris using *relationships*. Thus, for example, the fact that a person has a name is represented as a relationship connecting the person object and the name object. This approach is different from that of the Entity-Relationship (E-R) model [7], which allows objects to have attributes. The attribute concept is modeled in Iris by using functions whose values are derived from the relationships. Given a relationship called person-age, which connects persons and their ages, we can represent this relationship as a Boolean-valued function:

NEW FUNCTION person-age(p/Person, a/Integer) = Boolean

where person-age(John, 31) is true if the person specified has the age specified. We may then derive the functions

age(Person) = Integer
person-with-age(Integer) = Person

which are inverses of each other. The age function can be regarded as an attribute of person.

Relationships can be *n*-ary; for example, a relationship between mother, father, and child can be represented as a Boolean function with three parameters. An *n*-ary relationship can be used to derive a family of related functions, for example,

father(Person) = Person
child(Person) = Person
parents(Person) = (Person, Person)

and so on. In general, an *n*-ary relationship has 2^n related functions. The related functions may be derived using the DEFINE operation described previously.

2.4 Query Processing

Iris queries are implemented by compiling the queries into relational algebra representations, which are then interpreted. Some examples of queries are given in Section 3, where we discuss the interface to the Iris system.

Stored queries are implemented as functions; the query is compiled, and the compiled representation is stored in the database for later interpretation.

3. IRIS INTERFACES

The Iris DBMS may be accessed via both interactive and programmatic interfaces. These interfaces are implemented using the library of C subroutines that define the Iris Object Manager interface. The library is intended to be a platform upon which stand-alone interfaces and interfaces to various programming languages are built. In addition, programmers may use this library directly.

The following subsections discuss the design and functional capabilities of existing interactive and programmatic interfaces to Iris. The OSQL interface discussed first is implemented both as a stand-alone interactive interface and as a language extension. OSQL is currently embedded in Common LISP via macro extension.

3.1 Object SQL Interface

The initial interface to Iris stayed quite close to the atomic level of the operations supported by the Object Manager and was very useful in debugging the system. For more general use, however, it was decided to develop a higher level interface that would take the primitive notion of an atomic object and combine it with the set of property functions (or attributes) that the user considered to be intrinsic to the nature of the object. This is much like the treatment of entities and their attributes in the E-R model, or like one use of the tables in the relational model [9], where a row represents an object and each column represents a property. It is also close to the concept of an abstract type or class in an object-oriented programming language.

Given the definitions of two types of objects, such as Person and Document, simple means are needed to create instances of these types and to introduce relationships such as "is author of" or "has approval rights over" between persons and documents. This corresponds to the relationship sets in the E-R model and to the other usage of relational tables to relate objects (rows in other tables) by referring to their key values. Note that programming languages tend to lack high-level support for relationship sets of this kind.

The functional emphasis in Iris suggests the use of a functional style of interface for navigating around the relationships between interconnected objects. We therefore examined such languages as DAPLEX [30], GORDAS [15], and IDM [4]. However, because of the strong similarities of these languages to a relational language such as SQL [12], we also explored possible extensions to SQL to accommodate the object model and a more functional style. As a result of the study, we concluded that an Object SQL (OSQL) interface would be feasible and fairly attractive, and we decided to develop OSQL.

The two main extensions we have made beyond SQL to adapt it to the object and function model are

—Direct references to objects are used rather than their keys. Interface variables may be bound to objects on creation or retrieval and may then be used to refer to the objects in subsequent statements.

—User-defined functions and Iris system functions may appear in WHERE and SELECT clauses to give concise and powerful retrieval.

We have not included the GROUP BY and HAVING clauses on SELECT, since their effect can be achieved in other ways and they are difficult for users to understand [12].

There are also a few keyword differences from existing SQL. It should be possible to reinterpret all existing keywords mechanically, but for human users some of the keywords would be found very misleading when applied to the object model.

A few examples should illustrate both the general similarity of OSQL to SQL and the advantages of an object-based query language.

Suppose that we wish to automate some office procedures for obtaining approvals for documents. Some of the actions and corresponding OSQL statements could be as follows:

Start a new database called Approvals:

```
START Approvals;
```

Connect to the Approvals database and start a new session. This implicitly begins a new transaction:

```
CONNECT Approvals;
```

Create a new type called Person, with property functions called name, address, netaddress, and phone. Each Person object must have a value for the name function:

```
CREATE TYPE Person
 (name Charstring REQUIRED,
  address Charstring,
  netaddress Charstring,
  phone Charstring);
```

Create a new type called Approver as a subtype of Person. The type has a single property function called expertise (where we assume Topic has been created as a type), in addition to the four properties inherited from Person. The new property function is multivalued:

```
CREATE TYPE Approver SUBTYPE OF Person
 (expertise Topic MANY);
```

Create a new type called Author as a subtype of Person:

```
CREATE TYPE Author SUBTYPE OF Person;
```

Create a new type called Document:

```
CREATE TYPE Document
 (title Charstring REQUIRED,
  authorOf Author REQUIRED MANY,
  prim Topic,
  sec Topic,
  status Charstring REQUIRED,
  approverOf Approver MANY);
```

Create a stored function called grade which for a given document and a given approver returns the grade assigned to the document by the approver:

```
CREATE FUNCTION grade (Document, Approver) → Integer;
```

Create three instances of the type Approver and assign values to the property functions name (inherited from the type Person) and expertise. Bind the interface variables Smith, Jones, and Robinson to the objects created:

```
CREATE Approver (name, expertise)
INSTANCES Smith ('Albert Smith', software)
 Jones ('Isaac Jones', (finance, marketing)),
 Robinson ('Alan Robinson', (hardware, marketing, manufacturing, personnel));
```

Add the type Author to the two objects referred to by the interface variables Smith and Robinson. This shows objects being given multiple types:

```
ADD TYPE Author TO
 Smith,
 Robinson;
```

Enter documents written by Smith and Robinson:

```
CREATE Document (title, authorOf, status)
INSTANCES d1 ('The Flight from Relational', Smith, 'Received'),
 d2 ('Workstation Market Projections', Robinson, 'Received');
```

Assign approvers to the document d1:

```
SET approverof(d1) = (Jones, Robinson);
```

Assign to the document d1 the grade given by Jones:

```
SET grade(d1, Jones) = 3;
```

Make a type for approved documents:

```
CREATE TYPE ApprovedDocument SUBTYPE OF Document;
```

Approve the document d1:

```
ADD TYPE ApprovedDocument TO d1;
```

Commit the current transaction and start a new one:

```
COMMIT;
```

Get the title of document d5:

```
SELECT title(d5);
```

Get the titles of all the approved documents:

```
SELECT title
FOR EACH ApprovedDocument;
```

Find the titles of all the documents Robinson is approving:

```
SELECT title
FOR EACH Document d
WHERE Robinson = approverOf(d);
```

End the current session. This implicitly commits the current transaction:

```
END;
```

It is interesting to consider OSQL as a potential evolutionary growth path for SQL. It would be possible to use a subset of OSQL that is very similar to SQL, or to begin to make sparing use of new features such as the implicit keys, or to move to a style that takes full advantage of derived and nested functions in queries. Some of the new features of OSQL could be supported in a straightforward way on a relational system, whereas others would require a more ambitious object manager. Migration is never easy, but the OSQL approach could smooth the path for migration of both users and programs from SQL to the object world.

```
p1: Iris object "#(IRIS-HANDLE 2008,800000BA1FA814C7)"
|Type: "PAPER"
|  "TITLE": "A Unified Field Theory"
|  "PAPNO": 1
|  "PRIM": Iris object "#(IRIS-HANDLE 2008,800000A51FA814C7)"
|    |Type: "TOPIC"
|    |  "TNAME": "Physics"
|    |  "RELEVANT": T
|  "SEC": Iris object "#(IRIS-HANDLE 2008,800000A61FA814C7)"
|  "STATUS": "A"
|  "AUTHOROF":
|    Iris scan#(
|    " 0: "Iris object "#(IRIS-HANDLE 2008,800000B41FA814C7)"
|    |Supertype of REVIEWER: "PERSON"
|    |  "NAME": "Albert Einstein"
|    |  "ADDRESS": NIL
|    |  "NETADDRESS": "albert@ias.EDU"
|    Type: "REVIEWER"
|    |  "EXPERTISE":
|    |    Iris scan#(
|    |    " 0: "Iris object "#(IRIS-HANDLE 2008,800000A51FA814C7)"
|    |    |Type: "TOPIC"
|    |    |  "TNAME": "Physics"
|    |    |  "RELEVANT": T
|    |    " 1: "Iris object "#(IRIS-HANDLE 2008,800000A61FA814C7)"
|    |    ")
|  )
|  "REVIEWEROF": (IRIS-SCAN)"
```

Figure 3

3.2 Iris Inspector

The Iris Inspector provides a mechanism for a LISP user to examine Iris database entities in the same manner in which the usual LISP values would be examined [33]. The Iris Inspector is an extension of the Inspector utility in the Hewlett-Packard Artificial Intelligence Workstation environment [2].

The Inspector is given an arbitrary LISP value and provides a *browser* (i.e., screen-oriented textual display) of the value. The user can increase or decrease the level of detail of the display. For example, at a given level of detail, the components of the value being *inspected* may be displayed only as internal names; the user can put the cursor on such a component and issue the *more detail* command, and the display of that component will be made more verbose.

The Iris Inspector provides type-specific handling of the Iris types in much the same manner as the basic Inspector provides special handling for the primitive types from which LISP Objects are built.

An example of an Inspector display is shown in Figure 3.

3.3 Iris Database Object

An object-oriented interface to Iris from Common LISP that presents the model of an *Iris database object* to the LISP programmer has been implemented. The various entities in the interface are implemented as LISP Objects [32], the methods of which are the C functions in the subroutine library defining the Object Manager interface. These types encapsulate various state information that is needed to support the methods but that does not need to be exposed to the user, such as the underlying byte patterns of the database data structures. For example, there is a *:find* method on *iris-db* that returns an object of type *iris-scan*, which, in turn, has a *:next* method to fetch the items referred to by the scan, and so forth. The arguments to all of these methods are normal LISP values; for example, the predicate for a *:find* is a list that looks like a LISP form, with the semantic difference being that the functions are Iris, not LISP, functions.

The Iris Database Object interface presents to the LISP user a family of types and their methods, which can be manipulated and examined in the same way as any other LISP Object types. This interface is in the "middle ground" of programming language/database integration, in that the database is explicitly manipulated, but the manipulation is done with the usual syntax and mechanisms of the programming language. This approach would work equally well with other object-oriented languages.

3.4 Persistent Objects

The approach of providing a database sublanguage, like our OSQL, that is embedded in host programming languages seems inappropriate if an object-oriented database is to be accessed from an object-oriented programming language. One would like to hide at least syntactic differences between in-memory and database objects, and, if possible, to hide semantic differences as well. In general, it will not be possible to hide all of the semantic differences, especially if the database is to be accessed from more than one object-oriented programming language and if the various programming languages are based on different object models. On the other hand, it is remarkable how much alike most programming

languages are when they are stripped of syntactic differences and specialist features. Thus it seems possible that a well-chosen object-oriented data model will be able to support a fairly wide variety of object-oriented programming languages, and that interfaces to these languages that hide most of the differences between language objects and database objects can be provided. We are currently investigating this hypothesis.

Our first step in this investigation was to provide a DBMS interface to LISP. The interface provides the LISP programmer with "persistent objects", which are syntactically and semantically very like the transient objects already provided by the language. There are only two differences visible to the user. The first is that some restrictions have been imposed on persistent objects for reasons of efficiency and simplicity. The other is the addition of a tag field in the type definition that is used to specify that members of the type are persistent.

Any object-oriented programming language provides four basic mechanisms for operating on objects. These are

—the creation of a type and its placement in the type hierarchy;
—the creation of an operation for one or more types, with its associated data structures;
—the creation of a new object (and its later destruction);
—the application of an operation to one or more objects.

It is therefore necessary that an object-oriented DBMS be able to support these four mechanisms in their various guises. In particular, various programming languages bundle the first and second items in various ways (e.g., Simula puts them both together, whereas they are quite separate in LISP with flavors). Thus the DBMS must provide operations for each of the individual steps that make up the creation of a type with its operations. Once these basic operations are provided by the DBMS, it is possible to put around them a syntactic layer that makes the database objects look very much like programming-language objects.

It should be noted, however, that algorithms that are appropriate for random-access memory may be highly inappropriate for disk-based storage. This means that, whatever the syntactic similarities, the programmer must be aware sometimes of whether or not an object is persistent. Furthermore, the streaming, indexing, and filtering operations that are provided by database management systems have seldom been provided by, or indeed needed by, programming languages, because their storage is truly random access and the amounts of in-memory data manipulated by programs have been relatively small. It is therefore necessary to add extra operators for persistent objects in order to provide access to these facilities. We note that some expert-systems languages such as Prolog [8] and HPRL [29], already contain elaborate filtering and searching mechanisms (rules and inheritance), so that interfacing database searching mechanisms to such languages should be quite natural.

4. IRIS STORAGE MANAGER

The Iris prototype is built on top of a conventional relational storage manager, namely, that of Hewlett-Packard's Allbase relational DBMS. Some of the OSQL examples in Section 3.1 suggest how all instances of a type with some selected functions can be clustered in a relation. For example, all objects of type Person will be stored with their name, address, netaddress, and phone functions in one relation. The Allbase storage manager is very similar to System R's RSS [3]. Relations can be created and dropped at any time. The system supports transactions with "savepoints" and "restores to savepoints," concurrency control, logging and recovery, archiving, indexing, and buffer management. It provides tuple-at-a-time processing with commands to retrieve, update, insert, and delete tuples. Indexes and threads (links between tuples in the same relation) allow users to access the tuples of a relation in a predefined order. Additionally, a predicate over column values can be defined to qualify tuples during retrieval.

4.1 Transaction Management

One of the major goals of the Iris project is to provide concurrent database access to a diverse set of applications not currently well supported by existing database management systems. A characteristic of these applications is the prolonged access to and manipulation of database elements. Such interactions may last

from minutes to days or even weeks, thereby precluding the use of conventional strictly two-phase transaction management techniques. That is, since conventional techniques require the holding of locks until termination of the transaction, concurrency would be drastically reduced. Thus we are exploring modifications to the transaction management system that provide increased concurrency for such applications.

These applications can be categorized into three general classes:

(1) Applications in which a unit of work comprises a collection of conventional transactions against a multitude of databases, and where this unit of work is likely to span several days. A typical example of such an application would be the arrangements for a trip that might involve airline, car, and hotel reservations, and where the cancellation of the trip would require the individual cancellation of all the relevant reservations [17]. This action can be modeled as an umbrella transaction of long duration comprising several low-level conventional transactions against the airline, car rental, and hotel reservation databases. The general effect is that, at the termination of each of the low-level transactions, the locks on the entities in the respective databases are released and the changes become visible to other independent transactions resulting in maximal concurrency. In such applications, therefore, a transaction abort or undo at the application level, for example, a trip cancellation, would result in the execution of compensating low-level transactions against the target databases, logically undoing the committed results of the previous low-level transactions.

(2) AI-based application environments whose queries against the database translate into several concurrent and interrelated transactions. An interesting discussion of the differences between the particular demands of this application area and those of the previously mentioned application and of conventional applications appears in [6]. Such an environment is characterized by its highly interactive nature and the large number of read-only applications. Such interactive transactions are potentially of moderately long duration (possibly hours). Employing a conventional transaction mechanism on a shared database will cause an effectively serialized access pattern to the database and will drastically reduce concurrency. It appears that a multilayered transaction mechanism, where the higher layers provide abstract locks and employ a different concurrency control mechanism than lower layer transactions, would provide for increased concurrency [27].

(3) Design applications such as document design, CAD, and software development. Transactions in this environment could potentially involve manipulation of large and complex objects and are likely to last several days to weeks. Although in the first two application areas there is only one valid state of the world (the rest being past history), this application area requires simultaneous existence of several valid states of the world; for example, several correct alternatives of a particular design can exist simultaneously in the database. Because of this fact, the requirements imposed on the DBMS by this application area are the most rigorous as compared with the others.

Since our initial focus is on providing support for the third area, we elaborate on the imposed requirements of these applications. Traditional databases take a global and static view of the world. At any one time there is only one current value for any entity, and this value is changed in a very regular way. Although previous values of a particular entity may be accessible, for example, through the log file, it is the current value for the entity that is of primary importance. In contrast, design databases take a dynamic and temporal view of the world; an entity may simultaneously have several alternate values or representations in the database. Past values of an entity may be equally important to a user of a design database and may be frequently accessed.

The simultaneous presence of alternative values for a particular entity necessitates the existence of an object versioning mechanism in order to provide controlled access to these values [19, 20, 23, 24]. A version control mechanism is being explored as an integral part of the Iris Object Manager, which would form the basis for the implementation of concurrency control in this application environment. We are exploring a versioning model in which the user can create a tree of versions for any object. When we provide for merging of versions, this will be a more general version graph. The version control mechanism will dovetail with our transaction management approach, in which the user is allowed to *check out* one or more object versions for extended manipulation.

We require a new object locking mechanism that can put long-term locks on objects in persistent storage. This locking mechanism is employed at the design transaction level and is at a higher level than the traditional locks held in volatile memory by conventional transactions. This higher level lock mechanism provides a hierarchical lock structure with intention locks, as well as share and exclusive locks much like its lower level counterpart [16]. The object hierarchy and the dependencies and overlaps between object hierarchies need to be known to the lock manager so that the proper intention locks can be set.

The design database comprises a public and logically private databases. The same mechanism for long transactions also controls concurrency in the private databases [24]. When a version of an object is checked out, this version of the object, together with all the objects in its subtree, is locked in the public database and logically becomes part of a private database. The lock in the public database prevents further access to this object by others, although access to all other versions is possible. Once the object is checked out, versions of referenced objects can be made in the private database. All revisions to the private versions will be reflected in the public database at the time the entire subtree is checked back in.

On the basis of the above discussion, a multilayered transaction mechanism appears to be the appropriate solution for these diverse environments, where each application environment sees a different transaction interface. For example, a CAD application will call *checkout* to access a group of objects, whereas an AI application will call *begin_transaction* to perform a sequence of queries. We are actively evaluating the conceptual and implementational aspects of this scheme.

4.2 Extensible Types

The ability to add new data types, operations, and access methods is a desirable property of a DBMS. This ability allows one to model more easily and precisely a given application domain. For instance, a Date data type could be useful *in* a payroll application. In addition, this ability introduces the potential *for*

performance improvements. Operations on new types (e.g., subtraction of Dates) can be handled directly by the DBMS. Given the increased ability of the DBMS in handling new types, efficiency is increased, since the transfer of control and the movement of data between the application and the DBMS need not occur so frequently. Efficiency also results from the introduction of custom access methods, for example, as derived from a special collating sequence defined on a new type. Installing new types could be put to advantage by the DBMS authors, OEMs, and Database Administrators (DBAs) as well as users.

Stonebraker [34] points out that to support abstract data types, the DBMS must provide the user (most likely a DBA) with a mechanism for each of the following:

(1) declaring the existence of a new type and providing filters to translate between character strings and the new type's internal representation—this is needed at the user interface level to translate between a printable representation of a type and its internal representation;

(2) defining operations on the new types;

(3) implementing new access methods for newly created types.

Item (1) is fairly straightforward. Item (2), defining an operation, entails several tasks. A syntax for how the operation will be used in expressions must be presented, and the parser modified accordingly. Any context sensitive rules, such as precedence, must be incorporated. Additionally, a procedure to execute the operation must be presented and then stored where it can be accessed by the query interpreter. In its first implementation, we plan to require that the presentations of syntax and procedures be done at DBMS compile time so that the parse table and operation table become part of the DBMS executable. Operation installation utilities will be provided to eliminate the need to modify DBMS source code directly. Another concern is operator name overloading; for example, the operator symbol "+" may have different definitions and meanings for different types. Some of the techniques used in the Object Manager to resolve overloaded functions will be used in interpreting the meaning of an operator for an abstract data type.

Item (3), allowing the user to implement new access methods that would be linked with and interact with the existing storage manager, presents a greater challenge. The implementation of an access method interacts directly or indirectly with the concurrency control mechanism, with logging, and with the buffer and record manager. One would like to minimize the requisite interaction with logging and concurrency control, since these services are complicated and essentially unrelated to the access method from an algorithmic point of view. By virtue of its design, we believe that the Iris Storage Manager is amenable to these goals. The interaction between these modules in the Iris Storage Manager is shown in Figure 4.

The Index Manager (IM), must know how to interface to the Lock Manager (LM), the Buffer Manager (BM), and the Record Manager (RM). All interactions to the Log Manager (LG) are done through the Record Manager and the Buffer Manager. Consequently, it is not necessary for the implementor of an access method to understand the interaction with the Log Manager. In addition, the essentially unmodified), called Allbase-Core, is the Storage Manager of Hewlett Packard's Allbase DBMS product. This is an RSS-like storage subsystem, augmented with parent-child links, to support both a relational and a network query processor. The extensions discussed in the Storage Manager section are still in the design stage.

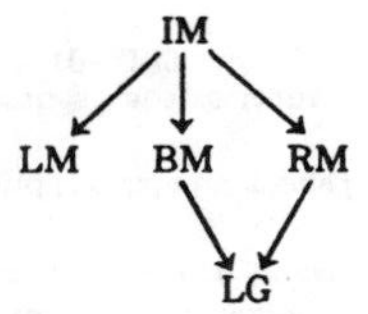

The Object Manager is entirely new code. It consists of an implementation of the model discussed in Section 2 and its associated query processor. Implemented features of the model include types and type hierarchies, including multiple supertypes, (atomic) objects, and operations. Only functions (operations without side effects) have been implemented thus far. Functions may be defined in terms of other functions via function composition and Boolean combination (currently only AND). Recursive function definitions are not yet supported. Also implemented are the functors SET, ADD, and REMOVE for altering the values returned by stored functions. Capabilities that have not yet been implemented include richer operations, recursive function definitions, and versioning. Designs for these capabilities are actively being pursued.

The interfaces that have thus far been implemented for Iris include the OSQL and Inspector interactive interfaces, OSQL embedded in LISP, and the "Iris database object" whose "methods" are precisely the operations supported by the Object Manager interface. Of course, there is also the C subroutine library that is the Object Manager interface, the use of which is required to implement all Iris interfaces.

ACKNOWLEDGMENTS

The authors wish to thank the referees for providing numerous comments and suggestions for improving the presentation of this paper. However, the authors take responsibility for any mistakes that remain.

REFERENCES

1. ABRIAL, J. R. Data semantics. In *Data Base Management*, J. W. Klimbie, and K. L. Koffman, Eds. North-Holland, Amsterdam, 1974, pp. 1–59.
2. HP AI workstation debugger. Internal Hewlett-Packard Laboratories Rep., Palo Alto, Calif, 1985.
3. ASTRAHAN, M. M., BLASGEN, M. W., CHAMBERLIN, D. D., ESWARAN, K. P., GRAY, J. N., GRIFFITHS, P. P., KING, W. F., LORIE, R. A., MCJONES, P. R., MEHL, J. W., PUTZOLU, G. R., TRAIGER, G. R., WADE, B. W., AND WATSON, V. System R: A relational data base management system. *ACM Trans. Database Syst. 1*, 2 (June 1976), 97–137.
4. BEECH, D., AND FELDMAN, J. S. The integrated data model—A database perspective. In *Proceedings of the 9th International Conference on Very Large Databases* (Florence, Italy, 1983). VLDB Endowment, Saratoga, Calif.
5. BRODIE, M. L. On modeling behavioral semantics of data. In *Proceedings of the 7th International Conference on Very Large Data Bases* (Cannes, France, Sept. 9–11). ACM, New York, 1981.
6. CAREY, M. J., DEWITT, D. J., AND GRAEFE, G. Mechanisms for concurrency control and recovery in Prolog—A proposal. In *Expert Database Systems—Proceedings of the 1st International Workshop*, L. Kerschberg, Ed. The Benjamin/Cummings Publishing Co., Inc, Menlo Park, Calif.
7. CHEN, P. P. The entity-relationship model: Toward a unified view of data. *ACM Trans. Database Syst. 1*, 1 (Mar. 1976), 9–36.
8. CLOCKSIN, W. F., AND MELLISH, C. S. *Programming in Prolog*. Springer-Verlag, New York, 1981.
9. CODD, E. F. A relational model of data for large shared data banks. *Commun. ACM 13*, 6 (June, 1970), 377–387.

Figure 4

interface to the Lock Manager is through a single procedure that merely specifies the object requested (relation, page, or tuple) and the lock mode. We believe that this is exactly the right level of interaction with the system. The Log Manager is entirely shielded from the application programmer. Interaction with the Lock Manager is simple, yet still under access method control. This is desirable since indexing techniques may have concurrency control requirements that are less stringent than a default, system imposed method.

4.3 Multimedia Objects

In addition to such data types as Date, Money, and Matrix, office and engineering applications require the storage and manipulation of large unstructured literal types, such as text and voice data. The rigid structure of conventional DBMSs makes these systems unsuitable for multimedia applications. The Iris Object Manager plans to support vector and raster graphics, text, and voice literal types, and the Storage Manager will offer specialized storage and search solutions for processing such data types. Multimedia data will not necessarily reside on the same storage medium as the conventional data, nor will they necessarily be managed (e.g., updates logged) in the same way. Some multimedia data, for example, text, may reside in conventional files, whereas others, text or speech data, may reside on special devices, such as optical disks. Specialized hardware, for example, text search engines or voice input/output devices, may be employed to search and manipulate such data.

We envision the Iris DBMS controlling several specialized DBMSs, each dedicated to handling a specific type of data. The central DBMS knows about objects, their relationship to other objects, and associated types. A multimedia object, for example, a document, may consist of text, image, and voice subobjects. The central DBMS knows of and delegates the storage and management of these multimedia data types to the appropriate specialized DBMSs. The central DBMS also coordinates the specialized databases. A transaction spanning different types of data will begin in the central DBMS, with subtransactions spawned to each appropriate specialized DBMS. The central DBMS will coordinate the commits. The specialized DBMSs will have query processing, access methods, concurrency control, and recovery and versioning techniques that are appropriate to the data they are handling. The multimedia data types will need appropriate query interfaces and data representation and display. These will be left to application programs that interface to the central DBMS.

5. CURRENT STATUS

The Iris prototype is being implemented in C on HP-9000/320 UNIX[1] workstations. These are MC68020-based computers. The Storage Manager (still

[1] UNIX is a trademark of AT&T Bell Laboratories.

32. SNYDER, A. CommonObjects: An overview. *SIGPLAN Not. 21*, 10 (Oct. 1986) 19–28.

33. STEEL, G. L. *Common Lisp: The Language.* Digital Press, Burlington, Mass., 1984.

34. STONEBRAKER, M. Inclusion of new types in relational data base systems. In *Proceedings of the 2d International Conference on Data Base Engineering* (Los Angeles, Calif., Feb.). IEEE Computer Society Press, Washington, D.C., 1986.

35. STROUSTRUP, B. *The C++ Programming Language.* Addison-Wesley, Reading, Mass., 1986.

Received August 1986; revised September 1986; accepted November 1986

10. Cox, B. J. *Object Oriented Programming: An Evolutionary Approach.* Addison-Wesley, Reading, Mass., 1986.

11. DATE, C. J. Referential integrity. In *Proceedings of the 7th International Conference on Very Large Data Bases* (Cannes, France, Sept. 9–11). ACM, New York, 1981.

12. DATE, C. J. *A Guide to DB2.* Addison-Wesley, Reading Mass., 1984.

13. DERRETT, N., KENT, W., AND LYNGBAEK, P. Some aspects of operations in an object-oriented database. *Database Eng. 8*, 4 (1985), 66–74.

14. DERRETT, N., FISHMAN, D. H., KENT, W., LYNGBAEK, P. AND RYAN, T. A. An object-oriented approach to data management. In *Proceedings of Compcon 31st IEEE Computer Society International Conference* (San Francisco, Calif., Mar. 1986). IEEE Computer Society Press, Washington, D.C.

15. ELMASRI, R., AND WIEDERHOLD, G. GORDAS: A formal high-level query language for the entity–relationship model. In *Entity–Relationship Approach to Information Modeling and Analysis.* P. P. Chen, Ed Elsevier, New York, 1981.

16. GRAY, J. N. Notes on database operating systems. In *Lecture Notes in Computer Science 60, Advanced Course on Operating Systems.* R. Bayer, R. M. Graham, and G. Seegmuller, Eds. Springer-Verlag, New York, 1978.

17. GRAY, J. N. The transaction concept: Virtues and limitations. In *Proceedings of the 7th International Conference on Very Large Data Bases* (Cannes, France, Sept. 9–11). ACM, New York, 1981.

18. HAMMER, M., AND McLEOD, D. Database description with SDM: A semantic database model. *ACM Trans. Database Syst. 6*, 3 (Sept. 1981), 351–386.

19. KATZ, R. H. *Information Management for Engineering Design.* Springer-Verlag, New York, 1985.

20. KATZ, R. H., CHANG, E., AND BHATEJA, R. Version modeling concepts for computer-aided design databases. In *Proceedings of the International Conference on Management of Data* (Washington, D.C., May 28–30). ACM, New York, 1986.

21. KING, R., AND McLEOD, D. The event database specification model. In *Proceedings of the 2d International Conference on Databases: Improving Usability and Responsiveness* (Jerusalem, Israel, June). Academic Press, New York, 1982, pp. 299–322.

22. KULKARNI, K. G. Evaluation of functional data models for database design and use. Ph.D. dissertation. Department of Computer Science, Univ. of Edinburgh, 1983.

23. LANDIS, G. S. Design evolution and history in an object-oriented CAD/CAM database. In *Proceedings of Compcon 31st IEEE Computer Society International Conference* (San Francisco, Calif., March). IEEE Computer Society Press, Washington, D.C., 1986.

24. LORIE, R., AND PLOUFFE, W. Complex objects and their use in design transactions. In *Proceedings of the Conference on Databases for Engineering Applications*, Database Week, 1983 (ACM), May 1983.

25. LYNGBAEK, P., AND KENT, W. A data modeling methodology for the design and implementation of information systems. In *Proceedings of the International Workshop on Object-Oriented Database Systems* (Pacific Grove, Calif., Sept.), IEEE Computer Society Press, Washington, D.C., 1986, pp. 6–17.

26. LYNGBAEK, P., AND McLEOD, D. A personal data manager. In *Proceedings of the 10th International Conference on Very Large Data Bases* (Singapore, Aug.) VLDB Endowment, Saratoga, Calif., 1984.

27. MOSS, J. E. B., GRIFFITH, N. D., AND GRAHAM, M. H. Abstraction in recovery management. In *Proceedings of the International Conference on Management of Data* (Washington, D.C., May 28–30). ACM, New York, 1986.

28. MYLOPOULOS, J., BERNSTEIN, P. A., AND WONG, H. K. T. A language facility for designing database-intensive applications. *ACM Trans. Database Syst. 5*, 2 (June 1980), 185–207.

29. ROSENBERG, S. T. HPRL: A language for building expert systems. In *Proceedings of the International Joint Conference on Artificial Intelligence* (Karlsruhe, West Germany). William Kaufmann, Inc., Los Altos, Calif., 1983.

30. SHIPMAN, D. The functional data model and the data language DAPLEX. *ACM Trans. Database Syst. 6*, 1 (Mar. 1981), 140–173.

31. SMITH, J. M., AND SMITH, D. C. P. Database abstractions: Aggregation and generalization. *ACM Trans. Database Syst. 2*, 2 (June 1977), 105–133.

O$_2$, an Object-Oriented Data Model

Christophe Lécluse
Philippe Richard
Fernando Velez

GIP Altaïr,
Domaine de Voluceau, B.P. 105,
78153, Le Chesnay Cedex, France.

Abstract

The *Altaïr* group is currently designing an object-oriented data base system called O$_2$. This paper presents a formal description of the object-oriented data model of this system. It proposes a type system defined in the framework of a set-and-tuple data model. It models the well known inheritance mechanism and enforces strong typing.

1. Introduction

One of the objectives of the *Altaïr* Group is to develop a new generation database system. The target applications are traditional business applications, transactional applications (excluding very high performance applications), office automation and multi-media applications.

The system we are designing is object-oriented. We briefly recall the main features of the object-oriented paradigm:

(i) Object identity. Objects have an existence which is independent of their value. Thus, two objects can be either identical, that is, they are the same object, or they can be equal, i.e., they have the same value.

(ii) The notion of *type*[1]. A type describes a set of objects with the same characteristics. It describes the structure of data carried by objects as well as the operations (*methods* in the object-oriented terminology) applied to these objects. Users of a type only see the interface of the type, that is, a list of methods together with their signatures (the type of the input parameters and the type of the result): this is called *encapsulation*.

(iii) The notion of *inheritance*: it allows objects of different structures to share methods related to their common part. Types are organized in an inheritance (or *subtype*) hierarchy which factorizes common structure and methods at the level at which the largest number of objects can share them[2].

(iv) *Overriding* and *late binding*. The body of a method in a given type may be redefined at any moment in any of its subtypes, yet keeping the same name. This frees the programmer from remembering the name of an overriden method in a given type, and therefore, the code is simpler and reusable because it is independent of the types that existed at the time the program was written. To offer this functionnality, the system has to bind method names to binary code at run time.

There is a clear interest in the database community for the object-oriented technology. First of all, types and inheritance are a powerful tool to model the real world. They also make systems extensible: by adding new types in a system, one can extend its capabilities. Object identity allows modeling object sharing and provides a natural semantics for object updates [Copeland & Khoshafian 86]. Second, this technology provides a framework to represent and manage both data and programs. It is a promising paradigm to solve the so-called *impedance mismatch*: the awkward communication

---

[1] The term *class* is frequently used; however, in addition to the intensional notion of type, it contains an extensional aspect, as it denotes the set of all objects of the system which conforms to the type at a given time.

[2] Another mechanism allowing objects to share operations is called *delegation*. It is the basis of the so-called "Actor languages". We will not consider it in this paper.

between a query language and a programming language that results when developing applications with a database system. Third, it provides good software engineering tools that make the programming task much easier.

Object-oriented database systems are being currently built. Most of them are prototypes [Banerjee & al 87], [Zdonik 84], [Nixon & al 87], [Bancilhon et al 87] and few of them are commercial products [Copeland & Maier 84], [Andrews & Harris 87]. The overall objective of these systems is to integrate database technology (such as data sharing, data security, persistency, disk management and database query languages) with the object-oriented approach in a single system.

However, there is a lack of a strong theoretical framework for object-oriented systems. This paper is a step in this direction. It proposes the data model foundations for an object-oriented database system. The originality of this model, called O_2, is its type system defined in the framework of a set and tuple data model. We think that what makes our approach different from other object-oriented approaches is that we use set and tuple constructors to deal with arbitrary complex objects, and the type system enforces strong typing, yet overriding is allowed.

There already exist models dealing with inheritance such as [Bruce & Wegner 86] and [Cardelli 84]. In [Bruce and Wegner 86] types are modeled as many-sorted algebras. A type is a subtype of another if their exist suitable (not necessarily injective) "coercion" operators which behave as homomorphisms between the algebras. In [Cardelli 84], a safe, strongly typed system is proposed in which the semantics of subtyping for tuple-structured types corresponds to set inclusion between the corresponding type interpretations (this semantics is different from the previous one). Functions are typed and rules for subtyping among functional types are also given.

We have borrowed Cardelli's interpretation for tuple types, as it leads to an intuitive notion of subtyping of tuple structures. Our model is different to these proposals in that (i) we propose a different rule for inheritance of methods (for functional subtyping, in Cardelli's terms), (ii) set-structured objects are introduced, and objects may form a directed graph in which cycles are allowed, and (iii) methods can be directly attached to objects.

Our "tuple-and-set" construction of objects is similar to that of [Bancilhon and Khoshafian 86] and specially to that of [Kuper and Vardi 84] where identifiers (called addresses) are also introduced.

This paper is organized as follows. Section 2 gives an informal overview of our approach and exposes it through examples. Section 3 gives a definition of objects. Section 4 gives the semantics of types and inheritance relationship. Finally, the notion of database is intro-duced in Section 5. Section 6 contains some concluding remarks and open problems.

2. Informal Overview

Let us introduce some of the notions of this model using examples. Objects represent our (computer) world. They are made up of an object identifier (a name for the object) and a value. Values can be atomic (string, integers, reals,...), tuple-structured or set-structured.

$(ob_1, <$name: "Smith", age: 32$>)$
$(ob_2, <$name: "Doe", age: 29, salary: 9700$>)$
$(ob_3, \{ob_1, ob_2\})$

The first two objects are examples of tuple objects and the last one is a set object. Atomic objects here are ages and names (they actually also have identifiers, as shown later). Objects can, of course, reference other objects and this allows the definition of complex objects. We can have mutually referencing objects, as shown in the following example:

$(ob_4, <$name: "john", spouse: $ob_5>)$
$(ob_5, <$name: "mary", spouse: $ob_4>)$

This possibility makes our objects more general than the simple nested tuple-and-set-objects.

A type has a name and it contains a structure and a set of methods, applying to these objects. A structure will be either a basic structure (String, Integer, Real for example), tuple structures and set structures. The following example of type structures will be used throughout the paper:

Person $= <$name: String, age: Integer, sex: String$>$
Employee $= <$name: String, age: Integer, sex: String,
                salary: Integer$>$
Male $= <$name: String, age: Integer, sex: "male"$>$
Persons $= \{$Person$\}$
Employees $= \{$Employee$\}$
Married-Person $= <$name: String, spouse: Married-
                Person, children: Persons$>$

The type structure of "Person" represents the set of all tuple objects having a name field which is a string, and an age field which is an integer. The type structure of "Male" is as "Person" except that the sex field is restricted to contain the string "male". The type structure of "Persons" represents all objects which are sets of persons. Given a set of objects Θ, we shall call the interpretation of a type structure (say "Person") the set of all objects of this set having the corresponding structure. If Θ is the set of all objects ob_1 to ob_5, then the interpretation of "Persons" will be the object ob_3, whereas the interpretation of "Person" will be the two objects ob_1 and ob_2. Indeed, these two objects have name and age fields with the corresponding structures (string and integers). Notice that we allow the objects to have additional fields (the object ob_2 also have a salary field). In the same manner, the interpretation of the "Employee" structure is the set containing only the ob_2 object. So the interpretation of "Employee" is included in the interpretation of type structure "Person". This is an intuitive result, because we want to say that every employee is a person. This "is-a" relationship between type structures is what is called inheritance in the object-oriented terminology.

The notion of inheritance also deals with methods. As employees are persons, a method defined for every person can be applied to an employee. Moreover, if a method (say "name") is defined for both persons and employees, then we shall put some constraint on these methods, in order to make them "compatible". Such a compatibility is necessary to be able to perform type checking.

3. Objects

In this section, we define the notion of objects. We suppose given:

- A finite set of *domains* $D_1, ..., D_n, n \geq 1$ (for example, the set Z of all integers is one such domain). We note D the union of all domains $D_1, ..., D_n$. We suppose that the domains are pairwise disjoint.

- A countably infinite set A of symbols called *attributes*. Intuitively, the elements of A are names for structure fields as we shall see later.

- A countably infinite set ID of symbols called *identifiers*. The elements of ID will be used as identifiers for objects.

Let us now define the notion of *value*.

Definition 1: Values

(i) The special symbol *nil* is a value, called a *basic value*.

(ii) Every element v of D is a value, called a *basic value*.

(iii) Every finite subset of ID is a value, called a *set-value*. Set-values are denoted in the usual way using brackets.

(iv) Every finite partial function from A into ID is a value, called a *tuple-value*. We denote by $<a_1 : i_1 , ..., a_p : i_p>$ the partial function t defined on $\{a_1, ..., a_p\}$ such that $t(a_k) = i_k$ for all k.

We denote by V the set of all values. □

We can now define the notion of object.

Definition 2: Objects

(i) An *object* is a pair o = (i, v), where i is an element of ID (an identifier) and v is a value.

(ii) We define, in an obvious way, the notion of *basic objects*, *set-structured* objects and *tuple-structured*

objects.

(iii) O is the set of all objects, that is $O = ID \times V$. □

This "tuple-and-set" construction of objects is similar to that of [Bancilhon and Khoshafian 86] and specially to that of [Kuper and Vardi 84] where identifiers (called addresses) were also introduced.

In the following, we need some technical notations: If o = (i,v) is an object then *ident*(o) denotes the identifier i and *value*(o) denotes the value v. We will denote by *ref* the function from O in 2^{ID} which associates to an object the set of all the identifiers appearing in its value, i.e., thode referenced by the object. We can use a graphical representation for objects as follows :

Definition 3: Object graph

If Θ is a set of objects, then the graph *graph(Θ)* is defined as follows:

(i) If o is a basic object of Θ then the graph contains a vertex with no outgoing edge. The vertex is labeled with the value of o.

(ii) If o is a tuple-structured object .br (i, $<a_1:i_1,..., a_p:i_p>$), the graph of o contains a vertex, say v, represented by a dot (•) and labeled with i, and p outgoing edges from v labeled with $a_1, ..., a_p$ leading respectively to the vertex corresponding to objects $o_1, ..., o_p$, where o_k is an object identified by i_k (if such objects exist).

(iii) if o is a set-structured object .br (i, $\{i_1,..., i_p\}$), the graph of o contains a vertex, say v, represented by a star (*) and labeled by i, and p unlabeled outgoing arcs from v leading respectively to the vertex corresponding to objects $o_1,..., o_p$, where o_k is an object identified by i_k (if such objects exist). □

We illustrate this definition with an example. Let Θ be the set consisting of the following objects:

$o_0 = (i_0, <\text{spouse} : i_1, \text{name} : i_3, \text{children} : i_2>)$
$o_1 = (i_1, <\text{spouse} : i_0, \text{name} : i_4, \text{children} : i_2>)$
$o_2 = (i_2, \{i_5, i_6\}), o_3 = (i_3, \text{"Fred"}), o_4 = (i_4, \text{"Mary"})$
$o_5 = (i_5, \text{"John"}), o_6 = (i_6, \text{"Paul"})$

Θ is represented by the following graph:

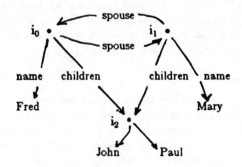

It is important to note that, referring to Definition 3, we cannot build the graph representation of any set of objects. For example, if an identifier i appears in a value, there must be an object identified by it. Intuitively speaking, identifiers are pointers on objects and there must be no dangling pointers in our set of objects. This leads us to introduce the notion of consistency for a set of objects.

Definition 4: Consistent set of objects

A set Θ of objects is consistent iff :

(i) Θ is finite,

(ii) The *ident* function is injective on Θ (i.e, there is no pair of objects with the same identifier),

(iii) for all $o \in \Theta$, $ref(o) \subseteq ident(\Theta)$ (i.e every referenced identifier corresponds to an object of Θ). □

In the following, we denote by $\Theta(i)$ the value v such that the object (i, v) is in Θ.

In value-based systems (i.e, in systems where no object identity exists, such as relational systems) there is no need to distinguish between identical objects and equal objects since the two notions are the same. On the contrary, object-oriented systems need to distinguish them as there is a sharp distinction between values and objects.

Definition 5: Equalities

(i) *0-equality*: two objects o and o' are 0-equal (or *identical*) iff o=o' (in the sense of mathematical pair equality),

(ii) *1-equality*: two objects o and o' are 1-equal (or simply *equal*) iff value(o) = value(o'),

(iii) *ω-equality*: two objects o and o' are ω-equal (or *value-equal*) iff span-tree(o) = span-tree(o') where span-tree(o) is the tree obtained from o by recursively replacing an identifier i (in a value) by the value of the object identified by i. □

Equality implies value-equality, but the converse is not true since many distinct objects may have the same span tree. These definitions of equality correspond to identity, shallow-equality and deep-equality of Smalltalk 80 [Goldberg and Robson 83]. We must notice that the span-tree build from an object may be infinite (in the case of cyclic objects). So, this construction cannot be used (directly) as a decision procedure for testing value-equality.

4. Types

A type is an abstraction that allows the user to encapsulate in the same structure data and operations. In our model, the static component of a type is called a type structure. As we shall see later, our notion of type bears some similarity to abstract data types. Users of a type

only see its abstract part, that is, the interface of its methods, whereas the programmer of the type is concerned with the implementation. However, a type has only one implementation.

In what follows, we shall decompose the process of defining the syntax, semantics and subtype relationship among types in two steps. First, in section 4.1, we shall define the syntax of type structures as well as the notion of schema. Then, we shall give the semantics of a schema with respect to a consistent set of objects. A partial order among type structures will be defined using this semantics. Second, in section 4.2, the same treatment will be given to methods. We shall bring up pieces together in section 4.3 with the notion of "type systems". We begin by defining the set of type names.

Definition 6: Type names

Bnames is the set of names for basic types containing :

(i) the special symbols *Any* and *Nil*,

(ii) a symbol d_i for each domain D_i. We shall note $D_i = dom(d_i)$,

(iii) a symbol 'x for every value x of D.

Cnames is a set of names for constructed types which is countably infinite and disjoint with *Bnames*. *Tnames* is the union of *Bnames* and *Cnames* and it is the set of all names for types. □

In order to define types, we assume that there is a finite set *MT* whose elements are called methods and which shall play the role of operations on our data structures. For the moment, we can think of the elements of *MT* as uninterpreted symbols. We shall define them in section 4.2

Definition 7: Types

Basic type (Btypes) : a basic type is a pair (n,m) where n is an element of *Bnames* and m a subset of MT[3].

Constructed types (Ctypes) : A constructed type is either

(i) a triple (s,t,m) where s is an element of Cnames, t is an element of Tnames, m a subset of *MT*. We shall denote such a type by (s = t,m).

(ii) a triple (s, t, m) where s is an element of Cnames and t is a finite partial function from A to Tnames and m a subset of *MT*. We shall denote such a type by (s $=<a_1:s_1, ..., a_n:s_n>$, m) where $t(a_k)=s_k$ and call it a *tuple structured type*,

(iii) a triple (s, s', m) where s is an element of Cnames and s' an element of Tnames and m a finite subset of *MT*. We shall denote such a type by (s={s'}, m) and call it a *set structured type*.

---

[3] The link between basic types and domains D_i will be given in the following section, in the definition of interpretations.

A *type* is either a basic or a constructed type. The set of all types is denoted by **T**. □

4.1. Type structures

In this subsection we are interested in the static part of a type, i.e. in its structure.

4.1.1. Definitions

Definition 8: Type structures

Basic type structure: let t=(n,m) be a basic type, we call n the *basic type structure* associated to t.

Constructed type structure: let t=(s=x,m) be a constructed type, we call "s=x" the *constructed type structure* associated to t.

Given a type t, its structure part will be denoted by *struct*(t) and its methods part by *Methods*(t). Intuitively, a type structure is a type in which the methods part is hidden, i.e it is the data part of the type. Note that recursion (or transitive recursion) is allowed in type definitions, that is, one of the s_i may be s. The type structure "Married-Person" is an example of recursively defined type.

Type structures are analogous to GALILEO's concrete types [Albano & al 85] except that type structures only exist within types.

For the same reasons as in section 2, we need a notion of consistency for a set of expressions defining type structures. In order to define it formally, we need some technical notations:

(1) If t is a type, then *name*(t) is the name of the type, that is the first component in its definition.

(2) If st is a type structure associated to the type t, we call "name of the type structure" st, the name of t and we note *name(st)*=name(t).

(3) If st is a type structure (associated to a type t), we call "set of types references for st" and denote by *refer(st)* the set of all types names appearing in the structure st.

Definition 9: Schemas

A set Δ of constructed type structures is a *schema* iff

(i) Δ is a finite set,

(ii) *name* is injective on Δ (only one type structure for a given name),

(iii) for all st ∈ Δ, *refer*(st) ∩ Cnames ⊆ *name*(Δ) (i.e. there are no dangling identifiers). □

Nota Bene : In a schema, we can identify a *type name* of name(Δ) with the corresponding type structure in Δ, and we shall use this convention in the sequel of the paper.

We illustrate the notion of a schema with two examples : Let Δ be the set consisting of the following type structures :

age = integer,
person = <name : string, age : age>

Δ is a schema. If we take off the type structure "age" from Δ, it is no longer a schema. On the other hand, the following set of type structures is also a schema:

person = human
human = person

This set of type structures may be not useful but it is well defined and has an interpretation as we shall see in the next section.

4.1.2. Interpretation

This section deals with the definition of the semantics of the type structure system presented above. It will be given by a particular function which associates subsets of a consistent set of objects to type structure names.

Definition 10: Interpretations

Let Δ be a schema and Θ be a consistent subset of the universe of objects O. An *interpretation* I of Δ in Θ is a function from Tnames in $2^{ident(\Theta)}$[4], satisfying the following properties:

Basic Type Names

1) I(Nil) ⊆ {i ∈ ident(Θ)[4] / (i, Nil) ∈ Θ}

2) $I(d_i)$ ⊆ { id ∈ ident(Θ) / Θ(id) ∈ D_i } ∪ I(Nil)

3) I('x) ⊆ { id ∈ ident(Θ) / Θ(id) = x } ∪ I(Nil)

Constructed Type Names

4) if s = $<a_1 : s_1, ... , a_n : s_n>$ is in Δ then
   I(s) ⊆ { id ∈ ident(Θ) / Θ(id) is a tuple structured value defined (*at least*) on $a_1,...,a_n$ and Θ(id) (a_k) ∈ $I(s_k)$ for all k} ∪ I(Nil)

5) if s = { s' } is in Δ then
   I(s) ⊆ { id ∈ ident(Θ) / Θ(id) ⊆ I(s') } ∪ I(Nil)

6) if s = t is in Δ then I(s) ⊆ I(t)

Undefined Type Names

7) if s is neither a name of basic type nor a name of the schema Δ, then I(s) ⊆ I(Nil) □

Definition 11: Model of a schema

(i) *Partial order on interpretations*: An interpretation I is *smaller* than an interpretation I' iff for all s ∈ Tnames , I(s) ⊆ I'(s)

(ii) *Model*: Let Δ be a schema and Θ be a consistent set of objects. The model M of Δ in Θ is the greatest interpretation of Δ in Θ. □

As we shall show later, this definition is well founded. Some important remarks are in order at this point. Intuitively, the model M(s) of a constructed type structure of

---

[4] Recall that ident(Θ) denotes the set of the identifiers of all objects of Θ and that Θ(id) denotes the (only) value v such that (id, v) is in Θ.

name s is the set consisting of all objects (identifiers of objects) having this structure. For example, if Θ is the set

$$\{(i_0,\text{Nil}),(i_1,\{i_2,i_3\}),(i_2,1),(i_3,4),(i_4,<a:i_2>),(i_5,<a:i_2,b:i_3>)\}$$

and Δ is the schema

$\{s_1 = <a:\text{Integer}>, \quad s_2 = <a:\text{Integer}, \quad b:\text{Integer}>,$
$s_3=\{\text{Integer}\}\}$

then $M(s_1) = \{ i_0, i_4, i_5\}$
$\qquad M(s_2) = \{ i_0, i_5\}$
$\qquad M(\text{Integer}) = \{i_0, i_2, i_3\}$
$\qquad M(s_3) = \{ i_0, i_1 \}$

We can notice that the value of an interpretation of a *Basic type name* does not depend on Δ which is an intuitive result. Moreover, if (the identifier of) an object belongs to the model $M(s)$ of a tuple structure, then it also belongs to the models of tuple type structures which are sub-structures of s. In the example below, i_5 is in $M(s_2)$ but also in $M(s_1)$. This property will allow us to give a simple set-inclusion semantics for the sub-typing relation among type structures defined in the following subsection. This interpretation is derived from an interpretation which was originally proposed in [Cardelli 84]. Note that any attribute could be added to a tuple-structured object and the latter would still have a well-defined type. Such "added" attributes will be referred to as "exceptional", and their manipulation is considered in section 4.4.

We now have to prove that our definition of the model of a schema is well founded. Given a schema Δ and a consistent set of objects Θ, there is a finite number of interpretations of Δ defined on Θ. Therefore, in order to prove that the greatest interpretation exists, we just have to prove that the union of two interpretations is an interpretation.

Let I_1 and I_2 be two interpretations, and I be the function defined by $I(s) = I_1(s) \cup I_2(s)$, for every type name s. This function I clearly verifies properties 1, 2 and 3 of the Definition of interpretations. If $s=<a_1:s_1,...,a_n:a_n>$ and id is an element of $I(s)$, (for example, an element of $I_1(s)$), then $\Theta(id)(a_k)$ is in $I_1(s_k)$ for all k, because I_1 is an interpretation. So $\Theta(id)(a_k)$ is in $I(s_k)$ for all k, and I verifies the property 4) of Definition 10. We can show in the same manner that I also verifies properties 5 and 6.

In conclusion, there is a greatest interpretation M, and we have:

$$M(s) = \bigcup_{I \in \text{INT}(\Delta)} I(s),$$

for every type name s, where $\text{INT}(\Delta)$ denotes the set of all interpretations of Δ (in Θ).

4.1.3. Partial Order Among Type Structures
Definition 12: Partial order $\leq_{st}$

Let s and s' be two type structures of a schema Δ. We say that s is a substructure of s' (denoted by $s \leq_{st} s'$) iff $M(s) \subseteq M(s')$ for all consistent set Θ. $\square$

For example, if Δ consists of the following type structures :

$\quad s_1 = <a:\text{Integer}>,$
$\quad s_2 = <a:\text{Integer}, b:\text{Integer}>,$
$\quad s_3 = <c:s_1>, s_4 = <c:s_2>,$
$\quad s_5 = \{s_1\}, s_6 = \{s_2\}, s_7 = <a:'1>$

then the following relationships holds among these structures :

$$s_2 \leq_{st} s_1 \qquad\qquad s_4 \leq_{st} s_3$$
$$s_7 \leq_{st} s_1 \qquad\qquad s_6 \leq_{st} s_5$$

The first relationship $(s_2 \leq_{st} s_1)$ comes from the interpretation of tuple type structures. Let us establish the second one $(s_4 \leq_{st} s_3)$. Let id be the (identifier of an) object belonging to $I(s_4)$. We know from the definition that $\Theta(id)(c)$ belongs to $I(s_2)$ and so to $I(s_1)$ because we have $s_2 \leq_{st} s_1$. We conclude that id belongs to $I(s_3)$ and so $I(s_4) \subseteq I(s_3)$. The inequality $s_6 \leq_{st} s_5$ can be established in the same manner and the relation $s_7 \leq_{st} s_1$ is obviously true.

Definition 12 gives a semantic definition for the subtyping relationship $\leq_{st}$. The following theorem gives a syntactic characterization of it.

Theorem 1:

Let s and s' be two type structures of a schema Δ. s is a substructure of s' $(s \leq_{st} s')$ iff

(i) either s and s' are tuple structures $s = t$ and $s' = t'$, such that t is more defined than t' and for every attribute "a" such that t' is defined, we have $t(a) \leq_{st} t'(a)$.

(ii) or s and s' are set structures $s = \{s_1\}$ and $s' = \{s'_1\}$ and we have $s_1 \leq_{st} s'_1$.

(iii) or $s = 'x$, s' is a basic type structure and x is in dom(s'). $\square$

Proof:
The validity of this characterization can be easily established by induction. The completeness can be established with a case study, inspecting successively tuple structured types, set structured types and basic types. $\square$

This theorem gives a syntactical means for checking type structure subtyping.

4.2. Methods

In Section 4.1, we have presented the syntax and semantics of type structures. In this subsection, we define, in the same way, the syntax and semantics of operations, which we call methods in this context. These operations will consist of (first order) functions.

4.2.1. Definition

We assume that we have a countable set Mnames of symbols that will be used as names for methods.

Definition 13: Signatures

Let Δ be a schema. A *signature* over Δ is an expression of the form:

$$s_1 \times s_2 \times ... \times s_n \longrightarrow s$$

where s_1, s_2,..., s_n, and s are types names corresponding to type structures in Δ or basic types names.

A *method* m is a pair m$=$(n,σ) where n is a method name (an element of Mnames) and σ is a signature. We shall denote by *name*(m) the name of the method m and by *sign*(m) the signature of the method m. □

In the object-oriented formalism, methods are related to types (or type structures) using the first argument of their signature, so we have:

Definition 14: Methods

Let m$=$(n, $s_1 \times ... \times s_n \longrightarrow$ s) be a method. We say that m *is defined on* s_1. □

4.2.2. Interpretation

In this subsection, we define the model of a signature σ

Definition 15: Model of a signature

Let Δ be a schema and σ a signature over Δ ($\sigma = s_1 \times ... \times s_n \longrightarrow$ s). If Θ is a consistent set of objects, then the *model of σ in Θ* is the set of all **partial** functions from $M(s_1) \times ... \times M(s_n)$ into $M(s)$ where $M(s_k)$ is the model in Θ of the structure of Δ identified by s_k. □

Let us illustrate these definitions by an example. Let Δ be the schema introduced in section 2 restricted to the type structures "Person", "Persons", "Employee", "Employees" and "Male". We consider now the following signatures:

$\sigma_1 =$ Persons $\times$ Person $\longrightarrow$ Boolean

$\sigma_2 =$ Employees $\times$ Employee $\longrightarrow$ Boolean

$\sigma_3 =$ Person $\longrightarrow$ Person

$\sigma_4 =$ Male $\longrightarrow$ Employee

$\sigma_5 =$ Employee $\longrightarrow$ Integer

We shall take the following set of objects Θ as interpretation domain:

(i_0,nil), (i_1, <name: i_{16}, age:i_7 sex:i_8>),
(i_2, <name: i_{17}, age:i_9, sex:i_{10}>)
(i_3, <name: i_{18}, age:i_9, sex:i_8, salary: i_{11}>),
(i_4, <name: i_{19}, age:i_{13}, sex:i_{12}, salary:i_{11}>)
(i_5, {i_1, i_2}), (i_6, {i_3, i_4}), (i_7, 20), (i_9, 25), (i_{11}, 130000),
(i_{13}, 35), (i_8, "male"), (i_{10}, "varying"), (i_{12}, "female"),
(i_{14}, false), (i_{15}, true), (i_{16}, "Smith")
(i_{17}, "Blake"), (i_{18}, "Jones"), (i_{19}, "Nash")

Using definition 11 in the previous subsection, we can build the models of the type structures defined in Δ:

$M(\text{Person}) = \{i_0, i_1, i_2, i_3, i_4\}$

$M(\text{Persons}) = \{i_0, i_5, i_6\}$

$M(\text{Employee}) = \{i_0, i_3, i_4\}$

$M(\text{Employees}) = \{i_0, i_6\}$

$M(\text{Male}) = \{i_0, i_1, i_3\}$

$M(\text{"male"}) = \{i_0, i_8\}$

$M(\text{String}) = \{i_0, i_8, i_{10}, i_{12}, i_{16}, i_{17}, i_{18}, i_{19}\}$

$M(\text{Integer}) = \{i_0, i_7, i_9, i_{11}, i_{13}\}$

$M(\text{Boolean}) = \{i_0, i_{14}, i_{15}\}$

The model of the signature σ_1 is the set of all **partial** functions from $\{i_0, i_5, i_6\} \times \{i_0, i_1, i_2, i_3, i_4\}$ into $\{i_0, i_{14}, i_{15}\}$. Intuitively, the model of the signature σ_1 is the set of functions assigning a boolean object to some pairs (i,j) where i is (the identifier of) a set of person objects and j is (the identifier of) a person object.

We shall use this interpretation of signatures in the following subsection which introduces an ordering among signatures.

4.2.3. Partial order among signatures.

Definition 16: Partial order $\leq_m$

Let Δ be a schema and f and g two signatures over Δ. We say that f is smaller than g (or that *f refines g*) iff $M(f) \subseteq M(g)$ for all consistent set Δ. This ordering will be denoted by $\leq_m$. □

Looking at the schema of the previous example , we can see that the following inequalities hold:

$$\sigma_2 \leq_m \sigma_1 \qquad \text{and} \qquad \sigma_4 \leq_m \sigma_3$$

In fact, let Θ be any consistent set of objects and f be a partial function in $M(\sigma_2)$. f is a (partial) function from $M(\text{employees}) \times M(\text{employee})$ in $M(\text{Boolean})$. We have seen in subsection 4.1.3 that employees $\leq_{st}$ persons and employee $\leq_{st}$ person, and hence, $M(\text{employees}) \subseteq M(\text{persons})$ and $M(\text{employee}) \subseteq M(\text{person})$. So f is also a partial function from $M(\text{persons}) \times M(\text{person})$ in $M(\text{boolean})$, so f is in $M(\sigma_1)$. A similar proof can be constructed for the inequality $\sigma_4 \leq_m \sigma_3$.

Intuitively, $\sigma \leq_m \sigma'$ means that we can use a method of signature σ' "in place of" a method of signature σ. In the example above, we can apply a method of signature σ_1 to a set of employees and an employee because, employees are persons. This partial order models inheritance of methods, just as the ordering $\leq_{st}$ models inheritance of data structures. In the following section, we put data structures and methods together to define type systems and we use the ordering $\leq_{st}$ and $\leq_m$ to define inheritance of types. The following theorem gives an easy syntactical equivalence to the definition of the partial order $\leq_m$ among signatures.

Theorem 2

Let f and g be two signatures over a schema Δ. Then, f

$\leq_m$ g iff:

$$f = s_1 \times ... \times s_n \rightarrow s$$
$$and \quad g = s'_1 \times ... \times s'_n \rightarrow s'$$
$$and \quad s_k \leq_{st} s'_k \text{ for } k=1,2,...,n$$
$$and \quad s \leq_{st} s'. \square$$

Proof :

In order to clarify the proof, we assume, without loss of generality, that the methods signatures are of the form: $\sigma = s_1 \rightarrow s$, and $\sigma' = s'_1 \rightarrow s'$. Suppose that $\sigma \leq_m \sigma'$. Every partial function from $M(s_1)$ to $M(s)$ is then a partial function from $M(s'_1)$ to $M(s')$. So, we necessarily have $M(s_1) \subseteq M(s'_1)$ and $M(s) \subseteq M(s')$.

Conversely, if these two inclusions hold, then every partial function from $M(s_1)$ to $M(s)$ is clearly also a partial function from $M(s'_1)$ to $M(s')$. $\square$

In the part concerning methods, our definition differs from the "classical" definitions of data type theory [Bruce & Wegner 86], [Cardelli 84], [Albano & al 85]. In these settings, functional types may be constructed: the type $r \rightarrow s$ has as instances functions having r as domain and s as co-domain. The general rule of subtyping among functional types can be expressed as follows:

$$\text{if } r' \leq r \text{ and } s \leq s' \text{ then } r \rightarrow s \leq r' \rightarrow s'$$

This means that a function with domain r and codomain s can always be considered as a function from some smaller domain r' to some larger codomain s'. This is a necessary condition for the type system to be *safe*, that is, to guarantee that a run-time error will never be caused by a syntactically well-typed expression. If we had adopted this rule in our framework, the subtype relation would be inverted between the right-hand sides of the signatures in theorem 2, i.e., $s' \leq s$ instead of $s \geq s'$.

Our choice leads to a less restrictive type system, but we give up safety. There are three main reasons for such a choice. First, we want to be able to inherit an "add" method defined on sets. Suppose there are two types S and T such that $S \leq_{st} T$ then we have $\{S\} \leq_{st} \{T\}$. Let add_S be a method of signature $\{S\} \times S \rightarrow \{S\}$, and add_T be a method of signature $\{T\} \times T \rightarrow \{T\}$, then we want $add_S \leq_m add_T$, which is a necessary condition to have $\{S\} \leq \{T\}$ (see definition 18). Second, this model is intended to be a foundation for an object-oriented layer on top of C which itself is not type safe. Third, we shall implement run-time checking for the cases where static type checking is not sufficient.

4.3. Type systems

Definition 17: Type systems
A set of types Π is a *type system* iff

(i) the set of structures associated to Π is a schema

(ii) for all type $t \in \Pi$, and for all method $m \in$ Methods(t)[5], m is defined on struct(t). $\square$

---
[5] We recall that Methods(t) denotes the set of methods of the type t.

Now, given a type system Π, we must be able to compare two types t and t', with respect to their structures and to the methods they contain.

Definition 18: Subtyping
Let Π be a type system and t and t' two types of Π. We say that *t is a subtype of t'* and we note $t \leq t'$ iff

(i) struct(t) $\leq_{st}$ struct(t')

(ii) for all m $\in$ Methods(t), there exist m' $\in$ Methods(t') such that name(m) = name(m') and sign(m) $\leq_m$ sign(m'). $\square$

We illustrate this by the following example : Let Π be the type system of the example of section 4.2.2. where

$$Methods(Person) = \{(husband, \sigma_3)\}$$
$$Methods(Persons) = \{(parent, \sigma_1)\}$$
$$Methods(Employee) = \{(husband, \sigma_3), (salary, \sigma_5)\}$$
$$Methods(Employees) = \{(parent, \sigma_1),(manager,\sigma_2)\}$$
$$Methods(Male) = \{(hire, \sigma_4), (husband, \sigma_3)\}$$

In this type system, the following subtype relationships hold : employee $\leq$ person, male $\leq$ person and employees $\leq$ persons

4.4. Objects revisited

We shall now extend the definition of an object in order to encapsulate in the same structure data and operations.

Definition 19: Objects revisited

An *object* o is a triple (i, v, m) where i and v are as in Definition 2 and m is a set of methods. The first component of the signature of every method of m is a type structure whose interpretation contains o. $\square$

The set of methods of an object can be empty, and in this case, it will be manipulated through the methods of the type it possesses. This notion is useful in the following cases:

(i) When handling exceptions. For example, let us assume that we define in type "Employee" a method "increase salary" to compute the salary of an employee. Suppose that one of these employees is the CEO and that his salary has to be computed in different way than for regular employees. One could create a specific subtype of employee in order to override the "increase salary" method of type employee. This would be heavy and it is more natural to define a specific method for the CEO object.

(ii) "Exceptional" attribute handling (see section 4.1.2) As full encapsulation is preserved, the only way to access and/or modify an exceptional attribute of an object is via a method attached to the object.

(iii) Still another application is when representing the data model in terms of itself. This kind of self-representation is very frequent in object-oriented frameworks (the predefined classes "class" and

"metaclass" of Smalltalk 80 are a good example).
Types could be represented as objects belonging to a
predefined type "type" and "type methods" could
be easily defined attaching them to these objects. An
example of a type method for a type T is a customized method for instanciating instances of T.

5. Databases

In this section, we introduce the notion of database.
Informally, a database is a type system together with a
consistent set of objects representing the instances of the
types at a given moment.

Definition 20: Databases

A database is a tuple $(\Pi, \Theta, <_{db}, \text{ext}, \text{impl})$ where

(i) Π is a type system, and Δ is the associated schema,

(ii) Θ is a consistent set of objects,

(iii) $<_{db}$ is a strict partial order among Π,

(iv) ext is an interpretation of Δ in Θ.

(v) impl is a function assigning a function to every
method m of a type t.

Moreover, we impose that the following properties hold:

(1) $t <_{db} t'$ implies $t \leq t'$.

(2) If $t <_{db} t'$ and $t <_{db} t''$ then t' and t'' are comparable.

(3) $\Theta = \bigcup_{t \in \Pi} \text{ext}(t)$.

(4) $\text{ext}(t) \cap \text{ext}(t') = \varnothing$ if t and t' are not comparable.

(5) If t is a type of Π and m a method of t having signa-
ture $t \times ... \times s_n \rightarrow s$, then $\text{impl}(m)$ is a function
defined at least from $\text{ext}(t) \times ... \times \text{ext}(s_n)$ in $\text{ext}(s)$.
□

This definition deserves some comments. The extension
of a type is an interpretation but may not be a model.
Indeed, a model contains all the possible objects which
satisfy a given structure. For example, there may be two
types of structure "integer" (say age and weight) in a
data base. These types have the same model but a given
extension as defined by an user will not contain the same
objects. The $\leq$ ordering of definition 18 models the
notion of subtyping. That is, two types t and t' are comparable using $\leq$ if one *can be* a subtype of the other.
The ordering $<_{db}$ is the actual inheritance types hierarchy, as *defined* by the user. This ordering must satisfy
property (1), that is, the user can declare that t is a subtype of t' ($t <_{db} t'$) only if it is allowed by the model (t
$\leq$ t'). For example, the type system may contain the
types:

>   Age = (Integer, {+,-}) and
>   Weight = (Integer, {+,-})

with corresponding signatures for the methods + and -.
We have the inequalities (Age $\leq$ Weight) and (Weight

$\leq$ Age) but the user does not intend to consider an age
as a weight nor a weight as an age, and Age and Weight
will be incomparable for $<_{db}$. Property (2) says that we
do not allow multiple inheritance. This is a constraint we
introduced for the O_2 system because it is still an open
problem to decide whether multiple inheritance is a useful modelization tool. In any case, our semantics would
still be valid in the context of multiple inheritance. Property (3) says that Θ is the union of all type extensions.
There are no database objects not belonging to any type
extension. Property (4) says that an object o cannot
belong to the extension of two types t and t' if they are
incomparable for $<_{db}$. Consider the types Age and
Weight above. The object $(i_1, 1)$ belongs to the model of
Age and to the model of Weight, but if we allow this
object to belong to both ext(Age) and ext(Weight), we
violate the user intention which was to isolate these two
types.

6. Concluding Remarks

The main contribution of this paper is to propose a data
model for an object-oriented data base system. The
model includes the following features:

(i) Objects may have a tuple or set structure (or be
atomic). They form a directed graph in which cycles
may appear. Consistent sets of objects are used as
interpretation domains for type structures and
method signatures.

(ii) Types consist of a type structure and a set of
methods. Their structure may be recursively defined.
The interpretation of tuple-structured types is
unusual in the database world and follows the original
proposal of [Cardelli 84]. It allows to give a simple set
inclusion semantics to the partial order among type
structures ($\leq_{st}$). Methods are defined as a name
together with a signature and are interpreted as a
function. The interpretation of method signatures
allows again a simple set inclusion semantics for the
partial order among signatures ($\leq_m$). The subtyping
relationship is defined using the ordering $\leq_{st}$ and
$\leq_m$ Notice that although our database definition restrict inheritance to simple inheritance, our model
deals with multiple inheritance.

(iii) The $\leq_m$ relation differs from other proposals ([Car-
delli 84], [Bruce & Wegner 86]) in that it is less restrictive, but the type system is no longer safe (that
is, run-time errors may be caused by a syntactically
well-typed expression). This decision was mainly
motivated because of its increased flexibility and by
the fact that we are not building a new language,
but rather an object layer according to this model on
top of existing programming languages with unsafe
type systems, such as C and Lisp.

(iv) The notion of "database" is introduced. A database is a type system, together with a consistent set of objects (database instances) and a subtyping relationship satisfying some constraints.

We are currently working on some extensions of the model. The first one concerns object naming. Up to here, the only handle that a programmer has on a object is through the name of one of its types. So, to retrieve an object of the database, the programmer has to send a message to the extension of the type with some key as argument. Such a problem is introduced by persistency: in standard programming languages, we name objects using temporary variable names. Object names seem to be needed, and they have to be introduced in the model.

A second extension concerns the introduction of variables in the construction of types in order to model genericity (also called "parametric polymorphism") of types and methods. Genericity can be simulated with inheritance [Meyer 86], but in a heavy and non-intuitive way.

A third extension is to increase the modeling power of the model: a list constructor should be included in order to model ordered collections of data (it could be implemented as a recursive tuple type, but we would lose expressiveness). Finally, in this model, we made the simplifying assumption that the methods are not objects of the model. So methods have to be modeled as first order functions. It should be interesting to extend the model to treat methods as objects and to allow higher order methods.

Acknowledgements

Most of the ideas presented here were generated with F. Bancilhon. This paper also benefits from the careful reading of S. Abiteboul and our colleagues from *Altaïr*, in particular D. Excoffier. Thanks also go to P. Buneman, A. Borgida and D. DeWitt for the fruitful discussions we had on this model.

References

[Albano & al 85], "GALILEO: A Strongly Typed, Interactive Conceptual Language", A. Albano, L. Cardelli and R. Orsini, *ACM TODS, Vol 10 No. 2, March 85*.

[Andrews & Harris 87], "Combining Language and Database Advances in an Object-oriented Development Environment", T. Andrews and C. Harris, *Proc. OOPSLA, 1987.*

[Bancilhon and Khoshafian 86], "A Calculus for Complex Objects", F. Bancilhon, S. Khoshafian, *ACM PODS Conference, 1986*

[Bancilhon & al 87b], "The O_2 Object Manager Architecture", F. Bancilhon, V. Benzaken, C. Delobel, F. Velez, *Altaïr Technical Report,14/87, Nov, 87.*

[Banerjee & al 87], "Data Model Issues for Object-Oriented Applications", J. Banerjee & al., ACM TOOIS, Vol 5, No 1, Jan 1987.

[Bruce & Wegner 86], "An Algebraic Model of Subtypes in Object-Oriented Languages", K., B. Bruce, P. Wegner, *SIGPLAN notices V21 #40, October 86.*

[Cardelli 84], "A Semantics of Multiple Inheritance", L. Cardelli, *in Semantics of Data Types, Lecture notes in Computer Science, Vol 173 pp. 51-67, Springer Verlag, 84*

[Copeland & Maier 84], "Making Smalltalk a Database System", G. Copeland and D. Maier, *ACM-SIGMOD, 1984.*

[Copeland and Khoshafian 86], G. Copeland and S. Khoshafian, "Object Identity", *OOPSLA 86, Portland, Oregon, Sept 86.*

[Goldberg and Robson 83], "Smalltalk 80: The Language and its Implementation", A. Goldberg, D. Robson, *Addison-Wesley, Reading, Mass., 83*

[Kuper and Vardi 84], "A new Approach to Database Logic", G. M. Kuper, M. Y. Vardi, *ACM PODS Conference, Waterloo, Canada, 84*

[Meyer 86], "Genericity versus inheritance", B. Meyer, *OOPSLA 86, Portland, Sept 86.*

[Nixon & al 87], "Implementation of a Compiler for a Semantic Data Model: Experience with Taxis", B. Nixon et al, *ACM SIGMOD 1987.*

[Zdonik 84], "Object Management System Concepts,", S. Zdonik, *Proc. ACM SIGOA on Office Systems, Toronto, 1984.*

Chapter 4

Implementation

Introduction

This chapter covers implementation techniques for object-oriented databases. Several of the papers we include cover the implementation of systems that do not pass the conditions of the threshold model. We include them because the techniques they set forth are applicable to OODB implementation.

As we mentioned in *Fundamentals of Object-Oriented Databases* in this volume, most object-oriented database systems are split into two major subsystems, an *interpreter* running on top of a *storage manager*. The storage manager is typically concerned with the placement of objects in secondary storage, movement of data between secondary storage and main memory, creation of new objects, recovery, concurrency control, and sometimes indexing and authorization. The interpreter provides the operational semantics of the data model; it understands the details of the data model, enforces encapsulation of objects, and executes methods. The interpreter calls the storage manager for physical data access and manipulation. The Encore/Observer system [HZ87] shows perhaps the purest example of this architecture of systems represented in the papers here.

The interpreter-storage manager architecture is not the only one that has been proposed to provide persistent objects. Thatte [Th86] describes a recoverable virtual memory as a layer in a persistent object system. Object semantics are provided not in the virtual-memory layer, but rather in layers above it. Thatte also points out a useful distinction between *persistence* and *resilience* of objects. Persistence in his sense means only that an object can live beyond the scope of the process that created it. Resilience goes further, in that the object can survive process and system failure. Resilience is sometimes called *permanence*. However, the term *persistent* in the literature sometimes has Thatte's meaning and sometimes has a meaning more like Thatte's notion of persistence plus resilience.

A chief architectural question in designing an OODBMS is how much semantics to put in the storage manager. That is, how much does the storage manager know about the data model of the database? The Observer storage manager has a primitive view of objects as uninterpreted blocks of data with identifiers. The Loom [KK83] and GemStone [MS87] storage managers understand the internal structure of objects, and something about object classes. Emerald's [JL+88] storage-management functions even understand something about the execution behavior of objects, being able to move activation records. Low semantics in the storage manager certainly simplifies implementation of that component, but also means that the storage manager can support multiple data models, as it internalizes the semantics of none. However, without understanding interobject references, the storage manager cannot manage garbage collection, index maintenance, or constraint enforcement. Most storage managers, even if they understand some of the data model, only provide operations for structural

237

access. A few, such as Trellis/Owl's [OBS86] persistent storage, can evaluate simple queries.

An engineering question related to the storage manager is whether to custom build one or to use an existing one. The IRIS [LD+87] project has used a relational storage subsystem as the storage manager. The question is whether the design decisions and tuning of an existing system will match the access patterns for an OODB.

If the storage manager does understand the structure of objects, then there are decisions regarding how each object is represented. The most straightforward representation is to have the state of an object stored contiguously, but (possibly) apart from the state of component objects, which is the strategy used by POMS [CA+84]. The Postgres [Sto87] storage system uses basically this approach, with each tuple stored contiguously. However, when there are multiple versions of a tuple, not all of them are stored in their entirety. Some versions are stored as "deltas" (differences) from previous versions, and are reconstituted as needed.

Alternatively, object states can be subdivided, perhaps on the basis of the types to which they belong, or at an even finer granularity, as in the storage structures for the ADAPLEX language [ChD+82]. Copeland and Khoshafian [CK85] investigate some of the performance tradeoffs between storing objects in composed form versus decomposing them to the level of fields and storing all instances of a given field together. Breaking down objects to the field level means fewer pages have to be touched when objects on that field are searched. Retrieving all the fields of a single object, however, is much more expensive. Representing an object in both a decomposed and a composed fashion is possible, but then additional overhead is imposed on update.

Emerald goes a step further in the direction of more composition, letting private subobjects (those that have no external references to them) of objects be represented as part of the superobject. The layout of such groupings of objects is described by *templates*.

Another case to cope with is objects whose local states are longer than a page, such as large bitmaps or long arrays. Systems that support large objects generally do not try to represent their states contiguously in secondary storage. Instead, they build a tree structure indexed on byte or array position to break up the state into chunks, and permit partial retrieval of the state. Exodus [CaD+88] supports such a scheme for large byte strings, using a clever technique for node keys that permits insertions into byte strings to be done inexpensively. GemStone supports large arrays and also large sets (indexed on object identifier).

Related to the representation of individual objects is how objects or object fragments are clustered and placed on disk. The main reason for clustering is to increase the likelihood that when an object is read into main memory, objects that it references or that are likely to be used with it are loaded at the same time or can be gotten quickly, by virtue of being on the same page (or other unit of physical transfer) or in a nearby cylinder. The chief problem is that not every object can be clustered with the objects it references, because those objects can be referenced from other places as well. A design decision is how automatic or manual such clustering should be. The CACTIS [HK] system gathers statistics on traversals between objects, and attempts to shift objects around such that objects used together are stored together. GemStone allows a user to specify that objects should be reclustered in a breadth- or depth-first manner. Not a lot is known about optimal static clustering strategies for objects. Stamos [Sta84] experimented with various kinds of object clustering in LOOM. The ADAPLEX storage system breaks objects into fragments, one per type in which the object participates. These fragments can be further partitioned. ADAPLEX provides for the fragments to be grouped by object or by type. Observer provides a visible unit of clustering, the *segment*, into which users and the program place objects. When one object in a segment is retrieved, the whole segment is loaded. GemStone also provides segments for grouping objects. One difference between Observer and GemStone is that in Observer, multiple copies of the same object can go into different segments, and segments may contain other segments. In GemStone, the segments form a flat partition of object space.

Another decision to face is how to implement object identifiers. They can be a logical or a physical address, as in LOOM or POMS. The problem with using addresses is that objects become pinned by their references, and cannot be moved easily—for example, for clustering or changing the size of an object. The alternative is an *object table* to translate references to object IDs into addresses. The advantage of having references go through an object table is that there is only one address reference to the state of the object, so that state is moved easily. The disadvantage is that the object table introduces a level of indirection, which means that the object reference costs more to follow. Also, the object table is a shared resource that can become a hot spot in concurrency control or recovery.

The ADAPLEX and Emerald storage systems combine the two approaches. In ADAPLEX, references to entities (objects) always use an *entity identifier*, which is mapped through the *entity directory*. However, a reference may also incorporate a physical address (forming a *hybrid pointer*). The physical address is treated as a hint about where the state of an object is stored. So that a hint can be checked, the state of an object must contain the entity identifier. Emerald supports two forms of object reference: one that gives a direct address, and one that maps through an object descriptor. (The main use of the indirection in Emerald is to reference objects that reside on other machines.)

The form of object references in main memory does not need to be the same as that used on disk. Disk-based references can be translated into a different format for objects in memory. This operation has the sobriquet of *pointer swizzling* (possibly bestowed by the implementors of Tektronix Smalltalk). LOOM swizzles disk references into short object identifiers, which are then mapped through a *resident object table* on dereferencing. POMS swizzles object IDs into main memory addresses. The advantage to swizzling pointers is that the mapping from object reference to memory address is done just once—subsequent accesses can be as fast as indirect addressing on the supporting hardware architecture. Swizzling presents some difficulties. One such problem is when to do the translation. If all the references in an object state are translated on its entry into memory, much of that work may be wasted if those references are never accessed. Also, some references might be to objects not in memory. (LOOM solves the latter problem by the use of a special *lambda* value to indicate reference to a nonresident object.) The alternative is to swizzle references on first access, which is what POMS does. Without hardware support, however, time is consumed on every object reference, checking in what form the reference is. A second problem is movement of objects back to disk if main memory becomes filled. Direct addresses effectively pin objects in main memory. POMS writes all objects back to disk when memory is filled. LOOM solves the problem by converting a memory object into a *leaf*, which contains only a small amount of the state of the object (enough to allow it to be expanded again).

Maintaining a hash table from object identifiers to memory addresses is an alternative to swizzling. Hashing is more expensive than is following a direct memory address, but generally is not as expensive as translation through an object table.

A final question related to the movement of objects into memory is whether they remain in pages, or are copied out of pages and the pages re-leased. Stamos [Sta84] compares the two strategies.

The systems covered here represent a variety of approaches to removing items from the database. A basic choice is whether to support explicit deletion. If deletion is not explicit, the system must do garbage collection, as in Emerald, to reclaim the space for objects that are no longer referenced. If deletion is allowed, then the system must deal with references to the deleted objects. In Observer, references to deleted objects will lead to *tombstones*, which indicate that the desired object has "died." Other systems, such as the ADAPLEX storage system and the Relationship–Entity–Datum model [Ca83], track all references to an entity, and remove those references when the referenced entity is deleted. Postgres actually leaves deleted tuples, but timestamps them with a deletion time after which they are not considered valid.

OODBMSs show a wider variety of mechanisms for atomicity of transactions and recovery than is employed in commercial systems. Most current commercial systems use some variety of *write-ahead logging* (WAL) to deal with transaction rollbacks and recovery. With WAL, updates to data items are entered into a log (usually both old and new versions of the item), and the log entries for a transaction must be written to disk before the transaction commits. WAL is advantageous in transaction-processing systems, because the amount of disk I/O during the critical section of commit processing can be reduced to one disk write. (Some schemes can commit multiple transactions with one write.) However, many of the applications anticipated for OODBs do not have requirements for high transaction-throughput rates. Also, transactions may exhibit behavior that causes problems with WAL, such as updating the same data item multiple times. (See Maier [Ma89] for further discussion of recovery tradeoffs in OODBs.) For these reasons, or for simplicity of implementation, many OODBMSs have used other recovery mechanisms.

POMS uses *shadowing*, in which modified objects are written to shadow pages. At commit-time, shadow pages atomically replace their originals. GemStone also uses shadowing. Thatte's persistent virtual-memory uses a similar scheme, with virtual-memory pages being represented by a pair of pages on disk, which are written alternately. Thatte's method also introduces *checkpoints*, at which it is ensured that a current copy of every virtual-memory page is forced to disk. Postgres uses its tuple timestamping mechanism for recovery. Old tuple values are never overwritten in the database, but rather are marked as out of date, after which a new version is written. There is no need to log old values of changed tuples. An added advantage of this mechanism is that it supports queries over past states of the database. The Postgres paper contains a performance analysis of its scheme versus that of WAL.

There is not the variety of concurrency control schemes in OODBMSs that is seen for recovery mechanisms. Most OODBMSs use some form of locking. The rest use optimistic protocols, possibly handling conflicts at commit-time by forking alternative versions of objects, rather than aborting a transaction [EE+87]. Observer uses locking, but provides a number of novel lock modes. One is *notify* locks, whereby a session can learn of accesses to data items by other sessions. Notify locks make the database an active entity, capable of initiating communication with an application process. Most database systems are passive, responding only to direct calls. Notify locks are useful when one application actually makes use of multiple database sessions, say one per window, and these sessions want to synchronize their view of the data.

The last topic we cover is locus of execution and data. Does the interpreter have buffers for the objects it is using, or does the storage manager hold all object states? Commonly, there is one interpreter process for every user session, but just one storage manager process that all share. Having an interpreter buffer its own objects cuts down on the interprocess calls to the storage manager. However, it also means that the same data may be in memory multiple times, in different interpreter processes. In a workstation–server environment, the interpreter processes can be moved onto workstations, while only the storage manager remains on the central server. Buffering then becomes highly desirable, to reduce remote procedure-call traffic. A study by Rubenstein, Kubicar, and Cattell [RKC87] indicates that buffering at the workstation provides tremendous performance enhancement.

With the interpreter on the workstation, a problem arises in evaluating queries over large collections. If there is no index to help, then all the objects in the collection need to be transferred from the server to the workstation for processing. This transfer imposes a large penalty when the answer to the query is actually small. The O_2 [Ba+86] system provides interpreters on both the workstation and the server, and selection by the programmer of where to execute a method. Such a technique requires that updates made by each interpreter be propagated to the other.

Emerald deals with the distribution of execution through a network of processing nodes of roughly equal power (no client-versus-server distinction is made). It copes with problems such as getting the arguments of a message to the same place as a receiver, and the distribution of methods along with the objects that use them.

References

[Ba+86]   F. Bancilhon, et al. The Design and Implementation of O_2, an Object-Oriented Database System. *Proceedings of the 2nd International Workshop on Object-Oriented Databases*. K. Dittrich, ed. Springer-Verlag Lecture Notes in Computer Science 334, September 1988.

[Ca83]   R.G.G. Cattell. *Design and Implementation of a Relationship–Entity–Datum Model*. Xerox CSL Report 83-4, May 1983.

•[CA+84]   W.P. Cockshot, M.P. Atkinson, K.J. Chisholm, P.J. Bailey, and R. Morrison. Persistent Object Management System. *Software—Practice and Experience 14*, 14(1), January 1984.

•[CaD+88]   M.J. Carey, D.J. DeWitt, G. Graefe, D.M. Haight, J.E. Richardson, D.T. Schuh, E.J. Shekita, and S.L. Vandenberg. The EXODUS Extensible DBMS Project: an Overview. *University of Wisconsin at Madison, Computer Sciences Technical Report* 808, November 1988.

•[ChD+82]   A. Chan, A. Danberg, S. Fox, W.-T. Lin, A. Nori, and D. Ries. Storage and Access Structures to Support a Semantic Data Model. *Proceedings of the VIII International Conference on Very Large Databases*, Mexico City, September, 1982. Morgan Kaufmann Publishers, San Mateo, CA.

[CK85]   G. Copeland and S.N. Khoshafian. A Decomposition Storage Model. *Proceedings of the ACM SIGMOD International Conference on Management of Data*, Austin, TX, May 1985.

[EE+87]   D. Ecklund, E. Ecklund, B. Eifrig, and F. Tonge. DVSS: A Distributed Version Storage Server for CAD Applications. *Proceedings of the XII International Conference on Very Large Databases*, Brighton, England, September

1987. Morgan Kaufmann Publishers, San Mateo, CA.

[HK]   S. Hudson and R. King. CACTIS: A Self-Adaptive, Concurrent Implementation of an Object-Oriented Database Management System. *ACM Transactions on Database Systems* (in press).

•[HZ87]   M.F. Hornick and S.B. Zdonik. A Shared, Segmented Memory System for an Object-Oriented Database. *ACM Transactions on Office Information Systems*, 5:1, 1987.

•[JL+88]   E. Juhl, H. Levy, N. Hutchinson, and A. Black. Fine-Grained Mobility in the Emerald System. *ACM Transactions on Computer Systems*, 6(1):109–133, February 1988.

•[KK83]   T. Kaehler and G. Krasner. LOOM: Large Object-Oriented Memory for Smalltalk-80 Systems. In *Smalltalk-80: Bits of History, Words of Advice*. G. Krasner, ed. Addison-Wesley, Reading, MA, 1983.

[LD+87]   P. Lyngbaek, N. Derrett, D.H. Fishman, W. Kent, and T.A. Ryan. Design and Implementation of the IRIS Object Manager. *Proceedings of the Workshop on Persistent Object Systems: Their Design, Implementation and Use*, Appin, Scotland, August, 1987. Also HP Labs Technical Report STL-86-17, December 1986.

[Ma89]   D. Maier. Making Database Systems Fast Enough for CAD Applications. W. Kim and F. Lochovsky, eds. In *Object-Oriented Concepts, Applications and Databases*, ACM Press, New York, 1989.

•[MS87]   D. Maier and J. Stein. Development and Implementation of an Object-Oriented DBMS. B.D. Shriver and P. Wegner, eds. In *Research Directions in Object-Oriented Programming*, MIT Press, Cambridge, MA, 1987.

[OBS86]   P. O'Brien, B. Bullis, and C. Shaffert. Persistent and Shared Objects in Trellis/Owl. U. Dayal and K. Dittrich, ed. In *Proceedings of the International Workshop on Object-Oriented Databases*, Pacific Grove, CA, September 1986.

[RKC87]   W.B. Rubenstein, M.S. Kubicar, and R.G.G. Cattell. Benchmarking Simple Database Operations. *Proceedings of the ACM SIGMOD International Conference on Management of Data*, San Francisco, CA, May 1987.

[Sta84]   J.W. Stamos. Grouping Objects to Enhance Performance of a Paged Virtual Memory. *ACM Transactions on Computer Systems*, 1984.

•[Sto87]   M. Stonebraker. The Design of the POSTGRES Storage System. *Proceedings of the XIII International Conference on Very Large Databases*, Brighton, England, September 1987. Morgan Kaufmann Publishers, San Mateo, CA.

•[Th86]   S. Thatte. Persistent Memory: Merging AI-knowledge and Databases. *Texas Instruments Engineering Journal*, January–February, 151–159, 1986.

• indicates article included in this volume

Persistent Memory:
Merging AI-knowledge and Databases

As symbolic computing and artificial intelligence (AI) techniques move from research laboratories to industry, computer-based systems using these techniques to improve professional productivity are expected to represent a major use of computers in the late 1980's and 1990's. Computer-aided design (CAD) systems, knowledge-based expert systems, software development workstations, professional personal computers, engineering "workbenches," etc., will be the tools of professional productivity. Such tools will benefit from the next-generation symbolic computers, which will have to manipulate large knowledge/databases and support applications that draw on the strengths of AI and database technologies.

Many future applications will depend on a successful "marriage" of AI-knowledge and database technologies because significant improvements in productivity and functionality of information systems require rich knowledge representation techniques being proposed for knowledge-based and reasoning systems. At the same time, practical applications of the same AI technology require support from database technology in terms of long-term, reliable storage of information that can be efficiently stored, accessed, and easily shared among multiple users. The goals of information systems based on database technology have much in common with those of knowledge representation techniques in AI. Both attempt to provide tools for the representation of real-world knowledge such as concept definition,

assumptions, constraints, and event descriptions[1]. In fact, AI technology may offer solutions to complex data management problems in such applications as VLSI and VHSIC design.

In AI, a representation of knowledge is a combination of data structures and interpretive procedures that, if used in the right way in a program, will lead to a "knowledgeable" behavior[2]. The goals of AI systems can be described in terms of cognitive tasks like recognizing objects, answering questions, and manipulating robotic devices. A number of different knowledge representation schemes, such as state-space representation, logic, procedural representation, semantic nets, production sytems, and frames, have been developed by the knowledge representation community. The choice of the knowledge representation scheme very much depends on the application requirements. No matter which scheme is used, at some sufficiently low level of representation, the knowledge is represented by memory objects interconnected by pointers. These objects exhibit a structure, which is defined by the interconnection graph of pointers connecting the objects. The structure of objects created and manipulated by symbolic/AI applications is usually very rich and complex. Moreover, both the information in objects, as well as the structure of objects, undergo rapid changes. In contrast to knowledge bases, in the conventional database world, the structure of objects (defined by the database schema) changes only occasionally.

Symbolic computers, such as the TI Explorer™, Symbolics 3670, and Xerox 1108, are perhaps the best tools available today to support rich knowledge representation and inference techniques. These computers are single-user machines with powerful interactive

program development environments for symbolic computing. In these computers, all processes and objects share a single virtual address space[3]. Sharing of objects via pointer structures allows efficient and flexible representation of knowledge. The representation is also processed most efficiently by the machine because it is defined by the machine architecture, and hence is directly interpreted by hardware or microcode. Powerful object-oriented abstraction techniques and the treatment of procedural objects as "data"[4] further aid in knowledge representation. The pointers to objects serve as names that can be passed as procedure parameters, returned as procedure results and stored in other objects as components. A high proportion of data is pointers to other data and structures. This storage model requires automatically garbage collected memory — a feature supported by LISP machines.

In the future, as the users of such machines develop large-scale, knowledge-based applications, they are expected to encounter major problems arising out of storage* management problems in supporting large and complex knowledge/databases. The problems can be primarily attributed to the dichotomy in which today's computers, including the state-of-the-art symbolic computers, manage storage along two entirely different organizations. These organizations are called the computational storage and the long-term storage†.

The processor can create and manipulate complex structures of objects in an efficient fashion in the computational storage, which is implemented as a virtual memory. These objects that make a knowledge base modeling a real world

---

*The word *storage* is used in a broad sense to encompass virtual memory, file systems and databases.

†Our terminology of computational storage and long-term storage is borrowed from that of Denning[5].

Satish Thatte

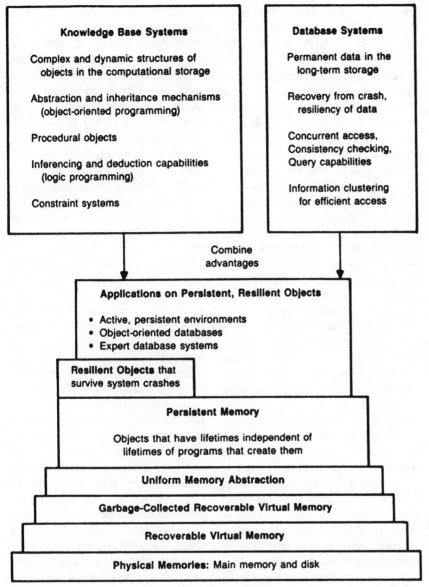

Figure 1. Our Approach to Persistent Memory

tation schemes. For example, procedural objects are very difficult to support in a file system or database without loss of efficiency. Also, the structure of a directory system or database schema is too simple and static to support the complex and dynamic structures of objects required for expert database systems.

The storage dichotomy puts a great burden on programmers of managing two entirely different storage models. The programmer has to cope with two disparate worlds of programming languages and data management, and transfer information to the computational storage for its manipulation and to the long-term storage for its long-term retention. This translation effort could be very substantial as the representations of information in these two worlds are very different from each other. This has an adverse effect on the programmer's productivity. Atkinson has reported that typically 30% of the total system code is required to map and transfer data between the computational and long-term storages in large data-intensive applications[6]. In addition, the storage dichotomy also adversely affects performance due to the space and time overhead of translating and transferring information between two very different storage organizations. The storage dichotomy is also an obstacle to programming generality and modularity as it increases potential types of interfaces among programs[7]. It also gives rise to much duplication of effort in operating system and database designs[8].

A persistent memory system eliminates the distinction between the computational and long-term storages and combines their advantages. Our approach to persistent memory is based on a uniform memory abstraction, which eliminates the distinction between transient and persistent objects, and therefore, allows the same set of powerful and flexible operations on transient and persistent objects from a single programming language, such as LISP or PROLOG. A persistent memory defines

domain may exist independently of programs which act on it. Therefore, they need to persist beyond the lifetimes* of the programs that create them. Unfortunately, objects in a knowledge base in the computational storage do neither exist beyond the lifetimes of the programs that create them, nor do they survive a system shutdown or crash.

Therefore, they are called short-lived or transient objects.

To store an object beyond the lifetime of the program that creates it, i.e., to make it persistent, it must first be mapped into a representation expected by the long-term storage, i.e., by a file system or an external database and then transferred to it. However, the types of objects in the long-term storage (essentially files, directories, relations, etc.) are too restrictive to efficiently support the rich variety of knowledge represen-

*The lifetime of a program indicates the time period in which the program is active, i.e., the time period from the invocation of the program to its termination.

a storage system architecture to support applications that combine the strengths of AI and database technologies. These applications, which include advanced file systems, active environments, and object-oriented databases, are expected to be implemented with greater ease, flexibility, and performance on persistent memory when compared to today's machines.

Critique of Existing Approaches to Persistent Memory

The current approach, taken by many researchers to facilitate knowledge-based applications, is based on connecting a symbolic comptuer to a database machine[9]. This approach is not based on persistent memory, as it neither addresses the storage dichotomy issues nor deals with the lifetime or interchangeability of procedure and data issues. There will be a mismatch between the data model requirements of symbolic/AI applications and the rigid data models supported by database machines. Therefore, the approach appears to be inadequate for large-scale knowledge-based applications. These reservations are shared by other researchers[10].

The persistent memory approach is based on a fundamentally different foundation. The literature on persistent* memory dates back to 1962,. when Kilburn proposed single-level storage, in which all programs and data are named in a single context[11]. Saltzer proposed a direct-access storage architecture, where there is only a single context to bind and interpret all objects[12]. Traiger proposed mapping databases into virtual address space[13]. It seems that simple data modeling requirements of the FORTRAN and COBOL worlds discouraged productization of these proposals because they are much more difficult to implement than the conventional virtual memory and database systems. We strongly believe that these proposals must be revived and adapted to the needs of knowledge-based symbolic computing if

we are to support their demanding requirements of data modeling and long-term storage of objects with rich types and structures.

The MIT MULTICS system[14] and the IBM System/38[15] have attempted to reduce the storage dichotomy. However, both have major shortcomings for symbolic computing; unlike LISP machines, each process has its own address space. All persistent information is in files. A file mapped into the address space of a process cannot hold a machine pointer to a file mapped in the address space of a different process. Thus, sharing of information among different processes is more difficult than with LISP machines. Furthermore, there is no automatic garbage collection, which is essential for supporting symbolic languages.

Recently, many researchers[16,17,18] have proposed implementing persistent objects on top of a file system provided by the host operating system. Though persistent and transient objects still reside in two separate storage organizations, persistent objects can be of any general type, such as number, vector, array, record, or list and can be manipulated with a common programming language such as Algol or LISP. However, there is a large overhead to access persistent objects because their pointers must be dereferenced by software, taking several machine cycles. In spite of their shortcomings, these recent approaches represent a step in the right direction, and our approach follows their spirit.

Our Approach to Persistent Memory

Our approach to the problem is based on eliminating the distinction between the computational and long-term storages and on combining their advantages. This is to be accomplished by means of a persistent memory system that allows complex and dynamic structures of objects to be reliably retained in virtual memory itself, for long periods of time, without resorting to a file system or a database

management system. Our implementation of the persistant memory system assures that all objects, both transient and persistent, can be manipulated with equal ease, flexiblity, and efficiency, independent of the types† and lifetimes‡, by means of adequate support in the architecture of the storage system itself.

Our approach to persistent memory is illustrated in Figure 1. Successively more powerful abstractions are created on top of the physical memory resources. The major contribution of this paper is a recovery scheme at the level of virtual memory itself, i.e., a recoverable virtual memory. A recoverable virtual memory is essential because no separate file system is assumed for the purpose of recovering permanent data. The recoverable virtual memory is based on an efficient checkpointing technique. The first layer of abstraction is a recoverable virtual memory. A garbage collector runs on top of it to reclaim space in inaccessible or garbage objects. Discussion on garbage collection is outside the scope of this paper. A good treatment can be found in McEntee[19].

A uniform memory abstraction is built on top of a garbage-collected recoverable virtual memory. In this abstraction, an object persists as long as it can be prevented from being garbage collected. The abstraction is implemented on a single, large virtual address space to support large knowledge-based applications. The persistent memory is based on the uniform memory abstraction. The concept of persistent memory, however, does not depend on the address space size.

---

*In the literature, terms such as permanent, stable, direct-access, or single-level storage are also used.

†The type of an object represents the generic class of the object. Different commonly used object types are integer, boolean, floating-point number, array, vector, procedure, relation, file, etc. For a given object type, there are usually several instances of the type in storage.

‡ The lifetime of an object indicates the time interval from the time it was created to the time it became inaccessible or garbage.

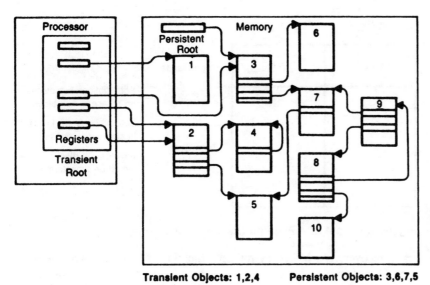

Transient Objects: 1,2,4   Persistent Objects: 3,6,7,5

Garbage Objects: 8,9,10

Figure 2. Uniform Memory Abstraction

Persistent objects created after the last checkpoint will not survive a system crash. Similarly, the checkpointed state will not reflect changes made to persistent objects after the checkpoint but before the crash. Resilient objects not only can survive beyond the lifetimes of programs that create them, but also survive crashes. Thus, resilience is a stronger property than persistence. Not all applications require resilient objects. A persistent memory system can support resilient objects with the help of a transaction* management package that keeps undo and redo logs to advance the state of the machine beyond the last checkpoint[21,22]. A detailed discussion of resilient objects is outside the scope of this paper; the details can be found in Thatte[21]. Various applications that combine the advantages of knowledge-based systems and database systems can be built on top of persistent or resilient objects.

Uniform Memory Abstraction

As shown in Figure 2, in the uniform memory abstraction a processor views memory as a set of variable-sized blocks

or objects interconnected by pointers. Pointers are typically implemented as virtual addresses. The abstraction provides an appropriate storage model for symbolic computing. The abstraction has the notion of persistent root, which is a distinguished object located at a fixed virtual address and disk location. All objects that are in the transitive closure of the persistent root, i.e., reachable from the persistent root by following pointers, are persistent. The persistent root survives system shutdowns or crashes. Typically, the persistent root may contain a pointer to a table that points to other tables or structures of persistent objects and so on. Thus, the persistent root anchors all persistent objects.

The persistence attribute of an object depends solely on whether that object can be prevented from being garbage collected even after the program that created it has terminated; this can be easily arranged by making that object a member of the set of objects in the transitive closure of the persistent root. Persistence based solely on the persistent root rather than the properties of the storage medium allows a complete separation of the persistence attribute of an object from its type or relationship with

other objects. Numbers, characters, lists, procedures, environments, etc., can be persistent objects while they exist in virtual memory. Therefore, an invocation of a procedure as a persistent object is as easy and efficient as its invocation as a transient object. In fact, from the machine point of view, transient and persistent objects are indistinguishable. From the user point of view, there is no need to treat transient and persistent objects differently; all the user needs to know is that to make an object persistent, it has to be in the transitive closure of the persistent root.

The processor contains a number of "registers."† The processor can access a memory object, i.e., read and write its individual words, if any of its registers holds a pointer to the object. These registers define the transient root of the memory system. They do not survive a system shutdown or crash. All objects that are in the transitive closure of the transient root, but not in the transitive closure of the persistent root, are called transient. All the remaining objects are garbage and are reclaimed by a garbage collector. Objects 1, 2, and 4 are transient; objects 3, 5, 6, and 7 are persistent; and objects 8, 9, and 10 are garbage.

Recoverable Virtual Memory

The most challenging problem in implementing persistent memory is how to maintain object consistency in the presence of system crashes. In fact, at least one project (Intel iMAX-432 object filing system) decided to live with the storage dichotomy due to a lack of crash recovery schemes[23]. Recovery becomes even more challenging in memory systems of symbolic computers: a page may contain multiple objects, and an object may span multiple pages. An object can point to any other object, and other objects can hold pointers to it.

---

*The notion of transactions is due to Eswaran, et al[20].

---

† The word *register* is used in a generic sense; it may be a hardware register or a scratch-pad memory in the processor.

Writing a single object to disk cannot maintain object consistency with respect to other objects unless the entire system state is captured on disk.

Failures dealt with by a recovery scheme can be classified as system crashes and disk crashes. A system crash can occur due to power failure, hardware failure, or software error. It is signalled by a power failure interrupt or hardware checking circuits or software error handling routines when they cannot handle a software error. It is assumed that the time interval between the system state corruption by a crash and the actual crash detection is quite small. Therefore, the probability of taking a checkpoint in this interval is also negligibly small. This assumption and its implementation are necessary to ensure that a checkpoint is not taken when the system has already reached a corrupted state. The rate of system crashes in a single-user machine is expected to be a few crashes per month, and the recovery time of several minutes is acceptable, assuming no permanent hardware failures. The recovery scheme for system crashes is described first, followed by the treatment of disk crashes.

Our recovery scheme is inspired from the study of recovery schemes known in the conventional database community[24,25]. However, the key difference between our recovery scheme and database recovery schemes is that our scheme is at the level of virtual memory itself. To our knowledge, no existing computers have a recovery capability at this level. Our recovery scheme is based on an efficient checkpointing technique that captures the entire system state and stores it on disk. Changes in the memory system following the last checkpoint are incrementally accumulated on disk in sibling pages. The correct sibling to be fetched on a page fault and the disk block on which it is to be written are identified by means of timestamps. The scheme keeps the entire machine state valid within the last few minutes on disk. After a system

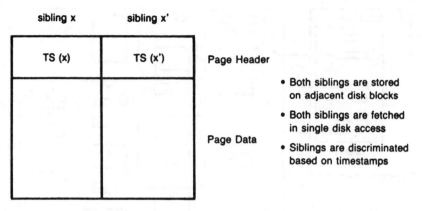

Figure 3. Layout of a Page on Disk in Sibling Form

- Both siblings are stored on adjacent disk blocks
- Both siblings are fetched in single disk access
- Siblings are discriminated based on timestamps

crash, recovery is achieved by rolling back the system state to the last checkpointed state. The recovery scheme is application-independent and user-transparent. For lack of space, the paper presents only the high-level salient features of the recovery scheme. Details can be found in Thatte[26].

Page and Timestamp Management
A virtual page is materialized on disk in either sibling or singleton form. In sibling form, two adjacent disk blocks are allocated to a virtual page. In singleton form, a single disk block is allocated. A page is materialized in sibling form if it is expected to contain data that is likely to be modified. To reduce the disk space requirement, a page is materialized in singleton form if it is unlikely to be modified in the future (for example, a page containing instructions). However, as in a conventional virtual memory system, a virtual page occupies only a single page frame when resident in main memory.

When a page is written to disk, it is stamped with the time of the disk write operation. The page header is a convenient place to record the timestamp. Timestamps survive system crashes because they are written to disk along with pages. Timestamps are derived from a timer that runs reliably even in the presence of system shutdowns and crashes. The granularity of timestamps need only be moderately smaller than

the time for a disk write operation because pages cannot be written faster than the disk write speed. With a 10 milliseconds granularity, a 64-bit timer can generate unique timestamps for over 5.8 billion years! Therefore, a 64-bit timestamp field in page headers is more than adequate.

When a page is materialized in sibling form, its siblings are initialized on disk with timestamps of -1 and -2, indicating that both are yet to be written*. When a page is materialized in singleton form, it is initialized on disk with timestamp of -1. All disk blocks that are modified since their initial materialization on disk will have unique timestamps within a machine.

Figure 3 shows a virtual page in sibling form. The siblings are denoted as x and x'. $TS(x)$ and $TS(x')$ denote the timestamps of x and x', respectively. As will soon become clear, siblings x and x' may exchange their roles when they are written to disk. A singleton page is denoted as s and its timestamp as $TS(s)$. The time of the last checkpoint operation is denoted as T_{chk}. It is stored in a reliable fashion at a known disk location.

For a singleton page s, if $TS(s) < T_{chk}$, then s belongs to the checkpointed state; if $T_{chk} < TS(s)$, s is outside the checkpointed state. For sibling

---

*This initialization scheme is not unique. Other schemes are possible.

pages x and x', if $TS(x) < TS(x') < T_{chk}$ or $TS(x') < TS(x) < T_{chk}$, the sibling with the smaller timestamp contains outdated information, and the sibling with the larger timestamp belongs to the checkpointed state; if $TS(x) < T_{chk} < TS(x')$ or $TS(x') < T_{chk} < TS(x)$, the sibling with the smaller timestamp belongs to the checkpointed state, and the sibling with the larger timestamp is outside the checkpointed state. Because of the way the timestamps are initialized and updated, "$T_{chk} < TS(x) < TS(x')$" or "$T_{chk} < TS(x') < TS(x)$" case is not possible.

On a page fault, if the missing page is in sibling form, both siblings are fetched in a single disk access to reduce the disk access time. The average additional time required to fetch both adjacent disk blocks of a siblng page is expected to be less than 10% over the time required to fetch a single disk block of a singleton page. For the TI Explorer LISP machine, the average additional time is less than 2%[27]. Four cases arise on a page fault depending on whether the page is in sibling or singleton form and its timestamp.

Case 1

Page fault on a sibling page, and $TS(x) < TS(x') < T_{chk}$ or $TS(x') < TS(x) < T_{chk}$: "$TS(x) < TS(x') < T_{chk}$" case is described here. The treatment of "$TS(x') < TS(x) < T_{chk}$" is analogous. The sibling with the larger timestamp, x', is kept in main memory, and the other sibling, x, is discarded. When the page is written to disk, it is written over the disk space of the discarded sibling x, because x contains useless information. Disk space of x' must not be written over because it would destroy the checkpointed state. Thus, x and x' exchange their roles. The timestamp relationship now becomes $TS(x') < T_{chk} < TS(x)$, i.e., case 2 below.

Case 2

Page fault on a sibling page, and $TS(x) < T_{chk} < TS(x')$ or $TS(x') < T_{chk}$

$< TS(x)$: "$TS(x) < T_{chk} < TS(x')$" case is described here. The treatment of "$TS(x') < T_{chk} < TS(x)$" is analogous. The sibling with the larger timestamp, x', is kept in main memory, and the other sibling, x is discarded. Unlike case 1, however, the page is written over its own disk space, i.e., over disk space of x', because x' is not part of the last checkpointed state and can be written over, while disk space of x belongs to the checkpointed state and must not be destroyed. The timestamp relationship remains "$TS(x) < T_{chk} < TS(x')$", i.e., case 2.

Case 3

Page fault on a singleton page and $TS(s) < T_{chk}$: If the singleton page is modified, at page-out time, it must be converted to a sibling form because the checkpointed state must not be overwritten. Sibling x retains the contents and timestamp of the original singleton, and sibling x' contains the modified contents and the timestamp of page-out time. The timestamp relationship becomes $TS(x) < T_{chk} < TS(x')$, i.e., case 2. The disk space for s is reclaimed.

Case 4

Page fault on a singleton page and $T_{chk} < TS(s)$: At page out time, no conversion to sibling form is needed because singleton s does not belong to the checkpointed state and can be written over its own disk space. The timestamp relationship remains $T_{chk} < TS(s)$, i.e., case 4.

Sibling to Singleton Conversion

To reduce the disk space requirement, a sibling page is converted back to singleton form when both siblings remain inactive for a long period, defined by a threshold parameter. The disk space manager hunts for such inactive sibling pages; if $TS(x) < TS(x') < T_{chk}$ and $T_{chk} - TS(x') <$ threshold, then the disk space for both siblings x and x' is reclaimed by converting them into singleton form. Singleton s contains the

original contents and timestamp of sibling x'. The treatment for "$TS(x') < TS(x) < T_{chk}$ and $T_{chk} - TS(x) <$ threshold" is analogous.

Expunge Log

All pages that were part of the checkpoint, but are modified after the checkpoint and before a crash, are in sibling form: $TS(x) < T_{chk} < TS(x')$ or $TS(x') < T_{chk} < TS(x)$. When the system state is rolled back during the post-crash recovery, the siblings with larger timestamps must be "expunged" from the system as they contain information written after the checkpoint. This is accomplished during the recovery process by demoting their timestamps to a large negative number (denoted by *) which renders them useless; they will be discarded from main memory if paged in during normal operation after the post-crash recovery (as in Case 1 above). If the timestamps are not demoted, the rollback process will fail to recreate the checkpointed state.

Siblings whose timestamps must be demoted during the post-crash recovery can be located using a log called the Expunge log. The Expunge log keeps track of a sibling page which is written out to disk if and only if it satisfied $TS(x) < TS(x') < T_{chk}$ or $TS(x') < TS(x) < T_{chk}$ before it was written out. Its virtual page id, v. and disk address d along with the time of its writing to disk, are appended to the end of the Expunge log. The Expunge log is maintained on disk and must be outside virtual memory to survive system crashes; otherwise, it too will be lost due to a system crash. To reduce the disk bandwidth requirement for maintaining the Expunge log, instead of writing an individual entry to the Expunge log each time a page is written out, entries for a number of pages can be queued and written into the Expunge log before the pages themselves are written out.

Checkpoint Process

The checkpoint process may be initiated by an application or the system. At checkpoint time, the checkpoint process saves all processor registers, i.e., the transient root into a snapshot object. The snapshot object is part of virtual memory. The page containing the snapshot object is writeen to disk; the snapshot object is in the transitive closure of the persistent root and resides at a fixed disk location. All dirty pages in main memory are then written to disk. Finally, T_{chk} is updated on disk to the current time, completing the checkpoint process. This update operation must be implemented as an atomic operation; T_{chk} is either successfully updated or it does not change at all. Right after the checkpoint completion, for all sibling pages, $TS(x) < TS(x') < T_{chk}$ or $TS(x') < TS(x) < T_{chk}$, and for all singleton pages, $TS(s) < T_{chk}$. Also, all previously transient objects become persistent as they become members of the transitive closure of the persistent root.

Dirty Page Clean-up

It is highly desirable to reduce the time required for the checkpoint operation so that the user processes are not suspended too long. This is achieved by keeping the fraction of dirty pages in main memory at the checkpoint time reasonably small with a background process that cleans up dirty pages between successive checkpoints. Additional details can be found in Thatte[28]. Dirty page clean-up requires disk bandwidth in addition to that needed for the normal paging activity. Our calculations show that for typical processors (speed: 1 to 4 million instructions per second), typical disk systems (access time: 30 to 50 milliseconds), and a moderte page fault rate (page fault period: 500K to 1M machine instructions per page fault), 50% to 80% disk bandwidth is available to clean-up dirty pages, maintain the Expunge log, and convert siblings to singletons. This bandwidth is judged to be adequate to support a recoverable virtual memory.

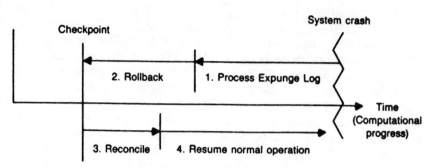

Figure 4. Post-Crash Recovery

Post-Crash Recovery

It is assumed that after a system crash diagnostics are run to detect permanent hardware failures and faulty hardware, if any, is already replaced. Figure 4 indicates the post-crash recovery process described below.

1. Process the Expunge log. Locate each page recorded in the Expunge log since the last checkpoint and expunge its sibling with higher timestamp by demoting its timestamp to *.
2. Rollback the system to the last checkpointed state by restoring the processor registers from the snapshot object on disk.
3. Reconcile with the external world. Part of the restored checkpointed state is related to the system configuration and I/O interfaces specific to the checkpoint time. This state must now be reconciled with the current time and configuration* (see footnote).
4. Resume the normal system operation.

Disk Crashes

Disk crashes arise from disk head crashes, deterioration of the magnetic media itself, or bugs in the disk driver software. The disk crash rate is expected to be a few failures per year, with the recovery time of a few hours. Disk crashes are treated differently from system crashes because they can corrupt the checkponted state on disk; therefore, the rollback technique used for recovery from system crash may not work. To deal with disk crashes, the last checkpointed state on disk needs to be archived on another media, such as a streaming tape. This operation is expected to be performed a few times a week, preferrably as an overnight operation. After a disk crash, a failed disk needs to be replaced with a new one, which is then initialized from the last archived checkpointed state.

Benefits of Persistent Memory

We are in the process of implementing a persistent memory prototype using the TI Explorer LISP machine. We plan to measure its behavior, both robustness and performance, and solicit users for evaluation under a variety of applications, some of which are described below. It should be noted that some of these applications can also be implemented on today's machines, but only with great difficulty and loss of efficiency. As with any new capability or function, applications that are very awkward to implement today, or are not even dreampt of, may emerge in the future with the availability of persistent memory. The use of persistent memory in

---

*For example, part of the restored checkpointed state may contain a timer variable, which reflects the time of the last checkpoint. The timer variable must be adjusted to reflect the current time. The state of I/O device registers and device control blocks may need to be adjusted so that the I/O devices become ready for normal operation.

network file systems, distributed data storage, and distributed computing raises many interesting opportunities for research, which is underway in our research group, as well as at other companies making symbolic computers[29].

Advanced "File" Systems

A persistent memory system subsumes many functions traditionally performed by a file system. Directories and files of a file system can be made persistent by simply making them reachable from the persistent root. In fact, to ensure survival against system crashes, files must be implemented as resilient objects with read and write operations on files implemented as transactions. If the virtual address space is too small to build an entire file system as a system of persistent objects, only its directory can be implemented as a persistent object and files can be kept otside the virtual address space.

However, if one were to use persistent memory to implement a conventional file system, it would represent a gross underutilization of the capabilities of persistent memory. A persistent memory can be used to support more advanced file systems. For example, a file object (implemented as a persistent object) need not be restricted to contain only a stream of bytes representing ASCII characters, but can contain arbitrary objects, including procedural objects, graphics, images, mail, and voice in a representation that can be directly interpreted by a processor.

Active Environments

Active environments are environments in which persistent procedural objects are activated as soon as interesting or noteworthy events occur or a database reaches a certain state. Such active environments exploit the duality of procedures and data common in symbolic computing. It must be pointed out that active environments do not provide any new capability which is impossible in today's "passive" systems, i.e., systems without persistent memory. However, things that are very awkward in a passive system can be very natural in an active environment built on top of a persistent memory.

As an example, consider a calendar manager, which is a very simple example of active objects. In today's passive systems, a calendar is implemented with "passive" techniques. Each time some event occurs which could affect the user's personal calendar, a calendar management program is invoked to make necessary updates and, if necessary, inform the user. The reason that a calendar manager is not too difficult to implement with passive techniques is that the environment being accessed (time and/or invocations of a calendar management program) is simple and can be easily monitored. As a second example, consider the reception of a mail message that automatically activates a deamon to sender an acknowledgement back to the sender of the mail.

However, as the events being monitored become more complex and dynamic (e.g., monitoring unexpected changes to a critical data structure), the functions doing the watching become more sophisticated; they need many complex "hooks" into the environment. Such active objects are very difficult to implement with passive techniques because programmers are forced to modify the system itself in order to achieve such active behavior. A persistent memory system provides a natural foundation to implement active environments.

Object-oriented Databases

With object-oriented programming systems, such as the Flavors system on LISP machines and the Smalltalk system, sophisticated and rich abstraction mechanisms are available to define abstract types and hide the implementation details of objects; similarly, powerful inheritance mechanisms are available to build higher levels of abstractions, i.e., higher level objects can inherit the properties of other objects. Large systems can be divided naturally into coherent parts, which can be developed and maintained separately. Also, specifying redundant information can be eliminated.

Many applications, such as VLSI CAD, have found the object-oriented programming style quite natural for their requirements[30]. However, these applications also require that objects persist beyond the lifetimes of programs that create them. For example, a VLSI CAD system user would like to have objects representing design entities (such as geometrical layouts, transistors) persist across his design sessions on a CAD workstation. In essence, what is needed here is an object-oriented database[31].

Unfortunately, in today's computers without persistent memory, objects can be made to "persist" only be translating them to a representation suitable for a file system or a database and then completing their transfer to it. As expected, these operations are quite expensive and time consuming in addition to the burden they impose on both the CAD system designer and the user[32].

A persistent memory system appears to be an ideal foundation to build object-oriented databases because objects can be left in the persistent memory across workstation sessions, as the design or development activity progresses over a period of time. There would be neither space or time penalty, nor burden on the programmer or user attributed to the storage dichotomy.

Conclusion

The storage dichotomy is expected to be a serious impediment in the development and use of large-scale, knowledge-based symbolic/AI applications. These applications require an effective marriage of AI-knowledge base and database technologies. The storage dichotomy puts a heavy burden of storage management on the programmer and causes a large space and time penalty due to the translation and transfer of information betweeen the computational and long-term storages. It was argued that the current approach in vogue to solve the storage management problem by connecting a symbolic computer to a database machine is inadequate because it does not address the fundamental issues arising from the storage dichotomy.

Our approach is based on persistent memory that eliminates the distinction between the computational and long-term storages. Implementation of persistent memory requires a recovery capability at the level of virtual memory itself. Our recovery scheme is based on the timestamp and sibling page techniques and has low space and time overheads. Resilient objects can be implemented on top of a persistent memory. Many applications that include advanced file systems, object-oriented databases, and active environments are expected to be implemented with far greater ease, flexibility, and performance on persistent, resilient objects than on a conventional file system or database.

Acknowledgements

I would like to thank Don Oxley of CRL-Computer Science Laboratory for many stimulating discussions that helped develop the concepts in this paper. Several members of the laboratory and Professor Randy Katz at University of California, Berkeley, reviewed an earlier draft of the paper. Their critique has been invaluable in improving the organization and clarity of the paper. Jerry Muscha served as an editor for the paper. His thoughtful feedback is greatly appreciated as it was very helpful in focusing the paper to the needs of TI engineers and scientists.

References

1. R. Yasdi. "A Conceptual Design Aid Environment for Expert-Database Systems," *Data and Knowledge Engineering*, Volume 1, No. 1, pp. 31-73, June 1985.
2. A. Barr and E.A. Feigenbaum, *The Handbook of Artificial Intelligence*, William Kaufman, Inc., 1981.
3. Texas Instruments Incorporated, Data Systems Group, "EXPLORER Technical Summary," Austin, Texas, May 1985, Part No. 2243189-0001.
4. H. Abelson and G.J. Sussman, *Structure and Interpretation of Computer Programs*, MIT Press, Cambridge, MA, 1985.
5. P.J. Denning, "Third Generation Computer Systems," *ACM Computing Surveys*, Volume 3, No. 4, pp. 175-211, December 1971.
6. M.P. Atkinson, et al, "An Approach to Persistent Programming," *The Computer Journal*, Volume 26, No. 4, pp. 360-365, December 1983.
7. G.J. Myers, *Advances in Computer Architecture*, Wiley-Interscience, New York, 2nd edition, pp. 91-989, 1982.
8. M. Stonebraker, "Operating System Support for Database Management," *CACM*, Volume 24, No. 7, pp. 412-148, July 1981.
9. H. Asio, "Fifth Generation Computer Architecture," In *Proc. 1981 Int. Conf. Fifth Generation Computers*, pp. 29-35, Japan Information Processing Development Center, 1981.
10. G.M.E. LaFue, "Basic Decision about Linking an Expert System with a DBMS: A Case Study," *IEEE Database Engineering*, Volume 6, No. 4, pp. 56-64, December 1983.
11. T. Kilburn, "One-Level Storage System," *IRE Trans. Electronic Comput.*, Volume EC-11, No. 2, April 1962.
12. J.H. Saltzer, "Naming and Binding of Objects," *Operating Systems: An Advanced Course*, p. 99, Springer-Verlag, New York, NY, 1978.
13. I.L. Traiger, "Virtual Memory Management for Database Systems," *ACM Operating System Review*, Volume 16, pp. 24-48, October 1982.
14. A. Bensoussan, C.T. Clingen, and R.C. Daley, "The MULTICS Virtual Memory," *Proc. 2nd Symp. Operating Systems Principles*, pp. 30-42, Princeton University, October 1969.
15. IBM General Systems Division, "IBM System/38 Technical Developments," Technical Report G580-237-1, IBM, July 1980.
16. M.P. Atkinson, et al, "Progress with Persistent Programming," Technical Report RPR-8-84, Department of Computer Science, University of Edinburgh, Edinburgh, Scotland, February 1984.
17. H. Lenz and M. Schoener. "Data Management Facilities for an Operating System Kernel." *ACM SIGMOD*, Volume 14, No. 2, pp. 58-69, August 1984.
18. N. Mishkin. "Managing Permanent Objects." Technical Report YALEU/DCS/RR-338, Department of Computer Science, Yale University, New Haven, CT, November 1984.
19. T.J. McEntee. "An Overview of Garbage Collection in Symbolic Computing." *Texas Instruments Engineering Journal*, Volume 3, No. 1, January-February 1986.
20. K.P. Eswaran, et al, "The Notions of Consistency and Predicate Locks in a Database System." *CACM*, Volume 19, No. 11, pp. 624-633, November 1976.
21. S.M. Thatte. "Persistent Memory for Symbolic Computers." Technical Report TR-08-85-21, Central Research Laboratories, Texas Instruments, Incorporated, Dallas, Texas, July 1985.
22. Thatte, ibid.
23. F.J. Pollack, K.C. Kahn, and R.M. Wilkinson. "The iMAX-432 Object Filing System." In *Proc. 8th ACM Symp. Operating Systems Principles — ACM SIGOPS Operating Systems Review*," pp. 137-147, ACM SIGOPS, Pacific Grove, CA, December 1981.
24. R.A. Lorie. "Physical Integrity in Large Segmented Database." *ACM-TODS*, Volume 2, No. 1, pp. 91-104, March 1977.
25. A. Reuter. "A Fast Transaction-Oriented Logging Scheme for UNDO Recovery." *IEEE Trans. Software Eng.*, Volume SE-6, No. 4, pp. 348-356, July 1980.
26. Thatte, ibid.
27. K. Johnson. Texas Instruments, Dallas, Texas, August 1985, Private communication with K. Johnson on disk access statistics for the TI Explorer Lisp machine.
28. Thatte, ibid.
29. R. Greenblatt. "MOBY Address Space." Lisp Machine Inc., Los Angeles, CA, August 1985, Seminar report on research in progress.
30. "DROID — An Object-oriented VLSI CAD System." In preparation at the TI-VLSI Design Lab, Dallas, Texas.
31. C.W. Thompson. "Object-oriented Databases." *Texas Instruments Engineering Journal*, Volume 3, No. 1, January-February 1986.
32. M.W. Wilkins and G. Wiederhold. "Relational and Entity-relational Model Database and VLSI Desing." *IEEE Database Engineering*, Volume 7, No. 2, pp. 61-66, June 1984. ⚡

Persistent Object Management System

W. P. COCKSHOT, M. P. ATKINSON AND K. J. CHISHOLM

Department of Computer Science, University of Edinburgh, Mayfield Road, Edinburgh EH9 3JZ, U.K.

AND

P. J. BAILEY AND R. MORRISON

Department of Computational Science, University of St. Andrews, North Haugh, St. Andrews KY16 8SX, U.K.

SUMMARY

This is a description of the integrated Persistent Object Management System (POMS) for the language PS-algol. The objective of POMS is to provide an implementation of the PS-algol persistent heap[1] entirely by means of procedures written in PS-algol.

KEY WORDS   Algols   Database   Persistent programming   PS-algol   Implementing heaps

INTRODUCTION

High level languages provide programmers with abstractions which allow them to organize the store of a computer without having to worry about how to allocate data items to storage locations. In languages with dynamic storage allocation, it is not even necessary to know, when writing an algorithm, just how much data it will use; instead, the algorithm itself decides this as it runs. As anyone who has used a language, such as Algol-68[2] or S-algol[3], which has fully dynamic storage allocation will realize, this adds greatly to the productivity of programmers.

The catch is that high level languages only organize one type of store: RAM. They ignore disk store, leaving that to the operating system to organize. But programmers cannot ignore disks. RAM is volatile, whereas one of the main uses of computers is to store information. As a result we have to spend a lot of time and energy organizing the preservation of data structures on disk. In RAM our favourite language allows us to easily build up complex logical structures which we are then forced to output to the essentially serial media of files. Direct access files are some help, but it is hard to map a RAM data structure containing pointers onto even a direct access file. One difficulty, at least with most operating systems, is ensuring that most transactions commit or leave the file unchanged.

It would be nice if we did not have to go to all the trouble of thinking how we were going to store our information on disk. It would be nice if the data structures that we were using in our program could somehow be saved on disk without our having to make any special effort. If a high level language can organize RAM it should be able to do the same for disk. There is no reason why we as programmers should have to treat the two types of store differently.

The persistent object management system (POMS for short) is a package that

0038–0644/84/010049–23$02.30   *Received 15 April 1983*
Revised 11 July 1983

allows programmers using PS-Algol[1] to write programs without being aware of the distinction between RAM and disk. Any data structure that they build up on the heap can be automatically transferred to disk at the end of a program and then brought back onto the heap the next time the data is used by a program. This enables us to abstract from the physical properties of disk store just as we already abstract from the physical properties of RAM, allowing us to view both with a uniform set of conceptual abstractions. Thus we have a uniform view of all the store available to the programmer.

The POMS is part of a research program to provide a persistent Von Neumann store for high level languages. Earlier implementations of such a store are documented in References 4 and 5. Language design issues for such an environment are discussed in Reference 6.

WAYS OF IMPLEMENTING PERSISTENT STORE

The mechanisms used by high level languages to organize RAM are quite complex, and have provided material for whole books.[7] Doing the same for disk store in a high level language is, as we shall see, perhaps even more complicated. This explanation of the POMS is therefore presented using the method of repeated elaboration. We start off by giving a simple and rather incomplete picture of the implementation and then present successively more complex pictures. This enables us to present the new concepts involved one at a time.

What to keep

Languages with a heap are already faced with the problem of deciding what to keep. When the heap fills up, they either behave irresponsibly or they face up to their responsibilities and carry out a garbage collection. In the latter case, they have to decide which objects on the heap to keep and which can have their space reclaimed. The guiding principle of garbage collection is that no object that is reachable from identifiers currently in scope may be reclaimed.

The same principle can be used for the run-time system of a language that organizes both volatile and persistent store. If we assume that at least one identifier has a scope that is global to all runs of a program, or even to all programs, then we can say that at the end of a program nothing reachable from this identifier must be allowed to evaporate. Conversely, everything reachable from it must be saved by being transferred to disk. How can this be done?

Copy the heap to a file

The simplest method of providing a language with a persistent store is to just copy the whole heap out to a file. This is often done in Lisp.[8] The fact that Lisp programmers can so easily store their data may be one reason for the popularity of the language. This method of providing persistent storage is simple. Simplicity is a vitrue, but it carries a price, with this technique for instance:

(a) The heap must always be loaded onto the same location, or pointers held on the heap become invalid. If the heap starts above the program, then any editing of the program which changes its size, will invalidate all of the pointers. In Lisp this is no problem as program and data both sit in the heap, but this means giving up the freedom that you get with an ordinary filing system of running several programs against one file or one program against several files.

(b) It is impossible to store more data than you can load onto the heap at any one time. Your maximum database is limited by your machine's physical or virtual memory. Although modern computers often have very large virtual address spaces, you may find that only a tiny fraction of this can actually be used, owing to the limited size of the page swapping files.

(c) Programs which make only a few small changes to a large body of stored data pay a high I/O penalty because they have to load the whole heap at the start and save it again at the end of a session.

In an attempt to get over these problems POMS uses an incremental loading and storing strategy.

Incremental loading and storing

In an incremental strategy, the run-time system maintains two separate heaps, one on disk and one in RAM. We will refer to a disk based heap as a database. Along with two types of heap come two types of address. The existence of and interaction between these two types of address are central to the operation of the POMS.

The first type of address we term a persistent identifier (abbreviated to PID). A PID describes where an object is to be found on disk. In its simplest form it is just an offset in words or bytes from the start of a file.

The second type of address is whatever the underlying machine supports, either a virtual or a physical address. We term these local addresses because their validity is localized in time and space to the particular machine and process on which the program runs.

In the incremental system, when a program has finished, or in database terms when it commits, the run-time system copies objects from the local heap in RAM to the persistent heap on disk. As each object is copied from RAM to disk all the pointers that it contains that are in the form of local addresses are converted to pointers in the form of PIDs.

When the same (or some other) program is run against this database on disk, a distinguished object is copied from the database to the local heap and assigned to a global pointer variable. This object, termed the *root* of the database, contains pointers to other items in the database. It might, for example, be the top of some sort of tree, or the head of a list. If the program tries to dereference a pointer field in the root, what it picks up is a PID, which points onto the disk. It is thus necessary that PIDs be distinguishable from local addresses.

Several ways of distinguishing the two are possible. You could make all local addresses word aligned and all PIDs odd byte aligned. In POMS we have chosen to make all PIDs negative and to locate our heap in the bottom half of our machine's address space ensuring that all local addresses will be positive, as shown in Figure 1.

A dereference instruction can therefore trap all negative addresses and escape into the POMS to deal with them. The POMS fetches the object from disk, loads it onto

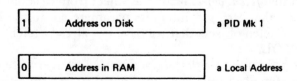

Figure 1. The essential difference between the two types of address

the heap and overwrites the negative address that had been dereferenced with the new local address of the object on the heap. The dereference instruction can then continue successfully. By this means objects are only brought in when needed and a program that only needs a few persistent objects will not pay a large I/O penalty.

You can also have a much bigger database than it is possible to load into RAM, as only parts of it need be loaded in any given session.

The PIDLAM

The kernel of the POMS is the process of translating PIDs to local addresses when address faults occur, and back again when objects are sent to disk. Two functions are used to do this translation:

$$loca.\ of.\ pid(\textbf{int}\ pid \rightarrow \textbf{int})$$
$$pid.\ of.\ loca(\textbf{int}\ loca \rightarrow \textbf{int})$$

which map from PIDs to local addresses and back again. These work by means of a data structure called the Persistent IDentifier to Local Address Map (PIDLAM for short). This is a two way index between the two types of addresses implemented by means of two hash tables from which intersecting linked lists are appended as shown in Figure 2.

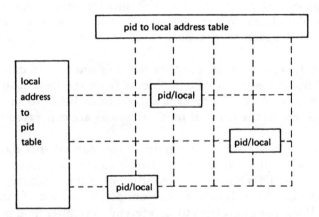

Figure 2. The organization of the PIDLAM

The cells on these links contain two fields, a PID and the equivalent local address. Given either of these, the other can be found by hashing into the appropriate table and following down a linked list until the matching entry is found. The linked lists are composed of the items that hash to a common table value. When an illegal local address is found the algorithm in Figure 3 is executed.

Here it is assumed that *fetch. object* loads the object from disk onto the heap returning its local address and that *Def. pid* enters its parameters into the PIDLAM. Observe that we only need to fetch objects that we have not already fetched and thus have not entered into the PIDLAM.

The legal address returned by *illegal. loca* is used to overwrite the PID in the field that was being dereferenced thus ensuring that the next time this path through the data is followed there will be no delays.

```
procedure illegal. loca(int pid→int)
begin
  let loca : = loca. of. pid(pid)
  if loca>0 then loca else begin
    loca: = fetch. object(pid)
    Def. pid(loca, pid)
    loca
  end
end
```

Figure 3. Dealing with illegal local addresses

Transactions

The incremental strategy outlined above gets over the problems involved in the simple technique of just copying the heap to a file, but does not support atomic transactions.

An atomic transaction is a transformation of a database from one consistent state to another. Clearly, in carrying this out it may be necessary to go through some inconsistent state or states but this must be hidden from the point of view of the external world. The external view of a transaction must be that it has either occurred or not occurred. This must remain true irrespective of possible hardware failures, or programs crashing.

In the model of persistence given above, what would happen if the program or machine failed while sending objects back to disk from the heap?

You could have a situation in which some of the data had been written back with new values, whereas other parts of the data still had their old values. The result would be an inconsistent state. If you were copying the whole heap back to a file it would be possible to get round this by always copying to a new file with a different name. Once the copy is complete you can delete the old file and give the new file the old name. How are we to achieve the same effects with the incremental strategy?

The general approach that is adopted in POMS to provide secure atomic transactions is to use shadow pages.[9] When data is written back to disk during a transaction it is written to different sites on disk to those from which it came. This means that no data that was valid at the start of the transaction is overwritten during the transaction. Thus if the transaction aborts, the previous consistent state is still available on disk. In doing this we exploit the fact that disk transfers occur in fixed sized units, the disk blocks. An address within a file can thus be thought of as having two components:

(i) the block number

(ii) the offset within the block

We now distinguish between *logical* blocks and *relative* blocks. A relative block occupies a fixed position within the file and is identified by a *relative block number* which is simply its offset from the start of the file. A logical block, characterized by a *logical block number*, may occupy different positions in the file. Suppose we have a table, the *LR. map*, which maps logical to relative block numbers such that, if L is a logical number, then $LR. map(L)$ is the corresponding relative block number.

We now refine the definition of a persistent identifier so that it looks like Figure 4. So we now address objects on disk in terms of their logical block and an offset from the start of that block.

In order to provide security, every transaction that modifies a logical block will

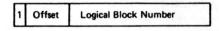

Figure 4. Persistent identifier mark II

cause it to be written back to a different relative block. The *LR. map* holds the currently valid mapping between logical and relative blocks within a database. In order to securely commit a transaction three phases are executed:

1. Determine which items on the heap have been changed in the course of a transaction.
2. Assign a new relative block to each logical block containing the modified items and write the block containing the updated item out to the new relative block.
3. Update the *LR. map* and write that back to disk.

Any failure in the first two phases will leave an unmodified *LR. map* on disk so that the transaction will not have occurred. Any program that now opens the database will see it through the old map which will not reveal any of the changes made in phase 2. This technique was originally proposed in reference 10.

By implementing an *LR. map* we create two types of address space on disk: relative and logical. Of these, the second has the vital property of being transactionally secure. Changes in the state of the logical address space occur as atomic transactions, so long as changes in the state of the *LR. map* are themselves atomic transactions.

What is the LR Map?

In principle the *LR. map* is just a large array acting as a lookup table. In practice this approach needs a slight modification. POMS allows approximately 2^{15} logical blocks in a database. If a single vector of this size was used to implement the map, small databases would carry an unnecessarily high mapping overhead. Moreover writing a large *LR. map* spread over several blocks back to disk would itself be an unsafe operation. If a failure occurred while it was being written you could get an *LR. map* some blocks of which belonged to a new and others of which belonged to an old state of the database.

The problem is solved by dividing the *LR. map* into two parts, a fixed part and an extensible part. The fixed part is small enough to fit into a single disk block. Then there is an extensible part. If the fixed part holds the first *n* blocks' LR mapping, then all logical blocks in the range *n* to *max. blocks* will be mapped via the extensible part.

PS-algol implements arrays as Illife vectors, that is, an *n* dimensional array is a vector of pointers to *n*–1 dimensional arrays. We can therefore represent the extensible part as a partially populated three dimensional array of integers.

> **let** *LR. map* = **vector** 1 . . 8 **of**
>   **vector** 0 . . *Ir. lev. size* **of**
>   **vector** 0 . . *Ir. lev. size* **of** 0

Where the *Ir. lev. size* is chosen so as to enable two of the subvectors of the array to fit into a disk block.

LR map in logical space

An important implication follows from the decision to implement the *LR. map* in two parts: the extensible part must exist in *logical* disk address space. In part this follows ineluctably from the decision to represent the *LR. map* as a PS-algol array.

On disk PS-algol objects have their pointers as PIDs. PIDs define points in logical disk address space. Thus the *LR. map* extension must exist in logical address space. But this also a necessity if transactions are to be safe.

Recall that all state changes of logical address space are atomic transactions. If we place the *LR. map* extension in logical rather than relative address space then changes in its state too will become atomic transactions.

But hold on! This argument seems recursive: logical space is transactionally secure if the *LR. map* is secure and the *LR. map* is made secure by being placed in logical space. Where is our fixed point?

It is the fixed portion of the *LR. map*. This all fits within one disk block. If we assume that writes of a single block to disk are transactions then changes in the state of the fixed portion of the *LR. map* will be atomic. If the transactional properties of the extensible part of the *LR. map* can be made to depend upon those of the fixed part we are safe.

To do this the following condition must hold:

If an object A is itself part of the mapping system, the lowest logical block number in whose mapping it participates must be higher than the logical block number of A itself.

This ensures the transactional security of the *LR. map* and thus of the whole logical disk address space.

In the POMS we chose to place the first *n* entries in the *LR. map* into the database root mentioned earlier. Given the depth of the *LR. map* tree and the size of its nodes, it turns out that an *n* of 3 will be enough to meet the security condition, because the *LR. map* is of depth 3. We only need to store information about the placement of the three nodes of the Illife vector tree that map the first *Ir. lev. size* elements. If we put each node in the tree in a distinct disk block then the first 3 entries enable us to get at mapping information that gets us to the next *Ir. lev. size* blocks.

TYPES

The persistent storage of program data creates problems for the typechecking mechanism of a language that supports it. In conventional programming languages the compiler writer can assume that any data encountered in RAM will belong to some type declared in the program under compilation or in some module to which it is going to be linked. It is thus possible to implement strong typing on the premise that the compiler is omniscient. Once you start storing data on disk, potentially for long time, this assumption breaks down. Data may persist on disk long after the program which operated on it has been deleted. The normal relationship between the durability of data and the durability of programs is inverted.

Unless we are just going to give up on type checking, we need to find new methods of implementing it. We have chosen to implement a more sophisticated run-time type checker than is normal, so that the run-time system takes over some of the responsibilities previously carried by the compiler.

S-algol type checking

PS-algol is based upon S-algol and its type checking system derives from that of S-algol. The S-algol type checking scheme is based upon a mixture of compile-time and run-time type checks. S-algol supports both what are termed types, and what are termed structure classes. It has an infinite set of types obtained from the base types integer, pointer, boolean, real, string, file under the operations of proceduring and vectoring.

The values assumed by expressions of type pointer are members of structure classes, which are tuples of named fields. A value of any structure class can be assigned to any pointer. It cannot be determined at compile time what class the value of an expression of type pointer will belong to. There are, however, operations in the language which require that the class membership of a pointer be known at compile time: the operations of field subscriptions and subscripted assignment.

The task of the type checking system in S-algol is to ensure that no identifier ever has a value assigned to it that is different from the type that it was declared to have. When a pointer is subscripted or has a field assigned to, it is necessary to be sure that the field has the type required in this context or else an assignment might occur that would violate the type rules.

In S-algol no two structure classes in the same scope can share a field name. The compiler can thus deduce from the field name used in a subscription what class the subscripted pointer will belong to, and plant code to carry out a run-time type check.

In the course of processing a program the compiler assigns to every structure class that it encounters a unique number termed a *trade mark*. In non-persistent implementations of the language, this trade mark is an adequate identifier for the class. The headers of instances of the class, in these implementations, incorporate a copy of the trade mark. When the compiler needs to check what class a pointer belongs to, it plants code to compare the header of the object pointed to with a known trade mark. In persistent implementations, this technique is not feasible, because it is a requirement that different programs, compiled independently, should be able to share data created at run-time. Since the S-algol compiler assigns trade marks in ascending order of the textual occurrences of structure class declarations, the only method of achieving type matching depends on ensuring that the same classes were declared in the same order in the two programs. This approach, used in early implementations of PS-algol, was judged to be unsafe for persistent data.

The database approach

An alternative approach, in line with conventional database practice, would be to maintain a schema database that the compiler would access and in which all past declarations of classes would be held. If the compiler found that a class in the program under compilation had already been inserted in the schema, it would obtain the trade mark previously associated with the class from the database, otherwise it would insert the class description into the database, increment a counter in the schema to obtain a new trade mark and use this in the program. This approach was rejected because:

(a) The PS-algol compiler is a slightly modified version of the S-algol compiler. It is itself implemented in S-algol, not PS-algol, and is thus incapable of accessing a PS-algol database.

(b) The use of such an approach might lead to undue contention in accessing the schema database.

(c) It would make PS-algol program object code and databases non-portable because the meaning of a trade mark would be specific to the schema on the machine on which the program was compiled.

The POMS approach

Instead, it was decided that both program object code and databases should carry complete descriptions of the classes declared or stored within them. POMS uses a tagged data architecture in which each object on the heap is either self describing or contains enough information to access a description of it. As Figure 5 shows, each object has a header word, the first few bits of which say if the object is a structure,

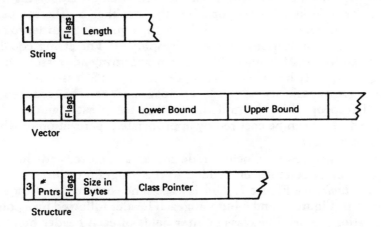

Figure 5. The format of objects on the PS-Algol heap

vector or string. The header word, or in the case of vectors the first 3 words, define the size of the object. In addition various bits are used as flags to be used in garbage collection and store management algorithms. By tagging objects it is easier to:

    (i) implement an element of run-time type checking
    (ii) implement a full garbage collector
    (iii) implement debugging aids.

Every instance of a structure class carries round with it a reference to its description.

The description chosen was a string containing a canonical form of the class declaration. This is shown in Figure 6. We term these strings *class ids*. Notice that in the canonical form of the class declaration the order of occurrence of fields does not correspond to that in the original declaration. In the example shown, the class

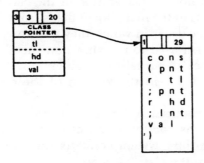

Figure 6. Each structure contains a pointer to a string containing its declaration

declared as:

structure *cons*(**pntr** *hd, tl*; **int** *val*)

has its fields reordered in the canonical description as *tl, hd, val*. This is a consequence of the rule that is used for evaluating the equivalence of class declarations. Classes are said to be equivalent if they have the same fieldnames and the fields have the same type, but the order in which the fields occur does not matter. By sorting the fields into a canonical order, checks for class membership, whether by the **is** operator or the implicit check at dereference, can be done by string equality. In order to minimize the cost of this, certain optimizations have to be employed. The string equality function operates on the addresses of strings. When given two string addresses it first compares the addresses for equality before comparing the strings. The essential thing is to make sure that the great majority of class comparisons can be reduced to address comparison. The proposition behind this is that the great majority of class comparisons succeed. This can be ensured by appropriate organization of what is termed the structure table.

The compiler continues to allocate trade marks as before, and these are used as indices into a set of three tables embedded in the program code.

   (i) *Structure table*: see Figure 7. This is a sequence of structure headers organized as shown in Figures 5 and 6 but with each header followed by a pointer into the permutations table. The class pointer fields of each header points into:

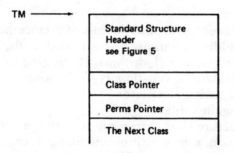

Figure 7. Structure table organization

  (ii) *Class id. table*: this is a sequence of string literals organized as shown in Figure 5 containing the canonical declaration of the classes.

 (iii) *Perms table*: consists of the mapping of fields from the order in which they have been declared to the order in which they are stored. This is necessary because in the syntactic form used to initialize new members of a structure class, the order of occurrence of initializing values must correspond to the order of occurrence of the fields in the version of the class declaration currently in scope.

The class pointer as produced by the compiler is an offset from the start of the *class id. table* and the perms pointer an offset from the start of the *perms. table*. At program startup the run-time system converts the class pointers into actual store addresses of the entries in the *class. id. table*.

In order to ensure that class membership checks can be reduced to address comparison when a structure is imported, the following algorithm is executed:

1. Check to see if a header for an equivalent class exists in the structure table. This check is optimized by keeping a vector of the addresses of the strings in the *class id. table* sorted alphabetically. A binary search is performed on this using the class declaration in the imported structure.

2. If there is an equivalent class then the class declaration field in the header is overwritten with the address of the equivalent string in the *class id. table*

Class fractions

It was explained earlier that in the POMS we take advantage of the fact that disk store is organized in terms of fixed size blocks to implement a transactionally secure storage system. Another factor that has to be taken into account is that disks are much slower than RAM. If you are using disks, it is wise to try and minimize the number of disk transfers that take place. In RAM there is no corresponding concept. You can follow a linked list equally well whether the nodes are adjacent in memory or widely spaced. On disk, however, it is much faster to follow a list whose elements are next to each other because several nodes can then be brought in with each disk transfer.

Since linked lists are a common class of data structures on heaps it was thought wise to design our placement algorithms to take this into account. We hypothesize that linked lists tend to be made up of objects of the same structure class and have therefore followed these rules in allocating PIDs to structures.

(a) Items of a given class are gathered together into a set of blocks which are termed the fractions of the class.

(b) Each logical block contains members of only one class.

(c) When allocating PIDs to cells on a linked list, try whenever possible to allocate adjacent cells to the same logical block, i.e. put them into the same fraction of their class.

Class descriptors

For every class in a database there is a class descriptor. This holds information that is common to the class as a whole, including:

(i) *Freelist*: a list of free PIDs available for the storage of new members of the class.

(ii) *Use list*: a list of the class fractions used to store this class.

The class descriptors are accessed via a table indexed on class identifiers and reachable from the database root. It is intended that the use list will enable fast access to all fractions of a class and thus allow the programming of bulk operations on all members of a class. For instance it would provide the access paths required for a query language interpreter program which allowed operations of selection and projection over classes.

Non-structure objects

In addition to structures, POMS supports the persistent storage of strings and vectors. Such objects do not fall into classes but they can still be grouped according to size so that objects of the same size can be clustered into single disk blocks just as with structures. However, in the case of strings and vectors the number of different sizes is likely to be greater than with structures. This could lead to the proliferation of disk blocks containing only one item—the only 43 character string in the database for example. So a compromise has been sought, objects for which the $\lceil \log_2 \rceil$ of their size is the same are grouped together. Thus there are logical blocks containing objects of size 2: 3 words, 4: 7 words, 8: 15 words, etc.

DATABASES

We are now in a position to summarize what a POMS database contains. A database is a named collection of PS-algol objects: strings, structures and vectors. It is the unit upon which program transactions are carried out:

At an implementation level a database effects three mappings:

(i) From relative block numbers (RBN) to physical block numbers. This mapping is analogous to that normally supported by a direct access file system. Its function is to make a set of non-contiguous disk extents look like a single contiguous address space.

(ii) From logical block numbers (LBN) to relative block numbers. As will be explained later, this mapping provides the mechanism for secure transactions.

(iii) From persistent identifiers (PID) to LBN + offset. This mapping takes us from a disk block based address space to a high level language object address space.

As far as possible, the data structures necessary to carry out these mappings have been implemented in terms of S-algol data structures. This is intended to make code more maintainable and more portable.

Root block

In logical block 1 of a database is the *root block* ROOT. This is a valid S-algol structure belonging to the class *opened. db* whose declaration is given in Figure 8.

```
structure opened. db (bool write. mode;
                ***int zLR. map;
                *int owner. dir;
                int db. no;
                pntr owner. toc;
                int zone1, zone2, zone3, zone4, zone5, zone6, zone7, zone8, zone9, zone10,
                    zone11, zone12;
                int LR1, LR2, LR3;
                pntr persistence. root;
                ***int BIT. map. tree;
                int Next. RBN, Max. RBN, Next. LBN, Max. LBN;
                pntr Class. table1, Class. table2, function. table;
                *pntr Non. struct;
                string path, db..name;
                int old. D, old. B
                )
```

Figure 8. The class of a root block

The *root block* contains pointers to all of the administrative data necessary to maintain the database, and a pointer to the root of whatever data particular applications programs have put in the database. This last pointer is the *persistence. root*. The first field of this *root block* is the *LR. map* which translates logical block numbers to relative block numbers.

Relative block numbers

We have already said that the relative block numbers to which the *LR. map* maps are analogous to record numbers within a direct access file. It would obviously be possible to implement these directly in terms of the record numbers of the filing system on top of which the POMS was running. It was decided not to do this in order to make the POMS more operating system independent. It is intended that POMS should be able to run as a stand alone system on single user machines where there may not be a suitable disk operating system beneath it. It therefore has provision to do its I/O directly in terms of physical disk blocks and disk addresses. This makes it necessary for the POMS to carry out the mapping from a contiguous set of relative blocks to a possibly non-contiguous set of physical blocks.

Zones 1 .. 12 are the data structure used to carry out the mapping from relative block numbers to physical block numbers. A zone is a contiguous set of physical blocks. The number of physical blocks in a zone z: 1 .. 12 is given by 2^{3+z}. A zone field contains the PBN of the first block in the zone. The mapping from RBN to PBN is shown in Figure 9.

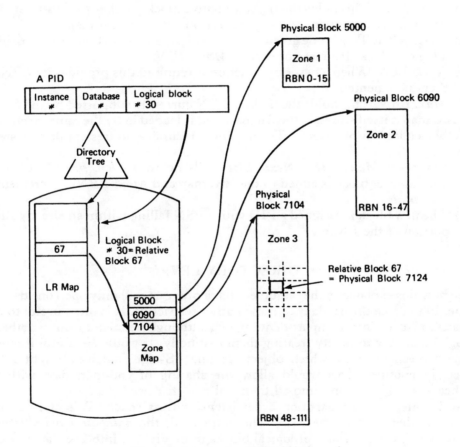

Figure 9. Interpreting a logical block number

The zones are held in 12 integer locations in the root structure. It is necessary that they be part of the *root block* to avoid an indefinite recursion when one attempts to get them in.

Block allocation

A pair of bit maps are maintained in each database to keep track of the free relative blocks. *bitmap* 1 is the current bit map, a bit is set in it for each relative block present in the database that is not currently assigned to a logical block. *bitmap* 2 is the future bit map, a bit is set in it for each relative block that will not be assigned to a logical block at the end of the current transaction. Whenever a new relative block is required, it is the first that corresponds to a set bit in bitmap 1 which is used. If none are set, another zone is added to the database, and all bits corresponding to it are set in both bit maps. The new zone will be twice the size of the last one allocated to this database. When the last zone has been added, a warning will be issued on commit that the database has now reached its maximum allocation. If the bit map was not empty, the first relative block found is allocated and the bits corresponding to it in both bit maps are cleared.

The database root block holds a number of registers associated with the allocation of blocks:

(a) *Max. RBN.* This holds the highest relative block number so far allocated in the database. It corresponds to the highest bit set in the bit map.

(b) *Next. RBN.* This is one greater than the highest relative block so far assigned to a logical block. It must not exceed *Max. RBN.*

(c) *Next. LBN.* When a new class fraction is required this provides its LBN and is then incremented.

(d) *Max. LBN.* This holds the highest LBN currently supported by the LR. map. The LR. map is itself stored in the database and is loaded in by the same mechanism as any other collection of objects. To prevent a recursive address fault two steps are taken:

(i) Whenever *Max. LBN* − *Next. LBN* falls below *Ir. lev. size* + 1, then a new bottom level block is added to the LR. map and *Max. LBN* is incremented by *Ir. lev. size.*

(ii) The new block is assigned a PID with a PSN falling within an already allocated portion of the LR. map

DIRECTORY LEVEL

Up to now this explanation has assumed that a program will only open one database at a time. In practice this is likely to prove rather restrictive. It is often useful to be able to partition data into compartments which although related to one another have enough autonomy to justify treating them distinctly. It would be useful if one could devise a mechanism by which objects in one PS-algol database might reference objects in another. This would allow the sharing of common data without the overheads of taking copies into all the databases that needed it.

To do this we must partition a persistent address space. This can be done by adding another field to the PID. The extra field, the *database number* (shown in Figure 10) allows the space of logical blocks to be divided into 256 databases.

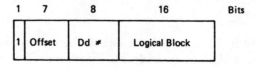

Figure 10. Persistent identifier mark III

To make this field meaningful it is necessary to impose a numbering system on the databases, so that when we encounter a database number we know which database this corresponds to. Organizing the interpretation of database numbers is the task of the POMS directory system.

At an abstract level a directory is an updateable function from strings to directories or databases. At an implementation level a directory serves further purposes.

(a) It acts as a means of finding directories and databases on disk.

(b) It acts as a means of distribution of disk resources.

(c) It is the basic support for atomic transactions.

In order for directories to act as a route map they must start in a known position. The starting point of the hierarchy will be located at physical block number 1.

Transactions

Directories provide the basic support for atomic transactions. To commit a transaction it is necessary to have some mechanism to cause the newly written set of pages to be treated as the currently valid set. In the POMS this mechanism is provided by the directories which contain pointers to the currently valid instantiations on disk of databases. When a transaction on a database completes, it is written back to a new location and its directory entry is updated to point to the physical disk address of its root block.

It is still necessary to be secure against the possibility of a hardware failure occurring during the course of a directory write. It is obviously impermissible to write the directory back to the same site that it came from, for if one did, an error during write could cause the old directory to be lost. The solution adopted is to write it back to alternating sites.

The physical implementation of a directory is as two contiguous versions each of which occupies two contiguous disk blocks as shown in Figure 11.

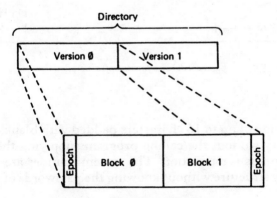

Figure 11. The format of a directory

The address of a directory is defined to be the PBN of the lowest numbered block in these two versions. The first and last 16-bit integer fields of a version are its epoch number. Before a version is written back to disk these epoch numbers must be incremented. A version is said to be valid if both of its epoch numbers are the same. In the event of a failure occurring between the output of the first and the second disk blocks, then this should be detected by the inconsistencies between the epoch numbers at the start and finish of the version. This method of consistency check is proposed in Reference 10.

Whichever of the two versions in a database has the higher epoch number is said to be the current version. If a version is not valid its epoch number is defined to be negative.

The operation of incrementing an epoch number is cyclical, so that the number following 10000 is 0. Given two epoch numbers a, b then

$$a < b \text{ iff } b = a + 1 \text{ or } a + 1 < b$$

If one version has been corrupted it is always possible therefore to recover the previous version.

A directory transaction comprises the following phases:

1. Read both versions.
2. Determine which is current.
3. Make any necessary changes to the in core copy of the current version.
4. Write the updated current version, with incremented epoch number back to the site of the non-current version.

Structure

The internal structure of a version occupies 510 16-bit integers disregarding the epoch numbers. These are divided into several fields as shown in Figure 12.

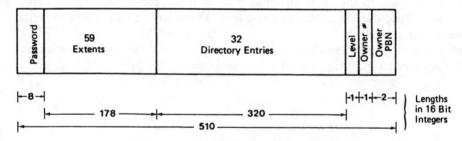

Figure 12. The format of a version

Password

A password is a string of up to 16 characters padded with blanks. No operations are allowed on a directory without the calling program supplying the correct password. The one exception to this is navigation. The system routines are allowed to navigate through the directory structure without knowing the passwords of intermediate levels.

Extent

An extent is three numbers that describe a contiguous area of disk. The first is the disk number, the second the starting block number on the disk, the third is the number of blocks in the extent.

The storage allocation system used in POMS is hierarchically distributed. Each directory is responsible for providing space for its subordinate databases or directories. If a directory runs out of space it asks its owner to allocate it extra space. Each time a directory demands space from its owner it asks for an amount equal to a fixed proportion of the total amount aquired so far. Currently this proportion is set to unity, so that the effect is to cause directories to grow by successive doublings of the amount of space allocated to them. The rationale behind this approach is twofold:

1. It is hoped to encourage locality of access to data that is likely to be accessed within a given transaction, thus reducing disk head movement.
2. By distributing the storage allocation it prevents over-locking of a single global block allocation structure.

A directory entry is a 20-byte field composed of the fields as shown in Figure 13.

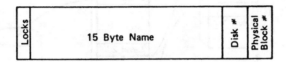

Figure 13. A directory entry

If the top bit of the lock is set then entry is open for writing. Otherwise the lock contains a count of the readers. If the lock is non-zero the entry cannot be opened for writing. The protocol is thus one writer many readers.

An entry may point at either another directory or at a database. If it points at a database this is indicated by a disk number ≥ 0 if it points at a directory the disk number is < 0. In the latter case, the absolute value of the disk number must be used for navigation.

The convention adopted in naming directory entries is to specify a path name whose components are separated by '/', so one might have a name such as 'poms/text/dictionary' to indicate a dictionary database that was in a directory 'text' in a directory 'poms'.

Database number

A database number identifies the database holding an object. The interpretation of this number depends upon the frame of reference in which it is situated. An absolute identification of a database can be achieved, using the path through the directory hierarchy from TOP to the database in question. Given that each level of the hierarchy can branch at most 32 ways, a database can be identified uniquely by a list of 5-bit numbers

$$(b_1, b_2, \ldots b_j) : j \to 1 \ldots n$$

where $n = $ max depth of hierarchy.

The absolute identification of a database requires $5n$ bits. If we impose a restriction on the set of objects that can be addressed from any one site, then we can in theory economize on the number of bits required. We have argued elsewhere[11] that it is desirable to restrict addressability in a persistent addressing system to the databases in nodes of the tree that form a path from the current node back up to the root of the tree. Thus, although for a tree of depth n and branching factor m there can be m^n databases, the number that can be addressed from within any one database would be mn. In our example $m = 32$ and $n = 8$. A POMS system can contain 2^{40} databases. The maximum that can be addressed from any given position is 256. If we are in database

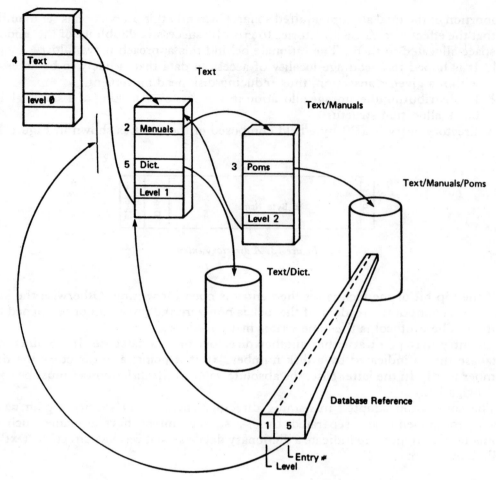

Figure 14. Interpretation of the database number field of a PID

$(b_1, b_2, \ldots, b_j): j \leqslant 8$, then this provides us with a frame of reference to interpret a database number $D:0 \,..255$: D refers to database D **rem** 32 in b_i where $i = D$ **div** 32.

An illustration of the interpretation of a database number is given in Figure 14. Our interpretation of PID is now given in Figure 15.

Owner

The owner field contains information necessary to locate the directory within the hierarchy. It points at the disk address of the owning directory.

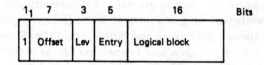

Figure 15. Persistent identifier mark IV

Operations

A number of operations on the directories are provided as transactions.

(i) *Space allocation*: transactions are provided to claim or release space.

(ii) *Entries*: transactions are provided to delete, lock and unlock entries and to change the disk address associated with a directory entry.

(iii) *Utilities*: various utility functions to search directories, create subdirectories and make enquiries about directories are available.

CLOSEDOWN

Currently it is only possible to commit a transaction on a single database: the one opened in write mode. The commit sequence is effected by the notional algorithm given in Figure 16. The procedures used in the algorithm are outlined below.

```
procedure commit
begin
  let the. db = Output. db
  let Bit. map = the. db(BIT. map. tree)
  let dn: = 0; let dc: = 0; BIT. map(1): = BIT. map(1)
  repeat {
       dc: = dn
       procedure keep(int i)
         if written(i) and marked(i) do {
             dc: = dc + 1; clear. flag (i, written. bit)
             mark. class. fraction. of(pid. of. lon(i), the. db)
         }
       app. to. dependents(Output. db, keep)
       }
  while dc > dn do dn: = dc
  purge. each. marked. class. fraction
  let disk. no = the. db(old. D)
  let block. no = PBN(RBN(PCN. of(pid. of. loca(pntr. to. loca(the. db)))))
  let root. loc = @1 of int[abs(disk. no), block. no]
       add. entry(db. file, the. db(owner. toc), root. loc, the. db(db. name))
end
```

Figure 16. The algorithm for committing a transaction on a database

Mark class fraction

The procedure *mark. class. fraction. of* maintains a hashed table of class fractions. Each time it is called, it checks to see if the class fraction of its parameter has been entered in the table and if not enters it into the table and updates the LR. map entry for that class fraction to point at a new relative block. The bit corresponding to the new relative block is cleared from the current bit map, and the bit corresponding to the old relative block is set in the future bit map.

Purge

The procedure *purge. each. marked. class. fraction* builds a list of class fractions in this hashed table sorted on their relative block numbers. It then traverses the list and executes the following algorithm
1. Fetch the old relative block.
2. Find all PIDLAM entries whose PIDs belong to this logical block.
3. Discard those that have not had their dump bit set.
4. Copy the objects refered to by the rest into the logical block buffer.
5. Write out the buffer to disk.
The initial sorting by relative block numbers is to minimize disk head movement. This could be thwarted by step (1) of the above algorithm. It will therefore be advisable to prefetch several of the old relative blocks at a time, and to fetch these in relative block order.

Bit Map

At the start of the close down the current bit map is assigned to itself. This apparently senseless assignment is intended to make sure that the top level of the bit map tree is written back to disk. The procedure *rotate. bit. maps* is shown in Figure 17.

```
procedure rotate. bit. maps(pntr db)
begin
    let bitmap = db(BIT. map. tree)
    let temp = bitmap(1)
    bitmap(1): = bitmap(2)
    bitmap(2): = temp
end
```

Figure 17. The bit maps must be swapped at the start of a transaction

PORTABILITY

The POMS is written in PS-algol in order to make the porting of PS-algol to new environments simple. An objective of POMS is to make it easy to implement PS-algol on any machine for which S-algol is already available.

New built in procedures

In order for an S-algol system to be able to run the POMS, several new procedures must be provided by the run-time system to communicate with the POMS, or to carry out operations required by POMS that are inefficient if written in standard S-algol.

Heap interface

(a) *HEAP*. This returns a vector which is the heap indexed by addresses divided by 4.

(b) *illegal. ion*. If the S-Algol system finds that it has been instructed to dereference a PID it calls the procedure *illegal. ion* with the illegal local address (PID) as parameter.

(c) *pntr. to. ion*. This coerces a pointer to a local address held in an integer.

(d) *int. to. pntr*. Used to set up initial data structure; just coerces an *int* to a *pntr*.

(e) *make. space*. Allocates a number of words on the heap and returns the local address.

(f) *block. move*. Given a source, a destination and a count, copies the requisite number of bytes from the source to the destination.

Bit twiddling

Some additional standard procedures to handle boolean operations have been added.

(i) *not*(**int** *word, bitno*→**int**). This complements an integer.

(ii) *test. bit*(**int** *word, bitno*→**bool**). This returns true if bit *bitno* in *word* is set.

(iii) *clear. bit*(**int** *word, bitno*→**int**). This returns the word with bit *bitno* cleared.

Disk interface

POMS is designed to work on either a bare machine on which it has total control of the disk drives or on a machine with a disk operating system interposed between it and the drives. In the second case a direct access file is to be used to mimic each drive.

The basic operations on the disk or erzatz disk are carried out by the procedures:

(a) *read. blocks*(**file** *f*; **int** *n* →***int**) ! *int parameter is block count*

(b) *write. blocks*(**file** *f*; ***int** *val*)

(c) *seek. blocks*(**file** *f*; **int** *block. number, disk. number*)

In the case of a system working at the level of the physical disk the filename will be ignored. *read. blocks* and *write. blocks* will transfer to or from the address provided by the previous seek operation.

A physical block number (PBN) is defined as being the identifier used by the procedure *seek. blocks* to identify which block transfers are to start at. Blocks are assumed to be 512 bytes. *seek. blocks* and the transfer routines must convert PBNs into the records of blocks used by the underlying system. Within an S-algol program the blocks are represented as vectors of integers.

PERFORMANCE

We have not yet seriously investigated the problem of defining performance metrics for PS-algol systems. It is difficult to make a direct comparison with other approaches to persistent storage, such as conventional network or hierarchical database systems because:

(a) Data structures may be arbitrarily divided between persistent and non-persistent store, tending to migrate into fast non-persistent store as a transaction progresses. Performance will therefore be heavily dependent upon the type of data structures set up by the applications programmer.

(b) There is no clear demarcation between work done to bring in objects needed by the POMS itself and objects directly needed by the application.

(c) The overall performance of the system is dominated by the efficiency of the code generated by the PS-algol compiler. Any improvement to the speed of the code generated by the compiler will accelerate both the POMS and the application program.

The system is still (as of June 1983) undergoing testing so that the body of performance data that has been collected is limited to that arising from the execution of the test suite. None of these programs stores very large bodies of data, the largest database so far set up was only 256K bytes. However, given the fixed depth of the access paths in the mapping structures it is to be expected that the time taken to fetch an object will be relatively independent of database size. Because of the growth of the PIDLAM with large transactions, we would expect performance to depend more closely upon the number of objects touched in a transaction.

With these reservations, we present data gathered from 4 sample transactions in Table I. these are:

A—a database create operation, this sets up all of the POMS type handling and mapping info and commits it to a new database; it is a write only transaction

B—a read only transaction that performs a query on some items in a database

C—a small read write transaction

D—a larger read write transaction

Table I. Table showing performance on a number of transactions

	A	B	C	D
Imported objects	—	45	41	145
Imported bytes	—	2336	2796	7404
Average import size	—	51	68	51
PIDS made	358	—	14	238
Export bytes	6740	—	2312	25,416
Block writes	29	0	12	79
Block reads	3	20	32	193
Objects in transaction	358	45	55	383
CPU time (s)	9·8	1·2	3·3	33·6
CPU time per object (s)	0·02	0·03	0·06	0·08

Bear in mind that the CPU time in all but the create transaction, is partially accounted for by the user program.

The implementation that gave these results was interpretive on a VAX 780. It used a PS-algol intermediate code interpreter. It is hoped that with a code generated or microcoded implementation of the algol an order of magnitude speed gain can be made.

CONCLUSION

POMS has been implemented on the VAX/VMS system. Work is currently under way transporting it to the ICL Perq, ICL 2900, Vax/Unix and Motorola 68000. In converting an existing S-algol system to PS-algol, additions to the compiler and interpreter do not exceed 10 per cent of the original source.

ACKNOWLEDGEMENTS

This work has been carried out at the Universities of Edinburgh and St. Andrews. The work at Edinburgh was supported in part by SERC grant GRA 86541. It is now supported at Edinburgh by SERC grants GRC 21977 and GRC 21960 and at St. Andrews by SERC grant GRC 15907. The work is also supported at both Universities by grants from ICL.

REFERENCES

1. M. P. Atkinson, K. J. Chisholm and W. P. Cockshott, 'PS-algol: an algol with a persistent heap', *ACM Sigplan Notices* **17** (7), 24–31 (1982).
2. A. Van Wijngaarden *et al.*, 'Revised report on the Algorithmic language Algol68', *Algol Bulletin*, No. 36, March 1974.
3. R. Morrison, 'S-algol reference manual', *Tech. report cs 79/1*, St. Andrews University, Department of Computer Science, 1979.
4. M. P. Atkinson, K. J. Chisholm, W. P. Cockshott and R. Marshall, 'Algorithms for a persistent heap', *Software—Practice and Experience*, **13**, 259–271 (1983).
5. M. P. Atkinson, K. J. Chisholm and W. P. Cockshott, 'CMS:—a chunk management system', *Software—Practice and Experience*, **13**, 273–285 (1983).
6. M. P. Atkinson, P. J. Bailey, K. J. Chisholm, W. P. Cockshott and R. Morrison, 'An approach to persistent programming', *The Computer Journal*, **26**, (4), 360–365 (1983).
7. P. Wegner, *Programming Languages Information Structures and Machine Organisation*, McGraw–Hill, Computer Science, New York, 1968.
8. W. Teitelman, *Interlisp Reference Manual*, Xerox, Palo Alto Research Center, 1974.
9. I. L. Traiger, 'Virtual memory management for database systems', *ACM Operating Systems Review*, **16**, October, 26–48 (1982).
10. M. F. Challis, 'Database consistency and integrity in a multi-user environment', in *Databases— Improving Usability and Responsiveness*, Academic Press, New York, 1978, pp. 245–270.
11. W. P. Cockshott, *'Orthogonal persistence'*, *PhD dissertation*, University of Edinburgh, November 1982.

A Shared, Segmented Memory System for an Object-Oriented Database

MARK F. HORNICK and STANLEY B. ZDONIK

Brown University

This paper describes the basic data model of an object-oriented database and the basic architecture of the system implementing it. In particular, a secondary storage segmentation scheme and a transaction-processing scheme are discussed. The segmentation scheme allows for arbitrary clustering of objects, including duplicates. The transaction scheme allows for many different sharing protocols ranging from those that enforce serializability to those that are nonserializable and require communication with the server only on demand. The interaction of these two features is described such that segment-level transfer and object-level locking is achieved.

Categories and Subject Descriptors: D.3.3 [Programming Languages]: Language Constructs—*abstract data types; data types and structures; modules and packages*; D.4.2 [Operating Systems]: Storage Management—*segmentation; virtual memory*; H.2.2 [Database Management]: Physical Design—*deadlock avoidance*; H.2.4 [Database Management]: Systems—*distributed systems; transaction processing*; H.3.2 [Information Storage and Retrieval]: Information Storage—*file organization*; H.3.3 [Information Storage and Retrieval]: Information Search and Retrieval—*clustering, retrieval models*

General Terms: Design, Experimentation, Languages, Performance

Additional Key Words and Phrases: Asynchronous communication, CAD transaction processing, data models, locking, object clustering, object-oriented databases, object server

1. INTRODUCTION

Modern workstation technology has made possible a new set of applications. These applications can be characterized as interactive and design based. The basic model is of a worker designing artifacts by using a set of intelligent tools. The artifacts will vary depending on the application, but the common activity seems to be design. Examples of these design environments are electronic and mechanical computer-aided design (CAD) programming environments and office information systems. For the latter, the office worker designs reports, graphics, slide presentations, and decision models.

This research was supported in part by the National Science Foundation under grant DCR 8605597, by the International Business Machines Corporation under contract 55917 and amendment contract 643513, by the Office of Naval Research under contract N00014-86-K-0621, and by DARPA under ONR contract N00014-83-K-0146, ARPA order 4786.

Authors' address: Brown University, Department of Computer Science, Providence, R.I. 02912. M. Hornick: mfh%cs.brown.edu; S. Zdonik; sbz%cs.brown.edu

In order to support the complex software tools that are needed in these environments, we need a powerful support platform. This platform must be capable of providing the glue that makes these applications function as an integrated unit. Database systems have been successful at providing this service for data processing applications. We strive to achieve the same goals for the domain of interactive design.

We believe that object-oriented databases are a step in this direction. They provide more flexible modeling tools than traditional database systems. They also incorporate some of the software engineering methodologies, such as data abstraction, that have proved to be effective in the design of large-scale software systems.

This paper describes one such system. It further raises a series of issues that must be addressed in building an object-oriented database. It sketches the solutions with which we are currently experimenting and focuses on the implementation of a sophisticated segmenting or data clustering scheme that we are using to achieve acceptable performance.

2. THE DATABASE MODEL

The database system that forms the basis for this work supports an object-oriented model of data [25]. It is in the tradition of much of the work on high-level semantic models [2, 3, 7, 12, 16, 20], but it takes a view of data that is very closely aligned with many of the object-oriented programming languages [1, 6, 10]. It illustrates a new direction in database research characterized as object-oriented databases [4, 5, 8, 9, 14, 22].

In the ENCORE database system [25], all objects are instances of some *type* that describes the behavior of its instances. A type T is a specification of behavior. As such, it describes a set of operations O, a set of properties P, and a set of constraints C that pertain to any of the instances of T. Intuitively, an operation is a program that is used to access or manipulate objects of the given type, a property relates objects of the given type to other objects in the database, and a constraint is a predicate that is used to restrict the legal states of objects. If x is an instance of T, any operation o in O can legally be applied to x, any property p in P is defined for x, and any constraint c in C must be satisfied for x. Types, operations, and properties are all objects in their own right and as such have a type that describes their behavior.

Types can be related to each other by means of a special property called *IS-A*. The IS-A property induces an inheritance relationship between types. If A IS-A B, then all operations, properties, and constraints that are defined on B will also be defined on A. In this case we say that A is a *subtype* of B and that B is a *supertype* of A. The system supports the ability for a type to have more than one subtype (i.e., multiple inheritance). It is possible for a subtype to redefine an operation or a property that is defined on its supertype. In this case, an instance of the subtype will not inherit that operation or property from its supertype.

Operations are active objects that are supported by code. Operation types correspond to a procedure definition, whereas instances of operation types correspond to procedure activations. All operation types have an *invoke* operation defined for them such that it is possible to invoke an operation defined on type

T on any object of type T. Operations are associated with a type. Each type defines a set of operation types that can be instantiated and invoked on its instances. A subtype may add operation types that are not defined on its supertype or may refine some of the operations that are defined on its supertype.

Operation refinement, as defined here, is distinguished from operation replacement, as in Smalltalk. In Smalltalk, a subtype method with the same name as a supertype method blocks the supertype method, thereby replacing it with the subtype method. In our system a subtype may provide an operation type that will substitute for an operation type that is defined on a supertype. Here, however, that operation type must be a subtype of the operation type that is being blocked in the supertype. The name of the refinement need not be the same as the operation type that it is refining. If the supertype A defines an operation f and the subtype B defines an operation g that is a subtype of f, an invocation of f on an instance of B will actually use the operation g.

Properties are objects that are used to relate other objects [23]. For example, a property called *works-for* might be defined on the type *Person*. Works-for would relate a given person to the company object for which he or she works. As a first-class object, it is possible for properties to have properties. A common constraint on property types limits the acceptable values for the property. We will call the set of all legal values for a property p its *value class*. Since properties are objects, there is a type called *Property* that describes how properties behave. There can be subtypes of this type, such as *Single-valued-properties* and *Multivalued-properties*. The first subtype restricts the value of the property to be a single entity, whereas the second allows a property value to be a set.

A subtype may refine a property that is defined by a supertype [23]. Just as in the case of operations, the property type that is defined on the subtype must be a subtype of the property type defined on the supertype.

Object-oriented databases are intended to support the development of large and complex applications. We believe that a strong view of encapsulation is essential for programming in the large. Each type has an implementation that is hidden. The implementation of a type includes a representation for instances and code that implements the operations and properties. Code outside of this type definition cannot access the representation of this type. Type definitions may only use the exported interface of other types. This includes a type and its subtypes. No subtype can make use of the implementation of any of its supertypes, and no supertype can make use of the implementation of any of its subtypes. A subtype may only interact with a supertype through the exported interface, just like any other type.

The concepts described above make up the kernel of the object-oriented database model. We view these as a minimal set of facilities for a database system of this kind. In addition to the kernel, we provide a set of facilities that are, in general, useful for design-oriented applications. These additional facilities are built out of the kernel facilities. The following paragraphs sketch a few of the additional facilities.

The ability to deal with change is one of the foremost requirements of any system that supports design activities. Change can occur at both the type level and the instance level. In order to deal with change at the instance level, we

introduce a version control mechanism [24]. This mechanism introduces two new types, *History-Bearing-Entity* (HBE) and *Version-Set*. HBE defines a set of properties that includes *next-version* and *previous-version*, which are used to express the appropriate temporal relationships between object versions. The *next-version* property can be multivalued, thereby allowing a given version object to have multiple successors. We call any version that is the value of a *next-version* property with cardinality greater than 1 an *alternative*. Any other type T can be defined to be a subtype of HBE (as well as any other logically related types), thereby giving instances of T the ability to record versions. *Version-Set* is a type that is used to collect all of the versions of an individual. It has an insert operation that can only add new versions at specific points in the version history. New versions can only be added at the end of a version sequence or as an alternative to an existing version.

The user-level transaction mechanism that is built on top of the kernel makes use of the version control mechanism. A transaction can add a new version to each of a set of version sets (i.e., its write set). This set of changes is called a *slice*, and only slices can be undone. The slice corresponds to a single atomic action, and undoing it corresponds to nullifying the effect of that transaction.

Since types are objects, we can use the version mechanism described above to keep track of changes to types. Each object retains its connection to the original version of the type under which it was created. If one needs to treat an object that is an instance of an old version of a type as if it were an instance of a newer version of that type, we use an exception-handling scheme [17, 18] to facilitate this operation. This scheme works equally well for the case in which we want to treat an object that is an instance of a new version of a type as if it were an instance of an older version of that type. We do not directly support the conversion of instances of old types to conform to new-type definitions. This process can cause old programs to stop working, is often very expensive, and, in some cases, loses information.

An object-oriented database needs to be able to model composite objects, that is, objects that are made up of other objects. In our view, there is a special property called *part-of* that is used to express this relationship. *Part-of* is a subtype of the type *Property*. The *part-of* property has special semantics. It is used by some operations to perform an action on an object and all of its pieces. An example of this is locking a whole object (e.g., a report) for update. This type of lock would first lock the high-level report object and then lock all other objects that are in the transitive closure of the *part-of* property. It is also used in the context of version sets to support version percolation [24].

It is important to realize that the model of data described above is part of a database system. As such, it governs the way in which persistent, sharable objects behave. Our system also addresses database notions of transaction, consistency, associative retrieval, and views.

It is also important to point out that in traditional data models there is always some fairly high level of abstraction below which programmers cannot have access. For example, with relational systems it is typically not possible to reprogram the basic file structures that are used to implement relations. In our view, an object-oriented database system should allow users to program at whatever level best suits their needs. Everything is represented by types, and all types exist at the same level. Levels of abstraction will certainly be encouraged, and, in fact, the system provides several very high-level abstractions such as version sets. However, the very lowest level types, like the type *byte-string*, are available to programmers to build their own abstract types as needed. This does not, however, mean that data abstractions can be compromised. This is critical in an environment like CAD where performance is key. Programmers have the choice of using the system-provided higher level abstraction, or, for cases in which the performance of these types is not adequate, they may choose to create structures that fit their application more closely.

3. THE ARCHITECTURE

The main focus of this paper is on the storage management aspects of an efficient object-oriented database. To achieve a better understanding of some of our choices, we also describe how the storage management function fits into our overall architecture. The rest of this section describes the main system modules and the way in which objects are mapped through the various levels of abstraction.

3.1 The Module Structure

The database system is decomposed into two distinct subsystems. One subsystem is a typeless backend that is responsible for managing the use of the persistent object store, and the other piece is responsible for the enforcement of the type system.

The OBject SERVER, known as ObServer, reads and writes chunks of memory from secondary storage. These chunks are used by the higher level module to store the state of objects. ObServer also has a primitive notion of transactions, which includes a subset of Moss's nested transactions [11]. Through the transaction mechanism, it is possible to lock and unlock objects to ensure an appropriate level of noninterference. The transaction mechansim can be used in a way that provides for resilient storage in that if it is used properly, it will not allow the changes of an aborted or crashed transaction to be permanently installed in the database.

The transaction scheme makes it possible to support a variety of shared memory applications. The server is currently being used at Brown University for two distinct purposes, the backend of an object-oriented database system and the storage system for an object-oriented, interactive programming environment. Other examples of systems that could be implemented on top of our server include mail or blackboard systems.

The type level is normally referred to as ENCORE (Extensible and Natural Common Object REsource). It is this level that deals with the semantics of objects through type definitions. This higher level module supports the type system that was described earlier as the ENCORE data model. It should be noted that ObServer can support other type systems as well. For example, the GARDEN programming environment defines its own type system, yet it uses the facilities of ObServer to store its persistent objects.

The type level communicates with the server through the UNIX[1] remote procedure call (RPC) mechanism. The communication channel is asynchronous in the sense that ENCORE (or any application process) sends messages to ObServer requesting services and does not wait for ObServer to reply. When ObServer replies, ENCORE may or may not choose to service the reply message.

A client sends a request to the server and is not suspended while the server processes the request. At a future time, the client takes reply messages from its message queue. Reply messages may be delivered soon after a request has been made or after some delay. For example, lock requests may be granted immediately, or they may wait in a queue and be granted or denied later. Similarly, messages for a client regarding changes in objects on which the client holds notify locks arrive periodically from the server.

3.2 Server Overview

The server is a resource for any application system that needs to manage chunks of memory allocated in a shared memory space. Here, a chunk is any contiguous string of bytes. The server must allocate space and a Unique IDentifier (UID) for each chunk that it stores. The UID is similar to a laundry ticket that is given out when the object is stored and that guarantees delivery of the same object when the UID is presented to the server. One of the principal functions of the server is to maintain the correspondence between UIDs and chunks of memory.

The setting for our system is a network of workstations (i.e., nodes), each running independent processes. We have adopted a model in which a server and its data reside on a single node. It is possible for processes on other nodes to access this server. Concurrent access to the shared memory is accomplished by means of UNIX remote procedure calls to possibly remote UNIX processes. The server also supports transaction processing in a manner that is flexible enough to handle long, interactive transactions, as well as the more traditional type. The nested transaction processing facility supports atomicity and recovery and deadlock detection. Our approach to locking has several novel features that are discussed in a later section.

Each process that wants to communicate with the server must bind a module called the *client* into its image. It is, therefore, possible for the client and the server to reside on different machines. When a process needs to request a service from the server, it makes a call on the client code that hides the details of the RPC interface. The ENCORE module uses the object server as a backend. It makes calls directly on its own copy of the client module. Notice that if there are two different processes on two different machines using the ENCORE database, separate copies of ENCORE must reside on each machine (see Figure 1). As will be seen (in a future section), we can achieve some performance enhancement by making the client an intelligent partner in the communication. It can often make certain decisions locally, thereby minimizing the amount of communication.

---

[1]UNIX is a trademark of AT&T Bell Laboratories.

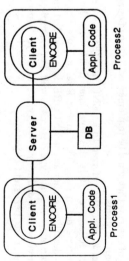

Fig. 1. The basic module structure.

3.3 ENCORE Overview

The chunks of memory that are managed by the server can be used to implement type objects as presented by the ENCORE interface. In an object-oriented database the type lattice introduces the problem of an object's being an instance of more than one type. If we have the type *Toyota* as a subtype of the type *Car*, then an instance *x* of the type *Toyota* is also an instance of the type *Car*. Since our system enforces a strong notion of data abstraction, there will be a chunk of storage that represents the part of *x* that is an instance of *Toyota*, and a chunk of storage that represents the part of *x* that is an instance of *Car*. We use the term *instance* to refer to each chunk and the term *object* to refer to the aggregate of all instances that make up *x*.

The system deals with object creation and modification in a way that is designed to optimize its interaction with the file system and the RPC facility. The reading and writing of objects is done on a block basis. That is, the application may request that an aggregate of UIDs be read or that a collection of objects be written in a single interaction with the server. This generates only one IPC transfer and also allows the server to optimize the way in which it interacts with the file system. Upon object creation, UID allocation is separated from storage allocation. This allows an application to request UIDs in anticipation of their use without reserving space for them in the file. Space is not allocated until objects are actually written.

3.4 Multiple Databases

In order to allow multiple databases to be accessed, we have adopted a scheme by which a separate *binder* process provides a client with a connection to the desired database. The interaction between the client, binder, and server allows both the creation of new databases and a connection to existing databases.

Each database that is being accessed will have a separate server process that mediates its requests. When a client wants to access a database, it issues a request to the binder. The binder returns enough information for the client to connect to the appropriate server. All further requests from the client will subsequently go directly to that server. The requests to a given server can come from any of several clients that are possibly on different machines.

3.5 Transaction Management

The transaction-processing facilities of the system were designed for transactions that are potentially long, interactive processes controlled by a user who is sitting at a workstation. Conventional transaction-processing schemes are designed for relatively short transactions that are implemented by a program. For this reason, we have made choices that are different from what one might expect of a database transaction facility. Our general philosophy is to provide the proper level of primitives so that applications built on top of our system can present the transaction mechanism that best suits their environment. For example, using our system it is possible to build a set of transactions that are serializable. It is also possible to use the primitives in a way that does not make such a strong guarantee about the results of a set of concurrent transactions.

A later section of this paper focuses on the transaction-processing capabilities provided by ObServer. ENCORE can make use of these primitives to construct transaction mechanisms of its own. We would model ENCORE transactions as instances of a type called *Transaction*. The type *Operation* would be a subtype of *Transaction*. We have not included definitions for the Transaction type in the current ENCORE kernel. If this type were to be built, it would make use of the ObServer facilities and may choose to let some or all of the transaction facilities show through.

3.6 Storage Mapping

ENCORE deals with abstract objects that are instances of types. These types participate in inheritance relationships and allow for the implementation of an object to be distributed across several type definitions. How are these levels of abstraction mapped onto the basic storage structures provided by ObServer?

At the type level, every object might consist of several instances, one for each type in which it participates. For example, if *Toyota* is a subtype of *Car*, *Car* is a subtype of *Vehicle*, and *Vehicle* is a subtype of *Object*, then a given Toyota will be an instance of all four types. Since each type has its own private representation, as required by our abstract data type scheme, the Toyota object would need four chunks of storage for its representation. Each of these chunks would be accessible through the operations of the corresponding type.

We must next ask how these chunks (i.e., one for each instance) are held together. A single UID is associated with each object. When a UID is dereferenced, it leads to a header block for that object. Conceptually, the header is a part of the chunk for the instance of type Object that every object must have. The header for object *x* contains some general bookkeeping information, as well as a set of pairs of the form (t, p), where *t* is a pointer to a type object, and *p* is a pointer to the beginning of the chunk that holds the representation for the instance of *t* that is a part of *x*.

Most often, these chunks are allocated contiguously such that the pointer *p* is the offset into that contiguous storage at which the chunk for *t* begins. In this case there would be a single UID for the large chunk that contains the instance chunks. This UID is the one that is used by ENCORE to represent object identity.

It is also possible for the chunks to be noncontiguous. Since *p* can be a UID, the chunks can be stored in any physical location. This allows for a vertical partitioning scheme in which instances of different types for the same object can be stored in different storage areas. The decision to perform this type of partitioning would depend on the access patterns for objects of the given type.

Every chunk that is stored by ObServer has an ObServer-level UID. Only some of these are exported by the ENCORE interface to application programs as object surrogates. If one of the internal pointers that binds together the type instances for an object is a UID, then this UID is never available to be passed to application programs. It is useful to allow ObServer to find the chunk, but since it does not represent a whole object, it has no semantic meaning at the ENCORE level.

Once we have an object decomposed into its proper storage pattern such that the chunk or chunks contain all of the necessary instance blocks, we can use ObServer to store those chunks with the appropriate UIDs. Notice that, if all the instances are stored contiguously, there is only one chunk to store, and the UID of the instance of Object is used.

4. SEGMENTS

In an environment in which many objects must be frequently accessed, efficiency becomes a principle design criterion. One approach to improving performance in a database involves clustering groups of related objects on the disk. The *segment* provides this facility. A segment contains objects that the object-oriented database management system expects a client to access during a transaction, thus eliminating frequent diskhead motion and single object transfers. Thus a segment clusters a logically related set of objects into a variable-sized single package. Since we expect a client to access other objects in a transferred segment, greater system performance results from preloading required objects. A segment is the unit of transfer for objects between client and server and from secondary storage to main memory.

Segment objects are only read or modified through the segment operators: install, find, update, delete. Find, update, and delete have the conventional meaning. Installing an object refers to inserting an object into a segment. Migrating an object involves deleting an object from one segment and installing it into another.

Once a client receives a segment, the objects are individually placed in an object hash table and the segment is freed. The client has no further use for the segment structure once it has acquired its objects. Part of the gain in performance involves the placement of objects on disk. Storing a segment's objects contiguously on disk allows faster disk access, since the segment may be read into main memory without random diskhead movement. Since the UNIX file system does not guarantee contiguous storage of segments, ObServer employs its own file mechanism.

The server receives a set of object changes from the client containing a client's operations (install, update, delete) and other information necessary (e.g., the object) to install the changes in the server's copy of the segment. By returning only the final changes to the server in one package, we minimize the amount of network traffic and reduce server processing. If changes are transmitted individ-

ually, the server not only installs the changes but must access the communication network for each change. It may seem that the entire segment should be sent to the server, thereby eliminating having the server install client changes into the server's segments. Since we wish to allow many clients to use copies of the same segment, the server would then have to merge the returned segments, which is a much more costly operation. As a result, our segment becomes a unidirectional unit of transfer, in the direction of the client, for reducing communication from the client to the server when objects are requested.

It is useful for a client to create different segment groupings or contexts in which to work. This allows individual segment sizes to remain small and at the same time define larger working sets above the level of transfer. To allow clients to retrieve different sets of related segments, we introduce the *segment group* (SG). To reference an SG, a unique name is assigned by the client creating the SG. This notion of grouping a set of segments facilitates having small, very strongly related sets of objects in segments, while allowing several alternative larger groupings to be specified. All segments are themselves uniquely named SGs, and an SG contains one or more SGs. Reading an SG provides a set of segments. As an example, Figure 2 illustrates nine segments that are involved in various groupings. Reading SG4 provides segments s2, s3, s4, s5, and s8. As indicated in Figure 2, a given segment may occur in several segment groups. Each database maintains its own SG forest, and an SG may only contain the segments within a database.

When a client requests an object, the server returns the segment s in which the object resides. The client may further specify an SG that indicates the context in which it is working. The SG may be selected by the ENCORE module on the basis of knowledge about how types are used and storage pragmas. In this case the server returns the other members of the SG asynchronously, while the client is working on the objects contained in the original segment s. This provides another level of preloading that can occur in the background.

4.1 Object Access

The object server maintains *master segments* containing the current versions of all objects resulting from committed object changes. A client obtains from the server *copy segments* that the client accesses locally. Clients may share the same copy segments by each having a copy at their location; however, object locks may prohibit specific object accesses.

Whereas segments provide access to objects in groups, the *unique identifier* (UID) provides individual object access. Our segmentation scheme employs two types of UIDs: *external* and *internal*. An external UID provides a user with a constant reference to a database object. When the server dereferences a valid external UID, there results an internal UID, manipulated by the system to locate an object physically. Both internal and external UIDs have the same length, but their internal structures differ. Each external UID maps either directly or indirectly onto one or more internal UIDs. A mapping to multiple internal UIDs results from replicating objects (discussed below). The server sequentially allocates external UIDs that are not recycled when objects are deleted. Deleted objects have external UIDs that map to a *tombstone* internal UID. This makes it

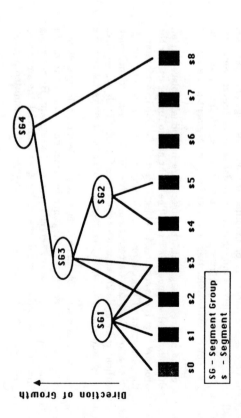

sG – Segment Group
s – Segment

Direction of Growth

Fig. 2. Example segment groups.

possible to detect a reference to an object that no longer exists. Figure 3 depicts the dereferencing process from an external UID to an object. The various mappings are maintained in files called the *Object Location Table* (OLT) and *Duplicate Object Table* (DOT). In Figure 3, the *code* field in the UID structure indicates the UID type, either internal or external. This information is used in both the client and server processes. The OLT maintains the external-to-internal UID mapping. The DOT is described in more detail in the next section.

4.2 Object Replication

In most clustering schemes, it is only possible to place an object in one group. The case may arise in which there is more than one reasonable way to cluster a given object. To resolve such conflicts, we provide an object replication facility. This scheme, of course, incurs a penalty for update but is extremely useful for objects that are either seldom updated or read only.

The implementation of replicated objects requires the introduction of a level of indirection between the external UID and the internal UID. Here, an external UID maps to an index in the *Duplicate Object Table* (DOT) that is maintained by the server and provides the internal UIDs with all copies of a replicated object. When dereferencing an external UID that maps to a replicated object, the system checks whether a client already has a segment containing the object. If so, the corresponding internal UID is returned.

Updating a replicated object is a more costly operation, since the server must update the object in each segment containing a copy. However, the decision to maintain multiple copies of an object rests with the database designer at the time the object is created. The system guarantees that the update of all copies of a replicated object occurs atomically. Thus a client cannot obtain a segment that contains a duplicate copy of x until all segments containing x have been updated.

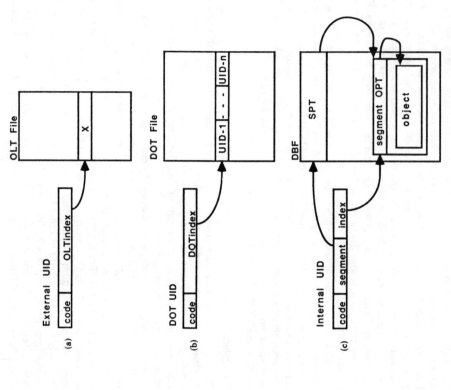

(a) External UID: code | OLTindex → OLT File: X

(b) DOT UID: code | DOTindex → DOT File: UID-1 - - |UID-n

(c) Internal UID: code | segment | index → DBF: SPT, segment OPT, object

Fig. 3. Server UID to object mapping. In (a) X is either an internal UID or a DOT UID. In (b) one of the n internal UIDs is selected on the basis of the status of the corresponding segments. In (c) the segment field corresponds to an index in the SPT. The index field corresponds to an object within the given segment.

Object-level locking, however, introduces a problem with updating replicated objects. If two clients, C_a and C_b, have copies of the same segment, and C_a updates an object that C_b will use after C_a commits, C_b now has an outdated copy of the object in its address space. To solve this problem, the server generates new timestamps for each object in the transferred segment and for the segment itself. If other clients have copies of the same objects, the update of these objects by any client causes new timestamps to be associated with them. The server determines whether a client has an old copy of an object in its address space by comparing the timestamp of the segment (when it was transferred) against that of the object. Timestamps are kept only for objects in use rather than for all database objects to reduce the amount of space required for timestamps in general. If a client tries to lock an object contained in a copy segment and the object is an old copy, the new object is sent to the client.

4.3 Clustering Objects

The segments collectively provide a *partition* of the objects within a database.[2] All database objects are contained in at least one segment. A *Database File* (DBF) represents a separate and independent set of objects and type specifications. It is often useful to partition objects by means of semantic properties. Some options for placement are the following:

—*One object per segment* is intended for very large objects, since they are costly to transfer and tend to be accessed individually.

—*Storing an object with its subobjects* transfers a package of related objects that are almost always accessed together.

—*Storing all instances of a type together* is used to satisfy queries requiring the search of all objects of a type.

—*Partitioning based on property values* is similar to indexing. In using properties, specific values, such as "red," or numeric intervals, such as $0 < n < 3$, may be specified. This method allows a client to separate objects containing a property value of particular interest into one segment.

At the discretion of the designer, any of these methods may be selected to tailor object placement to expected needs. Establishing an initial partition of objects, either through direct client specification (e.g., place object x into segment y) or by semantic criteria, a client may update an object, causing the original object placement to hold no longer. This mainly affects partitioning by property specifications. For example, changing an object's color from red to blue may violate the original specification of a segment whose objects were to have the COLOR property value of "red." We resolve this conflict of an inappropriate property value by specifying the *strictness* with which a segment adheres to the original specification. A segment designated to hold blue objects only holds blue objects if the segment is labeled as *strict*. If the object is updated with a property value violating the segment's strict specification, the object is moved to another, more appropriate segment. A segment labeled *nonstrict* accepts the appropriate objects when they are initially installed. However, updating the object does not cause the object to be moved out of the segment. Segments created by our automatic partitioning mechanism, the *Object to Segment Mapping* (OSM), have the segment specifications strictly enforced. Segments explicitly created by clients are labeled as nonstrict by default, yet may be altered by the client.

4.4 Segment Structure

A segment contains a pointer table and a set of objects. Each segment object is referenced by exactly one entry in the pointer table. Segments are stored in a *Database File* (DBF). The DBF structure is similar to that of the segment: a pointer table and a set of segments. The pointer table allows a reference to an object (or segment) without knowing its exact position. This makes it possible to move objects (or segments) within a segment (or DBF). The pointer table comprises one or more *pointer table blocks*, and additional fixed-size blocks are inserted as a segment acquires more objects. This feature reduces the frequency of segment expansion each time an object is installed. Figure 4 depicts the DBF and segment structures.

A DBF contains the number of *Segment Pointer Table Entries* (SPTEs), the *Segment Pointer Table* (SPT), and segments. The number of SPTEs represents the next available segment index to allocate. Each SPTE is composed of an *offset* and a *size*. The offset specifies the segment location within a file, and the size specifies the number of bytes occupied by the segment. The SPT index serves as the segment identification number and does not change for the life of the segment.

A segment in secondary storage likewise contains three sections: the number of *Object Pointer Table Entries* (OPTEs), an *Object Pointer Table* (OPT), and objects. The number of OPTEs represents the next available object index to allocate. Each OPTE contains an *offset*, *size*, and *OLTindex*, (Object Location Table index). The offset and size are the same as for the DBF. The OLT index provides a back pointer to the OLT that facilitates object migration.

Overflow blocks are main memory addenda to the segment structure. Upon the opening of a segment, space is allocated in main memory for the exact size of the segment. As new objects are installed or existing objects expanded, overflow blocks are allocated separately from the main segment. To reduce the frequency of creating overflow blocks, the system allocates enough memory so that several objects may fit in the same block. The allocation size is determined by a factor multiplied by the size of the first overflow object. Overflow blocks eliminate copying a segment each time objects are installed. Objects in overflow blocks are accessed as though the segment and overflow blocks were contiguous in main memory. When writing a segment back to its DBF, a new segment space is allocated in the file to reflect changes in the segment's size. If overflow blocks exist for a segment in main memory, the segment is first compacted in memory and then written to the disk.

The *Main Memory Segment Table* (MMST) contains information about an open segment throughout its duration in main memory. System routines referencing a segment use an MMST node as a *handle* for segment access. Upon opening a segment, an MMST node is created, initialized, and inserted into the MMST hash table. An MMST node maintains the overflow block information as objects are installed. Independent MMSTs are maintained at each client and at the server.

Object structure depends on the user-defined type specification, but this does not affect the object server since ObServer handles an object as a string of bytes when installing and retrieving objects.

---

[2] Our use of the term partition does not imply mutually exclusive sets of database objects but a lower level clustering of both replicated and nonreplicated objects.

Table I. Lock Modes and Compatibilities

Current lock	Lock request				
	NULL	NR-READ	R-READ	NR-WRITE	R-WRITE
NULL	T	T	T	T	T
NR-READ	T	T	T	T	T
R-READ	T	T	T	F	F
NR-WRITE	T	T	F	F	F
R-WRITE	T	F	F	F	F

5. SHARING

5.1 Lock Types

In conventional database systems, the lock set contains the generic read and write locks with well-defined protocols for their use (e.g., two-phase locking). The conventional lock types and protocols are too restrictive for the design environments that we want to support. For example, two-phase locking and serializability prevent a transaction from seeing the intermediate results of another transaction. Several designers who are in the middle of a design transaction (e.g., editing session) may need to share uncommitted results with their co-workers. Our objective is to provide a comprehensive lock set that allows users to define new protocols freely and easily.

We have identified two dimensions for lock definitions: *lock mode* and *communication mode*. Our scheme employs five lock modes, NULL, NR-READ, R-READ, NR-WRITE, and R-WRITE. NR stands for nonrestrictive and R for restrictive, in the sense of what they allow and disallow. The above ordering of the lock modes indicates their respective strengths from least to greatest. Their compatibility is specified in Table I.

The NR-READ lock mode allows a client to read an object without prohibiting the access privileges of other clients. The R-READ lock mode restricts other clients from writing to an object for the duration of the lock. The NR-WRITE lock mode prohibits other clients from obtaining R-READ or R-WRITE lock-mode locks but allows the reading of an object through the NR-READ lock mode. The R-WRITE lock provides a client with exclusive access to an object, which in essence removes the object from the database while the lock holder uses the object. This lock type is particularly useful when an object or operations on an object are malfunctioning. As an example, consider an operation that inadvertently overwrites random elements in main memory. To prevent further damage as a result of other clients invoking the operation, a system programmer wishes to stop all access to this operation while it is being updated. The lock mode NULL is useful when specifying soft locks (see below) or in conjunction with the communication-mode dimension.

The communication-mode dimension refers to communication between clients as the result of another client's action. Lock holders may wish to be notified of the status of an object, including requests from other clients for that object or committed updates from another client. The five communication modes are

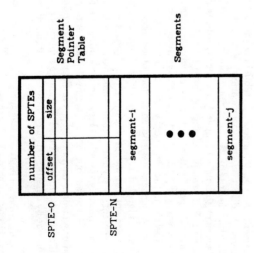

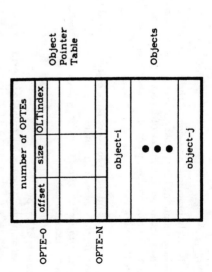

Fig. 4. Database file and segment structures.

would like to update their screens when this occurs. If all transactions hold a NR-READ/U-NOTIFY lock on their objects, then one of the transactions may convert its NR-WRITE lock to a N-NOTIFY lock. When it writes x, the other transactions will be sent a notification of the change, and they can reread x and reset the new value on their displays.

A rich lock set provides flexibility to the user but also greater responsibility to select a lock subset and consistently use locks from that subset. A lock subset is equivalent to the complete lock set with the undesirable lock types filtered out, so we now introduce a lock *filter*. Lock subsets are specified by selecting from one of the system-predefined filters (e.g., to ensure serializable transactions) or by dynamically creating such a filter. Filters guarantee that the specified lock environment is maintained and allows only the permissible lock requests to reach the server. Hence, the user has the ability to tailor an environment with the exact lock desired. A client may set a filter as part of a normal transaction operation. Later versions of the system will allow a database server to have many filters that apply to various user categories (e.g., read-only users or full-privileged users).

U-NOTIFY—notify lock holder upon update, *R-NOTIFY*—notify lock holder if another client requests the object for reading, *W-NOTIFY*—notify lock holder if another client requests the object for writing, *RW-NOTIFY*—notify lock holder if another client requests the object for reading or writing, and *N-NOTIFY* indicating no notification.

By taking the cross product of the lock modes and communication modes, 25 locks result, as depicted in Table II. Of the 25, 11 are nonfunctional, in that the lock mode prohibits the associated communication mode. As an example, consider the NR-WRITE/U-NOTIFY combination. An object locked as such could never be updated while the NR-WRITE was held; hence, notification on update is meaningless. By using various subsets of the remaining 14 locks, applications from cooperative programming design environments to those requiring full serializability may be satisfied.

As an example, the GARDEN [13] system currently uses a hybrid lock, *WRITE-KEEP* [19] that, among its other semantics, informs the owner of the lock of other clients' lock requests on the locked object. This WRITE-KEEP lock is used in conjunction with a NOTIFY lock. From our lock set, the subset NR-WRITE/RW-NOTIFY and NR-READ/U-NOTIFY provides the same functionality. GARDEN uses a NOTIFY lock in place of a read lock and a WRITE-KEEP lock in place of a write lock. This establishes a demand-driven communication scheme. When an object that GARDEN has read is updated, GARDEN is notified, and it can reread the object if necessary. When an object that GARDEN has for writing purposes is needed, GARDEN is notified, and it can return the object if desired.

For a more traditional lock environment, the subset R-READ/N-NOTIFY, NR-WRITE/N-NOTIFY provides the basics for serializable transactions when used with the proper transaction options (see below). By allowing a rich lock set, applications may tailor a locking environment to their requirements for sharing. In an interactive, cooperative design environment, one may wish to employ only locks with the RW-NOTIFY communication mode. Lock holders, not wishing to impede other client's productivity by keeping locks on objects not currently in use, are notified of other client's lock requests. Consequently, the lock holder may opt to free the lock or commit the current object changes, thus allowing the other users to lock the object.

As another example of the use of the communication mode, consider several transactions cooperating on a task, each of which has an object x displayed on its screen. Any one of the transactions is allowed to change x, but the others

5.2 Processing Lock Requests

The server interacts with the client to process both object and nonobject operations and maintains the files necessary for accessing master segments (see Section 6). Commands processed from clients involve DBF operations such as create and open, segment and segment group operations and lock requests. In satisfying client lock requests, the server must determine three things: (1) Does the client already have the object requested in the client's copy segment? (2) Does the client have the most recent copy of the object? (3) If the client has neither (1) nor (2), which segment should be sent to the client? We assume that a client locking an object does so only if it intends to use the object within the current transaction. Therefore, the object is sent in its segment if the lock is granted. The server answers the first question by checking the *Client Segment List* (CSL) maintained at the server for all clients. If the client already holds the required segment, the client receives only the object-access information. Otherwise, the client acquires an appropriate segment from the server. If the client has an outdated local copy of the object as determined by the object timestamp, the server sends the current copy of the object to the client and replaces the local copy.

5.3 Deadlock Detection

Deadlock can occur whenever two conflicting locks have been requested on the same object from two distinct transactions. This situation requires that one transaction wait until the other commits. In our model, the lock compatibilities that conflict are given in Table I. Our definition of deadlock is somewhat different from the usual definition. The server allows certain cycles to remain in the waits-for graph. Here, a deadlock requires that the deadly embrace be between two transactions that have actually been granted locks for each other's objects. If there is a cycle between two transactions that are queued, this cycle is allowed to remain. The system will not grant a lock request if that request would cause a

Table II. Locks and Validity of Mode Combinations

Lock modes	Communication modes				
	U-NOTIFY	R-NOTIFY	W-NOTIFY	RW-NOTIFY	N-NOTIFY
NULL	V	I	I	I	I
NR-READ	V	I	V	I	V
R-READ	I	I	V	I	V
NR-WRITE	I	V	V	V	V
R-WRITE	I	V	V	V	V

Note: V = valid; I = invalid.

deadlock. This potential for deadlock could happen at the time that the lock is requested, or it could happen at the time that a pending request is finally serviced (i.e., removed from the queue). Queued lock requests are serviced whenever a transaction commits or aborts and its locks are released, making them available to other waiting transactions.

Consider the following example. Transaction T_c has objects x_1 and x_2 locked in write mode. Transactions T_a and T_b request locks for x_1 and are queued in that order. Similarly, transactions T_a and T_b request locks for x_2 and are queued in the opposite order. The system will not consider this to be a deadlock, since T_a, T_b, or both of them may abort before T_c completes. If they do not abort, the system will detect deadlock when T_c completes, and either T_a or T_b will be informed that its lock request has been dequeued. Notice that in an interactive environment it is important that a deadlock not cause a transaction to abort.

6. LOCK AND SEGMENT INTERACTION

In our segmentation scheme, we present two levels of granularity for locking: *object-level* and *segment-level*. Locking at the object level implies that a client must request locks on individual UIDs, whereas when locking at the segment level, the client could lock all the objects in a segment with a single specification. Note that, locking an object by its UID locks all copies of the object. Since our system allows replicated objects to reside in separate segments, it would be possible with segment-level locking to lock large sections of the database by locking a single object. In the general case concurrency among clients is significantly reduced with segment-level locking, since a client using a single object in a segment prohibits other clients from obtaining other objects in that segment.

Locking purely at the object level allows clients to share segments, thus increasing concurrency. Our system supports object-level locking with the additional facility for locking all objects in a segment easily. This is more efficient from the user's standpoint in that procuring locks on all segment objects at the outset eliminates having the client repeatedly ask the server for locks or individually specify locks for each object in a segment. To lock all the objects within a segment, each object must acquire the desired lock. Locks that cannot be granted are queued, and the segment is sent with the objects that have acquired their locks.

Recall that our segmentation scheme sends a client an entire segment when the client requests even a single object. This clustering provides objects expected to be used by the client during a transaction. Because client/server interaction is asynchronous, frequent requests to the server for locks impedes client productivity, since the client must wait for the server to reply. Frequent requests also increase the work load at the server, hence reducing performance for all clients.

The server makes a distinction between objects explicitly requested by a client and objects in the remainder of a segment. Objects explicitly requested use *hard locks*, and the remaining segment objects in the segment use *soft locks*. In specifying a lock mode for the remainder of objects in a segment, the client does not know exactly which objects it will be getting. Therefore, we view soft locks as a convenience rather than a necessity (from the client's point of view). If a hard lock cannot be granted, it is queued; soft locks are not queued. The client

requesting a hard lock is notified whether the lock was granted or denied, but is only notified if the lock was granted for soft locks. Using soft locks, we reduce the size of the lock queue and minimize the amount of information returned to the client.

When requesting objects, the object and segment-lock specifications need not be alike, and all locks from the current lock filter are valid for either. A client specifies a lock request as a quadruple: the object UID to be locked, its lock, a segment, and the lock for the remainder of the objects in the segment.

7. TRANSACTION MODEL

The traditional transaction model [6] has well-defined features, such as two-phase locking, that arise from the guarantee that all transactions are atomic. The measure of correctness here is that all resulting schedules are serializable. We attempt to identify the basic building blocks that can be used to build all interesting transaction schemes. We begin by defining a transaction as a series of operations that occur during some period of time in a *well-defined* frame, that is, a frame that is marked by specific delimiters (e.g., *begin* and *end*). These transactions may be nested [11]. All operations occur during a transaction and are associated with an individual transaction. Since transactions at the same client may have different restrictions and allowable lock modes, the operation must be screened to determine whether it is using a validly locked object for that transaction and whether the operation itself is valid (e.g., unlocking an object in the middle of a transaction).

We introduce a set of constraints that may be applied to the skeleton transaction to tailor it to the environment in which it is used. The two essential facilities that a transaction provides are acquiring or releasing a lock and making changes visible (i.e., committed).

With respect to locking, unlock all objects associated with a transaction when it ends with the following two options:

—allow explicit unlocking of objects during a transaction,
—disallow explicit unlocking during a transaction.

With respect to committing, atomically commit all object changes at the end of a transaction with the following two options:

—allow explicit committing of objects during a transaction,
—disallow explicit committing during a transaction.

In general, all explicitly committed object changes are made visible and cannot be aborted. A transaction may be aborted at any time such that any changes not committed are thrown away and all objects are unlocked. From these building blocks, many transaction environments may be created. It should be obvious how the conventional transaction model can be created out of these options.

8. AN EXAMPLE

Figure 5 is an example depicting the role of hard and soft locks, the reduction of communication between the client and server as a result of segment transfers, and the general procedure for accessing objects. Note the following abbreviations:

access information is sent to the client. Having completed the locking phase, S_1 is sent to the client.

At the client, the object O_2 may be accessed using the call OBJECTread (O_2, O_2-buffer). Suppose C_2 wanted to access O_4. C_2 makes the call LOCKquery (O_4) in T_2 and finds that it has an $L_{2,0,S}$ lock on it, which is sufficient for its current needs. Since the object is already at the client, and the lock is valid, the client need not request it from the server, thus giving the client instant access to the object.

If T_2 further wants to write to O_1, it finds that it does not have the appropriate lock. Making the lock request LOCKobjects (O_1, $L_{3,0,H}$, ANY_SEGMENT, and $\bar{L}_{0,0,S}$) involves the following operations: The server finds that T_1 committed and freed the lock it had on O_1. T_2 is granted the lock and, through the timestamp mechanism, it is found to have an outdated copy of the object, so the server sends the individual updated object to C_2. If O_1 had not been updated, then the server informs the client that the lock is granted.

9. ATTAINING AN OPTIMAL PARTITION

The optimal partition of objects within a database results in the transfer of only those objects a user will access in one transaction. Although users provide a partition for objects either by *Object-Segment Mapping* (OSM) or manual specification, these may not result in an optimal partition. Therefore, heuristics provide a more flexible approach to maintaining an optimal object partition based on observations of object usage over time. The heuristics employ a *migration* facility for moving objects from one segment to another. The object migration process involves the system's monitoring object usage within segments and moving objects from one segment to another within the same DBF to aid database performance.

When objects are created, OSM partitions them by semantic criteria or user-specified segments. If an object changes logical association with the other objects in its segment, it needs to migrate or move to another segment to reduce the number of segments transferred, that is, to improve performance. The database administrator and system are responsible for this process.

We consider two types of heuristics, *transaction-oriented* and *single-object* evaluation of object usage. Transaction-oriented heuristics involve monitoring object usage within the context of a transaction. That is, transaction-oriented heuristics involve monitoring how objects are used together. Single-object heuristics involve monitoring using measurements amassed over a period of time. As an example of a time-interval heuristic, consider that natural partitions may form within a segment on the basis of an access count for individual objects, namely, some objects are used very frequently, and others not at all. If enough objects exist in each group so that creating another segment is justified, the objects in the smaller group migrate to the new segment.

Three measures are currently employed for monitoring: the *access count*, *open count*, and *access ratio*. The access count refers to the number of times an object was accessed in a given segment. The open count refers to the number of times the segment was opened. The access ratio is the quotient between the access count and the open count.

```
LOCK MODES          COMMUNICATION MODES
0—NULL              0—N-NOTIFY
1—NR-READ           1—U-NOTIFY
2—R-READ            2—R-NOTIFY
3—NR-WRITE          3—W-NOTIFY
4—R-WRITE           4—RW-NOTIFY

SERVER STRUCTURES
Master Segments:
  Segment Sₓ contains object Oy
  S₁: O₁, O₂, O₃, O₄
  S₂: O₁, O₅, O₆
  S₃: O₃, O₇

Lock Table:
  Transaction Tₓ locks object Oy with lock Lᵢ,ⱼ,ₖ
  T₁: (O₁, L₃,₂,ₕ), (O₅, L₂,₃,ₕ), (O₆, L₂,₀,ₛ)
  T₂: (O₃, L₁,₀,ₕ)

Client Segment List
  Client Cw has segment Sₓ
  C₁: S₂
  C₂: S₃
```

Figure 5

S, segment; O, object; T, transaction; C, client; $L_{i,j,k}$, $0 < i < 4$ lock modes, $0 < j < 4$ communication modes; k: H hard; S soft.

The following are a subset of the client operations that are relevant to this example: LOCKquery (O_y) returns the type of lock $L_{i,j,k}$ currently held on the object or a NO-LOCK signal if no lock is held. LOCKobjects (O_y, O, S_x, S) make the request for object O_y, with the lock O-$L_{i,j,k}$ and lock the accompanying segment S_x with the lock S-$L_{i,j,k}$. This operation informs the server of the request to which the server later responds. The client then takes the segment and the corresponding object-access information into its address space. OBJECTread (O_y, buffer) finds the object O_y in the client's address space and places it in the provided buffer. Not finding the object results in an error signal. SEGMENTfind (O_y) is separate from the standard routines in that it maintains a mapping, possibly at the type level, of where objects are stored. Hence, it determines which segment to request. This provides the client with an *intelligent* segment choice rather than a less informed choice from the server.

From here, client C_2 in transaction T_2 requires object O_2 and checks whether it has a lock on it by making the local procedure call LOCKquery (O_2). Since it does not have the lock and is interested in working on other objects in a specific segment, T_2 finds the segment it wants by the call SEGMENTfind (O_2) and makes a lock request LOCKobjects (O_2, $L_{3,0,H}$, S_1, $L_{2,0,S}$), asking for a specific object O_2 and segment S_1. If the client had not specified a segment, one would have been selected by the server.

At the server, the hard lock for O_2 is granted. The remaining objects on which to acquire soft locks are O_1, O_3, O_4. The soft lock on O_1 is denied, since T_1 holds the lock $L_{3,2,H}$. The soft lock on O_3 is not granted, since a hard lock already exists on the object. If O_3 had been soft locked by T_2, then, if possible, the existing lock would have been upgraded. In either case no additional information needs to be sent to the client about O_3. Object O_4 acquires the soft lock, and the corresponding

Some of these heuristics require keeping detailed statistics on both segments and objects. These are maintained in files at the server and used initially to fine-tune the database.

10. RELATED WORK

Attaining an optimal data organization to minimize retrieval costs is certainly not a new idea [21]. Schkolnick devised a clustering algorithm to perform this task [15]. Although our desired result is the same, our data structures (hierarchical data represented in a tree versus objects), work environment, and means are quite different.

Schkolnick chose to group all instances of a type into a segment. These segments were then grouped in a hierarchical tree structure. To apply his algorithm, Schkolnick obtains usage patterns of data access that are basically the most frequently used access paths in the hierarchy. Examining these patterns allows the algorithm to determine a partition of the tree segments. Once subtrees have been produced, the available disk space is divided into linear address spaces (LASs), one for each partition. The instances of all segments for a given partition are placed in their corresponding LASs in the same order as they appear in the hierarchical order. This idea is equivalent to our method of storing objects with their subobjects. Next, each LAS is divided into blocks of equal length called pages. The objective is to minimize page faults. The system paging mechanism acquires the data from secondary storage, and the data are accessed directly through these pages. A page fault is noted whenever a record is not found on a page already in the buffer pool. Schkolnick has shown that, for a given access pattern, the access time can be minimized on the basis of the storage method for a hierarchical structure. He states, "The predicted optimal storage allocation does in fact significantly reduce the average number of page faults over that obtained when the structure is stored in the conventional hierarchical order" [15, p. 43-44].

This method has several similarities to our segmentation scheme. As mentioned, the notion of storing objects with their subobjects is a common thread. In terms of accessing data, we read a set of related objects expected to be accessed during a transaction. In our method of fathoming a better partition, we analyze usage patterns amassed over time. To clarify the term *segment* in the two contexts, we allow a melange of instances of object types to reside within a segment, whereas Schkolnick's segments are a grouping of type instances which themselves are grouped into LASs. This latter grouping into LASs is similar to our use of *segment groups*, where related segments can be accessed as one larger unit. However, our segment groups maintain their individual segment identities. With Schkolnick's LASs, objects along the same access path within a subtree are stored contiguously, which shatters the original segment boundaries.

We allow more options for object grouping; hence, a more tailored set of objects may be placed in one segment. However, the option for all instances of a type is also provided. Since we devised our method for an object-oriented system, we pose virtually no restrictions on the overall data configuration and dependencies between objects. Our method has no immediate concern for the underlying paging mechanism, which makes it freer from hardware idiosyncracies. We also provide specific segment operators that give exclusive access to database objects.

11. SUMMARY

In this paper we have given an overview of our object-oriented database system. Within that discussion, our central focus has been the implementation of a typeless object server that is used as the backend. Specifically, we have described our segmentation scheme and the mechanisms that are used for controlled sharing. In a final section we have pointed out the interactions and problems encountered in building these two facilities, and we have sketched our solution.

A prototype of this system has been implemented. We have linked the prototype of ObServer with the GARDEN [11] programming environment. GARDEN is a system for visual programming. It allows programmers to construct their programs in terms of pictures. GARDEN also contains a set of tools for easily constructing new pictorial languages. GARDEN treats everything as an object and, as such, provides an excellent testbed for our system. GARDEN views static program pieces, such as modules, statements, and variables, as objects. It also views dynamic structures, such as stack frames, as objects as well. Future versions of GARDEN will make use of the ENCORE database system to take advantage of some of the more advanced features, such as version control.

There are many important research issues that need to be investigated. We view implementation issues as among the most important. This technology will only succeed to the extent that it can be made to operate efficiently. Many of the ideas expressed in this paper were derived from experience with our prototype in the GARDEN environment. We expect this kind of refinement to continue.

The issue of being able to handle objects of widely differing sizes is very important. How can we manage huge objects, such as bit maps or large programs, in a homogeneous way with small objects, such as characters or integers? The data model presents no problem here, but the implementation problems of managing these objects on a disk are yet to be solved.

At the model level, it is tempting and useful to be able to treat everything as an object. For example, we might treat paragraphs, sentences, and characters as objects. It is not unreasonable to incur the overhead associated with an object for paragraphs and sentences, but this overhead at the character level would be completely unreasonable. We therefore need a scheme whereby characters can be conceptually stored as objects, but not as full-fledged objects at the implementation level. A scheme such as this would require that the container objects know something about the form of the objects that are contained in them, and that inbound references be handled specially.

Other research areas include topics like extending and enhancing the data model to include facilities like triggers and views and designing a more complete transaction management scheme that supports concurrency control and recovery differently for different types. The issues involved in effectively supporting the management of change still require further study. Designing a databased programming language whose model of data is precisely the model that we have described above is currently underway. We are also interested in extending our database system to operate in a distributed database environment and to run on parallel-processor machines.

ACKNOWLEDGMENTS

The authors wish to thank David Babson, Steve Reiss, and Andrea Skarra for many invaluable discussions about the design of this system. We would also like to recognize their help, as well as the help of Mark Lellouch and Wlodek Nakonieczey, in implementing the prototype.

REFERENCES

1. BOBROW, D., AND STEFIK, M. The Loops Manual. Xerox Corp., Palo Alto, Calif, 1983.

2. CHEN, P. P. S. The entity-relationship model: Towards a unified view of data. *ACM Trans. Database Syst. 1*, 1 (Mar. 1976), 9–36.

3. CODD, E. F. Extending the database relational model to capture more meaning. *ACM Trans. Database Syst. 4*, 4 (Dec. 1979), 397–434.

4. COPELAND, G., AND MAIER, D. Making smalltalk a database system. In *Proceedings of the ACM SIGMOD* (Boston, June 18–21). ACM, New York, 1984, 316–325.

5. DITTRICH, K., GOTTHARD, W., AND LOCKEMANN, P. C. DAMOKLES—A database system for software engineering environments. In *Proceedings of the IFIP 2.4 Workshop on Advanced Programming Environments* (Trondheim, Norway, June), 1986.

6. GRAY, J. The transaction concept: Virtues and limitations. In *Proceedings of the Very Large Database Conference* (Cannes, France, Sept.), 1981.

7. HAMMER, M., AND MCLEOD, D. Database description with SDM: A semantic database model. *ACM Trans. Database Syst. 6*, 3 (Sept. 1981), 351–387.

8. MAIER, D., AND STEIN, J. Indexing in an object-oriented DBMS. Tech. Rep. CS/E-86-006, Oregon Graduate Center, Univ. of Oregon, Beaverton, Oreg., (May, 1986).

9. MAIER, D., STEIN, J., OTIS, A., AND PURDY, A. Development of an object-oriented DBMS. Tech. Rep. CS/E-86-005, Oregon Graduate Center, Univ. of Oregon, Beaverton, Oreg., (Apr. 1986).

10. MOON, D., STALLMAN, R., AND WEINREB, D. The Lisp Machine Manual, chap 20. MIT AI Laboratory, Jan. 1983, 321–361.

11. MOSS, E. The theory of nested transactions. Tech. Rep., University of Massachusetts, 1986.

12. MYLOPOULOS, J., BERNSTEIN, P. A., AND WONG, H. K. T. A language facility for designing database-intensive applications. *ACM Trans. Database Syst. 5*, 2 (June 1980), 185–207.

13. REISS, S. P. An object-oriented framework for graphical programming. *SIGPLAN Not. 21*, 10 (Oct. 1986) 49–57.

14. RUDMIK, A. Choosing an environment data model. In *Proceedings of the IFIP 2.4 Workshop on Advanced Programming Environments* (Trondheim, Norway, June), 1986.

15. SCHKOLNICK, M. A. A clustering algorithm for hierarchical structures. *Trans. Database Syst. 12*, 1 (Mar. 1977) 27–44.

16. SHIPMAN, D. W. The functional data model and the data language DAPLEX. *ACM Trans. Database Syst. 6*, 1 (Mar. 1981), 140–173.

17. SKARRA, A. H., AND ZDONIK, S. B. The management of changing types in an object-oriented database. In *Proceedings of the First Annual Conference on Object-Oriented Programming Systems, Languages, and Applications* (Portland, Oreg., Sept. 29–Oct. 2). ACM, New York, 1986, 483–495.

18. SKARRA, A. H., AND ZDONIK, S. B. Type evolution in an object-oriented database. In *Research Directions in Object-Oriented Programming*. Addison-Wesley, Reading, Mass., 1987.

19. SKARRA, A. H., ZDONIK, S. B., AND REISS, S. P. An object server for an object-oriented database system. In *International Workshop on Object-Oriented Database Systems* (Pacific Grove, Calif., Sept.). ACM, New York, 1986, pp. 196–204.

20. SMITH, J. M., FOX, S., AND LANDERS. T. *ADAPLEX: Rational and Reference Manual.* 2nd ed. Computer Corporation of America, Cambridge, Mass., 1983.

21. STAMOS, J. W. On object grouping experiments in LOOM. Xerox PARC report SC 6-82-2, Xerox Corp., Palo Alto, Calif.

22. ZDONIK, S. B. Object management system concepts. In *Proceedings of the 2nd ACM-SIGOA Conference on Office Information Systems* (Toronto, Canada, June 25–27). ACM, New York, 1984, 13–19.

23. ZDONIK, S. B. Why properties are objects or some refinements of Is-a. In *Proceedings of the National Computer Conference* (Austin, Tex.). ACM, New York, 1986.

24. ZDONIK, S. B. Version management in an object-oriented database. In *Proceedings of the International Workshop on Advanced Programming Environments* (Trondheim, Norway, June), 1986.

25. ZDONIK, S. B., AND WEGNER, P. Language and methodology for object-oriented database environments. In *Proceedings of the Nineteenth Annual Hawaii International Conference on System Sciences* (Honolulu, Jan.) 1986, 378–387.

Received September 1986; revised December 1986; accepted December 1986

THE DESIGN OF THE POSTGRES STORAGE SYSTEM

Michael Stonebraker

EECS Department
University of California
Berkeley, Ca., 94720

Abstract

This paper presents the design of the storage system for the POSTGRES data base system under construction at Berkeley. It is novel in several ways. First, the storage manager supports transaction management but does so without using a conventional write ahead log (WAL). In fact, there is no code to run at recovery time, and consequently recovery from crashes is essentially instantaneous. Second, the storage manager allows a user to optionally keep the entire past history of data base objects by closely integrating an archival storage system to which historical records are spooled. Lastly, the storage manager is consciously constructed as a collection of asynchronous processes. Hence, a large monolithic body of code is avoided and opportunities for parallelism can be exploited. The paper concludes with a analysis of the storage system which suggests that it is performance competitive with WAL systems in many situations.

1. INTRODUCTION

The POSTGRES storage manager is the collection of modules that provide transaction management and access to data base objects. The design of these modules was guided by three goals which are discussed in turn below. The first goal was to provide transaction management without the necessity of writing a large amount of specialized crash recovery code. Such code is hard to debug, hard to write and must be error free. If it fails on an important client of the data manager, front page news is often the result because the client cannot access his data base and his business will be adversely affected. To achieve this goal, POSTGRES has adopted a novel storage system in which no data is ever overwritten; rather all

This research was sponsored by the Navy Electronics Systems Command under contract N00039-84-C-0039.

updates are turned into insertions.

The second goal of the storage manager is to accomodate the historical state of the data base on a write-once-read-many (WORM) optical disk (or other archival medium) in addition to the current state on an ordinary magnetic disk. Consequently, we have designed an asynchronous process, called the **vacuum cleaner** which moves archival records off magnetic disk and onto an archival storage system.

The third goal of the storage system is to take advantage of specialized hardware. In particular, we assume the existence of non-volatile main memory in some reasonable quantity. Such memory can be provide through error correction techniques and a battery-back-up scheme or from some other hardware means. In addition, we expect to have a few low level machine instructions available for specialized uses to be presently explained. We also assume that architectures with several processors will become increasingly popular. In such an environment, there is an opportunity to apply multiple processors to running the DBMS where currently only one is utilized. This requires the POSTGRES DBMS to be changed from the monolithic single-flow-of-control architectures that are prevalent today to one where there are many asynchronous processes concurrently performing DBMS functions. Processors with this flavor include the Sequent Balance System [SEQU85], the FIREFLY, and SPUR [HILL85].

The remainder of this paper is organized as follows. In the next section we present the design of our magnetic disk storage system. Then, in Section 3 we present the structure and concepts behind our archival system. Section 4 continues with some thoughts on efficient indexes for archival storage. Lastly, Section 5 presents a performance comparison between our system and that of a conventional storage system with a write-ahead log (WAL) [GRAY78].

2. THE MAGNETIC DISK SYSTEM

2.1. The Transaction System

Disk records are changed by data base **transactions**, each of which is given a unique **transaction identifier** (XID). XIDs are 40 bit unsigned integers that are sequentially assigned starting at 1. At 100 transactions per second (TPS), POSTGRES has sufficient XIDs for about 320 years of operation. In addition, the remaining 8 bits of a composite 48 bit interaction identifier (IID) is a command identifier (CID) for each command within a transaction. Consequently, a transaction is limited to executing at most 256 commands.

In addition there is a **transaction log** which contains 2 bits per transaction indicating its status as:

> committed
> aborted
> in progress

A transaction is **started** by advancing a counter containing the first unassigned XID and using the current contents as a XID. The coding of the log has a default value for a transaction as "in progress" so no specific change to the log need be made at the start of a transaction. A transaction is **committed** by changing its status in the log from "in progress" to "committed" and placing the appropriate disk block of the log in stable storage. Moreover, any data pages that were changed on behalf of the transaction must also be placed in stable storage. These pages can either be forced to disk or moved to stable main memory if any is available. Similarly, a transaction is aborted by changing its status from "in progress" to "aborted".

The **tail** of the log is that portion of the log from the oldest active transaction up to the present. The **body** of the log is the remainder of the log and transactions in this portion cannot be "in progress" so only 1 bit need be allocated. The body of the log occupies a POSTGRES relation for which a special access method has been built. This access method places the status of 65536 transactions on each POSTGRES 8K disk block. At 1 transaction per second, the body increases in size at a rate of 4 Mbytes per year. Consequently, for light applications, the log for the entire history of operation is not a large object and can fit in a sizeable buffer pool. Under normal circumstances several megabytes of memory will be used for this purpose and the status of all historical transactions can be readily found without requiring a disk read.

In heavier applications where the body of the log will not fit in main memory, POSTGRES applies an optional compression technique. Since most transactions commit, the body of the log contains almost all "commit" bits. Hence, POSTGRES has an optional bloom filter [SEVR76] for the aborted transactions. This tactic compresses the buffer space needed for the log by about a factor of 10. Hence, the bloom filter for heavy applications should be accomodatable in main memory. Again the run-time system need not read a disk block to ascertain the status of any transaction. The details of the bloom filter design are presented in [STON86].

The tail of the log is a small data structure. If the oldest transaction started one day ago, then there are about 86,400 transactions in the tail for each 1 transaction per second processed. At 2 bits per entry, the tail requires 21,600 bytes per transaction per second. Hence, it is reasonable to put

the tail of the log in stable main memory since this will save the pages containing the tail of the log from being forced to disk many times in quick succession as transactions with similar transaction identifiers commit.

2.2. Relation Storage

When a relation is created, a file is allocated to hold the records of that relation. Such records have no prescribed maximum length, so the storage manager is prepared to process records which cross disk block boundaries. It does so by allocating continuation records and chaining them together with a linked list. Moreover, the order of writing of the disk blocks of extra long records must be carefully controlled. The details of this support for multiblock records are straightforward, and we do not discuss them further in this paper. Initially, POSTGRES is using conventional files provided by the UNIX operating system; however, we may reassess this decision when the entire system is operational. If space in a file is exhausted, POSTGRES extends the file by some multiple of the 8K page size.

If a user wishes the records in a relation to be approximately clustered on the value of a designated field, he must declare his intention by indicating the appropriate field in the following command

> cluster rel-name on {(field-name using operator)}

POSTGRES will attempt to keep the records approximately in sort order on the field name(s) indicated using the specified operator(s) to define the linear ordering. This will allow clustering secondary indexes to be created as in [ASTR76].

Each disk record has a bit mask indicating which fields are non-null, and only these fields are actually stored. In addition, because the magnetic disk storage system is fundamentally a versioning system, each record contains an additional 8 fields:

OID	a system-assigned unique record identifier
Xmin	the transaction identifier of the interaction inserting the record
Tmin	the commit time of Xmin (the time at which the record became valid)
Cmin	the command identifier of the interaction inserting the record
Xmax	the transaction identifier of the interaction deleting the record
Tmax	the commit time of Xmax (the time at which the record stopped being valid)
Cmax	the command identifier of the interaction deleting the record
PTR	a forward pointer

When a record is inserted it is assigned a unique OID, and Xmin and Cmin are set to the identity of the current interaction. the remaining five fields are left blank. When a record is updated, two operations take place. First, Xmax and Cmax are set to the identity of the current interaction in the record being replaced to indicate that it is no longer valid. Second, a new record is inserted into the data base with the proposed replacement values for the data fields. Moreover, OID is set to the OID of the record being replaced, and Xmin and Cmin are set to the identity of the current interaction. When a record is deleted, Xmax and Cmax are set to the identity of the current interaction in the record to be deleted.

When a record is updated, the new version usually differs from the old version in only a few fields. In order to avoid the space cost of a complete new record, the following compression technique has been adopted. The initial record is stored uncompressed and called the **anchor point**. Then, the updated record is differenced against the anchor point and only the actual changes are stored. Moreover, PTR is altered on the anchor point to point to the updated record, which is called a **delta record**. Successive updates generate a one-way linked list of delta records off an initial anchor point. Hopefully most delta record are on the same operating system page as the anchor point since they will typically be small objects.

It is the expectation that POSTGRES would be used as a local data manager in a distributed data base system. Such a distributed system would be expected to maintain multiple copies of all important POSTGRES objects. Recovery from hard crashes, i.e. one for which the disk cannot be read, would occur by switching to some other copy of the object. In a non-distributed system POSTGRES will allow a user to specify that he wishes a second copy of specific objects with the command:

> mirror rel-name

Some operating systems (e.g. VMS [DEC86] and Tandem [BART81]) already support mirrored files, so special DBMS code will not be necessary in these environments. Hopefully, mirrored files will become a standard operating systems service in most environments in the future.

2.3. Time Management

The POSTGRES query language, POSTQUEL allows a user to request the salary of Mike using the following syntax.

> retrieve (EMP.salary) where
> EMP.name = "Mike"

To support access to historical tuples, the query language is extended as follows:

> retrieve (EMP.salary) using EMP[T]
> where EMP.name = "Mike"

The scope of this command is the EMP relation as of a specific time, T, and Mike's salary will be found as of that time. A variety of formats for T will be allowed, and a conversion routine will be called to convert times to the 32 bit unsigned integers used internally. POSTGRES constructs a query plan to find qualifying records in the normal fashion. However, each accessed tuple must be additionally checked for validity at the time desired in the user's query. In general, a record is **valid at time T** if the following is true:

> $Tmin < T$ and Xmin is a committed
> transaction and either:
>   Xmax is not a committed transaction or
>   Xmax is null or
> $Tmax > T$

In fact, to allow a user to read uncommitted records that were written by a different command within his transaction, the actual test for validity is the following more complex condition.

> Xmin = my-transaction and Cmin !=
> my-command and T = "now"
>   or
> $Tmin < T$ and Xmin is a committed
> transaction and either:
>   (Xmax is not a committed transaction and
>   Xmax != my-transaction) or
>   (Xmax = my-transaction and Cmax =
>   my-command) or
>   Xmax is null or
> $Tmax > T$ or

If T is not specified, then T = "now" is the default value, and a record is valid at time, "now" if

> Xmin = my-transaction and Cmin !=
> my-command
>   or
> Xmin is a committed transaction and either
>   (Xmax is not a committed transaction and
>   Xmax != my-transaction) or
>   (Xmax = my-transaction and Cmax =
>   my-command) or
>   Xmax is null

More generally, Mike's salary history over a range of times can be retrieved by:

> retrieve (EMP.Tmin, EMP.Tmax, EMP.salary)
> using EMP[T1,T2] where EMP.name = "Mike"

This command will find all salaries for Mike along with their starting and ending times as long as the salary is valid at some point in the interval, [T1, T2]. In general, a record is **valid in the interval [T1,T2]** if:

> Xmin = my-transaction and Cmin !=
> my-command and T2 >= "now"
>   or
> $Tmin < T2$ and Xmin is a committed
> transaction and either:
>   (Xmax is not a committed transaction and
>   Xmax != my-transaction) or
>   (Xmax = my-transaction and Cmax =
>   my-command) or
>   Xmax is null or
> $Tmax > T1$

Either T1 or T2 can be omitted and the defaults are respectively T1 = 0 and T2 = +infinity

Special programs (such as debuggers) may want to be able to access uncommitted records. To facilitate such access, we define a second specification for each relation, for example:

> retrieve (EMP.salary) using all-EMP[T] where EMP.name = "Mike"

An EMP record is in all-EMP at time T if

> Tmin < T and (Tmax > T or Tmax = null)

Intuitively, all-EMP[T] is the set of all tuples committed, aborted or in-progress at time T.

Each accessed magnetic disk record must have one of the above tests performed. Although each test is potentially CPU and I/O intensive, we are not overly concerned with CPU resources because we do not expect the CPU to be a significant bottleneck in next generation systems. This point is discussed further in Section 5. Moreover, the CPU portion of these tests can be easily committed to custom logic or microcode or even a co-processor if it becomes a bottleneck.

There will be little or no I/O associated with accessing the status of any transaction, since we expect the transaction log (or its associated bloom filter) to be in main memory. We turn in the next subsection to avoiding I/O when evaluating the remainder of the above predicates.

2.4. Concurrency Control and Timestamp Management

It would be natural to assign a timestamp to a transaction at the time it is started and then fill in the timestamp field of each record as it is updated by the transaction. Unfortunately, this would require POSTGRES to process transactions logically in timestamp order to avoid anomolous behavior. This is equivalent to requiring POSTGRES to use a concurrency control scheme based on timestamp ordering (e.g. [BERN80]. Since simulation results have shown the superiority of conventional locking [AGRA85], POSTGRES uses instead a standard two-phase locking policy which is implemented by a conventional main memory lock table.

Therefore, Tmin and Tmax must be set to the commit time of each transaction (which is the time at which updates logically take place) in order to avoid anomolous behavior. Since the commit time of a transaction is not known in advance, Tmin and Tmax cannot be assigned values at the time that a record is written.

We use the following technique to fill in these fields asynchronously. POSTGRES contains a TIME relation in which the commit time of each transaction is stored. Since timestamps are 32 bit unsigned integers, byte positions 4*j through 4*j + 3 are reserved for the commit time of transaction j. At the time a transaction commits, it reads the current clock time and stores it in the appropriate slot of TIME. The tail of the TIME relation can be stored in stable main memory to avoid the I/O that this update would otherwise entail.

Moreover, each relation in a POSTGRES data base is tagged at the time it is created with one of the following three designations:

no archive: This indicates that no historical access to relations is required.

light archive: This indicates that an archive is desired but little access to it is expected.

heavy archive: This indicates that heavy use will be made of the archive.

For relations with "no archive" status, Tmin and Tmax are never filled in, since access to historical tuples is never required. For such relations, only POSTQUEL commands specified for T = "now" can be processed. The validity check for T = "now" requires access only to the POSTGRES LOG relation which should be contained in the buffer pool. Hence, the test consumes no I/O resources.

If "light archive" is specified, then access to historical tuples is allowed. Whenever Tmin or Tmax must be compared to some specific value, the commit time of the appropriate transaction is retrieved from the TIME relation to make the comparison. Access to historical records will be slowed in the "light archive" situation by this requirement to perform an I/O to the TIME relation for each timestamp value required. This overhead will only be tolerable if archival records are accessed a very small number of times in their lifetime (about 2-3).

In the "heavy archive" condition, the run time system must look up the commit time of a transaction as in the "light archive" case. However, it then writes the value found into Tmin or Tmax, thereby turning the read of a historical record into a write. Any subsequent accesses to the record will then be validatable without the extra access to the TIME relation. Hence, the first access to an archive record will be costly in the "heavy archive" case, but subsequent ones will incur no extra overhead.

In addition, we expect to explore the utility of running another system demon in background to asynchronously fill in timestamps for "heavy archive" relations.

2.5. Record Access

Records can be accessed by a sequential scan of a relation. In this case, pages of the appropriate file are read in a POSTGRES determined order. Each page contains a pointer to the next and the previous logical page; hence POSTGRES can scan a relation by following the forward linked list. The reverse pointers are required because POSTGRES can execute query plans either forward or backward. Additionally, on each page there is a line table as in [STON76] containing pointers to the starting byte of each anchor point record on that page.

Once an anchor point is located, the delta records linked to it can be constructed by following PTR and decompressing the data fields. Although decompression is a CPU intensive task, we feel that CPU resources will not be a bottleneck in future computers as noted earlier. Also, compression and decompression of records is a task easily committed to microcode or a separate co-processor.

An arbitrary number of secondary indexes can be constructed for any base relation. Each index is maintained by an **access method**. and provides keyed access on a field or a collection of fields. Each access method must provide all the procedures for the POSTGRES defined abstraction for access methods. These include get-record-by-key, insert-record, delete-record, etc. The POSTGRES run time system will call the various routines of the appropriate access method when needed during query processing.

Each access method supports efficient access for a collection of operators as noted in [STON86a]. For example, B-trees can provide fast access for any of the operators:

$$\{=, <=, <, >, >=\}$$

Since each access method may be required to work for various data types, the collection of operators that an access methods will use for a specific data type must be **registered** as an **operator class**. Consequently, the syntax for index creation is:

> index on rel-name is index-name
> ({key-i with operator-class-i})
> using access-method-name and
> performance-parameters

The performance-parameters specify the fill-factor to be used when loading the pages of the index, and the minimum and maximum number of pages to allocate. The following example specifies a B-tree index on a combined key consisting of an integer and a floating point number.

> index on EMP is EMP-INDEX (age with
> integer-ops, salary with float-ops)
> using B-tree and fill-factor = .8

The run-time system handles secondary indexes in a somewhat unusual way. When a record is inserted, an anchor point is constructed for the record along with index entries for each secondary index. Each index record contains a key(s) plus a pointer to an entry in the line table on the page where the indexed record resides. This line table entry in turn points to the byte-offset of the actual record. This single level of indirection allows anchor points to be moved on a data page without requiring maintenance of secondary indexes.

When an existing record is updated, a delta record is constructed and chained onto the appropriate anchor record. If no indexed field has been modified, then no maintenance of secondary indexes is required. If an indexed field changed, then an entry is added to the appropriate index containing the new key(s) and a pointer to the anchor record. There are no pointers in secondary indexes directly to delta records. Consequently, a delta record can only be accessed by obtaining its corresponding anchor point and chaining forward.

The POSTGRES query optimizer constructs plans which may specify scanning portions of various secondary indexes. The run time code to support this function is relatively conventional except for the fact that each secondary index entry points to an anchor point and a chain of delta records, all of which must be inspected. Valid records that actually match the key in the index are then returned to higher level software.

Use of this technique guarantees that record updates only generate I/O activity in those secondary indexes whose keys change. Since updates to keyed fields are relatively uncommon, this ensures that few insertions must be performed in the secondary indexes.

Some secondary indexes which are hierarchical in nature require disk pages to be placed in stable storage in a particular order (e.g. from leaf to root for page splits in B+-trees). POSTGRES will provide a low level command

> order block-1 block-2

to support such required orderings. This command is in addition to the required **pin** and **unpin** commands to the buffer manager.

3. THE ARCHIVAL SYSTEM

3.1. Vacuuming the Disk

An asynchronous demon is responsible for sweeping records which are no longer valid to the archive. This demon, called the **vacuum cleaner**, is given instructions using the following command:

> vacuum rel-name after T

Here T is a time relative to "now". For example, the following vacuum command specifies vacuuming records over 30 days old:

> vacuum EMP after "30 days"

The vacuum cleaner finds candidate records for archiving which satisfy one of the following conditions:

> Xmax is non empty and is a committed
> transaction and "now" - Tmax >= T
> Xmax is non empty and is an aborted
> transaction
> Xmin is non empty and is an aborted
> transaction

In the second and third cases, the vacuum cleaner simply reclaims the space occupied by such records. In the first case, a record must be copied to the archive unless "no-archive" status is set for this relation. Additionally, if "heavy-archive" is specified, Tmin and Tmax must be filled in by the vacuum cleaner during archiving if they have not already been given values during a previous access. Moreover, if an anchor point and several delta records can be swept together, the vacuuming process will be more efficient. Hence, the vacuum cleaner will generally sweep a chain of several records to the archive at one time.

This sweeping must be done very carefully so that no data is irrecoverably lost. First we discuss the format of the archival medium, then we turn to the sweeping algorithm and a discussion of its cost.

3.2. The Archival Medium

The archival storage system is compatible with WORM devices, but is not restricted to such systems. We are building a conventional extent-based file system on the archive, and each relation is allocated to a single file. Space is allocated in large extents and the next one is allocated when the current one is exhausted. The space allocation map for the archive is kept in a magnetic disk relation. Hence, it is possible, albeit very costly, to sequentially scan the historical version of a relation.

Moreover, there are an arbitrary number of secondary indexes for each relation in the archive. Since historical accessing patterns may be different than accessing patterns for current data, we do not restrict the archive indexes to be the same as those for the magnetic disk data base. Hence, archive indexes must be explicitly created using the following extension of the indexing command:

> index on {archive} rel-name is index-name
> ({key-i with operator-class-i})
> using access-method-name and
> performance-parameters

Indexes for archive relations are normally stored on magnetic disk. However, since they may become very large, we will discuss mechanisms in the next section to support archive indexes that are partly on the archive medium.

The anchor point and a collection of delta records are concatenated and written to the archive as a single variable length record. Again secondary index records must be inserted for any indexes defined for the archive relation. An index record is generated for the anchor point for each archive secondary index. Moreover, an index record must be constructed for each delta record in which a secondary key has been changed.

Since the access paths to the portion of a relation on the archive may be different than the access paths to the portion on magnetic disk, the query optimizer must generate two plans for any query that requests historical data. Of course, these plans can be executed in parallel if multiple processors are available. In addition, we are studying the decomposition of each of these two query plans into additional parallel pieces. A report on this subject is in preparation [BHID87].

3.3. The Vacuum Process

Vacuuming is done in three phases, namely:

> phase 1: write an archive record and its associated index records
> phase 2: write a new anchor point in the current data base

phase 3: reclaim the space occupied by the old anchor point and its delta records

If a crash occurs while the vacuum cleaner is writing the historical record in phase 1, then the data still exists in the magnetic disk data base and will be revacuumed again at some later time. If the historical record has been written but not the associated indexes, then the archive will have a record which is reachable only through a sequential scan. If a crash occurs after some index records have been written, then it will be possible for the same record to be accessed in a magnetic disk relation and in an archive relation. In either case, the duplicate record will consume system resources; however, there are no other adverse consequences because POSTGRES is a relational system and removes duplicate records during processing.

When the record is safely stored on the archive and indexed appropriately, the second phase of vacuuming can occur. This phase entails computing a new anchor point for the magnetic disk relation and adding new index records for it. This anchor point is found by starting at the old anchor point and calculating the value of the last delta that satisfies

$$\text{"now"} - Tmax >= T$$

by moving forward through the linked list. The appropriate values are inserted into the magnetic disk relation, and index records are inserted into all appropriate index. When this phase is complete, the new anchor point record is accessible directly from secondary indexes as well as by chaining forward from the old anchor point. Again, if there is a crash during this phase a record may be accessible twice in some future queries, resulting in additional overhead but no other consequences.

The last phase of the vacuum process is to remove the original anchor point followed by all delta records and then to delete all index records that pointed to this deleted anchor point. If there is a crash during this phase, index records may exist that do not point to a correct data record. Since the run-time system must already check that data records are valid and have the key that the appropriate index record expects them to have, this situation can be checked using the same mechanism.

Whenever there is a failure, the vacuum cleaner is simply restarted after the failure is repaired. It will re-vacuum any record that was in progress at some later time. If the crash occurred during phase 3, the vacuum cleaner could be smart enough to realize that the record was already safely vacuumed. However, the cost of this checking is probably not worthwhile. Consequently, failures will result in a slow accumulation of extra records in the archive. We are depending on crashes to be infrequent enough that this is not a serious concern.

We now turn to the cost of the vacuum cleaner.

3.4. Vacuuming Cost

We examine two different vacuuming situations. In the first case we assume that a record is inserted, updated K times and then deleted. The whole chain of records from insertion to deletion is vacuumed at once. In the second case, we assume that the vacuum is run after K updates, and a new anchor record must be inserted. In both cases, we assume that there are Z secondary indexes for both the archive and magnetic disk relation, that no key changes are made during these K updates, and that an anchor point and all its delta records reside on the same page. Table 1 indicates the vacuum cost for each case. Notice that vacuuming consumes a constant cost. This rather surprising conclusion reflects the fact that a new anchor record can be inserted on the same page from which the old anchor point is being deleted without requiring the page to be forced to stable memory in between the operations. More-over, the new index records can be inserted on the same page from which the previous entries are deleted without an intervening I/O. Hence, the cost PER RECORD of the vacuum cleaner decreases as the length of the chain, K, increases. As long as an anchor point and several delta records are vacuumed together, the cost should be marginal.

4. INDEXING THE ARCHIVE

4.1. Magnetic Disk Indexes

The archive can be indexed by conventional magnetic disk indexes. For example, one could construct a salary index on the archive which would be helpful in answering queries of the form:

retrieve (EMP.name) using EMP [,] where EMP.salary = 10000

However, to provide fast access for queries which restrict the historical scope of interest, e.g:

retrieve (EMP.name) using EMP [1/1/87,] where EMP.salary = 10000

a standard salary index will not be of much use because the index will return all historical salaries

	whole chain	K updates
archive-writes	1+Z	1+Z
disk-reads	1	1
disk-writes	1+Z	1+Z

I/O Counts for Vacuuming
Table 1

of the correct size whereas the query only requested a small subset. Consequently, in addition to conventional indexes, we expect time-oriented indexes to be especially useful for archive relations. Hence, the two fields, Tmin and Tmax, are stored in the archive as a single field, I, of type **interval**. An R-tree access method [GUTM84] can be constructed to provide an index on this interval field. The operators for which an R-tree can provide fast access include "overlaps" and "contained-in". Hence, if these operators are written for the interval data type, an R-tree can be constructed for the EMP relation as follows:

index on archive EMP is EMP-INDEX (I with interval-ops)
using R-tree and fill-factor = .8

This index can support fast access to the historical state of the EMP relation at any point in time or during a particular period.

To utilize such indexes, the POSTGRES query planner needs to be slightly modified. Note that POSTGRES need only run a query on an archive relation if the scope of the relation includes some historical records. Hence, the query for an archive relation must be of the form:

...using EMP[T]

or

...using EMP[T1,T2]

The planner converts the first construct into:

...where T contained-in EMP.I

and the second into:

...where interval(T1,T2) overlaps EMP.I

Since all records in the archive are guaranteed to be valid, these two qualifications can replace all the low level code that checks for record validity on the magnetic disk described in Section 2.3. With this modification, the query optimizer can use the added qualification to provide a fast access path through an interval index if one exists.

Moreover, we expect combined indexes on the interval field along with some data value to be very attractive, e.g:

index on archive EMP is EMP-INDEX
(I with interval-ops, salary with float-ops)
using R-tree and fill-factor = .8

Since an R-tree is a multidimensional index, the above index supports intervals which exist in a two dimensional space of time and salaries. A query such as:

retrieve (EMP.name) using EMP[T1,T2] where EMP.salary = 10000

will be turned into:

retrieve (EMP.name) where EMP.salary = 10000

and interval(T1,T2) overlaps EMP.I

The two clauses of the qualification define another

interval in two dimensions and conventional R-tree processing of the interval can be performed to use both qualifications to advantage.

Although data records will be added to the archive at the convenience of the vacuum cleaner, records will be generally inserted in ascending time order. Hence, the poor performance reported in [ROUS85] for R-trees should be averted by the nearly sorted order in which the records will be inserted. Performance tests to ascertain this speculation are planned. We now turn to a discussion of R-tree indexes that are partly on both magnetic and archival mediums.

4.2. Combined Media Indexes

We begin with a small space calculation to illustrate the need for indexes that use both media. Suppose a relation exists with $10**6$ tuples and each tuple is modified 30 times during the lifetime of the application. Suppose there are two secondary indexes for both the archive and the disk relation and updates never change the values of key fields. Moreover, suppose vacuuming occurs after the 5th delta record is written, so there are an average of 3 delta records for each anchor point. Assume that anchor points consume 200 bytes, delta records consume 40 bytes, and index keys are 10 bytes long.

With these assumptions, the sizes in bytes of each kind of object are indicated in Table 2. Clearly, $10**6$ records will consume 200 mbytes while $3 \times 10**6$ delta records will require 120 mbytes. Each index record is assumed to require a four byte pointer in addition to the 10 byte key; hence each of the two indexes will take up 14 mbytes. There are 6 anchor point records on the archive for each of the $10**6$ records each concatenated with 4 delta records. Hence, archive records will be 360 bytes long, and require 2160 mbytes. Lastly, there is an index record for each of the archive anchor points; hence the archive indexes are 6 times as large as the magnetic disk indexes.

Two points are evident from Table 2. First, the archive can become rather large. Hence, one should vacuum infrequently to cut down on the number of anchor points that occur in the archive. Moreover, it might be desirable to differentially code the anchor points to save space. The second point to notice is that the archive indexes consume a large amount of space on magnetic disk. if the target relation had three indexes instead of two, the archive indexes would consume a greater amount of space than the magnetic disk relation. Hence, we explore in this section data structures that allow part of the index to migrate to the archive. Although we could alternatively consider index structures that are entirely on the archive, such as those proposed in [VITT85], we believe that combined media structures will substantially outperform structures restricted to the archive. We plan performance comparisons to demonstrate the validity of this hypothesis.

Consider an R-tree storage structure in which each pointer in a non-leaf node of the R-tree is distinguished to be either a magnetic disk page pointer or an archive page pointer. If pointers are 32 bits, then we can use the high-order bit for this purpose thereby allowing the remaining 31 bits to specify $2**31$ pages on magnetic disk or archive storage. If pages are 8K bytes, then the maximum size of an archive index is $2**44$ bytes (about 1.75 $\times 10**13$ bytes), clearly adequate for almost any application. Moreover, the leaf level pages of the R-tree contain key values and pointers to associated data records. These data pointers can be 48 bytes long, thereby allowing the data file corresponding to a single historical relation to be $2**48$ bytes long (about 3.0 $\times 10**14$ bytes), again adequate for most applications.

We assume that the archive may be a write-once-read-many (WORM) device that allows pages to be initially written but then does not allow any overwrites of the page. With this assumption, records can only be dynamically added to pages that reside on magnetic disk. Table 3 suggests two sensible strategies for the placement of new records when they are not entirely contained inside some R-tree index region corresponding to a magnetic disk page.

Moreover, we assume that any page that resides on the archive contains pointers that in turn point only to pages on the archive. This avoids having to contend with updating an archive page which contains a pointer to a magnetic disk page that splits.

Pages in an R-tree can be moved from magnetic disk to the archive as long as they contain only archive page pointers. Once a page moves to the archive, it becomes read only. A page can be moved from the archive to the magnetic disk if its parent page resides on magnetic disk. In this case, the archive page previously inhabited by this page becomes unusable. The utility of this reverse migration seems limited, so we will not consider it further.

We turn now to several page movement policies for migrating pages from magnetic disk to the

object	mbytes
disk relation anchor points	200
deltas	120
secondary indexes	28
archive	2160
archive indexes	168

Sizes of the Various Objects
Table 2

P1   allocate to the region which has to be

P2   expanded the least
      allocate to the region whose maximum time
      has to be expanded the least

Record Insertion Strategies
Table 3

archive and use the parameters indicated in Table
4 in the discussion to follow. The simplist policy
would be to construct a system demon to
"vacuum" the index by moving the leaf page to the
archive that has the smallest value for Tmax, the
left-hand end of its interval. This vacuuming
would occur whenever the R-tree structure
reached a threshold near its maximum size of F
disk pages. A second policy would be to choose a
worthy page to archive based both on its value of
Tmax and on percentage fullness of the page. In
either case, insertions would be made into the R-
tree index at the lower left-hand part of the index
while the demon would be archiving pages in the
lower right hand part of the index. Whenever an
intermediate R-tree node had descendents all on
the archive, it could in turn be archived by the
demon.

For example, if B is 8192 bytes, L is 50 bytes
and there is a five year archive of updates at a frequency, U of 1 update per second, then $1.4 \times 10^{**}6$
index blocks will be required resulting in a four
level R-tree. F of these blocks will reside on magnetic disk and the remainder will be on the
archive. Any insertion or search will require at
least 4 accesses to one or the other storage
medium.

A third movement policy with somewhat
different performance characteristics would be to
perform "batch movement". In this case one
would build a magnetic disk R-tree until its size
was F blocks. Then, one would copy the all pages
of the R-tree except the root to the archive and
allocate a special "top node" on magnetic disk for
this root node. Then, one would proceed to fill up

F   number of magnetic disk blocks usable for
     the index
U   update frequency of the relation being
     indexed
L   record size in the index being constructed
B   block size of magnetic disk pages

Parameters Controlling Page Movement
Table 4

a second complete R-tree of F-1 pages. While the
second R-tree was being built, both this new R-
tree and the one on the archive would be searched
during any retrieval request. All inserts would, of
course, be directed to the magnetic disk R-tree.
When this second R-tree was full, it would be
copied to the archive as before and its root node
added to the existing top node. The combination
might cause the top node to overflow, and a conventional R-tree split would be accomplished.
Consequently, the top node would become a conventional R-tree of three nodes. The filling process would start again on a 3rd R-tree of F-3
nodes. When this was full, it would be archived
and its root added to the lower left hand page of
the 3 node R-tree.

Over time, there would continue to be two R-
trees. The first would be completely on magnetic
disk and periodically archived. As long as the
height of this R-tree at the time it is archived is a
constant, H, then the second R-tree of height, H1,
will have the bottom H-1 levels on the archive.
Moreover, insertions into the magnetic disk portion of this R-tree are always on the left-most
page. Hence, the pages along the left-side of the
tree are the only ones which will be modified;
other pages can be archived if they point entirely
to pages on the archive. Hence, some subcollection of the pages on the top H1-H+1 levels remain
on the magnetic disk. Insertions go always to the
first R-tree while searches go to both R-trees. Of
course, there are no deletions to be concerned
with.

Again if B is 8192 bytes, L is 50 bytes and F is
6000 blocks, then H will be 3 and each insert will
require 3 magnetic disk accesses. Moreover, at 1
update per second, a five year archive will require
a four level R-tree whose bottom two levels will be
on the archive and a subcollection of the top 2
levels of 100-161 blocks will be on magnetic disk.
Hence, searches will require descending two R-
trees with a total depth of 7 levels and will be
about 40 percent slower than either of the single
R-tree structures proposed. On the other hand,
the very common operation of insertions will be
approximately 25 percent faster.

5. PERFORMANCE COMPARISON

5.1. Assumptions

In order to compare our storage system with a conventional one based on write-ahead logging (WAL), we make the following assumptions:

1) Portions of the buffer pool may reside in non-volatile main memory

2) CPU instructions are not a critical resource, and thereby only I/O operations are counted.

The second assumption requires some explanation. Current CPU technology is driving down the cost of a MIP at a rate of a factor of two every couple of years. Hence, current low-end workstations have a few MIPs of processing power. On the other hand, disk technology is getting denser and cheaper. However, disks are not getting faster at a significant rate. Hence, one can still only expect to read about 30 blocks per second off of a standard disk drive. Current implementations of data base systems require several thousand instructions to fetch a page from the disk followed by 1000-3000 instructions per data record examined on that page. As a simple figure of merit, assume 30000 instructions are required to process a disk block. Hence, a 1 MIP CPU will approximately balance a single disk. Currently, workstations with 3-5 MIPs are available but are unlikely to be configured with 3-5 disks. Moreover, future workstations (such as SPUR and FIREFLY) will have 10-30 MIPs. Clearly, they will not have 10-30 disks unless disk systems shift to large numbers of SCSI oriented single platter disks and away from current SMD disks.

Put differently, a SUN 3/280 costs about $5000 per MIP, while an SMD disk and controller costs about $12,000. Hence, the CPU cost to support a disk is much smaller than the cost of the disk, and the major cost of data base hardware can be expected to be in the disk system. As such, if an installation is found to be CPU bound, then additional CPU resources can be cheaply added until the system becomes balanced.

We analyze three possible situations:

large-SM: an ample amount of stable main memory is available

small-SM: a modest amount of stable main memory is available

no-SM: no stable main memory is available

In the first case we assume that enough stable main memory is available for POSTGRES and a WAL system to use so that neither system is required to **force** disk pages to secondary storage at the time that they are updated. Hence, each system will execute a certain number of I/O operations that can be buffered in stable memory and written out to disk at some convenient time. We count the number of such **non-forced** I/O operations that each system will execute, assuming all writes cost the same amount. For both systems we assume that records do not cross page boundaries, so each update results in a single page write. Moreover, we assume that each POSTGRES delta record can be put on the same page as its anchor point. Next, we assume that transactions are a single record insertion, update, deletion or an aborted update. Moreover, we assume there are two secondary indexes on the relation affected and that updates fail to alter either key field. Lastly, we assume that a write ahead log will require 3 log records (begin transaction, the data modification, and end transaction), with a total length of 400 bytes. Moreover, secondary index operations are not logged and thereby the log records for 10 transactions will fit on a conventional 4K log page.

In the second situation we assume that a modest amount of stable main memory is available. We assume that the quantity is sufficient to hold only the tail of the POSTGRES log and the tail of the TIME relation. In a WAL system, we assume that stable memory can buffer a conventional log turning each log write into one that need not be synchronously forced out to disk. This situation (small-SM) should be contrasted with the third case where no stable memory at all is available (no-SM). In this latter cases, some writes must be forced to disk by both types of storage systems.

In the results to follow we ignore the cost that either kind of system would incur to mirror the data for high availability. Moreover, we are also ignoring the WAL cost associated with checkpoints. In addition, we assume that a WAL system never requires a disk read to access the appropriate undo log record. We are also ignoring the cost of vacuuming the disk in the POSTGRES architecture.

5.2. Performance Results

Table 5 indicates the number of I/O operations each of the four types of transactions must execute for the assumed large-SM configuration. Since there is ample stable main memory, neither system must force any data pages to disk and only non-forced I/Os must be done. An insert requires that a data record and two index records be written by either system. Moreover, 1/10th of a log page will be filled by the conventional system, so every 10 transactions there will be another log page which must be eventually written to disk. In POSTGRES the insertions to the LOG relation and the TIME relation generate an I/O every 65536 and 2048 transactions respectively, and we have ignored this small number in Table 5. Consequently, one requires 3 non-forced I/Os in POSTGRES and 3.1 in a conventional system. The next two columns in Table 1 can be similarly computed. The last column summarizes the I/Os for an aborted transaction. In POSTGRES the updated page need not be rewritten to disk. Hence, no I/Os are strictly necessary; however, in all liklihood, this optimization will not be implemented. A WAL system will update the data and construct a log record. Then the log record must be read and the data page returned to its original value. Again, a very clever system could avoid writing the page out to disk, since it is identical to the disk copy. Hence, for both systems we indicate both the optimized number of writes and the non-optimized number. Notice in Table 5 that POSTGRES is marginally better than a WAL system except for deletes where it is dramatically better because it does not delete the 2 index records. We now turn to cases where POSTGRES is less attractive.

	Insert	Update	Delete	Abort
WAL-force	0	0	0	0
WAL-no-force	3.1	1.1	3.1	0.1 or 1.1
POSTGRES-force	0	0	0	0
POSTGRES-non-force	3	1	1	0 or 1

I/O Counts for the Primitive Operations
large-SM Configuration
Table 5

Table 6 repeats the I/O counts for the small-SM configuration. The WAL configuration performs exactly as in Table 5 while the the POSTGRES data pages must now be forced to disk since insufficient stable main memory is assumed to hold them. Notice that POSTGRES is still better in the total number of I/O operations; however the requirement to do them synchronously will be a major disadvantage.

Table 7 then indicates the I/O counts under the condition that NO stable main memory is available. Here the log record for a conventional WAL system must be forced to disk at commit time. The other writes can remain in the buffer pool and be written at a later time. In POSTGRES the LOG bit must be forced out to disk along with the insert to the TIME relation. Moreover, the data pages must be forced as in Table 6. In this case POSTGRES is marginally poorer in the total number of operations; and again the synchronous nature of these updates will be a significant disadvantage.

	Insert	Update	Delete	Abort
WAL-force	0	0	0	0
WAL-no-force	3.1	1.1	3.1	0.1 or 1.1
POSTGRES-force	3	1	1	0 or 1
POSTGRES-non-force	0	0	0	0

I/O Counts for the Primitive Operations
small-SM Configuration
Table 6

	Insert	Update	Delete	Abort
WAL-force	1	1	1	1
WAL-no-force	3	1	3	0 or 1
POSTGRES-force	5	3	3	1
POSTGRES-non-force	0	0	0	0 or 1

I/O Counts for the Primitive Operations
no-SM Configuration
Table 7

In summary, the POSTGRES solution is preferred in the large-SM configuration since all operations require less I/Os. In Table 6 the total number of I/Os is less for POSTGRES; however, synchronous I/O is required. Table 7 shows a situation where POSTGRES is typically more expensive. However, group commits [DEWI84] could be used to effectively convert the results for either type of system into the ones in Table 6. Consequently, POSTGRES should be thought of as fairly competitive with current storage architectures. Moreover, it has a considerable advantage over WAL systems in that recovery time will be instantaneous while requiring a substantial amount of time in a WAL architecture.

6. CONCLUSIONS

This paper has described the storage manager that is being constructed for POSTGRES. The main points guiding the design of the system were:

1) instantaneous recovery from crashes

2) ability to keep archival records on an archival medium

3) housekeeping chores should be done asynchronously

4) concurrency control based on conventional locking

The first point should be contrasted with the standard write-ahead log (WAL) storage managers in widespread use today.

In engineering application one often requires the past history of the data base. Moreover, even in business applications this feature is sometimes needed, and the now famous TP1 benchmark assumes that the application will maintain an archive. It makes more sense for the data manager to do this task internally for applications that require the service.

The third design point has been motivated by the desire to run multiple concurrent processes if there happen to be extra processors. Hence storage management functions can occur in parallel on multiple processors. Alternatively, some functions can be saved for idle time on a single processor. Lastly, it allows POSTGRES code to be a collection of asynchronous processes and not a single large monolithic body of code.

The final design point reflects our intuitive belief, confirmed by simulations, that standard locking is the most desirable concurrency control strategy. Moreover, it should be noted that read-only transactions can be optionally coded to run as of some point in the recent past. Since historical commands set no locks, then read-only transactions will never interfere with transactions performing updates or be required to wait. Consequently, the level of contention in a POSTGRES data base may be a great deal lower than that found in conventional storage managers.

The design of the POSTGRES storage manager has been sketched and a brief analysis of its expected performance relative to a conventional one has been performed. If the analysis is confirmed in practice, then POSTGRES will give similar performance compared to other storage managers while providing the extra service of historical access to the data base. This should prove attractive in some environments.

At the moment, the magnetic disk storage manager is operational, and work is proceeding on the vacuum cleaner and the layout of the archive. POSTGRES is designed to support extendible access methods, and we have implemented the B-tree code and will provide R-trees in the near future. Additional access methods can be constructed by other parties to suit their special needs. When the remaining pieces of the storage manager are complete, we plan a performance "bakeoff" both against conventional storage managers as well as against other storage managers (such as [CARE86, COPE84]) with interesting properties.

REFERENCES

[AGRA85] Agrawal, R. et. al., "Models for Studying Concurrency Control Performance Alternatives and Implications," Proc. 1985 ACM-SIGMOD Conference on Management of Data, Austin, Tx., May 1985.

[ASTR76] Astrahan, M. et. al., "System R: A Relational Approach to Data," ACM-TODS, June 1976.

[BART81] Bartlett, J., "A Non-STOP Kernel," Proc. Eighth Symposium on Operating System Principles," Pacific Grove, Ca., Dec. 1981.

[BERN80] Bernstein, P. at. al., "Concurrency Control in a System for Distributed Databases (SDD-1)," ACM-TODS, March 1980.

[BHID87] Bhide, A., "Query processing in Shared Memory Multiprocessor Systems," (in preparation).

[CARE86] Carey, M. et. al., "Object and File Management in the EXODUS Database System,"

Proc. 1986 VLDB Conference, Kyoto, Japan, August 1986.

[COPE84] Copeland, G. and D. Maier, "Making Smalltalk a Database System," Proc. 1984 ACM-SIGMOD Conference on Management of Data, Boston, Mass. June 1984.

[DEC86] Digital Equipment Corp., "VAX/VMS V4.0 Reference Manual," Digital Equipment Corp., Maynard, Mass., June 1986.

[DEWI84] Dewitt, D. et. al., "Implementation Techniques for Main Memory Database Systems," Proc. 1984 ACM-SIGMOD Conference on Management of Data, Boston, Mass., June 1984.

[GRAY78] Gray, J., "Notes on Data Base Operating Systems," IBM Research, San Jose, Ca., RJ1879, June 1978.

[GUTM84] Gutman, A., "R-trees: A Dynamic Index Structure for Spatial Searching," Proc. 1984 ACM-SIGMOD Conference on Management of Data, Boston, Mass. June 1984.

[HILL85] Hill, M., et al. "Design Decisions in SPUR," Computer Magazine, vol.19, no.11, November 1986.

[ROUS85] Roussoupoulis, N. and Leifker, D., "Direct Spatial Search on Pictorial Databases Using Packed R-trees," Proc. 1985 ACM-SIGMOD Conference on Management of Data, Austin, Tx., May 1985.

[SEQU85] Sequent Computer Co., "The SEQUENT Balance Reference Manual," Sequent Computers, Portland, Ore., 1985.

[SEVR76] Severence, D., and Lohman, G., "Differential Files: Their Application to the Maintenance of large Databases," ACM-TODS, June 1976.

[STON76] Stonebraker, M., et. al. "The Design and Implementation of INGRES," ACM-TODS, September 1976.

[STON86] Stonebraker, M. and Rowe, L., "The Design of POSTGRES," Proc. 1986ACM-SIGMOD Conference on Management of Data, Washington, D.C., May 1986.

[STON86a]
Stonebraker, M., "Inclusion of New Types in Relational Data Base Systems," Proc. Second International Conference on Data Base Engineering, Los Angeles, Ca., Feb. 1986.

[VITT85] Vitter, J., "An Efficient I/O Interface for Optical Disks," ACM-TODS, June 1985.

LOOM—Large Object-Oriented Memory for Smalltalk-80 Systems

Ted Kaehler
Glenn Krasner
Software Concepts Group
Xerox Palo Alto Research Center
Palo Alto, California

Introduction

The Smalltalk-80 virtual machine is specified as a memory-resident system containing up to 2^{15} objects. When full, it typically occupies about 2M bytes of memory. Unfortunately, many machines do not have this capacity in main memory, and many applications require, or will require, more than this capacity. To solve this space problem, one typically uses a virtual memory system in which the resident, "real" memory is used as a cache for the larger mass storage, "virtual" memory. LOOM, Large Object-Oriented Memory, is a virtual memory system designed and implemented for the Smalltalk-80 system. The most important feature of the LOOM design is that it provides virtual addresses that are much wider than either the word size or the memory address size of the computer on which it runs.

LOOM is a single-user virtual memory system that swaps objects and operates without assistance from the programmer. Virtual memory systems may be characterized by the amount of attention that the programmer must pay to the transfers between virtual and real memories, and by the extent to which the memory is shared among users, and by the granularity of transfer between memory levels. Overlay mechanisms are an example of systems that require much programmer attention, while all common paging systems require none[1]. Databases may be viewed as the extreme in allowing sharing; the virtual memory for Interlisp-D[2] is one example of a single-user virtual memory. Most overlay systems transfer program segments, while paging systems transfer disk pages, and a few systems such as the OOZE virtual memory for Smalltalk-76[3] transfer objects.

The LOOM Design

We view virtual memory design as a process of trying to determine what happens most often, making it go fast, and hoping that it will continue to be what happens most often. Our experience with previous Smalltalk systems gave us three major assumptions on which we based the LOOM design: programmers and users have a large appetite for memory, object-swapping is an efficient and effective scheme, and the Smalltalk-80 design for handling resident objects is worth keeping. From these assumptions and the desire to provide a large number of objects on a machine with a narrow word width, we created the major design decisions.

• LOOM assumes that the object is the unit of locality of reference. It swaps individual objects between primary and secondary memory, and allows into main memory only those objects actually needed by the interpreter. Unlike paging systems, LOOM packs objects in main memory at maximum density.

• LOOM is designed for machines with 16-bit words. Fields of objects in main memory are 16 bits wide.

• The address space of the secondary memory is large. LOOM allows as many as 2^{31} objects.

• The interpreter accesses objects in main memory exactly as it does in a resident Smalltalk-80 interpreter. When the necessary objects are already in main memory, the interpreter runs as fast as it did in the resident system.

In order to allow the large number of possible objects, and yet treat the resident objects in the same way they are treated in a non-LOOM Smalltalk-80 implementation, we decided to create two different name spaces. The same object is identified by names from different spaces when it resides in different parts of the system, as shown in Fig. 14.1. The identifier of an object is called an *Oop*, which stands for "object pointer." An object in secondary storage has a 32-bit Oop (a long Oop), and each of its fields containing a pointer to another object holds that

The LOOM Details

The important issues in the LOOM design implementation are:

- The representation of resident objects,
- The representation of objects in secondary memory,
- The translation between representations, and
- The identification of times when the translations must occur.

The Representation of Resident Objects

Resident objects are represented in a manner similar to their representation in a resident Smalltalk-80 system. Each object has as its name in main memory, a short (16-bit) Oop. The Oop indexes the ROT in order to provide the starting address of the object's body, as shown in Fig. 14.2. The ROT entry also has reference-count bits, and a few other bits, described later. The body of each object contains a word for the length of the body, a pointer to the object's class, and the object's fields. Each field is either a pointer to another object or a collection of "bits", in the same manner as resident Smalltalk-80 fields. We will only deal with pointer fields here. Each field (as well as the class pointer) that refers

Format of Objects in Main Memory

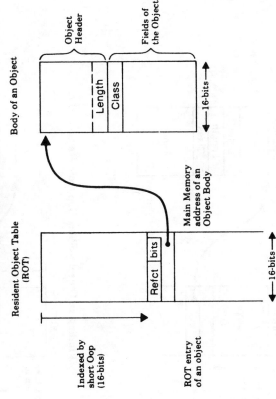

Figure 14.2

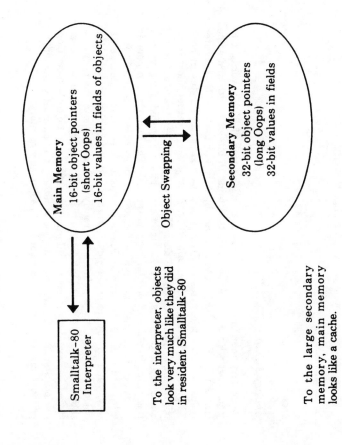

To the interpreter, objects look very much like they did in resident Smalltalk-80

Object Swapping

To the large secondary memory, main memory looks like a cache.

Figure 14.1

pointer as a 32-bit Oop. An object cached in main memory has a 16-bit Oop (a short Oop) and 16-bit fields. As in the resident Smalltalk-80 implementation, main memory has a resident object table (*ROT* or sometimes called an *OT*), which contains the actual main memory address of each resident object. An object's short Oop is an index into the ROT, so that the object's address can be determined from its Oop with a single addition and memory reference. When an object is brought into main memory from disk, it is assigned a short Oop, and those of its fields that refer to other objects in main memory are assigned the appropriate short Oop. Fields pointing to objects that are not resident are handled specially, the details of which make up the crux of LOOM.

Thus, when all objects in the working set are in main memory, LOOM behaves just like a resident Smalltalk-80 implementation—all objects have short Oops that index the ROT, providing their actual core address. When an object in core must access one of its fields that refers to an object that is not in core, something special must happen. LOOM brings that object into core, assigns it a short Oop, and resumes normal Smalltalk execution. The main memory resident space of 2^{15} objects acts as a cache for up to 2^{31} objects on the disk.

to another resident object contains the short Oop of that object. Fields that refer to non-resident objects (objects on secondary storage) contain a short Oop of one of two types, a *leaf* or a *lambda.*

In addition to these fields, resident objects in a LOOM system have three extra words. Two of these fields contain the long (32-bit) Oop of that object. The third word, known as the delta word, contains a delta reference count and some other bits. The short Oop of an object is not only an index into the ROT for that object's address, but is also the result of a hash function applied to that object's long Oop. See Fig. 14.3, p. 256. The algorithm for translating an object's short Oop to its long Oop is:

1. Index the ROT with the short Oop to get the body address

2. Load the long Oop from the first two words of the body

The algorithm for translating an object's long Oop to its short Oop is:

1. Convert the long Oop into a short Oop by applying the hash function

2. Index the ROT with this short Oop to get a body address

3. Look at the first two words of the body

4. If they match the long Oop, then the short Oop is correct

5. If not, create a new short Oop from the current one with a reprobe function (e.g., add 1), and go to step 2

---

*The
Representation of
Objects in
Secondary Memory*

Secondary memory is addressed as a linear space of 32-bit words. Objects start with a header word that contains 16 bits of length and some status bits. Each pointer field in the object is 32 bits wide. Non-pointer fields (such as the bytes in Strings) are packed, with 4 bytes in each 32-bit word. Resident SmallInteger-80 SmallIntegers are rather short to be occupying a full word on the disk. However, since they represent legitimate object pointers, their 15 significant bits are stored along with a flag value in a 32-bit pointer field on the disk. The long Oops in pointer fields are 31-bit disk pointers, addressing as many objects as will fit into 2^{31} disk words (32-bit words). Fields of objects on secondary storage always refer to objects in secondary storage and do not change when the object to which they point is currently cached in main memory. As shown in Fig. 14.4, no information about primary memory is ever stored in secondary memory. Information such as an object's short Oop, its location in primary memory, or whether it is currently cached in primary memory are never recorded in secondary memory.

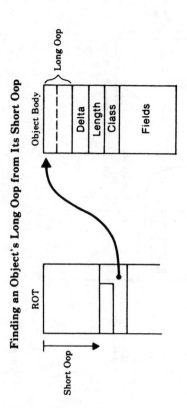

Finding an Object's Long Oop from Its Short Oop

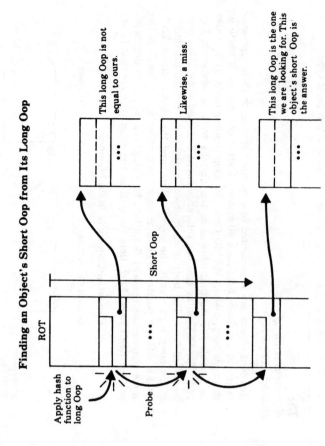

Finding an Object's Short Oop from Its Long Oop

Figure 14.3

How Objects in Primary and Secondary Memory Refer to Other Objects.

Hash a long Oop into the ROT and see if the object is cached in primary memory

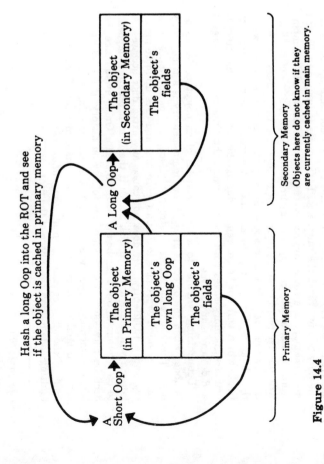

Primary Memory

The object (in Primary Memory) — The object's own long Oop — The object's fields

A Short Oop   A Long Oop

The object (in Secondary Memory) — The object's fields

Secondary Memory
Objects here do not know if they are currently cached in main memory.

Figure 14.4

When an object on secondary storage is brought into main memory, its fields must be translated from the long form to short form. The object is assigned an appropriate short Oop (one to which its long Oop hashes), a block of memory is reserved for it, and all of its fields are translated from long Oops to short Oops. Those fields that point to objects already in main memory are given the short Oops of those objects; those that point to objects not in main memory are handled in one of two ways, with leaves or with lambdas.

□ *Leaves* Leaves are pseudo-objects that represent an object on secondary storage. They have a short Oop hashed by that object's long Oop and a ROT entry. Their image in memory only contains a length word, disk address words, and the delta word. Their image contains no class word or fields, as shown in Fig. 14.5. Leaves therefore, only take up 4 words of memory, whereas the average object takes up 13. Leaves are created without looking at that object's image on secondary storage.

This is very important, since a major cost in virtual memories is the number of disk accesses. The short Oop of the leaf may be treated as if it were the short Oop of the object; it may be pushed and popped on the stack, stored into fields of other objects, without ever needing the actual contents of that object. Its reference count can be incremented and decremented (see p. 262).

A Leaf

ROT   Primary Memory   Secondary Memory

Leaf bit

Long Oop — Delta — Length (4)

The object in Secondary Memory

Figure 14.5

An object is always in one of three states. Either the entire object is in main memory, a leaf for the object is in main memory, or the object exists only on the disk. See Fig. 14.6. When the interpreter needs a field from an object which is represented by a leaf, the entire object with its fields must be brought into main memory from disk. Since the leaf contains the disk Oop, the body is easy to find. After the body is translated into main memory form, its core address is stored into the leaf's OT entry, and the leaf body is discarded. Short Oop references to the object remain the same, but now the full object is actually there. Since a leaf can be substituted for an object body and vice versa with no effect on pointers to the object, LOOM is always free to make more room in main memory by turning resident objects into leaves.

□ *Lambdas* Lambdas are the second way to represent fields of resident objects that refer to objects on secondary storage. Lambda is a place holder for a pointer to an object which has not been assigned a short Oop. Its purpose is to reduce the number of leaves in the system. Lambda is a pseudo-Oop, a reserved short Oop (the Oop 0) which is not the name of any resident object. Consider an object which has a lambda in one of its fields. To discover the actual value of that field, LOOM must go back to the object's image on secondary storage, look in that

States of an Object in LOOM

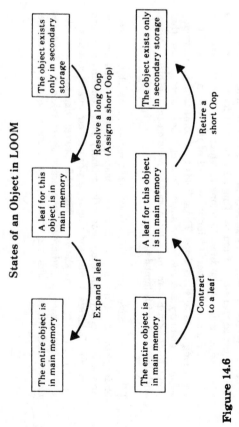

| The entire object is in main memory | A leaf for this object is in main memory | The object exists only in secondary storage |

Expand a leaf

Resolve a long Oop (Assign a short Oop)

| The entire object is in main memory | A leaf for this object is in main memory | The object exists only in secondary storage |

Contract to a leaf

Retire a short Oop

Figure 14.6

field for a long pointer, and create a leaf or resident object. This means that the cost of fetching a lambda field is an extra disk reference. However, unlike leaves, lambdas do not take up any ROT entries (they all use the single pseudo-ROT entry at 0) and they do not take up any main memory storage. Since the number of ROT entries is limited to 2^{15}, and main memory is a somewhat scarce resource, this saving can be important. During an object's typical stay in main memory, some of its fields will not be referenced. If leaves are created for the values in those fields when the object is swapped in, and then destroyed again when the object is thrown out, much work is wasted. Putting lambdas into primary memory saves both the space and the time needed to create and destroy many leaves.

Determining whether to make the fields of an object be leaves or lambdas when the object is brought into main memory is a tricky business. The choice of strategy strongly affects the performance of a LOOM system. Creating a leaf takes more time and uses up more memory and a ROT entry, but does not cause any extra disk accesses. A lambda will cause an extra disk access if the field it occupies happens to be referenced, but a lambda is faster to create. One way to make the decision between leaf and lambda is to rely on history; if a field was a lambda when this object was written to the disk one time, it is likely to remain a lambda during its next trip into main memory. Each pointer field of the disk contains a hint, the *noLambda* bit, and the object faulting code follows the advice of the hint.

The Translation Between Object Representations

Translating between the memory-resident and secondary-storage representations of an object is straightforward. For those fields that contain

short Oops, the Oop refers to an object or a leaf. The corresponding long Oop can be found in the header of the object or leaf. If the field refers to an object which has not yet been assigned a long pointer, a long pointer is assigned to the object and a copy is installed in the field. For those fields that contain lambdas, the field is guaranteed not to be changed from the object's previous disk image. (The object's disk image is read before it is written). If the object being translated still has some short pointers to it (has a positive in-core reference count), then it must be converted to a leaf instead of being deleted completely from core.

When to Translate

We have already mentioned when the translation between representations must occur. When a field of an object being brought into main memory has the noLambda bit set, and that field refers to a non-resident object, then a leaf is created. A leaf is also created when a field of a resident object containing a lambda is accessed. When the interpreter needs to access a field in a leaf, the flow of control in LOOM begins (see Fig. 14.7). The leaf is expanded into a resident object; its fields are translated from long form to short form. This is called an *object fault* (because the similar situation in paging virtual memory systems, trying to access a page that is not resident, is called a *page fault*). The inverse operation, *contracting* an object into a leaf, may be done at any time. The final part of an object's journey into primary memory consists of destroying the leaf and reusing its short Oop and memory space. This can only be done when there are no longer any fields in any resident objects pointing to the leaf.

Lambdas may be resolved into leaves and leaves may be expanded into full objects before they are needed, and this is called a *prefetch*. The complementary operations of contraction and prefetch of objects can both be done in the background. The exact order and mix of objects to prefetch or contract can be adjusted at run-time to optimize the performance of secondary storage (disk head movement or network traffic).

LOOM Implementation Details

In this section, we provide some details of how LOOM may be implemented. In particular we discuss the discovery of object faults, reference-counting, and the assignment of the extra bits in the ROT entry and the delta word.

Object Faults

Object faults occur when the interpreter tries to access a field in a leaf or a field in an object whose value is lambda. By the time the interpreter scrutinizes them, all objects must be full resident objects. How can leaves and lambdas be discovered without greatly slowing the speed of the interpreter?

It has been our experience that implementations tend to have a single subroutine (or expanded macro) that takes an Oop and sets up some base register to point to the actual address of that object. We call this subroutine "Otmap." It corresponds roughly to the ot:bits: method of the memory manager in the formal specification of the Smalltalk-80 virtual machine, in *Smalltalk-80: The Language and its Implementation*. Otmap is called if and only if you want to fetch or store a field of an object. Note that this is exactly the condition where you must test for the object being a leaf. (Otmap may sometimes be used for other purposes—for example a compaction routine may call Otmap to get the main memory address of the object in order to move it, but it wants to treat leaves and objects the same. These cases tend to be rare, so it is worth having a second subroutine for them.) We reserve one bit of the ROT entry to say whether the entry is for an object or a leaf. The Otmap subroutine tests this bit and calls the LOOM routines when the entry is a leaf. Since both words of the ROT entry are fetched anyway, this extra test usually only costs one or two extra instruction executions.

Testing for lambda however, must be done on *every* field reference. In the worst case, this would mean testing occurs every time a field is fetched from an object and every time an object is pushed onto the stack. To decrease the number of tests, we include one bit in each resident object called "holds lambda." It is set by the LOOM routines whenever that object has a field that is a lambda. The interpreter guarantees that the current context, the home context, the current method, and the receiver all have no lambdas in them. If any of them does contain a lambda, then the LOOM routines are called to make those fields into leaves. In this way, the most common fields fetched and all stack operations can work without testing for lambda. Note that these objects must be cleared of lambdas only when the active context changes. This occurs during message sends, returns, process switches, and during the execution of BlockContext value and value:.

It is useful to note that the LOOM design actually will work with leaves alone, and without lambdas. When the expand routine brings an object into main memory, it turns all the fields into leaves and never creates a lambda. This approach tends-to use more short Oops and main memory than the full LOOM design, but could be an intermediate stage in the implementation; providing a working virtual memory system with only the modification to the Otmap subroutine.

Reference Counting

Although some Smalltalk-80 implementations use mark/sweeping garbage collection, most implementations so far, including ours, use reference counting to identify garbage. Therefore we will describe the reference-counting scheme as it applies to LOOM. Reference counting serves two different purposes. One purpose is to detect when the total count of any object goes to zero. The other is to detect when the last short pointer to any object disappears so that the short pointer may be

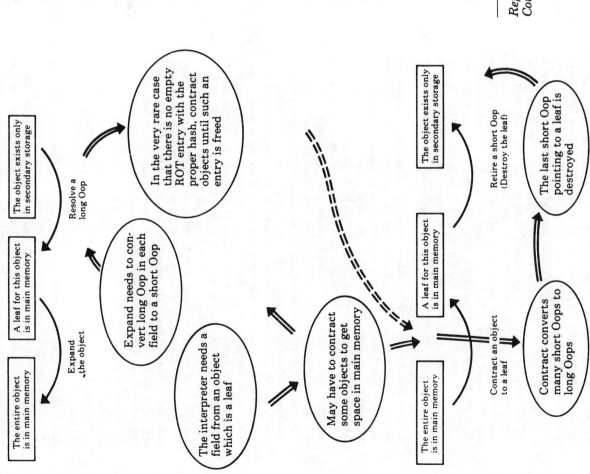

The Flow of Control in LOOM

Figure 14.7

The Three Types of Reference Counts

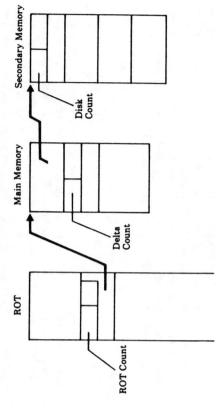

Example Reference Counts

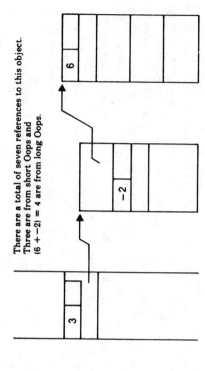

There are a total of seven references to this object. Three are from short Oops and (6 + −2) = 4 are from long Oops.

Figure 14.8

reused. The resident Smalltalk-80 interpreter keeps reference counts of short pointers. This count is kept in the ROT. LOOM uses the ROT reference count to keep the number of short pointers to an object. In addition, every object on the disk contains a reference count which is the number of long pointers to the object. The total count is the sum of the number of short and long pointers to an object. Whenever a long Oop is converted to a short Oop and installed in a field in main memory, both counts for the object pointed at must change. To avoid a disk access to find and modify the long Oop count every time a field is converted, LOOM keeps a "delta" or running change in the long Oop reference count for each object in main memory. The true long pointer reference count of any object is the count found on the disk in the object's header plus the count found in the "delta" part of the object's delta word in main memory. Fig. 14.8 shows the ROT entry, object body, and disk image of an object. The object has three short Oops pointing at it. It used to have pointers from 6 long Oops, but two were destroyed recently (they were probably converted to short Oops). The total number of references to the object is seven.

There are three sources of reference-count changes. One pointer can be stored over another, a long pointer can be converted to a short pointer, and a short pointer can be converted back. Since the interpreter only deals with short Oops, every store consists of a short pointer replacing another short pointer. This high-bandwidth operation touches only the short pointer reference counts, so the existing code in the interpreter does not need modification. When a leaf expands to a normal object, pointers in its fields change from long Oops to short ones. The expand-a-leaf routine increments the short count of that object and decrements the delta of its long count. The inverse happens when the routine which shrinks objects into leaves converts short Oops to long ones.

Consider the case when the short Oop count of an object goes to zero. The reference-count routine then looks at the object's long Oop count to see if the total count of the object is zero. If it is zero, the object is truly free, and its storage can be recycled. If not, the object is still held by some long pointers. When the short Oop reference count goes to zero, and the delta reference count goes to zero, then the object's long Oop count on disk need not change. Thus if the ultimate long pointer count of a leaf can be guessed correctly when the leaf is created, the disk count and delta count can be adjusted so that the leaf disappears from main memory without further disk references.

Other Data
LOOM Holds for
Each Object

As a help to the LOOM system, two other bits are added to the ROT entry for any object—"clean" and "unTouched." Clean is cleared whenever a field of the object is changed; unTouched is cleared whenever a field of the object is read or changed. Clean tells the LOOM system that it need not rewrite the object's image on disk (unless, of course, its true reference count changed). Clean is set when the object is newly created or swapped in. UnTouched is set by a routine that sweeps core whenever space is needed. Any object that the routine finds with unTouched still set has not been touched in an entire pass through memory, and is thus a candidate for being *contracted* (turned into a leaf).

The activity which is most likely to cause LOOM to thrash is the resolution of lambdas. When a lambda needs to be resolved (turned into a leaf or discovered to be an existing short Oop), LOOM must first look at the disk image of the parent object. If the pattern of computation is such that the noLambda hint does not correctly predict which fields are needed by the interpreter, lambdas would have to be resolved often. Even so, lambda resolution is likely to happen soon after the parent was expanded, so keeping the most recently fetched disk pages in a cache relieves the need to go to the disk. When a lambda needs to be resolved, the LOOM procedure looks first in the cache of pages that is called the *disk buffer*. If it finds the object in the buffer, it can directly retrieve the long Oop for the lambda, saving one disk access.

LOOM Implemented in the Smalltalk-80 Language

The LOOM design, though based on only a couple of simple principles, has a number of reasonably complex algorithms that require a substantial amount of code. We were faced with the problem of whether to implement LOOM's object swapping algorithms in a low-level language or a high-level language. Low-level implementations typically provide better performance at the cost of some flexibility.

We opted to implement the LOOM system in our favorite high-level system, the Smalltalk-80 system. A number of factors influenced this choice. The overriding factor was that for us, the Smalltalk-80 language was the most natural way to express and understand complex algorithms. We are implementing LOOM on the Xerox Dorado computer[5] (see also Chapter 7). We believe that the Dorado has sufficient performance and memory space so that the LOOM system will not be called very often. When LOOM is called, it will run with acceptable performance. Also, once the system is up and running, we will have a complete, debugged high-level description of the algorithms. Should we decide to reimplement LOOM on the Dorado or another machine in a lower-level language, only a translation of the code would be required. In addition, we designed LOOM not only as a working virtual memory system for our Smalltalk-80 work, but also as a test-bed for virtual memory techniques. Jim Stamos' master's thesis[6] is an example of one experimental technique based on simulation. We want further studies to use a real virtual memory system.

Deciding to implement LOOM in the Smalltalk-80 language itself led to problems that might not be encountered in a low-level language implementation. In particular, the amount of "machine state" that needs to be saved when switching between running the Smalltalk-80 interpreter for "user" and for LOOM was quite large. The amount is much larger than the amount of Smalltalk-80 virtual machine state that would have to be saved to run the LOOM code written in machine language. Also, to avoid a fault on the faulting code, all of the code and other objects which comprise the implementation of LOOM must be guaranteed to stay in main memory at all times.

We handled the first problem, saving state, by reworking our interpreter. It now obeys the convention that within the execution of a bytecode, an object fault is possible only before any "destructive" operations occur. In other words, before the interpreter writes into a field of any object or changes the reference count of any object, it reads fields from all objects needed by the current bytecode. In this way, the state we needed to save was only the "permanent" state that exists between bytecodes. Temporary state within a bytecode is not saved. In our system then, if an object fault occurs, we back up the Smalltalk program counter, switch the interpreter to the LOOM system, handle the fault, and then restart the bytecode.

The second problem, insuring that no object faults occur during the execution of the LOOM algorithms themselves, went through a couple of different designs. The first method we tried was to have the LOOM objects and the user's objects in the same Smalltalk-80 space, but to mark all the objects LOOM would ever need "unpurgable", and to guarantee that free space never went below a certain level. We made an almost-complete implementation of LOOM using this method on the Xerox Alto computer[7] before moving onto the Dorado. The problem with LOOM and the user sharing the same Smalltalk is retaining the marks on objects that LOOM needs. If the user adds many methods to class SmallInteger and its method dictionary grows, how does the new array in the dictionary get marked "unpurgable"? There are many similar cases.

The LOOM implementation on the Dorado has two separate Smalltalk-80 systems in the same machine: a full-size system for user's programs, and a smaller one for LOOM. The LOOM system has some primitives that enable it to manipulate the bits inside of objects in the user system. (Note that because they use the same interpreter, the user system has these primitives also. However, they make no sense in the user system, so are never used.) Because the LOOM system uses only a small subset of the Smalltalk-80 system, it can be much smaller, and can be guaranteed to fit entirely within its portion of main memory and never cause an object fault. Fig. 14.9 provides a view of the communication between the systems.

Alternative Smalltalk Virtual Memory Designs

The LOOM virtual memory design is only one of many ways to implement a virtual memory for a Smalltalk-80 system. The advantages of the LOOM design are:

1. It runs as fast as a resident Smalltalk-80 interpreter when the working set is in core,

2. It uses 16-bit fields in core to conserve space,

3. It allows the interpreter to avoid handling 32-bit Oops, which makes the interpreter smaller and faster on 16-bit machines,

4. It only uses memory for objects that are actually referenced, and

5. It provides a large, 32-bit virtual address space.

Its major disadvantages are:

1. It relies on fairly complicated algorithms to translate between the address spaces,

2. It takes no advantage of current hardware technology for memory fault detection, and

3. It must move objects between disk buffers and their place in memory.

There are alternatives to many of the design decisions within LOOM and to using the LOOM design itself.

LOOM was designed specifically to experiment with various methods of "grouping" objects on disk pages. If objects which are likely to be faulted on at the same time live on the same disk page, only the first fault actually has to wait for the disk. Static grouping restructures the arrangement of objects on disk pages while the system is quiescent. It reduces the number of disk accesses for both paged virtual memories and object swapping systems. Stamos extensively studied the advantages of static grouping and compared LOOM to paged virtual memories[8]. LOOM is also designed for experiments in dynamic grouping. We have several algorithms in mind for moving objects on the disk while Smalltalk is running. These algorithms will endeavor to reduce faulting by dynamically placing related objects on the same disk page.

We also mentioned that a LOOM system can be built that only uses leaves and not lambdas. Another alternative that we did not pursue is to use a marking garbage collection scheme for resident objects and reference counting for disk references. This should be possible using the delta reference-count scheme.

LOOM is currently intended for use over a local area network. The design could be extended to bring many users, many machines, and large quantities of immutable data into the same large address space. If 32-bit long Oops are not big enough, objects in secondary memory could be quad-word aligned, giving 2^{36} bytes of address space. The LOOM algorithms are parameterized for the width of long pointers, so that a change to 48-bit wide long Oops would not be difficult to do.

The LOOM design may be used for non-Smalltalk systems. In particular, we have proposed a LOOM-like design to extend the address space of Interlisp-D. The design adds another level of virtual memory to the

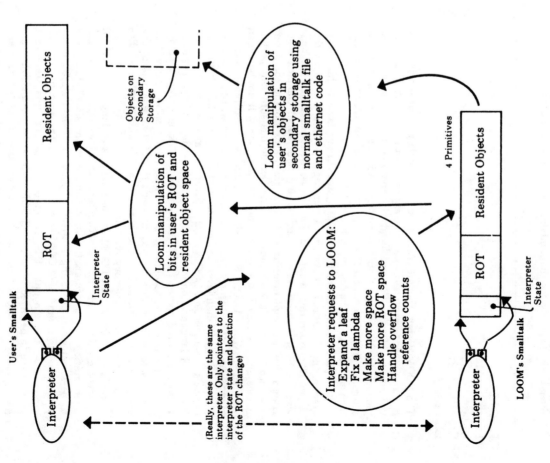

Two Separate Smalltalks in the Same Machine

Figure 14.9

existing Interlisp-D paging system by treating a page as a single object and an existing page address as a short pointer.

Learning from LOOM

Our LOOM virtual memory system is in its infancy. We are only beginning to make measurements on its performance. The design choices of the LOOM system are based on the belief that the way to design good virtual memory systems is to determine what happens most of the time, make it go fast, and hope it continues to happen most of the time. Many trade-offs were made to meet this goal. Some of the design choices we made apply to almost all Smalltalk-80 implementations and some were determined by our hardware/software environment. For example, the general idea that object swapping saves main memory over paging applies to all Smalltalk-80 systems, but the relative cost of object swapping versus paging can be heavily influenced by hardware support for one or the other. Since we know of no current hardware that supports object swapping, but we do know that a great deal of current hardware supports paging, paging has a tremendous advantage. Many of the costs of paging are hidden, such as the address computation on every memory reference, and the "built in" paging hardware on many machines. If those costs were brought into the open, and the same amount were spent on assisting object references, object oriented virtual memories might have better cost-performance than paging systems.

The LOOM design uses two levels of object addressing and translates between address spaces when necessary. Up to 2^{31} objects residing in secondary storage are represented by a cache of 2^{15} objects in main memory. These behave almost identically to resident Smalltalk-80 objects. When a reference from an object in main memory to one in secondary memory is made, an object fault occurs, the latter is brought into main memory, and processing continues. This design allows for a large virtual address space and a space- and speed-efficient resident space. Because the major algorithms in LOOM are written in Smalltalk itself, LOOM will be a major test-bed for new swapping algorithms and for new ways of reducing page faults by grouping objects in secondary storage.

Acknowledgments

The design of LOOM was a true group effort. Jim Althoff and Steve Weyer proposed an early version to improve the speed of their work on programmer directed object overlays. Peter Deutsch worked out a design for an early version of the dual name spaces (short and long Oops).

Dan Ingalls, Glenn, and Ted designed the three kinds of reference counts. Danny Bobrow said that leaves were not enough, and Larry Tesler suggested lambdas from the design of his operating system called Caravan. Ted, Dan, and Glenn worked out the final system design, and Ted and Diana Merry built a test version of the LOOM algorithms. Ted and Glenn did the Alto and Dorado implementations.

References

1. Denning, Peter J., "Virtual Memory", *Computing Surveys* vol. 2, no. 3, Sept. 1970.

2. Burton, Richard R., et al, (The Interlisp-D Group), Papers on Interlisp-D, Xerox PARC CIS-5, July 1981; (a revised version of Xerox PARC SSL-80-4).

3. Kaehler, Ted, "Virtual Memory for an Object-Oriented Language", *Byte* vol. 6, no. 8, Aug. 1981.

4. Goldberg, Adele, and Robson, David, *Smalltalk-80: The Language and Its Implementation*, Addison-Wesley, Reading, Mass., 1983.

5. Lampson, Butler W., and Pier, Kenneth A., "A Processor for a High-Peformance Personal Computer", Seventh International Symposium on Computer Architecture, SigArch/IEEE, La Baule, France, May 1980; (also in Xerox PARC CSL-81-1, Jan. 1981.)

6. Stamos, James W., "A Large Object-Oriented Virtual Memory: Grouping Strategies, Measurements, and Performance," Xerox PARC SCG-82-2, May 1982.

7. Thacker, C. P., et al., "Alto: A Personal Computer", in *Computer Structures: Readings and Examples*, 2nd Edition, Eds. Sieworek, Bell, and Newell, McGraw-Hill, New York, 1981; (also Xerox PARC CSL-79-11, Aug. 1979.

8. See reference 6.

Storage and Access Structures to Support a Semantic Data Model

Arvola Chan
Sy Danberg
Stephen Fox
Wen-Te K. Lin
Anil Nori
Daniel Ries

Computer Corporation of America
575 Technology Square
Cambridge, Massachusetts 02139

Abstract

This paper describes the design of storage and access structures for a high performance Ada* compatible database management system. This system supports the database application programming language ADAPLEX [Smith81, Smith82], which is the result of embedding the database sublanguage DAPLEX [Shipman81] in the general purpose language Ada [DoD80]. A prominent feature of the underlying data model is its support for generalization hierarchies [Smith77] which are intended to simplify the mapping from conceptual entities to database objects. An in-depth discussion of the rationale behind our choice of storage and access structures to support semantics intrinsic to the data model and to permit physical database organization tuning is provided in this paper.

1. INTRODUCTION

We are presently engaged in the development of a distributed database management system that is compatible with the programming language Ada [DoD80]. This system supports the general purpose database application programming language ADAPLEX [Smith82], which is the result of embedding the database sublanguage DAPLEX [Shipman81] in Ada. This DBMS is intended to go beyond systems like INGRES and System R, which are based on the older relational technology, in terms of modelling capabilities and ease of use. Two versions of the DBMS are being developed. A centralized DBMS, called the Local Database Manager (LDM), is designed for high performance and for use as a stand-alone system. A distributed DBMS, called the Distributed Database Manager (DDM), interconnects multiple LDMs in a computer network in order to provide rapid access to data for users who are geographically separated. This paper describes the set of storage and access structures supported in the LDM implementation.

The version of DAPLEX used in the formation of ADAPLEX is a simplification of the language described in [Shipman81]. However, all the key concepts have been retained. The semantics of database structure is defined in terms of entity types and relationships between entity types. Aside from the use of functional notations for expressions that significantly enhance the naturalness and readability of programs, the most prominent language feature that distinguishes ADAPLEX from other database languages is its support for the notion of generalization hierarchies [Smith77]. In this paper, we present our design for a set of storage and access structures that supports semantics intrinsic to the data model and permits the tuning of physical database organization. Section 2 provides a summary of the data model underlying the ADAPLEX language. Section 3 identifies our design objectives and presents an in-depth discussion of the rationale behind our design decisions.

2. DATA MODEL SUMMARY

The basic modelling constructs in ADAPLEX are entities and functions. These are intended to correspond to conceptual objects and their properties. Entities with similar generic properties are grouped together to form entity sets. Functions may be single-valued or set-valued. They may also be total or partial. Each (total) function, when applied to a given entity, returns a specific property of that entity. Each property is represented in terms of either a single value or a set of values. Such values can be drawn from noncomposite, Ada-supported data types and character strings, or they can refer to (composite) entities stored in the database as values.

This research was jointly supported by the Defense Advanced Research Projects Agency of the Department of Defense and the Naval Electronic Systems Command under Contract Number N00039-80-C-0402. The views and conclusions contained in this paper are those of the authors and should not be interpreted as necessarily representing the official policies, either expressed or implied, of the Defense Advanced Research Projects Agency, the Naval Electronic Systems Command, or the U.S. Government.

*Ada is a trademark of the Department of Defense (Ada joint program office).

Consider a university database modelling students, instructors, departments, and courses. Figure 2.1 is a graphical representation of the logical definition for such a database in ADA-PLEX. The big rectangles depict (composite) entity types and the smaller rectangles indicate (noncomposite) Ada data types. The single and double arrows represent respectively single-valued and set-valued functions that map entities from their domain types into their corresponding range types.

One notable difference between the data model underlying ADAPLEX and the relational data model is that referential constraints [Date81], which are extremely general and fundamental in database applications but not easily specifiable in relational contexts, are directly supported in ADAPLEX. In other words, the definition of the range of a function in our model is much more precise than the definition of the domain of a column in the relational model. At the same time, for functions that range over noncomposite values, we are able to exploit Ada's type definition facilities and avoid the need to introduce a separate domain definition facility [McLeod76], as has been proposed for a relational environment.

In relational systems, a real-world entity that plays several roles in an application environment is typically represented by tuples in a number of relations. In the example university database, we might have an instructor named John Doe and a student also named John Doe, who are in fact the same person in real life. In this case, we might want to impose the constraint that the age of John Doe as an instructor should agree with the age of John Doe as a student. This con-

straint can be more simply expressed in ADAPLEX by declaring a new entity type called person, indicating that student and instructor are subtypes of person, and that age is a function applicable to person. The function inheritance semantics of ADAPLEX automatically guarantees the consistency of age information on student and age information on instructor since age is a function inherited from the supertype person. At the same time, inherited functions can be applied directly to an entity in ADAPLEX data manipulation constructs, without the need for tedious explicit joining operations. Figure 2.2 is a graphical representation of the revised database definition. The double-edged arrows represent is-a relationships (e.g., each student is-a person). A person entity has properties common to both student and instructor entities, specifically name and age. Each student entity not only possesses properties specific to student (i.e., enrollments and advisor), but also inherits the properties of name and age by virtue of being a person. Similarly, each instructor entity has properties specific to instructor (i.e., dept and rank), in addition to the properties name and age inherited from being a person. The actual ADA-PLEX syntax used in the definition of this database is shown in Figure 2.3. Notice that the degree of overlap between the extents of two entity types is explicitly constrained. Such overlaps can be total or partial. The overlapping of the person, student, and instructor entity sets in the above example is illustrated graphically in Figure 2.4. The outer circle represents the set of person entities. The two inner circles represent the subset of person entities that are also student entities and instructor entities, respectively. The intersection of these two inner circles represents the

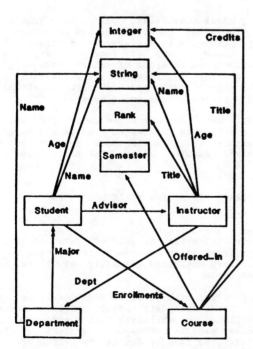

Figure 2.1 An ADPAPELX Database

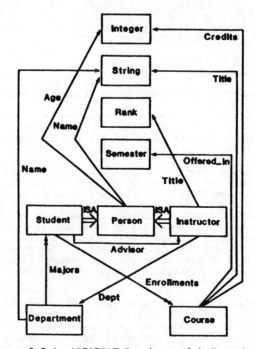

Figure 2.2 An ADPAPELX Database with Type Overlap

```
       database UNIVERSITY is

       type RANK is
       (ASST_PROF, ASSOC_PROF, FULL_PROF);

       type SEMESTER is
       (F, W, S);

       type DEPARTMENT;

       type COURSE;

       type PERSON is entity
        NAME: STRING(1..30);
        AGE: INTEGER;
       end entity;

       type INSTRUCTOR is entity
        TITLE: RANK;
        DEPT: DEPARTMENT;
       end entity;

       type STUDENT is entity
        ADVISOR: INSTRUCTOR partial;
        ENROLLMENTS: set of COURSE;
       end entity;

       type COURSE is entity
        TITLE: STRING(1..30);
        OFFERED_IN: SEMESTER;
        CREDITS: INTEGER range 1..4;
       end entity;

       type DEPARTMENT is entity
        NAME: STRING(1..30);
        MAJORS: set of STUDENT;
       end entity;

       unique NAME within PERSON;
       unique NAME within DEPARTMENT;
       unique TITLE within COURSE;
       contain INSTRUCTOR in PERSON;
       contain STUDENT in PERSON;
       share INSTRUCTOR with STUDENT;

       end UNIVERSITY;
```

Figure 2.3 Definition of an Example Database

subset of person entities that are both student entities and instructor entities.

Aside from general integrity constraints that may be explicitly declared as part of the database definition and that are enforced at the end of each database transaction, there are a number of invariant properties implied by the data model. These latter are in some sense treated as being more fundamental. Their validity is enforced at the end of each user-specified database interaction, rather than at the grosser transaction level. These fundamental constraints include:

● Referential/range constraint. The range of an entity-valued function may be another entity type in the database. When an entity of the latter type is deleted, it is necessary to ensure that there are no dangling references. For scalar and string functions, Ada provides the facilities for constraining the range of

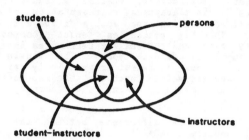

Figure 2.4 Example of Entity Set Overlap

possible values in the underlying value set. For example, the range of integers, the precision of real numbers, and the enumeration of values in a discrete type can all be defined.

● Extent overlap constraint. An entity can be included into the extent of an entity type only if overlaps among the extents of all of the types to which it currently belongs, and the extent of the type to which it is to be included, are permissible. At the same time, excluding an entity from the extent of a specified type will also exclude it from the extent of all subtypes whose extents are completely contained in the extent of the type in question.

● Totality constraint. A total function must be defined for all elements in its domain at all times; when a new entity is created, all of its values for various total functions must be known.

● Uniqueness constraint. One or more groups of single-valued functions within an entity type may optionally be declared to be unique. That is, each group of functions will yield distinct combinations of values when applied to distinct entities of the underlying type. This type of constraint is enforced automatically on insertions and updates.

This concludes our overview of the ADAPLEX data model. The interested readers are referred to [Smith81, Smith82] for more details on the syntax and semantics of the ADAPLEX language.

3. STORAGE AND ACCESS STRUCTURE DESIGN

Our choice for the set of data structures and implementation options to incorporate in the LDM has been motivated primarily by three considerations:

● Support for high-level ADAPLEX modelling constructs. Our data model provides several functional capabilities not supported by models used in contemporary systems. In particular, we need to devise new structures to efficiently represent information concerning entities that belong to multiple overlapping entity types.

- Maintenance of fundamental semantic integrity constraints. The underlying data model implies several fundamental constraints that must be enforced on database updates. Because of the universal nature of these constraints, it is desirable to design special structures to facilitate their enforcement.

- Performance tuning. Since different structures and implementation options are best suited for different patterns of use, efficiency can be attained only through organization tuning. We seek to achieve good performance by providing the database designer with a good range of implementation alternatives that he can choose to match against the requirements of his applications.(1)

We are assuming an environment where the bulk of the database is stored on conventional block-oriented storage devices. In this context, two fundamental design issues are: the appropriate clustering of information often used together to maximize the locality of reference, and the efficient support for frequently traversed associative access paths to minimize the amount of sequential searching required. More specifically, we are concerned with:

- Grouping of information concerning entities into logical records. Logical records of the same type are assumed to store the same set of fields.

- Placement of logical records into physical files. Each file is a linear address space that is mapped into physical blocks of storage devices. Logical records of the same type may optionally be divided into groups, each of which may then be stored in different files, possibly using different placement strategies. We will refer to each of these groups of logical records as a storage record type. Different storage record types that originate from the same generalization hierarchy may also be stored in the same file to achieve the desired clustering of information.

- Support for efficient associative access to stored records. The primary organization or placement strategy for the stored records in a file will determine the primary access path to these records. In addition, auxiliary access structures can be maintained in order to provide direct access based on secondary key fields that are not used to determine record placement.

3.1 Representing Entities and Entity Functions

The basic modelling concepts in ADAPLEX are those of entities and entity functions. To represent entity functions (in particular, entity-valued functions), it is important that entities be uniquely identifiable. However, the data model does not require that each entity be uniquely identifiable externally. That is, for entities of a given type, there does not necessarily exist a function (or a combination of functions) that yields a distinct value (or a distinct combination of values) when applied to each of the entities. Therefore, for internal unique identification purposes, an entity identifier is assigned to each entity upon creation. This entity identifier then serves to stand for the entity in the representation of functions.(2)

The set of functions that are applicable to an entity depends on the entity type(s) to which it belongs. Three different categories of information about an entity need to be stored:

- Values for applicable functions. This corresponds to values for attributes relevant to the entities in question and is typical of information accessed by applications in current database systems.

- Typing information. Given an entity, it is often necessary to determine the set of entity types (among a set of overlapping types) to which it belongs. Such a capability is essential for determining whether a function can legally be applied to the entity on hand. For example, in looping through entities of the type person, it is legal to apply the enrollments function to an entity only if that entity is also included in the type student.

- Additional control information. The deletion semantics of ADAPLEX requires that upon excluding an entity from an entity type, that entity must no longer be referenced by other entities (i.e., it is no longer in the active range of entity-valued functions). An efficient way to check for the satisfaction of such constraints is through the maintenance of reference counts that indicate the number of times each entity is referred to by entity functions, one for each entity type to which it belongs.(3)

Below, we describe our representation schemes for the above categories of function. We will first describe the mapping of entity functions into logical records and then introduce the notion of an entity directory as a receptacle for the remaining typing and reference count information.

3.1.1 Mapping Function Values Into Logical Records

As mentioned earlier, an important performance consideration is the clustering of information often needed together. In terms of the representation of functions, there are a number of obvious clustering alternatives:

---

(1) Our desire for tunability must, however, be balanced against the complexity and size of required software. Besides, in the absence of powerful design aids, we must ensure that the design freedom we provide to designers can be exploited effectively.

(2) Of course, given an entity identifier, it should be possible to obtain efficiently all information known about the corresponding entity.

(3) An exclusion operation is legal only if the corresponding reference count is zero.

● The no grouping approach. Each entity function is stored as a binary relation (i.e., a
two-attribute file).

● The complete grouping approach. The values
for all functions that are applicable to an
entity (independent of entity types within a
generalization hierarchy) are stored in the
same record.

● The semantic grouping approach. The values
for all (noninherited) functions applicable to
an entity from the viewpoint of a particular
entity type are stored in the same record.

● The arbitrary grouping approach. The values
for functions applicable to an entity are
stored in an arbitrary number of records to
suit the usage pattern.

Our decision here is to use a combination of
the semantic grouping approach and the no grouping approach. As a default, we will use the
semantic grouping approach and store values for
all noninherited applicable functions from the
same entity-type viewpoint in the same record.
In cases where we have arbitrarily long
(repeating/varying length) fields that might complicate storage allocation, we provide for the
option of storing such fields as individual
secondary records. Our rationale for such a
choice is that while the no grouping approach
results in an overly fragmented database,(4) the
complete grouping approach has the opposite
effect.(5) As we shall see later, when coupled
with the horizontal partitioning and clustering
options, our approach is flexible enough to permit the grouping together of all information
known about all entities of a given type, while
being completely isolated from other irrelevant
information.(6) By clustering all of the record
types that store information on a set of entities
from different viewpoints, an organization that
approximates the complete grouping approach can
also be obtained as a special case. Finally, we
disallow arbitrary grouping of functions because
we fear that this may result in too enormous a
physical design space, one which a human database
designer may not be able to utilize effectively.
Besides, a significant increase in software complexity may also result.

In summary, to store the values of functions
applicable to entities, there will be one primary
logical record type corresponding to each entity
type. Typically, each primary logical record
includes one field for the identifier of the

---

(4) It is frequently true that values for multiple functions applied to the same entity are
often needed together.

(5) The end result is that unnecessary data
transfers often have to be made.

(6) An entity type that is lower in a generalization hierarchy conceptually inherits all the
functions applicable to its ancestors in the
hierarchy. Rather than duplicating such information, we allow the use of clustering to appropriately juxtapose the related information.

entity being represented, and a number of repeating or nonrepeating fields for each set-valued or
single-valued function (as applied to the entity
in question and not specified for separate
representation). In addition, there may be zero
or more secondary logical records for separately
represented functions. Only the primary logical
records may be considered for further horizontal
partitioning and clustering. Each type of secondary logical record will be stored as a separate
two-attribute file(7) that will permit efficient
associative access based on entity identifiers.
In case an entity belongs to multiple entity
types, there will be one primary logical record
for each entity type to which it belongs.

3.1.2 Entity Directory

To keep the remaining information concerning
entities, an entity directory is maintained for
each generalization hierarchy. The information
stored in the entity directory is essentially
redundant and can be obtained through sequential
searching of logical records that represent entities. The purpose of the entity directory, however, is to centralize all information known
about entities in order to permit efficient
access. In the entity directory, there will be
one entry for each entity that belongs to at
least one of the types in the underlying generalization hierarchy. In addition to the typing
information and the reference count information,
the directory entry for each entity will also
contain physical pointers to the primary storage
records that store values for applicable functions, one for each entity type to which it
belongs. Thus, given an entity identifier, all
stored information concerning the entity can be
located either directly in the entity directory
itself or indirectly through it.

Occasionally, an entity may belong to an
arbitrary number of types in a generalization
hierarchy. Thus, an entry in an entity directory
may have to store a varying number of pointers.
We use a varying length record representation for
the entries to reduce storage overhead. The
organization of the entries also must support
efficient associative access based on entity
identifiers. Furthermore, to permit the inclusion of new entities and to reuse the space occupied by entries for defunct entities, it is
important that a dynamic file organization be
used. For this reason, we choose to organize the
entity directory using linear hashing [Larson80,
Litwin80]. Each associative retrieval of an
entry based on entity identifier can typically be
made in one page access, regardless of growth or
shrinkage of the directory.

3.2 Horizontal Partitioning of Primary
Logical Records

In order to achieve better inter and intra
entity type information clustering, we support

---

(7) That is, the entity identifier will be included as one of the attributes.

the options of mapping one primary logical record type into several disjoint storage record types, and also the option of clustering multiple storage record types originating from the same generalization hierarchy in the same file.

Consider the following generalization hierarchy involving the entity types persons, students, and instructors.(8) Assume that students and instructors do not overlap (i.e., a person cannot be both a student and an instructor). An alternative to storing all the person records in the same file is to divide the person records into disjoint groups, and to store the groups of records in different files. If we view all of the logical records of a given type as a table, then the grouping may be viewed as partitioning this table horizontally. Instead of horizontal partitioning based on arbitrary criteria, we require that the partitioning be based on properties of overlapping type membership only. In the above generalization hierarchy, we can divide person records into records for:

● person who is a student
● person who is an instructor
● person who is neither a student nor an instructor

Alternatively, to suit a different usage pattern, we can divide the person records into records for:

● person who is an instructor
● person who is not an instructor

Now consider a generalization hierarchy where student and instructor do overlap. Here we may want to divide person records into:

● person who is a student but is not an instructor
● person who is an instructor but is not a student
● person who is both a student and an instructor.
● person who is neither a student nor an instructor.

In essence, the blocks of a horizontal partitioning scheme are defined by a number of nonoverlapping block definition predicates. Each block definition predicate may consist of a conjunction of type inclusion/noninclusion conditions involving types that overlap with the type in question.(9) In addition to the blocks defined by each of these predicates, a complementary block is also induced by the complement of their disjunction when this complement is satisfiable. That is, records that do not satisfy any of the block definition predicates will be stored in the complementary block.

---

(8) That is, each student is also a person and each instructor is also a person.

(9) The use of disjunction of subtype membership properties to define blocks is in effect supported since we allow the placement of two or more blocks from the same horizontal partitioning scheme in the same file.

3.3 Placement of Storage Records

The primary organization of a file determines how records are to be positioned within the file. In general, the placement criteria may be based on:

● The entity identifier of the record
● One or more other fields stored in the record
● The positioning of related records

Typical file organizations may be dichotomized as static versus dynamic. In a static organization, records do not move once they have been inserted in the file. When the original (primary) space assigned to the file runs out, overflow space (typically additional pages chained onto the original pages) is used to accommodate the subsequently inserted records.(10) Contrarily, in a dynamic organization, the amount of primary space assigned to a file grows or shrinks dynamically in response to insertions and deletions. Records are moved as a result of page splitting and merging operations (used to maintain a certain loading factor) and to guarantee a certain level of associative access efficiency and uniformity.

For an infrequently updated file, a static organization typically is faster than a dynamic organization. However, the amount of overflow in a statically organized file is liable to become excessive and unbalanced, requiring costly periodic reorganization of the whole file. This will result in the file's inaccessibility while reorganization is in progress. In a dynamically organized file, reorganization is performed incrementally and continuously, so that performance and accessibility tends to be more uniform. The drawback with having to move records around in response to insertions and deletions is that pointers to these records cannot readily be maintained. On the other hand, the storage of such pointers is often necessary in auxiliary access structures in order to provide additional access paths to the records. As we shall see in subsequent discussions, it is possible to replace physical pointers to records with logical pointers consisting of entity identifiers in order to minimize the impact of record relocation. However, this will require indirection through the entity directory for each access.

It is our belief that there will be situations where a static organization is more desirable than a dynamic one, and vice versa. However, in an attempt to limit the size and complexity of the system, we have decided to support dynamic organizations only in the initial implementation. Our rationale is that stability is often more critical than performance, and that the need to initiate reorganization is too much of a burden on users in many applications [Stonebraker80]. As will be discussed in Section 3.6,

---

(10) The distinction between primary and overflow is that access to a record in the overflow space can be made only by first accessing other records in the primary space. Thus, it is more expensive to access a record in the overflow space.

we have an optimization scheme for approximating the performance characteristics of static file organizations through the storage of hybrid pointers (combination of logical and physical pointers).

From an alternate viewpoint, we can distinguish between organizations based on address calculation (randomization) and those that use tree-structured directories. Typically, a tree-structured organization provides the capability of accessing records in key order, which is not feasible in randomized organizations. On the other hand, a randomized organization is usually more efficient for accessing individual records. To accommodate a range of applications, we have decided to support both randomized and tree-structured organizations. Thus, the dynamic organizations we support initially will include B*-tree [Bayer72, Comer79] and linear hashing [Larson80, Litwin80].

It should be noted that the choice of primary organization is allowed for only in the case of primary storage records. Secondary storage records will always be organized using linear hashing since the predominant access mode will be keyed on individual entity identifiers.

3.4 Clustering of Storage Record Types

In addition to positioning criteria based purely on record contents, we also support the placement of records dependent on the position of related records. For example, we may want to store a student storage record next to a person storage record when they represent the same underlying entity. In particular, we may combine clustering with horizontal partitioning to achieve better juxtapositioning of information within the same generalization hierarchy. For example, we may map person logical records into storage records for person who is also an instructor, and storage records for person who is not an instructor, and then cluster the instructor storage records with the first group of person storage records. In this way, all the information concerning instructor entities will be readily accessible together.

In the above example, the clustering is based on a one-to-one relationship, namely, records representing the same entity are to be stored close to each other. In this case, we require the related records to be stored adjacently on the same page, so that a single page access will suffice for their simultaneous access.(11) We will call such clustering contiguous. As a special case, if we cluster both student records and instructor records with the corresponding person records, we effectively have

a scheme very similar to one that is obtained by storing values for all applicable functions in the same record.(12) In general, we allow multiple storage records representing the same underlying entity to be clustered together. We also allow multiple storage record types that originate from the the same logical record type to provide the functions for determining record placement.

Besides contiguous clustering based on one-to-one relationships, it is possible to perform clustering based on one-to-many relationships. For example, if there is a one-to-many relationship between department and employee (department is a single-valued function applicable to employee entities), we may require each employee record to be stored close to the corresponding department record. In this case, it may not always be possible to store all of the employee records related to a particular department record on the same page. Rather, it may be more reasonable to require that they be stored only in the same general vicinity (a small fraction of the file space). We will call this type of clustering noncontiguous. One practical way to implement noncontiguous clustering is in conjunction with a static file organization. Instead of requiring that all related records be found on the same page, related records are localized only on pages assigned to the same bucket. In this case, all related records can be located by a sequential scan of the entire bucket. As in contiguous clustering, multiple types of records may be clustered. For example, we may want to store Employee records close to the related Department records, and to store Dependent records close to corresponding Employee records. However, in view of our decision not to support static organization initially, we must also postpone support for noncontiguous clustering.

3.5 Auxiliary Access Structures

In addition to primary access paths provided by record placement strategies, often it is desirable to support associative access based on additional criteria. As in conventional systems, we permit the maintenance of simple and combined indices on logical records of a given type. Conceptually, an index provides a mapping from an indexed key value (or combination of values) to a set of pointers to the storage records that contain the indexed value (or combination of values). (As will be seen in the next section,

---

(11) In fact, we will construct a hybrid record to combine the information from the original records representing the same underlying entity. In general, a (hybrid or nonhybrid) record may consist of a fixed length portion followed by a varying length portion. We require only that the fixed length portion of the combined record not span page boundaries.

(12) A single record header is used to describe a group of records that represent the same underlying entity that is being clustered together. This header will also replicate the typing information in order to eliminate access to the entity directory when it is necessary to obtain information about an entity from the viewpoints of several overlapping entity types, and this information is already clustered in the same hybrid record. Pointers from the entity directory point to the combined record instead of to the individual records.

we will use only logical and hybrid pointers to point to dynamically organized records.) As for the organization for the index file(13) the options of using either a B*-tree organization or a linear hashing organization may both be useful. (There is no advantage for using a static organization for the index file since records in this file are not pointed to by records in other files.) A linear hashing organization provides more efficient access based on an equality search. Typically, a single access is all that is needed to locate a particular index entry. A B*-tree organization, on the other hand, requires one access for each level of the tree, while providing a fuller range of functional capabilities: the ability to access index entries in key order makes it useful in the resolution of range queries. In addition, it is also possible to use such an index to retrieve all records in key order. Both types of organizations are allowed for in the LDM implementation.

Another relevant organizational issue is how a pointer list should be represented. While most contemporary systems use a sorted array representation, there are also some which automatically convert an array representation to a bit-map representation when a list gets long. The advantage of the latter scheme is that it results in a much more compact representation on which bitwise operations can be performed in order to implement set operations on pointer lists. However, it may be more difficult to intersect pointer lists that use different representation. For the sake of software simplicity, we restrict our initial implementation to the array representation only.

3.6 Hybrid Pointers

Pointers in data structures are essential for supporting associative access. These pointers may be of a logical nature, or they may be physically oriented. A logical pointer has the advantage of providing a higher level of data independence. However, once a logical pointer is obtained, an extra level of searching must be performed to acquire an actual physical pointer to the desired information. In our context, the entity identifier serves as a logical pointer, with the entity directory providing the indirection. When a storage record that stores information concerning an entity has to be relocated, only the corresponding entry in the entity directory needs to be updated; all other records that store the entity identifier of the affected entity need not be modified. For indices that point to dynamically organized records, it would be appropriate to store logical pointers to simplify pointer maintenance.

As a physical pointer, we use the page

number together with the direct or indirect(14) offset of the record within the page. Physical pointers have the advantage of directness. However, the price we pay is pointer maintenance when records are relocated. Since we support only dynamic organizations, we do not permit the use of physical pointers in isolation in secondary indices or in the representation of functions.

As an optimization, however, we support the option of combining a physical pointer with a logical pointer to form a hybrid pointer. For example, when representing a function from course to student, it may be useful to store both the student entity identifier, and the physical pointer to the student record. The rationale is that often when the student function is applied to the course entity, one is interested only in the student aspects of the target entity. Similarly, in the index on age for the student record type, we can store both the entity identifiers and the physical pointers to the student records. In general, we can follow the physical portion of a hybrid pointer to find the pointed-to record, and then compare the entity identifier stored there against the logical pointer portion of the hybrid pointer on hand. If the two entity identifiers do not match, we know that the pointed-to record has been relocated. In this case, the corresponding entry in the entity directory should be examined to determine the new address of the relocated record, and the hybrid pointer should be updated. The advantage of this scheme is that records can be relocated without regard to the pointers that point to them. Only the entity directory needs to be updated. The hybrid pointers are revalidated when they are next used. Thus in a high update situation, a record may be relocated many times before pointers pointing to it need be updated.

4. SUMMARY

We have presented a set of storage and access structures for supporting a semantic data model. The prominent features of this data model, which are intended to capture more application semantics than constructs found in conventional data models, include the notions of generalization hierarchies and referential constraints. Our design allows for the flexible tuning of database organizations to match application requirements. The design space encompasses such options as horizontal and vertical partitioning of information within an entity type, as well as the clustering of information across entity types within the same generalization hierarchy. Dynamic file organizations are used for the storing of data records, and the concept of hybrid pointers is introduced for the

---

(13) Each record in this file consists of an indexed key value and an associated pointer list.

(14) In the case of varying length records, it is often desirable to be able to relocate a record within a page without having to update all pointers that point to the relocated record. The indirection of the physical pointer can solve the problem by means of indexing information stored at the bottom of the same page.

purpose of pointing to dynamically relocatable records in the representation of inverted lists in secondary indices, and in the representation of interentity relationships. The underlying DBMS that supports the discussed set of storage and access structures is being developed by the Computer Corporation of America. It is scheduled to be completed in 1983.

5. ACKNOWLEDGEMENTS

We are indebted to Professor Philip Bernstein, Professor Nathan Goodman, Dr. Randy Katz, Terry Landers, Frank Manola, Dr. James Rothnie, Dr. Diane Smith, and Dr. John Smith for providing us with invaluable input and feedback during the design of the Local Database Manager to support the ADAPLEX language.

6. REFERENCES

[Bayer72]
Bayer, R., C. McCreight, "Organization and Maintenance of Large Ordered Indexes," _Acta Informatica_, Vol. 1, No. 3, 1972.

[Comer79]
Comer, D., "The Ubiquitous B-Tree," _ACM Computing Surveys_, Vol. 11, No. 2, June, 1979.

[Date81]
Date, C. J., "Referential Integrity," _VLDB Conference Proceedings_, 1981.

[DoD80]
United States Department of Defense, "Reference Manual for the Ada Programming Language," Proposed Standard Document, July 1980.

[Larson80]
Larson, P., "Linear Hashing With Partial Expansions," _VLDB Conference Proceedings_, 1980.

[Litwin80]
Litwin, W., "Linear Hashing: A New Tool for File and Table Addressing," _VLDB Conference Proceedings_, 1980.

[McLeod76]
McLeod, D. J., "High Level Domain Definition in a Relational Database," _Proceedings for ACM SIGPLAN/SIGMOD Conference on Data: Abstraction, Definition, and Structure_, 1976.

[Shipman81]
Shipman, D., "The Functional Data Model and the Data Language DAPLEX," _ACM Transactions on Database Systems_, Vol. 6, No. 1, March 1981.

[Smith77]
Smith, J. M., D. C. P. Smith, "Database Abstractions: Aggregation and Generalization," _ACM Transactions on Database Systems_, Vol. 2, No. 2, June, 1977.

[Smith81]
Smith, J. M., S. Fox, T. Landers, "Reference Manual for ADAPLEX," Technical Report CCA-81-02, Computer Corporation of America, January 1981.

[Smith82]
Smith, J. M., S. Fox, T. Landers, "ADAPLEX: The Integration of the DAPLEX Database Language with the Ada Programming Language," Technical Report, Computer Corporation of America, in preparation.

[Stonebraker80]
Stonebraker, M., "Retrospection on a Database System," _ACM Transactions on Database Systems_, Vol. 5, No. 2, June 1980.

Fine-Grained Mobility in the Emerald System

ERIC JUL, HENRY LEVY, NORMAN HUTCHINSON, and ANDREW BLACK

University of Washington

Emerald is an object-based language and system designed for the construction of distributed programs. An explicit goal of Emerald is support for object mobility; objects in Emerald can freely move within the system to take advantage of distribution and dynamically changing environments. We say that Emerald has fine-grained mobility because Emerald objects can be small data objects as well as process objects. Fine-grained mobility allows us to apply mobility in new ways but presents implementation problems as well. This paper discusses the benefits of fine-grained mobility, the Emerald language and run-time mechanisms that support mobility, and techniques for implementing mobility that do not degrade the performance of local operations. Performance measurements of the current implementation are included.

Categories and Subject Descriptors: C.2.4[Computer-Communications Networks]: Distributed Systems—*distributed applications, network operating systems*; D.3.3[Programming Languages]: Language Constructs—*abstract data types, control structures*; D.4.2[Operating Systems]: Storage Management—*distributed memories*; D.4.4[Operating Systems]: Communications Management—*message sending*; D.4.7[Operating Systems]: Organization and Design—*distributed systems*

General Terms: Design, Languages, Measurement, Performance

Additional Key Words and Phrases: Distributed languages, object-oriented languages, object-oriented systems, process mobility

1. INTRODUCTION

Process migration has been implemented or described as a goal of several distributed systems [8, 11, 16, 20, 23, 24, 28]. In these systems, entire address spaces are moved from node to node. For example, a process manager might initiate a move to share processor load more evenly, or users might initiate remote execution explicitly. In either case, the running process is typically ignorant of its location and unaffected by the move.

This work was supported in part by the National Science Foundation under grants MCS-8004111, DCR-8420945 and CCR-8700106, by Københavns Universitet (University of Copenhagen), Denmark under grant J.nr. 574-2.2, by a Digital Equipment Corporation External Research Grant, and by an IBM Graduate Fellowship.

Authors' current addresses: E. Jul, DIKU, Dept. of Computer Science, University of Copenhagen, Universitetsparken 1, DK-2100 Copenhagen, Denmark; H. Levy, University of Washington, Dept. of Computer Science, FR-35, Seattle, WA 98195; N. Hutchinson, Dept. of Computer Science, University of Arizona, Tucson, AZ 85721; A. Black, Digital Equipment Corporation, 550 King St., Littleton, MA 01460.

During the last three years, we have designed and implemented Emerald [6, 7], a distributed object-based language and system. A principal goal of Emerald is to experiment with the use of mobility in distributed programming. Mobility in the Emerald system differs from existing process migration schemes in two important respects. First, Emerald is object-based, and the unit of distribution and mobility is the object. Although some Emerald objects contain processes, others contain only data: arrays, records, and single integers are all objects. Thus, the unit of mobility can be much smaller than in process migration systems. Object mobility in Emerald subsumes both process migration and data transfer. Second, Emerald has language support for mobility. Not only does the Emerald language explicitly recognize the notions of location and mobility, but the design of conventional parts of the language (e.g., parameter passing) is affected by mobility.

The advantages of process migration, which have been noted in previous work, include

(1) *Load sharing*—By moving objects around the system, one can take advantage of lightly used processors.

(2) *Communications performance*—Active objects that interact intensively can be moved to the same node to reduce the communications cost for the duration of their interaction.

(3) *Availability*—Objects can be moved to different nodes to provide better failure coverage.

(4) *Reconfiguration*—Objects can be moved following either a failure or a recovery or prior to scheduled downtime.

(5) *Utilizing special capabilities*—An object can move to take advantage of unique hardware or software capabilities on a particular node.

Along with these advantages, fine-grained mobility provides three additional benefits:

(1) *Data Movement*—Mobility provides a simple way for the programmer to move data from node to node without having to explicitly package data. No separate message-passing or file-transfer mechanism is required.

(2) *Invocation Performance*—Mobility has the potential for improving the performance of remote invocation by moving parameter objects to the remote site for the duration of the invocation.

(3) *Garbage Collection*—Mobility can help simplify distributed garbage collection by moving objects to sites where references exist [16, 29].

To our knowledge, the only other system that implements object mobility in a style similar to Emerald is a recent implementation of distributed Smalltalk [4]. In addition to mobility and distribution, we intend that Emerald provide efficient execution. We want to achieve performance competitive with standard procedural languages in the local case and standard remote procedure call (RPC) systems in the remote case. These goals are not trivial in a location-independent object-based environment. To meet them, we have relied heavily

Table I. Timings of Local Emerald Invocations

Emerald operation	Example	Time/μs
Primitive integer invocation	$i \leftarrow i + 23$	0.4
Primitive real invocation	$x \leftarrow x + 23.0$	3.4
Local invocation	localobject.no-op	16.6
Resident global invocation	globalobject.no-op	19.4

on an appropriate choice of language semantics, a tight coupling between the compiler and run-time kernel, and careful attention to implementation.

Emerald is not intended to run in large, long-haul networks. We assume a local area network with a modest number of nodes (e.g., 100). In addition, we assume that nodes are homogeneous in the sense that they all run the same instruction set and that they are trusted.

In this paper we concentrate primarily on the language and run-time mechanisms that support fine-grained mobility while retaining efficient intranode operation. First, we present a brief overview of the Emerald language and system and its mobility and location primitives. A more detailed description of object structure in Emerald can be found in [6] and of the type system in [7]. Second, we discuss the implementation of fine-grained mobility in Emerald and new problems that arise from providing such support. Third, we present measurements of the implementation and draw implications from the measurements and our design experience.

2. OVERVIEW OF EMERALD

As previously stated, an important goal of Emerald is explicit support for mobility. From a conceptual viewpoint, a more important goal is a single-object model. Object-based systems typically lie at the ends of a spectrum: object-based languages such as Smalltalk [13] and CLU [22] provide small, local data objects; object-based operating systems like Hydra [30] and Clouds [1] provide large, active objects. Distributed systems such as Argus [21] and Eden [3] that support both kinds of objects have a separate object definition mechanism for each. Choosing the right mechanism requires that the programmer know ahead of time all uses to which an object will be put; the alternative is to accept the inefficiency and inconvenience of using the "wrong" mechanism or to reprogram the object later as needs change. For example, while programming a Collaborative Editing System in Argus, Greif, Seliger, and Weihl have observed that a designer can be forced to use a Guardian where a cluster might be more appropriate [14].

The motivation for two distinct definition mechanisms is the need for two distinct implementations. In distributed object-based systems such as Clouds and Eden, a *local* execution of the general invocation mechanism can take milliseconds or tens of milliseconds [26]. A more restrictive and efficient implementation is appropriate for objects that are known to be always local; for example, shared store can be used in preference to messages.

Although we believe in the importance of multiple implementations, we do not believe that these need to be visible to the programmer. In Emerald, programmers use a single object definition mechanism with a single semantics for defining all objects. This includes small, local data-only objects and active, mobile distributed objects. However, the Emerald compiler is capable of analyzing the needs of each object and generating an appropriate implementation. For example, an array object whose use is entirely local to another object will be implemented differently from an array that is shared globally. The compiler produces different implementations from the same piece of code, depending on the context in which it is compiled [18].

The motivation for designing a new language, instead of applying these ideas to an existing language, is that the semantics of a language often preclude efficient implementation in either the local or remote case. In designing Emerald, we kept both implementations in mind. Moreover, Emerald's unique type system allows the programmer to state either nothing or a great deal about the use of a variable; in general, the more information the compiler has, the better the code that it generates.

We believe that the current Emerald implementation demonstrates the viability of this approach and meets our goal of local performance commensurate with procedural languages. Table I shows the performance of several local Emerald operations executed on a MicroVAX II;[1] more details on the compiler and its implementation can be found in [18]. The "resident global invocation" time is for a global object (i.e., one that can move around the network) when invoked by another object resident on the same node.

For comparison with procedural languages, a C procedure call takes 13.4 microseconds, while a Concurrent Euclid procedure call takes 16.4 microseconds. Concurrent Euclid is slower because, like Emerald, it must make explicit stack overflow checks on each call.

2.1 Emerald Objects

Each Emerald object has four components:

(1) A unique network-wide name;
(2) A representation, that is, the data local to the object, which consists of primitive data and references to other objects;
(3) A set of operations that can be invoked on the object;
(4) An optional process.

Emerald objects that contain a process are active; objects without a process are passive data structures. Objects with processes make invocations on other objects, which in turn invoke other objects, and so on to any depth. As a consequence, a thread of control originating in one object may span other objects, both locally and on remote machines. Multiple threads of control may be active concurrently within a single object; synchronization is provided by monitors.

Figure 1 shows an example definition of an Emerald object, in this case a simple directory object called *aDirectory*. The representation of the object

[1] Micro VAX is a trademark of Digital Equipment Corporation.

```
object aDirectory
    export Add, Lookup, Delete
    monitor
        const DirElement == record DirElement
            var name : String
            var obj : Any
        end DirElement
        const a == Array.of[DirElement].empty
        function Lookup[n : String] → [o : Any]
            var element : DirElement
            var i : Integer ← a.lowerbound
            loop
                exit when i > a.upperbound
                element ← a.getelement[i]
                if element.getname = n then
                    o ← element.getobj
                    return
                end if
                i ← i + 1
            end loop
            o ← nil
        end Lookup
        % Implementation of Add and Delete
    end monitor
end aDirectory
```

Fig. 1.   An Emerald directory object definition.

consists of an array a of directory elements. The object exports three operations: Add, Lookup, and Delete. The array a and the operations are defined within a monitor to guarantee exclusive access to the array.

2.2 Types in Emerald

The Emerald language supports the concept of *abstract type* [7]. The abstract type of an object defines its interface: the number of operations that it exports, their names, and the number and abstract types of the parameters to each operation. For example, consider the abstract type definition for *SimpleDirType* below:

```
const SimpleDirType == type SimpleDirType
    operation Lookup[String] → [Any]
    operation Add[String, Any]
end SimpleDirType
```

This abstract-type definition has two operations, *Lookup* and *Add*. *Lookup* has an input parameter of abstract type **String** and returns an object of abstract type **Any**. We say that an object *conforms* to an abstract type if it implements at least the operations of that abstract type and if the abstract types of the parameters conform in the proper way. When an object is assigned to a variable, the abstract type of that object must conform to the declared abstract type of the variable. All objects conform to type **Any** since **Any** has no operation.

Abstract types permit new implementations of an object to be added to an executing system. To use a new object in place of another, the abstract type of the new object must conform to the required abstract type. For example, we could assign the object *aDirectory* in Figure 1 to a variable declared to have abstract type *SimpleDirType* because *aDirectory* conforms to *SimpleDirType*. Note that each object can implement a number of different abstract types, and an abstract type can be implemented by a number of different objects.

2.3 Primitives for Mobility

Object mobility in Emerald is provided by a small set of language primitives. An Emerald object can

—*Locate* an object (e.g., **"locate X"** returns the node where X resides).
—*Move* an object to another node (e.g., **"move X to Y"** colocates X with Y).
—*Fix* an object at a particular node (e.g., **"fix X at Y"**).
—*Unfix* an object and make it mobile again following a fix (e.g., **"unfix X"**).
—*Refix* an object by atomically performing an Unfix, Move, and Fix at a new mode (e.g., **"refix X at Z"**).

The move primitive is actually a hint; the kernel is not obliged to perform the move, and the object is not obliged to remain at the destination site. Fix and refix have stronger semantics; if the primitives succeed, the object will stay at the destination until it is explicitly unfixed.

Central to these primitives is the concept of location, which is encapsulated in a *node* object. A node object is an abstraction of a physical machine. Location may be specified by naming either a node object or any other object. If the programmer specifies a nonnode object, the location implied is the node on which that object resides. These concepts are similar to the location-dependent primitives in Eden [5].

A crucial issue when moving objects containing references is deciding how much to move [25]. An object is part of a graph of references, and one could move a single object, several levels of objects, or the entire graph. The simplest approach—moving the specified object alone—may be inappropriate. Depending on how the object is implemented, invocations of the moved object may require remote references that would have been avoided if other related objects had been moved as well.

Emerald has no class/instance hierarchy, in contrast to Smalltalk. Objects are not members of a class; conceptually, each object carries its own code. This distinction is important in a distributed environment where separating an object from its code would be costly. However, identically implemented Emerald objects on each node do share code. In the implementation, the code is stored in a *concrete type object*. Because concrete type objects are immutable, they can be freely copied. When an object is moved to another node, only its data are moved. If the object contains a process, part of that data will include the process's stack, but no code is transferred.

When a kernel receives an object, it determines whether a copy of the concrete type object implementing that object already exists locally; if it does not, the kernel obtains a copy of it by finding one on another node using the location algorithm (described in Section 3.2). Typically, the concrete type will be available from the node that sent the object. When a concrete type object arrives, it is dynamically linked into the kernel—the compiler generates relocatable code and sufficient symbol table information to make such dynamic linking possible. This scheme makes it possible to add dynamically new concrete types that implement existing abstract types. Concrete type objects are kept on a node for as long as there are objects referencing them, after which they are garbage collected.

The Emerald programmer may wish to specify explicitly which objects move together. For this purpose, the Emerald language allows the programmer to *attach* objects to other objects. When a variable is declared, the programmer can specify the variable to be an "attached variable."

For example, in the Emerald mail system, mail messages have four fields: a sender, an array of destination mailboxes, a subject line, and a text string. It makes sense for the array of destination mailboxes to be attached to the mail message, and this could be specified as

attached var *ToList: Array.of[Mailbox]*

When the mail message is moved, the array pointed to at that time by *ToList* is moved with it. This may affect the performance of invocations on *ToList* but not their semantics.

Attachment is transitive: any object attached to *T.List* will also be moved. For example, linked structures may be moved as a whole by attaching the link fields. Attachment is not symmetric; the object named by *T.List* can itself be moved, perhaps before it is invoked, and no attempt will be made to move the mail message with it.

2.4 Parameter Passing

An important issue in the design of distributed, object-based systems (as well as RPC systems) is the choice of parameter passing semantics. In an object-based system, all variables refer to other objects. The natural parameter-passing method is therefore call-by-object-reference, where a reference to the argument object is passed. This is, in fact, the semantics chosen by CLU (where it is called *call by sharing*) [22] and Smalltalk [13].

In a distributed object-oriented system, the desire to treat local and remote operations identically leads one to use the same semantics. However, such a choice could cause serious performance problems: On a remote invocation, access by the remote operation to an argument is likely to cause an additional remote invocation. For this reason, systems such as Argus have required that arguments to remote calls be passed by value, not by object-reference [15]. Similarly, RPC systems require call-by-value since addresses are context dependent and have no meaning in the remote environment.

The Emerald language uses call-by-object-reference parameter-passing semantics for all invocations, local or remote. In both cases, the invoking code constructs an activation record that contains references to the argument objects. In the local case, the invoked object is called directly and receives a pointer to the activation record for the invocation. In the remote case, the activation record must be reconstructed on the remote system, but the basic operation and semantics are identical.

Because Emerald objects are mobile, it may be possible to avoid many remote references by moving argument objects to the site of a remote invocation. Whether this is worthwhile depends on (1) the size of an argument object, (2) other current or future invocations of the argument, (3) the number of invocations that will be issued by the remote object to the argument, and (4) the relative costs of mobility and local and remote invocation.

In the current Emerald prototype, arguments are moved in two cases. First, on the basis of compile-time information, the Emerald compiler may decide to move an object along with an invocation. For example, small immutable objects are obvious candidates for moving because they can be copied cheaply. Obviously, it makes little sense to send a remote reference to a small string or integer. Second, the Emerald programmer may decide that an object should be moved on the basis of knowledge about the application. To make this possible, Emerald provides a parameter-passing mode that we call *call-by-move*. Call-by-move does not change the semantics, which is still call-by-object-reference, but at invocation time the the argument object is relocated to the destination site. Following the call, the argument object may either return to the source of the call or remain at the destination site (we call these two modes *call-by-visit* and *call-by-move*, respectively).

Call-by-move is a convenience and a performance optimization. Arguments could instead be moved by explicit move statements. However, providing call-by-move as a parameter-passing mode allows packaging of the argument objects in the same network packet as the invocation message.

As an example, consider another mail system example. After composing a mail message (whose fields were described previously), the user invokes the message's *Deliver* operation:

```
operation Deliver
  var aMailbox: Mailbox
  if ToList.length = 1 then
    aMailbox ← Tolist.getelement[ToList.lowerbound]
    aMailbox.Deliver[move self]
  else
    var i: Integer ← ToList.lowerbound
    loop
      exit when i > ToList.upperbound
      aMailbox ← ToList.getelement[i]
      aMailbox.Deliver[self]
      i ← i + 1
    end loop
  end if
end Deliver
```

This operation delivers the message to all the mailboxes on the *ToList*. However, in the common case in which there is only one destination, call-by-move is used to colocate the mail message with the (single) destination mailbox.

2.5 Processes, Objects, and Mobility

An Emerald process is a thread of control that is initiated when an object with a process is created. A process can invoke operations on its object or on any object that it can reference. We think of a process as being a stack of activation records, as shown in Figure 2. The thread of control of one object's process may pass through other objects; in the case of Figure 2, the process owned by object A invokes operations in objects *A, B,* and *C*.

One can think of remote invocations in several ways. In the traditional remote operation model [27], the sending process blocks, and an existing remote process executes the operation, possibly returning a value to the caller, which then

In a distributed object-based system, this problem may be somewhat simplified. Objects cleanly define the boundaries of all system entities. Furthermore, since all resources are objects, addressing is standardized and location independent. All objects, whether user-implemented or kernel-implemented, are addressed indirectly using an object ID. Operations are performed through a standard invocation interface.

Although distribution and mobility increase the generality of a system, they often reduce its performance. Anyone building an object-based system must be sensitive to performance because of the generally poor performance of such systems. The implementation of mobility in Emerald involves trade-offs between the performance of mobility and that of more fundamental mechanisms, such as local invocation. Where possible, we have made these trade-offs in favor of the performance of frequent operations, and we would typically be willing to increase the complexity of mobility to save a microsecond or two on local invocation. Furthermore, it takes 100 times longer to move an object than to perform a local invocation; adding 5 microseconds to the object move time makes little relative difference, whereas 5 microseconds is 25 percent of the local invocation time. The result of this philosophy is that, to a great extent, the existence of mobility and distribution in Emerald do not interfere with the performance of objects on a single node.

In the following sections, we describe some of the implementation of the Emerald kernel that is relevant to mobility and some of the trade-offs that we have made in this design.

3.1 Object Implementation and Addressing

To meet our goal of building a distributed object-based system with efficient local execution, the Emerald implementation relies heavily on shared memory. We have implemented a prototype of Emerald on top of DEC's Ultrix system (which is based on UNIX 4.2BSD) running on five DEC MicroVAX II workstations.[2] The Emerald kernel and all Emerald objects on a single node execute within a single Ultrix address space. Emerald processes are lightweight threads scheduled within that address space. Protection among objects is guaranteed by the compiler both through type checking and through run-time checks inserted into the code. Objects that are resident on the same node address each other directly—an implementation style that has implications for mobility.

As previously stated, all objects are coded using a single object definition mechanism. However, based on its knowledge of an object's use, the compiler is free to choose an appropriate addressing mechanism, storage strategy, and invocation protocol [18]. The Emerald compiler uses three different styles of object implementation:

(1) A *global* object can be moved independently, can be referenced globally in the network, and can be invoked by objects not known at compile time. Global objects are heap allocated. An invocation of such an object may require a remote invocation. In Figure 1, the object *aDirectory* is implemented as a global object.

---

[2] UNIX is a trademark of AT&T Bell Laboratories. Ultrix is a trademark of Digital Equipment Corporation.

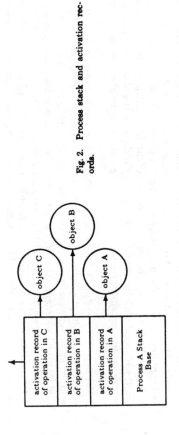

Fig. 2.   Process stack and activation records.

continues execution. In Emerald, when a remote invocation occurs, we think of the process moving to the destination node and invoking the object there. Or, alternatively, the new activation record moves to the destination node to become the base of a new segment of the process stack on that node. The invocation stack of a single Emerald process can therefore be distributed across several nodes.

Mobility presents a special problem to this process structure. For example, given the process activation stack in Figure 2, suppose that object *B* is moved to another node. In that case, the part of the thread that is executing in *B* must move along with *B*; that is, the activation record must move. Furthermore, when the operation in *C* terminates, it must now return to a different node. If object *C* were to move to a different node from *B*, we would have three parts of the process stack on three different nodes. Invocation returns would propagate control back from node to node.

One could imagine a different scheme that left the stack intact, with invocations always returning to the node on which the root process resides; at that point the situation could be analyzed and control passed to the proper location. The problem with this design is that it leaves *residual dependencies*. In the situation in which objects *C* and *B* have moved to different nodes, it should be possible for control to return from *C* to *B* even if *A* is temporarily unreachable. Depending on *B*'s behavior, it may, in fact, be some time before a return to *A* or its node is actually required. Moving invocation frames along with the objects in which they execute ensures that execution can continue as long as possible and removes the computational burden from nodes that do not need to be involved in a communication.

3. IMPLEMENTING MOBILITY IN EMERALD

Adding process mobility to existing systems often proves to be a difficult task. One problem is extracting the entire state of a process, which may be distributed through numerous operating system data structures. Second, the process may have variables that directly index those operating system data structures, such as open file descriptors, window numbers, and so forth.

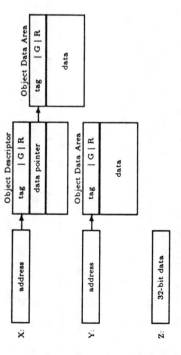

Fig. 3. Emerald addressing structures.

(2) A *local* object is completely contained within another object; that is, a reference to the local object is never exported outside the boundary of the enclosing object. Such objects cannot move independently; they always move along with their enclosing object. Local objects are heap allocated. An invocation is implemented by a local procedure call or in-line code. The array *a* in Figure 1 is not used outside of the directory and can thus be implemented as a local object.

(3) A *direct* object is a local object whose data area is allocated directly in the representation of the enclosing object. Direct objects are used mainly for primitive built-in types, structures of primitive types, and other simple objects whose organization can be deduced at compile time. For example, all integers are direct objects.

Figure 3 shows the various implementation and addressing options used by Emerald. Variable X names a global object, and the value stored in X is the address of a local *object descriptor*. Each node contains an object descriptor for every global object for which references exist on that node. When the last reference to object *m* is deleted from node *k*, *k*'s object descriptor for *m* can be garbage collected.

An object descriptor contains information about the state and location of a global object. The first word of the object descriptor identifies it as a descriptor and contains control bits indicating whether the object is local or global (the *G* bit) and whether or not the object is resident (the *R* bit). If the resident bit is set, the object descriptor contains the memory address of the object's data area; otherwise, the descriptor contains a forwarding address to the object as described in Section 3.2.

Variable Y in Figure 3 names a local object. The value stored in Y is the address of the object's data area. The first word of this data area, like the first word of an object descriptor, contains fields identifying the area and indicating that this is a local object, that is, the data area acts as its own descriptor. Finally, a variable Z names a direct object that was allocated within the variable itself.

Notice that within a single node, all objects can be addressed directly without kernel intervention. Emerald variables contain references that are location

dependent, that is, they have meaning only within the context of a particular node. For invocation of global objects, compiled code first checks the *resident* bit to see if a local invocation can be performed directly. If the target object is not resident, the compiled code will trap to the kernel so that a remote invocation can be performed. In this way, global objects can be invoked locally in time comparable to a local procedure call.

3.2 Finding Objects

Since objects are allowed to move freely, it is not always possible to know the location of a given object, for example, when invoking it. The run-time system must keep track of objects or at least be able to find them when needed. Keeping every node in the system up-to-date on the current location of every object is expensive and unnecessary. Instead, we use a scheme based on the concept of *forwarding addresses* as described in Fowler [12].

Each global object is assigned a unique network-wide *Object Identifier (OID)*, and each node has a hashed *access table* mapping OIDs to object descriptors. The access table contains an entry for each local object for which a remote reference exists and each remote object for which a local reference exists.

As previously described, an object descriptor contains a *forwarding address* as well as the object's OID. A forwarding address is a tuple $\langle timestamp, node \rangle$ in which the node is the last known location of the object and the timestamp specifies the age of the forwarding address. Fowler [12] has shown that it is sufficient to maintain the timestamp as a counter incremented every time the object moves. Given conflicting forwarding addresses for the same object, it is simple to determine which one is most recent. Every reference sent across a node boundary contains the OID of the referenced object and the latest available forwarding address. The receiving node may then update its forwarding address for the referenced object, if required.

If an object is moved from node A to node B, both A and B will update their forwarding addresses for the object. No action is taken to inform other nodes. Should node C try to invoke the object at A, A will forward the invocation message to B. When the invocation completes, B will send the reply to C with the new forwarding address piggybacked onto the reply message.

An alternative strategy, which we did not adopt, would be to keep track of all nodes that have references to a particular object. Should that object move, update messages could be sent to those nodes. However, these extra messages could significantly increase the cost of move and of passing references. For example, when an object reference is passed to a node for the first time, that node would have to register with the node responsible for the object. The DEMOS/MP system used a forwarding address update scheme, and updating forwarding addresses was shown to incur significant overhead [23]. In addition, sending update messages on every move will not avoid the need for invocation forwarding, since update messages do not arrive immediately at all destinations. Our scheme places the cost of forwarding-address maintenance on the current users of a forwarding address.

When it is necessary to locate an object, for example when the *locate* primitive is used, we apply the following algorithm. If the kernel has a forwarding address for the object, it asks the specified node whether the object is resident there; if it is, we are done. Otherwise, if that node has a newer forwarding address, then we start over using that forwarding address. However, if that node is unreachable or has no better information, we resort to a broadcast protocol.

The broadcast protocol is used whenever the previous step has failed to find the object. The searching kernel sends a first broadcast message to all other nodes seeking the location of the object. To reduce message traffic, only a kernel that has the specified object responds to the broadcast. If the searching kernel receives no response within a time limit, it sends a second broadcast requesting a positive or negative reply from all other nodes. All nodes not responding within a short time are sent a reliable, point-to-point message with the location request. If every node responds negatively, we conclude that the object is unavailable.

When performing remote invocations, the invocation message is sent without locating the target object first. Only if there is a lost forwarding address somewhere along the path will the location algorithm be used. This optimizes for the common case in which the object has not moved or where a valid forwarding address exists.

3.3 Finding and Translating Pointers

The use of direct memory addresses in Emerald (as opposed to indirect references, such as those used in the standard Smalltalk implementation [13]) increases the performance of local invocations. Consequently, movement of an object involves finding and modifying all of the direct addresses, which increases the cost of mobility. We feel that this is reasonable, since motion is less frequent than invocation. This design places the price of mobility on those who use it.

Finding and translating references could be done in several ways. For example, a *tag* bit in each word could indicate whether or not the word contains an object reference. Smalltalk 80 uses such bits to distinguish integers from references, but using tags increases the overhead of arithmetic operations and complicates the implementation in general.

Instead, the Emerald compiler generates *templates* for object data areas describing the layout of the area. The template is stored with the code in the concrete type object that defines the object's operations. Each object data area contains a reference to the concrete type object so that the code and the template can be found, given only the data area. In addition to their use for mobility, templates are used for garbage collection and debugging, since these tasks must also understand an object's data area.

As an example, consider the Emerald program shown in Figure 4 that defines a single object containing three variables inside a monitor. The variable *myself* contains a pointer to its own object descriptor. The variable *name* is initialized to point to a local string object. The variable *i* does not contain a pointer, since integers are implemented as direct objects. The corresponding object data area and template are shown in Figure 5.

The data area for *simpleobject* contains

—control information as described earlier,
—a pointer to the code for *simpleobject*,

—a lock for the monitor,
—the variable *i* allocated as 4 bytes of data, and
—the variables *myself* and *name*, each allocated as a pointer to an object.

The template does not describe the first two items since every data area contains them. Each template entry contains a count of the number of items described and the types of the items (called *template-types*). Typical template-types are

—*Pointer*, which is the address of an object; pointers must be translated if the object is moved.
—*Data*, which are direct data (e.g., integers) stored as numbers of bytes; these are not translated.
—*MonitorLock*, which controls access to the object's monitor. Monitors are implemented as a Boolean and a queue of processes awaiting entry to the monitor. A monitor must be translated if the object is moved.

Attached objects, which must move along with an object being moved, are indicated simply by a bit in the template entry. The compiler contiguously allocates variables that can be described by identical template entries. Therefore, the average template contains only two or three entries.

In addition to data areas, the compiler must produce templates to describe activation records so that active invocations can be moved along with objects.

```
const simpleobject == object simpleobject
  monitor
    var myself : Any — simpleobject
    var name : String — "Emerald"
    var i : Integer — 17
    operation GetMyName → [n : String]
      n — name
    end GetMyName
        :
  end monitor
end simpleobject
```

Fig. 4. Simple Emerald object definition.

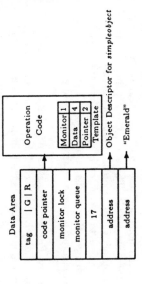

Fig. 5. Data area and template structure.

A template for an activation record describes three things: the parameters to the operation, the local variables used by the operation, and the contents of the CPU registers.

To simplify activation-record templates, the Emerald compiler does not permit registers to change their template-type during an operation. A register that contains a pointer must contain a pointer for the lifetime of the invocation; however, the pointer register can point to different objects during its lifetime. This restriction is similar to the segregation of address and data registers in some architectures but is more dynamic since the division is made for each specific operation. Without this restriction, we would need to have different templates at different points in an operation's execution—a design considered early in the project but later abandoned as unnecessary.

3.4 Moving Objects

Using the addressing and implementation structure described above, the actual moving of an object is rather straightforward. Although some systems precopy objects to be moved for performance reasons [28], we do not believe this is necessary in the Emerald environment for several reasons. First, unlike process mobility systems, we do not copy entire address spaces. Second, many objects contain only a small amount of data. Third, even when an object with an active process is moved, we may not need to copy any code.

3.4.1 Moving Data Objects. Objects without active invocations are the simplest ones to move. For these, the Emerald kernel builds a message to be transmitted to the destination node. At the head of this message is the data area of the object to be moved. As we previously described, this data area is likely to contain pointers to both global and local objects. Following the data area is translation information to aid the destination kernel in mapping location-dependent addresses. For global object pointers, the kernel sends the OID, the forwarding address, and the address of the object's descriptor on the source node. For local objects, the data area is sent along with its address.

On receipt of this information, the destination kernel allocates space for the moved objects, copies the data areas into the newly allocated space, and builds a translation table that maps the original addresses into addresses in the newly allocated space. OIDs are used to locate object descriptors for existing global objects, or new object descriptors are created where necessary. The kernel then locates the template for each moved object, traverses its data area, and replaces any pointers with their corresponding addresses found in the translation table.

3.4.2 Moving Process Activation Records. As previously described in Section 2.5, when an object is moved, the activation records for processes executing its operations must also move. This presents a particularly difficult problem: Given an object to move, how do we know which activation records need to move with it? Finding the correct activation records requires a list of all active invocations for a particular object.

Several solutions are possible, but all have potentially serious performance implications. The simplest solution is to link each activation record to the object on each invocation and unlink it on invocation exit. Unfortunately, this would increase our invocation overhead by 50 percent in the current implementation. On the other hand, finding the invocations to move would require only a simple list traversal.

A second solution is to create the list only at move time. This would eliminate the invocation-time cost but would require a search of all activation records on the node. Although we believe that mobility should not increase the cost of invocation, exhaustive search seems to be an unacceptable price to pay on every move.

We have therefore adopted an intermediate solution. We do maintain a list of all activation records executing in each object, as in the first solution above. However, on invocation, the activation record is not actually linked into this structure. Instead, space is left for the links, and the activation record is marked as "not linked," which is an inexpensive operation. When an Emerald process is preempted, its activation stack is searched for "not linked" activation records, and these are then linked to the object descriptors of their respective objects.

The search stops as soon as an activation record is found that has been linked previously. In this way, the work is only done at preemption time, and its cost is related to *the difference* in stack depth between the start and end of the execution interval, not to the number of invocations performed.

An operation must still unlink its activation record when it terminates. Each return must check for a queued activation record and dequeue it before freeing the record. However, most returns will find a "not linked" activation record, in which case no work need be done.

Therefore, when an object moves we can find all activation records that must move with it merely by traversing the linked list associated with the object. These activation records are moved in a manner similar to moving data areas as described above.

If necessary, the activation records are removed from the stack containing them. This is accomplished by splitting the stack into (at most) three parts: the "bottom" part that remains on the source node, the "middle" part that is moved to the destination node, and the "top" part that is copied onto a new stack segment on the source node. The stack break points are found by using the templates for the activation records. At each of the two stack breaks, invocation frames are modified to appear as if remote invocations had been performed instead of local invocations. Figure 6 shows the structure that would exist if object B from Figure 2 were moved from node α to node β.

3.4.3 Handling Processor Registers. An additional complexity in moving Emerald processes and activation records is the management of processor registers. The Emerald compiler attempts to optimize the addressing of objects by storing local variables in registers instead of in the activation record. In this way, some of the processor registers may contain machine-dependent pointers, and these must be translated when the activation record moves.

Unfortunately, the registers for a given activation record are not kept in one place. Each invocation saves in its activation record a copy of registers that will be modified by that invocation. Referring back to Figure 2, suppose that the first invocation (of A) and the third invocation (of C) both use register 5. In this case, a copy of A's register 5 is saved in C's activation record, as it would be in any conventional stack-based language implementation.

If object A moves, its activation record will move with it. The stack will be segmented, and the rest of the stack will be left behind. Furthermore, the copy of A's register stored in C's activation record will be incorrect when C returns because the data that it refers to will be at a different location on a different node.

To handle this situation, the kernel sends a copy of the registers used in an invocation along with the moving activation record. First, the kernel finds the template for the activation record in the concrete type object of the invoked object. Second, it determines which registers are used as pointers in an activation record by looking at its template. The templates for activation records have special entries for registers and for the area of the activation record where registers are saved. Third, the kernel scans the invocation stack and looks for the next activation record that has saved each of the registers. This enables copies of the current values of the registers to be sent along with the record. On the destination node, the registers are modified using the translation table (as described in Section 3.4.1) and stored with the newly created stack segment.

For each stack segment of an Emerald process, there is a separate image of the registers. When an invocation return crosses a stack segment boundary, the registers used are those stored with the stack segment receiving control. These are the possibly translated values of registers that were computed when the stack was segmented.

3.5 Garbage Collection

As with any object-based system, Emerald must rely on garbage collection to recover memory occupied by objects that are no longer reachable. Furthermore, Emerald must deal with the problems of garbage collection in a distributed environment. Although our garbage collector is not yet fully implemented, we describe its general design in this section.

The principal problem with distributed garbage collection is that object references can cross node boundaries. The system must ensure that it does not delete

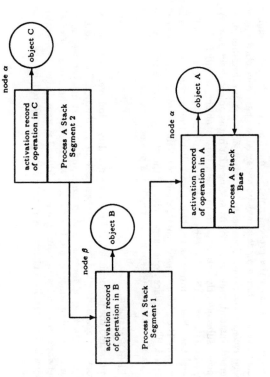

Fig. 6. Process stack after object move.

an object that can still be referenced. In a distributed system, a reference to an object could be on a node different from the object, on a node that is unavailable, or "on the wire" in a message. While Emerald has mobile objects, this presents no special difficulty; other distributed object-based systems may not have mobile objects, but they all have mobile references, which are the root of the problem. In fact, if an Emerald object moves, we know implicitly that it cannot be garbage, since either the object is actively executing or someone with a reference to that object must have requested the move. Furthermore, garbage collection is simplified by the presence of object descriptors. Each node retains a descriptor for every nonresident object that it has referenced since the last collection.

The Emerald garbage collection design calls for two collectors: a node-local collector that can be run at any time independently of other nodes and a distributed collector that requires the nodes to cooperate in collecting distributed garbage. Both are mark-and-sweep collectors modified to operate in parallel with executing Emerald processes.

We expect most garbage to consist of objects that are created and disposed of on a single node with no reference ever leaving that node. To know which objects can be collected by the node-local collector, each object descriptor has a flag called the *RefGivenOut* bit. The kernel sets this bit in an object's descriptor whenever a reference to the object is passed to another node. The kernel also sets this bit in the descriptor for a moving object that has arrived at its destination, since the source node retains a reference to the object. When the node-local collector finds an object with the *RefGivenOut* bit set, it considers the object to be reachable. The node-local collector ignores every reference to a nonresident object.

Distributed collection is performed using a modified mark-and-sweep collection algorithm. In the conventional mark-and-sweep, all objects are initially marked as *white*, indicating that they are not yet known to be reachable. Then, objects that are known to be reachable, for example, containing executable processes, are marked *gray*. A gray object is reachable, but its references need to be scanned to mark gray all objects reachable from that object; once this is done the original object is marked *black*. When all gray objects have been scanned, the system consists of black objects that are reachable and white objects that are garbage and can be deleted.

To perform a distributed collection in Emerald, a collecting process is started on each node, and all global collectors proceed in parallel. All global objects, that is, all objects with the *RefGivenOut* set, are first marked as being unreachable, **as** in the traditional mark-and-sweep scheme. Each global collector marks all of its explicitly reachable global objects gray. When attempting to scan a gray object, a global collector may find that the object resides on another node. In that case, it sends a mark-gray message to the node where the object resides. The collector on the receiving node adds the object to its gray set and sends back an object-is-black message when the object has been traversed and marked. Upon receiving an object-is-black message, a collector removes the object from its gray set and marks it black. The collection is complete when all nodes have exhausted their gray sets.

To prevent an object from "outrunning" traverse-and-mark requests by moving often, objects are traversed and marked black when moved. This is done even for objects currently marked white, since any moved object is a priori reachable—the object would eventually be marked anyway.

If a node is currently unavailable (e.g., has crashed) when a mark-gray message is sent to it, then the reference is ignored for the moment. Eventually the only gray references left are to objects on unreachable nodes. At this point, the collectors exchange information about the remaining gray objects so that every collector knows which objects still need to be scanned.

When an unavailable node becomes available again, the collectors continue marking gray objects until either the collection is done or there is a gray reference to an object on an unavailable node. The collectors again exchange gray sets and wait for a node to become available. This process is repeated until the collection completes, at which point garbage objects and object descriptors can be collected. Note that it is not necessary for all nodes to be up simultaneously—it is only necessary for each node to be available long enough for the collection to make progress over time.

Finally, a major problem with the traditional mark-and-sweep scheme is that all other activity must be suspended while collecting. In a distributed system, this is obviously not acceptable. There have been several suggestions for making mark-and-sweep collectors operate in parallel with the garbage-generating processes [10, 19], some of which have been implemented [4, 9]. Typically, parallel mark-and-sweep requires processes to cooperate with the collector by setting coloring bits of referenced objects when performing assignments.

Emerald avoids this extra work on assignment by using a scheme proposed by Hewitt [17]. At the start of the marking phase, each executable process is marked before being allowed to run again. Marking a process means marking the objects reachable from the activation records of the process and, transitively, any object reachable from such objects. After an individual process has been marked, it can proceed in parallel with the rest of the collection even though not all objects and processes have been marked. Should a process become executable (e.g., after waiting for entry to a monitor) then that process must be marked before being allowed to execute.

This scheme allows our collectors to proceed in parallel with executing processes, but there is a high initial cost when making a process executable: All objects reachable from the process must be marked. To reduce the number of objects traversed before a process may be restarted, we have developed a *faulting garbage collection* scheme. Reachable global objects are marked but are not traversed. Instead, they are *frozen* by setting a bit in the object descriptor. When a process subsequently attempts to invoke a frozen object, it will fault to the kernel exactly as if the object had been remote. The kernel lets the collector traverse the object, unfreezes the object, and allows the invocation to continue. Thus, only the global objects immediately reachable from the process need be traversed. This replaces one large delay at the start of garbage collection by a number of smaller delays spread throughout a process's execution.

4. PERFORMANCE

We measured the performance of Emerald's mobility primitives on 4 MicroVAX II workstations connected by a 10 megabit/second Ethernet. These primitives have been operational for only a short time, and no effort has yet been made to optimize their implementation. In addition, we measured the impact of mobility on network message traffic using the Emerald mail system driven by a synthetic workload. The results of these measurements are reported in the following sections.

4.1. Emerald Mobility Primitives

Table II shows the elapsed time cost of various Emerald operations. The measured performance figures are averages of repeated measurements. For the simplest remote invocation, the time spent in the Emerald kernel is 3.4 milliseconds. For historical reasons, we currently use a set of network communications routines that provide reliable, flow-controlled message passing on top of UDP datagrams. These routines are slow: The time to transmit 128 bytes of data and receive a reply is about 24.5 milliseconds. Hence, the total elapsed time to send the invocation message and receive the reply is 27.9 milliseconds.

Table III shows the benefit of call-by-move for a simple argument object. The table compares the incremental cost of call-by-move and call-by-visit with the incremental cost of call-by-object-reference. The additional cost of call-by-move was 2 milliseconds, whereas call-by-visit costs 6.4 milliseconds. These are computed by subtracting the time for a remote invocation with an argument reference that is local to the destination. The call-by-visit time includes sending the invocation message and the argument object, performing the remote invocation (which then invokes its argument), and returning the argument object with the reply. Had the argument been a reference to a remote object (i.e., had the object not been moved), the incremental cost would have been 30.8 milliseconds. These measurements are of a somewhat lower bound because the cost of moving an object depends on the complexity of the object and the types of objects it names.

Compared with the cost of a remote invocation, call-by-move and call-by-visit are worthwhile for even a single invocation of the argument object. As previously stated, the advantage of call-by-move depends on the size of the argument object, the number of invocations of the argument object, and the local and remote invocation costs. Emerald's fast local invocation time, about 20 *microseconds*, easily recaptures the time for the move. Even with the current unoptimized implementation, call-by-move and call-by-visit would be worthwhile for a remote invocation cost of under 10 milliseconds.

Table II. Remote Operation Timing

Operation type	Time/ms
Local invocation	0.019
Kernel CPU time, remote invocation	3.4
Elapsed time, remote invocation	27.9
Remote invocation, local reference parameter	31.0
Remote invocation, call-by-move parameter	33.0
Remote invocation, call-by-visit parameter	37.4
Remote invocation, remote reference parameter	61.8

Table III. Incremental Cost of Remote Invocation Parameters

Parameter passing mode	Time/ms
Call-by-move	2.0
Call-by-visit	6.4
Call-by-remote-reference	30.8

Moving a simple data object, such as the object in Figure 4, takes about 12 milliseconds. This time is less than the round-trip message time because the reply messages are "piggybacked" on other messages (i.e., each move does not require a unique reply). Moving an object with a process is more complex; as previously stated, although Emerald does not need to move an entire address space, it must send translation data so that the object can be linked into the address space on the destination node. The time to move a small process object with 6 variables is 40 milliseconds. In this case, the Emerald kernel constructs a message consisting of about 600 bytes of information, including object references, immediate data for replicated objects, a stack segment, and general process-control information. The process-control information and stack segment together consume about 180 bytes.

4.2 Message Traffic In The Emerald Mail System

The elapsed time benefit of call-by-move, as shown in Table III, is due primarily to the reduction in network message traffic. We have measured the effect of this traffic reduction in the Emerald mail system, an experimental application modeled after the Eden mail system [2]. Mailboxes and mail messages are both implemented as Emerald objects. In contrast to traditional mail systems, a message addressed to multiple recipients is not copied into each mailbox. Rather, the single mail message is shared between the multiple mailboxes to which it is addressed.

In a workstation environment, we would expect each person's mailbox normally to remain on its owner's private workstation. Only when a person changes workstations or reads mail from another workstation would the mailbox be moved. However, we expect mail messages to be more mobile. When a message

Table IV. Mail System Traffic

	Without mobility	With mobility
Total elapsed time (in seconds)	71	55
Remote invocations	1,386	666
Network messages sent	2,772	1,312
Network packets sent	2,940	1,954
Total bytes transferred	568,716	528,696
Total bytes moved	0	382,848

message, these four remote invocations are replaced by a move followed by four local invocations. However, additional effort may be required by other mailboxes to find the message once it has moved.

To facilitate comparison, a synthetic workload was used to drive each of the mail system implementations. Ten short messages (about one hundred bytes) and ten long messages (several thousand bytes) were sent from a user on each of four nodes to various combinations of users on other nodes; the recipients then read the mail that they received.

Table IV shows some of the measurement data collected by the Emerald kernel. As the Table shows, the use of mobility more than halved the number of remote invocations, reduced the number of network packets by 34 percent, and cut the total elapsed time by 22 percent. The number of network messages sent is exactly twice the number of invocations; each invocation requires a send and a reply. The number of packets is slightly higher than the number of network messages because the long mail messages require two packets. Note that the number of packets required per invocation is higher with mobility because mobile mail messages cause subsequent message readers to follow forwarding addresses.

Moving the mail messages reduces the total number of bytes transferred only slightly, by seven percent. Although the same data must eventually arrive at the remote site, whether by remote invocation or by move, the per-byte overhead of move is slightly less than that of invocation. In applications in which only a small portion of the data in an object is required at the remote site, invocation might still be more efficient than move.

Finally, it is interesting to note that the 22 percent execution time difference was achieved by simply adding the word "move" in two places in the application.

5. SUMMARY

We have designed and implemented Emerald, an object-based language and system for distributed programming. Emerald is operational on a small network of VAX computers and has recently been ported to the SUN 3.[3] Several applications have been implemented including a hierarchical directory system, a replicated name server, a load-sharing application, a shared appointment calendar system, and a mail system.

The goals of Emerald included

—support for fine-grained object mobility,

—efficient local execution, and

—a single object model, suitable for programming both small, local data-only objects and active, mobile distributed objects.

This paper has described the language features and run-time mechanisms that support fine-grained mobility. Although *process* mobility (i.e., the movement of complete address spaces) has been previously demonstrated in distributed systems, we believe that *object* mobility, as implemented in Emerald, has additional benefits. Because the overhead of an Emerald object is commensurate with its complexity, mobility provides a relatively efficient way to transfer fine-grained data from node to node.

The need for semantic support for mobility, distribution, and abstract types led us to design a new language, and language support is a crucial part of mobility in Emerald. Although invocation is location independent, language primitives can be used to find and manipulate the location of objects. The programmer can

is composed, it will be invoked heavily by the sender (in order to define the contents of its fields) and should reside on the sender's node. In section 2.4 we discussed how mail messages may utilize call-by-move to colocate themselves with a single destination mailbox upon delivery. If there are multiple destinations it is reasonable for the message to stay at the sender's node, but when the message is read it may be profitable to colocate the message with the reader's mailbox.

To measure the impact of mobility in the mail system, we have implemented two versions: one which does not use mobility, and one which uses mobility in an attempt to decrease message traffic. In the Emerald mail system, the reading of a mail message takes five invocations: one to get the mail message from a mailbox, and four to read the four fields. If the mail message is remote, then reading the message will take four remote invocations. By moving the mail declare "attached" variables; the objects named by attached variables move along with the objects to which they are attached. More important, on remote invocations a parameter-passing mode called call-by-move permits an invocation's argument object to be moved along with the invocation request. Our measurements demonstrate the potential of this facility to improve remote invocation performance while retaining the advantages of call-by-reference semantics.

Implementing fine-grained mobility, while minimizing its impact on local performance, presents significant problems. In Emerald, all objects on a node share a single address space and objects are addressed directly. Invocations are implemented through procedure call or in-line code where possible. The result is that pointers must be translated when an object is moved. Addresses can appear in an object's representation, in activation records, and in registers. The Emerald run-time system relies on compiler-produced templates to describe the format of these structures. A combination of compiled invocation code and run-time support is responsible for maintaining data structures linking activation records and run-time addresses to the objects they invoke. A lazy evaluation of this structure helps to reduce the cost of its maintenance.

Through the use of language support and a tightly coupled compiler and kernel, we believe that our design has been successful in providing generalized mobility without much degradation of local performance.

ACKNOWLEDGMENTS

We would like to thank Edward Lazowska and Richard Pattis for extensive reviews of early versions of this paper. We also thank Brian Bershad, Carl Binding, Kevin Jeffay, Rajendra Raj, and the referees for their helpful comments.

REFERENCES

1. ALLCHIN, J. E., AND MCKENDRY, M. S. Synchronization and recovery of actions. In *Proceedings of the 2nd ACM SIGACT/SIGOPS Symposium on Principles of Distributed Computing* (Montreal, Aug. 17–19, 1983). ACM, New York, 1983, pp. 31–44.

2. ALMES, G. T., BLACK, A. P., BUNJE, C., AND WIEBE. D. Edmas: A locally distributed mail system. In *Proceedings of the 7th International Conference on Software Engineering* (Orlando, Fla, Mar. 26–29, 1984). ACM, New York, 1984, pp. 56–66.

3. ALMES, G. T., BLACK, A. P., LAZOWSKA, E. D., AND NOE, J. D. The Eden system: A technical review. *IEEE Trans. Softw. Eng. SE-11*, 1 (Jan. 1985), 43–59.

4. BENNETT, J. K. Distributed Smalltalk. In *Proceedings of the 2nd ACM Conference on Object-Oriented Programming Systems, Languages, and Applications* (Orlando, Fl., Oct. 1987). ACM, New York, 1987, pp. 318–330.

5. BLACK, A. P. Supporting distributed applications: Experience with Eden. In *Proceedings of the 10th ACM Symposium on Operating System Principles* (Orcas Island, Wash., Dec. 1–4, 1985). ACM, New York, 1985, pp. 181–193.

6. BLACK, A., HUTCHINSON, N., JUL, E., AND LEVY. H. Object structure in the Emerald system. In *Proceedings of the 1st ACM Conference on Object-Oriented Programming Systems, Languages, and Applications* (Portland, Ore., Oct. 1986). ACM, New York, 1986, pp. 78–86.

7. BLACK, A., HUTCHINSON, N., JUL, E., LEVY, H., AND CARTER, L. Distribution and abstract types in Emerald. *IEEE Trans. Softw. Eng. 13*, 1 (Jan. 1987).

8. BUTTERFIELD, D. A., AND POPEK, G. J. Network tasking in the Locus distributed UNIX system. In *USENIX Summer 1984 Conference Proceedings* (Salt Lake City, Ut., June 1984), USENIX Association, pp. 62–71.

9. CHANSLER, R. J., JR. Coupling in systems with many processors. PhD dissertation, Dept. of Computer Science, Carnegie Mellon Univ., Pittsburgh, Pa., Aug. 1982.

10. DIJKSTRA, E. W., LAMPORT, L., MARTIN, A. J., SCHOLTEN, C. S., AND STEFFENS. E. F. M. On-the-fly garbage collection: An exercise in cooperation. *Commun. ACM 21*, 11 (Nov. 1978), 966–975.

11. DOUGLIS, F. Process migration in the Sprite operating system. Tech. Rep. UCB/CSD 87/343, Computer Science Division, Univ. of California, Berkeley, Feb. 1987.

12. FOWLER, R. J. Decentralized object finding using forwarding addresses. PhD dissertation, Univ. of Washington, Seattle, Wash., Dec. 1985. Also available as Dept. of Computer Science Tech. Rep. 85-12-1.

13. GOLDBERG, A., AND ROBSON, D. *Smalltalk-80: The Language and Its Implementation.* Addison-Wesley, Reading, Mass., 1983.

14. GREIF, I., SELIGER, R., AND WEIHL, W. Atomic data abstractions in a distributed collaborative editing system. In *Proceedings of the 13th Symposium on Principles of Distributed Computing* (Jan. 1986). ACM, New York, 1986.

15. HERLIHY, M., AND LISKOV, B. A value transmission method for abstract data types. *ACM Trans. Program. Lang. Syst. 4*, 4 (Oct. 1982), 527–551.

16. HEWITT, C. The Apiary network architecture for knowledgeable systems. In *Conference Record of the 1980 Lisp Conference* (Palo Alto, Calif., Aug. 1980). Stanford Univ., 1980, pp. 107–118.

17. HEWITT, C., AND BAKER, H. Actors and continuous functionals. In *IFIP Working Conference on Formal Description of Programming Concepts* (St. Andrews, N.B., Aug. 1977). North-Holland, Amsterdam, pp. 16.1–16.21.

18. HUTCHINSON, N. C. Emerald: An object-based language for distributed programming. PhD dissertation, Univ. of Washington, Seattle, Jan. 1987. Also available as Dept. of Computer Science Tech. Rep. 87-01-01.

19. KUNG, H. T., AND SONG, S. W. An efficient parallel garbage collection system and its correctness proof. In *Proceedings of the 18th Annual Symposium on the Foundations of Computer Science* (Providence, R.I., Oct. 1977). IEEE Computer Society, New York, 1977, pp. 120–131.

20. LAZOWSKA, E. D., LEVY, H. M. ALMES, G. T., FISCHER, M. J., FOWLER, R. J., AND VESTAL, S. C. The architecture of the Eden system. In *Proceedings of the 8th Symposium on Operating Systems Principles* (Pacific Grove, Calif., Dec. 1981). ACM, New York, 1981, pp. 148–159.

21. LISKOV, B. Overview of the Argus language and system. Programming Methodology Group Memo 40, MIT Laboratory for Computer Science, MIT, Cambridge, Mass., Feb. 1984.

22. LISKOV, B., ATKINSON, R., BLOOM, T., MOSS, E., SCHAFFERT, C., SCHEIFLER, B., AND SNYDER, A. CLU reference manual. Tech. Rep. MIT/LCS/TR-225, MIT Laboratory for Computer Science, MIT, Cambridge, Mass., Oct. 1979.

23. POWELL, M. L., AND MILLER, B. P. Process migration in DEMOS/MP. In *Proceedings of the 9th ACM Symposium on Operating Systems Principles* (Bretton Woods, N.H., Oct. 11–13, 1983). ACM/SIGOPS, New York, 1983, pp. 110–119.

24. RASHID, R. F., AND ROBERTSON, G. G. Accent: A communication oriented network operating system kernel. In *Proceedings of the 8th Symposium on Operating System Principles* (Pacific Grove, Calif., Dec. 14–16, 1981). ACM, New York, 1981, pp. 64–75.

25. SOLLINS, K. R. Copying complex structures in a distributed system. Master's thesis, MIT/LCS/TR-219, MIT, Cambridge, Mass., May 1979.

26. SPAFFORD, E. H. Kernel structures for a distributed operating system. PhD dissertation, School of Information and Computer Science, Georgia Institute of Technology, Atlanta, Ga., May 1986. Also available as Georgia Institute of Technology Tech. Rep. GIT-ICS-86/16.

27. SPECTOR, A. Z. Performing remote operations efficiently on a local computer network. *Commun. ACM 25*, 4 (Apr. 1982), 246–260.

28. THEIMER, M. M., LANTZ, K. A., AND CHERITON, D. R. Preemptable remote execution facilities for the V-system. In *Proceedings of the 10th ACM Symposium on Operating Systems Principles* (Orcas Island, Wash., Dec. 1–4, 1985). ACM/SIGOPS, New York, 1985, pp. 2–12.

29. VESTAL, S. Garbage collection: An exercise in distributed, fault-tolerant programming. PhD dissertation, Univ. of Washington, Seattle, Jan. 1987. Also available as Dept. of Computer Science Tech. Rep. 87-01-03.

30. WULF, W. A., LEVIN, R., AND HARBISON, S. P. *HYDRA/C.mmp: An Experimental Computer System.* McGraw-Hill, New York, 1981.

Received May 1987; revised August 1987; accepted September 1987

Chapter 5

Transaction Processing

Introduction

In traditional database systems, *transactions* provide control of the concurrent execution of independently prepared units of code. A transaction is viewed as an atomic, recoverable unit of work. This allows the system to interleave the steps of several transactions indiscriminately. The results can be quite unexpected. Normally, a transaction-processing system will allow only interleavings that produce a *serializable* result, that is, a result equivalent to some noninterleaved execution.

Serializability follows naturally from the requirement that transactions be *atomic*. Conceptually, atomic units can have no discernable substructure. Therefore, it makes sense to define correctness only in terms of results that are obtained by executing the transactions without any interleaving (i.e., serially—one after the other). Serializability simplifies the way we reason about programs. If the code of a transaction is correct in isolation, then it will remain correct in a concurrent execution environment. Programmers do not need to concern themselves with interference from other programs.

Transactions also are concerned with the correctness of executions in the presence of failures. Again, because of the atomicity requirement, the transaction becomes the unit of recovery. That is, if a failure occurs before a transaction T can complete, then the system ensures that any changes made by T are removed from the system

and that no other transactions could have formed a dependency on (i.e., read) any results of T.

To achieve these synchronization and recovery properties, a transaction system must carefully control when and to which other transactions new data values become visibile. One way to control the visibility of values is to institute a locking protocol that must be obeyed by all transactions. For example, if one transaction $T1$ holds a write lock on a data item x, then a second transaction $T2$ will not be allowed to obtain a read lock on x until $T1$ completes. In this way, $T2$ will have to wait for $T1$, so that a read dependency is not created between these two transactions.

We might ask whether there are any differences between transaction processing in an object-oriented database and transaction processing in a more traditional relational database. On the surface, both support access from programs that would be defined as transactions, and these transactions are both serializable and recoverable.

If we step back far enough, this view is correct. An object-oriented database could certainly be built with a traditional transaction-processing mechanism. The real issue is whether there are opportunities in the object-oriented approach to do something better. In fact, by having a system that captures more application-level semantics in terms of the user-defined types and operations, we can apparently exploit some of this information to acheive more concurrency than could be offered by viewing all operations as only reads and writes.

As an example, consider a **Directory** type that supports two operations, *Enter* and *List*. *Enter* inserts a new entry into a given directory, and *List* produces an alphabetical listing of the entries in a given directory. If we consider these operations as only reads and writes, then *Enter* is a write operation that conflicts with other *Enters*, and *List* is a read operation that conflicts with *Enter*. If we consider the actual semantics of *Enter* and *List*, then as long as the implementations avoid conflicts at the level of internal pointers, two transactions that perform only *Enter* operations on the same directory can be arbitrarily interleaved. The **Directory** type might be implemented as a linked list, and *Enter* might append new items to this list. Although the order of the items in the list will depend on the interleaving order of the transactions, this ordering cannot be observed, since there is no operation that reports this information.

Semantic approaches to concurrency control can be divided into two main approaches: those that associate concurrency information with the data (the *data approach*), and those that associate concurrency information with the transactions that are being interleaved (the *transaction approach*).

Schwarz and Spector [SS84] and Herlihy [He87] both take the data approach. The data approach is more modular in that concurrency information is specified once for each data type, independently of the application. The control mechanism is decentralized in the sense that we need to consider only information about other operations that have been executed on data item x to decide whether or not to allow another operation on x to proceed.

Conflict relations are typically defined over the operations of a type. The pair (o_1, o_2) is in the conflict relation R for a type **T** when o_1 cannot execute concurrently with o_2. It is generally true that operations conflict when the result of $o_1\ o_2$ is different from the result of $o_2\ o_1$. From this, we can see that conflicting operations in a serializable schedule must appear in the same order as they do in the equivalent serial schedule.

Herlihy uses a serial dependency relation as the basis for defining operation conflicts. In this type of scheme, conflict is defined when the existence of one operation in a history invalidates another later operation in that history. For example, bank accounts support a deposit and a withdraw operation. An unsuccessful withdraw operation by transaction $T1$ can depend on the existence of a deposit by transaction $T2$ earlier in the history, since when $T2$ commits, $T1$'s withdraw might no longer be unsuccessful.

For a discussion of the transaction approach, see [Gm83], [GS87], or [Ly83]. In short, concurrency control in this approach is based on the particular collection of transactions in a given application.

Stemple, Sheard, and Bunker [SSB86] take a different approach to managing transactions in an object-based setting. They concentrate on transactions as units of consistency: The transaction should take a database from one consistent state to another consistent state. Their view is that, by choosing an appropriate type system, it is possible to prove the correctness of the code that implements a transaction. The ADABTPL type system allows for the expression of constraint information. The system proves that a piece of transaction code must maintain the invariant (i.e., constraints). The authors do this by using a Boyer–Moore style theorem prover.

Most transaction-management systems do not get involved in the maintenance of constraints, outside of field types and bugs. The standard view is that the programmer who writes the transaction code is aware of the constraints and will ensure that, when the code terminates, the constraints have been satisfied. In other words, any constraint satisfaction is done explicitly by the transaction itself. Stemple, Sheard, and Bunker add to this the ability to detect transactions that will not maintain the constraints.

This treatment of transactions as verifiable units is made possible by the choice of a type system that is grounded on sound semantic principles. The ADABTPL type system is based on those of functional programming languages. Object-oriented features are introduced into this setting by mapping them onto the basic functional primitives, and by hiding some of the aspects of functional programming that make it difficult to use with databases (i.e., no update).

The Weihl and Liskov paper [WL85] discusses how database notions of serializability and recovery can be supported in a programming language with abstract data types. The authors do this by defining abstract data types that are *atomic* and *resilient*. Atomicity is defined to be a property of the objects. An activity is atomic if all of the objects that are shared are atomic. Resilient data are data for which the probability of losing them due to a failure is acceptably low.

The notion of atomicity used is more general than that provided by conventional database systems. It is more consistent with the point of view offered by the semantic concurrency-control mechanisms. Weihl and Liskov [WL85] adopt an approach, called *dynamic atomicity*, that takes into account the state of the object. In simple read/write transaction-processing schemes, if there is any chance that one operation could rely on the result of another, or if one operation could invalidate the effect of another, then the two operations are said to *conflict*. Dynamic atomicity looks at the shared object to see whether either of these dependencies is actually formed. For example, if one operation is putting elements into a list at one end and the other is taking elements out from the other, there is no conflict as long as they are separated by a nonzero-length interval.

Weihl and Liskov are primarily concerned with how to implement such resilient, atomic data types. They discuss additions to the Argus programming language that enable the implementation of such types.

References

[Al83]   J.E. Allchin. *An Architecture for Reliable Decentralized Systems*. PhD Dissertation. Technical Report GIT-ICS-83/23, School of Information and Computer Science, Georgia Institute of Technology, September 1983.

[AM83]   J.E. Allchin and M.S. McKendry. Synchronization and Recovery of Actions. *Proceedings of the Second Annual ACM Symposium on Principles of Distributed Computing*, Montreal, Quebec, August 1983.

[BHG87]   P.A. Bernstein, V. Hadzilacos, and N. Goodman. *Concurrency Control and Recovery in Database Systems*, Addison-Wesley, Reading, MA, 1987.

[GK87]   J.F. Garza and W. Kim. *Transaction Management in an Object-Oriented Database System*. Technical Report ACA-ST-292-87, Microelectronics and Computer Technology Corporation, September 1987.

[Gm83]   H. Garcia-Molina. Using Semantic Knowledge for Transaction Processing in a Distributed Database, *ACM Transactions on Database Systems*, 8(2):186–213, 1983.

[GS87]   H. Garcia-Molina and K. Salem. *Sagas*. Technical Report CS-TR-070-87, Department of Computer Science, Princeton University, January 1987.

• [He87]   M. Herlihy. Optimistic Concurrency Control for Abstract Data Types. *Proceedings of the Fifth ACM Symposium on the Principles of Distributed Computing*, Calgary, Alberta, August 1986.

[Ly83]   N.A. Lynch. Multilevel Atomicity—A New Correctness Criterion for Database Concurrency Control, *ACM Transactions on Database Systems*, 8(4):485–502, 1983.

• [SS84]   P.M. Schwarz and A.Z. Spector. Synchronizing Shared Abstract Types, *ACM Transactions on Computer Systems*, 2(3):223–250, 1984.

• [SSB86]   D. Stemple, T. Sheard, and B. Bunker. Abstract Data Types in Databases: Specification, Manipulation and Acess. *IEEE Second International Conference on Data Engineering*, Los Angeles, CA, February 1986.

[We88]   W.E. Weihl. Data-dependent Concurrency Control and Recovery. *Proceedings of the Second Annual ACM Symposium on Principles of Distributed Computing*, Toronto, Ontario, August 1988.

• [WL85]   W. Weihl and B. Liskov. Implementation of Resilient, Atomic Data Types. *ACM Transactions on Programming Languages and Systems*, 7(2):244–269, 1985.

Implementation of Resilient, Atomic Data Types

WILLIAM WEIHL and BARBARA LISKOV
M.I.T. Laboratory for Computer Science

A major issue in many applications is how to preserve the consistency of data in the presence of concurrency and hardware failures. We suggest addressing this problem by implementing applications in terms of abstract data types with two properties: Their objects are atomic (they provide serializability and recoverability for activities using them) and resilient (they survive hardware failures with an acceptably high probability). We define what it means for abstract data types to be atomic and resilient. We also discuss issues that arise in implementing such types, and describe a particular linguistic mechanism provided in the Argus programming language.

Categories and Subject Descriptors: C.2.4 [Computer-Communication Networks]: Distributed Systems—*distributed applications; distributed databases*; D.1.3 [Programming Techniques]: Concurrent Programming; D.3.3 [Programming Languages]: Language Constructs—*abstract data types; concurrent programming structures; modules, packages*; D.4.5 [Operating Systems]: Reliability—*checkpoint/restart; fault-tolerance*; H.2.4 [Database Management]: Systems—*distributed systems; transaction processing*

General Terms: Concurrency, Languages, Reliability

Additional Key Words and Phrases: Atomic actions, atomic objects, resilient objects

1. INTRODUCTION

There are many applications in which the manipulation and preservation of long-lived, on-line data is of primary importance. Examples of such applications include banking systems, airline reservation systems, office automation systems, and various components of operating systems. A major issue in such systems is preserving the consistency of on-line data in the presence of concurrency and hardware failures. This paper is concerned with how to define and implement data objects that help provide needed consistency.

To support consistency it is useful to make the concurrent activities that use and manipulate the data *atomic*. Atomic activities are referred to as *actions* or *transactions*; they were first identified in work on databases [5, 6, 8]. An atomic action is distinguished by two properties, serializability and recoverability. *Serializability* [8, 24] means that the execution of one action never appears to overlap (or contain) the execution of any other action, even when the actions are run concurrently. In other words, the effect of running the actions concurrently is the same as if they had been executed serially in some order. *Recoverability* means that the overall effect of an action is all-or-nothing: either all changes made to the data by the action happen, or none of these changes happen. An action that completes all its changes successfully *commits*. Otherwise it *aborts*, and whatever changes it made are discarded. Recoverability allows the user on whose behalf an action runs to decide to discard the effects of that action. In addition, it allows an action to work properly even if there is a hardware failure during its execution, and allows the system to abort an action if necessary (e.g., to resolve a deadlock).

In this paper we explore an approach in which atomicity is achieved through the shared data objects, which must be implemented in such a way that the actions using them appear to be serializable and recoverable. Data objects that support atomicity are referred to as *atomic objects*, and data types whose objects are atomic as *atomic types*. Atomicity of activities is guaranteed only when all objects shared by activities are atomic objects.

Atomicity alone is not sufficient to provide consistency, because it only concerns running actions. In addition, the data must be *resilient*: the probability of loss of data due to a hardware failure such as a node or media crash must be acceptably small. Resilient data are needed to ensure (with high probability) that effects of committed actions are not lost in crashes that occur later.

Up to now, consistency has been provided only in database systems (e.g., see [11]) and a few file systems [25, 28]. In these systems, implementors of applications are limited to using just those types of atomic objects provided by the system (e.g., database relations or files). These objects are not always the most convenient (or efficient) for implementing applications. We advocate a different approach: Implementors should be free to implement their applications in terms of whatever types of data objects they find convenient. By choosing types that are most natural for the application, it is often possible to achieve greater concurrency than can be obtained when applications are restricted to using only the types provided by the system. Of course, implementations that permit this extra concurrency are often more complex than implementations that permit relatively limited concurrency.

In the remainder of this paper we discuss how to implement resilient atomic types, focusing on how implementations that permit high levels of concurrency can be constructed. We begin in Section 2 by discussing what it means for an object to be atomic. In Section 3 we introduce a model of computation to serve as a basis for discussing the implementation of atomic objects; this model is taken from the Argus programming language [22]. In Sections 4 and 5 we describe the linguistic constructs provided by Argus for implementing resilient atomic types, and illustrate their use with two examples. In Section 4 we assume that hardware failures never occur and focus on atomicity. Then, in Section 5, we

A preliminary version of this paper appeared in the Conference Record of the ACM SIGPLAN Symposium on Programming Language Issues in Software Systems, June 1983 [29].

This research was supported in part by the Advanced Research Projects Agency of the Department of Defense, monitored by the Office of Naval Research under contract N00014-75-C-0661, and in part by the National Science Foundation under grant MCS79-23769. Partial support for the first author was also supplied by a graduate fellowship from the Fannie and John Hertz Foundation.

Authors' address: Laboratory for Computer Science, Massachusetts Institute of Technology, 545 Technology Square, Cambridge, MA 02139.

admit the possibility of failures and discuss implementing resilience. Finally, we conclude with an evaluation of the mechanisms and techniques presented in this paper and a discussion of open problems.

2. ATOMIC TYPES

An atomic data type, like an ordinary abstract data type [19], provides a set of objects and a set of operations. As with ordinary abstract types, the operations provided by an atomic type are the only way to access or manipulate the objects of the type. Unlike regular types, however, an atomic type provides serializability and recoverability for actions that use objects of the type. For example, relations in most relational databases provide operations to add and delete tuples and to test for the existence of tuples; these operations are synchronized (for example, using two-phase locking [8]) and recovered (for example, using logs [11]) to ensure the atomicity of actions using the relations. In this section we discuss the constraints placed on atomic types to ensure that actions sharing atomic objects are serializable and recoverable. Our approach is informal, and intended primarily to enhance the reader's intuition; a more precise treatment can be found in [30] and [31].

In writing specifications for atomic types, we have found it helpful to pin down the behavior of the operations by initially assuming no concurrency and no failures, and to deal with concurrency and failures later. In other words, we imagine that the objects exist in an environment in which all actions are executed sequentially, and in which actions never abort. This approach is particularly useful in reasoning about an action that uses atomic objects. The atomicity of actions means that they are "interference-free," so we can reason about the partial correctness of an individual action without considering the other actions that might be sharing objects with it [3]. This reasoning process is essentially the same as for sequential programs; the only information required about objects is how they behave in a sequential environment. As an example, an informal sequential specification of some operations on atomic arrays in Argus is described in Figure 1. These arrays are similar to CLU arrays [21], and bear some resemblance to files in that they can grow and shrink.

A description of a type's behavior in the absence of concurrency and failures is only part of the type's specification, however. It is also necessary to describe the kinds of concurrent executions permitted by the type and how the type handles failures. For the type to be atomic, these executions must be constrained so that actions using objects of the type are serializable and recoverable.

The constraints imposed by atomicity are a kind of *safety* requirement: Atomicity ensures that nothing bad ever happens. In describing the kinds of concurrent executions permitted by a type, it is also possible to require that something good will eventually happen. Such requirements are often referred to as *liveness* requirements. In this section we focus on the constraints imposed by atomicity. In Section 4 we give an example of a liveness requirement.

Atomicity of actions is a global property because it is a property of all of the actions in a system. However, atomicity for a type must be a local property: It deals only with the events (invocations and returns of operations and commits and aborts of actions) involving the particular type. Such locality is essential if

atomic types are to be specified and implemented independently of each other and of the actions that use them.

We have identified several local atomicity properties that result in global atomicity [30, 31]. For example, one local atomicity property, called *dynamic atomicity*, characterizes the behavior of a class of types that ensures serializability dynamically based on the order in which actions execute operations provided by the type. Another local atomicity property, called *static atomicity*, characterizes the behavior of a class of types that ensures serializability statically based on some predetermined order of actions. Dynamic atomic types can be implemented with protocols like two-phase locking [8]; static atomic types can be implemented with protocols like Reed's multiversion timestamp protocol [26]. A detailed discussion of these and other local atomicity properties can be found in [30, 31].

Each of these local atomicity properties is adequate to ensure global atomicity of actions. For example, if all types shared by actions are dynamic atomic, actions are guaranteed to be serializable and recoverable. However, different local properties may be incompatible. For example, if some types shared by actions are dynamic atomic and others are static atomic, nonserializable executions of the actions can result. (See [31] for detailed examples.) Thus, in any system, it is necessary to choose a particular local atomicity property that will be used for all

---

In the following T is an arbitrary Type.

new = **proc** ( ) **returns** (atomic-array[T])
  effect Returns a new, empty atomic array with low bound 0, high bound −1, and size 0.

low = **proc** (a: atomic-array[T]) **returns** (int)
  effect Returns the current low bound of a.

high = **proc** (a: atomic-array[T]) **returns** (int)
  effect Returns the current high bound of a.

size = **proc** (a: atomic-array[T]) **returns** (int)
  effect Returns the current size of a.

addh = **proc** (a: atomic-array[T], x: T)
  effect Extends a by appending x on the high end; the current high bound and size of a increase by 1.

addl = **proc** (a: atomic-array[T], x: T)
  effect Extends a by appending x on the low end; the current low bound of a decreases by 1, and the size of a increases by 1.

remh = **proc** (a: atomic-array[T]) **returns** (T) **signals** (bounds)
  effect If a is empty signals bounds; otherwise removes and returns the element at the high end of a; the size and high bound of a decrease by 1.

reml = **proc** (a: atomic-array[T]) **returns** (T) **signals** (bounds)
  effect If a is empty signals bounds; otherwise removes and returns the element at the low end of a; the low bound of a increases by 1, and the size decreases by 1.

store = **proc** (a: atomic-array [T], i: int, x: T) **signals** (bounds)
  effect If i is outside the bounds of a, signals bounds; otherwise stores x in the ith location of a.

fetch = **proc** (a: atomic-array [T], i: int) **returns** (T) **signals** (bounds)
  effect If i is outside the bounds of a, signals bounds; otherwise returns the object stored in the ith location of a.

Fig. 1. Partial sequential specification of atomic arrays.

shared types in the system. In this paper we use dynamic atomicity, which has been adopted as the standard in the Argus programming language.

Dynamic atomicity defines limits on the concurrency that can be permitted by an atomic type. These limits can be stated informally as follows: If the sequences of operations executed by two concurrent actions on a type conflict, then some operation executed by one of the actions must be delayed until the other has completed (i.e., committed or aborted). Two actions are said to conflict if one has observed the effects of the other, or if one has invalidated the results of the other's operations.

For example, consider an atomic array of integers a, and suppose that an action A performs $store(a, 3, 7)$, and then a second action B calls $fetch(a, 3)$. If B receives the result "7" from this invocation, then B has observed the effects of A, and A must be serialized before B. If A has not yet committed when B observes its effects, A and B could exchange roles and execute operations on a second atomic array (B executing $store$ and then A executing $fetch$), giving the conflicting constraint that B must be serialized before A. The resulting execution is not serializable. Since A and B conflict (B observes the effects of A), dynamic atomicity requires B's call of $fetch$ to be delayed until A has completed, thus preventing this kind of nonserializable behavior.

As another example, suppose an action A executes the *size* operation on an atomic array object, receiving n as the result. Now suppose another action B executes *addh*. The *addh* operation changes the size of the array, so B has invalidated the results of an operation executed by A. Thus, A must be serialized before B. As in the previous example, if A has not yet completed when B executes *addh*, A and B could exchange roles at another object, resulting in nonserializable behavior. Since A and B conflict (B invalidates the results of an operation executed by A), dynamic atomicity prevents this situation from arising by requiring B's call of *addh* to be delayed until A has completed.

Dynamic atomicity defines the limits on concurrency that an atomic type can permit. However, the implementation of an atomic type need not allow all of the concurrency permitted by dynamic atomicity. Indeed, it is often too expensive and too complicated to provide all of the permissible concurrency. For example, strict two-phase locking [2, 8, 15] is a reasonably systematic and efficient method for implementing serializability for dynamic atomicity, but the proposed protocols do not allow all of the permitted concurrency. Under strict two-phase locking, an action must acquire a lock on an object in the appropriate mode before executing an operation on the object. If the lock needed by an action conflicts with a lock held by some other action, the requesting action is forced to wait. Locks acquired by an action are held until an action completes.

One reason the two-phase locking protocols described in [2, 8, 15] do not provide all the concurrency permitted by dynamic atomicity is that they allow operations to be executed by concurrent actions only if the operations *commute* [2] (i.e., do not conflict in any state of the locked object). For example, consider the *addh* and *reml* operations on atomic arrays. Two actions executing *addh* and *reml* operations on an empty array conflict, and therefore these operations do not commute. The actions do not conflict when they execute the operations on a nonempty array, since in this case the *reml* operation cannot observe the effects

of the *addh* operations, and the *addh* operation cannot invalidate the results of the *reml* operation. Therefore, dynamic atomicity permits these operations to be performed concurrently on a nonempty array, but the above protocols do not. A similar situation arises with any type whose objects behave like a pool of resources: Operations to remove resources from the pool do not always commute with operations to add resources to the pool, yet, if the pool is nonempty, then actions can be allowed to execute these operations concurrently.

Previously existing concurrency control protocols are also limited in that they require operations to be total functions. Dynamic atomicity, however, allows types to have both partial and nondeterministic operations. Nondeterministic operations are especially important because they increase the permitted concurrency. The semiqueue type, to be presented in Section 4, has such a nondeterministic operation.

3. MODEL OF COMPUTATION

In the remainder of the paper we discuss implementations of atomic objects. In this section we describe the model of computation on which the rest of the paper is based. Our model is taken from Argus [22], a new language we are developing that provides a number of built-in atomic objects and supports the implementation of user-defined atomic objects. Argus is based on a number of decisions about how to implement atomicity and resilience. For example, we require all atomic types to be dynamic atomic, we do not support optimistic [16] implementations of atomic types, and we keep redundant information in stable storage to achieve resilience.

Argus is a language and system that supports distributed programs (i.e., programs that run on a distributed hardware base). Each node in this base is an independent computer consisting of one or more processors and some local memory; the nodes may differ in the number and types of processors, the amount of memory, and in the attached I/O devices. The nodes can communicate only by sending messages over the network; we make no assumptions about the network topology, except that every node can communicate with every other node. We assume such a base in this paper because this allows us to address the consistency problem in its most general form.

In Argus, an application is implemented from one or more modules, called *guardians*. Each guardian consists of some data objects and some processes to manipulate those objects. A guardian can be thought of as "owning" the objects that it contains; each object belongs to exactly one guardian. Processes within a guardian can share objects directly, but sharing of objects between guardians is not permitted. Instead, a guardian provides access to its objects via a set of operations called *handlers* that can be called from other guardians.[1] Arguments to handler calls are passed by value; it is impossible to pass a reference to an object in a handler call. This rule ensures that all references to an object are within that object's guardian.

Each guardian resides at a single physical node, although a node may support several guardians. Guardians survive crashes of their nodes of residence and

---

[1] In this regard a guardian is similar to a Simula class instance [4].

other hardware failures with high probability, and are therefore resilient. When a guardian's node crashes, all processes within the guardian are lost, but a subset of the guardian's objects, referred to as the guardian's *stable state*, survives. After a crash, the guardian recovers with its stable state intact; it then runs a special recovery process to recover the remainder of its objects. Resilience is accomplished by periodically copying the guardian's stable objects to stable storage [18], as discussed further in Section 5.

In addition to guardians, Argus also provides atomic actions and atomic data types. Actions are the primary method of carrying out computations in Argus. Actions terminate by either committing or aborting, and are serializable and recoverable provided that the only data shared among them is atomic. An action starts at one guardian but can spread to other guardians by means of handler calls. When an action completes it either commits at all guardians or aborts at all guardians. The Argus implementation uses a commitment protocol such as two-phase commit [10, 18] to ensure this latter property.

Argus provides a number of built-in atomic data types, for example, atomic arrays and atomic records. We have chosen implementations for the built-in atomic types in Argus that are efficient but provide for less than maximal concurrency. For atomic arrays and the other built-in atomic types, operations are classified as readers and writers, and readers and writers exclude one another in the usual way. For example, the array *addh* and *addl* operations are both writers, and therefore exclude each other even though they do not conflict.

Serializability for atomic arrays and the other built-in types is implemented using strict two-phase locking [8]. The locks are acquired automatically when a primitive operation (like *addh*) is called by an action, and are held until the calling action terminates (commits or aborts). Recoverability is implemented by making a copy the first time an action executes a writer operation. All changes are made to this copy. The copy replaces the original if the action commits; if the action aborts the copy is discarded. If an action modifies a stable object, the new value of the object is copied to stable storage as part of the commitment protocol for the action.

4. USER-DEFINED ATOMIC TYPES

The built-in atomic types in Argus are limited in their provision of concurrency. Users may very well define new atomic types that permit a great deal of concurrency. Although an implementation of an atomic type need not allow all of the concurrency permitted by the type's specification, for performance reasons it may be desirable to allow much of the permitted concurrency. If users were constrained to implementing new atomic types in terms of the built-in atomic types only, the desired concurrency could not be achieved. In this section we describe the tools provided by Argus to support highly concurrent implementations of atomic types and illustrate their use with an example. We defer a discussion of resilience to Section 5.

To understand the problems arising from constraining users to implement new atomic types only in terms of the built-in atomic types, consider the *semiqueue* data type. Semiqueues are similar to queues, except that dequeuing happens in a nondeterministic rather than in a strict FIFO order. They have three operations:

create, which creates a new, empty semiqueue; *enq*, which adds an element to a semiqueue; and *deq*, which removes and returns an arbitrary element that was enqueued previously and has not yet been dequeued.

Semiqueues have very weak concurrency constraints. Two *enq* operations do not conflict with each other, nor do an *enq* and a *deq* operation or two *deq* operations, as long as they involve different elements. Thus, many different actions can *enq* concurrently, or *deq* concurrently. Furthermore, one action can *enq* while another *deqs*, provided only that the latter not return the newly *enqd* element.

We impose the following liveness requirement on semiqueues: *deq* must eventually remove an element *e* that is eligible for dequeuing. The semiqueue could be used in a printer subsystem, in which actions submit files to be printed, and the subsystem prints a file once the action that submitted it has committed. The liveness constraint on the element returned by *deq* is enough for the printer subsystem to guarantee that each file submitted by an action that later commits will eventually be printed.[2]

The semiqueue data type could be implemented using an atomic array as a representation, for instance:

rep = atomic_array[elem].

In this case the implementation of *enq* would simply be to *addh* the new element to the atomic array. Since *addh* is a writer, an *enq* operation performed on behalf of some action A would exclude *enq* and *deq* operations from being performed on behalf of other actions until A completed. As observed above, the specification of the semiqueue permits much more concurrency than this. Note that the potential loss of concurrency is substantial since actions can last a long time. For example, an action that performed an *enq* may also do a lot of other things (to other objects at other guardians) before committing.

To avoid loss of concurrency, users need a way to implement new atomic types directly from nonatomic types. Such users will face a number of new problems, however, and these problems influence the design of a linguistic mechanism to support user-defined atomic types.

In the remainder of this section we describe how user-defined atomic types can be implemented in Argus. We view our mechanism as a first attempt to address the issues in this area. Some related work [27] addresses only the problem of achieving proper synchronization of actions, and not recovery or process synchronization issues.

Our mechanism was influenced primarily by considerations of efficiency and expressive power, and trade-offs were made that favored these goals over simplicity and ease of use. Our assumption is that new atomic types are rarely implemented in terms of nonatomic types, and it is therefore reasonable to require considerable sophistication of the programmer attempting such an implementation.

---

[2] This is not quite true when we consider failures: the action that dequeues a file to print it could abort every time, preventing any progress from being made. As long as failures do not occur sufficiently often to cause this situation, every file will eventually be printed. An interesting open question is how to state service requirements for systems that can fail.

To some extent the issues involved in implementing an atomic type are similar to those that arise in implementing other abstract types. The implementation must define a representation for the atomic objects, and an implementation for each operation of the type in terms of that representation. However, the implementation of an atomic type must solve some problems that do not occur for ordinary types, namely: interaction synchronization, making visible to other actions the effects of committed actions, and hiding the effects of aborted actions.

A way of thinking about the above set of problems is in terms of events that are of interest to an implementation of an atomic type. Like implementations of regular types, these implementations are concerned with the events corresponding to operation calls and returns; here, as usual, control passes to and from the type's implementation. In addition, however, events corresponding to termination (commit and abort) of actions that had performed operations on an object of the type are of interest to the type's implementation.

In our approach, implementations of user-defined atomic types are not informed about commit and abort events, but must instead find out about them after the fact through the use of objects of built-in atomic types. The representation of a user-defined atomic type is therefore a combination of atomic and nonatomic objects, with the nonatomic objects used to hold information that can be accessed by concurrent actions, and the atomic objects containing information that allows the nonatomic data to be interpreted properly. The built-in atomic objects can be used to ask the following question: Did the action that caused a particular change to the representation commit (so that the new information is now available to other actions), did it abort (so that the change is forgotten), or is it still active (so that the information cannot be released as yet)? The operations available on built-in atomic objects have been extended to support this type of use, as illustrated below.

The use of atomic objects permits operation implementations to discover what happened to previous actions and to synchronize concurrent actions. However, the implementations also need to synchronize concurrent operation executions. Here we are concerned with *process concurrency* (as opposed to action concurrency): two or more processes are executing operations on the same object at the same time.

We provide process synchronization by means of a new data type called *mutex*. Mutex objects provide mutual exclusion, as implied by their name. A mutex object is essentially a container for another object. This other object can be of any type, and mutex is parameterized by this type. An example is

mutex[array[int]]

where the mutex object contains an array of integers. Mutex objects are created by calling operation

create = **proc** (x: T) **returns** (mutex [T])

which constructs a new mutex object containing x as its value. The contained object can be retrieved later via operation

get_value = **proc** (m: mutex [T]) **returns** (T)

This operation delivers the value of the mutex object, namely (a pointer to) the contained T object, which can then be used via T operations. *Get_value* can be called via the syntactic sugar *m.value*, where *m* is a mutex object.

The **seize** statement is used to obtain exclusive use of a mutex object:

seize *expr* do *body* end

Here *expr* must evaluate to a mutex object. If that object is not now in the possession of a process, the process executing the **seize statement** *gains possession* and executes the *body*. Possession is *released* when control leaves the *body*. If some process has possession, this process waits until possession is released.[3] If several processes are waiting, one is selected fairly as the next to gain possession. The **seize** statement as explained above is semaphore-like: it could be translated to

P(m.sem)
body
V(m.sem)

where *m* is the mutex object obtained by evaluating *expr*, and we imagine this object has a semaphore as a component. However, the **seize** statement is more powerful than this because inside its *body* it is possible to release possession temporarily. This is done by executing the **pause** statement:

pause

Execution of this statement releases possession of the mutex object that was obtained in the smallest statically-containing **seize** statement. The process then waits for a system-determined amount of time, after which it attempts to regain possession; any competition at this point is resolved fairly. Finally, once it gains possession it starts executing in the *body* at the statement following the **pause**.

The combination of **seize** with **pause** gives a structure that is similar to monitors [14]. For example, the use of invariants is similar in the two mechanisms: An invariant can be assumed to hold at the beginning of the body of the **seize** and after a **pause**; the code must ensure that the invariant holds at the end of the body and before executing **pause**. However, **pause** is simply a delay; there is no guarantee that when the waiting process regains possession, the condition it is waiting for will be true.[4] The combination of **seize** and **pause** also differs from monitors in that the programmer has no control over the scheduling of processes. The reason why we do not provide an analog of a monitor's condition variables is the following: Often, the conditions processes are waiting for concern commit and abort events. These are not events over which other user processes in **seize** statements have any control. Therefore, it would not make sense to expect user processes to signal such information to each other.

4.1 Implementation of Semiqueues

In this section we present an example implementation of the semiqueue data type described earlier. For simplicity, we assume that the elements in the

---

[3] A runtime check is made to see if possession is held by this process. In this case, the **seize** statement fails with the exception *failure* ("deadlock").

[4] In Mesa [17], there is similarly no guarantee when a waiting process awakens.

semiqueue are integers. We use this example to illustrate how objects of built-in atomic types can be used to find out about the completion of actions, and how mutex can be used to synchronize user processes. As mentioned earlier, we defer discussing how to implement resilience until Section 5.

The plan of this implementation is to keep the enqueued integers in a regular (nonatomic) array. This array can be used by concurrent actions, but it is enclosed in a mutex object to ensure proper process synchronization. Any modification or reading of the array occurs inside a **seize** statement on this containing mutex object.

To determine the status of each integer in the array, we associate with each integer an atomic object that tells the status of actions that inserted or deleted that item. For this purpose we use the built-in atomic type, **atomic_variant.** Atomic variant objects are similar to variant records. An atomic variant object can be in one of a number of states; each state is identified by a tag and has an associated value. Thus we represent semiqueues by objects of type

mutex[buffer]

where

buffer = **array**[qitem]
qitem = **atomic-variant**[present: **int**, absent: **nil**].

If the qitem is in the "present" state, then the associated value is the enqueued integer. In the "absent" state, the value of the qitem does not matter, so we use type **null**, which has a single object **nil**.

Atomic_variants provide operations to create new objects and to read and modify existing objects. For each tag t, operation *make_t* creates a new variant object in the t state; this state is the object's "base" state, and the object will continue to exist in this state even if the creating action aborts. For example,

qitem$make_absent(nil)

creates a new *qitem* object in the "absent" state. Operation *change_t* changes the tag and the value of the object; this change will be undone if the calling action aborts. For example,

qitem$change-present(q, 3)

will cause q to be in the "present" state with associated value 3 (provided the calling action commits). There are also operations to decompose atomic variant objects, although these are usually called implicitly via special statements. Atomic variant operations are classified as readers and writers; for example, *change_t* is a writer, while *make_t* is a reader. We discuss the motivation for this classification in Section 4.2.

In this paper, atomic variant objects are decomposed using the **tagtest** statement.

tagtest *expr*
  |*tagarm*|
  [**others:** *body*]
  end

where

tagarm ::= *tagtype idn* [(*decl*)]: *body*
tagtype ::= **tag** | **wtag**

(In the syntax, optional clauses are enclosed with [ ], zero or more repetitions are indicated with { }, and alternatives are separated by | .) The *expr* must evaluate to an atomic variant object. Each *tagarm* lists one of the possible tags; a tag can appear on at most one arm. An arm will be selected if the atomic variant object has the listed tag, and the executing action can obtain the object in the desired mode: read mode for **tag** and write mode for **wtag**. If an arm can be selected, the object is obtained in the desired mode. Then, if the optional declaration is present, the current value of the atomic variant object is assigned to the new variable. Finally, the associated *body* is executed. If no arm can be selected and the optional **others** arm is present, the *body* of the **others** arm is executed; if the **others** arm is not present, control falls through to the next statement.

An Argus cluster (taken from CLU [20, 21], of which Argus is an extension) implementing semiqueue appears in Figure 2. (The keyword cvt in the interface of an operation indicates that the given argument or result object is viewed as an object of the representation type inside the cluster, and as an object of the type defined by the cluster outside the cluster.) The semiqueue operations are implemented as follows. The *create* operation simply creates a new empty array and places it inside of a new mutex object. The *enq* operation associates a new atomic variant object with the incoming integer; this variant object will have tag "present" if the calling action commits later, and tag "absent" if it aborts. Then *enq* seizes the mutex and adds the new item to the contained array.

The *deq* operation seizes the mutex and then searches the array for an item it can dequeue. If an item is enqueued and the action that called *deq* can obtain it in write mode, that item is selected and returned after changing its status to "absent". Otherwise, the search is continued. If no suitable item is found, **pause** is executed and the search is done again later.

Proper synchronization of actions using a semiqueue is achieved by using the *qitems* in the buffer. An *enq* operation need not wait for any other action to complete. It simply creates a new *qitem* and adds it to the array. Of course, it may have to wait for another operation to release the mutex object before adding the *qitem* to the array, but this delay should be relatively short. A *deq* operation must wait until some *enq* operation has committed; thus it searches for a *qitem* with tag "present" that it can write.

The *qitems* are also used to achieve proper recovery for actions using a semiqueue. Since the array in the mutex is not atomic, changes to the array made by actions that abort later are not undone. This means that a *deq* operation cannot simply remove a *qitem* from the array, since this change could not be undone if the calling action later aborted. Instead, a *deq* operation changes the state of a *qitem*; the atomicity of *qitems* ensures proper recovery for this modification. If the action that called *deq* aborts, the *qitem* will revert to the "present" state; if that action commits, the *qitem* will have tag "absent" permanently.

Qitems that are permanently in the "absent" state are also generated by *enq* operations called by actions that later abort. They have no effect on the abstract

Cleanup cannot run in the calling action because then its view of what the semiqueue contained would not be accurate. For example, if the calling action had previously executed a *deq* operation, that *deq* would appear to have really happened to a later operation execution by this action. But of course the *deq* really has not happened, because the calling action has not yet committed.

To get a true view of the state of the semiqueue, *cleanup* runs as an independent action. This action has its own view of the semiqueue, and since it has not done anything to the semiqueue previously, it cannot obtain false information. The independent action is started by the **enter** statement:

enter topaction *body* **end**

It commits when execution of the *body* is finished.

An independent action such as *cleanup* commits while its calling action is still active. The calling action may later abort. Therefore, the independent action must not make any modifications that could reveal intermediate states of the calling action to later actions. The *cleanup* action satisfies this condition because it performs a *benevolent side effect*: a modification to the semiqueue object that cannot be observed by its users.

4.2 Discussion

The representation of semiqueue is fairly typical of implementations of atomic types in Argus. It is a combination of atomic data (the *qitems*) with nonatomic data (the *buffer* array); the atomic data is used to interpret the nonatomic data (e.g., only "present" *qitems* that were added to the buffer by committed actions are considered by the *deq* operation to be in the semiqueue).

The entire representation is enclosed in a mutex, which is used to provide mutual exclusion for user processes. It is important to realize that there are two kinds of concurrency in a system like Argus: action concurrency and process concurrency. Locks on built-in atomic objects are used to synchronize actions, while mutex is used to synchronize processes. Action concurrency is much more important for performance than process concurrency. Critical sections are typically small, so the amount of time one process locks out another (assuming the programs are correct) is small. However, actions may last a very long time, so it is crucial that actions do not exclude one another unnecessarily.

The definition of atomic variants has been specially tailored to meet the needs of implementors of atomic types. Two examples of this tailoring are the **tagtest** statement and the semantics of newly created objects. The **tagtest** statement permits programs to avoid waiting to examine data in an "uninteresting" state. For example, in *deq*, only writable *qitems* in the "present" state are interesting. Suppose that the first item in the queue had been dequeued by an action that was still active; *deq* need not wait for that action to commit before going on to the next item.

In Argus, a reference to a newly created object may continue to exist even though the creating action aborted. For example, a reference to a newly created *qitem* continues to exist in the *buffer* even if the enqueuing action that created the *qitem* aborts. (Note that if a reference to the *qitem* were placed in an atomic object, like an atomic array, the reference would be deleted if the creating action aborted.) In such a case, the object referred to must have some value. Our

```
semiqueue = cluster is create, enq, deq
qitem = atomic_variant[present: int, absent: null]
buffer = array[qitem]
rep = mutex[buffer]

create = proc ( ) returns (cvt)
    return(rep$create(buffer$new( )))
    end create

enq = proc (q: cvt, i: int)
    item: qitem := qitem$make_absent(nil) % "absent" if action aborts
    qitem$change_present(item, i) % "present" if action commits
    seize q do
        buffer$addh(q.value, item) % add new item to buffer
    end
    rep$changed(q) % notify system of modification to buffer (this will be explained later)
    end enq

deq = proc (q: cvt) returns (int)
    cleanup(q)
    seize q do
        while true do
            % look at all items in the buffer
            for item: qitem in buffer$elements(q.value) do
                tagtest item % see if item can be dequeued by this action
                    wtag present (i: int): qitem$change_absent(item, nil)
                        return(i)

                    end % tagtest
                end % for
            pause
            end % while
        end % seize
    end deq

cleanup = proc(q: rep)
    enter topaction % start an independent action
    seize q do
        b: buffer := q.value
        for item: qitem in buffer$elements(b) do
            tagtest item
                tag absent: buffer$reml(b) % remove only qitems in the "absent" state
                others: return
                end % tagtest
            end % for
        end % seize
    end % enter—commit cleanup action here
    end cleanup

end semiqueue
```

Fig. 2.   Implementation of the semique type.

state of the semiqueue, but leaving them in the array wastes storage, so the internal procedure *cleanup*, called by *deq*, removes them from the low end of the array.[5] It seems characteristic of the general approach used here that reps need periodically to be garbage-collected in this fashion.

---

[5] A more realistic implementation would call *cleanup* only occasionally.

definition of atomic variants states that this value is the object's initial value. Another possibility is for the object to have a special "undefined" value. However, the system must then check every use of an object for this special value. The check is expensive, but omitting it destroys the type-safety of the language. Furthermore, user programs must be prepared on each use of an object to handle an exception indicating that the object is undefined; this leads to verbose and error-prone programs. In contrast, we have found that the use of an initial value is quite natural, since it often coincides with another state (e.g., a *qitem* is initially in the "absent" state, and is also in this state after it has been dequeued).

Make_t operations are classified as readers, so that an action that creates an atomic variant object obtains a read lock on that object. Again, this definition enhances the convenience of atomic variants. Sometimes a read lock is all that is wanted; an example is given in the next section. If a write lock is needed, the creating action has no difficulty obtaining it. This need usually manifests itself in the need to change the value of the object, as was the case in the implementation of the *enq* operation. Note that a lock is needed on a newly created atomic variant only if the atomic variant is stored in nonatomic data, as in the representation of semiqueues. If all references are to a newly created atomic variant are stored in atomic objects, then the references are not visible to other actions until the creating action commits, so no other action can obtain a lock on the atomic variant while the creating action is running.

It is worth noting that although semiqueues are atomic, their representations are not. For example, two *enqs* by concurrent actions do not conflict with respect to the semiqueue, but do conflict with respect to the representation. Their order of execution determines the order in which their items appear in the buffer. This order is not significant to the user of the semiqueue, since it is hidden by the nondeterministic specification of *deq*. It is, however, significant within the semiqueue cluster, where it is used to satisfy the service requirement for semiqueues.

5. RESILIENCE

Consistency requires that objects be both atomic and resilient. In the previous section we discussed how to implement atomicity. In this section we discuss how to implement resilience.

If hardware were highly reliable, that is, reliable enough that the probability of loss of information were extremely small, then the mechanism described above would be sufficient for implementing resilient atomic objects. It may be that hardware will be this reliable in the future, but it is not today: node and storage media failures are likely to lead to loss of information. Therefore, some method of implementing data resilience in software is needed.

Various methods of achieving resilience can be imagined. For example, every object might have one or more copies existing at different locations in the network, and actions would read and update the multiple copies in accordance with one of the known algorithms (e.g., [9, 13]). If one of the copies became unavailable because of a failure, some method of restoring that copy from one of the existing copies would be needed.

We are using a different approach, based on stable storage [18], which has the property that information entrusted to it is extremely unlikely to be lost. Each guardian can specify that some of its objects are *stable objects*. Each stable object has a backup copy kept on stable storage. New backup copies must be written to stable storage for all stable objects modified by committed actions. This copying can happen when the change takes place or after the change takes place; it must happen before an action can commit.

Objects are kept in volatile memory while they are used by actions, as are locks for built-in atomic objects and the copies of these objects made by writers. If a node crashes, the locks and copies will be lost for all objects at that node. In this case, any action that used objects at that node and had not yet committed must be forced to abort. To ensure that the action will abort, a standard two-phase commit protocol [10] is used. In the first phase, an attempt is made to verify that all locks are still held and to record the new state of each modified stable object on stable storage. If the first phase is successful, then in the second phase the locks are released, the recorded states become the current states, and the previous states are forgotten. If the first phase fails, the recorded states are forgotten and the action is forced to abort, restoring the objects to their previous states.

When a node crashes, all copies of a guardian's stable objects residing at that node become inaccessible. However, since copies of a guardian's stable objects reside on stable storage, a guardian is not destroyed by a crash. Instead, when a node recovers, its guardians restart; the information in stable storage is used to restore the states of the stable objects.

Both built-in and user-defined atomic objects can be stable, and thus must be copied to stable storage when the actions that modified them commit. This requirement raises the question of how an object's implementation ensures that the right information is written to stable storage when one of its objects is copied. We provide this control by extending the meaning of mutex. So far, mutex has been used only for synchronization of user processes. It will now be used for three additional functions: notifying the system when information needs to be written to stable storage, defining what information is written to stable storage, and ensuring that information is written to stable storage in a consistent state.

The system knows when a built-in atomic object needs to be copied to stable storage. This can happen for one of two reasons: either the committing action holds a write lock on the object, or it created the object. New mutex objects are also written to stable storage when the creating action commits. In addition, we provide mutex operation

changed = **proc** (m: **mutex**[T])

for notifying the system that an existing mutex object should be written to stable storage. Calling this operation will cause *m* to be written to stable storage by the time the action that executed the *changed* operation commits. Note that *changed* is not really needed; the system could keep track of all mutex objects used by an action (via the *get_value* operation) and write these to stable storage. But writing to stable storage is expensive and therefore should be avoided if possible. The *changed* operation allows the user to avoid copying of mutex objects that need not be copied (e.g., were only read).

Copying a mutex object involves copying the contained object. By choosing the proper granularity of mutex objects the user can control how much is written to stable storage. For example, a large database can be broken into partitions that are written to stable storage independently by partitioning it among several mutex objects. The *changed* operation can be used to limit writing to stable storage to just those partitions actually modified by a committing action.

In defining what is copied, we must consider the case of mutex and built-in atomic objects that refer to one another. Suppose the system is copying a mutex object that contains as a component a mutex or built-in atomic object. Should that contained object be copied to stable storage too? And, if so, in what order are the two objects copied? Our solution is to copy objects to stable storage *incrementally*: All portions of the contained object are copied except for contained mutex and atomic objects. These are copied separately if they were modified or are new. The system copies the objects in any convenient order.

Finally, the system gains possession of a mutex object before writing it to stable storage. By making all modifications to these objects inside *seize* statements, the user's code can prevent the system from copying the object when it is in an inconsistent state.

In the semiqueue example in the previous section, the addition of a new *qitem* to the array by an *enq* operation certainly needs to be stably recorded if the calling action commits; otherwise no permanent record of the *enq* operation would exist. Thus the *enq* operation uses the *changed* operation (see Figure 2) to notify the system of this fact. Then, when the enqueuing action commits, the system gains possession of the mutex and copies the contained array to stable storage. In copying the array, only the names (but not the values) of the contained *qitems* are written to stable storage. Those *qitems* that were modified by the committing action, or that are new (e.g., the newly enqueued *qitem*) are also written to stable storage, but this is done independently of the copying of the array state. In particular, the system does not have possession of the mutex object while copying the *qitems* to stable storage. Furthermore, the order in which these various objects are written to stable storage is undefined; the system might copy the array state first and later a contained, modified *qitem*, or vice versa.

A *deq* operation modifies an existing *qitem*; this change will be stably recorded since *qitems* are atomic. The effect of a *deq* operation on the array does not, however, need to be stably recorded. A *deq* operation only modifies the array in an invocation of *cleanup*. If these changes are forgotten in a failure that restores an earlier state of the array, the presence of the extra *qitems* in the array will not affect later operations, and *cleanup* will remove them again the next time it is executed. Thus, the modification made by *cleanup* need not be recorded stably (though it will be when the next action that executes *enq* commits).

The incremental copying scheme has the following impact on programs. The true state of an object usually includes the states of all contained objects, and a predicate expressing a consistency condition on an object state would normally constrain the states of contained objects (this predicate is usually referred to as the *representation invariant* [12]). For example, suppose we had an atomic type *doublequeue* that (for some reason) kept two copies of the semiqueue and was represented by

rep = record [first, second: semiqueue]

where the representation invariant required that the states of the two semiqueues be the same. Now suppose that the system is handling the commit of some action

A that modified both semiqueues contained in the doublequeue and, while this is happening, a second action *B* is modifying those semiqueues. Then it is possible that when the *first* semiqueue is written to stable storage it contains *B*'s changes, but when the *second* semiqueue is written to stable storage it does not contain *B*'s changes. Therefore, the information in stable storage appears not to satisfy the representation invariant of the doublequeue.

However, the representation invariant of the doublequeue really is satisfied, for the following reason. First note that the information in stable storage is only of interest after a crash. Suppose there is a crash. Now there are two possibilities:

(1) Before that crash, *B* also committed. In this case the data read back from stable storage is in fact consistent, since it reflects *B*'s changes to both the *first* and *second* semiqueues.
(2) *B* aborted or had not yet committed before the crash. In either case, *B* aborts. Therefore, the changes made to the *first* semiqueue by *B* will be hidden by the semiqueue implementation: At the abstract level, the two semiqueues *do* have the same state.

The point of the above example is that if the objects being written to stable storage are atomic, then the fact that they are written incrementally causes no problems.

On the other hand, when an atomic type is implemented with a representation consisting of several mutex objects, the programmer must be aware that these objects are written to stable storage incrementally, and care must be taken to ensure that the representation invariant is still preserved and that information is not lost in spite of incremental writing. We have explored several atomic type implementations that use more than one mutex. Often, incremental writing is not a problem; for example, this is the case when a database is implemented as a number of partitions. Sometimes implementations are more complex because of incremental writing. We have developed a general method that seems to work well in managing this complexity. To ensure that various mutexes are written to stable storage in the proper order, separate actions are used. For example, for a write-ahead-log [10], the implementation might make changes to the log in one action *A*, and change the database by a separate action *B* that runs only after *A* has committed. This technique is illustrated below.

5.1 The Amap Example

In this section we show an implementation of an atomic type that uses more than one mutex. The example chosen is a user-defined type *amap* (for atomic map) that can be used to remember information associated with names (*uids*). We begin by describing the semantics of amaps, including the concurrency constraints required for the type to be atomic. Then we present the implementation.

Amaps are like databases in which one field of the stored records is designated as a key; they act like associative memories, binding uids (the keys) to other objects (the database records). In different amaps, the uids can be bound to different types of objects. Therefore, the definition of amap is parameterized by the type of the bound object. For a particular object type, vtype, the type amap[vtype] provides four operations: *create*, *insert*, *delete*, and *lookup*. *Create* takes no arguments; it returns a new empty amap (one with no bindings). *Insert* takes an amap, a uid, and an object of type vtype. If there is already a binding for the uid, it signals *duplicate*; otherwise it binds the uid to the vtype object in the amap. *Delete* takes an amap and a uid. If the uid is not bound in the amap, it signals *not_found*; otherwise it deletes the binding for the uid from the amap. *Lookup* similarly takes an amap and a uid; if the uid is not bound in the amap, it signals *not_found*; otherwise it returns the vtype object bound to the uid.

Amaps permit a substantial amount of concurrency. *Insert*, *delete*, and *lookup* operations involving different uids do not conflict, and so can be used concurrently by different actions. Not much concurrency, however, is possible among operations involving the same uid. For example, if an action succeeds in inserting a binding for a uid, then concurrent actions cannot perform *insert*, *delete*, or *lookup* on that uid, although the *lookup* operation could be performed concurrently if that *insert* had failed (i.e., signalled *duplicate*). If a *lookup* succeeds, a concurrent action cannot *delete* that uid, while if the *lookup* fails a concurrent action cannot *insert* the uid.

Amap could be represented by an array of triples. Each triple would contain the uid, its mapping, and also its status. The status would be an atomic variant and would serve much the same purpose as the *qitem* in the semiqueue; it would contain information about the action that last modified or examined information about the uid. The problem with such an implementation is that it is expensive to keep status information about every uid if the amap is large.

Our implementation of amap removes this status information from most uids. The representation is organized as a large table plus a log. Information about all recent changes to the amap (i.e. insertions and deletions) is kept in the log, not in the table. In addition, information about *lookups* is kept in the log; this information is needed to synchronize with later *inserts* and *deletes*. As a result of this organization, status information is needed only in the log.

Only the log and not the table needs be written to stable storage when a binding changes. Since the log is frequently written to stable storage, it is important that it not get too big; this is achieved by periodically cleaning up the log, removing all entries for aborted actions, and copying changes made by committed actions into the table. Then the table must be written to stable storage. The cost of writing to stable storage could be reduced by partitioning both the log and the table. To simplify the presentation, we do not include partitioning in our implementation.

Both the log and the table are implemented using abstract type *map*. Maps are just like amaps, except they are not atomic, so no synchronization or recovery is provided for actions calling map operations. Maps provide the four operations *create*, *insert*, *delete*, and *lookup* and, in addition, operations *alter*, *size*, and *pairs*. *Alter*, like *insert*, takes a map, a uid, and a vtype object as arguments. If the uid is already bound to the vtype object, it signals *unchanged*; otherwise it binds the uid to the vtype object, deleting any existing binding. *Size* takes a map as an argument; it returns the number of uids that are bound in the map. *Pairs* is an iterator that takes a map as an argument; it yields all ⟨uid, vtype⟩ pairs such that the uid is bound to the vtype object in the map. We do not show a map implementation, but the *lookup* operation, especially, should be efficient since it will be used frequently. Maps could be implemented using hashing.

Thus, the representation of amap has two components, the *intentions* log and the *items* table:

rep = record[items: **mutex**[table], intentions: **mutex**[log]]

where

```
table  = map[vtype]
log    = map[status]
status = atomic_variant[present: vtype, absent: null].
```

Each component has its own mutex object, so it can be written to stable storage independently. The *intentions* log associates status information with uids. The status may be "absent," meaning either that the uid has been deleted or a call of *delete* or *lookup* observed that the uid is not in the amap. Or the status may be "present," either because the uid was inserted recently or because a call of *insert* or *lookup* observed the uid to be present; in either case, the associated vtype object is remembered in the status. The status is an atomic variant, so changes made to it will be undone automatically when actions abort. The status objects thus contain the information needed to synchronize and recover active actions. As was mentioned earlier, status information is not needed in the *items* table, thus saving substantial space in both stable and volatile storage.

The implementation of amap appears in Figure 3. Operations *insert*, *delete*, and *lookup* all make use of the internal routine *find_status*, which determines whether there is a binding for a given uid by examining both *intentions* and *items*. *Find_status* gives the illusion that a status object exists for all uids. It uses the internal routine *rebuild* to do garbage collection; we defer discussing *rebuild* until later.

Find_status checks *intentions* for a status object for the given uid. It returns the status object if one is found. Otherwise, it creates a new status object, inserts it in *intentions*, and returns it. This status object is in the "present" state if the uid is in the *items* table; otherwise it is in the "absent" state.

The implementations of *insert*, *delete*, and *lookup* are all similar. First, *intentions* is seized and then *find_status* is called to get the status object for the uid. Next, if the status object can be locked appropriately, its tag is checked, and then either information is returned about the binding for the uid or the status object is modified to reflect a change in the binding. If the status object cannot be locked appropriately, the operation pauses, releasing possession of *intentions*. When possession is regained, the status object obtained in the last call of *find_status* may have been removed from the log by *rebuild* (see below), so the operation calls *find_status* again.

Note that the *lookup* operation, by calling *find_status*, may add a new status object to *intentions*. This prevents the "phantom record" problem [8], in which one action observes the absence of a binding for a given uid, and another action adds a binding for the uid before the first action completes; the first action may then observe the state of the amap both before and after the second action, thus violating serializability.

Also note that we have been careful to avoid unnecessary copying of the *intentions* log to stable storage. For example, calls of *lookup* can modify *intentions*, as explained above, but these changes need not be copied to stable storage, since

```
amap = cluster [vtype: type] is create, insert, delete, lookup
status = atomic_variant[present: vtype, absent: null]
table = map[vtype]
log = map[status]

rep = record[items: mutex[table], intentions: mutex[log]]

create = proc ( ) returns (cvt)
    return(rep${intentions: mutex[log]$create(log$create( )),
        items: mutex[table]$create(table$create( ))})
end create

insert = proc (m: cvt, u: uid, v: vtype) signals (duplicate)
    seize m.intentions do
        while true do
            s: status := find_status(m, u)
            tagtest s
                tag present: signal duplicate
                wtag absent: status$change_present(s, v)
                    mutex[log]$changed(m.intentions)
                    return
                end % tagtest
            pause % couldn't lock s; wait and try again
        end % while
    end % seize of intentions
end insert

delete = proc (m: cvt, u: uid) signals (not_found)
    seize m.intentions do
        while true do
            s: status := find_status(m, u)
            tagtest s
                wtag present: status$change_absent(s, nil)
                    mutex[log]$changed(m.intentions)
                    return
                tag absent: signal not_found
            end % tagtest
            pause % couldn't lock s; wait and try again
        end % while
    end % seize of intentions
end delete

lookup = proc (m: cvt, u: uid) returns (vtype) signals (not_found)
    seize m.intentions do
        while true do
            tagtest find_status(m, u)
                tag present (v: vtype): return(v)
                tag absent: signal not_found
            end % tagtest
            pause % couldn't lock status object; wait, and try again
        end % while
    end % seize of intentions
end lookup

find_status = proc (m: rep, u: uid) returns (status)
    % m.intentions has been seized in caller
    l: log := m.intentions.value
    if log$size(l) > 1000
        then rebuild(m) end % garbage collection
    return(log$lookup(l, u))
```

Fig. 3.   (Continued on facing page)

```
    except when not_found: end
    s: status
    seize m.items do
        s := status$make_present(table$lookup(m.items.value, u))
        end except when not_found: s := status$make_absent(nil) end
    log$insert(i, u, s)
    return(s)
end find_status

rebuild = proc (m: rep)
    % m.intentions has been seized in caller
    l: log := m.intentions.value
    enter topaction % start a new "rebuild" action
        seize m.items do
            t: table := m.items.value
            for u: uid, s: status in log$pairs(l) do
                tagtest s
                    wtag present (v: vtype):
                        log$delete(l, u)
                        table$alter(t, u, v)
                        mutex[table]$changed(m.items)
                    wtag absent:
                        log$delete(l, u)
                        table$delete(t, u)
                        mutex[table]$changed(m.items)
                    end% tagtest
                    except when unchanged, not_found: end
                end % for
            end % seize
        end % enter—rebuild action commits here
    end rebuild
end amap
```

Fig. 3.   Implementation of the amap type.

they are of interest only while the action is active. The log needs to be copied to stable storage only when it is modified to contain information that is not simply a copy of information in *items*. This can happen only when inserting a new binding or deleting an old binding; *insert* and *delete* contain calls of the mutex operation *changed* in these two cases, respectively.

As mentioned above, we maintain status objects in *intentions* for uids that have been recently accessed. Periodically, we run the internal procedure *rebuild*, whose job is to update *items* to reflect the contents of status objects that are not being used by active actions, and to delete such status objects from *intentions*. We assume that at any point in time there are relatively few active actions that have accessed the amap. Thus, running *rebuild* should keep *intentions* small. *Rebuild* should not be run too often, however; it causes *items* to be copied to stable storage, and *items* may be large. (This cost can be reduced by partitioning *items*, as mentioned above.) *Rebuild* is run whenever *intentions* contains at least 1000 bindings.

Rebuild works in the following way. First, it starts a new action of its own. This is necessary because it must find all status objects that are not being used by active actions, including the calling action. (Notice the similarity with the *cleanup* procedure in the semiqueue implementation.) Such objects are precisely those that the independent action created by the **enter** statement is able to modify. Then *rebuild* loops through all (uid, status) bindings in *intentions*. For each binding it can modify, it deletes the binding from *intentions* and updates *items* appropriately. Note that *items* is modified only if the information in *intentions* is new; for example, if the information in *intentions* came from a *lookup* operation, *items* will not be modified. When the *rebuild* action commits, *items* is copied to stable storage if it was modified.

Suppose a crash occurs while the *rebuild* action is committing. Depending on when the crash occurs, the stable *copy* of *items* may be in either the old or the new state. Which state does not matter since *intentions* is not copied to stable storage by *rebuild*, and, furthermore, it will not be copied to stable storage for any other action while the *rebuild* action is committing (since this is done while in posession of *intentions*). Thus, after a crash, the old state of *intentions* will be recovered. The information in the status objects deleted by *rebuild* (but recovered after the crash) is needed if the stable copy of *items* is in the old state, and is redundant if *items* is in the new state. No information is lost in either case.

Note that *rebuild* may run while an *insert*, *delete*, or *lookup* operation pauses, and may remove from the log the status object obtained by the operation before it paused. This is why each operation, on regaining possession, calls *find_status* again. However, once an action has obtained a lock on a status object, *rebuild* cannot delete the object from *intentions* as long as the action is active.

5.2 Remarks

The implementation shown above controls writing to stable storage by controlling the order in which actions commit. The changes made by an action A to an amap are recorded in stable storage in three steps:

(1) A's changes to *intentions* are written to stable storage.
(2) A's changes are moved to *items* (and deleted from *intentions*), and the changes to *items* are written to stable storage.
(3) A new version of *intentions* in which A's changes are deleted is written to stable storage.

For the implementation to be correct, it is essential that these changes happen in the order shown. For example, if step 2 occurred and then the node crashed before step 1 happened, it would be impossible to undo A's changes if A aborted.

The steps happen in the right order for the following reasons. Step 1 occurs when A commits. Since A's changes are visible to other actions only after A commits, the rebuild action R that moves A's changes from *intentions* to *items* must run after A commits. Step 2 occurs when R commits, and therefore step 2 happens after step 1. Step 3 will happen when some other action, B, which modified *intentions*, commits. B might run after R, or it might overlap R. In the latter case, the committing of B is delayed until R has committed because, while R is running and committing, *intentions* is locked. Therefore, step 3 happens after step 2.

A problem with the implementation is that it will continually call *rebuild* if *intentions* is large due to the activity of active actions. A better method would be to call *rebuild* only if *intentions* is large and some number of operation calls have occurred since the last time *rebuild* was called.

A simple approach to implementing amap, while still limiting the amount of writing to stable storage, is to get rid of *intentions* and keep all the information in *items*, but to partition the data among several mutexes. The problem in this approach is that, as mentioned earlier, it is necessary to store status objects in *items*, thus consuming extra space in both stable and volatile storage. The *intentions* log is essentially a device for limiting the amount of status information that needs to be remembered. Partitioning could be combined with the implementation shown; *items*, and even *intentions*, could be partitioned.

6. CONCLUSIONS

Atomicity is a useful organizational concept for reducing the complexity of a concurrent system. If activities are atomic, concurrency can be ignored when checking the partial correctness of each individual activity. In this paper we have discussed how to implement resilient atomic data types, which support atomicity of activities. We have argued that user-defined atomic types, for which the applications programmer rather than the underlying system ensures appropriate synchronization and recovery, are essential for achieving adequate performance for some applications. We have also presented the constructs provided by the Argus programming language to support the implementation of resilient atomic types.

A system design methodology based on the use of atomic actions and atomic types results in systems with useful modularity properties. As noted above, the partial correctness of an individual action can be verified independently of the other actions in the system and of the implementations of the atomic types. Similarly, an implementation of an atomic type can be verified independently of which actions use objects of the type and of other types shared by those actions. This independence is especially useful if a system performs poorly because of internal concurrency limitations. In such a case, it may be possible to identify certain shared objects as bottlenecks and to substitute more concurrent (albeit more complex) implementations for the types defining those objects. Thus, it may be possible to systematically trade simplicity for concurrency.

It should be clear from the example implementations presented in this paper that implementing a resilient atomic type is a difficult task. Perhaps a different mechanism could make this task easier. We have investigated an alternative approach [31] that has better expressive power than our current mechanism; however, that approach seems to lead to even more complicated implementations, although it appears that the implementations are produced more systematically. Thus, further work is needed in designing and evaluating alternative approaches. In addition, approaches that support local properties other than dynamic atomicity are needed. Our hope in writing this paper is to interest others in this area of research.

ACKNOWLEDGMENTS

The authors gratefully acknowledge the contributions made by members of the Argus design group, especially Maurice Herlihy, Paul Johnson, and Bob Scheifler. This paper was improved by the comments of the referees and many others.

REFERENCES

1. BERNSTEIN, P., AND GOODMAN, N. Concurrency control algorithms for multiversion database systems. In *ACM Symposium on Principles of Distributed Computing*, (Ottawa, Aug. 1982), ACM, New York, 209–215.

2. BERNSTEIN, P., GOODMAN, N., AND LAI, M. Two-part proof schema for database concurrency control. In *Proceedings of the 5th Berkeley Workshop on Distributed Data Management and Computer Networks*, (Feb. 1981), 71–84.

3. BEST, E., AND RANDELL, B. A formal model of atomicity in asynchronous systems. *Acta Inf. 16* (1981), 93–124.

4. DAHL, O.-J., ET AL. The Simula 67 common base language. Publication No. S-22, Norwegian Computing Center, Oslo, 1970.

5. DAVIES, C. T. Recovery semantics for a DB/DC system. In *Proceedings of the 1973 ACM National Conference*, (1973). ACM, New York, 136–141.

6. DAVIES, C. T. Data processing spheres of control. *IBM Syst. J. 17*, 2 (1978), 179–198.

7. ELLIS, C. Concurrent search and insertion in 2-3 trees. *Acta Inf. 14* (1980), 63–86.

8. ESWARAN, K. P., GRAY, J. N., LORIE, R. A., AND TRAIGER, I. L. The notion of consistency and predicate locks in a database system. *Commun. ACM 19*, 11 (Nov. 1976), 624–633.

9. GIFFORD, D. Weighted voting for replicated data. In *Proceedings of the 7th ACM SIGOPS Symposium on Operating Systems Principles*, (Dec. 1979), ACM, New York, 150–162.

10. GRAY, J. N., Notes on database operating systems. In *Lecture Notes in Computer Science 60*, Goos and Hartmanis, Eds., Springer-Verlag, Berlin, 1978, 393–481.

11. GRAY, J. N., ET AL. The recovery manager of the System R database manager. *ACM Comput. Surv. 13*, 2 (June 1981), 223–242.

12. GUTTAG, J., HOROWITZ, E., AND MUSSER, D. Abstract data types and software validation. *Commun. ACM 21*, 12 (Dec. 1978), 1048–1064.

13. HERLIHY, M. P. Replication methods for abstract data types. Ph.D dissertation, Tech. Rep. MIT/LCS/TR-319, MIT Laboratory for Computer Science, May 1984.

14. HOARE, C. A. R. Monitors: An operating system structuring concept. *Commun. ACM 17*, 10 (Oct. 1974), 549–557.

15. KORTH, H. F. Locking primitives in a database system. *J. ACM 30*, 1 (Jan. 1983), 55–79.

16. KUNG, H. T., AND ROBINSON, J. T. On optimistic methods for concurrency control. *ACM Trans. Database Syst. 6*, 2 (June 1981), 213–226.

17. LAMPSON, B., AND REDELL, D. Experience with processes and monitors in Mesa. *Commun. ACM 23*, 2 (Feb. 1980), 105–117.

18. LAMPSON, B. Atomic transactions. In *Distributed Systems: Architecture and Implementation. Lecture Notes in Computer Science 105*, Goos and Hartmanis, Eds., Springer-Verlag, Berlin, 1981, 246–265.

19. LISKOV, B. AND ZILLES, S. N. Programming with abstract data types. In *Proceedings ACM SIGPLAN Conference on Very High-Level Languages. SIGPLAN Not. 9*, 4 (Apr. 1974), 50–59.

20. LISKOV, B., SNYDER, A., ATKINSON, R. R., AND SCHAFFERT, J. C. Abstraction mechanisms in CLU. *Commun. ACM 20*, 8 (Aug. 1977), 564–576.

21. LISKOV, B., ET AL. CLU reference manual. In *Lecture Notes in Computer Science 114*, Goos and Hartmanis, Eds., Springer-Verlag, Berlin, 1981.

22. LISKOV, B., AND SCHEIFLER, R. Guardians and actions: Linguistic support for robust, distributed programs. *ACM Trans. Programm. Lang. Syst. 5*, 3 (July 1983), 381–404.

23. MOSS, J. E. B. Nested transactions: An approach to reliable distributed computing. Ph.D dissertation. Tech. Rep. MIT/LCS/TR-260, MIT Laboratory for Computer Science, 1981.

24. PAPADIMITRIOU, C. H. The serializability of concurrent database updates. *J. ACM 26*, 4 (Oct. 1979), 631–653.

25. PAXTON, W. A client-based transaction system to maintain data integrity. In *Proceedings of the 7th ACM SIGOPS Symposium on Operating Systems Principles*, (Dec. 1979), ACM, New York, 18–23.

26. REED, D. P. Naming and synchronization in a decentralized computer system. Ph.D dissertation. Tech. Rep. MIT/LCS/TR-205, MIT Laboratory for Computer Science, 1978.

27. SCHWARZ, P., AND SPECTOR, A. Synchronizing shared abstract types. *ACM Trans. Comput. Syst. 2*, 3 (Aug 1984), 223–250.

28. STURGIS, H., MITCHELL, J., AND ISRAEL, J. Issues in the design and use of a distributed file system. *Oper. Syst. Rev. 14*, 3 (July 1980), 55–69.

29. WEIHL, W. E., AND LISKOV, B. H. Specification and implementation of resilient, atomic data types. In *Proceedings of the SIGPLAN '83 Symposium on Programming Language Issues in Software Systems*, (San Francisco, June 1983), ACM, New York, 53–64.

30. WEIHL, W. E. Data-dependent concurrency control and recovery. In *Proceedings of the 2nd Annual ACM Symposium on Principles of Distributed Computing* (Montreal, Aug. 1983), ACM, New York, 63–75.

31. WEIHL, W. E. Specification and implementation of atomic data types. Ph.D dissertation. Tech. Rep. MIT/LCS/TR-314, MIT Laboratory for Computer Science, Mar. 1984.

Received April 1983; revised July 1984; accepted January 1985

Abstract Data Types in Databases: Specification, Manipulation and Access

David Stemple
Tim Sheard
Ralph Bunker

Department of Computer and Information Science
University of Massachusetts at Amherst

ABSTRACT

The basic data types from which records can be constructed in most database management systems are limited to a few simple types such as integers, reals, and character strings. There are many applications, exemplified by office automation, computer-aided design and geographic information systems, that could benefit from management of databases containing the complex objects typically used in programming these systems. We call databases that contain user defined abstract data types *object-extended* databases. In this paper we examine three aspects of providing support for object-extended databases: their specification, their manipulation by transactions, and access to them via queries. We show that a database specification scheme grounded formally in three abstract data types, finite sets, tuples and lists, accommodates the integration of databases and arbitrary abstract data types from the points of view of database designers, transaction programmers, and query writers and implementers.[1]

1.0 INTRODUCTION

The basic data types from which records can be constructed in most database management systems is limited to a few simple types such as integers, reals, and character strings. There are many applications, exemplified by office automation, computer-aided design and geographic information systems, that could benefit from management of databases containing the complex objects typically used in programming these systems. The application of the abstract data type paradigm to database systems has been discussed at length.[1,2,3,4,5,6,7,8,9,10,11,12,13,14,15] However, practical use of abstract data types in the full specification of a database system/application still awaits realization. This paper reports on one part of an effort to use abstract data types in both the formalization of database

systems and in the specification of database applications, the latter including embedded user-defined types. One goal of our effort is to enable the use of automatic theorem proving in multiple aspects of database systems. In this paper, we do not deal with the theorem proving problem, but address instead three aspects of embedding user-defined abstract data types in databases – the specification of the database together with included abstract data types, the writing of transactions that intermix database and abstract data type operations, and the writing and implementation of queries which refer to the embedded types.

The specification techniques we present in this paper are based on our adaptation of the specification-based software development paradigm presented by Balzer to database system development.[16] Using our paradigm, a designer starts by describing the real world entities and relationships using some *semantic data model* such as the entity-relationship model[17] or the semantic hierarchy model.[13] This level of specification is translated into a specification of information structures and transitions, i. e., a schema and transactions, with the possible addition of constraints not specifiable in the semantic model. This information level specification is expressed in a high level programming language, ADABTPL[18,19], and it is in this language that users can specifiy abstract data types as components of databases. Specifications i ADABTPL are analyzed by an inference mechanism, Boyer-Moore style theorem prover[20], the results being used along with implementation choices, e. g., file structures, to generate optimized implementations in some programming language and database management system. The information level specification is also executable as a prototype prior to the system's implementation. The observable behavior of the prototype and the results of the formal analysis are valuable feedback to the designer on the quality of both schema and transaction designs. A further discussion of our development method has been presented elsewhere.[19]

[1] This material is based upon work supported by the National Science Foundation under Grant No. DCR-8503613.

We call a database which includes a user-defined abstract data type an *object-extended database*. In this paper we present an example of an object-extended database which contains an abstract data type as a relational tuple component domain. We use this example to explain our specification techniques, demonstrating the integrated specification of abstract data types and database, showing how transactions are written, and discussing the effect of object-extension on database queries. The implementation of object-extended database systems is obviously a difficult problem and one which we will not address in any depth in this paper. Some of the implementation problems have been addressed elsewhere.[21,22,14,31,32]

2.0 AN EXAMPLE SPECIFICATION OF AN OBJECT-EXTENDED DATABASE SYSTEM

In this section, we give an example of a specification of a simple object-extended database with an imbedded abstract data type, priority queue. Our database consists of an employees relation and a set of prioritized job assignments for the employees. We show how to specify, in an integrated manner, the database and the priority queue abstract data type to be used for job assignments in the database.

The language used in the example is ADABTPL, a language we developed for the specification of database systems.[18,33] The language is formally based on three abstract data types, finite sets, lists, and tuples, whose combined theories we have built using an extended Boyer-Moore theorem prover. Notable features of the language are:

- It is essentially a functional language, though its appearance is very similar to typical non-applicative languages.

- It uses Pascal-like type construction combined with arbitrary constraint predicates relating components of type instances. (In the database context these predicates include integrity constraints such as referential integrity and other interrelational constraints.)

- The declaration part culminates in a database declaration in which a database type is defined and a database variable is given.

- The procedural part addresses the database directly as a globally accessible entity; there are no reads and writes to the database.

- Relational capabilities are achieved by straightforward functional abstraction techniques and include relational algebras as well as relational calculus.

In addition to the ordinary primitive sets of integer, real, and character string, ADABTPL includes finite sets, lists, and tuples. The operations on finite sets are

emptyset: → **fsets**
insert: elements × fsets → fset
choose: fsets → elements
rest: fsets → fsets
empty: fsets → boolean
before: elements × elements → boolean

The *choose* of a set is the first in an arbitrary order defined by the hidden *before* relation. The boolean function *before* is an arbitrary total order, used for technical reasons, and is hidden from users of the finite set abstract data type. The *rest* of a set is the set with the *choose* removed. A further discussion of finite sets can be found elsewhere.[23]

The list (stack) operations are
emptylist: → list
add_to_front: list_element × list → list
first: list → list_element
tail: list → list
empty: list → boolean

The *first* is the last added to the list. The *tail* is the list with its *first* removed, (LISP CDR).

Tuples have a constructor function named in the underlying theory by the tuple type name but written with enclosing brackets in ADABTPL. Component selector functions are named by the component names and are written using a post-fix dot with the component name. For example, E.NAME in ADABTPL maps into the functional NAME(E) where E stands for a tuple.

2.1 An Object-extended Schema

We will now present the different parts of our example specification and explain the different constructs as we proceed. Figure 1 gives a definition of a generic (or parameterized) queue type we will use to build a priority queue.

This definition consists of several parts. The first is the **structure** part. This is used to base the new type on predefined types and the parameter types, in this case predefined *list* and parameter *queue_element*.

```
Begin generic type queue:

{ Defines generic type queue with operations empty, enqueue, first,
  qtail, and empty_queue }

    structure queue(queue_element) = list of queue_element;

    constant empty_queue = emptylist;

    rename qtail = tail;

    operation enqueue queue_element × queue = queue;

REFINEMENTS:

    enqueue(e,q) =
      if q = emptylist
         then add_to_front(e, emptylist)
         else add_to_front(first(q), enqueue(e, tail(q)));

    suppress add_to_front, tail, emptylist;

End queue;
```

Figure 1: Definition of Type Queue.

The **structure** statement causes the generation of axioms about the type being defined and specifies the basic set of operations usable on the new type. Some of the operations may be discarded by later statements in the definition. After a **structure** statement, the operations of the component types mentioned can be used. In this case the list operations are legally usable in the remainder of the queue specification.

The next three statements, **constant**, **rename**, and **operation**, all serve the same purpose, namely to define legal operation syntax for the type. The first is to redefine the nullary operator, *emptylist*, to allow it to be called *empty_queue* for purposes of clarity. We use **constant** in this case since nullary operators are not normally considered operations by non-algebraicists.

The **rename** statement is used to rename operations that have parameters without having to specifiy parameter variables. The **operation** statement is used to introduce new operators for the type. The semantics for operations introduced by **operation** statements can be specified by either axioms or functional extension. The latter is accomplished by giving a function definition, possibly recursive, in terms of the operators introduced by the **structure** statement. This is basically a version of abstract data type definition by abstract model[24,25,26] and is also essentially the same as that proposed by Burstall and Goguen,[27,28] though the style of written specifications are more in the database tradition (without any loss of formality). It is this method which we will use in our example. The section headed by REFINEMENTS contains the recursive definition of enqueue in terms of the list operations. Such function definitions have been demonstrated to be very effective in providing the basis for the effective proving of properties of complex types using our extended Boyer-Moore prover.[29]

```
Begin generic type priority_queue:

    structure  priority_queue(queue_element, priority_integer) =
                   set of [priority: priority_integer, que: queue(queue_element)]
                   where key(priority) and not empty(que);

    expose before {only for purposes of refinement};

    constant empty_pr_queue = emptyset; rename top_pq = choose;

    operation pq_insert: queue_element × priority_integer × priority_queue
                   → priority_queue;

    operation pq_remove: priority_integer × priority_queue → priority_queue;

REFINEMENTS:

    before(pq_el1, pq_el2) = pq_el1.priority < pq_el2.priority;

    pq_insert(e, p, pq) =
      if pq = empty_pr_queue
         then insert([p, enqueue(e, empty_queue)], empty_pr_queue)
         else if choose(pq).priority = p
                 then insert([p, enqueue(e, choose(pq).que)], rest(pq))
                 else if choose(pq).priority > p
                         then insert([p, enqueue(e, empty_queue)], pq)
                         else insert(choose(pq), pq_insert(e, p, rest(pq)));

    pq_remove(p, pq) =
      if empty(pq) = empty_pr_queue
         then empty_pr_queue
         else if choose(pq).priority = p
                 then if qtail(choose(pq).que) = empty_queue
                         then rest(pq)
                         else insert([p, qtail(choose(pq).que)], rest(pq))
                 else if choose(pq).priority < p
                         then insert(choose(pq), pq_remove(p, rest(pq)))
                         else pq;

    suppress insert, choose, rest, before, emptyset;

End priority_queue;
```

Figure 2: Definition of Type Priority-queue.

The **suppress** statement allows us to restrict the operations which can be used on objects of the type.

In figure 2 we give a more complex example defining a priority queue type. The **structure** statement declares that a priority queue is a set of tuples, and that one component of each tuple is a queue. Thus, since a queue is an extended list, priority queue is composed of all three of the primitive abstract data types of ADABTPL. The **where** clause of the **structure** statement introduces additional axioms. These are written in terms of either the primitive operations of the constituent types or predefined functions, e. g., *key*. Here we see the predicate function *key* used to specify that a priority queue will contain at most one queue paired with each unique priority. Other predicate functions include set membership and containment and universal and existential quantification in sets. These have been defined in terms of the primitive operations of finite sets. We have proven large numbers of theorems about these functions and have made them known to our theorem prover. [23]

```
name = string 30; job_name = string 50;

emp = [emp_name: name, job: job_name, salary: integer];

emp_rel = set of emp where key(emp_name);

task_descr = string 30; p_range = 1..5;

employee_sheet = [emp_name: name,
                  task_list: priority_queue(task_descr, p_range)];

task_queues = set of employee_sheet
              where key(emp_name);

{DATABASE DECLARATION}

Job_database = [emps:emp_rel, work_load:task_queues]

              where emps.emp_name contains work_load.emp_name;

{ The dot notation is overloaded to also mean relational projection. }

Database: Job_database.
```

Figure 3: Database Type Definition.

The **expose** statement is used to expose a suppressed operation of a constituent type in order to use it in a refinement. The boolean function *before* is used in the finite set axioms in a technical manner to allow us to choose an arbitrary member of a finite set in a manner which enables the use of structural induction in mechanical proofs.[30] It encapsulates an arbitrary order which is unobservable directly by users of the finite set type. However, in this case we wish to associate it with a particular order, namely the priority order. Thus we expose it temporarily and refine it by an additional axiom. We must of course prove that the additional axiom is consistent with the previous axioms. This is easily done for this case.

The two operations of insertion and removal from priority queues, *pq_insert* and *pq_remove*, are defined in the refinement section. Remember that though *choose(pq)* appears in several places in each function, it returns the same element of the set each time since it is a function and we make the assumption that operations run *atomically*, i. e., without interference from any concurrently executing operation. Properties of these operations can be stated as theorems, proven mechanically from the definitions, and added to the specification. The most important properties these functions must have is that of obeying the where clause of the **structure** statement. Proof of such properties in our system is the same as proving the consistency or "safety" of database transactions with respect to database integrity constraints, on which we have reported elsewhere.[29]

In figure 3 we give the remainder of the database declaration. The first three statements define a keyed relation type for employees, first giving the domain definitions (name and job_name), followed by a tuple type (emp), and finally the derived relation type

(emp_rel), which is fully axiomatized by the combined finite set and tuple axioms. We then introduce a task description type and a priority range. These are used to define an employee work sheet type (employee_sheet) which uses the previous two types as arguments to the generic priority_queue type. Work_sheet is then used to define a non-first normal form relation type (task_queues) which includes the abstract data type priority_queue.

The next to last statement in figure 3 defines the database type. The database state is a tuple of relations. The database type declaration includes any interrelational integrity constraints in the where clause. In this example, the contains predicate is used to express referential integrity of the employee name column of the work load relation. The database type inherits all the axioms of its constituent types along with all the defined operations of the types. These operations can be used to succinctly write high level transactions on the database. In the next section we discuss three such transactions.

2.2 Transactions for Object-extended Databases

In this section we give three transactions in which the operations of the priority queue are freely intermixed with the operations on the database. The simple form of the transactions demonstrate the benefits accruing to the programmer through the use of embedded abstract data types.

In figure 4 we see the definition of a transaction which adds tasks to employees' work sheets. The inputs to the transaction are typed by types introduced in the declarations of the database type. (Input types which are not component types of the database can also be used, of course.) Input is addressed by input parameter name. There are no read statements in ADABTPL, either of input or of the database. Assignment of input parameters to terminals or files is relegated to lower level specifications just as the location and form of the database is specified by the internal schema.

There is a preconditions statement specifiying conditions that must be met for the transaction to be run. The basic control structures are the *if-then-else* and *for* (ADABTPL is case insensitive with respect to reserved words). The *for* statement can be used with sets or lists as well as types refined from them. The *for-the* can be used when the where clause provably defines at most one member of a set. In both forms of the *for* statement, if the where clause is not met by any member of the set (or list) through which the program is iterating the body of the statement is not executed. The operations usable in transactions are

TRANSACTION SECTION;

{ Variables which are not input parameters are implicitly prefixed with "Database.". }

Transaction

Add_to_tasks (e_name: name, job: task_descr, pr: priority_integer)

{ Adds a job to an employee's work sheet }

Preconditions:
    e_name in emps.emp_name;

Begin

If not e_name in work_load.emp_name
    then
        insert [e_name, pq_insert(job, pr, empty_pq_queue)] into work_load
    else
        For the sheet in work_load where sheet.emp_name = e_name
            do update sheet using
                [task_list = pq_insert(job, pr, task_list)]

End Add_to_tasks.

Figure 4: Definition of Add-to-tasks Transaction in ADABTPL.

exactly those defined in the abstract data types of the database and input types. There is some syntactic sugaring of this fact such as the update statement. For example, an update can be used to change a tuple's components which involves the tuple constructor and selection operations and replace it in a set which involves the delete and insert operations. The equation in brackets specifies the update changes. Unmentioned parts of the tuple remain unchanged. See the example in figure 4.

In figure 5 we see both *for* statements used. The *for-each* statement is used to examine each employee's jobs and to run through the employee's queue (a list) if there is one paired with a priority of 1.

In figure 6 we see the finite set operation *choose*, renamed *top_pq*, used to select the top priority jobs of each employee. The *choose* operation is driven by the refined *before* relation of priority queues to choose the highest priority queue.

The transactions presented here demonstrate the ability to use the concepts built on the basic abstract types of ADABTPL, exemplified by *for*, *choose*, and tuple updating, together with their extensions such as the priority queue insert, in an integrated and complexity reducing fashion when defining a database system.

3.0 QUERYING OBJECT-EXTENDED DATABASES

There are a number of ways in which databases can be queried. One is to express some predicate whose variables range over objects in the database. The

Transaction Print_priority_1_jobs

{ Prints all the priority 1 jobs queued }

Begin

For each emp_sheet in work_load do

    begin
        print(emp_sheet.emp_name);
        For the job_queue in emp_sheet.task_list
            where job_queue.priority = 1
        do
            For each job in job_queue.que do print(job)
    end

End Print_priority_1_jobs

Figure 5: Transaction Print-priority-1-jobs in ADABTPL.

system searches the database for objects that obey the predicate and returns them as the answer to the query. Relational calculus oriented query systems such as QUEL are of this type. Another query specification technique is to give an algebraic expression whose variables are bound to database objects and to let the system evaluate the algebraic expression to produce the query result. Obviously relational agebra based query languages follow this form. A third way is to write a program or function in a programming language and to execute the program to find the query result. Such a program would contain calls (explicitly or implicitly) to a database manager in order to access the database. Hybrids of these three techniques are possible, e. g., PL/I with embedded SQL.

Object-extended databases can be queried in any of these manners. The second and third transactions in the previous section are queries of the third type where the programming language is ADABTPL. ADABTPL access to the database manager is implicit since access to the input variables and the database are identical in form. We will now turn to the other forms of database query, namely predicate-based, algebra-based and hybrid.

Transaction Print_top_priority_jobs

{ Prints the top priority jobs for all employees }

Begin

For each emp_sheet in work_load do

    print(emp_sheet.emp_name);

    if empty(emp_sheet.task_list)
        then print("No current jobs")
        else
            begin
                print(top_pq(emp_sheet.task_list).priority);
                For each job in top_pq(emp_sheet.task_list).que
                    do print(job)
            end;

End Print_top_priority_jobs

Figure 6: Transaction Print-top-priority-jobs in ADABTPL.

Predicate-based queries which integrate abstract data types in the relational calculus are discussed by Ong and others in the context of INGRES. [32] The basic issue here is how the query processor is to evaluate predicates which involve boolean operations from the embedded abstract data type. This can be done as simply as calling a designated subroutine implementing the boolean function using a predefined calling protocol. If instances of the type are to be delivered as a result of the query then the system must be given rules or routines for converting from the internal to the external form. Of course, the query manager must be flexible enough to accommodate such additions.

Predicate-based query specification naturally supports sophisticated query optimization techniques based on high level transformations using the semantics of the database.[34] If such methods are to be used on object-extended databases, then formal capture of the embedded abstract data types is needed. In this case, type specification techniques beyond those used by Ong are required. The specification techniques presented in this paper are formal enough to support such optimization methods as well as integrity checking optimization in transactions based on mechanical theorem proving.[18] Relational algebra based query methods are easily accommodated in databases extended by the specification technique presented in this paper. In fact, ADABTPL relations are treated as extended abstract data types based on the finite set and tuple abstract data types. Selection, project, join, and grouping are defined as ADABTPL functions using the primitives of ADABTPL. Non-normal form relations are just one of the possible extensions of the ADABTPL types.

Relational algebra based optimization techniques are usable in the ADABTPL context and can be proven correct by our theorem prover using theorems about the relational algebra functions which we have already proven.

Hybrid techniques are interesting because they allow query expressions which are often easier to write and understand. Such queries can arise naturally when querying in the context of a view, where the view (essentially a query itself) is defined by predicates and the query is framed algebraically (or vice versa). Since ADABTPL is essentially a functional language, intermixing functions and predicates (which are only special functions) as well as embedding predicates and functions in ADABTPL transaction programs presents no special problem.

4.0   CONCLUSION

We have presented a method of specifying database systems which allows arbitrary embedding of user-defined abstract data types in databases. We have called such databases object-extended databases. An example of an object-extended database specification was presented in order to demonstrate our integrated database and abstract data type specification technique. We then gave three transaction definitions which showed the degree to which transactions involving complex types in the database could be handled succinctly and easily. In the last section we discussed querying object-extended databases and concluded that this presented no special linguistic difficulty and afforded theoretical support for various query optimization techniques.

REFERENCES

[1] Brodie, M. L. "The Application of Data Types to Database Semantic Integrity." Information Systems 5, pp. 287-296, 1980.

[2] Brodie, M. L. "Association: A Database Abstraction for Semantic Modeling." In Entity-Relationship Approach to Information Modeling and Analysis, P. P. Chen, Ed., pp. 583-608, 1981.

[3] Casanova, M. A. and Bernstein, P. A. "A Logic of a Relational Data Manipulation Language." Sixth ACM Symposium on Principles of Programming Languages, Jan., 1979, pp. 101-120.

[4] Casanova, M. A., Veloso, P. A. S., and Furtado, A. L. "Formal Data Base Specification - An Eclectic Perspective." Proceeding of the Third ACM SIGACT-SIGMOD Symposium on Database Systems, Waterloo, Ontario, Apr. 1984, pp. 110-118. ACM Transactions on Database Systems, Vol. 6, No. 4, Dec. 1981, pp. 576-601.

[5] Ehrig, H., Kreowski, H. J., and Weber, H. "Algebraic Specification Schemes for Data Base Systems." Proceedings of the 4th International Conference on Very Large Data Bases, 1978, pp. 427-444.

[6] Furtado, A. L. and Veloso, P. A. S. "Procedural Specifications and Implementations for Abstract Data Types." ACM SIGPLAN Notices, Vol. 16, No. 3, Mar. 1981, pp. 53-62.

[7] Gerhart, S. "Formal Validation of a Simple Database Application." Proceedings of the Sixteenth Hawaii International Conference on System Sciences, 1983, pp. 102-111.

[8] Lockemann, P. C., Mayr, H. C., Weil, W. H. and Wohleber, W. H. "Data Abstractions for Database Systems." ACM Trans. on Database Syst., Vol. 4, No. 4, Mar. 1978, pp. 30-59.

[9] Neuhold, E. J. and Olnhoff, T. "Building Database Management Systems through Formal Specifications." in *Formalization of Programming Concepts*, J. Diaz and I. Ramos, Eds., Springer Verlag, Berlin, 1981.

[10] Santos, C. S. dos, Neuhold, E. J. and Furtado, A. L. "A Data Type Approach to the Entity-relationship Model." In *Entity-Relationship Approach to Systems Analysis and Design*, P. P. Chen, Ed., North-Holland, Amsterdam, 1980.

[11] Scheuermann, P., Schiffner, G., and Weber, H. "Abstraction Capabilities and Invariant Properties Modelling within the Entity-Relationship Model." *In Entity-Relationship Approach to Systems Analysis and Design*, P. P. Chen, Ed., North-Holland, Amsterdam, 1980.

[12] Schmidt, J. "Some High Level Constructs for Data of Type Relation." ACM Transactions on Database Systems. Vol. 2, No. 3, Sep. 1977. pp. 247-261.

[13] Smith, J. M. and Smith, D. C. P. "A Data Base Approach to Software Specification" In *Software Development Tools*, Riddle and Fairley, Eds., Springer-Verlag, 1980, pp. 176-204.

[14] Weber, H. "A Software Engineering View of Data Base Systems." Proceedings of the 4th International Conference on Very Large Data Bases, Sep. 1978, pp. 36-51.

[15] Yeh, R. T., Baker, J. W. "Toward a Design Methodology for DBMS: A Software Engineering Approach." Proceedings of the 3rd International Conference on Very Large Data Bases, Oct. 1977, pp. 16-27.

[16] Balzer, R., Cheatham, T. E., Jr., and Green, C. "Software Technology in 1990's: Using a New Paradigm." Computer, Vol. 16, No. 16, November, 1983.

[17] Chen, P. P. "The Entity-Relationship Model - Toward a Unified View of Data." ACM Transactions on Database Systems, Vol. 1, No. 1, Mar. 1976, pp. 9-36.

[18] Stemple, D. and Sheard, T. "Specification and Verification of Abstract Database Types", Proceedings of the Third ACM SIGACT-SIGMOD Symposium on Database Systems, Waterloo, Ontario, Apr. 1984, pp. 248-257.

[19] Stemple, D., Sheard, T. and Bunker, R. "Incorporating Theory into Database System Development." to be published in Information Technology, available as University of Massachusetts COINS Dept. Technical Report 85-08, Mar. 1985.

[20] Boyer, R. S. and Moore, J. S. *A Computational Logic*, Academic Press, New York, 1979.

[21] Stemple, D. "A Database Management Facility for Automatic Generation of Database Managers." ACM Transactions on Database Systems, vol. 1, no. 1, Mar. 1976, pp. 79-94.

[22] Stemple, D. "A Database Management Facility and Architecture for the Realization of Data Independence." Ph.D. thesis, Universtiy of Massachusetts at Amherst, Feb. 1977.

[23] Stemple, D. and Sheard, T. "Database Theory for Supporting Specification-based Database System Development." to be presented at the Eighth International Software Engineering Conference, Aug. 1985.

[24] Liskov, B. and Zilles, S. "Specification Techniques for Data Abstractions", IEEE Transactions on Software Engineering, Vol 1, No. 1, Mar. 1975, pp. 7-19.

[25] Berzins, V. A. "Abstract Model Specifications for Data Abstractions." Massachusetts Institute of Technology, MIT/LCS/TR-221, July, 1979.

[26] Claybrook, B. G. "A Specification Method fof Specifying Data and Procedural Abstractions." IEEE Transactions on Software Engineering, Vol. SE-8, No. 5, Sep. 1982, pp. 449-459.

[27] Burstall, R. M. and Goguen, J. A. "Putting Theories together to Make Specifications." Fifth International Joint Conference on Artificial Intelligence, Cambridge, Massachusetts, Aug., 1977, pp. 1045-1058.

[28] Goguen, J. A. and Burstall, R. M. "Introducing Institutions." in *Lecture Notes in Computer Science 164, Logics of Programs*, E. Clarke and D. Kozen, Eds., Springer Verlag, Berlin, 1983.

[29] Sheard, T and Stemple, D. "Coping with Complexity in Automated Reasoning about Database Systems." to be presented at the Eleventh International Conference on Very Large Data Bases, Aug. 1985.

[30] Burstall, R. M. "Proving Properties of Programs by Structural Induction." Computer Journal, Vol. 12, No. 1,pp. 41-48, Feb., 1969,

[31] Barroody, A. J. and DeWitt, D. J. "An Object-oriented Approach to Database System Implementation." [**Guttag 80**]Guttag, J. "Notes on Type Abstractions (Version 2)." IEEE Transactions on Software Engineering, Vol 6, No. 1, Jan. 1980, pp. 13-23.

[32] Ong, J., Fogg, D. and Stonebraker, M. "Implementation of Data Abstraction in the Relational Database System INGRES." ACM SIGMOD Record, Vol. 14, No. 1, Mar. 1984, pp. 1-14.

[33] Sheard, T. "Proving the Consistency of Database Transactions." Ph. D. Thesis, Dept. of Computer and Information Science, University of Massachusetts, Aug. 1985.

[34] King, J. J. "Query Optimization by Semantic Reasoning." Ph. D. Thesis, Dept of Computer Sciences, Stanford University, May 1981.

Synchronizing Shared Abstract Types

PETER M. SCHWARZ and ALFRED Z. SPECTOR
Carnegie-Mellon University

The synchronization issues that arise when transaction facilities are extended for use with shared abstract data types are discussed. A formalism for specifying the concurrency properties of such types is developed, based on dependency relations that are defined in terms of an abstract type's operations. The formalism requires that the specification of an abstract type state whether or not cycles involving these relations should be allowed to form. Directories and two types of queues are specified using the technique, and the degree to which concurrency is restricted by type-specific properties is exemplified. How the specifications of types interact to determine the behavior of transactions is also discussed. A locking technique is described that permits implementations to make use of type-specific information to approach the limits of concurrency.

Categories and Subject Descriptors: D.2.1 [**Software Engineering**]: Requirements/Specifications—*methodologies*; D.3.3. [**Programming Languages**]: Language Constructs—*abstract data types; concurrent programming structures*; D.4.1. [**Operating Systems**]: Process Management—*concurrency; synchronization*; H.2.4 [**Database Management**]: Systems—*transaction processing*

General Terms: Design, Reliability, Theory

Additional Key Words and Phrases: Transactions serializability, dependencies, locking

1. INTRODUCTION

Transaction facilities, as provided in many database systems, permit the definition of *transactions* containing operations that read and write the database and that interact with the external world. The transaction facility of the database system guarantees that each invocation of a transaction will execute at most once (i.e., either commit or abort) and will be isolated from the deleterious effects of all concurrently executing transactions. To make these guarantees, the transaction facility manages transaction synchronization, recovery, and, if necessary,

intersite coordination. Many papers have been written about transactions in the context of both distributed and nondistributed databases [3, 6, 9, 14, 15].

There are a number of ways in which transaction facilities could be extended to simplify the construction of many types of reliable distributed programs. Extensions that allow a wider variety of operations to be included in a transaction would facilitate manipulation of shared objects other than a database. Extensions that permit transaction nesting would facilitate more flexible program organizations, as would extensions allowing some form of intertransaction communication of uncommitted data. Although the synchronization, recovery, and intersite coordination mechanisms needed to support database transaction facilities are reasonably well understood, these mechanisms require substantial modification to support such extensions. For example, they must be made compatible with the abstract data type model and with general implementation techniques such as dynamic storage allocation.

Lomet [19] has considered some of the problems encountered in developing general-purpose transaction facilities, but more recently much of the research in this area has been done at M.I.T. Moss and Reed have discussed nested transactions and other related systems issues [20, 22]. As part of the Argus project, extensions to CLU have been proposed that incorporate primitives for supporting transactions [17, 18]. Additionally, Weihl has considered transactions that contain calls on shared abstract types such as sets and message queues and has discussed their implementation [26, 27]. Transactions will also be available in the Clouds distributed operating system [1].

This paper focuses on one important issue that arises when extending transaction facilities: the synchronization of operations on shared abstract data types such as directories, stacks, and queues. After a presentation of background material in the following section, Section 3 introduces some tools and notation for specifying shared abstract types. Section 4 describes three particular data types and uses the tools to specify how operations on these types can interact under conditions of concurrent access by multiple transactions. The specifications that are developed make explicit use of type-specific properties, and it is shown how this approach permits greater concurrency than standard techniques that do not use such information. Section 5 discusses how the specifications of individual types interact to determine global properties of groups of transactions. Section 6 proposes an extensible approach to locking that can be used for synchronization in implementations intended to meet these specifications. Finally, Section 7 summarizes the major points of this paper and concludes with a brief discussion of other considerations in the implementation of user-defined, shared abstract data types.

2. BACKGROUND

Transactions aid in maintaining arbitrary application-dependent *consistency constraints* on stored data. The constraints must be maintained despite failures and without unnecessarily restricting the concurrent processing of application requests.

This research was sponsored in part by the U.S. Air Force Rome Air Development Center under Contract F30602-81-C-0297, in part by the U.S. Naval Ocean Systems Center under Contract N66001-81-C-0484 N65, and in part by the Defense Advanced Research Projects Agency, ARPA Order 3597, monitored by the Air Force Avionics Laboratory under Contract F33615-81-K-1539.
Authors' address: Department of Computer Science, Carnegie-Mellon University, Pittsburgh, PA 15213.

In the database literature, transactions are defined as arbitrary collections of database operations bracketed by two markers: *BeginTransaction* and *EndTransaction*. A transaction that completes successfully *commits*; an incomplete transaction can terminate unsuccessfully at any time by *aborting*. Transactions have the following special properties:

(1) Either all or none of a transaction's operations are performed. This property is usually called *failure atomicity*.

(2) If a transaction completes successfully, the effects of its operations will never subsequently be lost. This property is usually called *permanence*.

(3) If a transaction aborts, no other transactions will be forced to abort as a consequence. *Cascading aborts* are not permitted.

(4) If several transactions execute concurrently, they affect the database as if they were executed serially in some order. This property is usually called *serializability*.

Transactions lessen the burden on application programmers by simplifying the treatment of failures and concurrency. Failure atomicity makes certain that when a transaction is interrupted by a failure, its partial results are undone. Programmers are therefore free to violate consistency constraints temporarily during the execution of a transaction. Serializability ensures that other concurrently executing transactions cannot observe these inconsistencies. Permanence and prevention of cascading aborts limit the amount of effort required to recover from a failure. Transaction models that do not prohibit cascading aborts are possible, but we do not consider them.

Our model for using transactions in distributed systems differs from this traditional model in several ways. The most important difference is that we incorporate the concept of an *abstract data type*. That is, information is stored in typed *objects* and manipulated only by *operations* that are specific to a particular object type. The users of a type are given a *specification* that describes the effect of each operation on the stored data, and new abstract types can be implemented using existing ones. The details of how objects are represented and how the operations are carried out are known only to a type's implementor. Abstract data types grew out of the *class* construct in Simula [4] and are supported in many other programming languages including CLU [16], Alphard [29], and Ada [5], as well as in operating systems, e.g., Hydra [28]. In our system model, transactions are composed of operations on objects that are instances of abstract types. Of particular interest are those objects that are not local to a single transaction. These are instances of *shared abstract types*.

We assume that the facilities for implementing shared abstract types and for coordinating the execution of transactions that operate on them are provided by a basic system layer that executes at each node of the system. This *transaction kernel* exports primitives for synchronization, recovery, deadlock management, and intersite communication. In some ways, a transaction kernel is similar to the RSS of System R [10]. A transaction kernel, however, is intended to run on a bare machine and must supply primitives useful for implementing arbitrary data types, whereas the RSS has the assistance of an underlying operating system and only provides specialized primitives tailored for manipulating a database.

Another difference between our system model and the traditional transaction model is that we do not necessarily require that transactions appear to execute serially. Serializability ensures that if transactions work correctly in the absence of concurrency, any interleaving of their operations that is allowed by the system will not affect their correctness. Sometimes, however, serializability is too strong a property, and requiring it restricts concurrency unnecessarily. For example, it is usually unnecessary for two letters mailed together and addressed identically to appear in their recipient's mailbox together. However, serializability is violated if the letters do not arrive contiguously, because there is no longer the appearance that the sender has executed without interference from other senders. Thus it may be desirable for some shared abstract types to allow limited nonserializable execution of transactions. This idea has also been investigated by Garcia-Molina [7] and Sha et al. [25].

Serializability guarantees that an ordering can be defined on a group of transactions. If the transactions share some common objects, serializability requires that these objects be visited in the same order by all the transactions in the group. In Section 3, a more general ordering property of transactions is defined, of which serializability is a special case. We show that it is possible to prove that transactions work correctly in the presence of concurrency, even if they do not appear to execute serially.

In order to maintain the special properties of transactions in our model, the operations on shared abstract types that compose them must meet certain requirements. To guarantee the failure atomicity of transactions, it must be possible to undo any operation upon transaction abort. Therefore, an *undo operation* must be provided for each operation on a shared abstract type. Recovery is not the main concern of this paper, and we consider undo operations only as they pertain to synchronization issues. Further discussion of recovery issues can be found in a related paper [24].

Operations on shared abstract types must also meet three synchronization requirements:

(1) Operations must be protected from anomalies that could be caused by other concurrently executing operations on the same object. Freedom from these concurrency anomalies ensures that an invocation of an operation on a shared object is not affected by other concurrent operation invocations. This is the same property that monitors provide [11].

(2) To preclude the possibility of cascading aborts, operations on shared objects must not be able to observe information that might change if an uncommitted transaction were to abort. This may necessitate delaying the execution of operations on behalf of some transactions until other transactions complete, either successfully or unsuccessfully.

(3) When a group of transactions invokes operations on shared objects, the operations may only be interleaved in ways that preserve serializability or some weaker ordering property of the group of transactions. The synchronization needed to control interleaving cannot be localized to individual shared objects, but rather requires cooperation among all the objects shared by the transactions.

Traditional methods for synchronizing access to an instance of a shared abstract type are designed solely to ensure the first goal: correctness of individual operations on an object. This paper is concerned with the second and third goals. We examine the problem of specifying the synchronization needed to achieve them, as well as the support facilities that the transaction kernel must provide to implementors of shared abstract types.

3. DEPENDENCIES: A TOOL FOR REASONING ABOUT CONCURRENT TRANSACTIONS

This section introduces a theory that can be used to reason about the behavior of concurrent transactions. It allows the standard definition of serializability to be recast in terms of shared abstract types and provides a convenient way of expressing other ordering properties. The theory is also useful in understanding cascading aborts.

3.1 Schedules

Schedules [6, 8] can be used to model the behavior of a group of concurrent transactions. Informally, a schedule is a sequence of ⟨transaction, operation⟩ pairs that represent the order in which the component operations of concurrent transactions are interleaved. Schedules are also known as *histories* [21] and *logs* [2]. In some of the traditional database literature, the operations in schedules are assumed to be arbitrary; no semantic knowledge about them is available [6]. In this case, a schedule is merely an ordered list of transactions and the objects they touch:

$T_1: O_1$
$T_2: O_1$
$T_2: O_2$
$T_1: O_2$

In other work, operations are characterized as Read (R) or Write (W) [8], in which case the schedule includes that semantic information:

$T_1: R(O_1)$
$T_2: R(O_1)$
$T_2: W(O_2)$
$T_1: R(O_2)$

To analyze transactions that contain operations on specific shared abstract types, we consider schedules in which these operations are characterized explicitly. For example, a schedule may contain operations to enter an element on a queue or to insert an entry into a directory. We call these *abstract schedules*, because they describe the order in which operations affect objects, regardless of any reordering that might be done by their implementation.[1] Given the initial state of a set of objects, an abstract schedule of operations on these objects, and specifications for the operations in the schedule, the result of each operation and the final state of the objects can be deduced. For instance, consider the following abstract schedule, which is composed of operations on Q, a shared object of type FIFO Queue. The operations **QEnter** and **QRemove**, respectively, append an

element to the tail of a FIFO Queue and remove one from it's head. Assume Q to be empty initially.

$T_1: \texttt{QEnter(Q, X)}$
$T_2: \texttt{QEnter(Q, Y)}$
$T_3: \texttt{QRemove(Q)}$

From this abstract schedule and the initial contents of the Queue, one can deduce the state of Q at any point in the schedule. Thus one may conclude that the **QRemove** operation returns X, and that only Y remains on the Queue at the end of the schedule.

3.2 Dependencies and Consistency

By examining an abstract schedule, it is possible to determine what *dependencies* exist among the transactions in the schedule. The notation $D: T_i;X \rightarrow_O T_j;Y$ is used to represent the dependency D formed when transaction T_i performs operation X and transaction T_j subsequently performs operation Y on some common object O. The object, transaction, or dependency identifiers may be omitted when they are unimportant. The set of ordered pairs $\{\langle T_i, T_j \rangle\}$ for which there exist X, Y, and O such that $D: T_i;X \rightarrow_O T_j;Y$ forms a relation, denoted $<_D$. If $T_i <_D T_j$, T_i *precedes* T_j and T_j *depends* on T_i under the dependency D.

Examples of dependencies and their corresponding relations can be drawn from traditional database systems. For instance, consider a system in which no semantic knowledge, either about entire transactions or about their component operations, is available to the concurrency control mechanism. The only requirement is that each individual transaction be correct in itself: it must transform a consistent initial state of the database to a consistent final state. Under these conditions, only serializable abstract schedules can be guaranteed to preserve the correctness of individual transactions.

Since all operations are indistinguishable, only one possible dependency D can be defined: $T_1 <_D T_2$ if T_1 performs any operation on an object later operated on by T_2. Now, consider $<_D^*$, the transitive closure of $<_D$. A schedule is *orderable* with respect to $\{<_D\}$ iff $<_D^*$ is a partial order. In other words, there are no cycles of the form $T_1 <_D T_2 <_D \cdots <_D T_n <_D T_1$. In general, a schedule is orderable with respect to S, where S is a set of dependency relations, iff each of the relations in S have a transitive closure that is a partial order. The relations in S are referred to as *proscribed* relations, and we use orderability with respect to a set of proscribed dependency relations to describe ordering properties of groups of transactions. Abstract schedules that are orderable with respect to a specified set of proscribed relations are called *consistent* abstract schedules.

It can be shown that orderability with respect to $\{<_D\}$ is equivalent to serializability [6]. Given a schedule orderable with respect to $\{<_D\}$, a transaction T, and the set O of objects to which T refers, every other transaction that refers to an object in O can unambiguously be said either to precede T or to follow T. Thus T depends on a well-defined set of transactions that precede it, and a well-defined set of transactions depend on T. Each transaction sees the consistent database state left by those transactions that precede it and (by assumption) leaves a consistent state for those that follow. The set of schedules for which

---

[1] In Section 4.4 we define a second kind of schedule, the *invocation schedule*, which reflects the concurrency of specific implementations.

$<_t$ is a partial order constitutes the set of consistent abstract schedules for a system that employs no semantic knowledge.

The scheme described above prevents cycles in the most general possible dependency relation; hence it maximally restricts concurrency. By considering the semantics of operations on objects, it is possible to identify some dependency relations for which cycles may be allowed to form. For example, consider a database with a Read/Write concurrency control. Such systems recognize two types of operations on objects: Read (R) and Write (W). Thus there are four possible dependencies between a pair of transactions that access a common object:

D_1: $T_i;R \to_O T_j;R$. T_i reads an object subsequently read by T_j.
D_2: $T_i;R \to_O T_j;W$. T_i reads an object subsequently modified by T_j.
D_3: $T_i;W \to_O T_j;R$. T_i modifies an object subsequently read by T_j.
D_4: $T_i;W \to_O T_j;W$. T_i modifies an object subsequently modified by T_j.

The earlier scheme, by not distinguishing between these dependencies, prevents cycles from forming in the dependency relation $<_D$, which is the union of all four individual relations. By contrast, Read/Write concurrency controls taken into account the fact that $R \to R$ dependencies cannot influence system behavior. That is, given a pair of transactions, T_1 and T_2, and an abstract schedule in which both T_1 and T_2 perform a Read on a shared object, the semantics of Read operations ensure that neither T_1, T_2, nor any other transaction in the schedule can determine whether $T_1 <_{D_1} T_2$ or $T_2 <_{D_1} T_1$. Since these dependencies cannot be observed, they cannot compromise serializability, nor can they affect the outcome of transactions. We call dependencies meeting this criterion *insignificant*. Korth has also noted that when operations are commutative, their ordering does not affect serializability [12].

For the Read/Write case, the necessary condition for serializability can be restated as follows in terms of dependency relations: a schedule is serializable if it is orderable with respect to $\{<_{D_2 \cup D_3 \cup D_4}\}$ [8]. By allowing multiple readers, Read/Write schemes permit the formation of cycles in the $<_{D_1}$ dependency relation, and in relations that include $<_{D_1}$, while preventing cycles in the relation that is the union of $<_{D_2}$, $<_{D_3}$, and $<_{D_4}$. For example, consider the following schedules, which have identical effects on the system state:

```
T₁: R(O₁)     T₂: R(O₁)
T₂: R(O₁)     T₁: R(O₁)
T₁: W(O₁)     T₁: W(O₁)
```

In the first schedule, $T <_{D_1} T_2$ and $T_2 <_{D_2} T_1$. Hence there is a cycle in the relation $<_{D_1 \cup D_2}$, although $<_{D_2 \cup D_3 \cup D_4}$ is cycle free. In the second schedule, the first two steps are reversed and neither cycle is present.

On the other hand, the following two schedules are not necessarily identical in effect:

```
T₁: R(O₁)     T₂: W(O₁)
T₂: W(O₁)     T₁: R(O₁)
T₁: W(O₁)     T₁: W(O₁)
```

In this case, the first schedule is not serializable because $T_1 <_{D_1} T_2$ and $T_2 <_{D_4} T_1$, thus forming a cycle in the relation $<_{D_2 \cup D_4}$, which is a subrelation of $<_{D_2 \cup D_3 \cup D_4}$. T_1 observes O_1 before it is written by T_2, but the final state of O_1 reflects the Write of T_1 rather than T_2, implying that T_1 ran after T_2. The second schedule has no cycle and is serializable.

In summary, orderability with respect to a set of proscribed dependency relations provides a precise way to characterize consistent schedules. For a concurrency control that enforces serializability with no semantic knowledge at all about operations, the set of proscribed relations must contain $<_D$, which is equivalent to the union of every possible dependency relation. For a Read/Write database scheme, the set contains the $<_{R \to W \cup W \to R \cup W \to W}$ relation. When type-specific semantics are considered, type-specific dependency relations can be defined for each type. In Section 4, dependencies are used to define *interleaving specifications* for various abstract types. These specifications provide the information needed to determine how an individual type can contribute toward maintaining a global ordering property such as serializability. If a specification guarantees orderability with respect to the union of all significant dependency relations for a given type, then it is strong enough to permit serializability. In general, however, more concurrency can be obtained when only weaker ordering properties are guaranteed. The way in which the interleaving specifications of multiple types interact to preserve global ordering properties is discussed in Section 5.

3.3 Dependencies and Cascading Aborts

Dependencies are also useful in understanding cascading aborts. A cascading abort is possible when a dependency forms between two transactions, the first of which is uncommitted. An abort by this uncommitted transaction may cascade to those that depend on it. Whether or not a cascade actually must occur depends on the exact type of dependency involved and the properties of the object being acted upon. For example, consider the four general dependency relations that arise in Read/Write database systems. $R \to R$ dependencies are insignificant and can never cause cascading aborts. This is analogous to the role of the dependencies in determining orderability. Likewise, $R \to W$ and $W \to W$ dependencies need not cause cascading aborts, because in both cases the outcome of the second transaction does not depend on data modified by the first.[2] By contrast, $W \to R$ dependencies represent a transfer of information between the two transactions. In the absence of any additional semantic information, it must be assumed that an abort of the first transaction will affect the outcome of the second, which must therefore also be aborted.

Once the dependencies that could lead to cascading aborts have been identified, their formation must be controlled. Stated in terms of abstract schedules: starting from the first of the two operations that form the dependency, there must be no overlapping of the two transactions in the schedule, with the prior transaction

---

[2] It may be necessary to control the formation of these dependencies if an insufficiently flexible recovery strategy is used.

in the dependency relation completing first. Such schedules are called *cascade free*. Note that some consistent schedules may not be cascade free, and vice versa.

4. SPECIFICATION OF SHARED ABSTRACT TYPES

This section focuses on the typed operations that make up transactions and discusses how to specify their local synchronization properties. The traditional specification of an abstract type describes the behavior of the type's operations in terms of preconditions, postconditions, and an invariant. This specification must be augmented in several ways to complete the description of a shared abstract type in our model. In the first place, the undo operation corresponding to each regular operation must be specified in terms of preconditions, postconditions, and the invariant. Specification of the undo operations themselves is not considered further in this paper. It is important to note, however, that the set of consistent abstract schedules defined by the interleaving specification for a type also implicitly includes schedules in which undo operations are inserted at all possible points after an operation has been performed but prior to the end of the invoking transaction. This reflects the assumption that it must be possible to undo any operation prior to transaction commitment. As is shown in Section 4.3, this is especially important for types that do not attempt to enforce serializability of transactions.

The specification of a shared abstract type must also include a description of how operations on behalf of multiple transactions can be interleaved. This *interleaving specification* can be used by application programmers to describe their needs to prospective type implementors or to evaluate the suitability of existing types for their applications. The specification of a shared abstract type must also list those dependencies that will be controlled to prevent cascading aborts. This part of the specification is used mainly by the type's implementor.

When specifying how operations on a shared object may interact, the amount of concurrency that can be permitted depends in part on how much detailed knowledge is available concerning the semantics of the operations [13]. We have shown how concurrency controls that distinguish those operations that only observe the state of an object ("Reads") from those that modify it ("Writes") can achieve greater concurrency than protocols not making this distinction. To increase concurrency further while still providing serializability, one can take advantage of more semantic knowledge about the operations being performed [12]. Section 4.1 illustrates how this is done in specifying Directories, using the concepts and notation of Section 3.

When enough concurrency cannot be obtained even after fully exploiting the semantics of the operations on a type, it is necessary to dispense with serializability and substitute orderability with respect to some weaker set of proscribed dependency relations. Sections 4.2 and 4.3 illustrate this by comparing a serializable Queue type with a variation that preserves a weaker ordering property.

Finally, Section 4.4 discusses how implementations may reorder operations to obtain even more concurrency and the steps that type implementors must take to demonstrate the correctness of an implementation.

4.1 Directories

As a first example, consider a Directory data type that is intended to provide a mapping between text strings and capabilities for arbitrary objects. The usual operations are provided:

DirInsert(dir, str, capa) inserts **capa** into Directory **dir** with key string **str** and returns **ok** or **duplicate key**. The undo operation for **DirInsert** removes the inserted entry if the insertion was successful.

DirDelete(dir, str) deletes the capability stored with key string **str** from **dir** and returns **ok** or **not found**. The undo operation for **DirDelete** restores the deleted capability if the deletion was successful.

DirLookup(dir, str) searches for a capability in **dir** with key string **str** and returns the capability **capa** or **not found**. The undo operation is null, because **DirLookup** does not modify the Directory.

DirDump(dir) returns a vector of ⟨**str, capa**⟩ pairs with the complete contents of the Directory **dir**. The undo operation for **DirDump** is null.

Suppose one wishes to specify the Directory type so as to permit serialization of transactions that include operations on Directories. One approach would be to model each **DirInsert** or **DirDelete** operation as a Read operation followed by a Write operation and to model each **DirLookup** or **DirDump** operation as a Read operation. The Directory type could then be specified using the Read/Write dependency relations discussed previously.

The difficulty with using such limited semantic information is that concurrency is restricted unnecessarily. For example, suppose Directories have been implemented using a standard two-phase Read/Write locking mechanism. Consider the operation **DirLookup(dir, "Foo")**, which will be blocked trying to obtain a Read lock if another transaction has performed **DirDelete(dir, "Fum")** and holds a Write lock on the Directory object. The outcome of **DirLookup(dir, "Foo")** does not depend in any way on the eventual outcome of **DirDelete(dir, "Fum")** (which may later be aborted), or vice versa, so this blocking is unnecessary. Because **DirDelete(dir, "Fum")** may be part of an arbitrarily long transaction, the Write lock may be held for a long time and severely degrade performance.

The unnecessary loss of concurrency in this example is not the fault of this particular implementation. It is caused by the lack of semantic information in the Directory specification. By using more knowledge about the operations, this problem can be alleviated. Instead of expressing the interleaving specification for this type in terms of Read and Write operations, the type-specific Directory operations can be employed to define dependencies and the interleaving specifications can be expressed in terms of these type-specific dependencies.

To keep the number of dependencies to a minimum, the operations for the Directory data type will be divided into three groups:

(1) *Those that modify a particular entry in the Directory.* **DirInsert** and **DirDelete** operations that succeed are in this class. These are Modify (M) operations.

(2) *Those that observe the presence, absence, or contents of a particular entry in the Directory.* **DirLookup** is in this class, as are **DirInsert** and **DirDelete** operations that fail. These are Lookup (L) operations.

(3) *Those that observe properties of the Directory that cannot be isolated to an individual entry.* **DirDump** is the only operation in this class that we have defined: an operation that returned the number of entries in the Directory would also be in this class. These are Dump (D) operations.

Note that in some cases operations that fail are distinguished from those that succeed. In addition to the operations and their outcomes, the dependencies also taken into account data supplied to the operations as arguments or otherwise specific to the particular object acted upon. In the following list of dependencies, the symbols σ and σ' represent distinct key string arguments to Directory operations.

The complete set of dependencies for this type is

D_1: T_i:$M(\sigma) \rightarrow T_j$:$M(\sigma')$. T_i modifies an entry with key string σ, and T_j subsequently modifies an entry with a different key string, σ'.

D_2: T_i:$M(\sigma) \rightarrow T_j$:$M(\sigma)$. T_i modifies an entry with key string σ, and T_j subsequently modifies the same entry.

D_3: T_i:$M(\sigma) \rightarrow T_j$:$L(\sigma')$. T_i modifies an entry with key string σ, and T_j subsequently observes an entry with a different key string, σ'.

D_4: T_i:$M(\sigma) \rightarrow T_j$:$L(\sigma)$. T_i modifies an entry with key string σ, and T_j subsequently observes the same entry.

D_5: T_i:$L(\sigma) \rightarrow T_j$:$L(\sigma')$. T_i observes an entry with key string σ, and T_j subsequently observes an entry with a different key string σ'.

D_6: T_i:$L(\sigma) \rightarrow T_j$:$L(\sigma)$. T_i observes an entry with key string σ, and T_j subsequently observes the same entry.

D_7: T_i:$L(\sigma) \rightarrow T_j$:$M(\sigma')$. T_i observes an entry with key string σ, and T_j subsequently modifies an entry with a different key string σ'.

D_8: T_i:$L(\sigma) \rightarrow T_j$:$M(\sigma)$. T_i observes an entry with key string σ, and T_j subsequently modifies the same entry.

D_9: T_i:$D \rightarrow T_j$:$M(\sigma)$. T_i dumps the entire contents of the Directory, and T_j subsequently modifies an entry with key string σ.

D_{10}: T_i:$D \rightarrow T_j$:$L(\sigma)$. T_i dumps the entire contents of the Directory, and T_j subsequently observes an entry with key string σ.

D_{11}: T_i:$M(\sigma) \rightarrow T_j$:$D$. T_i modifies an entry with key string σ, and T_j subsequently dumps the entire contents of the Directory.

D_{12}: T_i:$L(\sigma) \rightarrow T_j$:$D$. T_i observes an entry with key string σ, and T_j subsequently dumps the entire contents of the Directory.

D_{13}: T_i:$D \rightarrow T_j$:D. T_i dumps the entire contents of the Directory, and T_j subsequently dumps the Directory as well.

This list is long, but it is actually quite simple to derive. There is a family of dependencies for each pair of operation classes. The key to defining the specific dependencies is the observation that when two operations refer to different strings, the relationship between the transactions that invoked them is not the same as when they refer to identical strings. Those families of dependencies for

which both operation classes take a string argument therefore have two members, corresponding to these two cases. The families for which one of the operation classes is Dump have only a single member. In general, insight into the semantics of a type is needed to define the set of possible dependencies.

Like the R → R dependency, many of the Directory dependencies are insignificant and cannot affect the outcome of transactions. Hence they may be excluded from the set of proscribed dependencies for this type. The dependencies that may be disregarded are those for which neither operation in the dependency modifies the Directory object: D_6, D_{10}, D_{12}, and D_{13}—these are directly analogous to the R → R dependency; and those for which the two operations in the dependency refer to different key strings: D_1, D_3, D_5, and D_7.

In terms of the remaining dependencies, the interleaving specification for Directories states that an abstract schedule involving Directories is consistent if it is orderable with respect to $\{<_{D_2} \cup_{D_4} \cup_{D_8} \cup_{D_9} \cup_{D_{11}}\}$. The abstract Directory thus defined behaves like a collection of associatively addressed elements, with serializability preservable independently for each element. Transactions containing operations that apply to the entire Directory, such as **DirDump**, may also be serialized, as may those that refer to multiple elements or elements that are not present.

Only two of the Directory dependencies have the potential to cause cascading aborts. These are D_4 and D_{11}. In both cases, the first operation in the dependency modifies an entry and the second operation observes that modification.

4.2 FIFO Queues

Similar specifications can be developed for other data types. The FIFO Queue provides an interesting example. We consider only two operations:

QEnter(queue, capa) adds an entry containing the pointer **capa** to the end of **queue**. The undo operation for **QEnter** removes this entry.

QRemove(queue) removes the entry at the head of **queue** and returns the pointer **capa** contained therein. If **queue** is empty, the operation is blocked and waits until **queue** becomes nonempty. The undo operation for **QRemove** restores the entry to the head of **queue**.

In order to permit serialization of transactions that contain operations on strict FIFO Queues and to prevent cascading aborts, numerous properties must be guaranteed. For instance,

—if a transaction adds several entries to a Queue, these entries must appear together and in the same order at the head of the Queue;

—any entries added to a Queue by a transaction may not be observed by another transaction unless the first transaction terminates successfully;

—if two transactions each make entries in two Queues, the relative ordering of the entries made by the two transactions must be the same in both Queues.

It is very easy to destroy these properties if unrestricted interleaving of operations is allowed. For instance, if **QEnter** operations from different transactions are interleaved, the entries made by each transaction will not appear in a block at the head of the Queue.

In defining the dependencies for the Queue type, it is necessary, as it was in the case of Directories, to distinguish individual elements in the Queue. It is assumed that each element is assigned a unique identifier[3] when it is entered on the Queue. The symbols σ and σ' are used to represent the distinct identifiers of different elements, and the **QEnter** and **QRemove** operations are abbreviated as E and R, respectively. The complete set of dependencies for Queues is

D_1: T_i:$E(\sigma) \rightarrow_Q T_j$:$E(\sigma')$. T_j enters an element σ' into the queue Q after T_i has previously entered an element σ.
D_2: T_i:$E(\sigma) \rightarrow_Q T_j$:$R(\sigma')$. T_j removes element σ' after T_i entered element σ.
D_3: T_i:$E(\sigma) \rightarrow_Q T_j$:$R(\sigma)$. T_j removes the element σ that was entered by T_i.
D_4: T_i:$R(\sigma) \rightarrow_Q T_j$:$E(\sigma')$. T_j enters element σ' after T_i removed element σ.
D_5: T_i:$R(\sigma) \rightarrow_Q T_j$:$R(\sigma')$. T_j removed element σ' after T_i removed element σ.

In a Read/Write synchronization scheme, **QEnter** must be modeled as a Write operation, and **QRemove** must be modeled as a Read followed by a Write. Recall that such a scheme must prevent cycles in the $<_{R \rightarrow W} \cup_W \rightarrow_R \cup_W \rightarrow_W$ dependency relation. In this case, preventing cycles in this general dependency relation is unnecessarily restrictive. Consider dependency D_2, which is formed when a transaction removes a Queue element after another transaction has previously entered a different Queue element. Neither of the transactions performing the operations can detect their ordering, nor can a third transaction. The same applies to dependency D_4, which is the inverse of D_2. As was the case for Directories, concurrency can be increased by disregarding insignificant dependencies.

To provide a strictly FIFO Queue, one must guarantee that abstract schedules are orderable with respect to the compound $<_{D_1 \cup D_3 \cup D_5}$ relation, but cycles may be permitted to form in relations that include D_2 or D_4 as long as this property is not violated. For example, consider the following schedule, in which two transactions operate on a Queue that initially contains |A, B|:

```
T_1:  QEnter(Q, X)
T_2:  QRemove(Q) returns A
T_i:  Qenter(Q, Y)
```

At step 2 of this schedule, a D_2 dependency is formed; hence $T_1 <_{D_2} T_2$. At step 3, however, a D_4 dependency is formed with $T_2 <_{D_4} T_1$. Clearly a cycle exists in the compound relation $<_{D_2 \cup D_4}$. It is easy to create other examples of consistent abstract schedules that demonstrate a cycle in the basic $<_{D_2}$ (or $<_{D_4}$) relation, or in a compound relation formed from D_2 or D_4) together with D_1, D_3, and D_5.

The dependency relations can also be used to characterize schedules susceptible to cascading abort. Dependency relation $<_{D_1}$ is similar to the $W \rightarrow W$ dependency. Since entries made by an aborted transaction can be transparently removed from the Queue, there is no danger of cascading abort. Relations $<_{D_3}$ and $<_{D_5}$ are more similar to $W \rightarrow R$ dependencies. In a D_3 dependency, information is transferred between the transactions in the form of the queue element σ; this dependency

clearly can cause cascading aborts. A D_5 dependency can also cause cascading aborts, because the removal of an element by the first transaction affects which element is received by the second transaction.

While this definition of consistency for Queues is an improvement over a Read/Write scheme, it is still very restrictive of concurrency. It allows, at most, two transactions to access a Queue concurrently, one performing **QEnter** operations and one performing **QRemove** operations. Unlike the Directory, the Queue is intended to preserve a particular ordering of the elements contained in it. A system based on serializable transactions guarantees that transactions can be placed in some order; by enforcing a particular order, data types such as queues (and stacks) restrict concurrency.

4.3 Queues Allowing Greater Concurrency

The preceding examples show how the use of semantic knowledge about operations on a shared abstract type permits increased concurrency. Once such knowledge is incorporated, the limiting factor in permitting concurrency becomes knowledge about the consistency constraints that the operations in a transaction attempt to maintain [13]. This knowledge concerns the semantics of groups of operations rather than individual ones. For example, a consistency constraint might state that every Queue entry of type A is immediately followed by one of type B. The potential for such constraints was the cause of the concurrency limitations observed above.

If it is possible to restrict the consistency constraints that a programmer is free to require, types guaranteeing ordering properties weaker than serializability may be acceptable. This may permit further increases in concurrency. A variation of the queue type can be used to demonstrate this.

One of the most common uses for a queue is to provide a buffer between activities that produce and consume work. Frequently, the exact ordering of entries on the queue is not important. What is crucial is that entries put on the rear of the queue do not languish in the queue forever; they should reach the head of the queue "fairly" with respect to other entries made at about the same time. A data type having this nonstarvation property can be defined: the *Weakly FIFO Queue* (WQueue for short). A similar type, the *Semi-Queue*, has been defined by Weihl [27].

The operations on WQueues and their corresponding undo operations are similar to those for Queues, but the interleaving specification for WQueues allows more concurrency. The dependencies for the WQueue type are the same as for the strict Queue. However, where the strict Queue required that consistent abstract schedules be orderable with respect to $\{<_{D_1} \cup_{D_3} \cup_{D_5}\}$, the WQueue permits cycles to occur in all the dependency relations save one: $<_{D_3}$. By allowing cycles in $<_{D_1}$, the interleaving of entries by multiple transactions becomes possible. Similarly, removing D_5 from the set of proscribed dependency relations permits **WQRemove** operations to be interleaved.

To take full advantage of the greater concurrency allowed by this interleaving specification, the semantics of **WQRemove** differ slightly from those of **QRemove**. If the transaction that inserted the headmost entry in the queue has not committed, that entry cannot be removed without risking the possibility of a

---

[3]The identifier need not be globally unique, just unique among those generated for the particular Queue object.

cascading abort. Instead, **WQRemove** scans the WQueue and removes the headmost entry for which the inserting transaction has committed. If no such element can be found, any elements inserted by the transaction doing the **WQRemove** become eligible for removal. If neither a committed entry nor one inserted by the same transaction is available, the operation is blocked until an inserting transaction commits.

Modifying the semantics of **WQRemove** in this way does not destroy the fairness properties of the WQueue. No entry will remain in the WQueue forever if

(1) the transaction that entered it commits in a finite amount of time;
(2) transactions that remove it terminate after a finite amount of time;
(3) only a finite number of transactions remove the entry and then abort.

The behavior of the WQueue is best illustrated by example. In what follows, a WQueue is represented by a sequence of letters, with the left end of the sequence being the head of the WQueue. Lowercase italic letters (a) are used to denote entries for which the **WQEnter** operation has not committed (i.e., the transaction that performed **WQEnter** is incomplete). Uppercase bold letters (**A**) are used to represent entries that have not been removed and for which the entering transaction has committed. Uppercase italic letters are used for entries that have been removed by an uncommitted **WQRemove**. Superscripts on entries identify the transaction that performed the operation.

Assume that the WQueue is initially empty. If transaction T_1 and T_2 perform **WQEnter(WQ, a)** and **WQEnter(WQ, b)** respectively, the WQueue's state becomes

$$\{a^1, b^2\}.$$

Since cycles in $<_{D_i}$ are permitted, T_1 may also add another entry, yielding

$$\{a^1, b^2, c^1\}.$$

If T_1 and T_2 both commit, the state becomes

$$\{\mathbf{A}, \mathbf{B}, \mathbf{C}\}.$$

Note that the serializability of T_1 and T_2 has *not* been preserved. Now suppose that T_3 performs **WQRemove** and another transaction T_4 removes two more elements:

$$\{A^3, B^4, C^4\}.$$

If T_3 now aborts and T_4 commits, the final state becomes

$$\{\mathbf{A}\}.$$

In this case, A and C have effectively been reversed, even though they were inserted initially by the same transaction! This example illustrates an important difference between shared abstract types that attempt to preserve serializability and those that do not: when a type permits nonserial execution of transactions, invoking an operation and subsequently aborting it is not necessarily equivalent to not invoking the operation at all. While we do not explicitly consider the undo operations in defining dependencies or interleaving specifications, the underlying assumption that aborts can occur at any time prior to commit implies that undo operations can be inserted at any point in a schedule between the invocation of an operation and the time at which the invoking transaction commits.

Another example indicates what happens when an uncommitted entry reaches the head of the Queue. Suppose the initial state is

$$\{a^5, b^6\}.$$

If T_6 commits but T_5 remains incomplete, the state becomes

$$\{a^5, \mathbf{B}\}.$$

If T_7 removes an element at this time, B will re returned, leaving

$$\{a^5\}$$

after T_7 commits. On the other hand, if T_5 commits after T_6, but before the remove by T_7, A will be returned even though its insertion was committed after B's.

To summarize the comparison between the WQueue and the ordinary Queue, note that two properties of the regular Queue have been sacrificed. First, strict FIFO ordering of entries is not guaranteed, because aborting **WQRemove** operations can reorder them. Second, transactions that operate on WQueues are not necessarily serializable with respect to all transactions in the system. Some other crucial properties, however, are preserved. The WQueue will not starve any entry, and it enforces an ordering of those transactions that communicate through access to a common element of the queue. This is ensured by orderability with respect to $\{<_{D_i}\}$. These modifications greatly increase concurrency, while still providing a data type that is useful in many situations.

4.4 Proving the Correctness of Type Implementations

Whereas the user of a type may employ the specified properties of abstract schedules (along with the rest of the type's specification) to reason about the correctness of transactions, the implementor of a type must prove the correctness of an implementation given the order in which operations are actually invoked. Real implementations may reorder the operations on an object to improve concurrency without changing the type's interleaving specification. Consider an implementation of the Queue type in which elements to be entered by a transaction are first collected in a transaction-local cache and entered as a block at end-of-transaction. This implementation allows any number of transactions to invoke the **QEnter** operation simultaneously, provided care is taken to serialize correctly transactions involving multiple Queues. By actually performing the insertions as a block, this implementation effectively reorders the individual **QEnter** operations to preserve consistency. It is possible to reorder **QEnter** operations in this way because **QEnter** does not return any information to its caller. Formation of any dependencies that might result from its invocation can therefore be postponed. The ultimate ordering of operations in the abstract schedule is determined by the implementation once all the **QEnter** operations to be performed by a given transaction are known. Thus this implementation has the benefit of more knowledge about transactions than has the standard implementation.

Invocation schedules list operations in the order in which they are actually invoked, rather than in order of their abstract effects.[4] For example, the following is a possible invocation schedule for a **Queue** implemented using the block-insertion technique described above:

```
T₂: QEnter(Q, Y)
T₁: QEnter(Q, X)
T₃: QRemove(Q)
```

If T_1 commits before T_2, the implementation reorders the two **QEnter** operations, resulting in the abstract schedule:

```
T₁: QEnter(Q, X)
T₂: QEnter(Q, Y)
T₃: QRemove(Q)
```

The mapping between invocation schedules and abstract schedules is many-one; each invocation schedule implements exactly one abstract schedule, but an abstract schedule may be implemented by multiple invocation schedules. The synchronization mechanism used by an implementation determines a set of invocation schedules, called *legal schedules*, that are permitted by the implementation. The implementor must show that all legal invocation schedules map to consistent abstract schedules. To prevent cascading aborts as well, implementors must use a synchronization strategy that restricts the set of legal invocation schedules to those that map to abstract schedules that are in the intersection of the consistent and cascade free sets.

5. ORDERABILITY OF GROUPS OF TRANSACTIONS

The preceding section described how the standard specification of an abstract type, which only seeks to characterize the type's invariants and the postconditions for its operations, can be augmented with an interleaving specification that describes the local synchronization properties of objects. In this section, we broaden our focus from the properties of the typed objects that are manipulated by transactions to the properties of entire transactions. We first examine how to generalize the definition of consistent abstract schedules to schedules that include operations on more than one object type, and then we consider how ordering properties of groups of transactions can be used to show their correctness.

5.1 How the Specifications of Multiple Types Interact

Guaranteeing orderability with respect to the proscribed relations of a collection of individual types is not sufficient to ensure global ordering properties of transactions, such as serializability. Consider the following schedule, which contains transactions that operate both on Queues and Directories. Each of these types preserves orderability with respect to the union of all significant depend-

encies for the individual type, in order that transactions involving the type may potentially be serialized. However, this property alone does not guarantee serializability of the transactions. For example, the following schedule is not serializable:

```
T₁: QEnter(Q, X)
T₂: QEnter(Q, Y)
T₂: DirInsert(D, ''A'', Z)
T₁: DirDelete(D, ''A'')
```

Let $<_{Dir}$ stand for the $<_{D_1 \cup D_2 \cup D_8 \cup D_9 \cup D_{11}}$ relation, defined earlier for type Directory. Let $<_Q$ stand for the $<_{D_1 \cup D_2 \cup D_3}$ relation, defined earlier for Queues. Although the schedule is orderable with respect to $\{<_{Dir}, <_Q\}$, it is not serializable. To achieve serializability, the Queue and Directory types must cooperate to prevent cycles in the relation $<_{Dir \cup Q}$. The schedule is not orderable with respect to this compound dependency.

This example indicates how to generalize the definition of consistency to apply to abstract schedules containing operations on multiple types. Assume the interleaving specification for type Y_1 guarantees orderability with respect to $\{<_{D_1}\}$, the interleaving specification for type Y_2 guarantees orderability with respect to $\{<_{D_2}\}$, etc. The set of consistent abstract schedules involving types Y_1, $Y_2, \ldots Y_n$ is defined as those abstract schedules that are orderable with respect to $\{<_{D_1 \cup D_2 \cup \ldots \cup D_n}\}$: the union of the proscribed dependency relations of the individual types. A set of types whose implementations satisfy this property is called a set of *cooperative types*.

The need for cooperation among types does not necessarily imply that whenever a system is extended by the definition of a new type, the synchronization requirements of all existing types must be rethought. When designing a system, however, the implementors of cooperative types must first agree on a synchronization mechanism that is sufficiently flexible and powerful to meet all of their requirements. A poor choice of mechanism for fundamental building block types will have an adverse effect on the entire system. Section 6 describes a mechanism based on locking that permits highly concurrent implementations of a large variety of shared abstract types.

5.2 Correctness of Transactions

When all of the types involved in a group of transactions cooperate to preserve an ordering property equivalent to serializability, it is easy to show that the correctness of transactions is not affected by concurrency. Because transactions are completely isolated from one another, a transaction can be proven correct solely on the basis of its own code and the assumption that the system state is correct when the transaction is initiated.

It is much more difficult to prove the correctness of transactions when they include operations on types that permit nonserializable interaction among transactions. One must consider the possible effects of interleaving each transaction with any other transaction, subject to the constraints of whatever ordering property is guaranteed by the collection of types. Nevertheless, in many practical situations, this task should not be insurmountable. We give two examples of situations where it is possible to make useful inferences about the behavior of

---

[4] It is assumed that the actual concurrent execution of the transactions can be modeled by a linear ordering of their component operations. This requires that the primitive operations be (abstractly) atomic. In the multiprocessor case, all linearizations of operations that could occur simultaneously yield distinct invocation schedules.

transactions even though they preserve an ordering property weaker than serializability.

Users often invoke the **DirDump** operation on a Directory when they are "just looking around." In such cases, users would like to see a snapshot of the Directory's contents at an instant when the status of each entry is well defined, but they don't care what happens to the Directory thereafter. If all Directory operations attempt to enforce serializability, using **DirDump** in this way could greatly restrict concurrency. This problem can be alleviated by modifying the specification of the Directory type to permit limited nonserializable behavior.

Suppose dependency relations containing D_9: $T_i : D \rightarrow T_j ; M(\sigma)$ are removed from the set of proscribed relations for the modified Directory type. That is, the interleaving specification for Directories only requires orderability with respect to $\{<_{D_2 \cup D_4 \cup D_8 \cup D_{11}}\}$ instead of $\{<_{D_2 \cup D_4 \cup D_8 \cup D_9 \cup D_{11}}\}$. Although this modified Directory allows nonserializable behavior, one can still guarantee that certain consistency constraints are not violated. For example, if a transaction replaces a group of entries in a Directory, one can still prove that no other transaction doing **DirLookup** operations will observe an incompatible collection of entries.

The WQueue of Section 4.3 provides another example of a useful type that permits nonserializable interaction of transactions. Although the ordering property for WQueues is weaker than the one for strict Queues, some interesting properties can still be deduced based only on orderability with respect to $\{<_{D_3}\}$. Consider two transactions, T_1 and T_2, and two WQueues, Q_1 and Q_2. Suppose T_1 is intended to move all elements from Q_1 to Q_2, and T_2 is intended to move all elements from Q_2 to Q_1. If these transactions are run concurrently, the elements should all wind up in one WQueue or the other. This can guaranteed only if $<_{D_3}$ is proscribed; otherwise elements could be shuffled endlessly between Q_1 and Q_2 and the transactions might never terminate.

6. A TECHNIQUE FOR SYNCHRONIZING SHARED ABSTRACT TYPES

We have developed a formalism for specifying the synchronization of operations on shared abstract types, and interleaving specifications for some example types have been given. This section outlines a synchronization mechanism that can be used in implementations of these types. While we do not describe a particular syntax or implementation for this mechanism, we show how it can be used to prevent cascading aborts and control the interleaving of operations. We show how it provides the cooperation among types that is needed to preserve serializability or a weaker ordering property of a group of transactions. Implementation sketches for the shared abstract types specified in Section 4 are given as examples of its use.

As indicated in Section 4.4, the implementor of a type must take the following steps to demonstrate the correctness of an implementation:

(1) characterize the set of legal invocation schedules, that is, those invocation schedules allowed by the synchronization mechanism used in the implementation;

(2) give a mapping from invocation schedules to abstract schedules and prove that the implementation carries out this mapping;

(3) prove that every legal invocation schedule yields a consistent abstract schedule under this mapping.

This three-part task is simplest for implementations that are idealized in that they do not reorder operations on objects. Under these conditions, invocation schedules and abstract schedules are equivalent, and the second step in this process can be eliminated. The examples in this section discuss such idealized implementations of types.

6.1 Type-Specific Locking

The proposed synchronization technique is based on *locking*, which is used in many database systems to synchronize access to database objects. There are many variations on locking, but the same basic principle underlies them all: before a transaction is permitted to manipulate an object, it must obtain a *lock* on the object that will restrict further access to the object by other transactions until the transaction holding the lock releases it.

Locking restricts the formation of dependencies between transactions by restricting the set of legal invocation schedules. Whenever one transaction is forced to wait for a lock held by another, the formation of a dependency between the two transactions is delayed until the first transaction releases the lock. Under the well-known *two-phase locking* protocol [6], no transaction releases a lock until it has already claimed all the locks it will ever claim. This has the effect of converting potential cycles in dependency relations into deadlocks instead. These can be detected, and because no dependencies have yet been allowed to form, either transaction can be aborted without affecting the other.

Locking is a conservative policy, because it delays the formation of any dependency that is part of a proscribed relation, not just those that eventually lead to cycles. This is not as significant a disadvantage as it might appear, however, because formation of those dependencies that transfer information (see Section 3.3) must be delayed anyway to prevent cascading aborts. In fact, the even more restrictive strategy of holding certain locks until end-of-transaction must often be employed to ensure that schedules are cascade free. Furthermore, it is the conservative nature of locking protocols that makes them a suitable mechanism for sets of cooperative types. By preventing the formation of any dependencies local to a single object, cycles in proscribed relations that involve multiple types are automatically avoided without explicit communication between type managers. This is an important advantage, because it allows type managers to be constructed independently, as long as they correctly prevent the local formation of dependencies.

The chief disadvantage of many locking mechanisms is that they sacrifice concurrency by making minimal use of semantic knowledge about the objects being manipulated. The simplest locking schemes use only one type of lock and hence cannot distinguish between significant and insignificant dependencies. Read/Write locking schemes use some semantic information, but are not flexible enough to take advantage of the extra concurrency specifiable in terms of type-specific dependencies. It has been shown [13] that two-phase locking is optimal under such conditions of limited semantic knowledge, but much more concurrency

Table I. Lock Compatibility Table for Directories

Lock requested	Lock held		
	DirModify(σ)	DirLookup(σ)	DirDump
DirModify(σ)	No	No	No
DirModify(σ')	OK	OK	No
DirLookup(σ)	No	OK	OK
DirLookup(σ')	OK	OK	OK
DirDump	No	OK	OK

can be obtained if more semantic information is used. The locking technique described here generalizes the ideas behind Read/Write locking. It permits the definition of type-specific locking rules that reflect the interleaving specifications of individual data types. More restrictive type-specific locking schemes have previously been investigated by Korth [12].

Two observations can be made concerning type-specific dependencies. First, they specify the way in which type-specific operations on behalf of different transactions may be interleaved. Analogously, the generalized locking scheme requires the definition of type-specific *lock classes*, which correspond roughly to the operations on the type. Second, in addition to the operations, the dependencies reflect data supplied to the operations as arguments or data that is otherwise specific to the particular object acted upon. Therefore, an instance of a lock in the generalized locking scheme consists of two parts: the type-specific lock class and some amount of instance-specific data. It is the inclusion of data in the lock instance that differentiates our technique from Korth's. We use the notation {LockClass(data)} to represent an instance of a lock.

Once the lock classes for a type have been defined, a Boolean function must be given that specifies whether a particular new lock request may be granted as a function of those locks already held on the object. In accordance with the practice in database literature, this function will be represented by a *lock compatibility table*. Only those locks held by other transactions need be checked for compatibility; a new lock request is always compatible with other locks held by the same transaction.

To complete the description of a type's locking scheme, one must specify the protocol by which each of the type's operations acquires and releases locks. Although two-phase locking can be used with type-specific locks, the locking protocol may also be type-specific. A uniform two-phase protocol is simplest to understand, but the added flexibility of type-specific protocols can allow increased concurrency. The exact nature of a type-specific protocol depends not only on the semantics of the type, but also on the particular representation and implementation chosen.

6.2 Directories

A simple idealized implementation of the Directory type specified in Section 4.1 illustrates the basics of type-specific locking. In this example, it is assumed that the Directory operations have been implemented in a straightforward fashion with no attempt at internal concurrency. It is further assumed that the operations act under the protection of a monitor or other mutual exclusion mechanism during the actual manipulation of Directory objects. Locking is used exclusively to control the sequencing of Directory operations on behalf of multiple transactions. The locking and mutual exclusion mechanisms cannot be completely independent, however, because mutual exclusion locks must be released when waiting for a lock within the monitor. This is a standard technique in systems that use monitors for synchronization [11].

Because the mapping from invocation schedules to abstract schedules is trivial for this implementation, the second step of the validation process is eliminated. The discussion of the locking scheme for Directories therefore focuses on the first and third steps: informal characterization of the set of legal schedules, and comparison of this set with the set of consistent schedules.

As was noted in Section 4.1, the operations for the Directory data type can be divided into three groups:

(1) Modify operations, which alter the particular Directory entry identified by the key string σ;
(2) Lookup operations, which observe the presence, absence, or contents of the particular Directory entry identified by the key string σ;
(3) Dump operations, which observe properties of the Directory that cannot be isolated to an individual entry.

Corresponding to these groups, three lock classes can be defined:

(1) {DirModify(σ)}, which indicates that an incomplete transaction has inserted or deleted an entry with key string σ;
(2) {DirLookup(σ)}, which indicates that an incomplete transaction has attempted to observe the entry with key string σ;
(3) {DirDump}, which indicates that an incomplete transaction has performed a DirDump of the entire directory.

The lock compatibility table for Directories can be found in Table I. Since there are a potentially infinite number of strings, the symbols σ and σ' are used to represent two arbitrary nonidentical strings.

Each entry in this table reflects the nature of one of the type-specific dependency relations for Directories. Compatible entries represent dependency relations in which cycles are allowed to occur: for example, the entry in row 2, column 2 is "OK" because cycles are permitted in the $<_{M(\sigma) \to M(\sigma')}>$ dependency relation. Incompatible entries reflect proscribed relations, such as the entry in row 1, column 2, which is due to the proscribed $<_{M(\sigma) \to M(\sigma)}>$ relation.

The protocol used by the Directory operations for acquiring and releasing locks is as follows:

(1) DirInsert or DirDelete operations that specify the key string σ obtain a {DirModify(σ)} lock on the Directory. If the operation succeeds, the lock is held until end-of-transaction. If the operation fails, and the transaction was not holding a {DirModify (σ)} lock as a result of another operation, the lock is converted to a {DirLookup(σ)} lock, which is held until end-of-transaction.

(2) **DirLookup** operations that specify the key string σ obtain a {DirLookup(σ)} lock on the Directory that is held until end-of-transaction.

(3) **DirDump** operations obtain a {DirDump} lock on the Directory that is held until end-of-transaction.

The following example demonstrates how the components of the locking scheme interact. Suppose a Directory D is initially empty. If a transaction T_1 performs the operation **DirDelete(D, "Zebra")**, this operation will fail by returning **not found** and leave a {DirLookup("Zebra")} lock on the Directory until the termination of T_1. Now suppose a second transaction T_2 performs the operation DirInsert(D, "Zebra", capa). According to the protocol, **DirInsert** must first obtain a {DirModify("Zebra")} lock. Because the dependency relation $<_{L(\sigma)\rightarrow M(\sigma')}>$ is proscribed, this lock is incompatible with the {DirLookup("Zebra")} lock already held by T_1 (see row 1, column 3 of the compatibility table). Therefore, T_2 will be blocked. If T_1 subsequently becomes blocked while attempting to access an object already locked by T_2, a deadlock will occur. Both transactions are then blocked attempting to form dependencies that are part of proscribed relations. Although these relations may involve different objects, or even different types, a cycle in the union of the two relations is effectively prevented. This is exactly the behavior required to achieve consistency among cooperative types. On the other hand, if T_1 completes successfully the lock is released and the dependency of T_2 on T_1 is permitted to form. Since the $L(\sigma) \rightarrow M(\sigma)$ dependency cannot lead to cascading aborts, one may conclude (after the fact) that delaying T_2 was unnecessary.

By contrast, a transaction T_3 that performs the operation **DirInsert(D, "Giraffe", capa)** need not be blocked because the $<_{L(\sigma)\rightarrow M(\sigma')}>$ dependency relation is not proscribed. Accordingly, row 2, column 3 of the compatibility table indicates that a {DirModify("Giraffe")} lock is compatible with a {DirLookup("Zebra")} lock.

Although not a formal proof, this example characterizes the set of legal schedules permitted by the implementation and shows how the lock classes, compatibility table, and locking protocol combine to guarantee that the legal schedules correspond to the consistent schedules defined in Section 4.1. They capture the idea that, for this abstract data type, synchronization of access depends on the operations being performed, the particular entries in the Directory they attempt to reference, and their outcome. Because locks are on Directory objects, not components of directories, the technique also handles phantoms: entries that are mentioned in operations but are not present in the Directory.

6.3 Strictly FIFO Queues

Type-specific locking can also be used in implementations of the Queue data type of Section 4.2. As in the preceding example, assume an idealized implementation operating under conditions of mutual exclusion. To implement strictly FIFO Queues supporting only **QEnter** and **QRemove** operations, two lock classes are sufficient: {QEnter(σ)} and {QRemove(σ)}. As in the case of Directories, locks on Queues identify the particular entry to which the operation requesting the lock refers. Since Queue entries are not identified by key strings, it is assumed that at QEnter time, each element is assigned an identifier unique

Table II. Lock Compatibility Table for Queues

Lock requested	Lock held	
	QEnter(σ)	QRemove(σ)
QEnter(σ)	NA	NA
QEnter(σ')	No	OK
QRemove(σ)	No	NA
QRemove(σ')	OK	No

to the Queue instance. These identifiers correspond to those used in defining the dependency relations. Thus a {QEnter(σ)} lock indicates that an element with identifier σ has been entered into the Queue by an incomplete transaction. Likewise, a {QRemove(σ)} lock indicates that the element with identifier σ has been removed from the Queue by an incomplete transaction. The protocol for the Queue operations is

(1) **QEnter** operations must obtain a {QEnter(σ)} lock, where σ is the newly assigned identifier for the entry to be added. This lock is held until end-of-transaction.

(2) **QRemove** operations must obtain a {QRemove(σ)} lock, where σ is the identifier of the entry at the head of the Queue. This lock is held until end-of-transaction. Note that obtaining a {QRemove(σ)} lock does not necessarily imply that an entry σ is actually in the Queue, because the transaction that made the entry may have since been aborted. If so, the **QRemove** operation must request a {QRemove(σ')} lock on the new headmost entry σ'.

Table II shows the lock compatibility table for Queues. As usual, the symbols σ and σ' represent the identifiers of two different elements. Because the element identifiers are unique, certain situations (e.g., attempting to enter an element with the same identifier as an element already removed) cannot occur. The compatibility function is undefined in these cases, so the table entries are marked NA for "Not Applicable."

The lock compatibility tables reflects the limited concurrency of this type. Once a **QRemove** operation has retrieved the entry with identifier σ, some entry with identifier σ' becomes the head element of the Queue. But other transactions will be blocked trying to obtain the {QRemove(σ')} lock needed to remove it, until the first transaction completes. Multiple **QEnter** operations on behalf of different transactions interact in the same way. The incompatibility of {QRemove(σ)} with {QEnter(σ)} ensures that an uncommitted entry cannot be removed from the Queue, thereby eliminating a potential cause of cascading aborts.

6.4 WQueues

For a comparable idealized implementation of WQueues supporting only **WQEnter** and **WQRemove**, the same lock classes may be used as for FIFO Queues. The major difference between the two types shows up in the lock compatibility function, given by Table III. To reflect the allowability of interleaved **WQEnter** operations by different transactions, the table entry in row 2, column 2 defines

Table III. Lock Compatibility Table for WQueues

Lock requested	Lock held	
	WQEnter(σ)	WQRemove(σ)
WQEnter(σ)	NA	NA
WQEnter(σ')	OK	OK
WQRemove(σ)	No	NA
WQRemove(σ')	OK	OK

{WQEnter(σ)} and {WQEnter(σ')} locks to be compatible. Similarly, the entry in row 4, column 3 now permits multiple transactions to perform **WQRemove** operations. The only remaining restriction is the one in row 3, column 2 that prevents uncommitted entries from being removed. This prevents cycles in the proscribed $<_{E(\sigma) \to R(\sigma)}$ dependency relation and, because the lock is held until end-of-transaction, also prevents cascading aborts.

The locking protocol for the WQueue operations is substantially the same as the one for the Queue operations. The only difference is that a **WQRemove** operation that is unable to obtain the required {WQRemove(σ)} lock on the element at the head of the WQueue does not block. Instead, **WQRemove** searches down the WQueue for some other element with identifier σ', for which a {WQRemove(σ')} lock can be obtained. This reflects the property of WQueues that permits elements farther down the WQueue to be removed when the head element is uncommitted. If no element can be found, the operation is blocked until an inserting transaction commits.

6.5 Summary

The examples in this section have shown how type-specific locking can be used for synchronization in implementations of several data types. The examples show how locking can be used to prevent cycles in proscribed dependency relations, including cycles containing several types of objects. They also indicate how locking can be used to prevent cascading aborts.

A full discussion of the syntax and implementation of type-specific locking mechanisms is beyond the scope of this paper. Further work is needed to determine the specific primitives required for definition of new object types, locking, unlocking, conditional locking, etc. Another area requiring further study is the relationship between the locking mechanism and other synchronization mechanisms that are used for mutual exclusion and to signal events. It appears, however, that implementation of a type-specific locking mechanism is often no more complex or expensive than implementations of standard locking. Unlike predicate locking schemes [6], the set of locks that apply to a particular object can easily be determined. It is also not difficult to determine what processes may be awakened in response to an event such as transaction completion.

7. CONCLUSIONS

This paper has been concerned with synchronizing transactions that access shared abstract types. In our model, four properties distinguish such types from others:

(1) operations on them are permanent;
(2) they support failure atomicity of transactions;
(3) they do not permit cascading aborts;
(4) they contribute to preserving ordering properties of groups of transactions.

These properties are not independent, and the mechanisms that are used to achieve them are therefore related as well.

Schedules and dependencies are useful in understanding the interaction between concurrent transactions. The well-known consistency property of serializability can be redefined as a special case of orderability with respect to a dependency relation. The specific dependency relation depends on how much semantic knowledge is available concerning operations on objects. When Read operations are distinguished from Write operations, serializability requires orderability with respect to a less restrictive dependency relation than when this distinction is not made. Dependencies can also be used to characterize schedules that are not prone to cascading aborts.

Additional type-specific semantic knowledge about operations can allow additional concurrency. The interleaving specifications for Directories and Queues developed in Sections 4.1 and 4.2 were stated in terms of orderability with respect to type-specific dependencies. To increase concurrency further, the WQueue sacrifices serializability while preserving orderability with respect to a less restrictive dependency. When several abstract types are combined in a transaction, orderability must be guaranteed with respect to the relation that is the union of the proscribed relations of the individual types.

Section 6 described a locking mechanism for implementing the synchronization required by the types described in Section 4. By allowing locks that consist of a type-specific lock class and instance-specific data, the mechanism provides a powerful framework for using type-specific semantics in synchronization. This mechanism is suitable for use in transactions containing multiple types, and it can also be used to prevent cascading aborts. The implementation of Directories shows how type-specific locking permits a uniform treatment of the problem of phantoms. Locks need not be directly associated with particular components of objects, which facilitates the separation of synchronization from other type representation issues. The examples of various Queue types show the mechanism's flexibility.

This paper has not provided a complete discussion of the issues involved in the specification and implementation of shared abstract types. For example, we have not discussed the construction of compound shared abstract types, which use other shared abstract types in their implementation. (However, Schwarz [23] gives an example of this.) In addition, we have hardly mentioned recovery considerations, though we believe logging mechanisms as described by Lindsay et al. [15] can be extended to meet the needs of shared abstract types. Recovery is discussed more fully in a related paper [24]. Finally, we have not discussed specific algorithms for coping with deadlocks.

Clearly, the definition and implementation of shared abstract types is more difficult than the definition and implementation of regular abstract types. However, once these types are implemented, programmers can construct arbitrary transactions that invoke operations on the types. These transactions should greatly simplify the construction of reliable distributed systems. Though this paper has focused entirely on synchronization, we believe that this topic is central to understanding how transactions can be used as a basic building block in the implementation of distributed systems.

ACKNOWLEDGMENTS

We gratefully acknowledge the helpful technical and editorial comments that were made by Dean Daniels, Cynthia Hibbard, Andy Hisgen, Bruce Lindsay, and Irving Traiger. We also gratefully acknowledge the Archons Project at Carnegie-Mellon University for providing the framework in which we conducted this research.

REFERENCES

1. ALLCHIN, J.E., AND MCKENDRY, M.S. Synchronization and recovery of actions. In *Proceedings of the Second Principles of Distributed Computing Conference* (Aug. 1983), pp. 31–44.
2. BERNSTEIN, P.A., SHIPMAN, D.W., AND WONG, W.S. Formal aspects of serializability in database concurrency control. *IEEE Trans. Softw. Eng. SE-5,* 3(May 1979), 203–216.
3. BERNSTEIN, P.A., AND GOODMAN, N. Concurrency control in distributed database systems. *ACM Comput. Surv. 13,* 2(June 1981), 185–221.
4. DAHL, O.-J., AND HOARE, C.A.R. Hierarchical program structures. In *Structured Programming,* C.D.R. Hoare Ed., Academic Press, New York, 1972, ch. 3, pp. 175–220.
5. *Reference Manual for the Ada Programming Language,* July 1982 ed., Department of Defense, Ada Joint Program Office, Washington, D.C., 1982.
6. ESWARAN, K.P., GRAY, J.N., LORIE, R.A., AND TRAIGER, I.L. The notions of consistency and predicate locks in a database system. *Commun. ACM 19,* 11(Nov. 1976), 624–633.
7. GARCIA-MOLINA, H. Using semantic knowledge for transaction processing in a distributed database. *ACM Trans. Database Syst. 8,* 2(June 1983), 186–213.
8. GRAY, J.N., LORIE, R.A., PUTZOLU, G.R., AND TRAIGER, I.L. Granularity of locks and degrees of consistency in a shared data base. IBM Res. Rept. RJ1654, IBM Research Lab., San Jose, Calif., Sept. 1975.
9. GRAY, J. A transaction model. IBM Res. Rept. RJ2895, IBM Research Lab., San Jose, Calif., Aug. 1980.
10. GRAY, J.N., MCJONES, P., BLASGEN, M., LINDSAY, B., LORIE, R., PRICE, T., PUTZOLU, F., AND TRAIGER, I. The recovery manager of the system R database manager. *ACM Comput. Surv. 13* 2(June 1981), 223–242.
11. HOARE, C.A.R. Monitors: An operating system structuring concept. *Commun. ACM 17,* 10 (Oct. 1974), 549–557.
12. KORTH, H.F. Locking primitives in a database system. *J. ACM 30,* 1(Jan. 1983), 55–79.
13. KUNG, H.T., AND PAPADIMITRIOU, C.H. An optimality theory of concurrency control for databases. In *Proceedings of the 1979 SIGMOD Conference* (Boston, Mass., May 1979). ACM, New York, pp. 116–126.
14. LAMPSON, B.W. Atomic transactions. In *Distributed Systems—Architecture and Implementation: An Advanced Course,* G. Goos and J. Hartmanis (Eds.), Springer-Verlag, New York, 1981, ch. 11, pp. 246–265.
15. LINDSAY, B.G., ET AL. Notes on distributed databases. IBM Res. Rept. RJ2571, IBM Research Lab., San Jose, Calif, July 1979.
16. LISKOV, B., SNYDER, A., ATKINSON, R., AND SCHAFFERT, C. Abstraction mechanisms in CLU. *Commun. ACM 20,* 8(Aug. 1977), 564–576.
17. LISKOV, B. On linguistic support for distributed programs. *IEEE Trans. Softw. Eng. SE-8,* 3(May 1982), 203–210.
18. LISKOV, B., AND SCHEIFLER, R. Guardians and actions: Linguistic support for robust, distributed programs. In *Proceedings of the Ninth ACM SIGACT-SIGPLAN Symposium on the Principles of Programming Languages* (Albuquerque, N. Mex., Jan. 1982), pp. 7–19.
19. LOMET, D.B. Process structuring, synchronization, and recovery using atomic actions. In *ACM SIGPLAN Notices 12,* 3(March 1977).
20. MOSS, J.E.B. Nested transactions: An approach to reliable distributed computing. Ph.D. dissertation, Massachusetts Institute of Technology, Cambridge, Mass., April 1981.
21. PAPADIMITRIOU, C.H., BERNSTEIN, P.A., AND ROTHNIE, J.B. Some computational problems related to database concurrency control. In *Proceedings of the Conference on Theoretical Computer Science* (Waterloo, Ont., Canada, Aug. 1977).
22. REED, D.P. Naming and synchronization in a decentralized computer system. Ph.D. dissertation, Massachusetts Institute of Technology, Cambridge, Mass., Sept. 1978.
23. SCHWARZ, P.M. Building systems based on atomic transactions. Ph.D. thesis proposal, Carnegie-Mellon University, Pittsburgh. Pa. (Feb. 1982).
24. SCHWARZ, P.M. AND SPECTOR, A.Z. Recovery of shared abstract types. Carnegie-Mellon Rept. CMU-CS-83-151, Carnegie-Mellon University, Pittsburgh, Pa., Oct. 1983.
25. SHA, L., JENSEN, E.D., RASHID, R.F., AND NORTHCUTT, J.D. Distributed cooperating processes and transactions. In *Proceedings of the ACM SIGCOMM Symposium* (1983). ACM, New York, pp. 188–196.
26. WEIHL, W.E. Data dependent concurrency control and recovery. In *Proceedings of the Second Principles of Distributed Computing Conference* (Aug. 1983), pp. 73–74.
27. WEIHL, W., AND LISKOV, B. Specification and implementation of resilient, atomic data types. Presented at the Symposium on Programming Language Issues in Software Systems, June 1983.
28. WULF, W.A., COHEN, E., CORWIN, W., JONES, A., LEVIN, R., PIERSON, C., AND POLLACK, F. HYDRA: The kernel of a multiprocessor operating system. *Commun. ACM 17,* 6 (June 1974), 337–345.
29. WULF, W.A., LONDON, R.L., AND SHAW, M. An introduction to the construction and verification of Alphard programs. *IEEE Trans. Softw. Eng. SE-2,* 4 (Dec. 1976).

Received October 1982, revised December 1983; accepted May 1984

Optimistic Concurrency Control
for Abstract Data Types

Maurice Herlihy
Computer Science Department
Carnegie-Mellon University
Pittsburgh, PA 15213
8 May 1986

Abstract

A concurrency control technique is optimistic if it allows transactions to execute without synchronization, relying on commit-time validation to ensure serializability. This paper describes several new optimistic concurrency control techniques for objects in distributed systems, proves their correctness and optimality properties, and characterizes the circumstances under which each is likely to be useful. These techniques have the following novel aspects. First, unlike many methods that classify operations only as reads or writes, these techniques systematically exploit type-specific properties of objects to validate more interleavings. Necessary and sufficient validation conditions are derived directly from an object's data type specification. Second, these techniques are modular: they can be applied selectively on a per-object (or even per-operation) basis in conjunction with standard pessimistic techniques such as two-phase locking, permitting optimistic methods to be introduced exactly where they will be most effective. Third, when integrated with quorum-consensus replication, these techniques circumvent certain trade-offs between concurrency and availability imposed by comparable pessimistic techniques. Finally, the accuracy and efficiency of validation are further enhanced by some technical improvements: distributed validation is performed as a side-effect of the commit protocol, and validation takes into account the results of operations, accepting certain interleavings that would have produced delays in comparable pessimistic schemes.

This research was sponsored by the Defense Advanced Research Projects Agency (DOD), ARPA Order No. 4976, monitored by the Air Force Avionics Laboratory Under Contract NOOO39-85-C-0134.

1. Introduction

Informally, *optimistic* concurrency control is based on the premise that it is more effective to apologize than to ask permission. Transactions execute without synchronization, but before a transaction is allowed to commit, it is *validated* to ensure that it preserves atomicity. If validation succeeds, the transaction commits; otherwise the transaction is aborted and restarted. This paper proposes new optimistic concurrency control techniques for objects in distributed systems, proves their correctness and optimality properties, and characterizes the circumstances under which each is likely to be useful.

In conventional optimistic techniques, operations are classified simply as reads or writes, and transactions are validated by analyzing read/write conflicts between concurrent transactions. These techniques are intended only for applications where reads predominate; they are poorly suited for general-purpose applications such as banking or reservations where write operations occur frequently at "hot spots" such as counters, account balances, or queues. A novel aspect of the techniques proposed here is that they validate more interleavings by systematically exploiting type-specific properties of objects to recognize when concurrent "write" operations need not conflict. An object's validation conditions are derived directly from its data type specification, and the derivation technique is applicable to objects of arbitrary type. These techniques are optimal in the sense that no method using the same information can validate more interleavings.

Any optimistic scheme, however clever, is cost-effective only if validation succeeds sufficiently often. Numerous studies (cited below) have shown that the success rate of validation depends critically on the nature and frequency of transaction conflict. In large systems, it is reasonable to expect that different objects will have different patterns of conflict, and that individual objects' patterns may change over time. These observations suggest that optimistic techniques are cost-effective only under specialized circumstances, while pessimistic techniques are more robust. If optimistic techniques are to be useful in general-purpose systems, it must be possible to apply them selectively in conjunction with appropriate pessimistic techniques. (See Lausen [19] for a similar argument.) Even for pessimistic techniques, however, the compatibility of distinct mechanisms is a non-trivial question. For example, two-phase locking [8] and multiversion timestamping [24] cannot be used together in a single system, because they may serialize transactions in incompatible orders. A novel aspect of the techniques proposed here is that they are compatible with a large class of standard pessimistic techniques, including two-phase locking, thus they can be applied selectively on a per-object (or even per-operation) basis exactly where they are most cost-effective.

Optimistic and pessimistic methods behave differently when integrated with quorum-consensus replication [15]. Pessimistic techniques trade concurrency for availability; weakening the constraints on one may tighten the constraints on the other [13, 14]. Optimistic techniques are different: enhancing validation to accept more interleavings has no effect on availability.

The accuracy and efficiency of validation are further enhanced by two technical improvements. First, distributed validation requires no additional messages, since it is performed as a side-effect of the commit protocol. Second, because operations are validated after they have occurred, validation can take into account the results of invocations, permitting certain interleavings to be validated that would have produced delays in comparable locking schemes.

This paper is organized as follows. Section 2 surveys some related work, and Section 3 describes a model of computation. Section 4 describes *conflict-based* validation, a simple validation technique based on predefined conflicts. Section 5 describes a scheme that permits pessimistic and optimistic techniques to be combined in a single object. Section 6 describes *state-based* validation, a more complex scheme that validates additional interleavings by exploiting knowledge about the object's state. Section 7 examines how optimism interacts with replication, and Section 8 closes with a discussion.

2. Related Work

Perhaps the earliest concurrency control scheme to use validation is that of Thomas [26]. Kung and Robinson [17] have proposed a centralized optimistic method based on Read/Write conflicts. Ceri and Owicki [4] have extended Kung and Robinson's method to permit validation in distributed systems. Lausen [19] has proposed a centralized optimistic scheme integrating two-phase locking with Kung and Robinson's scheme, and has also shown that several general formulations of the validation problem are NP-complete [20]. Härder [12] has distinguished between *backward* validation, in which each transaction checks that its own results have not been invalidated by concurrent transactions, and *forward* validation, in which each transaction checks that its own effects will not invalidate any concurrent transaction's results.

IMS/VS [10] uses an optimistic technique to reduce contention for shared counters. Like the more general techniques proposed in this paper, IMS/VS mixes pessimistic and optimistic techniques, and exploits type-specific properties of counters to make validation effective.

A system of *logical clocks* [18] keeps track of orderings and dependencies among events. Timestamps generated by logical clocks provide a simple and efficient technique for extending the natural partial order of events in a distributed system to an arbitrary total order. The distributed validation protocol used in this paper generalizes Kung and Robinson's centralized transaction numbering scheme, and it is simpler and requires fewer messages than that of Ceri and Owicki [4].

Numerous studies have compared the performance of pessimistic and optimistic techniques [1, 2, 3, 9, 21, 25]. These studies have yielded a variety of conclusions, some in apparent disagreement. Nevertheless, one particular conclusion seems justified: the effectiveness of optimistic techniques depends on the distribution of conflicts in subtle and complex ways. In general-purpose distributed systems, where such predictions may be difficult and miscalculation expensive, optimistic techniques are most likely to be useful if they can be applied to individual objects rather than to entire systems.

Weihl [27] has developed analytic techniques for characterizing when atomicity mechanisms are compatible. The techniques proposed here satisfy *hybrid atomicity*, and are compatible with a wide variety of pessimistic techniques, including two-phase locking [8, 16, 22], as well as schemes that combine locking with timestamps [5, 6, 14].

3. Assumptions and Definitions

Distributed systems are subject to two kinds of faults: sites may crash and communication links may be interrupted. A widely-accepted technique for preserving consistency in the presence of failures and concurrency is to organize computations as sequential processes called *transactions*. Transactions are *atomic*, that is, serializable and recoverable. Serializability means that transactions appear to execute in a serial order [23], and recoverability means that a transaction either succeeds completely, or has no effect. A transaction that completes all its changes successfully *commits*; otherwise it *aborts*, and any changes it has made are undone. A transaction that has neither committed nor aborted is *active*. Some form of atomic commitment protocol [7, 11] ensures that commits are atomic, and non-volatile storage ensures that changes are not destroyed by later failures.

The basic containers for data are called *objects*. Each object has a *type*, which defines a set of possible *states* and a set of primitive *operations* that provide the (only) means to create and manipulate objects of that type. An *event* is a pair consisting of an operation invocation and a response. For example, a bank account might be represented by an object of type Account whose state is given by a non-negative dollar amount, initially zero. The Account data type provides Credit and Debit operations. Credit increments the account balance:

```
Credit = Operation(sum: Dollar).
```
Debit attempts to decrement the balance:
```
Debit = Operation(sum: Dollar) Signals (Overdraft).
```
If the amount to be debited exceeds the balance, the invocation signals an exception, leaving the balance unchanged. For brevity, a debit that returns normally is referred to as a *successful debit*, otherwise it is an *attempted overdraft*.

An object's state is modeled by a sequence of events called a *history*. For example,

    Credit($5)/Ok()
    Credit($6)/Ok()
    Debit($10)/Ok()
    Debit($2)/Overdrawn()

is a history for an Account. A *specification* for an object is the set of permissible histories for that object. For example, the specification for an Account object consists of histories in which the balance covers any successful debit, and fails to cover all unsuccessful debits. A *legal history* is one that is included in the object's specification. Histories are denoted by lower-case letters.

In the presence of failure and concurrency, an object's state is given by a *schedule*, which is a sequence of operation executions, *transaction commits*, and *transaction aborts*. To keep track of interleaving, a transaction identifier is associated with each step in a schedule. For example, the following is a schedule for an Account:

    Credit($5)/Ok() A
    Credit($6)/Ok() B
    Commit A
    Debit($10)/Ok() B
    Commit B

Here, A and B are transaction identifiers. The ordering of operations in a schedule reflects the order in which the object returned responses, not necessarily the order in which it received invocations. Schedules are denoted by upper-case letters.

(Serial) histories and (concurrent) schedules are related by the notion of *atomicity*. Let $\gg$ denote a total order on committed and active transactions, and let H be a schedule. The *serialization* of H in the order $\gg$ is the history h constructed by reordering the events in H so that if $B \gg A$ then the subsequence of events associated with A precedes the subsequence of events associated with B. H is *serializable in the order* $\gg$ if h is legal. H is *serializable* if it is serializable in some order. H is *atomic* if the subschedule associated with committed transactions is serializable. An object is atomic if all of its schedules are atomic.

A *system* encompassing multiple objects is atomic if all component objects are atomic and serializable in a common order. The optimistic mechanisms introduced in this paper serialize transactions in the order they commit (as observed by a system of logical clocks [18]), and are thus compatible with pessimistic methods that induce the same ordering (e.g., [5, 6, 8, 14, 16, 22]). Following the terminology of Weihl [27], a schedule is *hybrid atomic* if it is serializable in commit order.

4. Conflict-Based Validation

This section introduces *conflict-based validation*, an optimistic concurrency control mechanism which uses predefined conflicts between pairs of events for validation. This approach is the optimistic analog of locking mechanisms, which use similar predefined conflicts to introduce delays. A precise definition of conflict is given below, but for now it is enough to say that two transactions that execute no conflicting events can be serialized in either order, thus neither can invalidate the other. (This notion is weaker than commutativity, which requires that both serializations define equivalent states.)

Internally, an object is implemented by two components: a *permanent state* that records the effects of committed transactions, and a set of *intentions lists* that record each active transaction's tentative changes. When a transaction commits, the changes in its intentions list are applied to the permanent state. For example, a bank account's permanent state is the current balance, and its intentions lists record each active transaction's net credit or debit.

Each transaction is validated during the first phase of commitment. When an object receives the prepare message, it validates the transaction locally (using techniques described below) before recording the transaction's intentions list on non-volatile storage. If all participants validate the transaction, the co-ordinator issues the timestamped commit messages. An object can validate transactions concurrently if neither transaction's events conflict with the other's, but the object must apply the intentions lists in the order of commit. Validation requires no messages in addition to those needed for the standard commit protocol.

The following extension to the two-phase commit protocol ensures that intentions lists are applied in the proper order. When a site receives the *prepare* message from the coordinator, it generates a *prepared timestamp* for that transaction before responding with its acknowledgment. After the coordinator has received acknowledgments from all participants, it generates a *commit timestamp*, which is later than any of its prepared timestamps. The commit timestamp is forced to stable storage along with the commit record, and is included with each *commit* message to participants. A site may apply a transaction's intentions as soon as it has processed commit or abort messages from all transactions with earlier prepared timestamps. Note that no messages have been added to the standard commit protocol.

This section considers two distinct validation techniques [12]: *backward* validation ensures that the transaction's results have not been invalidated by the effects of a recently committed transaction, while *forward* validation ensures that the transaction's effects will not invalidate the results of any active transaction. Under conflict-based validation, the two approaches have comparable run-time costs.

4.1. Serial Dependency

This section gives a formal characterization of what it means for events to conflict. Let $\succ$ be a relation between pairs of events, and let *h* be a legal history. A legal subhistory *g* of *h* is *closed* under $\succ$ if whenever it contains an event *e* it also contains every earlier event *e'* of *h* such that $e \succ e'$. A subhistory *g* is a *view* of *h* for *e* under $\succ$ if *g* is closed under $\succ$, and if *g* contains every *e'* of *h* such that $e \succ e'$. Informally, $\succ$ is a *serial dependency* relation if whenever an event is legal for a view, it is legal for the complete history. More precisely, let "•" denote concatenation:

> **Definition 1:** A relation $\succ$ is a *serial dependency* relation if *g* • *e* is legal implies that *h* • *e* is legal, for all events *e* and all legal histories *h*, such that *g* is a view of *h* for *e* under $\succ$.

The optimistic techniques proposed here are correct if and only if conflict between events is defined by a serial dependency relation. Of primary interest are *minimal* relations, having the property that no smaller relation is also a serial dependency relation. As discussed below in Section 7, serial dependency is also important for quorum-consensus replication.

The Account data type has a unique minimal serial dependency relation, shown in Table 4-1. Here, successful debits do not depend on prior credits, because the debit cannot be invalidated by increasing the balance. Attempted overdrafts do depend on prior credits, however, because the Overdraft exception can be invalidated by increasing the balance. The FIFO Queue data type has two distinct minimal serial dependency relations, shown in Tables 4-2 and 4-3. (Here, Deq blocks when the queue is empty.) In the first relation, Enq events depend on no other events, but Deq events depend on all other events. In the second relation, Enq events depend on one another, Deq events depend on one another, but Enq events do not depend on Deq events, and vice-versa.

The next two sections present formal models for forward and backward validation, together with proofs of correctness and optimality. Correctness means that an object whose conflict relation is a serial dependency relation will validate only hybrid atomic schedules, and optimality means that an object whose conflict relation is *not* a serial dependency relation will validate some schedule that is not hybrid atomic.

4.2. Forward Validation

Forward validation ensures that a committing transaction cannot invalidate any active transactions. When a transaction executes an event at an object, the object grants an *optimistic lock* for that event. That object will validate a transaction *A* if and only if there is no other active transaction that holds an optimistic lock for an event that conflicts with an event in the intentions list for *A*. A transaction's

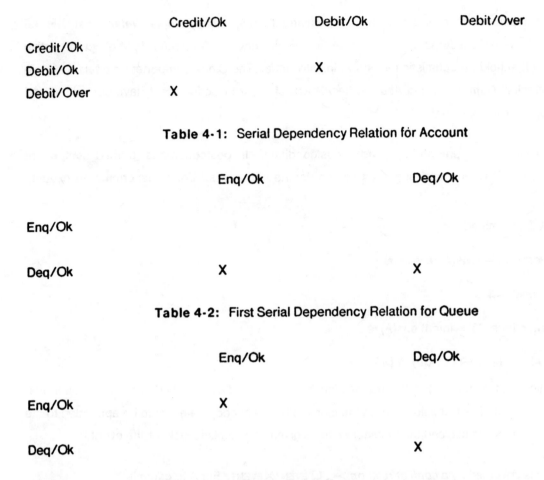

	Credit/Ok	Debit/Ok	Debit/Over
Credit/Ok			
Debit/Ok		X	
Debit/Over	X		

Table 4-1: Serial Dependency Relation for Account

	Enq/Ok	Deq/Ok
Enq/Ok		
Deq/Ok	X	X

Table 4-2: First Serial Dependency Relation for Queue

	Enq/Ok	Deq/Ok
Enq/Ok	X	
Deq/Ok		X

Table 4-3: Second Serial Dependency Relation for Queue

optimistic locks are released when it commits or aborts.

An object is modeled by an automaton that accepts certain schedules. The automaton's state is defined using the following primitive domains: TRANS is the set of transaction identifiers, EVENT is the set of events, TIMESTAMP is a totally ordered set of timestamps with minimal element $\perp$. The derived domain HISTORY is the set of sequences of events. $X \to Y$ denotes the set of partial maps from X to Y.

A *forward validation automaton* has the following state components:

Perm: HISTORY

Intentions: TRANS $\to$ HISTORY

O-Lock: EVENT $\to 2^{TRANS}$

Clock: TIMESTAMP

Committed: 2^{TRANS}

Aborted: 2^{TRANS}

The *Perm* component represents the object's permanent state, initially empty. *Intentions(A)* is the sequence of events executed by transaction A, initially none. *O-Lock(e)* is the set of active transactions that hold an optimistic lock for e, initially none. The *Clock* component models a system of logical clocks. *Committed* and *Aborted* keep track of the transactions that have committed and aborted; each is initially empty.

Each transition has a precondition and a postcondition. In postconditions, primed component names denote new values, and unprimed names denote old values. For transaction A to execute event e,

Pre: $A \notin$ Committed.

           Perm•Intentions(A)•e is legal.

Post: Clock' > Clock

           Intentions'(A) = Intentions(A)•e

           O-Lock'(e) = O-Lock(e) $\cup$ {A}.

The transition can occur only if the transaction has not already committed, and if the operation appears to be legal. The transition causes the clock to be advanced, the event to be appended to the transaction's intentions list, and the transaction to be given an optimistic lock for the event.

Validation is governed by a *conflict relation* $\succ_0 \subseteq$ EVENT$\times$EVENT. For A to commit,

Pre: $A \notin$ Committed $\cup$ Aborted.

           If e is in Intentions(A) and $e \succ_0 e'$ then O-Lock(e')—{A} = $\emptyset$.

Post: Clock' > Clock

           Perm' = Perm•Intentions(A)

           O-Lock'(e) = O-Lock(e)—{A}

A transaction may commit only if it has not already committed or aborted, and only if no other transaction holds an optimistic lock for a conflicting event. Afterwards, the clock is advanced, the transaction's intentions list is appended to the permanent state, and the optimistic locks are released. Finally, a transaction may abort only if it has not already committed. When a transaction aborts, it is added to the set of aborted transactions and its optimistic locks are released.

The first step toward proving correctness is the following lemma, which states that any sequence of events can be inserted into the middle of a history provided no later event serially depends on an inserted event.

Lemma 2: If $\succ$ is a serial dependency relation, f, g, and h histories such that $f{\bullet}g$ and $f{\bullet}h$ are legal, and there is no e in h and e' in g such that $e \succ e'$, then $f{\bullet}g{\bullet}h$ is legal.

Proof: The proof is by induction on the length of h. If h is empty, the result is immediate. Otherwise, let $h = h'{\bullet}e$. $f{\bullet}h'$ is a view of $f{\bullet}g{\bullet}h'$ for e, because $f{\bullet}g{\bullet}h'$ is legal by the induction hypothesis and $f{\bullet}h'$ is legal by assumption. Because $f{\bullet}h'{\bullet}e$ is legal and $\succ$ is a serial dependency relation, $f{\bullet}g{\bullet}h'{\bullet}e = f{\bullet}g{\bullet}h$ is legal.

The following lemma states that forward validation ensures that no active transaction can be invalidated by the commit of another transaction. Moreover, no active transaction ever sees an inconsistent state:

Lemma 3: For any forward validation automaton whose conflict relation is a serial dependency relation, $Perm{\bullet}Intentions(A)$ is legal for all active A.

Proof: The argument proceeds by induction on the number of transactions that have committed, showing that $Perm{\bullet}Intentions(A)$ remains legal when another transaction A' commits. By the induction hypothesis, $Perm' = Perm{\bullet}Intentions(A')$ is legal. The precondition for the commit of A' implies that there is no e in $Intentions(A)$ and e' in $Intentions(A')$ such that $e \succ_O e'$. Because $\succ_O$ is a serial dependency relation, $Perm'{\bullet}Intentions(A)$ is legal by Lemma 2.

The correctness theorem for forward validation is a direct consequence of Lemma 3:

Theorem 4: A forward validation automaton whose conflict relation is a serial dependency relation will accept only hybrid atomic schedules.

Proof: $Perm$ is the serialization in commit order of the schedule accepted by the automaton, and Lemma 3 implies that each commit carries $Perm$ from one legal state to another.

Serial dependency is optimal in the following sense: if a forward validation automaton's conflict relation is not a serial dependency relation, then it will accept some schedule that is not hybrid atomic. The proof is based on the following lemma, which states that if $\succ$ is *not* a serial dependency relation, then there exists a counterexample in which the view is missing exactly one event.

Lemma 5: If $\succ$ is not a serial dependency relation, then there exist a history h and an event e such that h has a view g of e missing exactly one event, $g{\bullet}e$ is legal, but $h{\bullet}e$ is not.

Proof: If $\succ$ is not a serial dependency relation, then there exist a history h and an event e such that h has a view g of e where $g{\bullet}e$ is legal, but $h{\bullet}e$ is not. Suppose g is missing k events of h. Consider the sequence of histories $\{h_i | i = 0,...,k\}$, where $h_0 = g$, $h_k = h$, and h_{i+1} is derived from h_i by restoring its earliest missing event.

If there exists an i such that h_i is legal but h_{i+1} is not, then there exist histories a, b, and c, and events e_1 and e_2 such that h_i can be written as $a{\bullet}b{\bullet}e_2{\bullet}c$, and h_{i+1} as $a{\bullet}e_1{\bullet}b{\bullet}e_2{\bullet}c$, where $a{\bullet}e_1{\bullet}b$ is legal, and $a{\bullet}e_1{\bullet}b{\bullet}e_2$ is not. But $a{\bullet}b$ is a view of $a{\bullet}e_1{\bullet}b$ for e_2, proving the lemma.

Otherwise, suppose h_i is legal for all i between 0 and k. Because $h_0 \bullet e$ is legal and $h_k \bullet e$ is not, there must exist an i such that $h_i \bullet e$ is legal but $h_{i+1} \bullet e$ is not. This h_i is a view of h_{i+1} for e, proving the lemma.

Lemma 5 provides a simple proof of optimality.

Theorem 6: Any forward validation automaton whose conflict relation is not a serial dependency relation will accept a schedule that is not hybrid atomic.

Proof: Since $\succ_O$ is not a serial dependency relation, there exist by Lemma 5 an event e and a legal history h such that g is a view of h for e missing exactly one event e', $g \bullet e$ is legal, but $h \bullet e$ is not. Let $g = a \bullet b$ and $h = a \bullet e' \bullet b$. Transaction A executes a and commits, leaving $Perm = a$. B executes b followed by e, and C executes e'. C commits, followed by B. Both B and C are validated, but the final value of $Perm$ is the illegal history $a \bullet e' \bullet b \bullet e = h \bullet e$.

4.3. Backward Validation

Backward validation ensures that the committing transaction has not been invalidated by the recent commit of another transaction. Each object keeps track of $Last(e)$, the most recent commit timestamp for a transaction that executed the event e. For each active transaction A, each object also keeps track of $First(A,e)$, the logical time when A first executed e. An object will validate A if and only if $Last(e') < First(A,e)$ for each event e' that conflicts with each event e executed by A. This condition ensures that A has not been invalidated by a transaction that committed since A executed e.

To model backward validation, the *O-Lock* component is replaced by:

First: TRANS $\times$ EVENT $\rightarrow$ TIMESTAMP

Last: EVENT $\rightarrow$ TIMESTAMP

The precondition for A to execute e is unchanged. The postcondition is slightly different: instead of granting an optimistic lock to A, $First(A,e)$ is updated if necessary.

$$First'(A,e) = \text{if } (First(A,e) = \perp) \text{ then Clock}$$
$$\text{else } First(A,e)$$

For A to commit,

Pre: $A \notin$ Committed $\cup$ Aborted.

If e is in Intentions(A) and $e \succ_O e'$ then $First(A,e) > Last(e')$.

Post: Clock' > Clock

Perm' = Perm$\bullet$Intentions(A)

If e is in in Intentions(A) then Last'(e) = Clock.

A transaction may commit only if no recently committed transaction has executed a conflicting event. Afterwards, the *Last* timestamp is updated for each event executed by the transaction.

An active transaction is defined to be *valid* if the precondition for its commit is satisfied. Backward validation ensures that all valid transactions view consistent states:

> **Lemma 7:** For any backward validation automaton whose conflict relation is a serial dependency relation, *Perm•Intentions(A)* is legal for any valid *A*.
>
> **Proof:** It is enough to show that if the commit of *A'* does not invalidate *A*, then *Perm•Intentions(A)* remains legal. If *A* remains valid, there is no *e* in *Intentions(A)* and *e'* in *Intentions(A')* such that $e \succ_O e'$, therefore *Perm'•Intentions(A)* is legal by Lemma 2.

The basic correctness theorem for backward validation is a direct consequence of Lemma 7:

> **Theorem 8:** Any backward validation automaton whose conflict relation is a serial dependency relation will accept only hybrid atomic schedules.
>
> **Proof:** *Perm* is the serialization in commit order of the schedule accepted by the automaton, and Lemma 7 implies that each commit carries *Perm* from one legal state to another.

Serial dependency is also optimal for backward validation:

> **Theorem 9:** Any backward validation automaton whose conflict relation is not a serial dependency relation will accept a schedule that is not hybrid atomic.
>
> **Proof:** By the same scenario constructed for Theorem 6.

4.4. Discussion

The Account data type illustrates how a type-specific definition of conflict allows more transactions to commit. Under conventional schemes employing Read/Write conflicts, both Credit and Debit would be classified as a combination of Read and Write operations, hence any transaction to access the account would either invalidate or be invalidated by any concurrent transaction. Here, there are fewer conflicts to invalidate transactions: a credit can invalidate an overdraft, and a successful debit can invalidate another successful debit.

It is difficult to judge whether forward or backward validation is preferable for conflict-based validation. The run-time costs of both techniques are comparable. An advantage of forward validation is that all transactions observe serializable states, even those for which validation fails. Also, asymmetric conflicts can sometimes be resolved by postponing rather than by denying validation. For example, if a transaction that credited an Account discovers that an active transaction has attempted an overdraft, the crediting transaction might choose to postpone validation until the other has had a chance to commit. The principal drawback of forward validation is its extreme optimism: while backward validation restarts active transactions in favor of committed transactions, forward validation restarts active transactions in favor of other active transactions, which themselves may never commit.

How do these optimistic techniques compare to pessimistic locking schemes? In most pessimistic schemes, a lock is acquired before invoking an operation, thus conflicts are typically defined between invocations, not between complete events. In optimistic schemes, by contrast, validation occurs after the invocations' results are known, thus conflicts can be defined between complete events. This additional information can be used to validate interleavings that would be prohibited by invocation locking. For example, compare the event/event conflict relation for Account in Table 4-1 and the invocation/invocation conflict relation in Table 4-4. Invocation locks for credit and debit must conflict, but conflict-based validation will permit a credit to occur concurrently with a successful debit (but not an attempted overdraft), a useful distinction if most debits are expected to be successful.

Optimistic schemes can also exploit knowledge about the order in which transactions commit. For example, under backward validation, a transaction that executed an unsuccessful debit will be allowed to commit before (but not after) a concurrent transaction that executed a conflicting credit, while pessimistic locking would have introduced a delay.

	Credit/Ok	Debit/Ok	Debit/Over
Credit/Ok		X	X
Debit/Ok	X	X	X
Debit/Over	X	X	X

Table 4-4: Invocation/Invocation Conflict for Account

5. Mixing Pessimistic and Optimistic Methods

The previous section showed that objects employing optimistic and pessimistic techniques can be used together in a single system. This section shows that optimistic and pessimistic techniques can also be combined within a single object. For example, consider an Account whose balance is expected to cover all debits, but for which concurrent debits are frequent. Optimistic techniques are well suited for resolving the infrequent conflicts between credits and debits, but poorly suited for the more frequent conflicts between debits. A mixed scheme could exploit the strengths of each method by using pessimistic techniques to prevent "high-risk" conflicts, reserving optimistic methods to detect "low-risk" conflicts.

Mixed conflict-based validation is implemented as follows. After a transaction executes an operation, but before it updates its intentions list, it requests a *pessimistic lock* for that event. Pessimistic locks are related by a *pessimistic conflict* relation. If any other transaction holds a conflicting lock, the lock is refused, the event is discarded, and the operation is later retried. (The invocation may return a different result when it is retried.) If the lock is granted, the intentions list is updated, and the response is returned to the client. A transaction's pessimistic locks are released when it commits or aborts. When the transaction commits, validation proceeds as before.

Unlike optimistic conflict relations, pessimistic relations must be symmetric, since the order in which transactions eventually commit is unknown when pessimistic conflicts are detected. The fundamental constraint governing an object's optimistic and pessimistic conflict relations is the following: their union must be a serial dependency relation. An empty pessimistic relation yields the conflict-based validation scheme of Section 4, and an empty optimistic relation yields a type-specific two-phase locking scheme. Numerous possibilities lie between these two extremes; the appropriate balance between pessimism and optimism depends on the expected frequency of each conflict.

The mixed protocol is modeled by adding the following state component to both the forward and backward validation automata:

$$\text{P-Lock: EVENT} \rightarrow 2^{\text{TRANS}}$$

P-Lock(e) is the set of transactions that hold pessimistic locks for *e*. Initially, all such sets are empty. Pessimistic lock conflicts are governed by a pessimistic conflict relation $\succ_p \subseteq \text{EVENT} \times \text{EVENT}$. The precondition for *A* to execute *e* has an additional clause:

If $e \succ_p e'$ or $e' \succ_p e$ then $\text{P-Lock}(e') - \{A\} = \emptyset$.

Note that lock conflicts are determined by the symmetric closure of $\succ_p$. Afterwards, the transaction is granted a pessimistic lock for the event.

$$\text{P-Lock}'(e) = \text{P-Lock}(e) \cup \{A\}$$

Finally, a transaction's pessimistic locks are released when it commits or aborts.

Pessimistic conflicts prevent concurrent transactions from executing conflicting events:

Lemma 10: For a mixed (forward or backward) validation automaton, if *A* and *A'* are concurrent active transactions, and *e* is an event in *Intentions(A)*, then there is no *e'* in *Intentions(A')* such that $e \succ_p e'$.

Proof: The precondition for *A* to execute *e* ensures that the property holds initially, and it prevents any other transaction from violating the property while *A* is active.

Define a mixed automaton's conflict relation to be $\succ_p \cup \succ_o$.

Lemma 11: For any mixed forward validation automaton whose conflict relation is a serial dependency relation, *Perm•Intentions(A)* is legal for all active *A*.

Proof: As before, it is enough to show that *Perm•Intentions(A)* remains legal after the commit of a distinct transaction *A'*. By the induction hypothesis, *Perm'* = *Perm•Intentions(A')* is legal. There is no *e* in *Intentions(A)* and *e'* in *Intentions(A')* such that $e \succ_o e'$ (Lemma 3) or $e \succ_p e'$ (Lemma 10). Because $\succ_p \cup \succ_o$ is a serial dependency relation, *Perm'•Intentions(A)* is legal by Lemma 2.

Lemma 12: For any mixed backward validation automaton whose conflict relation is a serial dependency relation, *Perm•Intentions(A)* is legal for all valid *A*.

Proof: If *A'* commits without invalidating *A*, there is no *e* in *Intentions(A)* and *e'* in *Intentions(A')* such that $e \succ_o e'$ (Lemma 7) or $e \succ_p e'$ (Lemma 10), therefore *Perm'•Intentions(A)* is legal by Lemma 2.

The proofs of the remaining correctness and optimality theorems are omitted for brevity, since they are almost identical to their analogs in the previous section.

> **Theorem 13:** A mixed forward validation automaton whose conflict relation is a serial dependency relation will accept only hybrid atomic schedules.

> **Theorem 14:** A mixed forward validation automaton whose conflict relation is a not serial dependency relation will accept a schedule that is not hybrid atomic.

> **Theorem 15:** A mixed backward validation automaton whose conflict relation is a serial dependency relation will accept only hybrid atomic schedules.

> **Theorem 16:** A mixed backward validation automaton whose conflict relation is a not serial dependency relation will accept a schedule that is not hybrid atomic.

6. State-Based Validation

Although conflict-based validation accepts more interleavings than other optimistic schemes, it will nevertheless restart certain transactions unnecessarily. For example, one debiting transaction need not be invalidated by another if the balance covers both debits. The optimality proofs given above imply that no scheme, optimistic or pessimistic, can permit concurrent debits simply on the basis of conflicts between pairs of events. Instead, the accuracy of validation can be enhanced only by taking objects' states into account, as in the optimistic counter management scheme of IMS/VS [10]. Such *state-based* validation may be more expensive than conflict-based validation, since it may (at worst) amount to re-executing part of the transaction. Nevertheless, state-based validation may be cost-effective in special cases where predefined conflicts are too restrictive, and where validation conditions can be evaluated efficiently.

Both forward and backward validation can exploit state information. For forward validation, *A* may commit only if:

For all *A'* active and distinct from *A*, Perm•Intentions(A)•Intentions(A') is legal.

For backward validation, *A* may commit only if:

Perm•Intentions(A) is legal.

These formulations reveal an important practical asymmetry between forward and backward state-based validation: forward validation is strictly more expensive. This observation is in contrast to conflict-based validation, where forward and backward validation are roughly equivalent in run-time cost. Consequently, only backward validation is considered in this section.

A predicate *P[e]* on histories is a *validating predicate* for *e* if:

$P[e](h) \Rightarrow h \cdot e$ is legal.

A validating predicate is *optimal* if the implication is mutual. Validating predicates can be extended to histories in the obvious way:

$P[g \cdot e](h) = P[g](h) \wedge P[e](h \cdot g)$

As it executes, each transaction builds up a validating predicate for its intentions list. The transaction is validated by applying this predicate to the object's permanent state.

The cost of conflict-based validation is largely type-independent, but the cost of state-based validation depends on type-specific properties: how compactly validating predicates can be represented, how efficiently they can be evaluated, and how many additional interleavings they validate. The following idealized implementation of an Account provides an "existence proof" that state-based validation can be effective for certain data types. An Account is modeled as an automaton with the following components:

Bal: INT

Low: TRANS → INT

High: TRANS → INT

Change: TRANS → INT

Clock: TIMESTAMP

Committed: 2^{TRANS}

Aborted: 2^{TRANS}

Bal is the object's permanent state, represented here as a balance. Each transaction's validating predicate is encoded by two quantities: Low(A) is the transaction's lower bound on the current balance (initially zero), and High(A) is the transaction's current upper bound (initially unbounded). Change(A) is the transaction's intentions list, represented here simply as a net change to the balance.

Account events have the following pre- and postconditions. For A to execute Debit(k)/Ok(),

Pre: Bal + Change(A) $\geq$ k

Post: Change'(A) = Change(A)—k

           Low'(A) = max(Low(A),k—Change(A)),

for Debit(k)/Overdraft(),

Pre: Bal + Change(A) $<$ k

Post: High'(A) = min(High(A),k—Change(A))

and for Credit(k)/Ok(),

Pre: true

Post: Change'(A) = Change(A) + k.

A will be validated if and only if the committed balance lies between the observed upper and lower bounds:

           Low(A) $\leq$ Bal $<$ High(A)

After A commits, its changes are applied to the balance.

           Bal' = Bal + Change(A)

An inductive argument (not given) shows that the validating predicates employed by this automaton are correct and optimal. Moreover, the run-time cost of validation is comparable to the cost of conflict-based validation for this particular data type.

7. Interaction With Replication

This section gives a brief informal summary of how optimistic techniques interact with quorum-consensus replication [15, 14]. Conflict-based validation extends readily to replication, supporting availability properties identical to those supported by pessimistic conflict-based techniques. State-based validation, however, has an interesting property: it places fewer constraints on availability than pessimistic state-based techniques.

A *replicated object* is an object whose state is stored redundantly at multiple sites. Replicated objects are implemented by two kinds of modules: *repositories* and *front-ends*. Repositories provide long-term storage for the object's state, while front-ends carry out operations for clients. A client executes an operation by sending the invocation to a front-end. The front-end merges the data from an *initial quorum* of repositories, performs a local computation, and records the response at a *final quorum* of repositories. A *quorum* for an operation is any set of sites that includes both an initial and a final quorum for that operation. Each operation's availability is determined by its set of quorums, thus constraints on quorum assignment determine the range of availability properties realizable by replication.

Because state information for replicated objects is distributed, it is convenient for validation to use conflicts between invocations and events rather than between pairs of events. Validation based on invocation/event conflict is less effective, since it uses less information, but it requires less message traffic. The notion of serial dependency is extended to relations between invocations and events as follows. A relation $\succ$ between invocations and events induces a relation $\succ'$ between pairs of events: $e \succ' e'$ if $e.inv \succ e'$, where $e.inv$ denotes the invocation part of the event e. $\succ \subseteq$ INVOCATION $\times$ EVENT is an (invocation/event) *serial dependency relation* if the induced relation between events is an (event/event) serial dependency relation.

For forward validation, each repository maintains an optimistic lock for each invocation. A transaction acquires an optimistic lock at each repository in the invocation's initial quorum. A transaction is validated if and only if no other transaction holds a conflicting optimistic lock at any repository in the transaction's final quorums. For backward validation, each repository keeps track of $First(A,i)$, the logical time when A first executed the invocation i at that repository, and $Last(e)$, the commit timestamp of the most recent transaction to execute e at that repository. A transaction is validated if and only if for each invocation i of A and each conflicting event e: $Last(e) < First(A,i)$ at each repository in the transaction's initial quorums.

The following is a necessary and sufficient correctness condition for both schemes: the intersection of the conflict relation with the quorum intersection relation must be an (invocation/event) serial dependency relation. (In practice, they would be identical.) This requirement ensures that any conflict will be detected at the non-empty intersection of two quorums, causing validation to fail. This condition is identical to that imposed by *consensus locking* [14], a conflict-based pessimistic scheme.

While conflict-based validation can be done at repositories, state-based validation must done at front-ends, because the state information at any individual repository may be incomplete. For simplicity, assume that each transaction uses a single front-end for each object. A transaction is validated by reconstructing the permanent state from the transaction's initial quorums and applying the validation predicate for its intentions list. Here, a necessary and sufficient correctness condition is that the quorum intersection relation be a serial dependency relation.

State-based validation provides a way to circumvent certain trade-offs between concurrency and availability imposed by pessimistic state-based methods. Using pessimistic techniques, concurrency is enhanced at the cost of tightening constraints on quorum assignment. This trade-off is best illustrated by an example; a systematic treatment appears elsewhere [13, 14]. Consider an Account replicated among n identical sites. Consensus locking permits $\lceil n/2 \rceil$ distinct quorum assignments: Debit requires any m sites, where $m > n/2$, and Credit requires any $n-m+1$ sites. A more complex pessimistic scheme that takes full advantage of state information permits exactly one quorum assignment: both Credit and Debit require a majority of sites. The interesting observation here is that state-based validation permits all $\lceil n/2 \rceil$ quorum assignments, yet it validates every interleaving permitted by the more restrictive pessimistic scheme. The disadvantage of pessimistic schemes is that they must perform the equivalent of both forward and backward validation: each event must be legal when appended to its transaction's view, and the event must not invalidate any concurrent transaction's view. In short, after-the-fact conflict detection places fewer constraints on quorum assignment than dynamic conflict avoidance.

8. Conclusions

I have proposed two reasons why conventional optimistic techniques are inappropriate for general-purpose distributed systems. First, such techniques are typically designed for database applications in which read operations predominate, an implausible assumption for many non-database applications. Second, such techniques are typically monolithic, applying to all the data encompassed within a system, an undesirable property in an open-ended, decentralized distributed system. This paper has proposed new techniques to address these limitations:

- Conflict-based validation systematically exploits type-specific properties to provide more effective validation than conventional techniques employing a simple model of read/write conflicts. The problem of identifying a correct and minimal set of conflicts for an object is shown to be equivalent to the algebraic problem of identifying a minimal serial dependency relation for the data type.

- The optimistic techniques proposed here are modular, permitting individual objects to choose independently from optimistic, pessimistic, or mixed techniques. Optimistic techniques can be used to resolve "low-risk" conflicts, while standard pessimistic techniques such as two-phase locking can be used to resolve "high-risk" conflicts.

- Besides permitting more accurate validation, the notion of serial dependency also provides an "upper bound" on the concurrency realizable by conflict-based validation. An application that needs additional concurrency must use a validation technique that takes the object's state into account. *State-based* validation is a general technique that can validate any interleaving permitted by a pessimistic method, although its run-time cost is type-dependent.

- Forward and backward conflict-based validation have comparable run-time costs, but backward state-based validation is easier than forward state-based validation.

- Conflict-based validation is readily integrated with quorum-consensus replication, at a slight loss in concurrency. State-based validation, however, places fewer constraints on availability than pessimistic methods that support a comparable level of concurrency.

These results suggest that optimistic concurrency control may yet have a place in general-purpose distributed systems.

Acknowledgments

I would like to thank Beth Bottos, Dean Daniels, Dan DuChamp, Ellen Siegel, and Bill Weihl for comments and for help in tracking down citations.

References

[1]   R. Agrawal.
        Concurrency control and recovery in multiprocessor database machines: design and performance evaluation.
        PhD thesis, University of Wisconsin, 1983.

[2]   D. Z. Badal.
        Concurrency Control overhead or closer look at blocking vs. non-blocking concurrency control mechanisms.
        In *Proceedings of the 5th Berkeley Workshop*, pages 55-103. 1981.

[3]   M. Carey.
        Modeling and Evaluation of Database Concurrency Control Algorithms.
        PhD thesis, University of California, Berkeley, September, 1983.

[4]   S. Ceri and S. Owicki.
        On the use of optimistic methods for concurrency control in distributed databases.
        In *Proceedings of the 6th Berkeley Workshop*, pages 117-130. 1982.

[5]   A. Chan, S. Fox, W. T. Lin, A. Nori, and D. Ries.
        The implementation of an integrated concurrency control and recovery scheme.
        In *Proceedings of the 1982 SIGMOD Conference.* ACM SIGMOD, 1982.

[6]   D. J. Dubourdieu.
        Implementation of distributed transactions.
        In *Proceedings 1982 Berkeley Workshop on Distributed Data Management and Computer Networks*, pages 81-94. 1982.

[7]   C. Dwork and D. Skeen.
       The Inherent Cost of Nonblocking Commitment.
       In *Proceedings of the Second Annual Symposium on Principles of Distributed Computing*,
            pages 1-11. ACM, August, 1983.

[8]   K. P. Eswaran, J. N. Gray, R. A. Lorie, and I. L. Traiger.
       The notion of consistency and predicate locks in a database system.
       Communications ACM 19(11):624-633, November, 1976.

[9]   P. Franaszek, and J. T. Robinson.
       Limitations of concurrency in transaction processing.
       ACM Transactions on Database Systems 10(1):1-28, March, 1985.

[10]   D. Gawlick.
       Processing 'hot spots' in high performance systems.
       In *Proceedings COMPCON'85*. 1985.

[11]   J. Gray.
       Notes on Database Operating Systems.
       Lecture Notes in Computer Science 60.
       Springer-Verlag, Berlin, 1978, pages 393-481.

[12]   T. Härder.
       Observations on optimistic concurrency control schemes.
       Information Systems 9:111-120, June, 1984.

[13]   M. P. Herlihy.
       Comparing how atomicity mechanisms support replication.
       In *Proceedings of the 4th annual ACM SIGACT-SIGOPS Symposium on Principles of
            Distributed Computing*. August, 1985.

[14]   M. P. Herlihy.
       Availability vs. atomicity: concurrency control for replicated data.
       Technical Report CMU-CS-85-108, Carnegie-Mellon University, February, 1985.

[15]   M. P. Herlihy.
       A quorum-consensus replication method for abstract data types.
       ACM Transactions on Computer Systems 4(1), February, 1986.

[16]   H. F. Korth.
       Locking primitives in a database system.
       Journal of the ACM 30(1), January, 1983.

[17]   H. T. Kung and J. T. Robinson.
       On optimistic methods for concurrency control.
       ACM Transactions on Database Systems 6:213-226, June, 1981.

[18]   L. Lamport.
       Time, clocks, and the ordering of events in a distributed system.
       Communications of the ACM 21(7):558-565, July, 1978.

[19]   G. Lausen.
       Concurrency control in data base systems: a step towards the integration of optimistic
            methods and locking.
       In *Proceedings of ACM '82*. 1982.

[20]   G. Lausen.
        Formal Aspects of optimistic concurrency control in a multiversion data base system.
        Information Systems 8(4):291-301; 1983.

[21]   D. A. Menasce, and N. Nakanishi.
        Optimistic versus pessimistic concurrency control mechanisms in data base management
            systems.
        Information Systems 7(1):13-27, 1982.

[22]   J. E. B. Moss.
        Nested Transactions: An Approach to Reliable Distributed Computing.
        Technical Report MIT/LCS/TR-260, Massachusetts Institute of Technology Laboratory for
            Computer Science, April, 1981.

[23]   C. H. Papadimitriou.
        The serializability of concurrent database updates.
        Journal of the ACM 26(4):631-653, October, 1979.

[24]   D. Reed.
        Implementing atomic actions on decentralized data.
        ACM Transactions on Computer Systems 1(1):3-23, February, 1983.

[25]   Y. C. Tay, N. Goodman, and R. Suri.
        Performance evaluation of locking in databases: a survey.
        Technical Report TR-17-84, Harvard Aiken Laboratory, 1984.

[26]   R. H. Thomas.
        A solution to the concurrency control problem for multiple copy databases.
        In *Proc. 16th IEEE Comput. Soc. Int. Conf. (COMPCON)*. Spring, 1978.

[27]   W. Weihl.
        Data-Dependent concurrency control and recovery.
        In *Proceedings of the 2nd annual ACM SIGACT-SIGOPS Symposium on Principles of
            Distributed Computing*. August, 1983.

Chapter 6

Special Features

Introduction

The papers in this chapter cover special features of database systems that fit in well with an object-oriented model, or that support the kinds of applications OODBs are designed to serve. The first three deal with features aimed at computer-aided design (CAD): complex objects, propagation of changes, and "designer transactions" (our thanks to Dave Stryker for the final term). The last paper concerns derived data.

Every variety of CAD—electrical, mechanical, software, architectural—deals with designs as complex objects: composite objects consisting of multiple subcomponents, which may themselves be complex objects. Entities recursively composed of simpler entities arise in many other application domains as well: office information systems, document management, and graphics, to name three. Different approaches to database support for complex objects have emphasized different aspects, depending on the proclivities of the researchers and on what these people thought most important for their applications. Those aspects include the following:

- *Arbitrary levels of structure*: There is often no a priori bound on the number of levels of hierarchical decomposition in design artifacts. However, many record-based systems support direct modeling of only one level of structure (relational) or a fixed number of levels (hierarchical). *Non–first-normal-form* (NFNF) or *nested* relational databases [Da+86; SS86] support relations as attribute values, thus getting away from the single level of structure in the relational model. Some NFNF databases do bound the depth of

nesting in a given relation. All object-oriented databases can support arbitrary levels of nesting, through types whose instances can directly reference other instances of the type.

- *Manipulation as a unit*: A problem in the relational model is that a complex object typically must be decomposed into tuples over several relations, and there is no data item that represents the object as a whole. Hence, some approaches concentrate on treating the complex object as a single unit for purposes of query, copying, locking or physical placement. Lorie and Plouffe [LP83] made extensions to the relational model to treat a group of related tuples as a unit for certain operations. The ORION project [KB+87] has looked at locking schemes for gaining control of a complex object without obtaining explicit locks on all that object's subcomponents.

- *Sharing of subparts*: Other projects have focused on the ability of complex objects to share subparts. In most record-based database systems, there is no sharing of records between aggregate structures (as in the relational and hierarchical models), or a record can participate in a fixed number of aggregates (as in the network model). CAD environments often provide libraries of components, and the expectation is that a design can make unlimited use of them. Object identity obviously supports shared subparts, and a number of data models that predated OODBs provided sharing through object or entity identity. Functional data models such as DAPLEX [Sh81] have functions on entities whose values are other entities or sets of entities. The hybrid model of Haynie [Ha81] is a variation on the relational model in which tuples have identity and can participate in multiple relations.

- *A distinguished Component-of relationship*: Some data-model designers believe that the component-of or subpart-of relationship between a composite object and its constituents is important enough to be made a primitive concept in their models. That relationship is thus distinguished from general interobject reference, and often has special operation or constraint semantics. The Version Server of Katz, Chang, and Bhateja [KCB86] has *configuration* as a basic modeling unit, to represent the grouping of design components into a consistent whole.

- *Hiding detail*: The *molecular-object* model [BKi85] focuses on the distinction between interface and implementation of complex objects. The subparts of a complex objects are segregated into those that can be referenced from outside and those that are hidden. For example, a complex object representing an integrated-circuit chip might show only its **Pin** objects, and hide its **Gate** and **Wire** objects. Information hiding serves to shield parts of a design from changes. As long as the interface objects stay the same, the internal implementation of the complex object can change without affecting other parts of the design (at least structurally). The developers of the PROBE Data Model (PDM) [DM+87] argue that multiple interfaces to or abstractions of a complex object might be needed, and can be handled more uniformly with views.

- *Collective properties*: Values of properties can be propagated from the parts to the whole and from the whole to the parts in a complex object. For example, a **Road** may derive its length from the combined lengths of its **RoadSegment** components, and a **RoadSegment** might inherit its name from the name of the **Road** in which it is located. PDM emphasizes the procedural aspects of complex objects, to deal with such derived information.

- *Algebraic or logical operations*: Still other efforts have concentrated on algebras or logics for building, manipulating, and querying collections of complex objects [BKh86; Za85].

Katz and Chang [KC87] consider the interaction of complex design objects with versions of components and with equivalences declared between components. The equivalences arise from two components being descriptions of the same piece of the design, such as an electrical schematic and a VLSI mask layout for the same circuit. Creating a new version of a component A can entail creating new versions of another component B, either because A is part of a design configuration represented by complex object B, or because B is an equivalent representation of the design artifact described by A. The authors point out a number of ways ambiguity can arise in how far to propagate version changes, and how many versions to create when multiple objects are changed in one transactions. They propose a number of mechanisms to remove ambiguity and to limit the propagations of changes, such as performing group check-in and check-out, flagging objects as dependent and independent, and doing timestamp comparisons.

The requirements for concurrency control and recovery in design databases are different from those for business data processing. Traditional transaction processing emphasizes large numbers of short, simple transactions issued on behalf of users who are oblivious of one another. Design applications have groups of cooperating users who need parts of the database for long periods and who make complex updates. Transactions in business data processing are the unit of atomicity, recovery, integrity, and visibility by other users. The trend in transaction support for design is to provide these capabilities at different levels of granularity. For example, a designer may be involved in a long design session, where she does not want to make her work visible to other users yet, but wants to take *savepoints* to avoid losing her work in a system crash. The nested transaction model of Moss [Mo81] separates atomicity from visibility. A transaction can have any number of subtransactions that each execute atomically relative to one another, but no changes are visible to other users until the top-level transaction commits. Korth, Kim, and Bancilhon [KKB88] propose *cooperative transactions* for groups of designers working together on a task. All the designers have mutual visibility for their work within the cooperative transaction, but no other users see the changes until the cooperative transaction commits. The authors also propose several other variations on transactions for design applications, most of which exploit the fact that the decomposition of a design effort into project and teams gives natural divisions of data and transactions. Their hierarchy of transaction types, workspace model for concurrency control, and multigranularity locking takes advantage of this decomposition.

The CACTIS system [HK86] emphasizes efficient support for derived data. In the CACTIS model, objects are attributed nodes in a graph in which the edges are named relationships. The values for computed attributes can depend on the values of attributes at adjacent nodes (objects), similarly to the way attributes are computed from values at parent and children nodes in attributed trees used in parsing. However, the CACTIS model allows general graph structures rather than trees, so a more sophisticated attribute evaluation algorithm is needed. Attribute updating is done selectively in CACTIS, making sure that any attribute has its values computed at most once because of a change, and delaying reevaluation of attributes that do not participate in the current query.

Although all OODBs can provide computed attributes via methods, most compute such values on demand, whereas CACTIS computes and stores such values. If a computed attribute is likely to be read several times before it gets a new value, on average, then the CACTIS approach can save computation time in exchange for more storage space.

References

[BKh86]   F. Bancilhon and S. Khoshafian. A Calculus for Complex Objects. *Proceedings of the ACM SIGACT-SIGMOD Symposium on Principles of Database Systems*, Boston, March 1986.

[BKi85]   D.S. Batory and W. Kim. Modeling Concepts for VLSI CAD Objects. *ACM Transactions on Database Systems*, 10(3), 1985.

[Da+86]   P. Dadam, et al. A DBMS Prototype to Support Extended NF2 Relations: An Integrated View on Flat Tables and Hierarchies. *Proceedings of the ACM SIGMOD International Conference on Management of Data*, Washington, D.C., May 1986.

•[DM+87]   U. Dayal, F. Manola, A. Buchman, U. Chakravarthy, D. Goldhirsch, S. Heiler, J. Orenstein, and A. Rosenthal. Simplifying Complex Objects: The PROBE Approach to Modelling and Querying Them. *Proceedings of the German Database Conference*, Burg Technik und Wissenschafts, Darmstadt, April 1987.

[Ha81]   M.N. Haynie. The Relational/Network Hybrid Data Model for Design Automation Databases. *Proceedings of the 18th Design Automation Conference*, Nashville, TN, July 1981.

•[HK86]   S.E. Hudson and R. King. CACTIS: A Database System for Specifying Func-

tionally-Defined Data. K. Dittrich and U.Dayal, eds. In *Proceedings of the International Workshop on Object-Oriented Database Systems*, Pacific Grove, CA, September 1986.

[KB+87]   W. Kim, J. Banerjee, H.-T. Chou, J.F. Garza, and D. Woelk. Composite Object Support in an Object-Oriented Database System. *ACM Conference on Object-Oriented Programming Systems, Languages, and Applications*, Orlando, FL, October 1987.

•[KC87]   R.H. Katz and E. Chang. Managing Change in a Computer-Aided Design Database. *Proceedings of the XIII International Conference on Very Large Databases*, Brighton, England, September 1987. Morgan Kaufmann Publishers, San Mateo, CA.

[KCB86]   R.H. Katz, E. Chang, and R. Bhateja. Version Modelling Concepts for Computer-Aided Design Databases. *Proceedings ACM SIGMOD International Conference on Management of Data*, Washington, D.C., May 1986.

•[KKB88]   H. Korth, W. Kim, and F. Bancilhon. On Long-Duration CAD Transactions. *Information Science*, 1988.

[LP83]   R.A. Lorie and W. Plouffe. Complex Objects and Their Use in Design Transactions. *Proceedings of the ACM Workshop on Engineering Design Applications*, San Jose, CA, May 1983.

[Mo81]   J.E.B. Moss. *Nested Transactions: An Approach to Reliable Distributed Computing*. Ph.D. Thesis, Laboratory for Computer Science, MIT, April 1981. Available as Technical Report MIT/LCS/TR-260.

[SS86]   H.-J. Schek and M.H. Scholl. The Relational Model with Relation-Valued Attributes. *Information Systems*, 11:(4), 1986.

[Sh81]   D. Shipman. The Functional Data Model and the Data Language DAPLEX. *ACM Transactions on Database Systems*, 6:1, 1981.

[Za85]   C. Zaniolo. The Representation and Deductive Retrieval of Complex Objects. *VLDB XI*, Stockholm, August 1985. Morgan Kaufmann Publishers, San Mateo, CA.

• indicates article included in this volume

Simplifying Complex Objects:
The PROBE Approach to Modelling and Querying Them *

Umeshwar Dayal, Frank Manola, Alejandro Buchmann, Upen Chakravarthy,
David Goldhirsch, Sandra Heiler, Jack Orenstein, Arnon Rosenthal

Computer Corporation of America, Cambridge, Massachusetts U.S.A.

ABSTRACT

Several recent papers have described application requirements, data model capabilities, or implementation approaches for supporting objects with a complex internal structure. These "complex objects" are interesting because they are often found in interesting new applications of databases, such as engineering. Unfortunately, the requirements for complex objects have typically been described without relating them to specific new capabilities required from the DBMS, and frequently the extensions have been tied to the relational model. This paper attempts to clarify the requirements for such capabilities in a model-independent way. It shows that a (relatively) small number of capabilities are really needed, and outlines how we are trying to incorporate many of them into PROBE, an object-oriented DBMS being developed at CCA.

1. Introduction

The application of database technology to new application domains, such as CAD/CAM, geographic information systems, software engineering, and office automation, is an extremely active area of database research. Many of these new applications deal with highly structured objects that are composed of other objects. For example, a part in a part hierarchy may be composed of other parts; an integrated circuit module may be composed of other modules, pins, and wires; a complex geographic feature such as an industrial park may be composed of other features such as buildings, smokestacks, and gardens; a program module may be composed of other program modules, each with a declaration part and a body; a document may be composed of sections and front matter, and the sections themselves may be composed of section headings, paragraphs of text, and figures.

In many applications these complex objects are the units for storage, retrieval, update, integrity control, concurrency control, and recovery. For instance, in a design application, it may be necessary to lock an entire part assembly (i.e., a part together with its component parts) if the part is to be redesigned. Similarly, if an instance of an integrated circuit module is deleted from a design, the deletion must be propagated atomically to all its components.

The basic problem is that in conventional (e.g., relational) database systems, a complex object is typically represented by many tuples scattered among several relations. Consider, for example, a 4-input AND gate built up of three 2-input AND gates [LOR183].

Gate Type	GT	description
	2AND	"C = A & B"
	4AND	"E = A&B&C&D"

Pin Type	GT	PT	I/O
	2AND	A	I
	2AND	B	I
	2AND	C	O
	4AND	A	I
	4AND	B	I
	4AND	C	I
	4AND	D	I
	4AND	E	O

Gate Instance	GT	GI	Parent
	2AND	C1	4AND
	2AND	C2	4AND
	2AND	C3	4AND
	4AND	P	---

Wire Instance	WI	GT1	GI1	Pin1	GT2	GI2	Pin2	Parent
	W1	4AND	P	A	2AND	C1	A	4AND
	W2	4AND	P	B	2AND	C1	B	4AND
	W3	4AND	P	C	2AND	C2	A	4AND
	W4	4AND	P	D	2AND	C2	B	4AND
	W5	2AND	C	C	2AND	C3	A	4AND
	W6	2AND	C	C	2AND	C3	B	4AND
	W7	2AND	C	C	4AND	P	E	4AND

Figure 1.1 Relational Representation of a Complex Object

This object and a collection of relations to represent it are shown in figure 1.1. The Gate Type and Pin Type relations describe the two types of gates and the pins for each gate type, respectively. The Gate Instance relation indicates that each instance of a 4-input AND gate is built up of three instances of 2-input AND gates. The Wire Instance relation shows that each instance of a 4-input AND gate contains seven wires, each connecting a pair of pins. For instance, wire W1 connects the (external) input pin A of the 4-input AND gate to pin A of its first component 2-input AND gate.

* This work was supported by the Defence Advanced Research Projects Agency and by the Space and Naval Warfare Systems Command under Contract No. N00039-85-C-0263. The views and conclusions contained in this paper are those of the authors and do not necessarily represent the official policies of the Defense Advanced Research Projects Agency, the Space and Naval Warfare Systems Command, or the U.S. Government.

The tuples in these different relations that together constitute the complex object have toPbe logically linked together by value (in this case, by values of the parent attributes of the Gate Instance and Wire Instance relations). There is no way to explicitly specify to the DBMS that all these linked tuples form a single, complex object. Thus, operations on the complex object as a whole must typically consist of several relational commands.

The focus of previous work on complex objects was largely to overcome this deficiency of the relational model. [HASK82, LORI83] propose enhancements to the relational model to represent entities and hierarchical relationships. The proposed enhancement is to provide links between tuples comprising a "complex object". This is accomplished by first introducing system-generated identifiers or surrogates [CODD79] of tuples. The GT, GI, and WI attributes will be automatically generated by the system when tuples are stored in these relations and these values are system-wide unique and never reused. Then, the Parent attributes are declared to be COMPONENT-OF of the Gate Type relation; the values of these attributes will be identifiers connecting to the Gate Type relation. Although operations on these linked relations are not explicitly described, it is not too hard to imagine how the system can trace these links to propagate retrieval, deletion, locking requests, etc. to all the components of a complex object.

More recently, the relational model has been extended to more directly represent hierarchical structures through the notion of nested (or non first normal form) relations, i.e.. relations whose attribute values may themselves be relations. The relational algebra and calculus have correspondingly been extended to manipulate and retrieve such hierarchically structured objects [SCHE86, FISC83, BANC86a]. Storage structures and query processing techniques for non first normal form relations are currently being investigated [DEPP86, KHOS87].

Other requirements of complex objects have been studied in [BATO84, BATO85, KATZ86]. This has led to the introduction of some additional modelling concepts. [BATO84] introduced the concept of *molecular aggregation*. The motivation for this concept was to represent a complex object at different levels of abstraction. Specifically, a complex object was defined to have an *interface*, describing its external characteristics, and an *implementation*. describing its internal structure. In our example. the interface of the 4-input AND gate would consist of the second tuple in the Gate Type relation and the last five tuples of the Pin Type relation shown in figure 1.1. The implementation would consist of all the tuples of the Gate Instance and Wire Instance relations. Four categories of molecular aggregation were identified. The result was a framework that distinguishes between objects that share and that do not share structure; and between objects in which instances of a type (e.g., Part) can appear as components of other instances of the same type, and those in which this cannot happen.

In [BATO85], additional concepts for modelling objects in VLSI CAD applications were introduced. These new concepts are: *version generalization*, which permits versions of a complex object to inherit its interface (but not its implementation): *component instantiation*, which permits more than one instance of a component to be used in the implementation of a complex object (the instances may differ in some attribute values, e.g., the three 2-input AND gate instances that are used in the 4-input AND gate are all at different locations): and *parametrized versions*, which permits a designer to identify the component types that are used to implement complex objects without specifying which versions of these components are to be used.

[KATZ86] adopts a similar approach, introducing modelling constructs for representing three distinguished relationships: COMPONENT-OF. IS-A (generalization). and VERSION-OF.

In the course of developing an advanced DBMS, PROBE, aimed at these new applications. we naturally studied the various published concepts of "complex objects". Understanding these concepts was made difficult by several problems. First. the requirements were often identified in application-oriented terms without translating them into data-model-oriented terms. This sometimes made it unclear whether what was required was actually an enhancement to the data model or other DBMS capabilities, or just a particular database design technique, or perhaps a well-designed set of view definitions.

Second, the requirements were usually described as enhancements to the relational data model. This made it hard to determine whether enhancements would be needed if some *other* data model was used or were due solely to limitations of the relational model.

Third, the specific enhancements proposed were sometimes special cases of more general facilities. Given the applications involved, it seemed likely that these facilities would have to be provided in their full generality anyway.

This paper attempts to more precisely identify the requirements for complex objects that arise in many new DBMS applications. We also survey requirements that almost invariably accompany complex objects, yet are often omitted from papers on the subject. We argue that support for complex objects per se imposes few new requirements. Most of the required data modeling features are already provided in entity-based semantic data models, such as DAPLEX [SHIP81], which serves as the starting point for our investigations. Those that are not (such as special operations) are not readily definable by a simple operation propagation facility associated with a special type of relationship (viz., the COMPONENT-OF relationship); rather, a general facility for defining tailored operations is needed.

Specifically, the PROBE approach is to provide general capabilities rather than introduce *ad hoc* special-purpose constructs. We believe that an object-oriented database approach [DITT86, LOCH86] provides most of the requisite general capabilities. Such an approach allows other related requirements of the applications, not dealt with directly by previous approaches to complex objects, to be satisfactorily supported.

This approach of providing general rather than special capabilities is also being pursued by the POSTGRES group [STON86]. [ROWE86] describes how hierarchical objects can be implemented using the general facilities of POSTGRES. However, while POSTGRES extends a relational DBMS, PROBE starts with a semantic data model that already provides many of the necessary basic features (entities, functions, and inheritance).

The rest of this paper is organized as follows. Section 2 lists the requirements for modelling complex objects and associated relationships, and describes the approaches that we are exploring for meeting these requirements in PROBE. Section 3 addresses issues in querying and manipulating complex objects, and describes an object-oriented algebra that we have developed for this purpose. Section 4 briefly comments on implementation issues.

2. Complex Objects and Relationships

This section identifies the data model requirements for complex objects. For each requirement, we describe how we propose to meet it in PROBE. We start from DAPLEX, a se:..antic data model and query language [SHIP81, SMIT81], which already provides some of the necessary basic features, and enhance it to a full object-oriented data model. We refer to the enhanced model as PDM (PROBE Data Model).

Entity Identity:

Supporting complex objects first requires supporting some notion of "entity" or "object" to which components and attributes can be related. The primary characteristic of an entity is its existence distinct from that of any other entity known to the system, or of any collection of attribute values. Since entities are distinct from ordinary values, special operators are required to deal with them (e.g. to specify that a new entity is to be created, to compare entities for identity, to create entity relationships).

PDM, like DAPLEX and other semantic data models, directly supports the notion of entities to model real-world objects, and provides the necessary operators. (We defer discussion of the operators to the next section.) Properties of entities, relationships between entities, and operations on entities are all uniformly represented in PDM as *functions*. Functions may be single-valued or set-valued, and either scalar-valued or entity-valued. Also, functions are allowed to have multiple input arguments and multiple output arguments. Entities that have the same functions are grouped into *entity types*. For the example of Figure 1.1, we can define the following entity type and functions on it:

    entity GATE TYPE is ENTITY
        function Name (GATE TYPE) --> STRING
        function Description (GATE TYPE) --> STRING
        function Pins (GATE TYPE) --> set of PIN TYPE
        function Gate Components (GATE TYPE) --> set of GATE INSTANCE
        function Wire Components (GATE TYPE) --> set of WIRE INSTANCE

Here, Name and Description are single-valued, scalar-valued functions, and Pins is a set-valued, entity-valued function. (Each of these functions has a single input argument and a single output argument.) Later we shall see examples of functions with more than one input or output argument.) Unlike the relational model, or extensions to it [CODD79, HASK82, LORI83], no "primary key" attributes or "surrogate" attributes have to be explicitly defined. The system automatically generates and maintains internal identifiers for each entity.

Object-Component Relationships:

A complex object is composed of other objects, and the relationship between the complex object and its components must be modelled.

In the relational representation of figure 1.1, the object-component relationship is modelled through the foreign key attribute, Parent, of the Wire Instance and Gate Instance relations. In [HASK82, LORI83], these foreign key attributes are specified to be COMPONENT-OF attributes; the system maintains *referential integrity*, i.e., when the parent object is deleted, the deletion is propagated automatically to the component objects. In [BATO84, BATO85], the component objects are hidden inside the implementation part of the molecular aggregate.

However, all models support some means of representing relationships among model objects. And so one must determine what special requirements, if any, exist for *component* relationships. In general, any special requirements must be either at the logical level (e.g., propagating deletions from the complex object to its components) or at the physical level (e.g., clustering of the components near the "parent" object). Our observation is that such requirements exist for a variety of relationships, not just for the COMPONENT-OF relationship associated with complex objects, and that the requirements may differ from one occurrence of a relationship to another. For example, in some applications it may be desirable to cluster objects based not on the COMPONENT-OF relationship, but on some other relationship (e.g., DESIGNED-BY). Similarly, in some applications it may be mandated that the deletion of a complex design cause the deletion of all subdesigns; in other applications, the subdesigns may be important in their own right and should not be deleted.

This suggests that a general facility for specifying arbitrary relationships and their behavioural properties is needed, instead of some small number of distinguished relationships with fixed semantics.

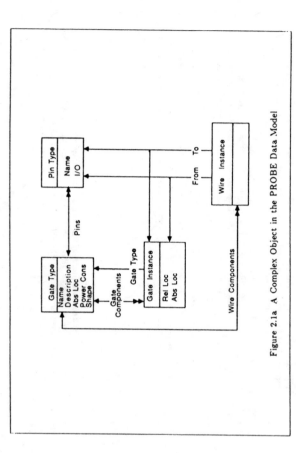

Figure 2.1a A Complex Object in the PROBE Data Model

In PDM, the complex object *and* its components are modelled as entities; relationships between the complex object and its components, and among components, are modelled by entity-valued (possibly set-valued) functions. Thus, the schema includes both the interface and the implementation (to use the terminology of [BATO84, BATO85]) of a complex object, together with one or more explicit functions that represent the relationship(s) between them. This is illustrated in figure 2.1, which corresponds to the complex object shown in the relational representation of figure 1.1 (plus some additional functions). (Figure 2.1a shows the schema in diagram form: entity types are depicted by boxes; entity-valued functions by arrows. Figure 2.1b lists the entity types and functions in this schema.)

Incidentally, figure 2.1 also illustrates that we can model more than one named relationship (Gate Components and Wire Components) between a complex object and its components, something that is not conveniently supported by the more rigid models of [HASK82, LORI83, BATO84, BATO85].

Entities and entity-valued functions can also be used to emulate the other modelling constructs for VLSI CAD objects, introduced in [BATO85, KATZ86]. Figure 2.2 illustrates how this is done for parameterized versions.

Our point here is that, like molecular aggregation itself, concepts such as COMPONENT-OF and parameterized versions are application-specific "packages" of capabilities. Instead of "building in" these specific packages, more generality can be obtained by breaking the packages down into their component facilities, and providing generalizations of these individual facilities. These generalized facilities can then be combined in powerful ways to meet the requirements of many other applications.

Derived Values in Complex Objects and Components:

Although a complex object will probably have attributes distinct from those of its components, some attribute values of the complex object may be derived from attribute values of its components. For example, the weight of a part assembly is the sum of the weights of its component parts; the delay through a circuit may be computed from the delays through its components; the earliest completion time of a task schedule is the sum of the start time and the durations of the tasks on the critical path. Conversely, some attribute values of the components may be derived from attribute values of the parent complex object. For example, the absolute location of a part in an assembly may be derived recursively from its relative location with respect to its parent, and so on up the part hierarchy.

```
for gt in GATE TYPE
  define
    Power Cons (gt) := sum (Power Cons (gt:2 in GATE TYPE
      where gt:2 isin Gate Type (Gate Components (gt))))
end

for gi in GATE INSTANCE
  define
    Abs Loc (gi) := transformation (Rel Loc (gi),
      Abs Loc (gt in GATE TYPE where
      gi isin Gate Components (gt)))
end
```

Figure 2.3 Derived Functions

Though a facility for derived data computation is clearly useful for complex objects. its usefulness is hardly *restricted* to complex objects. Data model designers have frequently observed the need to provide facilities for deriving data in "both directions" along 1-n relationships among data objects of conventional types. For example, one might wish to aggregate the salaries of employees in a department. Even in an engineering database. many of the computations that might be invoked are rather general (e.g. test and analysis procedures), rather than simple aggregate computations over the components of a single object. Thus, the new applications justify providing a general derived data definition facility, as opposed to some special bundling with "complex objects".

In PDM, because a complex object and its components are all represented as entities, it is easy to specify arbitrary functions over them. Although DAPLEX supports only *extensionally defined* functions i.e., functions whose values are "stored" in the database, PDM has been extended to include *intensionally defined* functions, i.e., functions whose values are derived from other values or are computed by arbitrary procedures. These intensionally defined functions can be used to specify that some attributes of a complex object are derived from attributes of its components and vice versa. Figure 2.3 illustrates this capability, using DAPLEX-like syntax. The Absolute Location of a Component Instance entity is defined to be a geometric

```
entity    GATE TYPE is ENTITY
function  Name (GATE TYPE) → STRING
function  Description (GATE TYPE) → STRING
function  Abs Loc (GATE TYPE) → POINT
function  Rel Loc (GATE TYPE) → POINT
function  Shape (GATE TYPE) → BOX
function  Pins (GATE TYPE) → set of PIN TYPE
function  Gate Components (GATE TYPE) → set of GATE INSTANCES
function  Wire Components (GATE TYPE) → set of WIRE INSTANCES

entity    PIN TYPE is ENTITY
function  Name (PIN TYPE) → STRING
function  I/O (PIN TYPE) → "I", "O"

entity    GATE INSTANCE is ENTITY
function  Gate Type (GATE INSTANCE) → GATE TYPE
function  Rel Loc (GATE INSTANCE) → POINT
function  Abs Loc (GATE INSTANCE) → POINT

entity    WIRE INSTANCE is ENTITY
function  From (WIRE INSTANCE) → (GATE INSTANCE, PIN TYPE)
function  To (WIRE INSTANCE) → (GATE INSTANCE, PIN TYPE)
```

Figure 2.1b Entity Types and Functions for the Complex Object

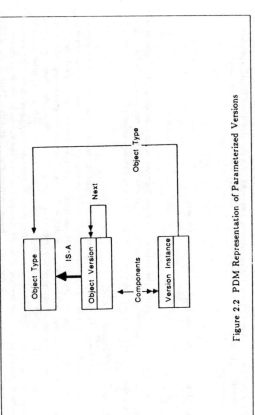

Figure 2.2 PDM Representation of Parameterized Versions

transformation of its Relative Location and the Absolute Location of its parent Gate entity. Conversely, the Power Consumption of a Gate entity is defined to be the sum of the Power Consumptions of its components. (Note that these may be recursive computations, in general, if we think of more than two levels of the component hierarchy. We describe the PROBE approach to recursion in the next section.) This capability is also not described in previous papers on complex objects.

3. Operations and Constraints on Complex Objects

In this section, we identify the requirements for querying or manipulating complex objects. As in the previous section, we argue that these requirements are best met through facilities that are useful in general, not just for some restricted notion of complex objects.

Operations on Complex Objects:

Perhaps the most fundamental requirement of a complex object is that the user be allowed to manipulate it as a whole. This requirement can be broken down into three sub-requirements. First is the ability to apply generic DBMS operations (such as deletion or display) to enire complex objects. Second is the ability to define arbitrary, application-specific operations on objects. The new applications generally require a variety of specialized operations associated with aspects of objects not considered in conventional applications, such as the orientation of objects in space and time. For example, it frequently is necessary to express operations such as geometric rotations and intersection of objects in space, search conditions based on geometric or pattern-oriented conditions, and constraints based on timing requirements. Third is the ability to automatically propagate operations to the components along relationships.

Operations on complex objects and propagation rules have been around since AUTOMATIC set membership was included in the CODASYL model. The model of [HASK82, LORI83] supports the propagation of retrieval, deletion, and lock operations. The IPIP system supports the definition and propagation of global operations, such as deletion, on CODASYL structures [JOHN83]; [BATO85] describes various deletion propagation rules for the modelling constructs it introduces for VLSI CAD objects.

However, it does not seem possible to attach a single fixed semantics for propagating operations along any of these relationships, because the semantics of these relationships are application-dependent. In some applications, it may be mandated that the latest version of an object be used in a design. As a new version is released, it may be important to replace automatically all instances of old versions in a design with the new version, or at least to alert designers that a new version has been released. In other applications, once a version is selected for a design, it may never be changed, except through a special authorized operation. For derived properties of a complex object, it may be important in some cases to propagate changes immediately; in other cases, it may be desirable to defer the propagation.

For PROBE, we have developed an algebra (the PDM algebra) that (a) provides generic operations on entities and functions, (b) permits the definition of application-specific operations, and (c) permits the specification of rules for propagating operations along relationships.

The algebra is a modification of relational algebra, and contains operations such as selection, projection, Cartesian product, and set operations. For purposes of the algebra, functions are viewed as relations, and entity types are viewed as zero-argument functions (i.e., unary relations containing all the entities of the type). The operations are viewed as operating on functions and producing functions. For example, the selection operation Select(F, P) selects those tuples of function F that satisfy predicate P (predicates are viewed as Boolean-valued functions). Project(F, L) projects the tuples of F on the functions in list L. Instead of a join operation, the algebra contains an "apply and append" operation: Apply-Append(F, G) applies function G to arguments taken from the tuples of function F; the result is a new function formed by appending to F columns containing the results of evaluating G on the tuples of F.

Given the schema of Figure 2.1, the query "Retrieve the names of the pins of a 4-input AND gate", would be expressed by the following sequence of statements in the PDM algebra:

```
T1 := Apply-Append (, GATE TYPE: GT)
T2 := Apply-Append (T1, Name(GATE TYPE: GT, STRING: S))
T3 := Select (T2, EQ(S, "4AND"))
T4 := Apply-Append (T3, Pins(GATE TYPE: GT, PIN TYPE: P))
T5 := Apply-Append (T4, Name(PIN TYPE: P, STRING: N))
T6 := Project (T5, N)
```

(Labels such as GT are used to relate arguments of the functions referenced in the various operations.)

The algebra also contains aggregation operations, update operations, and metadata operations for creating new entities and functions. For example, in Figure 3.1, we show how the two derived functions of Figure 2.3 can be expressed in the algebra. The interested reader is referred to [MANO86b] for more details of PDM algebra.

```
a. Definition of Power Cons (GATE TYPE) --> REAL:
T0 := Apply-Append (, GATE TYPE: GT)
T1 := Apply-Append (T0, Gate Components (GATE TYPE: GT1, GATE INSTANCE: GI))
T2 := Apply-Append (T1, Gate Type (GATE INSTANCE: GI, GATE TYPE: GT2))
T3 := Apply-Append (T2, Power Cons (GATE TYPE: GT2, REAL: R))
T4 := ggregate (T3, [GT1], Sum (R, REAL: RSUM))
     The tuples of of T3 are first grouped by GT1, then aggregated.
T5 := Project (T4, [GT1, RSUM])

b. Definition of Abs Loc (GATE INSTANCE) --> POINT:
T0 := Apply-Append (, GATE TYPE: GT)
T1 := Apply-Append (T0, Gate Components (GATE TYPE: GT, GATE INSTANCE: GI))
T2 := Apply-Append (T1, Rel Loc (GATINSTANCE: GI, POINT: P1))
T3 := Apply-Append (T2, Abs Loc (GATE TYPE: GT, POINT: P2))
T4 := Apply-Append (T3, Transformaion (POINT: P1, POINT: P2, POINT: RES))
T5 := Project (T4, [GI, RES])
```

Figure 3.1 Using the PDM Algebra to Define Derived Functions

PDM algebra is not intended to be an end-user query language; rather, it can serve as the basis for defining the semantics of query languages, and for studying query processing issues.

Additional operations on specific entity types can be introduced via intensionally defined functions, whose values are computed by procedures (written in some suitable programming language), rather than being stored in the database. Examples of such operations are "the center of gravity of a part" (computed from the shape of the part), "rotate part X through angle A", and the "transformation" function in Figure 2.3. Since these application-specific operations are modelled by functions, they, too, are evaluated over a set of entities through the Apply-Append operation of the PDM algebra, as illustrated by the second example of Figure 3.1. Furthermore, like all functions, operations, too, are inherited by subtypes from their supertypes.

Constraints on Component Relationships:

Not only is it important to model the components of a complex object, but it is equally important to capture any constraints on their interrelationships. In some cases, it is possible to capture such constraints within the DBMS. For example, the components of a circuit must satisfy connectivity constraints; the tuples of the Wire Instance relation in Figure 1.1 in effect establish these constraints. However, many of these constraints are too complex to be succinctly expressed and efficiently verified and enforced by a general-purpose DBMS. For example, there may be design constraints on the total power consumption of a circuit: the various components of the boundary representation of a 3D solid must be connected in a structure satisfying various geometric and graph-theoretic constraints. In such cases, it may be necessary to implement these constraints by special procedures (e.g., VLSI design rule checkers) outside the DBMS. However. it may still be desirable to declare these procedures to the DBMS. which can then automatically invoke the appropriate procedure when an operation that potentially violates a constraint is to be executed.

The DBMS response to a constraint violation is also an issue. Existing DBMSs always abort requests that violate constraints. This may be too restrictive for many design, decision support, and military command and control applications. Some constraints may be physically inviolable, e.g., absolute temperatures cannot be negative. Others may be design guidelines that are generally to be enforced. but may be violated in special cases (particularly when contradictory rules may be applicable). Facilities for specifying the action to be taken when a constraint is violated and for handling exceptions are necessary. These may involve notifying or alerting users, invoking compensatory procedures or exception handlers [BORG85, BUCH85].

In PROBE, the rules for specifying how and when to check constraints, and the rules for invoking exception handlers. are incorporated into the procedures that implement the various operations. Hence, like the operations themselves, these rules are definable by the user or application developer.

Multiple Levels of Abstraction:

A frequent requirement of modelling complex objects is the ability to view them at different levels of abstraction. The concept of molecular aggregation distinguishes two levels: the interface (at which only the aggregate characteristics of the object are visible) and the implementation (which describes the internal structure of the object in terms of its components).

In practice, however, the two-level concept of molecular aggregation may be too restrictive – arbitrary views may have to be supported. For example, an application that lists components of circuits may not need to "see" the WIRE INSTANCE entities of figure 2.1. An application that tests for short circuits may need to "see" only the WIRE INSTANCE entities and not the GATE INSTANCE entities. Another example occurs in geographic information processing. where entirely independent representations of objects (e.g., maps) at different levels of resolution have to coexist.

Furthermore, the interface or external properties of an object type that are exported to other types may need to change over time. For instance, the definers of the POINT and BOX entity types may initially suppress all representation information. However, if later an operation POINT-IN-BOX is to be defined, the implementor of this operation may need to access some details of the internal representations of the POINT and BOX types. These details (previously hidden in the implementation parts of the types) may now have to be added to the interface.

Again, the need to look at objects at multiple levels of abstraction or to support evolution is hardly limited to complex objects. Moreover, for the reasons cited above, the facility required is rarely as simple as that supported by molecular aggregation.

With the enhancements described here, DAPLEX becomes an "object-oriented" data model, because entities of a given type can be accessed and manipulated only through the functions (operations) that have been defined for that type. Moreover, PROBE objects (entities) not only encapsulate behavior, but can be interrelated through entity-valued functions to construct arbitrarily complex structures.

Because a complex object is itself modelled as an entity of some defined entity type, the generic operations of PDM can be applied to the complex object. In addition, application-specific data types and operations can be added by defining them as new entity types and functions.

Recognizing that many of the objects that occur in the applications to be supported by PROBE deal with spatial and temporal data, we have given special treatment to spatial and temporal semantics. This is accomplished through the definition of special *point set* entities and operators for manipulating them. A point set is a member of the PTSET type, which is a subtype of the root type ENTITY. Further specializations for PTSETs of different dimensions and for space and time domains of different characteristics (e.g. discrete or continuous) can be defined. The Box and Point entity types of Figure 2.1 are defined as specializations of the generic PTSET type:

```
entity    BOX is PTSET
function  Bottom Left (BOX) → POINT
function  Top Right (BOX) → POINT

entity    'Point is PTSET
function  X (POINT) → REAL
function  Y (POINT) → REAL
```

In this model, object versions (which have received special treatment in [BATO85, KAT286]) are treated as temporal objects. The model is general enough to support many different notions of space and time. For example, the Next function in Figure 2.2, which orders the Object Versions, may be defined to be a partial order. The spatial and temporal aspects of PDM are described in more detail in [MANO86].

The rules for propagating operations along relationships are incorporated into the procedures defining the operations. This general mechanism is illustrated in Figure 3.2. Here, the delete-complex function on GATE TYPE is defined to delete not just the particular GATE TYPE entity, but also the related PIN, GATE INSTANCE, and WIRE INSTANCE entities.

```
Delete_complex (GATETYPE, P) :=

    for gt in GATE TYPE where P(gt)
    begin
        delete Pins(gt)
        delete gi in Gate Components(gt)
        delete wi in Wire Components(gt)
        delete gt
    end for
```

Figure 3.2 Expressing Operation Propagation Rules

View mechanisms appear to already provide much of the required functionality. In PROBE, the PDM algebra can be used to restructure the entities and functions in the database for inclusion in views. Thus. we can define one view that includes only the GATE TYPE and PIN TYPE entity types and the Pins function relating them, and another view that includes all of the schema of figure 2.1. That is, the interface and implementation parts of a complex object are easily defined as views. However, unlike many other views could be defined, as needed. The multiple representations problem is also easily solved: The entities and functions needed for the different representations are all included in the database, and are related to the "native" entity type (e.g., MAP) via appropriate functions (e.g., a set-valued REPRESENTATIONS function). The representations may themselves be related via functions (to show, for example, that a representation at a finer resolution can be transformed into one at a coarser resolution by an aggregation operation, or vice-versa by a zoom operation). Finally, the problem of evolution can also be easily solved by defining a new view that includes more detail.

In conventional DBMSs. operations on a view are translated automatically into operations on the underlying database; most update operations are prohibited because unique automatic translations may not exist. In PROBE, because arbitrary operations can be specified for entity types, the view definition can include rules for translating operations on the view entities into operations on the underlying entities. The same mechanism is used for this purpose as for specifying the propagation of operations among related entities or for computing derived values; essentially, our viewpoint is that view entities are (implicitly) related to the underlying entities from which they are derived.

The connection between views and complex objects was also explored in [WIED86]. However, the model there was that the database contains relations (as in Figure 1.1), and objects are defined as views. In contrast, our approach is object-oriented: complex objects, their components, relationships, operations, etc., are all specified in the database schema; views are used as an abstraction device to suppress detail or to tailor the objects for use by an application.

Recursion:

Complex objects that are composed of sub-objects to an arbitrary number of levels require recursion to permit traversal of the entire object. Examples of such objects abound in CAD/CAM (part hierarchies), cartography (feature hierarchies). planning and scheduling (task networks), information retrieval (hierarchically organized subject indices), software engineering (nested program structures), and deduction (proof trees).

Recursion requires both self-referencing types and support for recursive queries over them. While self-referencing entity types can be stored in records in existing database systems, operations over them cannot be defined in the first-order query languages of these DBMSs [AHO79], nor can derived data be defined recursively. The complex object types of [HASK83, LORI83] cannot even be self-referencing nor is recursive processing possible in SQL, the query language of the underlying DBMS. The molecular aggregates of [BATO84, BATO85] allow recursion, but no query language is described. It is, of course, always possible to implement recursive computations in the host application programming languages supported by most DBMSs. However, [DAYA85, DAYA86] show that several orders of magnitude performance improvement can be obtained if the DBMS is enhanced to directly support some forms of recursion.

The inclusion of recursion in DBMSs, especially to support PROLOG-style deduction over relational databases, has become an extremely active area of research [BANC86b]. Rather than adding general recursive PROLOG-style rule processing, which is potentially inefficient and not guaranteed to terminate, to a DBMS, we have identified a special class of recursion, called *traversal recursion*, that has two crucial properties. First, it is powerful enough to express the recursive computations needed for complex objects. Second, very efficient algorithms, based on graph traversal, exist for performing these computations. Traversal recursions generalize transitive closure computations on the database viewed as a labelled directed graph. For these examples, the nodes of the graph to be traversed are the GATE TYPE entities and the edges are the

GATE INSTANCE entities. Given an Absolute Location of one GATE TYPE, a traversal recursion can specify the computation of the Absolute Locations of all its components. then of their components, and so on down the hierarchy. Conversely, the computation of Power Consumption can be specified by a traversal recursion that proceeds "up" the component hierarchy.

PDM algebra is augmented with a traversal recursion operator. To use this operator in a query, various parameters have to be specified: the node and edge entities of the graph to be traversed; the functions of the nodes or edges to be computed recursively; a recipe for computing each of these functions in terms of the function values computed for the immediate predecessors or successors (e.g., the expressions in Figure 2.3); and any selection conditions on the nodes, edges, or paths traversed (e.g., compute the power consumption of only the 4-input AND gate; find the shortest path from Boston to New York that does not include more than 50 miles of secondary highways).

We have defined different flavours of traversal recursion, which differ depending upon properties of the graph (is it acyclic or cyclic? is it reconvergent or not?), properties of the functions (e.g., Power Consumption is monotonic, component objects are spatially enclosed within their parent objects), and properties of the computations (how are the values of the predecessors' functions aggregated?) See [ROSE86] for details of traversal recursion.

Flexible Transaction Management

The traditional methods of transaction management have been found to be inappropriate for many applications that manipulate complex objects. Instead, techniques that permit the extraction of a complex object into a private workspace, and the subsequent restoration of the object into the public database have been described in [LORI83] and elsewhere. However, it is not clear that these techniques are general enough for all applications. For example, in a military application it may be important to immediately propagate certain updates on the shared database to an extract, and vice versa; changes to one extract may have to be propagated to other extracts within a given time window. In design applications, if one part of a design is changed, other designers may have to be notified; it may sometimes be acceptable to permit concurrent activity on different parts of a design, and provide means to reconcile inconsistencies before the designs are reinstalled in the database; and so on.

The general problem of extract management, change notification, and version control to support cooperative work has not yet been solved. It may be that for complete flexibility, a rule-based mechanism is necessary.

4. Implementation Issues

In this section we briefly examine approaches to efficiently supporting the requirements identified in Sections 2 and 3. First, we consider physical data structures and access methods for complex objects. Then, we discuss query optimization issues. Many of these issues have not been addressed in detail for the design of the PROBE breadboard (currently under implementation), which will be used to demonstrate some of the concepts discussed in this paper. These issues may be addressed more fully in the future. PROBE's architecture is deliberately designed to be extensible, so that as new access methods or query processing techniques are developed in the future, they can be incorporated into the system.

Physical Data Structures

Because complex objects may be represented by links between entities, the system must implement links efficiently, especially under update. One such mechanism for strictly hierarchical complex objects is described in [LORI83]. A more general mechanism for implementing links uses entity directories and hybrid pointers [CHAN81]. Other mechanisms are described for

a. Query against Complex Object:

```
for g in GATE TYPE where Name(g) = '4AND'
    retrieve Complex(g)
end for
```

b. Multiple Queries:

```
for gt in GATE TYPE where Name(gt) = '4AND'
    retrieve Description(gt)
end for

for pt in PIN TYPE where for some gt in GATE TYPE: Name(gt) = '4AND'
    and pt is in Pins(gt)
    retrieve Name(pt), I/O(pt)
end for

for gi in GATE INSTANCE where for some gt in GATE TYPE: Name(gt) = '4AND'
    for gt2 in Type(gi)
    retrieve Name(gt2), Description(gt2)
    end for

for wi in WIRE INSTANCE where for some gt in GATE TYPE: Name(gt) = '4AND'
    retrieve From(wi), To(wi)
end for
```

Figure 4.1 Replacing a Complex Query with Multiple Queries

```
for gt in GATE TYPE where Name(gt) = '4AND'
    retrieve Description(gt)
    for pt in Pins(gt)
        retrieve Name(pt), I/O(pt)
    end for
    for gi in Gate Components(gt)
        for gt2 in Type(gi)
            retrieve Name(gt2), Description(gt2)
        end for
    end for
    for wi in Wire Components(gt)
        retrieve From(wi), To(wi)
    end for
end for
```

Figure 4.2 A Single Hierarchical Retrieval Query

It may seem that this problem arises because PDM algebra (and the DAPLEX-like language we have used in our examples) are based on first normal form relations. It is not too difficult to extend the algebra and the DAPLEX-like syntax along the lines suggested in [SCHE86, FISC83, BANC86a] to express the retrieval of hierarchical objects in a single query (in fact, DAPLEX already has this capability [SMIT82] - see figure 4.2). However, we believe that the problem of

non-first normal form relations in [DEPP86, DADA86, VLDB86, MAIE86]. Not surprisingly, these mechanisms are adapted from storage structures and access methods (e.g., physical clustering of components along 1:n relationships, pointer arrays, hierarchical indexed sequential files) that were prevalent in older, hierarchical or network DBMSs (e.g., IMS, CODASYL). An access method for large, untyped objects is described in [CARE86].

The most promising of these approaches appears to be the use of entity directories and hybrid pointers to support links, together with physical clustering for frequently accessed 1:n relationships, hierarchical indices for use when physical clustering is inappropriate or impossible (e.g., when sub-objects are shared), and support for large objects. We believe that a full prototype of an object-oriented DBMS should include at least these mechanisms.

In addition, the PROBE architecture permits the inclusion of functionally specialized hardware or software processors (e.g., geometry modellers) for application-specific data types.

Query Optimization

Very little previous work on optimizing queries over complex objects has been reported (with the exception of [KHOS87], which looks only at very restricted special cases). The PDM algebra is based upon the relational algebra, and so relational query optimization techniques may be expected to apply. However, major extensions of these techniques are necessary. We discuss these extensions below.

1. Optimizing recursion: Because PDM algebra contains recursion operators, we have to optimize recursive queries. Our approach is to tailor fast graph traversal algorithms for the various flavours of traversal recursion. There are three generic classes of algorithms: breadth first search, one-pass traversal, and main memory techniques. The optimizer uses information gleaned from the user's query and from metadata about the size and properties of the graph to be traversed, the properties of the functions, and the properties of the computations to be performed, to select the best algorithm for a given query. It also uses heuristics to truncate the computation when certain monotonicity properties hold, and to reduce the volume of data returned by a query. Details of these techniques are described in [ROSE84, ROSE86].

2. Optimizing spatial and temporal queries: Point set entities and operations are generally useful abstractions for a wide variety of spatial and temporal applications. PROBE offers good performance for these applications through the use of a *geometry filter*, a dimension- and representation-independent processor that implements the point set abstractions. The geometry filter uses simple approximate geometric representations (based on space-filling curves) and corresponding fast query processing algorithms that produce approximate answers to spatial queries. To use PROBE for a spatial application, it usually is necessary to add an object class that provides a specific detailed representation for individual spatial objects (e.g., a boundary representation of POLYGON), and that implements operations on individual instances of the representation. Spatial queries are first processed by the geometry filter and then by the specialized processor. Because the filter works with a set of objects at a time, it can dramatically reduce the number of objects that must subsequently be examined by the specialized processor, which manipulates one or two instances at a time of the detailed representation. For details, see [OREN86].

3. Optimizing multiple queries: Because operations can be propagated along relationships, a single query against a complex object may spawn a collection of interrelated queries. For example, the query (in figure 4.1a) to retrieve the 4-input AND gate, its pins, gate components, and wire components, and their details, will result in the collection of queries shown in figure 4.1b. (For succinctness, we have used DAPLEX-like syntax, instead of the PDM algebra.) Multiple query optimization has only recently received some attention [CHAK85, SELL86]. The richer set of data structures (e.g., physical clustering) makes the optimization problem even harder. For our example, if the PIN TYPE entities, GATE INSTANCE entities, and WIRE INSTANCE entities are physically clustered near their parent GATE TYPE entities, the optimizer must recognize that several of the "joins" in the queries can be solved simultaneously in one scan of the file.

optimizing such queries is no easier than the multiple query optimization problem. Furthermore, these languages cannot specify the manipulation of non-hierarchical objects.

4. Optimizing user-defined operations: Traditional query optimization techniques assume complete knowledge of the file structures and access methods, and cost statistics of alternative implementation methods for the operators of the query language. For the PDM algebra, however, the optimization of queries that include the Select and Apply-Append operators is a difficult problem, in general, because these operators can reference user-defined functions. In the pure object-oriented approach, the implementations of these functions (perhaps by specialized hardware or software processors) would be treated as black boxes. No optimization would then be possible.

For object-oriented DBMSs, we believe that the right approach is to strike a balance between the conflicting requirements of information hiding (data independence) and performance. While implementation details are still hidden from the end user, some information about the entity types and functions is revealed to the optimizer through a separate interface. This information includes the algebraic properties (e.g., commutativity, associativity, distributivity) of the operations supported, and cost and result size estimates. (Other physical information such as the property that the result is left in a sorted state may also be important.) This extensible query optimization problem is still the subject of active research.

In some cases, it is too expensive to compute an intensionally-defined function on demand (i.e., at query execution time). It may be cheaper to precompute and cache its values, instead. For query processing purposes, then, the function may be treated as an extensionally-defined function. However, updates to the function's arguments may cause the cached values to become obsolete, requiring propagation of the updates. [STON86, ROWE86, LIND86, HUDS86] describe techniques for maintaining these computed values. Of course, these same techniques can be used for maintaining materialized views and derived values (the motivation for materializing views is the same as for precomputing functions -- improving the response time for selected queries).

5. Summary and Conclusions

We have attempted to identify the requirements for complex objects, and to survey other requirements that almost invariably arise in applications of complex objects (but that have largely been ignored in previous work on complex objects). These requirements were then related to specific capabilities for data modelling and manipulation.

Many of the necessary data modelling features were shown to exist in entity-based semantic data models such as DAPLEX. In particular, the semantic models support definition of and generic operations on entities, relationships between entities, and constraints on these entities and relationships. Other necessary features, such as user-defined operations and operation propagation, are part of more general capabilities or general data model requirements, rather than specific requirements associated only with complex objects. Once these features are provided in their more general forms, the requirements for complex objects can be handled as special cases. We described the PROBE Data Model and Algebra and showed how they satisfy the general requirements.

The modelling requirements also imply extended requirements on DBMS implementation facilities. We discussed approaches to providing these extended capabilities.

We have attempted to apply this interpretation of requirements in developing PROBE, in terms of choosing an existing data model to start with, in determining what enhancements to make to the data model, and in designing an open architecture that facilitates the integration of new applications and new implementation methods, and the evolution of old ones.

6. References

[BANC86a] Bancilhon, F., and S. Khoshafian, "A Calculus for Complex Objects," Proc. ACM SIGACT-SIGMOD Symposium on Principles of Database Systems, 1986.

[BANC86b] Bancilhon, F., and R. Ramakrishnan, "An Amateur's Introduction to Recursive Query Processing Strategies," Proc. ACM SIGMOD International Conference on Management of Data, 1986.

[BATO84] Batory, D.S., and A.P. Buchmann, "Molecular Objects, Abstract Data Types, and Data Models: A Framework," 10th Intl. Conf. on Very Large Data Bases, Singapore, 1984.

[BATO85] Batory D.S., and W. Kim. "Modeling Concepts for VLSI CAD Objects," ACM Trans. Database Systems, 10 No. 3 (September 1985).

[BORG85] Borgida, A. "Language Features for Flexible Handling of Exceptions in Information Systems," ACM Trans. Database Systems, 10 No. 4 (December 1985).

[BUCH85] Buchmann, A., and C. Perez de Celis, "An Architecture and Data Model for CAD Databases," 11th Intl. Conf. on Very Large Data Bases, Stockholm, Sweden, 1985.

[CARE86] Carey, M., et. al.. "Object and File Management in the EXODUS Extensible Database System," Proc. International Conference on Very Large Databases, 1986.

[CHAK86] Chakravarthy, U.S., and J. Minker, "Multiple Query Processing in Deductive Databases Using Query Graphics," Proc. International Conference on Very large Databases, 1986.

[CHAN82] Chan, A., et al. "Storage and Access Structures to Support a Semantic Data Model," 8th Intl. Conf. on Very Large Data Bases,. Mexico City, 1982.

[CODD79] Codd, E.F., "Extending the Database Relational Model to Capture More Meaning," ACM Trans. Database Systems, 4. No. 4 (December 1979).

[DADA86] Dadam, P., et. al.. "A DBMS Prototype to Support Extended NF2 Relations: An Integrated View On Flat Tables and Hierarchies," Proc. ACM SIGMOD International Conference On Management of Data, 1986.

[DAYA85] Dayal, U., et.al.. "PROBE - A Research Project in Knowledge-Oriented Database Systems: Preliminary Analysis," Technical Report CCA-85-03, Computer Corporation of America, July 1985.

[DAYA86] Dayal, U., and J.M. Smith. "PROBE: A Knowledge-Oriented Database Management System," in M.L. Brodie and J. Mylopoulos (eds.), On Knowledge Base Management Systems: Integrating Artificial Intelligence and Database Technologies, Springer-Verlag, 1986.

[DEPP86] Deppisch, U., H-B Paul, and H-J Schek, "A Storage System for Complex Objects," Proc. International Workshop on Object-Oriented DBMS, 1986.

[DITT86] Dittrich, K. and U. Dayal (eds). *Proceedings International Workshop On Object-Oriented Database Systems*, 1986.

[FISC83] Fischer, P., and S. Thomas, "Operators for Non-First-Normal Form Relations," *Proc. COMPSAC*, November 1983.

[HUDS86] Hudson, S.E., and R. King. "CACTIS: A Database System for Specifying Functionally Defined Data." 1986.

[JOHN83] Johnson, H.R., J.E. Schweitzer, and E.R. Warkentine. "A DBMS Facility for Handling Structured Engineering Entities." *Proc. Database Week: Engineering Design Applications.* IEEE Computer Society. 1983.

[KATZ86] Katz, R.H., E. Chang, R. Bhateja. "Version Modelling Concepts for Computer-Aided Design Databases." *Proc. ACM SIGMOD International Conference on Management of Data*, 1986.

[KHOS87] Khoshafian, S., et. al., "A Query Processing Algorithum for the Decomposed Storage Model." *Proc. International Conference on Data Engineering*, 1987.

[LIND86] Lindsay, B., et. al., "A Snapshot Differential Refresh Algorithm," *Proc. ACM SIGMOD International Conference on Management of Data*, 1986.

[LOCH86] Lochovsky, F. (ed.), *Database Engineering*, Vol. 8, No. 4, Special Issue on Object-Oriented Systems. 1986.

[LOR182] Lorie, R.A., "Issues in Database for Design Applications." in J. Encarnacao and F.-L. Krause (eds.), *File Structures and Data Bases for CAD*. North-Holland. 1982.

[LOR183] Lorie, R.A., and W. Plouffe, "Complex Objects and Their Use in Design Transactions," Proc. 1983 ACM Engineering Design Applications. San Jose, CA (May 1983).

[MAIE86] Maier, D., and J. Stein, "Indexing in an Object-Oriented DBMS," *Proc. International Workshop on Object-Oriented Database Systems*, 1986.

[MANO86] Manola. F.A., and J.A. Orenstein, "Toward a General Spatial Data Model for an Object-Oriented DBMS." *Proc. International Conference on Very Large Databases*, 1986.

[MANO86G] Manola, F., and U. Dayal. "PDM: An Object-Oriented Data Model." *Proc. International Workshop on Object-Oriented Databases*, 1986.

[OREN86] Orenstein, J., "Spatial Query Processing in an Object-Oriented Database System," *Proc. 1986 ACM-SIGMOD Intl. Conf. on Management of Data.*

[ROSE86] Rosenthal, A., et al., "A DBMS Approach to Recursion," *Proc. 1986 ACM-SIGMOD Intl Conf. on Management of Data.*

[ROSE84] Rosenthal, A., S. Heiler, and F. Manola. "An Example of Knowledge-Based Query Processing in a CAD/CAM DBMS," *Proc. International Conference on Very Large Databases*, 1986.

[ROWE86] Rowe, L.A., "A Shaped Object Hierarchy," *Proc. International Workshop on Object-Oriented DB Systems*, 1986.

[SCHE86] Schek, H-J., and M.H. Scholl, "The Relational Model with Relation-Valued Attributes," *Information Systems*, 11, no. 4, (1986).

[SELL86] Sellis, T.K., "Global Query Optimization," *Proc. ACM SIGMOD International Conference on Management of Data*, 1986.

[SHIP81] Shipman, D., "The Functional Data Model and the Data Language DAPLEX." *ACM Trans. Database Systems*, 6,1 (March 1981).

[SMIT81] Smith, J.M. et al., "ADAPLEX Rationale and Reference Manual," Technical Report CCA-83-08. Computer Corporation of America (May 1983).

[STON83] Stonebraker, M., B. Rubenstein, and A. Guttman. "Application of Abstract Data Types and Abstract Indices to CAD Databases," *Proc. Database Week: Engineering Design Applications*, IEEE Computer Society, 1983.

[STON86] Stonebraker, M., "Object Management in POSTGRES Using Procedures." *Proc. International Workshop on Object-Oriented DB Systems*. 1986.

[VALD86] Valduriez, P., S. Khoshafian, and G. Copeland, "Implementation Techniques for Complex Objects," *Proc. International Conference on Very Large Databases*, 1986.

[WIED86] Wiederhold, G. "Views, Objects, and Databases," *IEEE Computer*, 19, no. 12, (December 1986).

Managing Change in a Computer-Aided Design Database[1]

R. H. Katz and E. Chang

Computer Science Division
Electrical Engineering and Computer Science Department
University of California, Berkeley
Berkeley, CA 94720

Abstract: Object-oriented concepts can make a design database more *reactive* to changes in its contents. By embedding change semantics in the database model, the design engineer can be relieved of managing the detailed effects of changes. However, mechanisms are needed to limit the scope of change propagation and to unambiguously identify the objects to which propagated changes should apply. We propose new mechanisms, based on group check-in/check-out, browser contexts and paths, configuration constraints, and rules, to support a powerful automatic change capability within a design database.

Key Words and Phrases: Object-oriented data models; Computer-aided design databases; Inheritance; Change propagation; Constraint propagation

1. Introduction

Object-oriented [GOLD83] concepts, as embodied in such systems as Smalltalk-80, LOOPS, and Flavors, are becoming pervasive throughout computer science. They provide an appealing way to structure applications and their data. An emerging consensus is that an object-oriented approach can simplify the applications that create and manipulate computer-aided design data. Several groups are using these concepts to structure a CAD database (e.g., [ATWO85, BATO85, HARR86, LAND86]), as well as databases for office applications [ZDON84].

The elements of the object-oriented approach appear to include: (i) types (classes), in which operations (methods) on data are packaged with the data itself, (ii) inheritance, in which default procedure definitions and values are propagated from types to instances, and (iii) generic operation invocation, via message passing. For us, the first two concepts are the most important: "object-oriented" means abstract data types with inheritance.

Inheritance provides scoping for data and operation definitions through a taxonomic hierarchy of instances belonging to types, which in turn belong to supertypes (i.e., types of types). If a variable is accessed from an instance, and is not defined there, then its associated type is searched for the definition. If it is not defined in the type, the process recurses to the supertype and so on until the root of the lattice. More advanced models allow types to be instances of multiple supertypes (i.e., "mix-ins"), where one supertype's definition of a common variable must be specified to dominate the others.

In this paper, we are particularly interested in how object-oriented concepts can be used to manage change and constraint propagation in a design database. For example, inheritance provides an ability to define default values (for example, in a type) that can be locally overridden (in an instance). It can also be used to determine the constraints that apply to new versions. The goal is to embed change semantics within the database structure, so the system can react to changes automatically.

[1]Research supported under N.S.F. grants ECS-8403004 and ECS-8352227, with matching support from the Microelectronics and Computer Technology Corporation.

Most previous work has dealt with change *notification* rather than *propagation*. [NEUM82] defined a transaction model for a database of independent and derived design objects. The database is not consistent until changes to independent objects are propagated to their associated derived objects, although the system does not propagate these itself. [WIED82] proposed a mechanism for flagging records that might be affected by a change in a CODASYL-structured design database. It works by traversing backwards from a changed record, recursively marking its ancestors up to the roots of any hierarchies that contain it. [BATO85b, CHOU86] developed a more sophisticated change notification mechanism within an object-oriented data model. It uses time stamps to limit the range of objects to be flagged in response to a change. A related object is flagged only if it has an older timestamp. In these works, only very limited change propagation is supported. For example, a change propagates from a component to its immediate composite, but no further. There has been little discussion of how to handle ambiguity in the set of propagated changes. We concentrate on these new issues in this paper.

The rest of the paper is organized as follows. Section 2 contains an overview of a version data model, implemented in our prototype Version Server. In Section 3, we describe changes in a computer-aided design databases in terms of default values, change propagation, and constraint propagation. An example demonstrating the interplay among these concepts is given in Section 4. Ways of disambiguating the required set of changes are given in Section 5. Section 6 discusses some implementation issues. Section 7 contains our summary and conclusions.

2. A Version Data Model

The model described in this section has been implemented in a system called the *Version Server* [KATZ86a, KATZ86b]. It manages units of design called *design objects*, which roughly correspond to the named design files found in conventional design environments. In the following discussion, we call these "representation objects". They are uniquely denoted by *object-name[version#].type*. In addition, the Version Server introduces special "structural objects" with which to organize these representational objects, much as directories are used to organize files in file systems.

The Version Server recognizes three possible relationships among design objects: *version histories, configurations,* and *equivalences*. Version histories maintain **is-a-descendent-of** and **is-an-ancestor-of** relationships among version instances of the same real world object (e.g., ALU[4].layout **is-a-descendent-of** ALU[3].layout, both of which are versions of ALU.layout). A structural *version object* is associated with each collection of version instances. Structural *configuration objects* relate composite representational objects to their components via **is-a-component-of** and **is-composed-of** relationships. Finally, equivalences identify objects across types that are constrained to be different representations of the same real world object, e.g., ALU[2].layout **is-equivalent-to**

ALU[3].schematic if these are different representations of the same ALU design. More generally, equivalences can denote arbitrary dependencies among representational objects. They are explicitly represented by structural *equivalence objects*. The Version Server relationships are summarized in Figure 2.1 and the associated data structure is given in Figure 2.2.

Operationally, the Version Server supports a workspace model. Designers *check-out* objects from shared archives into their private workspaces. Changes made in private workspaces are not visible to other designers until such objects are *checked-in* to a shared group workspace, where the changes can be integrated with other designers' work. Finally, the modified object is returned as a new version to the shared archive. The Validation Subsystem, invoked on object check-in, analyzes a log of verification events to ensure that the object has been successfully validated before it can be added to the archive. A Browser supports the interactive examination of Version Server databases.

3. Reacting To Changes

3.1. Scope and Ambiguity

Database system implementors have always been reluctant to provide automatic change propagation, because users rarely understand the full (and potentially dangerous) effects of spawned changes. However, aspects of design databases can simplify these problems. Since the design database is append-only, the correct response to change is to spawn new versions of related objects and to incorporate these into new configurations. Note that any new objects are created in private or group workspaces, never in an archive space. Since validation must be performed before these new versions are added to an archive, change propagation can never corrupt the "released" copies that reside there.

However, it is still possible to create a large number of useless intermediate versions. Mechanisms are needed to *limit the scope* of the propagation and *disambiguate* its effects. Ideally, the scope should be limited to the smallest set of objects "directly" affected by the change. Ambiguity is introduced if there is more than one way to incorporate the new versions into configurations. In the worst case, the cross-product of possible configurations could be added to the database, wasting both time and space.

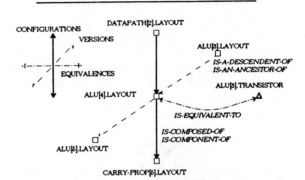

Figure 2.1 -- Version Server Logical Data Model

Design data is organized as a collection of typed and versioned design objects, interrelated by configuration, version, and equivalence relationships. Only representational objects are shown. For example, ALU[4].layout is descended from ALU[3].layout and is the ancestor of ALU[5].layout. It is also a component of DATAPATH[2].layout and is composed of CARRY-PROPAGATE[5].layout. Additionally, ALU[4].layout is equivalent to other objects, such as ALU[3].transistor.

3.2. Default Values

One of the simplest ways to change a design database is by adding to it a new version of an existing object. The designer can fill in its attributes and relationships at its creation time, but it is better if the system can fill these in automatically. Inheritance provides the necessary mechanism. For example, consider the "type" of ALU layouts. All instances of ALU layouts share much in common, perhaps their interface descriptions, or the operations (i.e., add, subtract, etc.) they support. This common data can be factored out of the instances and stored with the type. In creating new instance of the ALU layout, these common attributes can be inherited without being explicitly specified.

However, Smalltalk-style type-instance inheritance provides only one of many possible ways to propagate defaults to a new ver-

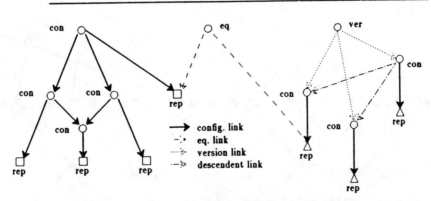

Figure 2.2 -- Version Server Physical Data Structure

Circular objects are structural; square and triangular objects are representational. Relationships are actually implemented by interconnected structural objects, which indirectly reference representation objects. The structural objects are *con*, *ver*, and *eq*, for configuration, version, and equivalence relationships respectively. The configuration and equivalence links are self-explanatory. Version links tie together the versions of the same logical object. Descendent links implement the explicit ancestor-descendent connections of a version history.

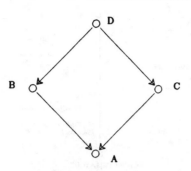

Figure 3.1 -- Configuration Example

Object D is composed of objects B and C. Both B and C use instances of A. Only configuration objects are shown to keep the figures simple. Note that each would contain a reference to a particular representation object.

sions. There are four different kinds of inheritance within the Version Server data model, which can conceivably vary on an instance by instance basis: (i) from version objects to version instances (i.e., the type-instance inheritance mentioned above), (ii) from ancestor to descendent (this is how the Version Server currently operates, since a new version begins as a copy of its ancestor), (iii) from composite object to component (where a version is used within the design hierarchy can determine the value of some of its attributes), and (iv) from equivalent to other equivalents. The propagation of information need not be limited to data; new object instances can inherit constraints, such as equivalence constraints, from their related objects.

3.3. Change Propagation

Once a new version instance is created, it must be incorporated into new configurations to be made part of the design. In most systems (including our prototype Version Server), these new configurations must be laboriously constructed by hand. *Change propagation* is the process that incorporates new versions into configurations automatically. Consider an object A that has been checked out from the archive to create a new version A'. At check-in

time, new configuration objects could be created, that form a new configuration of the objects that formerly contained A as a component or subcomponent, but should now contain A'. If the propagations only go up a single level in the configuration hierarchy, then this is essentially the proposal of [CHOU86].

However, it is desirable to propagate changes even further, but this requires additional mechanisms to limit the extent of changes and to keep them unambiguous. For example, consider the configuration of Figure 3.1. Object D is configured from objects B and C, which in turn share an object A (only configuration objects are shown). If a new version of object A is created, and changes are naively propagated along both paths, then there are two possible resulting configurations shown in Figure 3.2. This has been called the "multiple path problem" in [MITT86]. Either both paths of changes are merged into a single new configuration of D or two separate new configurations are spawned, one incorporating A' in each of the two original uses of A (i.e., the use of A in B and in C respectively). In general, the former is to be preferred, but there are cases when the latter is what the designer intended. For example, some integrated circuit layout editors support editing in context, which allows a cell to be changed everywhere it is used, or alternatively, just within its current editing context. We will discuss mechanisms to disambiguate changes in Section 5.

3.4. Constraint Propagation

Equivalence relationships model dependency constraints among objects, especially across representations. A new version inherits the equivalences of its ancestor at check-out time. Equivalence is interpreted in terms of the execution of a sequence of CAD verification programs whose success demonstrates that the objects are indeed equivalent. This condition is checked by the Version Server's validation subsystem [BHAT86].

The system currently supports passive enforcement: object check-in fails if any equivalence constraints are left unsatisfied. The obvious extension is to support *active* enforcement by actually executing the validation script to create a new version of the constrained object. For example, if a schematic object and a netlist object are *actively constrained* to be equivalent, then equivalence is enforced by executing a netlist generator to create a new netlist version when the revised schematic is checked-in. The spawned netlist version becomes a descendent of the original netlist object. Changes to actively enforced constraints are the only kinds allowed to propagate to

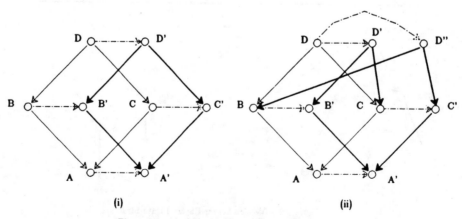

(i)   (ii)

Figure 3.2 -- Ambiguous Change Propagation

A new version of A, A', causes new configurations of B and C to be created through change propagation. Configuration (i) has merged these new objects into a single new configuration of D. Configuration (ii) has evolved separate configurations of D to incorporate the changed components B and C. D' contains the new B and the old C, while D'' contains the new C and the old B. The broken arrows represent descendent linkages.

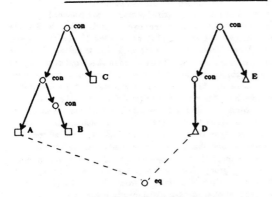

Figure 4.1 – Initial Conditions

The initial condition has two simple configuration hierarchies, of square and triangle objects respectively, and a single *active* equivalence constraint between them.

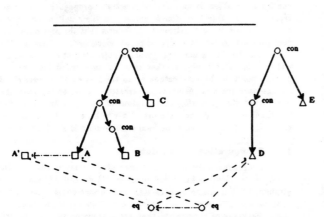

Figure 4.2 – New Version of Object A

A new version of A is created, A'. Note how A' *inherits* the equivalence constraint from its version ancestor.

configurations of other representations.

4. A Detailed Example

The ideas presented above are developed more formally in the process of working through a specific example. Figure 4.1 shows initial configurations of square and triangle objects. These are used as icons for representational types, while circles stand for structural objects. Descendent linkages are not shown, to keep the figures uncluttered. The first step is for a designer to check-out A to create a new version A'. A' will *inherit* certain attributes and relationships from its ancestor or objects related to it. Figure 4.2 shows that A' has inherited the equivalence relationship between A and D. We will assume that this relationship represents an active constraint between square objects and triangle objects, i.e., there is a procedure (or set of rules) that describes how to create a new triangle object from a changed square object.

The check-in of the new version A' causes *change propagation*. New configuration objects are spawned to incorporate A' and affect composites up through the root of the configuration hierarchy. The effects are shown in Figure 4.3. Since the constraint between A' and D is actively enforced, a new version of D, D', must be generated. The equivalence relationship is modified to reference this new version. The result is given in Figure 4.4. Finally change propagation must

be performed for the configurations that contain D. This is shown in Figure 4.5.

In addition to the multiple path problem already described, the interaction between change and constraint propagation can result in ambiguous configurations. Consider what would happen if object A and E are both checked out for update. If A' and E' are checked back independently, two new triangle configurations will be created: one containing the old D and the new E' and another containing the new D' and the old E. Note that the resulting configurations are independent of the order of the check-ins. However, if A' and E' are checked in as a group, then a single new configuration containing both D' and E' should be made. Group check-in as a method for disambiguating changes will be discussed in Section 5.2.

5. Handling Ambiguity

5.1. Introduction

The system has several options when faced with ambiguity: (1) do not propagate changes if there is any ambiguity, (2) create the

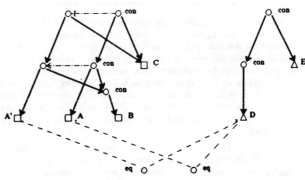

Figure 4.3 – New Configuration Incorporating A'

Change propagation is realized by spawning new configuration objects upwards towards the root of the square configuration hierarchy. Note that only new configuration objects are created, and that only new descendent links are shown. Existing representational objects are not modified.

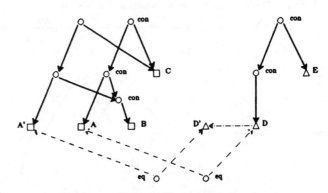

Figure 4.4 – Constraint Propagation to D

Since the equivalence constraint is *actively* enforced, a new version of D must be spawned. Note how the equivalence object now points to D'. Only the new D -> D' descendent link is shown.

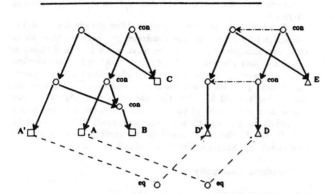

Figure 4.5 -- New Configuration Incorporating D'

Finally, change propagation is once again invoked to spawn new configurations incorporating D'. Only the new descendent links are shown.

cross product of all possible unambiguous configurations, (3) only perform change propagation for the subset that is unambiguous, or (4) provide the designer with the appropriate operational mechanisms to unambiguously describe the effect s/he desires; if that fails, use the browser interface to disambiguate the changes. Choice (1) is the way most systems are built today: they do not support any change propagation. Choice (2) is not really a solution, although some systems have essentially proposed this method [ATWO85]. The systems that do support change propagation usually make the third choice (e.g., [CHOU86]).

In this section, we examine the possible mechanisms for the last choice. Rather than propose a single general purpose approach, we concentrate on more specific "user-oriented" mechanisms. The idea is to provide change propagation effects that make sense to the designers who will be using the system. These may be implemented on top of the same underlying general purpose mechanisms, for example, the events and triggers of [DITT84].

5.2. Group Check-in/Check-out

When a single object is checked-out to create a new version, it automatically inherits the equivalence relationships of its ancestor, unless explicitly overridden by the designer. However, consider the situation in which a layout is constrained to be equivalent to a given schematic, and a major design change is underway that will affect both. There is no reason to constrain the new layout to be

equivalent to the original schematic, and similarly for the old layout and the new schematic. The desired semantics are provided by *group check-out*. Constraints that range over objects solely within the group lead to new constraints that are limited to the checked-out versions of those objects. Constraints with objects outside the group are inherited in the usual way. Thus, a group check-out of the layout and schematic objects would yield an equivalence constraint between the new versions of the layout and schematic, but no constraints would exist between them and the original versions in the archive.

Group check-in is like a transaction, in that the objects in the group should be added to the database as an atomic unit. In effect, any spawned configurations should merge changes from all members of the group, rather than create new configurations for each. In other words, no more than one new version of a configuration object is created during group check-in, no matter how many change paths touch the configuration it is derived from. The difference between group and conventional check-ins is shown in Figure 5.1.

As long as there is at most one new version of each representation object being checked-in, group check-in is guaranteed to result in an unambiguous final configuration. The sketch of the proof is as follows. At most one new instance can be added for each existing object, either as the result of change propagation (i.e., a new configuration object is spawned) or constraint propagation (i.e., a new representation object version is created as the result of an actively enforced equivalence constraint). It follows that the arcs out of new configuration instances can change at most once. There are two cases. At the time a new configuration object is first created, its arcs either point at old objects that may be superceded later or they already point at the new instances. In the first case, the arcs should change once the new instances are created. In the second case, they need never change during the duration of the check-in. Since each arc changes at most once, the order in which new instances are generated is irrelevant. The same final configuration is obtained.

5.3. Configuration Constraints

A mechanism for limiting change propagation is *configuration constraints*. Several kinds are possible: (1) dependency status constraints, (2) timestamp constraints, (3) interface constraints, and (4) containment and partitioning constraints. This list is meant to illustrate the kinds of constraints that are reasonable to associate with configuration objects. It is not meant to be exhaustive. Of course it possible to associate more than one such constraint with a configuration object. We will discuss each kind in turn.

The simplest kind of configuration constraint relies on a simple status attribute associated with each configuration object. The value of this attribute can either be *dependent* or *independent*, not unlike independent and derived representations in [NEUM82]. A dependent configuration is one that cannot exist outside another configuration.

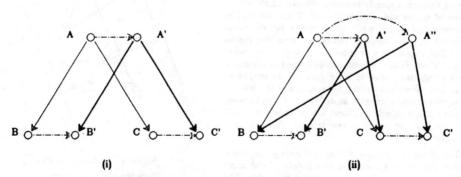

Figure 5.1 -- Group vs. Non-Group Check-ins

Configuration (i) illustrates the result of Check-in (B', C'). Configuration (ii) shows what happens when Check-in (B') is followed by Check-in (C').

Change propagation proceeds through dependent configurations, stopping at the first independent configuration it encounters. The designers must incorporate new independent configurations into higher level composites by hand. The first instance of a configuration defaults to being independent, unless explicitly overridden by the designer. Spawned instances can inherit the value of their dependency status in any of the ways described in Section 3.2. Unless changed by the designers, the default inheritance is from their immediate ancestor configurations.

A second kind of constraint depends on timestamps to limit change propagation, as in [BATO85b, CHOU86]. Objects have timestamps that indicate the time at which they were last updated. A configuration's timestamp is inherited from its associated representation object, and is not related to the time at which it was created. A configuration is *timestamp consistent* if its timestamp is newer than any of its components, i.e., the composite representation object was last updated after any of its component representation objects. Change propagation proceeds as long as it creates new configurations that are timestamp consistent. This mechanism is well-suited to constructing a valid configuration from a check-in group. However, it explicitly disallows the replacement of a component by a new version within an existing configuration, since the timestamp of the composite representation object will be older than the new version.

Interface constraints depend on the internal details of representation objects. We say that the interface of a new version is *compatible* with its ancestor's interface if it is possible to replace the ancestor in any existing configuration with the new version. The easiest way to ensure compatibility is for the designers to guarantee that the interface portion of the object has not changed across versions. This may be overly conservative since minor changes may not result in an incompatible interface. One can imagine representation-dependent programs that could determine the compatibility of a new version's interface. Change propagation stops when it would attempt to create a configuration from a version whose interface is incompatible with its ancestor.

The last constraint is *representation-dependent containment*. In general, a composite object's configuration is consistent if its components are properly contained within it. This is easy to verify if the representation type defines intersection operations: the intersection of each component with the composite should be the component itself. For example, consider a design type that associates a bounding box with each object, and defines an intersection operation on that box. If a component's bounding box is not properly contained within its associated composite, then the configuration is inconsistent. A related concept is a *partitioning constraint*, i.e., the pairwise intersection of each component is the empty set. Change can be propagated up the configuration hierarchy as long as these constraints are satisfied, and stopped as soon as a violation is detected.

5.4. Browser Paths and Contexts

The propagation of changes is unambiguous as long as each node along the path to the root of the configuration is not referenced from more than one place. When a node is used more than once, as for A in Figure 3.1, then information from the context in which the original was checked-out can be used to disambiguate the change propagation. *Check-in (A')*, without further specification, would result in configuration (i) of Figure 3.2. If A were checked-out along the path D-->B-->A, then a *Check-in (A') along check-out path* would create the configuration rooted at D' in configuration (ii). If the check-out had been along the path D-->C-->A, then the configuration rooted at D'' would be the result. A designer can specify a path explicitly or s/he can select it graphically by using the browser to choose the appropriate configuration arcs. Using the latter method, it is possible to check-in an object along multiple paths. This is particularly useful for objects that are used many places in the design, but the change should be propagated to only a portion of these. An example is shown in Figure 5.2.

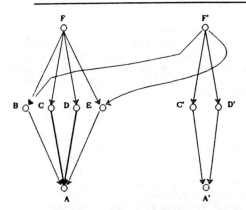

Figure 5.2 -- Check-in Along Selected Paths

Object A is used in four places in the configuration. A new version A' is created, but is to be checked in along the selected paths, which are highlighted (it is possible to select these paths by interacting with the browser prior to check-in). The resulting configuration, rooted at D', is shown on the right. Only the two middle uses of A have been replaced by A'.

Besides disambiguating the path of changes, browser information can limit the scope of changes through the *browser context*. The browser already implements mechanisms for pruning the complex design structure before presentation to the designer. Taking into account the structure of the configuration hierarchy, the browser heuristically determines the neighborhood of interest around an object being browsed. Change propagation can be limited to this neighborhood by issuing a *check-in within context* command.

Figure 4.5 demonstrates that the browsing context by itself is not enough to limit change propagation, because of the effects of constraint propagation across representations. In the figure, the triangle objects need not have been involved in any browser operations involving the original square object A. Mechanisms like configuration constraints must work with contexts to limit the propagation.

5.5. Rule-based Methods

There remains one case in which group check-in does not guarantee an unambiguous result. Consider the example of Section 4, and the case where A and D are checked-out for change, even though D is normally derived from A through an active constraint. A hand-crafted version D'' will be created in parallel with the automatically propagated D'. Even if A' and D'' are checked-in as a group, the system needs to disambiguate which of D' or D'' to incorporate into the new configuration. For example, the system could be given the rule that "a checked-out version always supercedes a spawned version in propagated configurations". Then in the example, D'' would be incorporated in new configurations rather than D'. A smart enough system could avoid generating D' altogether.

6. Implementation Issues

6.1. Algorithm for Group Check-in

The semantics of group check-in is that the objects in the group must be merged into a common configuration as the result of the check-in. Note that in Figure 6.1, A' is configured from the old B and C, and the system must build a new configuration if a group check-in of A', C', and D' is issued. Further, if a high-level component and a primitive component are checked-in together, then objects on the path between them must also be contained in any spawned configuration, even if they are not mentioned in the group.

The group check-in algorithm from a source workspace to an archive proceeds as follows:

(1)   To keep the discussion simple, we assume each check-in group has a single object that dominates the rest, such as object A' does in the check-in group A', C', and D' in Figure 6.1. This dominating object forms the root of a minimum spanning graph that covers the ancestors of the remaining objects within the group (see Figure 6.2).

(2)   Any objects found in this subgraph that do not also have descendents in the check-in list should be marked (e.g., B).

(3)   Starting from the configuration of the root object (A'), recursively examine its components and subcomponents: (i) if a node is not marked and does not have a descendent in the check-in list, then the system can ignore the node and any of its components; (ii) if a node is marked, then the system creates a new configuration for it in the source workspace (even though it references a rep object in the archive); (iii) if a node's descendent is in the check-in list, the system will link its descendent's configuration to the configuration being formed in the source workspace.

If there are "holes" in the configurations that need to be filled in this way, then it is likely that the validation subsystem will veto the movement of the resulting configuration into the archive space. However, the full configuration is left in the source workspace, where it can be reverified, and successfully checked-in as a group at a later time.

If the browsing path is specified, the change algorithm is similar to the one above. However, the subgraph would cover only the paths among checked-in objects and the objects specified in the browsing path.

6.2. Algorithm for Group Check-out

The problem of rebuilding the configuration at check-in time can be avoided if the appropriate group of objects was checked-out together. Once again, the appropriate configuration relationships need to be constructed in the target workspace, even if there are "holes" in the group. The basic algorithm is described below:

(1)   Determine the root object within the check-out group.

(2)   Determine the minimum spanning subgraph that covers the configuration nodes of the checked-out objects and all the paths among them, starting with the configuration of the root object.

(3)   Mark all the configuration nodes covered by the subgraph.

(4)   Examine the configuration hierarchy, creating configuration objects in the the workspace as follows: (i) if a node is marked, create a configuration object for it; (ii) if a node is also in the check-out list, a new version node is created for it; (iii) if a node is not marked, then it is skipped by the system.

7. Summary and Conclusions

In this paper, we have described some of the issues in making a design database more adaptive to changes in its structure. Previous work has focused on change notification, i.e., marking objects that might be affected by a change, rather than actually propagating changes automatically. To do so requires new mechanisms for disambiguating what changes are to take place, and for limiting the scope of change propagation. We described specific operational mechanisms that address these issues: group check-in/check-out and browser paths to disambiguate the effects of changes; configuration constraints and browser contexts to limit the scope of these effects. We are implementing these mechanisms in a second edition of the Version Server.

An object-oriented approach helps to limit much of the complexity of change propagation and design evolution. Inheritance makes it possible to identify default values and constraints. By hav-

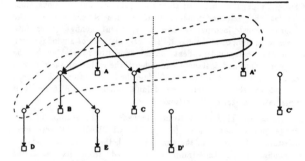

Figure 6.1 – Before Group Check-in (A', C', D')

The original configuration is shown on the left. Objects A, C, and D have been individually checked out into a workspace on the right, yielding the new versions A', C', and D'. The figure shows the configurations before the execution of *group check-in (A', C', D')*. The minimum spanning configuration subgraph that covers this check-in group is circled in the figure.

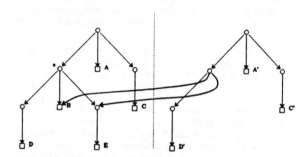

Figure 6.2 – After Group Check-in (A', C', D')

The configuration node associated with B is marked, because a new configuration node must be introduced into the workspace to complete the configuration. The final configuration is shown on the right.

ing types with intersection operations, it is possible to support representation-dependent configuration constraints, such as containment and partitioning, without the system needing to know representation details.

We gratefully acknowledge the assistance of Rhajiv Bhateja, David Gedye, and Vony Trijanto, who as members of our research group contributed to the discussions that led to the work reported here. We also thank Thomas Atwood and the other referees for their constructive comments and suggestions.

8. References

[ATWO85] Atwood, T., "An Object Oriented DBMS for Design Support Applications," Proc. IEEE COMPINT 85, Montreal, Canada, (Sept. 1985).

[BATO85a] Batory, D., W. Kim, "Modeling Concepts for VLSI CAD Objects," ACM Trans. on Database Systems, V 10, N 3, (Sept. 1985).

[BATO85b] Batory, D., W. Kim, "Supporting Versions of VLSI CAD Objects," M.C.C. Technical Report, Austin, TX, (1985).

[BHAT86] Bhateja, R., R. H. Katz, "A Validation Subsystem of a Version Server for Computer-Aided Design Data", submitted to ACM/IEEE 25th Design Automation Conf., Miami, Fl, (June 1987). Also available as UCB CSD Technical Report 87/317, (October 1986).

[CHOU86] Chou, H-T, W. Kim., "A Unifying Framework for Versions Control in a CAD Environment," 12th VLDB, Kyoto, Japan, (August 1986).

[DITT84] Dittrich, K. R., A. M. Kotz, J. M. Mulle, "An Event/Trigger Mechanism to Enforce Complex Consistency Constraints in Design Databases," University of Karlsruhe Technical Report, Karlsruhe West Germany, (November 1984).

[GOLD83] Goldberg, A., D. Robson, *Smalltalk-80: The Language and its Implementation*, Addison-Wesley, Reading, MA, (1983).

[HARR86] Harrison, D., et. al., "Data Management and Graphics Editing in the Berkeley Design Environment," Proc. ICCAD, Santa Clara, CA, (November 1986).

[KATZ86a] Katz, R. H., E. Chang, R. Bhateja, "Version Modeling Concepts for Computer-Aided Design Database," ACM SIGMOD Conf., Washington, DC, (May 1986).

[KATZ86b] Katz, R. H., E. Chang, M. Anwarrudin, "A Version Server for Computer-Aided Design Databases," ACM/IEEE 24th Design Automation Conf., Las Vegas, NV, (June 1986).

[LAND86] Landis, G., "Design Evolution and History in an Object-Oriented CAD/CAM Database," Proc. IEEE COMPCON, San Francisco, CA, (March 1986).

[MITT86] Mittal, S. J., D. G. Bobrow, K. M. Kahn, "Virtual Copies: At the Boundary Between Classes and Instances," Proc. OOPSLA'86 Conference, Portland, OR, (Sept. 1986).

[NEUM82] Neumann, T., C. Hornung, "Consistency and Transactions in CAD Databases," Proc. 8th VLDB, Mexico City, Mexico, (Sept. 1982).

[WIED82] Wiederhold, G., et. al., "A Database Approach to Communication in VLSI Design", *I.E.E.E. Transactions on Computer-Aided Design*, V CAD-1, N 2, (April 1982).

[ZDON84] Zdonik, S. B., "Object Management System Concepts," Proc. 2nd ACM SIGOA Conference on Office Information Systems, Toronto, Canada, (June 1984).

On Long-Duration CAD Transactions

Henry F. Korth[*], *Won Kim,*[**] *François Bancilhon*[***]

[*] *Dept. of Computer Sciences*
University of Texas
Austin, Texas 78712-1188

[**] *Microelectronics and Computer Technology Corporation*
3500 West Balcones Center Drive
Austin, Texas 78759

[***] *INRIA*
B.P. 105
78150 Le Chesnay
France

ABSTRACT

The conventional model of transactions is based on the notions of serializability and atomicity. This transaction model has served conventional data-processing applications well. However, it is not appropriate for a CAD environment. Transactions in a CAD environment are of long duration and represent interactive modifications to a complex design. Application of the standard techniques to ensure atomicity and serializability results in intolerably long waits or the undoing of a significant amount of work.

In this paper, we first review a model of CAD transactions which allows a group of cooperating designers to arrive at a complex design without being forced to wait over a long duration, and which also allows a group of designers to collaborate on a design with another group by assigning subtasks. We then discuss concurrency control and recovery schemes that implement the model. We also propose a number of significant extensions to the current theory of concurrency control to achieve a high degree of parallelism among transactions, while preserving database consistency.

1. Introduction

A computer-aided design (CAD) environment, such as VLSI circuit design, mechanical parts design, or software development, typically requires a group of designers to complete a complex design by closely interacting among themselves and dynamically sharing design data and data about design data. During the past few years, we have studied various aspects of transactions within CAD environments. We have modeled a CAD environment and the characteristics of the database in a CAD environment. We have developed a general model of transactions which can be specialized to a CAD environment. Further, we have studies implementation issues for the concurrency control and recovery aspects of our model of transactions. We have also developed a number of significant extensions to the current theory of concurrency control which can significantly increase the amount of parallelism among transactions in a CAD environment.

This paper is intended to be a compendium of our work on CAD transactions. Our model of transactions in a CAD environment, as well as our characterization of a CAD database and CAD environments, has been presented in [BANC85]. For completeness, we will include a summary of the results here. However, the focus of this paper is the presentation of implementation issues for our model of transactions, and the extensions to the current theory of concurrency control to exploit the the opportunities for increased concurrency which is inherent in our model of transaction. The extensions include multiple granularity DAG of [GRAY76] to include design objects and versions of design objects, an extended set of lock modes to accommodate the database operations associated with design objects and versions of design objects. We also define new criteria for the correctness of a database concurrency scheme which does not use serializability as the notion of correctness.

This paper is organized as follows. In Section 2 we provide an overview of CAD environments with respect to their transaction requirements. We review our model of transactions and its application to CAD environments in Section 3. Section 4 is concerned with implementation issues of our transaction model. In particular, we discuss implementation of the concurrency control requirements of the cooperating transactions and client/subcontractor transactions, and recovery of transactions. In Section 5 we propose extensions to the current theory of concurrency control, which allow increased parallelism among transactions which do not require serializability.

2. CAD Transaction Requirements

In this section, we review the transaction requirements in a CAD environment that provided the basis of our model of CAD transactions. This section is taken from [BANC85].

2.1. CAD Transaction Environment

In this subsection, we summarize several observations about the way in which large design projects are carried out. The first observation is that a partitioning of a design database is induced by the partitioning of a large design effort into a number of projects. Each data partition consists of design data and some data about design data, for each project. CAD transactions from distinct project require shared access to certain classes of data, such as the database directory (catalog). We interpret this observation to mean that long duration waits (due, for example, to the use of two-phase locking) may be acceptable for cases where project transactions attempt to access another project's database partition.

Our second observation is that a transaction hierarchy is induced naturally from the interaction of a designer and the *window system* on most of the workstations commercially available today. A designer may create and manipulate multiple windows, executing multiple tasks concurrently. The sequence of transactions initiated from the same window implies a user-defined ordering of transactions. However, this ordering is only a partial ordering of transactions. For this reason, we model a designer's transaction as a *set* rather than a *sequence* of short-duration transactions as in [KATZ84b, LORI83, KIM84].

The third observation is that each project has a number of designers who further subdivide the project into a number of subtasks. As the designers work on a well-defined, fairly small subtask, there is a far greater need for shared access to the project's database, than that among projects. This leads to the notion of cooperating transactions. A *cooperating transaction* is a set of designer's transactions. Each designer's short-duration transaction needs to wait only until any currently-executing, conflicting short-duration transactions of other designer's transactions complete. From the point of view of database consistency, it is immaterial how many designers participate in the same cooperating transaction; all the short-duration transactions of all the designers' transactions are to be treated just as if they were issued by a single designer.

The fourth, and final, observation is that in a complex design project, it is often the case that some tasks are subcontracted to other (groups of) designers. The client specifies tasks to be completed, and grants the subcontractor limited access to the client's database. For example, a client may allow a subcontractor to access a file describing the interface (i.e., I/O pins and functional specification) of a circuit, and specify that the subcontractor provide the implementation details of the circuit.

We represent the notion of subcontracted work by defining the notion of a *client/subcontractor transaction* pair. A subcontractor transaction is a cooperating transaction which exists solely to work on behalf of a cooperating client transaction. A subcontractor transaction may itself subcontract work, thus becoming a cleint of one transaction while being a subcontractor of another transaction. The result is a hierarchy of client/subcontractor transactions in which a transaction is a subcontractor of its parent and a client of its children. From here on, we will use the term *cooperating transaction* to mean an entire hierarchy of client/subcontractor transactions. Where distinction is necessary, we shall use the term *client/subcontractor transaction* to refer to a node of this hierarchy.

We can combine the above observations to derive the following intuitive model of CAD transactions. A design environment consists of a number of project transactions, each of which may consist of a set of cooperating transactions. Each cooperating transaction is a hierarchy of client/subcontractor transactions. Each client/subcontractor transaction is a set of designer's transactions, which in turn is a set of short-duration transactions. A short-duration transaction is initiated from a window of the designer's workstation. Figure 1 illustrates our intuitive model.

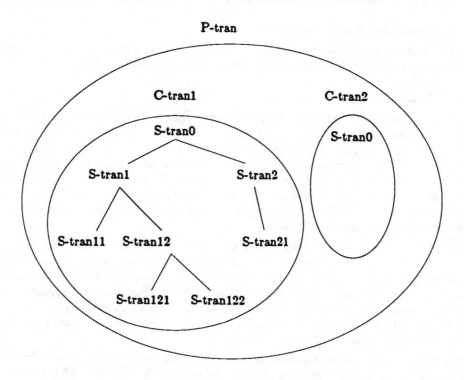

legend: P-tran -- project transaction
         C-tran -- cooperating transaction
         S-tran -- client/subcontractor transaction

Figure 1. Intuitive model of CAD transactions

2.2. CAD Database Hierarchy

For performance reasons, the system configuration often envisioned for CAD systems consists of a public system (central server) and a collection of private systems connected to the public system [HASK82, KATZ84b, LORI83, KIM84]. The public system manages the public database of stable design data and design control data. A private system manages the private database of a designer on a design workstation. A CAD transaction, initiated on a private system, consists of

- checking out of design data from the public system and their insertion into the private database,
- checking in of updated design data to the public database, and
- reading and writing of both the private database and the public database.

Our model of transactions leads to a logical partitioning of the global database of such a distributed CAD system into a set of databases, consisting of the public database, private databases, and project databases. The public database holds released design objects and data about design objects and design status. A released design has two properties: it cannot be updated or deleted, and it is accessible to all authorized designers within a CAD environment. The data about design objects and design status include the directory of design objects, checkout/checkin status, etc. They are also accessible to all authorized designers. Further, they can be updated by the public database system and authorized users.

A project database serves as the repository of design objects that are being passed back and forth among designers within a project. It contains those designs and data about designs that are accessible only to cooperating designers within a project and specified subcontractor transactions. The design objects in a project database are considered stable; however, the assumption is that they have not gone through validation tests and, as such, they cannot be released to the public. The project transaction will have the database administrator privileges over the project databases of the subcontractor hierarchy it spawns. In particular, it can delete design objects in the project databases of its subcontractor hierarchy.

A client may place design objects in its project database, from where a subcontractor may check them out. The subcontractor updates the objects, and returns (checks) them in its own project database. The client then checks out the updated design objects from the subcontractor's project database.

A private database exists in a workstation and contains non-released designs, on which a designer is currently working, and any additional information the designer wishes to maintain. It contains copies of data checked out of either a project database or the public database. The designer who creates the private database is the owner and administrator of the database. A private database of a designer is not accessible to any other designer.

3. CAD Transaction Model

In [BANC85], we defined a formal model of nested transactions that includes the various transaction requirements discussed in Section 2. The model has provided a framework for the exploration of alternative concurrency control schemes for the management of transactions in a CAD environment. We present several such schemes in subsequent sections. In order to motivate properly the discussions of these issues, we include a summary of our formal model of transactions in this section.

3.1. Definitions

Our notion of transaction is a generalization of that of Gray [GRAY81a]. We allow nesting of transactions to arbitrary depth, as in the nested-transaction model of [MOSS81]. Transactions in our model may themselves be parallel programs, subject to limitations we shall discuss. The nesting and parallelism allow us to capture the notions of client/subcontractor transactions and cooperating transactions, as we shall see in the next subsection.

Transactions are mappings from the set S of all database states to S. The simplest form of these mappings are the atomic database operations that are provided as primitives of database systems. The following definition shows how we represent these mappings.

Definition: A *transaction* is a 3-tuple (T,O,C) where

- T is a set of transactions or operations
- O is a partial order on T
- C is the consistency constraint (invariant) preserved by the transaction

We require that for all transactions (t,o,c) in T, C implies c. In other words, nested transactions may have weaker constraints than their ancestors, but not vice-versa. Note that this definition of transaction is recursive. We shall assume that the depth of nesting is finite. Thus, at the deepest levels of nesting, transactions consist solely of operations. A transaction represents a set of possible mappings from S to S. When the transaction is run, exactly one of these mappings will be chosen. Such a choice is called an *execution* of T.

[LYNC83] proposes a transaction model which allows a transaction to specify a set of "breakpoints". The equivalent of atomic execution is guaranteed only between breakpoints, and interleaving of transactions occurs at breakpoints. Our model may be viewed as a scheme for the implementation of a restricted form of this model.

To simplify the presentation that follows, we assume that each transaction or operation has a globally unique name. In practice, this can be accomplished by using a hierarchical naming scheme in which each transaction or operation is prefixed by the names of its containing transactions. We use M to denote the set of all operation names.

It is possible to represent any nesting of transaction in an equivalent unnested form, consisting only of operations, which we call the *closure*.

Definition: The *closure* $(T,O,C)^*$ of a transaction (T,O,C) is the transaction (T^*,O^*,C) where

- $$T^* = (M \cap T) \cup (\cup_X (t^*,o^*,c)^*) \qquad \text{and}$$
  $$X = {}^{"}\{^{"}(t^*,o^*,c) \mid (t^*,o^*,c) \in T - M^{"}\}^{"}$$

- O^* is the partial order induced on T^* defined as follows: Let a and b be operations in T^*. In O^*, $a < b$ if one of the following holds:

  1. $a,b \in T$ and $a < b$ in O
  2. There exist a pair of transactions (t_1,o_1,c_1) and (t_2,o_2,c_2) in T such that $a \in t_1^*$, $b \in t_2^*$ and $t_1 < t_2$ in O
  3. There exists a transaction (t_1,o_1,c_1) in T such that $a,b \in t_1^*$ and $a < b$ in o_1^*.

The nested form of a transaction is more natural than its closure for most applications. However, the notion of closure is useful in the development of the formal model. The closure of a transaction represents all possible partial orderings of operations at any level of nesting in the transaction, that is, any ordering consistent with the orderings specified in the transaction definition. When the closed transaction is run, one of these orderings will be chosen.

Definition: An *execution* e of a transaction $t = (T,O,C)$ is a transaction (T^*,O',C) where O' is a total order such that O' implies O^*. That is, if $a,b \in T^*$, and $a < b$ in O^*, then $a < b$ in O'. We denote the set of all executions of t by E_t.

Definition: Let S_c denote the set of database states satisfying consistency constraint C. An execution e of (T,O,C) is *correct* if for all states $s \in S_C$, $e(s) \in S_C$.

The transaction definitions we expect most users of our model to define will permit incorrect executions. That is, we do not expect the orderings O to constrain E_t sufficiently to ensure preservation of consistency. Therefore, it will be the responsibility of the system to ensure that, given an consistency constraint C, only correct executions are permitted. This is analogous to the situation we encounter in the traditional transaction model: individual transactions preserve consistency, but the closure of a set of transactions (called a *schedule* in the traditional model) may not preserve consistency unless special action is taken by the system.

A protocol is a set of rules that restricts the set of admissible executions. Typically, a protocol is implemented by a set of rules that all "well-formed" transactions follow and by an algorithm executed by the system scheduler.

Definition: A *protocol* P is a mapping from the set E_t of executions of t to {TRUE, FALSE}. If e is an execution, then $P(e)$ if and only if e is an execution *legal* under P. A protocol P is *correct* if for all executions $e \in E_t$, $P(e)$ implies e is correct.

3.2. Application of Our Model to CAD

In [BANC85] we showed that our model is sufficiently general to include the standard model of transaction. The notion of serializability needs to be available in the CAD version of the model since there are occasions where we require serializable actions on a CAD database. The model allows us to describe a wide variety of concurrency control schemes. Indeed, the degree of freedom allowed by the model may be too great for most users. Furthermore, a fully general implementation of the model may involve considerable overhead.

In this subsection we present an example instance of the formal model suitable for a CAD environment. First, we will show how the model captures the various types of transaction identified for a CAD environment in Section 2. Then we define the correctness requirements for each type of transaction.

At the root of our nested-transaction hierarchy is a *global,* or *root transaction.* Immediately below this transaction is a set of project transactions. These represent different groups of people, working on the same design. As noted in Section 2, each project is independent of the work of other projects, though they may access shared data. Each project therefore would maintain database consistency just as if no other concurrent project transactions exist in the system. Thus, a global transaction P is described by (T,O,C) where T is a set of *project* transactions, O is the empty order, and C is the database consistency constraint. The concurrency control protocol requires that the schedule for the set of project transactions be serializable (the protocol will be discussed later).

Each project transaction consists of a set of *cooperating transactions.* These transactions, as a whole, maintain database consistency but no order is specified among them. Transactions within a cooperating transaction (i.e., designer's transactions) are aware of one another's presence and cooperate to maintain the overall consistency of the database. Since (T,O,C) is a set of cooperating transactions,

- T is a set of transactions of the form (t,o,c)

- O is the empty order

- C is the set of consistency constraints that we wish to enforce on the entire database.

Each transaction (t,o,c) is a cooperating transaction. The concurrency control protocol at this level requires the atomicity of any subcontractor transactions (to be defined formally below) in each (t,o,c) in T.

In the simplest case in which cooperating transactions consist solely of database operations (i.e., there is only one designer's transaction and it has no subtransactions), all that the protocol requires is atomicity of database operations. In this case, a complete definition of a set (T,O,C) of cooperating transactions is as follows:

- T is a set of transactions of the form (t,o,c) where

- t is a set of transactions of the form (t',o',c') where
    - t' is a set of operations
    - o' is some total order
    - c' is TRUE
- o is some partial order
- c is TRUE
- O is the empty order
- C is the set of consistency constraints that we wish to enforce on the entire database.

Observe that the deepest level of nesting represents the atomic operations provided to the designers. Each transaction at the second level of nesting represents an individual cooperating designer. At the top level of nesting, transaction T represents the work being performed by the group of designers within a project.

In general, each transaction within a cooperating transaction (i.e., a designer's transaction) is a hierarchy of clients/subcontractors. This situation is represented by (T_c,o,c), where T_c is a set of operations and subcontractors, o specifies when each subcontractor is initiated relative to the other members of T_c, and c is some local consistency constraint. The concurrency control protocol requires that every client sees every subcontractor as an atomic step executed immediately after the step that initiated it.

Let (T_c,O,C) be a transaction where

- T_c contains T_s, where T_s represents a subcontractor of (T_c,O,C) (i.e., (T_c,O,C) is a client of T_s). Transaction $T_s = (t',o',c')$
- O is some partial order.
- C is the set of consistency constraints that we wish to enforce on the entire database.

We say that T_s is a *subcontractor* of *client* T_c under protocol P if $P(e)$ is true only if e is equivalent to a correct execution of $((T_c - T_s) \cup t',O',C)$, where O' contains:

- All elements $a < b$ of O such that $a,b \in T_c - T_s$
- All elements $a < b$ of o'
- All orderings of the form $a < b$ where $a \in T_c - T_s$ and $a < T_s$ appears in O, and $b \in t'$.
- All orderings of the form $a < b$ where $b \in T_c - T_s$ and $T_s < b$ appears in O, and $a \in t'$.

The ordering O' above represents the original ordering for the client and the original ordering for the subcontractor. We add the constraint that any operation or transaction within the client that came before the subcontractor in O comes before all operations or transactions of the subcontractor in O'. Similarly, we require that any operation or transaction within the client that came after the subcontractor in O, comes after all operations or transactions of the subcontractor in O'.

In other words, a client/subcontractor relationship holds under a protocol if all executions are *equivalent* to a "macro expansion" of the subcontractor's operations at some point within the client. The use of subcontractors accomplishes more than the use of subroutines in standard programming languages. Unlike a normal subroutine, the subcontractor transaction is able to run in parallel with its client.

Each client or subcontractor consists of a set of *short-duration transactions*, together with some order defined on them. A subcontractor is (t,o,c) where t is a set of short-duration transactions, o is a user-defined order, and c is the user's notion of consistency. The concurrency control protocol at this level requires that short-duration transactions be executed in a serializable fashion (this is to be expressed at some lower level).

A short-duration transaction consists of a sequence of database operations which include reads and updates. Thus, a short-duration transaction is (r, o, c) where r is a set of reads and updates, o is the user-defined sequential order, and c is the trivial consistency constraint that is always TRUE. Concurrency control at this level requires atomicity (which is equivalent to serializability).

And finally, a *database operation* consists of a set of system operations (catalog access, index reads and writes, page accesses, etc.) which are sequentially ordered. Thus we have (r, o, c) where r is a set of system operations, o is a sequential order, and c is trivial. Each system operation is atomic by definition.

From the discussion thus far in this subsection, we conclude that a CAD environment consists of

- a set of concurrent project transactions, where a project transaction is
- a set of cooperating transactions, where a cooperating transaction is
- a hierarchy of clients/subcontractors, where a client/subcontractor transaction is
- a directed acyclic graph of short-duration transactions, where a short-duration transaction is
- a sequence of database operations, where a database operation is
- a sequence of system operations.

At each level of nesting, the system must enforce transaction atomicity, the consistency constraints, and the partial order. In Section 4 we present protocols to accomplish this. For now, we summarize the concurrency control requirement at each level.

- Serializability of concurrent project transactions can be enforced at the database operation level by a two-phase (potentially long-duration) locking algorithm.
- Cooperating transactions require atomicity of constituent short-duration transactions. A two-phase (short-duration) locking algorithm can enforce this.
- Subcontractor hierarchies require a multilevel concurrency control scheme, implemented at the database operation level. In Section 4.2, we will describe two algorithms for supporting the atomicity requirements of client/subcontractor hierarchies.
- Database operations must be executed in an atomic fashion. This must be enforced at the system operation level by guaranteeing serializability through a two-phase locking algorithm.

The heavy reliance on two-phase locking in the above example may have adverse effects on performance. Predicatewise two-phase locking (Section 5.1) can be used to reduce our reliance on standard two-phase locking. We shall see that this allows us improved performance while retaining consistency.

4. Implementation of Nested CAD Transactions

In this section, we describe implementation techniques for the concurrency control and recovery of nested CAD transactions in our model of transactions. In particular, we are concerned with two types of transaction nesting. One is the nesting of short-duration transactions within a project transaction. Another is the recursive nesting of subcontractor transactions as the children of a client transaction.

4.1. Concurrency Control for Cooperating Transactions

The project transactions logically partition the database, such that each project transaction in effect reserves a partition of the database for shared access among CAD transactions belonging to the same project. The motivation for this is that each CAD transaction need only wait for the termination of the short-duration transactions comprising the CAD transactions within the same project. We impose standard two-phase locking at the level of project transactions, so that a lock request by a transaction belonging to one project transaction is rejected if it conflicts with a lock held by a different project transaction.

A project transaction establishes its partition of the database, by dynamically acquiring and releasing locks on the database. A project transaction locks a data item, not to access it directly, but to allow its constituent CAD transactions to access the data. In other words, a lock taken by a project transaction is intended to restrict access to the data by other project transactions. Since a project transaction has many short-duration transactions executing concurrently, it js necessary to impose locking at the short-duration transaction level. Although a lock taken by one short-duration transaction must conflict with an incompatible lock requested by another short transaction, it must not conflict with the lock held by the project transaction, as long as the short transaction requests an equal or weaker lock.

We implement locking in our model by defining nested protocols. Conceptually, there is a separate lock manager for each level of nested transactions. A lock request is *legal* if all ancestors of the transaction making the request already hold the lock being requested. A lock request is granted if the lock manager for the appropriate nesting level allows it. In other words, a legal lock request is checked only against requests made by other transactions at the same level of nesting within the same parent.

In practice, it is undesirable to implement multiple lock managers, because of excessive performance overhead. Instead, we use a hierarchical transaction naming scheme that allows a single lock manager to simulate the lock managers required by our scheme. Let t_1, t_2, ..., t_n denote the set of project transactions. Each subtransaction of a project transaction is named uniquely within its project. The globally unique name of the transaction is the concatenation of its parent's name and its own locally unique name. Thus, the cooperating transactions within project transaction t_1 are named $t_{1,1}$, $t_{1,2}$, ..., $t_{1,m}$. Using this naming scheme, it is a simple matter for a single lock manager to perform the following functions:

- check legality of requests: If the lock manager is designed to accept only legal requests, then to verify the legality of a new request it suffices to see that the parent of the requesting transaction has the appropriate lock.

- check legality of lock release requests: If a transaction attempts to release a lock, the lock manager can check to see if a subtransaction still holds a lock on the data. If so, the lock manager should disallow the request.

- simulate a set of nested lock managers: A legal lock request is checked for compatibility in the same way as a standard lock manager would. However, if the request turns out not to be compatible with one or more currently held locks, the name of the transaction holding the lock is compared with the name of the transaction requesting the lock. If the name of the transaction holding the lock is a prefix of the name of the transaction requesting the lock, then the incompatibility is ignored.

It should be noted that the above technique is based on the assumption that the lock manager being simulated at each level of nested transactions follows the same set of protocol rules.

As we have seen, a CAD transaction consists of a set of short-duration transactions, and for access to data shared by a number of CAD transactions belonging to the same project, each CAD transaction need only wait until the termination of the short transactions of the CAD transactions within the same project. Therefore, a CAD transaction whose lock request is denied, because another transaction belonging to the same project already holds a conflicting lock, has three options. It can wait for the lock to be grantable, or be notified of the denial of the request and be allowed to continue, or the short-duration transaction which issued the lock request on behalf of the CAD transaction can be rolled back. However, if the request is denied because another project holds a conflicting lock, the requesting transaction should not be made to wait, since the wait may be for a long duration. Instead, either it should be notified of the conflict, or the short-duration transaction that issued the lock request can be rolled back.

4.2. Concurrency Control for Subcontractor Transactions

In this section we present two protocols that may be used to implement the client/subcontractor transaction nesting in our model. We presented these protocols in [BANC85]; however, for completeness, we include them here. Each of these protocols resolves the difficulty with database consistency in the nested-transaction model proposed in [KIM84]. The first protocol pertains to the case in which the client's partial ordering places no constraints on the point at which the "subroutine call" to the subcontractor appears within the execution of the client. The second, a timestamp algorithm, is suitable for situations in which there is a partial ordering in the client that constrains acceptable subcontractor executions.

4.2.1. A Two-Phase Checkout Algorithm

We say that a client or subcontractor transaction has associated with it a client space, a private space, and a subcontractor space. The *private space* of a transaction is not shared with any other transaction. A transaction can read and update data in its private space. The *subcontractor space* is where a transaction places private data that subtransactions may check out. A transaction has a unique subcontractor space. The *client space* of a transaction is the subcontractor space of its client, if there is one; otherwise, it is the public database. As a cooperating transaction is in general a hierarchy of client/subcontractor transactions, more than one transaction may share the same client space.

Definition: A *checkout* is the moving of data by a transaction from its client space to its private space. The converse of a checkout is a *checkin*, whereby a transaction moves data from its private space to its client space. A *checkout enable* is the moving of data by a transaction from its private space to its subcontractor space. A *checkout disable* is the moving of data from a transaction's subcontractor space back to its private space.

Definition: We say that a client/subcontractor transaction is observes the *two-phase checkout protocol*, if it checks out data from its client space during one phase and checks them back in during the next phase, such that once it checks in any data, it cannot check out any more data.

In the two-phase checkout protocol, a checkout is analogous to a lock request and a checkin is analogous to a lock release. To illustrate the operation of this protocol, let t_1 be a transaction, and let t_2 be a subcontractor of t_1. When t_1 wishes to assign a subtask to t_2, it checkout-enables the necessary data into its subcontractor space (i.e., the client space of t_2). t_2 checks out the data, moving it from its client space to its private space. We emphasize that our two-phase checkout protocol does not impose any restrictions on the order in which t_1 may checkout-enable data or in which t_2 checks them out. In other words, t_2 may dynamically check out data it needs, possibly over a long duration; likewise, t_1 may dynamically checkout enable data, as t_2's needs become clear. Once t_2 does not need any more data, it may enter the second phase of the two-phase checkout protocol and start to check data back into its client space.

We can now make the connection between two-phase checkout and two-phase locking more precise. In order to check out data, a transaction needs an R mode lock. In order to checkin data, a W mode lock is needed. This upgrading of an R lock to W is consistent with the first phase of two-phase locking. The W lock is released immediately after the checkin. The prohibition of checkout after any checkin thus follows from the requirement in two-phase locking that no lock requests follow an unlock request.

The semi-public database protocol presented in [KIM84] is similar to our protocol. However, it does not enforce two-phase checkout/checkin: it allows subcontractors to check in and check out data any time.

4.2.2. A Virtual Timestamp Algorithm

Sometimes a subcontractor must appear as a subroutine call to its client. This means that a particular partial order must be enforced among the operations of the client and subcontractor. *Virtual timestamping* is a technique to achieve this. Each subtransaction in a client/subcontractor hierarchy is assigned a timestamp that conforms to the partial order. We resort to *virtual* timestamps, since the depth of the hierarchy may be arbitrarily large and system-clock-based timestamps in general do not provide the time granularity we need. The version of virtual timestamping we present here enforces a linear ordering on subcontractors of a client transaction. Its extension to partial ordering is straightforward.

When we begin a client/subcontractor transaction T, we assign to it *a start time* ST and a *duration* D. If that transaction consists of a sequence of short-duration transactions 1, 2, ..., n, we will assign to each short-duration transaction i a start time $st(i)$ and a duration $d(i)$. Then the following equations have to be satisfied.

$$ST \leq st(1) < st(2) < \cdots < st(n) < +ST + D \tag{1}$$

$$st(i) + d(i) \leq st(i+1) \tag{2}$$

When a short-duration transaction i of T spawns a subcontractor T', it assigns to it a start time ST' and a duration D' such that:

$$st(i) < ST' < ST' + D' < st(i+1) \tag{3}$$

The above is repeated recursively for the depth of the client/subcontractor hierarchy.

Atomicity of subcontractors is guaranteed, if equations (1), (2), and (3) above are satisfied. Now we describe how the start times and durations of subcontractors in these equations may be assigned. Assume that transaction T has start time ST and duration D. Then, we assign start time and duration to its subcontractors by:

$$st(1) = ST \qquad d(1) = D/2$$

$$st(2) = st(1) + d(1) \qquad d(2) = d(1)/2$$

$$\cdots$$

$$st(i) = st(i-1) + d(i-1) \qquad d(i) = d(i-1)/2$$

Let transaction i with start time $st(i)$ and duration $d(i)$ spawn subcontractor T'. We assign a start time ST' and a duration D' defined by:

$$ST' = st(i) + \epsilon \qquad D' = st(i+1) \ ST'$$

The above scheme satisfies equations (1), (2) and (3) and does not require an *a priori* knowledge of the number of subcontractors of any client.

We characterize a database operation by a pair $(t\#, st)$ where $t\#$ is the identifier of the immediate client of the subcontractor transaction that issues the operation, and st is the start time of the short-duration transaction that belongs to the subcontractor transaction. Then access to data is granted if the data is stamped with a different transaction identifier, or, if already stamped with the same transaction identifier, it has an earlier start time. When access is granted, the data is stamped with the couple $(t\#, st)$. This algorithm guarantees that each object is processed by clients and subcontractors in the correct order. The details of the algorithm are analogous to standard timestamp techniques as described in [BERN81].

If we use the timestamp-ordering protocol to enforce the partial order on a client/subcontractor transaction hierarchy, we will need two different types of concurrency managers. This will present problems of integrating them in one database system. Because of the absence of waits in timestamp schemes, it is never necessary to involve the timestamp scheme in the deadlock detection algorithm of the lock manager. However, each concurrency manager must inform the other of any transaction aborts that it initiates. Within the timestamp scheme, a transaction must not be given access to data that is not locked by its closest ancestor running under a locking protocol. Similarly, a transaction controlled by a locking protocol must not be given a lock that its closest ancestor running under a timestamping scheme could not access. These two conditions are easy to test via simple queries of the concurrency manager's internal data structures.

4.3. Recovery of Nested Transactions

Now we address the issue of recovery technique for CAD databases. The techniques most widely used for transaction recovery in database systems are shadowing and logging [GRAY81c]. The shadow mechanism keeps two copies of the data pages that a transaction updates; the current copy of updated pages and the shadow copy of pages before the update. When the transaction successfully finishes (commits), the shadow copy is discarded and the current copy becomes the shadow. If the transaction fails (aborts), however, the current copy is dropped.

The log mechanism records the before and after values (UNDO and REDO logs, respectively) of the updated fields of each record. These logs are used to either back out any changes to the database if the transaction fails, or to re-compute the changes if the transaction committed but the database changes were not written to the disk.

CAD database systems must support multiple concurrent transactions. The difficulty in supporting concurrent transactions using only the shadow mechanism [GRAY81c] quickly leads us to the logging approach.

In traditional database systems, crash recovery requires that all transactions active at the time of a crash be aborted. This presents a severe problem in systems that include long-duration transactions, including work done by designers. The amount of work that is lost in aborting a long-duration transaction is significant. Abortion of long-duration transactions is undesirable not only from a performance standpoint, but also from a human-factors standpoint.

To minimize the amount of work that is lost due to a crash, the notion of a *save point* is proposed in [GRAY78] and [GRAY81c]. Under the save-point scheme, a transaction may request that the system save the internal state of the transaction. In the event of a crash, the transaction is restarted from the most recent save point possible. However, the implementation of save points is very complex. Not only must the internal state of the transaction be saved, but also all subsystems of the database system must save all data pertaining to the transaction. For example, the lock manager must save all locks taken by the transaction requesting a save.

Moreover, at recovery time, it may not be possible to restart the transaction from the most recent save point prior to the crash. Let us consider transaction t_2, which at time T_2 has read data written by transaction t_1 at time T_1. If t_1 had not yet committed, and cannot be restarted at a point between T_1 and T_2, then it is not possible to restart t_2 at any point *after* T_2. One way to deal with this problem is to use a locking scheme which delays all lock releases until the end of the transaction. Then it is always possible to restart a transaction from its most recent save point.

In our model of CAD transactions, long-duration transactions are composed of a set of short-duration transactions. This fact allows us to solve the transaction-restart problem simply. If a long-duration transaction is active at the time of a crash, any active short-duration subtransactions of the long transaction are aborted. The results of all committed subtransactions are restored (by means of a REDO operation if necessary). Thus, in effect, the termination of a short-duration transaction represents a save point for the long-duration transaction that contains it.

The state of a long-duration transaction consists of a record of which subtransactions have been completed. This information is obtained from the log at recovery time by checking for commit records for subtransactions [GRAY81c]. This data represents most of the long-duration transaction's state, so the overhead of implementing a save point at the termination of each subtransaction is minimal. To restart the database system, however, it is necessary to restore the lock manager's record of locks held by long-duration transactions. Locks held by short-duration transactions need not be restored, since those transactions will be aborted.

Our lock manager will have two separate data structures for locks: one for project transactions, and another for short-duration subtransactions. For short-duration transactions, the data structure for locks will be the conventional, main-memory resident structure. However, the data structure for locks acquired and released by project transactions will be a part of the database (in the form of a lock table), so that we can treat locks taken or released on behalf of a long-duration transaction as we treat database accesses. Any updates to this long-duration lock table will be recorded in log records, which are forced to disk in accordance with the *write-ahead log protocol* [GRAY78] used to commit short-duration subtransactions.

5. Enhancing Concurrency in CAD Transactions

In this section, we propose a number of significant extensions to the current theory of concurrency control to increase the amount of parallelism in CAD transactions that a database system can exploit. First, we extend the granularity DAG with nodes which will represent design objects and versions of design objects. Then we define an extended set of lock modes which will directly accommodate database operations against design objects and versions of design objects. Then we examine the notion called *predicatewise two-phase locking* which weakens the two-phase locking, by applying two-phase locking to only selected partitions of the database. Finally, we propose the use of update-mode locks to prevent deadlocks during lock-mode conversion, without restricting the degree of parallelism in transactions.

5.1. Extending the Granularity DAG

In this section, we review the directed acyclic graph (DAG) used by [GRAY76] and [KORT83] to represent multiple granularities of data. We then show how this approach can be extended to represent design objects and versions of design objects.

5.1.1. Review of the Granularity DAG

Multiple-granularity locking is motivated by the fact the different transactions require different units of data. Some may need a few records chosen randomly from a relation; others may need a whole relation, etc. In a design database, design objects may consist of tuples stored in several distinct relations. Many transactions will access data in object units rather than in relation or tuple units. It is possible to implement a locking scheme using only one lock granularity. However, such a scheme imposes inefficiencies on the system:

- Transactions that access data in large units (e.g., design objects or relations) need to take a large number of locks. This increases the amount of overhead imposed by locking.

- Transactions that access data in small units (e.g., records) may have to lock a larger unit of data than is actually needed. This has the effect of reducing the amount of potential concurrency in the system.

Multiple-granularity locking is a technique that allows a transaction to lock data using a granule size that corresponds closely to that with which the transactions accesses data.

We describe a collection of lock granularities by defining a *granularity scheme*, which specifies the types of granularity (e.g., record, file, relation) that we shall allow. A granularity scheme also gives a sub-granule relationship between pairs of granularities (e.g., record is a sub-granule of file). Typically, we represent a granularity scheme by a directed graph. Figure 2 shows a granularity scheme for a simple data-processing database.

The database is partitioned into a collection of areas. Areas are partitioned in several ways:

- An area contains a collection of files. Although every record is contained in some file, it may be the case that records of a particular relation are spread over many files.

- An area contains a collection of database relations. Records of a relation may appear in several different files.

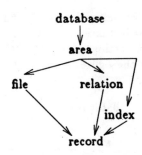

Figure 2.   Granularity DAG for a Conventional Database

Having defined a granularity scheme, we may construct an *instance* of this scheme for any given instance of the database. An instance is a directed acyclic graph (DAG) that shows the sub-granules and super-granules for each granule of data in the database. There is a one-to-one correspondence between the nodes of the DAG and the granules of data in the instance. An edge (a,b) appears in the DAG if and only if the granule associated with node b is a subgranule of the granule associated with node a. Thus, the leaves of the DAG represent the smallest units of data at which we are willing to allow locking. The multiple-granularity locking protocol uses the granularity-scheme instance.

The directed-graph for an instance is necessarily acyclic, since it represents the notion of sub-granule. Since the granule representing the entire database contains all other granules as sub-granules, the database granule serves as the root of this DAG. Figure 3 shows a sample instance for the scheme of Figure 2.

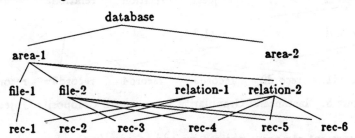

Figure 3.   Instance of Granularity Scheme of Figure 2.

We review briefly the locking protocol of [GRAY76] using the instance of Figure 3 as our example. The database is split into 2 areas. Area-1 holds 2 relations (rel-1 and rel-2), and 2 files (file-1 and file-2). The records contained within the relations, and files of area-1 and records rec-1, rec-2, ..., rec-n. We have not shown the structure of area-2 in our figure due to space considerations.

We use the DAG of Figure 3 to explain the semantics of locking in a multiple-granularity scheme. A lock on file file-1, for example, locks all the records within file-1, but does so with only one lock request. In such a case, we say that the records of file-1 (rec-1 and rec-2) are locked *implicitly*. Similarly, a lock on area-1 locks all the files and relations in area-1 implicitly, and thus locks all records contained in area-1 implicitly.

5.1.2. Design-Objects and Versions of Design Objects

The granularity scheme of Figure 2 needs to be augmented in order to describe granularities appropriate for CAD transactions. We need to include a granularity that represents *design objects*. A design object consists of records from several relations and several files [HASK82]. Thus, the design-object granularity is neither a sub-granule nor a super-granule of either the file or record granularities. This leads to a granularity scheme as shown in Figure 4.

The scheme of Figure 4 is not sufficiently general to represent design hierarchies of composite objects. In general, an object may contain other objects. That is, objects may be composite.

Sub-objects may be shared among several objects. We do not know, in general, how many sub-objects an object might have in a particular instance, nor is there any fixed bound on the depth of nesting. Figure 5 shows an example of a nesting of objects. (Note that we have omitted the structure of area2 and object2 to simplify the figure. Also, we have not shown the file granularity.)

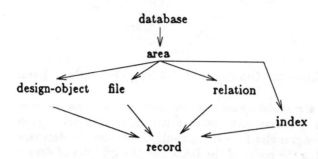

Figure 4.   Granularity Scheme for a CAD database (without composite objects)

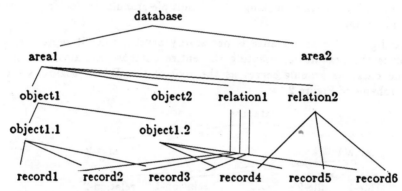

Figure 5.   Instance of Granularity Scheme with Composite Objects.

In order to represent composite objects, we add an edge in the directed graph from a design object to itself, thus creating a cycle. This edge indicates that an object granule may be a sub-granule of another object granule. Although the resulting granularity scheme is cyclic, we restrict *instances* of granularity scheme to be acyclic. This does not constrain our model in any practical sense, since our condition of acyclicity simply requires that no design object contain itself. Figure 6 shows our granularity scheme for composite objects. Figure 5 is, in fact, a sample instance of the granularity scheme of Figure 6.

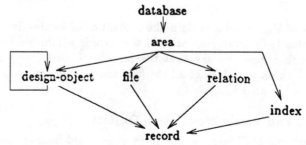

Figure 6.   Granularity Scheme for a CAD database (with composite objects)

We consider the question of allowing multiple *versions* of data [KATZ84]. The idea of versions has been used previously in concurrency-control schemes. In [BERN81], versions are used in conjunction with timestamp-ordering for concurrency control. Versions in schemes such as those in [BERN81] are not visible to users and exist solely to assist in concurrency control. In a CAD environment, versions are a natural consequence of the design process. Versions may represent released designs as well as modifications of existing designs. Thus, the distinction among versions must be visible to the user.

We do not set an a priori bound on the number of versions and seek an approach that will accommodate however many versions we are willing to allocate space for. In general, we can represent versions in an instance of our granularity scheme as follows: Let n be a node of the DAG. If n represents a data granule for which multiple versions exist, create a node n_i for each version v_i of the data. Add an edge (n, n_i) for each node n_i. Create a copy of the subtree of node n for each version and associate one copy with each of the n_i. Mark node n as representing a multiversion granule.

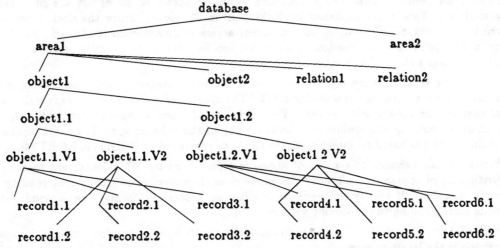

Figure 7.   Instance of Granularity Scheme with Composite Objects and Multiple Versions.

Thus, we have a two-level scheme for representing a multiversion datum in a DAG. The higher level represents the datum itself (all its versions). The lower level represents the individual versions. In order to model a practical CAD environment, it is sufficient to allow versions only for design objects. However, we do not need to make this restriction a requirement of our model.

Figure 7 shows the instance of Figure 5 extended to include several versions of the design objects.

5.2. Extending the Lock Modes

There are several types of access to CAD data that may be required. Often, design data is "checked out" of a design database, operated on by the transaction in a designer's private database, and then "checked in", perhaps as a new version [KATZ84]. Below, we list four lock modes and show intuitively how these modes can be used to provide access to CAD data under different requirements for transaction isolation.

- X – Exclusive
- W – Write
- R – Read
- D – Read dirty snapshot

Figure 8 shows a *lock compatibility matrix* for our set of lock modes. To determine if a lock in mode a can be granted to a transaction despite another transaction already holding a b mode lock on the same datum, we look in the row for a and the column for b. If the entry is *true* then the request is allowed. Otherwise the lock request is denied.

We now show to which of several modes of access to a CAD database these lock modes correspond. In what follows, for a data item n for which versions exist, we shall use n_i to denote the node corresponding to a particular version. We assume that if $i < j$, version n_i is older than

	X	W	R	D
X	false	false	false	false
W	false	false	false	true
R	false	false	true	true
D	false	true	true	true

Figure 8. Compatibility Matrix

version n_j.

- Protect all versions: This means obtaining exclusive access to all of the n_is of a version granule n. This is accomplished by locking n in X mode. Since this lock provides an implicit X lock on all versions, no concurrent access to any version is allowed. An X lock on n also precludes the creation of a new version by another transaction, since a new version becomes a child of n.

- Create new version: When a new version of a datum is created, a node corresponding to it must be inserted into the granularity DAG. The creator of a new version needs write access to that version (or exclusive access). Thus, creation of a new version will conflict with an X lock on n, but will not conflict with locks on any of the existing n_is. The exact mechanism of the conflict is based on intention mode locks, as presented in [GRAY76, KORT83].

- Write specific version: This mode of access is represented by W. Concurrent reading and writing is, of course, not allowed. W mode does, however, allow concurrent reading of a dirty snapshot. If the writer needs to disallow such accesses, it may use X mode on the node corresponding to the specific version.

- Write latest: This mode of access is the same as "write specific version", where the specific version is the latest version.

- Read specific version: This mode of access is represented by R.

- Read latest: This mode is implemented using "read specific version" in a manner similar to the implementation of "write latest".

- Read latest available: This mode uses R mode. The system needs to determine the latest version on which no locks other than R and D locks are held. This information is available in the lock manager's state information.

- Read dirty snapshot: This mode of access is represented by D mode. A dirty snapshot is a copy of the datum that may contain uncommitted changes by concurrent transactions.

Note that the presence of D mode implies that we allow for non-serializable schedules even if two-phase locking is used. In what follows, we shall pay little attention to D mode under the assumption that it will be used only by read-only transactions. Thus, transactions that use D mode will not generate an inconsistent database.

Suppose that we support the granularities shown in Figure 6. Consider the case of a transaction checking a design object out of the design database. The checkout operation amounts to a read (R), on one of the versions. The version read is copied into the transaction's private database. The transaction has write access to the newly created private version. Eventually, the transaction will check in the object to the design database, thereby creating a new version. Concurrent checkout requests are allowed since they correspond to concurrent R lock requests.

Note that the approach to checkout and checkin presented above allows for the generation of non-serializable schedules, since two checkin operations on the same datum do not conflict. When we require serializability, we need to regulate further legal operations on versions. Among the rules we can add to the protocol for version creation are the following:

- Before a transaction may create a new version of a datum, it must hold the latest version of that datum in W mode.

- Before a transaction may create a new version of a datum, it must hold an X mode lock on the node representing all versions of the datum.

5.3. Locking Protocols

In this section, we propose new protocols based on the notion of *predicatewise two-phase locking* that preserve database consistency as defined in [BANC85].

5.3.1. Review of the Granularity Locking Protocols

In the previous section, we defined a lock compatibility function for the modes X, W, R, and D. We gave an intuitive argument justifying our choice of compatibility function. We now state precisely what we require of lock compatibility functions. Each lock mode that we have defined (X, W, R, D) corresponds to a database operation. For this reason, we call them *operational* modes. The operational lock modes define the amount of semantic information available for concurrency control. Although we are not, in general, interested in serializability for CAD transactions, we shall see that the notion of correctness remains useful in defining the class of "acceptable" lock compatibility functions.

Definition: A transaction is *well-formed* if it locks data it accesses in the operational lock mode corresponding to the desired form of access.

That is, a reader must acquire a R or D lock, and an updater must request a W or X lock.

Definition: A lock compatibility function is *correct* if, given a set of well-formed transactions that observe two-phase locking, the scheduler can generate only serializable schedules.

Because of the inclusion of D mode, the compatibility function of Figure 8 is *not* correct. However, if we consider the restriction of COMPAT to X, W, R, then the function is correct.

We define intention mode locks in order to ensure that locks taken at different granularities do not conflict. For example, we must avoid a situation in which a transaction is allowed an X mode lock on a relation while another transaction holds a W mode lock on one record of the relation. We define one intention mode for each operational mode. We then construct a lock compatibility matrix for this extended set of modes.

Let INITIAL denote our initial set of lock modes. For each mode a in INITIAL, we define a new mode called *intend-a* mode, denoted I_a. Let INTENT denote the union of INITIAL and the set of intention modes constructed from INITIAL. Let COMPAT be the initial lock compatibility function mapping INITIAL x INITIAL to {*true, false*}. The first argument to COMPAT signifies the mode of lock being *requested*. The second argument signifies the mode of lock *already held* on the data item in question. We extend COMPAT to INTENT as follows: Let p and q be two lock modes. Then COMPAT(p,q) is

- *true* if both p and q are intention modes, that is, if there is a mode P and Q in INITIAL such that $p = I_P$ and $q = I_Q$.
- COMPAT(P,q) if q is in INITIAL and there is a mode P in INITIAL such that $p = I_P$.
- COMPAT(p,Q) if p is in INITIAL and there is a mode Q in INITIAL such that $q = I_Q$.

To illustrate the intuition behind the use of intention modes, consider the special case in which the granularity DAG happens to be a tree. We require all transactions to observe the following rule, called the *tree/parent rule*.

Definition: A transaction observes the *tree/parent rule* if it does not request a lock on a node unless it already holds a lock on the parent of the node in the corresponding intention mode. This rule does not apply to the root of the tree (since the root has no parent).

Thus, if transaction t is to be allowed to lock a node n in mode a, t must already hold an I_a lock on the parent of n. The tree/parent rule implies that transactions must begin locking at the root and take intention locks along tree paths to those nodes that it needs to lock in one of the operational modes (X, W, R, D).

The above rule is not sufficient to ensure a correct concurrency scheme. Suppose transaction t_1 follows the tree/parent rule to lock relation rel-1 in X mode and then releases all of its I_X mode locks. Another transaction t_2 could take an X mode lock on the root, thus locking the entire database implicitly. Therefore, we impose the *leaf-to-root node release rule* [GRAY76, KORT82]:

Definition: A transaction t observes the *leaf-to-root node release rule* in a DAG G if:

- for each node n of G, t is two-phase with respect to n. (i.e., no node is locked, unlocked, and re-locked).

- for each node n of G, t does not unlock n while it holds a lock on a child of n in G.

These definitions allow us to characterize the correctness of a lock compatibility function as follows:

Definition: A lock compatibility function is *tree-correct* if given a set of transactions that

- are well-formed

- observe two-phase locking

- follow the tree/parent rule

- follow the leaf-to-root node release rule

the scheduler can generate only serializable schedules.

Theorem: The lock compatibility function for INTENT (X, W, R) is tree correct.

Proof: This is a corollary to a theorem in [KORT83].

In order to extend this locking scheme to DAGs, we need to replace the tree/parent rule. Since a DAG node may have many parents, we need to define the number of parents that must be locked. The most general form of the requirement that must be satisfied is that for any two conflicting INITIAL modes a and b, the number of parents that must be locked in I_a mode plus the number of parents that must be locked in I_b mode must be greater than the number of parents. For our purposes, we shall use only the following rule. We require intention mode locks on only one parent for R and D, but we require locks on all parents for W and for X. Furthermore, we restrict implicit locking. In order for a node to be locked implicitly, in R or D mode, only one parent of the node need be locked. However, all parents are required for implicit locking in W or X mode. We call our DAG analog of the tree/parent rule the *biased-parent rule* since we are "biased" in favor of readers. We choose to favor readers in this way because reading is a more frequent activity than writing. Thus, we anticipate that providing fewer requirements for reading will result in improved system performance.

Definition: A transaction observes the *biased-parent rule* if it does not request a lock on a node n in modes R, I_R, D, or I_D unless it already holds a lock on a parent of the node in the corresponding intention mode and it does not request a lock on a node n in modes X, I_X, W, or I_W unless it already holds a lock on all parents on the node in the corresponding intention mode.

The above rule leads to a notion of DAG-correctness:

Definition: A lock compatibility function is *DAG-correct* if given a set of transactions that

- are well-formed

- observe two-phase locking

- follow the biased-parent rule

- follow the leaf-to-root node release rule

the scheduler can generate only serializable schedules.

The following theorem follows directly from [KORT83]:

Theorem: INTENT (X, W, R) is DAG-correct.

5.3.2. Predicatewise Two-Phase Locking

We relax our requirement of *serializability* by replacing it with a requirement of *preservation of the consistency constraint*. In the model of [BANC85], the definition of each transaction includes an invariant and a partial order on the steps and sub-transactions of the transaction. We require that a transaction preserve its invariant if it is run alone.

Although we refer to the invariant as *the* consistency constraint, many practical invariants are a conjunction of relatively simple consistency constraints. This motivates us to put each invariant C into *conjunctive normal form*, that is, we write C as a conjunction of predicates $c_1, c_2, ..., c_n$, such that the c_i do not contain any "ands". It is an elementary fact of mathematical logic that we can put any C into this form. We refer to each c_i as a *conjunct*.

Before we introduce our main protocol, we present a special case in which each conjunct is expressed in terms of an individual object. We do not claim that this is frequently true in practice; rather we wish to illustrate the technique we shall use in the general protocol. Consider the history of accesses to one particular object by a set of transactions. If we can show that this history is equivalent to one created by a serial execution of the transactions, then we know that our consistency constraint is preserved. Note that this does *not* imply serializability since the equivalent serial ordering may be different for different objects. In this case, we can consider the following protocol:

- Two-phase locking with respect to versions: A transaction is required not to request any lock on any node pertaining to a multiversion granule after it has released a lock on that granule.

Note that this is a very weak two-phase requirement. That is, this requirement imposes fewer limitations on the legality of schedules than does standard two-phase locking. It is applied to each multiversion granule *individually*.

Although the above rule is not very general, it suggests a fruitful approach to concurrency control without global serializability. We define localized sections of the database on which two-phase locking is required. To the extent that these sections of the database are small, we have gained in potential concurrency over standard two-phase locking.

For example, in CAD applications, it is often possible to divide a database into possibly overlapping partitions and consider the question of consistency in each partition individually. Let us consider an example. Suppose a designer designs a circuit component A by first partitioning it into two sub-components, A_1 and A_2. For CAD applications, it is often advantageous to define separately the *interface* part and the *implementation* part of a CAD object, such as a circuit component [BATO85]. The interface part describes the input/output ports of the circuit, and the implementation part gives details of the configuration of the circuit and the interconnection of the components of the circuit among themselves and with the input/output ports of the circuit.

We should be able to allow a designer of our example circuit A to lock separately the interface part and the implementation part of the circuit subcomponent A_1. Once the interface is completed, the designer may release the lock on it, but then acquire locks on the interface and implementation parts of the subcomponent A_2. This will allow other designers to read the circuit component A_1 in their designs of other circuits, without having to wait until the design of the implementation part of A_1 is completed.

In the above example, the criterion for partitioning a database was the interface and implementation distinction in the database representation of CAD objects. We can generalize this, and express the consistency constraint for the database as a conjunction of predicates on the partitions. Since it is always possible to put a predicate into conjunctive normal form, we will assume that our consistency constraints are expressed in this form. Then we can define two-phase locking with respect to a set of predicates (predicatewise 2PL) as follows:

- For each conjunct c_i of a predicate c, let d_i denote the set of data items associated with c_i. We observe two-phase locking only with respect to each set d_i individually.

Predicatewise 2PL allows transactions to release locks prior to the last lock request. Thus, it allows greater concurrency than standard 2PL. Later in this section, we will prove formally that although predicatewise 2PL allows non-serializable schedules, it ensures preservation of database consistency. Note that this is weaker than standard 2PL, but stronger than two-phase locking with respect to versions.

We now introduce a new notion of correctness and a new multiple-granularity locking protocol based upon predicatewise 2PL, the leaf-to-root node release rule, and the biased-parent rule. We begin by defining a notion of correctness for a single-granularity locking scheme.

Definition: A lock compatibility function is *predicatewise correct* with respect to a consistency constraint C if given a set of transactions that

- are well-formed

- observe predicatewise two-phase locking

the scheduler may generate only schedules that preserve C.

Now, we extend the above notion to a multiple-granularity locking scheme represented by a DAG:

Definition: A lock compatibility function is *predicatewise-DAG correct* with respect to a consistency constraint C if given a set of transactions that

- are well-formed

- observe predicatewise two-phase locking

- follow the biased-parent rule, and

- follow the leaf-to-root node release rule

the scheduler may generate only schedules that preserve C.

When we use the term *predicatewise correct* without reference to a specific constraint C, we mean predicatewise correct with respect to all possible constraints C. We are now able to justify our original choice of a lock compatibility function:

Theorem: The compatibility function of Figure 6 for (X, W, R) is a predicatewise correct compatibility function.

Proof: Let s be a schedule. Let C be the consistency constraint and let c_i $(i=1,...,n)$ denote the conjuncts in a conjunctive normal form representation of C. For each set d_i of data items referenced by conjunct c_i, let s_i denote a schedule formed from s as follows: Take those steps from s that access a data item in d_i and list those steps in the same order in which they appear in s. Note that a particular step in s may appear in several of the s_is. Since all transactions in the set T that generated s are predicatewise two-phase, they are two-phase with respect to d_i. For each transaction t in T, let t_i denote a transaction formed by taking only those steps of t that appear in s_i. Since, t_i accesses only data items in d_i, and t_i is two-phase with respect to d_i, t_i is a two-phase transaction. Therefore, s_i is a schedule for a set of two-phase transactions. Since we know that the compatibility function is correct, and is observed in s_i, s_i must be serializable. Each s_i thus preserves c_i. Furthermore, since the steps in s_i include exactly the steps in s that access a data item in d_i, it follows that s must preserve c_i as well. Since i was chosen arbitrarily, s preserves c_i for all i and therefore, s preserves the conjunction of the c_is, which is C.

We generalize the proof of the above theorem to show the following more general result.

Theorem: If a lock compatibility function is correct, then it is predicatewise correct.

Proof: Let C be a consistency constraint and let c_i $(i=1,...,n)$ denote the conjuncts in a conjunctive normal form representation of C. Let d_i denote the set of data items referenced by conjunct c_i. Assume that COMPAT is not predicatewise correct with respect to C. Then there is a schedule s for a set T of predicatewise two-phase transactions such that s fails to preserve some c_i. Each t in T must preserve c_i if there is no concurrency since C is the consistency constraint. Define a set R of transactions as follows: For each t in T, create a transaction r

consisting of those steps of t that access data in d_i. R is the set of all such transactions r. Define a schedule p for R by deleting from s those steps that do not pertain to data in d_i. Since s does not preserve c_i, neither does p. However, all transactions in R are two-phase since all transactions in T are two-phase with respect to d_i. But then p is a counterexample to the assertion that COMPAT is correct.

The above theorem implies that we can use any correct compatibility function for predicatewise two-phase locking, regardless of the consistency constraint. However, since in a CAD database, we are interested in multiple granularities of locking, we must consider the extension of a predicatewise correct compatibility function to a predicatewise DAG-correct compatibility function. In [KORT83], it was shown that the extension of correct compatibility functions to INTENT results in a DAG-correct compatibility function. The following theorem is an analogous result for predicatewise correctness.

Theorem: Let INITIAL be a set of basic lock modes and let COMPAT be a given lock compatibility function for INITIAL. If COMPAT is predicatewise correct, then the extension of COMPAT to INTENT, as defined above, is predicatewise-DAG correct.

Proof: Let s be a schedule for a set T of two-phase biased-parent rule observing transactions. Construct a schedule p from s as follows: Delete all steps involving the request or release of intention mode locks. Replace each step that locks a granule of data in an operational mode with a series of steps that locks explicitly all granules (at the finest granularity) locked implicitly by the step being replaced. Schedule p is equivalent to s since there is no change to steps that result in modification to the database. Furthermore, if the compatibility function INTENT was observed in s, then COMPAT must be observed in p. Since COMPAT is predicatewise correct, p must preserve the consistency constraint and thus, so must s.

We note without proof that the above theorems still hold if we used an unbiased parent rule rather than a biased parent rule as the basis of our definition of predicatewise correctness. This follows from a theorem of [KORT83].

We now consider the practical issues in implementing predicatewise 2PL. First, we consider the tradeoff between serializability and concurrency. We observed earlier that two-phase locking leads to long duration waits in CAD transactions. These long duration waits result from a transaction being unable to release any locks until all locks are acquired. Predicatewise 2PL allows earlier release of locks. The partitions used in predicatewise 2PL reflect the semantics of the database. Each partition reflects a set of closely-related collections of data items. Thus, we anticipate that transactions operate on only a few partitions at a time. Once a transaction has completed its work on a partition, it may release its locks on that partition while continuing to acquire locks in other partitions.

The price of this advantage is that nonserializable schedules are possible. This may be unacceptable in traditional financial database applications in which a serial audit trail is required. In CAD, the crucial issues are correctness and acceptable performance. Since the consistency constraint is preserved in all cases, correctness is ensured even if the result is one that could not be generated by a serial schedule. Indeed, current design environments involve concurrent human interactions with no attempt to ensure serializability. Correctness is ensured by design rule checkers, etc., that test what in our model would be called consistency constraints.

In order to implement predicatewise 2PL, we can use the same lock manager that we would use for standard 2PL. (This fact follows from the theorems presented above.) The challenge in taking optimal advantage of the concurrency potential of predicatewise 2PL is to insert unlock statements into transactions as early as possible. This can be done for compiled transactions using standard compilation techniques. For ad-hoc interactive transactions, an explicit statement must be added to the user interface.

5.4. Conversions and Deadlock

It is often the case that a transaction will read a datum, do some computation and some other database accesses, and then write that datum. If we require that a write lock be used for this purpose, we reduce potential parallelism. Yet, if we allow conversions from read mode to write mode, we may introduce deadlocks involving updaters. A simple example of this is two transactions that obtain read locks on a datum and both wish to convert the read lock to a write lock. [GRAY81a] reports on experiments that show that a large percentage (97 percent) of real-world deadlocks may result from such conversions. The class of *update-mode* locks [KORT83] is designed to eliminate most (though, unfortunately, not all) deadlocks resulting from conversions, while minimizing the impact that this has on the amount of parallelism. Given a set of lock modes (such as INITIAL or INTENT) we generate an update mode for every pair of lock modes in our given set. If a and b are given lock modes, then U_a^b is a mode which allows exactly the privileges of a mode but indicates that the transaction plans to convert this lock to b mode at some point in the future.

As an example, consider U_R^W mode (called *update* mode). This mode allows its holder the privileges of R mode, that is, the right to read the locked datum. This mode is not compatible with itself, thereby avoiding the simple deadlock scenario we noted above. However, update mode is designed to allow the update transaction to read the datum concurrent with transactions holds a R mode lock. [KORT83] defines COMPAT(U_R^W, R) to be true, but COMPAT(R, U_R^W) to be false. This prevents a series of readers from delaying the updater indefinitely. In the experiments of [GRAY81], approximately 76 percent of the observed deadlocks could have been avoided by the use of update modes.

The notion of update mode that we have just defined appears to be the appropriate form of update mode for short-duration transactions. We conjecture that for long-duration updaters, it makes sense for COMPAT(R, U_R^W) to be true. Consider, for example, a case in which a long-duration transaction has checked out an object and will be overwriting the object upon checkin of the object (i.e., it will not be creating a new version). In such a case, we wish to allow short duration transaction to have read access to the object without waiting for the object to be checked back in. If the long-duration transaction uses update mode, read access may proceed concurrently with the long-duration transaction until the point that the long-duration transaction upgrades its lock via a lock conversion in order to be able to check in its updated version. However, transactions that need to modify the datum locked in update mode will be forced to wait.

We now give a general definition of an extension of a compatibility function COMPAT to the update modes. Let UPDATE denote the set of lock modes consisting of our given set of lock modes and all update modes U_a^b for which a is a weaker lock mode that b. Then, using the definition of [KORT83], COMPAT(U_a^b, U_c^d) = COMPAT(a, d).

Theorem: Let MODES be a set of lock modes with a predicatewise-DAG-correct compatibility function COMPAT. Then the extension of COMPAT to UPDATE is also predicatewise-DAG-correct.

Proof (sketch): The proof follows directly from the observation that for all mode a and b, U_a^b is a mode that allows the same accesses as a but is strictly more restrictive that a. Thus any counterexample to the predicatewise DAG correctness of UPDATE would also be a counterexample to the predicatewise DAG correctness of COMPAT.

6. Summary and Conclusion

In this paper, we first provided a formal development of a general model of CAD transactions, and then outlined implementation considerations for the transaction model.

Our model is designed to support a design environment in which a group of cooperating designers can complete a design without being forced to wait over a long duration, and in which a group of designers can collaborate on a design with another group by assigning subtasks. The model maps each of the projects comprising a design project into a set of cooperating transactions. A cooperating transaction is a hierarchy of client/subcontractor transactions, each node of which in turn consists of a set of cooperating designers' transactions. A cooperating designer's transaction is a set of conventional short-duration transactions, initiated from a window of the designer's workstation. The client/subcontractor relationship supports the notion that all actions of a subcontractor are logically executed atomically immediately after its initiation by the client.

Next, we outlined schemes for implementing the concurrency control and recovery for the nested transactions suggested in our model of CAD transactions. In particular, we considered two types of nested transactions. One is for the short-duration transactions comprising long-duration CAD transactions, a number of which constitute a project transaction. Another is for a client/subcontractor transaction hierarchy spawned by a client transaction.

Finally, we explored some techniques for increasing the degree of parallelism in concurrently executing transactions, when we remove serializability as the criterion for database consistency. These included predicatewise two-phase locking, update-mode locks for lock conversions, and read-only checkout of versions. Predicatewise two-phase locking serves in our model a role analogous to that of two-phase locking in the traditional model. It is a protocol that ensures consistency without requiring serializability. We gave an example to show how predicatewise two-phase locking can be applied in practice to enhance potential parallelism in a CAD database system.

References

[BANC85] Bancilhon, F., W. Kim, and H.F. Korth. "A Model of CAD Transactions," Proc. Intl. Conf. on Very Large Data Bases, August 1985.

[BATO85] Batory, D. and W. Kim. "Modeling Concepts for VLSI CAD Objects," ACM Trans. on Database Systems, 10:3 (Sept. 1985).

[BERN81] Bernstein, P.A, and N. Goodman "Concurrency Control in Distributed Database Systems," ACM Computing Surveys, 13:2 (June 1981), pp. 185-221.

[GARC83] Garcia-Molina, H "Using Semantic Knowledge for Transaction Processing in a Distributed Database," ACM Transactions on Database Systems 8:2, 1983 pp. 186-213

[GRAY76] Gray, J.N., R.A. Lorie, G.R. Putzolu, I.L. Traiger, "Granularity of Locks and Degrees of Consistency in a Shared Data Base," in Nijssen, G.M., ed. *Modeling in Data Base Management Systems*, pp. 365-394, also RJ1606, IBM Research Laboratory, San Jose, CA.

[GRAY78] Gray, J. "Notes on Data Base Operating Systems," IBM Research Report: RJ2188, IBM Research, Calif., February 1978.

[GRAY81a] Gray, J.N. "The Transaction Concept: Virtues and Limitations," 7th VLDB Conf. pp. 144-154 (1981).

[GRAY81b] Gray, J.N., P. Homan, H. F. Korth and R. Obermarck, "A Straw Man Analysis of the Probability of Waiting and Deadlock," Oral presentation, *5th Berkeley Workshop on Distributed Databases and Computer Networks* , also, RJ3066 IBM Research Laboratory, San Jose, CA.

[GRAY81c] Gray, J.N., P. McJones, M. Blasgen, R. Lorie, T. Price, G.R.. Putzolu, and I.L. Traiger, "The Recovery Manager of a Data Management System," *ACM Computing Surveys, vol. 13, no. 2* , June 1981, pp. 223-242.

[HASK82] Haskin, R. and R. Lorie. "On Extending the Functions of a Relational Database System," in Proc. ACM SIGMOD Conf., June 1982, pp. 207-212.

[KATZ84a] Katz, R. and T. Lehman. "Database Support for Versions and Alternatives of Large Design Files," IEEE Trans. on Software Engineering, vol. SE-10, no. 2, March 1984, pp. 191-200.

[KATZ84b] Katz, R. and S. Weiss, "Design Transaction Management," Proc. 19th Design Automation Conf., June 1984

[KIM84] Kim, W., R. Lorie, D. McNabb, and W. Plouffe. "A Transaction Mechanism for Engineering Design Databases," in Proc. Intl. Conf. on Very Large Data Bases, August 1984.

[KORT82] Korth, H.F., "Deadlock Freedom Using Edge Locks," *ACM Transactions on Database Systems*, **7:4**, (Dec 1982), pp. 632-652.

[KORT83] Korth, H. F., "Locking Primitives in a Database System," *Journal of the ACM* , 30:1 (Jan 1983), pp. 55-79.

[KORT85] Korth, H. F. and W. Kim, "A Concurrency Control Scheme for CAD Transactions," TR-85-34, Department of Computer Sciences, The University of Texas at Austin (1985).

[LORI83] Lorie, R. and W. Plouffe. "Complex Objects and Their Use in Design Transactions," in Proc. Databases for Engineering Applications, Database Week 1983 (ACM), May 1983, pp. 115-121.

[LYNC83] Lynch, N.A., "Multilevel Atomicity — A New Correctness Criterion for Database Concurrency Control," ACM Transactions on Database Systems, 8:4 (Dec 1983), pp. 484-502.

[MOSS81] Moss, J.E. "Nested Transactions: An Approach to Reliable Distributed Computing," Ph.D. dissertation, Dept. of Electrical Engineering and Computer Science, MIT, April 1981.

CACTIS: A Database System
for Specifying Functionally-Defined Data

Scott E. Hudson

Roger King

University of Colorado
Department of Computer Science
Boulder, Colorado, 80309

Abstract

Cactis is an object-oriented database management system being developed at the University of Colorado. The data model underlying Cactis is based on a principle we call *active semantics,* and is designed to support complex functionally-defined data. In an active semantics database, each entity is assigned a behavioral specification which allows it to respond to changes elsewhere in the database. Each entity may be a piece of non-derived or (possibly complex) derived data, and may have constraints associated with it. Derived data and constraint specifications are maintained automatically and efficiently by the system. Furthermore, the active semantics data model supports an efficient rollback and recovery mechanism, which enables the user to freely explore the database. An in-memory version of Cactis exists and a full DBMS is near completion.

1. Active Semantics

The purpose of this paper is to describe an on-going research project at the University of Colorado. We are developing a database management system called Cactis, which supports a data model based on what we call *active semantics.* The goal of Cactis is to allow a user to model and manipulate real world situations in an efficient fashion. In order to provide this capability, the Cactis data model supports complex derived information. In this way, the user can safely deal with one small part of the database and know that the rest remains consistent and correct. A secondary goal of Cactis is to reduce the burden of learning to use the database, by allowing the user to effectively explore and experiment. Thus, Cactis provides a powerful user recovery and reversal (often called Undo) mechanism.

Many attempts have been made at creating powerful data models which represent derived information. A large class of such models are commonly called semantic models. A complete discussion of semantic modeling and its relationship to traditional modeling may be found in [8]. Briefly, traditional database models support record-like structures and/or inter-record links (e.g., the relational, hierarchical, and network models). Semantic models support expressive data relationships; a typical semantic model allows a designer to specify complex objects, and also supports at least one form of derived relationship, generalization (sometimes called subtyping). With generalization, one sort of object can be defined as belonging to a subcategory of a larger category of objects.

Very few semantic models have been actually implemented, although one of the authors of this paper was involved in a semantic database implementation called Sembase (see [5, 7]). While this implementation did succeed in providing an effective means of implementing objects and subtyping, it only supports a restricted class of first order predicate-defined subtypes. Sembase did not provide the generalized tool we wanted to support a wide class of derived information. Further, the algorithms which support derived subtypes in Sembase, although they are quite efficient, are not as elegant as we would like. In this paper, we present a data model which is much more generalized in its capability to represent derived information than typical semantic database systems. The mechanism used to keep derived data up to date is also simple and easy to program. (For a full discussion of semantic models and the various experimental implementations, see [6].)

One of the primary goals of Cactis is to support database exploration. Researchers have taken different

This work is being supported in part by NSF under grant DMC-850516, and in part by Hewlett Packard under an American Electronics Association Faculty Development Program fellowship, and in part by ONR under contract N00014-86-K-0054.

directions in providing this capability. Hypothetical databases (see [16, 17, 19]) allow the user of a relational database to pose "what if" questions. Different update paths may be pursued, and the various versions of the original database are supported by a differential file mechanism. In this paper, we present an idea which is similar philosophically, but takes a completely different approach in answering "what if" questions. Database exploration is centered around an efficient means of maintaining constraints and derived data, and an efficient rollback and recovery facility. The effectiveness of this last capability is quite important, as databases with complex derived data have the potential of being very difficult to rollback.

Other researchers have stressed the importance of derived data in knowledge based databases [11, 12, 15]. Much of the previous work in this area has come from AI research towards constraint based programming systems [1]. While this work shares many common goals with Cactis, it takes a slightly different conceptual outlook as well as a considerably different algorithmic approach.

Essentially, the Colorado ACTIve Semantics data model (CACTIS) extends techniques from attribute grammers (see [9, 10]) and incremental attribute evaluation (see [4, 14]) to construct what we call *active semantics* databases. The term active semantics implies that the various pieces of data in the database are *active*, that is each understands its own local semantics and how its local values can be derived from the rest of the database. Such a database supports a powerful data model, capable of representing complex derived data and constraints.

In the next section, the active semantics data model is briefly described. In section three, an example is used to illustrate the utility of the Cactis system. Section four discusses the implementation of Cactis, and section five gives closing remarks, including a discussion of ongoing enhancements to Cactis.

2. The Cactis Data Model

In a Cactis database, the semantics of the database are described by an unusual data model. In this section, we briefly and informally present this model, which extends techniques derived from Knuth's attribute grammars [9, 10] as well as from more recent work on incre-

mental attribute evaluation [4, 14] used in syntax directed editors. These techniques have been used extensively in compiler construction to represent the semantics of programming language text. In a Cactis database, the data of the database is held in an *attributed graph*. At a high level, an attributed graph is structured like a conventional network model. Each node in the graph is an instance of a particular named type of data. Each such instance represents some semantically meaningful entity and contains a number of named attributes which describe the entity represented by that instance. Each instance in the database can also be connected to other instances in the database by named relationships of various types.

In addition to this conventional entity-relationship style of modeling, the Cactis model allows *attribute evaluation rules* to be attached to certain attributes. These rules allow attributes to be derived from other attributes within a given instance and from the values contained in related instances. Thus, entities may be active in responding to changes in their environment rather than simply passively storing data. Since attribute evaluation rules can be constructed from arbitrary functions of attributes, it is possible to model and manipulate the complicated semantics that real world entities often possess. It should be noted that, in an attributed graph, the attributes of a given instance may be derived only in terms of attribute values passed to it from instances the given instance is directly related to via named relationships. However, attribute values may be passed transitively from instance to instance. Thus, if the data instance A is related to instance B and instance B is related to instance C, A's attributes may derived in terms of C's attribute values.

There are two kinds of attributes in the attributed graph, derived and intrinsic. Derived attributes have an attribution rule attached to them, while intrinsic attributes do not. This means that only intrinsic attributes may be given new values directly. Derived attributes are only changed indirectly by computations resulting from changes to intrinsic attributes.

An additional property of the Cactis data model is the ability to attach constraints to attributes. In the data model, a constraint is implemented as a derived attribute value which computes a boolean value indicating whether the constraint has been violated. The attribute evaluation rule in this case is simply the predi-

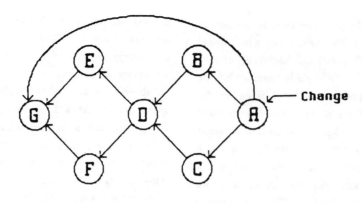

Figure 1.

cate defining the constraint. Whenever an attribute which is designated as testing a constraint evaluates to true, rollback of the current transaction is performed. Since constraint predicates are handled in the same manner as normal derived attribute values, the constraint predicate may be formed using any expression which returns a boolean value.

A number of data models have made provisions for functionally derived data. However, the actual implementations of most of these systems use techniques equivalent to triggers [2] attached to data. While this method is adequate for sparsely interconnected data, it can present problems for more highly interconnected data. Since there is no restriction on the kinds of actions performed by triggers, the order of their firing can change their overall effect. While this allows triggers to be extremely flexible, it can also become very difficult to keep track of the interrelationships between triggers. Hence, it is easy for errors involving unforeseen interrelationships to occur, and much more difficult to predict the behavior of the system under unexpected circumstances.

By contrast, the effects of attribute evaluation computations used in the Cactis system are much easier to isolate and understand. Each data type in the system can be understood in terms of the attribute values it stores, the values it transmits out across relationships, and the values it receives across relationships. This allows the schema to be designed in a structured fashion and brings with it many of the advantages of modern structured programming techniques.

Even if we can adequately deal with the unconstrained and unstructured nature of triggers, they can also be highly inefficient. Figure 1 shows the interrelationships between seven pieces of data. The arcs in the graph represent the fact that a change in one piece of data invokes a trigger which modifies another piece of data. For example, modifying the data marked A affects the data items marked B and C. If we choose a naive ordering for recomputing data values after a change, we may waste a great deal of work by computing the same data values several times. For example, a simple trigger mechanism might work recursively, invoking new triggers as soon as data changes. However, in our example, this simple scheme would result in recomputing data value G five times, once for each path from the original change to the data item. In fact, only a few of the many possible orderings of computations does not recompute some data values. Any trigger mechanism which uses a fixed ordering of some sort (e.g depth first or breadth first) can needlessly recompute some values; in fact, in the worst case can recompute an exponential number of values.

On the other hand, the attribute evaluation technique used in the Cactis system will not evaluate any attribute that is not actually needed, and will not evaluate any given attribute more than once.

While a formal data manipulation language has not yet been defined, Cactis does provide a series of data manipulation primitives which can be used to construct such a language. These primitives include creating and deleting data instances, establishing and breaking relationships between instances, and primitives for retrieving and replacing attribute values. These primitive actions are augmented by the meta-action *Undo*. Undo has the effect of forcing the rollback of one transaction. This meta-action allows the user to freely explore the database, knowing that no actions need have permanent effect.

Whenever changes are made to a database using one of the primitive data manipulation actions, Cactis must ensure that all attribute values in the database retain a value which is consistent with the attribute rules of the system. This requires some sort of attribute evaluation strategy or algorithm. One approach would be to recompute all attribute values every time a change is made to any part of the system. This is clearly too expensive. What is needed is an algorithm for incremental attribute evaluation, which computes only those attributes whose values change as a result of a given database modification. This problem also arises in the area of syntax directed editing systems, so it is not surprising that algorithms exist to solve this problem for the attribute grammars used in that application. The most successful of these algorithms is due to Reps [13]. Reps' algorithm is optimal in the sense that only attributes whose values actually change are recomputed.

Unfortunately, Reps' algorithm, while optimal for attributed trees, does not extend directly to the arbitrary graphs used by Cactis. Instead, a new incremental attribute evaluation algorithm has been designed for Cactis. This new algorithm exhibits performance which is similar to Reps' algorithm, but does have a slightly inferior worst case upper bound on the amount of overhead incurred.

The algorithm works by using a strategy which first determines what work has to be done, then performs the actual computations. The algorithm uses the *dependencies* between attributes. An attribute is *dependent* on another attribute if that attribute is mentioned in its attribute evaluation rule (i.e. is needed to compute the derived value of that attribute). When the value of an intrinsic attribute is changed, it may cause the attributes which depend on it to become out of date with respect to their defining attribute evaluation rules. Instead of immediately recomputing these values, we simply mark them as *out of date*. We then find all attributes which are dependent on these newly *out of date* attributes, and mark them *out of date* as well.

This process continues until we have marked all affected attributes. During this process of marking, we determine if each marked attribute is *important*. Attributes are said to be *important* if they have a constraint predicate attached to them, or if the user has asked the database to retrieve their values. When we have completed marking attributes during the first phase of the algorithm, we will have obtained a list of attributes which are both *out of date* and *important*. We can then use a demand driven algorithm to evaluate these attributes in a simple recursive manner. The calculation of attribute values which are not *important* may be deferred, as they have no immediate affect on the database. If the user explicitly requests the value of attributes (i.e. makes a query) they become *important,* and new computations of *out of date* attributes may be invoked in order to obtain correct values. A similar implementation approach using lazy evaluation is described in [3].

Reps' algorithm, which is not demand-driven, has a worst case cost of $O(|\text{attributes-changed}|)$, where **attributes-changed** is the set of all attributes whose values actually change, and $|X|$ represents the cardinality of set X. Note that this cost analysis is in terms of the number of attributes (not instances) changed. The Cactis algorithm has two phases: marking out of date attributes and reevaluating attribute values. Phase one has worst case cost of $O(|\text{could-change}|)$, where **could-change** is the transitive closure of the attribute dependencies starting at the nodes whose primitive values have been updated. Phase 2 also has worst case $O(|\text{could-change}|)$.

The above cost analysis gives a worst case for the algorithm. In actual practice the algorithm will often perform much better. In particular, attributes which are not important and have not been accessed (directly or indirectly) can remain in the database with out of date values indefinitely. This means that the first marking phase need not remark these attributes nor any attributes that depend on them when changes are made. This allows computations involving parts of the database which are not currently of interest to be deferred until their values are actually needed. Also, if a given attribute is changed as a result of two different primitive updates to intrinsic attributes, the given attribute will only be reevaluated once (unless of course, the given attribute has been accessed before the second primitive

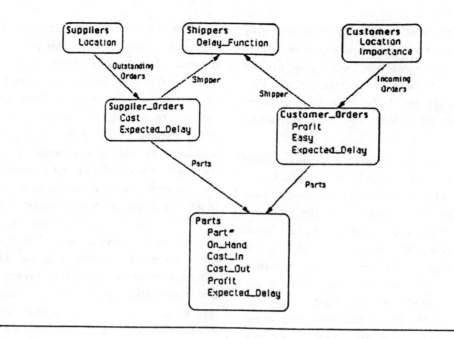

Figure 2.

update is performed). As a final note on cost analysis, what we clearly need to develop for the future is a cost measure based on instance fetches, not on attribute reevaluations.

In order to support the primitives which break and establish relationships, a process similar to that used for intrinsic attribute changes is used. When a relationship is broken, the system determines which derived attributes depend on values that are passed across the relationship. These attributes are marked out of date just as if an intrinsic attribute had changed. When a relationship is established, the second half of the attribute evaluation algorithm is invoked to evaluate attributes which are out of date and important. In order to ensure that derived attributes can always be given a valid value, the database ensures that relationships are not left dangling across attribute evaluations. This is either done explicitly by the transaction, or where necessary the system will provide special dummy instances to tie off any dangling relationships. As a final note, please notice that the primitive to delete an instance can be treated the same as breaking all relationships to the instance, and the primitive to create a instance does not affect attribute evaluation until relationships are established.

During the evaluation of attributes, certain attributes will have constraint predicates attached to them. After an attribute is evaluated, this constraint predicate is tested. If it evaluates false, a constraint violation exists. By default, this causes the transaction invoking the evaluation to fail and be rolled back or undone. Optionally, a special recovery action associated with the constraint can be invoked to attempt to recover from the violation. In either case, the constraint must be satisfied or the transaction invoking the evaluation will fail and be undone (rollback and recovery will be discussed in section 4).

3. A Sample Session

Figure 2 is a Parts/Suppliers schema in the Cactis data model. In this application, a middleman buys parts, marks them up, and sells them to his customers. The supplier orders are orders to his supliers, and customer orders are from his customers. The middleman also has a certain amount of stock on hand, which represents parts that have already been purchased from suppliers, but not delivered to or ordered by any customers yet.

```
┌─────────────────────────────────────────────────────────────┐
│  Supplier_Orders                                            │
│     Cost  ←  Σ over Parts of (Parts . Cost_in)              │
│     Expected_Delay  ←                                       │
│     Apply Shipper.Delay_Function(Outstanding_Orders.Location)│
└─────────────────────────────────────────────────────────────┘


┌─────────────────────────────────────────────────────────────┐
│  Customer_Orders                                            │
│     Profit  ←  Σ over Parts of (Parts . Profit)             │
│     Easy   ←  AND over Parts of (Parts . On_Hand)           │
│     Expected_Delay  ←                                       │
│        Apply Shipper.Delay_Function(Incoming_Orders.Location)│
│      + Max over Parts of (Parts . Expected_Delay)           │
└─────────────────────────────────────────────────────────────┘


┌─────────────────────────────────────────────────────────────┐
│  Customers                                                  │
│     Location      «Intrinsic»                               │
│     Importance   ←                                          │
│        Σ over Incoming_Orders of (Incoming_Orders . Profit) │
└─────────────────────────────────────────────────────────────┘


┌─────────────────────────────────────────────────────────────┐
│  Parts                                                      │
│     Part                                                    │
│     On_Hand                                                 │
│     Cost_In                                                 │
│     Cost_Out  «Intrinsic»                                   │
│     Profit    ←  (Cost_Out - Cost_In)                       │
│        Constraint  Profit > 0                               │
│     Expected_Delay  ←                                       │
│        Max over Parts of (In_Parts  Expected_Delay)         │
└─────────────────────────────────────────────────────────────┘
```

Figure 3.

3.1. Supporting Derived Data and Constraints

Figure 3 shows some detail concerning the definition of the derived attributes of Figure 2. As a simple example, consider the profit attribute of parts. This attribute is defined to be the selling price (Cost Out) less the purchase price (Cost In). Similarly, the profit of a customer order is defined as the sum of the profits for its parts, and the cost of a supplier order is defined as the sum of the cost of its parts. Finally, an attribute is defined for customers which gives their *importance* (computed as the sum of the profits of their orders).

To illustrate the utility of derived information, consider what happens when the middleman changes the selling price of some part. We can expect that this person will be able to find and change the Cost Out attribute of the appropriate part. However, we should not force the user to understand the rest of the database as well. When the user changes the Cost Out attribute of some part, the database will automatically update the profit for that part, as well as the profit for any Customer Order that contains that part, and finally, the database will recompute the Importance attribute of each Customer which is affected. All of this occurs without user intervention, or even user awareness unless a constraint predicate is violated.

If a constraint is violated, the transaction causing the violation fails and is rolled back. In the case of our example, there is a constraint predicate attached to the Profit of Parts. This ensures that a profit is made on each part. As an example, this predicate would fail if the user accidently changed the Cost In attribute when in fact they had intended to change the Cost Out attribute. This sort of a constraint mechanism is particularly important in the case of derived data, since transactions can have wide ranging effects.

```
Parts
    Part⬦
    On_Hand
    Cost_In
    Min_Cost  ≪Intrinsic≫
    Cost_Out  ← Max ( 1.5*Cost_In, Min_Cost )
    Profit    ← (Cost_Out - Cost_In)
      Constraint  Profit > 0
    Expected_Delay ←
      Max over Parts of (In_Parts  Expected_Delay)
```

Figure 4.

```
Customer_Orders
    Profit ← Σ over Parts of (Parts . Profit)
    Easy   ← AND over Parts of (Parts . On_Hand)
    Expected_Delay ←
      Apply Shipper.Delay_Function(Incoming_Orders.Location)
    + Max over Parts of (Parts . Expected_Delay)
    Emergency_Filling_Order ←
      If Easy Then Profit Else ∞
```

Figure 5.

3.2. Exploring the Database

As an example of more complex derived informa-tion, let's suppose that our middleman is having finan-cial problems. His business is in trouble, and he is look-ing for a way to cut costs and increase the cash flow into the company. One of the first things he might think of is to adjust his shipper contracts. If he can speed up deliveries. some of his current clients will probably give him more business. So, the middleman tries assigning different shippers to different customer orders. Notice that shippers have an intrinsic attribute: Delay Function. This attribute is in fact a representation of a function which, when given a location, will compute the delay expected for delivery to or from that location. As shown in Figure 3, this attribute is used to compute an expected delay for each supplier order, then for each part, and finally for each customer order. Each time the middleman assigns a new shipper, Cactis automatically brings the Expected Delay attribute up to date for each

order, and if the result is not satisfactory, the middle-man may quickly reverse the effects of a change by using the Undo command.

The middleman sees another opportunity for improvement when he notices that often, the Cost In attribute for some part changes. This cuts into his profit. He often does not notice the declining profit for a part until the constraint forcing non-zero profit is violated. Then, the trigger notifies him. Now, with his serious concern over profits, the middleman changes an attribute definition. In figure 4, we see he now has defined Cost Out as 1.5 * Cost In or, an assigned non-derived value, which ever is greater. This ensures him that he will make a significant profit on any part. He no longer needs the constraint on profit.

Both of the above changes will only provide long term help. In order to get his company over the current rough period, the middleman has a smart idea. He will

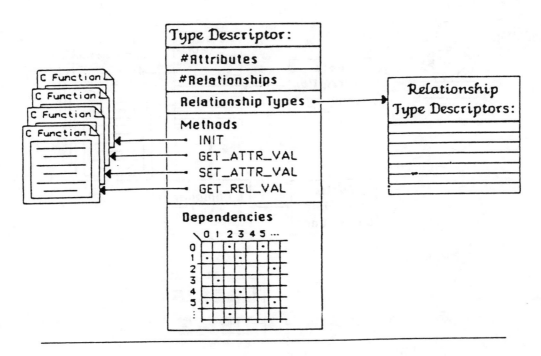

Figure 6.

fill the most profitable orders first. However, he realizes that many of his outstanding customer orders require parts that are not on hand. And, of course, buying any new parts would use up what little cash reserve he has.

The attribute Easy already tells the middleman if an order is made up of parts which are all on hand, so, as shown in Figure 5, he creates a new attribute of Customer Orders called Emergency Filling Order. It is defined as the Profit of the order as long as the Easy attribute is yes; otherwise the Filling Order is infinity. The middleman may now use this new attribute whenever the company has cash problems. It should be noted that as an order is filled and stock on hand is removed, the Easy attribute of other orders will change, but the system will automatically compensate and update the corresponding Filling Order attributes. This implements a greedy algorithm, which while not optimal, is a natural hueristic.

4. The Cactis Implementation

Up to now, our work has been primarily concerned with how to effectively utilize the capabilities of the Cactis data model. To gain experience with the data model, an in memory prototype implementation has been constructed. This prototype consists of approximately 6000 lines of C code and runs on a variety of Unix machines. In addition, a full mass storage version of the system is currently being implemented. This version is also being implemented in C and will run on a variety of Unix machines.

4.1. Data Structures

The implementation of the data model at a low level is fairly straightforward. Each instance is given a unique integer identifier. Instances on mass storage are referenced by this identifier using a simple hashed access method. Each instance in the system is structured both in memory and on disk as a header, a block of relationship pointers, and a block of storage for attribute values. The header of each instance contains an index into the schema type table. As would be expected, the schema for the database is kept in memory while the DBMS is running. However, the organization of the schema differs from a conventional database.

A Cactis schema consists of a table of type descriptors. As shown in Figure 6, these type descriptors encode information about the number of attributes in instances of the type, the number of values transmitted into and out of a instance of this type, and the number and type of relationships that a instance of this type may have with other instances. Type descriptors also contain information about how attributes of an instance

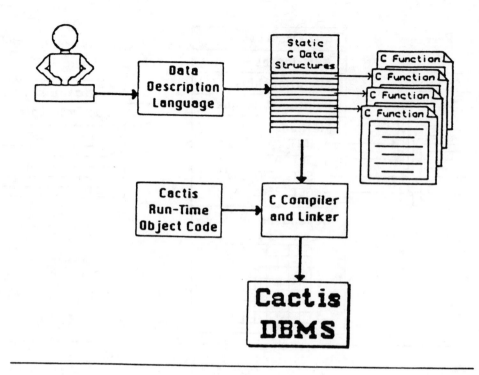

Figure 7.

of this type are dependent on other attributes within the instance and on values transmitted into the instance across relationships. However, the schema does not directly encode any information about how the storage of attribute values is actually organized (other than the total size of the block of storage that holds the attribute values). Instead, this information is held in compiled code which is responsible for the actual access to information.

In a Cactis database, each instance is implemented as an object which responds to a standard predefined set of messages. These messages include:

Initialize -
assign initial values to attributes of a newly created instance.

Get_Attr_Val -
return the value of an attribute within the instance.

Set_Attr_Val -
assign an attribute within the instance a new value.

Get_Rel_Val -
return a value transmitted out of the instance across a relationship.

All instances respond to this same set of messages, but instances of different types will respond to the same

message in different ways. One of the primary tasks of the schema in a Cactis database is to provide the actual methods which respond to these messages for each type in the system. All information about how the data is stored is implicitly encoded in the method routines which are responsible for manipulating the data. In fact, it is not necessary to actually store all attribute values so long as these values can be computed when asked for. Consequently, other parts of the schema, such as the attribute dependency information, need only refer to attributes by an index and can remain ignorant of the actual storage arrangement used by the instance.

Because a Cactis schema contains not only conventional information but also method routines, it is implemented as statically initialized data stored in an object file. With this arrangement, the method routines can be implemented as pointers to C functions. The attribute evaluation rules described in some data definition language can then be compiled directly into C functions as shown in Figure 7. This allows the attribute evaluation rules to use the full power of the C language without reimplementing a special programming language within the database itself.

4.2. Rollback and Recovery

Since Cactis databases are intended to be used in an exploratory manner, they provide a rollback and recovery (or undo) mechanism. The task of rollback and recovery in the presence of complex derived data would seem to be difficult. However, because of the nature of the attribute evaluation algorithms used, Cactis databases can provide this capability with very little additional effort.

The key to rollback and recovery in a Cactis database is that all changes to derived data occur as a result of the automatic attribute evaluation process that is invoked whenever intrinsic attributes are changed. Because of this fact, we can completely reverse the effects of a change to an intrinsic attribute simply by restoring the old value. The same attribute evaluation process that was used to derive information in the first place can be used to un-derive the information when rollback and recovery is performed. Because of this, the system need only retain the old value of any changed intrinsic attributes to be able to completely undo the changes. Just as the user can ignore the automatic information derivation process, the system need only concern itself with restoring intrinsic attributes, and need not try to retain information about how these attributes affect other parts of the database.

Because rollback and recovery uses precisely the same mechanisms as the original update process, it is equally efficient. In addition, very little complexity is added to the database. The database need only remember a series of old values and the location of changes along with a (nested) set of markers which delineate the boundaries of (nested) transactions. When a transaction fails, or the user explicitly requests an undo, the system simply restores the saved values back to the appropriate transaction boundary marker. The normal attribute evaluation mechanism then automatically restores the effected derived information.

5. Directions

If we ignore the process of attribute evaluation required for updates, a Cactis database can be seen as a simple object-oriented database. Consequently, many of the standard optimization techniques for databases, such as algebraic query manipulation, indexing and clustering [18], can be used for a Cactis database. Below, we discuss how the known techniques of deferred updates, batching, and clustering can be used to address the specific performance problems associated with the Cactis attribute update algorithm.

Although the attribute evaluation algorithm discussed in section 2 is efficient in terms of the number of attribute evaluations, it was originally designed for use with a relatively small amount of data residing in high speed memory. The rest of this section discusses optimization techniques that can be used with large amounts of data residing in slower (disk based) storage. We are now in the process of completing the implementation of these techniques.

5.1. Deferred Computations

Recall that the attribute evaluation algorithm has two phases: first, a series of attributes are marked *out of date;* then, an evaluation is made of attributes which are *out of date* and *important*. Note that attributes which are not of immediate interest to the user nor have constraint predicates attached (i.e. not *important*) need not be evaluated. Once they have been marked as *out of date* they may remain in the database with their old invalid values until they are actually needed. Only then will they be actually evaluated. In this way, we can defer a significant amount of computation. In addition, this avoids the inefficiency of updating a value several times even though intermediate values are never actually used.

In addition to deferring computations in a long term sense, a Cactis database also defers computations in the short term by using the common technique of batching. Batching is done on a sub-transaction level. The actual transactions given by the user are broken into *transaction fragments*. These transaction fragments are such that the intermediate results of the fragment are not needed until after the fragment has been executed. An example of this would be a series of updates, without intervening queries. No actual attribute evaluations occur until the end of a transaction fragment is reached. Only at the end of a fragment do we begin to mark attributes as *out of date* or perform any actual evaluations. By using batching, we are able to make a more intelligent selection of update ordering, as we will see below.

5.2. Using Concurrency to Improve Evaluation Efficiency

Evaluation of functionally defined data in a Cactis DBMS is performed in a purely applicative manner. By using this applicative model we are not constrained to perform evaluations in a fixed order but need only observe the partial order required by attribute dependencies. Conceptually, many computations may be done concurrently. Even when only one processor is available we may perform the evaluations in the order which is most efficient.

At any one time the system will have a set of values that are *pending*. These are values which are needed to complete some computation(s). Since the order in which these computations are performed cannot effect the result the system may choose to perform them in the order which is most efficient. For example, to evaluate an attribute A we may need the values of attributes B, C, and D while to evaluate an attribute E we may the the values of attributes F, G, and H. If the system can determine that evaluating attributes B, C, and D would likely be inexpensive (e.g. the values happened to already be cached in memory) it can choose to evaluate A first.

In general the system will choose to perform computations involving values that are currently cached in memory first. When all such computations have been performed the system will choose computations which appear to be least expensive based on some hueristic. We are currently experimenting with several such hueristics with the goal of minimizing the number of disk reads needed to complete the computation. For example, we are keeping dynamic statistics about the past I/O cost for computing a particular attribute value and then use this to estimate how much new I/O is likely to take place if we choose to evaluate this attribute next. Using this scheme the system can be self-adaptive using past performance information to choose the most efficient evaluation order.

In addition to information about I/O performance for computing particular attribute values, the system also keeps statistics about the frequency of traversal of relationships in the database. This information is then used to periodically reorganize the database to improve its clustering using a simple greedy algorithm. With a well clustered database, when we are forced to read a new block into memory, there is some likelyhood that a number of computations may be performed involving that block before it must be replaced by another.

While this sort of clustering will improve the performance of attribute evaluations, it should be noted that it may conflict with the clustering that might be used in a normal network database to optimize frequently executed queries. A tradeoff may be necessary to balance fast updates with fast query response. This tradeoff will be governed by the relative frequency of updates, and the importance of answering "what if" types questions.

5.3. Final Remarks

Cactis is a DBMS that has been developed at the University of Colorado. The goal of Cactis is to support very complex derived information in as efficient a fashion as possible. In this paper, we have tried to establish the generality of the Cactis model, the power it provides, and its efficiency.

As a last note, we have not yet begun to design a concurrency control mechanism for Cactis. Because of the possibility of an update causing a large part of the database to become out of date, a locking mechanism might be very costly. We are considering a timestamping technique (see [18]), whereby during the first phase of the incremental attribute evaluation algorithm, any attribute that is being marked out of date would have its write time compared to the timestamp of the transaction. If these times conflict, rollback is performed.

Acknowledgements

The authors would like to thank Dan Olsen of BYU. The original form of the incremental attribute evaluation algorithm we use in the Cactis system emerged from a long discussion between Dan and one of the authors. We would especially like to thank the Cactis implementation team: Michael Carter, Pam Drew, Shehab Gamalel-din, Carla Mowers, Loraine Neuberger, Evan Patten, Tom Rebman, Jerry Thomas, and Gary Vanderlinden.

References

1. A. Borning, "The Programming Language Aspects of ThingLab, a Constraint-Oriented Simulation Laboratory", *ACM Transactions on Programming Languages and Systems 3* (October 1981), 353-387.

2. O. P. Buneman and E. K. Clemons, "Efficiently Monitoring Relational Databases", *Trans. Database Systems 4* (Sept. 1979), 368-382.

3. P. Buneman, R. E. Frankel and R. Nikhil, "An Implementation Technique for Database Query Languages", *ACM Transactions on Database Systems 7* (June 1982), 164-186.

4. A. Demers, T. Reps and T. Teitelbaum, "Incremental Evaluation for Attribute Grammars with Application to Syntax Directed Editors", *Conference Record of the 8th Annual ACM Symposium on Principles of Programming Languages*, Jan. 1981, 105-116.

5. D. Farmer, R. King and D. Myers, "The Semantic Database Constructor", *IEEE Transactions on Software Engineering SE-11* (July 1985), 583-590.

6. R. Hull and R. King, "Semantic Database Modeling: Survey, Applications, and Research Issues", *USC Technical Report Tech. Rep.-86-201* (April 1986).

7. R. King, "Sembase: A Semantic DBMS", *Proceedings of 1st Int'l Workshop on Expert Database Systems*, Kiawah Island, South Carolina, Oct. 1984, 151-171.

8. R. King and D. McLeod, "Semantic Database Models", in *Database Design*, S. B. Yao (editor), Prentice Hall, 1985.

9. D. E. Knuth, "Semantics of Context-Free Languages", *Math. Systems Theory J. 2* (June 1968), 127-145.

10. D. E. Knuth, "Semantics of Context-Free Languages: Correction", *Math. Systems Theory J. 5* (Mar. 1971), 95-96.

11. G. M. E. Lafue and R. G. Smith, "Implementation Of A Semantic Integrity Manager With A Knowledge Representation System", *Proc. First International Worksohop on Expert Database Systems*, Kiawah Island, South Carolina, Oct. 24-27, 1984, 172-185.

12. M. Morgenstern, "The Role of Constraints in Databases, Expert Systems, and Knowledge Representation", *Proc. First International Worksohop on Expert Database Systems*, Kiawah Island, South Carolina, Oct. 24-27, 1984, 207-223.

13. T. Reps, "Optimal-time Incremental Semantic Analysis for Syntax-directed Editors", *Conference Record of the 9th Annual ACM Symposium on Principles of Programming Languages*, Jan. 1982, 169-176.

14. T. Reps, T. Teitelbaum and A. Demers, "Incremental Context-Dependent Analysis for Language-Based Editors", *Trans. Prog. Lang and Systems 5* (July 1983), 449-477.

15. A. Shepherd and L. Kerschberg, "Constraint Management in Expert Database Systems", *Proc. First International Worksohop on Expert Database Systems*, Kiawah Island, South Carolina, Oct. 24-27, 1984, 522-546.

16. M. Stonebraker and K. Keller, "Embedding Expert Knowledge and Hypothetical Databased into a Database System", *Proc. ACM SIGMOD Conf.*, 1980.

17. M. Stonebraker, "Hypothetical Databases as Views", *Proc. ACM SIGMOD Conf*, 1981.

18. J. Ullman, *Principles of Database Systems*, Computer Science Press, Rockville, Maryland, 1982.

19. J. Woodfill and M. Stonebraker, "An Implementation of Hypothetical Relations", *Proc. of the International Conference on Very Large Data Bases*, 1983.

Chapter 7

Relational Extensions and Extensible Database Systems

Introduction

The *raison d'être* of OODBs is to provide database support for applications that are not well served by conventional record-oriented systems. OODBs provide for direct representation of complex data structures and for new database types to be created by the database programmer. Extended relational systems and extensible database systems are two other approaches seeking to serve nontraditional applications.

Extended relational systems support higher-level modeling features, such as are found in semantic data models, plus some capabilities found in OODBs: adding new scalar types, set- or array-valued attributes and DML stored in the database.

The GEM data language [Za83] can be viewed as providing syntactic extensions to the relational model. In fact, the initial implementation of GEM [TZ84] mapped GEM constructs into the Quel language. GEM took common relational programming idioms, and gave them language support. GEM has a generalization hierarchy of relation schemes (called *entities*, presumably from similarity to entities in the Entity-Relationship model [Ch76]). This hierarchy supports the addition of attributes in subschemes, and of disjoint subschemes. GEM provides *reference attributes*, which serve much as object identifiers, except references from any one attribute are restricted to tuples from a single relation (and its subscheme relations). Thus, GEM could support a **RoadSegments** relation with attributes **START** and **END** that reference tuples in an **Intersection** relation. A path notation is provided to tra-

verse reference attributes. So, if *r* is a tuple variable ranging over **RoadSegments**, and **POSITION** is an attribute of **Intersection**, then *r*.**START**.**POSITION** is a legal path description, referring to the position of the start intersection referenced by a **RoadSegments** tuple. Path notation is a shorthand form for a join operation, and probably in excess of 80 percent of the joins in relational queries can be handled by paths. GEM also provides for set-valued attributes and for set-comparison operators, which are useful for queries involving quantification ("for-all" or "for-some" conditions).

A more recent system with many similarities to GEM is SIM [JG+88], which is a database system from Unisys based on the semantic model SDM [HM81]. Rather than translating features into relational form, SIM implements many of them directly.

The Postgres data model [RS87] also incorporates a hierarchy of relations, where subrelations can add attributes. However, the semantics of this hierarchy differ from those of the GEM hierarchy. In GEM, an entity belonging to a relation is viewed as also being an element of all relations above it in the hierarchy. In Postgres, the relations in the hierarchy are hold entities. The language for Postgres, Postquel, gives the choice of querying just a single relation, or a relation and all its subrelations.

Postgres allows users to add new base types to the system, by providing information on storage requirements, literal formats, comparison operators, and evaluation costs. Postgres also allows attributes that are arrays of base types. Perhaps the most powerful extension in Postgres is allowing a field of a tuple to contain a Postquel statement. A Postquel field can have a different statement for every tuple in a relation, or the statement can be given with the relation scheme, and the tuples can provide parameters to that statement. Postquel fields can be used to represent attributes whose values are heterogeneous sets (sets composed of tuples from several relations) and also to support reference attributes similar to those in GEM. Postquel provides a path syntax similar to that of GEM. Postgres also has database procedures, which are defined on tuples of a relation, and can be inherited by tuples in subrelations, in much the way methods are inherited in OODBs.

We now turn to extensible database systems. The goal of such systems is to provide a ready means for constructing a database systems tuned or biased toward a particular domain of applications. Much of the work in this field can be characterized as software engineering: trying to produce clean specifications of database components and their interfaces, so that those components can be easily interchanged or modified.

This chapter includes papers on two such systems, the EXODUS [CD+88] and GENESIS [BB+88] systems. EXODUS provides a kernel of DBMS functions, a language (E) for writing database systems, and a variety of tools for implementing a full database system. EXODUS provides a storage manager, a library of access methods and operator algorithms, a query-optimizer generator, and a tool for query-language construction. It has been used to implement a relational database system, and also an object-oriented data model and language, called EXTRA and EXCESS. GENESIS emphasizes a library of components that have standard interfaces, and that can be layered on one another to produce a database system with little writing of new code. The components include a library of *transformers*, which provide mappings from abstract file and link structures to more concrete forms of those structures. Those structures can in turn be transformed to even more concrete structures, and so on, eventually ending up at basic access methods. Other components include *expanders*, which express operations on abstract structures as one or more operations on their concrete implementations; the *Grand Central* component, which dispatches the correct expander for an operation, and a file system, *Jupiter*. Other extensible database systems are Starburst [LMP87], PROBE [DS86], and DMC (Data Model Compiler) [MB+86].

To give you a feeling for the range of possibilities for extensible database systems, we consider here the who, what, when, how, where, and why of extensibility:

- *Who* does the extending? This task might be performed by the end user of a database application, by an application programmer, by a database administrator (DBA), or by a database-system programmer. The GENESIS project posits a new role: the *database implementor* (DBI). The DBI lies somewhere between a database administrator and the programmers of the database system. In the GENESIS model, the system programmers produce a collection of components. A DBI selects and combines those components into a database systems by writing an *architecture program*. The architecture program then processes specific database schema definitions written by database administrators. The EXODUS project tailors its tools for a *database engineer* (DBE), who is roughly equivalent to the DBI of GENESIS. The Starburst project is aimed more at supporting the database-system programmers through product release and maintenance cycles. Object-oriented databases are designed to allow extensibility by the database administrator or application programmer, as is the extensible base-type capability of Postgres. A key point in determining the necessary sophistication of the extender is the language in which the extension is written. In OODBs, new types or classes are coded using the DML of the database system. Base-type extension in Postgres requires a more sophisticated programmer, as it must be done in the implementation language of the database rather than in Postquel.

  Generally, an extension can be more inclusive, the earlier it appears in the production chain. OODBs provide for extending the set of types available for an application, whereas the extensible systems described here extend access methods, storage mappings, and query optimization. Sometimes, earlier extension will make a performance difference, such as if a type definition is compiled into the database system code, instead of being interpreted at run-time.

- *What* part of the database system is being extended? OODBs concentrate on the set of types available to the application programmer. Type extensions come in different flavors. The simplest is adding new base types, out of which other database structures, typically records, can be built. In the roads example, we might want to have

Coordinate as a new base type. Base types are distinguished by having reps that are not decomposable (as far as the database system is concerned). Their reps do not reference other database items. Postgres supports the addition of new base types. Next simplest is adding abstract types whose reps can use other type definitions and reference other objects. All behavioral OODBs allow adding abstract types. The most complex kind of type extension is the ability to add type constructors, parameterized types, or generic types. All are forms of type generators. They cannot have instances created directly; they must be specialized first with one or more component types to form a type definition that can have instances. For example, consider a parameterized type **Dictionary[*KeyType*, *ValueType*]** that provides for accessing objects of the ***Value-Type*** via keys of the ***KeyType***. A specialization of this type would be **Dictionary[String, RoadSegment]**, whose instances are dictionaries mapping strings to **RoadSegment** objects. The E language of EXODUS supports *generic classes*, which act as class generators for specific classes. The architecture program that a DBI writes in GENESIS in essence implements a number of parameterized aggregate types. The architecture program creates specific aggregate types once the DBA gives information on the types of fields in each aggregate. (Note that "relation" in a relational database system is a parameterized type. The database designer provides a relation scheme before an instance of the relation type is created.)

There are other parts of a DBMS that can be extended. The query language can have new operators added to deal with new base types. The collection of data-access methods and operator algorithms can be augmented. It is on such extensibility that PROBE and Starburst concentrate. The PROBE project has dealt extensively with access-method extensions for multidimensional data (such as geographic regions or three-dimensional mechanical parts). In the EXODUS or GENESIS scenario, adding new access methods or operators would be done primarily by the database system programmers, to enrich the library of components available to DBEs or DBIs. Starburst deals also with extensions to data-management facilities, such as concurrency control, recovery, authorization, index maintenance, derived data, and integrity constraints. These extensions are all handles via *attachments*. An attachment is a group of routines associated with one or more relations. A particular routine in the attachment is invoked for each different operator on the relations, such as adding a tuple, modifying a tuple, and so forth.

- *When* are the extensions made to the database? In the Starburst model, extensions are made "at the factory," and the purchaser of the DBMS is presented with a fixed set of features. In the GENESIS, EXODUS, and DBC models, the extensions are made "in the field," where database components and descriptions are compiled, and are linked to generate a particular DBMS. The extensions in OODBs and in Postgres happen mainly when the database schema is defined for a particular application. (But note that schema definition is an ongoing process over the life of a database.) Finally, some databases support creation of new types by executing commands at run-time. For example, as part of a new application, an end user could define a data-entry form, which could cause the creation of a new data type.

- *How* are the extensions carried out? In OODBs, writing type definitions and their methods is the approach used. In DBC and also the ADABTPL system [SSB86], writing a database specification and type translations in a special language and having it compiled is the technique. GENESIS promotes the view of extensibility through component assembly. In EXODUS, there is more of a view that the extensions are accomplished through writing in a database implementation language, linking in existing libraries of access methods and operators, and using custom-tailored components.

  There are two approaches to providing custom-tailored components. One is to have a component generator that takes a component specification and produces a specialized instance of the component. The other is to have a generic component that is custom-tailored through some type of configuration file. For example, both EXODUS and Starburst provide for custom-tailored query optimizers. EXODUS uses a query-optimizer generator that takes a set of rules as input and produces an optimizer incorporating those rules [GD87]. Starburst uses a generic optimizer that takes as input both a rule base and a query to be optimized [Lo88].

- *Where* (in which system layer) are the extensions made? Are they made at the storage manager, at the interpreter (or query evaluator), or at the virtual image? (The virtual image is the current collection of types, method definitions, and system objects in an OODB.) Extensible database systems make most of their extensions in the storage-manager and query-evaluation layers, whereas OODBs mainly extend the virtual image. Some OODBs allow the interpreter to be extended with new *primitive methods*, which are methods internal to the interpreter that do not send any messages themselves. Other layers for extension are the parsers for DDL and DML, or a command preprocessor.

- *Why* are the extensions made? The principal reasons are application support and performance. *Application support* involves providing types and data-management features (such as concurrency control protocols) that make a particular domain of database applications easier to produce. *Performance extensions* are aimed at causing a class of applications or queries to run faster, through specialized access methods, more semantics knowledge in the query optimizer, tuning of transaction management, and so forth.

References

•[BB+88]   D.S. Batory, J.R. Barnett, J.F. Garza, K.P. Smith, K. Tsukuda, B.C. Twitchell, and T.E. Wise. GENESIS: An Extensible Database Management System. *IEEE Transactions on Software Engineering* 14(11), 1988.

•[CD+88]   M.J. Carey, D.J. DeWitt, G. Graefe, D.M. Haight, J.E. Richardson, D.T. Schuh, E.J. Shekita, and S.L. Vandenberg. *The EXODUS Extensible DBMS Project: an Overview.* University of Wisconsin, Madison Computer Sciences Technical Report 808, November 1988.

[Ch76]   P.P. Chen. The Entity-Relationship Model—Toward a Unified View of Data. *ACM Transactions on Database Systems* 1(1), 1976.

[DS86]   U. Dayal, J.M. Smith. PROBE: A Knowledge-Oriented Database Management System. M.L. Brodie and J. Mylopoulos, eds, in *On Knowledge Base Management Systems*, Springer-Verlag, New York, 1986.

[GD87]   G. Graefe and D. DeWitt. The EXODUS Optimizer Generator. *Proceedings of the ACM-SIGMOD International Conference on Management of Data*, San Francisco, CA, May 1987.

•[HM81]   M. Hammer and D. McLeod. Database Description with a Semantic Data Model: SDM. *ACM Transactions on Database Systems* 6(3), 1981.

[JG+88]   D. Jagannathan, R. Guck, B. Fritchman, J. Thompson, and D. Tolbert. SIM: A Database System Based on the Semantic Data Model. *Proceedings of the ACM SIGMOD International Conference on the Management of Data*, Chicago, June 1988.

[LMP87]   B. Lindsay, J. McPherson, and H. Pirahesh. A Data Management Extension Architecture. *Proceedings of the ACM-SIGMOD International Conference on Management of Data*, San Francisco, May 1987.

[Lo88]   G. Lohman. Grammar-Like Functional Rules for Representing Query Optimization Alternatives. *Proceedings of the ACM-SIGMOD International Conference on Management of Data*, Chicago, June 1988.

[MB+86]   F. Maryanski, J. Bedell, S. Hoehlscher, S. Hong, L. McDonald, J. Peckman, and D. Stock. The Data Model Compiler: A Tool for Generating Object-Oriented Database Systems. K.R. Dittrich and U. Dayal, eds, in *Proceedings International Workshop on Object-Oriented Database Systems*, Pacific Grove, CA, September 1986.

•[RS87]   L. Rowe and M. Stonebraker. The Postgres Data Model. *Proceedings of the XIII International Conference on Very Large Databases*, Brighton, England, September 1987. Morgan Kaufmann Publishers, San Mateo, CA

•[SSB86]   D. Stemple, T. Sheard, and R. Bunker. Abstract Data Types in Databases: Specification, Manipulation and Access. *Proceedings of the IEEE Second International Conference on Data Engineering*, Los Angeles, CA, February 1986.

[TZ84]   S. Tsur and C. Zaniolo. An Implementation of GEM—Supporting a Semantic Data Model on a Relational Back-End. *ACM International Conference on the Management of Data*, Boston, MA, June 1984.

•[Za83]   C. Zaniolo. The Database Language GEM. *Proceedings of the ACM-SIGMOD International Conference on Management of Data*, San Jose, CA, May 1983.

• indicates article included in this volume

The Database Language GEM

Carlo Zaniolo

Bell Laboratories
Holmdel, New Jersey 07733

ABSTRACT

GEM (an acronym for General Entity Manipulator) is a general-purpose query and update language for the DSIS data model, which is a semantic data model of the Entity-Relationship type. GEM is designed as an easy-to-use extension of the relational language QUEL, providing support for the notions of entities with surrogates, aggregation, generalization, null values, and set-valued attributes.

1. INTRODUCTION

A main thrust of computer technology is towards simplicity and ease of use. Database management systems have come a long way in this respect, particularly after the introduction of the relational approach [Ullm], which provides users with a simple tabular view of data and powerful and convenient query languages for interrogating and manipulating the database. These features were shown to be the key to reducing the cost of database-intensive application programming [Codd1] and to providing a sound environment for back-end support and distributed databases.

The main limitation of the relational model is its semantic scantiness, that often prevents relational schemas from modeling completely and expressively the natural relationships and mutual constraints between entities. This shortcoming, acknowledged by most supporters of the relational approach [Codd2], has motivated the introduction of new *semantic data models*, such as that described in [Chen] where reality is modeled in terms of entities and relationships among entities, and that presented in [SmSm] where relationships are characterized along the orthogonal coordinates of *aggregation* and

generalization. The possibility of extending the relational model to capture more meaning — as opposed to introducing a new model — was investigated in [Codd2], where *surrogates* and *null values* were found necessary for the task.

Most previous work with semantic data models has concentrated on the problem of modeling reality and on schema design; also the problem of integrating the database into a programming environment supporting abstract data types has received considerable attention [Brod, KiMc]. However, the problem of providing easy to use queries and friendly user-interfaces for semantic data models has received comparatively little attention[1]. Thus the question not yet answered is whether semantic data models can retain the advantages of the relational model with respect to ease of use, friendly query languages and user interfaces, back-end support and distributed databases.

This work continues the DSIS effort [DSIS] to enhance the UNIX* environment with a DBMS combining the advantages of the relational approach with those of semantic data models. Thus, we begin by extending the relational model to a rich semantic model supporting the notions of entities with surrogates, generalization and aggregation, null values and set-valued attributes. Then we show that simple extensions to the relational language QUEL are sufficient to provide an easy-to-use and general-purpose user interface for the specification of both queries and updates on this semantic model.

---

1. To the extent that the functional data model [SiKe] can be viewed as a semantic data model, DAPLEX [Ship] supplies a remarkable exception to this trend.

* UNIX is a trademark of Bell Laboratories.

ITEM(Name: c, Type: c, Colors: {c})   **key**(Name);

DEPT (Dname: c, Floor: i2)   **key**(Dname) ;

SUPPLIER (Company: c, Address: c)   **key**(Company);

SALES (Dept: DEPT, Item: ITEM, Vol: i2)   **key**(Dept, Item) ;

SUPPLY (Comp: SUPPLIER, Dept: DEPT, Item: ITEM, Vol: i2) ;

EMP (Name: c, Spv: EXMPT **null allowed**, Dept: DEPT,

     [EXMPT(Sal: i4), NEXMPT(Hrlwg: i4, Ovrt: i4)],

     [EMARRIED (Spouse#: i4), **others**])   **key** (Name), **key** (Spouse#) ;

Figure 1.   *A GEM schema describing the following database:*

ITEM:	*for each item, its name, its type, and a set of colors*
DEPT:	*for each department its name and the floor where it is located.*
SUPPLIER:	*the names and addresses of supplier companies.*
SALES:	*for each department and item the volume of sales.*
SUPPLY:	*what company supplies what item to what department in what volume (of current stock).*
EMP:	*the name, the supervisor, and the department of each employee;*
EXMPT:	*employees can either be exempt (all supervisors are) or*
NEXMPT:	*non-exempt; the former earn a monthly salary while the latter have an hourly wage with an overtime rate.*
EMARRIED:	*Employees can either be married or not; the spouse's social security number is of interest for the married ones.*

2. THE DATA MODEL

Figure 1 gives a GEM schema for an example adapted from that used in [LaPi]. The attributes Dept and Item in SALES illustrate how an aggregation is specified by declaring these two to be of type DEPT and ITEM, respectively. Therefore, Dept and Item have occurrences of the entities DEPT and ITEM as their respective values. The entity EMP supplies an example of generalization hierarchy consisting of EMP and two generalization sublists shown in brackets. The attributes Name, Spv and Dept are common to EMP and its subentities in brackets. The first generalization sublist captures the employment status of an employee and consists of the two mutually exclusive subentities EXMPT and NEXMPT (an employee cannot be at the same time exempt and nonexempt). The second generalization sublist describes the marital status of an employees who can either be EMARRIED or belong to the **others** category. Although not shown in this example, each subentity can be further subclassified in the same way as shown here, and so on.

The Colors attribute of entity ITEM is of the set type, meaning that a set of (zero of more) colors may be associated with each ITEM instance; each member of that set is of type c (character string).

Name and Spouse# are the two keys for this family. However, since the uniqueness constraint is waived for keys that are partially or totally null Spouse# is in effect a key for the subentity EMARRIED only.

We will next define GEM's Data Definition Language, using the same meta-notation as in [IDM] to define its syntax. Thus {...} denote a set of zero or more occurrences, while [...] denotes one or zero occurrences. Symbols enclosed in semiquotes denote themselves.

A GEM *schema* consists of a set of uniquely named entities.

1. <Schema>: { <Entity> ; }

An *entity* consists of a set of one or more attributes and the specification of zero or more keys.

2. <Entity>: <EntName> (<AttrSpec>
           { , <AttrSpec> }) { Key }

Attributes can either be single-valued, or be a reference (alias a link) attribute, or be set-valued or represent a generalization sublist.

3. <AttrSpec>: <SimpleAttr> | <RefAttr>
      | <SetAttr> | <Generalization sublist>

4. <SimpleAttr>: <DataAttr> [<null spec>]

5. <DataAttr>: <AttrName> ':' <DataType>

GEM's data types include 1-, 2- and 4-byte integers (respectively denoted by i1, i2 and i4), character strings (denoted by c) and all the remaining IDM's types [IDM].

The user can allow the value of a data attribute to be null either by supplying a regular value to serve in this role, or by asking the system to supply a special value for this purpose (additional storage may be associated with this solution).

6. <null spec>: **null**':' <datavalue> | **null**':' **system**

The option **null allowed** must be entered to allow a null link in a reference attribute.

7. <RefAttr>:
      <AttrName>':' <EntName> [**null allowed**]

Set-valued attributes are denoted by enclosing the type definition in braces.

8. <SetAttr>: <AttrName>':' '{' <DataType>'}'

A generalization sublist defines a choice between two or more disjoint alternatives enclosed in brackets. The keyword **others** is used to denote that the entity need not belong to one the subentities in the list.

9. <Generalization sublist>:
      '[' <Entity> {, <Entity>} , <Entity> ']'
      | '[' <Entity> {, <Entity> } , **others** ']'

Repeated applications of this rule produce a hierarchy of entities called an *entity family*. We have the following conventions regarding the names of a schema.

Names: All entity names must be unique within a schema. Attribute names must be unique within an entity-family (i.e., a top level entity and its subentities). Attributes and entities can be identically named.

Any subset of the attributes from the various entities in a family can be specified to be a key; no two occurrences of entities in the family can have the same non-null key value.

The DDL above illustrates the difference between the relational model and the GEM model. Productions 1 and 2 basically apply to GEM as well as to the relational model, with relations corresponding to entities. In the declaration of

attributes, however, a relational system would be limited to the pattern:

$$<AttrSpec>: <SimpleAttr>$$

$$<SimpleAttr>: <DataAttr>$$

Instead GEM's data model is significantly richer than the relational one. However, we will show that it is possible to deal with this richer semantics via simple extensions to the QUEL language and also to retain the simple tabular view of data on which the congeniality of relational interfaces is built.

3. A GRAPHICAL VIEW of GEM SCHEMAS

DBMS users' prevailing view of schemas is graphical, rather than syntactic. IMS users, for instance, perceive their schemas as hierarchies; Codasyl users view them as networks. Relational users view their database schema and content as row-column tables; this view is always present in a user's mind, and often drawn on a piece of paper as an aid in query formulation. Moreover, relational systems also use the tabular format to present query answers to users. For analogous reasons, it would be very useful to have a graphical — preferably tabular — representation for GEM schemas. A simple solution to this problem is shown in Figure 2.

There is an obvious correspondence between the inline schema in Figure 1 and its pictorial representation in Figure 2; all entity names appear in the top line, where the nesting of brackets defines the generalization hierarchy. A blank entry represents the option "others". Under each entity-name we find the various attributes applicable to this entity. For reasons of simplicity we have omitted type declarations for all but reference attributes. However, it should be clear that these can be added, along with various graphical devices to represent keys and the option "null allowed" to ensure a complete correspondence between the graphical representation and the in-line definition such as that of Figure 1. Such a representation is all a user needs to realize which queries are meaningful and which updates are correct, and which are not[2].

---

2. A network-like representation can be derived from this by displaying the reference attributes as arrows pointing from one entity to another. The result is a graph similar to a DBTG data structure diagram with the direction of the arrows reversed. More alluring representations (e.g., using double arrows and lozenges) may be useful for further visualizing the logical structure of data (e.g., to represent the generalization hierarchies); but they do not help a user in formulating GEM queries.

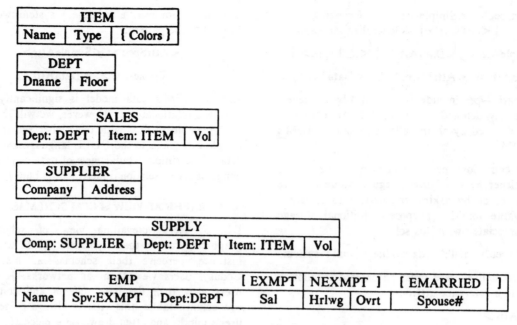

Figure 2. A graphical representation of the GEM schema of Figure 1.

Query results of GEM are also presented in output as row-column tables derived from these tables.

4. THE QUERY LANGUAGE

GEM is designed to be a generalization of QUEL [INGR]; both QUEL and IDM's IDL are upward-compatible with GEM. Whenever the underlying schema is strictly relational (i.e., entities only have data attributes):

<AttrSpec> → <SimpleAttr> → <DataAttr>,

GEM is basically identical to QUEL, with which we expect our readers to be already familiar. However, GEM allows entity names to be used as range variables without an explicit declaration. Thus the query, "Find the names of the departments located on the third floor," that in QUEL can be expressed as

range of dep **is** DEPT
retrieve (dep.Dname)
where dep.Floor=3

Example 1. List each department on the 3rd floor.

in GEM can also be expressed as:

retrieve (DEPT.Dname) **where** DEPT.Floor = 3

Example 2. Same as Example 1.

The option of omitting range declarations improves the conciseness and expressivity of many queries,

particularly the simple ones; nor does any loss of generality occur since range declarations can always be included when needed.

The query of Example 2 is therefore interpreted by GEM as if it were as follows:

range of DEPT **is** DEPT
retrieve (DEPT.Dname)
where DEPT.Floor=3

Example 3. Same as examples 1 and 2.

Thus in the syntactic context of the **retrieve** and **where** clauses, DEPT is interpreted as a range variable (ranging over the entity DEPT).

Besides this syntactic sweetening, GEM contains new constructs introduced to handle the richer semantics of its data model; these are discussed in the next sections.

5. AGGREGATION and GENERALIZATION

A *reference* (alias *link*) attribute in GEM has as value an entity occurrence. For instance in the entity SALES, the attribute Dept has an entity of type DEPT as value, and Item an entity of type ITEM, much in the same way as the attribute Vol has an integer as value. Thus, while SALES.Vol is an integer, SALES.Dept is an entity of type DEPT and SALES.Item is an entity of type ITEM. An entity occurrence cannot be printed as such. Thus, the statement,

range of S **is** SALES
retrieve (S)

Example 4. A syntactically incorrect query.

is incorrect in GEM (as it would be in QUEL). Therefore, these statements are also incorrect:

range of S **is** SALES
retrieve (S.Dept)

Example 5. An incorrect query.

and

retrieve (SALES.Item)

Example 6. A second incorrect query.

Thus, reference attributes cannot be printed. However both single-valued and set-valued attributes can be obtained by using QUEL's usual dot-notation; thus

retrieve (SALES.Vol)

Example 7. Find the volumes of all SALES.

will get us the volumes of all SALES. Moreover, since SALES.Dept denotes an entity of type DEPT, we can obtain the value of Floor by simply applying the notation ".Floor" to it. Thus,

retrieve (SALES.Dept.Floor)
where SALES.Item.Name="SPORT"

Example 8. Floors where departments selling items of type SPORT are located.

will print all the floors where departments that sell sport items are located. The importance of this natural extension of the dot notation cannot be overemphasized; as illustrated by the sixty-six queries in Appendix II of [Zani3], it supplies a very convenient and natural construct that eliminates the need for complex join statements in most queries. For instance, the previous query implicitly specifies two joins: one of SALES with DEPT, the other of SALES with ITEM. To express the same query, QUEL would require three range variables and two join conditions in the **where** clause.

A comparison to functional query languages may be useful here. Reference attributes can be viewed as functions from an entity to another, and GEM's dot-notation can be interpreted as the usual dot-notation of functional composition. Thus GEM has a functional flavor; in particular it shares with languages such as DAPLEX [Ship] the convenience of providing a functional composition notation to relieve users of the burden of explicitly specifying joins. Yet the functions used by GEM are strictly

single-valued non-redundant functions; multivalued and inverse functions and other involved constructs are not part of GEM, which is based on the bedrock of the relational theory and largely retains the "Spartan simplicity" of the relational model.

Joins implicitly specified through the use of the dot notation will be called *functional joins*. An alternative way to specify joins is by using *explicit entity joins*, where entity occurrences are directly compared, to verify that they are the same, using the *identity test operator*, **is**[3]. For instance the previous query can also be expressed as follows:[4]

range of S **is** SALES
range of I **is** ITEM
range of D **is** DEPT
retrieve (D.Floor)
where D **is** S.Dept **and** S.Item **is** I
              and I.Type="SPORT"

Example 9. Same query as in example 8.

Comparison operators such as =, !=, >, >=, <, and <= are not applicable to entity occurrences.

The names of entities and their subentities — all in the top row of our templates — are unique and can be used in two basic ways. Their first use is in defining range variables. Thus, to request the name and the salary of each married employee one can write:

range of e **is** EMARRIED
retrieve (e.Name, e.Sal)

Example 10. Find the name and salary of each married employee.

or simply,

retrieve (EMARRIED.Name, EMARRIED.Sal)

Example 11. Same as in example 10.

Thus all attributes within an entity can be applied to any of its subtypes (without ambiguity since their names are unique within the family).

---

3. The operator **isnot** is used to test that two objects are not identical.

4. queries in Examples 8 and 9 are equivalent only under the assumption that the Dept attribute in SALES cannot be null. If some SALES occurrences have a null Dept link, then the results of the two queries are not the same, as discussed in detail in the section on null values.

Subentity names can also be used in the qualification conditions of a **where** clause. For instance, an equivalent restatement of the last query is

>**retrieve** (EMP.Name, EMP.Sal)
>**where** EMP **is** EMARRIED

Example 12. Same as example 11.

(Retrieve the name and salary of each employee who is an employee-married.) For all those employees who are married but non-exempt this query returns their names and a null salary. Thus, it is different from

>**retrieve** (EXMPT.Name, EXMPT.Sal)
>**where** EXMPT **is** EMARRIED

Example 13. Find all exempt employees that are married.

that excludes all non-exempt employees at once. The query,

>**retrieve** (EMP.Name) **where**
>EMP **is** EXMPT **or** EMP **is** EMARRIED

Example 14. Find all employees that are exempt or married.

will retrieve the names of all employees that are exempt or married.

In conformity to QUEL, GEM also allows the use of the keyword **all** in the role of a target attribute. Thus to print the whole table ITEM one need only specify,

>**retrieve** (ITEM.**all**)

*Example 15. Use of **all**.*

In the presence of generalization and aggregation the **all** construct can be extended as follows. Say that t ranges over an entity or a subentity E. Then "t.**all**" specifies *all simple and set-valued attributes in E and its subentities.* Thus,

>**retrieve** (EMP.**all**)
>**where** EMP.Sal > EMP.Spv.Sal

*Example 16. Extended use of **all**.*

returns the name, the salary, the hourly wage and overtime rate, and the spouse's social security number of every employee earning more than his or her supervisor (the values of some of these attributes being null, of course); while

>**retrieve** (EXMPT.**all**)
>**where** EXMPT.Sal > EXMPT.Spv.Sal

*Example 17. Use of **all** with subentities.*

returns only the salaries of those employees.

The following query gives another example of the use of entity joins and the use of subentity names as default range variables (EMP and EMARRIED are the two variables of our query).

>**retrieve** (EMARRIED.Name)
>**where** EMP.Name="J.Black"
>**and** EMP.Dept **is** EMARRIED.Dept

Example 18. Find all married employees in the same department as J.Black.

6. NULL VALUES

A important advantage of GEM over other DBMSs is that it provides for a complete and consistent treatment of null values. The theory underlying our approach was developed in [Zani1, Zani2], where a rigorous justification is given for the practical conclusions summarized next.

GEM conveniently provides several representations of null values in storage and in output tables; at the logical level, however, all occurrences of nulls are treated according to the no-information interpretation discussed in [Zani1].

A three-valued logic is required to handle qualification expressions involving negation. Thus, a condition such as,

>ITEM.Type= "SPORT"

evaluates to **null** for an ITEM occurrence where the Type attribute is null. Boolean expressions of such terms are evaluated according to the three-valued logic tables of Figure 3. Qualified tuples are only those that yield a TRUE value; tuples that yield FALSE or the logical **null** are discarded.

It was suggested in [Codd2] that a **null** version of a query should also be provided to retrieve those tuples where the qualification, although not yielding TRUE, does not yield FALSE either. By contrast it was shown in [Zani2] that the TRUE version suffices once the expression "t.A **is null**" and its negation "t.B **isnot null**" are allowed in the qualification expression. Therefore, we have included these clauses in GEM. Thus, rather than requesting a null version answer for the query in Example 2, a user will instead enter this query:

OR	T	F	null
T	T	T	T
F	T	F	null
null	T	null	null

AND	T	F	null
T	T	F	null
F	F	F	F
null	null	F	null

NOT	
T	F
F	T
null	null

Figure 3. Three-valued logic tables.

range of dep **is** DEPT
retrieve (dep.Name)
where dep.Floor **is null**

Example 19. Find the departments whose floors are unspecified.

Indeed, this query returns the names of those departments that neither meet nor fail the qualification of Example 2 (dep.Floor $=$3).

In [Zani2] it is shown that a query language featuring the three-valued logic with the extension described above is complete — relational calculus and relational algebra are equivalent in power, as query languages. GEM, which is also complete, consists of a mixture of relational calculus and algebra, just like QUEL. In particular, both languages draw from the relational algebra inasmuch as they use set-theoretic notions to eliminate the need for universal quantifiers in queries. The treatment of set and aggregate operations in the presence of null values will be discussed in the next section.

R	
#	A
1	a1
2	a2
3	a3

S			
#	B	Ref1:R	Ref2:R
6	b1	1	2
7	b2	2	null

Figure.4.: A database.

Null values make possible a precise definition of the notion of implicit join defined by the dot-notation. For concreteness consider the database of Figure 4. On this database, the query

retrieve (S.B, S.Ref1.A)

Example 21. Implicit join without nulls.

produces the following table. (For clarity we show the reference columns although they are never included in the output presented to a user.)

#	B	Ref1	A
6	b1	1	a1
7	b2	2	a2

Figure 5. The result of example 21.

However, the query

retrieve (S.B, S.Ref2.A)

Example 22. Implicit join with nulls.

generates the table,

#	B	Ref2	A
1	b1	2	a2
2	b2	null	null

Figure 6. Result of example 22.

We can compare these queries with the explicit-join queries:

retrieve (S.B, R.A) **where** S.Ref1 **is** R

Example 23. Explicit join without nulls.

and

retrieve (S.B, R.A) **where** S.Ref2 **is** R

Example 24. Explicit join with null.

Since two entities are identical if and only if their surrogate values are equal, these queries are equivalent (in a system that, unlike GEM, allows direct access to surrogate values) to:

retrieve (S.B, R.A) **where** S.Ref1=R.#

Example 25. Implementing Example 23 by joining on surrogates.

and,

retrieve (S.B, R.A) **where** S.Ref2=R.#

Example 26. Implementing Example 24 by joining on surrogates.

Applying the three-valued logic described above, one concludes that the queries of Examples 21 and 25 return the same result; however, the query of Example 22 produces the table of Figure 6, while that of Example 26 produces the same table but without the last row.

It can be proved that an implicit functional join, such as the one of Figure 6, corresponds to a semi-union join [Zani1], alias a semi-outer join [Codd2], which is in turn defined as the union of S with the entity join, S ⋈ R. Therefore, implicit functional joins are equivalent to explicit entity joins whenever the reference attributes are not null. Therefore, queries of Examples 8 and 9 are equivalent only under the assumption that SALES.Dept is not allowed to be null. However, nulls in SALES.Item would have no effect, since such tuples are discarded anyway because of the qualification, I.Type="SPORT".

7. SET-VALUED ATTRIBUTES and OPERATORS

The availability of set-valued attributes adds to the conciseness and expressivity of GEM schemas and queries. For instance, in the schema of Figure 2, we find a set of colors for each item:

ITEM (Name, Type, {Colors})

This information could also be modeled without set-valued attributes, as follows,

NewITEM (Name, Type, Color)

However, Name is a key in ITEM, but not in NewITEM, where the key is the pair (Name, Color). Thus the functional dependency of Type (that denotes the general category in which a merchandise ITEM lies) on Name is lost with this second schema.

A better solution, from the modeling viewpoint, is to normalize NewITEM to two relations: an ITEM relation without colors, and a COLOR relation containing item identifiers and colors. But this would produce a more complex schema and also more complex queries.

Thus inclusion of set-valued attributes is desirable also in view of the set and aggregate functions already provided by QUEL. In QUEL, and therefore in GEM, the set-valued primitives are provided through the (grouped) **by** construct. For example, a query such as, "for each item print its name, its type and the number of colors in which it comes" can be formulated as follows:

range of I **is** NewITEM
retrieve (I.Name, I.Type,
    Tot=**count**(I.Color **by** I.Name, I.Type))

Example 27. Use of **by**.

(Since Type is functionally dependent on Name, I.Type can actually be excluded from the **by** variables without changing the result of the query above.)

Using the set-valued Colors in ITEM, the same query can be formulated as follows:

range of I **is** ITEM
retrieve (I.Name, I.Type, Tot=**count**(I.Colors))

Example 28. Example 27 with a set-valued attribute.

Thus, ITEM basically corresponds to NewITEM grouped by Name, Type. Therefore, we claim that we now have a more complete and consistent user interface, since GEM explicitly supports as data types those aggregate and set functions that QUEL requires and supports as query constructs.

In order to provide users with the convenience of manipulating aggregates GEM supports the set-comparison primitives included in the original QUEL [HeSW]. Thus, in addition to the set-membership test operator, **in**, GEM supports the following operators:

=	(set) equals
!=	(set) does not equal
>	properly contains
>=	contains
<	is properly contained in
<=	is contained in

These constructs were omitted in recent commercial releases of QUEL [QUEL]. This is unfortunate, since many useful queries cannot be formulated easily without them — as demonstrated by the sixty-six queries in Appendix II of [Zani3].

Unfortunately, set operators are also very expensive to support in standard relational systems. Our approach to this problem is two-fold. First we plan to map subset relationships into equivalent aggregate expressions that are more efficient to support. Then we plan to exploit the fact that set-valued attributes can only be used in this capacity, so that substantial improvements in performance can be achieved by specialized storage organizations. Performance improvements obtained by declaring set-valued attributes may alone justify their addition to the relational interface.

In the more germane domain of user convenience, set-valued attributes entail a more succinct and expressive formulation of powerful queries. For instance, the query "Find all items for which there exist items of the same type with a better selection of colors," can be expressed as follows:

> **range of** I1 for ITEM
> **range of** I2 for ITEM
> **retrieve** (I1.**all**) **where**
> I1.Type = I2.Type **and** I1.Colors < I2.Colors

> *Example 29. Items offering an inadequate selection of colors (for their types).*

Thus, set-valued attributes can only be operands of set-valued operators and aggregate functions. The latter, however, can also apply to sets of values from single-valued attributes and reference attributes. Thus, to find all the items supplied to all departments one can use the following query:

> **retrieve** (SUPPLY.Item.Name) **where**
> {SUPPLY.Dept **by** SUPPLY.Item} >= {DEPT}

> *Example 30. Items supplied to all departments.*

Observe that sets are denoted by enclosing them in braces. Also, GEM enforces the basic integrity tests on set and aggregate functions (sets must consist of elements of compatible type).

In the presence of null values, the set operators must be properly extended. A comprehensive solution of this complex problem is presented in [Zani1]; for the specific case at hand (sets of values rather than sets of tuples), that reduces to the following simple rule: Null values are excluded from the computation of all aggregate functions or expressions; moreover, they must also be disregarded in the computation of the subset relationship.

8. UPDATES

GEM supports QUEL's standard style of updates, via the three commands *insert*, *delete* and *replace*. Thus,

> **append to** DEPT (Dname="SHOES", Floor= 2)

> *Example 31. Add the shoe department, 2nd floor.*

adds the shoe department to the database.

To insert a soap-dish that comes in brass and bronze finishes, one can write:

> **append to** ITEM (Name="Soap-dis",
>   Type="Bath", Colors={brass, bronze})

> *Example 32. Inserting a new item.*

Attributes that do not appear in the target list are set to **null** if single-valued; if set-valued, they are assigned the empty set.

The statement,

> **append to** ITEM (Name= "towel-bar",
>   Type= ITEM.Type, Colors= ITEM.Colors)
> **where** ITEM.Name = "Soap-dish"

> *Example 33. Completing our bathroom set.*

allows us to add a towel-bar of the same type and colors as our soap-dish. (According to the syntax of the **append to** statement, the first occurrence of "ITEM" is interpreted as an entity name, while the others are interpreted as range variables declared by default.)

Hiring T. Green, a new single employee in the shoe department under J. Black, with hourly wage of $ 5.40 and overtime multiple of 2.2, can be specified by the statement,

> **append to** EMP (Name="T.Green", Spv=
>   EXMPT, Dept = DEPT, Hrlwg=5.40, Ovrt=2.2)
> **where** EXMPT.Name="J.Black"
> **and** DEPT.Dname= "SHOE"

> *Example 34. Adding a new single non-exempt employee.*

In this statement, we can replace EMP by NEXMPT without any change in meaning since the fact that Hrlwg and Ovrt are not null already implies that the employee is non-exempt. Moreover, since no attribute of EMARRIED is mentioned in the target list, the system will set the new EMP to **others**, rather than EMARRIED. (If no attribute of either EXMPT or NEXMPT were in the target list an error message would result, since **others** is not allowed for this generalization sublist.)

If after a while T. Green becomes an exempt employee with a salary of $12000 and a supervisor yet to be assigned, the following update statement can be used:

replace EMP (Spv = null, Sal= 12000)
where EMP.Name = "T.Green"

*Example 35. Tom Green becomes exempt and
loses his supervisor.*

Note that the identifier following a **replace** is a
range variable, unlike the identifier following a
append to. The fact that salary is assigned a new
value forces an automatic change of type from
NEXMPT to EXMPT. Finally, note the assignment
of **null** to a reference attribute.

GEM also allows explicit reassignment of entity
subtypes. Thus the previous query could, more
explicitly, be formulated as follows:

replace NEXMPT
with EXMPT (Spv=null, Sal= 12000)
where NEXMPT.Name= "T.Green"

Example 36. Same as Example 35.

Say now that after being married for some time,
T. Green divorces; then the following update can be
used:

replace EMARRIED with EMP
where EMP.Name= "T.Green"

Example 37. T. Green leaves wedlock.

This example illustrates the rule that, when an
entity e1 is replaced with an ancestor entity e2, all
the entities leading from e1 to e2 are set to **others**.
Thus the EMP T. Green will be set to **others** than
EMARRIED.

The deletion of an entity occurrence will set to **null**
all references pointing to it. Thus the resignation of
T. Green's supervisor,

delete EMP.Spv
where EMP.Name = "T.Green"

Example 38. T. Green's supervisor quits.

causes the Spv field in T. Green's record, and in the
records of those under the same supervisor, to be set
to **null** (if null were not allowed for Spv, then the
update would abort and an error message be
generated), and then the supervisor record is
deleted[5].

---

5. Of course, according to standard management practices T.
Green's people may instead be reassigned to another
supervisor, e.g. Green's boss; this policy can be implemented
by preceding the deletion of Green's record with an update
reassigning his people.

A request such as,

delete EXMPT
where   EXMPT.Name="T.Green"

Example 39. T. Green goes too.

is evaluated as the following:

delete EMP
where EMP.Name="T.Green"
and EMP is EXMPT

Example 40. Same as above.

Thus, since T., Green is exempt, his record is
eliminated; otherwise it would not be.

9. CONCLUSION

A main conclusion of this work is that relational
query languages and interfaces are very robust. We
have shown that with suitable extensions the
relational model provides a degree of modeling
power that matches or surpasses those of the various
conceptual and semantic models proposed in the
literature. Furthermore, with simple extensions, the
relational language QUEL supplies a congenial
query language for such a model. The result is a
friendly and powerful semantic user interface that
retains, and in many ways surpasses, the ease of use
and power of a strictly relational one. Because of
these qualities, GEM provides an attractive interface
for end-users; moreover, as shown in [Andr], it
supplies a good basis on which to build database
interfaces for programming languages.

The approach of extending the relational model is
preferable to adopting a new semantic model for
many reasons. These include compatibility and
graceful evolution, since users that do not want the
extra semantic features need not learn nor use them;
for these users GEM reduces to QUEL. Other
advantages concern definition and ease of
implementation. As indicated in this paper and
shown in [Tsur, TsZa], all GEM queries can be
mapped into equivalent QUEL expressions. In this
way a precise semantic definition and also a notion
of query completeness for GEM can be derived
from those of QUEL, which in turn maps into the
relational calculus [Ullm]. This is a noticeable
improvement with respect to many semantic data
models that lack formal, precise definitions. Finally,
the mapping of GEM into standard QUEL supplies
an expeditious and, for most queries, efficient means
of implementation; such an implementation, planned
for the commercial database machine IDM 500, is
described in [Tsur, TsZa].

Acknowledgments

The author is grateful to J. Andrade and S. Tsur for helpful discussions and recommendations on the design of GEM. Thanks are due to D. Fishman, M. S. Hecht, E. Y. Lien, E. Wolman and the referees for their comments and suggested improvements.

References

[Andr] Andrade J. M. "Genus: a programming language for the design of database applications," Internal Memorandum, Bell Laboratories, 1982.

[Brod] Brodie, M.L., "On Modelling Behavioural Semantics of Databases," *7th Int. Conf. Very Large Data Bases*, pp. 32-42, 1981.

[Codd1] Codd, E.F., "Relational Database: A Practical Foundation for Productivity" *Comm. ACM*, 25,2, pp. 109-118, 1982.

[Codd2] Codd, E.F., "Extending Database Relations to Capture More Meaning," *ACM Trans. Data Base Syst.*, 4,4, pp. 397-434, 1979.

[Chen] Chen, P.P., "The Entity-Relationship Model — Toward an Unified View of Data," *ACM Trans. Database Syst.*, 1, 1, pp. 9-36, 1976.

[DSIS] Lien, Y.E., J.E. Shopiro and S. Tsur. "DSIS — A Database System with Interrelational Semantics," *7th Int. Conf. Very Large Data Bases*, pp. 465-477, 1981.

[HeSW] Held, G.D, M.R. Stonebraker and E. Wong, "INGRES: a Relational Data Base System," *AFIPS Nat. Computer Conf.*, Vol. 44, pp. 409-416, 1975.

[KiMc] King, R. and D. McLeod, "The Event Database Specification Model," *2nd Int. Conf. Databases — Improving Usability and Responsiveness*, Jerusalem, June 22-24, 1982.

[IDM] IDM 500 Software Reference Manual. Ver. 1.3, Sept 1981. Britton-Lee Inc., 90 Albright Way, Los Gatos, CA, 95030.

[INGR] Stonebraker, M., E. Wong, P. Kreps and G. Held. "The Design and Implementation of INGRES", *ACM Trans on Database Syst.* 1:3, pp. 189-222, 1976.

[LaPi] Lacroix, M. and A. Pirotte, "Example queries in relational languages," MBLE Tech. note 107, 1976 (MBLE, Rue Des Deux Gares 80, 1070 Brussels).

[QUEL] Woodfill, J. et al., "INGRES Version 6.2 Reference Manual," Electronic Research Laboratory, Memo UCB/ERL-M78/43, 1979.

[Ship] Shipman, D.W., "The Functional Model and the Lata Language DAPLEX," *ACM Trans. Data Base Syst.*, 6,1, pp. 140-173, 1982.

[SiKe] Sibley, E.H. and L. Kershberg, "Data Architecture and Data Model Considerations," *AFIPS Nat. Computer Conf.*, pp. 85-96,1977.

[SmSm] Smith, J.M. and C.P. Smith, "Database Abstractions: Aggregation and Generalization," *ACM Trans. Database Syst.*, 2, 2, pp. 105-133, 1977.

[Tsur] Tsur, S., "Mapping of GEM into IDL," internal memorandum, Bell Laboratories, 1982.

[TsZa] Tsur, S. and C. Zaniolo, "The Implementation of GEM — Supporting a Semantic Data Model on a Relational Backend", submitted for publication.

[Ullm] Ullman, J., "Principles of Database Systems," Computer Science Press, 1980.

[Zani1] Zaniolo, C., "Database Relations with Null Values," *ACM SIGACT-SIGMOD Symposium on Principles of Database Systems*, Los Angeles, California, March 1982.

[Zani2] Zaniolo, C., "A Formal Treatment of Nonexistent Values in Database Relations," Internal Memorandum, Bell Laboratories, 1983.

[Zani3] Zaniolo, C., "The Database language GEM," Internal Memorandum, Bell Laboratories, 1982.

Appendix I: GEM SYNTAX

This syntax is an extension of, and use the same metanotation as, that of [IDM]. Thus {...} denote a set of zero or more occurrences, while [...] denotes one or zero occurrences. Symbols enclosed in semiquotes denote themselves.

retrieve [**unique**] (<query target list>) [**where** <qualification>]

<query target list>	: <query target element> '{' , <query target element> '}'
<query target element>	: <attribute> /* a simple or set-valued attribute*/
	| <name> = <expression>
	| <name> = <set>
<attribute>	: <variable> . <name>
<variable>	: <variable> { . <name> } /* every <name> must denote a reference attribute/*
	| <range variable> /* declared in the range statement/*
	| <entity name> /* range variable by default/*
<expression>	: <aggregate> /* count(), average(), etc. /*
	| <attribute> /* a simple attribute/*
	| <constant>
	| - <expression>
	| (<expression>)
	| <function> /* see [IDM] for a definition of functions /*
<set>	: <attribute> /* a set-valued attribute/*
	| '{' <extended expr> [**by** <extended expr> { , <extended expr> }]
	[**where** <qualification>] '}'
	| <constants set>
<extended expr>	: <expression> | <variable>
<constants set>	: '{' '}' | '{' <constant> {, <constant>} '}'
<qualification>	: (<qualification>)
	| **not** <qualification>
	| <qualification> **and** <qualification>
	| <qualification> **or** <qualification>
	| <clause>
<clause>	: <expression> <relop> <expression>
	| < extended expr> **in** <set>
	| <set> <relop> <set>
	| <attribute> <identity test> **null**
	| <variable> <identity test> <variable>
<relop>	: = | != | < | <= | > | >=
<identity test>	: **is** | **isnot**

append [**to**] <entity name> (< update target list>)

delete <variable> [**where** <qualification>]

replace <variable> [**with** <entity name>] (<update target list>)

<update target list> : <update target element> '{' , <update target element> '}'

<update target element>	: <name> = <expression> /* <name> of a simple attribute */
	| <name> = <variable> /* <name> of a reference attribute*/
	| <name> = <set> /* <name> of a set attribute */
	| <name> = **null** /* <name> of a simple or reference attribute/*

The POSTGRES Data Model[†]

Lawrence A. Rowe
Michael R. Stonebraker

Computer Science Division, EECS Department
University of California
Berkeley, CA 94720

Abstract

The design of the POSTGRES data model is described. The data model is a relational model that has been extended with abstract data types including user-defined operators and procedures, relation attributes of type procedure, and attribute and procedure inheritance. These mechanism can be used to simulate a wide variety of semantic and object-oriented data modeling constructs including aggregation and generalization, complex objects with shared subobjects, and attributes that reference tuples in other relations.

1. Introduction

This paper describes the data model for POSTGRES, a next-generation extensible database management system being developed at the University of California [23]. The data model is based on the idea of extending the relational model developed by Codd [5] with general mechanisms that can be used to simulate a variety of semantic data modeling constructs. The mechanisms include: 1) abstract data types (ADT's), 2) data of type procedure, and 3) rules. These mechanisms can be used to support complex objects or to implement a

† This research was supported by the National Science Foundation under Grant DCR-8507256 and the Defense Advanced Research Projects Agency (DoD), Arpa Order No. 4871, monitored by Space and Naval Warfare Systems Command under Contract N00039-84-C-0089.

shared object hierarchy for an object-oriented programming language [17]. Most of these ideas have appeared elsewhere [21,22,24,25].

We have discovered that some semantic constructs that were not directly supported can be easily added to the system. Consequently, we have made several changes to the data model and the syntax of the query language that are documented here. These changes include providing support for primary keys, inheritance of data and procedures, and attributes that reference tuples in other relations.

The major contribution of this paper is to show that inheritance can be added to a relational data model with only a modest number of changes to the model and the implementation of the system. The conclusion that we draw from this result is that the major concepts provided in an object-oriented data model (e.g., structured attribute types, inheritance, union type attributes, and support for shared subobjects) can be cleanly and efficiently supported in an extensible relational database management system. The features used to support these mechanisms are abstract data types and attributes of type procedure.

The remainder of the paper describes the POSTGRES data model and is organized as follows. Section 2 presents the data model. Section 3 describes the attribute type system. Section 4 describes how the query language can be extended with user-defined procedures. Section 5 compares the model with other data models and section 6 summarizes the paper.

2. Data Model

A database is composed of a collection of *relations* that contain tuples which represent real-world entities (e.g., documents and people) or relationships (e.g., authorship). A relation has attributes of fixed types that represent properties of the entities and relationships (e.g., the title of a document) and a primary key. Attribute types can be atomic (e.g., integer, floating point, or boolean) or structured (e.g., array or procedure). The primary key is a sequence of attributes of the relation, when taken together, uniquely identify each tuple.

A simple university database will be used to illustrate the model. The following command defines a relation that represents people:

```
create PERSON ( Name = char[25],
    Birthdate = date, Height = int4,
    Weight = int4, StreetAddress = char[25],
    City = char[25], State = char[2])
```

This command defines a relation and creates a structure for storing the tuples.

The definition of a relation may optionally specify a primary key and other relations from which to inherit attributes. A primary key is a combination of attributes that uniquely identify each tuple. The key is specified with a key-clause as follows:

```
create PERSON ( . . .)
key (Name)
```

Tuples must have a value for all key attributes. The specification of a key may optionally include the name of an operator that is to be used when comparing two tuples. For example, suppose a relation had a key whose type was a user-defined ADT. If an attribute of type *box* was part of the primary key, the comparison operator must be specified since different *box* operators could be used to distinguish the entries (e.g., area equals or box equality). The following example shows the definition of a relation with a key attribute of type *box* that uses the area equals operator (AE) to determine key value equality:

```
create PICTURE(Title = char[25], Item = box)
key (Item using AE)
```

Data inheritance is specified with an **inherits**-clause. Suppose, for example, that people in the university database are employees and/or students and that different attributes are to be defined for each category. The relation for each category includes the *PERSON* attributes and the attributes that are specific to the category. These relations can be defined by replicating the *PERSON* attributes in each relation definition or by inheriting them for the definition of *PERSON*. Figure 1 shows the relations and an inheritance

hierarchy that could be used to share the definition of the attributes. The commands that define the relations other than the *PERSON* relation defined above are:

```
create EMPLOYEE (Dept = char[25],
    Status = int2, Mgr = char[25],
    JobTitle = char[25], Salary = money)
inherits (PERSON)

create STUDENT (Sno = char[12],
    Status = int2, Level = char[20])
inherits (PERSON)

create STUDEMP (IsWorkStudy = bool)
inherits (STUDENT, EMPLOYEE)
```

A relation inherits all attributes from its parent(s) unless an attribute is overriden in the definition. For example, the *EMPLOYEE* relation inherits the *PERSON* attributes *Name*, *Birthdate*, *Height*, *Weight*, *StreetAddress*, *City*, and *State*. Key specifications are also inherited so *Name* is also the key for EMPLOYEE.

Relations may inherit attributes from more than one parent. For example, *STUDEMP* inherits attributes from *STUDENT* and *EMPLOYEE*. An inheritance conflict occurs when the same attribute name is inherited from more than one parent (e.g., *STUDEMP* inherits *Status* from *EMPLOYEE* and *STUDENT*). If the inherited attributes have the same type, an attribute with the type is

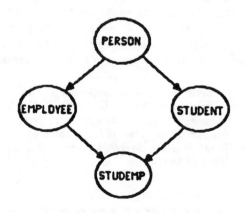

Figure 1: Relation hierarchy.

included in the relation that is being defined. Otherwise, the declaration is disallowed.[1]

The POSTGRES query language is a generalized version of QUEL [13], called *POSTQUEL*. QUEL was extended in several directions. First, POSTQUEL has a from-clause to define tuple-variables rather than a range command. Second, arbitrary relation-valued expressions may appear any place that a relation name could appear in QUEL. Third, transitive closure and **execute** commands have been added to the language [14]. And lastly, POSTGRES maintains historical data so POSTQUEL allows queries to be run on past database states or on any data that was in the database at any time. These extensions are described in the remainder of this section.

The from-clause was added to the language so that tuple-variable definitions for a query could be easily determined at compile-time. This capability was needed because POSTGRES will, at the user's request, compile queries and save them in the system catalogs. The from-clause is illustrated in the following query that lists all work-study students who are sophomores:

```
retrieve (SE.name)
from SE in STUDEMP
where SE.IsWorkStudy
    and SE.Status = "sophomore"
```

The from-clause specifies the set of tuples over which a tuple-variable will range. In this example, the tuple-variable *SE* ranges over the set of student employees.

A default tuple-variable with the same name is defined for each relation referenced in the target-list or where-clause of a query. For example, the query above could have been written:

---

[1] Most attribute inheritance models have a conflict resolution rule that selects one of the conflicting attributes. We chose to disallow inheritance because we could not discover an example where it made sense, except when the types were identical. On the other hand, procedure inheritance (discussed below) does use a conflict resolution rule because many examples exist in which one procedure is prefered.

```
retrieve (STUDEMP.name)
where STUDEMP.IsWorkStudy
    and STUDEMP.Status = "sophomore"
```

Notice that the attribute *IsWorkStudy* is a boolean-valued attribute so it does not require an explicit value test (e.g., *STUDEMP.IsWorkStudy = "true"*).

The set of tuples that a tuple-variable may range over can be a named relation or a relation-expression. For example, suppose the user wanted to retrieve all students in the database who live in Berkeley regardless of whether they are students or student employees. This query can be written as follows:

```
retrieve (S.name)
from S in STUDENT*
where S.city = "Berkeley"
```

The "*" operator specifies the relation formed by taking the union of the named relation (i.e., *STUDENT*) and all relations that inherit attributes from it (i.e., *STUDEMP*). If the "*" operator was not used, the query retrieves only tuples in the student relation (i.e., students who are not student employees). In most data models that support inheritance the relation name defaults to the union of relations over the inheritance hierarchy (i.e., the data described by *STUDENT** above). We chose a different default because queries that involve unions will be slower than queries on a single relation. By forcing the user to request the union explicitly with the "*" operator, he will be aware of this cost.

Relation expressions may include other set operators: union ($\bigcup$), intersection ($\bigcap$), and difference ($-$). For example, the following query retrieves the names of people who are students or employees but not student employees:

```
retrieve (S.name)
from S in (STUDENT ∪ EMPLOYEE)
```

Suppose a tuple does not have an attribute referenced elsewhere in the query. If the reference is in the target-list, the return tuple will not contain the attribute.[2] If the reference is in

---

[2] The application program interface to POSTGRES allows the stream of tuples passed back to the program to have dynamically varying columns and types.

the qualification, the clause containing the qualification is "false".

POSTQUEL also provides set comparison operators and a relation-constructor that can be used to specify some difficult queries more easily than in a conventional query language. For example, suppose that students could have several majors. The natural representation for this data is to define a separate relation:

```
create MAJORS(Sname = char[25],
    Mname = char[25])
```

where *Sname* is the student's name and *Mname* is the major. With this representation, the following query retrieves the names of students with the same majors as Smith:

```
retrieve (M1.Sname)
from M1 in MAJORS
where {(x.Mname) from x in MAJORS
        where x.Sname = M1.Sname}
  ⊂ {(x.Mname) from x in MAJORS
        where x.Sname = "Smith"}
```

The expressions enclosed in set symbols ("{...}") are relation-constructors.

The general form of a relation-constructor[3] is

```
{(target-list)  from from-clause
        where where-clause}
```

which specifies the same relation as the query

```
retrieve (target-list)
from from-clause
where where-clause
```

Note that a tuple-variable defined in the outer query (e.g., M1 in the query above) can be used within a relation-constructor but that a tuple-variable defined in the relation-constructor cannot be used in the outer query. Redefinition of a tuple-variable in a relation constructor creates a distinct variable as in a block-structured programming language (e.g., PASCAL). Relation-valued expressions (including attributes of type procedure described in the next section) can be used any place in a query that a named relation can be

---

[3] Relation constructors are really aggregate functions. We have designed a mechanism to support extensible aggregate functions, but have not yet worked out the query language syntax and semantics.

used.

Database updates are specified with conventional update commands as shown in the following examples:

```
/* Add a new employee to the database. */
append to EMPLOYEE(name = value,
    age = value, ...)
```

```
/* Change state codes using
    MAP(OldCode, NewCode). */
replace P(State = MAP.NewCode)
from P in PERSON*
where P.State = MAP.OldCode
```

```
/* Delete students born before today. */
delete STUDENT
where STUDENT.Birthdate < "today"
```

Deferred update semantics are used for all updates commands.

POSTQUEL supports the transitive closure commands developed in QUEL* [14]. A "*" command continues to execute until no tuples are retrieved (e.g., **retrieve***) or updated (e.g., **append***, **delete***, or **replace***). For example, the following query creates a relation that contains all employees who work for Smith:

```
retrieve* into SUBORD(E.Name, E.Mgr)
from E in EMPLOYEE. S in SUBORD
where E.Name = "Smith"
    or E.Mgr = S.Name
```

This command continues to execute the retrieve-into command until there are no changes made to the *SUBORD* relation.

Lastly, POSTGRES saves data deleted from or modified in a relation so that queries can be executed on historical data. For example, the following query looks for students who lived in Berkeley on August 1, 1980:

```
retrieve (S.Name)
from S in STUDENT["August 1, 1980"]
where S.City = "Berkeley"
```

The date specified in the brackets following the relation name specifies the relation at the designated time. The date can be specified in many different formats and optionally may include a time of day. The query above only examines students who are not student employees. To search the set of all students, the **from**-clause would be

...**from** S in STUDENT*["August 1, 1980"]

Queries can also be executed on all data that is currently in the relation or was in it at some time in the past (i.e., all data). The following query retrieves all students who ever lived in Berkeley:

    retrieve (S.Name)
    from S in STUDENT[]
    where S.City = "Berkeley"

The notation "[]" can be appended to any relation name.

Queries can also be specified on data that was in the relation during a given time period. The time period is specified by giving a start- and end-time as shown in the following query that retrieves students who lived in Berkeley at any time in August 1980:

    retrieve (S.Name)
    from S in STUDENT*["August 1, 1980",
                       "August 31, 1980"]
    where S.City = "Berkeley"

Shorthand notations are supported for all tuples in a relation up to some date (e.g., *STUDENT*[,"August 1, 1980"]*) or from some date to the present (e.g., *STUDENT*["August 1, 1980",]*).

The POSTGRES default is to save all data unless the user explicitly requests that data be purged. Data can be purged before a specific data (e.g., before January 1, 1987) or before some time period (e.g., before six months ago). The user may also request that all historical data be purged so that only the current data in the relation is stored.

POSTGRES also supports versions of relations. A version of a relation can be created from a relation or a snapshot. A version is created by specifying the base relation as shown in the command

    create version MYPEOPLE from PERSON

that creates a version, named *MYPEOPLE*, derived from the *PERSON* relation. Data can be retrieved from and updated in a version just like a relation. Updates to the version do not modify the base relation. However, updates to the base relation are propagated to the version unless the value has been modified. For example, if George's birthdate is changed in *MYPEOPLE*, a replace command that changes his birthdate in *PERSON* will not be propagated to *MYPEOPLE*.

If the user does not want updates to the base relation to propagate to the version, he can create a version of a snapshot. A snapshot is a copy of the current contents of a relation [1]. A version of a snapshot is created by the following command:

    create version YOURPEOPLE
    from PERSON["now"]

The snapshot version can be updated directly by issuing update commands on the version. But, updates to the base relation are not propagated to the version.

A merge command is provided to merge changes made to a version back into the base relation. An example of this command is

    merge YOURPEOPLE into PERSON

that will merge the changes made to *YOUR-PEOPLE* back into *PERSON*. The merge command uses a semi-automatic procedure to resolve updates to the underlying relation and the version that conflict [10].

This section described most of the data definition and data manipulation commands in POSTQUEL. The commands that were not described are the commands for defining rules, utility commands that only affect the performance of the system (e.g., **define index** and **modify**), and other miscellaneous utility commands (e.g., **destroy** and **copy**). The next section describes the type system for relation attributes.

3. Data Types

POSTGRES provides a collection of atomic and structured types. The predefined atomic types include: *int2*, *int4*, *float4*, *float8*, *bool*, *char*, and *date*. The standard arithmetic and comparison operators are provided for the numeric and date data types and the standard string and comparison operators for character arrays. Users can extend the system by adding new atomic types using an abstract data type (ADT) definition facility.

All atomic data types are defined to the system as ADT's. An ADT is defined by specifying the type name, the length of the internal representation in bytes, procedures for converting from an external to internal representation for a value and from an internal to external representation, and a default value. The command

```
define type int4 is (InternalLength = 4,
    InputProc = CharToInt4,
    OutputProc = Int4ToChar, Default = "0")
```

defines the type *int4* which is predefined in the system. *CharToInt4* and *Int4ToChar* are procedures that are coded in a conventional programming language (e.g., C) and defined to the system using the commands described in section 4.

Operators on ADT's are defined by specifying the the number and type of operands, the return type, the precedence and associativity of the operator, and the procedure that implements it. For example, the command

```
define operator " +"(int4, int4) returns int4
    is (Proc = Plus, Precedence = 5,
        Associativity = "left")
```

defines the plus operator. Precedence is specified by a number. Larger numbers imply higher precedence. The predefined operators have the precedences shown in figure 2. These precedences can be changed by changing the operator definitions. Associativity is either left or right depending on the semantics desired. This example defined an operator denoted by a symbol (i.e., "+"). Operators can also be denoted by identifiers as shown below.

Another example of an ADT definition is the following command that defines an ADT that represents boxes:

Precedence	Operators
80	↑
70	not − (unary)
60	* /
50	+ − (binary)
40	< ≤ > ≥
30	= ≠
20	and
10	or

Figure 2: Predefined operators precedence.

```
define type box is (InternalLength = 16,
    InputProc = CharToBox,
    OutputProc = BoxToChar, Default = "")
```

The external representation of a box is a character string that contains two points that represent the upper-left and lower-right corners of the box. With this representation, the constant

"20,50:10,70"

describes a box whose upper-left corner is at (20, 50) and lower-right corner is at (10, 70). *CharToBox* takes a character string like this one and returns a 16 byte representation of a box (e.g., 4 bytes per x- or y-coordinate value). *BoxToChar* is the inverse of *CharToBox*

Comparison operators can be defined on ADT's that can be used in access methods or optimized in queries. For example, the definition

```
define operator AE(box, box) returns bool
    is (Proc = BoxAE, Precedence = 3,
        Associativity = "left", Sort = BoxArea,
        Hashes, Restrict = AERSelect,
        Join = AEJSelect, Negator = BoxAreaNE)
```

defines an operator "area equals" on boxes. In addition to the semantic information about the operator itself, this specification includes information used by POSTGRES to build indexes and to optimize queries using the operator. For example, suppose the *PICTURE* relation was defined by

create PICTURE(Title = char[], Item = box)

and the query

```
retrieve (PICTURE.all)
where PICTURE.Item AE "50,100:100,50"
```

was executed. The *Sort* property of the *AE* operator specifies the procedure to be used to sort the relation if a merge-sort join strategy was selected to implement the query. It also specifies the procedure to use when building an ordered index (e.g., B-Tree) on an attribute of type *box*. The *Hashes* property indicates that this operator can be used to build a hash index on a *box* attribute. Note that either type of index can be used to optimize the query above. The *Restrict* and *Join* properties specify the procedure that is to be called by the query optimizer to compute the restrict and join selectivities, respectively, of a clause involving the operator. These selectivity properties specify procedures that will return a floating point value between 0.0 and 1.0 that indicate the attribute selectivity given the operator. Lastly, the *Negator* property specifies the procedure that is to be used to compare two values when a query predicate requires the operator to be negated as in

retrieve (PICTURE.all)
where not (PICTURE.Item
                AE "50,100:100,50")

The **define operator** command also may specify a procedure that can be used if the query predicate includes an operator that is not commutative. For example, the commutator procedure for "area less than" (*ALT*) is the procedure that implements "area greater than or equal" (*AGE*). More details on the use of these properties is given elsewhere [25].

Type-constructors are provided to define structured types (e.g., arrays and procedures) that can be used to represent complex data. An *array* type-constructor can be used to define a variable- or fixed-size array. A fixed-size array is declared by specifying the element type and upper bound of the array as illustrated by

create PERSON(Name = char[25])

which defines an array of twenty-five characters. The elements of the array are referenced by indexing the attribute by an integer between 1 and 25 (e.g., "*PERSON.Name[4]*" references the fourth character in the person's name).

A variable-size array is specified by omitting the upper bound in the type constructor. For example, a variable-sized array of characters is specified by "char[]." Variable-size arrays are referenced by indexing the attribute by an integer between 1 and the current upper bound of the array. The predefined function *size* returns the current upper bound. POSTGRES does not impose a limit on the size of a variable-size array. Built-in functions are provided to append arrays and to fetch array slices. For example, two character arrays can be appended using the concatenate operator ("+") and an array slice containing characters 2 through 15 in an attribute named x can be fetched by the expression "x[2:15]."

The second type-constructor allows values of type procedure to be stored in an attribute. Procedure values are represented by a sequence of POSTQUEL commands. The value of an attribute of type procedure is a relation because that is what a **retrieve** command returns. Moreover, the value may include tuples from different relations (i.e., of different types) because a procedure composed of two **retrieve** commands returns the union of both

commands. We call a relation with different tuple types a *multirelation*. The POSTGRES programming language interface provides a cursor-like mechanism, called a *portal*, to fetch values from multirelations [23]. However, they are not stored by the system (i.e., only relations are stored).

The system provides two kinds of procedure type-constructors: variable and parameterized. A variable procedure-type allows a different POSTQUEL procedure to be stored in each tuple while parameterized procedure-types store the same procedure in each tuple but with different parameters. We will illustrate the use of a variable procedure-type by showing another way to represent student majors. Suppose a *DEPARTMENT* relation was defined with the following command:

create DEPARTMENT(Name = char[25],
        Chair = char[25], ...)

A student's major(s) can then be represented by a procedure in the *STUDENT* relation that retrieves the appropriate *DEPARTMENT* tuple(s). The *Majors* attribute would be declared as follows:

create STUDENT(..., Majors = postquel, ...)

Data type *postquel* represents a procedure-type. The value in *Majors* will be a query that fetches the department relation tuples that represent the student's minors. The following command appends a student to the database who has a double major in mathematics and computer science:

append STUDENT(Name = "Smith", ...,
    Majors =
        "retrieve (D.all)
        from D in DEPARTMENT
        where D.Name = "Math"
        or D.Name = "CS"")

A query that references the *Majors* attribute returns the string that contains the POSTQUEL commands. However, two notations are provided that will execute the query and return the result rather than the definition. First, nested-dot notation implicitly executes the query as illustrated by

retrieve (S.Name, S.Majors.Name)
from S in STUDENT

which prints a list of names and majors of students. The result of the query in *Majors* is implicitly joined with the tuple specified by the rest of the target-list. In other words, if a student has two majors, this query will return two tuples with the *Name* attribute repeated. The implicit join is performed to guarantee that a relation is returned.

The second way to execute the query is to use the **execute** command. For example, the query

```
execute (S.Majors)
from S in STUDENT
where S.Name = "Smith"
```

returns a relation that contains *DEPARTMENT* tuples for all of Smith's majors.

Parameterized procedure-types are used when the query to be stored in an attribute is nearly the same for every tuple. The query parameters can be taken from other attributes in the tuple or they may be explicitly specified. For example, suppose an attribute in *STUDENT* was to represent the student's current class list. Given the following definition for enrollments:

```
create ENROLLMENT(Student = char[25],
    Class = char[25])
```

Bill's class list can be retrieved by the query

```
retrieve (ClassName = E.Class)
from E in ENROLLMENT
where E.Student = "Bill"
```

This query will be the same for every student except for the constant that specifies the student's name.

A parameterized procedure-type could be defined to represent this query as follows:

```
define type classes is
    retrieve (ClassName = E.Class)
    from E in ENROLLMENT
    where E.Student = $.Name
end
```

The dollar-sign symbol ("$") refers to the tuple in which the query is stored (i.e., the current tuple). The parameter for each instance of this type (i.e., a query) is the *Name* attribute in the tuple in which the instance is stored. This type is then used in the **create** command as follows

```
create STUDENT(Name = char[25], ...,
    ClassList = classes)
```

to define an attribute that represents the student's current class list. This attribute can be used in a query to return a list of students and the classes they are taking:

```
retrieve (S.Name, S.ClassList.ClassName)
```

Notice that for a particular *STUDENT* tuple, the expression "*$.Name*" in the query refers to the name of that student. The symbol "$" can be thought of as a tuple-variable bound to the current tuple.

Parameterized procedure-types are extremely useful types, but sometimes it is inconvenient to store the parameters explicitly as attributes in the relation. Consequently, a notation is provided that allows the parameters to be stored in the procedure-type value. This mechanism can be used to simulate attribute types that reference tuples in other relations. For example, suppose you wanted a type that referenced a tuple in the *DEPARTMENT* relation defined above. This type can be defined as follows:

```
define type DEPARTMENT(int4) is
    retrieve (DEPARTMENT.all)
    where DEPARTMENT.oid = $1
end
```

The relation name can be used for the type name because relations, types, and procedures have separate name spaces. The query in type *DEPARTMENT* will retrieve a specific department tuple given a unique object identifier (*oid*) of the tuple. Each relation has an implicitly defined attribute named *oid* that contains the tuple's unique identifier. The *oid* attribute can be accessed but not updated by user queries. *Oid* values are created and maintained by the POSTGRES storage system [26]. The formal argument to this procedure-type is the type of an object identifier. The parameter is referenced inside the definition by "*$n*" where *n* is the parameter number.

An actual argument is supplied when a value is assigned to an attribute of type *DEPARTMENT*. For example, a *COURSE* relation can be defined that represents information about a specific course including the department that offers it. The **create** command is:

```
create COURSE(Title = char[25],
    Dept = DEPARTMENT, ...)
```

The attribute *Dept* represents the department that offers the course. The following query adds a course to the database:

```
append COURSE(
    Title = "Introductory Programming",
    Dept = DEPARTMENT(D.oid))
from D in DEPARTMENT
where D.Name = "computer science"
```

The procedure *DEPARTMENT* called in the target-list is implicitly defined by the "define type" command. It constructs a value of the specified type given actual arguments that are type compatible with the formal arguments, in this case an *int4*.

Parameterized procedure-types that represent references to tuples in a specific relation are so commonly used that we plan to provide automatic support for them. First, every relation created will have a type that represents a reference to a tuple implicitly defined similar to the *DEPARTMENT* type above. And second, it will be possible to assign a tuple-variable directly to a tuple reference attribute. In other words, the assignment to the attribute *Dept* that is written in the query above as

... Dept = DEPARTMENT(D.oid) ...

can be written as

... Dept = D ...

Parameterized procedure-types can also be used to implement a type that references a tuple in an arbitrary relation. The type definition is:

```
define type tuple(char[], int4) is
    retrieve ($1.all)
    where $1.oid = $2
end
```

The first argument is the name of the relation and the second argument is the *oid* of the desired tuple in the relation. In effect, this type defines a reference to an arbitrary tuple in the database.

The procedure-type *tuple* can be used to create a relation that represents people who help with fund raising:

```
create VOLUNTEER(Person = tuple,
    TimeAvailable = integer, ...)
```

Because volunteers may be students, employees, or people who are neither students nor employees, the attribute *Person* must contain a reference to a tuple in an arbitrary relation. The following command appends all students to *VOLUNTEER*:

```
append VOLUNTEER(
    Person = tuple(relation(S), S.oid))
from S in STUDENT*
```

The predefined function *relation* returns the name of the relation to which the tuple-variable *S* is bound.

The type *tuple* will also be special-cased to make it more convenient. *Tuple* will be a predefined type and it will be possible to assign tuple-variables directly to attributes of the type. Consequently, the assignment to *Person* written above as

... Person = tuple(relation(S), S.oid) ...

can be written

... Person = S ...

We expect that as we get more experience with POSTGRES applications that more types may be special-cased.

4. User-Defined Procedures

This section describes language constructs for adding user-defined procedures to POST-QUEL. User-defined procedures are written in a conventional programming language and are used to implement ADT operators or to move a computation from a front-end application process to the back-end DBMS process.

Moving a computation to the back-end opens up possibilities for the DBMS to precompute a query that includes the computation. For example, suppose that a front-end application needed to fetch the definition of a form from a database and to construct a main-memory data structure that the run-time forms system used to display the form on the terminal screen for data entry or display. A conventional relation database design would store the form components (e.g., titles and field definitions for different types of fields such as scalar fields, table fields, and graphics fields) in many different relations. An example database design is:

```
create FORM(FormName, ...)

create FIELDS(FormName, FieldName,
    Origin, Height, Width,
    FieldKind, ...)

create SCALARFIELD(FormName,
    FieldName, DataType,
    DisplayFormat, ...)

create TABLEFIELD(FormName,
    FieldName, NumberOfRows, ...)

create TABLECOLUMNS(FormName,
    FieldName, ColumnName, Height,
    Width, FieldKind, ...)
```

The query that fetches the form from the database must execute at least one query per table and sort through the return tuples to construct the main-memory data structure. This operation must take less than two seconds for an interactive application. Conventional relational DBMS's cannot satisfy this time constraint.

Our approach to solving this problem is to move the computation that constructs the main-memory data structure to the database process. Suppose the procedure *MakeForm* built the data structure given the name of a form. Using the parameterized procedure-type mechanism defined above an attribute can be added to the *FORM* relation that stores the form representation computed by this procedure. The commands

```
define type formrep is
    retrieve (rep = MakeForm($.FormName))
end
addattribute (FormName, ...,
    FormDataStructure = formrep)
to FORM
```

define the procedure type and add an attribute to the *FORM* relation.

The advantage of this representation is that POSTGRES can precompute the answer to a procedure-type attribute and store it in the tuple. By precomputing the main-memory data structure representation, the form can be fetched from the database by a single-tuple retrieve:

```
retrieve (x = FORM.FormDataStructure)
where FORM.FormName = "foo"
```

The real-time constraint to fetch and display a form can be easily met if all the program must do is a single-tuple retrieve to fetch the data structure and call the library procedure to display it. This example illustrates the advantage of moving a computation (i.e., constructing a main-memory data structure) from the application process to the DBMS process.

A procedure is defined to the system by specifying the names and types of the arguments, the return type, the language it is written in, and where the source and object code is stored. For example, the definition

```
define procedure AgeInYears(date) returns int4
    is (language = "C", filename = "AgeInYears")
```

defines a procedure *AgeInYears* that takes a *date* value and returns the age of the person. The argument and return types are specified using POSTGRES types. When the procedure is called, it is passed the arguments in the POSTGRES internal representation for the type. We plan to allow procedures to be written in several different languages including C

and Lisp which are the two languages being used to implement the system.

POSTGRES stores the information about a procedure in the system catalogs and dynamically loads the object code when it is called in a query. The following query uses the *AgeInYears* procedure to retrieve the names and ages of all people in the example database:

```
retrieve (P.Name,
        Age = AgeInYears(P.Birthdate))
from P in PERSON*
```

User-defined procedures can also take tuple-variable arguments. For example, the following command defines a procedure, called *Comp*, that takes an EMPLOYEE tuple and computes the person's compensation according to some formula that involves several attributes in the tuple (e.g., the employee's status, job title, and salary):

```
define procedure Comp(EMPLOYEE)
    returns int4 is (language = "C",
    filename = "Comp1")
```

Recall that a parameterized procedure-type is defined for each relation automatically so the type *EMPLOYEE* represents a reference to a tuple in the *EMPLOYEE* relation. This procedure is called in the following query:

```
retrieve (E.Name, Compensation = Comp(E))
from E in EMPLOYEE
```

The C function that implements this procedure is passed a data structure that contains the names, types, and values of the attributes in the tuple.

User-defined procedures can be passed tuples in other relations that inherit the attributes in the relation declared as the argument to the procedure. For example, the *Comp* procedure defined for the *EMPLOYEE* relation can be passed a *STUDEMP* tuple as in

```
retrieve (SE.Name,
        Compensation = Comp(SE))
from SE in STUDEMP
```

because *STUDEMP* inherits data attributes from *EMPLOYEE*.

The arguments to procedures that take relation tuples as arguments must be passed in a self-describing data structure because the procedure can be passed tuples from different relations. Attributes inherited from other relations may be in different positions in the relations. Moreover, the values passed for the same attribute name may be different types (e.g., the definition of an inherited attribute may be overridden with a different type). The self-describing data structure is a list of arguments, one per attribute in the tuple to be passed, with the following structure

(AttrName, AttrType, AttrValue)

The procedure code will have to search the list to find the desired attribute. A library of routines is provided that will hide this structure from the programmer. The library will include routines to get the type and value of an attribute given the name of the attribute. For example, the following code fetches the value of the *Birthdate* attribute:

GetValue("Birthdate")

The problem of variable argument lists arises in all object-oriented programming languages and similar solutions are used.

The model for procedure inheritance is nearly identical to method inheritance in object-oriented programming languages [20]. Procedure inheritance uses the data inheritance hierarchy and similar inheritance rules except that a rule is provided to select a procedure when an inheritance conflict arises. For example, suppose that a *Comp* procedure was defined for *STUDENT* as well as for *EMPLOYEE*. The definition of the second procedure might be:

define procedure Comp(STUDENT)
 returns int4 **is** (language = "C",
 filename = "Comp2")

A conflict arises when the query on *STUDEMP* above is executed because the system does not know which *Comp* procedure to call (i.e., the one for *EMPLOYEE* or the one for *STUDENT*). The procedure called is selected from among the procedures that take a tuple from the relation specified by the actual argument *STUDEMP* or any relation from which attributes in the actual argument are inherited (e.g., *PERSON*, *EMPLOYEE*, and *STUDENT*).

Each relation has an *inheritance precedence list* (IPL) that is used to resolve the conflict. The list is constructed by starting with the relation itself and doing a depth-first search up the inheritance hierarchy starting with the first relation specified in the inherits-clause. For example, the inherits-clause for *STUDEMP* is

... inherits (STUDENT, EMPLOYEE)

and its IPL is

(STUDEMP, STUDENT,
 EMPLOYEE, PERSON)

PERSON appears after *EMPLOYEE* rather than after *STUDENT* where it would appear in a depth-first search because both *STUDENT* and *EMPLOYEE* inherit attributes from *PERSON* (see figure 1). In other words, all but the last occurrence of a relation in the depth-first ordering of the hierarchy is deleted.[4]

When a procedure is called and passed a tuple as the first argument, the actual procedure invoked is the first definition found with the same name when the procedures that take arguments from the relations in the ILP of the argument are searched in order. In the example above, the Comp procedure defined for *STUDENT* is called because there is no procedure named *Comp* defined for *STUDEMP* and *STUDENT* is the next relation in the IPL.

The implementation of this procedure selection rule is relatively easy. Assume that two system catalogs are defined:

PROCDEF(ProcName, ArgName, ProcId)
IPL(RelationName, IPLEntry, SeqNo)

where *PROCDEF* has an entry for each procedure defined and *IPL* maintains the precedence lists for all relations. The attributes in *PROCDEF* represent the procedure name, the argument type name, and the unique identifier for the procedure code stored in another catalog. The attributes in *IPL* represent the relation, an IPL entry for the relation, and the sequence number for that entry in the IPL of the relation. With these two catalogs, the query to find the correct procedure for the call

Comp(STUDEMP)

is[5]

```
retrieve (P.ProcId)
from P in PROCDEF, I in IPL
where P.ProcName = "Comp"
  and I.RelationName = "STUDEMP"
  and I.IPLEntry = P.ArgName
  and I.SeqNo = MIN(I.SeqNo
    by I.RelationName
    where I.IPLEntry = P.ArgName
      and P.ProcName = "Comp"
      and I.RelationName = "STUDEMP")
```

---

[4] We are using a rule that is similar to the rule for the new Common Lisp object model [4]. It is actually slightly more complicated than described here in order to eliminate some nasty cases that arise when there are cycles in the inheritance hierarchy.

[5] This query uses a QUEL-style aggregate function.

This query can be precomputed to speed up procedure selection.

In summary, the major changes required to support procedure inheritance is 1) allow tuples as arguments to procedures, 2) define a representation for variable argument lists, and 3) implement a procedure selection mechanism. This extension to the relational model is relatively straightforward and only requires a small number of changes to the DBMS implementation.

5. Other Data Models

This section compares the POSTGRES data model to semantic, functional, and object-oriented data models.

Semantic and functional data models [8,11,16,18,19,27] do not provide the flexibility provided by the model described here. They cannot easily represent data with uncertain structure (e.g., objects with shared subobjects that have different types).

Modeling ideas oriented toward complex objects [12,15] cannot deal with objects that have a variety of shared subobjects. POSTGRES uses procedures to represent shared subobjects which does not have limitation on the types of subobjects that are shared. Moreover, the nested-dot notation allows convenient access to selected subobjects, a feature not present in these systems.

Several proposals have been made to support data models that contain non-first normal form relations [3,7,9]. The POSTGRES data model can be used to support non-first normal form relations with procedure-types. Consequently, POSTGRES seems to contain a superset of the capabilities of these proposals.

Object-oriented data models [2,6] have modeling constructs to deal with uncertain structure. For example, GemStone supports union types which can be used to represent subobjects that have different types [6]. Sharing of subobjects is represented by storing the subobjects as separate records and connecting them to a parent object with pointer-chains. Precomputed procedure values will, in our opinion, make POSTGRES performance competitive with pointer-chain proposals. The performance problem with pointer-chains will be most obvious when an object is composed of a large number of subobjects. POSTGRES will

avoid this problem because the pointer-chain is represented as a relation and the system can use all of the query processing and storage structure techniques available in the system to represent it. Consequently, POSTGRES uses a different approach that supports the same modeling capabilities and an implementation that may have better performance.

Finally, the POSTGRES data model could claim to be object-oriented, though we prefer not to use this word because few people agree on exactly what it means. The data model provides the same capabilities as an object-oriented model, but it does so without discarding the relational model and without having to introduce a new confusing terminology.

6. Summary

The POSTGRES data model uses the ideas of abstract data types, data of type procedure, and inheritance to extend the relational model. These ideas can be used to simulate a variety of semantic data modeling concepts (e.g., aggregation and generalization). In addition, the same ideas can be used to support complex objects that have unpredicatable composition and shared subobjects.

References

1.   M. E. Adiba and B. G. Lindsay, "Database Snapshots", *Proc. 6th Int. Conf. on Very Large Databases*, Montreal, Canada, Oct. 1980, 86-91.

2.   T. Anderson and et. al., "PROTEUS: Objectifying the DBMS User Interface", *Proc. Int. Wkshp on Object-Oriented Database Systems*, Asilomar, CA, Sep. 1986.

3.   D. Batory and et.al., "GENESIS: A Reconfigurable Database Management System", Tech. Rep. 86-07, Dept. of Comp. Sci., Univ. of Texas at Austin, 1986.

4.   D. B. Bobrow and et.al., "COMMONLOOPS; Merging Lisp and Object-Oriented Programming", *Proc. 1986 ACM OOPSLA Conf.*, Portland, OR, Sep. 1986, 17-29.

5. E. F. Codd, "A Relational Model of Data for Large Shared Data Bases", *Comm. of the ACM*, JUNE 1970.

6. G. Copeland and D. Maier, "Making Smalltalk a Database System", *Proc. 1984 ACM-SIGMOD Int. Conf. on the Mgt. of Data*, June 1984.

7. P. Dadam and et.al., "A DBMS Prototype to Support Extended NF2 Relations: An Integrated View on Flat Tables and Hierarchies", *Proc. ACM-SIGMOD Conf. on Mgt. of Data*, Washington, DC, May 1986.

8. U. Dayal and et.al., "A Knowledge-Oriented Database Management System", *Proc. Islamorada Conference on Large Scale Knowledge Base and Reasoning Systems*, Feb. 1985.

9. U. Deppisch and et.al., "A Storage System for Complex Objects", *Proc. Int. Wkshp on Object-Oriented Database Systems*, Asilomar, CA, Sep. 1986.

10. H. Garcia-Molina and et.al., "DataPatch: Integrating Inconsistent Copies of a Database after a Partition", Tech. Rep. Tech. Rep.# 304, Dept. Elec. Eng. and Comp. Sci., Princeton, NJ, 1984.

11. M. Hammer and D. McLeod, "Database Description with SDM", *ACM-Trans. Database Systems*, Sep. 1981.

12. R. Haskins and R. Lorie, "On Extending the Functions of a Relational Database System", *Proc. 1982 ACM-SIGMOD Conference on Management of Data*, Orlando, FL, JUNE 1982.

13. G. Held, M. R. Stonebraker and E. Wong, "INGRES -- A Relational Data Base System", *Proc. AFIPS NCC*, 1975, 409-416.

14. R. Kung and et.al., "Heuristic Search in Database Systems", *Proc. 1st International Workshop on Expert Data Bases*, Kiowah, SC, Oct. 1984.

15. R. Lorie and W. Plouffee, "Complex Objects and Their Use in Design Transactions", *Proc. Engineering Design Applications Stream of ACM-IEEE Data Base Week*, San Jose, CA, May 1983.

16. J. Myloupoulis and et.al., "A Language Facility for Designing Database Intensive Applications", *ACM-Trans. Database Systems*, JUNE 1980.

17. L. A. Rowe, "A Shared Object Hierarchy", *Proc. Int. Wkshp on Object-Oriented Database Systems*, Asilomar, CA, Sep. 1986.

18. D. Shipman, "The Functional Model and the Data Language Daplex", *ACM-Trans. Database Systems*, Mar. 1981.

19. J. Smith and D. Smith, "Database Abstractions: Aggregation and Generalization", *ACM Trans. Database Systems*, JUNE 1977.

20. M. Stefik and D. G. Bobrow, "Object-Oriented Programming: Themes and Variations", *The AI Magazine* 6, 4 (Winter 1986), 40-62.

21. M. R. Stonebraker and et. al., "QUEL as a Data Type", *Proc. 1984 ACM-SIGMOD Conf. on the Mgt. of Data*, May 1984.

22. M. R. Stonebraker, "Triggers and Inference in Data Base Systems", *Proc. Islamorada Conference on Large Scale Knowledge Base and Reasoning Systems*, Feb. 1985.

23. M. R. Stonebraker and L. A. Rowe, "The Design of POSTGRES", *Proc. 1986 ACM-SIGMOD Int. Conf. on the Mgt. of Data*, June 1986.

24. M. R. Stonebraker, "Object Management in POSTGRES Using Procedures", *Proc. Int. Wkshp on Object-Oriented Database Systems*, Asilomar, CA, Sep. 1986.

25. M. R. Stonebraker, "Inclusion of New Types in Relational Data Base Systems", *Proc. Second Int. Conf. on Data Base Eng.*, Los Angeles, CA, Feb. 1986.

26. M. R. Stonebraker, "POSTGRES Storage System", Submitted for publication, 1987.

27. C. Zaniola, "The Database Language GEM", *Proc. 1983 ACM-SIGMOD Conference on Management of Data*, San Jose, CA., May 1983.

The EXODUS Extensible DBMS Project: An Overview

Michael J. Carey, David J. DeWitt,
Goetz Graefe, David M. Haight,
Joel E. Richardson, Daniel T. Schuh,
Eugene J. Shekita, and Scott L. Vandenberg

Computer Sciences Department
University of Wisconsin
Madison, WI 53706

ABSTRACT

This paper presents an overview of EXODUS, an extensible database system project that is addressing data management problems posed by a variety of challenging new applications. The goal of the project is to facilitate the fast development of high-performance, application-specific database systems. EXODUS provides certain kernel facilities, including a versatile storage manager. In addition, it provides an architectural framework for building application-specific database systems; powerful tools to help automate the generation of such systems, including a rule-based query optimizer generator and a persistent programming language; and libraries of generic software components (e.g., access methods) that are likely to be useful for many application domains. We briefly describe each of the components of EXODUS in this paper, and we also describe a next-generation DBMS that we are now building using the EXODUS tools.

1. INTRODUCTION

Until fairly recently, research and development efforts in the database systems area have focused primarily on supporting traditional business applications. The design of database systems capable of supporting non-traditional application areas, such as computer-aided design and manufacturing, scientific and statistical applications, large-scale AI systems, and image/voice applications, has now emerged as an important research direction. Such new applications differ from conventional database applications and from each other in a number of important ways. First of all, their data modeling requirements vary widely. The kinds of entities and relationships relevant to a VLSI circuit design are quite different from those of a banking application. Second, each new application area has a different, specialized set of operations that must be efficiently supported by the database system. For example, it makes little sense to talk about doing joins between satellite images. Efficient support for such specialized operations also requires new types of storage structures and access methods. For applications like VLSI design, involving spatial objects, R-Trees [Gutt84] are a useful access method for data storage and manipulation; to manage image data efficiently, the database system needs to provide large arrays as a basic data type. Finally, a number of new application areas require support for multiple versions of their entities [Snod85, Daya86, Katz86].

A number of research projects are addressing the needs of new applications by developing approaches to making a database system *extensible* [DBE87]. These projects include EXODUS[1] at the University of Wisconsin [Care86a, Carey86c], PROBE at CCA [Daya86, Mano86], POSTGRES at UC Berkeley [Ston86b, Rowe87], STARBURST at IBM Almaden Research Center [Schw86, Lind87], and GENESIS at the University of Texas-Austin [Bato88a, Bato88b]. Although the goals of these projects are similar, and each uses some of the same mechanisms to provide extensibility, their overall approaches are quite different. For example, POSTGRES is a complete

This research was partially supported by the Defense Advanced Research Projects Agency under contract N00014-85-K-0788, by the National Science Foundation under grant IRI-8657323, by IBM through two Fellowships, by DEC through its Incentives for Excellence program, and by donations from Apple Corporation, GTE Laboratories, the Microelectronics and Computer Technology Corporation (MCC), and Texas Instruments.

[1] EXODUS: A departure; in this case, from traditional approaches to database management. Also an EXtensible Object-oriented Database System.

database management system, with a query language (POSTQUEL), a predefined way of supporting complex objects (through the use of procedures as a data type), support for "active" databases via triggers and alerters, and inferencing. Extensibility is provided via new data types, new access methods, and a simplified recovery mechanism. A stated goal is to "make as few changes as possible to the relational model." The PROBE system, on the other hand, is an advanced DBMS with support for complex objects and operations on them, dimensional data (in both space and time dimensions), and a capability for limited recursive query processing. Unlike POSTGRES, PROBE provides a mechanism for directly representing complex objects; the PROBE query language is an extension of DAPLEX [Ship81]. STARBURST is an extensible DBMS based on the relational data model, and its design is intended to allow knowledgeable programmers to add extensions "on the side" in the form of abstract data types, access methods, and external storage structures. Like EXODUS, STARBURST uses a rule-based approach to query optimization to enable it to handle such extensions [Lohm88].

In contrast to these efforts, EXODUS and GENESIS are modular and modifiable systems, rather than being complete, end-user DBMSs for handling all new application areas. The GENESIS project is aimed at identifying primitive building blocks, together with facilities for describing how to combine building blocks, in order to allow a new DBMS to be automatically composed from a library of existing database components. The goal of the EXODUS project (which is in some sense a "database software engineering" project) is to provide a collection of kernel DBMS facilities together with software tools to enable the semi-automatic construction of an application-specific DBMS for a given new application area. Included in EXODUS are tools intended to simplify the development of new DBMS components (e.g., a new access method or a new query language operator).

In this paper we describe the EXODUS approach to achieving extensibility. Section 2 of the paper provides an overview of the various components of EXODUS. Section 3 describes the lowest level of the system, the Storage Manager. Section 4 discusses the EXODUS approach to handling two difficult tasks involved in extending a database system: implementing new access methods, and implementing new, application-specific database operations. EXODUS simplifies these tasks by providing a programming language called E, which extends C++ [Stro86] with facilities for persistent systems programming. Section 5 describes the rule-based approach to query optimization employed in EXODUS. Section 6 describes EXTRA and EXCESS, a data model and query language that we are now building using the aforementioned tools. Finally, Section 7 summarizes the paper and discusses the implementation status of the various components of the EXODUS project.

2. AN OVERVIEW OF THE EXODUS ARCHITECTURE

Since one of the principal goals of the EXODUS project is to provide extensibility without sacrificing performance, the design of EXODUS reflects a careful balance between what EXODUS provides for the user[2] and what the user must explicitly provide. Unlike POSTGRES, PROBE, or STARBURST, EXODUS is not intended to be a complete system with provisions for user-added extensions. Rather, it is intended more as a "toolkit" that can be easily adapted to satisfy the needs of new application areas. In this section we summarize our overall approach and briefly introduce each of the key components and tools of EXODUS.

2.1. The EXODUS Approach

Two basic mechanisms are employed in EXODUS to help achieve our extensibility and performance goals: First, where feasible, we furnish a generic solution that should be applicable to database systems for most any application area. As an example, EXODUS supplies at its lowest level a layer of software termed the Storage Manager which provides support for concurrent and recoverable operations on storage objects of any size. Our feeling is that this level provides sufficient capabilities such that user-added extensions will not be necessary. However, due to both generality and efficiency considerations, such a single, generic solution is not possible for every component of a database system.

---

[2] Our use of the word *user* will be more carefully explained in the paragraphs ahead.

In cases where a single, generic solution is inappropriate, EXODUS instead provides either a *generator* or a *library* to aid the user in constructing the appropriate software. As an example, we expect EXODUS to be used for a wide variety of applications, each with a potentially different query language. As a result, it is not possible for EXODUS to furnish a single, generic query language; this also makes it impossible for a single query optimizer to suffice for all applications. Instead, we provide a generator for producing query optimizers for algebraic query languages. The EXODUS query optimizer generator takes as input a collection of rules regarding the operators of the query language, the transformations that can be legally applied to these operators (e.g., moving selections before joins in a relational algebra query), and a description of the methods that can be used to execute each operator (including their costs and side effects). As output, it produces an optimizer for the application's query language in the form of a C program.

In a conventional database system environment it is customary to consider the roles of two different classes of individuals: the database administrator and the user. In EXODUS, a third type of individual is required to customize EXODUS into an application-specific database system. While we referred to this individual loosely as a "user" in the preceding paragraphs, he or she is not a user in the normal sense (i.e., an end user, such as a bank teller or a cartographer). Rather, this user of the EXODUS facilities is a "database engineer" or DBE; our goal has been to engineer EXODUS so that only a moderate amount of database expertise is needed in order for a DBE to architect a new system using the tools. Once EXODUS has been customized into an application-specific database system, the DBE's initial role is completed and the role of the database administrator begins. Thereafter, the DBE's role is to provide incremental improvements (if any), such as more efficient access methods or faster operator implementations.

2.2. EXODUS System Architecture

We present an overview of the design of EXODUS in the remainder of this section. While EXODUS is a toolkit and not a complete DBMS, we find it clearer to describe the system from the viewpoint of an application-specific database system that was constructed using EXODUS. In doing so, we hope to make it clear which pieces of the system are provided without modification, which can be generated automatically, and which must be directly implemented by the DBE using the E programming language.

Figure 1 presents the general structure of an application-specific database management system implemented using EXODUS. The major facilities provided to aid the DBE in the task of generating such a system are as follows:

(1)   The Storage Manager.

(2)   The E programming language and its compiler.

(3)   A library of type-independent Access and Operator Methods.

(4)   A rule-based Query Optimizer Generator.

(5)   Tools for constructing query language front-ends.

At the bottom level of the system is the Storage Manager. The basic abstraction at this level is the storage object, which is an untyped, uninterpreted, variable-length byte sequence of arbitrary size. The Storage Manager provides capabilities for reading and updating storage objects without regard for their size. To further enhance the functionality provided by this level, buffer management, concurrency control, and recovery mechanisms for operations on shared storage objects are also provided. Finally, a versioning mechanism that can be used to support a variety of application-specific versioning schemes is provided. A more detailed description of the Storage Manager is presented in Section 3.

Although not shown in Figure 1, which really depicts the run-time structure of an EXODUS-based DBMS, the next major component is the E programming language and its compiler. E is the implementation language for all components of the system for which the DBE must provide code. E extends C++ by adding generic classes, iterators, and support for persistent object types to the C++ type facilities and control constructs. For the most part, references to persistent objects look just like references to other C++ objects; the DBE's index code can thus deal

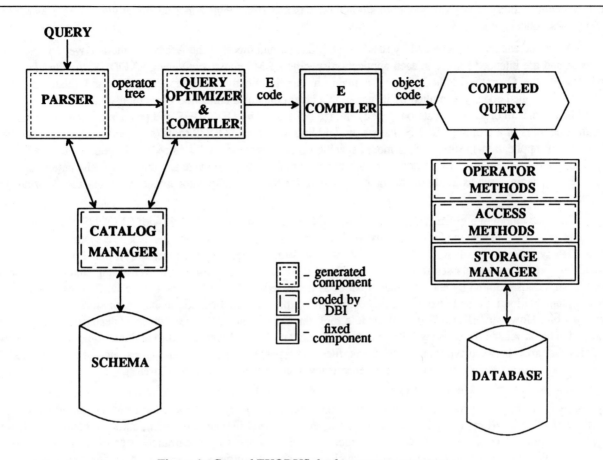

Figure 1: General EXODUS database system structure.

with index nodes as arrays of key-pointer pairs, for example. Where persistent objects are referenced, the E compiler is responsible for inserting calls to fix/unfix buffers, to read/write the appropriate portions of the underlying storage objects, and to handle other such low-level details. Thus, the DBE is freed from having to worry about the internal structure of persistent objects. In order to regain performance, E will also enable the DBE to provide guidance to the compiler in certain ways (e.g., by providing information to aid it in doing buffer management). E should not be confused with database programming languages such as Pascal/R [Schm77] or RIGEL [Rowe79], as these languages were intended to simplify the development of database applications code through a closer integration of database and programming language constructs. Similarly, despite its object-orientedness (stemming from C++), it should not be confused with object-oriented database languages such as OPAL [Cope84, Maie87] or COP [Andr87]. The objective of E is to simplify the development of *internal* systems software for a DBMS.

Layered above the Storage Manager is a collection of access methods that provide associative access to files of storage objects and further support for versioning (if desired). For access methods, EXODUS will provide a library of type-independent index structures such as B+ trees, Grid files [Niev84], and linear hashing [Litw80]. These access methods will be written using the generic class capability provided by the E language, as described in Section 4. This capability enables existing access methods to be used with DBE-defined abstract data types without modification — as long as the capabilities provided by the data type satisfy the requirements of the access methods. In addition, a DBE may wish to implement new types of access methods in the process of developing an application-specific database system. Since new access methods are written in E, the DBE is shielded from having to map main memory data structures onto storage objects and from having to deal directly with other low-level details of secondary storage.

While the capabilities provided by the Storage Manager and much of the Access Methods Layer are general-purpose and are intended for use in each application-specific DBMS constructed using EXODUS, the third layer in the design, the Operator Methods Layer, contains a mix of mostly DBE-supplied code and relatively little EXODUS-supplied code. As implied by its name, this layer contains a collection of methods that can be combined with one another in order to operate on (typed) storage objects. While EXODUS will provide a library of methods for the operators of a prototype DBMS that we are building with the EXODUS tools (see Section 6), we expect that a number of application-specific or data-model-specific operator methods will be needed. In general, the DBE will have to implement one or more methods for each operator in the query language associated with the target application. E will again serve as the implementation language for this task. Operator methods are discussed further in Section 4.

The data model of a given application-oriented DBMS is defined by the DBE, with EXODUS providing what amounts to an internal data model via the type system of the E programming language. E's type system includes the basic C++ types (e.g., int, float, char) and type constructors (e.g., class, struct, union, array), plus it provides additional support for generic classes and typed files. These facilities provide sufficient power to implement the higher-level abstractions required by end-user data models, as discussed further in Section 4. The DBE is responsible for this implementation task, and also for implementing (in E) the associated catalog manager for storing user schema information. However, EXODUS does provide a tool, the Dependency Manager, which is designed to help keep track of schema-related dependency information. In particular, this tool is intended to maintain type-related dependencies that arise between types and other types, files and types, stored queries and types, etc., at the data model level. More information about the EXODUS dependency manager can be found in [Care87].

The execution of a query in EXODUS follows a set of transformations similar to that of a relational query in System R [Astr76]. The parser is responsible for transforming the query from its initial form into an initial tree of database operators. After parsing, the query is optimized, converted into an E program, and then compiled into an executable form. The output produced by the query optimizer consists of a rearranged tree of operator methods (i.e., particular instances of each operator) to which query specific information such as selection predicates (e.g., name = "Mike" and salary > $200,000) will be passed as parameters. As mentioned earlier, EXODUS provides a generator for producing the optimization portion of the query compiler. To produce an optimizer for an application-specific database system, the DBE must supply a description of the operators of the target query language, a list of the methods that can used to implement each operator, a cost formula for each operator method, and a collection of transformation rules. The optimizer generator will transform these description files into C source code for an optimizer for the target query language. At query execution time, this optimizer behaves as we have just described, taking a query expressed as a tree of operators and transforming it into an optimized execution plan expressed as a tree of methods. Section 5 describes the optimizer generator in greater detail.

Finally, the organization of the top level of a database system generated using EXODUS depends on whether the goal is to support some sort of interactive interface, a query facility embedded in a programming language, or an altogether different kind of interface. In the future we would like to provide tools to facilitate the creation of interactive interfaces. We are currently implementing one such interface for the object-oriented data model and query language described in Section 6. Through doing so, we hope to gain insight into the kind of tools that would be helpful at the interface level of the system (in addition to learning how effective the current tool set is).

3. THE STORAGE MANAGER

In this section we summarize the key features of the EXODUS Storage Manager. We begin by discussing the interface that the Storage Manager provides to higher levels of the system, and then we describe how arbitrarily large storage objects are handled efficiently. We discuss the techniques employed for versioning, concurrency control, recovery, and buffer management for storage objects, and we close with a brief discussion about files of storage objects. A more detailed discussion of these issues can be found in [Care86b].

3.1. The Storage Manager Interface

The Storage Manager provides a procedural interface. This interface includes procedures to create and destroy files and to open and close files for file scans. For scanning purposes, the Storage Manager provides a call to get the object ID of the next object within a file. It also provides procedures for creating and destroying storage objects within a file. For reading storage objects, the Storage Manager provides a call to get a pointer to a range of bytes within a given storage object; the desired byte range is read into the buffers, and a pointer to the range is returned to the caller. Another call is provided to inform the system that these bytes are no longer needed, which "unpins" them in the buffer pool. For writing storage objects, a call is provided to ask the system to modify a subrange of the bytes that were read. For shrinking/growing storage objects, calls to insert bytes into and delete bytes from a specified offset in a storage object are provided, as is a call to append bytes to the end of an object. Finally, for transaction management, the Storage Manager provides begin, commit, and abort transaction calls; additional hooks are planned to aid in implementing concurrent and recoverable operations for new access methods efficiently.

In addition to the functionality outlined above, the Storage Manager is designed to accept a variety of performance-related hints. For example, the object creation routine mentioned above accepts hints about where to place a new object (i.e., "place the new object near the object with object ID X"). The buffer manager accepts hints about the size and number of buffers to use and what replacement policy to employ; these hints are supported by allowing a *buffer group* to be specified with each object access, and having the buffer manager accept these hints on a per-buffer-group basis. Buffer management policies ranging from simple schemes like global LRU to complex schemes such as DBMIN [Chou85] are thus easily supported.

3.2. Storage Objects and Operations

As described earlier, the *storage object* is the basic unit of data in the Storage Manager. Storage objects can be either small or large, a distinction that is hidden from higher layers of EXODUS software. Small storage objects reside on a single disk page, whereas large storage objects occupy potentially many disk pages. In either case, the object identifier (OID) of a storage object has the form (*volume #*, *page #*, *slot #*, *unique #*), with the *unique #* being used to make OID's unique over time (and thus usable as surrogates). The OID of a small object points to the object on disk; for a large object, the OID points to its *large object header*. A large object header can reside on a slotted page with other large object headers and small storage objects, and it contains pointers to other pages involved in the representation of the large object. Other pages in a large object are private rather than being shared with other objects (although pages are shared between versions of an object). When a small object grows to the point where it can no longer be accommodated on a single page, the Storage Manager automatically converts it into a large object, leaving its object header in place of the original small object. We considered the alternative of using purely logical surrogates for OID's rather than physical addresses, as in other recent proposals [Cope84, Ston86b], but efficiency considerations led us to opt for a "physical surrogate" scheme — with logical surrogates, it would always be necessary to access objects via a surrogate index.

Figure 2 shows an example of our large object data structure. Conceptually, a large object is an uninterpreted byte sequence; physically, it is represented as a B+ tree-like index on byte position within the object plus a collection of leaf blocks (with all data bytes residing in the leaves).[3] The large object header contains a number of (*count*, *page #*) pairs, one for each child of the root. The count value associated with each child pointer gives the maximum byte number stored in the subtree rooted at that child, and the rightmost child pointer's count is therefore also the size of the object. Internal nodes are similar, being recursively defined as the root of another object contained within its parent node, so an absolute byte offset within a child translates to a relative offset within its parent node. The left child of the root in Figure 2 contains bytes 1-421, and the right child contains the rest of the object (bytes 422-786). The rightmost leaf node in the figure contains 173 bytes of data. Byte 100 within this leaf node is byte $192 + 100 = 292$ within the right child of the root, and it is byte $421 + 292 = 713$ within the object as a whole.

---

[3] This data structure was inspired by the ordered relation index of [Ston83], but our update algorithms are quite different [Care86b].

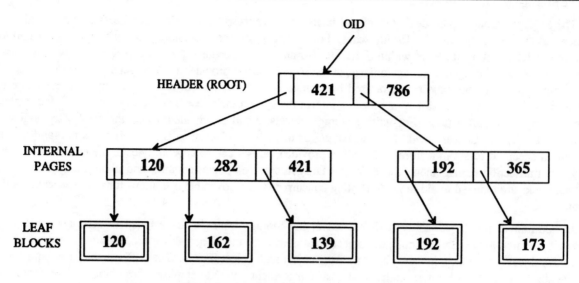

Figure 2: An example of a large storage object.

Searching is accomplished by computing overall offset information while descending the tree to the desired byte position. As described in [Care86b], object sizes up to 1 GB or so can be supported with only three tree levels (header and leaf levels included).

Associated with the large storage object data structure are algorithms to *search* for a range of bytes (and perhaps update them), to *insert* a sequence of bytes at a given point in the object, to *append* a sequence of bytes to the end of the object, and to *delete* a sequence of bytes from a given point in the object. The insert, append, and delete operations are novel because inserting or deleting an arbitrary number of bytes (as opposed to a single byte) into a large storage object poses some unique problems compared to inserting or deleting a single record from a B+ tree or an ordered relation. Algorithms for these operations are described in detail in [Care86b] along with results from an experimental evaluation of their storage utilization and performance characteristics. The evaluation showed that the EXODUS storage object mechanism can provide operations on very large dynamic objects at relatively low cost, and at a reasonable level of storage utilization (e.g., 80% for large dynamic objects, and very close to 100% for large static objects).

3.3. Versions of Storage Objects

The Storage Manager provides primitive support for versions of storage objects. Versions of objects are identified simply by OIDs. A storage object can have both *working* (current) versions and *frozen* (old) versions; this distinction is recorded in each version's object header. Working versions may be updated by transactions, while frozen versions are immutable. A working version of an object can be made into a frozen version, and new working versions can be derived from frozen versions as desired. It is also possible to delete a version of an object when that particular version is no longer of interest. The reason for providing this rather primitive level of version support is that different EXODUS applications may have widely different notions of how versions should be supported [Ston81, Dada84, Clif85, Klah85, Snod85, Katz86]. We do not omit version management altogether for efficiency reasons — it would be prohibitively expensive, both in terms of storage space and I/O cost, to maintain versions of large objects by maintaining entire copies of objects.

Versions of large objects are maintained by copying and updating the pages that differ from version to version. Figure 3 illustrates this by an example. The figure shows two versions of the large storage object of Figure 2,

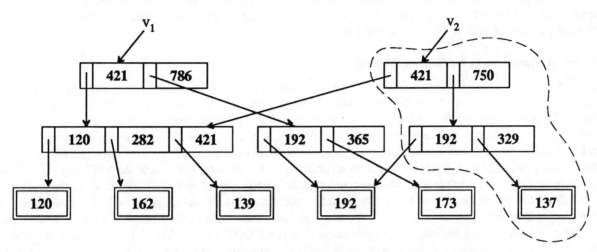

Figure 3: Two versions of a large storage object.

the original (frozen) version, V_1, and a newer (working) version, V_2. In this example, V_2 was created by deriving a working version from V_1 and subsequently deleting its last 36 bytes. Note that V_2 shares all pages of V_1 that are unchanged, and it has its own copies of each modified page; each page pointer has a bit associated with it (not shown in the figure) that distinguishes pointers to shared pages from pointers to unshared pages. Deriving a new version of a large storage object creates a new copy of the root of the object, with subsequent updates leading to the creation of copies of other nodes as needed. Since the number of internal pages in an actual large object is small relative to the number of data pages in the object (due to high fanout for internal nodes), the overhead for versioning large objects in this scheme is small — it is basically proportional to the difference between adjacent versions, and not to the overall size of the objects. In the case of small objects, versioning is accomplished by simply copying the entire object when creating a new version.

A working version such as V_2 may be updated via the insert, append, delete, and write operations provided for all storage objects, and the Storage Manager also supports the deletion of unwanted versions of objects, as noted above. When deleting a version of a large object, however, we must be careful — we must avoid discarding any of the object's pages that are shared (and thus needed) by other versions of the same object. An efficient version deletion algorithm that addresses this problem, providing a safe way to delete one version with respect to a set of other versions that are to be retained, is presented in [Care86b].[4]

3.4. Concurrency Control and Recovery

The Storage Manager provides concurrency control and recovery services for storage objects. Two-phase locking [Gray79] of storage objects and files is used for concurrency control. For recovery, small storage objects are handled using before/after-image logging and in-place updating at the object level [Gray79]. Recovery for large storage objects is handled using a combination of shadowing and logging — updated internal pages and leaf blocks are shadowed up to the root level, with updates being installed atomically by overwriting the old object header with

---

[4] The notion of frozen/working versions was not present in [Care86b], but its version deletion algorithm is still applicable. The frozen/working version distinction was added in order to allow versions of a large object to be updated by a series of transactions without forcing each one to derive a new version of the object.

the new header [Verh78]. The name and parameters of the operation that caused the update are logged, and a log sequence number [Gray79] is maintained on each large object's root page; this ensures that operations on large storage objects can be undone or redone as needed.

3.5. Buffer Management for Storage Objects

An objective of the EXODUS Storage Manager design is to minimize the amount of copying from buffer space that is required. A related objective is to allow sizable portions of large storage objects to be scanned directly in the buffer pool by higher levels of EXODUS software, but without requiring that large objects be small enough to fit entirely in the buffer pool. To accommodate these needs, buffer space is allocated in variable-length *buffer blocks*, which are integral numbers of contiguous pages, rather than in single-page units. When an EXODUS client requests that a sequence of N bytes be read from an object X, the non-empty portions of the leaf blocks of X containing the desired byte range are read into one contiguous buffer block by obtaining a buffer block of the appropriate size from the buffer space manager and then reading the pages into the buffer block in (strict) byte sequence order, placing the first data byte from a leaf page in the position immediately following the last data byte from the previous page. (Recall that leaf pages of large storage objects are usually not entirely full.) A descriptor is maintained for the current region of X in memory, including such information as the OID of X, a pointer to its buffer block, the length of the actual portion of the buffer block containing the bytes requested by the client, a pointer to the first such byte, and information about where the contents of the buffer block came from. The client receives a pointer to the descriptor through which the buffer contents may be accessed.[5] Free space for the buffer pool is managed using standard dynamic storage allocation techniques, and buffer block allocation and replacement is guided by the Storage Manager's hint mechanism.

3.6. Files of Storage Objects

Files are collections of storage objects, and they are useful for grouping objects together for several purposes. First, the EXODUS Storage Manager provides a mechanism for sequencing through all of the objects in a file, so related objects can be placed in a common file for sequential scanning purposes. Second, objects within a given file are placed on disk pages allocated to the file, so files provide support for objects that need to be tightly clustered on disk. A file is identified by a file identifier (FID) that points to its root page. Like large storage objects, files are represented by an index structure similar to a B+ tree, but the key for the index is different — a file index uses *disk page number* as its key. Each leaf page of the file index contains a collection of page numbers for slotted pages contained in the file. (The pages themselves are managed separately using standard disk allocation techniques.) The file index thus serves as a mechanism to gather the pages of a file together, and it also enables rapid scanning of all of the objects within a given file. Rapid scanning is a consequence of the fact that the file B+ tree is keyed on page number, meaning that a scan of the objects in a file will access them in *physical order*. Note that since all of the objects in a file are directly accessible via their OIDs, a file is *not* comparable to a surrogate index — secondary indices on the objects in a given file will contain OID entries, which point *directly* to the objects being indexed; this is important from a performance standpoint. Further discussion of file representation, operations, concurrency control, and recovery may be found in [Care86b].

4. METHOD IMPLEMENTATION SUPPORT

As described in Section 2, application-specific database systems include access methods and operator methods appropriate for their intended class of applications, and these will undoubtedly vary from one application area to another. For example, while B+ trees and hashing are usually sufficient as access methods for conventional business database systems, a database system for storing and manipulating spatial data is likely to need a spatial access method such as the KDB tree [Robi81], R tree [Gutt84], or Grid file [Niev84]. Unfortunately, such structures, being highly algorithmic in nature, require the DBE to implement them rather than simply specifying them in

---

[5] As is discussed in Section 4, the E language hides this structure from the DBE.

some high-level form. A complication is that a given index structure often needs to handle data of a variety of types (e.g., integers, reals, character strings, and various ADTs) as long as they satisfy the requirements for correct operation of the index structure. For instance, a B+ tree should work for all key types that provide an appropriate comparison operator [Ston86a]; this includes working for data types that are not defined by the DBE until after the index code has been completely written and debugged. Similar issues arise for operator methods, which must also be written in a general manner in order to handle new, unanticipated data types.

In adding a new access method to a DBMS, sources of complexity include (i) coding and verifying the new algorithms, (ii) mapping the new data structure onto the primitive objects provided by the storage system of the DBMS, (iii) making the access method code interact properly with the buffer manager, and (iv) ensuring that concurrency control and recovery are handled correctly. Although access method designers are mostly interested in item (i), this can comprise as little as 30% of the actual code that must be written; items (ii)-(iv) comprise the remaining 70% or so of the overall code needed to add an access method to a typical commercial DBMS [Ston85]. Items (i)-(iii) are all issues for operator methods as well, and again (i) is the issue that the DBE would presumably like to focus on. To improve this situation, EXODUS provides a programming language, E, for the DBE to use when implementing new methods. E is intended to shield the DBE from items (ii)-(iv), so the E compiler produces code to handle these details based on the DBE's index code (plus some declarative "hints").

In the remainder of this section, we describe the E language and how its various features simplify the DBE's programming tasks. E was designed with the DBMS architecture of Section 2 in mind, so the access methods, operator methods, and utility functions of the DBMS are all intended to be written in E. In addition to these components, the DBMS includes the Storage Manager and the E compiler itself. At runtime, database schema definitions (e.g., "create relation" commands) and queries are first translated into E programs and then compiled. One result of this architecture is a system in which the "impedance mismatch" [Cope84] between type systems is reduced. Another is that the system is easy to extend. For example, the DBE may add a new data type by coding it as an E class. The E programming language is an upward-compatible extension of C++ [Stro86]; E's extensions include both new language features and a number of predefined classes. We present the major features of E briefly here, and refer to the reader to [Rich87, Rich89a, Rich89b] for additional details and examples of how E constructs apply to DBMS implementation problems.

4.1. Persistence in E

In order to provide support for persistence, shielding the DBE from having to interact directly with the low-level, typeless view of storage objects provided by the Storage Manager, the E language mirrors the existing C++ type system with constructors having the *db* (database) attribute. Informally, a db type is defined to be:

(1)   A fundamental db type, including *dbshort, dbint, dblong, dbfloat, dbdouble, dbchar*, or *dbvoid*.

(2)   A *dbclass, dbstruct,* or *dbunion*. Such classes may have data members (fields) only of other db types, but the argument and return types of member functions (methods) are not similarly restricted.

(3)   A pointer to a db type object.

(4)   An array of db type objects.

An object that is to be persistent is required to be of a db type. However, a db type object can be either persistent or non-persistent. Note that any type definable in C++ may be analogously defined as a db type. Furthermore, since persistence is orthogonal [Atki87] over db types, one could program exclusively in db types and achieve the effect of strict orthogonality if so desired.[6] Db types were introduced in E so that the compiler can always distinguish between objects that can only reside in memory and those that generally reside on disk (but may also reside in memory), as their underlying implementation is very different; this distinction is made so that critical, main-memory-only types can be implemented every bit as efficiently as normal C++ types.

---

[6] Note that one could even use macros to redefine the keywords *class* to mean *dbclass*, *struct* to mean *dbstruct*, *union* to mean *dbunion*, *int* to mean *dbint*, etc.

Given db types for describing the type structure of objects that may be persistent, E supports the declaration of actual persistent objects via a new storage class called *persistent*; this is in addition to the usual C++ storage classes (extern, automatic, static, and register). For example, to declare a persistent object named emp of a dbclass named Employee in an E program, one would simply write:

```
persistent Employee emp;
```

This declaration causes the name emp to become a handle for a persistent Employee object; the object itself will reside in the Storage Manager. Uses of the object then look exactly like they would if emp were an instance of a normal C++ class. Similarly, member functions of the Employee dbclass are coded just as if it were an equivalent non-db class. The E compiler is implemented as an E-to-C translator, and it translates references to portions of persistent objects into C code that calls the Storage Manager as needed to manipulate the contents of persistent objects. Persistent E objects are mapped one-to-one onto storage objects, and pointers to db type objects are actually OIDs; thus, in E the DBE retains control over the format of persistent objects without having to explicitly make calls to the Storage Manager.

4.2. Generic Classes for Unknown Types

As described earlier, many of the types involved in database programming are not known until well after the code needing those types is written by the DBE. Access method code does not know what types of keys it will contain, nor what types of entities it will index, and the code implementing a join algorithm does not know what types of entities it will be called upon to join.

To address this problem, E augments C++ with *generic* (or generator) classes, which are very similar to the parameterized clusters of CLU [Lisk77]. Such a class is parameterized in terms of one or more unknown types; within the class definition, these (formal) type names can be used freely as regular type names.[7] This mechanism allows one to define, for example, a class of the form Stack[T] where the specific class T of the stack elements is not known. The user of such a class can then *instantiate* the generic class by providing actual type parameters to the class. For example, one may define a stack class IntStack for handling integer data and then declare an integer stack x by saying:[8]

```
class IntStack: Stack[int];
IntStack x;
```

Similarly, the DBE can implement a B+ tree as a generic dbclass BTree[KeyType, EntityType] where both the key type and the type of entity being indexed are dbclass parameters. Later, when a user wishes to build an index over employees on social security number, the system will generate and compile a small E program that instantiates and uses the dbclass:

```
Emp_BTree: BTree[SSNo_type, Emp_type];
persistent Emp_BTree EmpSSNoIndex;
```

Such instantiations are dealt with efficiently via a linking process along the lines of that used in the implementation of CLU [Atki78].

Figures 4a and 4b give a partial example of a generic dbclass, BTreeNode, to illustrate the flavor of how such classes are described in E. This dbclass represents the node structure of a B+ tree index, and once defined it could be used in writing the generic B+ tree dbclass discussed above (as we will show shortly). The interface portion of the dbclass is shown in Figure 4a. The dbclass has two dbclass parameters, KeyType and EntityType, and the dbclass KeyType is required to have a compare member function. KeyType and EntityType are

---

[7] In addition to type parameters, generic classes and dbclasses can also have constant and function parameters.

[8] We chose this syntax over Stack[int] x to maintain compatibility with the existing C++ class derivation syntax.

```
enum status { FOUND, NOT_FOUND };


dbclass BTreeNode
[
    dbclass KeyType{                    // type of keys in tree
        int   compare(KeyType);         // (compare function needed)
    },
    dbclass EntityType{ }               // type of indexed entities
]

{

public:

    // type for key-pointer pairs
    dbstruct KPpair {
      KeyType  keyVal;
      dbunion {
          EntityType*  entityPtr;       // used in leaf nodes
          BTreeNode*   childPtr;        // used in interior nodes
      } ptr;
    };

    // internal structure of a B+ tree node, consisting of the
    // node height (which is 0 for leaf nodes), the number of
    // keys currently in the node, and an array of key/pointer
    // pairs of the appropriate size
    dbint    height;
    dbint    nKeys;
    KPpair   kppArray[(PAGESIZE - 2*sizeof(int)) / sizeof(KPpair)];

    // binary search function for a single node
    status searchNode(KeyType key, int& index);

    // etc.  ...  (other node member functions)  ...

}; // dbclass BTreeNode
```

Figure 4a: The generic dbclass BTreeNode.

the key and entity types for the node, and the compare member function compares two keys[9] and returns -1, 0, or 1 depending on their relative order. The structure of a B+ tree node is described as having a height, a count of the keys in the node, and an array of key-pointer pairs. The size of the array is determined by the constant PAGESIZE, which is the maximum object size (in bytes) that will fit on one Storage Manager disk page, together with the size of

[9] It compares the key to which the function is applied with the key passed as an explicit function argument, as illustrated in Figure 4b.

```
// binary search of B+ tree node

status BTreeNode::searchNode(KeyType key, int& index) {

    int min = 0;
    int max = nKeys - 1;
    int mid;
    int cmpVal;

    while (min <= max) {

      mid = (min + max) / 2;
      cmpVal = kppArray[mid].keyVal.compare(key);

      if (cmpVal < 0)
          { min = mid + 1; }
      else if (cmpVal == 0)
          { index = mid; return FOUND; }
      else
          { max = mid - 1; }

    } // while

    return NOT_FOUND;

} // BTreeNode::searchNode
```

Figure 4b: Code for BTreeNode's searchNode member function.

a key-pointer pair.[10] The searchNode member function in Figure 4b shows that the code for potentially persistent (i.e., dbclass) objects looks just like normal C++ code.

4.3. Fileof[T] for Persistent Collections

In addition to providing support for persistent objects, and providing generic dbclasses for programming in the face of missing type information, E also provides support for handling large, scannable *collections* of persistent objects of similar type. E's provision here is a built-in generic dbclass, fileof[T], where T must be a dbclass. As an example, if Department is a dbclass, a useful new dbclass can be created via the declaration:

```
dbclass DeptFile: fileof[Department];
```

Objects of type DeptFile can now be used to hold entire sets of Department objects (including objects of any subclass of Department). The operational interface of the generic fileof class allows the user to bind typed pointers to objects in a file, to create and destroy objects in a file, etc. A file can also be viewed as a "persistent heap" in a sense, as the new statement for dynamically allocating persistent objects requires the specification of a

---

[10] This is not particularly elegant, but it is necessary for performance.

file in which to create the object.

As an example, the following function returns the sum of the budgets of the departments in a file of `Depart-ment` objects. The file is passed by reference, and we assume that `Department` objects have a public data member called `budget`:

```
float TotalBudget(DeptFile& depts)
{
    Department* d;
    float sum = 0.0;
    for(d = depts.get_first(); d != NULL; d = depts.get_next(d)) {
        sum += d->budget;
    }
    return sum;
}
```

While this example is extremely simple, it illustrates how easy it can be to scan the contents of a file of objects. No typecasting is needed to use the pointer d, and no buffer calls are necessary. Each instance of the `fileof` dbclass is implemented as a Storage Manager file and represented by its associated FID; the DBE is shielded from file-related Storage Manager calls by the `fileof` dbclass interface. Finally, for cases where the restriction of storing only instances of a type `T` and its subtypes in a file is too limiting, an untyped, byte-oriented `file` dbclass is also provided.

4.4. Iterators for Scans and Query Processing

A typical approach for structuring a database system is to include a layer which provides *scans* over objects in the database. A scan is a control abstraction which provides a state-saving interface to the "memoryless" storage systems calls. Such an interface is needed for the record-at-a-time processing done in higher layers. A typical implementation of scans will allocate a data structure, called a scan descriptor, to maintain all needed state between calls to the storage system; it is then up to the user to pass the descriptor with every call.

The control abstraction of a scan is provided in EXODUS via the notion of an *iterator* [Lisk77]. An iterator is a coroutine-like function that saves its data and control states between calls; each time the iterator produces (*yields*) a new value, it is suspended until it is resumed by the client. Thus, no matter how complicated the iterator may be, the client only sees a steady stream of values being produced. The client can invoke an iterator using a new kind of control statement, the *iterate* loop of E (which generalizes the *for ... in* loop of CLU).

The general idea for implementing scans should now be clear. For example, to implement a scan over B+ trees, one can write an iterator function for the `BTree` class that takes a lower bound and an upper bound as arguments. The scan will begin by searching down to the leaf level of the tree for the lower bound, keeping a stack of node pointers along the way. It will then walk the tree, yielding object references one at a time, until reaching the upper bound; alternatively, if leaves were linked together, it could walk through the sequence set. The iterator will then terminate. Figure 5 shows what the interface definition for such a generic `BTree` class might look like, including a constructor function to initialize a newly created B+ tree index, a destructor function that is invoked to clean up when a B+ tree is destroyed, member functions to insert and delete index entries, and the `scan` iterator that we just described.

Iterators can also be used to piece executable queries together from an access plan tree. If one views a query as a pipeline of processing filters, then each processing stage can be implemented as an iterator which is a client of one or more iterators (upstream in the pipe) and yields result tuples to the next stage (downstream in the pipe). Execution of the query pipeline will be demand-driven in nature. For example, the DBE for a relational DBMS would write various operator methods for the select, project, and join operations as iterators in this fashion. Given the access plan tree that results from optimizing a user query, it is not difficult to produce E code that implements the pipeline by plugging together instances of these iterators. This approach to forming queries is further described in [Rich87], and it was also the basis for a relational DBMS prototype that we developed using the EXODUS tools for a demonstration at SIGMOD-88. The idea is illustrated by the following excerpt from our relational DBMS prototype. This code is an iterator member function from a (generic) class that provides a method for the equi-join operator:

```
iterator DstType* index_join::next_tuple()
{
    DstType   rslt;
    AttrType  joinVal;

    iterate(SrcType1* outer = outerQuery->next_tuple()) {
        extract(outer, &joinVal);
        iterate(SrcType2* inner = innerIndex->scan(joinVal, joinVal)) {
            concatenate(outer, inner, &rslt);
            yield(&rslt);
        }
    }
}
```

This code implements the next_tuple iterator for computing a join via an index-based algorithm. SrcType1, SrcType2, and DstType are the outer, inner, and result tuple types (respectively), and AttrType is the type of the join attribute. The join method iterates over a stream of outer relation tuples using the iterator next_tuple provided by the subquery (outerQuery) feeding the join, and for each tuple it extracts its join attribute value using the function extract. It then scans the inner relation via a B+ tree index on the join attribute

---

```
dbclass BTree [
    dbclass KeyType{                        // type of keys in tree
        int  compare(KeyType);              // (compare function needed)
    },
    dbclass EntityType{ }                   // type of indexed entities
]
{
    // instantiate types used for B+ tree index
    dbclass Node: BTreeNode[KeyType, EntityType];
    dbclass NodeFile: fileof[Node];

    // represent B+ tree as file of nodes plus root pointer
    NodeFile       tree;
    Node*          root;

public:
    BTree();        // constructor function
    ~BTree();       // destructor function
    EntityType* insert(KeyType, EntityType*);
    EntityType* delete(KeyType, EntityType*);
    iterator EntityType* scan(KeyType, KeyType);
}; // dbclass BTree
```

Figure 5: Interface for the generic dbclass BTree.

(innerIndex), using the B+ tree's scan iterator to find matching inner tuples. Each time it finds a matching tuple it calls the concatenate function to concatenate the outer and inner tuples, forming a result tuple, and yields the result tuple to the next operator method in the query stream. (The extract and concatenate functions and the outerQuery and innerIndex pointers are initialized based on arguments passed to the index_join class constructor, as shown in a more complete example in [Rich87].)

4.5. Method Performance Issues

Since E is the language used by the DBE to implement key portions of the code for a DBMS, performance is clearly an important issue. One performance issue related to E is how frequently the code produced by the E compiler issues calls to the Storage Manager. We are currently working on an optimization pass for the E compiler that will perform transformations to reduce this frequency. For example, if a number of fields of an object are referenced, the compiler should generate a single call to retrieve the relevant portion of the object all at once (as opposed to a series of individual calls). Or, if an object is a large array (e.g., an image), it may be useful/necessary to transform a loop that processes all of the elements in the array into a nested loop that processes a block of array elements at a time. We also plan to add "hint" facilities to E in order to allow the DBE to guide the E compiler in making performance-related decisions (e.g., by specifying buffer group sizes and replacement policies for critical operations).

A second performance issue, relevant especially to access method code, is that of specialized locking and recovery schemes (e.g., B+ tree locking protocols [Baye77]). While the two-phase locking and log-based recovery mechanisms employed by the Storage Manager will ensure the correct and recoverable operation of E programs, these mechanisms are likely to prove too restrictive for a truly high-performance DBMS. Our long-term goal is to add transaction control facilities to E in order to permit clever DBEs to implement index-specific concurrency control and recovery algorithms when they are needed.

4.6. Modeling End-User Schemas

As discussed briefly in Section 2, the type system of the E language can in some sense be viewed as the internal type system of EXODUS: To support a target end-user data model, the DBE must thus develop mappings from the data model's type system to E's type system; the collection of available primitive internal EXODUS types thus includes integers, floating point numbers, characters, and enumerations, and the available type constructors include pointers, arrays, structures, and unions. New abstract data types (e.g., rectangle, complex number, or image) and their associated operations can be defined as E dbclasses. In addition, new data model type constructors (e.g., list or set) can be modeled by implementing them as parameterized E dbclasses. Since E provides pointers together with a rich collection of type constructors, even complex, recursive, end-user object types can be modeled in E without too much difficulty. We thus expect that the internal type system of EXODUS will be powerful enough to satisfactorily model most any application area's type system.

5. QUERY OPTIMIZATION AND COMPILATION

Given the unforeseeably wide variety of data models we hope to support with EXODUS, each with its own operators (and corresponding methods), EXODUS includes a query optimizer *generator* that produces an application-specific query optimizer from an input specification. The generated optimizer repeatedly applies algebraic transformations to a query and selects access paths for each operation in the transformed query. This transformational approach is outlined by Ullman for relational DBMSs [Ullm82], and it has been used in the Microbe database project [Nguy82] with rules coded as Pascal procedures. We initially considered using a rule-based AI language to implement a general-purpose optimizer, and then to augment it with data model specific rules. Prolog [Cloc81] and OPS5 [Forg81] seemed like interesting candidates, as each provides a built-in "inference engine" or search mechanism. However, this convenience also limits their use, as their search algorithms are rather fixed and hard to augment with search heuristics (which are very important for query optimization). Based on this limitation, and also on further considerations such as call compatibility with other EXODUS components and optimizer execution speed, we decided instead to provide an optimizer generator [Grae87a, Grae87b] which produces an optimization procedure in the C programming language [Kern78].

The generated optimization procedure takes a query as its input, producing an access plan as its output. A query in this context is a tree-like expression with logical operators as internal nodes (e.g., a join in a relational DBMS) and sets of objects (e.g., relations) as leaves. It is not part of the optimizer's task to produce an initial algebraic query tree from a non-procedural expression; this is done by the user interface and parser. An access plan is a tree with operator methods as internal nodes (e.g., a nested loops join method) and with files or indices as leaves. Once an access plan is obtained, it is then transformed into an iterator-based E program by a procedure that walks the access plan tree (in a manner loosely related to that of [Frey86]).

5.1. Basic Optimizer Generator Inputs

There are four key elements which the optimizer generator requires in a description file in order to generate an optimizer: (1) the operators, (2) the methods, (3) the transformation rules, and (4) the implementation rules. Operators and their methods are characterized by their name and arity. Transformation rules specify legal (equivalence-preserving) transformations of query trees, and consist of two expressions and an optional condition. The expressions contain place-holders for lower parts of the query which are unaffected by the transformation, and the condition is a C code fragment which is inserted into the optimizer at the appropriate place. Finally, an implementation rule consists of a method, an expression that the method implements, and an optional condition. As an example, here is an excerpt from the description file for a prototype relational query optimizer:

```
%operator 2 join
%method 2 nested-loops-join merge-join
join (1, 2) <-> join (2, 1);
join (1, 2) by nested-loops-join (1, 2);
```

In this example, join is declared to be a binary operator, and nested-loops-join and merge-join are declared to be two binary methods. The symbol <-> denotes equivalence (i.e., a potential two-way transformation) in the context of a transformation rule, and *by* is a keyword used for implementation rules. The transformation rule in the above example states that join is commutative, and the implementation rule says that nested loops-join is a join method. If merge-join is a method that is only useful for joining sorted relations, then its implementation rule would have to include a condition to test whether or not each input relation is sorted appropriately.

5.2. Optimizer Support Functions

In addition to a declarative description of the data model, the optimizer generator requires the DBE to provide a collection of support procedures in a code section of the optimizer description. These procedures are C routines that access and/or manipulate the optimizer's data structures. The generated optimization procedure employs two principal data structures, *MESH* and *OPEN*. *MESH* is a directed acyclic graph that holds all of the alternative operator trees and access plans that have been explored so far, employing a rather complex pointer structure to ensure that transformations can be identified and performed quickly (and also that equal subexpressions will be processed only once). *OPEN* is a priority queue containing currently applicable transformations, as described further in Section 5.3.

The overall cost of an access plan is defined as the sum of the costs of the methods involved, and the objective of optimization is to minimize this sum. Thus, for each method, the DBE must provide a cost function for calculating the cost of the method based on the characteristics of the method's input. The method's cost function will be called by the generated optimizer whenever it considers using the method for implementing an operator (or a pattern of operators). The input arguments for method cost functions are pointers to the root node of the relevant portion of the query tree in *MESH* and to the nodes in *MESH* that produce the input streams according to the associated implementation rule.

In addition to method cost functions, a property function is needed for each operator and each method. The DBE is permitted to define properties (as C structures) that are to be associated with each operator and method node in *MESH*. Operator properties are logical properties of intermediate results, such as their cardinalities and schemas. Method properties are physical properties (i.e., method side effects), such as sort order in our merge-join example. Operator property functions are called by the generated optimizer when transformations are applied, and method propery functions are invoked when methods are selected.

Each node in *MESH* contains arguments associated with the operator represented by the node and with the best method that has been found for the subquery rooted at the node. In a relational optimizer, for example, the select and join operators have predicates as arguments, and the project operator has a field list as an argument. A method that implements a combined select-project operation would have both a predicate and a field list as arguments. As with properties, it is necessary for the DBE to define this data-model-dependent aspect of a node (typically as a C union). By default, operator and method arguments are copied automatically between corresponding *MESH* nodes, which is fine for many simple transformation and implementation rules (e.g., join commutativity, which simply reorders operators in the query tree). However, for rules where such copying is insufficient, the DBE must provide argument transfer functions to manipulate the arguments. For example, consider the following transformation rule:

```
select 9 (product (1, 2)) -> join (select(1), select(2)) xpj_arg_xfer
{{
    if (no_join_predicate(OPERATOR_9.oper_argument))
      REJECT;
}};
```

This (one-way) transformation rule replaces a selection over a cross-product with a join of two selections. The function `xpj_arg_xfer`, which the DBE must provide, will be called when the rule is applied by the generated optimizer in order to rearrange the operators' predicate arguments; it will need to split the predicate associated with the select operator on the left-hand side of the rule into a join predicate and two select predicates for the operators on the rule's right-hand side. This example also illustrates several other features that were mentioned earlier. First, it shows how a condition can be associated with a rule, as the transformation will be rejected if the `no_join_predicate` function provided by the DBE determines that no join predicate exists. Second, it shows how access is provided to operator arguments. The select operator on the left-hand side of the example rule is numbered to identify it uniquely within the rule so that its `oper_argument` field can be passed to the function employed in the condition. Method arguments and properties of operators and methods can be accessed in a similar manner.

Finally, in some cases the DBE may wish to assist the optimizer in estimating the benefit of a given transformation before the transformation is actually performed. A function can be named in the transformation rule using the keyword *estimate*, in which case this function will be called by the optimizer to estimate the expected cost of a transformed query based on the relevant portion of the query tree, the operator arguments, and the operator and method properties.

At first glance, it may appear that there is quite a bit of code for the DBE to write. However, not all of the functions outlined above are required. In particular, only the cost functions are absolutely necessary. If the DBE does not specify a type for operator property fields, then operator property functions are not necessary; similarly, method property functions are only needed if a method property type is specified. Argument transfer functions and estimation functions are optional, and need not be specified except for rules where their functionality is required. Finally, remember that a key design goal for the EXODUS optimizer generator was data model independence, so these functions really cannot be built into the optimizer generator. However, we do intend to provide libraries of generally useful functions (such as predicate manipulation routines) that the DBE can use in cases where they are appropriate.

5.3. Operation of the Generated Optimizer

The generated optimization procedure starts by initializing the MESH and OPEN data structures. MESH is set up to contain a tree with the same structure as the original query. The method with the lowest cost estimate is then selected for each node in MESH using the implementation rules. Finally, the transformation rules are used to determine possible transformations which are inserted into OPEN. Once MESH and OPEN have been initialized in this manner, the optimizer repeats the following transformation cycle until OPEN is empty: The most promising transformation is selected from OPEN and applied to MESH. For all nodes generated by the transformation, the optimizer tries to find an equal node in MESH to avoid optimizing the same expression twice. (Two nodes are equal if they have the same operator, the same argument, and the same inputs.) If an equal node is found, it is used to replace the new node. The remaining new nodes are matched against the transformation rules and analyzed, and the methods with the lowest cost estimates are selected.

This algorithm has several parameters which serve to improve its efficiency. First, the *promise* of each transformation is calculated as the product of the top node's total cost and the *expected cost factor* associated with the transformation rule. To insure that a matching transformation rule with a low expected cost factor will be applied first, entries in OPEN are prioritized by their expected cost decrease. Expected cost factors provide an easy way to ensure that restrictive operators are moved down in the tree as quickly as possible; it is a general heuristic that the cost is lower if constructive operators such as join and transitive closure have smaller inputs. Second, it is sometimes necessary to apply equivalence transformations even if they do not directly yield cheaper solutions, as they may be needed as intermediate steps to even less expensive access plans. Such transformations represent hill climbing, and we limit their application through the use of a *hill climbing factor*. Lastly, when a transformation results in a lower cost, the parent nodes of the old expression must be reanalyzed to propagate any cost advantages; a *reanalyzing factor*, similar to the hill climbing factor, limits this propagation in cases where the new plan's cost is worse than the best equivalent subquery by more than this factor.

It is a non-trivial problem to select values for the optimization parameters so as to guarantee optimal access plans together with good optimizer performance. Thus, it is would be nice if they could be determined and adjusted automatically. We have not yet automated the selection of the hill climbing or reanalyzing parameter values, but we have successfully automated the choice of expected cost factors. Our current prototype initializes the expected cost factors of all transformation rules to 1, the neutral value, and then adjusts them using sliding geometric averages. This has turned out to be quite effective in experiments with several prototype relational optimizers [Grae87a, Grae87b]; our experience has been that generated optimizers are fast enough for production use, and that the access plans that they produce are consistently very close to optimal. We have also found that the EXODUS optimizer generator provides a useful, modular framework for breaking the data-model-dependent code of a query optimizer into small but meaningful pieces, which aids in the rapid prototyping and development of new query optimizers.

6. A DBMS SUPPORTING COMPLEX OBJECTS AND OBJECT ORIENTATION

As a number of the components of EXODUS are now ready for an initial trial, we recently turned our attention to the process of selecting a target data model to implement using the EXODUS toolkit. The goals of this implementation effort are to validate the EXODUS approach to DBMS development, to serve as a forcing function for developing a library of access methods and operator methods, and to provide a system that can serve as a demonstration of the use of EXODUS for potential users. Since no single data model and query language was quite what we were looking for (in terms of our goals), we decided to design our own data model and query language. The EXTRA data model and EXCESS query language are the result of this design effort. The EXTRA data model includes support for complex objects with shared subobjects, a novel mix of object- and value-oriented semantics for data, support for persistent objects of any type in the EXTRA type lattice, and user-defined abstract data type extensions (ADTs). The EXCESS query language provides facilities for querying and updating complex object structures, and it can be extended through the addition of ADT functions and operators (written in E) and procedures and functions for manipulating EXTRA schema types (written in EXCESS). This section of the paper presents an overview of the key features of EXTRA and EXCESS; more details can be found in [Care88].

6.1. The EXTRA Data Model

An EXTRA database is a collection of named persistent objects of any type that can be defined using the EXTRA type system. EXTRA separates the notions of type and instance. Thus, users can collect related objects together in semantically meaningful sets and arrays, which can then be queried, rather than having to settle for queries over type extents as in many other data models (e.g., [Mylo80, Ship81, Bane87, Lecl87, Rowe87]). EXTRA provides a collection of type constructors that includes tuple, set, fixed-length array, and variable-length array. In addition, there are four flavors of instance values, **own**, **ref**, **own ref**, and **own unique ref** (although casual users such as query writers need not be concerned with this distinction). Combined with the EXTRA type constructors, these provide a powerful set of facilities for modeling complex object types and their semantics. Finally, EXTRA provides support for user-defined ADTs, derived attributes, and automatic maintenance of inverse relationships among attributes.

Figure 6 shows a simple database defined using the EXTRA data model. In EXTRA, the tuple, set, and array constructors for complex objects are denoted by parentheses, curly braces, and square brackets, respectively. The figure should be fairly self-explanatory, with the exception of the keywords **own**, **unique**, and **ref**. In EXTRA, subordinate entities are treated as values (as in nested relational models [Sche86]), not as objects with their own separate identity, unless prefaced by **ref**, **own ref**, or **own unique ref** in a type definition or an object creation statement. The declaration **ref x** indicates that **x** is a reference to an extant object. **Own ref x** indicates that **x** has object identity but its existence is dependent on the existence of at least one object that refers to it via an **own ref** reference. **Own unique ref x** indicates that **x** has object identity but its existence is dependent on a unique owning object.

Briefly, Figure 6 defines four types, all of which happen to be tuple types in this example: Person, Student (a subtype of Person), Employee (another subtype of Person), and Department. It then defines a university database consisting of two named, persistent objects: Students, which is a set of Student objects, and Departments, which is a set of Department objects. Since both are of the form "{ **own unique ref** ... }", these two sets own their member objects and these member objects will be deleted when their owning sets are subsequently **destroyed**. Each Department object in the set Departments contains a set of Employee objects that work in that Department, and it owns these objects (i.e., a given Employee object can be thought of as being part of a "composite" [Bane87] Department object). Both Employee and Student objects contain (references to) a Department object that they work for or major in, respectively, and the management structure for the employees is captured by the manager and sub_ords attributes of Employee objects.

Two concepts are central in the design of EXTRA/EXCESS: extensibility and support for complex objects. In addition, the model incorporates the basic themes common to most semantic data models [Hull87, Peck88]. Extensibility in EXTRA/EXCESS is provided through both an abstract data type mechanism, where new types can be written in the E programming language and then registered with the system, and through support for user-defined functions and procedures that are written in the EXCESS query language and operate on user-defined EXTRA types. Complex objects are objects in the database, possibly composed of other objects, that have their own unique identity. Such objects can be referenced by their identity from anywhere in the database. In [Bato84], four useful varieties of complex objects are identified: disjoint-recursive, disjoint-nonrecursive, nondisjoint-recursive, and nondisjoint-nonrecursive.[11] The EXTRA data model is capable of modeling all four varieties.

EXTRA also provides many of the capabilities found in semantic data models. Four primitive modeling concepts fundamental to most semantic data models [Hull87, Peck88] are: the *is-a* relationship (also known as generalization), the *part-of* relationship (often called aggregation), the *instance-of* relationship (also referred to as classification), and the *member-of* relationship (called association in some models). Each of these concepts is easily modeled using the facilities of EXTRA. Generalization is modeled in EXTRA by using the **inherits** keyword to indicate that a type inherits attributes and functions from another type. For example, an Employee is a Person in Figure 6. (Note that our notion of generalization is often called "specialization" in the semantic modeling literature.) Aggregation is easily modeled using the tuple constructor — for instance, a Department is an aggregation of its employees, its manager, etc. (We ignore the distinction between attributes, which merely describe an object, and components of an object). Classification is simply the notion of type-instance dichotomy, and is present in EXTRA in the distinction between the **define type** and **create** statements in Figure 6. Finally, association is modeled by the set constructor of EXTRA. An example of this is the set of employees which are subordinate to a manager.

6.2. The EXCESS Query Language

EXCESS queries range over objects created using the **create** statement. EXCESS is based on QUEL [Ston76], GEM [Zani83], POSTQUEL [Rowe87], and SQL extensions for nested relations [Dada86, Sche86]. EXCESS is designed to provide a uniform query interface to sets, arrays, tuples, and single objects, all of which can

---

[11] Two objects are disjoint if they share no subobjects; an object is recursive if it contains other objects of the same object type.

```
define type Person:
(
        ssnum:          int4,
        name:           char[ ],
        street:         char[20],
        city:           char[10],
        zip:            int4,
        birthday:       Date
)

define type Student:
(
        gpa:            float4,
        dept:           ref Department
)
inherits Person

define type Employee:
(
        jobtitle:       char[20],
        dept:           ref Department,
        manager:        ref Employee,
        sub_ords:       { ref Employee },
        salary:         int4,
        kids:           { own Person }
)
inherits Person

define type Department:
(
        name:           char[ ],
        floor:          int4,
        employees:      { own unique ref Employee }
)

create Students:         { own unique ref Student }
create Departments:      { own unique ref Department }
```

Figure 6: A simple EXTRA database.

be composed and nested arbitrarily. In addition, user-defined functions (written both in E and in EXCESS) and aggregate functions (written in E) are supported in a clean and consistent way. A few examples should suffice to convey the basic flavor of the language.

As a first example, the following query finds the names of the children of all employees who work for a department on the second floor:

```
range of E is Employees
retrieve (C.name) from C in E.kids where E.dept.floor = 2
```

Our second example illustrates the use of an aggregate function over a nested set of objects. The following query retrieves the name of each employee, and for each employee it retrieves the age of the youngest child among the children of all employees working in a department on the same floor as the employee's department.

> **range of** EMP **is** Employees
> **retrieve** (EMP.name, min(E.kids.age
> **from** E **in** Employees
> **where** E.dept.floor = EMP.dept.floor))

In this example, the variable E ranges over Employees within the scope of the min aggregate, and within the aggregate it is connected to the variable EMP through a join on Employee.dept.floor. The query aggregates over Employee.kids, which is a set-valued attribute. Here, age is assumed to be defined by a function that computes the age of a Person from the current date and their birthday, so it is a virtual field of Person objects.

User-defined functions and procedures written in EXCESS are supported, and are handled uniformly in the syntax (as illustrated by the use of the age function in the example above). Functions can be invoked using either the syntax for denoting attributes (for functions defined on particular types) or the user-defined function syntax (which is similar to the aggregate function invocation syntax shown in the previous example). EXCESS procedures are invoked in a manner consistent with the EXCESS syntax for performing updates. Procedures differ from functions in that functions return a value and have no side-effects, while procedures usually have side-effects and return no value. Further details and examples are presented in [Care88].

6.3. The EXTRA/EXCESS System Architecture

The EXTRA/EXCESS environment will consist of a frontend process and a backend process, as illustrated in Figure 7 (which is essentially an EXTRA/EXCESS-specific version of Figure 1). The frontend process parses a query, converts it to an optimizable form, optimizes it, converts the optimized query to E, and sends this E program to the backend for execution.[12] The optimizer will be generated using the EXODUS Optimizer Generator. The frontend also interfaces with the EXTRA/EXCESS data dictionary for processing data definition language requests, performing authorization, etc. The data dictionary is itself designed as an EXTRA database, and thus will be stored by the EXODUS Storage Manager like all other data. It is drawn separately in Figure 7 simply to clarify its function.

The backend process consists of several components. The E compiler compiles E code into executables which contain calls to the EXODUS Storage Manager. There is also a loader to dynamically load compiled queries into the E run-time system (ERTS). ERTS contains operator methods and access methods written in E by the DBE as well as methods taken from the generic method libraries provided by EXODUS. The EXODUS Storage Manager is also part of the backend, as it serves as the repository for persistent E objects; it is the only component of the system which directly manipulates persistent data. Finally, the backend will send query results to the frontend for formatting and output.

7. SUMMARY AND CURRENT STATUS

In this paper we have described EXODUS, an extensible database system project aimed at simplifying the development of high-performance, application-specific database systems. As we explained, the EXODUS model of the world includes three classes of database experts — ourselves, the designers and implementors of EXODUS; the database engineers, or DBEs, who are responsible for using EXODUS to produce various application-specific DBMSs; and the database administrators, or DBAs, who are the managers of the systems produced by the DBEs. In addition, of course, there must be users of application-specific DBMSs, namely the engineers, scientists, office workers, computer-aided designers, and other groups that the resulting systems will support. The focus of this paper has been the overall architecture of EXODUS and the tools available to aid the DBE in his or her work.

---

[12] We also plan to support precompiled queries, but their execution path is not shown in Figure 7.

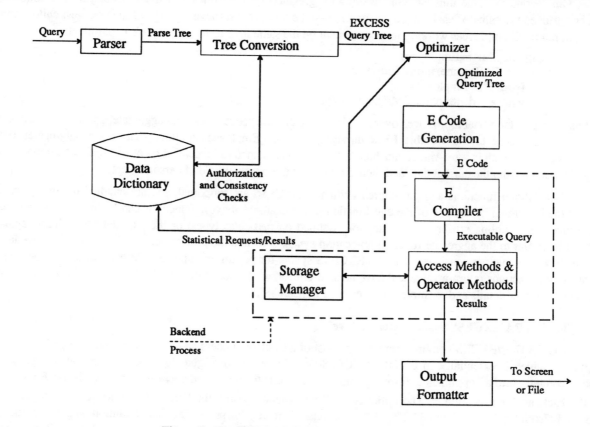

Figure 7: The EXTRA/EXCESS system architecture.

As we described, EXODUS includes one component that requires no change from application area to application area — the Storage Manager, a flexible, low-level storage manager that provides concurrent and recoverable access to storage objects of arbitrary size. In addition, EXODUS provides libraries of database system components that are likely to be widely applicable, including various useful access methods and operator methods. The corresponding system layers are constructed by the DBE through a combination of borrowing components from the libraries and writing new components. To make writing new components as painless as possible, EXODUS provides the E database implementation language to largely shield the DBE from many of the low-level details of persistent programming. E is also the vehicle provided for defining new ADTs, which makes it easy for the DBE to write operations on ADTs even when they are very large (e.g., an image or voice ADT). At the upper level of the system, EXODUS provides a generator that produces a query optimizer from a description of the available operations and methods. Finally, we described EXTRA/EXCESS, a next-generation data model and query language with an object-oriented flavor that will drive further EXODUS developments.

An initial implementation of the EXODUS tools is basically complete, including all of the components described here. A single-user version of the Storage Manager is running, providing excellent performance for both small and large storage objects; work on versions, concurrency control, and recovery is underway. The implementation of the rule-based query optimizer generator was completed over a year ago, and it has been used to generate most of a full relational query optimizer. The E compiler is coming along nicely, with virtually all of the language features (except hints) working at this time; the E effort is currently focused on optimization issues (e.g., coalescing storage manager calls and improving our implementation of generic classes). At SIGMOD-88 we demonstrated a relational DBMS prototype that was implemented using the EXODUS tools, and we are now working on an initial EXTRA/EXCESS implementation.

REFERENCES

[Andr87]   Andrews, T., and Harris, C., "Combining Language and Database Advances in an Object-Oriented Development Environment," *Proc. of 1987 OOPSLA Conf.*, Orlando, FL, Oct. 1987.

[Astr76]   Astrahan, M., et. al., "System R: A Relational Approach to Database Management," *ACM Trans. on Database Sys. 1, 2*, June 1976.

[Atki87]   Atkinson, M., and Buneman, O.P., "Types and Persistence in Database Programming Languages," *ACM Comp. Surveys, 19, 2*, June 1987.

[Atki78]   Atkinson, R., Liskov, B., and Scheifler, R., "Aspects of Implementing CLU," *ACM National Conf. Proc.*, 1978.

[Bane87]   Banerjee, J., et. al., "Data Model Issues for Object-Oriented Applications," *ACM Trans. on Office Info. Sys. 5, 1*, Jan. 1987.

[Bato84]   Batory, D., and Buchmann, A., "Molecular Objects, Abstract Data Types, and Data Models: A Framework," *Proc. of the 1984 VLDB Conf.*, Singapore, Aug. 1984.

[Bato88a]   Batory, D., "Concepts for a Database System Compiler," *Proc. of the 1988 ACM Principles of Database Sys. Conf.*, Austin, TX, March 1988.

[Bato88b]   Batory, D., et al, "GENESIS: An Extensible Database Management System," *IEEE Trans. on Software Eng. 14, 11*, Nov. 1988.

[Baye77]   Bayer, R., and Schkolnick, M., "Concurrency of Operations on B-trees," *Acta Informatica 9*, 1977.

[Care86a]   Carey, M., and D. DeWitt, "Extensible Database Systems," in *On Knowledge Base Management: Integrating Artificial Intelligence and Database Technologies*, M. Brodie and J. Mylopoulos, eds., Springer-Verlag, 1986.

[Care86b]   Carey, M., et al, "Object and File Management in the EXODUS Extensible Database System," *Proc. of the 1986 VLDB Conf.*, Kyoto, Japan, Aug. 1986.

[Care86c]   Carey, M., et al, "The Architecture of the EXODUS Extensible DBMS" *Proc. of the Int'l. Workshop on Object-Oriented Database Sys.*, Pacific Grove, CA, Sept. 1986.

[Care87]   Carey, M., and DeWitt, D., "An Overview of EXODUS," in [DBE87].

[Care88]   Carey, M., DeWitt, D., and Vandenberg, S., "A Data Model and Query Language for EXODUS," *Proc. of the 1988 SIGMOD Conf.*, Chicago, IL, June 1988.

[Chou85]   Chou, H.-T., and D. DeWitt, "An Evaluation of Buffer Management Strategies for Relational Database Systems," *Proc. of the 1985 VLDB Conf.*, Stockholm, Sweden, Aug. 1985.

[Clif85]   Clifford, J., and A. Tansel, "On An Algebra for Historical Relational Databases: Two Views," *Proc. of the 1985 SIGMOD Conf.*, Austin, Texas, May 1985.

[Cloc81]   Clocksin, W. and C. Mellish, *Programming in Prolog*, Springer-Verlag, New York, 1981.

[Cope84]   Copeland, G. and D. Maier, "Making Smalltalk a Database System," *Proc. of the 1984 SIGMOD Conf.*, Boston, MA, May 1984.

[DBE87]   *Database Engineering 10, 2*, Special Issue on Extensible Database Systems, M. Carey, ed., June 1987.

[Dada84]   Dadam, P., V. Lum, and H-D. Werner, "Integration of Time Versions into a Relational Database System," *Proc. of the 1984 VLDB Conf.*, Singapore, Aug. 1984.

[Dada86]   Dadam, P., et al, "A DBMS Prototype to Support Extended NF^2 Relations: An Integrated View of Flat Tables," *Proc. of the 1986 SIGMOD Conf.*, Washington, DC, May 1986.

[Daya86]   Dayal, U. and J. Smith, "PROBE: A Knowledge-Oriented Database Management System," in *On Knowledge Base Management: Integrating Artificial Intelligence and Database Technologies*, M. Brodie and J. Mylopoulos, eds., Springer-Verlag, 1986.

[Feld79]   Feldman, S., "Make — A Program for Maintaining Computer Programs," *Software — Practice and Experience* 9, 1979.

[Forg81]   Forgy, C.L. "OPS5 Reference Manual," Computer Science Technical Report 135, Carnegie-Mellon Univ., 1981.

[Frey86]   Freytag, C.F. and Goodman, N., "Translating Relational Queries into Iterative Programs Using a Program Transformation Approach," *Proc. of the 1986 ACM SIGMOD Conf.*, May 1986.

[Grae87a] Graefe, G., and DeWitt, D., "The EXODUS Optimizer Generator," *Proc. of the 1987 SIGMOD Conf.*, San Francisco, CA, May 1987.

[Grae87b] Graefe, G., "Rule-Based Query Optimization in Extensible Database Systems," Ph.D. Thesis, Comp. Sci. Dept., Univ. of Wisconsin, Madison, 1987.

[Gray79]   Gray, J., "Notes On Database Operating Systems," in *Operating Systems: An Advanced Course*, R. Bayer, R. Graham, and G. Seegmuller, eds., Springer-Verlag, 1979.

[Gutt84]   Guttman, A., "R-Trees: A Dynamic Index Structure for Spatial Searching," *Proc. of the 1984 SIGMOD Conf.*, Boston, MA, May 1984.

[Hull87]   Hull, R., and King, R., "Semantic Database Modeling: Survey, Applications, and Research Issues," *ACM Comp. Surveys* 19, 3, Sept. 1987.

[Katz86]   Katz, R., E. Chang, and R. Bhateja, "Version Modeling Concepts for Computer-Aided Design Databases," *Proc. of the 1986 SIGMOD Conf.*, Washington, DC, May 1986.

[Kern78]   Kernighan, B.W. and D.N. Ritchie, *The C Programming Language*, Prentice-Hall, Englewood Cliffs, N.J., 1978.

[Klah85]   Klahold, P., et al, "A Transaction Model Supporting Complex Applications in Integrated Information Systems," *Proc. of the 1985 SIGMOD Conf.*, Austin, TX, May 1985.

[Lecl87]   Lecluse, C., et. al., "O_2, An Object-Oriented Data Model," *Proc. of the 1988 SIGMOD Conf.*, Chicago, IL, June 1988.

[Lind87]   Lindsay, B., McPherson, J., and Pirahesh, H., "A Data Management Extension Architecture," *Proc. of the 1987 SIGMOD Conf.*, San Francisco, CA, May 1987.

[Lisk77]   Liskov, B., et al, "Abstraction Mechanisms in CLU," *Comm. ACM* 20, 8, Aug. 1977.

[Litw80]   Litwin, W., "Linear Hashing: A New Tool for File and Table Addressing," *Proc. of the 1980 VLDB Conf.*, Montreal, Canada, Oct. 1980.

[Lohm88]   Lohman, G., "Grammar-Like Functional Rules for Representing Query Optimization Alternatives," *Proc. of the 1988 SIGMOD Conf.*, Chicago, IL, June 1988.

[Maie87]   Maier, D., and Stein, J., "Development and Implementation of an Object-Oriented DBMS," in *Research Directions in Object-Oriented Programming*,, B. Shriver and P. Wegner, Eds., MIT Press, 1987.

[Mano86]   Manola, F., and Dayal, U., "PDM: An Object-Oriented Data Model," *Proc. of the Int'l. Workshop on Object-Oriented Database Sys.*, Pacific Grove, CA, Sept. 1986. Grove, CA, Sept. 1986.

[Mylo80]   Mylopoulos, J., et. al., "A Language Facility for Designing Database-Intensive Applications," *ACM Trans. on Database Sys.* 5, 2, June 1980.

[Nguy82]   Nguyen, G.T., Ferrat, L., and H. Galy, "A High-Level User Interface for a Local Network Database System," *Proc. of the IEEE Infocom Conf.*, 1982.

[Niev84]   Nievergelt, J., H. Hintenberger, H., and Sevcik, K.C., "The Grid File: An Adaptable, Symmetric Multikey File Structure," *ACM Trans. on Database Sys.* 9, 1, March 1984.

[Peck88] Peckham, J., and Maryanski, F., "Semantic Data Models," *ACM Comp. Surveys* 20, 3, Sept. 1988.

[Rich87] Richardson, J., and Carey, M., "Programming Constructs for Database System Implementation in EXODUS," *Proc. of the 1987 SIGMOD Conf.*, San Francisco, CA, May 1987.

[Rich89a] Richardson, J., and Carey, M., "Implementing Persistence in E," *Proc. of the Newcastle Workshop on Persistent Object Sys.*, Newcastle, Australia, Jan. 1989.

[Rich89b] Richardson, J., and Carey, M., "The Design of the E Programming Language," Tech. Rep., Computer Sciences Dept., Univ. of Wisconsin, Madison, Jan. 1989.

[Robi81] Robinson, J.T., "The k-d-B-tree: A Search Structure for Large Multidimentional Dynamic Indexes," *Proc. of the 1981 SIGMOD Conf.*, June 1981.

[Rowe79] Rowe, L. and K. Schoens, "Data Abstraction, Views, and Updates in RIGEL, *Proc. of the 1979 SIGMOD Conf.*, Boston, MA., 1979.

[Rowe87] Rowe, L., and Stonebraker, M., "The POSTGRES Data Model," *Proc. of the 13th VLDB Conf.*, Brighton, England, Aug. 1987.

[Sche86] Schek, H.-J., and Scholl, M., "The Relational Model with Relation-Valued Attributes," *Information Sys.*, 11, 2, 1986.

[Schm77] Schmidt, J., "Some High Level Language Constructs for Data of Type Relation," *ACM Trans. on Database Sys.* 2, 3, Sept. 1977.

[Schw86] Schwarz, P., et al, "Extensibility in the Starburst Database System," *Proc. of the Int'l. Workshop on Object-Oriented Database Sys.*, Pacific Grove, CA, Sept. 1986.

[Ship81] Shipman, D., "The Functional Data Model and the Data Language DAPLEX," *ACM Trans. on Database Sys.* 6, 1, March 1981.

[Snod85] Snodgrass, R., and I. Ahn, "A Taxonomy of Time in Databases," *Proc. of the 1985 SIGMOD Conf.*, Austin, TX, May 1985.

[Ston76] Stonebraker, M., Wong, E., and Kreps, P., "The Design and Implementation of INGRES," *ACM Trans. on Database Sys.* 1, 3, Sept. 1976.

[Ston81] Stonebraker, M., "Hypothetical Data Bases as Views," *Proc. of the 1981 SIGMOD Conf.*, Boston, MA, May 1981.

[Ston83] Stonebraker, M., et al, "Document Processing in a Relational Database System", *ACM Trans. on Office Info. Sys.* 1, 2, April 1983.

[Ston85] Stonebraker, M., personal communication, July 1985.

[Ston86a] Stonebraker, M., "Inclusion of New Types in Relational Data Base Systems," *Proc. of the 2nd Data Engineering Conf.*, Los Angeles, CA., Feb. 1986.

[Ston86b] Stonebraker, M., and L. Rowe, "The Design of POSTGRES," *Proc. of the 1986 SIGMOD Conf.*, Washington, DC, May 1986.

[Stro86] Stroustrup, B., *The C++ Programming Language*, Addison-Wesley, Reading, MA, 1986.

[Ullm82] Ullman, J.D., *Principles of Database Systems*, Computer Science Press, Rockville, MD., 1982.

[Verh78] Verhofstad, J., "Recovery Techniques for Database Systems," *ACM Comp. Surveys* 10, 2, June 1978.

[Zani83] Zaniolo, C., "The Database Language GEM," *Proc. of the 1983 SIGMOD Conf.*, San Jose, CA, May 1983.

GENESIS: An Extensible Database Management System

D. S. BATORY, J. R. BARNETT, J. F. GARZA, K. P. SMITH, K. TSUKUDA, B. C. TWICHELL, AND
T. E. WISE

Abstract—We present a novel yet simple technology which enables customized database management systems to be developed rapidly. Over the last few years, a theory of database implementation was developed to explain the storage architectures of many commercial DBMS's (i.e., how these systems store and retrieve data) [5]. The theory identified basic components of DBMS software, required all components to have the same interface, and showed that component composition can be achieved in a simple manner. We are designing an extensible DBMS, called GENESIS, which is based on this theory. This paper gives a detailed description of our first operational prototype.

DBMS software components in GENESIS can be written in a few months. When all components for a target DBMS are present, writing the architecture specification of the DBMS and reconfiguring GENESIS takes a few hours and can be accomplished with negligible cost. Building the same DBMS from scratch can take many man-years and cost hundreds of thousands of dollars.

We believe that the extensible software technology proposed herein embodies an important advance in tailoring database management systems to specialized applications. We also outline a way that our technology might impact software development beyond the confines of a DBMS setting.

Index Terms—Extensible DBMS's, software building blocks, software reusability, transformation model, unifying model.

I. INTRODUCTION

DATABASE management systems (DBMS's) have proven to be cost-effective tools for organizing and maintaining large volumes of data. In recent years it has become evident that there are many important database applications that do not conform to the familiar debit–credit scenario of business-oriented transactions. Statistical databases CAD and engineering databases [25], [28], textual databases [47], [21], and databases for artificial intelligence [26] are examples. Owing to their unusual requirements, it is not surprising that existing "general-purpose" DBMS's do not support these applications efficiently. Special-purpose database management systems are needed.

DBMS's are presently customized in one of two ways: systems are developed from scratch [30], [53] or existing systems are enhanced [24], [47]. It is well-known that both approaches are exceedingly difficult, costly, and not always successful. There is a definite need for tools that

Manuscript received June 30, 1986; revised March 20, 1987. This work was supported by the National Science Foundation under Grants MCS-8317353 and DCR-86-00738.

The authors are with the Department of Computer Science, University of Texas at Austin, Austin, TX 78712.

IEEE Log Number 8823664.

simplify and aid the development of database system software.

A number of researchers have begun to address these problems in the context of specific DBMS's [18], [11], [49], [43]. Concurrent with their work, our research has concentrated on the development of an encompassing and practical theory of DBMS implementation [2], [3], [5], [6]. The theory provides a common framework to relate disparate results on a wide range of topics on database research, and reveals the basic components of DBMS software to be modules that realize simple files (file structures), linksets (record linking structures), and elementary transformations (conceptual-to-internal mappings). The storage architectures of commercial DBMS's (i.e., how systems store and retrieve data) are explained by compositions of these building blocks.

This paper documents the design of GENESIS, the first operational system that is based on this theory. GENESIS can be reconfigured into a DBMS that stores and retrieves data according to a specified storage architecture. Reconfiguration is accomplished by synthesizing the target DBMS from a library of software modules that correspond to the components of the theory. The library is extensible, so new modules can be added as needed.

Once a storage architecture has been designed, only the modules that are not present in the library must be written. As all modules are reusable, we anticipate the need for adding new modules will decrease as the library enlarges. When all modules are present, the time it takes to write the specification and to reconfigure GENESIS is a matter of hours, and can be done with negligible cost. This is in sharp contrast to the way customized DBMS's are presently developed. If the same DBMS was built from scratch, it could take many man-years and cost hundreds of thousands of dollars.

Constructing software from existing components is an old idea, and certainly every DBMS has been developed in a modular fashion. However, what distinguishes our approach from others is the way we define modules. Every module in our system is plug compatible with all other modules in that all support exactly the same interface. This enables modules to be composed quickly in many different ways by a simple linking process.

The boundaries of modules that comprise existing DBMS's are drawn differently than ours, and reflect the ad hoc nature of DBMS software design. Adding new capabilities to an existing DBMS quite often requires significant rewriting of modules. In contrast, new capabilities are usually encompassed by a single module in GENESIS, and adding new module/layer to a storage architecture is a simple task because of plug-compatible interfaces.

The theory behind reconfigurable database systems is not yet widely known. We review the theory in Section II, and illustrate it with the storage architecture of the MRS database management system [33]. An in-depth presentation of the theory is given in [5], along with examples of other storage architectures.

We present the design and mechanics of GENESIS in Section III by showing how the MRS architecture has been implemented. (Other storage architectures would be realized in an identical manner.) Future work is outlined in Section IV. We specifically examine how concurrency control and query processing fit into our framework. The MRS architecture is used to illustrate these extensions. We also outline a way that our technology might impact software development beyond the confines of a DBMS setting.

II. Background

Files and links are fundamental concepts in databases. A *file* is a set of records that are instances of a single record type. A relationship between two or more files is a *link*, which is a generalization of a CODASYL set. Each link relates records of one file, called the *parent file*, to records of other files, called *child files*. Links are more general than CODASYL sets in that they can express $M:N$ relationships and that a file can serve as both parent and child in the same link.

Files and links are logical concepts; that is, their implementation is unspecified. To explain the spectrum of their implementations, two models are used: the *Transformation Model (TM)* and the *Unifying Model (UM)*. The TM formalizes the notion of conceptual-to-internal mappings and the UM codifies file structures and record linking mechanisms.

A. The Transformation and Unifying Models

A primary function of a DBMS is to map conceptual files and operations to their internal counterparts. INGRES [46], for example, maps relations to inverted files. RAPID [53] and SYSTEM R [1] also begin with relations, but RAPID maps to transposed files and SYSTEM R maps to inverted files with record clustering. The software that performs conceptual-to-internal mappings is the physical database component of a DBMS.

An intuitive understanding of conceptual-to-internal mappings is gained by recognizing that a mapping is a sequence of database definitions that are progressively more implementation-oriented. The sequence begins with definitions of conceptual files and conceptual links, and ends with definitions of internal files and internal links. Each intermediate definition contains both conceptual and internal elements, and can be identified with a *level of abstraction* that lies *between* the conceptual and internal levels. We apply the terms *abstract* and *concrete* to files and links that are defined in adjacent levels/definitions, where an abstract file or link is realized by its concrete counterparts. Thus the terms *conceptual* and *internal* represent the most abstract and most concrete representations of files and links in a DBMS.

Distinguishing different levels in a DBMS and mapping from one level to an adjacent level is usually straightforward. In the DBMS's that we have studied, only ten different primitive mappings, henceforth called *elementary transformations*, have been used. Elementary transformations map abstract files and abstract links to concrete files and concrete links. Classical transformations include indexing, encoding, transposition, segmentation, record fragmenting (also called division), the CODASYL representation of $n:m$ relationships, and horizontal partitioning. It follows that the conceptual-to-internal mappings of a software-based DBMS can be modeled by 1) taking a description of the conceptual files and conceptual links that the DBMS supports, and 2) applying a well-defined sequence of elementary transformations to produce the generic internal files and internal links of the DBMS. In the case of INGRES, SYSTEM R, and RAPID, all begin with the same conceptual files (i.e., relations), but each is distinguished by different sequences of transformations and hence different sets of internal files and internal links. Modeling storage architectures using elementary transformations is the basis of the *Transformation Model (TM)* [5].

Once the internal files and internal links are known, the storge structures of the DBMS's internal database are specified using the *Unifying Model (UM)* [2], which distinguishes file structures from link structures. A *simple file* is a storage structure that organizes records of one or more internal files. Classical simple files include hash-based, indexed-sequential, B+ trees, dynamic hash-based, and unordered files. A *linkset* is a storage structure that implements one or more internal links. Classical linksets include pointer arrays, inverted lists, ring lists, hierarchical sequential lists, and record clustering (i.e., "store near" [17]). It follows that the storage structures of an internal database are specified by assigning each internal file to a simple file and each internal link to a linkset. Catalogs of recognized simple files and linksets are given in [5].

It is important to recognize that conceptual-to-internal mappings and elementary transformations are not artificial concepts. Each elementary transformation can be realized by a simple layer of software (i.e., and abstract data type). In turn, the physical database software of a DBMS can be seen as a composition of these layers, where the software of different DBMS's are described by different compositions (i.e., different nestings of abstract data types). The idea of level of abstraction corresponds to the files and links of a DBMS that are *visible at a particular layer in its software*. Thus, conceptual-to-internal mappings and elementary transformations are fundamental to the way DBMS software is actually written *or can be written*.

We illustrate the TM and UM by modeling the MRS database system [33]. Models of INQUIRE, ADABAS, SYSTEM 2000 are given in [5], IDMS is described in [3], INGRES and RAPID are found in [6], and preliminary models of DMS-1100, IMS, TOTAL, SPIRES, and CREATABASE are outlined in [6] and [12].

As aids to explain the transformation model of MRS, we will use three different diagrams: *data structure diagrams* (*dsd*) show the relationships among files and links at a particular level of abstraction, *field definition diagrams* (*fdd*) indicate the fields of record types for each file shown in a dsd, and *instance diagrams* (*id*) illustrate both dsds and fdds (see Figures 2–4 for examples). Boxes in dsds represent files and arrows are links. Boxes in fdds represent record types. (There are no arrows in fdds.) And boxes in ids represent record instances and arrows are pointers.

In addition to the usual conventions for drawing dsds, we use two others. First, abstract objects (typically files) are indicated by dashed outlines in data structure diagrams. Fig. 1 shows a data structure diagram of an abstract file W and its materialization as the concrete files F and G and concrete link L.

Second, pointers to abstract records arise naturally in storage architectures. In order to give such pointers a physical realization (i.e., a physical address or symbolic key), they must ultimately reference internal records. To define how pointer references are mapped, we rely on the orientation of record types within a dsd. The orientation of F and G in Fig. 1 shows that file F is above file G. We say that F *dominates* G. This means that a pointer to an abstract record of type W will actually reference its corresponding concrete record of type F. For almost all transformations, there is a $1:1$ correspondence between abstract records and their dominant concrete records: the only exception of which we are aware is full transposition (see [5]). Note that the dominance concept is recursive, that is, a pointer to a W record is the same as the pointer to its F record, which is the same as the pointer to the dominant record of the F record, and so on. In this way, pointers to abstract records are mapped to internal records.

B. A Model of the MRS Database System

MRS is a relational database management system that was implemented at the University of Toronto [33]. MRS creates a distinct internal database for each conceptual file that is defined by a user. Relationships between different conceptual files are realized by joins rather than by storage structures. The underlying storage architecture of MRS, therefore, can be revealed by examining how records of a single conceptual file are stored.

The generic CONCEPTUAL record type that is sup-

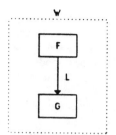

Fig. 1. Materialization of abstract file W.

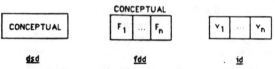

Fig. 2. The CONCEPTUAL record type of MRS.

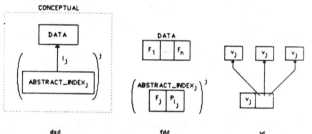

Fig. 3. Indexing of CONCEPTUAL fields.

ported by MRS is shown in Fig. 2. It consists of n data fields, $F_1 \cdots F_n$, where n is user definable. Each data field has a fixed length, so CONCEPTUAL records have fixed lengths. CONCEPTUAL files are the files that are defined in MRS schemas: CONCEPTUAL records are the records that are processed by MRS users. The id of Fig. 2 shows a CONCEPTUAL record with the value v_1 in field F_1 and value v_n in field F_n.

The internal files of MRS are materialized in the following way. MRS first maps CONCEPTUAL files to inverted files. The mapping produces a DATA file, where DATA records are in one-to-one correspondence with CONCEPTUAL records. In addition, for each field F_j that is to be indexed, an ABSTRACT_INDEX$_j$ file is created. It is connected to the DATA file by link I_j (see Fig. 3). I_j is implemented by an inverted list.

If r fields are indexed, there will be one DATA file and r ABSTRACT_INDEX files each connected to the DATA file by precisely one link. The dsd of Fig. 3 shows this relationship. (Note the notation $(\;)^j$ in Fig. 3 means that zero or more fields may be indexed, each with a different value for j.) In the case that no fields are indexed, CONCEPTUAL records are mapped directly to DATA records.

Note that an ABSTRACT_INDEX$_j$ record type has fields F_j and P_{I_j}. P_{I_j} called the *parent field* of linkset I_j; it contains the inverted list of link I_j.

ABSTRACT_INDEX$_j$ records are unbounded in length. As the file structures that MRS uses cannot store arbitrarily long records, ABSTRACT_INDEX$_j$ records are *di-*

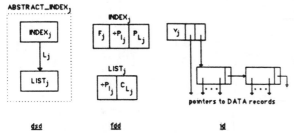

Fig. 4. Division of ABSTRACT_INDEX.

vided into one or more fixed-length fragments. The first fragment, called an $INDEX_j$ record, contains the data field F_j and the first pointer of the inverted list. The other fragments, called $LIST_j$ records, contain the remaining pointers. (A motivation for this division was that if the data value was a primary key, no $LIST_j$ records would be needed.) $INDEX_j$ is connected to $LIST_j$ by link L_j. L_j is implemented as a linear list. The id of Fig. 4 shows a division of an $ABSTRACT\_INDEX_j$ record that resulted in three fragments: an $INDEX_j$ record and two $LIST_j$ records. Note that the fragments of field P_{I_j} are noted by $\div P_{I_j}$ in the fdd of Fig. 4. Also note that P_{L_j} is the parent field of link L_j (it contains the pointer to the first $LIST_j$ record) and C_{L_j} is the *child field* of link L_j (it contains a pointer to the next $LIST_j$ record).

DATA, $INDEX_j$, and $LIST_j$ are the internal files of MRS and I_j and L_j are the internal links. As mentioned earlier, the I_j links are implemented by inverted lists and the L_j links by linear lists. Each internal file is stored in its own file structure. DATA records are organized by an unordered file. For each j, $INDEX_j$ and $LIST_j$ records are, respectively, organized by a B-tree and unordered file. Thus, if r fields are indexed, there would be a total of $2*r + 1$ file structures.

Fig. 5 summarizes the storage architecture of MRS. The four tables list how abstract files are mapped to concrete files [Fig. 5(b)], and how internal files and internal links are mapped to simple files and linksets [Fig. 5(c)–(e)].

C. Comments

The model of MRS accounts for a considerable amount of implementation detail, all of which are essential to the construction and function of MRS software. It is this level of detail that enables our models to be used as blueprints for DBMS storage architectures.

Architecture models express the conceptual-to-internal mappings of data in a DBMS. They also can be used to explain the mappings of operations. MRS, for example, maps operations on CONCEPTUAL files to operations on DATA and ABSTRACT_INDEX files; operations on ABSTRACT_INDEX files are mapped to operations on INDEX and LIST files.

We are familiar with many database storage and retrieval algorithms that have been published in the last fifteen years, and are not aware of any practical example that does not fit our layered paradigm. We are convinced that layering has been an implicit part of explaining and

developing database algorithms in the past. Our research demonstrates the importance of explicit layering.

In the next section, we show how GENESIS implements the TM and UM.

III. THE GENESIS PROTOTYPE

A fundamental precept of the TM is the uniformity with which abstract and concrete files and links are treated. That is, the record types that can be defined and the operations that can be performed at the conceptual level are exactly the same as those at the internal and intermediate levels. Thus, a single DDL and DML is sufficient to express the files, links, and operations that occur at every level of abstraction.

Defining a DDL and DML that is suitable for use at every level is perhaps the most important and difficult task in the design of GENESIS because not just any interface can be used. The DDL and DML of existing systems (e.g., CODASYL) are much too specific or clumsy. For this reason, the present GENESIS interface is synthetic. The DDL is based on an amalgam of concepts taken from existing DDL's and programming languages. The DML is primarily based on embedded-SQL [13], [23] and the extension of SQL to handle long fields [24].

We begin with an overiview of the GENESIS prototype. We then outline the interface that is shared by every layer of software that realizes an elementary transformation, and explain the implementation of each layer in terms of data mappings and operation mappings. We conclude by showing how the composition of mappings is achieved.

The basic ideas of each section are summarized in the introductory paragraphs. Further details, for those who are interested, are presented in the paragraphs that follow the bullet (•) marker.

A. Organization and Overview

Fig. 6 shows the components of the GENESIS prototype. Their function and relationship, in addition to the people who interact with GENESIS, are summarized below.

The *Database Implementor (DBI)* is responsible for designing a storage architecture for the target DBMS. He specifies this architecture by writing an *architecture program*, which compiles conceptual schemas using the *DDL compiler* and maps the data definitions of conceptual files and conceptual links to their internal counterparts. The mappings are accomplished by prewritten procedures called *transformers* which realize the abstract-to-concrete data definition mappings of elementary transformations. Unless the DBMS architecture needs to be changed, there is no need to alter an architecture program once it is written. Different storage architectures are realized by different architecture programs.

The *Database Administrator (DBA)* is responsible for database design. He develops conceptual schemas in terms of the GENESIS DDL, and runs the architecture program to convert these schemas into an internal representation called *storage architecture tables*.

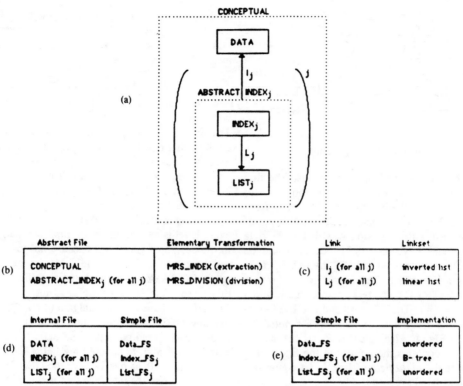

Fig. 5. The storage architecture of MRS.

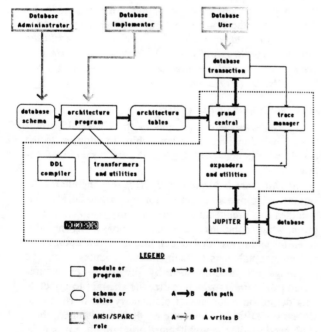

Fig. 6. The organization of the GENESIS prototype.

Database users write transactions to process database retrievals and updates. The host language is C [31]. The record types that can be defined in GENESIS are more general than those supported by C, so users are supplied routines to read and manipulate buffer-resident GENESIS records. These are the routines of the *trace manager*.

Records are transferred between main memory buffers and secondary storage by *file operations* which are accessed via the Grand Central module.

Grand Central serves as a routing circuit to modules called *expanders*. Each expander defines the abstract-to-concrete operation mappings for an elementary transformation. The number of expanders equals the number of elementary transformations needed by a storage architecture. When an operation O on an abstract file is to be executed and the abstract file is materialized by the elementary transformation T, Grand Central causes operation O_T of the expander for T to be executed. Every expander calls the trace manager to aid in the reading and manipulation of main-memory resident GENESIS records.

Abstract operations are eventually mapped to operations on internal files, which are processed by JUPITER, the file management system of GENESIS. JUPITER supports both single-keyed and multikeyed simple files through a single interface, and handles all I/O between main-memory and secondary storage.

In summary, data definition mappings of elementary transformations are handled by transformers. Operation mappings are handled by expanders. A database schema is compiled and mapped by an architecture program, which calls the DDL compiler and transformers. A transcript of these mappings is stored in architecture tables. A transaction initiates operations on conceptual files and conceptual links. Grand Central uses the contents of architecture tables to direct the translation of conceptual operations to their internal counterparts. Expanders are called to perform the level-by-level mappings.

The ANSI/SPARC role of database users, who write and execute transactions, and the DBA, who designs and writes database schemas, remain unchanged [51]. Extensible DBMS's, such as GENESIS, requires an additional party, the DBI, who is responsible for the construction and customization of a DBMS.

We estimate that it may take several days or weeks for the DBI to determine a satisfactory storage architecture for a given class of applications. It has been our experience that a typical expander and its transformer can be designed, coded, and debugged in several months. Once a storage architecture has been chosen, and when all the expanders and transformers that are needed are available, GENESIS can be reconfigured to store and retrieve data according to the target architecture in the time it takes to write the DBMS's storage architecture program. This can be done in hours.

B. The Layer Interface

1) DDL: The GENESIS DDL is a mixture of record structuring concepts taken from the C, Pascal, and Cobol programming languages, and the set constructs of DBTG. GENESIS record types can contain fixed-length and variable-length fields, scalar and set-valued attributes (henceforth called *scalar fields* and *repeating fields*), nested scalar and nested repeating fields, and matrices. These constructs underly *non-first normal form relations* [16], [38], [40], [29]. Links support $N:M$ relationships, information carrying sets [50], and multimember sets [17].

As mentioned earlier, the GENESIS DDL is used to declare schemas from the conceptual level through the internal level. As an example of a conceptual schema, Fig. 7 shows a typical MRS (relational) schema, i.e., one that contains no nested definitions, LINK, or SET constructs. Fig. 8 is an example of an internal schema which describes an inverted file (at a level of detail comparable to Fig. 3).

• A schema consists of a sequence of four statements: OPTIONS, TYPES, FILES, and LINKS [45]. The OPTIONS statement declares tags that can be associated with individual fields, files, or links. Tags are used as architecture directives. In Fig. 8, "bplus" and "unordered" are used to tag files that are to be stored in B+ trees and unordered file structures, respectively, and "primary_key" tags key fields.

User-defined types are listed in the TYPES statement, and files are declared in the FILES statement. For the most part, the syntax is conventional. However, note that the SET (n) OF x construct declares repeating fields to contain up to n elements of type x, and SET (*) OF x permits an unbounded number of elements.

Links are declared in the LINKS statement. In Fig. 8, Ename_Index is the parent file and Employee is the child of link EI. The link key [2], [5] for both files is Ename, and the parent field of link EI is Inverted_List.

2) DML: The basic objects in a database are records,

```
DATABASE      MRS_schema
{
    OPTIONS
        primary_key;      /* primary key option */
        indexed;          /* index option       */
    TYPES
        Professor_Type =
        {
            Pname          STRING (10) OF CHAR   primary_key indexed;
            Office#        INT;
            Building       STRING (4) OF CHAR    indexed;
            Campus_Phone   INT;
        };
    FILES
        Professor          Professor_Type;
}.
```

Fig. 7. An MRS (relational) schema.

```
DATABASE      Inverted_File
{
    OPTIONS
        primary_key;      /* primary key option            */
        bplus;            /* b+ tree implementation        */
        unordered;        /* unordered file implementation */
    TYPES
        Dependent_Type =
        {
            First_Name     STRING (8) OF CHAR;
            Age            INT;
        };

        Employee_Type =
        {
            Emp#           INT                    primary_key;
            Ename          STRING (12) OF CHAR;
            Salary         FLOAT;
            Offspring      SET (20) OF Dependent_Type;
        };

        Ename_Index_Type =
        {
            Ename          STRING (20) OF CHAR    primary_key;
            Inverted_List  SET (*) OF POINTER;
        };
    FILES
        Employee           Employee_Type          unordered;
        Ename_Index        Ename_Index_Type       bplus;
    LINKS
        EI =
        {
            PARENT.LKEY  = Ename_Index.Ename;
            PARENT.FIELD = Ename_Index.Inverted_List;
            CHILD.LKEY   = Employee.Ename;
        };
}.
```

Fig. 8. An example GENESIS schema.

files, and links. Each has its own data retrieval and manipulation operations. Record operations process records that are in main-memory, file operations transfer main-memory records to and from secondary storage, and link operations traverse and alter link occurrences.

Cursors are run-time mechanisms that are used to reference objects and to express operations on objects [23]. Records, files, and links have their own types of cursors.

In GENESIS, only record and file cursors are explicitly supported. A link cursor can be realized by one or more file cursors, and link operations are primarily accomplished by calls to file operations. For this reason, ad hoc

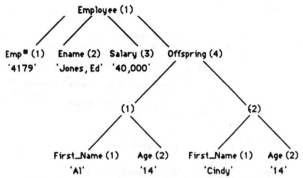

Fig. 9. A tree representation of an employee record.

Operation Type	Trace Operation	Semantics
Navigation		
	LEFT(trace)	reposition trace to left sibling
	RIGHT(trace)	reposition trace to right sibling
	UP(trace)	reposition trace to parent node
	DOWN(trace, nth_child)	reposition trace to the nth child
Manipulation		
	RD(trace, buffer)	read scalar field into buffer
	WR(trace, buffer)	write buffer into scalar field
	AD(trace, buffer)	add element in buffer to repeating field
	DL(trace, nth_child)	delete nth_element of repeating field
Utility		
	MAKE_TRACE(trace, field_name)	create trace to specified field
	DROP_TRACE(trace)	deallocate trace
	INIT_FIELD(trace, buffer)	initialize field in buffer
	COUNT_CHILDREN(trace)	return number of subfields of given field
	LEN(trace)	return length of field
	LOC(trace)	return starting address of field

Fig. 10. A partial list of trace operations.

Operation	Semantics
MAKE_FILE_CURSOR(F_cursor, mt_id)	create file cursor for file with handle mt_id
DROP_FILE_CURSOR(F_cursor)	delete file cursor
REASSIGN(F_cursor, new_mt_id)	reassign file cursor to another file
RET(F_cursor, query, into_list, position)	prepare F_cursor for record retrieval. query is a selection predicate, into_list contains trace-buffer pairs for the input and output of individual fields, position specifies initial positioning of F_cursor (before_first or at_first record)
ADV(F_cursor)	advance F_cursor to point to next record to be retrieved
INIT(F_cursor, query, into_list)	prepare F_cursor for pointer following
ACC(F_cursor)	follow pointer in F_cursor to access record
REM(F_cursor)	delete record referenced by F_cursor
UPD(F_cursor)	update record referenced by F_cursor; trace-buffer pairs that are flagged on F_cursor's into_list indicate the fields to be updated and the buffers containing their new values
INS(F_cursor, hold_option)	insert record into the file of F_cursor; field values of record are referenced in F_cursor's into_list; hold_option is true if record is to be updated shortly after insertion
MAKE_FIELD_CURSOR(F_cursor, trace, L_cursor)	create a cursor to a long field
DROP_FIELD_CURSOR(L_cursor)	delete cursor to long field
GET(L_cursor, #_of_elements, buffer, buf_size)	long field retrieval
PUT(L_cursor, #_of_elements, buffer)	long field update

Fig. 11. A partial list of file operations.

support of links will suffice for the short-term. However, a general-purpose link manager is a long-range goal.

The cursors and operations that are supported by GEN-ESIS are reviewed in the remainder of this section.

a) Traces and Record Operations: A GENESIS record is an unnormalized relational tuple and is structured as an ordered tree of fields. The root represents an entire record. Its children are its immediate subfields, their children are their subfields, and so on. The ordering of nodes reflects the ordering in which fields appear in the record. Leaves correspond to scalar fields defined over primitive types, such as characters, bytes, floats, and integers, or strings of these types. Repeating groups and matrices are represented by nonleaf nodes, where their elements are treated as subfields.

Fig. 9 shows a tree representation of an Employee record, where the Employee type was defined in Fig. 8. Beside each node is the name of the corresponding field and its ordinal number in parentheses. Under each leaf node is the data value that is contained in the field. The depicted record has Emp# = 4179, Ename = "Jones, Ed," Salary = 40,000, and two Offspring: Al and Cindy, both of age 14.

The field name of a node cannot be used as its identifier, as many nodes may share the same name. Instead, nodes are identified by their *trace*, i.e., the path from the root to the node in question. The ordinal trace to the field containing "Cindy" in Fig. 9 is (1, 4, 2, 1). Traces serve as cursors to fields of records in GENESIS.

Unlike many DDL's where there is compatibility of the record types of the host language and DBMS, GENESIS record types are more general than those provided by the C language. Special routines, called *trace operations*, are used to read and update fields in GENESIS records *that are buffer resident*. The collection of all trace operations is the *trace manager*.

• There are three different groups of trace operations: navigational, manipulation, and utility. *Navigational* operations position traces, *manipulation* operations read and update individual fields, and *utility* operations create and delete traces dynamically and provide encoding information (e.g., the number of elements in a repeating field, the field length in bytes, etc.). A partial list of trace operations is given in Fig. 10. A detailed description of the trace manager is given in [45].

b) File Cursors and File Operations: GENESIS operations on files are patterned after embedded SQL [13] and operations on long fields [24]. A partial list of operations is given in Fig. 11.

• Every file in a GENESIS database is assigned an identifier called a *file handle* or *mt_id*, which is used to identify a cursor with a file. Cursors can be dynamically allocated, deallocated, and reassigned to different files.

Records of a file that satisfy a query can be retrieved in two different ways. One way is to initialize a cursor for file searching (using the RET operation) and to advance the cursor repeatedly (using ADV) to return the sequence of qualified records one at a time. Queries involving joins are handled by the JOIN operation, which is discussed later in Section IV-B.

A second way to retrieve records is to follow pointers. The INIT operation prepares a cursor for direct accessing, and the ACC operation retrieves a record given its pointer. The procedure to follow an inverted list, for example, is accomplished by INITializing a cursor, storing a pointer in the cursor, and ACCessing the record. The latter two steps are repeated for each pointer on the list.

Other file operations include modification (UPD) and deletion (REM) of the current record of a cursor, and record insertion (INS), which repositions a cursor to the inserted record. GET and PUT operations are used to retrieve and update an integral number of elements within repeating groups (i.e., long fields).

C. The Layer Implementation

Every layer of software that realizes an elementary transformation features the interface described in Section III-B. We explain in the following sections how layers are implemented.

We begin with a brief description of JUPITER, the file management system and the lowest layer of GENESIS. Implementing elementary transformations requires the abstract-to-concrete mappings of both data definitions and operations. We show how data definitions are mapped by procedures called transformers, and how file operations are mapped by procedures called expanders. We conclude by explaining how expanders relate to software layers and how operation mappings are composed.

1) The JUPITER File Management System: JUPITER is a general-purpose file management system [22], [54]. It is composed of five layers and resides on UNIX (see Fig. 12). The bottom layer is the *buffer manager*. It handles block I/O and coordinates the usage of buffers via an LRU or CLOCK replacement strategy. The next higher layer is the *recovery manager*, which uses Lorie's shadowing algorithm [34], DB-cache [20], or before-image page-logging. (The actual algorithm used is declared at JUPITER compilation time.) Above the recovery manager is the *block manager*. It handles the storage and retrieval of records within buffer-resident blocks. Records can either be fixed-length or variable-length, and can be either anchored (i.e., have fixed storage locations) or unanchored. In all, four different block formats are handled.

A *node* or *frame* is a logical sequence of records. Nodes (frames) have been shown to be the basic components of file structures [37], [2]. The *node manager* provides nodes and operations on nodes as primitives, and relies on the block and recovery managers for lower-level support. Four different types of node implementations are available: 1) primary block only, 2) primary block with unshared overflow blocks, 3) primary block with shared overflow blocks, and 4) shared overflow blocks only. (Unshared overflow blocks contain records of a single node; shared overflow blocks contain records of multiple nodes.)

The highest layer is the *file manager*. It presents a uniform interface to all single-keyed and multikeyed file

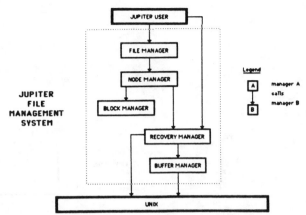

Fig. 12. The organization of JUPITER.

structures. By doing so, a measure of data independence is achieved. Simple file implementations in a DBMS storage architecture can be changed without forcing modifications to the software that reference them. JUPITER presently features indexed-sequential, indexed aggregate. B+ tree, deferred B+ tree, unordered, hash-based, heap, and multikeyed hashing file structures. (Useful variations of these structures can be generated by altering their node and block implementations. This is easily done by resetting the block and node implementation flags prior to file creation.)

JUPITER is extensible. Different buffer and recovery management algorithms, such as those described in [20], [19], can be introduced by replacing the existing algorithms while retaining the same interface. New file structure algorithms can be added easily because many of the difficult-to-write primitives are already provided by lower-level managers. A detailed description of JUPITER is forthcoming [54].

2) Transformers and Architecture Programs: A formal specification of conceptual-to-internal data mappings is an *architecture program*, which translates the data definitions of conceptual files to their internal counterparts using *transformers* [52]. Transformers are procedures that handle the details of entering architecture specifications into tables, called *storage architecture tables*. These tables are used to direct the conceptual-to-internal mappings of file operations.

An architecture program for MRS, written in C [31], is shown in Fig. 15. All architecture programs are very simple and very short, and can be written quickly. An explanation of this program and architecture programs in general is given below.

• There are five different types of objects that architecture programs deal with: record type definitions, volumes, JUPITER files, file implementation types, and file types. Objects of each type are respectively identified with rows in the following architecture tables: the FDT, VT, JFT, FIT, and MT. The row numbers that are identified with these objects are their *handles* (*ids*).

When a schema is compiled, an internal representation of each record type is entered into a row of the *field def-*

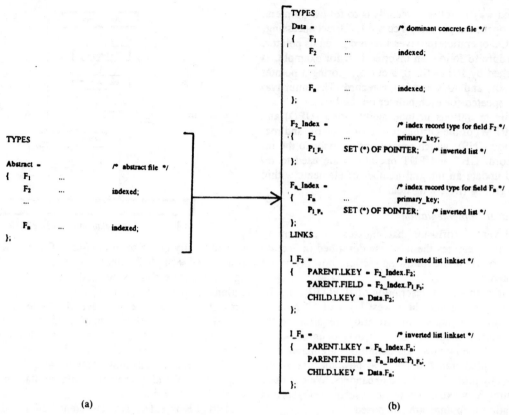

(a)   (b)

Fig. 13. Data mappings of MRS_INDEX.

inition table (*FDT*). A *volume* in GENESIS is an area of secondary storage. (Presently, volumes are identified with UNIX files). Every volume of a database is described in a row of the *volume table* (*VT*). A volume can contain one or more JUPITER files. Every JUPITER file has a row entry in the *JUPITER file table* (*JFT*). (A subentry in a JFT row lists the volume handle (vt_id) of the volume that contains the JUPITER file.) Every JUPITER file has a simple file implementation. As many JUPITER files can have the same implementation, all implementation descriptions are factored into a separate table, called the *file implementation table* (*FIT*). (Again, a subentry in a JFT row lists the file implementation (fit_id) of the JUPITER file.) Finally, files are generated by transformers during conceptual-to-internal mappings. Every file that is created is described in a row of the *mapping table* (*MT*). (As we saw in Section III-B-2-b (File Cursors), the row number of a file is its file handle or mt_id.)

Given the above, a typical architecture program performs the following five steps: 1) initialization of the architecture tables, 2) compilation of the conceptual schema, 3) mapping each conceptual file to its internal files, 4) assigning an implementation to each internal file, and 5) saving a transcript of these steps.

Using the MRS architecture program of Fig. 15 as an example, Steps 1 and 2 are straightforward. There is only one volume for the entire database, and all JUPITER files will be stored in that volume.

Steps 3 and 4 are interleaved in Fig. 15, and require

some explanation. Each conceptual file is mapped to an inverted file by the MRS_INDEX transformer. This transformer creates a data file and one abstract index file for each field of the conceptual file that is to be indexed, and enters their definitions into the FDT and MT. Fig. 13(b) shows the schema mappings that are generated by MRS_INDEX given the abstract record type definition of Fig. 13(a). (A field of the abstract definition is indexed if it is tagged with the appropriate OPTIONS; this tag is input to the MRS_INDEX transformer.)

Each abstract index file is mapped to an index file and list file by the MRS_DIVIDE transformer, and the definitions of these files are entered into the FDT and MT. Fig. 14(b) shows the schema mappings that are generated by MRS_DIVIDE given the abstract record type definition of Fig. 14(a).

Finally, each internal file (data, index, and list) is assigned to a distinct JUPITER file. This creates entries in the JFT. The above mappings are accomplished in two nested loops in Fig. 15. The last step is to write the architecture tables to a disk file (''mrs_schema_tables'') for later reference.

As an example of how an architecture program maps the record types of a specific schema, Fig. 16 illustrates the mapping of the Professor record type defined in the MRS schema of Fig. 7. A more detailed explanation of this example, including a listing of architecture tables, is given in Appendix I.

It is worth noting that unless a storage architecture is

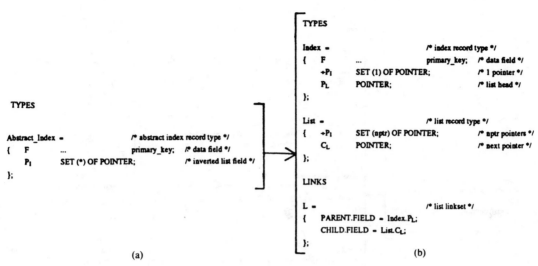

(a)   (b)

Fig. 14. Data mappings of MRS_DIVIDE.

Fig. 15. An architecture program for MRS.

modified, an architecture program does not change once it is written. Different architectures are described by different architecture programs.

MRS has a rather simple architecture. Although other DBMS's can be considerably more complicated (e.g., IDMS), their architecture programs are only a few lines longer than the one presented. It is because of this simplicity that architecture programs can be developed and modified very quickly.

3) Expanders: An *expander* is a procedure that maps an operation on an abstract file to a sequence of operations on concrete files, as prescribed by an elementary transformation. The mapping algorithm that is encapsulated by an expander does *not* rely on how concrete operators are realized at lower levels. (As we noted in Section II-C, this is simple to do.) It is this independence which permits radically different DBMS storage architectures to be constructed from a common pool of components.

Again consider MRS. The MRS_INDEX transformation maps an abstract file to an inverted file (i.e., a concrete data file and concrete index files). Operations on inverted files are well-understood. When abstract records are retrieved their corresponding (dominant) data records are retrieved, along with zero or more index records. (The index records were used to locate the data records.) When an abstract record is updated or deleted, its corresponding data record is updated or deleted, in addition to the modification of affected index records.

The MRS_DIVIDE operation mappings are also straightforward. Retrieving an abstract index record involves the retrieval of its (dominant) index record and the following of a linear-list linkset to access all of its list records. By concatenating these records, the abstract index record is reconstructed. An update or deletion of an abstract index record requires the update or deletion of its corresponding index and list records.

The INTERNAL transformation translates operations on files directly to operations on JUPITER files. As such, operations on internal files are treated as primitives. (Actually, JUPITER has a slightly more primitive set of operations than the operations listed in Section III-B-2-b. INTERNAL algorithms perform this translation.)

In the remainder of this section, we show the MRS_INDEX, MRS_DIVIDE, and INTERNAL expanders for a simple operation: MAKE_FILE_CURSOR. Expanders for the more complicated retrieval operations RET and ADV are given in Appendix II.

• We will use the following notation to express oper-

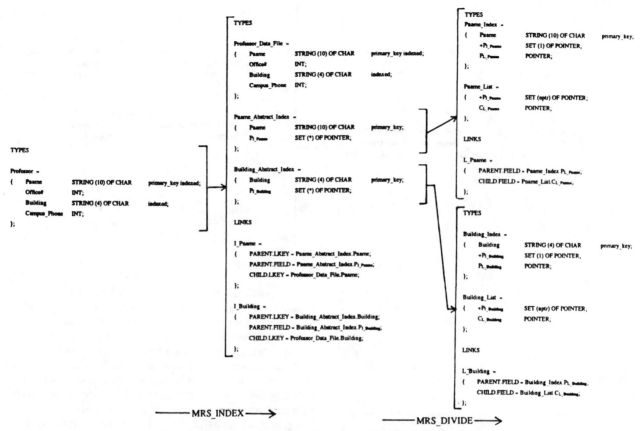

Fig. 16. MRS conceptual-to-internal mapping of the professor record type.

ation mappings:

OPERATION$_{transformation}$ →
    OPERATION-1;
    OPERATION-2;
    . . .
    OPERATION-n;

The operation to the left of → is an operation on an abstract file. Its subscript indicates which elementary transformation produces this mapping. The sequence of operations to the right of → are operations on concrete files and have unspecified transformation subscripts (to denote no reliance on how concrete operations are implemented at lower levels).

Consider the mapping of the MAKE_FILE_CURSOR operation by MRS_INDEX. Suppose that at most two cursors are needed at any one time to process operations on an inverted file; one is permanently assigned to the data file and the other is reassignable to any of the index files. It follows that when a cursor is created for the abstract file, a data file cursor and an index file cursor are also created. The mapping for this operation is:

MAKE_FILE_CURSOR$_{MRS\_INDEX}$(A_cursor, A_mtid) →
    MAKE_FILE_CURSOR(D_cursor, D_mtid);
    MAKE_FILE_CURSOR(X_cursor, X_mtid);

A_mtid and D_mtid denote the handles of the abstract file and the data file, and X_mtid is the handle of one of the index files. (Note that the mapping table MT provides the means to determine D_mtid and X_mtid from A_mtid.)

Although not shown, D_cursor and X_cursor are actually linked as "subcursors" to A_cursor. Subsequent transformations may create subcursors to D_cursor and X_cursor, giving rise to a tree of cursors rooted at A_cursor. The leaves of the tree are cursors on internal (JUPITER) files. With this construction, it is possible to find the concrete cursors of any abstract cursor quickly. We show an example cursor tree at the end of the next section (Grand Central).

Now consider the mapping of MAKE_FILE_CURSOR by MRS_DIVIDE. Creating a cursor on an abstract index file requires the creation of cursors on the corresponding concrete index and concrete list files. Again, we have a simple expansion:

MAKE_FILE_CURSOR$_{MRS\_DIVISION}$(X_cursor, X_mtid) →
    MAKE_FILE_CURSOR(I_cursor, I_mtid);
    MAKE_FILE_CURSOR(L_cursor, L_mtid);

X_mtid is the handle of the abstract index file, and I_mtid and L_mtid are the handles of the index and list files.

As mentioned earlier, MAKE_FILE_CURSOR$_{INTERNAL}$ along with other INTERNAL operations are treated as primitives. Thus, no explicit expansions for these operations are necessary.

4) *Grand Central:* Conceptual-to-internal mappings of operations are realized as a composition of abstract-to-concrete mappings of operations. This composition is accomplished at run-time by routing the output of one expander to the input of another. The mapping table (MT) contains the routing information. The routing procedures are collectively called *Grand Central*. A more advanced method of composition is discussed in Section IV-C.

• Grand Central is a set of procedures, one procedure for each file operation. Each procedure is a case statement, where the case indicator identifies an elementary transformation. The number of cases equals the number of expanders that are needed for a specific architecture. Suppose an abstract file A has handle A_mtid. Let XFORM(A_mtid) be the identifier of the elementary transformation which maps A to its concrete counterparts. (XFORM is a trivial lookup function; it returns the "xform" column value of row A_mtid in table MT.) The Grand Central procedures for MAKE_FILE_CURSOR and RET look like:

```
MAKE_FILE_CURSOR(A_cursor, A_mtid)
{
  switch(XFORM(A_mtid))
  {
  case MRS_INDEX:
    MAKE_FILE_CURSOR_MRS_INDEX(A_cursor,
      A_mtid);
  case MRS_DIVIDE:
    MAKE_FILE_CURSOR_MRS_DIVIDE(A_cursor,
      A_mtid);
  case INTERNAL:
    MAKE_FILE_CURSOR_INTERNAL(A_cursor,
      A_mtid);
  };

RET(A_cursor, A_query, A_into_list, position)
{
  switch(XFORM(A_cursor.mtid))
  {
  case MRS_INDEX:
    RET_MRS_INDEX(A_cursor, A_query, A_into_list,
      position);
  case MRS_DIVIDE:
    RET_MRS_DIVIDE(A_cursor, A_query, A_into_list,
      position);
  case INTERNAL:
    RET_INTERNAL(A_cursor, A_query, A_into_list,
      position);
  };
};
```

Procedures for other operations follow the same pattern.

Here's how Grand Central works. Each procedure of Grand Central directs the expansion of an operation on abstract files. If an abstract file is materialized by the MRS_INDEX transformation, then the RET, ADV, etc., operations on the abstract file would be translated into the RET_{MRS_INDEX}, ADV_{MRS_INDEX}, etc., operations on con-

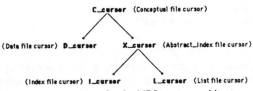

Fig. 17. A cursor tree for the MRS storage architecture.

crete files. In general, if an abstract file is materialized by transformation T, the abstract operation O on this file is mapped to operation O_T by Grand Central.

Users issue operations on conceptual files in the MRS architecture. These operations are translated by MRS_INDEX mappings to operations on abstract index files and data files. Operations on abstract index files are translated by MRS_DIVIDE mappings to operations on index and list files. Operations on data, index, and list files are translated by INTERNAL to operations on JUPITER files. All of these translations are directed by Grand Central.

As mentioned in Section III-C-3 (Expanders), a tree of file cursors is created when a cursor on a conceptual file in an MRS database is created. Fig. 17 shows an instance of this tree. Again, it is a result of composing $MAKE\_FILE\_CURSOR_{MRS\_INDEX}$, $MAKE\_FILE\_CURSOR_{MRS\_DIVIDE}$, and $MAKE\_FILE\_CURSOR_{INTERNAL}$. As mentioned earlier, the leaves of the cursor tree are JUPITER cursors (i.e., cursors on INTERNAL files).

IV. FUTURE RESEARCH

Extensible database systems require a technology that will take years to perfect. We have taken the first steps to consolidate theoretical results and practical achievements. The next steps will require basic research both in databases and software development.

Among the outstanding database issues that remain to be incorporated into the prototype are concurrency control, query processing, and customized end-user interfaces. Although we are investigating all three, we discuss the first two in Sections IV-A and IV-B to show how layering forces a novel interpretation and generalization of existing results.

Customizing end-user interfaces is an essential feature of extensible DBMS's. It can take the form of allowing alternative data models and data languages, allowing new data types and operators to be defined, or both. Our research on this topic has lead us to the development of a functional data model and data language as the basis for end-user interface customizing to GENESIS. Details of this research are explained in [7].

From the side of software development, a technology is needed to compose layers of software at compile time (not at run-time as we are now doing). Compile-time composition has the potential of eliminating unneeded generality in expanders through code simplification. Furthermore, there is the possibility of applying our technology to other areas of software development. These topics are the subject of Section IV-C.

As before, the basic ideas of each section are summa-

rized in the introductory paragraphs. Additional details follow the bullet (•) marker.

A. Concurrency Control

Concurrency control is an integral component of multiuser database systems. The most common method to achieve concurrency control is locking; i.e., a transaction can access a data item only if it holds an appropriate lock on that item [32]. As a general rule, locking protocols have been developed for reading and writing objects that are visible through a single interface. Extensible database technology requires more sophistication because a series of interfaces are crossed in conceptual-to-internal mappings. At each interface, objects in addition to conceptual objects may appear (e.g., indexes, fragment files, etc.), and protocols for reading and writing them are needed. It is often the case that protocols, such as two-phase locking (2PL), which are appropriate at the conceptual level may not be optimal at the internal level.

A way to explain the locking protocol that is used by a DBMS is by a composition of the protocols that are enforced at each layer of its architecture. This concept is illustrated below.

• Placing and releasing locks on records are special database operations. Consequently, they are subject to mappings. It is not unusual, for example, that locking a conceptual record may generate locks on one or more internal records. A simple set of rules appears to govern the mapping of record locks, so that consistency at a higher level is preserved at lower levels [15]:

1) A lock on an abstract record is always mapped to a lock on its dominant concrete record.

2) A record lock becomes a page lock if mapped by the internal or layering transformation.

3) Secondary records created by division and segmentation are indirectly locked by locking their primary record. That is, locking the primary path to secondary records prevents them from being accessed by others.

Note that these rules do not say *when* locks should be placed or released (this is the responsibility of the locking protocol), but rather *how* a lock on an abstract object is inherited by concrete objects. Thus we distinguish between locking protocols and lock mappings.

Lock mapping in MRS occurs in the following way (see Fig. 18). A lock on a CONCEPTUAL record becomes a lock on its DATA record by rule 1). A lock on an ABSTRACT_INDEX record becomes a lock on its INDEX record, again by rule 1). LIST records need not be locked, even if they are read or updated, by rule 3). Locks on DATA and INDEX records are locks on internal records. Lock mappings can either stop here, or they can be translated into page locks by rule 2). (This means that two different versions of the MRS architecture could be constructed, each with a different lock granularity, i.e., records versus pages.)

MRS uses 2PL for concurrency control at the conceptual level. However, a non-2PL protocol is used for locking ABSTRACT_INDEX records and their corresponding

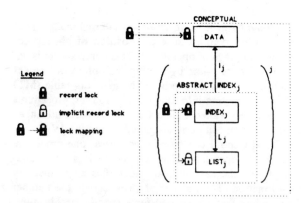

Fig. 18. Conceptual-to-internal lock mappings in MRS.

INDEX records. As mentioned above, LIST records are not locked at all. Thus, if the locking protocol of MRS were explained solely in terms of internal records, it would be an odd mixture of rules which would not correspond at all with recognized protocols. Viewed in a layered manner, where the semantics of the objects that are being locked are taken into account, the MRS protocol can be easily seen as a composition of familiar results.

An extensible DBMS should provide a selection of protocols at any given layer. System R, for example, has a software layer similar to MRS_INDEX. However, it uses 2PL to lock ABSTRACT_INDEX records. IDMS uses a variant of 2PL at the conceptual level.

It appears possible to integrate concurrency control into expanders, so that multiuser DBMS's can be constructed from components just as easily as that for single user systems. A general theory of lock mappings will be needed to provide the required groundwork.

B. Query Processing

Query processing is a fundamental area of database research. The seminal results have concentrated on relational DBMS's (e.g., [44], [57]). Extensions have generalized their scope so that query processing in network, hierarchical, and relational databases are subsumed as special cases (e.g., [14], [56], [39]). Current research addresses the challenges of non-1NF relations, abstract data types, complex objects, and recursive queries (e.g., [41], [48], [35], [58]).

Extensible DBMS technology requires query processing algorithms to be consolidated and recast into a layered framework. This calls for known algorithms to be decomposed into layers, so that each processing strategy and optimization strategy is localized to a specific layer. Thus, a query processing algorithm which covers multiple layers would be reconstructed by the composition of the optimization and strategies of the layers that it references.

Queries are posed at the external level; it is the responsibility of the DBMS to map queries to the internal level. A layered model of query processing must account for *external-to-internal* mappings in a unified way. An example of layered decomposition is given below.

• Consider the conceptual Employee and Department record types (relations) which both have indexes on the

Dept. field:

```
TYPE      Employee =
{
    E#        INT                        primary_key;
    Ename     SET (10) OF CHAR;
    Salary    FLOAT;
    Dept      SET (8) OF CHAR           indexed;
};

TYPE      Department =
{
    D#        INT                        primary_key;
    Dept      STRING (8) OF CHAR         indexed;
    Building  STRING (10) OF CHAR;
    City      STRING (10) OF CHAR;
};
```

A view file (relation) of the equi-join of Employee and Department is declared in SQL as:

```
DEFINE VIEW Empdept AS
SELECT  E#, Ename, Salary, Employee.Dept, D#, Building, City
FROM    Employee, Department
WHERE   Employee.Dept. = Department.Dept
```

The query to retrieve employee names and department numbers of employees who earn more than $30,000 and work in Denver is expressed through this view as:

```
SELECT  Ename, D#
FROM    Empdept
WHERE   Salary > 30000 AND City = "Denver"
```

One way that this query could be processed is by a merge-join of the Dept. indexes [9]. That is, a Dept index record of the Employee file is joined with a Dept index record of the Department file if both have the same Dept value. The join produces pairs of inverted lists; one list points to Employee records and the other points to Department records. An inverted list pair is processed by following the pointers of each list and applying the restriction predicates to the referenced records. The Employee and Department records that qualify are joined unconditionally, and the Ename and D# attributes are projected. The query is evaluated by processing each inverted list pair in the above manner.

Decomposing this algorithm into layers requires us to introduce a new layer to the MRS architecture and a new file operation. The new layer is called VIEW and is responsible for external-to-conceptual mappings. It resides on top of MRS_INDEX and incorporates standard query modification and query simplification algorithms to map operations on view relations to operations on conceptual relations.[1] Fig. 19 is a dsd that shows the *external-to-internal* data mappings of the Empdept view relation.

[1]The implementation of the VIEW layer may be different than other MRS layers. A preprocessor can accomplish the external-to-conceptual mappings for embedded DML statements at program compile time. In such cases, the VIEW "layer" is actually in the preprocessor expansions. For high-level query languages, the VIEW expansions are done at run-time. The VIEW layer would then constitute part of the query language subsystem of the DBMS.

The new file operation is called JOIN. It binds a cursor to a "view" file which is produced by the join of two concrete files. A parametric definition of JOIN is given in Fig. 20. A cursor initialized by JOIN can be ADVanced, in the same way as RET, to read records of a view file one at a time.

Fig. 21 shows how the RET operation at the external level is mapped to operations at the internal level. Each step in the mapping is highlighted below.

1) External Level: A user initiates a RET on the Empdept view relation. Grand Central translates this operation into RET_{VIEW} [Fig. 21(a)].

2) External-to-Conceptual Mappings: VIEW maps the RET on Empdept relation to a JOIN of the Employee and Department files [Fig. 21(b)]. The mapping is accomplished by view substitution algorithms.

3) Conceptual-to-Inverted_File Mappings: MRS_INDEX maps the JOIN of Employee and Department to a JOIN of the abstract Dept index files, and an INITialization of the cursors on the internal Employee_Data and internal Department_Data files [Fig. 21(c)]. The data file cursors are used for following pointers of inverted lists and applying restriction predicates to data file records. It is in MRS_INDEX where the algorithm to process inverted list pairs, which was described above, resides.

4) Abstract_Index-to-Internal Mappings: MRS_DIVIDE maps the JOIN of the abstract Dept index files to a JOIN of the internal index files, and an INITialization of cursors to the internal list files [Fig. 21(d)]. The INITed cursors are used for pointer following to access list file records. It is in MRS_DIVIDE that inverted lists are reconstructed from their fragments.

5) Internal Level: INTERNAL materializes the JOIN of the internal index files by the merge-join algorithm.

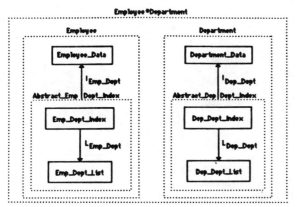

Fig. 19. External-to-internal mapping of data in MRS.

Operation:

    JOIN(J_cursor,
          mtid₁, query₁, into_list₁,
          mtid₂, query₂, into_list₂,
          join_clause, position)

Semantics:

    join concrete file mtid₁ with concrete file mtid₂.
    J_cursor is a cursor over the records of the joined files.
    query₁ and into_list₁ are the qualification predicate
    and field-buffer pairs for data input and output for file mtid₁
    join_clause gives the joining condition, and
    position specifies initial positioning of J_cursor
    (before_first or at_first record).

Fig. 20. A parametric definition of the JOIN operation.

(a) operation at the external level:

     RET$_{VIEW}$(V_cursor, 'Salary > 30,000 and City = Denver', V_into_list, position)

(b) RET$_{VIEW}$ expansion:

     JOIN$_{MRS\_INDEX}$(J_cursor,
          Employee_mtid, 'Salary > 30000', Employee_into_list,
          Department_mtid, 'City = Denver', Department_into_list,
          'Employee.Dept = Department.Dept', position)

(c) JOIN$_{MRS\_INDEX}$ expansion:

     JOIN$_{MRS\_DIVIDE}$(JAX_cursor,
          Abstract_Emp_Dept_Index_mtid, null, Abs_Emp_Dept_Index_into_list,
          Abstract_Dep_Dept_Index_mtid, null, Abs_Dep_Dept_Index_into_list,
          'Abstract_Emp_Dept_Index.Dept = Abstract_Dep_Dept_Index.Dept', position);

     INIT$_{INTERNAL}$(Employee_Data_cursor, 'Salary > 30000', Employee_Data_into_list);
     INIT$_{INTERNAL}$(Department_Data_cursor, 'City = Denver', Department_Data_into_list);

(d) JOIN$_{MRS\_DIVIDE}$ expansion:

     JOIN$_{INTERNAL}$(JX_cursor,
          Emp_Dept_Index_mtid, null, Emp_Dept_Index_into_list,
          Dep_Dept_Index_mtid, null, Dep_Dept_Index_into_list,
          'Emp_Dept_Index.Dept = Dep_Dept_Index.Dept', position);

     INIT$_{INTERNAL}$(Emp_Dept_List_cursor, null, Emp_Dept_List_into_list);
     INIT$_{INTERNAL}$(Dep_Dept_List_cursor, null, Dep_Dept_List_into_list);

Fig. 21. External-to-internal mapping of JOIN's in MRS.

Once an external cursor has been bound to the view file (which is what the above mappings accomplish), view records are read one at a time by ADVancing the external cursor. The mapping of this operation is straightforward and is not presented here.

As indicated earlier, there are many other ways of processing this query; each would have its own distinctive

external-to-internal mappings. Although it may not be obvious from this example, specific strategies and optimization decisions can be identified with each layer. The VIEW layer, for example, determines the ordering in which conceptual files are to be joined. (No decision was necessary in our example.) The MRS_INDEX layer determines whether or not indexes should be used. (An alternative to the one considered above would be to ignore indices altogether and to perform a JOIN on the Employee_Data and Department_Data files directly. A JOIN of the conceptual files would still result, but perhaps at a cost of lower performance.) Some layers, such as MRS_DIVIDE, do not involve optimization of JOIN's as there is only one obvious strategy to pursue.

A layered model of query processing, based on the above approach, is forthcoming [8].

C. Software Development Technologies

Our work opens up two interesting areas of research in software development. One is to apply our ideas to data structures, the other is to compose layers at compile time. We discuss each in turn.

The technology that we have described so far has applications beyond the development of DBMS software. To understand this possibility, recognize that data structures are main-memory storage structures. Layering occurs in data structures much in the same way as it does in secondary storage structures. Thus, there should be data structure counterparts to the UM and TM. As data structures are used in virtually every major software application (of which DBMS's are a small subset), it seems reasonable to believe that a companion technology to GENESIS can be devised to handle a much broader scope of software development problems than we are presently considering.

Performance is a key issue in DBMS's. If one compares the code that GENESIS produces with the actual handwritten code of MRS, one finds substantial differences. GENESIS code has a considerable amount of layering between the conceptual and internal levels, whereas handwritten code has minimal layering. GENESIS code relies heavily on intermediate results (such as cursors to ABSTRACT_INDEX files in Fig. 17), whereas handwritten code does not. GENESIS layers (expanders) embody generalized algorithms, whereas handwritten code embodies subalgorithms.[2] The overhead of extra layering, materialization of intermediate results, and algorithm generality causes GENESIS code to be more verbose and to run slower than handwritten code. Despite these differences, both accomplish exactly the same mappings.

The drawbacks of GENESIS-produced code are not intrinsic to extensible DBMS technology; they are actually a consequence of composing modules at run-time. Com-

---

[2]The MRS_INDEX module in the GENESIS prototype, for example, handles the inversion of both scalar and repeating fields. Although repeating fields in conceptual records are excluded from the MRS architecture, they may be featured in other architectures. The extra generality enables the MRS_INDEX module to be used in the construction of radically diverse DBMS's.

pile-time composition of modules offers a means by which these problems can be eliminated.

• Handwritten code expresses a compact form of conceptual-to-internal mappings. We are convinced that programmers are mentally composing the mappings of expanders and simplifying the resulting compositions without realizing the layering processes that are involved. Preliminary investigations support the hypothesis that just as arithmetic equations can be expanded and simplified by plugging in definitions of lower-level functions and collecting terms, so too can efficient code—resembling handwritten—be produced by macro-expanding expanders and then simplifying. Obvious simplification techniques are the elimination of dead code and the replacement of unnecessary computations with their resulting values. Such techniques have been used optimizing compilers [36], [10], [42].

V. Conclusions

Database systems have largely been built in an ad hoc manner. Typical DBMS software is monolithic; to affect modifications and upgrades is either very costly or impractical. Constructing DBMS's has been more of an art practiced by few, rather than a science understood by many.

We have developed a novel, yet simple, technology which enables customized DBMS's to be produced cheaply and quickly. Our technology for extensible DBMS's is based on theoretical models [2], [5] which 1) identified basic building blocks of DBMS software, 2) revealed that all building blocks could be referenced through a common interface, and 3) showed that operational DBMS's could be described by compositions of these building blocks. An operational prototype, called GENESIS, is an implementation of these ideas.

The merit of our research lies in both its practical and theoretical contributions. From a practical perspective, once a storage architecture has been designed, the software to support it can be produced rapidly. If a prototype architecture does not work out, it can be changed easily. Both capabilities are in stark contrast to the present state-of-the-art where the exact opposite is true.

Another practical advantage is the method by which basic software components of DBMS's can be developed. Each component (e.g., an expander–transformer pair) describes simple data and operation mappings and can be coded and debugged in isolation. This contrasts with current methods of DBMS software construction where many of our components (layers) are fused and therefore must be debugged simultaneously.

From a theoretical perspective, our research points a way to which disparate academic results and practical achievements on database implementation (i.e., storage structures, query processing, concurrency control, etc.) can be unified. Furthermore, we see the potential of our technology to be generalized to areas of software development beyond DBMS's.

We believe that the development of an extensible

fdt_id	opt_flags	type	bounds	1st_child	n_child	name
0		DB		1	1	MRS_Schema
1		FILE		2	4	Professor
2	F1+F2	STRING	10	6	1	Pname
3		INT				Office
4	F1	STRING	4	6	1	Building
5		INT				Campus_Phone
6		CHAR				
7		FILE		2	4	Professor_Data_File
8		FILE		9	2	Pname_Abstract_Index
9	F1	STRING	10	6	1	Pname
10		SET	*	11	1	/* pointer array */
11		POINTER				/* pointer type */
12		FILE		13	2	Building_Abstract_Index
13		STRING	4	6	1	Building
14		SET	*	11	1	/* pointer array */
15		FILE		16	3	Pname_Index
16	F1	STRING	10	6	1	Pname
17		SET	1	11	1	/* set (1) of pointer */
18		POINTER				/* next child pointer */
19		FILE		20	2	Pname_List
20		SET	nptr	11	1	/* set (nptr) of pointer */
21		POINTER				/* next child pointer */
22		FILE		23	3	Building_Index
23	F1	STRING	4	6	1	Building
24		SET	1	11	1	/* set (1) of pointer */
25		POINTER				/* first child pointer */
26		FILE		27	2	Building_List
27		SET	nptr	11	1	/* set (nptr) of pointer */
28		POINTER				/* next child pointer */

note: F1 denotes the 'indexed' option and F2 denotes the 'primary_key' option.

Fig. 22. The field definition table (FDT).

DBMS technology will result in a fundamental advance in understanding and simplifying the construction of database systems.

Appendix I
Storage Architecture Tables

The five most important storage architecture tables are the field definition table (FDT), the mapping table (MT), the volume table (VT), the file implementation table (FIT), and the Jupiter file table (JFT). There are other tables, but they are not relevant here. In the following paragraphs, we show the contents of five tables for the MRS schema of Figs. 7 and 16 after it has been processed by the architecture program of Fig. 15.

Field definitions are stored in the FDT. Each row of the FDT of Fig. 22 describes a single field by its option flags, type, bounds (if any array or repeating group), the row of the FDT of its first subfield, the number of subfields, and the name of the field itself. Row 0 always contains the name of the conceptual schema. The rows whose type is "FILE" contain record type definitions. For example, the Professor record type is stored in row 1 and the Pname_Abstract_Index record type is stored in row 8. Rows 0–6 were entered by the DDL compiler when the MRS schema of Fig. 7 was processed. Rows 7–14 were added by the MRS_INDEX transformer.

Files are defined in the MT. Each row of the MT of

mt_id	file_name	fdt_id	xform	1st_child	n_child	jft_id
0	Professor	1	MRS_INDEX	1	3	
1	Professor_Data_File	7	INTERNAL			5
2	Pname_Abstract_Index	8	MRS_DIVIDE	4	2	
3	Building_Abstract_Index	12	MRS_DIVIDE	6	2	
4	Pname_Index	15	INTERNAL			1
5	Pname_List	19	INTERNAL			2
6	Building_Index	22	INTERNAL			3
7	Building_List	26	INTERNAL			4

Fig. 23. The mapping table (MT).

VT		FIT		JFT		
vt_id	vname	fit_id	file_type	jft_id	simple_file_name	vt_id	fit_id
1	mrs_vol	1	unordered	1	Pname_Index_SF	1	2
		2	b+ tree	2	Pname_List_SF	1	1
				3	Building_Index_SF	1	2
				4	Building_List_SF	1	1
				5	Professor_Data_File	1	1

Fig. 24. The volume table (VT), file implementation table (FIT), and Jupiter file table (JFT).

and B+ trees. They are defined in the FIT. The MRS database of Fig. 7 generates five internal files: two index files, two list files, and one data file. They are defined in consecutive rows of the JFT.

APPENDIX II
RET AND ADV OPERATION EXPANDERS FOR THE MRS ARCHITECTURE

Consider the MRS_INDEX transformation and its mapping of the RET and ADV operations. For purposes of simplicity, we will assume that queries are single clauses of the form (field = value). Algorithms for processing/mapping more complicated queries are given in [44] and [1].

When RET prepares an abstract cursor A_cursor for retrieval, a strategy for processing the specified query is decided. The data file is scanned if there is no index to process the query, else the index record identified by the query is retrieved and the pointers of its inverted list are followed. This strategy is expressed by:

RET_MRS_INDEX(A_cursor, A_query, A_into_list, position) →

 if A_query can be processed by indices then

  {
(1)   X_into_list := (inverted_list_trace, inverted_list_buffer);
(2)   RET(X_cursor, A_query, X_into_list, at_first);
(3)   INIT(D_cursor, null, A_into_list);
  }
 else /* scan data file */
  {
(4)   RET(D_cursor, A_query, A_into_list, before_first);
  };
(5) if position = at_first then ADV_MRS_INDEX(A_cursor);

Fig. 23 describes a file by its name, the row of the FDT at which its record type is stored, the identifier of the elementary transformation that maps it to its concrete counterparts, the row of its dominant concrete file, the number of concrete files to which it is mapped, and the row of the JFT specifying where records of this file are stored (applicable if the file is internal). For example, the Professor file (row 0) is mapped by the MRS_INDEX transformation to the Professor_Data_File (row 1) and the abstract index files for Pname and Building (rows 2 and 3).

The tables of Fig. 24 are relevant to JUPITER. MRS databases are stored in a single volume. The VT of Fig. 24 contains only one volume definition ("mrs_vol"). Two different file structures are used by MRS: unordered

Lines (1–3) deal with the case of processing A_query using an index. At line (1), "inverted_list_buffer" is declared to be the buffer that is to contain the inverted list of the retrieved index record. The record (and its inverted list) is retrieved at line (2), where the index record satisfies A_query (i.e., "field = value"). The D_cursor is initialized for pointer following in line (3). Note that the fields to return are the same as that for the abstract file.

Line (4) handles the case of data file scanning. D_cursor is initialized by using the query and into_list specified for the abstract file. (Again, data records are identical to their abstract record counterparts.)

At line (5), if A_cursor is to be positioned at the first qualified record, ADV_MRS_INDEX is called. The expansion of ADV_MRS_INDEX is:

ADV_MRS_INDEX(A_cursor) →
 if A_query can be processed using indices then
  {
(1) loop: get next pointer p from inverted_list_buffer;
(2)   if no more pointers exist, set STATUS := EOF and return;
(3)   D_cursor.pointer := p; /* D_cursor now points to record p */
(4)   ACC(D_cursor); /* follow pointer */
  }
 else /* scan data file */
  {
(5)   ADV(D_cursor);
  };

Lines (1–4) get the next pointer from the inverted_list-_buffer and access the referenced record. At line (5), an advance of an abstract cursor translates to an advance of the data file cursor.

MRS_INDEX mappings for other operations (e.g., INS, REM, UPD, etc.) can be written in an analogous manner. We omit their details.

Now consider the MRS_DIVIDE transformation. Retrieving an abstract index record involves the retrieval of its (dominant) index record and the following of a linear-list linkset to access all of its list records. The index and list records are concatenated to reconstruct the abstract index record. Let X_mtid be the mtid of an abstract index file, and I_mtid and L_mtid be the mtids of its index and list files. The retrieval algorithm for MRS_DIVIDE is expressed by:

such as $RET_{INTERNAL}$ and $ADV_{INTERNAL}$, are primitives and are not given expansions.

ACKNOWLEDGMENT

We thank H. Korth and A. Keller for their comments on an earlier draft of this paper.

REFERENCES

[1] M. M. Astrahan, *et al.*, "System R: A relational approach to database management," *ACM Trans. Database Syst.*, vol. 1, no. 2, pp. 97–137, June 1976.

[2] D. S. Batory and C. C. Gotlieb, "A unifying model of physical databases," *ACM Trans. Database Syst.*, vol. 7, no. 4, pp. 509–539, Dec. 1982.

[3] D. S. Batory, "Conceptual-to-internal mappings in commercial database systems," *ACM PODS*, pp. 70–78, 1984.

$RET_{MRS\_DIVIDE}(X\_cursor, X\_query, X\_into\_list, position) \rightarrow$

```
(1)   I_into_list := (trace to entire index record, index_buffer);
(2)   RET(I_cursor, X_query, I_into_list, before_first);
(3)   L_into_list := (trace to entire list record, list_buffer);
(4)   INIT(L_cursor, null, L_into_list);
(5)   if position = at_first then ADV_MRS_DIVIDE(X_cursor);
```

$ADV_{MRS\_DIVIDE}(X\_cursor) \rightarrow$

```
(1)    ADV(I_cursor);
(2)    if STATUS = EOF then return;
(3)    get child pointer p from index record (in index_buffer);
(4)    while p < > null do
(5)    {  L_cursor.pointer := p;   /* L_cursor now points to record p */
(6)       ACC(L_cursor);
(7)       add pointers of list record (in list_buffer) to the pointers
             of the index record (in index_buffer);
(8)       get next child pointer p from list record (in list_buffer);
       };
(9)    return fields of the abstract index record (reconstructed in
          index_buffer) that are specified in X_into_list;
(10)   set STATUS := successful;
```

In RET_{MRS_DIVIDE}, the index cursor I_cursor is prepared for record retrieval, where a RETrieved index record is to be placed in index_buffer [lines (1–2)]. The list cursor L_cursor is prepared for pointer following in lines (3–4), where an ACCessed list record is to be placed in list-_buffer. ADV_{MRS_DIVIDE} is performed in line (5) if the first abstract index record is to be retrieved.

In ADV_{MRS_DIVIDE}, lines (1–3) retrieve an index record and make preparations to follow a chain of list records. Lines (4–8) follow the chain and concatenate the pointers of list records onto the index record. The abstract index record is reconstructed in the index_buffer. Lines (9–10) return the fields requested by X_into_list and set a successful status code.

MRS_DIVIDE mappings for other operations can be written in a straightforward manner, and will not be presented here.

As mentioned earlier, INTERNAL level operations,

[4] —, "Notes on commercial DBMS architectures," unpublished manuscript, 1984.

[5] —, "Modeling the storage architecture of commercial database systems," *ACM Trans. Database Syst.*, vol. 10, no. 4, pp. 463–528, Dec. 1985.

[6] —, "Progress toward automating the development of database systems software," in *Query Processing in Database Systems*, W. Kim, D. Reiner, and D. S. Batory, Eds. New York: Springer-Verlag, 1985, pp. 261–296.

[7] D. S. Batory and T. Y. Leung, "Implementation concepts for an extensible data model and data language," Univ. Texas, Austin, Tech. Rep. TR-86-24, 1986.

[8] D. S. Batory, "An algebra for database system design," to be published.

[9] M. W. Blasgen and K. P. Eswaren, "Storage and access in relational database systems," *IBM Syst. J.*, vol. 16, no. 4, pp. 363–377, 1977.

[10] J. L. Carter, "A case study of a new code generation technique for compilers," *Commun. ACM*, vol. 20, no. 12, pp. 914–920, Dec. 1977.

[11] M. Carey *et al.*, "The architecture of the EXODUS extensible DBMS," in *Proc. Int. Workshop Object-Oriented Database Systems*, 1986, pp. 52–65.

[12] I. R. Casas, "Performance prediction of data base systems," Ph.D. dissertation, Comput. Sci., Univ. Toronto, 1986.

[13] D. D. Chamberlin et al., "SEQUEL 2: A unified approach to data definition, manipulation, and control," IBM J. Res. Dev., vol. 20, no. 6, pp. 560–575, Nov. 1976.

[14] H. Chen and S. M. Kuck, "Combining relational and network retrieval methods," in Proc. ACM SIGMOD, 1984, pp. 131–142.

[15] R. E. Culler, "Locking and the transformation model," M.Sc. thesis, Dep. Comput. Sci., Univ. Texas, Austin, 1985.

[16] P. Dadam et al., "A DBMS prototype to support extended NF2 relations: An integrated view on flat tables and hierarchies," in Proc. ACM SIGMOD, 1986, pp. 356–367.

[17] C. J. Date, An Introduction to Database Systems. Reading, MA: Addison-Wesley, 1982.

[18] U. Dayal and J. Smith, "PROBE: A knowledge-oriented database management system," in Proc. Islamorda Workshop Large Scale Knowledge Base and Reasoning Systems, Feb. 1985, pp. 103–138.

[19] W. Effelsberg and T. Haerder, "Principles of Database Buffer Management," ACM Trans. Database Syst., vol. 9, no. 4, pp. 560–595, Dec. 1984.

[20] K. Elhard and R. Bayer, "A database cache for high performance and fast restart in database systems," ACM Trans. Database Syst., vol. 9, no. 4, pp. 503–525, Dec. 1984.

[21] C. Faloutsos, "Signature files: Design and performance comparison of some signature extraction methods," in Proc. ACM SIGMOD, 1985, pp. 63–83.

[22] J. F. Garza, "Design and implementation of Jupiter: A general file management system," M.Sc. thesis, Dep. Comput. Sci., Univ. Texas, Austin, 1985.

[23] J. Gray, "Notes of database operating systems," IBM Laboratory, San Jose, CA, Res. Rep. RJ2188, 1978.

[24] R. L. Haskin and R. A. Lorie, "On extending the functions of a relational database system," in Proc. ACM SIGMOD, 1982, pp. 207–212.

[25] R. Katz, Ed., Design Data Management, IEEE Database Engineering, June 1982.

[26] W. Kim, Ed., Expert Systems and Database Systems, IEEE Database Engineering, Dec. 1983.

[27] D. Batory, Ed., Statistical Database Management, IEEE Database Engineering, Mar. 1984.

[28] R. Katz, Ed., Engineering Database Management, IEEE Database Engineering, June 1984.

[29] G. Jaesche and H. Schek, "Remarks on the algebra of non first normal form relations," ACM PODS, pp. 124–138, 1982.

[30] H. R. Johnson, J. E. Schweitzer, and E. R. Warkentine, "A DBMS facility for handling structured engineering entities," in Proc. ACM Database Week: Engineering Design Applications, 1983, pp. 3–12.

[31] B. W. Kernighan and D. M. Ritchie, The C Programming Language. Englewood Cliffs, NJ: Prentice-Hall, 1978.

[32] H. F. Korth and A. Silberschatz, Database System Concepts. New York: McGraw-Hill, 1986.

[33] J. Z. Kornatowski, The MRS User's Manual, Computer Systems Research Group, Univ. Toronto, 1979.

[34] R. A. Lorie, "Physical integrity in a large segmented database," ACM Trans. Database Syst., vol. 2, no. 1, pp. 91–104, Mar. 1977.

[35] R. A. Lorie et al., "Supporting complex objects in a relational system for engineering databases," in Query Processing in Database Systems, W. Kim, D. S. Reiner, and D. S. Batory, Eds. New York: Springer-Verlag, 1985, pp. 145–155.

[36] D. B. Loveman, "Program improvement by source to source transformation," JACM, vol. 24, no. 1, pp. 121–145, Jan. 1977.

[37] S. T. March, D. G. Severance, and M. Wilens, "Frame memory: A storage architecture to support rapid design and implementation of efficient databases," ACM Trans. Database Syst., vol. 6, no. 3, pp. 441–463, Sept. 1981.

[38] Z. M. Ozsoyoglu and L.-Y. Yuan, "A normal form for nested relations," ACM PODS, pp. 251–260, 1985.

[39] A. Rosenthal and D. Reiner, "An architecture for query optimization," in Proc. ACM SIGMOD, 1982, pp. 246–255.

[40] M. A. Roth, H. F. Korth, and A. Silberschatz, "Theory of non-first-normal-form relational database," Dep. Comput. Sci., Univ. Texas at Austin, Tech. Rep. 84-36, 1984.

[41] M. A. Roth, H. F. Korth, and D. S. Batory, "The SQL/NF query language," Dep. Comput. Sci., Univ. Texas at Austin, 1985.

[42] R. W. Scheifler, "An analysis of inline substitution for a structured programming languages," Commun. ACM, vol. 20, no. 9, pp. 647–654, Sept. 1977.

[43] P. Schwarz, et al., "Extensibility in the Starburst database system," in Proc. Workshop Object-Oriented Database Systems, 1986, pp. 85–93.

[44] P. G. Selinger, et al., "Access path selection in a relational database management system," in Proc. ACM SIGMOD, 1979, pp. 23–34.

[45] K. Smith, "Design and implementation of the GENESIS record manager," M.Sc. thesis, Dep. Comput. Sci., Univ. Texas, Austin, 1985.

[46] M. Stonebraker, E. Wong, P. Kreps, and G. Held, "The design and implementation of INGRES," ACM Trans. Database Syst., vol. 1, no. 3, pp. 189–222, Sept. 1976.

[47] M. Stonebraker, B. Rubenstein, and A. Guttman, "Application of abstract data types and abstract indices to CAD data bases," ACM Database Week: Engineering Design Applications, 1983, pp. 107–114.

[48] M. Stonebraker, "Inclusion of new types in relational data base systems," Electron. Res. Lab., Univ., California, Berkeley, Rep. UCB/ERL M85/67, 1985.

[49] M. Stonebraker and L. Rowe, "The design of POSTGRES," in Proc. ACM SIGMOD, 1986, pp. 340–355.

[50] D. C. Tsichritzis and F. Lochovsky, Data Base Management Systems. New York: Academic, 1977.

[51] D. C. Tsichritzis and A. Klug, "The ANSI/X3/SPARC DBMS framework: Report of the study group on database management systems," Inform. Syst., vol. 3, pp. 173–191, 1978.

[52] K. Tsukuda, "Mapping of record types in the GENESIS database management system," M.Sc. thesis, Dep. Comput. Sci., Univ. Texas, Austin, 1985.

[53] M. T. Turner, R. Hammond, and P. Cotton, "A DBMS for large statistical databases," in Proc. Conf. VLDB, 1979, pp. 319–327.

[54] B. C. Twichell, "Design concepts for an extensible file management system," M.Sc. thesis, Comput. Sci., Univ. Texas, Austin, 1987.

[55] G. Wiederhold, Database Design. New York: McGraw-Hill, 1983.

[56] K.-Y. Whang, "A physical database design methodology using the property of separability," Ph.D. dissertation, Dep. Comput. Sci., Stanford Univ., Stanford, CA, 1983.

[57] E. Wong and K. Youssefi, "Decomposition—A strategy for query processing," ACM Trans. Database Syst., vol. 1, no. 3, pp. 223–241, Sept. 1976.

[58] J. D. Ullman, "Implementation of logical query languages for databases," ACM Trans. Database Syst., vol. 10, no. 3, pp. 289–321, Sept. 1985.

D. S. Batory, photograph and biography not available at the time of publication.

J. R. Barnett, photograph and biography not available at the time of publication.

J. F. Garza, photograph and biography not available at the time of publication.

K. P. Smith, photograph and biography not available at the time of publication.

K. Tsukuda, photograph and biography not available at the time of publication.

B. C. Twichell, photograph and biography not available at the time of publication.

T. E. Wise, photograph and biography not available at the time of publication.

Chapter 8

Interfaces

Introduction

Interfaces to database systems are an important area for further development, but have regrettably received only a small amount of attention from the research community. Over the past 10 years, high-performance graphics-based workstations have become commonplace, and working environments that are based on visual metaphors have appeared. Consider the kinds of tools that a designer of a complex electrical circuit will use, and the desktop metaphors that have been developed for Macintoshes.

Although some work has been done in the area of graphical interfaces for relational databases [SK82; WK82; Zl75], the use of graphics for database access is in its infancy. One of the best-known projects is Query-by-Example [Zl75] which has actually been made into a product. G-Whiz [HR85] extends the query by example style to complex and recursive structures. Another effort that was designed to stretch the limits of I/O technology is SDMS [He80] from CCA and MIT. In SDMS, the user is presented with multiple screens, eye-position–tracking hardware, a joystick, and a special chair with tactile sensors mounted in the arms. Users are able to view iconic representations of a large data space in which zooming the current view toward a particular position reveals more detail about the objects displayed there. The multiple screens provided a multiple windowing capability long before the advent of window-management software such as the X Window System.

Databases have largely grown up in environments in which they were available only through complex program-level interfaces. Users typically interacted with their IMS database in terms of very detailed subroutines with long argument lists. The databases were thought of as application-development platforms more than as end-user tools. Relational systems brought with them the possibility for end-user access through ad hoc query languages such as SQL, but these were textually based and turned out to be more of a high-level programming tool than a way for end users to interact with their databases. Most relational systems now have application development tools for producing form-based user interfaces.

But there is still a technology gap between the kinds of things that end-users would like to do with their databases and the kinds of easy-to-use workstation interfaces that they are receiving for their editors and their spreadsheets. The papers in this chapter describe experimental systems that move the state of the art in that direction.

Graphical interfaces for databases must address several fundamental problems.

1. How do you access huge databases with possibly millions of objects on a small piece of real estate (e.g., a 1024-by-1024-pixel display)?

2. How do you graphically represent declarative structures such as a query or a constraint?

3. How do you display schema information (what you can ask about the data) in a way that retains its connection with the actual stored data?

There is little agreement on the best ways to address these issues, but the following papers do suggest some commonalities. The use of certain graph structures to represent the metadata, for example, is a common thread. All the systems represented here have a way to access and browse through the schema information apart from the instances. This schema information usually is displayed as a directed graph (or hierarchy).

Both ISIS [GG+85] and SNAP [BH86] are interfaces for semantic data models, whereas SIG [MNG85] is an interface for object-oriented systems that have type models like that of Smalltalk. All these interfaces are attached to database systems that include a notion of identity and are, therefore, concerned with displaying graph structures. Each has its own way of displaying an object and the objects that are related to it.

SNAP provides functionality for the basic activities of schema design, schema browsing, and query formulation. All three of these functions involve constructing and inspecting pictures at the schema level. A query is a graph template expressed in terms of schema-level (i.e., type-level) constructs. It can include constants and comparator arcs, as well as type nodes that mirror the structure of the schema.

The results of a query are returned in an answer window. The answer is given in terms of a report in the form of a nested table. The answer window provides the report for inspection by the user, but it is not graphical and it cannot be used for browsing.

The ISIS system provides the capability to do schema design, schema browsing, query, and instance-level browsing. The schema design and browsing capability is much like that of SNAP. A query is built up out of terms. The terms involve a path expression ($x.p.q$ where x is an object and p and q are appropriate attribute names) that the user specifies graphically by pointing to attribute names on a type icon, a comparator operation, and either a constant or another path expression (also specified graphically).

The result of a query in ISIS is a new subclass, and like any subclass it can have its membership inspected from the interface. If a particular object in the membership display is interesting, the user can look at it in more detail, and can browse from that entity to a related object. The theory here is that a good way to use the limited screen space is to use queries to restrict the view and then to use browsing to inspect the narrower object space returned by the query. In this way, query and browsing are natural tools to use together. The KIVIEW system [Mo88] also combines selection and browsing

The SIG system allows users to custom-tailor the display of objects. Each type can have its own display type (format) or types. The system allows the user to traverse a graph at the object level revealing displays for each object that meet the specifications of the display types. There is no direct support for querying. There is also no direct support for schema design, although SIG does include a display-type editor that helps a user through the steps of creating a new display type.

SIG provides support for keeping the displays up to date in the face of updates. Neither of the other two systems includes this type of facility. If the same object is displayed multiple times, the SIG system will propagate any change through one of these displays to the other displays via a notification mechanism. Moreover, update operations can be invoked by selecting items from a menu through the interface. The change appears on the SIG screen, and additional data can be entered through these screens.

There has been a great deal of interest in hypermedia-style systems lately [DS88]. Such a system presents the user with a complex interconnected web that can be browsed by following links from a node of one type to a node of a possibly different type. This activity is very much like browsing an object database. In fact, there are many people who believe that the hypermedia movement could benefit by building their systems on top of object-oriented databases. It might also turn out that the object-oriented database movement will benefit from the interface results that come from hypermedia systems.

Also, there has been a lot of work recently on interfaces for object-oriented systems in general [SBY87]. The characteristics of these systems include icons, menus, and pointing devices. Perhaps some of the experience gained in this area will filter over to the object-oriented database area. Of course, for databases, the major additional problem will concern interfacing to huge numbers of objects.

References

• [BH86]   D. Bryce and R. Hull. SNAP: A Graphics-Based Schema Manager. *IEEE Conference on Data Engineering*, Los Angeles, CA, February 1986.

[Ca80]   R.R.G. Cattell. An Entity-Based User Interface. *ACM SIGMOD Proceedings of the International Conference on the Management of Data*, Santa Monica, CA, May 1980.

[DS86]   N. Delisle and M. Schwartz. Neptune: a Hypertext System for CAD Applications. *ACM SIGMOD Proceedings of the Conference on the Management of Data*, Washington, D.C., May 1986.

[Fo84]   D. Fogg. Lessons from "Living in a Database" Graphical Query Interface. *ACM SIGMOD Proceedings of the Conference on the Management of Data*, Boston, May 1984.

• [GG+85]   K.J. Goldman, S.A. Goldman, P.C. Kanellakis, and S.B. Zdonik. ISIS: Interface for a Semantic Information System. *ACM SIGMOD Proceedings of the International Conference on the Management of Data*, Austin, TX, May 1985.

[HR85]   S. Heiler and A. Rosenthal. G-Whiz, a Visual Interface for the Functional Model with Recursion. *Proceedings of the XI International Conference on Very Large Databases*, Stockholm, Sweden, August 1985. Morgan Kaufmann Publishers.

[He80]   C. Herot. SDMS: A Spatial Data Management System. *ACM Transactions on Database Systems*, 5(4):493–513, December 1980.

• [MNG85]   D. Maier, P. Nordquist, and M. Grossman. Displaying Database Objects. *Proceedings of the First International Conference on Expert Database Systems*, Charleston, SC, April 1986.

[MO88]   A. Motro. Extending the Relational Database Model to Support Goal Queries. K.R. Dittrich and U. Dayal, eds, in *Proceedings of the First International Conference on Expert Database Systems*. Benjamin Cummings, Menlo Park, CA, 1988.

[SBY87]   R.G. Smith, P.S. Barth, and R.L. Young. A Substrate for Object-Oriented Interface Design. B. Shriver and P. Wegner, eds, in *Research Directions in Object-Oriented Programming*. MIT Press, Cambridge, MA, 1987.

[SK82]   M. Stonebraker and J. Kalash. TIMBER: A Sophisticated Relational Browser. *Proceedings of the VIII International Conference on Very Large Databases*, Mexico City, September 1982. Morgan Kaufmann Publishers, San Mateo, CA.

[WK82]   H.K.T. Wong and I. Kuo. GUIDE: Graphical User Interface for Database Exploration. *Proceedings of the VIII International Conference on Very Large Databases*, Mexico City, September 1982. Morgan Kaufmann Publishers, San Mateo, CA.

[Zl75]   M.M. Zloof. Query by Example. *Proceedings of the National Computer Conference*, May 1975.

• indicates article included in this volume

ISIS:

Interface for a Semantic Information System

Kenneth J. Goldman   Sally A. Goldman
Paris C. Kanellakis[1]   Stanley B. Zdonik

Brown University

Abstract

ISIS is an experimental system for graphically manipulating a database. The system is based on a simply specified high-level semantic data model. It demonstrates the capabilities of a workstation environment by integrating three aspects of database programming in one graphical setting. Namely, it permits database construction and modification, it allows browsing at the schema and data levels, and provides a graphical query language. In all of these activities it maintains uniform graphical representations and consistent user interaction techniques.

1. Introduction

ISIS is a system that exploits the visual dimension for database programming. It allows users to construct, maintain, and query a database using a graphics interface and a consistent operational paradigm. Based on a high-level semantic data model, ISIS is an experiment in integrating several forms of database programming into a single interface that is rich in capability yet intuitive

[1] On leave from Brown University; current address: Laboratory for Computer Science, Massachusetts Institute of Technology, Cambridge, Mass. 02139

This research was supported in part by the Office of Naval Research and the Defense Advanced Research Projects Agency under contract N00014-83-K-0146 and ARPA Order No. 4786.

enough for non-experts to use.

The construction of database retrievals constitutes a very important part of programming in commercial data processing. A system like ISIS allows a broad class of users to become "database programmers" and can substantially reduce the amount of time required to construct programs of this type.

1.1. Visual Query Languages

Many of the database query languages that have appeared suffer from the fact that they are textually oriented and very formal. Although simple queries are reasonably straightforward, slightly more complex queries exceed the capabilities of a novice user. The use of the visual dimension seems to hold promise as a way of providing a more intuitive interface in the context of a two-dimensional syntax.

ISIS uses the visual dimension to integrate three aspects of database programming. With ISIS, a user is able to build a databasse or modify an existing one, to browse through the contents of a database in order to answer questions about the data or the schema, and to construct queries that can be saved for later use. All of these activities are accomplished using the same style of interface and the same iconic representations, so that a user is able to move easily from one activity to another at any time.

Other efforts [Zl, MS, He, Ki] have made some progress in this direction. Query by Example (QBE) [Zl] is a relational query language that allows a user to fill example values into templates of relations. The system then determines which tuples satisfy this pattern and prints the specified results. Cupid [MS] is a graphical query facility to a relational database that allows users to construct a two-dimensional picture that can be interpreted as a query. The system represents a relation with a picture of a representative tuple from that relation (one slot per field). One draws labeled arcs between fields to indicate the constraints that should hold on the answer. The arcs are labeled with comparison operators. SDMS [He] is a very highly-developed browser that allows a user to navigate with a joy stick through a space of icons that represent the entities in the database. It is possible to zoom in on an entity at any time to obtain more details of that entity. SKI [Ki] is a system that allows a user to build a query graphically. Like ISIS, it is based on a semantic data model; however, unlike ISIS, it does not provide the integrated facilities for schema construction and for browsing at the entity level. A number of browsers using high powered graphics, but with limited query capabilities have also been developed [Fo,Ca,SK].

1.2. Semantic Data Models

The relational data model [Co1] has recently achieved a great deal of popularity. This is largely due to the simplicity and uniformity of the model. It is easy to learn and has successfully isolated semantic issues from implementation concerns. At the same time it has been recognized that the relational model does not have sufficient expressive power to specify directly some of the complex data relationships that one encounters in applications modeling. Recently, a great deal of work has been done on the development of higher-level data models that have more expressive capability than pure relations; [BF, BN, Ch, Co2, HM, HY, MBW, S, SS, TL, WMy, Zd] are only some of the efforts in this direction.

The Semantic Data Model (SDM) [HM] is one such high-level model, and it provides the underpinnings for this work. ISIS supports a graphical interface to a modified subset of the features of the SDM. We will informally summarize the main features of the SDM in this section and describe the ISIS subset in the section that follows.

Users create and manipulate *entities* when using an SDM database. An entity corresponds to anything in the application that is semantically meaningful. The most central concept in the SDM is that of a *class*. A class is a collection of entities, all of a similar type. Entities have associated *attributes*. An attribute is defined to have a *name*

and a *value class*. A value class is some class in the SDM database from which the values of the attribute are drawn. All members of a class have a common set of attributes.

Classes can be related to each other via *interclass connections*. The two most common interclass connections are *subclass connections* and *grouping connections*. A subclass connection indicates a relationship between some class S and a class T that is constrained to contain a subset of the elements of S. T is said to be a *subclass* of S, and S is said to be a *superclass* of T. The subset can be defined by enumeration of the members, or by a predicate such that T contains exactly those members of S that satisfy the predicate. Some classes are distinguished as *baseclasses*. A baseclass is one that has no superclasses. A grouping connection is one that relates a class S to a grouping class T, where T contains sets of entities from S as members.

Members of a class are said to *inherit* the attributes from all of their superclasses. That is to say, if T is a subclass of S, all members of T will automatically be defined to have all those attributes that are defined on S (as well as the attributes of all the superclasses of S).

In order to make the construction of the initial experimental version of ISIS more tractable, we have selected a modified subset of the SDM as our data model. For this subset, we chose those features that would make our system relationally complete and useful. One major point of departure is the way that the our data model handles groupings. In ISIS a grouping is only allowed on common values of an attribute. Another is that we limit the inheritance behavior of a subclass to single parent inheritance.

It should be noted that ISIS views the construction of a query as equivalent to defining a new derived class. The derived class is specified in terms of a predicate that corresponds to the query expression of more traditional languages. ISIS allows users to build this predicate using graphical means.

The basic semantic model constructs used are in Section 2. Their graphical representations are contained in Section 3.2 and an extended example is in Section 4. A measure of the success of the ISIS interface is the degree in which the example of Section 4 suffices to demonstrate most of the system's non-trivial features.

2. Basic Concepts

The basic concepts presented in this section are the building blocks of our data model, and are sufficient to describe most of the present capabilities of ISIS. They correspond to essential features of existing semantic data models, and, in particular, reflect the basic design principles of SDM.

Entity: An entity corresponds to an object in the application environment. Each entity has a unique name, which is a string.

Class: A class is a named set of entities. The set of all entities is partitioned into disjoint classes called *baseclasses*. If class C is not a baseclass, it is associated with a single other class *parent*(C), where $C \subseteq$ parent(C). We then say that C is a *subclass* of parent(C). There are four predefined baseclasses: the *Integers*, the *Reals*, the *Booleans (Yes/No)*, and the *Strings*.

Attribute: Let C, V be classes, then attribute A of C with *value class* V is a function from C to the subsets of V. We say that A is *multivalued* (A: C $\rightarrow\rightarrow$ V) unless this function is constrained to map each element of C to a singleton subset of V; then we say A is *singlevalued* (A: C $\rightarrow$ V). In the singlevalued case, A defines a function from C to V.

Map: Let x be an entity of C_1 and $A_i : C_i \rightarrow C_{i+1}$, $1 \leq i \leq n$, then $A_1 A_2 ... A_n(x) = \{ e \mid$ there exists a sequence of entities $x_1, x_2, ..., x_n, x_{n+1}$, such that, x_1 is in C_1, $x = x_1$, $e = x_{n+1}$, and $x_{i+1} = A_i(x_i)$, $1 \leq n \}$. We call $A_1 A_2 ... A_n$, $(n \geq 1)$ a map *(from C_1 to C_{n+1})*. For n = 0 we have the *identity map from C to C* (i.e., x is mapped to $\{x\}$).

Grouping: Let A be an attribute of a class C with value class V, then grouping G of C on A is the following family of subsets of C indexed by the members of V, $G = \{ S_e \mid$ entity e in V, and entity x of C is in S_e if and only if e is in A(x)$\}$. We call class C the *parent*(G). Unlike classes, groupings have no attributes, subclasses or groupings. However, we do want groupings to be ranges of attributes. For this we allow attribute B to be a function from a class S to a grouping G. This attribute B is treated as B: S$\rightarrow\rightarrow$ parent(G).

Inheritance: Let class C be a subclass of parent(C), then every attribute A of parent(C) is also an attribute A of C. Since $C \subseteq$ parent(C), a function defined on parent(C) has a natural restriction on C. Inheritance of attributes is from the one parent class to the child class. Note that a class could be a subset of another class without being its subclass; in this case, attributes are not inherited.

Given a collection of classes, attributes, and groupings one can naturally define two directed graphs, whose nodes correspond to the given classes and groupings:

The inheritance forest, with arc (X,Y) iff X = parent(Y). The inheritance forest is easily seen to be a collection of directed trees, where each tree contains exactly one baseclass node, its root. A grouping node can only be a leaf in these trees.

The semantic network, with arc (X,Y) labeled A iff A is attribute of class X with value class Y. The semantic network is a standard construction: we use a single arrow for singlevalued and a double one for multivalued attributes. Note that in it no grouping node has outgoing arcs. The outgoing arcs of a class node correspond to its attributes, including those that are inherited. If a grouping node corresponds to a grouping on attribute A, we label it with A.

Remark: We limit our description to *single parent inheritance*. This is because this type of inheritance combines a wide range of applictions with a single tree representation. This is also for ease of exposition; the system is currently being extended to handle *multiple parent inheritance*.

Schema: A schema is an inheritance forest and a semantic network on the same set of nodes. These nodes are either class nodes or grouping nodes.

Data: Let D be a schema, we associate:
(1) a baseclass with each root of the inheritance forest;
(2) a class C with every class node, such that $C \subseteq$ parent(C);
(3) a (singlevalued) attribute with every (single arrow) arc of the semantic network;
(4) the grouping G on A of parent(G) with every grouping node labeled A.

We assume that the standard baseclasses, *Integers, Booleans, Reals,* and *Strings,* are always in our schema and contain as data all integers, booleans, reals and strings of interest. We also assume that entity names are determined by a special singlevalued naming attribute of each baseclass.

Remark: We have defined a syntactic notion, the schema, and a semantic notion, the data. To guarantee an acceptable level of *integrity* we require that the data be *consistent* with the schema. This notion of integrity represents a reasonable requirement we impose on the system at low computational cost.

Data is consistent with the schema in the sense that each entity is in one baseclass only, each subclass is a subset of its parent, a singlevalued attribute defines a function, and each grouping is completely determined from its parent class and an attribute.

We allow arbitrary modifications of the data and/or the schema, such as *insertions, deletions* and *updates*, as long as the data remains consistent with the schema. For example, in the data level, we can insert an entity in a class, provided we also insert it in its parent and specify a value for its naming attribute. If we do not specify a value for any other singlevalued attribute, the default is the *null* entity, which we assume to be a member of every class. If we do not specify a value for a multivalued attribute of an entity the default is the empty set. In the schema level, we may delete a class, provided it is not the parent of some other class or the value class of some attribute.

The insert, delete, and update facilities are simple but do not provide for querying the database. In order to build queries we use:

Derived Subclasses: Let V be a class in the schema. A derived class S can be defined from V using a predicate P on the entites of class V, which becomes parent(S). $S = \{ e \mid e$ in V and $P(e) =$ true$\}$

Derived Attributes: Let V,C be classes in the schema. A derived attribute A can be defined from C to V. If x is an entity in C, $A(x)$ is defined using a predicate P_x on the entities of V. Formally, for x in C, $A(x) = \{ e \mid e$ in V and $P_x(e) =$ true$\}$

Predicates $P(e)$ and $P_x(e)$, x in C, e in V, can be constructed from *atoms* using the boolean connectives **and, or**. The atoms of $P(e)$ are of the form (a) or (b), and the atoms of $P_x(e)$ are of the form (a), (b) or (c):

(a) $<mapv_1(e)> <operator> <mapv_2(e)>$
(b) $<mapv(e)> <operator> <mapc(w)>$, $w \subseteq C$
(c) $<mapv(e)> <operator> <mapc(x)>$

The *mapv* and *mapc* are maps from classes V,C respectively (they could be the identity maps). Set comparison *operators* used are: set equality ($=$), subset and superset operators ($\subseteq, \supseteq, \subset, \supset$), and a weak match operator ($\approx$) to determine if two sets have a common element. In addition, ordering operators ($\leq, \geq$) are available for comparing singleton sets. The negations of all these operators are also available. Finally, there is a shorthand unary operator (represented by the hand icon) for assigning some $<mapv(e)>$ to be the derivation of an attribute. These predicates provide the full

power of relational algebra, and other operators can be easily added to enhance data manipulation capabilities.

Derived subclasses and attributes are examples of schema and data modifications that do not violate any consistency requirements. We transform old data, consistent with an old schema, into new data, consistent with a new schema. However, the predicates of derived subclasses and attributes do not (at present) form part of the consistency requirements of the system.

3. System Description

In this section we describe the various ISIS features and capabilities. ISIS provides multiple views of the database schema, as well as views of the data itself.

A *view* corresponds to an entire workstation screen. A view could contain: (1) *menus*, (2) *textwindows*, and/or (3) *windows*. All of these are disjoint rectangular areas within the view.

Menus are standardized commands for each view. These commands are consistent within the various views. That is, commands in different views with the same names have the same semantics. Selection of the menu commands is made with a one-button mouse and, in some cases, can also be made through function keys. This last deviation from mouse purity is a simple convenience, which greatly speeds up interaction.

Text windows are areas used for textual input (from the keyboard) and for textual ouput. A text window can be used for: (1) system error warnings, (2) system prompts for user input from the keyboard, mouse, or function buttons, and (3) system text ouput.

Windows are areas containing graphical representations of subsets of the schema or the data. The metaphor here is that the graphical representations of the schema and the data exist in their respective *planes*. The windows show us a piece of these planes; some of the decisions for window positioning over the planes are made automatically by the system. Commands are always provided for manually changing the window position (e.g., *panning* commands). Where appropriate, a *graphical editor* is provided for changing the graphical representations. The one-button mouse is used for selecting rectangular areas inside the windows.

3.1. A Two-Level Approach

ISIS operates at two levels, the *schema level* and the *data level*. Diagram 1 illustrates how one moves among these levels during a database session. The schema level provides views of the schema plane. These views are the *semantic network*, the *inheritance forest*, and the *predicate worksheet*. The data level provides views of the data plane.

In both levels, *navigation* is possible using the maps formed by attributes in the schema. The state of ISIS consists of a *schema selection* (the class, attribute, or grouping being examined) and a *data selection*. Schema selection can be changed (S ← S') at both levels as part of navigating through the schema. Data selection can be changed (D ← D') at the data level. When one switches levels temporarily to select a constant or create a user-defined subclass (see loop arrows in Diagram 1), neither the schema selection nor the data selection are changed upon returning from the temporary visit to the other level.

3.2. Graphical Representations

Classes have three parts: (1) a class name section; for baseclasses this is in reverse video, (2) a characteristic fill pattern unique to the class, which is provided automatically by the system, and (3) an attribute section containing a number of attributes.

Attributes, in the class attribute sections, contain their name and the fill pattern of their value class. If an attribute is multivalued, this fill pattern is shown with a white border to signify that the attribute value is a set. The first attribute in a baseclass is the naming attribute.

Maps are represented by a stack of classes. These are the classes linked by the map attributes.

Groupings are represented in the same way as classes, but they have no attribute sections and their characteristic fill patterns have a white border to signify that their members are sets.

Inheritance of attributes is explicitly represented in one view, and implicitly in the others; through their automatic addition to the attribute section of a class.

Schema Level:

In the inheritance forest view (see Figure 1), lines connect parent classes to their children and the system enforces some of the placement decisions. Namely, groupings always appear above their parent class and subclasses below. In this

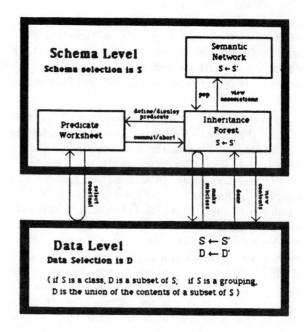

Diagram 1. Interconnections of ISIS components

view classes do not contain inherited attributes, which appear automatically in all other views. A hand icon is used to point to the schema selection. An editing menu is available at the right for panning within the view, moving classes and groupings, deleting classes, attributes and groupings, and undoing and redoing actions.

The inheritance forest view provides variants of a menu of commands: for (re)naming the selection, going to the semantic network view (view associations), going to the predicate worksheet (define), and going to the data level (view contents). Schema selection is changed by picking some other object with the mouse. The commands on the menu vary according to whether the schema selection is a class, an attribute or a grouping. For example if the schema selection is a class then a subclass or attribute can be created. If the schema selection is an attribute then a list of all classes can be created, as a pop-up menu, for selecting the value class. This selection can also be made with the mouse in the view.

An alternate view at the schema level, the semantic network, consists of one window, in which there are classes, groupings, and arcs as defined in section 2 (see Figure 2). The semantic network may be used for navigation in the schema. At any point one may pop back to the inheritance forest view with the new schema selection.

The predicate worksheet consists of several windows (see Figure 9). The atom construction window at the lower right contains three subwindows: for the left hand side, the operator, and the right hand side. Maps are specified by choosing the map attributes with the mouse and forming a stack of classes. The four right hand side options are: **map**, for constructing a map from the entity, as on the left hand side; **map starting at class**, for contructing a map starting at an arbitrary class chosen from the class list window on the right; **constant**, which temporarily takes the user into the data level, where he may select or create a constant in the class at which the left hand side mapping terminates; **constant starting at class**, which allows the user to select the class (from the class list window) in which he would like to start searching for the constant at the data level. As atoms are being constructed, feedback is provided above the atom creation window in the atom list window, which contains atoms that have been constructed or are being constructed. These atoms may be edited and placed in clauses (the set of windows on the left) in disjunctive or conjunctive normal form.

Data Level:

The view here contains a number of overlapping pages (see Figure 3). The top page contains the schema selection, a class or grouping and the data selection, some of its members. Each page contains a class, with all of its attributes including inherited ones, or a grouping. To the right of each class or grouping is a pannable list of its members. Selected members are highlighted with bold text. Navigation is possible at the data level by following attributes. It is also possible to pop backwards. At the data level one can change the schema selection, assign/modify attribute values, and create new entities and new classes. The latter is performed by manually selecting entities and using the make subclass menu command to temporarily visit the inheritance forest to name and position the new class. Returning to the inheritance forest correctly sets the hand icon pointing at the new schema selection.

4. Example

The following example illustrates the major functionality of the interface. We assume an existing database (schema plus data), described in section 4.1. Then, in section 4.2, we describe an ISIS session that makes use of the existing database. Although the example does not illustrate building a database from the beginning, the techniques used in section 4.2 for adding to and modifying the database may be used equally well for schema definition and data entry.

4.1. Sample Schema

The database *Instrumental_Music* has baseclasses *musicians*, *instruments*, *music_groups*, and *families* (see Figure 1).

The *musicians* baseclass has three attributes: *stage_name*, providing names for the entities; *plays*, which is a multivalued attribute with the value class *instruments*, and is the set of instruments that each musician plays; and *union*, which maps into the *YES/NO* class and indicates whether or not the given musician belongs to the musicians' union. The groupings *by_instrument* and *work_status* group the entities in *musicians* according to the instruments they play and according to whether or not they are union members. The subclass *play_strings* contains those musicians who play at least one intrument whose attribute *family* has the value stringed. This subclass has an attribute, *in_group*, which maps into the *YES/NO* class and indicates whether or not the string player is the value of the *members* attribute of some entity in the class *music_groups*. The *play_strings* subclass also has an associated grouping, *by_in_group*, which groups musicians on the basis of the attribute *in_group*. The subclass *soloists* is user-defined (i.e., formed by hand-picking entities from the parent class.

The baseclass *music_groups* has four attributes: *name*, the name of the music group; *members*, a multivalued attribute, which maps into the class *musicians* and represents the members of the given music group; *size*, which has the value class *INTEGER* and is the number of members in the group; and *includes*, which maps into the class *families* and contains the families of instruments that are played by the music group.

The baseclass *instruments* has three attributes: *name*, the name of the given instrument; *family*, which maps into the class *families* and is the family of the instrument; and *popular*, an attribute mapping into the *YES/NO* class. The grouping *by_family* partitions the instruments into sets according to their *family* attribute.

The baseclass *families* contains types of instruments (e.g., brass) and has attribute *name*.

4.2. Sample Session

The user desires to find entertainment for a department holiday party. Upon entering ISIS, he loads the database *Instrumental_Music* and begins by familiarizing himself with the database. Upon loading the database, he sees the inheritance forest view of the database. Since there is no schema selection, he chooses an object on which to focus his attention. With entertainment in mind, he moves the cursor to the class *soloists* and clicks the mouse button (this action will be referred to as **picking**). *Soloists* becomes the schema selection, identified by the hand icon as in Figure 1.

In order to find out more about the information associated with soloists, he chooses the function button, **view associations**. (Note: Although functions need not be picked with the mouse, example figures often show the cursor on the chosen function key description for clarity.) Upon examining the semantic network for soloists, the user becomes interested in the multivalued attribute *plays* and picks its value class, *instruments*. This causes the *instruments* class to become the new schema selection and its semantic network to be displayed as in Figure 2.

Deciding that he wants to see the contents of *instruments*, he picks the **pop** button to return to the inheritance forest, where *instruments* is now the schema selection, and then presses the function button, **view contents**, which takes him into the data level. He now sees *instruments* with all its attributes and a list of its member entities. Using **select/reject**, he can choose members on which to focus his attention; these are highlighted with a large boldface type. In Figure 3, he has already selected the flute and is selecting the oboe.

Next he wants to find the families associated with these entities. Upon pressing the **follow** function key, he is prompted to choose an attribute, and picks *family*. The selected entities from *instruments* are listed in boldface type under that class, and an arrow is drawn from the followed attribute to its value class (Figure 4). Since brass is the only family highlighted on the new page, it appears that both flute and oboe are in the brass family. But the user knows that these instruments are both woodwinds and decides to correct the error. Using **select/reject**, he unhighlights brass and highlights woodwind. He then uses **(re)assign att. value** to update the family attribute for both flute and oboe simultaneously (Figure 5).

Deciding to find out more about families, the user returns to the inheritance forest and changes the schema selection from *families* to *by_family*. Wondering if this is related to the class *families*, he uses **display predicate** and finds that this grouping indeed contains sets of instruments

grouped by common value of their *family* attribute. He returns to the entity level in this grouping class and selects the percussion family (Figure 6). By pressing the **follow** function key he sees all instruments with the percussion instruments highlighted (Figure 7). When **follow** is applied to a grouping, obviously no attribute selection is required; we merely follow the selected set(s) into the parent class and highlight the members of the set(s).

Satisfied that he has browsed enough to familiarize himself with the database, he returns to the schema level to begin his query. Rather than randomly selecting a music group, he decides to form a subclass of *music_groups* that will satisfy his requirements: He desires a music group of four musicians because of the size of the gathering. He also has the special requirement that at least one of the musicians must play the piano, since a friend of his plans to sing at the party and will need an accompanist. After pressing the **create subclass** function key, he is presented with a box which he may drag into position (Figure 8). He names this new class *quartets* using **(re)name**.

He then selects **(re)define membership**, which takes him into the predicate worksheet. He begins by selecting atom A, which will specify that the size of the group is four. He puts this atom into the second clause and picks the **edit** button. He then picks the attribute *size* on the left hand side of the atom creation window and the predefined class *INTEGER* is added to the stack of classes on the left (since the attribute *size* maps into *INTEGER*). After picking the equality operator, he proceeds to the right hand side, where he picks **constant**. Since the left hand side map terminates in the *INTEGER* class, he is taken temporarily into the data level with the *INTEGER* class showing. After selecting the constant {4}, the user is returned to the predicate worksheet. Next, he edits atom E, which will require that at least one musician in the quartet plays the piano. He puts atom E in the first clause, specifies the left hand side map, and chooses the superset operator (Figure 9). After selecting the constant {piano} and changing the predicate to conjunctive normal form with the **switch and/or** button, he presses **commit**, which causes evaluation of the predicate and his return to the inheritance forest.

Now the user would like to know all instruments played by the members of each music group in the *quartets* subclass. To accomplish this, he creates an new attribute, names it *all_inst*, and then uses **(re)specify value class** to tell the system that the values of this attribute come from the class *instruments*. He then chooses **(re)define derivation**: except for the addition of the unary assignment operator (shown as a hand icon), he sees the same predicate worksheet as before. Using the same mechanisms as before, he specifies the attribute derivation, which is shown completed in Figure 10.

After returning to the inheritance forest, the user is ready to look at the entites in the *quartets* subclass and enters the data level. Finding only one quartet has met his requirements, he decides to examine it more closely.

He follows the attribute *members* to see who is in the quartet. After seeing the members he thinks that Edith sounds familiar and wants to focus on her. Therefore, he uses **select/reject** to unhighlight the other members (Figure 11). He follows *plays* and sees that she plays the viola and the violin. The user wants to remember this information so he presses **make subclass**, which takes him temporarily to the inheritance forest, where he names this new subclass *edith_plays* and positions it under *instruments*. (Note: this subclass automatically becomes the child of the class on the current page at the data level.) After more browsing, he is satisfied and returns to the inheritance forest, where he sees the subclass that he created (Figure 12).

Finally, he feels that he has seen enough for now and picks **stop**. In case he needs to come back and browse some more, he saves this new database as *entertainment*, and then phones LaBelle Musique.

In this session, the user was able to become familiar with the organization of a database, through browsing in both the schema level and the data level. As he browsed, he was able to modify the data to correct an error. He then added to the schema: in forming a query, he created a new subclass, and then added a derived attribute to that subclass. Finally, he was able to explore the result of his query at the data level and to create a user-defined subclass containing some information that he wanted to remember.

5. Summary

We have described an experimental system for graphically manipulating a database. This system integrates several aspects of database programming. In particular, it allows users to construct schemas, to browse through the database at both the schema and the data level, and to

formulate queries that can be stored as part of the schema and reused at some time in the future.

We feel that this system builds very strongly on previous work and contributes a paradigm of interaction that integrates more functionality than any of its predecessors. This integration is achieved by using a uniform model of data coupled with a simple set of functions and a single iconic representation.

ISIS is a part of a larger effort at Brown University to build a programming environment based on visualizations of the structures that are required to create programs. This effort stresses the need to view these program structures in multiple ways and to make changes to the underlying programs by directly manipulating the graphical images. Other components of this environment include PECAN [Re] and BALSA [BS]. ISIS is implemented on an Apollo workstation in the C programming environment. It uses the ASH graphics package and the APIO input package, both developed at Brown.

At this point, ISIS is only an experimental vehicle. We see several interesting directions in which this work could proceed. First, we would like to include additional SDM features into our system without disturbing the smoothness of the interface. For example, we are working on providing multiple inheritance. Second, we would like to be able to specify arbitrarily complex predicates in a similar graphical way as a part of an integrity constraint specification system. For example, how would a user specify that an employee cannot earn more than his/her manager using only a screen and a pointing device? Third, we would like to add features to assist users in the process of designing their schemas, as in [RBBCFKLR]. For example, it would be useful to be able to keep track of the history of a database design.

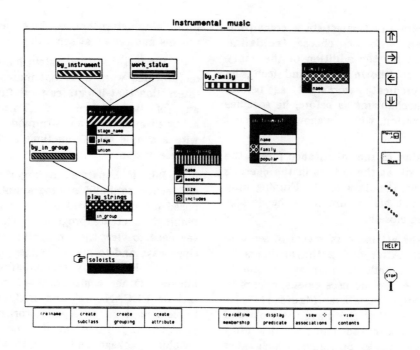

Figure 1. The inheritance forest view with *soloists* as the schema selection.

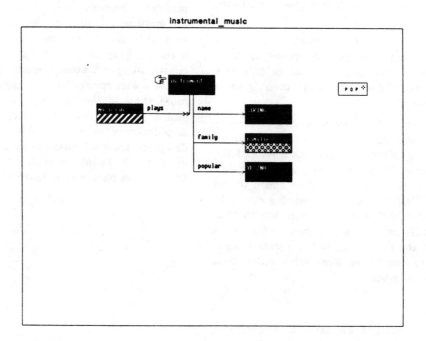

Figure 2. The semantic network view with *instruments* as the schema selection.

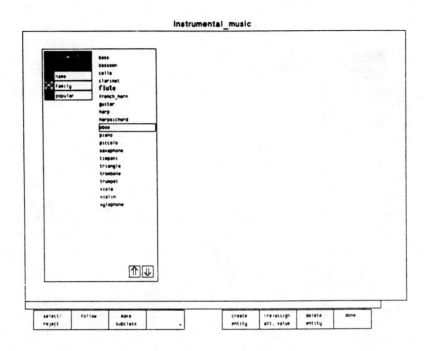

Figure 3. Selecting the entity *oboe* from the *instruments* class at the data level.

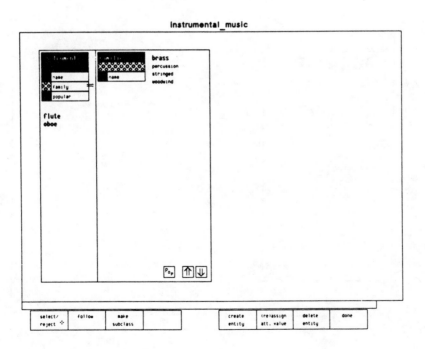

Figure 4. After following the *family* attribute for the entities *flute* and *oboe*.

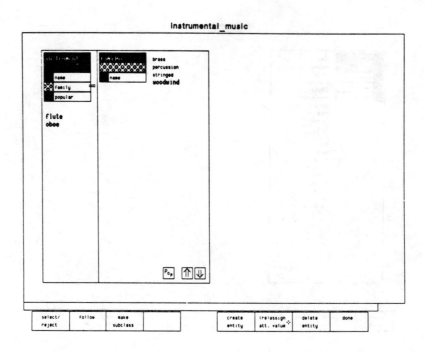

Figure 5. Updating the *family* attribute for both *flute* and *oboe*.

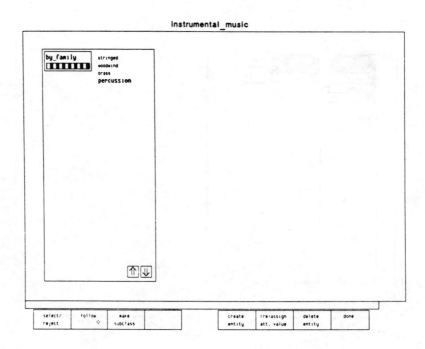

Figure 6. The *by_family* grouping at the data level.

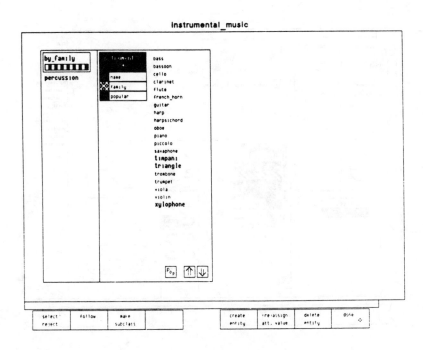

Figure 7. After following *percussion* (from the *by_family* grouping) into the *instruments* class.

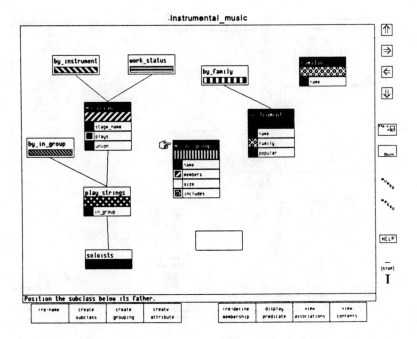

Figure 8. Creating a subclass of *music_groups*.

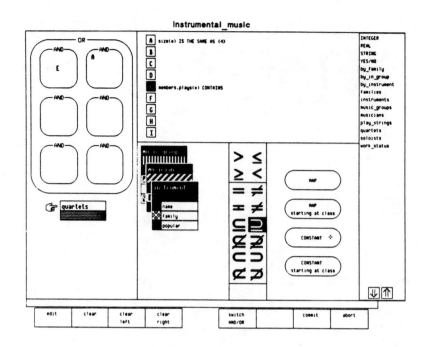

Figure 9. Constructing a predicate to define the membership of the *quartets* class.

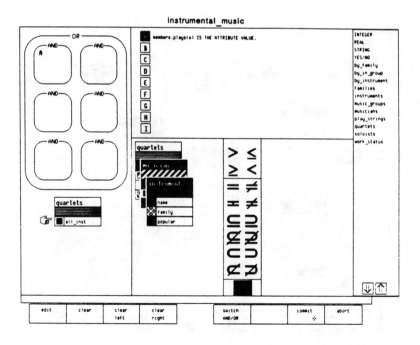

Figure 10. A completed derivation for the attribute *all_inst* in the *quartets* class.

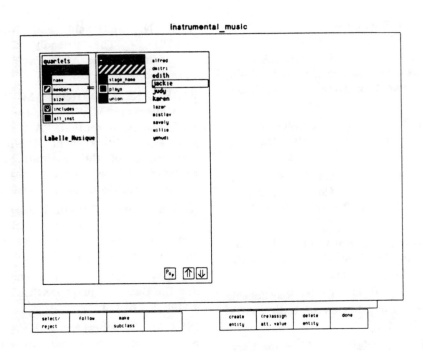

Figure 11. Changing the data selection.

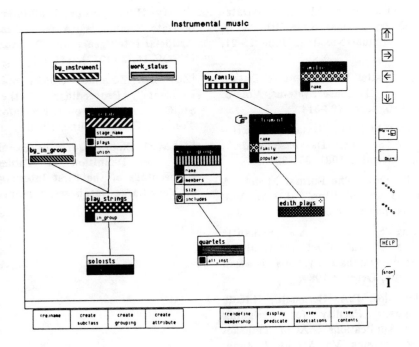

Figure 12. The inheritance forest with the new user-defined subclass *edith_plays* that was created at the data level.

References

[BF] P. Buneman, R.E. Frankel, "FQL – A Functional Query Language", In Proc. ACM SIGMOD Int. Conf. Management of Data, Boston, Mass., 1979.

[BN] H. Biller, E.J. Neuhold, "Semantics of Databases: The Semantics of Data Models", Inf. Syst. 3 (1978), 11-30.

[BS] M. Brown and R. Sedgewick, "A System for Algorithm Animation", Brown University, Department of Computer Science, Technical Report No. CS-84-01.

[Ca] R.G.G. Cattell, "An Entity-based Database User Interface", In Proc. ACM SIGMOD Conf. Management of Data, May, 1980.

[Ch] P.P.S. Chen, "The Entity-Relationship Model: Towards a Unified View of Data", ACM TODS 1, 1, March 1976.

[Co1] E.F. Codd, "A Relational Model for Large Shared Data Banks". Communications of the ACM 13, 6 (June 1970) 377-387.

[Co2] E.F. Codd, "Extending the Database Relational Model to Capture More Meaning". ACM Transactions on Database Systems 4, 4 (December 1979), 397-434.

[Fo] Fogg, D., "Lessons From "Living in a Database" Graphical Query", ACM SIGMOD, 14, 2, Proceedings of the Annual Meeting, June 18-21, 1984.

[He] C.F. Herot, "Spatial Managment of Data", ACM Transactions on Database Systems, Vol. 5, No. 4, December 1980, pages 493-514.

[HM] M. Hammer, D. McLeod, "Database Description with SDM: A Semantic Database Model", ACM TODS 6, 3, September 1981, 351-387.

[HY] R. Hull, C.K. Yap, "The Format Model: A Theory of Database Organization", JACM, Vol. 31, No. 3, July 1984, pages 518-537.

[Ki] R. King,"Sembase: A Semantic DBMS",Proceedings of the First International Workshop on Expert Database Systems, Kiawah Island, South Carolina, October 1984.

[MBW] J. Mylopoulos, P.A. Bernstein, H.K.T. Wong, "A Language Facility for Designing Database-Intensive Applications", ACM Transactions on Database Systems, Vol 5, No. 2, June, 1980, pages 185-207.

[MS] N. McDonald and M.R. Stonebraker, "CUPID - The Friendly Query Language", Proceedings of the ACM Pacific Conference, San Francisco, April, 1975.

[RBBCFKLR] D. Reiner, M. Brodie, G. Brown, M. Chilenskas, M. Friedell, D. Kramlich, J. Lehman, and A. Rosenthal, "A Database Design and Evaluation Workbench: Preliminary Report", Proceedings of the International Conference on Systems Development and Requirements Specification, Gothenburg, Sweden, August, 1984.

[Re] S. Reiss, "Graphical Program Development with PECAN Program Development System", Brown University, Department of Computer Science, Technical Report No. CS-84-04.

[S] D.W. Shipman, "The Functional Data Model and the Data Language DAPLEX", ACM TODS 6, 1 (1981), 140-173.

[SK] M. Stonebraker, J. Kalash, "TIMBER: A Sophisticated Relational Browser.", Technical Report, University of California, Electronics Research Laboratory, May, 1982.

[SS] J.M. Smith, D.C.P. Smith, "Database Abstractions: Aggregation", CACM 20, 6 (1977).

[TL] D.C. Tsichritzis, F.H. Lochovsky, "Data Models", Prentice-Hall, 1982.

[WMy] H.K.T. Wong, J. Mylopoulos, "Two Views of Data Semantics: A Survey of Data Models in Artificial Intelligence and Database Management", INFOR 15, 3 (1977), 344-382.

[Zd] S.B. Zdonik, "Object Mangement System Concepts", Proceedings of the Second ACM-SIGOA Conference on Office Information Systems, Toronto, Canada, June, 1984.

[Zl] M.M. Zloof, "Query by Example: The Invocation and Definition of Tables and Forms", Proceedings of the First International Conference on Very Large Databases, September, 1975.

SNAP: A Graphics-based Schema Manager

(Extended Abstract)

Daniel Bryce   Richard Hull[1]

Computer Science Department
University of Southern California
Los Angeles, CA 90089-0782
USA

Abstract

The SNAP system provides interactive, graphics-based access to schemas of the IFO database model, supporting the varied activities of schema design, schema browsing, and the specification of selection-type queries. The system uses a novel representation for schemas and includes a variety of abstraction mechanisms which encourage users to design and view schemas in a modular fashion. It also supports numerous capabilities for the simultaneous display of large amounts of information about the underlying schema, queries being specified, and answers to those queries. A prototype of the system which demonstrates the basic features of the user interface has been implemented.

1. Introduction

The primary objective of a database management system is to provide users with fast, easy access to large volumes of data. Over the past couple of decades a variety of sophisticated techniques have been developed to provide efficient physical storage structures and fast access mechanisms for manipulating the actual data. Considerably less progress has been made in the area of providing users with convenient access to database schemas. Most of the advances that have been made in this area are based on object-based, semantic database models. For example, the Entity-Relationship (ER) model [9] is widely used as a schema design aid, primarily at the conceptual level. Recently, systems have been developed which provide interactive design, browsing and querying capabilities to ER schemas [8, 11, 28]. More dramatically, the SKI [18, 20] and ISIS [12] systems provide these capabilities for semantic data models which are considerably richer than the ER model. In this paper we describe the SNAP[2] system, which provides the next step in this evolution of schema access support systems. In particular, the interactive graphics-based SNAP system is

a general-purpose schema manager for the IFO database model [2] which provides a coherent paradigm to support the three activities of schema design, schema browsing, and query specification. Furthermore, the system introduces a number of novel concepts which can be incorporated into extant and future database schema access packages.

Perhaps the single most important component of any graphics-based schema management system is the visual representation of schemas used. A number of basic criteria for this representation can be articulated. While the entire schema may not be shown at one time, the representation should

- permit the simultaneous, coherent display of all types of relationships arising in the underlying data model.

Also, natural clustering mechanisms should be provided so that the representation can

- permit a modular perspective of the schema; and
- display the schema at several levels of abstraction.

Finally, the system should

- permit flexible visual rearrangement of the schema; but also
- provide mechanisms for easily returning to visually familiar, essential static visual representations of schema components.

This last feature is important for providing users with a feeling of continuity and stability over the course of lengthy system interactions.

The visual representation of schemas in the SNAP system is based on the IFO database model, an object-based semantic database model which provides features for the representation of simple and constructed objects, functional relationships, and ISA relationships. In the formal definition of IFO [2], database schemas are directed graphs with certain properties; these graphs provide a coherent and unified framework in which the various types of data relationships are visually represented. Furthermore, two fundamental principles of

---

[1]Work by this author supported in part by the National Science Foundation grant IST-83-06517.

[2]"Schemas Notated As Pictures", or as Roger King suggested, "Semantic Navigation And Perusal".

IFO provide the basis from which SNAP satisfies the other criteria mentioned above. The first principle is

- the use of "fragment representations" as the basic building blocks for schemas.

As will be illustrated below, each fragment representation (or fragment "rep") depicts an entity set along with all of its attributes, and can serve as a visually familiar schema component to which users can easily return. The second principle of IFO is

- the use of distinct representatives (i.e., distinct nodes in the schema graph) for distinct roles of given entity sets.

This is illustrated, for example, by the different nodes labelled 'city' in Figures 1 and 2, and is discussed in Section 3 below. While this second principle marks a considerable divergence from other graph-based representations of database schemas [5, 9, 24], it permits the SNAP system to easily provide both modular views and levels of abstraction in the representation of schemas.

In addition to introducing a novel representation for schemas, the SNAP system makes a fundamental contribution in the area of graphics-based query specification. In particular, SNAP queries incorporate considerably more expressive power in a directly visual format than either the SKI or ISIS systems. To explain why, we note first that the query mechanisms of both SKI and ISIS appear to be visual, interactive realizations of an essentially linear, text-based query language. In both of these systems, query specification is based on forming derived data, that is, forming new subtypes and functions from existing entity types and functions. For example, to select all hotels with capacity $\geq$ 250 in these systems, a graph-based command is used to create a new subtype, perhaps called LARGE-HOTEL, and then a text-based language is used to specify that the new subtype is to be populated by all hotels with capacity $\geq$ 250. To form more complex queries, users may have to iteratively construct a number of new subtypes and functions. Thus, the specification of a query consists in an essentially linear sequence of steps which lead to the desired result.

In contrast with the SKI and ISIS systems, SNAP provides a fundamentally two dimensional, graph-based syntax for queries. To accomplish this, SNAP combines aspects of the philosophy of Query-By-Example [29] and CUPID [21] with the graph-based approach to schema representation found in semantic database models. Significantly, it appears that the representation of schemas in IFO (as opposed to those of SKI and ISIS) facilitates this combination of philosophies remarkably well. Speaking loosely, SNAP queries consist in portions of the underlying schema, which are qualified using restrictions such as "$\geq$ 250" and constructs called "comparitor arcs" (see Figures 4 through 7). Specific advantages of this approach include that

- simple queries can be expressed in simple ways; and

- complex queries can be displayed in their entirety.

However, it appears that the static, entirely graph-based framework described thus far is insufficient to capture the expressive power of the derived data paradigm of SKI and ISIS. Some of this expressive power is captured in SNAP because

- composed and inverse functions can be defined in an entirely visual manner.

It would also be easy to extend the system to support text-based specification of more involved types of derived data.

The SNAP query interface permits "wide" answers to queries, in the sense that answers can be conventional (first normal form) relations with any number of columns. The system also

- permits a variety of formats for answers.

In particular, answers can be displayed as non-first normal form relations using the "bucket" notation of [1], which allows users to group data in a variety of ways (see Figures 6 and 7).

A prototype implementation of the SNAP system is currently under development on a Symbolics 3600. In particular, the schema design, database creation, and schema browsing portions of the system have already been implemented, and the query specification and answering component of SNAP is currently under development. All of the figures included in this report were created using this prototype, although the query answering subsystem was not implemented at the time of writing.

This paper presents an overview of the SNAP system. In Section 2 the relevant parts of the IFO database model are introduced. Section 3 describes the capabilities of the SNAP system utilized in the schema design process, and Section 4 focusses primarily on the query specification subsystem of SNAP. Section 5 briefly discusses related systems described in the literature. Comments on the status of the implementation and some remarks concerning future research are made in Section 6. Due to space limitations in this abstract, much of the discussion will be brief; more complete motivation and details may be found in [6].

2. An overview of the IFO database model

The SNAP system is based on the IFO database model, a mathematically defined, object-based semantic database model which subsumes the structural components of most of the semantic database models currently found in the literature. In this section we present a brief overview of the IFO model based on several examples, and conclude with some general remarks. (A formal definition of the IFO model is presented in [2]; the discussion here is intended only to provide an introduction to the model sufficient for SNAP users.)

The IFO database model supports the representation of simple and complex object types, functional relationships, and ISA relationships. As such, it is similar in spirit to the Functional Data Model [17], especially as extended to incorporate ISA relationships in [10]. There is a natural graph-based representation of IFO schemas, in which entity sets are depicted using nodes, and functional and ISA relationships are depicted using directed edges of various types.

The various components of the IFO model are now introduced by a simple schema that might be used by a tourist agency which sponsors group trips to various cities. The full schema for this example is shown in Figure 2, and portions of the schema are shown in Figures 1 and 3.

Figure 1 shows three main clusters of information, one for the cities the tourist agency organizes tours of; one for the (tourist) traps visited; and one for the hotels used by the agency. As shown in the right part of Figure 1, the entity type CITY is shown using a diamond node, with three function arrows emanating from it. These correspond to three attributes of CITY: the name of the city (CNAME); the language of the city; and information about the climate of the city. A diamond node is used for CITY to indicate that the type CITY is an *abstract* type. Rectangles are used for CNAME and LANGUAGE to indicate that (for the purposes of this example) they are *printable* types. The CLIMATE node is a ⊗-node with printable children AVE-TEMP and AVE-RAINFALL, indicating that objects of type CLIMATE are ordered pairs of printables. Finally, we assume in this example that city names (CNAME) serve as "surrogate" identifiers for the cities, in the sense that they uniquely identify each city. This is indicated diagramatically by the ⇔ icon as opposed to the square icon in the function edge pointing to CNAME. As we shall see below, in formulating queries and viewing answers, users will be able to use surrogate values to refer to abstract objects. (Due to space limitations, we assume here that all abstract types have associated printable surrogates.)

The portion of the graph of Figure 1 just described is an example of a *fragment rep(resentation)* in the IFO model. This fragment rep consists of a *primary node* (in this case the one labeled CITY) and three associated function edges (and range nodes). Speaking informally, an *instance* of this fragment rep is a set of objects corresponding to the primary node, and three functions corresponding to the three function edges. In this instance, the actual cities are stored using internal identifiers which are essentially inaccessible to database users. (This corresponds to the intuition that objects of type CITY are physical things in the world, and cannot themselves be presented on a computer screen.) As we shall see, fragment reps can have a structure somewhat richer than the one just discussed.

Three fragment reps are shown in Figure 1, the one for CITY described above, and two others for TRAP and HOTEL. Considering TRAP for a moment, note that it has two printable attributes (TNAME, which serves as a surrogate, and TYPE, such as "amusement" or "historical"). It also has a third attribute, which is intended to specify the city that each trap is in. In IFO, this is represented by introducing a *derived* node which is depicted using a circle (in this case labelled 'city', although a different label is also permitted), along with an *ISA* edge (shown using the traditional double-shafted arrow [⇒]) connecting this derived node to the primary node for the type CITY.

The introduction of a new circular node labelled 'city' as part of the fragment rep of TRAP is a simple illustration of the fundamental principle in IFO of introducing distinct representatives for distinct roles of an entity type. This principle diverges from the graphical depictions associated with schemas from models such as the Entity-Relationship (ER) [9], Functional [17, 24] and Extended Semantic Hierarchy [5] models. In those models, there would be only one node for the type CITY, and a function arrow would be drawn directly from the TRAP node to the (unique) CITY node. While this provides a simpler representation for small schemas, it can be argued that in more realistic, larger schemas this leads to very confusing pictures in which there is considerable entanglement of function arrows. In the IFO representation, this entanglement is still present, but resides entirely in the ISA edges which qualify attribute ranges. And quite importantly, the SNAP system permits users to easily hide all or some of these ISA edges, thus removing the entanglement when desired (cf. Figures 2 and 3). Finally, because the nodes used to represent the ranges of functions mapping to abstract types are distinct from the primary nodes representing those types, the removal of these ISA edges does not affect the visual appearance of fragment reps. As a result, fragment reps naturally and easily serve as essentially static visual representations for reasonably sized portions of the overall schema. (Furthermore, if users desire both interactive and hard-copy versions of a schema, it would be natural to devote each page of the hard copy to a different fragment rep.)

Turning to Figure 3, we now discuss three additional features of IFO, these being the use of ISA edges to define subtypes; the capability to build complex object structures; and the representation of nested functions. In the upper left portion of this figure the entity type PERSON is depicted with a diamond node, and two subtypes GUIDE and TOURIST are depicted below that using derived nodes (shown as circles which are a bit larger than the derived nodes occuring as function ranges) and ISA edges. In this case, the attribute associating a PNAME with each person is automatically inherited by both subtypes.

The IFO model provides two mechanisms for constructing complex object types from simpler object types. The first, called "aggregation" [13, 25], is represented using the ⊗-node and is based on Cartesian product. This construct has already been illustrated by the CLIMATE attribute of CITY. The second mechanism is represented using a ⊕-node, and forms entities which are sets of an underlying entity type. This has been called "grouping" [13] and "association" [5] in the literature. For example, in Figure 2 the type TRIP has an attribute called GROUP, which associates a set of participants (which are from type TOURIST) to each trip. (Note that the representation of multivalued functions in IFO is different than in the Functional Data Model, which represents them using a function edge with a double head.) The ⊗-node and ⊕-node constructs can be applied recursively to construct complex data structures, as illustrated by the ITINERARY attribute of TRIP. Also, although not illustrated in this abstract, constructed object types may serve as the primary nodes fragment reps.

An example of a *nested function* is given in the fragment of GUIDE in Figure 3. Specifically, for each guide there is an associated set of languages, togther with a function assigning a proficiency to each language in that set. To illustrate this, suppose that these functions are named SPEAKS and WITH-PROF. Then it might be that SPEAKS(Jim) = {'French', 'Portuguese'} and SPEAKS(Gail) = {'French', 'Chinese', 'Japanese'}; and that SPEAKS(Jim)/WITH-PROF('French') = '3' and SPEAKS(Gail)/WITH-PROF('French') = '4'. (Speaking roughly, this direct representation of nested functions, which is not present in the Functional Model, corresponds to a certain type of non-first normal form relation, called V-relations [1] or "partitioned normal form" relations [23].) The fragment rep of the entity type TRIP includes other nested functions: each trip has an associated itinerary consisting of a set of stops; and relative to a given trip each stop has an associated hotel and set of traps to be visited.

Recall now that an instance of a fragment rep consists of a set of objects corresponding to the primary node of that fragment rep, and a function corresponding to each function edge of the fragment rep. Thus, an instance of the schema shown in Figure 2 consists of seven (fragment) instances, one for each fragment rep. Furthermore, the inclusion constraints implied by the ISA edges must be satisfied by these fragment instances. (For example,. the set of objects associated with the PARTICIPANT node must be contained the set associated with TOURIST; which in turn must be contained in the set associated with the PERSON node.)

We conclude this section with some general remarks about the IFO model. First, IFO schemas are graphs composed of five types of nodes and three types of edges (function, ISA,[3] and object construction) which satisfy a set of precisely defined rules [2]. Second, the IFO model subsumes the structural, static components of virtually all of the object-based, semantic database models found in the literature, including the Entity-Relationship, Event [19], Extended Hierarchy Semantic [5], Functional, Semantic Data [13] and Sembase [18] Models. The IFO model can also serve as a skeleton upon which constraint and transaction specification mechanisms, such as those found in other semantic models, can be added in a precise fashion.

Finally, we briefly mention how the IFO model, and hence the SNAP system, realize the various criteria for the visual representation of schemas mentioned in the introduction. It is clear that the representation used for IFO incorporates all of the representable types of data relationship in one coherent framework. A modular perspective of a schema is afforded by the use of fragment reps as building blocks of the schema. Different levels of abstraction are supported by the interactive hiding and unhiding of fragment reps, of attributes within fragment reps, and of the children of complex object structures. Finally, while the user can rearrange the visual layout of the schema in essentially any manner, he can also easily return to the initially defined fragment reps in order to obtain a visually familiar representation of portions of the schema.

3. Schema design in SNAP

The SNAP system supports three primary activities: schema design, schema browsing, and graphical query specification. This section focusses on schema design; the following two sections focus on browsing and query specification. In principle, different modes of SNAP operation supporting different subsets of these capabilities could be implemented for different user groups (e.g., database administrators, novice users, advanced users), but in the current SNAP implementation all capabilities are supported simultaneously.

SNAP utilizes a high resolution bit-mapped graphics display with a three button mouse to create a highly interactive environment. The user communicates with SNAP primarily through four windows: graphics windows for the schema and the query specification, an enhanced text-based window for displaying query results, and a text-based window for special user interactions. The user may freely size and position these windows to most efficiently utilize screen space.

---

[3]Technically, the IFO model supports two different types of ISA relationships, a feature necessitated primarily by the strong object-typing present in the model (see [2]). The second type of ISA relationship is useful for combining fundamentally different entity types (e.g., businesses and persons are both legal entities), and is not discussed further in this abstract.

In general, user requests are handled in two steps. First, the user identifies an object of interest by positioning the cursor over that object and pressing a mouse button. Second, the system displays a pop-up menu with the applicable options for the selected object, and the user picks the desired option with the mouse (cf. Figure 3). Selectable objects include schema nodes and edges, the various windows, and window borders.

We now illustrate the flavor of typical schema definition commands by mentioning briefly how a user can create the CITY fragment rep of the schema of Figure 2 (see also Figure 1). To begin, the user moves the cursor to the position where she wishes to create the CITY node and presses a mouse button. SNAP responds by presenting a pop-up menu offering options such as 'abstract', 'primary derived', 'primary cross', etc., corresponding to the various types of node that can be created. The user now moves the cursor up or down the menu to select the desired option (which in this case is to create an abstract node). SNAP then requests the name of the object in a pop-up box for text, into which the user types 'city'. In this manner she also creates the two printable object nodes corresponding to CNAME and LANGUAGE. The user is now ready to add the function arcs associated with these nodes, and therefore selects the CITY node. SNAP responds by presenting a pop-up menu offering the options 'delete', 'link', 'hide', 'edit label', and 'move'. After the user selects the link option, SNAP displays the CITY node in reverse video and asks her to select another object. At this point she can press the middle button to abort the operation or select another object node to complete the sequence. In this session she first selects the CNAME node, and SNAP responds by presenting a menu of possible types of links between the CITY node and the CNAME node, in this case including only 'function' and 'surrogate' edges. She selects the surrogate arc for CNAME, and repeats the above sequence of operations to create a function arc for LANGUAGE. The creation of other schema components, and in particular constructed objects and ISA arcs, is performed in the same manner.

Although not implemented in the SNAP prototype at this time, it would also be possible to develop a "hybrid" approach to schema definition, in which the user could initially specify a fragment rep using a compact, text-based syntax, and subsequently modify the graph corresponding to that specification using mouse-based commands.

As mentioned in the previous section, there are a number of precisely articulated rules concerning what constitutes a valid IFO schema [2]. A significant feature of the design component of the SNAP system is the way in which it prevents the violation of most of these rules during interactive schema design. To understand this feature, note that the rules concerning valid IFO schemas imply an associated set of rules defining the family of partial IFO schemas, that is, graphs which can be extended to be valid IFO schemas. (For example, in a valid IFO schema each ⊛-node must have exactly one child, but in a partial IFO schema each ⊛-node may have zero or one children.) During interactive schema design, users are permitted only those options which can be applied without violating the rules defining partial IFO schemas. Once design is (thought to be) complete, users may request that the system verify that the specified schema satisfies all of the rules for valid IFO schemas. An interactive dialogue subsystem is included to facilitate easy correction of rule violations. It should also be noted that some of the rules concerning schemas and partial schemas are essentially global in nature (e.g., that there are no directed cycles of ISA edges). In order to provide fast system response, these global rules are not enforced during design steps, but are included in the verification that a finalized schema is valid. Once the system has verified that a designed schema is valid, the system can create the data structures and files needed to store database instances. This feature and the mechanisms whereby data is entered and updated in the database are described in [6].

4. Schema browsing in SNAP

As is apparent from the full schema shown in Figure 2, the complete representation of even small schemas is too complex to comprehend easily. As noted previously, the visual representation of schemas in SNAP include fundamental features which support both modularity and levels of abstraction. The SNAP system combines these features with the power of interactive graphics to provide a rich set of basic commands for schema browsing.

Browsing in SNAP is accomplished primarily through simple, direct mechanisms for manipulating schemas and viewing them in different ways. In general terms, these include options to reposition objects, hide/redisplay objects, pan and zoom around the schema, and automatically reformat ISA hierarchies and complex object reps. Users can call these options relative to individual nodes, relative to entire fragment reps, or relative to object types along with all of their subtypes and associated fragment reps. As a result, there is often more than one specific mechanism for accomplishing many of these general capabilities. For example, there are four distinct methods for repositioning objects by dragging them with the mouse: move individual nodes; move fragment reps; move entire type-subtype lattices; or move all nodes in a specified region of interest (possibly with other nodes included or excluded the region). Users can also relocate a node or fragment rep by specifying a location and then requesting that the desired object(s) be placed there. This illustrates how SNAP typically provides a number of different methods for accomplishing similar tasks. Based on user experience with the system, this provision of both atomic commands and sometimes redundant meta-commands is necessary to provide a convenient interface with which users can quickly perform desired activities.

A second type of browsing capability supported by SNAP is that of finding and displaying nodes of particular interest. For example, if a node is currently off-screen, the user can request that the portion of the schema viewed by the window be moved to that the node is in view. The system also locates nodes related to given nodes. For example, if the user selects the primary node for CITY and asks to see the nodes connected to it by ISA arcs, the system will respond by highlighting those nodes for a few seconds, redisplaying them if they are hidden. Supertypes of a node can be found in a similar fashion. Users can also request that hidden ISA edges be selectively redisplayed to highlight certain connections.

5. Query specification in SNAP

As mentioned in the introduction, a primary contribution of the SNAP system is the development of a fundamentally two dimensional syntax for specifying queries in semantic databases. As will be illustrated shortly, this provides a rich basis for specifying a wide range of selection-type queries in a completely visual manner. Additional expressive power is incorporated into the query subsystem through visual mechanisms for defining composed and inverse functions. Another contribution of the SNAP system is to permit users to format answers so that data is clustered according to common values.

When specifying queries, the user interacts primarily with three types of window, these being for the schema, the query, and the answer. In order to facilitate multiple, simultaneous inquiries of the database, more than one query window can be associated with a given schema, and more that one answer window can be associated with each query window. Each query window is closely linked to its associated schema window; as a result manipulations in one window are easily translated into associated manipulations in the other. (For example, one can identify a node in the schema window and have that node replicated in a query window.) Answer windows are essentially text-based windows enhanced with scrolling and format specification capabilities.

Queries in SNAP are expressed using *query graphs* which are formed by combining one or more *query fragment reps*, which in turn are closely related to IFO fragment reps. Query fragment reps are constructed primarily from the fragment reps of a schema; a query graph can contain any number of query fragment reps, possibly including duplicates. The values which are to be associated with the query fragment reps are specified using three fundamental mechanisms. The first is called *node restriction*, and permits users to associate a restriction directly with a given node of a fragment rep. The second is based on *comparitor arcs*, which permit

users to indicate that a certain relationship must hold between values associated with different nodes. And the third mechanism permits users to construct new functions from existing ones in an entirely visual manner, and easily include them in query fragment reps. These mechanisms are now illustrated in four examples.

Figure 4 shows a simple query which requests a listing of information about all hotels in Beijing which have a capacity $\geq$ 250. This example illustrates three important points about the syntax for query specification used in SNAP. First, while the query is represented using most of the fragment rep for HOTEL, only two nodes are shaded, indicating that only values associated with these nodes are to be displayed in the answer. Second, although technically the occupants of the HOTEL and CITY nodes correspond to abstract, non-printable entities in the world, SNAP permits the use of printable surrogate values to identify these abstract entities. (As mentioned previously, we assume here that all entity types have unique printable surrogates.) And finally, the query includes two node restrictions, the first restricting output to only those hotels with capacity $\geq$ 250, and the second restricting to those hotels in Beijing. (At present only simple expressions are permitted in node restrictions, although it would be natural to extend this to permit the use of the propositional connectives 'and', 'or', and 'not'.) The answer to the query is displayed in an answer window, which is essentially a text-based window enhance by scrolling facilities.

The second example, shown in Figure 5, illustrates how comparitor arcs can be used. As part of the original schema, each tourist has an associated comfort-quotient (COMF-QUOTIENT), which is a number between 1 and 5 specifying how much comfort the tourist requires; and each hotel has an associated COMF-RATING. The query shown in Figure 5 asks to print tourist-city pairs, such that there is a hotel in the given city whose comfort-rating is $\geq$ the comfort-quotient of the tourist.

The comparitor arc in the query of Figure 5 specifies a restriction on printable (in fact, numerical) values. Comparitor arcs may also be used to compare abstract types, and to compare sets with sets (using e.g. $=$, $\leq$ [used to denote $\subseteq$], # [for has non-empty intersection], etc.), and individuals with sets (using $\in$ or $\notin$). A query graph can include several node restrictions and comparitor arcs; in answering the query SNAP uses the conjunction of all of the implied restrictions.

Before presenting the third example, we briefly describe the semantics associated with query graphs. We focus here on the formal (or "logical") specification of semantics, and do not discuss efficient ways for implementing this semantics. The formal semantics associated with a query graph is most easily understood in

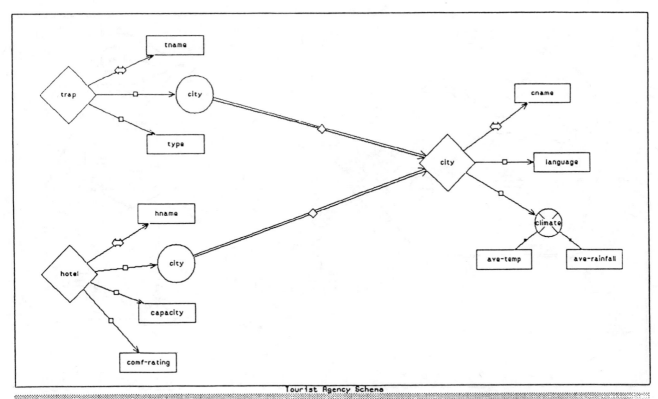

Figure 1: Three fragment reps

terms of a four step procedure for defining the answer to a query. Recall that a query graph consists of one or more query fragment reps, which are closely related to fragment reps. In the first step of defining the meaning of the query, a first normal form relation (possibly with null values) is associated with each of the query fragment reps in the query graph. (These relations will hold information corresponding to all of the data associated with the relevant fragment reps in the original instance.) This relation will include a column for each node of the query

fragment rep (including those of abstract types, which will have internal identifiers as column entries), and also columns for associated surrogate values if they are called for in the query answer. In the second step, a cross-product of these relations is formed, yielding a single first normal form relation. (Identical column names from different relations are renamed in this cross-product relation.) In the third step tuples are removed from the cross-product relation, according to the node restrictions and the comparitor arcs. (Node restrictions and some comparitor arcs can be viewed as simple relational selections on the cross-product relation; but the impact of other comparitor arcs involving sets will typically involve a consideration of the underlying instance.) And the

fourth step is to remove those columns of the resulting relation which are not specifically called for by shaded nodes in the query graph. (A final step to query answering involves formatting the answer, and will be discussed shortly.)

In the third example (Figure 6) we illustrate how users can define composed and inverse functions in a visual manner. In this example, the user is interested in creating a function mapping each trip to the set of languages that will be used during that trip, so that she can compare the languages needed for trips with the languages that guides can speak. To create this function

in the query window, the user first displays the TRIP node in the query window, and then relative to that node requests the function definition option. She then activates a path of nodes in the schema window corresponding to the path of functions which are to be composed to define the new function (as shown in Figure 6). The system responds by displaying the created function in the query window. In this case, the created function is multi-valued; in cases where the created function is single-valued the system would not include the ⊕-node. In this example the path from TRIP to LANGUAGE was used to

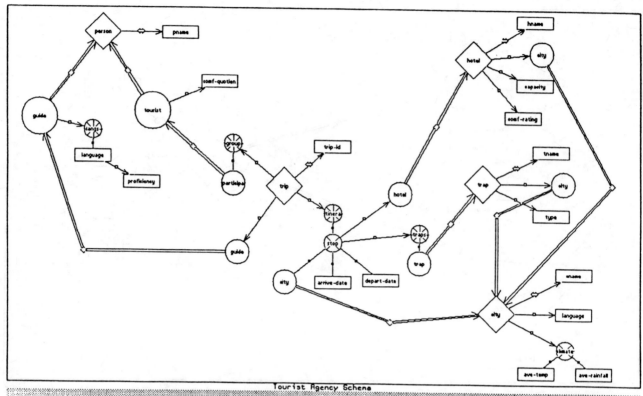

Figure 2: Tourist agency database schema

define a function from trips to sets of languages; this path could also be used to define the corresponding inverse function from languages to sets of trips. Also, paths involving both functions and inverse functions are permitted. Finally, although not currently supported in the SNAP system, it would be natural to permit users to incorporate constructed functions directly into the underlying schema.

Two answer windows are shown in Figure 6. The one on the left shows the answer in the form of a conventional (first normal form) relation. The other answer window provides a simple illustration of how the SNAP system permits users to group data using the "bucket" notation of [1] for non-first normal form relations [16]. In this case, the data is grouped by TRIP; for each trip the answer shows a bucket filled with the associated set of guides. The user could also request the answer to be grouped by guides.

Our final example (Figure 7) illustrates a final aspect of the graph-based syntax for queries used in SNAP, and also provides a more complex example of answer formatting. The query here requests information about pairs of traps and hotels in the same city. In the

query graph, the type TRAP has an attribute CITY as in the underlying schema, and that the derived node CITY has the *inherited* attribute LANGUAGE. This illustrates the general feature of SNAP queries, which is that all functions relevant to a derived node can be inherited to that node in a query fragment rep. (Indeed, it is for this reason that query fragment reps may not be, technically speaking, fragment reps.) We also note that the answer window in this example shows most aspects of answer formatting in SNAP, namely, that buckets can be nested, and that two or more buckets can occur at the same level.

When a query is specified, the SNAP system chooses a default format for the answer, and also provides a dialogue mechanism whereby users can select other formats. To illustrate, we describe the dialogue used to define the format of the answer of the last query. The user begins by choosing CITY as the top or "driving" attribute. The system makes two responses to this. First, since LANGUAGE is functionally determined by CITY in this query, it places LANGUAGE at the same level as CITY. Also, since for each city the group of hotels (and associated comfort-ratings) is independent of the group of traps (and associated types), it forms two buckets, one for HOTEL and COMF-RATING, and the other for TYPE and

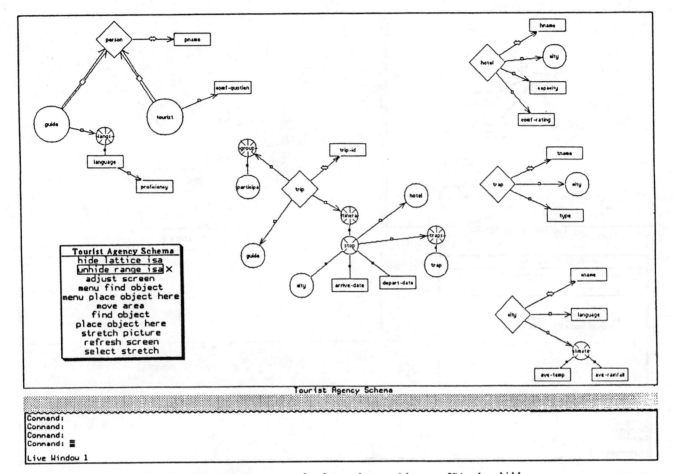

Figure 3: Tourist agency database schema with range ISA edges hidden

TRAP. The user leaves the HOTEL bucket alone, and chooses to make TYPE the driving attribute within the TRAP bucket. The system responds by forming the second-level bucket for TRAP. Although not illustrated here, it is also possible to chose two or more attributes as the driving attributes of a bucket.

The preceding examples have focussed primarily on the actual syntax for queries in the SNAP system, without mentioning how users construct these queries. As mentioned earlier, there are tight connections between a schema window and its associated query windows. To specify that a given node or fragment rep be included in a query graph, the user can select it in the schema window, or can request that it be replicated by specifying a location in the query window and either typing in the name of the node or selecting that name from a menu. Entire fragment reps can be replicated into the query window and then massaged, or nodes and edges can be replicated individually. If a derived node in the query window is selected, the user can chose to display its inherited attributes, either individually or all at once. Node restrictions are specified by selecting the node to be restricted, and comparator arcs are specified in the same

way that function edges are specified in schema construction. Most of the browsing and graph manipulation capabilities supported for schema windows are also available in query windows. Finally, users can name and save query graphs for future use and modification.

6. Survey of related systems

In this section we present a brief survey of other interactive systems for database access, with an emphasis on systems whose functionalities overlap those of SNAP. Speaking in general terms, this includes two systems based on an expressive semantic database model; four systems based on the ER model; and five systems essentially based on the relational model.

As described above, the two systems most closely related to the SNAP system are the SKI [18, 20] and ISIS [12] systems, both of which are essentially based on subsets of the Semantic Database Model [13]. The SKI system was the first interactive schema manager based on a rich semantic database model, and the first to embody the paradigm of expressing queries through the iterative

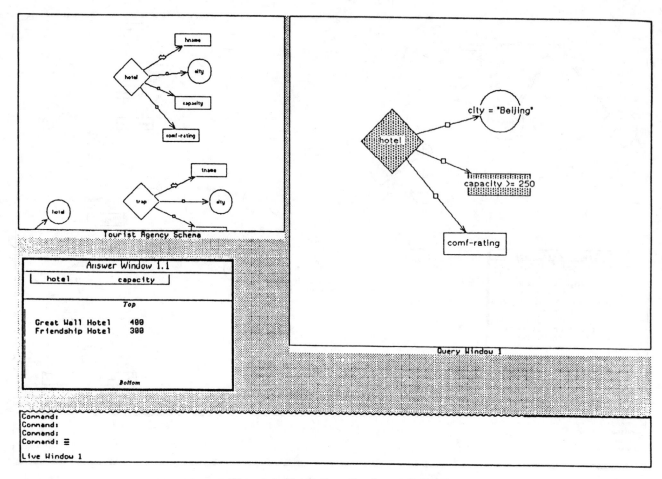

Figure 4: Illustration of node restriction

specification of derived data. An important contribution of the ISIS system is its sophisticated, mouse-based editor which permits users to build the predicates used in specifying derived data. While neither of these systems permit the visual representation of node restrictions or comparitor arcs as in SNAP, both provide the expressive power of these mechanisms in their predicate specification languages.

Turning to systems based primarily on the (ER) model, the GUIDE system [28] was the first to present a graph-based view of database schemas to users, and permits users to specify textual queries using a combination of text and graph manipulations. A system developed at the University of Toronto in 1979 [8] supports design and browsing of ER schemas. The Database Design and Evaluation Workbench (DDEW) [22] is a comprehensive schema design tool directed at the currently existing database user community; in this system a considerable effort went into the development of a coherent user interface which is easy to learn and use. Finally, the Living in a Database (LID) system [11] permits users to browse data organized by an ER schema. In this system, users "live" inside a database

instance, residing at a particular tuple in the database and viewing both data tuples and schema components which are associated with it.

We conclude our discussion by briefly mentioning five systems essentially based on the relational model. In the well-known Query-By-Example (QBE) language [29], queries are specified with tables which correspond to relations in the database, where variables used as entries in the tables indicate inter-relationships between the tuples which are to form the answer. Although defined in the context of the relational model, QBE appears to be the first system supporting a partially visual representation of database queries. The CUPID system [21] generalizes QBE in the sense that rather than using relational skeletons, CUPID uses icons to represent the relations, tuple components and comparison operators. SNAP is related to CUPID since many of the nodes of IFO schemas play essentially the same role as tuple components in the relational model; also, SNAP adopts the use of comparator edges from the CUPID system. The TIMBER system [26] allows users to browse in one or more specific relations of a relational database; in essence the TIMBER system brings the power of full-screen text editors to the relational database model. In the Spatial

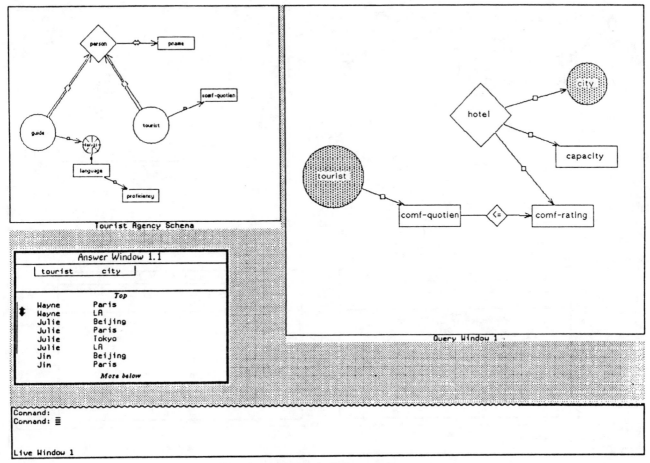

Figure 5: Illustration of comparitor arc

Data Management System [14], graphical icons which represent entities in the database are arranged in a two dimensional lay-out, over which users can scroll and zoom to examine different parts of the database at different levels of detail. And the RABBIT system [27] incorporates principles from psychology to provide a data browsing environment in which users view both a partially specified query and sample answers to it, and iteratively refine the query until the desired query is attained.

7. Concluding Remarks

In this section the current status of the prototype implementation of SNAP is described, and some research directions motivated by SNAP are mentioned.

As mentioned earlier, the SNAP system is being developed on a Symbolics 3600, and is built upon BOOGIE (Bell's Object-Oriented Graphics Interactive Executive), an object-oriented graph-based package (which was developed by Brigham Bell at the Information Sciences Institute, Marina Del Rey, California). The focus of the SNAP prototype is on demonstrating the features of the graphical user interface; efficiency is not an emphasis of the implementation. Thus, database instances are physically stored in straight-forward, list-based structures. (It should be noted, however, that the SNAP system does generate text-based schema specifications from the graph-based representations of IFO schemas; these could be used to create a substantially more efficient physical design.) At present, the schema design, schema browsing, and database creation capabilities of the SNAP system are implemented and running. The query specification component is currently under development.

It is our view that the IFO model and SNAP system demonstrate a number of novel concepts in the area of graphics interfaces to databases, and can serve as the skeleton for the development and demonstration of a wide variety of more advanced concepts for such systems. These would be especially useful in the context of database schemas having a realistic size of one or two hundred entity types, each with ten or twenty attributes. For example, in the interest of a more compact representation, it may be desirable to use a tabular format to list collections of printable attributes within one rectangle as found in the DDEW system, rather than

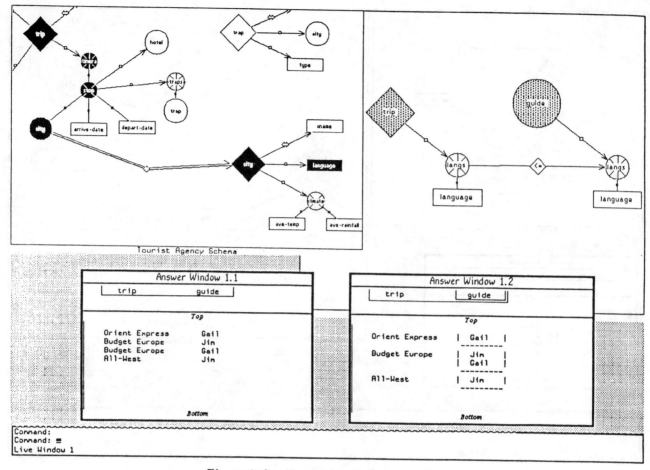

Figure 6: Specification of composed functions

using a separate node for each attribute. More significantly, experience with the SNAP system has shown that in order to provide a truly useful browsing system for such schemas, it will be necessary to incorporate meta-commands which combine SNAP's basic browsing capabilities in various ways. For example, it would be desirable to have a mechanism whereby users could focus on selected fragment reps of interest, and also see related schema components at levels of detail corresponding to their "distance" from the selected fragment reps. Another needed capability is that of showing the shortest connecting paths between a selected pair of fragment reps, as provided in the SKI system. It would also be useful to associate a level of significance to each node of the database as in the GUIDE system.

The query subsystem of SNAP also raises a number of interesting research questions. First, it would be useful to "measure" the expressive capability of SNAP by comparing it with other query languages (e.g., DAPLEX [24] or FQL [7]). It would also be interesting to consider various enhancements of the query language. One extension would be to permit variables in node restrictions, and possibly to permit condition boxes as in Query-By-Example. A second type of extension would be

to develop mechanisms whereby users could specify disjunctions between the restrictions in a query.

Another general approach to extending the SNAP query subsystem is based on the alternative structurings of data available in the IFO model. Simple mechanisms for restructuring data representations are already provided in SNAP through the mechanism for defining composed and inverse functions (cf. Figure 6). For example, given a function mapping each student to her set of courses, in the SNAP system users can visually define the inverse function mapping each course to its set of enrolled students. There is also a natural representation of this information using a set of student-course ordered pairs. It is easy to imagine data restructurings which are much more involved. This raises the questions: what is an appropriate general framework within which to understand this kind of data restructuring; and is there a natural visual representation for it? Initial work in this area [4] indicates that an algebra of simple, local restructurings generalizing those of [15] may provide the desired framework. It would also be interesting to incorporate node restrictions and comparitor arcs into such an algebra.

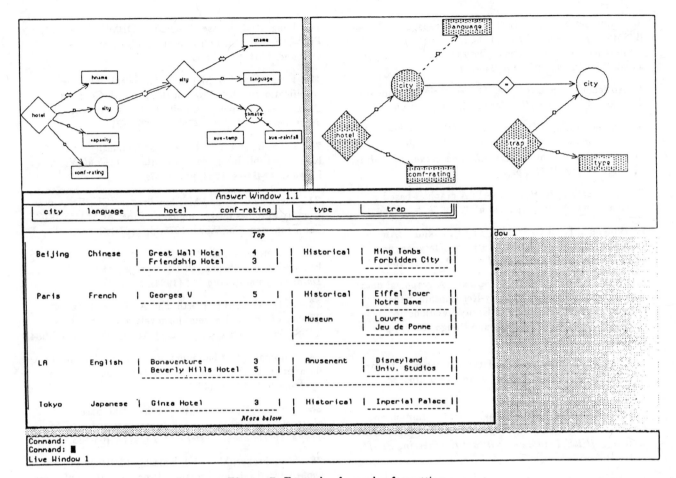

Figure 7: Example of complex formatting

A final general issue which can be investigated with the SNAP system involves the relationship between IFO and the relational model. In general terms, it appears that the SNAP system could serve as a useful front end to a relational database system. In particular, there is a relatively straightforward translation from a natural subset of IFO schemas into third normal form relational schemas (in much the same way that ER schemas can be translated into the relational model [9]). Thus, SNAP could be used as an aid in designing relational schemas. SNAP could also be used to gain information about a relational schema through browsing the associated IFO schema, and could be used to specify graphical queries against the relational schema. (Another specific benefit of this approach to relational design is that the theoretical results of IFO concerning update propagation [2, 3] could

be applied to the relational schema to ensure that functional and inclusion dependencies were not violated by updates.) A provocative research question in this area is motivated by the desire to use SNAP on existing relational databases: is there an automatic or semi-automatic methodology for associating natural IFO schemas with third normal form relational schemas?

Acknowledgement

The authors would like to thank Steve Crocker and Carl Kesselman of the Computer Science Laboratory within the Aerospace Corporation (El Segundo, California), for providing computing facilities and technical assistance in support of the SNAP prototype development.

Bibliography

1. Abiteboul, S. and N. Bidoit. Non first normal form relations to represent hierarchically organized data. Proc. ACM SIGACT-SIGMOD Symp. on Principles of Database Systems, 1984.

2. Abiteboul, S. and R. Hull. IFO: A formal semantic database model. TR-84-304, Department of Computer Science, Univ. of Southern Calif., April, 1984. Preliminary version appears in Proc. ACM SIGACT-SIGMOD Symp. on Principles of Database Systems, April, 1984, pp. 119-132.

3. Abiteboul, S. and R. Hull. Update propagation in the IFO database model. Proc. of the International Conference on Foundations of Data Organization, Kyoto, Japan. May 22-24, 1985, pp. 243-251.

4. Abiteboul, S. and R. Hull. Restructuring of semantic database objects and office forms. In preparation.

5. Brodie, M.L. and D. Ridjanovic. On the design and specification of database transactions. In Brodie, Mylopoulus, and Schmidt, Ed., *On Conceptual Modelling*, Springer-Verlag, 1984, pp. 277-306.

6. Bryce, D. and R. Hull. SNAP: A graphics-based schema manager. In preparation.

7. Buneman, P., R.E. Frankel, and R. Nikhil. "An implementation technique for database query languages". *ACM Trans. on Database Systems 7*, 2 (1982), 164-186.

8. Chan, E.P.R. and F.H. Lochovsky. A graphical data base design aid using the Entity-Relationship model. Proc. of the Intl. Conf. on the Entity-Relationship Approach to Systems Analysis and Design, 1979, pp. 303-318.

9. Chen, P.P. "The entity-relationship model -- toward a unified view of data". *ACM Trans. on Database Systems 1*, 1 (1976), 9-36.

10. Dayal, U. and H.-Y. Hwang. "View definition and generalization for database integration in a multidatabase system". *IEEE Trans. on Software Engineering SE-10*, 6 (1984), 628-644.

11. Fogg, D. Lessons from a "Living in a Database" graphical query interface. Proc. ACM SIGMOD Int. Conf. on the Management of Data, 1984, pp. 100-106.

12. Goldman, K.J., S.A. Goldman, P.C. Kanellakis and S.B. Zdonik. ISIS: Interface for a semantic information system. Proc. ACM SIGMOD Int. Conf. on the Management of Data, 1985, pp. 328-342.

13. Hammer, M. and D. McLeod. "Database description with SDM: A semantic database model". *ACM Trans. on Database Systems 6*, 3 (1981), 351-386.

14. Herot, C.F. "Spatial Management of Data". *ACM Trans. on Database Systems 5*, 4 (1980), 493-514.

15. Hull, R., and C.K. Yap. "The format model: A theory of database organization". *J. ACM 31*, 3 (1984), 518-537.

16. Jaeschke, B. and H.J. Schek. Remarks on the algebra of non first normal form relations. Proc. ACM SIGACT-SIGMOD Symp. on Principles of Database Systems, 1982.

17. Kerschberg, L. and J.E.S. Pacheco. A functional data base model. . Pontificia Universidade Catolica do Rio de Janeiro, Rio de Janeiro, Brazil, Feb., 1976.

18. King, R. Sembase: A semantic DBMS. Proc. of the First Intl. Workshop on Expert Database Systems, October, 1984, pp. 151-171.

19. King, R. and D. McLeod. The event database specification model. Proc. of the 2nd Intl. Conf. on Databases: Improving Usability and Responsiveness, Jerusalem, Isreal, June, 1982, pp. 299-321.

20. King, R. and S. Melville. The Semantics-Knowledgeable Interface. Proc. 10th Int. Conf. Very Large Data Bases, 1984, pp. 30-37.

21. McDonald, N. and M. Stonebraker. CUPID: A user friendly graphics query language. Proc. ACM-PACIFIC, San Francisco, Ca., April, 1975, pp. 127-131.

22. Reiner, D., et. al. "The Database Design and Evaluation Workbench (DDEW) Project at CCA". *IEEE Database Engineering 7*, 4 (1984), .

23. Roth, M.A., H.F. Korth, and A. Silberschatz. Theory of non-first-normal-form relational databases. TR-84-36, University of Texas at Austin, December, 1984.

24. Shipman, D. "The functional data model and the data language DAPLEX". *ACM Trans. on Database Systems 6*, 1 (1981), 140-173.

25. Smith, J.M. and D.C.P. Smith. "Database abstractions: Aggregation and generalization". *ACM Trans. on Database Systems 2*, 2 (1977), 105-133.

26. Stonebraker, M. and J. Kalash. TIMBER: A sophisticated relation browser. Proc. 8th Int. Conf. Very Large Data Bases, 1982, pp. 1-10.

27. Williams, M.D. "What makes RABBIT run?". *Int. J. Man-Machine Studies 21* (1984), 333-352.

28. Wong, H.K.T. and I. Kuo. GUIDE: A graphical user interface for database exploration. Proc. 8th Int. Conf. Very Large Data Bases, 1982, pp. 22-32.

29. Zloof, M. "Query-by-example: A data base language". *IBM Systems Journal 16* (1977), 324-343.

Displaying Database Objects

David Maier
Oregon Graduate Center
Peter Nordquist
Intel Corp.
Mark Grossman
Oregon Graduate Center

We outline the requirements for features and construction of interactive displays on complex database objects. Few systems to date meet these requirements, as they either do not support update through the display, or are not generated automatically from a specification. We present a system, SIG, for producing and interpreting high-level display specifications for complex objects. SIG supports *display types*, which are declarative descriptions of of interactive displays for classes of objects, and *abstract views*, which decode and implement display types, and which can dynamically change the format of a display to accommodate changes in the structure of an object.

1. Introduction

The study of database systems has largely overlooked the display of data, even though database applications typically contain more code for data display and entry than for data manipulation [Pilo83]. Relational technology provides a very workable abstraction of secondary storage; there is no analogous abstraction for user interfaces. With the advent of object-oriented database systems that support complex objects and multiple connectivity, a fixed format for displaying the results of queries is no longer adequate. We describe the SIG system for automatically generating interactive displays on structured objects. We look at the capabilities of the system, and the main concepts behind it. SIG is currently implemented in Smalltalk-80 (TM Xerox Corp.), but the design could be ported to other systems with window support. We conclude with our vision of how database applications should be assembled.

2. Requirements

We desire a tool for creating *interactive displays* (IDs) on complex database objects, in the environment of a personal workstation with bit-mapped graphics. An ID must not only provide a view of its object on the screen, but also allow a user to update the object by manipulating the view with a keyboard and mouse. We wanted a tool close to the level of abstraction that relational query languages provide for data manipulation. In particular, we tried to satisfy the following requirements:

1. IDs should be described declaratively, and generated automatically from their descriptions when needed. Ideally, no modifications to the object being displayed should be needed to define an ID on it.

2. IDs should dynamically reflect the structure of the object displayed. The number and location of the subviews in an ID can depend on the state of the object displayed. For example, Figures 1a and 1b are "before" and "after" snapshots of the same ID on a binary tree when a left subtree is added. Each subtree has its own sub-ID, which can contain sub-IDs for subtrees at lower levels. Four new sub-IDs were added because the added subtree itself had three subtrees.

3. IDs should accommodate arbitrary levels of structure in the objects they display. There should be no *a priori* bound on the depth of nesting of sub-IDs of a display. IDs should also accommodate multiple connectivity in objects, in that the same object can appear in multiple IDs, if it is a subpart of several objects. Updates to the object through one of these IDs should be reflected in them all.

Expert Database Systems; Larry Kerschberg, Editor. Copyright 1987 by The Benjamin/Cummings Publishing Company, Inc.

4. The system should support multiple display descriptions for a single type of objects. Figures 2a and 2b show two IDs for the same binary tree, but generated from different descriptions. Figure 2a shows a tree in a format similar to that of Figure 1, but with no arrows. Figure 2b portrays a tree in outline form, with subtrees indented below their parents.

5. The system should assist in the creation of display descriptions, and support a design methodology for building up complex IDs from simpler IDs. Once a display description is created on one class of objects, that description should be available for constructing displays for other classes.

3. Related Work

Previous works on displaying database objects and display generation mostly fail to meet our requirements because either

1. update through the display is not supported, or
2. the displays are written ad hoc, not generated automatically from descriptions.

The INCENSE system [Myer83] generates displays on data structures in the Mesa language. Each data type has an *artist* to render instances of the type on the screen, but data cannot be updated through the display. The Application Development Environment (ADE) being constructed at Burroughs [Ande85] supports *perspectives* for defining a printable format of a data item. Perspectives build up a rendering of a complex object from displays of its subparts, but do not provide for update of objects. The specifications of perspectives are stored as part of the database. Several researchers have proposed high-level languages for drawing pictures [Egge83, Hend82, Pere83, VanW82], but again, these languages provide rendering but not updating of objects. Also, certain document preparation systems [Furu82, Kimu83] can be viewed as displaying some document object on screen or paper, but without update capabilities.

One of the first graphical display systems for databases was the Spatial Data Management System [Hero80]. Another such system is included in the Sembase semantic database system [King84]. Sembase provides displays that dynamically keep up with added objects and changed attributes. Both systems, however, have a fixed set of formats for displaying a particular class of objects.

Program visualization systems, such as PECAN [Reis83], PV [Hero82, Kram83] and others [Fisc84], aid program development and debugging by displaying data structures associated with a program and its execution: parse tree, calling stack, variable bindings. Such systems provide dynamically changing displays, but for a fixed set of structures. Algorithm animations display the changes in an algorithm's data structures as the algorithm executes, for purposes of documentation, education and algorithms research. Such systems to date [Baec81, Brow84, Lond85] require that displays on new classes of data objects be generated manually as needed.

The Programming-by-Rehearsal system [Finz84] gives support for constructing an interactive display of a complex object from previously defined displays on its subobjects. However, each such display is constructed anew or copied from an existing display, not derived from a higher-level specification.

One example of where an interactive display has been constructed from a high-level specification is in the Crystal system for interpreting oil-well logs [Smit84]. For that project, the IMPULSE editor [Scho83] (used for editing knowledge bases described in the STROBE object representation language) was modified to accept declarations of specialized editors, and to produce editors from the declarations.

4. The Implementation Vehicle

The Smalltalk Interaction Generator (SIG) [Nord85] is a prototype ID generator for complex objects, as might be found in an object-oriented database system. SIG builds upon the model-view-controller (MVC) mechanism of Smalltalk [Gold83]. An MVC is a triad consisting of three objects: *model* to be displayed and possibly updated, a *view* responsible for displaying the model on the screen, and a *controller* for interpreting user inputs as updates to the model. The model can be an arbitrary Smalltalk object, but the view and controller must be appropriate to the class of the model. For example, different flavors of views exist for text, list and Boolean objects. A simple ID is constructed from a single MVS triad. An ID with sub-IDs uses an MVC triad for each sub-ID. The structure of the ID is maintained by the view objects, which know about their subviews.

SIG actually makes use of an enhancement of the MVC paradigm known as *pluggable views*. A pluggable view queries its model to determine the *aspect* of the model it should display. Pluggable views cut down the proliferation of types of views. Rather than constructing a new view class for each format and class of model, one view class suffices for displaying a certain aspect, such as the text, of any model. Pluggable views also make interactions among displays easier to program, as several displays can be linked by being views on different aspects of the same model. In a complex display, pluggable views cut out unnecessary redisplay, as a subview need repaint only if its aspect of the model changes.

The MVC mechanism, while providing many features needed for the prototype, does not by itself meet all the requirements for an ID generation system:

1. Defining an ID with the MVC mechanism is a procedural, not declarative, task. To produce an ID, the programmer must write code to sire together views of existing types, and possibly code new view classes.

2. IDs in the MVC paradigm usually have a fixed format; they do not dynamically adapt to changes in the structure of the model. Most Smalltalk-supplied IDs have only a two-level hierarchy of sub-views, and do not add or delete views while in use. Nothing prevents a Smalltalk ID from changing the number of subviews it has, but no tools are supplied to help construct dynamic IDs.

3. The MVC mechanism does not lend itself to a modular design methodology. Most IDs are a mass of interrelated pieces that are not easily separated. In adapting an existing ID, it is often difficult to locate the right piece of code to change a particular facet of the display. Design questions concerning which part (model, view or controller) should implement which functions are difficult to resolve. In the Smalltalk-supplied IDs, sometimes the view and controller store data to be displayed apart from the model, and the controller does some of the updating of the display.

5. SIG Capabilities

In database terms, Smalltalk objects are non-1NF tuples that have identity and that can share attribute values. *Classes* group objects with similar structure and behavior. An object is an *instance* of its class. Every Smalltalk object has a *protocol* of *messages* to which it responds by changing its state or returning information. The protocol to an object serves to encapsulate its internal state. An object may not, as a rule, manipulate or examine the internal state of another object directly, but may only do so indirectly through a message.

SIG uses a display description, called a *display type*, to define an ID for an object. Display types are associated with classes, and a class can have multiple display types, as witnessed by the various IDs on binary trees in Figures 1 and 2, which were defined in SIG. The IDs generated by SIG can adapt to changes in the state of the object displayed, as shown in Figures 3a and 3b. Those figures show an ID on an object of a class BooleanListTest. An instance of BooleanListTest contains a Boolean value and a list of strings. The list is only displayed when the Boolean value is true.

The next examples involve a class Employee. Instances of class Employee have a name and address field, a social security number field, a projects field, and a manager field. The first two fields hold strings, the project field holds an object from the class ProjectList, and the manager field holds another Employee object. A ProjectList is an array of projects.

Figure 4 shows a SIG-generated ID on an Employee object. It has four sub-IDs, one for each field, plus some labels. The labels are also IDs, but with no update capabilities. The sub-IDs on project and manager are further structured. The sub-ID on project was generated from a display type for the class ProjectList, and the sub-ID on manager was generated from the same display type that was used for the entire ID. Thus, display types can reference other display types. In particular, a display type can mention itself recursively.

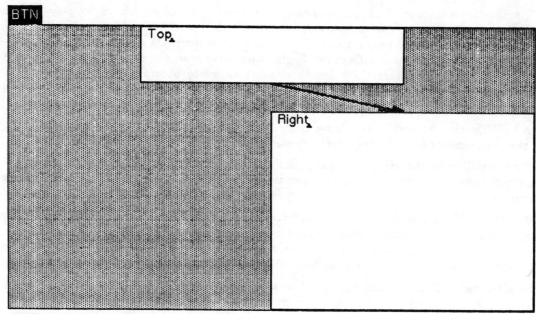

Figure 1a. Tree ID before adding left subtree.

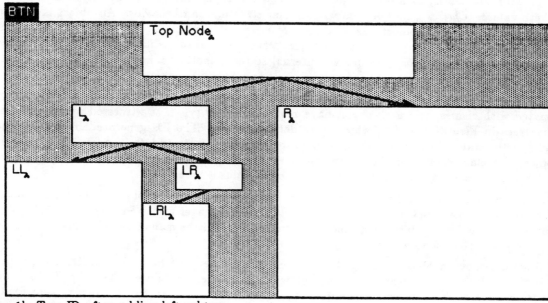

Figure 1b. Tree ID after adding left subtree.

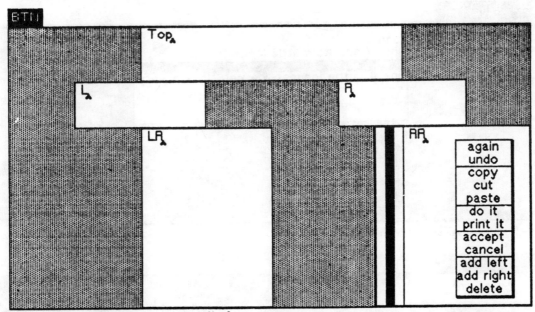

Figure 2a. Tree ID using 'without arrows' display.

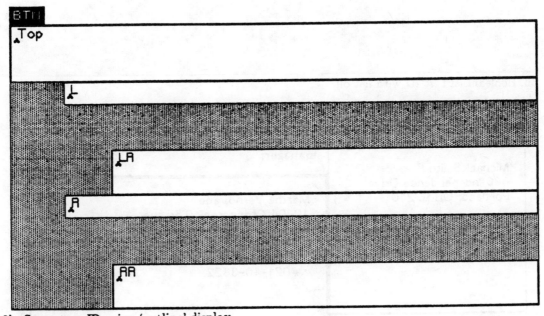

Figure 2b. Same tree ID using 'outline' display.

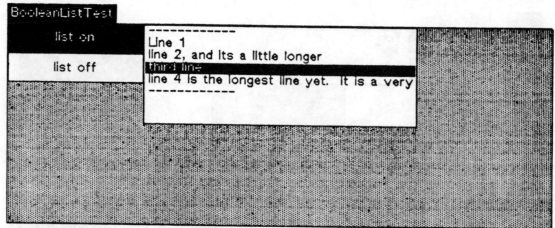

Figure 3a. BooleanListTest ID with list on.

Figure 3b. BooleanListTest ID with list off.

EmployeeDisplay			
Michael Smith 806 Independence Drive Portland, OR 97210	manager:		
	Martha Vernovage 10404 Crosscreek Terrace Portland, OR 97219		
#083-42-5312	#021-10-3322		
projects:	projects:		
Hudson Account	Jones Account	Michael Smith Annual Review	Salary Survey	Department Budget

Figure 4. ID on an employee object.

Part of a display type is a specification of a menu of update commands on each sub-ID. By associating a menu with sub-IDs rather than with the display type itself, one display type can support different kinds of update behavior in different contexts. In Figure 5a we see a menu in use to add a manager for the manager, thus updating the underlying employee object. That update to the employee object in turn causes the ID to change by adding a new sub-ID. In Figure 5b the new manager appears, and we can then add new information about him (Figure 5c).

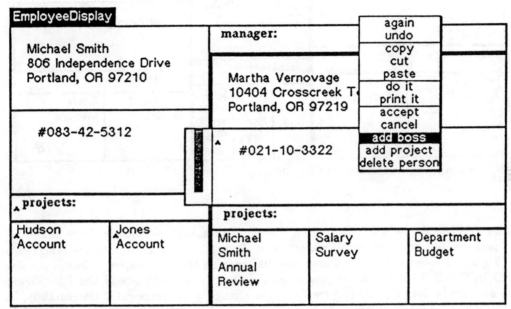

Figure 5a. Adding the manager's manager.

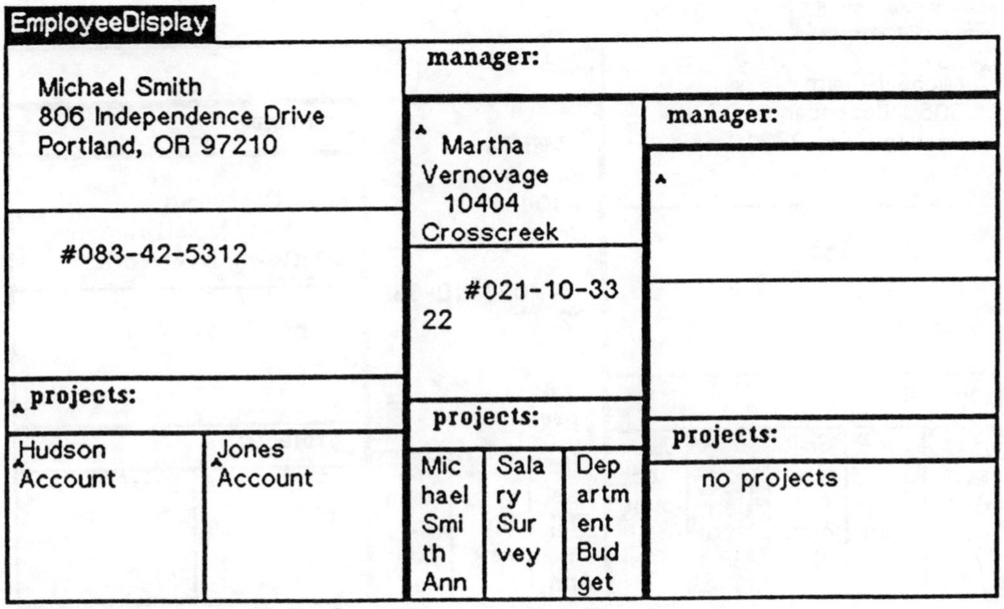

Figure 5b. New manager, uninitialized.

EmployeeDisplay

Michael Smith
806 Independence Drive
Portland, OR 97210

#083-42-5312

projects:

| Hudson Account | Jones Account |

manager:

Martha
Vernovage
10404
Crosscreek

#021-10-33 22

projects:

| Michael Smith Ann | Salary Survey | Department Budget |

manager:

Mark Grossman
118 Red Maple Drive
Levittown, New York
11756

#084-12-6214

projects:

| V.P. Monthly Report | Staff Meeting |

Figure 5c. New manager with information filled in.

SIG IDs can handle iteration in limited forms. The sub-ID on projects can adapt to different numbers of projects, but once the number grows past four, some of the projects are replaced by ellipses (Figure 6). Figure 7a shows that we can have two IDs open on the same object. (One of the IDs is a sub-ID of the ID in Figure 6.) If the underlying object is updated through one of the IDs (Figure 7b), the update also appears in the other ID (Figure 7c). The change is not propogated immediately, as the sub-ID involved supports a kind of commit-abort mechanism on changes. The changes are actually made to a copy of the model. The model is altered only when the user commits these changes.

EmployeeDisplay

Michael Smith
806 Independence Drive
Portland, OR 97210

#083-42-5312

projects:

| Hudson Account | Jones Account | Smith Account | ... | Jill Account |

manager:

Martha
Vernovage
10404
Crosscreek

#021-10-33 22

projects:

| Michael Smith Ann | Salary Survey | Department Budget |

manager:

Mark Grossman
118 Red Maple Drive
Levittown, New York
11756

#084-12-6214

projects:

| V.P. Monthly Report | Staff Meeting |

Figure 6. Elision of projects.

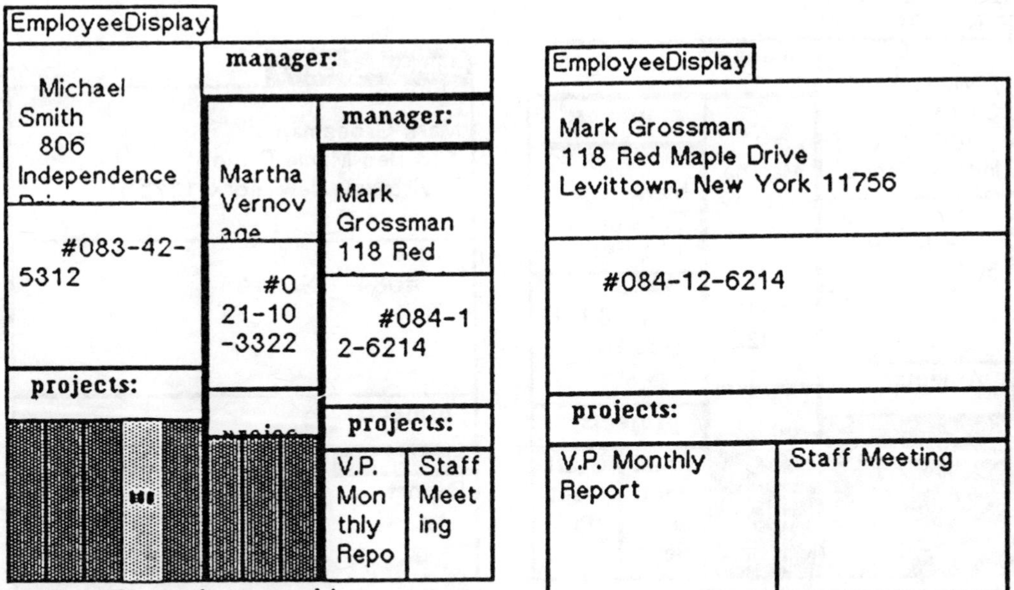

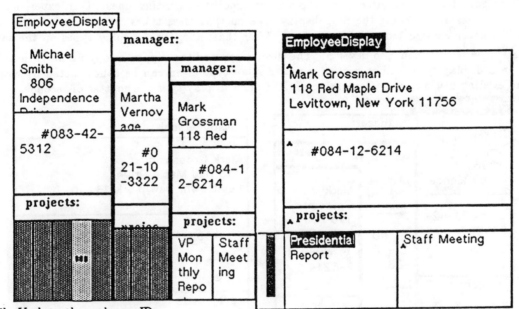

Figure 7a. Two IDs on the same object.

Figure 7b. Update through one ID.

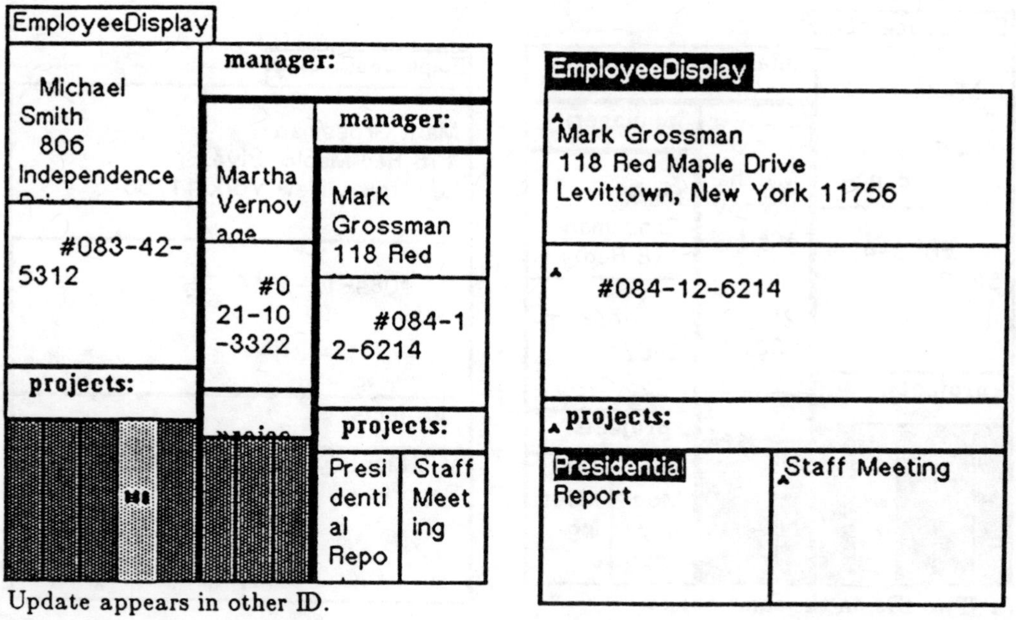

Figure 7c. Update appears in other ID.

A SIG ID can detect if the screen space allotted it is too small in which to display (Figure 8a). In that case the screen space is painted dark gray, and there is a menu option to spawn a new ID on the obscured object (Figure 8b).

Display types in SIG are created with the aid of a display-type editor, which guides a display developer through the various steps in describing a display. The display-type editor suggests a design methodology for IDs, by progression through its panes left to right, top down, filling in requested information. The editor has two modes: *display mode* (Figure 9a), for inspecting previously created displays, and *edit mode* (Figure 9b), for creating new displays, or modifying existing ones. Our experience is that adding a new class and defining the first display type on that class takes several days, for a Smalltalk user who has never constructed a display before. After that, additional display types on the same class take a half hour to four hours to develop. The display-type editor supports copying at various levels of structure in a display type. All or part of a new display type often can be concstructed by modifying a copy of an existing display type. Generating an ID from a display type is a matter of seconds.

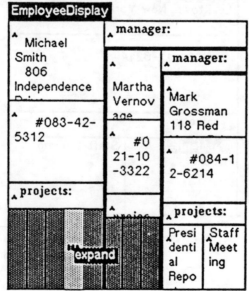

Figure 8a. Insufficient space to display ID on project.

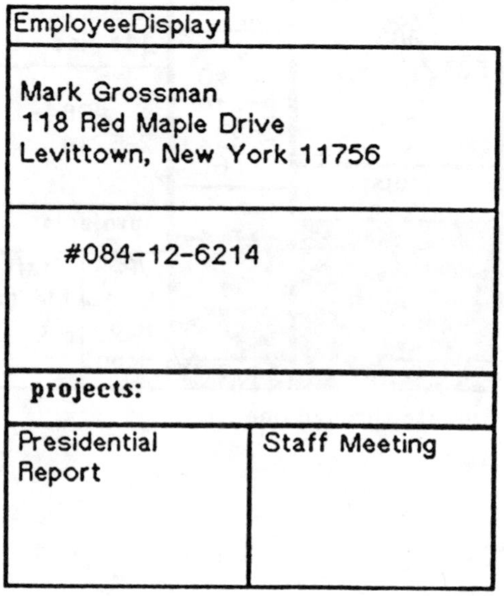

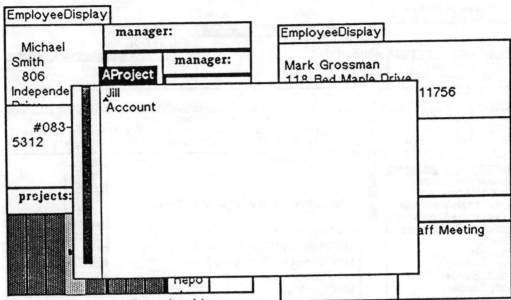

Figure 8b. Spawning a larger ID on the object.

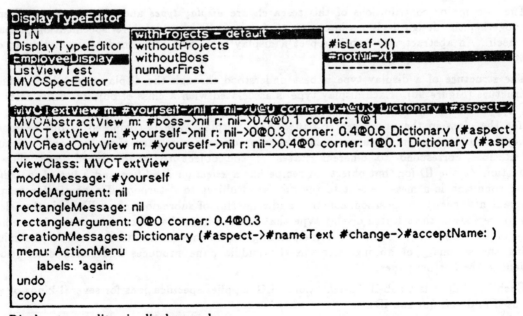

Figure 9a. Display-type editor in display mode.

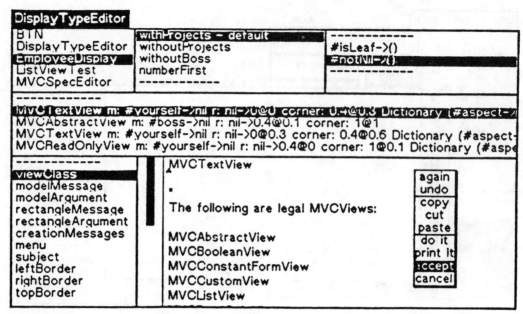

Figure 9b. Display-type editor in edit mode.

6. System Concepts

The two major contributions of this research are *display types* and *abstract views*. Display types gather together the design decisions in constructing a new ID into high-level specifications, separate from the ID itself. An abstract view can interpret a display type, and accommodate its display to changes in the state of the object displayed.

The structure of a display type is best understood through the display-type editor, which reflects that structure (Figure 9b). Each display type is associated with a class of objects. All classes that have display types are listed in the upper left pane. Selecting a class in that pane produces a list of display types for the class in the upper center pane. Each display type is composed of one or more *recipes*. Selecting a display type in the upper center pane produces a summary of its recipes in the upper right pane. Recipes correspond to different states of the object to be displayed, and allow different configurations of the ID for that object. A recipe has a *selection condition* and a list of *ingredients*. The selection condition is a message sent to the displayed object to determine if a particular recipe applies. The ingredients specify the position, contents and rendering of subregions of an ID. It is the selection conditions for recipes of the selected display type that are shown in the upper right pane of the editor. Picking one of the conditions causes the corresponding ingredients to be summarized in the middle pane. Selecting the summary of an ingredient in the middle pane produces a detailed description of that ingredient in the bottom panes.

Each ingredient is a sub-ID specification. SIG supplies specifications for several kinds of views commonly used in describing sub-IDs:

1. text views, which display and edit text,
2. read-only views, which display text, but do not support update,
3. list views, which support scrolling and selection in a list of items,
4. Boolean views, for displaying and toggling a Boolean value, and
5. constant form views, for scaling and displaying a fixed graphical image (a *form* in Smalltalk parlance).

These SIG-supplied view specifications are templates that must have some additional information filled in to describe the sub-ID fully. The lower left pane lists the slots that must be filled in to complete the specification of a sub-ID. Selecting one of those slots causes its current value to be listed in the lower right pane, along with information on permissible values for the slot. SIG fills in the slots with initial values that are appropriate for the kind of view selected. There are slots for the position of the view within the ID, what object is being displayed in the view, widths of borders, a menu for updates, and more. The right pane also provides a pattern for filling in a new value for the selected slot. An ingredient can also specify a user-supplied *custom view* for producing special graphic images. Custom views are used for graphic details that are not produced well by scaling a constant form, such as the arrows in Figure 1.

The last possibility for an ingredient is that it specify an abstract view. Specifying an abstract view defers most decisions on the format of a sub-ID to a display type on another object, usually a sub-part of the object being displayed at the highest level. In the display type we have been using for the Employee ID, abstract views were used for the projects and manager fields. (Note that not all the ingredients are visible in the center pane of Figure 9b.)

When an ID is created for an object from a display type, an abstract-view object is created by SIG. The abstract view has the object as its model, and also holds a copy of the display type to be used. The proper display type to be used is found in a dictionary that SIG maintains, which is keyed on class and names of display types. The abstract view generates an ID for the object by interpreting the display type. The abstract view queries the object about its state, to determine which recipe in the display type pertains. The query is performed by sending the selection condition messages in the recipes to the model until one returns true. Once the recipe is determined, the abstract view creates sub-IDs based on the kind of view and corresponding slot values for each ingredient in the recipe. It does so by creating a view object of the kind specified, and selecting an appropriate controller to go with it, and binding that view and controller to the correct model. If the ingredient calls for an abstract view on a subobject with a different (or the same) display type, the ID-generation process is repeated recursively. Thus, abstract views are the mechanism that permits modular description of an ID based on IDs for subparts of an object.

An abstract view interprets a display type dynamically. An ID using an abstract view monitors the object being displayed for significant changes. If changes occur and another recipe is called for, the abstract view reconstitutes itself with sub-IDs based on the ingredients in the new recipe. Parts of the ID that correspond to parts of the objects that did not change usually do not have to be repainted.

7. Work Outside of SIG

There are a few aspects of display development that currently must be dealt with outside of SIG. If a display designer wants to use a custom view, then he or she must implement a routine that draws the desired graphics in a given area. The designer then includes a message to invoke that routine in a display description.

For the class being displayed, the designer must write routines so that objects can process certain messages issued by the ID. Some messages request updates corresponding to items on the ID's menu. Many of those update messages will be implemented in any case when constructing a new class of objects. Usually the subregion of a display area that a sub-ID occupies is fixed in the ingredient for the sub-ID. If that subregion is to depend on some property of the model (such as the number of nodes in a subtree), the model must provide a *rectangle message* that returns that proper subregion in relative coordinates. Other messages are needed to support the pluggable view mechanism. The most important is the *aspect message*, which is sent by a view to a model to determine which aspect of the model to display. A model may require several aspect messages, if different views display different aspects of it.

While some Smalltalk code must be written to produce a display with SIG, that code need only be written once for a class, even if the class has multiple display types. Furthermore, all the code is associated with the class of the object being displayed. No view or controller code need be written, as contrasted to using the MVC mechanism directly.

8. System Construction

As mentioned before, SIG builds upon the MVC mechanism of Smalltalk. Models use a broadcast message to let views know that they have been updated. Smalltalk maintains a *dependencies list* telling which views are concerned with which models. When a model changes, the list is scanned, and the appropriate views are notified. If the model changes in only one aspect, it broadcasts that that aspect has changed. Only views concerned with that aspect respond. The views and controllers SIG uses to build IDs are adaptations of views and controllers supplied with Smalltalk, except for abstract views.

The display-type editor is itself a SIG-generated ID on an object of class DisplayBuilder.

9. What Next?

We believe more of the construction of a display type can be done graphically, rather than lexically. For example, the subregions of a display corresponding to different ingredients could be sketched on the screen, rather than specified via relative coordinates. Other parts of a display type, such as border width and the kind of view for an ingredient could be chosen off menus. We also need better support for iterative sub-IDs, such as a view that can scroll a sequence of subviews. Also, while we can spawn a new ID on a sub-ID that is too small to display, we have no facility to zoom in on one region of an ID.

We would like to specify the routines for messages to the model at a high level in a display type, rather than as Smalltalk code. Display types would then be self-contained descriptions of displays, which would make it easier to implement SIG on systems other than Smalltalk.

Ideally, we would like to create display types for a class with no modification of the class itself. The data modeling and computation portion of application development could proceed separately from the display design. We have experimented with an architecture for interactive applications called Humanizer [Gros85] that cleanly separates display modules from data access and computation modules in a database application. Figure 10 shows the layout of Humanizer. Display modules and other application modules communicate through shared objects held in a Data Access Manager (DAM). Display modules continually monitor the objects in the DAM for changes made by the other modules. In response to user input, display modules modify objects that the other application modules are monitoring. The DAM is an in-core database system that ensures serializable access of objects, enforces constraints, imposes authorization conditions, and maintains queues of interesting events for the various application modules. With Humanizer, it is easy to have two displays communicating with one computation module, or one display communicating with two computation modules, or even switch displays while an application is running.

Acknowledgements

We thank Harry Porter and Mark Ballard for help with the software for producing hard copies of screen images. This work was supported in part by NSF grant IST 83 51730, co-sponsored by Tektronix Foundation, Intel, Digital Equipment Corporation, Servio Logic, Mentor Graphics, Xerox, IBM and the Beaverton Area Chamber of Commerce.

Database Access Manager (DAM)

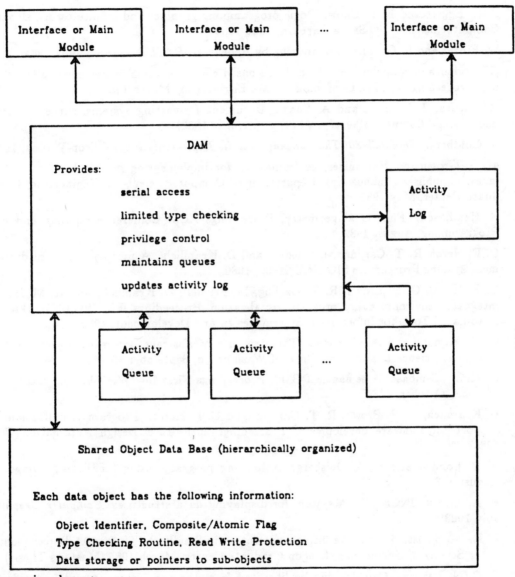

Figure 10. Humanizer layout.

10. Bibliography

[Ande85]   T. L. Anderson and B. B. Claghorn. ADE: Mapping between the external and conceptual levels. In *Information Systems: Theoretical and Formal Aspects*, (Proceedings of the IFIP WG 8.1
Working Conference on Theoretical and Formal Aspects of Information Systems, Sitges, Bar-
celona, Spain, 16-18 April, 1985), A. Sernadas, J. Bubenko, and A. Olive, eds. North Holland,
1985.

[Baec81]   R. Baecker. *Sorting Out Sorting*, 16mm color sound film, 25 minutes, SIGGRAPH '81, 1981.

[Brow84]   M. H. Brown and R. Sedgewick. A system for algorithm animation, *Computer Graphics 18* (3), July 1984.

[Egge83]   P. R. Eggert and K. P. Chow. Logic programming graphics and infinite terms, Department of Computer Science, UC Santa Barbara, June 1983.

[Finz84]   W. Finzer and L. Gould. Programming by Rehearsal, *BYTE Magazine*, June 1984.

[Fisc84]   G. Fischer and M. Schneider. Knowledge-based communication processes in software engineering, Proceedings 7th Int. Conf. on Software Engineering, March 1984.

[Furu82]   R. Furuta, J. Scofield, and A. Shaw. Document formatting systems: survey, concepts, and issues, *ACM Computing Surveys 14* (3), September 1982.

[Gold83]   A. Goldberg. *Smalltalk-80: The Language and its Implementation*, Addison-Wesley, 1983.

[Gros85]   M. B. Grossman. Humanizer—A framework for implementing flexible human-machine interfaces, unpublished manuscript, Department of Computer Science & Engineering, Oregon Graduate Center, May 1985.

[Hend82]   P. Henderson. Functional geometry, Proceedings ACM Conference on Lisp and Functional Programming, August 1982.

[Hero80]   C. F. Herot, R. T. Carling, M. Friedell, and D. Kramlich. A prototype spatial data management system, Proceedings SIGGRAPH '80, 1980.

[Hero82]   C. F. Herot, G. P. Brown, R. T. Carling, M. Friedell, D. Kramlich, and R. M. Baecker. An integrated environment for program visualization, Proceedings IFIP WG8.1 Working Conf. on Automated Tools for Information System Design and Development, 1982.

[Kimu83]   G. D. Kimura and A. C. Shaw. The structure of abstract document objects, TR 83-09-02, Computer Science Department, Univ. of Washington, September 1983.

[King84]   R. King. Sembase: A semantic DBMS, Proceedings First Int. Workshop on Expert Database Systems, October, 1984.

[Kram83]   D. Kramlich, G. P. Brown, R. T. Carling, and C. F. Herot. Program visualization: Graphics support for software development, Proceedings 20th IEEE Design Automation Conference, 1983.

[Lond85]   R. L. London and R. A. Duisberg. Animating programs using Smalltalk, *Computer 18* (8), August 1985.

[Myer83]   B. A. Myers. INCENSE: A system for displaying data structures, *Computer Graphics 17* (3), July 1983.

[Nord85]   P. R. Nordquist. Interactive display generation in Smalltalk, TR 85-009, Department of Computer Science & Engineering, Oregon Graduate Center, March 1985 (Master's Thesis).

[Pere83]   F. C. N. Pereira. Can drawing be liberated from the von Neumann style?, Artificial Intelligence Center, SRI International, March 1983.

[Pilo83]   M. Pilote. A data modeling approach to simplify the design of user interfaces, Proceedings 9th VLDB, October-November 1983.

[Reis83]   S. P. Reiss. PECAN: Program development systems that support multiple views, Proceedings 1983 International Conf. on Software Engineering.

[Scho83]   E. Schoen and R. G. Smith. IMPULSE: A display oriented editor for STROBE, AAAI '83.

[Smith84]   R. G. Smith, G. M. E. LaFue, E. Schoen, and S. C. Vestal. Declarative task description as a user-interface structuring machanism. *IEEE Computer 17* (9), September 1984.

[VanW82]   C. J. Van Wyk. A high-level language for specifying pictures, *ACM Transactions on Graphics 1* (2), April 1982.

Chapter 9

Applications

Introduction

This chapter looks at applications of object-oriented databases. The papers represent two approaches to OODB support for applications. One is to put features into a database system that are particularly useful for the application area. The other is to "build a model on a model"—to use the type- or class-definition facilities of an OODB to create abstractions useful in an application area.

The OPAL system ([AB+84], not to be confused with the GemStone system's data language OPAL) is an example of the first approach. It is an object-oriented database system with special features aimed at office information system. OPAL is based on *packets*, which share the characteristics of both objects and processes. Like objects in most OODBs, packets are instances of classes (where the classes are arranged in a hierarchy), have references to other objects, have local state, and are accessed through methods. However, each packet also has a *statement part*, with a *statement cursor* that captures a thread of execution, and thus can function as an independent process. This capability can be used a number of ways in office systems. One packet can send a message to another, and not wait for a response, thus effectively forking a subtask; for example, an **Order-entry** packet might start up a **Restock** packet when inventory of a particular item is low. Also one packet can act as a coroutine or server for several others; for example, one packet might serve as a registry for all **Pending-order** packets that represent orders

waiting to be filled. A packet can also suspend execution waiting for some external event, thus functioning as an exception handler or carrying out periodic batch processing.

Packets support constraints on their internal state, and derived attributes, similar to those in the CACTIS system [HK86]. OPAL supports two kinds of derived attributes—those that are updated immediately when the values on which they depend change, and others that are updated only by explicit request. A use of the former might be a **credit-available** attribute in a **Customer** packet, representing the difference between **credit-line** and **outstanding-bills**. An example of the latter is a packet representing the current price list. The prices of individual items might be calculated from current wholesale costs, but the price list might be revised on only a monthly basis.

OPAL also contains several features to aid user interaction. A packet can communicate with a user for input. It can also cede control to a user, and act as a workspace in which the user can cache values and can execute ad hoc expressions. A *scratchpad* is provided in each packet to preserve these values and expressions if desired. Certain packets are *templates* for viewing other packets or groups of packets, and also serve as a security and authorization mechanism. The part of a packet that contains references to other packets is called the *folio*. The folio is structured as a name-to-packet mapping. The folio section of a packet can be used as a directory, giving rise to a hierarchical name space for users to locate objects.

The Office Task Manager (OTM) [LH+88] is an example of an application-specific model implemented on top of a more general object-oriented database. OTM supports the Officeaid visual programming system, which allows users to specify office tasks by example. Officeaid supports the definition of office tasks that collect documents, act on those documents, set deadlines, and dispose of the documents on completion. The OTM language provides a task-execution model, with the decomposition of tasks into subtasks via iterative, conditional, and parallel evaluation constructs. It also supports as its basic types *documents* and *roles*. Documents are the entities acted on in Officeaid, whereas roles describe the actors.

OTM in turn is built on the OZ+ object-oriented database system [We85]. OZ+ has a data model like that of Smalltalk, with classes, instances, and inheritance between classes. However, the execution model of OZ+ departs from that of Smalltalk. Computation is specified by rules, which can be invoked in a variety of ways: in response to messages from other objects, or when triggered by internal or external changes. An object can also limit the set of other objects from which it will accept messages, which is useful in OTM and Officeaid for capturing constraints that only certain roles can perform certain actions on documents. Also, OZ+ objects can synchronize their activities in *events*, in which a group of objects evaluate rules simultaneously. A use of this feature is a group of **Time-schedule** objects for different employees collectively choosing a time for a meeting.

The paper by Woelk, Kim, and Luther [WLK86] discusses the database requirements for supporting multimedia document objects and proposes an object-oriented model for such objects. This document model could be either implemented directly or mapped onto types in an object-oriented database system. One interesting requirement the authors point out is that the class for a document not only will specify the structure of document instances and the types of their subparts, but also might specify data values common to all instances. Their example is strings such as "From:", "To:", "Subject:", and "Date:" in a memo document. Some OODBs can support this requirement through *class variables*. Class variables are variables stored by the class-describing object that can be accessed by all instances of the class. Another requirement that the authors point out is that document instances must be to some extent self-describing. A document class cannot specify a fixed structure for all its instances, as they will vary in the number of chapters, sections, paragraphs, and so forth.

The authors propose a nodes-and-arcs model for defining both document classes and instances of those classes. Nodes represent classes, instances, attributes, methods, and so on. Arcs capture relationships such as subpart, instance-of, and subclass-of. The model has the unusual capability of attribute inheritance at the instance level. A shared subobject will inherit different attribute values depending on the superobject through which it is viewed. For example, two documents might share a bibliography entry. When viewed in the first document, the entry might inherit attributes for doing single-spacing and for quoting the paper title. Through the other document, it could inherit attributes for doing double-spacing and for putting the title in boldface. The model also supports historical and alternative versions of documents.

The final paper concerns the application of an OODB to VLSI design [AK+85]. It gives a set of types defined in the 3DIS (three-dimensional information space) object model to support the ADAM design environment. The types deal with the complexity that arises from a VLSI component being viewable in a variety of ways: as a dataflow algorithm, as timing and sequencing behavior, as a circuit schematic, and as a physical layout. A component can be recursively defined as subcomponents in each of these domains. Although top-level components will probably have similar structural descriptions in each of these domains, by the time the lowest levels of detail are reached, there is likely to be little natural correspondence. Thus, the 3DIS model for ADAM has types for describing a component in each of these domains, plus *bindings* to capture relationships between pieces of the description in different domains.

Katz and Chang [KC87] are also concerned with supporting electronic-design applications. Their emphasis is on propagating changes from one part or representation of a design to another.

References

•[AB+84]   M. Ahlson, A. Björnerstedt, A. Britts, C. Hulten, and L. Söderlund. An Architecture for Object Management in OIS. *ACM Transactions on Office Information Systems* 2(3), 1984.

•[AK+85]   H. Afsarmanesh, D. Knapp, D. McLeod, and A. Parker. An Object-Oriented Approach to Extensible Databases for VLSI/CAD. *Proceedings of the XI International Conference on Very Large Databases*, Stockholm, September 1985. Morgan Kaufmann Publisher, San Mateo, CA.

•[HK86]   S.E. Hudson and R. King. CACTIS: A Database System for Specifying Functionally Defined Data. K. Dittrich and U.Dayal, eds. In *Proceedings of the International Workshop on Object-Oriented Database Systems*, Pacific Grove, CA, September 1986.

[KC87]   R. Katz and E. Chang. Managing Change in a Computer-Aided Design Database. *Proceedings of the XIII International Conference on Very Large Databases*, Brighton, England, September 1987. Morgan Kaufmann Publishers, San Mateo, CA.

[LH+88]   F.H. Lochovsky, J.S. Hogg, S.P. Weiser, and A.O. Mendelzon. OTM: Specifying Office Tasks. *Proceedings of the ACM Conference on Office Information Systems*, Palo Alto, CA, March 1988.

[We85]   S.P. Weiser. An Object-Oriented Protocol for Managing Data. *Database Engineering* 8(4), 1985.

•[WLK86]   D. Woelk, W. Kim, and W. Luther. An Object-Oriented Approach to Multimedia Databases. *Proceedings of the ACM SIGMOD International Conference on Management of Data*, Washington, D.C., May 1986.

• indicates article included in this volume

An Architecture for Object Management in OIS

MATTS AHLSEN, ANDERS BJÖRNERSTEDT, STEFAN BRITTS,
CHRISTER HULTEN, and LARS SÖDERLUND
SYSLAB

The design of an office information system (OIS) application development environment prototype, OPAL, is outlined. OPAL is based on an object management approach. The central concept is the *packet*, which is the principal data and action structuring device. The main ideas in OPAL are described, including novel data types, partitioned work spaces, object version management, multiple property inheritance, and incremental application development.

A scheme for naming objects is proposed and discussed. There are basically two large advantages to such a scheme—a very practical shorthand for referring to objects and a means for structuring information according to criteria not represented in the objects themselves. The latter property also supports viewing objects in different roles. Furthermore, the scheme is used to structure the whole object management system.

Categories and Subject Descriptors: D.3.3 [**Programming Languages**]: Language Constructs—*data types and structures*; H.2.1 [**Database Management**]: Local Design—*data models*; H.2.3 [**Database Management**]: Languages—*query languages*; H.4.1 [**Information Systems Applications**]: Office Automation

General Terms: Design, Languages

Additional Key Words and Phrases: Application development tools, OIS, object programming, object databases

1. INTRODUCTION

1.1 Motivation

In the field of Office Information Systems (OIS), the demands for high-level information system development tools are constantly increasing. In particular, the natural integration of many functions in an OIS leads to the need for application development tools which include implementation concepts that support the development of integrated systems. Such tools could facilitate

- fast development of reliable systems;
- incremental application development and prototyping;

This work was supported by the National Swedish Board for Technical Development (STU).
Authors' address: SYSLAB, Dept. of Information Processing and Computer Science, University of Stockholm, S-106 91, Stockholm, Sweden.

- production of extremely flexible systems; and
- development of customized applications for individual users.

In surveying the area of OIS development tools we found many interesting ideas [1]. However, we did not find any approach that would cover all the problems we wanted to address. Our approach, therefore, is to combine some ideas from previous research with some of our own, and in general to utilize ideas from programming languages, operating systems, databases and, to some extent, from artificial intelligence. The result is a combined development and run-time system named OPAL, which is currently in the design stage. One of its characteristics is that it generates target systems which are entirely built by object structures stored in a database. The objects represent programs as well as data, and are uniformly integrated into the database.

The aim of this paper is to present some of the ideas behind OPAL rather than to describe the user interface, either in an application design mode or in a production mode. We therefore show examples expressed in a linear (string) language rather the graphical language the user may be provided with.

1.2 Overview of the Paper

We start with a short, general (not specific to our approach) discussion on object-oriented systems and some important related concepts. Our object-oriented system, OPAL, is based on a concept we call *packet*, which is described in Section 2. In Section 3 object *versions* are introduced, and Section 4 covers the ideas of how to structure a packet-based application system. The paper concludes with sections on incremental application development, OPAL and OIS configuration, and a summary.

1.3 Object Management Systems

Recent proposals call for the integration of previously separated functions such as programming, database management, communications, and command language into uniform development environments [12, 21, 25, 36]. Such environments presume a uniformity in the syntax and semantics of the language used to express applications. To achieve this general uniformity, yet allow for local and application-dependent customization, there is a need for a unifying general concept such as the *object*. What any two objects have in common are the underlying mechanisms of how objects are defined, created, related, and how they interact.

An *object* is a "conceptually distinct unit that has some abstract significance to users of the system" [40]. The idea of object management systems and object-oriented programming is the result of a convergence of concepts from many areas of computer science, such as programming languages, artificial intelligence, databases, and operating systems. The programming language Simula [3], introduced the class concept, which captures the essence of what we see as object-oriented programming: abstraction, encapsulation, and independently active objects. The abstraction and encapsulation aspects were formalized into the concept of the abstract data type [24]. Smalltalk [15] is perhaps the best current example of an object-oriented programming language. But apart from consider-

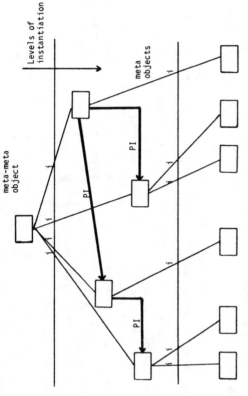

Fig. 0.   Instantiation is denoted by i; property inheritance by PI.

ations of virtual memory management [4, 22], not much attention has been paid to the need for an object database.

In the database field, data models using concepts such as entities [8], general-ization and aggregation [30], molecules [9], and objects [33], have been developed, and database management systems which support such higher level data models [17, 29, 38] have been created. However, the objects supported by these systems are pure data structures, that is, passive objects. Actors [18], on the other hand, are purely active objects; they do not recognize any data structures.

Operating systems have traditionally been the software component with the greatest degree of generality, since they are shared by all users of a system. It is not surprising then that general object-oriented methods have been used in the construction of operating systems for quite some time [20, 23, 27, 31, 37]. An object from the perspective of an operating system is simply a resource to be managed, for example, a file, a printer, a work space, or some user-defined object.

The object-oriented view as a synthesis of ideas from all these areas can be described by a few basic concepts.

Modularity. The general idea is that things which are related, such as data structures and procedures, should be kept together. Closely related to the concept of modularity is that of *encapsulation* or *information hiding*: Properties used only for purposes internal to the module are protected from outside access.

Instantiation. The object concept becomes a bit more useful if we make the distinction between object types and object instances. Every instance is generated and manipulated according to the cast represented by its type description. To be more general, we could regard object types as objects in themselves. An object type would then be a *metaobject* containing both its own data and the description of its instances. We would then be forced to recognize a *meta-metaobject*, to serve as the cast for the metaobject. We could continue in this way indefinitely, each level consisting of objects which are instantiations of the objects on the level above. In practice, three or four such levels of instantiation are sufficient. The top level is purely descriptive[1], while bottom-level objects are pure data containers. Objects on intermediate levels contain both a descriptive part and a data container part.

Property Inheritance and Subclassing. The class concept in Simula is an example of what we call a metaobject. A subclass C_s of a class C inherits the descriptions in C. In addition C_s has its own descriptions, some of which may "override" the inherited descriptions. In most systems (and in Simula), a subclass can only have one parent. Systems which allow multiple inheritance [6, 10] must have some mechanism for resolving name conflicts between properties inherited from more than one parent. Although property inheritance and subclassing are often taken to mean the same thing, there is a distinction to be made. Subclassing is a semantic notion which states that instances of a subclass C_s form a subset of the instances of a class C. Property inheritance, on the other hand, is simply a convenient mechanism useful for structuring descriptions. Descriptions which

several classes have in common can be placed in a common parent, thus giving the descriptions greater clarity and reduced redundancy on the description level. Property inheritance could be employed without connecting it to the semantic notion of subclassing, but in this paper we assume this connection. A subclass C_s of class C inherits *all* the descriptions of C, no selectivity is allowed.

Subclassing should not be confused with instantiation. The subclass C_s is *not* an instance X of its superclass C, it is only a refinement. Thus, if we create an instance X of C_s, then X will conform to the cast of both C_s and C (and any superclasses of C). In particular, if C_s "overrides" some property description in C (by redefining a name already defined in C), this will simply mean that X has two alternative implementations of the property. Which implementation is selected depends on whether X is used as an instance of C_s or C. To be precise, property inheritance should be called "property description inheritance." Property inheritance is orthogonal to instantiation. The difference between property inheritance and object instantiation is illustrated in Figure 0. The levels in Figure 0 are instantiation levels; that is, an object is molded according to its type-description object on the level above. Object instances on the lowest level have the properties defined by the descriptions in their type (metaobject), but they do not inherit any property descriptions. On other levels, instances have the properties defined by the description in their type (on the level above), and inherit the property descriptions of their superclasses (located on the same level in Figure 0). Thus, instantiation means generating an object according to the cast of its metaobject and assigning values to the properties of the object, whereas property inheritance means propagating property descriptions through a series of descriptive objects on the same instantiation level. In Figure 0 the bold line-arrows denote property inheritance and the thin line-arrows, instantiation.

[1]Top-level objects would also have to be self-descriptive in order to be handled as objects.

Active Objects. If we had *passive* objects only, then in order to get anything done we would need some other entity than an object to do the work. If work is to be *performed* by objects, they must be more than simple data structures. If work is to be *initiated* by objects, they must be able to communicate and pass control. The latter type of objects are called *active* objects. A central issue here is how to pass control between objects, hierarchically (procedure call) or freely (message passing), and whether different objects execute concurrently (as different processes) or sequentially (more than one object is executed in one process).

1.4 OIS-Modeling Tools

A number of graphical OIS-modeling tools have been reported in the literature. A graphical modeling language should be able to represent the interrelationships between the components of the modeled system in a clear and comprehensible way. A modeling language should preferably not only be an analysis and design tool, but also an effective means of communication between designers and end users.

A graphical model can be either control- or data-oriented. The former focuses on the control flow between processes in the model, whereas data-oriented models are primarily concerned with the flow of data between processes. Some models have both these capacities, in which case the processes are data driven (that is, triggered by data flow).

Many of the existing OIS-modeling languages are based on the theory of Petri nets [28], and are mainly control-flow oriented, for example, Augmented Petri Nets (APNs) [41] and Information Control Nets (ICNs) [13]. An example of a model which unifies the notions of control and data flow is the Document Flow Component (DFC) of the Business Definition Language (BDL) [16]. In this model the flow of data (documents) triggers the execution of processes.

An OIS-modeling tool being developed by the authors (the DISCO project) is inspired mainly by ICNs but is based on a process-oriented *data* flow model [32]. There are basically two types of objects represented in this model: data objects and process objects (processes). The processes are hierarchically decomposable into subprocesses so that a structured top-down design is facilitated. What is needed is a device for the implementation of these objects which will do the following:

- facilitate well-structured modular design;
- facilitate correctness validation by using abstract data-type concepts;
- enable piecemeal execution of modules for incremental application development;
- assist dialogue design;
- enable property (data and procedural) inheritance in generic structures;
- enable unification of data and action structures; and
- enable representation of metastructures.

In order to examine the benefits of object-oriented systems and to experiment with implementations of these ideas, we have developed the *packet* concept. A *packet* represents a type of *object* with a particular structure and properties (discussed in detail in Section 2).

A Packet
System Data
Folio
Scratch Pad
User Data/Procedures
Statement Body

Fig. 1.

2. THE PACKET CONCEPT

2.1 The Packet Structure

The packet is the principal data and action-structuring concept. Programs, data including large databases, system metadata as well as system-defined components are all represented as objects which in turn are implemented as packets. Since everything in the system is considered an object, it is possible to have uniform management of all these components, which in turn simplifies the system and makes it easy to use. Conceptually, a packet instance consists of

- *System-maintained data* (e.g., packet identifier, creation time, and so on).
- A *FOLIO* which can hold references to other packets (see below). The name *FOLIO* is used because a number of related objects (such as documents related to some activity) are collected in a container. The FOLIO is used for constructing aggregates of packets.
- A *scratch pad memory* for storage of data and procedures defined in the INTERACT mode (see below).
- *User attributes* characterized by data structures together with initialization procedures, access procedures, access privileges, and constraint definitions.
- *User-defined procedures.*
- A *user-defined statement body* for coroutine-style execution of the packet instance.

Procedures and the statement body do not, of course, actually reside in the instance, since they are common to all instances of the same packet type, and are therefore represented in the metapacket.

A packet instance is described by a packet type (or metapacket), which itself is represented as a packet instance. The meta-metapacket is built into the system. This means that packet types can be accessed just as any other packet instance and thereby function as a metadatabase. The packet type has attributes (described in the meta-metapacket) which hold the descriptions of its instances. The attribute values of a packet type thus describe the attributes, procedures, statement body, and so on of its instances. The application designer constructs packet types by working on them as instances.

2.2 Creating Packet Instances

When a packet instance is generated it is supplied with an identifier by the system. The identifier is unique over the entire system and is not reused, c.f. [9]. The attributes of a packet instance are assigned values at creation time.

(In the following we use the term packet and packet instance as synonyms. Analogously, a metapacket is the same as a meta-metapacket instance. Thus, a packet type is represented by a metapacket).

An initialization procedure may be defined which is executed automatically when the packet is created. This initialization procedure may also be explicitly called at a later point in time if desired. This is called "REFRESHING" the packet. Although the initialization procedure assigns values to attributes which may be derived from other packets in a packet database or be obtained from the environment (for instance, by terminal input), it is important to understand the independence of the generated packet. If the data which is used in the generation of the packet is updated at a later time in the database, these later updates will not be propagated to the packet.

In database terminology, packets correspond to a static snapshot rather than to a dynamic view. Attributes whose values have been obtained through a database or packet query may deviate from the originals at some point in time. In many applications such deviation is highly desirable; for example, if an order has been created based on the current product prices and the prices are later updated, the order and a subsequent invoice should probably reflect the former prices.

2.3 Data Types in Packets

The basic data types include the standard types:

INTEGER, REAL, TEXT, TEXTFILE, DOLLAR, DATE, TIME.

Furthermore, three additional data types are provided:

PACKETREF, TUPLE, and TABLE.

2.3.1 *The PACKETREF Data Type.* A *packetref* is a reference to a packet instance. Since symbolic references, or identifiers, are used and since they never change, the references can be used freely by the application designer and the end user. A variable of packet reference type may be typed or untyped. If it is untyped, it may reference an instance of an arbitrary packet type, but must on the other hand be qualified when accessing other than system attributes. For example, if we have the following declarations:

```
PACKET invoice; sum:DOLLAR; ENDPACKET invoice;
pacref:PACKETREF;
```

We can then use pacref to reference instances of arbitrary packet types (e.g., when browsing through a set of packets), but we must use qualification when accessing user attributes in the packet.

```
pacref ← some_invoice;
/* pacref can now be used to reference this invoice */
```

To access the attribute "sum" we must say pacref: invoice.sum. If a packetref variable is typed, that is:

```
pacref:PACKETREF (invoice);
```

A shorter notation may be used without losing any of the safety of strong typing when accessing attributes. To access the attribute "sum" we then merely say pacref.sum, c.f. Simula [3], where strong typing is used, or PLITS [14] where strong typing is relaxed. The flexible typing scheme for reference variables makes object handling much easier for the designer/user. The advantages of strong typing are still obtained in that type mismatches, which often reflect semantic errors, can be caught (in particular, a large class of such errors can be caught at compile time) and pinpointed. In other words, testing and debugging activities can be reduced for a given level of reliability.

2.3.2 *The TUPLE Data Type.* A *tuple* is defined as an ordered set of a predefined number of scalars of various types; that is, it is basically the same as a tuple in a First Normal Form (1NF) relation in the relational data model.

2.3.3 *The TABLE Data Type.* A *TABLE* is an *ordered* set of tuple type instances. The primary reason for differentiating between the types tuple and table is performance. The tuple can be seen as a table constrained to have cardinality equal to 1; but to gain efficiency, the system supports the tuple type directly. A TABLE will mostly be used for representing two-dimensional tables in "forms." For convenience, two access methods are available,

a content-oriented way, and

a position-oriented way

In the content-oriented way, data is accessed in an SQL-like manner [19]. In the position-oriented way, data is accessed through an indexing scheme. An example:

```
employee: TABLE(empno:INTEGER,
                empname:TEXT, salary:INTEGER;
```

employee	empno 1	empname 2	salary 3
1	234	Smith	43000
2	312	Jones	54000
3	444	Blake	99000
4	999	Brown	39000

```
SELECTTAB empno, empname FROM employee
                 WHERE salary < 50000
```

234	Smith
999	Brown

employee [2, 2]

Jones

employee [*, empname]

Smith
Jones
Blake
Brown

employee [2..3, *]

312	Jones	43000
444	Blake	99000

employee [3..MAX, 2..MAX]

Blake	99000
Brown	39000

office workers so that the processing history of an office object, particularly with regard to exceptional conditions, is saved.

The *FOLIO* attribute is fundamental for structuring both OPAL itself and in application systems. It is a system-controlled packet attribute which contains data and a set of operations to work on those data. The data in the *FOLIO* is an ordered set of packetrefs. In essence, it provides a means for building structures of packet instances (i.e., we can structure a whole system—programs, data metadata—with the *FOLIO:s* in packets).

The basic folio data structure is of the following form:

TABLE(name:TEXT, ref:PACKETREF);

The name attribute in a folio tuple may be null, in which case the data in the folio is only an ordered set of packet references. The packet query language is built around the folio (actually, it is closed on packets). A packet SELECT query takes a packet (with its folio) as an argument and produces as a result a packet with zero, one, or more references to packets in its folio. The WHERE clause of a packet SELECT is essentially a filter, which allows certain references in the folio of the source packet to pass on to the result packet. As a consequence it is possible to perform nested SELECT:s or explicitly store the result of a query and perform multistep operations. In combination with browsing of packet folios, the packet select provides a powerful information retrieval capability.

Folio operations are procedures that are defined on all packet types. Like all packet attribute operations, they are accessible from the outside, that is, from another packet by dot-notation. Each packet has a folio cursor associated with it, which can either be null or point to a specific tuple in the folio. Since the folio is ordered, we may speak of the cursor's relative position in the folio. Examples of these operations are NEXT, PREVIOUS, SORT, and APPEND (see the Appendix for a listing).

Example. Create an invoice for all current orders where the supplier's name is Smith.

Assumptions:

- There is a system procedure "READ" which copies attribute values from one packet to another where attribute names agree.
- The packet types "invoice" and "order" are defined.
- The user procedure "addorder", defined for invoices, adds the contents of an order to the invoice.

```
ord, inv, smithord:PACKETREF;
smithord ← SELECT order WHERE supplier = "Smith";
IF NOT smithord.EMPTY THEN
  BEGIN
    inv ← NEW invoice;
    inv.READ(smithord.FIRST);
       /* copies values with same attr.
              name for example
              suppliername, address, etc. */
```

Several TABLE:s (from arbitrary packets) may participate in a SELECTTAB access (i.e., there is an operation corresponding to the join operation in the relational model). The result of an access from a TABLE is a TABLE. There is also a "tuple at a time" interface, which the following example illustrates:

FOR EACH TUPLE IN
SELECTTAB empname, empno FROM employee
    WHERE salary < 50000 DO S;

where S denotes a set of statements.

2.3.4 *User-Defined Data Types.* Users can define their own data types by using the basic types and structuring them into tuples and tables. Constraints, initialization procedures, and access procedures can be defined for each data type. If this is not adequate, a new packet type can be introduced. Note that the difference between user-defined data types, in particular structured data types, and user-defined packets is minimal. The difference is basically that a packet is regarded as an object and must be explicitly generated (and attributes must be accessed through dot notation), whereas an attribute defined on a data type is "in-line." Conversely, a data-type "instance" does not have an independent existence; it must always be the value of some attribute in some packet. Note, however, that a data-type *definition* is represented as a packet, because we want data-type definitions to have an independent existence. One data type could be used in many packet-type definitions.

2.4 Packet Attributes

2.4.1 *System-Controlled Attributes.* A packet has a number of system-controlled attributes. Every packet, including metapackets, has these attributes; examples are

- *Identifier.* A system-unique symbolic packet identifier (PID).[2]
- *Type.* The type is actually represented by the PID of the metapacket.
- *Creator.* The PID of the packet that issued the creation.
- *Owner.* A reference to the user who owns the packet.
- *Creation_time, refresh_time, update_time.*
- *Statement_cursor.* Points to the next statement to be executed in the packet's statement body.
- *Folio.* A dynamic container of named references to other packets (see below).
- *Packet_log.* A notebook for comments.

The packet_log can, for example, be used for commenting on the life of an office object. Normally, the log is only augmented, that is, comments are added, but not deleted, to ensure that specific information is carried through a chain of

[2] The packet identifer is defined on a system data type: PID, which is not directly accessible to the user. The packetref data type holds the PID of some packet and some additional information regarding the access rights of the holder of the reference. The authorization mechanism of the system will be elaborated on in a forthcoming paper.

```
FOR EACH order ord IN smithord DO
    inv:invoice.addorder(ord);
END ELSE
    REPLY("No orders for Smith");
```

Note that the source packet in the packet SELECT is the "order" packet type. The folio of a packet type holds references to all of its available instances. Since a folio is present in every packet (that is, the folio concept along with the folio operations are structured into a packet which is in the prefix chain of all packets), a call on a folio procedure *within a packet* can be applied to the packet's own folio without using dot notation. For instance, if we want the first packetref in the built-in folio, we merely say FIRST. On the other hand, if *another packet* is referenced by a variable p, then, in order to get the first packetref in p's folio, we say p.FIRST.

2.4.2 *Application Attributes.* The application designer declares each application attribute of a packet type on some data type. Each application attribute may be connected to a generating expression; that is, an expression which, when evaluated, will result in a value which is assigned to the attribute. This expression will be reevaluated when the packet is refreshed. These expressions are called ATTRIBUTE SOURCES, and we distinguish between two kinds: An EXTERNAL SOURCE may contain any expression and is only used at generation or refresh time. An INTERNAL SOURCE is local to the packet and will automatically be evaluated whenever a source attribute is changed, for example:

$$c \leftarrow a * b$$

$$d \leftarrow c * 1.21$$

will propagate updates on a or b to c and d. The INTERNAL SOURCE concept provides the backbone for a powerful spreadsheet feature.

Example. Definition of an order (we only look at the interesting part) which consists of a varying number of orderlines. An orderline consists of the attributes: part number, price, quantity, and rowsum. The latter is the product of the price and quantity of the same orderline.

Finally, there is a packet attribute total, which should always contain the sum of the rowsums.

```
PACKET order;
ATTRIBUTE orderlines:
    TABLE[partno:INTEGER,price:DOLLAR,
        quantity:INTEGER,rowsum:DOLLAR);
    total:DOLLAR;
INTSOURCE BEGIN
    orderlines[#i,rowsum] ←
        orderlines[#i,price] *
        orderlines[#i,quantity];
    total ← SUM(orderlines[*,rowsum]);
END INTSOURCE;
ENDPACKET order;
```

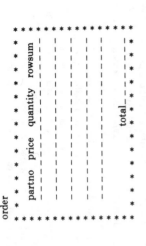

The $\#i$ in the source expression is an internal expression variable. Note that with this notation it is quite easy to express functions, for instance, accumulating rowsums. The layout of the packet is defined in a template (see below), and when the packet is displayed through the template on a CRT screen, and update operations are performed on some source attribute—for example, the price—the propagated updates on the packet will be reflected in real time on the screen.

It is also possible to connect a constraint procedure or expression to an attribute that is executed or evaluated each time the attribute is written (or read, if appropriate) by another packet. This is possible because external access is never done directly but rather through system procedures. A *constraint* consists of a constraint expression and a violation procedure. A *constraint expression* is a Boolean expression which, when evaluated to false, triggers the violation procedure. Constraint checking can be deferred by specifying transactions.

2.5 The SCRATCH PAD

The statement body of a packet is activated by an EXECUTE statement. An active packet can be in either of two modes, packet control or interactive control. The statements in the body are executed in packet control.

If an INTERACT statement is encountered while executing a packet, control is passed to the user at the terminal, and the user obtains interactive control. In this mode the terminal user can issue commands, do ad hoc queries, and so on, and eventually resume execution of the packet statements by issuing the statement PROCEED.

Space requirements are computed for the predefined attributes at code commit time, that is, when the code is committed to the system. However, for ad hoc interaction, memory is also needed. A user may often want to temporarily save some formated or unformated data as well as procedures.[3] The packet scratch pad is a storage space available for interactive usage. A user can dynamically name variables and assign values obtained through, for example, database queries. The scratch pad is similar to the work space of an APL, a Prolog, or a LISP system, and can be stored with the packet if necessary. Since procedures and variables can be defined dynamically, the scratch pad is considered to be *inner* to the static attribute definitions of the packet; that is, for an interactive operation, the variable names in the scratch pad override the static ones. A

---

[3] Here a *procedure* could simply be a labeled query.

scratch pad is only accessible *interactively*. Thus, variables or procedures defined in the scratch pad are not accessible from either the procedures defined in the packets' type nor from other packets.

2.6 Packet TEMPLATES

An OIS task, for example, creating orders or invoices, is accomplished by executing one or more packets defined for that purpose. In the execution, which typically is highly interactive, data in various packets is displayed on a user's CRT or hard-copied on some device. Since different users may want to view the packets in different ways, we need a transformation mechanism, which we call the *template*, similar to the templates in OFS [34]. A template type is a special packet type which is refined by a user (through property inheritance) and stored in the database. The template can then be referenced in the packet language. If the packet is to be updated through a template, the template must represent a simple view of the packet. A *simple view* is a mapping that is reversible in the sense that a data item piped through a template can be uniquely determined when piped the other way, similar to views in System R [11]. Templates serve not only as I/O filters, that is, as both views and display casts, but also as the vehicle for carrying the security and authorization mechanisms in OPAL. A template can be attached to either a particular packet instance or to a set of instances of different types (e.g., when a user wants to work (on a screen) with parallel display of several packets of different types).

2.7 Property Inheritance

The packet inheritance mechanism is based on *multiple inheritance*, and has simple rules for resolving name conflicts. Assume that we have the following definitions:

```
    PACKET a;
    ATTRIBUTE x, y:INTEGER;
      BODY s1; s2;
      END;
    PACKET b;
    ATTRIBUTE x, z:INTEGER;
      BODY s3; s4;
      END;
a, b  PACKET c;
    ATTRIBUTE y:INTEGER;
    BODY s5; s6;
    END;
    p:PACKETREF(c);
    p ← NEW c;
```

The syntax a, b PACKET c; ...; means that c inherits properties of a and b. The statements s_1, s_2, ..., s_6 form the statement bodies of the packets. The statements s_1, s_2, ..., s_6 assigned to p, can be seen from three different aspects, a, b, or c. The packet type c has inherited properties from a and b, so that when we say $p . z$, we refer to the attribute z described in the packet type b. We have two kinds of name conflicts—horizontal and vertical. The horizontal conflict occurs when we say $p . x$; we don't know if we get the x belonging to a or b. Our solution is to

have a default inheritance order defined by the prefix order, in this case a, b; which means that the expression $p . x$ evaluates to $p:a . x$. If we want to access the b belonging to x, we explicitly say $p:b . x$.

Vertical name conflicts arise when a packet type such as a, which is a prefix to packet type c, has the same attribute name defined as c does—in our example, $p . y$— which y do we mean, the one belonging to a or the one belonging to c? Our principle is that there is a default, just as in Simula, where the innermost attribute definition always overrides a superclass attribute definition when a name conflict arises. In other words, $p . y$ means the y belonging to c. If we want to refer to the y belonging to a, we will have to say $p:a . y$.

Since inheritance rules also cover procedures, a general or "standard" procedure defined in a packet type can be redefined or augmented in subpacket types. When a packet is executed the statements in the body are executed. The question then is: in what order are the statements in super- or subpackets executed? We have, as before, both a vertical and a horizontal order. The statements could be ordered a, b, c or b, a, c with respect to horizontal order. Our rule is that they be ordered left to right in the prefix definition, in this case a, b, c. We implicitly assume the vertical order a or b and thereafter c; this is also, quite naturally, our rule for vertical order.

Simula has a very useful option by which the statement execution order may be altered by use of the INNER statement. In OPAL, at most one INNER statement is allowed in the body of a packet type. It turns out to be very convenient to structure packet types so that they can have an initialization part and, possibly, a termination part. The initialization part is executed before the statements in the body of the subpackets, the termination part is executed after. This is a recursive process. In our example, suppose we want statements s_1, s_3, s_5, s_6, s_4, s_2 executed in that order. Then we would insert INNER between s_1 and s_2 in a, and also between s_3 and s_4 in b.

3. PACKET VERSIONS

3.1 Packet Type Versions

In organizations characterized by frequent change it is desirable to be able to change the structure of the objects (represented by packets in our system) with minimal repercussions for on-going work. However, change becomes a problem when the objects are stored in a database for access by many processes over long periods of time. If the system is distributed and the processes loosely coordinated, as is the case in our system, reorganization of the database may be impossible.

As explained, in our system, packet types are regarded as packets in themselves, that is, instances of a meta-metapacket. Changes in the structure of a packet type will then correspond to an update on a metapacket. The problem then is that instances of the packet type created before the update will usually not conform to the descriptions in the type after the update. To overcome this difficulty, without resorting to global restructuring of all instances, we introduce the concept of *packet type versions*— elaborated on in another paper [2]. The main idea is to have versions of packet types, instead of updating them directly. Old versions of a packet type are left intact in the system for as long as they are needed. Instead of reorganizing instances, a view mechanism is used to dynamically map instances, of different versions of the same type, to the type version which is used by the accessing packet or end-user. A goal is to make packet-type changes transparent from the point of view of end-users and accessing packets. The designer of the new type-version specifies mappings which the system can utilize, and thereby conceals the differences between the versions. Often, but not always, it is possible to avoid making explicit references to the different versions and avoid changing dependent packet types.

When type versions are not "compatible," instances from different versions must be processed separately. Since instances of different packet versions are distinguishable, when necessary, by means of a version number (or a version name given by the designer), conventional constructs can be utilized. The keywords TYPEVERSION IS are used to split action into different parts, depending on which type version the actual instance belongs to. For example, assume that a packet type "invoice" has been subject to a number of type changes, each of which has resulted in a type version. Assume further that the latest two versions, x and y, are incompatible to the earlier ones from some processing point of view.

```
f:PACKETREF;
f← SELECT invoice WHERE
        customername = "Smith Inc.";
FOR EACH invoice IN f DO
  WHEN TYPEVERSION IS x:
      /* Process instances of version x */
  WHEN TYPEVERSION IS y:
      /* Process instances of version y */
  OTHERWISE:
      /* Process other instances */
```

To summarize: the packet type version concept and its associated mechanisms permit:

- updates to packet types without affecting old instances, and often without affecting dependent (referencing) packet types;
- end-users not concerned with a change can avoid seeing it;
- smooth introduction of change to a distributed and loosely coordinated system.

3.2 Packet Instance Versions

In many applications it is necessary to keep track of updates to objects such as contract documents, articles, organization charts, and so on. One solution to this problem is to do away with updates for such objects by recording versions of the same object instance. We can exploit the uniformity of our object-oriented system by also introducing packet *instance* versions. With such an approach it is possible to record within the system all updates made to a packet instance. When some attribute values of an instance are to be changed, we add a new version of the instance. This strategy has some interesting theoretical and practical properties, and has been discussed in the database literature, see for example [5, 7].

Whether successive self-contained objects are to be generated or "increments" only stored (a delta change approach) is of course an implementation issue.

Nevertheless, in many cases, it is prohibitively wasteful to use a "don't-forget" approach, such a feature should be optional for every packet type. For example, it is easy to make sure that the ten last instance versions of a packet are kept, and that the older ones are successively removed. Another implementation issue is whether there should be an option for selectivity on the attribute level with regard to instance versions; that is, whether it should be possible to record old values for certain attributes and at the same time have conventional updates for others (an issue raised by Zdonik [39]).

It is quite natural that instance version handling here should also be as transparent as possible and that the default instance version of a packet should be the last instance version. The packet query language must be capable of expressing explicit searches for packet instance versions also. Note that we need the same facilities for querying the metasystem, that is, finding out about packet types, packet type versions, and so on.[4] We therefore add a few key words to our query language:

```
SELECT source-packet
WHERE qualification AND IVERSION IS
    instance-version-expression;
```

An instance-version expression is one of the key words FIRST, LAST, ALL, or a relational operator (one of the usual six, $=, <, >, <>, \leq, \geq$), or an instance-version number. We assume here that the system generates positive increasing integers as instance-version names. As mentioned, if the VERSION clause is omitted, the last instance version is assumed.

Case constructs can also be used to process instance versions:

```
f:PACKETREF;
f← SELECT invoice WHERE
        customername = "Smith Inc."  AND
        date = Feb 12 1983           AND
        IVERSION IS ALL;
FOR EACH invoice IN f DO
  WHEN IVERSION IS LAST: ...;
        OTHERWISE: ...;
```

The SELECT statement can consequently return not only different packet instances, but also different versions of packet instances. When packing the result from a SELECT statement into a folio, the result is an ordered set of packets. Packets may be of several instance versions, but may all be processed as individual objects having the attribute IVERSION with some specific value, that is, instance-version number.

A logical two-level store is used in the system. To save a packet in nonvolatile storage, an explicit *commit* must be made on the packet. New versions of a packet are created only when the packet is committed. Tentative operations on a packet, such as testing alternatives and letting them propagate through internal sources, do not generate new versions.

---

[4] Packet-type versions are actually the same as packet-instance versions, but on the metalevel.

4. STRUCTURING A SYSTEM

4.1 Packets—Programs and Data

An application is represented by one or more processes. A process corresponds to a process of the data-flow model in [32], and is implemented by one or more packets. A process (which is normally controlled by a human operator) executes the initial packet of an application, accesses and/or generates packets, and possibly transmits packets to other users. Control may be transferred to other packets, which start or resume execution.

As mentioned above (in connection with the SCRATCH PAD description), when the end-user executes a packet and an INTERACT statement is encountered, he or she has the option of issuing statements. It is then possible for the end-user to use most of the utilities present in the computer system, for example text editors, sort facilities, and so on.

A packet can define a grouping of actions, for example, an end-user dialogue concerning creation and shipment of a document. The statements of a packet are generally predefined by the application designer, who normally writes procedures and statements in PAL, the PAcket Language. However, it is possible to write closed procedures/programs in other languages, for example, Pascal or C. The application designer works with OPAL, the system we describe in this paper, in a design mode to define packet types. He or she may also execute any packet and thereby test the design in a piecemeal fashion. Changes to a packet type (new type versions) are not visible to other users of OPAL before the designer commits the (meta)packet. In a distributed system, for any node to be affected by the type change, a copy of the new type version must be sent to it.

4.2 The Notion of Control

A packet resembles a Simula class since it contains not only data structures and procedure definitions, but also an optional body of executable statements and the notion of a statement cursor.

A packet has two aspects. The *attribute* aspect and the *execution* aspect. The attribute aspect regards a packet as basically a data container with functions for operating on the data. The packet is a passive data object and is operated on from other packets. The second aspect is the execution aspect. When a packet is executed, the statements of the statement body are executed. The statement cursor determines where execution will commence. It is possible to send arguments when invoking the statement body; in fact, the statement body can be viewed as a nameless coroutine-style procedure. Control is passed in the following ways:

(1) A *subroutine call*. An executing packet p_1 calls a procedure (EXTERNAL or INTERNAL) local to p_1 or a procedure (EXTERNAL) in another packet, p_2. In the first case it is quite natural that control stays with p_1 and that the context is determined by the called procedure's textual environment, which, of course, is p_1. In the second case, control may seem to be transferred to p_2, however, p_2 functions as a data and procedure library only, and is not active. Again, the context is determined by the called procedure's static environment, this time p_2.

The statement cursor of p_2 is not affected, whereas the cursor of p_1 points to the executing statement in the procedure of p_2. This is equivalent to how it is done in Simula.

If p_2 has a procedure $proc_2$, this procedure can be called in two ways from p_1, depending on whether sequential or parallel execution is desired. The sequential

$p_2 . proc_2;$

will cause p_1 to wait until $proc_2$ is done before proceeding with the next statement. The parallel form:

$p_2 . proc_2\&;$

will permit p_1's next statement to be executed without waiting for $proc_2$ to finish; for example, if the remaining actions in p_1 are independent of $proc_2$ (the "&" notation is inspired by the UNIX Shell).[6]

(2) An *execution statement*. If a packet p_1 executes another packet p_2, p_2 will start executing the statement pointed to by p_2's statement cursor. Each packet with a statement body has a system-controlled packet reference variable (ACTIVATOR), which is set to reference the packet that issued the execution statement. Execution of a packet where no statements follow the cursor raises an exception.

An execution statement can also be issued as a sequential or parallel transfer of control. If p_1 is in control we have the sequential case:

EXECUTE p_2;

Or, if p_2 has the name "backorder" in p_1's folio:

EXECUTE backorder;

p_1 will not continue execution until p_2 has either terminated (executed its last statement) or been activated by p_2. The parallel case is

EXECUTE $p_2\&$; or EXECUTE backorder&;

where p_1 continues independently of p_2. In interactive mode, the explicit key word EXECUTE can be omitted.

(3) A *wait-until statement*. The calling packet is suspended until the condition in the argument has become true, for example,

WAIT-UNTIL(TIME = 0800) or
WAIT-UNTIL(ACTIVATOR = p_1).

In other words, a demon or trigger is activated to monitor this condition and wake the caller when the condition becomes true. The wait-until statement is used when the condition is known to the caller.

(4) A *sleep statement*. The calling packet sleeps until woken (activated) by another packet. Here the condition is determined externally to the caller. A

---

[6] UNIX is a trademark of the Bell Laboratories.

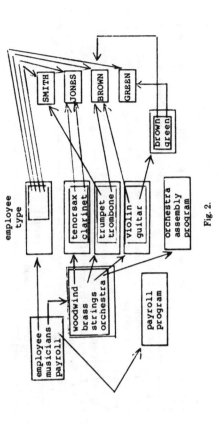

Fig. 2.

scheduling monitor is responsible for the system-controlled scheduling, which includes

- maintaining a real-time calibrated time variable (with user-controlled resolution);
- scheduling packets waiting for a timing signal (time demons);
- scheduling packets waiting for a general condition to become true (general demon);
- coping with error situations which the packet causing them cannot resolve.

As is evident, much of this resembles Simula class simulation concepts.

4.3 Name Structures

In order to structure a system effectively, we need a scheme for naming packet instances. The user of a packet database can access packets through its *identifier* (the PID) and its *content*. There are many cases in which it would be very valuable to access packets with respect to some quality (not represented in the packet) a particular user wants to associate with one packet or a group of them. It would therefore be convenient to give user-defined names to packets and to group groups of packets in a structure. In other words, a scheme for imposing structures of user semantics on packets in order to access packets by *name*. (It should be possible for a packet to have several names.) We propose such a scheme for building name structures for packet instances.

The scheme is, in fact, one for structuring the whole packet system. We, however, only outline the system structure in order to illustrate the naming scheme.

We know that packets contain folios. A *folio* is an ordered table with particular operations associated with it. The basic folio data structure is of the form:

FOLIO: TABLE (name:TEXT, ref:PACKETREF);

where *name* is an arbitrary character sequence given to a particular packet instance and *ref* is a symbolic packet identifier. Since the PACKETREF data type may hold a reference to packets of any type, the folio may hold references to packets of different types.

The name component of any folio entry may be omitted. A metapacket (representing a particular packet type) contains all the information about that particular packet type. The folio of a metapacket contains references to all available instances of that type, and normally does not use the name component. When a packet is created, a reference is automatically inserted into the folio of its metapacket.

We can now outline the structure of the system. Assume that we have an application with employee packets and that we want to structure these employees according to something that is not necessarily content-dependent, for example, according to musical skills. Figure 2 illustrates the relevant packets.

We have the following scheme, inspired by the UNIX file system: The top packet (the root) is called "/". The packets form a directed graph, and a complete packet name implies a path from the root to a node in the graph; for example, the guitar player BROWN has the complete name /musicians/strings/guitar/

brown. Every name refers to a packet, and since the packet has a folio which may contain references to other packets, we may use names to represent groups of packets. As in UNIX, we allow regular expressions so that wild cards can be used in names, for example:

/musicians/strings/guitar would evaluate to

| brown |
| green |

/musicians/strings/guitar/*gr** would evaluate to

| GREEN |

/musicians/strings/guitar/brown would evaluate to

| BROWN |

It is also possible to set one's environment in order to abbreviate names. If we say "change directory /musicians/woodwind" we could thereafter say "tenorsax", and the system would automatically expand it to "/musicians/woodwind/tenorsax". It is also possible to let the login procedure preset the environment so that the expected environment is selected by just signing on to the system or, as another example, by executing some packet which does an environment setting for some specific application.

As mentioned before, the SELECT statement has a packet as an argument. The selection of packets is made from the folio of the argument packet; that is, we can apply a SELECT statement to some user-named subset of the database. This gives uniformity with SELECT:s from a particular TYPE of packet; for instance,

SELECT employee WHERE ...

is analogous in form to

SELECT musicians/brass WHERE...

When a name is evaluated in a SELECT statement the result is a folio which is then searched. If a name is used as a procedure call, the packet is executed; for example, if p is a reference to a packet and "calculation" is a name for that packet, "execute p" is equivalent to "execute calculation;". If the packet is not executable, an error occurs. When "/musicians/orchestra" is evaluated it will result in the execution of the "program" orchestra (which could assemble some orchestra, see Figure 2). Just as in UNIX, this is a very useful feature, enabling a user to build his or her own commands. With this structuring facility it is very convenient to build application structures—data and programs.

Folios are not strongly typed (they can contain references to packets of different types) because it is very restrictive not to allow the directories in the naming structures to contain references to packets of different types (for example, other directories as well as user-defined packet types). The issue then is how to maintain a balance among considerations of safety, user flexibility, and efficiency in the design of a language. In order to gain safety we have adopted the approach of type qualification, implying that access to an attribute must always be qualified with the type of packet on some level (see the section on the PACKETREF data type). For example, assume that p references a packet in which the folio contains references to packets of type A and B. Assume further that type A has an attribute a_1 and that type B has an attribute b_1. Both attributes are integers. We can then execute the following query:

SELECT p WHERE A . a_1 = 1 OR B . b_1 = 0;

If B is a specialization of A (i.e., B inherits the descriptions of A), then we can also write:

SELECT p WHERE A . a_1 = 1 AND B . b_1 = 0;

The related issue of naming objects in a distributed environment is discussed in [26].

5. INCREMENTAL APPLICATION DEVELOPMENT

The packet concept is designed to support incremental development of applications. The design and implementation of an application can begin by defining a few central "office objects" which are shipped around in the system. At that point, before the actual processing needs are well known, the only statement in the body of the main "application program" is the statement "INTERACT"; that is, the end user has to perform all the work on the office objects in a nonautomatic way by using only system primitives as operations. As the processing requirements become better known, procedures can be written which are invoked interactively (by the user) or even automatically (by a packet). In this way applications can be incrementally implemented and the degree of automation can be customized from user to user, c.f., gradual automation in SBA (System for Business Automation) [42]. The incremental development of object types can be handled with a minimum of undesired repercussions due to the capabilities of the packet-type-version management system.

6. OPAL AND OIS-CONFIGURATION

OPAL supports OIS configurations consisting of

- a central node with an object database. The central node also holds a communication facility similar to the one in OFS [35], so that objects can be sent to remote nodes regardless of whether the nodes are disconnected or malfunctioning. Furthermore, the central node keeps track of where objects are located. There are also elementary functions for interfacing the object database with conventional databases.

- remote (or local) nodes which also maintain object databases. The central database is shared by all remote nodes (in accordance with access privileges, of course). Communication between nodes is controlled by the central node. This has the disadvantage of being dependent on the functioning of the central node, but also has many advantages, for example, less complex crash recovery.

The central and remote nodes are mapped to processors in a many-to-one fashion. The basis for the implementation is that the processors are UNIX machines.

7. SUMMARY

The DISCO project at the University of Stockholm is developing a prototype of an OIS application development environment on the basis of an object management approach. The central concept is the PACKET concept, which is the sole data and action structuring device. We have tried to convey some of the ideas of our approach, including novel data types, FOLIO:s, SCRATCH PAD:s, object version management, multiple inheritance, and incremental application development.

We have also discussed and proposed a scheme for naming packets. There are basically two large advantages to such a scheme: a very practical shorthand for referring to packets and a means for structuring information according to criteria not represented in the packets themselves. The latter property also supports viewing packets in different roles.

APPENDIX

f, f_i: PACKETREF;

f.CURR. Returns the current value of the folio cursor which is either a packetref or nil.

f.NEXT. Returns the next packetref in the folio. Nil is returned if there are no more packetrefs. The folio cursor is advanced one step if appropriate.

f.PREVIOUS. Returns the previous packetref in the folio. Nil is returned if the cursor is located on the first packetref or if the folio is empty. The folio cursor is backed-up one step if appropriate.

f.RESET. Resets the folio cursor so that the value of the cursor is nil, but a subsequent call on f.next will return the first (if any) of the p packetref:s contained in the folio.

f.FIRST. Returns the first packetref in the folio. If the folio is empty, nil is returned.

f.LAST. Returns the last packetref in the folio. If the folio is empty, nil is returned.

f.MORE. Returns true if there are more packetref:s left, that is, if a subsequent f.next would yield a non-nil result.

f.EMPTY. Returns true if the folio is empty.

f.CLEAR. Empties the folio and resets the cursor.

f.SORT(..sort list..). Sorts a folio according to the sort list.

f . APPEND(f₁). Appends the packetrefs of the folio in f_1 to f's folio. The appended packetrefs are located after the original ones.

f . EXCLUDE(f₁). Excludes the packetrefs of f_1's folio from f's folio. If the cursor had one of the excluded packetrefs as its value before the operation, it will have the value nil after the operation.

f . CARDINAL. Returns the number of packetrefs currently in the folio.

REFERENCES

1. AHLSEN, M., BJORNERSTEDT, A., BRITTS, S., HULTEN, C., AND SODERLUND, L. A survey of office information systems. WP No. 44, SYSLAB, Univ. of Stockholm, Mar. 1983.
2. AHLSEN, M., BJORNERSTEDT, A., BRITTS, S., HULTEN, C., AND SODERLUND, L. Making type changes transparent. In *Proceedings of IEEE Workshop on Languages for Automation*, (Nov. 7–9, 1983). Also available as SYSLAB Rep. No. 22.
3. BIRTWISTLE, G., DAHL, O.-J., MYHRHAUG, B., AND NYGAARD, K. *Simula Begin.* Auerbach, Philadelphia, Pa., 1973.
4. BLAU, R. Paging an object-oriented personal computer for Smalltalk. UCB/CSD 83/125, Univ. of California, Berkeley, Aug. 1983.
5. BOLOUR, A., ANDERSON, T., DEKEYSER, L., AND WONG, H. The role of time in information processing; A survey. *ACM SIGMOD Rec. 12*, 3 (Apr. 1982), 27–50.
6. BORNING, A.H., AND INGALLS, D.H.H. Multiple inheritance in Smalltalk-80. In *Proceedings IJCAI*, 1982.
7. BUBENKO, J.A. The temporal dimension in information modelling. In *Architecture and Models in Database Management Systems.* G.M. Nijssen, Ed., North Holland, 1977, 93–118.
8. CHEN, P.P.S. The entity relationship model—towards a unified view of data. *ACM Trans. Database Syst. 1*, 1 (1976), 9–36.
9. CODD, E.F. Extending the database relational model to capture more meaning. *ACM Trans. Database Syst. 4*, 4 (1979).
10. CURRY, G., BAER, L., LIPKIE, D., AND LEE, B. Traits: An approach to multiple-inheritance subclassing. In *Proceedings ACM SIGOA Conference on Office Information Systems.* (June 1982), 1–9.
11. DATE, C.J. *An Introduction to Database Systems.* 3rd ed., Addison-Wesley, Reading, Mass., 1981.
12. DENNING, P.J. Are operating systems obsolete? *Commun. ACM 25*, 4 (Apr. 1982), 225–227.
13. ELLIS, C.A. Information control nets: A mathematical model for office information flow. In *Proceedings ACM Conference on Simulation Modeling and Measurement of Computer Systems.* (Aug. 1979), 225–239.
14. FELDMAN, J.A. High-level programming for distributed computing. *Commun. ACM 22*, 6 (1979).
15. GOLDBERG, A. AND ROBSON, D. *Smalltalk-80: The Language and Its Implementation,* Addison-Wesley, Reading, Mass, 1983.
16. HAMMER, M., HOWE, W.G., KRUSKAL, V.J. AND WLADAVSKY, I. A very high-level programming language for data processing applications. *Commun. ACM 20*, 11 (1977).
17. HASKIN, R.L. AND LORIE, R.A. On extending the functions of a relational database system. In *Proceedings SIGMOD* (1982), 207–212.
18. HEWITT, C. Viewing control structures as patterns of passing messages. *Artif. Intell. 8*, 3 (June 1977), 323–364.
19. IBM. SQL/data system concepts and facilities. Program Product, GH24-5013-1, IBM, 1982.
20. JONES, A.K., CHANSLER, R.J., DURHAM, I., SCHWANS, K., AND VEGDAHL, S.R. StarOS, a multiprocessor operating system for the support of task forces. In *Proceedings of the 7th ACM Symposium on Operating Systems Principles* (Dec. 1979), 117–127.
21. KOFER, R. Some software integration technology concepts for saving money while doing empirical user research. In *Office Information Systems,* N. Naffah, Ed., North Holland, 1982, 217–232. Also in the *2nd International Workshop on Office Information Systems* (13–15 Oct. 1981).
22. KRASNER, G. *Smalltalk-80: Bits of History, Words of Advice.* Addison-Wesley, Reading, Mass., 1983.
23. LAMPSON, B.W., AND STURGIS, H.E. Reflections on an operating system design. *Commun. ACM 19* (May 1976), 251–265.
24. LISKOV, B., SNYDER, A., ATKINSON, R., AND SCHAFFERT, C. Abstraction mechanisms in CLU. *Commun. ACM 20*, 8 (Aug. 1977), 564–576.
25. NEWMAN, P.S. Towards an integrated development environment. *IBM Syst. J. 21*, (1982), 81–107.
26. OPPEN, D.C., AND DALAL, Y.K. The clearinghouse: A decentralized agent for locating named objects in a distributed environment. *ACM Trans. Office Inf. Syst. 1*, 3 (July 1983), 230–253.
27. OUSTERHOUT, J.K., SCELZA, D.A., AND SINDHU, P.S. Medusa: An experiment in distributed operating system structure. *Commun. ACM 23*, 2 (Feb. 1980), 92–105.
28. PETERSON, J.L. Petri nets. *ACM Comput. Surv. 9*, 3 (1977).
29. SHIPMAN, D.W. The functional data model and the language Daplex. *ACM Trans. Database Syst. 6*, 1 (Mar. 1981), 140–173.
30. SMITH, J.M., AND SMITH, D.C.P. Database abstractions: Aggregation and generalization. *ACM Trans. Database Syst. 2*, 2 (1977), 105–133.
31. SNODGRASS, R. An object-oriented command language. *IEEE Trans. Softw. Eng. SE-9*, 1 (Jan. 1983).
32. SODERLUND, L., AND HULTEN, C. A data flow model for application modeling in DISCO. SYSLAB WP No. 45, SYSLAB/ADB/Univ. of Stockholm, 1982.
33. SUNDGREN, B. Database design in theory and practice: Towards an integrated methodology. In *Proceedings 4th International Conference on Very Large Data Bases.* (Sept. 13–15, 1978), 3–16.
34. TSICHRITZIS, D. OFS: An integrated form management system. In *A Panache of DBMS Ideas, III.* D. Tsichritzis, Ed., Univ. of Toronto, Toronto, 1980.
35. TSICHRITZIS, D. Form management. *Commun. ACM 25*, 7 (July 1982), 453–477.
36. WASSERMAN, A.I. Toward integrated software development environments. In *Proceedings COMPSAC, Tutorial: Software Development Environments.* (Nov. 16–20, 1981), 15–35.
37. WULF, W.A. COHEN, E., CORWIN, W., JONES, A., LEVIN, R., PIERSON, C., AND POLLACK, F. HYDRA: The kernel of a multiprocessor operating system. *Commun. ACM 17*, 6 (June 1974), 337–345.
38. ZANIOLO, C. The database language GEM. In *Proceedings SIGMOD* (1983), 207–218.
39. ZDONIK, S.B. Private communication. Nov. 1983.
40. ZDONIK, S.B. Supporting integrated office applications via object management systems. Office Automation Group, MIT, Cambridge, Mass, June 1983. Lecture notes from MIT summer course on integrated office systems.
41. ZISMAN, M.D. Representation, specification, and automation of office procedures. Ph.D. dissertation, Dept. of Decision Sciences, Wharton School, Univ. of Pennsylvania, 1977.
42. ZLOOF, M.M., AND DEJONG, S.P. The system for business automation (SBA): Programming language. *Commun. ACM 20*, 6 (1972).

OTM: Specifying Office Tasks

F.H. Lochovsky, J.S. Hogg, S.P. Weiser, A.O. Mendelzon

Computer Systems Research Institute
Department of Computer Science
University of Toronto
Toronto, Canada
M5S 1A4

ABSTRACT

While there are many difficulties in computerizing office tasks, two of the major ones are a lack of appropriate end-user facilities for specifying office tasks and inadequate system-level support for managing office tasks. We are investigating these two issues within the Office Task Manager (OTM) project at the University of Toronto. To address the user-level aspects of specifying office tasks, we believe that a programming-by-example approach to office task specification holds much promise for providing office workers with facilities to help them computerize their own office activities. We outline our approach to such a facility in this paper. To address the system-level aspects of managing office tasks, we believe that object-oriented environments, because of their ability to combine data and operations on the data, can provide the support required for managing office tasks. In this paper, we also outline how office data and tasks are encoded and managed as objects. Initially, we are addressing the problem of supporting structured office tasks and our approach to this problem is the emphasis of this paper.

1. INTRODUCTION

Work that is performed in an organization can be viewed as consisting of various *tasks*. Each task can be decomposed into zero or more *subtasks*. These subtasks may be further decomposed resulting in a hierarchical task structure. This hierarchical view seems to be fairly natural for office tasks and can be found in other systems that support office tasks (e.g., [1, 3]).

Not all aspects of every office task are, or can be, left to the discretion of individual office workers. Many office tasks contain what we refer to as organization aspects and individual aspects. The *organization aspects* of a task may define the overall task structure and usually impose some global requirements on the task. They represent policy set by the organization to which all individuals using the task must adhere. The *individual aspects* of a task, on the other hand, specify how a specific office worker accomplishes a specific task assigned to him. They represent the office worker's personal preferences and know-how for accomplishing a task. This mix of organization and individual aspect of a task allows the organization to maintain some control over its tasks while still providing some freedom to the office workers performing the tasks.

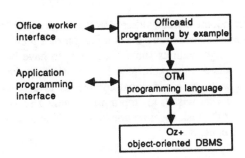

Fig. 1. Support for tasks in OTM.

We see the specification of the individual and the organization aspects of a task occurring as follows. The *task administrator* of the organization specifies the organization aspects of tasks. He determines the requirements for tasks, and specifies and decomposes tasks as required. A task can be specified either partially or completely by the task administrator. Specific tasks are associated with specific office workers in the organization. Office workers can add their own individual aspects to tasks by completing and/or modifying a task, where this is allowed by the organization, or by providing their own task specification in the case that a predefined task specification does not exist. Task specification by office workers may further decompose tasks. In general, office workers would be allowed to customize a task specification to suit their work requirements provided such customization does not violate any requirements established by the task administrator.

To allow office workers to specify tasks, they must basically be provided with a programming language. Yet, we do not want to require office workers to become programmers (at least explicitly). We believe that task specification facilities based on a programming by example paradigm are a promising approach to this problem [6]. In Section 2, we describe a programming by example system that allows office workers to specify office tasks[1]. In Section 3, we describe the underlying system support for this task specification facility which consists of an object-oriented programming language and an object-oriented DBMS. Figure 1 shows the relationships among these three facilities.

2. OFFICE WORKER TASK SPECIFICATION

Task specification is based on the folder model of office tasks proposed in [4] and enhanced in [15]. In the folder model, an office worker constructs an office task by assembling a folder of relevant documents required by the task and specifying various actions to be performed on these documents. There are four distinct stages to specifying a task: *collection*—the documents required by the task are gathered; *action*—the collected documents are manipulated, new ones created, or information external to the task is retrieved; *deadline*—the actions to perform when certain time constraints are exceeded are specified; *disposal*—what to do with the documents after all the processing is completed is specified.

Task specification takes place within the visual programming with examples (VPE) subsystem of Officeaid[2]. Task specifications appear within the user interface of Officeaid as *task folders*, much like document folders. Thus, to invoke Officeaid VPE, the office worker simply opens an existing task folder or creates a new one. A task folder may already exist for a task, having been defined by the task administrator. If the office worker can perform the task, then he has access to the task's folder and can change certain parts of it as allowed by the organization. Alternatively, the office worker can create a new task folder, called an *individual task folder*, using the facilities of the Officeaid interface. An individual task folder as well as a modified task folder, is initially accessible to, and can be used, only by the office worker who created it[3].

---

1. In many cases the same facilities can be used by a task administrator. For those cases where the programming by example facilities are inadequate for task specification, our system provides an object-oriented application programming interface, called the OTM language, discussed in section 3.
2. Officeaid provides an icon-based user interface similar to the Xerox Star or Apple Macintosh user interface [10].
3. In effect, such tasks become specializations of the original tasks (see Section 3). Also, individual aspects of a task can become organization aspects under certain circumstances (see [21]).

After a task folder has been opened or created, the office worker selects a stage of the task specification process to work on. Any stage can be selected, but some stages require the completion of a previous stage before anything meaningful can be specified (i.e., the disposal stage requires some documents to have been collected or created). Each stage of a task is specified by *recording* the actions performed by the office worker. The "statements" in a program are the normal Officeaid commands with some additional commands to give the office worker a fully functional programming system. If the office worker wishes to stop a programming session before he has actually completed the task specification, he can *suspend* the task specification and *continue* it at a later time. To review a task specification, parts or all of it can be *played back*.

2.1. Specifying the Collection

The purpose of the collection stage is to assemble the set of documents that are needed by the task. This set may have been partially or completely specified by the task administrator. For those cases where the office worker wants to add to the collection or define a collection for an individual task, he needs to follow three steps: find an example document to work with; specify the document selection criteria; and, indicate how the document is to be used. To illustrate how the office worker performs these steps, we will use a generic example.

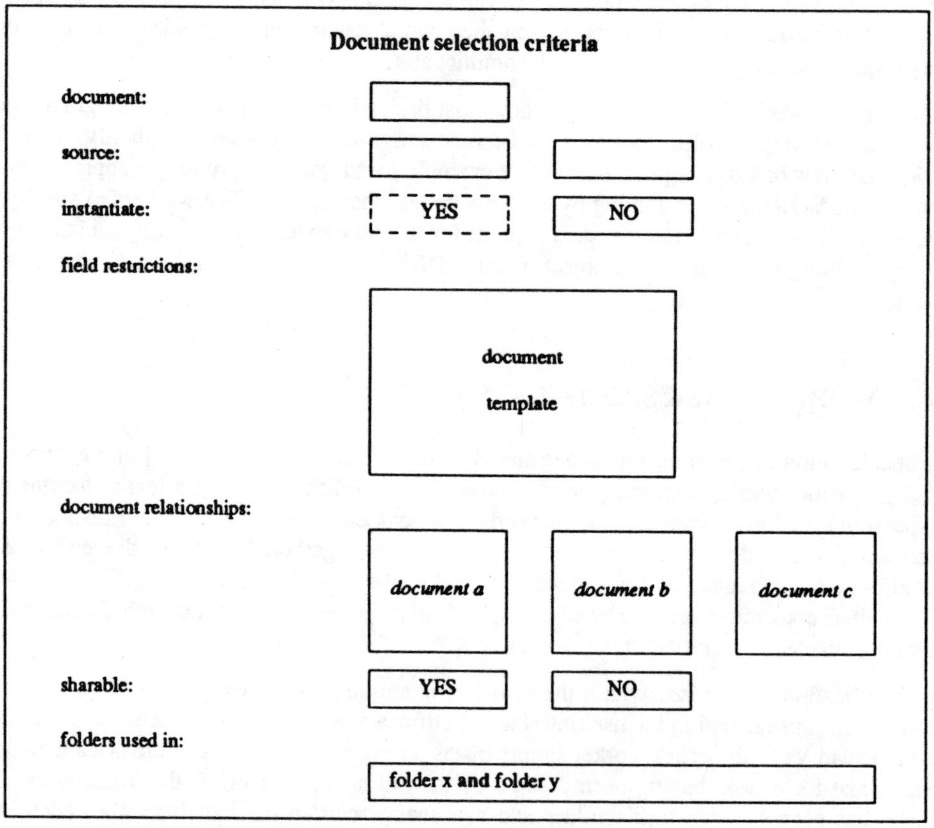

Fig. 2. The *document selection criteria* system-form.

Example documents to work with may come from a number of sources. Suppose the office worker finds an example of the document required for a particular task in his In malltray and places it in the task folder. The system responds by displaying the *document selection criteria* system-form[4] (Figure 2). In our example, the *source* attribute

---

4. As a general mechanism, system forms, which are completely analogous to option sheets in the Star [17], are used to provide a visual interface for eliciting arguments to some commands and for the specification of constraints when needed in the programming process.

of this form would already have a picture of the In malltray in it. Usually, the In malltray will be the sole source, however, additional sources can be specified. The office worker may indicate that this document can instantiate the task by setting the *instantiate* attribute to 'yes'[5].

Next, the office worker specifies the field value restrictions, if there are any, in a query-by-example fashion [22]. Relationships between documents (i.e., join-like conditions) are specified by forming predicates using examples from both documents also in a query-by-example fashion. The system form contains a template of each of the other documents in the collection that this document is related to. These templates are added dynamically as the collection for the task is specified.

Finally, the office worker can set the two options governing the use of the document. The *sharable* attribute requires a simple yes/no choice. This applies to the sharing of the document between instantiations of the same task folder. The *folders used in* attribute indicates whether the document selected can be used in more than one task folder. A boolean expression is constructed to indicate the folders in which it can be used in this case as shown in Figure 2. **And** is the default, meaning that the document is shared; **or** means that the first task to complete its collection is the only one that can use the document. In the latter case, the office worker can indicate an order in which the tasks are to be tried. Although quite complex expressions can be formed, the office worker will most likely designate the document as either sharable or non-sharable over all the task folders to which it is common.

2.2. Specifying Actions

The action stage is where the office worker can manipulate the documents he has assembled in the collection, create new ones, and retrieve additional information. This is the stage where the office worker requires the basic ingredients of a conventional programming language. Any program can be constructed out of suitable combinations of step-by-step (sequential) instructions, binary decisions (conditionals), and loops [2]. Facilities for realizing these three basic structures as well as other programming requirements are presented in this section.

Generalization

Using the basic commands of the Officeaid interface an office worker could start writing some tasks. The problem is that the tasks will always perform exactly the same actions on the same objects and accept no input from an office worker using the task. The office worker has no facility to generalize the task; everything is treated as a constant. Under these circumstances, the office worker can only specify fairly uninteresting tasks. Generalization supplies the office worker with a way to distinguish between constants and parameters. Three kinds of generalizations are possible: *same name* is used to generalize a selected icon; *same field value* refers to the value of the selected document field at run time; *ask for office worker input* will prompt the office worker for a value during task execution. There are a number of opportunities during and after the specification of a task for specifying generalization. In Officeaid VPE, generalization during task recording is used. In addition to being the quickest method, it is probably the easiest for non-programmers to learn. Generalizing after the task is written is essentially a form of program editing. We are investigating this latter method as part of a task browser and editor [12].

Retrieving stored data

When specifying a task, there may be a need to retrieve information from various files that are maintained in the office. Many of these retrievals will use information from fields in one of the documents in the collection to match an entry in a file of documents and obtain a value for a particular document field. For each document in Officeaid, there is a general *search template*. When the office worker selects a file, he is presented with a portion of the contents of the file and a search template for the document stored in that file. He specifies a retrieval from the file by filling in the document search template in a query-by-example fashion. The system presents those documents that match the completed fields of the search template. The office worker can then specify more fields to be matched, but only those fields that have not already been filled in. When more than one document matches the search template, the office worker is presented with a list of all the matching documents. He either picks one of the documents from the list or, if possible, specifies more fields of the search template and executes another match. A similar capability

---

5. This means that the presence of a document of this type, at the source indicated, will result in the creation of an instance of the task folder. The first document placed in the collection is the only document that has the *instantiate* attribute set to 'yes' by default.

is available while using a task. This means that incomplete patterns can be specified without repercussions. In addition to this query-based retrieval, the office worker can also select documents by browsing through filing cabinets and file drawers [12].

Conditionals

A way for specifying conditionals is an essential element of a task specification facility. There are two aspects to the specification of conditionals: the predicate and the action clauses. However, a basic problem is encountered when trying to mesh conditionals with a programming by example framework. Given the state of the world, a predicate is either true or false; when does one record the actions associated with the opposite state of the world? The technique adopted in Officeaid VPE is to use pictorial representations of the flow of task control. Such representations already exist for most programming constructs in the form of flowchart constructs. To demonstrate their use in Officeaid VPE, an example of specifying a conditional if-then-else construct is discussed below.

The conditional is selected from a menu by the office worker and the system constructs a diagram of it (see Appendix). Selecting either of the boxes or the diamond in the diagram opens a window within which actions appropriate for the selected item can be specified [12]. For example, selecting the diamond allows a predicate for the conditional to be specified. Suppose the predicate happens to evaluate to true. The office worker then proceeds to specify the actions associated with this branch by selecting the box on the branch labeled true. The office worker can either specify actions by example or he can enter the name of a previously defined task. In the latter case, the actions specified in the named task will be used as the actions for this branch of the conditional.

When the office worker wishes to specify the alternate action, this can be accomplished by selecting the box for the false branch of the conditional. To do this however, the predicate must evaluate to false so that appropriate examples can be used to specify the actions associated with the false branch. Thus, the office worker must change the state of the world so the alternate branch can be recorded or wait until such a condition arises.

Loops

There are three aspects that must be specified when defining a loop structure: the set of actions that are repeated, the set of data that the actions are performed on, and the stopping criterion. These aspects are specified differently depending on the type of loop used (i.e., loops that test a condition to determine if the loop body should be repeated (*while* loops and *until* loops) or loops that iterate over a set of data (*for* loops)). With the former type, the set of data is implicit in the actions of the loop body, while the stopping criterion is explicitly specified. With the latter type, the set of data is explicitly specified, while the stopping criterion is always 'when the set is finished.' Officeaid VPE provides facilities for specifying all three looping constructs. The type of loop desired is selected from a menu and the system constructs a diagram of the loop (see Appendix). Stopping conditions for loops are specified by constructing a predicate by example.

For loops are slightly more complex for two reasons. First, the set of data over which the loop is repeated, the iteration set, must be constructed. Second, the notion of "jumping back" in the task is hard for non-programmers to understand [6]. Although *while* loops also have this last characteristic, it is easier for the office worker to understand in this context, since a condition is explicitly controlling the flow of control. This is reinforced by the diagram that is displayed by the system. *For* loops, on the other hand, iterate until they have finished going through the set of data; the flow of control is implicit in the semantics of the *for* loop. Both of these problems are addressed by the use of a novel diagram to illustrate the *for* loop (see Appendix and [12]).

Parallel actions

Normally an office worker will specify a single thread of execution (i.e., a single task to be executed from start to finish). There are times, however, when it may be desirable to specify that a set of tasks should be executed in parallel. The pictorial representation for parallel actions is shown in the Appendix. Within each parallel task, the usual Officeaid VPE actions can be specified. Postconditions (see Section 3) are specified as predicates.

2.3. Specifying Deadlines

Officeaid VPE is designed to specify the routine processing of documents. Exceptions are left for the office worker to process. However, the office worker should be made aware of the occurrence of an exception. He will handle the exception appropriately and then let the system resume. When an exception becomes routine, he can write a new task to handle it. A deadline is an exception[6]. The office worker expected the task's full complement of documents to arrive within a reasonable time. The possible permutations of missing documents grows rapidly with the number of documents in the collection. The actions to be taken for each possible combination are left to the office worker to perform explicitly. The system only needs to inform the office worker that the task's collection has not completed within the specified time. The office worker specifies a deadline for a task folder's collection by indicating the amount of time it has to complete and the action(s) to be taken when the deadline is passed. The office worker can specify any action that is possible within Officeaid.

2.4. Specifying Document Disposal

Disposing of the documents of a task is the simplest of the four stages. The office worker must indicate a destination for each document in the collection and for any documents that were instantiated during the action stage. This is accomplished by performing the action on the example documents used in the task.

3. SYSTEM-LEVEL SUPPORT FOR OFFICE TASKS

Officeaid VPE task specifications are translated into a concurrent, object-oriented programming language called the OTM language [8] (see Appendix)[7]. Underlying the OTM language and providing basic support for task execution and persistent storage of office data and office tasks is OZ+ an object-oriented database system [13, 14, 20]. OZ+ is a general-purpose object-oriented DBMS whereas the OTM language is specifically designed for specifying and executing office tasks. In this section we will briefly describe the OTM language and the OZ+ DBMS and how they provide support for office tasks.

3.1. The OTM Language

The OTM language has the flavour of Smalltalk [5], but is most noticeable for the way it provides control over task creation and destruction [7]. It was designed to support office tasks, and therefore is structured to permit the simple specification of concurrent tasks in a hierarchical manner which allows responsibility for a task to be determined unambiguously. It also allows considerable external control over subtasks.

The basic units of the OTM language are *objects*. Each object is an instance of a *class* of objects. There are two types of classes: *primitive* and *compound*. The primitive classes are **boolean, integer, real** and **string**. Each of these has a set of associated *primitive tasks*; for instance, the task + may be applied to **integers**. These are directly implemented by the underlying interpreter, and their implementations are not visible to the programmer.

Compound classes are those defined by the users of the system. A compound class definition is made up of a set of *local* variables and a set of *methods*. A class may *inherit* the behaviour (variables and methods) of one or more *superclasses*, with simple rules for deciding which task definition to inherit if there are name collisions. The user must ensure that multiple superclasses use their variables in compatible ways. There is no notion of variable type: a variable is simply a pointer to any object. Thus, multiple inheritance of a single variable name is guaranteed not to cause type clashes; a single variable will appear in the new class. The Smalltalk notion of the variable **self** was used. This is always a pointer to the current object instance, and may not be assigned to. Objects are persistent; once created, they exist until they can no longer be accessed. Therefore, their local variables are also persistent. They maintain their values between invocations, and are shared by concurrent tasks.

The *tasks* of an object class definition correspond to *rules* or *methods* in other object-oriented languages. A task is composed of a set of parameters, a set of *temporary* variables, and a *statement*. Temporary variables have the scope of a single task invocation. Even if two tasks concurrently execute a single method, they will see different temporaries. The body of a task is a statement, which may be a block (of which more below). The simplest statements are *assignments* and *task invocations*. An assignment is of the form *<variable> := <expression>*. Every expression produces a *result*, which is an object; the assignment points the named variable at that object.

A task invocation is analogous to a procedure call. Examples are **x + y** and **printer Print doc**. (Variable names

---

6. For most tasks, deadline specifications would be specified by the task administrator.
7. Since the OTM language is a much more powerful programming language than Officeaid VPE, it is not the case that all OTM programs can be viewed as Officeaid VPE task specifications.

all start with lower-case letters, and task names start with an upper-case letter or are special symbols.) In the first example, the object pointed at by **y** is sent to the task **+** of the object pointed at by **x**. This results in a new object whose value will be the sum of the values of the other objects. The second case is similar, although the result will depend upon the implementation of **Print** for the class of **printer**, since that class is compound or user-defined.

Statements may be separated by semicolons and combined into *blocks*. In a *sequential* block (delimited by --{...}), the statements are executed in sequence. In a *parallel* block (delimited by ||{...}), they are executed concurrently. In the default case, the block will complete when all the component statements complete, and the statement following the block will then be executed. Statements and blocks may in turn be used in familiar control structures which will not be further discussed here: **if, while, foreach** and **parforeach**.

We have found it useful to have each task return not only a *result*, but also a *status*. This status is used to control execution. The simplest instance of this is a sequential block containing *alternate* tasks, which are statements separated by vertical bars ("|") instead of semicolons. The first task in the block is executed and, if it *succeeds*, the block as a whole succeeds and the remaining tasks are not tried. Otherwise, the following tasks are attempted until either one succeeds or there are no more left; in the latter case, the block as a whole *fails*. Normally, a sequential block succeeds iff all of its component tasks succeed. A parallel block normally succeeds iff one of its component tasks succeeds. However, more sophisticated control over task termination and status determination is possible through **when** and **check** clauses respectively, which appear at the end of a block.

A *label* of the form "*<labelName>*:" may be placed at the beginning of a task. A **when** clause conceptually executes continually while the block is being executed, and uses the label to refer to the status of the task. **When** (*OkToSales* or *OkToAccount*) **and** *FillAppl* **done** indicates that a block may terminate when either of the tasks labeled with *OkToSales* and *OkToAccount* has succeeded, and the task labeled *FillAppl* has completed. At that point, any tasks which have not yet completed are told to terminate. When a block terminates, the **check** clause determines what its status should be. In this example, a reasonable **check** clause would be **check** (*OkToSales* or *OkToAccount*) **and** *FillAppl*, which states that the application-filling task must not only have completed, but also succeeded.

To support the programming by example task specification facilities, two object classes are used: documents and roles. Document objects are used to store information (e.g., forms, reports, etc.). Role objects correspond to the various functions that office workers carry out in an office. Officeaid VPE task specifications are encoded as OTM tasks of document or role objects. Knowledge specific to a particular office worker is encoded in a special role object called an *agent*. An agent object inherits all of the capabilities of the role objects to which it is related. In particular, since office tasks are encoded as the tasks of objects, an agent object inherits all of the tasks to which it is related.

3.2. The OZ+ DBMS

The OZ+ object model is a general-purpose object model providing objects with contents (data) and rules (operations) in a manner analogous to Smalltalk objects [5]. While the OZ+ object model allows the natural representation of real world entities and the tasks associated with them, the database support provided by OZ+ ensures object persistency.

To capture natural structure, especially that associated with office objects (such as documents), OZ+ objects have a potentially hierarchical structure. An OZ+ object may contain other OZ+ objects. OZ+ objects may aggregate any number of *simple* objects. Simple objects are an abstraction of instance variables (such as those found in Smalltalk). In addition, OZ+ objects may also aggregate any number of non-simple or *complex* objects. Each complex object may itself, in turn, aggregate simple and complex objects. Simple and complex objects may also have set occurrences.

OZ+ rules, which correspond to Smalltalk operations, have a number of characteristics which distinguish them from rules in most other object-oriented languages. OZ+ rules may specify acquaintances. An acquaintance is an object from which a rule receives a message. A rule will only accept messages from objects which belong to a particular set of classes or types. This facilitates object independence. Objects "choose" whom they are willing to let invoke their rules. OZ+ rules may be self-triggering. A rule may invoke itself when a certain set of trigger conditions become true. These trigger conditions may test the state of the object containing the rule, or the state of other objects. The object containing a self-triggering rule appears to act spontaneously—it will perform an action or actions without having received a message to do so. Thus OZ+ objects exhibit a kind of autonomy not found in other object-oriented systems.

State changing rule actions are synchronized by *events*. The performance of the state changing actions of a rule do not occur independently but rather in concert with the performance of state changing actions in other objects. A group of communicating objects which "reaches an agreement" to perform their state changing actions together are said to participate in an event. Events can be viewed as an atomic change of state within the object universe. Any number of events may be active concurrently.

Since memory is volatile, information maintained exclusively in memory is lost in the event of the failure of a processor or its operating system. As we desire the OZ+ object state to be persistent, a version of this state is always available on disk, a relatively stable storage medium. However, it is not sufficient to maintain the OZ+ object universe state (the totality of OZ+ object states) exclusively on disk. Rule executions involve multiple accesses of object state. Such accesses are substantially more time consuming if the required object state exists on disk rather than in memory. As a compromise to the extremes of maintaining the object universe state exclusively in memory or in disk, we adopt the following scheme. At any point in time, the existence of a consistent, though not necessarily up to date, version of the object universe state on disk is guaranteed. When it is determined that a particular rule has a high likelihood of being executed in the near future, a copy of each of the objects[8] which it will need to access is brought into memory, unless such a copy already exists there. When the rule executes, it will access only memory-based objects and not their disk-based counterparts. Changes of state are induced on the "active" memory-based objects by the rules which access them. Disk is periodically updated to reflect these changes in a manner which guarantees the consistency of the disk-based object universe.

Once in memory, an object tends to remain there if it is periodically active. Each object is given an activity rating, which characterizes the frequency that an object is accessed by rule executions. Objects that are virtually inactive (i.e., those that have not been accessed over a long period of time) are deleted from memory (after making sure that their disk-based counterparts are up to date). This is effectively a method of "garbage collection" which provides room for new objects to be copied into memory. In consequence, the more active an object, the more likely it is to remain in memory indefinitely. In this way, we minimize the traffic *from* disk *to* memory.

Objects are managed on disk by the OZ+ object-oriented disk manager which ensures the integrity and consistency of OZ+ objects. The disk manager in turn is built on top of a relational data base management system (rDBMS). This was accomplished by the development of an algorithm which translates an OZ+ object into a set of relations, in which form the object is managed on disk, and back again into OZ+ objects, when the object is to participate in an event.

4. SUMMARY

The Office Task Manager project at the University of Toronto is investigating issues dealing with task storage representation, task definition, authorization, implementation environment, and execution strategies [11]. In this paper, we have outlined the end-user task specification facilities being implemented and their underlying system support. The task specification facility consists of a programming by example system that allows office workers to specify a task by "programming" an example of the task. The system support for tasks consists of a concurrent object-oriented programming language, specifically designed to support office tasks, and an object-oriented DBMS. The system is being implemented on Sun workstations [18]. It is written in the C programming language [9] under version 4.2 bsd of the UNIX operating system [19]. The Empress relational data base management system [16] is used as the underlying disk storage and access mechanism.

ACKNOWLEDGEMENTS

Many people have contributed to and worked on the design and implementation of Officeaid, the OTM language, and the OZ+ DBMS. David Propp did the initial design of Officeaid PBE. Thierry Mosser and Paolino Di Felice extended this design and implemented a prototype version of the system. Others who have contributed to these projects are Jimmy Chui, John DiMarco, Panos Economopoulos, John Empey, Mario Goldstein, Alison Lee, Murray Mazer, Hetty Ngo, Stephen Pollock, David Propp, Didier Trullard, Larry Williams, and Carson Woo. This research was supported by the Natural Sciences and Engineering Research Council of Canada under grant G1360 and by Bell-Northern Research Ltd.

---

8. For purposes of brevity, we will use "object" in place of "object state".

REFERENCES

[1]   Barber, G.R., "Supporting organizational problem solving with a workstation," *ACM Trans. on Office Inf. Sys.* 1(1), 1983, pp. 45-67.

[2]   Bohm, C., and Jacopini, G., "Flow diagrams, Turing machines, and languages with only two formulation rules," *Comm. ACM* 9(5), 1966, pp. 366-371.

[3]   Croft, W.B., and Lefkowitz, L.S., "Task support in an office system," *ACM Trans. on Office Inf. Sys.* 2(3), 1984, pp. 197-212.

[4]   Fong, A.C., "A model for automatic form-processing procedures," *Proc. 16th Hawaii Int. Conf. on System Sciences*, 1983, pp. 558-565.

[5]   Goldberg, A., and Robson, D., *Smalltalk-80: The Language and its Implementation.* Addison-Wesley, Reading, MA, 1983.

[6]   Halbert, D.C., *Programming By Example.* Ph.D. thesis, Dept. of Elec. Eng. and Computer Sc., Univ. of California, Berkeley, CA, 1984.

[7]   Hogg, J.S., "OTM: a language for representing concurrent office tasks," *Proc. IFIP WG8.4 Workshop on Office Knowledge: Representation, Management and Utilization*, 1987, pp. 10-12.

[8]   Hogg, J.S., and Weiser, S.P., "OTM: applying objects to tasks," *Proc. Object-Oriented Programming Systems, Languages and Applications Conf.*, 1987, pp. 388-393.

[9]   Kernighan, B.W., and Ritchie, D.M., *The C Programming Language.* Prentice-Hall, Inc., Englewood Cliffs, NJ, 1978.

[10]   Lee, A., Woo, C.C., and Lochovsky, F.H., "Officeaid: an integrated document management system," *Proc. ACM SIGOA Conf. on Office Information Sys.*, 1984, pp. 170-180.

[11]   Lochovsky, F.H., "Managing office tasks," *Proc. IEEE Office Automation Symp.*, 1987, pp. 247-249.

[12]   Mosser, T., Di Felice, P., and Lochovsky, F.H., "Specifying office tasks by example," *Proc. IFIP WG8.4 Working Conf. 'Office Information Systems: The Design Process'*, 1988.

[13]   Nierstrasz, O.M., "An object-oriented system", in *Office Automation Concepts and Tools*, (Tsichritzis, D.C., ed.), pp. 167-190. Springer-Verlag, Berlin, 1985.

[14]   Nierstrasz, O., Mooney, J., and Twaites, K., "Using objects to implement office procedures," *Proc. CIPS Conf.*, 1983, pp. 65-73.

[15]   Propp, D.L., *A Forms Programming By Example System for Non-programmers.* M.Sc. thesis, Dept. of Computer Sc., Univ. of Toronto, Toronto, Canada, 1983.

[16]   Rhodnius, Inc., *EMPRESS/32: Relational Data Base Management System.* Rhodnius, Inc., Toronto, Canada, 1986.

[17]   Smith, D.C., Irby, C., Kimball, R., and Harslem, E., "The Star user interface: an overview," *Proc. AFIPS NCC*, 1982, pp. 516-528.

[18]   *The Sun Workstation Architecture.* Sun Microsystems Inc., Mountain View, CA, 1986.

[19]   Thompson, K., and Ritchie, D., "The UNIX time-sharing system," *Bell Technical J.* 57(6), 1978, pp. 1905-1929.

[20]   Weiser, S.P., "An object-oriented protocol for managing data," *Database Engineering* 8(4), 1985, pp. 41-48.

[21]   Williams, L., and Lochovsky, F.H., "Knowledge migration in organizations," in *Office and Data Base Systems Research '88*, Lochovsky, F.H., and Mendelzon, A.O., eds., pp. ?-?. Tech. rep. CSRI-???, Computer Sys. Res. Inst., Univ. of Toronto, Toronto, Canada, 1988.

[22]   Zloof, M.M., "Query-by-example: a data base language," *IBM Sys. J.* 16(4), 1977, pp. 324-343.

Appendix

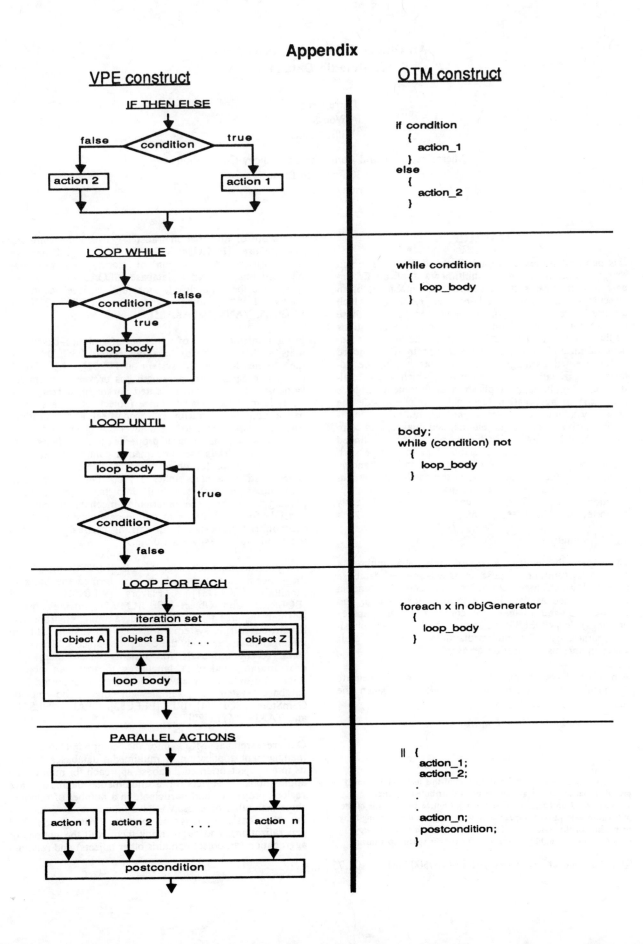

An Object–Oriented Approach to
Multimedia Databases

Darrell Woelk[*]

Won Kim

Willis Luther

Microelectronics and Computer Technology Corporation

9430 Research Blvd.

Austin, Texas 78759

ABSTRACT

This paper identifies data modelling and data access and sharing requirements which multimedia applications impose on a database system. It shows the capabilities of an object-based data model and indicates extensions which are needed to meet the data modelling aspects of these requirements. A logical implementation of the operations on the model is described. The model generalizes the notions of instantiation and generalization in the standard object-oriented paradigm, and augments it with the notions of aggregation and relationships which are specialized for a multimedia application environment. Objects may exist in aggregation hierarchies which provide the capability to integrate diverse types of multimedia information such as text, sound, bit-mapped images, and complex graphics drawings. Objects may also be linked through other user-defined relationships to capture such application functions as voice annotation and referencing of one document by another. Using this model, the semantics of aggregation and relationships in a multimedia application environment can be understood and efficiently supported by a database system.

1.0 Introduction

This paper will identify the requirements for a multimedia database system and propose an object-oriented database approach which meets these requirements. Multimedia data is defined as data in the form of text, sound, and images (digitized images and complex vector graphics drawings). In [WOEL85] we studied the logical and physical characteristics of multimedia data, as well as their usage in various application areas.

A number of systems have been developed which integrate graphical representation with a DBMS to broaden the

---

[*] On assignment from NCR Corporation

bandwidth of information transfer between the computer and the user [FOGG84, WILS80, WONG82]. Other systems provide the function of storing and retrieving digitized images from a database [SLOA82]. Some systems have the capability to store and retrieve documents composed of text, images, and audio [FORS84, CHRI84, POGG85, YANK85, SAKA85].

In the implementation of a number of graphics-based systems, such as the Xerox Smalltalk system [GOLD81] and the Apple MacIntosh system [APPL83], the object-oriented programming paradigm has proven to be highly valuable. In the object-oriented paradigm, a real-world entity is modeled as an instance (object) of a class which has a number of attributes (properties) and operations (methods) applicable to the objects. A class, and therefore an object, may inherit properties and methods from other classes. Thus the fundamental data modelling concepts instantiation (an object is an instance of a class) and generalization (a class inherits properties and methods from other classes) are built into the object-oriented paradigm. Further, the inheritance mechanism makes it possible for applications to define new classes and have them inherit properties from existing classes; this makes the applications easily extendible.

The programming language Simula [BIRT73] introduced the concept of a class, which later formed the basis of Smalltalk [GOLD81]. Flavors [WEIN81], LOOPS [BOBR83], and Object-LISP [LMI85] provide object-oriented features for the LISP programming environment. Frame-based rule systems [MINS75, FOX85] in artificial intelligence also embody the concept of objects. There are some recent proposals for systems which merge the programming and data languages to form an object-oriented programming environment that is supported by a database system. Examples of this trend include GemStone [COPE84], IRIS [BEEC83], OPAL [AHLS84], and TAXIS [MYLO80].

Our research at MCC into the compound document management application of multimedia databases has led us to an object-oriented database approach for multimedia applications. Objects in a multimedia database have various properties and participate in a number of relationships with other objects. We have found that by generalizing the basic notions of objects (instantiation and generalization), and augmenting them with the notions of aggregation (an object contains other objects) and relationships (an object is related to another object), we can capture the data modelling requirements of multimedia applications. Using this model, the semantics of aggregation and relationships in a multimedia application environment can be understood and efficiently supported by a database system.

In this paper, we first establish data modelling and data access and sharing requirements of multimedia applications. We then propose an object–oriented data model which meets the data modelling aspects of these requirements, and we describe a logical implementation of the operations on the data model. The remainder of this paper is organized as follows. In Section 2 we describe an example of a multimedia application drawn from a multimedia document management system under development. We present the functional requirements of a multimedia database system in Section 3. Section 4 describes our object–oriented data model for the support of multimedia applications. In Section 5 we present a logical implementation of the model, in terms of operations on a logical database design supporting the data model. Section 6 provides a summary and conclusion.

2.0 Description of a Representative Multimedia Application

Figure 1 presents a typical document which might be generated with a multimedia document manager. It contains three text paragraphs, a drawing in the middle of the page which has been created by combining primitive graphics shapes along with text, and an image at the bottom of the page which is a photograph stored as a bit-mapped image. The highlighting of the "From: D. Woelk" in Figure 1 will be a blinking highlight to draw attention. The small "speaker" icon next to the line indicates that there is a voice message associated with this line. The highlighted box in the drawing is another blinking highlight. The large arrow next to the box indicates that there is more detail concerning this object in another document.

The document in Figure 1 could have been created with a simple typewriter and some creative pasting. However, the power of the multimedia document system does not come from the creation of static documents which look nice. Rather, it will come from creating a body of information which can be shared by many users. Paper documents are a model of information transfer with which people are familiar today and, therefore, they make a reasonable metaphor for information transfer. This will change as the bandwidth of information transfer between humans and computers increases because of improved computer capability for processing (storage, reproduction, and recognition) of speech, images, and knowledge. The combination of these will create new techniques for human-to-human and human-to-computer information transfer. The data model proposed in this paper will support these new techniques.

Figure 2 presents a logical view of the information in the document in Figure 1. Notice that the information forms an *aggregation* (or *part-of*, or *containment*) *hierarchy* [SMIT77]. This should be intuitively obvious because even in this simple example, a person will naturally separate the body of a memo from the header information. The example of a book with a table of contents, chapters, sub-

chapters, and an index is also an obvious example. Note that there are seven types of information represented in Figure 2.

1. The connected Circles represent the logical parts of the document. They are connected to form the aggregation hierarchy. Unshaded Circles represent what we might consider to be part of a template for a Memo. For example, all Memos contain a Memo–Header, a Body, and a Memo–Trailer. This can be thought of as representing the schema for a memo. The schema can be used as a template for creating new Memos by enforcing constraints on the structure of the Memo (a Memo can only contain a Memo–Heading, Body, and Memo–Trailer), on the types of attributes which are allowable (a Memo–Logo can only contain Text), and on the relationships among parts of the Memo (a From–Line can be annotated by a Voice Message). Furthermore, the schema can be used for phrasing high level queries to access all or portions of one or more Memos ("Retrieve MEMO where MEMO.FROM–NAME = D. Woelk").

2. Shaded Circles represent the portion of the aggregation hierarchy which is unique to this particular Memo. For example, the Paragraphs contained in the Body of the Memo are unique to this particular Memo.

3. The Squares represent unformatted intrinsic data such as text, digitized images, complex vector graphics drawings, or sound. These Unshaded Squares represent data which is present for every Memo. For example, the word "FROM:" will occur in every Memo.

4. The Shaded Squares represent text, image, or audio data which we might consider to be unique to this particular Memo. For example, the words "D. Woelk" would only occur on this Memo.

5. The Ovals represent information about the data in the Shaded and Unshaded Squares as well as information about the Shaded and Unshaded Circles of the aggregation hierarchy. For example, all of the text in the Memo–Header is to be displayed in Font–Size = 14. The Memo node, however, also has a Font Size = 12 which is to be used for all text in the Memo except where over-ridden lower in the aggregation hierarchy. In this example, the Memo–Header Font–Size = 14 will over-ride the Memo Font–Size = 12.

6. The Rectangles represent operations on the data in the Squares, Circles, and Ovals of the aggregation hierarchy. For example, the Rectangle labelled SEND in Figure 2 contains procedural operations for sending the document to the people listed in the To-Line and in the CC-List.

7. The dotted lines represent relationships among nodes which are not represented in the aggregation hierarchy. For example, the dotted line from the first Group node under the Drawing node to the Workstation Manual node indicates that a workstation manual document contains more details concerning the abstract object represented by this group of graphic shapes.

3.0 Functional Requirements of Multimedia Applications

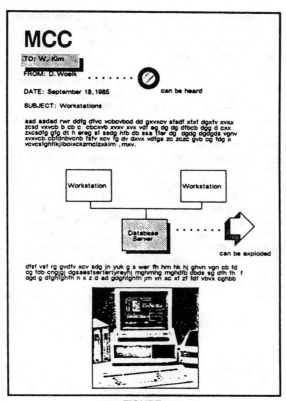

FIGURE 1
Example Document

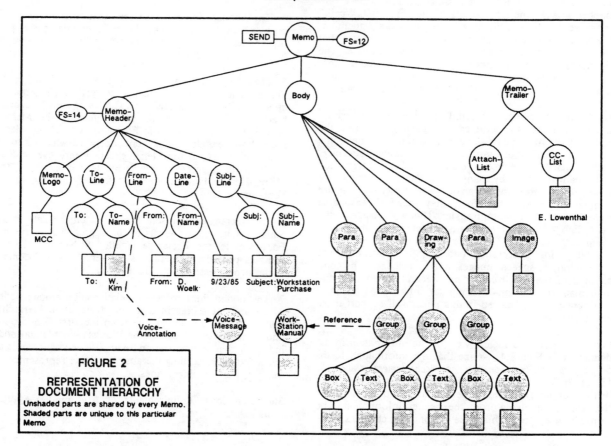

FIGURE 2

REPRESENTATION OF DOCUMENT HIERARCHY

Unshaded parts are shared by every Memo.
Shaded parts are unique to this particular Memo

The example application in Section 2, although rather simple, exposes a spectrum of requirements, many of which present problems for traditional database systems. These requirements are listed below.

1. The aggregation hierarchy presented in Figure 2 must be supported by the database system. Nodes at each level of the hierarchy represent an abstraction of all of the nodes below. This abstraction mechanism provides for the integration of diverse types of multimedia information. The flexibility of the aggregation hierarchy is also essential for the storage and manipulation of the vector graphics shapes shown under the Drawing node in Figure 2. Complex drawings may be represented by hierarchies of considerable depth where subtrees of the hierarchies may be shared among drawings [PHIG84]. The relational model of data does not support this type of structure directly. The application must take responsibility for tracing the hierarchy. This situation has been improved by enhancements to the relational model which allow definition of complex objects [KIM85a, LORI83].

Ordering is also necessary at some levels of the aggregation hierarchy. For example, the user may wish to express that a Memo will always contain exactly one Memo-Header, one Body, and one Memo-Trailer and they must always exist in that order. Another example is the Memo instance in Figure 2 where the particular ordering of the nodes under the Body node is an integral part of the representation of the Memo.

2. In addition to its place in the aggregation hierarchy, each node may also be a part of a *generalization hierarchy* [SMIT77]. A generalization hierarchy is used to define a node N as a subtype of some other node M such that N can inherit properties from M. For example, the Memo-Header node may be a *specialization* of a Header, where Headers always have a Font Size = 14. Then, the Font Size = 14 need not exist as an unshaded oval connected to the Memo-Header node in Figure 2. The value would be inherited from the Header class of objects and used to over-ride the Font Size = 12 in the unshaded oval of the Memo node. The notion of inheritance will become increasingly important in the compound document management environment as documents take on more properties and behavior.

3. Note that in addition to providing structural and domain constraints, the unshaded squares representing part of the schema in Figure 2 also include data which should be included in every Memo, such as the word "From:". There is no easy way to express this in the schema for the relational model. The application program must take responsibility for maintaining the data in the unshaded squares as data in separate relations and for presenting it as part of every Memo.

4. The properties associated with a node may be represented as either data (oval) or as procedural operations (rectangle). For example, instead of the Font Size = 14 oval, a procedure rectangle may be connected to the Memo-Header which calculates the optimum Font Size based on the resolution of the terminal being used and the other objects presently being displayed. If the user wishes to enter a Font Size value for a Memo-Header on a specific Memo, a procedure may constrain the selections available to the user. Both of these examples can also be viewed as constraints which are associated with the Memo-Header. Another example is the Rectangle labelled SEND in Figure 2. Access of this rectangle will cause the Memo to be sent to the persons listed in the shaded squares below the COPYEE node. The procedure may constrain the mode of delivery of the Memo to be decided on the basis of the addresses of the recipients, the size of the document (how large are the images?), the contents of the document (is audio included?), etc.

5. It is difficult to define a schema for the information within the Body of the Memo in Figure 2. For example, the Body can consist of any number of Paragraphs, Drawings, or Images in any order. Further, there may be constraints which are not easily expressed in a declarative manner. For example, the ordering of the Paragraphs, Drawings, and Images in the document may be dependent on the user's point of view or on the level of understanding which the user has of the information being presented. The system will use feedback from the user to determine constraints on the order of presentation. The best way to represent these constraints is through rules associated with the Body. These rules can be represented as procedural data as described in the previous paragraph. Rules of this complexity cannot be expressed in traditional database systems.

6. There is very little a priori knowledge of the structure of relationships (represented by dotted lines in Figure 2) among nodes. In general, any node can have a relationship with any other node regardless of type and position in the aggregation hierarchy. The database system must support this type of flexibility. There is also little a priori knowledge of the manner or order in which these relationships will be used for accessing information in the database. The relationships may actually be an integral part of the user's view of the document and they may be used extensively for navigation. This same behavior has also been observed in the mechanical CAD/CAM environment where there are many relationships such as "connected-to" and "on-top-of" which are not part of the normal aggregation hierarchy [CAMM84].

7. There is a need to dynamically modify the schema for Memo. This same requirement has been observed in engineering databases [KIM85a, REHF84]. For example, a new version of the Memo schema may be created which represents Database Department Memos. These are similar to Memos except that they contain a different version of the Memo-Logo and another node following the Subject node, called Priority Indicator. The Priority Indicator may contain a number indicating the importance of the document. Traditional concepts in schema definition would require entering a new static schema for Database Department Memo, with no simple way of indicating that a Database Department Memo is really just another kind of Memo. This semantic information would have to be maintained by the application.

8. In addition to the logical structure presented in Figure 2, there is also information concerning the physical presentation of the document. This has traditionally been viewed as the static mapping of the intrinsic data such as text or graphic drawings onto some physical display device (paper or display terminal). This mapping can be viewed

as a separate aggregation hierarchy of physical pages and rectangles for presentation, which ultimately has intrinsic data at the leaf nodes.

This mapping aggregation hierarchy can become much more complex when sound is added, allowing simultaneous presentation of both sound and images. Further complexity is added when the user is allowed to interactively modify aspects of the physical presentation, such as the physical location, orientation, or color of objects on a screen. The database system must manage this interactive modification of physical presentation information.

9. The creation and control of versions of documents is also an important part of this application. The decisions controlling the naming of versions, the selection of default versions, and the notification of documents which reference modified versions will vary with the environment. The database system should provide support for version creation, control, and change notification [KATZ84, KIM85a].

10. Concurrent access to the same data by multiple users must be controlled. For example, we may specify that changes made to a document will not be visible to other documents, until the changes are committed. If changes are being made to the Body of the Memo in Figure 2 and if another Memo is being read which references the Body, the viewer of the second Memo will see the most recent released version rather than the Body being updated. This is a straightforward method of concurrency control which suffices for many document management applications.

11. The unformatted intrinsic data represented by the Squares may consist of a large number of bytes. A bit-mapped still image may require as much as 4,000,000 bytes and one minute of digitized speech may require up to 480,000 bytes of storage. The movement of these large amounts of data in the system must be minimized and extra buffering of data must also be minimized. Special functions are necessary in the database system to support such requests as "Move backwards 15 seconds" in a voice message and "Replay" the message.

12. A document may contain text or complex graphics drawings which are generated based on the value of data items in a database. For example, a document may contain a bar chart which describes the average salaries of employees in each department. This document can be viewed as either a snapshot of the underlying data at some point in time or as a window into the underlying data. The selected view will determine whether the bar chart is updated when the salary of an employee changes. This is the snapshot and view mechanism found in conventional database systems.

13. The ability to share data among multiple documents is critical to this application. There are two primary motivations for this sharing; reduction in use of secondary storage and the ability to reference a specific version of another document. Reductions in the use of secondary storage come from sharing the data represented by the squares in Figure 2. For example, if the image in the document in Figure 2 is to be included in another document, it is only necessary to reference the Image node. The image need not be copied. An example of referencing

a specific version of a document is shown in the Reference Relationship from the first Group node under the Drawing node in Figure 2. This Reference is to a portion of another document and is assumed to point to the most recent version of that document.

14. Associative access to stored documents must be provided by the database system. This access may be based on document structure (all documents with images), document type (all memos), or document contents (all documents containing the word *database*).

15. As is the case with any type of application, database recovery [GRAY81] is an obvious requirement. This includes both secondary–storage recovery and transaction recovery. For recovery from secondary storage (e.g., disk-head crash), the database needs to be periodically dumped to tapes. Transaction recovery is important in maintaining mutual consistency of data across multiple documents that a user updates within a single transaction. In case of system crashes, all changes to all documents touched within a transaction must be committed or aborted together. As in CAD environments [BANC85a], a transaction in a multimedia–application environment will be a long–duration transaction, consisting of a set of conventional short–duration transactions, and involve more than one cooperating users.

While the requirements listed above are based on the example of a multimedia document system, they are also found in the much broader area of design applications. Research has revealed similar types of requirements in the CAD environment [HASK82, KIM85a, REHF84, CAMM84]. Applications in a CAD environment involve an attempt to iteratively capture a concept and translate it into engineering artifacts. The data model for these applications must be flexible enough to model both the concepts and the engineering artifacts and to document the iterative design steps.

The database approach described in this document will integrate many of the features of the systems described above into a single database system. This system will meet all of the functional requirements presented above. The object–oriented approach of the system will provide the flexibility of information representation and manipulation necessary for satisfying requirements 1–8. Requirements 12–15 will be met by adapting traditional database technology to the object–oriented approach. Requirements 9–11 will be met by adding new functions to the database system which are valuable regardless of whether or not the system is object–oriented.

4.0 Multimedia Application Model

The application will be described in terms of diagrams which are similar to semantic nets [NILS80] and entity-relationship diagrams [CHEN76]. The diagram is a directed acyclic graph containing nodes and directed arcs. The types of nodes and the legal directed arcs from each type of node are shown in Figure 3. There are six types of nodes represented in Figure 3: token objects representing classes, token objects representing instances, relationship objects, attributes, method objects, and intrinsic data objects. Every node (with the exception of Attributes) is labelled with a unique numeric identifier. This identifier

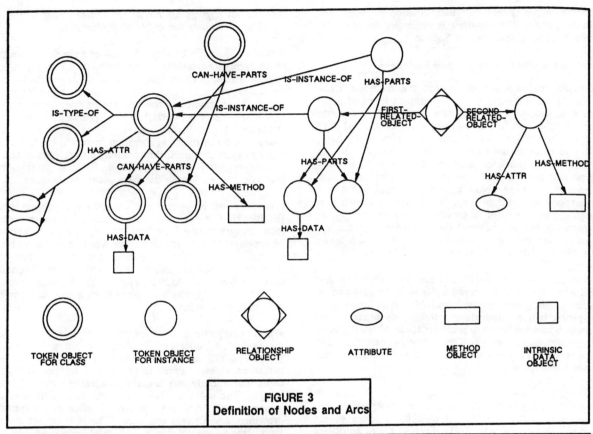

FIGURE 3
Definition of Nodes and Arcs

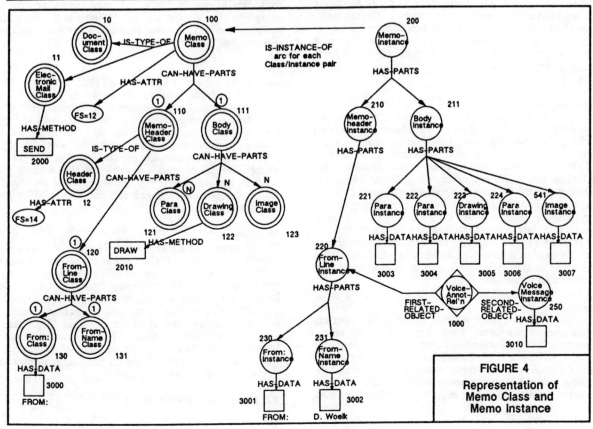

FIGURE 4

Representation of Memo Class and Memo Instance

provides a unique system wide identification for every object in the system. The identifier is important for the logical data structures described in Section 5.

4.1 Token Objects for Classes and Instances

Multimedia applications require that the database store and manipulate a diverse group of complex types of data. We have developed the concept of a *token object* to provide a single mechanism for representing diverse types of data and the relationships among these diverse types of data. The key to accomplishing this goal is the flexibility in the expression of *abstraction*. Smalltalk objects and LISP objects provide abstraction in the form of *generalization* and *instantiation*. A token object provides generalization and instantiation, but adds to these the power of abstraction through *aggregation*. A token object "stands-for" all of the token objects and intrinsic data beneath it in the aggregation hierarchy. This is similar to the approach taken in the Mosaic design support system [ATWO85].

A token object also differs from a Smalltalk object in that each token object can be stored independently and can be included in many aggregation hierarchies, thus creating an aggregation lattice. Methods are treated as separate objects which can be linked to multiple token objects, rather than belonging to classes. The following describes the legal directed arcs which are associated with a token object as shown in Figure 3.

Instantiation
Token objects are used to implement the concept of instantiation. Each instance is represented by a token object which has an **IS-INSTANCE-OF** directed arc to an object class represented by another token object. For example, the **IS-INSTANCE-OF** directed arc between the Memo instance node and the Memo class node in Figure 4 represents instantiation. The instance will inherit properties from the class unless over-ridden by the instance.

Generalization
Token objects are also used to implement generalization. An object class, represented by a token object, can have an **IS-TYPE-OF** directed arc to another token object representing another object class. In Figure 4, there is an **IS-TYPE-OF** directed arc between Memo-Header class and Header class. This arc indicates that Memo-Header is a sub-class of Header. It will inherit properties of Header, such as the Font Size = 14, unless over-ridden in the Memo-Header properties. An object may be a sub-class of more than one class. Therefore, the **IS-TYPE-OF** arc may refer to a set of objects. This creates a *generalization lattice* rather than a *generalization hierarchy*. This set is ordered so as to specify precedence if there is a conflict in inheritance of properties.

Aggregation
The implementation of aggregation is one of the most important uses of the token object. Aggregation can be expressed for both object classes and object instances. In Figure 4, there is a **HAS-PARTS** directed arc between the Body instance and the three Paragraph instances, the Drawing instance, and the Image instance. This arc indicates that the Body instance contains the other instances,

creating an *aggregation hierarchy*. The ordering of the instances determines the order of presentation.

A token object can be viewed as either a *simple token object* or an *aggregate token object*. An aggregate token object consists of a simple token object and all of its descendants in the aggregation hierarchy. The aggregate token object is important in modelling the multimedia document application and other engineering design applications which are structured hierarchically. An aggregate token object can share a subtree of its aggregation hierarchy with another aggregate token object, thus creating an *aggregation lattice*. The aggregation lattice is the basis for data sharing, version control, and some database access techniques.

Properties can be propagated down the aggregation lattice [BOBR83]. For example, if two documents share a common paragraph, the Font Size value for the paragraph will be propagated from the document which is presently being viewed. Note that the value of an attribute is propagated from the containing instance to the parts which it contains in the aggregation lattice. This differs from inheritance where a class inherits a property from a superclass in the generalization lattice.

When aggregation is used for classes of objects, the meaning is slightly different. In Figure 4, there is a **CAN-HAVE-PARTS** directed arc between the Body class and the three classes, Para, Drawing, and Image. This indicates that a Body can contain paragraphs, drawings, and images. The notation "N" next to the Para, Drawing, and Image classes indicates that any number of paragraphs, drawings, and images can occur. The N is circled for the Para class to specify that a Body *must* include at least one paragraph. The circled notation "1" next to the Body class specifies that a Memo must contain a Body and can contain *only one* Body.

Attributes
Each token object has a **HAS-ATTRIBUTES** arc which points to multiple *attributes* as shown in Figure 3. Both object classes and object instances may have these arcs. An example of an attribute is the Font Size = 14 in Figure 4. The Font-Size attribute can take its value from a restricted set of values specified by the user. Other examples of attribute data are physical location of a graphics object in some coordinate system, color of a graphic object, etc. An attribute is not considered to be an object. It has no unique identifier and can not be shared by more than one token object.

Methods
The operations on a token object are referred to as *methods* as in Smalltalk [GOLD81]. Each token object has a **HAS-METHODS** arc which points to one or more programs which are stored independently from the token object. Both object classes and object instances may have these arcs. The program will contain procedural statements in a selected programming language (such as Lisp). An example is the SEND method in Figure 4 which sends the Memo instance via electronic mail. Another example is the DRAW method which handles the physical presentation of instances of the Drawing class.

4.2 Intrinsic Data Objects

Intrinsic data is represented by squares at the leaf nodes of the aggregation hierarchy in the diagram in Figure 3. Above the level of intrinsic data, the system can manipulate token objects, which stand for the intrinsic data, without concern for the internal format of the intrinsic data. This provides great power and flexibility for manipulating different types of multimedia data. A special-purpose *media manager* for each type of media will manipulate the intrinsic data. Portions of this media manager will reside in the database system. For example, if a request is received to play 5 minutes of sound, the database system will translate this request and return the correct number of bytes of digitized sound to the speech output device.

4.3 Relationship Objects

While the token object formalizes the generalization, instantiation, and aggregation relationships which an object may have, there are many other relationships among objects which are necessary to model a multimedia application. These are modelled through the *relationship object* nodes in the diagram in Figure 3. These relationships can be named by the user and provide for functions such as annotation of text by sound and references to other documents. Figure 4 shows a From-Line instance related to a Voice-Message instance via a relationship object which represents a Voice-Annotation relationship. Since a relationship object is an object with a unique identity, a relationship object may also have relationships with other objects. For example, the Voice-Annotation relationship object described above could itself be annotated by another Voice-Message through a separate relationship object representing a separate Voice-Annotation relationship.

5.0 Logical Implementation

This section will describe the logical implementation of the database functions necessary to support the multimedia document application. These functions will first be described in terms of the diagrams which were introduced in the previous section. Then, in Section 5.5, the logical data structures for implementing the functions will be described.

5.1 Operations on Classes and Instances

5.1.1 Operations on Classes

The creation of either an object class or an object instance requires the creation of a token object. The left side of Figure 4 is a partial representation of the token objects which describe the Memo class. Classes can be created, modified and deleted dynamically at any time by the user. When a class is deleted, all of its instances are deleted as well. However, sub-classes of the class and their instances are not necessarily deleted. This is a research issue which is still under investigation.

Classes can be created as specializations of one or more other classes through IS-TYPE-OF links to other token objects. Classes can also be explicitly linked to other classes to form an aggregation lattice using the CAN-HAVE-PARTS link. Attributes for a class can be defined by specifying the attribute name, legal values which it may have, and an initial value. The generalization lattice will be

used extensively for inheritance of attributes, thus reducing work required to create new classes. Intrinsic data, such as the "FROM:" square in Figure 4, can be included with the class information to provide intrinsic data which is common to all instances of the class.

The class information may be modified. The user can create a new version of the class, which will be used for the creation of new instances. Versions will be discussed in more detail in Section 5.2.

5.1.2 Operations on Instances

The right side of Figure 4 depicts an instance of the Memo class. The Memo instance will inherit all of the attributes from the Memo class as well as the attributes from the Document class and the Electronic-Mail class. When the user requests the creation of a new Memo instance, token objects are created for the instances at all levels of the aggregation hierarchy. The class information on the left side of Figure 4 is used to constrain the selection of classes whose instances can be linked using a HAS-PARTS arc on the right side of Figure 4. For example, the Memo instance can only contain a Memo-Header instance and a Body instance.

A new version of a class can also be created during the generation of a document instance. For example, suppose the user wishes to add a Priority-Indicator to the Memo-Header. The Priority-Indicator will contain a number indicating the priority of the Memo. The user can create a new class called Priority-Indicator which can be linked to the Memo-Header class with a CAN-HAVE-PARTS arc. An instance of this class can be created and linked to the Memo-Header instance with a HAS-PARTS arc. The Memo-Header class has now been modified, thus creating a new version of Memo-Header class as described in Section 5.2.

5.2 Version Creation and Control

The control of the evolution of documents is an integral part of the conceptual view of this application environment. Version control in the document creation environment is similar to that in any design environment such as VLSI chip design or software system design. Version creation and control is implemented using versions of token objects. Since token objects are used to implement both classes and instances, version control applies to both classes and instances. Two types of versions will be discussed here. Historical versions represent a history of a document as it has evolved over a period of time. Alternative versions are different implementations or representations of the same abstract object [KATZ84].

5.2.1 Historical Versions

The user must explicitly request the creation of a new *historical* version. The length of time between the designation of historical versions by the user will vary with the specific application. The unshaded token objects in Figure 5 represent an instance of a Book as it exists at some point in time. Suppose that the Book is being created by multiple authors and that an author wishes to make changes to one of the Chapters. The author will retrieve the Chapter from

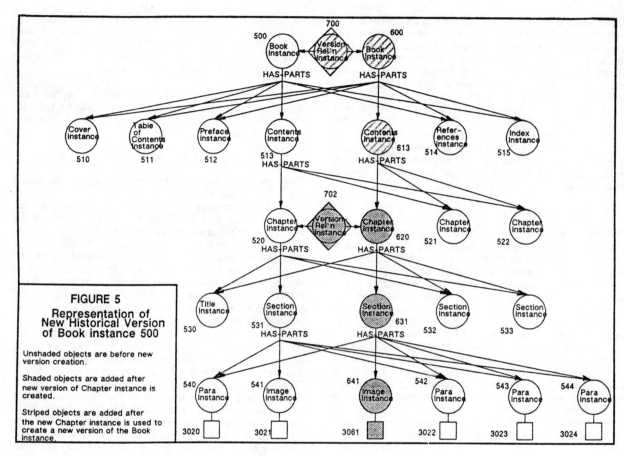

FIGURE 5

Representation of New Historical Version of Book instance 500

Unshaded objects are before new version creation.

Shaded objects are added after new version of Chapter instance is created.

Striped objects are added after the new Chapter instance is used to create a new version of the Book instance.

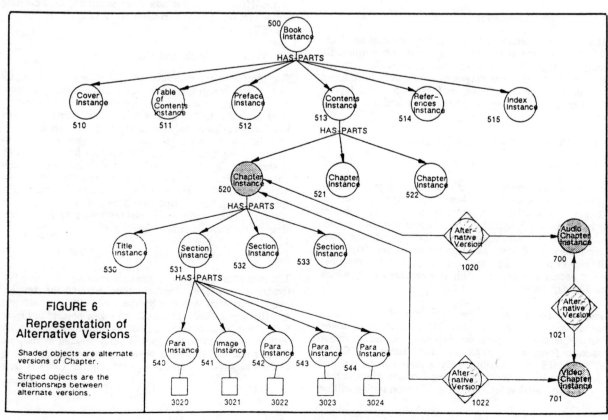

FIGURE 6

Representation of Alternative Versions

Shaded objects are alternate versions of Chapter.

Striped objects are the relationships between alternate versions.

the database and indicate that a new historical version of the Chapter is going to be created.

Suppose that the author wishes to make a modification to the Image instance 541 at the bottom of Figure 5. A copy of the token object representing Image instance 541 will be created and given a unique identifier. This new Image instance 641 is shown as shaded in Figure 5. The new copy of the image can now be modified by the author. The creation of Image instance 641 will cause the creation of new token objects upwards in the aggregation hierarchy. This is termed *percolation* in [ATWO85]. The shaded Section instance 631 will be created by this percolation. Percolation will stop at the Chapter instance 620. The shaded token objects in Figure 5 now represent the new version of the Chapter.

The author may now explicitly request that a new historical version of the Book instance 500 be created as Book instance 600. This will cause the creation of new token objects to percolate up to the Book instance level as shown in the striped token objects in Figure 5.

5.2.2 Alternative Versions

Historical versions imply sequential changes to an object. Alternative versions represent different implementations or representations of the same abstract object. For example, the shaded token objects in Figure 6 represent three completely different representations for a Chapter. There is a text, an audio, and a movie representation of the Chapter. There may also be multiple historical versions of each of these alternatives. The Book instance 500 in Figure 6 is linked through its aggregation hierarchy to one of the alternatives. The alternatives are linked to each other through relationship objects representing Alternative-Version-Relationships. These are shown as striped token objects in Figure 6. Authors can now create historical versions of the Book which combine different historical and alternative versions of the Chapter. At the implementation level, there is not a significant distinction between historical versions and alternative versions.

5.3 Sharing of Token Objects

The discussion of versions has shown how a token object or intrinsic data can become a member of more than one aggregation hierarchy implicitly as versions are formed. It is also possible to explicitly place a token object or intrinsic data into more than one aggregation hierarchy. There are two ways to do this depending on whether or not modifications made later to the object are to be seen.

5.3.1 Sharing by Deferred-Copy

A *deferred copy* is a logical copy which is used so that large intrinsic data objects need not be replicated. Suppose that a user wishes to copy an image from one document to another document. The user does not want to see any future changes in the image; the user only wishes to make a copy of it. This type of sharing of an object can be accomplished through the HAS-PARTS links. In Figure 7, the user issued a request to copy the shaded Image instance 541 from the Book into the Memo. Instead of making a physical copy, the Image instance 541 was linked to the Body instance 211 via the HAS-PARTS arc. As far

as the user is concerned, a new copy of the image has been created. If, as in Figure 5, Image instance 541 in the Book instance 500 is modified to create a new Image instance 641, the Memo will continue to include the old Image instance 541.

5.3.2 Sharing by Reference

Now suppose that the user wishes to include the image in a document, but always wants the document to contain the most recent version of the image. This time the user will request to include a *reference* to the image in the document. This will cause the creation of a Reference token object which will be used to link the image into the aggregation hierarchy of the Memo. Figure 8 shows the result of this reference. The shaded Image instance 541 has been linked to the Memo instance 200 via the striped token object representing the Reference instance 900. Now, when the Image instance 541 is modified, Memo instance 800 will contain the new version. An attribute of the Reference token object also contains a flag indicating whether the viewer should be notified that the image has been modified since the last time it was viewed [KIM85b].

5.4 Accessing Objects

The object-oriented model is associated with an interactive user-friendly environment. The model itself encourages and simplifies the concept of pointing at an object to find out the allowable operations on the object and then selecting a desired operation. Object-oriented models do not emphasize other modes of access. The approach proposed here will take advantage of the associative access which is inherent in instantiation, aggregation, generalization, and user-defined relationships. A number of different modes of access are outlined below.

Access to an Object Instance Through its Class
Every object is an instance of a class of objects. The token object implements this relationship with an IS-INSTANCE-OF directed arc from the instance to the class. The inverse of this arc will provide the identity of the instances of each class. For example, the Memo class 100 in Figure 4 can identify all of the Memo instances, such as Memo instance 200. The extent to which this access mode is used will have to be considered in designing the physical implementation of the system.

Access Through the Aggregation Hierarchy
A token object can be viewed as either a simple token object or an aggregate token object as described in Section 4.1. Therefore, classes and instances can be viewed as either simple or aggregate. A request to retrieve the simple Memo instance 200 in Figure 4 will return only one token object. Requests for descendants in the aggregation hierarchy, such as Memo-Header instance, can then be found through the HAS-PARTS arcs.

On the other hand, a request to retrieve the aggregate Memo instance 200 will return the token object for Memo instance 200, plus all of its descendants linked through the HAS-PARTS arcs. Higher level queries such as "Retrieve MEMO· where MEMO.FROM-NAME = D. Woelk" can also be expressed using the aggregation hierarchy.

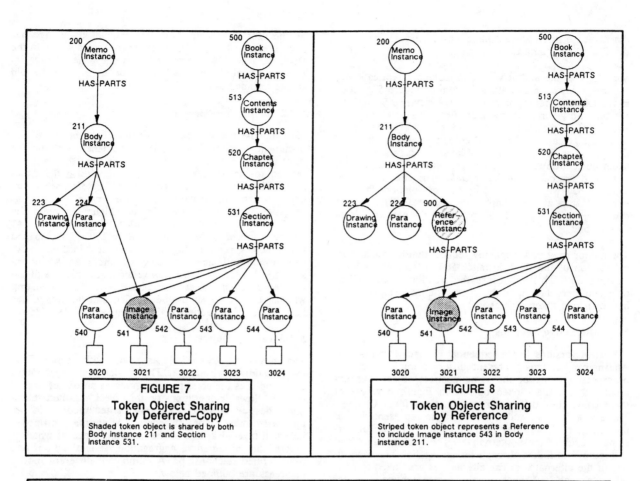

FIGURE 7
Token Object Sharing by Deferred-Copy
Shaded token object is shared by both Body instance 211 and Section instance 531.

FIGURE 8
Token Object Sharing by Reference
Striped token object represents a Reference to include Image instance 543 in Body instance 211.

			TOKEN OBJECTS for CLASSES								METHOD OBJECTS	
obj-id	class-name	is-type-of obj-id	can-have-parts			has-data obj-id	has-attributes	has-methods			obj-id	method
			min	max	obj-id							
100	Memo	10 (Document) 11 (Elect. Mail)	1 1	1 1	110 (Memo-Header) 111 (Body)		Font-Size=12				2000	(Send Program)
10	Document										2010	(Draw Program)
11	Electronic-Mail							2000 (Send)				
110	Memo-Header	12 (Header)		1	120 (From-Line)							
12	Header						Font-Size=14					
120	From-Line		1 1	1 1	130 (From:) 131 (From-Name)							
130	From:					3000						
131	From-Name											
111	Body		1 0 0	N N N	121 (Para) 122 (Drawing) 123 (Image)							
121	Para											
122	Drawing							2010 (Draw)				
123	Image											

FIGURE 9
Logical Data Structures

Logical data structures which represent the Memo class in Figure 4.

Comments enclosed in parentheses.

Access Through the Generalization Hierarchy

The generalization hierarchy contains valuable information which can be used for accessing objects. A request such as "Retrieve all Documents" can be answered by first finding all of the sub-classes of the Document class. In Figure 4, the Document class has only one sub-class which is indicated by the IS-TYPE-OF directed arc from the Memo class to the Document class. The inverse of this arc will provide a link between the Document class and the Memo sub-class. All Memo instances can then be returned using the inverse of the IS-INSTANCE-OF arc.

Access Through Relationships

Access to objects through instantiation, aggregation, and generalization paths all use information about structural relationships among objects which the user has provided. The user may also create other relationships among objects through the creation of relationship objects as described in Section 4.3. These relationships can be used to move from one object to another as in Figure 4, where a Voice-Annotation relationship object is used to link a From-Line instance and a Voice Message instance. Relationship objects may also be searched directly to provide associative access for a query such as "Retrieve all Voice-Annotations".

Access Through Feature Extraction from Intrinsic Data

Intrinsic data may exist at the leaf nodes of the aggregation lattice. Since the internal format and presentation characteristics of each type of intrinsic data is different, a special-purpose media manager will be needed for manipulating this data. For some types of media, it is possible to access a subset of the data based on certain *features* of the data. These features are not explicitly described as part of the data and must first be *extracted* from the data.

This extraction process may be very slow or even impossible in some cases. In speech recognition, for example, the feature extraction process is presently efficient only for limited vocabulary and limited number of independent speakers speaking slowly. Image recognition is equally restricted. Searching for patterns in text, on the other hand, is a common practice in text editors and information retrieval systems. This searching can also be accelerated through the use of specialized hardware [HASK83]. It would be possible, therefore, to pass a pattern to the Text media manager and have the media manager search for the pattern in all text passages or in some subset of text passages.

Combinations of Access Modes

Any of the access modes described above can be combined to create a query. An example is the query "Retrieve Memos which contain pictures of database machines and which reference the 1985 Database Program Plan". This query combines a number of access modes, and as such it consists of a number of sub-queries. The performance of the execution of the query may be dependent on the order in which the individual sub-queries are executed. One sequence of execution is to find the 1985 Database Program Plan, search for Reference relationship objects linked to the 1985 Database Program Plan, find the Memos which make reference to the 1985 Database Program Plan, search for those Memos which have pictures, and display these pictures for user recognition of a "database machine". Other sequences of sub-query execution are possible and may result in different performance.

Browsing as an Access Mode

Browsing is an important mode of accessing documents in a multimedia document management environment. Many times the user cannot precisely formulate a query using the access methods listed above which will result in a satisfactory answer. There may be too many documents which fit the selection criteria or there may be none at all. In either case the query must be reformulated to either expand or narrow the selection criteria. If many documents are returned as a result of a query, the user may wish to look at a few before deciding to narrow the selection criteria. As described in [CHRI84], the query may then be reformulated with a request that documents already viewed should not be viewed again. In addition, the user can organize and classify the documents which satisfy the selection criteria by interactively creating a temporary "document" which contains these documents.

5.5 Logical Data Structures

Figures 9 and 10 illustrate the logical data structures which are used to implement the functions described in the previous section. The data structures contain data which represent the Memo class and Memo instance that were described in Figure 4. Figure 11 represents the two Book instance versions described in Figure 5. (Text enclosed in parentheses in these structures are comments that we have added to aid the reader in understanding the example.)

The token object format used for representing classes is presented in Figure 9, where each row represents a class. The token object format for instances is presented in Figure 10 and Figure 11, where each row represents an instance. Note that the structures are similar since classes and instances are represented in a similar manner in the diagram of Figure 4. However, there are a few differences. A class does not have an IS-INSTANCE-OF field; whereas an instance does not have an IS-TYPE-OF field. Further, the semantics of the CAN-HAVE-PARTS field of the class and the HAS-PARTS field of the instance are different. The CAN-HAVE-PARTS field of a class specifies the classes of the objects which an instance of the class *may* contain in its next lower level in an aggregation hierarchy. The MIN value specifies the minimum number of instances of the class which can be contained. The MAX value is the maximum number of instances of the class that can be contained. The HAS-PARTS field of an instance, on the other hand, specifies the *actual* instances which are contained in the next lower level.

A couple of other observations can be made concerning the logical data structures of the token objects used to represent classes and instances. It is obvious that these tables are not normalized relations, due to the multiple values for some fields. For example, the HAS-PARTS field of the sixth row of the token object structure in Figure 10 contains an ordered list of five object identifiers.

The structures might be represented as complex objects as defined in [KIM85a, LORI83] or in the Set and Tuple Data Model of [BANC85b]. However, these models cannot represent the inheritance (or propagation) of properties through generalization (or aggregation).

TOKEN OBJECTS for INSTANCES

obj-id	is-instance-of obj-id	has-parts obj-id	has-data obj-id	has-attributes	has-methods
200	100 (Memo)	210 (Memo-Header), 211 (Body)			
210	110 (Memo-Header)	220 (From-Line)			
220	120 (From-Line)	230 (From:), 231 (From-Name)			
230	130 (From:)		3001		
231	131 (From-Name)		3002		
211	111 (Body)	221 (Para), 222 (Para), 223 (Drawing), 224 (Para), 541 (Image)			
221	121 (Para)		3003		
222	121 (Para)		3004		
223	122 (Drawing)		3005		
224	121 (Para)		3006		
541	123 (Image)		3007		
250	(Voice-Message)		3010		

RELATIONSHIP OBJECTS

obj-id	first-related-obj-id	second-related-obj-id	relationship-type
1000	220 (From-Line)	250 (Voice-Message)	Voice-Annotation
700	500 (Book)	600 (Book)	Historical-Version
702	520 (Chapter)	620 (Chapter)	Historical-Version

FIGURE 10
Logical Data Structures (cont'd)

Logical data structures which represent memo instance in Figure 4.

Comments enclosed in parentheses.

TOKEN OBJECTS for INSTANCES

obj-id	is-instance-of obj-id	has-parts obj-id	has-data obj-id	has-attributes	has-methods
500	(Book)	510 (Cover), 511 (T. of C.), 512 (Preface), 513 (Contents), 514 (References), 515 (Index)			
513	(Contents)	520 (Chapter), 521 (Chapter), 522 (Chapter)			
520	(Chapter)	530 (Title), 531 (Section), 532 (Section), 533 (Section)			
531	(Section)	540 (Para), 541 (Image), 542 (Para), 543 (Para), 544 (Para)			
541	(Image)		3021		
600	(Book)	510, 611, 512, 613, 514, 515			
613	(Contents)	620, 521, 622			
620	(Chapter)	530, 631, 532, 533			
631	(Section)	540, 641, 542, 643, 544			
641	(Image)		3061		

FIGURE 11
Logical Data Structures (cont'd)

Logical data structures which represent two versions of Book instance in Figure 5.

Comments enclosed in parentheses.

The creation of a new class will result in the insertion of a new row in the token object structure in Figure 9. The **IS–TYPE–OF** field will contain a list of the object identifiers for the classes of which this class is a sub–class. The creation of an instance of a class will result in the creation of a new row in the token object structure in Figure 10. The **IS–INSTANCE–OF** field will contain the object identifier of the class. If a class is deleted, all of the instances of this class must be deleted. Note that this will require searching of all the **IS–INSTANCE–OF** fields for the object identifier of the instances of the deleted class, unless an index of inverse pointers to instances is maintained for each class.

The creation of a relationship object will result in the creation of a new row in the relationship objects structure in Figure 10. The first row of that structure represents the Voice–Annotation relationship which was shown in Figure 4. The **FIRST–RELATED–OBJECT** and **SECOND–RELATED–OBJECT** fields contain the object identifiers for the token objects which are related, the From–Line instance 220 and the Voice–Message instance 250. An index of inverse pointers from token objects for instances to relationship objects are necessary to find the relationships in which a token object takes part if a full search of the relationship objects structure is to be avoided.

The unshaded portion of Figure 11 represents the Book instance 500 from Figure 5. The lightly shaded portion represents the new version of the book which is identified as Book instance 600. These two instances both contain many of the same object identifiers in their respective **HAS–PARTS** fields. The relationship object created to represent the version relationship between the two instances is also shown in Figure 10.

Figure 7 described the creation of a deferred–copy of Image instance 541 taken from Book instance 500 which was included in Memo instance 200. The entries in the **HAS–PARTS** fields which represent this deferred–copy are shown as darkly shaded in Figure 10 and Figure 11. Notice that in row 5 of Figure 11, the Image instance 541 entry does not include any indication of the identities of the aggregation hierarchies in which it exists. Here again an index of inverse pointers is necessary to eliminate the need for searching the **HAS–PARTS** fields of all of the token objects.

Inheritance of properties through the generalization lattice can cause extensive pointer chasing. For example, to find the Font–Size value for the Memo–Header instance 210 in Figure 10 (Row 2), the system must look at the Memo–Header class 110 in Figure 9 (Row 4) for a Font–Size attribute. Since no value exists for Font–size for Memo–Header class 110, the system must look at the Header class 12 (Row 5) where a Font–Size = 14 is found.

6.0 Concluding Remarks

In this paper, first we identified two types of requirements which multimedia (compound document management) applications impose on a database system. One is the requirement for a data model that allows a very natural and flexible definition and evolution of the schema that can represent the composition of compound documents and capture the complex relationships among parts of compound documents. Another is the requirement for sharing and manipulating (storage, retrieval, and transmission) compound documents containing images and voice as intrinsic data.

We then proposed an object–oriented data model which generalizes the notions of instantiation and generalization that form the basis of the current object–oriented systems, and which augments the conventional object–oriented paradigm with the notions of aggregation and relationships. We showed that this object–oriented data model is an elegant approach to addressing all data modelling requirements of the multimedia applications. Further, we showed, in terms of 'logical' data structures, how operations on the data model (e.g., creation and deletion of classes and instances) can be implemented in an object–oriented database system.

There are a number of important issues that require further research. First, property inheritance and constraints management is more complex in our system than in conventional object–oriented systems since our data model supports the notions of instantiation, generalization, and aggregation. We need more work on this. Second, we need to extend our 'logical' implementation of the data model to a 'physical' implementation. In particular, we need to address such issues as buffering techniques for transmitting the long intrinsic data, a cost model and a query processing strategy for complex associative search of the contents of compound documents, and storage structures for the 'logical' data structures we developed to support the operations on our data model.

REFERENCES

[AHLS84] Ahlsen M., A. Bjornerstedt, S. Britts, C. Hulten, and L. Soderlund. "An Architecture for Object Management in OIS," *ACM Trans. on Office Information Systems*, vol. 2, no. 3, July 1984, pp. 173–196.

[APPL83] *MACINTOSH*, by Apple Computer, Inc. Cupertino, Ca, 1983.

[ATWO85] Atwood, T.M. "An Object-Oriented DBMS for Design Support Applications," *Proc. IEEE COMPINT 85*, Montreal, Canada, pp. 299–307.

[BANC85a] Bancilhon, F., W. Kim, and H.F. Korth. "A Model of CAD Transactions," *Proc. VLDB*, 1985.

[BANC85b] Bancilhon, F. "A Set and Tuple Data Model," *MCC Technical Report DB–020–85*, June 1985.

[BEEC83] Beech, D. and S. Feldman. "The Integrated Data Model: A Database Perspective," *Proc. VLDB*, 1983, pp. 302–304.

[BOBR83] Bobrow, B. and M. Stefik. *The LOOPS Manual*, Xerox PARC, Palo Alto, CA., 1983.

[BIRT73] Birtwistle, G., O.J. Dahl, B. Myhrhaug, and K. Nygaard. *Simula Begin*, Auerbach Publishers, Philadelphia, Pa., 1973.

[CAMM84] Cammarata, S. and M. Melkanoff. "An Interactive Data Dictionary Facility for CAD/CAM Data Bases," *Proc. First Int'nl. Workshop on Expert Database Systems*, Oct. 1984, pp. 360–377.

[CHEN76] Chen, P.P.S. "The Entity–Relationship Model – Towards a Unified View of Data," *ACM Trans. on Database Systems*, vol. 1, no. 1, 1976, pp. 9–36.

[CHRI84] Christodoulakis, S., J. Vanderbroek, J. Li, S. Wan, Y. Wang, M. Papa, and E. Bertino. "Development of a Multimedia Information System for an Office Environment," *Proc. VLDB*, 1984, pp. 261–271.

[COPE84] Copeland, G. and D. Maier. "Making Smalltalk a Database System," *ACM SIGMOD*, June 1984, pp. 316–325.

[FOGG84] Fogg D. "Lessons from a 'Living in a Database' Graphical Query Interface," *ACM SIGMOD*, 1984, pp. 100–106.

[FORS84] Forsdick, H.C., R.H. Thomas, G.G. Robertson, and V.H. Travers. "Initial Experience with Multimedia Documents in Diamond," *IEEE Database Engineering Quarterly Bulletin*, vol.7 no. 3, Sept. 1984.

[FOX85] Fox, M., J. Wright, and D. Adam. "Experiences with SRL: An Analysis of a Frame–based Knowledge Representation," *Proc. First Int'nl. Workshop on Expert Database Systems*, Oct. 1984, pp. 224–237.

[GOLD81] Goldberg, A. "Introducing the Smalltalk–80 System," *Byte*, vol. 6, no. 8, August 1981, pp. 14–26.

[GRAY81] Gray, J.N., P. McJones, M. Blasgen, B. Lindsay, R. Lorie, T. Price, F. Putzola and I. Traiger. "Recovery Manager of a Data Management System," *ACM Computing Surveys*, vol. 13, no. 2, June 1981, pp. 223–242.

[HASK82] Haskin, R. and R. Lorie. "On Extending the Functions of a Relational Database System," in *ACM/SIGMOD*, June 1982, pp. 207–212.

[HASK83] Haskin, R. and L.A. Hollaar. "Operational Characteristics of a Hardware–Based Pattern Matcher," *ACM Trans. on Database Systems*, vol. 8, no. 1, March 1983, pp. 15–40.

[KATZ84] Katz, R. and T. Lehman. "Database Support for Versions and Alternatives of Large Design Files," *IEEE Trans. on Software Engineering*, vol. SE-10, no. 3, March 1984, pp. 191–200.

[KIM85a] Kim, W. "CAD Database Requirements – Rev. 1," *MCC Technical Report DB–058–85*, July 1985.

[KIM85b] Kim, W., H. Chou, and D. Woelk. "On Versions in a Distributed CAD System," *MCC Technical Report DB–60-85*.

[LMI85] *ObjectLISP User Manual*, LMI, Cambridge, MA, 1985.

[LORI83] Lorie, R. and W. Plouffe. "Complex Objects and Their Use in Design Transactions," *Proc. ACM Database Week: Engineering Design Applications*, May 1983, pp. 115–121.

[MINS75] Minsky M. "A Framework for Representing Knowledge," In *The Psychology of Computer Vision*, P. Winston (Ed.), New York: McGraw–Hill.

[MYLO80] Mylopoulos, J., P. Bernstein, and H. Wong. "A Language Facility for Designing Database-Intensive Applications," *ACM Trans. Database Systems*, vol. 5, no. 2, 1980, pp. 185–207.

[NILS80] Nilsson, N. *Principles of Artificial Intelligence*, Tioga Publishing Co., Palo Alto, Ca., 1980, pp. 370–378.

[PHIG85] *Programmers Hierarchical Interactive Graphics System (PHIGS)*, document X3H3/85-21, X3 Secretariat, CBEMA, 311 First St. NW, Suite 500, Washington, DC 20001, 1985.

[POGG85] Poggio, A., J.J. Garcia Luna Aceves, E.J. Craighill, D. Moran, L. Aguilar, D. Worthington, and J. Hight. "CCWS: A Computer–Based Multimedia Information System," *IEEE Computer*, vol. 18, no. 10, Oct. 1985, pp. 92–103.

[REHF84] Rehfuss, S., M. Freiling, and J. Alexander. "Particularity in Engineering," Proc. *First Int'nl. Workshop on Expert Database Systems*, Oct. 1984, pp. 677–684.

[SAKA85] Sakata, S. and T. Ueda. "A Distributed Interoffice Mail System," *IEEE Computer*, vol. 18, no. 10, Oct. 1985, pp. 106–116.

[SLOA82] Sloan, K.R. and A. Lippman. "Data Bases of / about / with Images," *IEEE Conf. on Pattern Recognition and Image Processing*, June 1982, pp. 441–446.

[SMIT77] Smith, J. and D.C.P. Smith. "Database Abstractions: Aggregation and Generalization," *ACM Trans Database Systems*, vol. 2, no. 2, 1977, pp. 105–133.

[WEIN81] Weinberg, D. and D. Moon. *Lisp Machine Manual*, Symbolics, Inc., July 1981.

[WILS80] Wilson, G. and C. Herot. "Semantics vs. Graphics –– To Show or Not To Show," *Proc. VLDB*, 1980, pp. 183–197.

[WOEL85] Woelk, D. and W. Luther. "Multimedia Database Requirements – Rev. 0," *MCC Technical Report DB–042–85* , July, 1985.

[WONG82] Wong, H. and I. Kuo. "GUIDE: Graphical UserInterface for Database Exploration," *Proc. VLDB*, 1982, pp. 22–32.

[YANK85] Yankelovich, N., N. Meyrowitz, and A. van Dam. "Reading and Writing the Electronic Book," *IEEE Computer*, vol. 18, no. 10, Oct. 1985, pp. 15–30.

An Extensible Object-Oriented Approach to Databases for VLSI/CAD[1]

Hamideh Afsarmanesh
Dennis McLeod

David Knapp
Alice Parker

Department of Computer Science
University of Southern California
Los Angeles, California 90089-0782

Department of Electrical Engineering
University of Southern California
Los Angeles, California 90089-0781

Abstract

This paper describes an approach to the specification and modeling of information associated with the design and evolution of VLSI components. The approach is characterized by combined structural and behavioral descriptions of a component. Database modeling requirements specific to the VLSI design domain are considered and techniques to address them are described. An extensible object-oriented information management framework, the 3DIS (3 Dimensional Information Space), is presented. The framework has been adapted to capture the underlying semantics of the application environment by the addition of new abstraction primitives. An example 3DIS database for a VLSI design system is presented.

1. Introduction

The Very Large Scale Integrated circuit (VLSI) design environment is characterized by a large volume of data, with diverse modalities and complex data descriptions [Bushnell 83], [Davis 82], and [Knapp 85]. Both data and descriptions of data are dynamic, as is the underlying collection of design techniques and procedures. Design engineers, who are normally not database experts, nevertheless become the designers, manipulators, and evolvers of their databases. A final distinctive property of VLSI design environments is a requirement to model both the dynamic behavior of a circuit and its static structure.

In this paper, we characterize a class of digital VLSI design environments, describe a unified system for VLSI design, and present an object-oriented information framework appropriate to model these environments. The remainder of this section concerns digital VLSI design application domains and their specific database modeling requirements. Section 2 briefly describes an extensible object-oriented framework suitable for modeling VLSI design environments, the 3DIS (3 Dimensional Information Space), which has been extended to capture the underlying semantics of circuit structure and behavior. Section 3 describes the modeling of VLSI circuits in the ADAM (Advanced Design AutoMation) system. An example 3DIS database for the ADAM VLSI design system is presented in Section 4 of this paper.

1.1. The VLSI Circuit Design Domain

The VLSI circuit design process typically begins with a descriptive high-level specification of the design, consisting primarily of dataflow and timing graphs, which together describe the data-transformation and timing behavior of the desired hardware. Less detailed structural (i.e. schematic) and physical specifications are given, describing static properties of the target circuit. The descriptive graphs are hierarchical in that their components can be recursively decomposed into simpler components. For example, a dataflow node "multiply" can be decomposed into simpler "shift" and "add" constructs.

Several relationships might be specified among the components of a high level design specification; e.g. among specific time intervals and data operations in the timing and dataflow graphs. Various constraints can be

[1]This research was supported by the National Science Foundation, #MCS-8203485, and the Joint Services Electronics Program through the Air Force Office of Scientific Research under contract # F49620-81-C-0070.

attached to the graphs; for example, the duration of a time interval can be limited, a schematic wire can be specified to be a bidirectional bus connection, and the area of a physical bounding box can be limited. The descriptive graphical representations contain both numeric and symbolic attributes on their arcs and vertices.

The descriptive specification is usually large and complex. Many kinds of data are involved and it is in a large part recursively defined. Furthermore, the specification must be checked for completeness and consistency before the design process begins.

VLSI circuit design typically utilizes a design library, which contains components to be used in the construction of new components. It can also contain designs that are themselves under construction; these may be subparts of a larger design (e.g. the control unit for a CPU), or independent projects. Selecting the appropriate library component may be difficult. For example, if an adder is desired, there might be several components named 'adder', a few named 'ALU', and a few 'complex standard' (i.e. microprocessors). In other situations, the behavior desired may not match the stated behavior of any component in the library without some transformation being applied.

The output of the design system includes a set of graphs, relationships, and constraints similar to those of the descriptive specification, but with a much more detailed physical description.

1.2. ADAM: A Unified System for VLSI Design

The ADAM (Advanced Design AutoMation) system [Granacki 85] is envisioned to become a unified system for VLSI design, starting with a functional and timing specification and proceeding to circuit layout via automatic synthesis routines. The ADAM system describes VLSI circuits by means of four recursively defined and explicitly interrelated hierarchies. In ADAM, the representational formalisms of the input descriptive specification, the library components, and the output design are identical. This in turn facilitates the task of design verification and validation, e.g. testing the equivalence of specified and implemented dataflow graphs.

ADAM supports several major circuit design activities. These activities comprise the main part of the process by which the dataflow and timing descriptive specifications are mapped into the physical output components [Parker 84], [Director 81]. An appropriate information modeling environment for ADAM must support these tasks:

- *Algorithm Synthesis*: The dataflow graph is transformed in order to optimize speed, area, power, and other tradeoffs.

- *Partitioning*: Some part of the specification is partitioned so that the parts can be dealt with separately.

- *Floor Planning*: Given partitions and constraints, high-level chip plans can be constructed that aid in the prediction and optimization of area and performance.

- *Data Path and Control Synthesis*: Data paths are allocated hardware resources and the order of operations is fixed. Controllers are specified and synthesized. Interconnections are synthesized.

- *Built-In Test Synthesis*: Hardware is added to make the end product testable.

- *Module Selection*: Design library elements are introduced to implement operators, memories, and random logic.

- *Placement and Routing*: Modules are allocated physical positions on the layout, and interconnect wires are routed.

- *Validation and Verification*: At any step of the design process, performance and function may be validated using an appropriate simulator or formal verification tool.

1.3. Information Management Requirements of VLSI Design Environments

Given the above general characterization of the VLSI design process, the fundamental characteristics of digital VLSI design environments can be summarized as follows:

- The design data is of large volume, and of various modalities and complexities, e.g. graphical, symbolic, numeric, textual and formatted data.

- Structural information (e.g. data-description, data-interrelation, and data-classification) is complex, of large quantity and must support dynamic use. Structures must allow programs, documents, messages, constraints, and graphs to coexist.

- The end-users, design engineers and CAD application programmers, are familiar with their application environment, but are not likely to have expertise in databases or programming.

2. Information Modeling for VLSI/CAD

Much of the reported work in the VLSI database design literature describes management of design information as collections of raw data in files. Interpretation of the stored design data is completely hidden in the application programs and the users' minds. These database systems are costly to maintain and evolve. Record-oriented database models, such as the relational data model has also been applied to VLSI/CAD design environments [Wong 79], [Eastman 80]. However, these models are of limited suitability for non-database-expert VLSI designers who intend to build, use, and maintain their own databases.

Recently, the suitability of the so-called *semantic database models* as tools to help in the construction and use of design databases has been examined [Katz 82], [McLeod 83], [Batory 84], and [Dittrich 85]. Some semantic database models are object-oriented in the sense that the modeling constructs and the construct manipulators of these models are defined as objects. In such systems objects can be defined to correspond to the concepts, entities, and activities of application environments.

2.1. A Brief Summary of the 3DIS

The 3 Dimensional Information Space (3DIS) [Afsarmanesh 84], and [Afsarmanesh 85a] is a simple but extensible object-oriented information management framework. The 3DIS is mainly intended for applications that have dynamic and complex structures, and whose designers, manipulators, and evolvers are non-database experts. As a step towards addressing the modeling needs of such application environments, the 3DIS unifies the view and treatment of all kinds of information including the structural (description and classification of data) and non-structural (data) database contents, which simplifies database manipulation and modification tasks.

3DIS databases are collections of interrelated objects, where an object represents any identifiable piece of information, of arbitrary kind and level of abstraction. For example, a VLSI component, a

component's attribute, a string of characters, a structural component (type), and a procedure defined on a component type are all modeled uniformly as objects in a homogeneous framework. Therefore, what distinguishes different kinds of objects is the set of structural and non-structural (data) relationships defined on them.

Each 3DIS object has a globally unique *object-id* that is an identifier generated by the system. An object can also have several user-specified surrogate *object-names* which also uniquely identify it. Objects may be referred to via their unique object-ids, object-names, or via their relationships with other objects. The 3DIS model supports the following kinds of objects:

- *Atomic objects* represent symbolic constants in databases. These objects carry their own information content in their object-ids. Atomic objects cannot be decomposed into other objects. The contents of atomic objects are uninterpreted, in the sense that they are either displayable or executable. Strings of characters, numbers, Booleans, text, messages, audio, and video objects, as well as behavioral (procedural) objects, are example atomic objects. Text objects and messages represent long character strings, while audio and video objects represent digitized voice and images. Behavioral objects represent the routines that embody database activities, representing objects that are executable. Behavioral objects accomplish modeling of data definition, manipulation, and retrieval primitives, e.g. **Insert-an-OEM-Component**[2].

- *Composite objects* describe non-atomic entities and concepts. The information content of these objects can be interpreted meaningfully by the 3DIS system through their decomposition into other objects. An example of a composite object is a component **H42paddr**. Composite objects are not displayable, except in terms of their relationships with atomic objects; for example, **Designer-names** for **H42padder** are **David** and **John**. If a composite object is related to certain other composite objects, e.g. **H42paddr** has the dataflow model **H42paddr-Dataflow**, then it may be displayed recursively in terms of the atomic

---

[2] Boldface is used to denote object-names.

objects related to those composite objects. Mapping objects are a special kind of composite objects. A mapping object is defined in terms of, and may be decomposed into, a domain type object, a range type object, an inverse mapping object, and the minimum and maximum number of the values it may return. Mappings model both the descriptive characteristics of an object, e.g. a component's name via **Component-Name**, and the associations defined among objects, e.g. a component's constituents via **Has-Link-Constituents**. Mappings also model both single and multi-valued relationships.

- *Type objects* specify classification information: a type object is a structural specification of a group of atomic or composite objects. It denotes a collection of database objects, called its *members*, together with the shared common information about these members. A type object is defined in terms of its members, a set of mappings shared by its members, the fundamental relationships between this type object and other type objects, and a set of operations shared by its members. A type object can be a *subtype* of another type object (*supertype*). Subtypes are defined by the enumeration of members of their supertypes and inherit some of their supertype's definition such as the mappings and operations shared by members (Enumeration may be accomplished through a behavioral object, i.e. a procedure defined on the supertype; this in effect supports predicate-defined subtypes). A type object can be the subtype of more than one type object. The subtype/supertype relationships among type objects can be represented by a directed acyclic graph (DAG). Examples of type objects are **In-House-Component** and **Dataflow-Model**.

Basic associations among objects in 3DIS databases are established through a set of predefined abstraction primitives. The 3DIS model has been extended to accommodate other kinds of abstractions that are useful in VLSI design applications. For example, abstraction primitives to support the definition of recursively defined entities and concepts such as sets, lists, and binary trees are included in the model. In particular, for the ADAM design database,

the 3DIS supports the recursive definition of VLSI components, as described in section **4**.

An integral part of the 3DIS model is its simple and multi-purpose geometric representation. This geometric framework graphically organizes both structural and non-structural database information in a 3-D representation space and supports their uniform handling. The framework reflects a mathematically founded definition for 3DIS modeling constructs in terms of the geometric components that represent them. The three axes in the space represent the domain (D), the mapping (M), and the range (R) axes. Relationships among objects are modeled by "domain-object, mapping-object, range-object" triples that represent specific points in the geometric space.

Figure 2-1 illustrates a perspective view of the geometric representation of an example 3DIS database. In this figure, **FA-1** and **FA-2** are members of the type object **Single-Node**, while they are also the **Model-Constituents** of **H42padder-Dataflow**. Figure 2-2 illustrates the right view of the geometric representation for the **H42padder-Dataflow**. Both figures have been simplified to represent only a part of the information in the database; the example is further described in Section 4.

Several geometric components such as points, lines, and planes play a meaningful role in representing certain abstractions of the data. For instance, in Figure 2-1, the vertical line emanating from the object **H42padder-Dataflow** represents all mappings defined on that object. Similarly, an orthogonal plane passing through the same object contains the information about all objects directly related to **H42padder-Dataflow**. The variety of information encapsulation supported by the geometric representation, is a unique feature of the 3DIS data model.

The geometric representation is also intended to provide a foundation for information browsing and serves as an environment for a simple graphics-based database user interface. A simple set of navigational operations is defined that consists of *viewing* and *moving* primitives. Viewing operations provide "display windows" to "information neighborhoods" of interest, such as the example views in Figures 2-1 and 2-2. Moving operations allow the information browsing and retrieval. Movements are defined between points on views in orthogonal directions, and they have unique meanings relative to their start position. However, moving in each direction has also a specific meaning that is independent of the start position. For example,

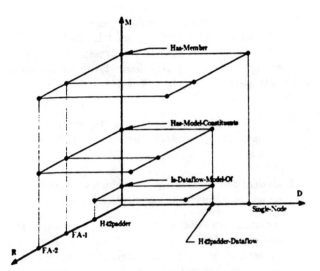

Figure 2-1: Perspective view of a part of information in a 3DIS database

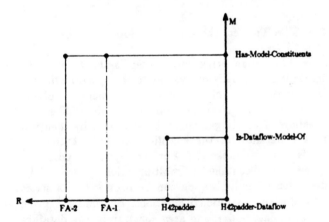

Figure 2-2: Right view of H42padder-Dataflow

moving parallel to the R-axis from any point to the next always returns the next range object for the same domain and mapping objects. Navigational operations support viewing, browsing, and retrieval of both structural and non-structural information. A further description of the 3DIS user interface is given in [Afsarmanesh 85a].

3. A 3DIS Database for VLSI

The digital circuit design process can be regarded as a search of a "design space" [Director 81] for a particular solution that meets constraints on functionality, timing, power, cost, etc. The entire design space can be broken down into subspaces which are near-orthogonal in the sense that decisions taken in one subspace affect decisions taken in another subspace weakly across some region of interest. For example, a single functional specification can be mapped into

several different implementations with varying speeds, power dissipations, and costs.

The 3DIS database described below is based on four hierarchical subspaces (also called *models*) chosen for their near-orthogonality [Knapp 83] and [Knapp 85]. For example, one of the subspaces is used to represent schematic (structural) information; this subspace is a hierarchy with block diagrams at the top, registers and ALUs at the middle, gates a little lower, and transistors at the bottom. Design entities are described in terms of these subspaces and a set of relationships across them.

3.1. The Definition of Component

The fundamental structure of the ADAM 3DIS database is the **component**. A component can represent either a specification, a design in progress, or a member of the design library. A specification is represented as an incomplete component. The information that is present in the specification usually represents the operations the target must perform and the constraints it must meet.

A design in progress is also an incomplete component. The design gradually becomes more and more complete, until it can be manufactured. In the initial stages of design, the target component contains primarily dataflow and timing information; in the later stages it contains more schematic information, and finally physical layout. The original dataflow, timing, and schematic information are preserved for documentation and verification/validation purposes.

The design library is used to store both procured components (OEM components) and "In-house" components. An in-house component may be either complete or incomplete.

3.2. The Four Models of a Component

A component is described in terms of four **models** and a set of relationships (**bindings**) across the constituents of the models. The models correspond to the four subspaces of the design space. The four models are:

1. *The dataflow model* describes the data transformation operations performed by the component. Its primitives are **nodes** and **values**. Nodes represent data transformations; values represent data passed between nodes.

2. *The timing and sequencing model* describes

time-domain and branching behavior of the component. Its primitives are **ranges and points**[3]. A range represents a time interval during which an operation can take place; points represent infinitesimal "events", which are partially ordered because the ranges have signs as well as durations.

3. *The structural model* describes the schematic diagram of the component. Its primitives are **modules and carriers**. A module represents a schematic block, gate, transistor etc.; a carrier represents a schematic wire.

4. *The physical model* describes the layout, position, size, packaging and power dissipation of the component. The primitive elements are **blocks and nets**, which represent layout cells and interconnect respectively.

For example, the OEM-component "74181", which is a 4-bit TTL ALU slice, has a dataflow model with **add**, **subtract**, **AND**, and **OR** nodes, which represent its data transformations. This component has a timing-and-sequencing model that describes its propagation delays for various combinations of inputs. It has a schematic diagram that either consists of a box with connection points or a gate diagram. It also has a physical description that signifies that its package is a 14-pin DIP.

3.2.1. Hierarchy within the Subspaces

The four models are each hierarchically structured. For example, a dataflow node is either primitive or it is defined recursively in terms of other nodes and values. Similarly, a value is either primitive or defined recursively in terms of other values. Similar recursive definitions are used in all four hierarchies.

3.2.2. Models and Links in the Four Subspaces

The generic name **Model** is used for nodes, ranges, modules, and blocks. The dataflow model of a component is therefore a **Node**, which can be recursively decomposed into **Nodes** and **Values**. The generic name **Link** is used for values, points, carriers, and nets. These too can be decomposed, with the exception of points, which represent atomic events of infinitesimal duration.

---

[3]These points (timing events) are not to be confused with the points of the 3DIS geometric representation.

3.2.3. Relationships across Subspaces

All relationships among models and links of different subspaces are explicitly represented by means of **bindings**. There are two basic types of bindings, which are general enough to cover all of the cases of interest:

1. *Operation bindings*, which relate dataflow elements to structural elements and time ranges.

2. *Realization bindings*, which relate structural elements to physical elements.

For example, an operation binding expresses the relationship between an **add** operation (dataflow), an ALU (structure), and the time interval during which it happens. A realization binding represents the correspondence between a particular layout region and the ALU.

3.3. The Target, the Specification, and the Library

The design being constructed is the *target*. The target is functionally equivalent to the *specification*; it is composed of primitive elements and members of the *design library*. Near the top of the hierarchies, the dataflow of the target might be syntactically identical to the dataflow of the specification, but at the low levels this is unlikely. For example, suppose the specification contains a multiplication node. The definition of multiplication can be regarded as a series of shifts and conditional additions. But under a given set of timing, power, and area constraints, the dataflow actually implemented might be radically different. Therefore, the specification and the target are considered to be two completely different components. In general the relationships among constituents of the target and the specification can be complex.

4. An Example

Consider the design of a particular component, a two-bit binary adder, which can be represented as in Figure 4-1. First the schema of the component is discussed; then the dataflow model of the component is examined in detail. The timing, structural, and physical models of the component are not detailed here; for further details please see [Afsarmanesh 85b]. Finally, the way in which bindings are used to unify the four subspaces is described.

4.1. The Component

The subtype/supertype (generalization) hierarchy

of component definitions is shown in Figure 4-2, where boxes represent type objects, the arrows represent subtype/supertype relationships, and the undirected lines that come out of the boxes lead to mappings (properties) that describe members of the types. The type **Component** has properties that denote its name, four **Models** of the component, and two sets of **Bindings**.

There are two subtypes of **Component**. The **OEM-Component** represents a component supplied by an OEM (Outside Equipment Manufacturer). As such it is characterized by the name of the manufacturer, the manufacturer's designation (**Kind**), and a list of **Suppliers**. Other properties, such as **Price**, have been omitted from the figure in the interest of simplicity.

In-House-Component represents a component that is manufactured in-house. It may not even be a

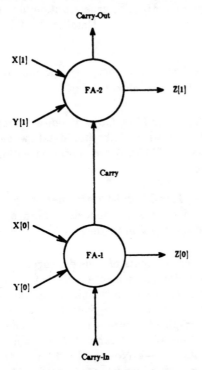

Figure 4-1: Two-bit adder example

complete design; that information is captured by the **Complete-Bit**[4]. The in-house component also has a set of **Designer-Names**, denoting the people responsible for its construction, a **Process**, which identifies a particular fabrication process, and a **Guru**.

---

[4]More complex historical information could be attached, e.g. a **Verification-History**.

The member of the **Component** type used for this example is shown in Figure 4-3. This **Component** is an **In-House-Component**. Its name, a property inherited from the supertype, is "H42padder". The four **Models** are similarly named; Figure 4-3 shows only the

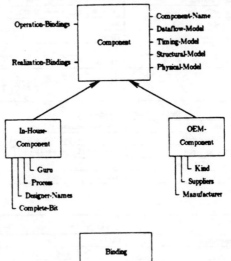

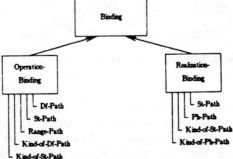

Figure 4-2: The generalization hierarchy of Components and Bindings

"H42padder.Dataflow" **Model** in detail, where again some mappings such as **Complete-Bit** and **Designer** have been omitted in the interest of simplicity[5]. **Operation-Bindings** and **Realization-Bindings** are also shown schematically as lists of logical references to the actual binding objects, as discussed in Section 4.3. The other properties of "H42padder" are self-explanatory. The dataflow graph of "H42padder" is given in Figure 4-1.

4.1.1. Models and Subspaces

In this example we examine only the dataflow subspace. The other models are similar to the dataflow model. The differences mainly consist of minor

---

[5]In figures 4-3 and 4-6, the use of parentheses ( ) denote objects whose details have been omitted in the interest of simplicity. Square brackets [ ] represent list delimiters.

In-House-Component 'H42padder'	
Component-Name	H42padder
Dataflow-Model	●
Timing-Model	●————▶ (H42padder.Timing)
Structural-Model	●————▶ (H42padder.Structure)
Physical-Model	●————▶ (H42padder.Physical)
Operation-Bindings	[●——▶ (OB1), ●——▶ (OB2), ...]
Realization-Bindings	[●——▶ (RB1), ●——▶ (RB2), ...]
Complete-Bit	false
Designer-Names	['David', 'John']
Guru	'Fadi'
Process	'MOSIS NMOS 3-micron'

Dataflow-Model 'H42padder-Dataflow'	
Model-Name	H42padder.Dataflow
Has-Model-Constituents	[●——▶ (FA2.Df), ●]
Has-Link-Constituents	[●——▶ (X), ●——▶ (Y), ...]
Has-Structural-Dimension	2
Function	'Two Bit Adder'

Single-Node 'FA1.Df'	
Component-Name	FA1.Df
Has-Kind	●————▶ (Full-Adder-Data-Flow)
Intended-Function	'Low Order Bit'

Figure 4-3:   A Component member and its partial
dataflow model

attributes. For example, the structural counterpart of
a dataflow **value** is the **carrier**. The carrier attribute
driver, which describes hardware implementation
attributes such as **tri-state, open-drain**, has no
counterpart in the dataflow model. The interested
reader is referred to [Afsarmanesh 85b] and [Knapp 85].

4.2. The Dataflow Subspace and Dataflow Models

The generalization hierarchy for the
Dataflow-Model is shown in Figure 4-4. Objects of
type **Model** each have a name, a **Complete-Bit**
similar to that of **Component**s, and a **Designer**.
There are four subtypes of **Model**, one for each
subspace. Shown in Figure 4-4 is the subtype
Dataflow-Model, also called **Node** for short. The
other three subtypes of **Model** are **Structural-Model**,
Timing-Model, and **Physical-Model**.

Dataflow-Model has the following properties:

● The **Function** property indicates the
overall function performed by the Node. For
example, in Figure 4-3 the function of
"H42padder-Dataflow" is that of "Two Bit
Adder".

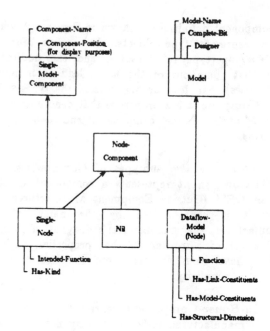

Figure 4-4:   The generalization hierarchy of
Dataflow Models

● The **Dimension** property specifies the bit
width of the Node.

● The **Has-Link-Constituents** property
indicates which links (for dataflow models,
links are **Values**) are contained within the
model.

● The **Has-Model-Constituents** property
specifies which models (**Nodes**) are
contained within the model.

The constituents of a model together express the
application domain semantics of that model, thereby
supporting its recursive definition. In the example of
Figure 4-3, which corresponds to the two-bit adder
dataflow graph of Figure 4-1, the link-constituents are
the input, output and carry **Values**; and the model-
constituents are the Nodes "FA-1" and "FA-2". The
constituents of a model are represented as lists of
logical references.

The objects that are logically referred to in
Has-Model-Constituents   are   of   type
Node-Component, which also designates that they
are either of type **Single-Node** or **Nil**[6]. If the

---

[6]This is accomplished via the definition of the recursion
abstraction described in [Afsarmanesh 85a].

reference is to **Nil**, then the constituent is not further defined, i.e. the **Node** is either a primitive or its definition does not exist at present. In either case the recursive definition of the model ends at this point. If the reference is to a **Single-Node**, as is the case in the example, the recursive definition of the model continues through it. In the example, the **Single-Nodes** are called "FA-1" and "FA-2". "FA-1" has the **Intended-Function** "Low Order Bit"; presumably "FA-2" is the high order bit of the adder. Both "FA-1" and "FA-2" could have the value "Full-Adder-Data-Flow" in their **Has-Kind** properties; that means they are both one-bit full adder nodes. "Full-Adder-Data-Flow" is itself a **Node**, and is represented by a **Dataflow-Model**; hence it is further defined in terms of its model and link constituents. This is the recursion abstraction at work: **Models** are defined in terms of other **Models**.

4.2.1. Dataflow Links

Figure 4-5 shows the subtype/supertype hierarchy of **Links** for the dataflow subspace. **Links** are more complicated than **Models**, because they bear the burden of representing connections between **Models**. A Dataflow **Link** is called a **Value**. A **Value** has a **Name**, such as "Carry", which is inherited from the supertype **Link**. It also inherits a **Complete-Bit** and a **Designer**, with meanings similar to those of the **Component**'s corresponding properties.

The reason a **Value** should have an explicitly mentioned **Designer** is that a **Value** is potentially a structured entity (for example a complex floating-point number). If the **Value** is a simple array, then the **Has-Structural-Dimension** property specifies the dimension of the array. If the **Value** is structured, then its **Has-Sublink-Constituents** property defines the structure. **Sublink-Constituents** are of type **Value-Component**, which also indicates that they are either of type **Nil**, or if they are of type **Single-Element** it signifies that they are again either of type **Single-Value** or **Sub-Value** (Figure 4-5).

For example, a floating-point number "Flonum" is a structured value consisting of two fields "Mantissa" and "Exponent". These are **Sub-Values**, which have **Has-Kind** properties of their own. The **Has-Kind** property of "Mantissa" might refer to a **Value** named "Long-Signed-Integer" and the **Has-Kind** property of "Exponent" might refer to "Excess-64-Integer".

The input "X" of Figure 4-1 is a **Single-Value**. Figure 4-6 shows "X" in more detail. The **Has-Kind** property of "X" points to the **Value** "Two-Bit-

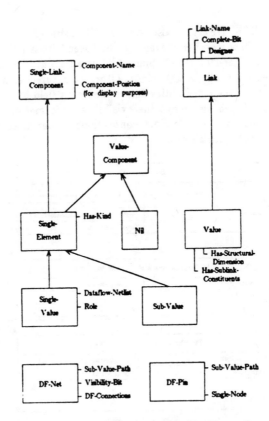

Figure 4-5: The generalization hierarchy of Dataflow Links

Integer". The **Value** "Two-Bit-Integer" has the **Structural-Dimension** 2. "Two-Bit-Integer" also has **Sublink-Constituents** consisting of two **Sub-Values**, named "High-Order-Bit" and "Low-Order-Bit" respectively. The **Has-Kind** properties of these bits have logical references to the primitive **Value** "Bit". The **Has-Sublink-Constituents** of the **Value** "Bit" is **nil**, so the recursive definition of "Two-Bit-Integer" ends at this point.

In addition, "X" has a **Role** which is "second vector input". Furthermore, it has connections, represented by a **Dataflow-Netlist**. The **Dataflow-Netlist** is a list of logical references to **DF-Nets**. In Figure 4-6, the two bits of the "Two-Bit-Integer" "X" are connected separately, only the connections of the "Low-Order-Bit" being shown.

The **DF-Net** has a **Sub-Value-Path**. This is a path into the structure of the value being connected. For example, if the high-order bit of the mantissa of a complex floating-point number "A" was connected individually, the path would be "A.Real.Mantissa.Bit63". In Figure 4-6, the path simply points to the low-order bit of "X".

The **DF-Net** also has a **Visibility-Bit**; this determines whether the bit can be "seen" from outside "H42padder-Dataflow". Since "X" is an input, this bit is **true** for all its **DF-Nets**. Other structured **Links** may have their visibilities determined on a field-by-field basis, which is why the visibility information is attached to the individual connections rather than to the **Single-Link** itself.

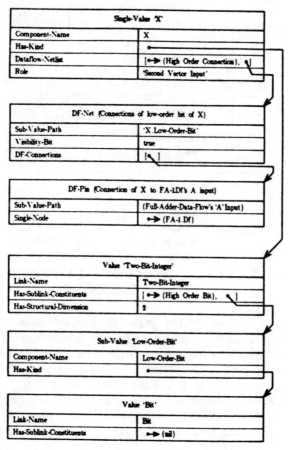

Figure 4-6:   The definition and connections of the Value "X".

DF-Connections are used to describe connections in the dataflow subspace. The **DF-Connections** of a **DF-Net** are references to **DF-Pins**. A **DF-Pin** refers to a **Single-Node**, e.g. "FA-1.Df", and a **Sub-Value-Path**, which represents a connection point on that **Single-Node**. In the example of Figure 4-6, the **Sub-Value-Path** of the "X" connection point is a path to the "A" input bit of the "Full-Adder-Data-Flow" model, which is given in parentheses in Figure 4-6 (recall that "Full-Adder-Data-Flow" is the **Has-Kind** property of "FA-1.Df").

Using both the **Sub-Value-Path** of a link, as expressed in the **DF-Net**, and the **Sub-Value-Path** of

a Single-Node connection point, as expressed in the **DF-Pin**, very general kinds of connections can be constructed.

For example, using both paths in their full generality would allow us to make arbitrary permutations of structured array values at connection points. If a two-bit **Value** "P" was to be connected to the "X" input of "H42padder.Dataflow", it would be possible to connect "P[1]" to "X[0]" and "P[0]" to "X[1]", thus achieving a bitwise reversal at the point of connection.

4.3. Bindings

The two binding sets represent the interrelationships between the elements of the models. **Operation-Bindings** show the relationship between an operation (or value), a structure, and a time interval; (for example, an addition, an adder, and a microcycle). Similarly, a different Operation-Binding might represent the relationship between a value, a bus or register, and a microcycle. **Realization-Bindings** are used to represent the relationships between structural elements and physical realizations (for example, between an adder's schematic and its layout).

Both kinds of **Bindings** have properties that represent paths into the four hierarchies, e.g. "St-Path" as shown in Figure 4-2. The reason paths must be used is that **Bindings** refer to unique **Single-Model-Components**. Such a **Single-Model-Component** may be deep down in the recursion hierarchy, and the only way to uniquely specify it is by giving a complete path down into the hierarchy, starting at the root **Component**.

The **Kind-of-Df-Path** property of **Operation-Binding** simply indicates whether the binding is to a **Node** or a **Value**; similarly the **Kind-of-St-Path** property indicates whether the binding is to a **Carrier** or a **Module**. These are examples of the use of a "*generic interrelation abstraction*"[7]. All combinations are permitted in the schema. Similar considerations apply to **Realization-Bindings**.

There is no **Kind-of-Range-Path** property for **Operation-Bindings** because the only valid timing element for a binding is a **Range**. **Points** have

---

[7]This abstraction primitive and the recursion abstraction mentioned earlier were specifically defined for the ADAM VLSI design database, and are supported by the 3DIS data model.

infinitesimal duration, and hence are never suitable for binding either operations or values to structural elements.

5. Conclusions

The 3DIS was introduced as an extensible information modeling framework that captures the underlying semantics of VLSI/CAD application environments, and supports requirements specific to this domain. The application of the 3DIS to the ADAM system was described. An example 3DIS database design for ADAM was presented.

The 3DIS database is object-oriented in that all data entities, relationships defined on entities, events and operations, as well as the description of data (meta-data) are modeled as objects. It provides a structured, unified view of the application information that reduces the required level of expertise for database manipulation and database development/evolution. The extension of the 3DIS model to support the specific modeling requirements of engineering design environments, such as modeling recursively defined entities and concepts, simplifies the task of database design.

The representation schema is based on the idea of unifying the design data in three major structures called the specification, the target, and the library, respectively. Each of these consists of a single component or a collection of components, where all components are modeled uniformly. A component is represented in terms of four orthogonal hierarchies: dataflow, timing, structural, and physical. The four hierarchies are linked by explicit relationships called bindings.

We expect significant benefits from the presented approach in construction of the overall ADAM system. Since the design data is unified by the database, adding application packages is greatly simplified. Since non-experts can access the underlying schema easily, the designers of CAD packages need not be database experts to use the system flexibly. The representation has several advantages. It cleanly represents the data of interest. Important relationships between specification and the target are not obscured. Designer freedom is limited to the degree permitted by the specification. The same concepts and techniques can be used to analyze and construct target designs, specifications, and library components. Finally, the design details are hidden until they are needed. The unification of the database with the synthesis and analysis tools results in an automated process from algorithm specification to circuit layout. This in itself is expected to simplify the design process and enhance design correctness.

A Pascal-based graphical interface to the 3DIS, implemented on an IBM PC/XT [Afsarmanesh 85a], has been designed and implemented. This interface provides an experimental vehicle for evaluation and improvement of the browsing capabilities of the 3DIS user interface. A Pascal-based graphical editor for an older, file-oriented version of the design data structure (DDS) has also been implemented.

Future work on this project includes integrating the system into a coherent whole. In particular the data structures of a number of synthesis packages must be changed from the DDS file format to the new 3DIS-oriented database support system in order for ADAM to function as a single unified system. The implementation of the 3DIS database system and its user interface must be completed. The definition and implementation of database activities, e.g. the invocation of semantic checking routines, must also be added.

References

[Afsarmanesh 84] Afsarmanesh, H., and Mcleod, D.
A Framework for Semantic Database Models.
In *Proceedings of NYU Symposium on New Directions for Database Systems*. New York, NY, May, 1984.

[Afsarmanesh 85a]
Afsarmanesh, H.
The 3 Dimensional Information Space (3DIS): An Extensible Object-Oriented Framework for Information Management.
PhD thesis, Department of Computer Science, University of Southern California, July, 1985.

[Afsarmanesh 85b]
Afsarmanesh, H., Knapp, D., McLeod, D., and Parker, A.
An Object-Oriented Approach to Databases for VLSI/CAD.
Technical Report, Department of Computer Science, University of Southern California, April, 1985.

[Batory 84] Batory, D.S. and Kim, W.
Modelling Concepts for VLSI CAD Objects.

technical report TR-84-35,
    Department of Computer Science,
    University of Texas at Austin,
    December, 1984.

[Bushnell 83]   Bushnell, M., Geiger, D., Kim, J.,
                  LaPotin, D., Nassif, S., Nestor,
                  J. Rajan, J., Strojwas, A., and
                  Walker, H.
                  *DIF: The CMU-DA Intermediate
                      Form.*
                  Technical Report CMUCAD-83-11,
                      CMU Center for Computer-Aided
                      Design, 1983.

[Davis 82]   Davis, R., Shrobe, H., Hamscher, W.,
                  Wieckert, K., Shirley, M., and Polit,
                  S.
                  Diagnosis Based on Description of
                      Structure and Function.
                  In *Proceedings of the National
                      Conference on AI*, pages 137-142.
                      AAAI, 1982.

[Director 81]   Director, S.W., Parker, A.C.,
                  Siewiorek, D.P., and Thomas, D.E.
                  A Design Methodology and Computer
                      Aids for Digital VLSI Systems.
                  *IEEE Transactions on Circuits and
                      Systems* CAS-28:634-645, July,
                      1981.

[Dittrich 85]   Dittrich, K.R., Kotz, A.M., and Mulle,
                  J.M.
                  *An Event/Trigger Mechanism to
                      Enforce Complex Consistency
                      Constraints in Design Databases.*
                  Technical Report, Institut fuer
                      Informatik II, Universitaet
                      Karlsruhe, West Germany, 1985.

[Eastman 80]   Eastman, C.M.
                  System Facilities for CAD Databases.
                  In *Proceedings of the 17th Design
                      Automation Conference.* 1980.

[Granacki 85]   Granacki, J., Knapp, D., and Parker,
                  A.
                  The ADAM Advanced Design
                      AutoMation System: Overview,
                      Planner, and Natural Language
                      Interface.
                  In *Proceedings of the 22nd Design
                      Automation Conference.* 1985.

[Katz 82]   Katz, R. H.
                  A Database Approach for Managing
                      VLSI Design Data.
                  In *Proceedings of the 19th Design
                      Automation Conference.* 1982.

[Knapp 83]   Knapp, D. and Parker, A.
                  *A Data Structure for VLSI Synthesis
                      and Verification.*
                  Technical Report DISC 83-6a, Digital
                      Integrated Systems Center, Dept.
                      of EE-Systems, University of
                      Southern California, October,
                      1983.

[Knapp 85]   Knapp, D. and Parker, A.
                  A Unified Representation for Design
                      Information.
                  In *Proceedings of the 1895
                      Conference on Hardware
                      Description Languages.* IFIP,
                      1985.

[McLeod 83]   McLeod, D., Bapa Rao, K. V., and
                  Narayanaswamy, K.
                  An Approach to Information
                      Management for CAD/VLSI
                      Applications.
                  In *Proceedings of the ACM SIGMOD
                      International Conference on
                      Management of Data.* San Jose,
                      California, May, 1983.

[Parker 84]   Parker, A.
                  Automated Synthesis of Digital
                      Systems.
                  IEEE Design and Test , November,
                      1984.

[Wong 79]   Wong, S. and Bristol, W.A.
                  A CAD Database.
                  In *Proceedings of the 16th Design
                      Automation Conference.* 1979.

Index

Afsarmanesh, H., Knapp, D., McCleod, D., Parker, A., "An Extensible Object-Oriented Approach to Databases For VLSI/CAD," *Proceedings of VLDB-85*, 13-24. © 1985, Morgan Kaufmann Publishers, Inc. All rights reserved. Reprinted with the permission of the publisher and the authors.

Ahlsen, M., Bjornerstedt, A., et al, "An Architecture for Object Management in OIS," *ACM Translation on OIS*, (2)3, 1984. © 1984, ACM. All rights reserved. Reprinted with the permission of the publisher and the authors.

Albano, A., Cardelli, L., and Orsini, R., "Galileo: A Strongly Typed, Interactive Conceptual Language," *Transactions on Database Systems*, 10(2), pp. 230-236, 1985. © 1985, ACM. All rights reserved. Reprinted with the permission of the publisher and the authors.

Andrews, T., Harris, C., "Combining Language and Database Advances in an Object-Oriented Development Environment," *Proceedings of the OOPSLA*, 1987. © 1987, ACM. All rights reserved. Reprinted with the permission of the publisher and the authors.

Atkinson, M.P., et al, "An Approach to Persistent Programming," *The Computer Journal*, 26:4, 1983. © 1983, Cambridge University Press. All rights reserved. Reprinted with the permission of the publisher and the authors.

Banerjee, J., et al, "Data Model Issues for Object-Oriented Applications," *ACM Transactions on Office Information Systems*, 5:1, 1987. © 1987 ACM. All rights reserved. Reprinted with permission of the publisher and the authors.

Batory, D.S., et al, "GENESIS: An Extensible Database Management System," *IEEE Transactions on Software Engineering*, IEEE. All rights reserved. Reprinted with the permission of the publisher and the authors.

Bryce, D., Hull, R., "SNAP: A Graphics-Based Schema Manager," *IEEE Conference on Data Engineering*, 1986. © 1986 The Institute of Electrical and Electronical Engineers, Inc. All rights reserved. Reprinted with the permission of the publisher and the authors.

Cardelli, L., "Semantics of Multiple Inheritance," *Information and Computation*, 76:138-164, 1985. © 1985, Academic Press. All rights reserved. Reprinted with the permission of the publisher and the author.

Carey, M.J., et al "The EXODUS Extensible DBMS Project: An Overview," unpublished technical report. All rights reserved. Reprinted with the permission of the authors.

Chan, A., Danberg, A., et al, "Storage and Access Structures to Support a Semantic Data Model," *Proceedings of the VLDB-82*, 122-130. © 1982, Morgan Kaufmann Publishers, Inc. All rights reserved. Reprinted with the permission of the publisher and the authors.

Cockshot, P. W., Atkinson, M.P., et. al., "Persistent Object Management System," *Software—Practice and Experience,* 14:49–71. © 1984, John Wiley and Sons Limited. All rights reserved. Reprinted with the permission of the publisher and the authors.

Copeland, G.P., Khoshafian, S. "Object Identity," *Proceedings of Object Oriented Programming Systems, Languages and Applications-86.* © 1986, ACM. All rights reserved. Reprinted with the permission of the publisher and the authors.

Dayal, U., Manola, F., et al "Simplifying Complex Objects: The Probe Approach to Modelling and Querying Them," *Proceedings of German Database Conference, Burg Technik and Wissenschaft-87.* © 1987 Springer-Verlag. All rights reserved. Reprinted with the permission of the publisher and the authors.

Fishman, D.H., Beech, D., et. al., "Simplifying Complex Objects: The Probe Approach to Modelling and Querying Them," *Proceedings of German Database Conference, Burg Technik and Wissenschaft-87.* © 1987 Springer-Verlag. All rights reserved. Reprinted with the permission of the publisher and the authors.

Goldman, K.J., Goldman, S.A., Kanellakis, P.C., Zdonik, S.B., "ISIS: Interface for a Semantic Information System," *Proceedings of SIGMOD-85.* © 1985, ACM. All rights reserved. Reprinted with permission of the publisher and the authors.

Hammer, M., McLeod, D., "Database Description with SDM: A Semantic Database Model," *ACM Transactions on Database Systems,* 1981. © 1981 ACM. All rights reserved. Reprinted with permission of the publisher and the authors.

Herlihy, M., "Optimistic Concurrency Control for Abstract Data Types," *5th ACM Principles of Distributed Computing Conference,* 1986. © 1986 ACM. All rights reserved. Reprinted with permission of the publisher and the author.

Hornick, M.F., Zdonik, S.B., "A Shared, Segmented Memory System for an Object-Oriented Database," *ACM Transactions on Office Information Systems,* 5:1, pp.70-85, 1987. © 1987, ACM. All rights reserved. Reprinted with permission of the publisher and the authors.

Hudson, S., King, R., "CACTIS: A Database System for Specifying Functionally Defined Data," *IEEE OODBS Workshop,* 1986. © 1986 the Institute of Electrical and Electronical Engineers, Inc. All rights reserved. Reprinted with permission of the publisher and the authors.

Jul, E., Levy, H., Hutchinson, A. "Fine-Grained Mobility in the Emerald System," *ACM Transactions on Programming Languages and Systems,* 7:244-269, 1985. All rights reserved. Reprinted with permission of the publisher and the authors.

Kaehler, T., Krasner, G., "LOOM: Large Object-Oriented Memory for Smalltalk-80 Systems," *Bits of History, Words of Advice.* Edited by G. Krasner, Xerox PARC, 1983. © 1983 Xerox PARC, Palo Alto. All rights reserved. Reprinted with permission of the publisher and the authors.

Katz, R.H., Chang, E., "Managing Change in a Computer-Aided Design Database," *Proceedings of the VLDB-87,* 455-462. © 1987 Morgan Kaufmann Publishers, Inc. All rights reserved. Reprinted with permission of the publisher and the authors.

Korth, H., Kim, W., Bancilhon, F., "On Long Duration CAD Transactions," *Information Sciences,* 1988. © 1988 ACM. All rights reserved. Reprinted with permission of the publisher and the authors.

Lecluse, C., Richard, P., Velez, F., "O2, An Object-Oriented Data Model," *Proceedings of SIGMOD,* 1988. © 1988 ACM. All rights reserved. Reprinted with permission of the publisher and the authors.

Liskov, B., Snyder, A., Atkinson, R., Schaffert, C., "Abstraction Mechanisms in CLU," *Communications of the ACM,* 20:564-576, 1977. © 1977 ACM. All rights reserved. Reprinted with permission of the publisher and the authors.

Lochovsky, F., Hogg, J.S., et al, "OTM: Specifying Office Tasks," *Conference on Office Information Systems,* 1988. © 1988 The Institute of Electrical and Electronical Engineers, Inc. All rights reserved. Reprinted with permission of the publisher and the authors.

Maier, D., Nordquist, P., Grossman, M., "Displaying Database Objects," *Proceedings of the 1st International Conference on Expert Database Systems,* 1985. © 1985 Benjamin-Cummings. All rights reserved. Reprinted with permission of the publisher and the authors.

Maier, D. and Stein, J., "Development and Implementation of an Object-Oriented DBMS," *Research Directions in Object-Oriented Programming.* Edited by B. Shriver and P. Wegner. © 1987 MIT Press. All rights reserved. Reprinted with permission of the publisher and the authors.

Manola, F., Dayal, U., "PDM: An Object-Oriented Data Model," *IEEE OODB Workshop-86.* © 1986 The Institute of Electrical and Electronic Engineers, Inc. All rights reserved. Reprinted with permission of the publisher and the authors.